A RURAL MANIFESTO

REALIZING INDIA'S FUTURE THROUGH HER VILLAGES

A RURAL MANIFESTO

REALIZING INDIA'S FUTURE THROUGH HER VILLAGES

FEROZE VARUN GANDHI

RUPA

Published by
Rupa Publications India Pvt. Ltd 2018
7/16, Ansari Road, Daryaganj
New Delhi 110002

Sales Centres:
Allahabad Bengaluru Chennai
Hyderabad Jaipur Kathmandu
Kolkata Mumbai

ISBN: 978-93-5333-309-6

First impression 2018

10 9 8 7 6 5 4 3 2 1

Printed at Thomson Press India Ltd., Faridabad

Book designed by Yamini Gandhi, Incarnations

In tribute to India's marginal farmer
whose daily toil is as much an act of
defiance as an article of faith.

CONTENTS

CHAPTER VII

PREFACE

The idea of writing a tome, nay, a dense synthesis of facts, forecasts and, at times, personal anecdotes, came from my travels in India's dusty hinterland. Whether it was campaigning in the deltaic regions of West Bengal, conducting field visits in the vicinity of Sultanpur and Pilibhit, or more simply, meeting students of provincial universities in states often forgotten by national media, the cause of marginal farmers and their current dismal condition struck a chord with me. This issue, once proudly espoused by all up-and-coming politicians, was at once an intellectual and emotional problem, and one with no easy solutions.

Farmers in Champaran district in Bihar, a century back, under the Tinkathia system, were forced to set aside 15 per cent of their land for the cultivation of indigo. Even after these were planted, the farmers were still subject to a variety of extortionist cesses, termed 'abwabs'—even the cost of an elephant for colonial shikaar was included. Farmers naturally rose in resistance in the thousands, but were crushed by the East India Company until the arrival of a barrister from South Africa, who fought for the cause of the harassed tillers of the soil. And yet, a century after the Mahatma sought freedom from exploitation for them, India's farmers remain a beleaguered lot.

In Majuli district of Assam, farmers are increasingly taking to eating beetles, as a way of beating back pests from their marginal farms. Meanwhile, in Maharashtra, onion farmers routinely see over 20 per cent of their produce wasting due to lack of cold storage facilities. Consider the landscape that India's farmers survive in. The country's heat-baked plains are criss-crossed by a range of turbulent rivers, many worshipped and dreaded since prehistory. Such rivers have repeatedly altered course, changing the way they deposit sediment during the monsoons, and overrunning ancestral fields. Even major distributaries would end up getting diverted—consider the case of the Bhagirathi in West Bengal, whence the main course of the Ganga shifted eastwards towards the Padma; and post the floods of 1770, even the Damodar witnessed a change of confluence point. For India's farmers, agricultural risk has been ever-present. They have to take a variety of decisions, right from choice of crops (annual or short-term) to time of tillage. The challenge is further exacerbated by rising prices of agricultural inputs, availability of water, soil suitability and pest management. All these decisions and uncertainties narrow the window of economic benefit for the marginal farmer. A faulty decision can wreak significant havoc. The viability of being a marginal farmer is further eroded due to macro developments.

This uncertainty is reflected in rural debt levels. Large farmers (>10 hectares) in Punjab typically have a debt-to-income ratio of 0.26, while medium farmers (4–10 hectares) and semi-medium farmers (2–4 hectares) have a debt-to-income ratio of 0.34—all seemingly affordable.[1] However, small (1–2 hectares) and marginal farmers (<1 hectare) face a greater burden of debt, with a debt-to-income ratio of 0.94 and 1.42, respectively, with over 50 per cent of their loans from non-banking sources.

With the average landholding size decreasing (from 2.3 hectares in 1971 to 1.16 hectares in 2011) and average input prices rising, the cost of cultivation has increased, and with it margins associated with farming have reduced. Media reports highlight that a farmer can now typically earn between ₹2,400–₹2,600 per hectare, tilling fields of paddy or wheat, while farm labourers can earn less than ₹5000 per month. Real farm wages have grown at an average annual growth rate of 2.9 per cent between 1991 and 2012, with farm wages actually declining between 2002 and 2007.[2] About 30.5 million peasants quit farming over 2004–05 and 2010–11, seeking employment in the secondary and tertiary sectors. The size of this agricultural workforce is expected to shrink to ~200 million by 2020. When we talk of rural distress, these are some of its symptoms.

Minimum support prices (MSPs) have also declined. Food inflation has declined significantly over the past year, with the price of arhar down by 45 per cent in April 2017 compared to the previous year, while the price of urad has declined by 29 per cent.[3] Soyabeans were down by 24 per cent, while potatoes were cheaper by 41 per cent in April 2017. Expansion in acreage, along with improvement in procurement, a rise in buffer stocks and imports, and global agro-commodity trends, along with fire sales during the demonetization period have combined to accentuate the fall in food prices, especially for pulses (13.64 per cent decline year over year [YOY])

---

1   Punjab Agricultural University, 2014

2   Gulati, 2013

3   Jethmalani, H., June 2017

and vegetables (7.79 per cent decline YOY).[4] Meanwhile, the average growth in minimum support prices of kharif crops has been ~4 per cent, compared to the ~13–15 per cent growth seen between 2010 and 2013.

The dismal consequence is—acutely depressed farmers committing suicide. Officially, around 12,602 individuals associated with the farm sector committed suicide in 2015, about 2 per cent more than 2014.[5] Farmer suicides have increased primarily in states with limited irrigation and variable rainfall (e.g. Maharashtra, Karnataka, Telangana, Chhattisgarh, Andhra Pradesh, Tamil Nadu and Madhya Pradesh), which contribute 87.5 per cent of total farmer suicides in 2015. Over 321,428 farmers have committed suicide in the past twenty years.

India's agricultural strategy has historically sought to raise productivity (through high-yield varieties) while seeking to keep input costs low (through fertilizer subsidies and seed grants), and attempting to guarantee a minimum return (through minimum support prices). Meanwhile, consumers were provided cheap food through the public distribution system. However, this strategy has outgrown its utility—India's agricultural inputs market is increasingly deregulated, with subsidies for fertilizers being cut. Public investment in irrigation, flood control and high-yielding varieties has been affected by a shift towards lessening the fiscal deficit. Liberalized imports of agricultural commodities have also done their bit to dampen domestic prices. The viability of being a marginal farmer in India has been eroded. Meanwhile, governments have sought to address production shortfalls and rising food inflation in urban markets by liberalizing imports and releasing buffer stocks into the market, further reducing prices. Thus, even in good harvest years, farmers end up with low minimum support prices and limited procurement of their produce. So, India's agriculture sector is increasingly exposed to market signals that it hasn't been prepared for.

Amidst this, access to agricultural inputs has become more fraught—large farmers in Maharashtra typically have access to modern pumps, thereby consuming large amounts of water, and leaving little, if any, for small and marginal farmers.[6] Fertilizer and pesticide prices have risen continuously over the past few years, causing marginal farmers to adopt organic means instead.[7] The high cost of high-yielding seed varieties, combined with limited availability in India, also hampers agricultural productivity. Given such constraints, farmers have limited scope for crop diversification. Unfortunately, there are limited capacity building programmes

---

4   CMIE, 2017

5   NCRB, 2015

6   Bhogal, P., Dec 2016

7   Mitral, N., Sept 2016

and extension services for farmers, with universal access far from being achieved.

Institutional support for mitigating the plight of such farmers has been provided in various forms since Independence. The National Bank for Agriculture and Rural Development (NABARD) was established in 1982, seeking to provide financing support to tube well irrigation, farm mechanization and other ancillary activities. The institution of a nationwide agriculture loan waiver in 1990 had a deleterious impact, breeding credit indiscipline and hampering rural credit growth. The 2004–05 Union budget sought to double agricultural credit, while a 2 per cent interest subvention was provided in 2006, allowing farmers to avail of Kisan Credit Card (KCC) loans at per cent per annum (up to 3 lakh). Another agricultural loan waiver was provided in 2009, just prior to the Lok Sabha elections. Small and marginal farmers certainly deserve greater support from the government. However, India's historic agricultural policy has disincentivized the creation of a formal credit culture amongst Indian farmers. If waivers are so common, why would any farmer seek to pay off their loan on time?

Ideally, India ought to have no rural distress—we have the second-largest quantity of arable land in the world. And yet, less than 35 per cent of this land is irrigated, with the remnant land subject to fluctuations in rainfall. Growth in agriculture and allied sectors has almost been offset by rural inflation. With small farm sizes and rising agricultural input costs, farmers have increasingly grown indebted. Rural India remains where it was, mired in its own abyss.

The writing is on the wall: India's small and marginal farmers will need another agricultural loan waiver. However, granted this once, it just cannot continue in the future. There are other ways to mitigate their plight. We need more subsidies on the purchase of agricultural equipment, fertilizers and pesticides, along with expanding medical insurance coverage. In addition, the scope of the Mahatma Gandhi National Rural Employment Guarantee Act (MGNREGA) could be increased. Allowing marginal farmers to be paid for tilling their own fields could reduce their input costs; they can't afford other agricultural labourers and find it socially awkward to till someone else's field. Such measures could increase their net income, while reducing the scope of rural distress. Small steps like these can make a meaningful contribution to their lot.

For centuries, India's economic strength was based on the agricultural surplus generated by its farmers, and the trade revenues brought in by its rural entrepreneurs in handicrafts, calico and metalworks. And yet, suddenly, over the past few centuries, India's natural competitive advantage vanished. Our agricultural techniques became outdated and our handicrafts, once pillaged by the British, found fewer and fewer markets as the years passed. Such a progression rouses natural questions—

how did India's demographic change transform its rural economy? How do we transition out of this to rural prosperity?

One requirement is retailoring our concepts. For centuries, we have been besotted by the notion of villages being self-sufficient and self-regulating. The idea that an Indian village was isolated and yet self-sufficient was first propounded by Charles Metcalfe in 1830—'The village communities are little republics, having nearly everything that they can want within themselves, and almost independent of any foreign relations. They seem to last where nothing else lasts. Dynasty after dynasty tumbles down; revolution succeeds to revolution; Hindoo, Pathan, Moghul, Mahratta, Sikh, English, are all masters in turn, but the village communities remain the same.' Karl Marx also popularized the idea of village self-sufficiency—'Under this form of municipal government, the inhabitants of the country have lived from time immemorial. The boundaries of the village have been but seldom altered, and though the villages themselves have been sometimes injured and even desolated by war, famine and disease, the same name, the same limits, the same interests, and even the same families have contributed for ages.'

Most writers of rural India have taken the idea of village autonomy and autarchy for granted, categorizing the village as a standalone community, with limited interaction with the wider economic, political and religious systems. More recently, questions have been raised about the idea of a nucleated village, with clear boundaries between one village and another. Migration patterns, farmer suicides and stagnating rural incomes, along with increasingly ad hoc land acquisition in the name of public good, have politicized the idea of rural economics.

Is a village simply a vertical economic unit composed of various castes, bound by ties of kinship, marriage and economic obligations? Or should we consider its deep dependence on towns for specialized services (construction, transportation, healthcare, education, etc.) as part of the hinterland's paradigm? How does economic policy at the village level result in sustainable and growing per capita income, while providing essential services and a safety net? How can agriculture be revived in an era of fragmented landholdings and rising input and fuel prices? Does the rural economy offer enough opportunities to quell rising discontent? Why does construction offer the only hope for rural youth, bereft as they are of any transferable skills in an urban context?

Furthermore, we need a national conversation on rural distress. Much like the decline of the peasant, the interest of historians and social policy observers has also dwindled with regard to capturing their fate. India's rich history has been illustrated with a range of tomes about kings, queens, nawabs and soldiers, and in some cases, even traders—and yet, the peasant himself, and the village economy he sustains, have drawn limited attention. As Eric Stokes, the most famed of agrarian historians at Cambridge, recognized, 'the balance of destiny in South Asia rests in peasant hands.' The challenge, however, has been to capture the travails and tragedies of a social group that resists classification and leaves little, if any, records. The 1970s and '80s saw renewed focus on empirical research that sought to provide a historical reconstruction of our agrarian economy, seeking correlations and dependencies on a range of social factors and social groups. In India, the history of land, especially in rural India, has somehow not gone alongside the history of capital, subsuming documentation about changes in the rural economy under the dialectic between capitalist development and the proletarian masses. Unlike during the Champaran Satyagraha, national attention has been curiously lacking. We must empathize with India's marginal farmers and we must make the choice to support them.

Policymaking in a country riven by rural poverty, social faultlines and inadequate infrastructure should be focused on alleviating rural hardships while building the infrastructure for future growth. The pursuit of grandiose urban infrastructure, and gigantic symbolic statues is a luxury for other nations. This book hopes, through a series of vignettes, to elucidate such issues, with their constraints and potential solutions. It hopes to highlight experiences from my decade-long public life, serving as a Member of Parliament (MP) for mostly rural constituencies, while drawing lessons from sociological experts and development policy. This set of experiences has been distilled into a rural manifesto, one that could help to shift the contours of the rural economy towards a more positive bearing for the marginal farmer.

In writing this heartfelt and, perhaps, timely set of essays on the village economy, I am deeply indebted to India's rich tradition of agricultural economists and agrarian historians, whose contribution is recognized through footnotes scattered across pages. Writing this book has been a learning experience for me as well, helping me understand India's rhythm, particularly of its villages and the aspirations of those living in them. I have travelled far and wide, across a multitude of Indian towns, villages and habitations, and everywhere I have heard stories of sorrow and yet been witness to the generosity and resilience that rural Indians possess. I have drawn on the resources and goodwill of a variety of people, including my research team. Finally, my mother and my wife have lent unstinting emotional and intellectual support, while providing me with a sense of empathy for the downtrodden. It is to them, and my daughter, that I dedicate this book.

CHAPTER I

ON AGRICULTURAL INPUTS

'A farmer cannot work without applying his mind. He must be able to test the nature of his soil, must watch changes of weather, must know how to manipulate his plough skilfully and be generally familiar with the movements of the stars, the sun and the moon. The farmer knows enough of astronomy, geography and geology to serve his needs. Physically, it goes without saying, he is always sturdy. He is his own physician, when ill. Thus, we can see, he does have an educated mind.' — Mahatma Gandhi[1]

In our quest for a shining India, apathy has killed our rural equilibrium. Sometimes, statistics help paint the context. According to a National Sample Survey Office (NSSO) survey, 33 per cent of all farm households have less than 0.4 hectares of land. In Sultanpur district, cultivation cost per hectare for wheat has increased by 33 per cent in five years. Such farmers face an uncertain Hobbesian life—poor, brutish and short. A sense of apathy stalks the hinterland. Changing this requires delving deep into the reasons why marginal agriculture is increasingly uneconomic; gaining a sense of how agricultural input costs simply make our existing cropping pattern unviable. In addition, we need to understand how the access to clean water, the availability of cheap electricity and cooking fuel, and the support of a robust agricultural marketing system enabling price discovery, will play a role in pushing the produce to the market.

It is often assumed that villages stand apart from external trade and commerce, ignored by regional, national and international trading routes. However, other than in non-tribal areas, this is patently untrue—consider villages in Gujarat, Kerala and the Coromandel region, which fostered maritime commerce with the West, trading indigo, cotton, wheat, rice, honey, ginger and spices. Inter-regional trade between villages too remains a historical fact, references to the Kabuliwallah aside. Gujarat

---

1   Mahatma Gandhi Writings, Vol 13: 12 March, 1913 - 25 December, 1913; p. 64

has historically purchased its wheat and opium from the Malwa plateau, rice and coconuts from the Konkan and drugs from the Himalayan foothills. Most Indian villages still produce commodities that are sold to the regional or national market, receiving various goods like salt, spices, clothing, metals and ornaments in return. The American Civil War led to a cotton boom in Gujarat and the former Central Provinces, bringing prosperity and technological advancement. The idea that villages, in this day and age, stand apart from macroeconomic and policy trends, is facile. Indian villages have always been part of a wider entity, affected by roughly built for unpaved roads, limited urban job creation and political dysfunction. This illusion needs to be dispelled.

―――――――

FARMING DECISIONS

Inder Singh, a marginal farmer near Orchha, in Tikamgarh district, amidst the Bundelkhand region of Madhya Pradesh, has a few critical decisions to make before the planting season each year. Bordering a picturesque landscape surrounded by monuments built by the Bundela Rajputs, he faces destitution on an annual basis. Last year's rabi crop was destroyed prior to harvesting, due to extremely hot weather and drought conditions. His loans, covering seeds, fertilizers, crop protection chemicals and machinery lease, required restructuring. Another fallow year could drive him to abandonment.

Bundelkhand's soil covers an impervious rock found at a depth of 6–15 m; it proffers little in organic content or moisture retention. Its soil type is variable, changing every 100 m, while the land is undulating. Some varieties of it, called pahari, found over granite, have little phosphorus or nitrogen content, rendering them unsuitable for farming. Another variety, the parua soil (a yellowish variety of red iron-rich soil) offers some clay and considerable sand—a challenge for all crops except wheat. Black soil, highly prized, is found in limited quantities—kabar, a variety with high clay content, offering greater adhesiveness and moisture retention, is ideal for gram and jowar. Mar, another variety, is prone to waterlogging but offers high organic content, enabling cropping without any fertilizers, and which supports wheat, rice and gram. The region also suffers from significant soil erosion, particularly in Banda, Datia and Hamirpur districts. Its numerous rivers and streams, bifurcated by many nullahs, cut away at the top soil. Of Banda district's 1,722,000 hectares of catchment area, 120,000 hectares were affected by soil erosion (Banda District Gazetteer, 1977, p. 93). With rainfall typically averaging just 930 mm, and most of it concentrated in the monsoon, Orchha and its surrounding areas are typically restricted in cropping choices.

For Inder Singh, there is a host of decisions to make. Should he consider planting annual crops, those producing seeds and dying within the season (e.g. rice, maize, wheat), or should he consider branching out to perennial crops like sugar cane, living for three to four years, and occupying fallow land for more than thirty months? Does he want shorter timelines—pulses only need seventy-five days to grow, but mustard and cotton can occupy nearly 150 days of the year. When should he time his initial tillage (the ideal timing for tillage is usually at 60 per cent of the field capacity)?

Any crop-selection decision would also require an identification of crop usability. To restore crop fertility, restorative crops such as legumes could be utilized to fix nitrogen in root nodules helping to enliven the soil conditions. Other crops can help prevent soil surface erosion through root mats and foliage (e.g. groundnut, sweet potato). Yet other crops could help guard his main produce from trespassing or wind damage (gram surrounded by safflower, cotton surrounded by sorghum). And others could help suppress weed growth through extensive foliage suffocating or obscuring any weeds (mustard, cowpea).

A slight mistake in decision-making can wreak significant havoc. Marginal farmers like Harishchandra Sapkal in Latur district, Maharashtra, planting sugar cane on plots no more than 1.5 acres, have had years of savings wiped out by a bad cropping decision. He invested nearly ₹4 lakh over three years, seeking to move away from risk-averse soyabean and tur to sugar cane, given the handsome returns from the nearby sugar mill. With Latur experiencing little, if any, rain over the past few years, his entire crop has failed, leaving him with little fodder to sustain his livestock. Over 5,000 farmers, spread across 45,000 hectares, are in a similar predicament in the district, with rainfall averaging 50 per cent less than normal.[2]

Even seemingly risk-averse crops can go wrong. Guar, a drought-tolerant crop, grown primarily in Rajasthan, Haryana and parts of Punjab, is typically sown towards July and harvested by November. In many ways, it is an ideal drought crop with little water requirement, a ninety-day maturation period and low input costs; it also fixes nitrogen level, boosting soil fertility. Its seeds contain about 35 per cent endosperm, which is ground and processed into a gum, while the remaining husk and germ are processed into cattle feed called korma and churi. The gum is used as a thickening agent for fracking fluid, a copious cocktail of water, suspended sands and chemicals, which is injected at high pressure into shale rock formations to

---

2 More, M.D., 'Wrong crop pattern, drought'; a farmer reveals why he wants to end his life, The Indian Express, 2 May 2016, Sourced from: http://indianexpress.com/article/india/india-news-india/farmer-suicide-marathwada-latur-drought-sugar cane-crop2781186/

induce oil and gas to flow out of them. Since 2012, guar was being stockpiled by oil servicing companies for the production of this thickening agent, resulting in guar prices rising from $2,000 per tonne to $30,000 per tonne. By 21 March, 2012, guar was costing ₹30,432 per quintal in Jodhpur. Planting of guar nearly doubled in acreage in Rajasthan over 2011–12 and 2013–14, rising from 30.94 lakh hectares to 50.70 lakh hectares. However, the collapse in oil price, along with a removal of export subsidies under the Gram Udyog Yojana led to a steep decline, with guar prices winding down to $1,200 per tonne. Meanwhile, seed prices had risen by 40 per cent in 2015[3] given fears of unseasonal rain and hail. Farmers like Hari Singh in Rajasthan who had benefited in the boom years, are now forced to store their guar crop in warehouses until markets recover.[4]

Meanwhile, Inder Singh's soil type remains a significant constraint. Edaphic factors such as soil moisture, soil air, soil temperature, its mineral matter, organic matter content, existing organisms and reaction can impact productivity. Moisture lost by transpiration can only be made up by absorption from the soil. The absorption rate from this soil depends on soil temperature, with the maximum absorption by roots generally occurring between 20°C and 30°C. The mineral content of the soil, derived from the weathering of rocks and minerals, is a significant source of plant nutrition (from nutrients such as silicon, calcium, magnesium, iron, sodium, etc.). Soil air remains essential for growth and water absorption, and oxygen is needed for respiration of roots and microorganisms. Organic matter content, widely variable (1 per cent in arid sandy soils; 90 per cent in well-developed soils), can have a significant impact on plant growth. If the soil holds enough moisture, he could consider planting potatoes, wheat or sugar cane. On the other hand, if he has built dykes or bunds around to hold stagnant water, he could consider rice or jute. Should his soil discourage water retention, he would have to consider crops tolerant of drought-like conditions, e.g. sorghum. Any sandy or sandy loam soil would support sunflower, potato or onion production. Clay loam would offer moisture to lentil, guinea grass and barley. Acidity in his soils would impose further constraints—acidic soils tend to favour potato or mustard; saline soils offer sustenance to wheat, chillies or bajra. If soil erosion is frequent, groundnut or black gram would be a suitable choice.

The wrong soil type can be a significant impediment. Fazilka district in Punjab, bordering Pakistan and the Sutlej river, typically endures a dry climate with a very hot summer, a short rainy season and a chilly winter. Its soil is sandy in nature,

---

3   Acharya, N., 'Guar seed prices spurt sharply on crop damage', Business Standard, 5 May 2015, sourced from: http://www.business-standard.com/article/markets/guar-seed-prices-spurt-sharply-on-crop-damage-115050500581_1.html

4   Singh, M.P., 'Rajasthan's guar farmers: A tale of interconnectedness', The Indian Express, 8 October 2015, sourced from: http://indianexpress.com/article/india/india-news-india/rajasthans-guar-farmers-a-tale-of-interconnectedness/

deficient in nitrogen, phosphorus and potassium, with wind erosion a significant problem in summer. In July 2016, residents of four border villages (Muthian Wali, Channan Wala, Chudiwala Chisti and Kerian) in this district announced a campaign for 'Vikta Punjab', seeking to sell all four villages and their associated land to the highest bidder, given the woeful scenario of poor soil and lack of irrigation. Ninety-nine per cent of the residents of the villages face heavy debt, with increasing crop failure pushing them to bankruptcy and potential suicide.[5]

The size, topology and geography of the farmer's plot of land also matters. If he has levelled his elevated land with drains all around, he could consider crops that cannot withstand waterlogging—cotton, sorghum, groundnut, etc. The current condition of his land also matters—weeds would require deep ploughing, which would raise costs. Primary tillage, cutting and inverting over 10–30 cm of soil with ploughs or tractors, would help control weeds and restore soil structure. Conducting secondary tillage, by incorporating fertilizers and manure, along with stirring the soil and conditioning it to break down the crust through levelling and pulverizing operations, would require additional effort. Should he wish to avoid preparatory tillage, para grass would be useful.

Intensive cropping can also be considered, subject to water availability and local weather conditions. Multicropping, where two or more crops are grown in a sequence on the same field in a year, can be considered (e.g. rice-rice-cotton). Overlapping cropping, where the crop is harvested in phases, while the vacated area is sown with new crops, is another option (e.g. forage crops with berseem). Intercropping (two or more crops being grown simultaneously), with the associated crop being complementary to the main crop, can offer a significant yield boost. Crops that have different growth habits and limited competition can yield bountiful harvests (e.g. soyabean with cotton) while other combinations can offer synergistic benefits (e.g. potato with sugar cane). Crop rotation can help maintain soil productivity while allowing exhaustive crops to be followed by less exhaustive ones. Such practices offer insurance against drought, while enabling better utilization of labourers.

However, limited water availability could put paid to all plans. If there is no irrigation, cultivation will depend on the quantity and timing of rainfall received, constricting his cropping pattern and the length of his crop season, and eventually impacting crop selection. Rainfall averaging 10–20 cm per month for three months is suitable only for bajra and small millets; heavier rainfall (>20 cm) encourages maize and rice. Irrigation, too, concerns significant uncertainty—the water release

---

5   Four Punjab border villages put on 'sale', farmers left in lurch, Punjab News Express, 9 July 2016, Sourced from: http://punjabnewsexpress.com/punjab/news/four-punjab-border-villages-put-on-sale-farmers-left-in-lurch-51291.aspx

in a canal can be early (allowing for a double crop) or late (allowing for just a single crop). A twenty to thirty-week crop season would enable him to plant a solo crop along with an inter crop, while thirty weeks would allow for a two-crop sequence. He would also have to make choices about which season to plant. Water-associated uncertainties can be equally significant. Farmers in Mandya, Karnataka, had to burn down their entire withered sugar cane crop in May 2016 due to lack of water release from dams and inadequate pre-monsoon rain. Irrigation authorities had stopped water flow from the Krishnarajasagara reservoir to the canals about two months earlier, leaving the sugar cane crop, requiring copious amounts of water, unable to survive in the drought-like conditions. Forced to choose between dying crops and clearing the land for the next cycle, the farmers reposed faith in continued uncertainty.[6]

Surface temperature variations, on a diurnal and annual basis, can play a crucial role in cropping decisions and subsequent yield. In March 2015, extreme weather conditions in Patiala damaged 30 per cent of the wheat crop in the district, with high-speed winds and showers leaving standing crops flattened and causing extensive waterlogging. For farmers like Davinder Singh, from Simbro village, a potentially bumper wheat crop was wiped out by windstorms, leaving him to await nominal compensation from the government.[7] Wheat, barley and oats germinate at an optimum temperature of 20°C with a cardinal temperature range of 4.5°C to 32°C, while maize and sorghum can withstand up to 40°C. Hot-climate plants when exposed to low temperatures can be injured significantly (e.g. a three-day winter spell of 2°C to 4°C would leave bands, a cholorotic condition, on the leaves of sorghum and sugar cane). Frost, seen in hilly areas, can dehydrate plant cell protoplasm, causing severe damage to crops like potato. Heat exposure, on the other hand, can halt growth and increase respiration rates, leading to rapid depletion of reserve food and eventual starvation for the plant. Flowers can be rendered sterile, and seedlings can suffer shrinkage of cambial tissues. With rising temperatures, bajra, jowar or castor are increasingly being planted, while a long winter spell, accompanied by cold or frost, would incentivize cabbage and sugar beet.

Availability and affordability of other agricultural inputs also affect cropping decisions. Inputs like pesticides and fertilizers, when utilized in time, can help improve agricultural yield. Having the right know-how through education, best-practice dissemination and government support are also important factors. To

---

6   TNN, 'Distraught farmers burn down sugar cane crop', The Times of India, 9 May 2016, sourced from: http://timesofindia.indiatimes.com/city/mysuru/Distraught-farmers-burn-down-sugarcane-crop/articleshow/52181623.cms

7   Khaira, H.S., 'Bad weather damages 30 percent of wheat crop in Patiala', Hindustan Times, Patiala, 14 March 2016, Sourced from: http://www.hindustantimes.com/punjab/bad-weather-damages-30-percent-of-wheat-crop-in-patiala/story-U34NTBs89mlcuqomqY9pPK.html

increase yield, hybrid varieties of staple crops (maize, wheat, sunflower, soyabean, etc.), depending on the farmer's economic condition, will warrant consideration.

Once crop selection is done, the timing of sowing is critical. Sowing of seeds is typically conducted after sufficient rainfall has been observed (~20–30 mm), especially in dryland areas. Where heavy monsoonal rains prevail, seeds are sowed seven to ten days before the expected arrival of rain. The depth of sowing would matter as well, with optimum depths typically at 2.5 to 3 cm—the deeper a seed is sowed, the longer the crop takes for maturation, while ensuring crop survival under bad weather conditions. The crop yield would be dependent on plant density and the cropping geometry. High crop density would easily deplete soil moisture, while low crop density would leave moisture, along with land, underutilized. However, yield would drop if crop density rises above the optimum level.

Seed selection is important as well. In 2016, farmers from Narayangaon who planted tomatoes over 20,000 acres in western Maharashtra with TO-1057 seeds provided by Sygenta, saw them ripen with green, yellow or red insides and then rot due to a viral infection. Other farmers from Pargaon, near Narayangaon, planted Sygenta seeds on 6 acres with expectations of 60 to 70 tonnes of tomatoes per acre—their yield was not even 10 tonnes.[8]

Once planting is done, the farmer has to then worry about weed removal. There are various options—manual weeding is arduous. Weeds, essentially undesirable plants that reduce land or water utilization, can easily take advantage of the long maturation time of various crops, competing with them for space, sunlight, soil nutrients and moisture, and leading to a reduction in crop yield (1 kg of weed growth typically leads to 1 kg of crop growth shortfall). Major staple crops can be significantly affected (rice can lose 9.1 to 51.4 per cent; sugar cane, 14.1 to 71.7 per cent; wheat, 6.3 to 34.8 per cent). During the critical period when weed growth rivals crop growth, typically the first thirty-five days for a crop of hundred days' duration, the field needs significant weeding, with concomitant economic returns. While eradication is unlikely, weed control can be conducted through mechanical means (tillage, hoeing, uprooting by hand, digging), cropping methods (crop rotation, mulching, intercropping) and biochemical methods (weedicides, bioherbicides). This would come with costs and the risk of eutrophication. Pests would also require similar application of pesticides.

With so many dynamic variables working favourably and with plant growth occurring, nutrient management becomes critical. Essential elements such as

---

8   Chari, M., 'Tomato price rise: Failed seeds have hurt production, not just extreme heat', Scroll.in, 17 June 2016, sourced from: http://scroll.in/article/810139/tomato-price-rise-failed-seeds-have-hurt-production-not-just-extreme-heat

phosphorus, potassium, magnesium, sulphur, iron, zinc, cobalt, manganese, calcium and so on are required to conduct photosynthesis, stimulate root and stem growth, fix nitrogen and help in protein synthesis, among other uses. A majority of soil tests have highlighted that over 98 per cent of Indian soils have limited phosphorus content, while 47 per cent have a zinc limitation and 60 per cent suffer from potassium deficit. Organic manures, often just plant and animal byproducts, in bulky (cattle manure, village compost or just sewage) and concentrated forms (oil cakes, guano, animal products) can offer varying quantities of plant nutrients and resultant yield improvement. Utilizing bio-fertilizers to encourage nitrogen fixation in the soil can often be a wise long-term choice. Fertilizer choices can be driven by affordability and availability issues, along with their chemical nature. The responsiveness of crops to fertilizer application can be affected by sowing timing, the cropping pattern, and the dosage and method of fertilizer application.

Having planted the crops, harvesting can require time or investments. Timing is again critical—harvesting early would lead to crops containing significant moisture and a larger proportion of immature and constricted grains or fruits. Harvest maturity symptoms need to be watched for—rice is typically harvested thirty-two days after flowering; wheat needs less than 15 per cent of moisture in its grains; groundnut depends on the yellowing of leaves and shedding. Harvesting is typically conducted when at least 75 per cent of the grains/fruits/pods are mature, to optimize yield.

Harvesting methods, ranging from manual to mechanical (combine harvester, threshers, rollers, etc.) require yield planning and equipment leasing. While harvesting and processing, yield losses can be significant: 1–3 per cent during harvesting, 2–6 per cent during threshing, 1–5 per cent during drying, 2–7 per cent during handling and 2–10 per cent during milling. Poor transport facilities to storage and market areas can lead to further losses (typically 2–3 per cent).

Post-harvest, storage/warehousing is critical, particularly for preventing losses (typically 10–25 per cent for cereals, 20–30 per cent for perishables). Moisture content of the produce can encourage pests and pre-germination. Ensuring the optimum storage moisture content assumes criticality (rice requires 14 per cent, wheat 12 per cent, groundnut 6 per cent). Storage options (mud bins, bukhari bins, metal bins), offering varying levels of moisture and pest protection, can become significant economic choices. Along this value chain, the farmer would also need to determine when and where to employ mechanization. From seed bed preparation (tractors, levellers, ploughs, dozers), to sowing and planting (seeder, planter, dibbler), plant protection (harrow, tiller, sprayer, duster), harvesting (harvester, thresher, digger, reaper) and post-harvest agroprocessing (extractor, dehusker, huller, grader), employing mechanization can lead to economies of scale. Farm mechanization can lead to significant input cost savings—seeds (15–20 per cent) and fertilizers (15–20 per cent), along with improving crop yield (5–20 per cent) and reducing farming time (15–20 per cent).[9] Mechanization can help limit post-harvest losses, improving product quality and farmer income, while helping in the conversion of barren land through modern techniques and tools. With a decrease in workload for women, given a rise in labour productivity along with safer farming practices, farming can end up becoming an avenue for growth.

All these decisions and uncertainties leave just a narrow window of economic benefit for the marginal farmers, particularly those living in dryland areas, like Inder Singh. For farmers like him, tracking agricultural input prices is a monthly activity, impacting choices, affecting yields and making the difference between penury and a robust harvest. Of course, managing these dynamic variables in a challenging environment requires an educated mind.

Even when such farmers make the right decisions, their wages can still lag—for a variety of systemic reasons, leading a search for supplementary income. Bijoy Dehri, a farmer from the Santhal Pargana region in Jharkhand, is an adivasi with a large family of ten members, including his parents, his kids and his brother's family. They collectively own about 5 acres of land, on half of which they cultivate green cowpea beans, while planting maize and bajra on the other half. With poor soil fertility and limited application of fertilizers, their crop yield is typically low, so much so that the maize and bajra harvested are not enough to meet the household needs. For him, given other expenses (medical, kids' education and daily expenses), distress sales of such crops at low prices is often required to maintain his working capital. When demonetization kicked in, such farmers were forced to accept far lower rates during distress sales as well. For adivasis like him, farming in arid regions of Jharkhand is inherently a loss-making proposition. Sometimes, given the low yield, farmers like him are unable to even save seeds for the next crop, forcing them to purchase seeds on loan from a local trader at usurious rates (sometimes even in kind at two and a half times the amount of grain borrowed). Instead, they seek to make do by working as agricultural labour in towns in Uttar Pradesh and in Kolkata. The technological advances in agriculture have passed them by, while government support remains lacking.

---

9   Kapur, R., Chouhan, S., Gulati, S., & Saxena, V., Transforming Agriculture Through Mechanization, Grant Thornton, FICCI, 2015

AGRICULTURAL PRODUCTIVITY

This set of uncertainties has consequences, leading to a history of underperformance and rising input prices. Our agricultural yields per hectare are amongst the lowest in the world—for chickpeas, the highest yield in India is recorded in Andhra Pradesh at 1,439 kg;[10] this is lower than that found in Ethiopia at 1,663 kg. Tamil Nadu produces 5,372 kg of maize per hectare, while the United States (US) produces 8,858 kg; Punjab produces 3,952 kg of rice per hectare, China is nearly double at 6,661 kg. Yields in India are ~3 tonnes/hectare, compared to a global average of 4 tonnes/hectare.[11] While yield gains were substantial from the 70's to the 70's, yield per hectare, across major crops, has essentially stagnated over the last decade (Table 1).

Even between states there remains a significant disparity in crop yields, e.g. differ glaringly between rainfall-rich states like Punjab and West Bengal.

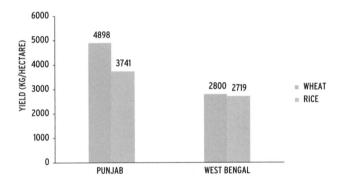

FIGURE 1: YIELD IN PUNJAB VS YIELD IN WEST BENGAL; SOURCE: AGRICULTURAL CENSUS

Some of this is due to the shrinking size of landholdings in India. The average size of landholdings has also declined from 2.28 hectares in 1970–71 to 1.16 hectares in 2010–11. As of 2010–11, 85 per cent of all operational landholdings are classified as small and marginal holdings—with 68 per cent of farms less than 2 acres in size, and 95 per cent less than five. While the number of such holdings is increasing, their average size is declining—a recipe for poor harvests, low incomes and dismal productivity.

---

10   Subramanian, A., A26, Economic Survey 2014-15, Ministry of Finance, February 2015

11   Agrochemicals Knowledge Report, FICCI, Tata Strategic Management Group, Nov 2015. Sourced from: http://ficci.in/spdocument/20662/Agrochemicals-Knowledge-report.pdf

TABLE 1: YIELD PER HECTARE OF MAJOR CROPS[12]

GROUP / COMMODITY	1970-71	1980-81	1990-91	2000-01	(KG / HECTARE) 2012-13	2013-14A
FOODGRAINS	872	1023	1380	1626	2128	2101
KHARIF	837	933	1231	1357	1892	1866
RABI	942	1195	1635	2067	2431	2387
CEREALS	949	1142	1571	1844	2449	2435
KHARIF	892	1015	1357	1512	2116	2084
RABI	1093	1434	2010	2438	2932	2933
PULSES	524	473	578	544	789	764
KHARIF	410	361	471	417	594	593
RABI	607	571	672	604	934	878
RICE	1123	1336	1740	1901	2462	2424
KHARIF	1100	1303	1670	1788	2374	2326
RABI	1625	2071	2671	3042	3353	3274
WHEAT	1307	1630	2281	2708	3117	3075
JOWAR	466	660	814	764	850	925
KHARIF	533	737	969	938	1171	1051
RABI	354	520	582	594	644	847
MAIZE	1279	1159	1518	1822	2566	2583
BAJRA	622	458	658	688	1198	1164
GRAM	663	657	712	744	1036	967
TUR	709	689	673	618	776	848
OILSEEDS	579	532	771	810	1168	1153
KHARIF	649	492	698	757	1135	1123
RABI	449	588	872	929	1244	1221
GROUNDNUT	834	736	904	977	995	1750
KHARIF	NA	629	751	861	811	1712
RABI	NA	1444	1611	1756	1910	1929
RAPESEED AND MUSTARD	594	560	904	935	1262	1188
SUGAR CANE (TONNES/HECT.)	48	58	65	69	70	70
COTTON	106	152	225	190	486	532
JUTE AND MESTA	1032	1130	1634	1867	2281	2449
JUTE	1186	1245	1833	2026	2396	2561
MESTA	684	828	988	1078	1237	1365
PLANTATION CROPS						
TEA	1182	1491	1794	1673	1730	1730
COFFEE	814	624	759	959	766	766
RUBBER	653	788	1076	1576	1206	1206
POTATO (TONNES/HECT.)	10	13	16	18	22	21

---

12 Subramanian, A., A26, Economic Survey 2014-15 Statistical Index, Ministry of Finance, February 2015.
    Sourced from: http://indiabudget.nic.in/es2014-15/estat1.pdf

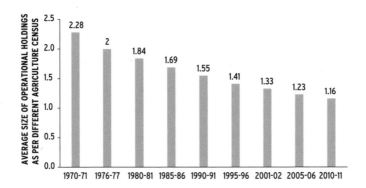

FIGURE 2: AVERAGE SIZE OF LANDHOLDINGS (HA) – ALL INDIA; SOURCE: AGRICULTURAL CENSUSES, ANALYSIS BY TATA STRATEGIC MANAGEMENT GROUP[13]

India's per capita arable land has also declined—from 0.34 hectare in 1950–51 to ~0.15 hectare in 2001; this is projected to decline to 0.07 hectare by 2030.

AGRICULTURAL EQUIPMENT

Limited mechanization is also a significant factor in keeping Indian agricultural yields low, but the reasons for this shortfall vary. Ramesh Meena, hailing from a pastoral adivasi tribe in Jhabua district of Madhya Pradesh, knits his brow when asked about mechanization. His only experience of it has been one of leasing a tractor for a cropping season this year, for the princely sum of ₹300. It certainly did reduce tilling and weeding time, helping him adjust quickly to variable showers this monsoon. Beyond that, he does not care for the range of equipment at the local custom hiring centre (CHC). The gods favour us when they will, he says, and our brute force and draught animals should be enough for ploughing.

Such views apart, mechanization and farming yields have an established link. Purchasing and leasing costs aside, farm mechanization can provide a significant level of input savings across seeds (15–20 per cent) and fertilizers (15–20 per cent)

---

13   Agrochemicals Knowledge Report, FICCI, Tata Strategic Management Group, November 2015. Sourced from: http://ficci.in/spdocument/20662/Agrochemicals-Knowledge-report.pdf

and a concomitant rise in cropping intensity (5–20 per cent).[14] It can improve the efficiency of local farm labour, while reducing drudgery and overall workloads, and cut tilling time by 15–20 per cent. When harvesting season comes, mechanization can help cut harvesting time while reducing post-harvesting losses, of which all allows farmers to earn more. Apart from this, 'banjar land', often found hard to till by hand, can be steered towards food production through assiduous use of mechanization, while encouraging the youth to stick with farming as a profession.

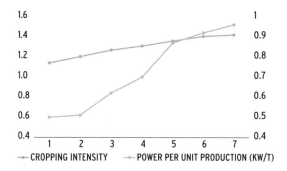

FIGURE 3: INCREASES IN CROPPING INTENSITY ARE CORRELATED WITH INCREASES IN POWER PER UNIT PRODUCTION[15]

However, despite such benefits, the mechanical tools in use are mostly antique. Our ancient text, *Krishi Parasara*, provides details of a basic plough, with mention of abadha (disc plough), phalika (a ploughing blade), vidhaka (spiked tooth) and madika (wooden plank), with Kashyapa advocating the use of strong wood like tinduka, tinisha or a sarjaka.[16] Kashyapa also refers to the dual worship of the plough and the bullocks. The basic plough has hardly undergone any fundamental design change since then. Hand tools have become prevalent; there were an estimated 809.22 million hand tools in 2010, serving an agriculture labour force of 269.74 million people, about three tools per labourer.[17] Such hand tools have significant disadvantages—accounting for 34.2 per cent of accidents in agriculture

14   Transforming Agriculture through mechanization, Grant Thornton. Sourced from: http://www.grantthornton.in/globalassets/1.-member-firms/india/assets/pdfs/cima_agrimach.pdf

15   Farm Mechanization in India, the custom hiring perspective, Yes Bank. Sourced from: https://www.yesbank.in/pdf/farm_mechanization_in_india_%E2%80%93_the_custom_hiring_perspective.pdf

16   Chandrasekaran, B., Annadurai, K., & Somasundaram, E. (2010). A textbook of agronomy. New Delhi: New Age International.

17   Shreshta S., Testing of Hand Tools and Non-Motorized Machines used in Agriculture in Asia Pacific Region, Nepal Agricultural Research Council, UNAPCAEM, 2012, Available at: http://www.unapcaem.org/Activities%20Files/A1205_AS/PPT/np.pdf

(Indian Council of Agricultural Research [ICAR], 2007) with 70 per cent of all such injuries taking more than a week to heal. Despite this, even now bullock-drawn implements evoke significant interest, with the wooden plough predominant.

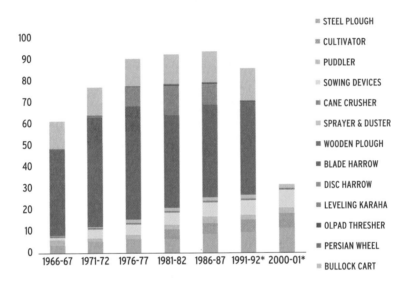

FIGURE 4: BULLOCK-DRAWN IMPLEMENTS CONTINUE TO EVOKE INTEREST. ANNUAL GROWTH IN NUMBER OF BULLOCK-DRAWN IMPLEMENTS IN INDIA[18]

It can be quite tough to afford modern farming equipment associated with animal labour. A simple 40 horsepower (hp) tractor, with a rotavator and a cultivator, can cost ₹8 lakh without subsidies.[19] Farmers in Khadki Budruk village of Jalgaon district, Maharashtra, face this problem annually, resulting in significant debt combined with high interest rates imposed by the local moneylender. Taking steps to improve their meagre agricultural yield of just 2 quintals of cotton using farm equipment is beyond their capacity. A pair of bulls can cost anything between ₹50,000 and ₹70,000, while hiring a pair for the day could cost up to ₹500—many marginal farmers choose to forgo both and use their own hands to till their

18   Agricultural Research Data Book, 2001, and Ministry of Agriculture, Govt. of India, Indiastat data

19   Urs, A., 'How a Karnataka experiment can revolutionise agriculture in India', Business Standard, 24 August 2015. Sourced from : http://www.business-standard.com/article/punditry/how-a-karnataka-experiment-can-revolutionize-agriculture-in-india-115082300320_1.html

land.[20] Even maintaining a pair of bullocks is now expensive, given the high price of fodder and the impact on horseshoes from metalled roads. A shoeing session can now cost ₹500 or so, and is usually required monthly. Purchasing tractors remains a long shot for most marginal farmers.

TABLE 2: ILLUSTRATIVE TABLE OF OPTIONS FOR FARM EQUIPMENT,
WITH EXAMPLE CHOICES SHOWN[21]

ACTIVITY	EQUIPMENT SELECTION				FINANCING
	BY HAND	ANIMAL-DRAWN	TRACTOR-OPERATED	POWER-OPERATED	LEASE OR BUY
LAND PREPARATION	√	X	NA		NA
SEEDBED PREPARATION		√		?	LEASE
SOWING	√			√	LEASE
PLANTING		√		?	LEASE
WEEDING	X		√	√	LEASE
FERTILIZER APPLICATION			√		LEASE
SPRAYING				X	BUY
IRRIGATION				X	BUY
HARVESTING		√	√		LEASE
THRESHING			√		LEASE
PACKAGING	√	X			LEASE
TRANSPORTATION TO MARKET				√	LEASE

And yet, at a relatively slow pace, India's agriculture sector is slowly moving towards significant mechanization (extent of mechanization across value chain levels: soil working and seed preparation—40 per cent, seeding and planting—29 per cent, plant protection—34 per cent, irrigation—37 per cent, harvesting and threshing—60–70 per cent) for wheat and rice.[22, 23]

---

20   Katoch, M., 'In the Face of Extreme Hardship, This Farmer Did Something Incredibly Brave to Till His Land', The Better India, 2 July 2016, Sourced from: http://www.thebetterindia.com/60318/vitthal-mandole-tilled-farm-with-cot-jalgaon/

21   'Farm Mechanization in India, the Custom Hiring Perspective', Yes Bank. sourced from: https://www.yesbank.in/pdf/farm_mechanization_in_india_%E2%80%93_the_custom_hiring_perspective.pdf

22   Kapur, R., Chouhan, S., Gulati, S., & Saxena, V., 'Transforming Agriculture Through Mechanization', Grant Thornton, FICCI, 2015

23   Singh, Dr S., Country Presentation Paper (India), Regional Roundtable of National Agricultural Machinery Associations in Asia and the Pacific—Connection for Cooperation and Development, Agricultural Machinery Manufacturers' Association (AMMA-India), 28-30 October 2014, Wuhan, China. Sourced from: http://un-csam.org/ppta/201410wuhan/3IN.pdf

TABLE 3: PRESENT STATUS OF MECHANIZATION OF CROPS (2013–14)[24]

CROPS	PER CENT OPERATIONS MECHANIZED			
	SEEDBED PREPARATION	SOWING/PLANTING/ TRANSPLANTING	WEED AND PEST CONTROL	HARVESTING AND THRESHING
PADDY	85–90	5–10	80–90	70–80
WHEAT	90–95	80–90	70–80	80–90
POTATO	90–95	80–90	80–90	70–80
COTTON	90–95	50–60	50–60	0
MAIZE	90–95	80–90	70–80	50–60
GRAM (CHICKPEA)	90–95	50–60	60–70	30–40

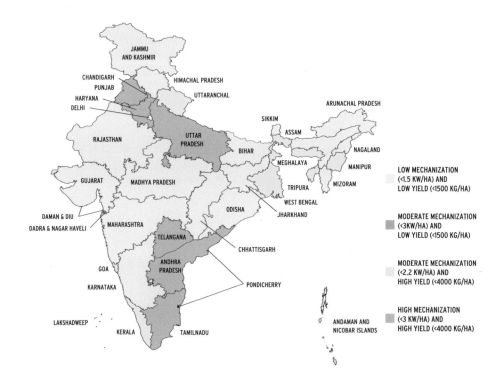

FIGURE 5: INDIA'S FARM MECHANIZATION STORY HAS A LONG WAY TO GO,
ESPECIALLY IN RAIN-DEFICIENT STATES (2010–11)[25]

24 Singh, Dr S., Country Presentation Paper (India), Regional Roundtable of National Agricultural Machinery Associations in Asia and the Pacific —Connection for Cooperation and Development, Agricultural Machinery manufacturers' Association (AMMA-India), 28-30 October 2014, Wuhan, China. Sourced from: http://un-csam.org/ppta/201410wuhan/3IN.pdf

25 Ministry of Agriculture, Government of India, 2010-11; 'Farm Mechanization in India, Custom Hiring Perspective', Yes Bank. Sourced from: https://www.yesbank.in/pdf/farm_mechanization_in_india_%E2%80%93_the_custom_hiring_perspective.pdf

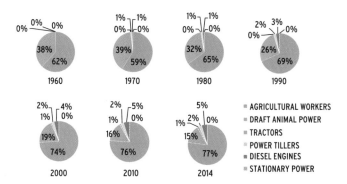

FIGURE 6: AGRICULTURAL WORKERS CONTINUE TO SUPPLY THE MAJORITY POWER SOURCE
(IN NUMBERS, NOT POWER) FOR FARM EQUIPMENT[26]

India purchased 747,826 units of farm equipment, worth $6.37 billion, in 2014,[27] buying tractors, rotavators, threshers, power tillers, combine harvesters and rice transplanters. India's domestic supply is provided by around 250 medium- to large-scale units, 2,500 small-scale units, 15,000 tiny industries and over 100,000 village-level artisans.[28] This is supported by a network of R&D and academic institutions (e.g. All India Coordinated Research Project on Spices, AICRPS).

Tractors account for the largest share (66.1 per cent in 2013)—over 697,695 tractors were sold in FY14 (including exports), with an expected growth of 8–9 per cent over the next five years. Penetration has grown to one per 30 acres, from one per 150 acres. The thresher and rotavator markets saw growth at 2 per cent and 21 per cent, respectively between 2008 and 2013. This growth has been encouraged by financing provided by non-banking financial companies (NBFCs), along with limited farm labour and shortening replacement cycle. In addition, the variation in minimum support price (MSP) rates has impacted farmer purchases, with lower MSPs leaving little discretionary income for such purchases. India's tractor penetration is still limited while marginal farmers own even less. With limited

26 'Farm Mechanization in India, the custom hiring perspective', Yes Bank. Sourced from: https://www.yesbank.in/pdf/farm_mechanization_in_india_%E2%80%93_the_custom_hiring_perspective.pdf

27 Kapur, R., Chouhan, S., Gulati, S., & Saxena, V., 'Transforming Agriculture Through Mechanization', Grant Thornton, FICCI, 2015

28 Singh, Dr S., Country Presentation Paper (India), Regional Roundtable of National Agricultural Machinery Associations in Asia and the Pacific—Connection for Cooperation and Development, Agricultural Machinery Manufacturers' Association (AMMA-India), 28-30 October 2014, Wuhan, China. Sourced from: http://un-csam.org/ppta/201410wuhan/3IN.pdf

purchases of other farming equipment, India has undergone 'tractorization',[29] instead of large-scale mechanization. India has ~3.1 million tractors representing a 10.7 per cent share in the global tractor market, next only to the US.

TABLE 4: NUMBER OF HOUSEHOLDS USING FARM IMPLEMENTS BY LAND-SIZE[30]

FARM SIZE GROUP	HAND-OPERATED		ANIMAL-OPERATED		POWER-OPERATED IMPLEMENTS		SHARE OF HIRED MACHINE HOURS (%)	
	1997	2007	1997	2007	1997	2007	1997	2007
MARGINAL	218.3	150.8	160.1	107	17.3	51	92	96
SMALL	83.6	47.6	75.9	47.1	9.9	23.7	83	89
SEMI-MEDIUM	59.2	29.4	58.9	30.2	10.4	19.8	57	63
MEDIUM	33.5	14.1	35.7	14.1	8.4	13.3	49	43
LARGE	9.8	2.8	10.7	2.2	2.6	3	33	27
ALL GROUPS	404.4	244.7	341.4	200.5	48.6	111	-	-

However, mechanization has a long way to go—China bought 4,213,212 units of farm equipment, worth $58.87 billion, in 2014, while exporting $9.38 billion worth of farming equipment. China has attained significant mechanization—ploughing is now 76 per cent mechanized while harvesting is 47 per cent mechanized. Canada has mechanized 95 per cent of all farming activities, while Canadian farmers buy farming equipment worth $2 billion, with an average of 19,000 tractors, 3,500 swathers and 4,000 grain combines, despite having just 2 per cent of its 35 million population in agriculture.

TABLE 5: ANNUAL MARKET OF MAJOR FARM MACHINERY USED IN INDIA[31]

ITEM	NO. OF UNITS SOLD IN INDIA IN FY14
TRACTORS	600,000-700,0001
MB PLOW	45,000-50,000
CULTIVATORS	150,000-200,000
SEED-FERTILIZER DRILLS	60,000-75,000
RICE TRANSPLANTERS	2,000-3,000
REAPERS	10,000-15,000
COMBINE HARVESTERS	3,500-4,000
SPRAYERS (TD)	10,000-15,000

29   Kapur, R., Chouhan, S., Gulati, S., & Saxena, V, 'Transforming Agriculture Through Mechanization', Grant Thornton, FICCI, 2015

30   Input Survey, Agriculture Census Division and plot level summary data under cost of cultivation, Directorate of Economics and Statistics, Ministry of Agriculture, Government of India, New Delhi.

31   Singh, Dr S., Country Presentation Paper (India), Regional Roundtable of National Agricultural Machinery Associations in Asia and the Pacific—Connection for Cooperation and Development, Agricultural Machinery Manufacturers' Association (AMMA-India), 28-30 October 2014, Wuhan, China. Sourced from: http://un-csam.org/ppta/201410wuhan/3IN.pdf

POTATO DIGGERS	25,000–30,000
POWER TILLERS	50,000–60,000
ROTAVATORS	100,000–120,000
HARROWS	120,000–150,000
PLANTERS	15,000–25,000
POWER WEEDERS	35,000–40,000
THRESHERS	60,000–75,000
TRAILERS	150,000–175,000
LASER LAND LEVELLERS	2,500–3,500
ROTARY HOES/POWER WEEDERS	20,000–25,000

This trend towards mechanization has been accompanied by an increase in farm power availability, despite issues in power transmission and distribution, rising from 1.05 kW/hectare in 1995–96 to 2.02 kW/hectare in 2013–14.[32]

TABLE 6: CROPPING INTENSITY, POWER AVAILABILITY ON INDIAN FARMS[33]

YEAR	CROPPING INTENSITY (%)	PRODUCTIVITY (T/HA)	POWER AVAILABLE (KW/HA)	POWER PER UNIT PRODUCTION (KW/T)	NET SOWN AREA PER TRACTOR (HA)
1965-66	114	0.636	0.32	0.5	2162
1975-76	120	0.944	0.48	0.51	487
1985-86	127	1.184	0.73	0.62	174
1995-96	131	1.5	1.05	0.7	84
2004-05	135	1.65	1.47	0.89	47
2009-10	130.2	1.85	1.73	0.96	36
2013-14	141	2.11	2.02	0.96	27

While mechanization is an obvious solution, for marginal farmers like Inder Singh economies of scale can be non-existent. The average Indian farm size is less than 2 acres (the US around 170 acres), and often non-contiguous, making it hard and in some cases impossible, to operate large farm machinery, particularly for land preparation or harvesting. In addition, agricultural equipment can prove unreliable, with poor after-sales service, and a limited feedback system. There are few mandatory safety standards for machinery usage and quality, providing limited incentives to manufacturers to invest in quality and modern technologies.

---

32   Singh, Dr S., Country Presentation Paper (India) Regional Roundtable of National Agricultural Machinery Associations in Asia and the Pacific—Connection for Cooperation and Development, Agricultural Machinery Manufacturers' Association (AMMA-India), 28-30 October 2014, Wuhan, China. Sourced from: http://un-csam.org/ppta/201410wuhan/3IN.pdf

33   Ibid

FARMER BEHAVIOUR

But beyond price, there are a lot of reasons why uptake for mechanized equipment has been constrained. While farmers purchase tractors for a variety of reasons, including brand name, price, fuel consumption efficiency, maintenance cost, resale value, colour, driving convenience and overall design, their usage of tractors can be atypical. While tractors are ideally suited for tillage, threshing and transportation of farm produce and inputs, many farmers are often seen putting tractors to other uses—transporting people and local materials, for one. Such activities can limit the life of a tractor (typically ten to fifteen years) and lower its overall utilization for agricultural activities. The returns on investment in a tractor can be impacted by the farm size, the type of cropping pattern, the cultivation technology utilized and lease/buy decisions.[34]

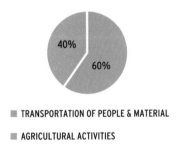

■ TRANSPORTATION OF PEOPLE & MATERIAL

■ AGRICULTURAL ACTIVITIES

FIGURE 7: LIFETIME USAGE—SPLIT BY ACTIVITIES[35]

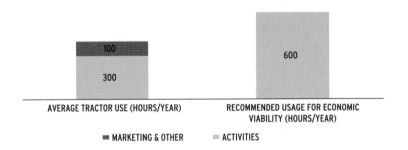

■ MARKETING & OTHER   ▩ ACTIVITIES

FIGURE 8: UTILIZATION OF TRACTORS—ACTUAL VS RECOMMENDED (IN HOURS/YEAR)[36]

---

34 Singh & Sidhu, 1990

35 Singh, S., Agricultural Machinery Industry in India, CMA Publication No. 230, April 2009
    Sourced from: http://www.iimahd.ernet.in/users/webrequest/files/
    cmareports/3AgriculturalMachineryIndustry.pdf

36 Singh, S., Agricultural Machinery Industry in India, CMA Publication No. 230, April 2009
    Sourced from: http://www.iimahd.ernet.in/users/webrequest/files/
    cmareports/3AgriculturalMachineryIndustry.pdf

Such behaviour can also vary by caste (with landed, upper castes and other backward classes (OBCs) typically seen as owning tractors)—only those with large, medium and small acreage holdings typically own tractors; marginal farmers are unlikely to come into play here. Similar variations can be seen across states, with Punjab and Haryana predominating.

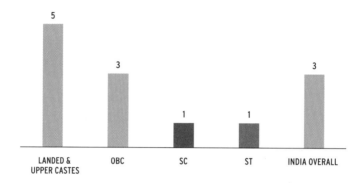

FIGURE 9: AVERAGE TRACTOR OWNERSHIP (NUMBER OF TRACTORS PER 100 HECTARES) ACROSS CASTE GROUPS, AS OF 2009[37]

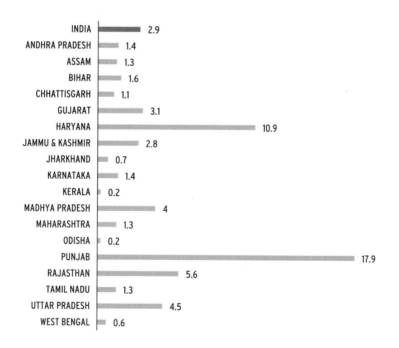

FIGURE 10: TRACTOR OWNERSHIP VARIES BY STATE (DATA AS OF 2009)[38]

37   Ibid

38   NSSO Report No. 497

PROCURING FARMING EQUIPMENT

Purchasing farm equipment on the basis of a government subsidy is a tedious and anguish-ridden process. A farmer needs to have his land records verified through various departments, along with additional checks by the District Agriculture Officer, to gain approval and clearance for purchase. In addition, tendering conducted by the government for bulk purchase can be prolonged and ill-timed. In certain states, tendering can lag until August and September-end, with the main cropping season ending. The absence of historical farm machinery tendering data, along with information on usage, breakdown patterns, and repair and management costs—all at a granular level—prevent market growth and financing expansion.

FIGURE 11: TYPICAL FARMING EQUIPMENT PROCUREMENT PROCESS FOR AN ELIGIBLE FARMER[39]

More important, any farming equipment, when bought upfront, is capital-intensive (~90 per cent of all tractors bought in India are done so with financing)[40]. As such, financing can prove to be a significant hurdle to increasing agricultural productivity. However, tractor loans are increasingly facing payment collection issues—almost 15 per cent of tractor loans distributed over 2014 and 2015 were due for payment for more than three months, compared with an average delinquency rate of 9 per cent in 2009. Average interest rates for such loans have risen from 17 per cent in 2010 to 21 per cent in 2014–15. Consequentially, we have witnessed a decline in medium- to long-term credit supply to the agriculture sector (such loans comprised

---

39   Singh, S., 'Agricultural Machinery Industry in India', CMA Publication No. 230, April 2009
      Sourced from: http://www.iimahd.ernet.in/users/webrequest/files/
      cmareports/3AgriculturalMachineryIndustry.pdf

40   Kapur, R., Chouhan, S., Gulati, S., & Saxena, V.,'Transforming Agriculture Through Mechanization',
      Grant Thornton, FICCI, 2015

25 per cent of total farm credit in 2014–15, versus 40 per cent in 2004–05).[41]

Despite such schemes and subsidies provided by the government, farmers continue to have limited options for financing. High collateral requirements, especially for loans of more than ₹1 lakh, along with short repayment periods (five to seven years) and high interest rates are hindrances to significant mechanization. Purchasing standalone equipment is seemingly frowned upon—many financial institutions insist on purchase of tractors along with other equipment, which discourages farmers. In addition, the presence of a 'pricing cartel'[42] is rife in the farming equipment sector—prices of equipment under subsidy are considered to be higher than the market price of such equipment. Manufacturers also face issues of excise duties on intermediate parts (e.g. high-quality gear boxes) that are imported for assembly and usage.

CUSTOM HIRING

India's farming sector has also seen the emergence of custom hiring of farming equipment since the late '80s. This provides a selection of farming machinery, tools and other equipment for hire on a rental basis to farmers who are unable to afford or finance the purchase of high-end machinery. Highly mechanized states like Punjab, Gujarat, Uttar Pradesh and Haryana have seen the development of a secondary market for equipment hire. This segment is significantly unorganized and regionally variant, with a long gestation period—given low asset utilization after periods of seasonal cropping. It has a limited scale, preventing efficient operation, and is constrained by capital intensiveness. With a significant barrier for small entrepreneurs, given poor creditworthiness and high collateral requirements (separate from any hypothecation of farming equipment), such centres cry out for policy intervention.

Madhya Pradesh implemented the Yantradoot Scheme for Promotion of Farm Mechanization in 2009. The scheme sought to establish mission villages across twenty-five districts, where district-level officers would provide information associated with mechanization of agricultural operations, along with on-site

---

41   Bera, S., 'Overdue tractor loans reveal stress in farm sector', Live Mint, 1 July 2016, Sourced from: http://www.livemint.com/Politics/abt2xZgZ65UbKoBAhJ60bJ/Overdue-tractor-loans-reveal-stress-in-farm-sector.html

42   Kapur, R., Chouhan, S., Gulati, S., & Saxena, V., 'Transforming Agriculture Through Mechanization', Grant Thornton, FICCI, 2015

demonstrations. They would also provide such machines for rent at a nominal rate through newly set up CHCs—enabling a farmer to, for instance, hire a tractor for an hour for ₹300, including the cost of diesel and the driver. Such rates are typically well below market rates (more than ₹500 per hour). In such villages farming has been transformed, with mechanization prevailing and agricultural productivity rising by 40 per cent. While soya, a mainstay of these villages, earlier had a production of 2 to 3 quintals per acre, it has now jumped to 15 to 16 quintals per acre.

In Punjab, agro service centres were established in 1972, with a focus on providing employment and the provision of custom hiring services to marginal farmers. With farmers growing richer and purchasing small-powered tractors, such centres were phased out. More recently, the Punjab State Farmers Commission sought to strengthen Primary Agriculture Cooperative Societies (PACS) through subsidies for purchasing costly farming machines and equipment, transforming them into Cooperative Agro-Service Centres (CASCs). This distribution model has helped reduce capital investment on machinery, with machines typically hired at 16 per cent lower rates than from private operators.

Tamil Nadu implemented the Agricultural Mechanization Programme in FY15, with funding assistance from both the centre and state, equally. The programme, with an outlay of ₹1,080 lakh in FY15, sought to increase the penetration of farm mechanization among small and marginal farmers, particularly in areas where availability of farm power was low, through subsidy assistance to farmers for purchasing tractors, power tillers, rice transplanters, animal-drawn implements, plant protection systems, etc.

Such custom hiring centres (CHCs) should be promoted and encouraged beyond their traditional outlook—they can serve to disseminate information about local, condition-specific equipment, along with helping to form cooperatives of marginal and small farmers. They can serve as markets for sale of second-hand equipment and any subsequent after-sales service. Small outlets of such CHCs, organized in a 'hub and spoke' model, can help provide last-mile outreach.[43] An institutional framework, for custom hiring to benefit farmers, is the need of the hour.

---

43 Kapur, R., Chouhan, S., Gulati, S., & Saxena, V., 'Transforming Agriculture Through Mechanization', Grant Thornton, FICCI, 2015

GOVERNMENT SUPPORT

India's agricultural policy provides limited support to such practices. The Rashtriya Krishi Vikas Yojana (RKVY), launched in 2007–08, sought to provide assistance for establishing CHCs. The Mission for Integrated Development of Horticulture (MIDH), a scheme focusing on the overall growth of the horticulture sector, seeks horticulture mechanization by providing assistance for procurement of power-operated machines and imports along with a 40 per cent subsidy to grower associations and farmer groups engaged in horticulture. The Sub-Mission on Agricultural Mechanization (SMAM), part of the National Mission on Agricultural Extension and Technology, has sought to increase the reach of farm mechanization to small and marginal farmers, while 'promoting custom hiring centres and financial incentives to offset the adverse economies of scale associated by the high cost of individual ownership and small landholding sizes'. It has sought to do this by creating hubs for hi-tech farm equipment ownership, designating testing centres for performance testing and certification, and creating awareness amongst farmers through demonstration and capacity-building activities.

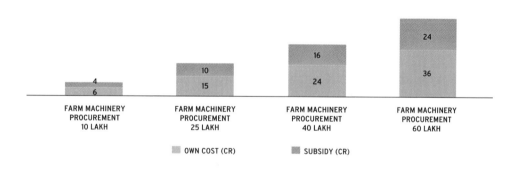

FIGURE 12: FINANCIAL ASSISTANCE UNDER SMAM FOR PROCURING
FARM MACHINERY FOR CHCS[44]

---

44   'Farm Mechanization in India, the Custom Hiring Perspective', Yes Bank, Sourced from: https://www.yesbank.in/pdf/farm_mechanization_in_india_%E2%80%93_the_custom_hiring_perspective.pdf

FIGURE 13: SMAM SUBSIDY ACROSS STATES IN FY16 IN LAKH[45]

All of this cumulatively leads to an effective subsidy of 25–50 per cent from the government for farming machinery/equipment purchase, subject to ceiling limits associated with the respective schemes (National Food Security Mission, RKVY, National Horticulture Mission, etc.). The Union Budget 2013–14 allocated ₹2,250 crore ($339.5 million) towards such schemes, seeking to encourage 5.79 lakh demonstrations of improved packaging practices for rice, wheat and pulses. Around 43,656 farmer field schools (FFS) were encouraged for capacity-building while nearly ₹30.16 lakh worth of farm machinery was distributed. The government allocated ₹3,707 ($559.4 million) towards RKVY and its sub-initiatives in 2015–16 and ₹2,000 ($300 milion) as a subsidy for farming equipment under SMAM.

---

45   'Farm Mechanization in India, the custom hiring perspective', Yes Bank. Sourced from: https://www.yesbank.in/pdf/farm_mechanization_in_india_%E2%80%93_the_custom_hiring_perspective.pdf

A brief look at all subsidy interventions in the state of Maharashtra

TABLE 7: MACHINERY & TECHNOLOGY—ASSISTANCE SCHEMES IN MAHARASHTRA.[46]

NO.	TYPE OF ASSISTANCE	QUANTUM OF ASSISTANCE	SCHEME
1	TRACTOR UP TO 40 HP	₹45,000 OR 25 PER CENT OF THE COST, WHICHEVER IS LESS	MACRO MANAGEMENT MODE OF AGRICULTURE (MMA)
2	POWER TILLER	₹45,000 OR 40 PER CENT OF THE COST, WHICHEVER IS LESS FOR 8 BHP AND ABOVE ₹25,000 OR 40 PER CENT OF THE COST, WHICHEVER IS LESS FOR 8 BHP	MMA
3	SELF-PROPELLED REAPER, PADDY TRANSPLANTER AND OTHER SIMILAR SELF-PROPELLED MACHINES	₹45,000 OR 25 PER CENT OF THE COST, WHICHEVER IS LESS	MMA
4	SPECIAL POWER-DRIVEN EQUIPMENT LIKE RAISED BED PLANTER, SUGAR CANE PLANTER, ETC.	₹20,000 OR 40 PER CENT OF THE COST, WHICHEVER IS LESS	MMA
5	SPECIAL POWER-DRIVEN IMPLEMENTS LIKE POTATO PLANTER, POTATO DIGGER. ETC.	₹15,000 OR 25 PER CENT OF THE COST, WHICHEVER IS LESS	MMA
6	MANUALLY OPERATED IMPLEMENTS	₹2,000 OR 25 PER CENT OF THE COST, WHICHEVER IS LESS	MMA
7	POWER THRESHER/ MULTI-CROP THRESHER	₹12,000 OR 25 PER CENT OF THE COST, WHICHEVER IS LESS	
8	MANUALLY OPERATED IMPLEMENTS/TOOLS	₹2,000 OR 25 PER CENT OF THE COST, WHICHEVER IS LESS	
9	ANIMAL-DRIVEN IMPLEMENTS	₹2,500 OR 25 PER CENT OF COST, WHICHEVER IS LESS	
10	DIESEL OR ELECTRIC PUMP SET FOR IRRIGATION	₹100,000 OR 50 PER CENT OF THE COST, WHICHEVER IS LESS	
11	AERO BLAST SPRAYER-PLANT PROTECTION EQUIPMENT	₹25,000 OR 25 PER CENT OF THE COST, WHICHEVER IS LESS	
12	TRACTOR-DRIVEN PLANT PROTECTION EQUIPMENT	₹4,000 OR 25 PER CENT OF THE COST, WHICHEVER IS LESS	
13	POWER-OPERATED PLANT PROTECTION EQUIPMENT	₹2,000 OR 25 PER CENT OF THE COST, WHICHEVER IS LESS	
14	MANUAL PLANT PROTECTION EQUIPMENT	₹800 OR 25 PER CENT OF THE COST, WHICHEVER IS LESS	
15	POWER-DRIVEN EQUIPMENT (TRACTOR-OPERATED)	₹10,000 OR 25 PER CENT OF COST, WHICHEVER IS LESS	
16	POWER TILLER-OPERATED EQUIPMENT	₹10,000 OR 25 PER CENT OF COST, WHICHEVER IS LESS FOR ONE SET OF IMPLEMENTS	
17	ROTAVATOR	₹20,000 OR 40 PER CENT OF THE COST, WHICHEVER IS LESS	MMA AND NFSM
18	ZERO TILL SEED DRILL/MULTICROP PLANTER/ SEED FERTILISER DRILL/ POWER WEEDER	₹15,000 OR 25 PER CENT OF THE COST, WHICHEVER IS LESS	NFSM AND MMA
19	CONO WEEDER AND OTHER FARM IMPLEMENTS	₹3,000 OR 50 PER CENT OF THE COST, WHICHEVER IS LESS	NFSM
20	PUMP SET (UP TO 10 HP)	₹10,000 OR 50 PER CENT OF THE COST, WHICHEVER IS LESS	NFSM

46   Krishi Handbook (English Version), Publication No. 1762, Department of Agriculture, Government of Maharashtra, August 2012

21	KNAP SACK SPRAYERS (MANUAL OR POWERED)	₹3,000 OR 50 PER CENT OF THE COST, WHICHEVER IS LESS	
22	ESTABLISHMENT OF PRIMARY POST-HARVEST UNIT BY GROUP OF FARMERS/ YOUTH.	₹2 LAKH OR 40 PER CENT OF THE COST, WHICHEVER IS LESS	POST-HARVEST MANAGEMENT
23	MANUAL / BULLOCK-DRIVEN IMPLEMENT FOR OILSEEDS, PULSES, OIL PALM AND MAIZE	₹2,500 PER IMPLEMENT	INTEGRATED SCHEME ON OILSEEDS, PULSES, OIL PALM AND MAIZE (ISOPOM)
24	POWER-DRIVEN IMPLEMENT FOR OILSEEDS, PULSES, OIL PALM AND MAIZE	₹15,000 PER IMPLEMENT	ISOPOM
25	SETTING UP PRIMARY AND SECONDARY PROCESSING OF MILLETS	₹4 LAKH FOR PRIMARY AND SECONDARY PROCESSING OF SORGHUM, PEARL MILLET AND RAGI. ₹2 LAKH PER PRIMARY UNIT OF SMALL MILLETS	INITIATIVE FOR NUTRITIONAL SECURITY THROUGH INTENSIVE MILLETS PROMOTION (INSIMP)
26	POWER-OPERATED MACHINES/TOOLS INCLUDING POWER SAW AND PLANT PROTECTION EQUIPMENTS	LIMITED TO ₹35,000 PLIER PER SET, 50 PER CENT OF THE COST (LIMITED TO ONE SET PER BENEFICIARY)	NHM
27	POWER MACHINE UP TO 20 BHP WITH ROTAVATOR/EQUIPMENT)	LIMITED TO ₹1.20 LAKH PER SET, 50 PER CENT OF THE COST (LIMITED TO ONE SET PER BENEFICIARY)	NHM
28	POWER MACHINE (20 BHP AND ABOVE) INCLUDING ACCESSORIES/EQUIPMENTS	LIMITED TO ₹3 LAKH PER SET, 50 PER CENT OF THE COST (LIMITED TO ONE SET PER BENEFICIARY)	NHM
29	IMPORT OF NEW MACHINES AND TOOLS FOR HORTICULTURE FOR DEMONSTRATION PURPOSE	LIMITED TO ₹50 LAKH PER MACHINE, 100 PER CENT OF THE TOTAL COST	NHM
30	ANIMAL-DRIVEN IMPLEMENTS	₹2500 OR 25 PER CENT OF THE COST, WHICHEVER IS LESS	MMA
31	ANIMAL-DRIVEN TOOL CARRIER	₹6,000 OR 25 PER CENT OF THE COST, WHICHEVER IS LESS	MMA
32	SETTING UP OF PRIMARY AND SECONDARY PROCESSING UNITS FOR MILLET CROPS	₹4 LAKH FOR PRIMARY AND SECONDARY UNITS	INITIATIVE FOR NUTRITIONAL SECURITY THROUGH INTENSIVE MILLETS PROMOTION (INSIMP)
33	MULTI-CROP THRESHER	50 PER CENT OF COST, LIMITED TO ₹24,000 PER UNIT	OILSEED PRODUCTION PROGRAMME (OPP)
34	BRUSH CUTTER WITH ACCESSORIES	50 PER CENT OF COST, LIMITED TO ₹30,000 PER UNIT	OPP
35	DISTRIBUTION OF PLANT PROTECTION EQUIPMENT (MANUALLY OPERATED)	50 PER CENT OF COST, LIMITED TO ₹800 PER EQUIPMENT	OPP
36	DISTRIBUTION OF PLANT PROTECTION EQUIPMENT (POWER-OPERATED)	50 PER CENT OF COST, LIMITED TO ₹2,000 PER EQUIPMENT	OPP
37	SUPPLY OF IMPROVED FARM IMPLEMENTS (MANUALLY OPERATED)	50 PER CENT OF COST, LIMITED TO ₹2,500 PER IMPLEMENT	OPP
38	SUPPLY OF IMPROVED FARM IMPLEMENTS (POWER-OPERATED)	50 PER CENT OF COST, LIMITED TO ₹15,000/IMPLEMENT	OPP
39	SUPPLY OF HDPE/PVC PIPES	ASSISTANCE OF 50 PER CENT OF COST OR ₹15,000 FOR WATER-CARRYING PIPES UP TO 800 M AND ALL TYPES OF PIPES I.E. PVC, HDPE, ETC. AND ALL SIZES AS PER THE REQUIREMENT OF THE FARMER	OPP
40	SUPPLY OF IMPROVED AGRICULTURAL IMPLEMENTS (TRACTOR-DRAWN/ POWER-DRIVEN)	25 PER CENT OF THE COST, LIMITED TO ₹15,000 PER UNIT	CENTRALLY SPONSORED SUSTAINABLE DEVELOPMENT OF SUGAR CANE-BASED CROPPING SYSTEM

Though India has made considerable progress, it pales in comparison to that made by other countries. In contrast, China has outlined responsibilities, with respect to custom hiring, for its entire gamut of agricultural and government authorities. It has encouraged the development of machinery cooperatives, along with supporting rental practices for leasing, contract management and maintenance—resulting in 5.24 million machinery service providing households and 201,000 machinery maintenance plants.[47]

There exist numerous business models that can be encouraged. A focus on tractors would see leasing out of tractors, along with other equipment, for basic agricultural services (land preparation, ploughing, harrowing, and planting). It would be a model best suited for those with limited financial resources. For those with greater financial wherewithal, an operational focus on a fleet of high-end machinery would be more suitable—such a business model would be able to work across states, while offering services for complex operations like harvesting and transplantation.

Olam, a conglomerate with sugar mill operations in Madhya Pradesh, has focused on running CHCs for harvesting sugar, partnering with local agri tech service providers, who purchase equipment using financial assistance from the company in addition to government subsidies. The company guarantees rental orders for the machines for a period of 5 years, with a focus on maximising utilization of the equipment. The result—40 per cent mechanization has been achieved through the initiative.

Escorts has sought to move from being a standalone tractor manufacturer to a farm solutions provider by adopting a CHC model. It has sought to tie up with five to six entrepreneurial and well-off farmers in certain areas (specifically in Odisha and Telangana), covering over 300 acres. It finances the purchase of equipment, while having the farmers put in seed money to cover margins and take out loans for other working capital. The company trains the farmers in business development of equipment rental services.

Mahindra & Mahindra has striven for a three-prolonged stretch across the farm equipment sector—utilizing its EPC arm for selling micro-irrigation equipment, its existing manufacturing set up for selling tractors, harvesters and transplanters, and Trringo, its farm rental aggregator, for collating demand.

—

47   Kapur, R., Chouhan, S., Gulati, S., & Saxena, V, Transforming Agriculture Through Mechanization, Grant Thornton, FICCI, 2015

CONSTRAINTS

Farm mechanization has its unique constraints and challenges which can leave a newly mechanizing farmer befuddled. Given the cost-conscious nature of the market, quality can often be a hit-or-miss situation. There is limited standardization of farming machinery, and little to no awareness and training about the proper usage of such machinery. There are few, if any, regulations governing farming equipment, letting manufacturers play at the low end of the market. Most equipment are based on external models, with limited adaptation for Indian conditions and local needs—India's range of farm sizes and soil types, across varying geological conditions, requires significant customization. Meanwhile, lack of water can act as a significant constraint for mechanization—not having irrigation facilities will hinder crop yield and limit the scope and affordability for mechanization. And, counterintuitively, mechanization would free up draught animals but deprive them of any purpose, leaving the farmer in hock for their upkeep. Given the cyclic nature of farming income, at once paying for this and for renting farm equipment might prove too much for some.

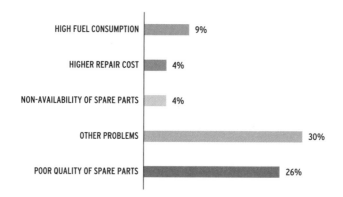

FIGURE 14: MAJOR PROBLEMS FACED BY TRACTOR-OWNING FARMERS[48]

After-sales service, particularly for tractors, is increasingly poor, with customer satisfaction dropping to 751 in 2016 from 774 in 2015.[49] Just 13 per cent of farmers reported having their tractors repaired on-site in 2016, and service quality tends to remain low (15 per cent of all farmers are unimpressed with the servicing work

48   Singh, S., 'Agricultural Machinery Industry' in India', CMA Publication No. 230, April 2009. Sourced from: http://www.iimahd.ernet.in/users/webrequest/files/cmareports/3AgriculturalMachineryIndustry.pdf

49   J.D. Power 2016 India Tractor Customer Service Index (CSI). Sourced from: http://india.jdpower.com/press-releases/2016-india-tractor-customer-service-index-csi-study

from OEM engineers).[50] The informal nature of the market also makes it highly concentrated. Tractor ownership is far higher among large farm owners than small or marginal farm owners, leaving 85 per cent of small farmers highly dependent on the 15 per cent pool of larger farmers and tractor owners for any potential hiring or sale.

For those farmers who are risk-tolerant enough to set up a CHC, there are many challenges to counter. The initial high capital cost can serve as a significant shock, while their limited knowledge about the maintenance and repair of such equipment can restrict overall utilization. In addition, the seasonal nature of demand, with low utilization during the rest of the year, ends up limiting the economic viability of any CHC, without scale. Finally, most farmers tend to be sceptical about custom hiring, given a lack of awareness about its benefits.

FOSTERING MECHANIZATION THROUGH POLICY

India's farm equipment policy needs to be retailored with a Make in India focus. The ICAR should be encouraged to establish standardized norms for farming equipment and implements. Testing procedures need to be refashioned, with removal of redundancies, and a focus on class-based testing (e.g. one test for 5- to 7-foot rotavators).[51] More certification centres need to be set up, with increased regional spread, along with greater funding for the development of local condition-specific farming implements. Any pricing cartel issues, as observed in the subsidized market, can only be resolved through an open list of manufacturers and their respective equipment prices on a central government tendering portal, available for state and panchayat-level access. Credit outflow in the machinery sector can be improved through creating a Credit Guarantee Fund. An on-the-spot subsidy provision should be introduced for purchase of tractors, farm machinery and equipment.[52] Taxation policy also needs to be redefined. Taxation should distinguish between implements used in the farming and automotive sector, with lower tax rates for the former.

50   Tractor service customer satisfaction down in 2016. Sourced from: http://auto.economictimes.indiatimes. com/news/automotive/off-highway/tractor-service-customer-satisfaction-down-in-2016/50959502

51   Kapur, R., Chouhan, S., Gulati, S., & Saxena, V., 'Transforming Agriculture Through Mechanization', Grant Thornton, FICCI, 2015

52   The Times of India, 16 June 2016. Sourced from: http://timesofindia.indiatimes.com/city/ludhiana/ Ailing-farm-equipment-sector-needs-subsidies/articleshow/52770901.cms

Examples of farmer support abound across states. In the late '80s, Karnataka sought to establish a CHC market, with each taluk having two to three centres with nine tractors for each. Given a labour surplus and limited partners, the programme failed, and most tractors were subsequently auctioned off. Now, with farm labour shortages looming, Karnataka has revamped its programme. Running under a public-private partnership (PPP) model, each CHC has an allocated subsidy (capped at ₹50 lakh) that can be used to purchase agricultural equipment and machinery required for local conditions.[53] A subsidy of ₹27.5 lakh is given by the government in the first year, with ₹12.5 lakh allocated for the second year—with the private partner providing the rest.[54] The CHC is required to run on internal accruals from the third year onwards for the contract period. Hiring and servicing charges are determined by considering the farmer's economic background, while keeping profitability in mind.[55] The impact has been profound—equipment rentals tend to be 10 to 20 per cent cheaper than market rates, with over 7,724 farmers utilizing the 18 CHCs' services in the 2015 summer season across three districts (Mysore, Chamarajanagar and Mandya). The Mysore regional office, running the eighteen CHCs, recorded revenue of ₹1.4 crore over just six months (February to August 2015). The CHCs rented out sixteen medium-powered tractors of 45 hp, eleven mini-tractors and other implements.[56] There have been pitfalls too—an 80 per cent credit policy has led to difficulties in recovering receivables. Certain equipment has proven to be irrelevant—a 5 hp diesel pump weighing 120 kg had significant mobility issues. Such CHCs can help de-risk farmers from accumulating debt to purchase farming equipment, while effectively deploying government funds to build a rental market for farming equipment.

Madhya Pradesh offers an interesting template.[57] Farmers in Vidisha district have benefitted from government incentives that have sought to encourage farmers to run CHCs, renting out machinery to small and marginal farmers. For the cost of setting up such a centre, typically ₹25 lakh, the government offers a ₹10 lakh subsidy (or 40 per cent of the cost of the CHC). Increasing the supply of machinery available for hire has helped reduce the need for manual labour, thereby lowering the cost

---

53 Madhusudan, M.K., 'Karnataka to hire out farm equipment', The Times of India, 15 March 2016. Sourced from: http://timesofindia.indiatimes.com/city/bengaluru/Karnataka-to-hire-out-farm-equipment/articleshow/51410961.cms

54 Kamila, R., 'Now, farm equipment on rent', The Hindu, 11 August 2014. Sourced from: http://www.thehindu.com/news/national/karnataka/now-farm-equipment-on-rent/article6301679.ece

55 Urs, A., 'How a Karnataka experiment can revolutionise agriculture in India', Business Standard, 24 August 2015. Sourced from: http://www.business-standard.com/article/punditry/how-a-karnataka-experiment-can-revolutionize-agriculture-in-india-115082300320_1.html

56 Ibid

57 Bera, S., 'A quiet revolution in farm mechanization', Live Mint, Sept 2016. Sourced from: http://www.livemint.com/Politics/GUjViqjuiAACb6e4lS5g7M/A-quiet-revolution-in-farm-mechanization.html

of cultivation, given the ongoing labour shortage; yields have naturally gone up by ~20 per cent. Fundamentally, a tractor needs 1,000 hours of operation a year to become economically sustainable. While a land parcel of two hectares typically requires 100 hours of tractor work, so a CHC can help increase its utilization rate without raising the debt of farm households. Madhya Pradesh's scheme has helped promote livelihoods for unemployed rural youth, with agriculture graduates preferred. Post-selection, such youth are often sent for technical training while being required to purchase a mandatory set of equipment. Such a scheme has served to give youth who may have a declining interest in farming, a chance to re-engage with agriculture while offering a sustainable livelihood. This scheme is being run in conjunction with Yantradoot, an initiative in which 200 villages are adopted every year as an effort to help farmers understand the benefits of mechanization. The introduction of better farm implements, like the deep plough, can help increase soil fertility, raising productivity. Even without such incentives, the increased availability of farming equipment will be beneficial. Subsidized machinery in Punjab is increasingly finding its way to Rajasthan and Haryana for rent, with a number of farmers and cooperative societies seeking to diversify from a farm equipment-surplus situation in Punjab.[58] However, done right, we would have laid the foundations of large-scale mechanization of Indian agriculture.

EFFECTIVE BUSINESS MODELS

Sometimes, the market itself can provide an answer. Marginal farmers in South Kamrup district in Assam have increasingly taken to small water pumps, of less than 2 hp capacity.[59] Such farmers typically engaged in backyard farming, with paddy cultivation dominant, while vegetables like tomato, brinjal, pumpkin, chillies, etc. are finding inroads. Typically, such farmers invested in shallow tube wells, with 4 to 6 hp pumps, despite water being available at a depth of less than 5 m. However, unsustainable withdrawal, especially for growing paddy, led to the disuse of the pumps, and a shift to small pumps which offer a lower capital cost (typically ₹8,000 for a 1.5 hp pump, which can run on a domestic power line). Such pumps are also lighter and can be easily transported from one marginal farm to another, and have lower operating costs than larger pumps. As farmers shift

58   Chaba, A.A., 'Agriculture Department seeks report on use of subsidized farm equipment in Punjab, The Indian Express, Oct 2017. Sourced from: http://indianexpress.com/article/india/agriculture-department-seeks-report-on-use-of-subsidized-farm-equipment-in-punjab-4881177/

59   Chamola, B., 'Village Square', Better India, May 2017. Sourced from: https://www.thebetterindia.com/98828/small-water-pumps-success-story-assam/

increasingly towards planting more vegetables, given better margins, they need less water, rendering smaller pumps sufficient. Subsidizing the spread of such pumps can help bring agricultural equipment cost down.

Meanwhile, other start-ups are focusing on becoming farm equipment aggregators, seeking to bring farmers and equipment owners together. Start-ups like Farmringg have sought to take equipment on hire, paying between ₹30,000–₹40,000 per month, and then sub-leasing it to needy farmers on a per-hour basis, at rates that are 20 to 30 per cent cheaper than informal mechanisms.[60] Farmringg started out in Siddipet district, where it can be accessed by a simple phone call, to hire equipment by the hour. Take-up has been quick, with the founders even being invited to local weddings frequently.

―

SEEDS

The quality of a seed has historically been considered key to a plant's productivity (accounting for ~20 to 25 per cent).[61] Farmers in the Krishna-Godavari Basin grew rice in nurseries and transplanted them over 10,000 years ago. The *Manusmriti* mentions it as 'Subeejam Sukshetre Jayate Sampadyate' ('a good seed in a good field will win and prosper').[62,63] Punishment was prescribed for traders selling inferior seeds as 'Seeds belong to no one, but are the gift of life to life itself.' Over 2,000 years ago, Sage Parashara recommended proper care for seeds, by drying them, segregating them by visual uniformity, keeping them free from pests and providing them proper storage in strong bags. Kautilya, in the *Arthashastra*, highlighted the time of seed-sowing, according to ongoing rainfall patterns. For farmers, passing down seeds is a historical rite, a tradition enshrined in ancient lore.

―

60 Krishnamoorthy, S., 'Farm Equipment too just a call away', The Hindu, September 2017. Sourced from: http://www.thehindu.com/news/cities/Hyderabad/farm-equipment-too-just-a-call-away/article19656857.ece

61 'Indian Agriculture: Performance and Challenges', State of Indian Agriculture 2012–13. Directorate of Economics and Statistics, Department of Agriculture and Cooperation,Ministry of Agriculture, Government of India, New Delhi, pp. 1-22.

62 Poonia, T. C. 2013. 'History of Seed Production and its Key Issues'.Inter. J. Food, Agri. and Vet. Sci, 3(1), pp.148–154.

63 Koundinya, A.V.V., Pradeep Kumar, P. 'Indian Vegetable Seeds Industry: Status & Challenges', International Journal of Plant, Animal and Environmental Sciences, Volume 4, Issue 4, Oct–Dec 2014. Sourced from: http://www.ijpaes.com/admin/php/uploads/705_pdf.pdf

INDIA'S SEED POLICIES

The importance of seeds was historically reflected in India's agricultural policy. The Famine Commission report (1871) resulted in the establishment of the Indian Agricultural Research Institute in Pusa, Bihar, along with six other colleges between 1905 and 1907. Sutton & Sons, the first private seed company in India, was established in 1912 in Calcutta, while the Royal Commission on Agriculture (1925) sought to introduce and spread improved crop practices through extensive commercialization. The establishment of the National Seed Corporation (1963) led to the certification of seeds, the enactment of the Seeds Act (1966) to ensure seed quality and the invocation of the Seed Rules (1968) to regulate seed issues. The Seeds Act defined the need for labelling or voluntary certification of seeds to conform to a minimum standard of physical and genetic purity, along with assured percentage of germination. The '60s saw the introduction of high-yielding varieties of cereals, particularly wheat and rice, along with the constitution of a Seed Review Team and the formation of the National Commission on Agriculture. The New Seed Development Policy (1988) gave Indian farmers access to foreign seeds and planting material. The policy allowed the private sector to import selected seeds (oilseed crops, pulses, coarse grains, vegetables, flowers, ornamental plants, tubers, bulbs, cuttings and saplings of flowers) under an Open General Licence (OGL).[64]

The National Seed Policy (2002) encouraged private sector participation in the research and development of new plant varieties—transgenic Bt cotton was first approved for cultivation in India under this policy. It established a National Seed Board in place of the Central Seed Committee and Central Seed Certification Board, making it responsible for seed certification, and seed planning and development.[65]

The draft Seed Bill (2004) sought to register all seeds for sale on their value of cultivation, while establishing a Central Seed Committee (in line with the National Seed Board and as advocated by the National Seed Policy, 2002) to set up minimum standards for seeds, along with harm identification. In the light of genetically modified (GM crops) concerns, it also advocated compulsory testing of all transgenic crop varieties under the AICCIP to determine their agronomic value and environmental impact, along with post-release performance monitoring for three to five years by the Ministry of Agriculture. It also sought to appoint seed inspectors, while establishing plant quarantine procedures associated with imported seeds.[66] The Protection of

---

64 Santhy, P.R.V. Kumari V., Vishwanatha, A., Deshmukh, R.K., 'Legislation for Seed Quality Regulation in India', Central Institute for Cotton Research Nagpur (CICR) Technical Bulletin No: 38. Sourced from: http://www.cicr.org.in/pdf/legislation_seed_quality.pdf

65 Ibid

66 Ibid

Plant Varieties and Farmers' Rights Act was also established to protect the rights of breeders and farmers, thereby promoting innovation.

A range of institutions was also set up—the ICAR promotes breeder seed programmes through the State Farms Corporation of India (SFCI), State Seeds Corporation (SSC) and the Krishi Vigyan Kendras (KVK).[67] The launch, in 1979, of the All India Coordinated Research Project (AICRP), termed the National Seed Project, across fourteen centres in different agricultural universities led to institutional support for seed innovation. Quality control and certification are conducted by twenty-two seed Certification Agencies, supported by 104 State Seed Testing Laboratories.

TABLE 8 SEEDS—TYPE OF ASSISTANCE IN MAHARASHTRA[68]

NO.	CROP	QUANTUM OF ASSISTANCE PER KG OF SEEDS	SCHEME/COMPONENT	
		ASSISTANCE ON DISTRIBUTION OF CERTIFIED SEEDS		
1	(I) PADDY AND WHEAT	(I) 50 PER CENT OF COST OR ₹5 PER KG, WHICHEVER IS LESS	INTEGRATED CEREALS DEVELOPMENT PROGRAMME, MACRO MANAGEMENT OF AGRICULTURE	
2	(I) BAJRA, SORGHUM, RAGI AND BARLEY	(I) 50 PER CENT OF COST OR ₹8 PER KG, WHICHEVER IS LESS	INTEGRATED CEREAL DEVELOPMENT PROGRAMME	
	(II) HYBRID BAJRA/SORGHUM	(II) ₹10		
3	ALL PULSES (ARHAR, MOONG, URAD, LENTIL, PEA, GRAM, RAJMA AND MOTH)	50 PER CENT OF COST OR ₹12 PER KG, WHICHEVER IS LESS	NATIONAL FOOD SECURITY MISSION	
4	ALL OILSEEDS (GROUNDNUT, SUNFLOWER, TOREA, SAFFLOWER, MUSTARD, RAPESEED, TIL, CASTOR) AND MAIZE	50 PER CENT OF COST OR ₹12 PER KG, WHICHEVER IS LESS	INTEGRATED SCHEME ON OILSEEDS, PULSES, OIL PALM AND MAIZE. (ISOPOM)	
5	OIL PALM SEEDLING	85 PER CENT OF THE COST OF OIL PALM SPROUTS FOR TOTAL LANDHOLDING OF THE FARMERS WITH A CEILING OF ₹1000 PER HECTARE	OIL PALM AREA EXPANSION PROGRAMME (RKVY)	
6	CERTIFIED SEEDS OF COTTON	₹20	COTTON TECHNOLOGY MISSION	
7	CERTIFIED SEEDS OF JUTE AND MESTA	50 PER CENT OF COST OR ₹12, WHICHEVER IS LESS	JUTE AND MESTA TECHNOLOGY MISSION	
	SUPPLY OF GREEN MANURING SEED	₹2,000 PER QUINTAL (25 PER CENT SUBSIDY)	WORK PLAN ORGANIC FARMING SCHEME	
	PLANTATION OF GLYRICIDIA/ SHEVARI	₹2 PER PLANT	WORK PLAN ORGANIC FARMING SCHEME	
8	FOR ALL CROPS DISTRIBUTION OF FOUNDATION/CERTIFIED SEEDS FOR PRODUCTION OF QUALITY SEEDS TO IMPROVE QUALITY OF FARM SAVED SEEDS	50 PER CENT OF COST OF THE SEEDS	SEED VILLAGE PROGRAMME	
		ASSISTANCE ON PRODUCTION OF FOUNDATION FOR CERTIFIED SEEDS		
9	SEED TREATMENT	25 PER CENT SUBSIDY LIMITED TO ₹50/HA	25 PER CENT GOVERNMENT OF MAHARASHTRA	

67 Poonia, T.C., History of Seed Production and its key issues, International Journal of Food, Agriculture and Veterinary Sciences ISSN: 2277-209X, 2013 Vol. 3 (1) January-April, pp. 148-154/Poonia. Sourced from: http://www.cibtech.org/J-FOOD-AGRI-VETERINARY-SCIENCES/PUBLICATIONS/2013/Vol_3_No_1/JFAV...30-014...Poonia....Seed...General%20Article...148-154.pdf

68 Krishi Handbook (English Version), Publication No. 1762, Department of Agriculture, Government of Maharashtra, August 2012.

10	DEMONSTRATION INPUTS	₹5000/HA. LIMIT		25 PER CENT STATE GOVT OF MAHARASHTRA
11	CULTIVATION COST AS ASSISTANCE FOR GESTATION PERIOD FOR OIL PALM	₹20000/HA IN FOUR YEARS	OIL PALM AREA EXPANSION PROGRAMME	
12	A. PEARL MILLET HYBRID	₹30	INITIATIVE FOR NUTRITIONAL SECURITY THROUGH INTENSIVE MILLETS PROMOTION (INSIMP)	
	B. HYVS OF OTHER MILLETS	₹10		
13	COTTON SEED		COTTON TECHNOLOGY MISSION	
	(I) FOUNDATION SEED PRODUCTION	(I) ₹50 OR 50 PER CENT OF COST, WHICHEVER IS LESS		
	(II) CERTIFIED SEED PRODUCTION	(II) ₹15 OR 25 PER CENT OF COST, WHICHEVER IS LESS		
14	JUTE AND MESTA		JUTE AND MESTA TECHNOLOGY MISSION	
	(I) FOUNDATION SEED PRODUCTION	(I) ₹30 OR 50 PER CENT OF COST, WHICHEVER IS LESS		
	(II) CERTIFIED SEED PRODUCTION	(II) ₹7 OR 25 PER CENT OF COST, WHICHEVER IS LESS		
15	ASSISTANCE FOR BOOSTING SEED PRODUCTION IN PRIVATE SECTOR INCLUDING INDIVIDUALS/ENTREPRENEURS, SELF-HELP GROUPS, ETC.	CREDIT-LINKED BACK-ENDED CAPITAL SUBSIDY AT THE RATE OF 25 PER CENT OF PROJECT COST LIMITED TO ₹25 LAKH PER UNIT	DEVELOPMENT AND STRENGTHENING OF INFRASTRUCTURE FOR PRODUCTION AND DISTRIBUTION OF QUALITY SEED	
	SEED MINI-KITS OF HIGH-YIELDING VARIETIES			
16	PADDY AND WHEAT MINI- KITS, ALL PULSES (ARHAR, MOONG, URAD, LENTIL, PEA, GRAM, RAJMA & MOTH)	FREE	NATIONAL FOOD SECURITY MISSION	
17	ALL OILSEEDS (GROUNDNUT, LINSEED, SUNFLOWER, TORIA, SAFFLOWER, MUSTARD, RAPESEED, CASTOR) AND MAIZE	FREE	INTEGRATED SCHEME ON OILSEEDS, PULSES, OIL PALM AND MAIZE (ISOPOM)	
18	PEARL MILLET HYBRIDS AND HYVS OF OTHER MILLETS FOR ALL CROPS	FREE	INITIATIVE FOR NUTRITIONAL SECURITY THROUGH INTENSIVE MILLETS PROMOTION (INSIMP)	
19	ASSISTANCE FOR TRAINING ON SEED PRODUCTION AND SEED TECHNOLOGY FOR A GROUP OF 50 TO 150 FARMERS	₹5000 PER TRAINING (FOR THREE-DAY TRAINING)	SEED VILLAGE PROGRAMMING	
		(I) AT THE TIME OF SOWING OF SEED CROP: TRAINING ON SEED PRODUCTION TECHNIQUE, ISOLATION DISTANCE, SOWING PRACTICES, OTHER AGRONOMIC PRACTICES		
		(II) AT THE TIME OF FLOWER INITIATION STAGE OF THE CROP		
		(III) AFTER HARVEST AND AT THE TIME OF SEED PROCESSING		
20	ASSISTANCE FOR PROCURING SEEDS STORAGE BIN OF 20 QTL CAPACITY	25 PER CENT OF THE COST SUBJECT TO A MAXIMUM OF ₹2,000 (AT 33 PER CENT OF THE COST SUBJECT TO A MAXIMUM OF ₹3,000 FOR SC/ST FARMERS)	SEED VILLAGE PROGRAMME	
21	ASSISTANCE FOR MAKING SEED STORAGE BIN OF 10 QTL. CAPACITY	25 PER CENT OF COST SUBJECT TO A MAXIMUM OF ₹1,000 (AT 33 PER CENT SUBJECT TO A MAXIMUM OF ₹1,500 TO SC/ST FARMERS)	SEED VILLAGE PROGRAMME	
22	DISTRIBUTION OF CERTIFIED SEEDS	50 PER CENT OF THE COST OF ALL CROP GROUPS OR ₹1200/QL, WHICHEVER IS LESS	OILSEED PRODUCTION PROGRAMME	
23	DISTRIBUTION OF CERTIFIED SEEDS (ARBORIUM & HERBACIUM)	25 PER CENT OF THE MARKET PRICE FOR HYBRID VARIETIES WHICH HAVE BEEN NOTIFIED DURING LAST 15 YEARS. PRODUCTION OF EXTRA LONG STAPLE COTTON WILL BE 50 PER CENT OF THE MARKET PRICE FOR VARIETIES/ HYBRIDS IRRESPECTIVE OF AGE LIMIT (₹2000 PER QL.) (ARBORIUM & HERBACIUM SP.)	CENTRALLY-SPONSORED INTENSIVE COTTON DEVELOPMENT PROGRAMME	
24	PRODUCTION OF CERTIFIED SEED(SVS)	₹1,000/QL	OILSEED PRODUCTION PROGRAMME	
25	FOUNDATION SEED PRODUCTION	10 PER CENT OF THE COST LIMITED TO ₹4,000/HA	CENTRALLY SPONSORED SUSTAINABLE DEVELOPMENT OF SUGAR CANE-BASED CROPPING SYSTEM	

26	CERTIFIED SEED PRODUCTION	10 PER CENT OF THE COST LIMITED TO ₹4,000/HA	CENTRALLY SPONSORED SUSTAINABLE DEVELOPMENT OF SUGAR CANE-BASED CROPPING SYSTEM	
27	A. SEED PRODUCTION OF HYBRID VARIETIES	₹3,000/QL	INTENSIVE FOR NUTRITIONAL SECURITY THROUGH INTENSIVE MILLETS PROMOTION (INSIMP)	
	B. SEED PRODUCTION OF IMPROVED VARIETIES	₹1,000/QL	- DO -	
28	SEED MINI-KIT JOWAR & OTHER MILLETS (PACK 4 KG) FOR 0.4 HA	₹200/ MINIKIT	INTENSIVE FOR NUTRITIONAL SECURITY THROUGH INTENSIVE MILLETS PROMOTION (INSIMP)	
29	SEED MINI-KIT BBAJRA (PACK OF 1.5 KG) FOR 0.4 HA	₹250/ MINIKIT	INTENSIVE FOR NUTRITIONAL SECURITY THROUGH INTENSIVE MILLETS PROMOTION (INSIMP)	

PROCURING SEEDS

However, each year, the process remains the same. Farmers wait in long queues outside seed supply centres to get seeds in exchange for cash, primarily raised from private moneylenders. When seeds are available and accessible, quality becomes a significant factor. Indigenous varieties with good germination potential have become increasingly scarce, while GM varieties come with their own baggage (high input costs, greater amount of pesticides needed, and newer pests). Farmers typically demand seed of specific varieties, especially high-yield ones, instead of saving on seed input costs. Reliable and current information, in an easy-to-understand manner, on seed varieties, their costing and associated pest risks is often not available, while a network of commission agents and seed companies brand their own products.

Seed production inherently remains a biological process, seeking to multiply small numbers of breeder seeds into larger quantities for commercial distribution, over planned stages across various cropping seasons. Seeds, unlike fertilizers, require far greater handling care, particularly during storage and transportation, along with regular testing for quality before actual sale. Each seed type has certain minimum standards for germination and purity.

Once bred, distribution can be a longwinded process. India currently has over fifteen state seed corporations and two national ones, namely the National Seed Corporation of India and the State Farms Corporation of India. However, such public institutions focus mainly on open pollinating varieties, with private players meeting the requirements for hybrid seeds and transgenic crops. Quality seeds tend to form just 30 per cent of the total seed demand, with farmers saving and breeding their own seeds. There remain significant constraints in the process—limited awareness of new technologies amongst hybrid seed producers, coordination issues between various seed-producing associations, and seasonal production trends (rabi production tends to be prevalent, while kharif production of seeds is rife with quality issues). The lack of a specific regulatory watchdog doesn't help either.

Seeds can now cost ~10 per cent of the total operational cost associated with cultivating a hectare of land. Regional prices can vary significantly. Consider sugar cane—seeds can cost 3 per cent of a farmer's total cost in Karnataka, while rising to 18 per cent for a farmer in Uttar Pradesh. A farmer in Assam or Odisha can cultivate paddy cheaply, at just 3 per cent of his total costs, while someone in Tamil Nadu would have to shell out 11 per cent for similar seed. This seed price rise, driven by a seed shortage, is despite an overall surplus (the 2012–13 National Report on requirement and availability of seeds suggested a surplus of 14 lakh quintals). Maize, jute, arhar and gaur face significant deficits while paddy and wheat have registered surpluses. This is reflected in projections of India's seed market, with the domestic vegetable seeds industry expected to double by 2023, hitting ₹8,000 crore.[69]

For genetically modified seeds, the royalty paid to an MNC like Monsanto can hike prices significantly. India's steps to impose cuts on such royalties, particularly for cotton seeds, are welcome—royalties were slashed by 70 per cent in 2016, with plans for an additional 20.4 per cent cut being finalized in 2018, effectively lowering the price of a GM cotton seed to ₹740 per 450-g pack.

SEED QUALITY AND HYBRIDS

Seed quality remains a consistent worry. Public institutions have focused on open pollinated seed varieties, while the private sector has focused on meeting hybrid and transgenic seed demand. Current quality requirements are typically met only to 20 per cent of the demand, with farmers meeting the balance through their own saved seeds with limited quality standards. The usage of such generic varieties can result in significant loss of crop productivity. India's seed/cultivar replacement rate (SRR, per cent of area sown out of the total crop area that uses certified quality seeds instead of saved seeds) remains around 25 per cent for self-pollinated crops (jumping from 10 per cent in the '90s). The average SRR rate for staple crops like wheat (18.37 per cent), paddy (21.70 per cent), maize (33.77 per cent) and soyabean (24.16 per cent) remains quite low. Pulses, having seen the development few innovative hybrid seeds have, are at the bottom of the scale (peanut – 9.6 per cent, chickpea – 8.76 per cent, etc.).

TABLE 9: ALL-INDIA SEED REPLACEMENT RATE (%) OF MAJOR CROPS[70]

ALL-INDIA SEED REPLACEMENT RATE (%) OF MAJOR CROPS									
CROPS	2001	2002	2003	2004	2005	2006	2007	2008	AVERAGE
WHEAT	13.04	13	13	16.48	17.64	21.76	25.23	26.84	18.37
PADDY	19.22	19.31	19.16	16.27	21.33	22.41	25.87	30.05	21.70
MAIZE	20.98	21.35	24.41	31.5	35.39	43.78	44.24	48.48	33.77
JOWAR	18.36	18.78	26.71	19.28	19.03	19.37	19.87	26.16	20.95
BAJRA	45.92	48.47	51.02	44.9	55.36	55.1	48.47	62.92	51.52
CHICKPEA	4.17	4.23	7.09	9.87	9.41	9.04	11.9	14.38	8.76
URDBEAN	16.55	17.06	20.48	17.24	15.7	13.65	23.89	26.31	18.86
ARHAR	8.71	8.84	13.6	9.8	10.48	11.56	16.05	16.02	11.88
PEANUT	5.2	5.5	11	7.11	6.89	9.79	14.29	17.04	9.60
RSM	38.39	44.64	66.96	58.48	55.36	60.71	58.62	52.67	54.48
SOYABEAN	12.44	12.45	15.58	27	28.88	28.4	33.39	35.12	24.16
SUNFLOWER	13.73	15.69	19.61	60.15	67.67	66.92	62.88	43.64	43.79
COTTON	21.21	21.86	19.84	20.73	21.78	19.84	15.3	12.07	19.08

TABLE 10: TRENDS IN BREEDER SEED PRODUCTION AND
QUALITY SEED DISTRIBUTION IN INDIA: 1995–2011[71]

YEAR	BREEDER SEED PRODUCTION (IN TONNES)				QUALITY SEED DISTRIBUTION (IN '000 QUINTALS)			
	CEREALS	PULSES	OILSEEDS	FIBRES	CEREALS	PULSES	OILSEEDS	FIBRES
1995-96	2645	339	992	19	4400	360	1260	260
1998-99	1874	416	595	25	5730	410	1380	290
2001-02	2154	579	1234	39	6560	470	1210	290
2004-05	3189	870	1927	33	8140	740	2340	280
2008-09	4833	1505	2676	20	14740	1450	3990	260
2009-10	5959	1995	3511	22	16520	1970	5070	270
2010-11	6167	1562	3729	80	18260	2080	5060	260
2011-12	6282	1428	3871	51	18450	1920	5840	340

70 Poonia, T.C., History of Seed Production and its key issues, International Journal of Food, Agriculture and Veterinary Sciences ISSN: 2277-209X, 2013 Vol. 3 (1) January-April, pp. 148-154/Poonia. Sourced from: http://www.cibtech.org/J-FOOD-AGRI-VETERINARY-SCIENCES/PUBLICATIONS/2013/Vol_3_No_1/JFAV...30-014...Poonia....Seed...General%20Article...148-154.pdf

71 Venkatesh P., Pal, S., Impact of Plant Variety Protection on Indian Seed Industry, Agricultural Economics Research Review Vol. 27 (No.1) January-June 2014 pp 91-102 DOI: 10.5958/j.0974-0279.27.1.008. Sourced from: http://ageconsearch.umn.edu/bitstream/170251/2/8-P-Venkatesh.pdf

TABLE 11: STATE-WISE SEED REPLACEMENT RATE FOR MAJOR CROPS IN INDIA[72]

YEAR	TN	AP	KT	GJ	MH	RJ	UP	PB	BH	INDIA
FOR PADDY										
2001	17	42	22	18	18	4	14	11	6	19
2005	55	61	29	21	19	5	20	19	12	21
2011	68	87	41	38	46	7	32	53	38	40
FOR MAIZE										
2001	8	48	100	100	53	2	7	42	21	21
2005	2	84	100	100	60	18	12	69	40	35
2011	98	100	100	100	93	53	31	99	100	57
FOR CORN										
2001	15	100	100	100	100	61	70	-	-	21
2005	14	84	100	100	100	51	64	-	-	22
2011	100	100	100	100	100	100	100	73	-	100
FOR PIGEON PEA										
2001	6	13	8	10	13	14	12	-	-	8
2005	3	33	14	15	13	9	18	-	-	10
2011	12	78	33	31	22	25	-	2		
FOR RAPESEED & MUSTARD										
2001	-	-	-	71	-	69	27	26	29	49
2005	-	-	-	100	-	48	52	21	30	55
2011	-	-	-	100	-	85	64	64	47	79

From a yield perspective, hybrid seeds offer a significant advantage. Cotton is typically best suited for black alluvial soil, but hybrids can help extend the soil domain. Hybrids are significantly prevalent in cotton—India jumped from a production of 14 million bales (278 kg/hectare) in 2000–01 to 38 million bales (511 kg/hectare) in 2015, emerging as the world's largest producer and second-largest exporter. The total area under hybrid cotton cultivation has jumped from 40 per cent in South/Central India in 2002 to 96 per cent by 2011. Hybrid seeds also offer significant trade-offs. Yield stagnation can often happen; given the ~1,000 brands of hybrid seeds, monitoring and certification remains an arduous task. They can tend to be cost-intensive, and often susceptible to other sap-insects and leaf-alterations. A lack of suitable cropping area and farmer habits that leave little time between seed harvest and its use for the next cropping season can also impact yields significantly.[73]

---

72   Venkatesh P., Pal, S., Impact of Plant Variety Protection on Indian Seed Industry, Agricultural Economics Research Review Vol. 27 (No.1) January-June 2014 pp 91–102 DOI: 10.5958/j.0974-0279.27.1.008. Sourced from: http://ageconsearch.umn.edu/bitstream/170251/2/8-P-Venkatesh.pdf

73   Poonia, T.C., History of Seed Production and its key issues, International Journal of Food, Agriculture and Veterinary Sciences ISSN: 2277-209X, 2013 Vol. 3 (1) January-April, pp. 148-154/Poonia. Sourced from: http://www.cibtech.org/J-FOOD-AGRI-VETERINARY-SCIENCES/PUBLICATIONS/2013/Vol_3_No_1/JFAV...30-014...Poonia....Seed...General%20Article...148-154.pd

Consider the case of Bollgard or BG-2, as Monsanto's second-generation cotton hybrid seeds are called. The seed was supposed to be able to protect crops against the pink bollworm, but the pest has grown resistant, leading to farmers spending more on pesticides to control such infestations. This is partially a result of the structure of India's hybrid seeds market. Monsanto's licencing of its BG and BG-2 traits to Indian seeds restricted their inclusion only to hybrid seeds.[74] Such seeds enable significant value capture as their progeny loses genetic stability, when seeds are replanted. Farmers are required to repurchase seeds every year, turning seeds sales effectively into an annuity. Upon the introduction of Bt cotton in India, farmers across India's central and western belts shifted en masse to hybrid seeds. This shift has led to farmers planting the cotton crop at low densities (the hybrids are bigger and bushier in nature), leading to just 11,000–16,000 crops per acre; compare this with Brazil's 100,000 crops per acre. To make up for this shortfall, farmers typically plant their crop for a longer period (between 160 days and 300 days), exposing them to pink bollworm.

Transgenic seeds (incorporating useful genes from distantly related species that normally do not sexually mate) by utilizing recombinant DNA technology, have been recognized as a key tool in the race to increase yields. India's Ministry of Science and Technology established the Department of Biotechnology in 1986, with a focus on biotechnological innovations in agriculture, animal science and human health. Their transgenic research is currently focused on popular field crops—cotton, mustard, brinjal, tomato, etc.—with emphasis on insect pest control, nutrition enhancement and hybridization. The ministry also established a Review Committee on Genetic Manipulation (RCGM) in 1989 for effective monitoring and evaluation which laid down guidelines for assessment of GM crops. An Institute of Bio-safety Committee was developed to monitor rDNA technology work, while a Special Monitoring cum Evaluation Committee under RCGM was announced to oversee the impact of transgenic plants on the environment. A Genetic Engineering Approval Committee was established to provide recommendations to the government for approval of a transgenic variety for commercial cultivation.

Bt cotton, one of the first GM crop technologies utilized in India, has provided significant benefits to farmers in India. On average, such farmers have cut pesticide usage by 40 per cent, while gaining yield advantages of 30–40 per cent and profit gains at $60 per acre.[74] Concerns, however, have remained over the sustainability of its benefits, with secondary pests associated with cotton turning into primary pests. In addition, the monopolistic pricing associated with Bt cotton has resulted in lower farm profits and restricted technology access (Lalitha, 2004; Qaim and De Javry, 2003).

---

74   Sadashivappa, P., Qaim, M., Bt Cotton in India: Development of Benefits and the Role of Government Seed Price Interventions, AgBioForum, 12(2): 172-183, 2009, AgBioForum. Sourced from: http://www.agbioforum.org/v12n2/v12n2a03-sadashivappa.pdf

India's regulatory authorities have hence intervened significantly in GM seed pricing—Bollgard seed prices have now been controlled, trait fees reduced by 67 per cent and the royalty slashed by 70 per cent due to MNCs. Such price control measures will have a positive impact on the availability and distribution of innovative seeds within India.

Other options are available as well. Veteran plant breeder K.K. Subramani has developed a hybrid variety of papaya seeds, which are native to India and can help lower the cost of cultivating papaya.[75] India annually imports over ₹100 crore of Red Lady Dwarf papaya seeds every year from Taiwan—this variant is famed for its short growing season, taking only eight months to fruit, and its fruit's condition remains good even fifteen days post-harvest. Papaya seeds typically have low germination rates and lose their efficacy quickly, while the crop is highly prone to viral diseases. Subramani's F1 hybrid variety is resistant to diseases like ringpot and mosaic viruses, with good feedback received from planters.

IMPROVING CROP YIELD

The seed replacement rate has a strong correlation with crop yield—the production and supply of quality seeds to induce a higher rate requires the amalgamation of technical know-how, with trained personnel and farmer awareness. Improper coordination between seed-producing associations, limited focus on innovation by current hybrid seed producers and the lack of an overarching industry regulator are key constraints to furthering this rate. Rising competition amongst seed producers has also led to a degradation of production practices, while structural seed production constraints (rabi seed production is much easier than kharif seed production) have impeded growth. A regulator should encourage greater public-private partnership to enforce seed quality standards, while encouraging farmers to plant specific quality seeds for certain crops. Seed movement should be minimized through the development of small-scale seed industries focused on seed production and the modification of the State Seed Plan towards full utilization of existing infrastructure and personnel.

The Protection of Plant Varieties and Farmers' Rights Act (2001) encouraged investment in the research and development of seed technology and new hybrid seeds. However, we need greater investment in agricultural research, with a focus on developing our own hybrid and transgenic varieties in cotton and other crops.

---

75   Bose, H., Better India, March 2018. Sourced from: https://www.thebetterindia.com/134292/farming-seeds-papaya-india/

Budgets for the ICAR, the Central Institute for Cotton Research and the University of Agricultural Sciences in Dharwad need to be increased—ICAR's 2014–15 budget was just $800 million; Monsanto spends double that on agricultural research annually. Meanwhile, China's ChemChina sought to spend $43 billion in 2016 to acquire Sygenta. India's private sector should receive due support from the government to enhance quality seed supply. Institutional R&D should instead be focused on the development of suitable varieties for upland, flood-prone and cold conditions.

Policy reform is essential. Precision farming techniques, like Systematic Rice Intensification (SRI), can help increase seed production in this regard.[76] The enactment of the Seed Bill (2004) would go a long way in promoting seed innovation. However, traditional seeds must not be allowed to fall by the wayside. Such seeds remain hardy, pest-resistant, and consume less resources—all while withstanding India's adverse local weather conditions and offering a unique flavour. With water tables falling and high-yielding seeds facing issues associated with new pest resistance, traditional seeds offer a useful hedge in the face of climate change.[77,78]

In Madurai district of Tamil Nadu, farmers are increasingly adopting a custodian role, seeking to preserve seed varieties of traditional paddy, mango and fruit.[79] Farmers should be encouraged to develop 'seed villages', with two to three villages selected for seed production for specific varieties on a regular basis. In situ biodiversity conservation should be encouraged, with pure lines sought to be conserved without significant amalgamation.

Consider the Indarsan variety of rice, grown primarily in Nainital district of Uttarakhand in the '80s. Acceptance of hybrid 'Pant-4' varieties by farmers has led to a high utilization of input resources (water and chemical pesticides). Heavy exploitation of groundwater lead to over 50 per cent of artesian wells going dry and witnessing pressure drops, while the nearby Haripura dam on the Bhakra river saw falling water levels.

---

76 Poonia, T.C., History of Seed Production and its key issues, International Journal of Food, Agriculture and Veterinary Sciences ISSN: 2277-209X, 2013 Vol. 3 (1) January-April, pp. 148-154/Poonia. Sourced from: http://www.cibtech.org/J-FOOD-AGRI-VETERINARY-SCIENCES/PUBLICATIONS/2013/Vol_3_No_1/JFAV...30-014...Poonia....Seed...General%20Article...148-154.pdf

77 Using Traditional Methods and Indigenous Technologies for Coping With Climate Variability, C. J. Stigter, Zheng Dawei, L. O. Z. Onyewotu, Mei Xurong, Climatic Change, May 2005, Volume 70, Issue 1, pp 255-271 Sourced from: http://link.springer.com/article/10.1007/s10584-005-5949-5

78 Assessing the vulnerability of traditional maize seed systems in Mexico to climate change, Mauricio R. Bellon, David Hodson, and Jon Hellin, Proceedings of the National Academy of Sciences of the United States of America, Vol 33. Sourced from: http://www.pnas.org/content/108/33/13432.full

79 http://www.thehindu.com/news/cities/Madurai/local-seeds-best-bet-against-climate-change/article5149009.ece

Some farmers, like Inder Singh (not related to our protagonist) who persevered with the traditional varieties of rice, saw high yields provided at a low cost of cultivation. One of them being the Indarsan variety (named after the eponymous Inder Singh) was adopted across the region over a period of six to seven years, with concomitant yield increases. A National Gene Fund has been constituted to provide payments for farmers who preserve a variety that is used as donor of genes for development of new varieties. A similar fund for farmers preserving traditional seeds should be constituted for promoting biodiversity. The future remains with such farmers adopting a mixed approach, using the best seeds on offer, while salvaging traditional seeds for adverse weather conditions.

FERTILIZERS

Akhilesh Rawat, a well-off farmer with 5 hectares of irrigated land in Haldwani district in Uttarakhand, has never heard of a soil test being done locally. Sure, he has heard the Prime Minister mention it, often, but he's never really felt the need to conduct a test. '*Yeh mitti upjao hai,*' he says, referring to the fertility of the land. Why bother?

Abhishek Vinnakota, from Bagalkot district, in northern Karnataka, casts a sweeping eye across his ancestral land, bemoaning its cracked, open plains in the ongoing drought and its consequences. His only recourse is to continue drilling for groundwater, while having his forehands take samples of soil to the district's soil testing laboratory nearby. Insights from such tests have made a significant difference to his margins, with fertilizer spend declining by 30 per cent and yields rising by 20 per cent. The proper application of manure, urea and other enriched fertilizers have helped him survive. With a significant lack of awareness, most farmers in the district continue to plough their fields, applying manure and urea, as they have done for eons, while remaining ignorant of the benefits of soil testing. Urea, instead, reigns supreme.

India offers a varying palate of soils to the aspiring farmer. Alluvial soils constitute the Indo-Gangetic Plain, while remaining deficient in nitrogen, phosphorus and organic matter, with near-neutral to slightly alkaline pH content. The Deccan Lava Tract, in parts of Maharashtra, Gujarat, Chhattisgarh, Madhya Pradesh and Andhra Pradesh, contains black soils with high clay content, high moisture retention—it has a reputation for being difficult to manage, yet is highly fertile. Its peninsular region (from Tamil Nadu in the south to Bundelkhand in the north) is composed primarily of red soils or Acrisols which have a low water and nutrient holding capacity, and are generally deficient in nitrogen, phosphorus, zinc and sulphur. The Eastern Ghats, in Odisha, and some parts of the Western Ghats are composed of laterites and lateritic soils which are deficient in potassium, phosphorus, zinc, boron and calcium, and are of acidic nature. Central Indian forest soils have high organic content while West Bengal's coastal saline and sodic soils have serious problems of high sodium content and nutrient deficiency. Peaty soils, distributed in coastal tracts of Odisha and West Bengal, typically require good drainage and fertilization (usually for paddy crop). Rajasthan's desert soils remain highly prone to wind erosion and have a general lack of water and are characterized by lack of vegetation. The Royal Commission on Agriculture (1928) mentions the poor soil fertility of India's major soil types, with a significant deficiency in nitrogen, phosphorus and potash. About a century later, the situation remains the same, with soil fertility reduced by a high cropping intensity and a fertilizer content imbalance.

—•—

OUR FIXATION WITH NITROGEN

For the majority of these soils, urea remains a favourite of Indian farmers, with its cheap and highly subsidized offering—farmers usually end up applying double the recommended amount and even more (10x–15x) particularly in areas such as Punjab, Rajasthan and Haryana. Urea is considered to be a one-stop solution to all soil fertility issues, whilst ignoring any phosphorus, nitrogen or micronutrient requirements. Marginal returns have started declining now, with crops responding more feebly to greater application of the said fertilizer. Crop yield per kg of fertilizer has declined from 13 kg in the '70s to 4 kg in 2010 while the fertilizer prices shift upwards.[80]

---

80   Bera, S., A soil health card not enough for balanced fertilizer use, Live Mint, 14 August 2015. Sourced from: http://www.livemint.com/Politics/1xM0dNr7g9BLYw5Rx45tvK/A-soil-health-card-not-enough-for-balanced-fertilizer-use.html

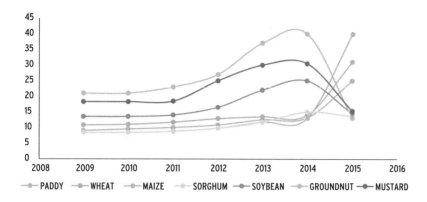

FIGURE 15: THE PRICE OF SULPHUR-BASED FERTILIZER HAS GROWN MORE
EXPENSIVE FOR STAPLE CROPS IN INDIA (₹/KG)[81]

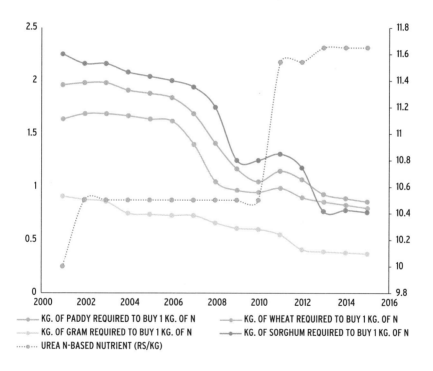

FIGURE 16: COST OF UREA-BASED N-FERTILIZERS FOR PADDY, WHEAT, GRAM AND SORGHUM HAS
GONE UP BUT MINIMUM SUPPORT PRICES FOR CROPS HAVE HELPED MITIGATE THIS[82]

---

81   Fertilizer Association of India. (15215) & (16851); IndiaStat Data

82   Ibid

Nitrogen fixation has been a policy mandate for Independent India. A recommended NPK ratio of 4:2:1, now standard across the land, was first established in the early '50s, from field trials (NAAS 2009). This ratio remains fixed now—ignoring soil content changes over the years. It also ignores two important factors—that farmers continued to apply farm yard manure on native soils rich in potassium and phosphorus content and that this ratio was relevant primarily for red and lateritic soils, which required phosphorus and potassium fertilizers. The ratio of NPK should ideally differ for different types of soils (NAAS 2009).[83] Fertilizer norms should ideally be dependent on cropping patterns, soil characteristics, crop yield and water availability. Field trials that were conducted in the '80s highlighted that phosphorus-rich fertilizers also provided a similar boost to yield for rice crops, while wheat crops showcased a far greater yield increase than with nitrogen-rich fertilizers.[84]

TABLE 12: INDIA'S DECADAL EVOLUTION OF NPK FERTILIZER CONSUMPTION ('000 TONNES) (ANNUAL REPORTS, DEPARTMENT OF FERTILIZERS, MINISTRY OF CHEMICALS & FERTILIZERS)

YEAR	NITROGEN %	PHOSPHORUS %	POTASSIUM %
1973-74	64	23	13
1983-84	68	22	10
1993-94	71	22	7
2003-04	67	25	9
2013-14	69	23	8

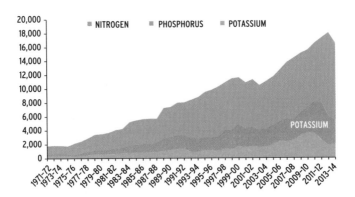

FIGURE 17: INDIA'S NITROGEN, PHOSPHORUS & POTASSIUM FERTILIZER CONSUMPTION ('000 TONNES) (ANNUAL REPORTS, DEPARTMENT OF FERTILIZERS, MINISTRY OF CHEMICALS & FERTILIZERS)

83   S.,Pavithra, Chand, Ramesh, Fertilizer Use and Imbalance in India, Economic & Political Weekly, vol l no 44, October 31, 2015. Sourced from: http://www.im4change.org.previewdns.com/siteadmin/tinymce/uploaded/Fertilizer_Use_and_Imbalance_in_India.pdf

84   Ibid

The norm of 4:2:1 implies that nitrogen should constitute 57.2 per cent and phosphorus and potassium should constitute 28.6 per cent and 14.2 per cent, respectively. However, in most years, nitrogen's share in the fertilizer mix has hovered around 65 per cent, over 8 per cent higher than the recommended norm. When the oil shock in the '70s hit, fertilizer prices rose, nitrogen spiked to 74 per cent in the fertilizer mix. Gradual reduction in share was witnessed later till the '90s, but deregulation of potassium and phosphorus prices favoured a rise in consumption of nitrogen-heavy fertilizers. By 2009–10, the NPK ratio was close to its optimum (NPK at 58.8 per cent, 27.5 per cent and 13.7 per cent, respectively) but the Nutrient Based Subsidy Policy (2010), introduced with the aim of achieving balanced fertilizer use, enhanced urea usage with the share of nitrogen rising to ~70 per cent again by 2012–13.[85] The Economic Survey (2014) called for a review of the Nutrient Based Subsidy (NBS) policy, highlighting a subsidy of ~₹8,500 crore on urea[86] (~₹2,680 crore by farmers and ~₹5,860 crore by the government) on account of urea purchases beyond what our soil requires.[87] While the government has expressed concern over the worsening of the NPK ratio, no significant study has been conducted to determine the optimal NPK ratio for different soil types across India. This recommended ratio needs a relook, the skew towards nitrogen-rich fertilizers in India needs correction.

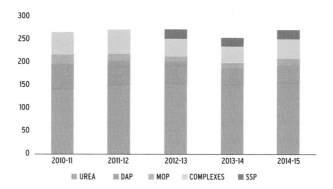

FIGURE 18: UREA DOMINATES PRODUCT-WISE PER HECTARE CONSUMPTION OF FERTILIZERS IN INDIA (IN KG/HA)[88]

85   Economic Survey 2014: Government, farmers waste funds about ₹8,500 crore on urea, Economic Times, Jul 9, 2014, Sourced from: http://articles.economictimes.indiatimes.com/2014-07-09/news/51248126_1_urea-price-p-and-k-fertilizers-fertilizer-subsidy

86   Economic Survey 2013-14, Chapter 2, Issues & Priorities. Sourced from: http://indiabudget.nic.in/budget2014-2015/es2013-14/echap-02.pdf

87   Economic Survey 2014: Government, farmers waste funds about ₹8,500 crore on urea, Economic Times, Jul 9, 2014, Sourced from: http://articles.economictimes.indiatimes.com/2014-07-09/news/51248126_1_urea-price-p-and-k-fertilizers-fertilizer-subsidy

88   Lok Sabha Unstarred Question No. 2710, dated 15.12.2015 & Lok Sabha Unstarred Question No. 1623, dated 08.03.2016; IndiaStat data

This overuse of urea is more pronounced in large states—especially Punjab, Haryana and Uttar Pradesh, where average consumption is significantly higher than other Asian economies. This skews the N:P and the N:K ratios significantly, affecting soil quality. In some states, the distortion in N:P ratio is more than 100 per cent, whereas it is even more in the case of N:K ratio—while on an average, India uses 100 per cent more nitrogen than recommended for given potash levels, the situation is grim in Rajasthan (~4,500 per cent more N than K), Punjab (~1,300 per cent more N than K) and Haryana (~1,200 per cent more N than K).

Changing fertilizer composition will require a significant revamp of the entire ecosystem, with urea pricing key. When the nutrient-based subsidy regime increased prices for all fertilizers except urea, farmers increased urea application.

Ensuring a balanced fertilizer use is not just about ensuring optimum NPK application. About 50 per cent of soil samples tested across the country (2 lakh samples) have recorded deficiency of zinc. Over 130 districts now suffer from deficiency of sulphur, which was once only limited to coarse soils under oilseed crop, with yield hikes with increased application of sulphur being recorded across forty crops. The application of magnesium (Mg) and boron (B) have also showcased significant yield increases.[89] These studies have highlighted that while yield enhancement from nitrogen-rich fertilizers can be a short-term gain, the long-term implications are usually detrimental—fields that were originally healthy can become deficient when cropped with only nitrogen-rich fertilizers.

SUPPORTING FERTILIZER UPTAKE

The Sivaraman Committee (1965) laid the foundation for the fertilizer sector regulations, encompassing production, promotion, distribution and consumption of fertilizers.[90] The Committee recommendations were made in the background of the Fertilizer (Control) Order, 1957/1985 (FCO) and the Fertilizer (Movement Control) Order, 1960/1973/2001 (FMCO). To ensure affordable availability of

---

89 Tiwari, K.N., The Changing Face of Balanced Fertilizer Use in India, Better Crops International Vol. 15, No. 2, November 2001. Sourced from: http://www.ipni.net/publication/bci.nsf/0/ B4EEDC01C4FCACD585257BBA006868BD/$FILE/Better%20Crops%20International%20 2001-2%20p24.pdf

90 Fertilizer Association of India (Sourced from: http://www.faidelhi.org/reports.htm)

fertilizers at the farm gate, the Marathe Committee (1976–78) was constituted, which equated a balance between affordability for farmers and return on investment for producers while upholding the ECA (Essential Commodities Act) Allocation Orders. The beast of subsidies is not new—the Singh Committee (1983) evolved a group retention price for existing units under different feedstock after taking into account various factors for rising cost of production, while recommending a uniform price later to contain the subsidies. However, none of the recommendations of the Singh Committee have been implemented. The GVK Rao Committee (1987) made recommendations for marginal increases in fertilizer prices (considering consumption spurt) for sustainable development, the Joint Parliamentary Committee (1991) on fertilizer pricing recommended price decontrol for P & K fertilizers while reducing urea prices—causing imbalance in incentives for balanced fertilizer use in the quest for managing subsidies and improving production sentiment, while completely ignoring any aspect of capital cost optimization. Fertilizer subsidies continued to rise, and the Expenditure Reforms Commission (2000) recommended decontrolled fertilizer industry, while fixing the farm gate prices of N, P and K fertilizers (including urea) to promote balanced fertilizer usage. The Gokak Committee, on recommendations of the ERC, suggested input energy consumption norms, with a view to replace the retention pricing system with the Group Concession Scheme. Thus, the fertilizer sector remains replete with policies and regulations with various Committee studies trying to achieve balanced fertilizer use, incentivize production and contain ever-rising fertilizer subsidies.

Our policies have pursued different objectives over various periods. Cost-effective urea production was discouraged through urea subsidies, provided to producers, under the Retention Price Scheme (RPS), effective till 2003, and its substitute, the New Pricing Scheme (NPS) and its various versions (NPS-I, NPS-II & NPS-III), ensuring that inefficient producers get more subsidies.[91] The subsidies misutilized in this process can be significant—about 24 per cent of urea subsidies in 2012–13 were misutilized to sustain inefficient production, a consequence of fixed retail prices. Over the last fifteen years, the fertilizer sector has not seen any significant new-field investments, with private sector participants routinely touting their intention to exit the sector.

---

91   Economic Survey 2015-16, Chapter 9, Reforming the Fertilizer Sector. Sourced from: http://indiabudget. nic.in/es2015-16/echapvol1-09.pdf

PRICING FERTILIZERS

By ignoring the 'one-product, one-price' principle, the government has also increased leakages to other industries and across borders. Urea is routinely smuggled across borders—with a 75 per cent subsidy, a 50-kg bag of urea costs ~₹268, it costs ~₹685 (800 takas) in Bangladesh and ~₹622 (996 Nepal rupees) in Nepal. About 41 per cent of urea allocated to agriculture is estimated to be diverted to industry and across borders, leading to ~51 per cent of Indian farmers buying urea at higher than MRP prices from the black market. Those closest to the borders are the hardest hit, ~100 per cent of farmers in Assam, West Bengal, Odisha and Bihar pay more than MRP rates, ~67 per cent of farmers in Uttar Pradesh pay more than MRP rates for a bag of urea. The development of this black market can have a significant impact on small and medium farmers—the share of additional expense borne by small farmers is 17 per cent higher than expense borne by large farmers, with small farmers in Punjab, Tamil Nadu and Uttar Pradesh being worse off—paying 60 per cent more than the large farmers.

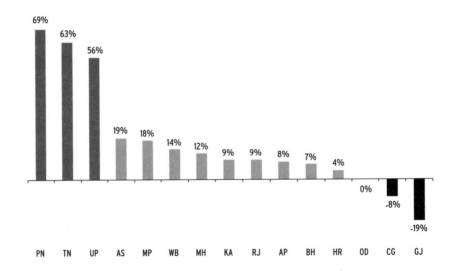

FIGURE 19: IMPACT OF BLACK MARKETING—SHARE OF ADDITIONAL EXPENDITURE BORNE BY SMALL FARMERS RELATIVE TO LARGE FARMERS

REINVIGORATING FERTILIZER UPTAKE

There are a few steps that the government can take to reinvigorate the fertilizer sector. We need to bolster the local fertilizer industry—timely delivery of subsidy would improve working capital requirements, enabling them to manage costs through internal sources rather than external loans. The average outstanding amount on a regular basis payable to the producers has led to an interest outgo of ₹3,500 crore itself, which causes companies to report losses each quarter on account of additional borrowing costs.[92]

We need to change the fixed price model in a cost-plus-margin policy that favours inefficient producers. We should set incentives that bring in production efficiencies—both in terms of quality and cost. With energy costs comprising ~75–80 per cent of the operational expenditure for a fertilizer plant, the establishment of fertilizer plants in countries with cheap gas prices (e.g. Oman, Iran) can provide cost-efficient fertilizer production.

In addition, urea should be brought under the Nutrient Based Subsidy scheme with a recalibration of urea, Di-Ammonium Phosphate (DAP) and Murate of Potash (MoP) prices—with urea prices rising and DAP+MoP prices falling, farmers would be encouraged to ensure balanced NPK consumption, with overall subsidy and farmer cost remaining the same.

Black marketing of urea needs to be restricted. The government's steps to encourage neem-coating of urea can add significant value—only 50 per cent of conventional urea is typically absorbed by the plant, with the remaining seeping into the bottom soil, causing groundwater contamination. Neem oil slows down the release of nitrogen by about 15 per cent with its 'slow release' mechanism, consequently reducing the fertilizer consumption and increasing yields. Field trials have shown significant benefits, with rice and wheat yields increasing by 10 per cent and 7 per cent, respectively. It can also reduce such illegal diversion, especially in the chemical industry (Punjab and Haryana) and dairy industry. It has the potential to save ~₹6,500 crore in subsidies—twice the interest outgo on account of delayed payment of subsidies to producers.

We should also free up urea imports—only three canalizing agents are allowed to import urea in the country, with specific directives on the quantity to be imported, consignment-wise subsidy and its intended destination. After the decision to import a specified quantity of urea is made, it takes as much as two months for the fertilizer

92   Datta, K., Neem-coated truth: Urea policy isn't a game-changer, Business Standard, 16 February 2016, Sourced from: http://www.business-standard.com/article/economy-policy/neem-coated-truth-urea-policy-isn-t-a-game-changer-116021601168_1.html

to reach the distribution centres—meanwhile, the farmer risks missing the critical weather window, forcing him to buy from the black market. Free import of urea by public and private agencies can relieve these supply issues and market distortions in the Indian fertilizer industry.

The Direct Benefit Transfer (DBT) mechanism should be utilized to distribute fertilizer subsidy, making use of the Jan Dhan Yojana. Such a move would however, need to be targeted at the poor; we need to ensure that tenant farmers tilling someone else's land are not missed out.[93] Soluble fertilizers can be an ideal solution—they can be bought under the NBS scheme, and fertigation can reduce overall fertilizer consumption, boosting agricultural productivity, improving soil health and providing better farm economics with long-term environmental sustainability.

Similar to how LPG subsidies were reformed, the government can also seek to cap the number of subsidized urea bags a household can purchase with biometric identification at point of sale making large-scale diversions difficult—all while poor farmers continue to avail of the benefit of cheaper urea. Pilot trials will be needed to develop the mechanism further, prior to national implementation. A software-based approach (proposed by Visakhapatnam DC) can also be explored—the software integrating all primary agricultural credit societies, fertilizer dealers (also sugar factory suppliers) and land details to ensure a farmer doesn't use more urea than the stipulated amount, improving compliance.

The Soil Health Card Scheme, launched as a corrective measure, is expected to help detect and correct the imbalance in fertilizer usage, while boosting productivity. The scheme seeks to provide ~140 million farmers with a soil health card over a period of three years—as of 2015-end, there were 1,244 government labs that could conduct testing for 9 million samples annually.[94] The eponymous soil health card will provide information on nutritional balance in their local soil, alongside fertilizer advice to obtain optimum yields. Farmers will have to renew the card every three years, giving them a chance to monitor their farm's soil health. The higher budget can cater to urgent requirements for more labs (approximately cost ₹3 crore per lab), a greater number of mobile facilities and a rise in technical staff, all to ensure adequate geographic coverage.

---

93   http://indiabudget.nic.in/es2015-16/echapter-vol1.pdf

94   Bera, S., A soil health card not enough for balanced fertilizer use, Live Mint, 14 August 2015. Sourced from: http://www.livemint.com/Politics/1xM0dNr7g9BLYw5Rx45tvK/A-soil-health-card-not-enough-for-balanced-fertilizer-use.html

CROP PROTECTION

Pest control matters. In 2016, the fear of the whitefly pest led farmers to cut down cotton cultivation in Punjab, with the area under cotton crop shrinking to 2.56 lakh hectares, compared to 4.5 lakh hectares in 2015 (a drop of 43.11 per cent; the lowest cultivated area since 1955–56) and cotton output dropping to 9 lakh bales, from 12 lakh bales in 2015. With whitefly instances observed in Mansa and Bathinda districts, farmers substituted paddy instead.[95]

Crop pests have historically had a major impact on rural societies. Wheat rust epidemics in India (1850–1950) led to the declaration of twenty-seven major famines and drove India to starvation. The famed potato leaf blight in Ireland (1845–46) left over 3 million people dead. Rice brown leaf spot in Bengal (1942–43) left another 2 million dead. Groundnut rosette virus disease in sub-Saharan Africa (1900 till date) has caused over fifteen epidemics in, with losses over $300 million per epidemic. Insect pests associated with rice, sorghum and maize regularly cause 10–35 per cent yield losses annually. In addition, weeds of cotton, rice and maize can cause an additional ~20 per cent yield loss annually.[96] Evolution continuously occurs—over the last few years, we have seen the emergence of many new pests in India (banana leaf roller), South-east Asia (cassava mealy bug), West Africa (tomato yellow leaf curl virus) and Bangladesh (cucumber mosaic virus).[97]

TABLE 13: CROP-WISE PEST INCREASE SINCE 1940 (SOURCE: AGRICULTURAL CENSUS, ANALYSIS BY TATA STRATEGIC MANAGEMENT LIMITED[98])

CROP	1940		AT PRESENT	
	TOTAL NO. OF PESTS	NO. OF SERIOUS PESTS	TOTAL NO. OF PESTS	NO. OF SERIOUS PESTS
RICE	35	10	240	17
WHEAT	20	2	100	19
SUGAR CANE	28	2	240	43
GROUNDNUT	10	4	100	12
MUSTARD	10	4	38	12
PULSES	35	6	250	34

95   Aujlal, I., Whitefly fear: Cotton acreage drops to 61-year low, Times of India, 10 July, 2016. Sourced from: http://timesofindia.indiatimes.com/city/chandigarh/Whitefly-fear-Cotton-acreage-drops-to-61-year-low/articleshow/53135445.cms

96   Lenne, J., Pests and poverty: the continuing need for crop protection research, Outlook on Agriculture, Vol 29, No 4, 2000, pp 235-250. Sourced from: http://www.envirobase.info/PDF/CPPPestsPoverty.pdf

97   Pretty, J., Bharucha, Z.P., Integrated Pest Management for Sustainable Intensification of Agriculture in Asia and Africa, , 5 March 2015, Insects 2015, 6(1), 152-182; doi:10.3390/insects6010152

98   Agrochemicals Knowledge Report, FICCI, Tata Strategic Management Group, Nov 2015. Sourced from: http://ficci.in/spdocument/20662/Agrochemicals-Knowledge-report.pdf

Farmers have witnessed a significant rise in number of pests attacking their crops—the number of pests harmful for rice increased from thirty-five to 240 and for wheat from twenty to 100. This damage illustrates the significant need for agrochemicals to power India's second green revolution.

PESTICIDES ARE NOT NOVEL

The application of pesticides to mitigate such threats is not a recent phenomenon. The Sumerians regularly used sulphur compounds for insect control in 2500 BC. Ancient Chinese farmers treated seeds with organic substances, mercury and arsenic compounds to combat natural pests and lice. Pliny regularly recommended the use of arsenic as an insecticide, while ancient Greece and Rome saw the use of a wide variety of fumigants, oil sprays and sulphur ointments.[99] References to plant protection can be found in the *Rigveda* (c. 3700 BC), *Krishi-Parashara* (c. 100 BC), *Agni Purana* (c. AD 400), Varaha Mihira's *Brhat-Samhita* (c. AD 500), Suprapala's *Vrikshayurveda* (c. 1000 BC), Sarangadhara's *Upavanavinoda* (c. AD 1300), *Tuzuk-e-Jahangiri* (c. AD 1600), Dara Shikoh's *Nuskha Dar Fanni–Falahat* (c. AD 1650) and Watt's *Dictionary of Economic Products of India* (1889–1893).[100] Kautilya proposed using seed dressers for better germination, with *Krishi-Parashara* mentioning even the pests such as pandarundi (rice stem borer). Jati Jaichand's diary (1658–1714) mentions possibly botrytis gray mould of chickpea and ear blight (Curvularia penniseti) of pearl millet (Javalia et al., 2001). The roots of vasika and branches of atimuktaka, mustard, bidanga, ash, mahua and custa—all had their uses in fighting pest proliferation in medieval times.

By the eighteenth century, widespread use of natural pesticides was common—nicotine, mercuric oxide and copper sulphate were commonly used as fungicides. The Bordeaux mixture (copper sulphate and lime) was found to be surprisingly effective against powdery mildew in 1882, while Paris Green (copper arsenite) was a common pesticide by the nineteenth century. By the advent of the twentieth century, calcium arsenate was replacing Paris Green, while synthetic organic compounds (alkyl thiocyanate insecticides, dichlorodiphenyltrichloroethane or DDT) were discovered. Organophosphates (parathion, malathion), carbamates and synthetic pyrethroids soon came into use. Modern pesticides, despite their

---

99 Pretty, J., Bharucha, Z.P., Integrated Pest Management for Sustainable Intensification of Agriculture in Asia and Africa, , 5 March 2015, Insects 2015, 6(1), 152-182; doi:10.3390/insects6010152

100 Chandrasekaran, B., Annadurai, K., & Somasundaram, E. (2010). A textbook of agronomy. New Delhi: New Age International.

deleterious side effects, have been shown to increase crop output substantially—an 1.8 per cent increase in pesticide usage typically leads to a 1 per cent increase in crop output per hectare.[101]

As such, India's domestic crop protection market is now worth $2.25 billion (₹14,000 crore), expected to grow at 8 per cent CAGR till 2019, with insecticides constituting 60 per cent of the market and herbicides 16 per cent.[102] This market is served by over 125 technical grade manufacturers, ~800 formulators and over 145,000 distributors. Andhra Pradesh (21 per cent of total market), Maharashtra and Punjab predominate, contributing to 45 per cent of India's pesticide consumption. And yet, India's per hectare pesticide consumption remains amongst the lowest in the world (0.6 kg/ha vs 13 kg/ha in China). Government incentives continue to encourage farmer uptake.

TABLE 14: PLANT PROTECTION—TYPE OF ASSISTANCE IN MAHARASHTRA[103]

NO	TYPE OF ASSISTANCE	QUANTUM OF ASSISTANCE	SCHEME
1	SUPPORT FOR DEMONSTRATION OF INTEGRATED PEST MANAGEMENT IN FARMER'S FIELD	MAXIMUM LIMIT PER HECTARE MUSTARD— TRICHODERMA, NEEM ₹1,500 GROUNDNUT- TRICHODERMA, CHRYSOPERLA, NPV, NEEM – ₹1,627; SOYABEAN - TRICHODERMA, NPV, NEEM – ₹1,500; SUNFLOWER -TRICHODERMA, CHRYSOPERLA, NPV, BT – ₹1,230; MAIZE - TRICHODERMA, CHRYSOPERLA, BT – ₹1,480	ISOPOM (FOR GROUNDNUT, SOYABEAN, NIGER, RAPESEED, MUSTARD, SUNFLOWER, SAFFLOWER, CASTOR, LINSEED, MAIZE)
2	DEMONSTRATION OF INTEGRATED PEST MANAGEMENT ON FARMER'S FIELD.	₹22,680 PER DEMONSTRATION	-DO-
3	DISTRIBUTION OF INSECTICIDES AND WEEDICIDES	50 PER CENT OF THE COST OR ₹500 PER HECTARE, WHICHEVER IS LESS	-DO-
4	SUPPORT FOR LPM, PESTICIDES, INTEGRATED NUTRIENT MANAGEMENT, FERTIGATION, TREE GUARD, ETC.	50 PER CENT OF THE COST LIMITED TO ₹5,000 PER HECTARE	SPECIAL PROGRAMME ON OIL PALM AREA EXPANSION.
5	SUPPORT FOR FUNGICIDES FOR SEED TREATMENT, PESTICIDES, BIO-CONTROL AGENTS, NPV (VIRUS), ORGANIC PESTICIDE PHEROMONE TRAP, ETC. FOR PULSE PRODUCTION	UP TO ₹860 TO ₹1,450 PER UNIT PER HECTARE	ACCELERATED PULSE PRODUCTION PROGRAMME. (A 3P)
6	DISTRIBUTION OF PLANT PROTECTION CHEMICALS AND ORGANIC PESTICIDES IN PADDY CROP	50 PER CENT OF THE COST OR ₹500 PER HECTARE, WHICHEVER IS LESS	NATIONAL FOOD SECURITY MISSION RICE
7	DISTRIBUTION OF CHEMICAL AND ORGANIC PESTICIDE FOR IPM IN PULSE CROPS	50 PER CENT OF THE COST OR ₹750 PER HECTARE, WHICHEVER IS LESS	NATIONAL FOOD SECURITY MISSION
8	INTEGRATED PEST MANAGEMENT IN HORTICULTURAL CROPS	LIMITED TO 4 HECTARE PER BENEFICIARY AT ₹1,000 PER HECTARE	NATIONAL HORTICULTURE MISSION AND HORTICULTURE MISSION FOR NORTHEASTERN AND HIMALAYAN STATES

101 Schreinemachersa, P.,Tipraqsab, P., Agricultural pesticides and land use intensification in high, middle and low income countries, Food Policy, Volume 37, Issue 6, December 2012, Pages 616-626

102 Agrochemicals Knowledge Report, FICCI, Tata Strategic Management Group, Nov 2015. Sourced from: http://ficci.in/spdocument/20662/Agrochemicals-Knowledge-report.pdf

103 Krishi Handbook (English Version), Publication No. 1762, Department of Agriculture, Government of Maharashtra, August 2012

9	SUPPLY OF BIO-AGENTS / BIO-PESTICIDES	25 PER CENT OF THE COST, LIMITED TO ₹500 /HA	MACRO MANAGEMENT OF AGRICULTURE
10	CROP PROTECTION IMPLEMENTS/ IMPROVED AGRI IMPLEMENTS	₹10,000 LIMIT	SCP, TSP & OTSP (STATE GOVT)
11	BIO-INTENSIVE AT DIFFERENT STAGES	BIO-INTENSIVE AT DIFFERENT STAGES OF CROP GROWTH; 50 PER CENT COST MUSTARD – ₹930, GROUNDNUT – ₹1627.50, SOYABEAN – ₹480, SUNFLOWER – ₹1,230	OILSEED PRODUCTION PROGRAMME
12	PLANT PROTECTION CHEMICALS	50 PER CENT COST OF CHEMICALS OR ₹500/ HA, WHICHEVER IS LESS	OILSEED PRODUCTION PROGRAMME
13	SUPPLY OF WEEDICIDES	50 PER CENT COST OF CHEMICALS OR ₹500/ HA, WHICHEVER IS LESS	OILSEED PRODUCTION PROGRAMME
14	SUPPLY OF RHIZO AND PSB	50 PER CENT COST OF CULTURE OR ₹100/HA, WHICHEVER IS LESS	OILSEED PRODUCTION PROGRAMME

POLICYMAKING FOR CROP PROTECTION

India's agricultural policy has been cognizant of pesticide usage. The manufacture, sale, distribution of pesticides is governed by the Insecticides Bill, 1968 and Insecticide Rules, 1971, broadly known as the Insecticides (Amendment) Act, 2000. Pesticide testing is a rigorous process, with forty-nine State Pesticide Testing Laboratories (SPTLs) located in twenty states and two Regional Pesticide Testing Laboratories (RPTLs) to bolster resources for SPTL and catering to states without any SPTL.[104] The Pesticide Management Bill, 2008 propagating the improved and safe use of pesticides including manufacturing, inspection, testing and distribution, and replace the Insecticide Act, 1968 still awaits approval.[105] The Bill aims to ensure availability of quality pesticides, and minimizing the contamination of agricultural commodities with pesticide residue. It also heralds a change in terms of types of substances covered, extending it to cover any substance of biological or chemical origin used to control pest proliferation. Inspection and testing would enable classification of pesticides—be it being misbranded, substandard or spurious (including imitations, expired and unregistered pesticides). The tolerance limit prescribed would have to be in line with the provisions of the Food Safety and Standards Act, 2006 (FSSA, 2006). Even for pests, the Government of India passed a comprehensive act in as early as 1914, the Destructive Insects and Pests (DIP) Act to regulate the import of any article into India likely to carry any pest that may be destructive to any crop. The DIP act complements with the Livestock Importation Act (LI Act), 1898 and the Prevention and Control of Infectious and

---

104 Agricultural Legislations. (n.d.). Retrieved from http://icar.org.in/files/Agril-Legislation.pdf

105 Source – PRS India – Pending Bills. Sourced from: http://www.prsindia.org/billtrack/the-pesticide-management-bill-2008-169/

Contagious Diseases in Animals Act, 2009 (PCDA Act), but with many players complaining about the ineffectiveness of these Acts, a modification to the DIP has been proposed, which involves establishing the Agricultural Biosecurity Authority of India (ABAI) to protect plants, animals and related products from pests and diseases to ensure agricultural biosecurity, in line with the recommendation of the National Commission on Farmers, 2007. The ABAI, proposed to function as an integrated national authority covering plant, animal and marine health with respect to biosecurity matters will be helpful to regulate biosecurity intra and inter-state. This also calls for greater state participation and a member from each state in the ABAI can be looked at (as recommended by the Standing Committee), besides cost recovery for action taken in controlled areas from the state exchequer.

MEETING EXPECTATIONS OF FARMERS

Despite this growth, the industry faces challenges in meeting farmer expectations. About 40 per cent of the pesticides sold in India are non-genuine (counterfeit, adulterated or sub-standard) formulations which are unable to kill pests effectively or efficiently. They also leave byproducts which can harm the environment, wreck soil fertility and potentially lead to eutrophication. Only 25–30 per cent of all farmers have any knowledge about agrochemicals and their benefits, along with the right dosage and frequency.[106] Most retailers have little to no knowledge about the product. There remains a long gestation period for new and innovative products, with underfunded regulatory bodies failing to conduct timely registration of new products.

In addition, the application of pesticides imposes significant trade-offs on farmers and consumers. Pesticides have proved harmful for bees[107] and have been proved to have a significant impact on human health, potentially causing deadly poisoning[108] and cancer in young children.[109] Glyphosate, a commonly used herbicide globally,

106 Agrochemicals Knowledge Report, FICCI, Tata Strategic Management Group, Nov 2015. Sourced from: http://ficci.in/spdocument/20662/Agrochemicals-Knowledge-report.pdf

107 EPA Releases the First of Four Preliminary Risk Assessments for Insecticides Potentially Harmful to Bees, EPA, 1 June 2016. Sourced from: https://yosemite.epa.gov/opa/admpress.nsf/eeffe922a687433c85257359003f5340/63e7fb0e47b1aa3685257f320050a7e3!OpenDocument

108 Highly hazardous pesticides should be phased out in developing countries, FAO, 30 July 2013, Sourced from: http://www.fao.org/news/story/en/item/180968/icode/

109 Guyton K.Z., Loomis, D., Grosse. Y., El Ghissassi, F., Benbrahim-Tallaa, L., Guha, N., Scoccianti, C., Mattock, H., Straif, K., Carcinogenicity of tetrachlorvinphos, parathion, malathion, diazinon, and glyphosate, The Lancet Oncology, Volume 16, No 5, p490-491, May 2015

has been declared 'probably carcinogenic' by the World Health Organization (WHO).[110] Farmers and labourers engaged in the application of pesticides are at risk of occupational exposure, with prenatal exposure to pesticides from mothers leading to visual memory impairment and motor task dysfunction in children.[111] Pesticide poisoning remains significantly underreported by 50–80 per cent worldwide[112] and risks increase when such hazardous chemicals are distributed without raising awareness about proper handling techniques and associated dangers.

MITIGATING PESTICIDE RUN-OFF

Despite all this, India's history with the hazards of pesticide use remains grim. In 1958, Kerala saw the death of over hundred people from consumption of wheat flour contaminated with parathion (Karanukaran, 1958). The Surveillance of Food Contaminants in India (1993) found DDT residues in 82 per cent of 2,205 samples of milk collected from twelve states, of which 37 per cent had residues over the tolerance limit (0.05 mg/kg of whole milk).[113] By 1992, the average total DDT and HCH consumed by Indians was reported to be 115 and 48 mg per person, much higher than in developed countries (Kannan et al, 1992). Fifty-eight per cent of drinking water samples drawn from various hand pumps and wells around rural Bhopal were contaminated with Organo Chlorine (OCs) pesticides, way above EPA standards (Kole & Bagchi, 1995).[114] The Ganga River Basin remains heavily polluted with pesticides and resulting effluents (Mohan, 1989) while several studies have reported the presence of OCs in humans and wildlife in India (Senthilkumar et al, 2000).

It can result in tragic incidents. Twenty-three children in the age range of five to twelve years died in 2013 in Dharmashati Gandaman village in Saran district of

---

110   Cressey, D., Widely Used Herbicide Linked to Cancer, Scientific American, 25 March 2015. Sourced from: http://www.scientificamerican.com/article/widely-used-herbicide-linked-to-cancer/

111   Harari, R., Julvez, J., Murata, K., Barr, D., Bellinger, D.C., Debes, F., Grandjean, P., Neurobehavioral Deficits and Increased Blood Pressure in School-Age Children Prenatally Exposed to Pesticides, Environ Health Perspect 118:890-896 (2010). http://dx.doi.org/10.1289/ehp.0901582 [online 25 February 2010]

112   The Atlas of Children's Health and Environment in the Americas (2011). Sourced from: http://www.paho.org/hq/index.php?option=com_docman&task=doc_view&gid=20365&Itemid=721

113   Aktar, Md. Wasim, Sengupta, Dwaipayan, Chowdhury, Ashim, Impact of pesticides use in agriculture: their benefits and hazards, Interdisc Toxicol. 2009; Vol. 2(1): 1–12. doi: 10.2478/v10102-009-0001-7. Sourced from: http://www.intertox.sav.sk/ITX_pdf/02_01_2009/10102-Volume2_Issue_1-01_paper.pdf

114   Ibid

Bihar after consuming a meal that was contaminated with monocrotophos. The students started vomiting soon after having their first bite of rice and potatoes that were provided at their local primary school. Children who had complained about the food were rebuked by the headmistress.[115]

India's continued use of poorly regulated generic pesticides has led to the 'lock-in' of several obsolete products. By 2011, global consensus had been reached on adding endosulfan to the list of banned substances and phasing it out as an agrochemical. However, India sought a further ten-year moratorium to phase out the chemical. Protective clothing remains mostly unknown, and poisoning and hospitalization is common.[116,117]

Government policy can be fine-tuned to encourage bio-pesticides—these are microbial biological pest control agents that are applied in a manner similar to chemical pesticides; however, they are biodegradable, leaving few, if any, harmful residues. There are more than 1,250 registered bio-pesticide products in the US currently.[118]

SAFETY FOR PESTICIDES

The registration process of the Central Insecticides Board and Registration Committee (CIBRC) is shambolic, with registration recommendations made by all agriculture departments, universities and boards exceeding the pesticides that CIBRC has approved for a crop.[119] Farmers are stuck between the two—following local state advice to use a specific pesticide, despite the CIBRC not registering it. Waiting periods associated with each pesticide need to be defined and data on the use of banned pesticides collected. Regulatory approvals should be fast-tracked for

115 Violent protests in India over school meal deaths, BBC, 17 July 2013. Sourced from: http://www.bbc. co.uk/news/world-asia-india-23342003

116 Pretty, Jules, Bharucha, Zareen Perves, Integrated Pest Management for Sustainable Intensification of Agriculture in Asia and Africa, , 5 March 2015, Insects 2015, 6(1), 152-182; doi:10.3390/insects6010152

117 Athukorala, W.; Wilson, C.; Robinson, T. Determinants of health costs due to farmers' exposure to pesticides: An empirical analysis. In Proceedings of the 85th Annual Conference of Western Economic Association, Hilton Portland and Executive Tower, Portland, OR, USA, 29 June–3 July 2010.

118 Bharadwaj, Tulsi, Sharma, J.P., Impact of Pesticides Application in Agricultural Industry: An Indian Scenario, International Journal of Agriculture and Food Science Technology. ISSN 2249-3050, Volume 4, Number 8 (2013), pp. 817-822. Sourced from: http://www.ripublication.com/ijafst_spl/ijafstv4n8spl_18. pdf

119 Bhushan, C., Bhardwaj, A. and Misra, S.S. 2013, State of Pesticide Regulations in India, Centre for Science and Environment, New Delhi, Sourced from: http://www.cseindia.org/userfiles/paper_pesticide.pdf

innovative, eco-friendly crop protection products that can help beat back pests and boost soil fertility. Tracking the sale of banned pesticide is almost impossible without any system in place—a crackdown on non-genuine pesticides is required, while farmer awareness about the deleterious impact of such products needs to be raised.

In addition, the minimum residue limits (MRLs) for pesticides need further definition. The recommendations of the 4th Joint Parliamentary Committee on Pesticide Residues and Safety Standards for Soft Drinks, Fruit Juice and Other Beverages , 2005, required MRLs of all registered and deemed pesticides to be set, along with a review of their compliance with the Acceptable Daily Intake (ADI).

INTEGRATED PEST MANAGEMENT

Our agricultural policy should also encourage integrated pest management (IPM), an approach that focuses on combining biological, chemical, mechanical and physical means to combat pests, with a long-term focus on eliminating or significantly reducing the need for pesticides. All pests have a natural predator—incorporating the latter's use in pest management can help minimize or potentially eliminate the use of chemical pesticides.

TABLE 15: IPM APPLICATIONS[120]

NO.	TYPE	EXAMPLES OF APPLICATION
1	SUBSTITUTION OF PESTICIDAL PRODUCTS WITH OTHER COMPOUNDS	SYNTHETIC PESTICIDE WITH HIGH TOXICITY SUBSTITUTED BY ANOTHER PRODUCT WITH LOW TOXICITY. USE OF AGROBIOLOGICALS OR BIOPESTICIDES (E.G. DERIVED FROM NEEM)
2	MANAGEMENT OF APPLICATION OF PESTICIDES	TARGETED SPRAYING. THRESHOLD SPRAYING PROMPTED BY DECISION-MAKING DERIVED FROM OBSERVATION/DATA ON PEST, DISEASE OR WEED INCIDENCE
3	CROP OR LIVESTOCK BREEDING	DELIBERATE INTRODUCTION OF RESISTANCE OR OTHER TRAITS INTO NEW VARIETIES OR BREEDS (E.G., RECENT USE OF GENETIC MODIFICATION FOR INSECT RESISTANCE AND/OR HERBICIDE TOLERANCE)
4	RELEASES OF ANTAGONISTS, PREDATORS OR PARASITES TO DISRUPT OR REDUCE PEST POPULATIONS	STERILE BREEDING OF MALE PEST INSECTS TO DISRUPT MATING SUCCESS AT POPULATION LEVEL. IDENTIFICATION AND DELIBERATE RELEASE OF PARASITOIDS OR PREDATORS TO CONTROL PEST POPULATIONS
5	DEPLOYMENT OF PHEROMONE COMPOUNDS TO MOVE OR TRAP PESTS	STICKY AND PHEROMONE TRAPS FOR PEST CAPTURE
6	AGROECOLOGICAL HABITAT DESIGN	SEED AND SEED BED PREPARATION. DELIBERATE USE OF DOMESTICATED OR WILD CROPS/PLANTS TO PUSH-PULL PESTS, PREDATORS AND PARASITES. USE OF CROP ROTATIONS AND MULTIPLE-CROPPING TO LIMIT PEST, DISEASE AND WEED CARRYOVER ACROSS SEASONS OR VIABILITY WITHIN SEASONS. ADDING HOST-FREE PERIODS INTO ROTATIONS. ADDING STAKES TO FIELDS FOR BIRD PERCHES

120 Pretty, J., Bharucha, Z.P., Integrated Pest Management for Sustainable Intensification of Agriculture in Asia and Africa, , 5 March 2015, Insects 2015, 6(1), 152-182; doi:10.3390/insects6010152

IPM has numerous examples that demonstrate its efficacy. Bangladesh was able to cut back its pesticide use against the melon fly (infecting watermelons)—instead of spraying pesticides fifteen times during the season, it sought to create pheromone traps (a male-scented lure, 'Cuelure', along with a small amount of insecticide, inside a bottle). The traps were highly effective, catching five to eighteen times as many flies as the original traps, with damage going down by 70 per cent. Yields rose by 40–130 per cent within two years, while insecticide use was eliminated completely.[121,122]

Kenya has piloted a 'push-pull system, vutu sukumu'—with farmers mixing maize with legumes and planting a variety of grasses on farm borders. The system has proven highly effective—legumes released natural chemicals that pushed away maize pests; the grass borders pulled in predators through natural chemical odours. The overall combination was also successful in combating striga (also termed witchweed), an invasive parasitic weed.[123]

A 'no spray rule' was adopted by over 20 lakh farmers in the Mekong delta of Vietnam—thereby restricting insecticide application for the first forty days of planting rice. Predatory beetles were sustained and helped in cutting insecticide usage by more than half.

Developing and deploying Farmer Field Schools (FFS) to spread IPM is an innovative outdoor experience that can boost ecological knowledge, organize farmers and teach them about new technology. Each FFS is typically a group of twenty-five to thirty farmers, working in sub-groups, with a focused field-based and season-long training. Over ninety countries have set up FFSs, with a huge number of farmers graduated (e.g. Bangladesh – 650,000; Vietnam – 930,000; Indonesia – 1,500,000).[124]

IPM can help reduce pesticide use significantly, without a concomitant impact on crop yield. Studies (University of Essex) have measured pesticide use and crop yield at 85 project sites practising IPM in twenty-four African and Asian countries—finding that crop yield increased by ~41 per cent while pesticide use dropped by

121 Fruit fly frenzy for pheromones in Bangladesh. Sourced from: http://www.oired.vt.edu/ipmil/success-and-impact/success-stories/fruit-fly-pheromones-bangladesh/

122 Bajak, A., The developing world is awash in pesticides. There may be a better way., Ensia, Vox.com, 3 July 2016, http://www.vox.com/2016/7/3/12085368/developing-world-pesticides

123 Pretty, J., Bharucha, Z.P., Integrated Pest Management for Sustainable Intensification of Agriculture in Asia and Africa, , 5 March 2015, Insects 2015, 6(1), 152-182; doi:10.3390/insects6010152

124 Pretty, J., Bharucha, Z.P., Cut pesticide use to boost yields? It's worked for millions of farmers in Asia and Africa, The Conversation, 30 April 2015, https://theconversation.com/cut-pesticide-use-to-boost-yields-its-worked-for-millions-of-farmers-in-asia-and-africa-38951

67 per cent once IPM was adopted.[125,126] A kg of pesticide can impose \$4–\$19 worth of external costs on human health, local wildlife and the environment—such costs are incurred whenever clean-up is conducted (e.g. water companies filtering polluted water, the loss of pollinating honeybees). IPM can deliver a significant reduction in pesticide usage, while improving public health, sustaining bio-diversity and promoting sustainability.

> 'Today our villages are half-dead. If we imagine we can just/continue to live, that would be a mistake. The dying can pull/the living only towards death.' —Rabindranath Tagore (The Neglected Villages, 1934)

Gentrified India has a warm, fuzzy, Gandhian-influenced nostalgia for its villages. India's policymaking elite believes in a simplistic, nostalgic, green, pollution-free India of villages with simple folk and traditions. While partly true, everyday life in rural India is a living story of economic deprivation and social injustice. This hopelessness, never really alleviated by innumerable government schemes, manifests itself in farmer suicides, landless labourers and a feudal outlook. With skeletal cattle lying down, the despondent farmer continues to stare upwards for heavenly succour. The idea of marginal farming as an economic activity is seemingly dead.

Consider the case of Ramchand, a Scheduled Caste farmer from the Kol peasant community in the vicinity of Varanasi, in Uttar Pradesh. With just under an acre of inherited land, he and his two brothers toil away on their one-third share, seeking to grow paddy and wheat. About 0.33 acres of land resulted in just 1 quintal of wheat and 3 quintals of rice in 2016, far lower than even his household requirement of 5 quintals. While fortunate to have his land irrigated from a nearby canal, his input costs have continued to rise—last year, he spent ₹3,700 on agricultural inputs (including seeds, DAP and urea) for wheat and paddy. Furthermore, when demonetization hit, any payments in ₹500 notes provided by Ramchand incurred a 20 per cent commission by agricultural input traders. Unable to afford an agricultural labourer, any tilling or harvesting work is typically done by him or his family members. Despite such a shoe-string budget, last year's paddy and wheat harvest netted him a loss of ₹6,000. Agricultural surplus is a myth in rural India, with farmers like Ramchand finding it hard to make ends meet. Such farmers are increasingly forced to work as labourers at local stone quarries, earning ₹3,500 for quarrying over 500 cubic feet stones (typically taking two to three weeks of back-breaking effort). Eventually, such farmers will be forced to mortgage their land to make ends meet, while being denied credit from formal financing mechanisms. In

---

125 Hoff, M., A Win for farmers and the environment, Ensia.com, May 8 2015, Sourced from: http://ensia.com/notable/a-win-for-farmers-and-the-environment/

126 Pretty, J., Bharucha, Z.P., Integrated Pest Management for Sustainable Intensification of Agriculture in Asia and Africa, , 5 March 2015, Insects 2015, 6(1), 152-182; doi:10.3390/insects6010152

rural India, mortgaging one's land can typically mean letting the lender use the land until the loan is repaid.

ESCALATING INPUT COSTS

Let's consider the impact of such trends. With seed application rising, given an intensified cropping pattern, farmers are also seeing a rise in seed costs. Arhar prices nearly tripled from ₹27/kg in 2004 to ₹73/kg in 2013. Cotton saw a massive five-times jump from ₹396/kg to ₹1,860/kg, courtesy of the switch to Bt cotton. Maize, riven with crop failure, saw a similar jump from ₹20/kg to ₹99/kg. Even staple crops like paddy (₹6/kg to ₹31/kg), soyabean (₹20/kg to ₹40/kg) and sugar cane (₹89/kg to ₹230/kg) have seen a significant increase. The longstanding tradition of farmers handing seeds to the next generation as family heirlooms is long gone.

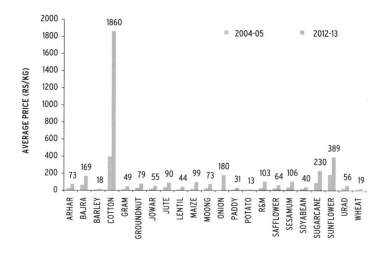

FIGURE 20: SEED PRICES (2004 VS 2013)[127]

Fertilizer prices have witnessed a comparable increase, with NPK fertilizers for cotton jumping from ₹14/kg to ₹26/kg, while plain barley saw a sudden jump from ₹9/kg in 2004–05 to ₹26/kg by 2012–13.

---

127   Adapted (averaged across states) from data sourced from the Department of Economics and Statistics. Sourced from: http://eands.dacnet.nic.in/Cost_of_Cultivation.htm

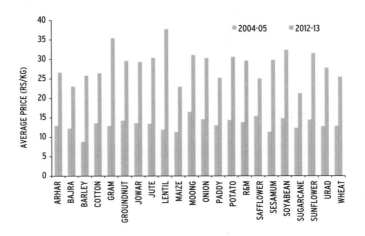

FIGURE 21: FERTILIZER PRICES (2004 VS 2013)[128]

The cost of human labour, a substitute often for agricultural machinery, has also shot up substantially.

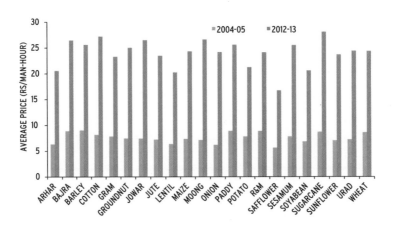

FIGURE 22: HUMAN LABOUR COST (2004 VS 2013)[129]

---

128 Ibid

129 Adapted (averaged across states) from data sourced from the Department of Economics and Statistics. Sourced from: http://eands.dacnet.nic.in/Cost_of_Cultivation.htm

The cost paid for ensuring plant protection through pesticides has gone through the roof, jumping nearly five times for arhar (from ₹281/hectare in 2004–05 to ₹1,138/hectare in 2012–13).

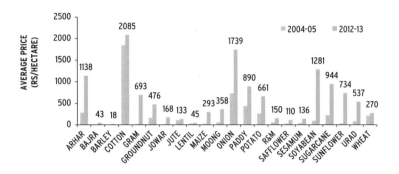

FIGURE 23: PESTICIDE COST (2004 VS 2013)[130]

The cost of labour, associated with both animal and machine labour, has also undergone a substantial jump. Hired animal labour for paddy cost ₹532/hectare in 2012–13 vs just ₹241/hectare in 2004–05. The cost of machine labour for wheat rose from ₹1,721/hectare in 2004–05 to ₹4,695/hectare in 2012–13.

130 Adapted (averaged across states) from data sourced from the Department of Economics and Statistics. Sourced from: http://eands.dacnet.nic.in/Cost_of_Cultivation.htm

TABLE 16: COST OF LABOUR (ANIMAL & MACHINE)[131]

	ANIMAL LABOUR				MACHINE LABOUR			
	HIRED (₹/HECTARE)		OWNED (₹/HECTARE)		HIRED (₹/HECTARE)		OWNED (₹/HECTARE)	
CROP TYPE	2004-05	2012-13	2004-05	2012-13	2004-05	2012-13	2004-05	2012-13
ARHAR	247	628	1343	1667	654	1845	86	189
BAJRA	311	202	654	726	1156	2936	141	217
BARLEY	163	16	1903	850	1172	3646	169	933
COTTON	178	403	1295	1885	797	2298	393	721
GRAM	91	140	533	520	922	3185	163	248
GROUNDNUT	572	587	876	1706	1087	2500	50	136
JOWAR	224	605	1127	1660	751	2532	20	60
JUTE	287	159	1461	2358	126	1728	8	107
LENTIL	61	287	328	721	965	2454	52	222
MAIZE	141	333	1193	951	493	3043	53	253
MOONG	98	243	1269	1467	539	1395	20	82
ONION	541	360	1479	543	958	2931	39	501
PADDY	241	532	1159	1490	1114	3695	368	361
POTATO	160	432	1473	948	883	2660	123	297
R&M	107	109	754	905	1036	3017	487	455
SAFFLOWER	177	0	869	2484	423	800	29	125
SESAMUM	123	295	474	748	681	1465	55	153
SOYABEAN	157	443	1422	1008	1030	3834	142	232
SUGAR CANE	345	1408	425	630	1675	3464	264	984
SUNFLOWER	557	1009	1219	1602	553	2664	27	165
URAD	96	238	793	1337	471	1718	22	202
WHEAT	95	301	893	483	1721	4695	359	479

On an overall basis, the cost of agricultural inputs, meanwhile, has risen substantially over the last decade.

---

131 Adapted (averaged across states) from data sourced from the Department of Economics and Statistics. Sourced from: http://eands.dacnet.nic.in/Cost_of_Cultivation.htm

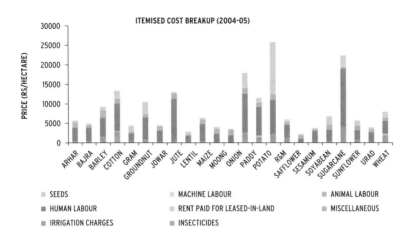

FIGURE 24: ITEMIZED COST BREAK-UP (2004-05)[132]

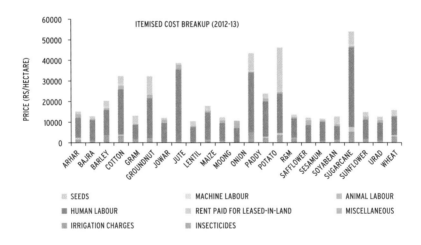

FIGURE 25: ITEMISED COST BREAKUP (2012-13)[133]

Amidst all this, agricultural input usage continues to rise.

132 Adapted (averaged across states) from data sourced from the Department of Economics and Statistics.
     Sourced from: http://eands.dacnet.nic.in/Cost_of_Cultivation.htm

133 Ibid

TABLE 17: USE OF INPUTS BY SIZE OF HOLDINGS[134]

FARM-SIZE GROUP	% OF OPERATIONAL HOLDINGS USING				% OF AREA TREATED WITH			
	CERTIFIED SEEDS		INSTITUTIONAL CREDIT		CHEMICAL FERTILIZERS		PESTICIDES	
	1997	2007	1997	2007	1997	2007	1997	2007
MARGINAL	30.4	32	9.5	19.6	64.1	73.6	17.3	73.6
SMALL	37.5	43.8	17.6	32.8	62.7	76.6	16.3	76.6
SEMI-MEDIUM	40.7	49.8	19.9	34.5	60.8	75.5	14.1	75.5
MEDIUM	43.4	54.2	23.1	39.4	57.4	71.5	12.4	71.5
LARGE	39.3	52.4	23	40.1	45	58.1	11.5	58.1
ALL GROUPS	34	37.5	13.4	25	58.8	72.6	14.4	72.6

ADAPTING TO RISING INPUT COSTS

Farmers are increasingly seeking solutions to manage such escalating input costs. Some have sought new technology and farming techniques. Jaspal Singh Munda, from Deoghar district in Jharkhand, used to struggle day and night to eke out some meagre earnings from his land, with crop failure common, and with some supplemental earnings from hard labour in the lean season.

However, a government-led training programme to improve his skills changed his focus from improving individual crop performance and increasing systemic productivity. The techniques taught him how to combine crops, develop limited horticulture as an alternative source of income, and seek to monetize livestock and aquaculture during the lean season. The focus was on developing a self-sustaining farm, by limiting the demand for agricultural inputs through recycling of materials. Bio-compost has substituted expensive fertilizers, prepared easily by digging a three-foot by six-foot pit, which is filled with dead plants, fallen leaves and dung, along with earthworms. Instead of plain tilling, he was trained in utilizing System of Wheat Intensification (SWI) and Kharif Paddy Stabilization (KPS), along with utilizing mixed cropping and inter-cropping to boost production. The result has been dramatic—his paddy yield has nearly doubled. Meanwhile, he has extra space now to grow potato, beans and pulses, allowing his family to have a wholesome meal at home.

---

134 Input Survey (various years), Agriculture Census Division, DAC, Ministry of Agriculture, Government of India, New Delhi.

Other farmers have sought a solution in organic farming. Agricultural scientists like Subhash Palekar, famous for the propagation of the idea of zero budget farming, have helped offer training to farmers in Sundargarh district in Odisha, in the production of 'Jeevamruta' (a concoction of cow dung, cow urine, jaggery, molasses and besan), and organic pesticides (from neem, karanja, calotropis and garlic leaves).[135] Farmers have been encouraged to go for multi-cropping, along with adoption of the System of Rice Intensification (SRI) method in cultivating staple crops like millets and mustard. Yields have improved substantially, rising 10–12x for the ragi crop in 2017. Young professionals have taken this idea forward in other districts of the country, particularly in villages in and around Latur in Maharashtra. Farmers have been encouraged to plant legumes to make the soil nitrogen-rich, while rotating crops to control pests and renew the soil.

Others, facing the rising input costs for certain crops, have sought to develop alternative revenue streams. The farmers in Valsad district in Gujarat have taken to bee-farming, realizing the role bees play as pollinators, while embracing a bee-friendly cropping pattern including secondary crops like gram, onions and hemp.[136] The impact of cultivating bees has been immediate, raising the yield of crops by 80 per cent amongst applicable farmers in the district, effectively an increase of ₹7,000–8,000 within a year in 2017. This has also led to income stability, with farmers being able to sell honey during the monsoon months when the land lies fallow.

In Assam's Gohainpukhuri village, in Lakhimpur district, the Mishing community has sought to scale up production from its fisheries—until recently, production remained low due to unavailability of quality fish seeds, infrastructure and limited awareness about scientific fish rearing.[137] Poor feeding practices, combined with the high cost of feeds, and limited pond management, also constrained production. Fish yield had hovered around 1 MT per hectare through traditional rearing methods. Entities like the Centre for Microfinance & Livelihood, along with the Mishing Autonomous Council, sought to establish promoters who could provide fish cultivation services to local fishermen, with the provision of good quality fry, fingerling and yearling. Such promoters were trained in fish seed cultivation, pond development, stocking, feed and pond management, and, finally, harvesting. At the end of the nine-month training cycle, local villagers were able to enhance the local

---

135 Village Square, Better India, July 2017. Sourced from: https://www.thebetterindia.com/108128/tribal-women-sundargarh-make-organic-farming-life-changing-economic-activity/

136 Pareek, S., Better India, March 2015. Sourced from: https://www.thebetterindia.com/21050/how-bee-keeping-is-positively-changing-indian-agricultural-scenario-mif-siap-utmt/

137 Mannan, A., "Assam youth are netting healthy incomes from fish seeds", Village Square, December 2017. Sourced from: https://www.villagesquare.in/2017/12/08/assam-youth-netting-healthy-incomes-fish-seeds/

fishing ecosystem, raising yields and improving their daily income.

In Maharashtra's Sindhudurg district, villages have started cultivating bamboo, instead of a focus on cotton, mango or palm trees, seeking to supplement their farm income.[138] The district itself annually receives around 2,000–4,000 mm of rainfall, with rice considered the primary crop. Bamboo, especially the Manga variety, when cultivated, requires little, if any, irrigation and is typically not susceptible to pests, offers protection from vertebrates required during the shoot growing season (a period of three months typically). Requiring minimum labour, and possessed with climatic hardiness, it can be easily marketed into a well-developed supply ecosystem. Farmers are increasingly cultivating bamboo as a tree-based intercrop, planting it around existing trees, where it tends to grow taller, seeking sunlight in a competitive environment.

Entrepreneurs have also sought to provide appropriate solutions—Kamal Kisan, a customized low-cost farm equipment firm, founded by engineer Devi Murthy, has sought to provide low-cost vegetable planters, power weeders, sugar cane planters, mulch layers and bed makers. Another start-up—FlyBird—has developed sensors that allow farmers to observe moisture content levels and highlight their irrigation requirements.[139] Such sensors have helped farmers in Karnataka and Tamil Nadu improve their crop yields by 15–20 per cent while reducing water requirements by 25–30 per cent.

THE COST OF CULTIVATION

However, this adaptation is not enough. Something is rotten in rural India. Input costs, for fertilizers, seeds and pesticides, have risen significantly, while food inflation ravages the rural markets.

Ramesh Yadav, a marginal farmer from Kaushambi district, in Uttar Pradesh, has trouble sleeping—with just 0.2 acres of land, typically irrigated by tube wells, he wonders about the fruits of his labour. He invested ₹4,000 on seeds, fertilizers and pesticides in the last season for his maize crop; it was an arduous struggle to till the land, with ploughing needed several times to de-clump it. Requiring careful

---

138   Bose, H.K., 'Konkan farms reap the bounty of bamboo', Village Square, December 2017. Sourced from: https://www.villagesquare.in/2017/12/18/konkan-farms-reap-bounty-bamboo/

139   Wangchuk, R.N., Better India, Dec 2017. Sourced from: https://www.thebetterindia.com/125044/5-agri-startups-farmers/

irrigation and weeding, the crop needed several weeks of effort for cultivation. However, when the harvest period arrived, the prices of maize crashed, so much so that the cost of harvesting and transport to Kaushambi's outlying markets was not feasible. He and his family had to settle for harvesting for their own use, with some given to relatives and friends. The rest was left to rot.

In the next cropping season, Ramesh tried to cultivate wheat—a crop that required hiring another labourer to help with tilling and harvesting. Given that he had spent a significant sum in purchasing fertilizer for his maize crop, he had to turn organic for wheat, tilling the land and harvesting the crop by hand. The harvest led to a marginal profit of just ₹2,000, after including the cost of labour, land and other resources. Meanwhile, marriage season had crept up and he had to take a loan of ₹60,000 from the local moneylender to fund his daughter's marriage, at a rate of 7.5 per cent for the current year. He doesn't know when he will pay off the principal—his wife works as a daily agricultural labourer to help them make ends meet. This is the reality of agriculture in India.

Given this jump in input costs, the cost of cultivation has gone up substantially, rising from ₹20,607 per hectare for paddy in 2004–05 to ₹47,644.5 per hectare in 2012–13. Fixed costs (cost of land, etc.) have had a significant part to play in this rise, along with a rise in variable costs like seeds, fertilizers and insecticides.

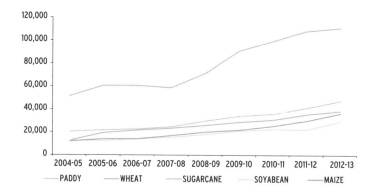

FIGURE 26: TOTAL COST OF CULTIVATION (PER HECTARE)[140]

---

140   Adapted (averaged across states) from data sourced from the Department of Economics and Statistics. Sourced from: http://eands.dacnet.nic.in/Cost_of_Cultivation.htm

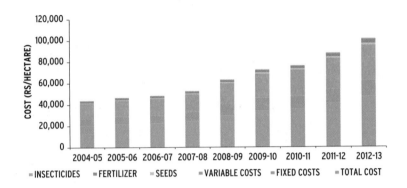

FIGURE 27: COST OF CULTIVATION FOR PADDY (PER HECTARE)[141]

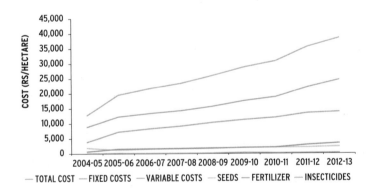

FIGURE 28: COST OF CULTIVATION (₹/HECTARE)[142]

---

141 Ibid

142 Adapted (averaged across states) from data sourced from the Department of Economics and Statistics.
      Sourced from: http://eands.dacnet.nic.in/Cost_of_Cultivation.htm

APPENDIX

Examples of agricultural input subsidies range across a variety of programmes through decades. The following shows examples in 2004 in Madhya Pradesh and Chhattisgarh:

TABLE 18: AGRICULTURAL INPUT SUBSIDIES UNDER INTEGRATED CEREALS DEVELOPMENT PROGRAMME[143]

NO.	ITEM	RATE OF SUBSIDY
1	CERTIFIED SEED DISTRIBUTION	A) CERTIFIED SEED DISTRIBUTION. 1. PADDY, WHEAT AND BARLEY–₹200 PER QUINTAL
		B) JOWAR, BAJRA AND OTHER MILLETS- ₹400 PER QUINTAL
		C) HYBRID PADDY- ₹500 PER QUINTAL
2	DEMONSTRATIONS	A) PRODUCTION TECHNIQUE DEMONSTRATIONS - 0.4 HECTARE DOUBLE/ SINGLE CROP DEMONSTRATIONS ₹2,000 / ₹1,000, RESPECTIVELY
		B) IPM DEMONSTRATIONS - (40 HECTARE OR ENTIRE VILLAGE)–₹6,000 PER DEMONSTRATION WITH TRAINING
3	AGRICULTURAL IMPLEMENTS	50 PER CENT OF THE COST OF IMPLEMENTS OR A MAXIMUM OF ₹1,500
4	POWER TILLER	50 PER CENT OF THE COST OF TILLER OR A MAXIMUM OF ₹30,000
5	SPRINKLER	A) 75 PER CENT OF THE COST APPROVED BY NABARD OR ₹15,000, WHICHEVER IS LESS, FOR FARMERS BELONGING TO SCHEDULED CASTES, SCHEDULED TRIBES AND WOMEN
		B) 50 PER CENT OF THE COST APPROVED BY NABARD OR ₹10,000,WHICHEVER IS LESS, FOR FARMERS BELONGING TO GENERAL CASTES
6	FARMERS' TRAINING	₹50 PER FARMER PER DAY FOR TWO DAYS FOR 50 FARMERS OR ₹5,000 PER TRAINING

---

143   Sharma, K.G., Agricultural Input Subsidies in India: Quantum of Subsidies to SC/ ST Farmers In Madhya Pradesh & Chhattisgarh, Agro Economic Research Centre for Madhya Pradesh and Chattisgarh J.N.K.V.V., Jabalpur (M.P.), June 2004. Sourced from: http://jnkvv.org/PDF/AERC/Study-90.pdf

TABLE 19: AGRICULTURAL INPUT SUBSIDIES UNDER NATIONAL
PULSES DEVELOPMENT PROGRAMME[144]

NO.	ITEM	RATE OF SUBSIDY		
1	SEED MINIKITS	100 PER CENT SUBSIDY ON THE VALUE FOR 0.2 HECTARE AREA		
2	CERTIFIED SEED DISTRIBUTION	₹300 PER QUINTAL SUBSIDY TO INSTITUTIONS DISTRIBUTING THE SEED		
3	BLOCK DEMONSTRATIONS	IN EVERY DEVELOPMENT BLOCK SEED DEMONSTRATIONS WILL BE CONDUCTED ON 10 HECTARES OR 5 HECTARES. SUBSIDY RATES WILL BE:		
		GRAM AND PEA- ₹1,400 PER HECTARE		
		ARHAR, MOONG AND URAD–₹900 PER HECTARE		
		LENTIL–₹1,000 PER HECTARE		
4	SEED VILLAGE PLAN	INSTITUTIONS WOULD BE ALLOWED SUBSIDY AT ₹200 PER QUINTAL. OUT OF THIS ₹150 PER QUINTAL WOULD BE ADMISSIBLE TO THE FARMERS		
5	MICRO NUTRIENTS	50 PER CENT OF THE COST OR MAXIMUM OF ₹100 PER HECTARE		
6	IPM DEMONSTRATIONS	FOR IPM DEMONSTRATIONS ON PULSES ON 10-HECTARE PLOT, SUBSIDY AT ₹1,500 PER HECTARE		
7	RHIZOBIUM CULTURE P.S.B. DISTRIBUTION	SUBSIDY AT ₹2 PER PACKET OR MAXIMUM OF ₹25 PER HECTARE		
		SUBSIDY AT ₹4 PER PACKET OR MAXIMUM OF ₹25 PER HECTARE		
8	SEED TREATMENT	A) SEED AND SOIL-BORNE DISEASES–50 PER CENT OF THE PRICE OF MEDICINE OR MAXIMUM OF ₹100 PER HECTARE		
	PLANT PROTECTION CHEMICALS/ WEEDICIDES	B) PLANT PROTECTION CHEMICALS/WEEDICIDES - 50 PER CENT OF THE VALUE OF CHEMICALS / WEEDICIDES WHICHEVER IS LESS, OR ₹100 PER HECTARE PER SPRAY FOR 2 SPRAYS		
9	IMPROVED AGRICULTURAL IMPLEMENTS	HAND / BULLOCK-DRAWN–SUBSIDY AT 50 PER CENT OF THE COST OR MAXIMUM OF ₹1,500		
		POWER-DRIVEN–SUBSIDY AT 30 PER CENT OF THE COST OR MAXIMUM OF ₹10,000 PER IMPLEMENT PER FARMER OR WHICHEVER IS LESS		
10	FARMERS' TRAINING	₹10,000 PER TRAINING FOR 50 FARMERS		
11	GYPSUM / PYRITE DISTRIBUTION	50 PER CENT OF MATERIAL COST INCLUDING TRANSPORTATION CHARGES TO A MAXIMUM OF ₹500 PER HECTARE		
12	NUCLEAR POLYHYDRAL VIRUS CULTURE DISTRIBUTION	50 PER CENT OF THE PRICE OR MAXIMUM OF ₹250 PER HECTARE, WHICHEVER IS LESS		

144 Sharma, K.G., Agricultural Input Subsidies in India : Quantum of Subsidies to SC/ ST Farmers In Madhya Pradesh & Chhattisgarh, Agro Economic Research Centre for Madhya Pradesh and Chattisgarh J.N.K.V.V., Jabalpur (M.P.), June 2004. Sourced from: http://jnkvv.org/PDF/AERC/Study-90.pdf

TABLE 20: AGRICULTURAL INPUT SUBSIDIES UNDER MODIFIED
COTTON DEVELOPMENT PROGRAMME[145]

NO	ITEM	RATE OF SUBSIDY
1	DISTRIBUTION OF CERTIFIED SEED	50 PER CENT OF SALE PRICE OR ₹1,000 PER QUINTAL, WHICHEVER IS LESS
2	FIELD DEMONSTRATIONS	MAXIMUM ₹2,500 PER HECTARE FOR CRITICAL INPUT MATERIAL
3	IPM DEMONSTRATIONS WITH ASSOCIATED TRAINING	EVERY DEMONSTRATION HAS TO BE OF 50 HECTARES OR FOR WHOLE VILLAGE; ₹85,000 SUBSIDY FOR ONE DEMONSTRATION WITH ASSOCIATED TRAININGS
4	DISTRIBUTION OF PLANT PROTECTION IMPLEMENTS	A) HAND DRAWN- SUBSIDY AT 50 PER CENT OF COST OR MAXIMUM OF ₹700 PER IMPLEMENT
		B) POWER DRIVEN- SUBSIDY AT 50 PER CENT OF COST OR MAXIMUM OF ₹1,500 PER IMPLEMENT
		C) TRACTOR MOUNTED - SUBSIDY AT 25 PER CENT OF COST OR MAXIMUM OF ₹4,000 PER TRACTOR-OPERATED UNIT
4	DISTRIBUTION OF BIO-AGENT	SUBSIDY AT 50 PER CENT OF COST OR MAXIMUM OF ₹300 PER HECTARE
5	FARMERS' TRAINING	₹10,000 PER TRAINING FOR 2 DAYS FOR 50 FARMERS

TABLE 21: AGRICULTURAL INPUT SUBSIDIES UNDER INTEGRATED
CEREALS (COARSE) DEVELOPMENT PROGRAMME[146]

NO	ITEM	RATE OF SUBSIDY
1	FIELD DEMONSTRATIONS	A) TECHNOLOGY DEMONSTRATION - SUBSIDY AT ₹2,000 PER ACRE PER DEMONSTRATION FOR KHARIF AND RABI, ₹1,000 FOR KHARIF OR RABI DEMONSTRATION INDIVIDUALLY
		B) IPM DEMONSTRATION – SUBSIDY AT ₹6,000 FOR ONE DEMONSTRATION OF 40 HECTARES WITH ASSOCIATED TRAINING
2	FARMERS' TRAINING	MAXIMUM OF ₹5,000 PER TRAINING FOR 2 DAYS FOR 50 FARMERS AT ₹50 PER FARMER PER DAY
3	DISTRIBUTION OF IMPROVED SEED	1) ₹200 PER QUINTAL FOR IMPROVED SEED OF PADDY, WHEAT AND BARLEY
		2) ₹400 PER QUINTAL FOR IMPROVED SEED OF JOWAR AND BAJRA
		3) ₹1,000 PER QUINTAL FOR HYBRID SEED OF JOWAR AND BAJRA. THIS IS APPLICABLE ONLY FOR SEED OF VARIETIES LESS THAN 10 YEARS OLD
4	AGRICULTURAL IMPLEMENTS	1) 50 PER CENT OF THE COST OR MAXIMUM OF ₹1,500 PER HAND OR BULLOCK-DRAWN IMPLEMENT PER FARMER
		2) 25 PER CENT OF THE COST OR MAXIMUM OF ₹5,000 PER POWER-DRIVEN IMPLEMENT PER FARMER
5	DISTRIBUTION OF SPRINKLER SETS	1) 75 PER CENT OF THE COST OR ₹15,000, WHICHEVER IS LESS FOR SMALL, MARGINAL, SCHEDULED CASTES, SCHEDULED TRIBES AND WOMEN FARMERS
		2) 50 PER CENT OF THE COST OR ₹10,000, WHICHEVER IS LESS, FOR FARMERS BELONGING TO GENERAL CATEGORIES

145 Sharma, K.G., Agricultural Input Subsidies in India : Quantum of Subsidies to SC/ ST Farmers In Madhya Pradesh & Chhattisgarh, Agro Economic Research Centre for Madhya Pradesh and Chattisgarh J.N.K.V.V., Jabalpur (M.P.), June 2004. Sourced from: http://jnkvv.org/PDF/AERC/Study-90.pdf

146 Ibid

REFERENCES

AGRICULTURAL EQUIPMENT

Subramanian, A. (2015). Economic Survey of India. Delhi: Ministry of Finance.

Kumar, A., Singh, J.K., Mohan, D., Varghese, M. (2008). Farm hand tools injuries: A case study from northern India. Safety Science 46 (2008) 54–65

Clarke, L. J. and Bishop C. (2002). Farm Power — Present and Future Availability in Developing Countries. ASAE Annual International Meeting/ CIGR World Congress, 30 July 2002, Chicago.

Day, L. 2009. Is it time for a coordinated international effort in agricultural health and safety research. Journal of Agricultural Safety and Health 15(2): 115–117.

Singh, G. 2005. Agricultural Machinery Industry in India (Manufacturing, marketing and mechanization promotion), Central Institute of Agricultural Engineering (CIAE), Bhopal, India, 2005.

ILO. (2000). Safety and Health in Agriculture. Geneva, Switzerland: International Labour Office. [On-line] Available at: www.ilo.org/public/english/ protection/safework/agriculture/brochure/ english/ agricult_e.pdf. Accessed 27 March 2009.

Mohan D., Patel R.1992. Design of safer agricultural equipment: application of ergonomics and epidemiology. Intern J Indus Ergon 10, 301–9.

Mufti I., Ahmad S.I., Majid A. 1989. Farm accidents in Pakistan. Agricultural Mechanization in Asia, Africa and Latin America (AMMA) 1989; 20: 73–75.

Yiha, O. and Kumie, A. 2010. Assessment of occupational injuries in Tendaho Agricultural Development S.C, Afar Regional State, Ethiop. J. Health Dev., Addis Ababa, Ethiopia, 2010.

Nag, P.K. & Nag, A. 2004. Drudgery, Accidents and Injuries in Indian Agriculture. Industrial Health 2004, 42, 149–162

Shrestha, S. 2008, Current Status of Agricultural Mechanization and its' Needs and Prospects in Nepal. Proceedings of National Workshop on Policy Issues and Need for Agricultural Mechanization in Nepal" 2008 Kathmandu

Tiwari P.S., Gite L.P., Dubey A.K.; Kot L.S. 2002. Agricultural injuries in Central India: nature, magnitude and economic impact. J Agric Safety Health 8, 95–111

Babu, S.C., Joshi, P.K., Glendenning, C.J., Asenso Okyere, K. and Rasheed, S.V. (2013) The state of agricultural extension reforms in India: Strategic priorities and policy options. Agricultural Economics Research Review, 26 (2): 159–172

Girabi, F. and Mwakaje, A.E.G. (2013) Impact of microfinance on smallholder farm productivity in Tanzania: The case of Iramba district. Asian Economic and Financial Review, 3(2): 227–242

GoI (Government of India) (2012) Indian Fertilizer Scenario 2012, Department of Fertilizers, Ministry of Chemicals and Fertilizers, New Delhi

GoI (Government of India) (2013) Agricultural Statistics at a Glance, Directorate of Economics and Statistics, Department of Agriculture and Cooperation, Ministry of Agriculture, New Delhi

Gordon, A. (2000) Improving Smallholder Access to Purchased Inputs in Sub-Saharan Africa. Policy Series 7. Natural Resources Institute, Chatham, UK

Goyal, A. (2010) Information, direct access to farmers, and rural market performance in central India. American Economic Journal: Applied Economics, 2(3): 22–45. Input Survey (various years), Agriculture Census Division, DAC, Ministry of Agriculture, Government of India

Mittal, S., Gandhi, S. and Tripathi, G. (2010) Socio-economic Impact of Mobile Phone on Indian Agriculture. ICRIER Working Paper No. 246. International Council for Research on International Economic Relations, New Delhi

NSSO (National Sample Survey Organization) (2005) Situation Assessment Survey of Farmers – Access to Modern Technology for Farming, 59th Round (January December 2003), Ministry of Statistics and Programme Implementation, Government of India, New Delhi

North, D.C. (1990) Institutions, Institutional Change and Economic Performance. Cambridge University Press, Cambridge

Pal, S., Mruthyunjaya, Joshi, P.K. and Saxena, R. (2003) Institutional Change in Indian Agriculture. National Centre for Agricultural Economics and Policy Research, New Delhi

Qaim, M., Subramanian, A., Naik, G. and Zilberman, D. (2006) Adoption of Bt cotton and impact variability: Insights from India. Review of Agricultural Economics, 28 (1): 48–58

Swaminathan, M. (1991) Segmentation, collateral undervaluation, and the rate of interest in agrarian credit markets: Some evidence from two villages in south India. Cambridge Journal of Economics, 15 (2): 161–178

Venkatesh, P. and Pal, S. (2014) Impact of plant variety protection on Indian seed industry. Agricultural Economics Research Review, 27(1): 91–102

Venugopal, P. (2004) State of the Indian farmer — A millennium study. Input Management Series, Vol. 8. Academic Foundation, New Delhi.

SEEDS

Heijbroek A.M.A. and Schutter E.M.L. (1996). The World Seed Market, Development and Strategies. Rabobank, Food and Agribusiness Research 19.

Conway, G. (1997). The Doubly Green Revolution Food for all in the 21st century Penguin London 334.

Paroda R.S. (1999). Biotechnology and future of Indian Agriculture keynote address at IIC New Delhi 24.

Swaminathan M.S. (1999). Cotton and Rural Livelihoods, Silver Jubilee Lecture Series– Indian Society for Cotton Improvement (ISCI) Mumbai 11–12.

Annual Report 2006-07 of Seed Production in Agricultural crops and fisheries, Directorate of Seed Research, Mau

Zaidi, A. (2005) Seeds of despair Frontline Vol.22. Issue 16

Gadwal, V.R. {2003) The Indian seed Industry: Its history, current status and future Current Science, 84 (3): 399–406

India Seed Bill, 2004, G.O I

National Seed Policy, 2002 G.O.I. 7. PPV & FR, Act, 2001

Brahmi, P., Saxena, S. and Dhillon, B.S. (2003) The Protection of Plant Varieties and Farmers Rights Act of India Current Science, 86, (3): 392–398

Ramamoorthy, K., Sivasubramaniam, K. and Kannan, A. (2006) Seed legislation in India Eds. Published by Agrobios

AP government moves MRTPC against Monsanto on Bt cotton royalty. (2006a, January 3). The Hindu Business Line. Available on the World Wide Web: http://

www.thehindubusinessline.com/2006/01/03/ stories/2006010301881200.htm.

Basu, A.K., & Qaim, M. (2007). On the adoption of genetically modified seeds in developing countries and the optimal types of government intervention. American Journal of Agricultural Economics, 89(3), 784–801.

Bennett, R., Ismael, Y., & Morse, S. (2005). Explaining contradictory evidence regarding impacts of genetically modified crops in developing countries: Varietal performance of transgenic cotton in India. Journal of Agricultural Science, 143, 35–41.

Bennett, R., Kambhampati, U., Morse, S., & Ismael, Y. (2006). Farm-level economic performance of genetically modified cotton in Maharashtra, India. Review of Agricultural Economics, 28(1), 59–71.

Bt cotton royalty issue: AP seeks PM's support. (2006, January 24). The Hindu Business Line. http://www. thehindubusinessline.com/2006/01/24/ stories/2006012401701900.htm.

Cotton Association of India (CAI). (2008, January 15) Cotton statistics and news (Issue No. 42). Mumbai, Maharashtra, India: Author. Chandrashekhar, G. (2006, June 3).

Are tech fees for Bt cotton seed really high? The Hindu Business Line. http://www. thehindubusinessline.com/2006/06/ 04/ stories/2006060402670400.htm.

Cooper, J.C., Hanemann, M., & Signorello, G. (2002). One-andone-half-bound dichotomous choice contingent valuation. The Review of Economics and Statistics, 84(4), 742–750.

Crost, B., Shankar, B., Bennett, R., & Morse, S. (2007). Bias from farmer self-selection in genetically modified crop productivity estimates: Evidence from Indian data. Journal of Agricultural Economics, 58(1), 24–36.

Farmers rush for Bt cotton seeds in Andhra Pradesh. (2007, May 29). The Hindu Business Line. http://www. thehindubusinessline.com/2007/05/29/ stories/2007052900791200.htm.

Fernandez-Cornejo, J., Klotz-Ingram, C., & Jans, S. (2002). Farmlevel effects of adopting herbicide-tolerant soyabeans in the U.S.A. Journal of Agricultural and Applied Economics, 34, 149–163.

Fukuda-Parr, S. (2007). Emergence and global spread of GM crops: explaining the role of institutional change.

In S. Fukuda-Parr (Ed.), The gene revolution: GM crops and unequal development (pp. 15–35). London, Sterling, VA: Earthscan.

Gandhi, V.P., & Namboodiri, N.V. (2006). The adoption and economics of Bt cotton in India: Preliminary results from a study (Working paper number 2006-09-04). Ahmedabad, India: Indian Institute of Management.

Huang, J., Hu, R., Rozelle, S., Qiao, F., & Pray, C.E. (2002). Transgenic varieties and productivity of smallholder cotton farmers in China. Australian Journal of Agricultural and Resource Economics, 46, 367–387.

Hubbell, B.J., Marra, M.C., & Carlson, G.A. (2000). Estimating the demand for a new technology: Bt cotton and insecticide policies. American Journal of Agricultural Economics, 82, 118–132.

James, C. (2007). Global status of commercialized biotech/GM crops: 2007 (ISAAA Brief No. 37). Ithaca, NY: International Service for the Acquisition of Agri-Biotech Applications.

Kambhampati, U., Morse, S., Bennett, R., & Ismael, Y. (2005). Perceptions of the impacts of genetically modified cotton varieties: A case study of the cotton industry in Gujarat, India. AgBioForum, 8(2&3), 161–171.

Khadi, B.M., Rao, M.R.K., & Singh, M. (2007). The Hindu survey of Indian agriculture 2007: Potential to improve lives of ryots. The Hindu.

Kuosmanen, T., Pemsl, D., & Wesseler, J. (2006). Specification and estimation of production functions involving damage control inputs: A two-stage, semiparametric approach. American Journal of Agricultural Economics, 88, 499–511.

Krishna, V.V., & Qaim, M. (2007). Estimating the adoption of Bt eggplant in India: Who benefits from public-private partnership? Food Policy, 32, 523–543.

Lalitha, N. (2004). Diffusion of agricultural biotechnology and intellectual property rights: Emerging issues in India. Ecological Economics, 49, 187–198.

AICRP- NSP (All India Coordinated Research Project - National Seed Project) (Crops) Annual Report (various years), Directorate of Seed Research, Mau, Uttar Pradesh.

Alston, J.M. and Venner, R.J. (2002) The effects of the US Plant Variety Protection Act on wheat genetic improvement. Research Policy, 31: 527–542.

CIPR (Commission on Intellectual Property Rights) (2002) Integrating Intellectual Property Rights and Development Policy. Report of the Commission on Intellectual Property Rights, London, U.K. Available at: http://www.iprcommission.org/papers/text/ final_report/chapter1 htmfinal.htm.

Correa, C.M. (2001) Review of the TRIPS Agreement: Fostering the Transfer of Technology to Developing Countries. Third World Network, 131 Jalan Macalister 10400 Penang, Malaysia.

Diez, M.C.F. (2002) The impact of plant varieties rights on research: The case of Spain. Food Policy, 27(2): 171–183.

Drew, J. (2010) An Economic Evaluation of the Roots and Fruits of Intellectual Property Rights for U.S. Horticultural Plants. Ph.D. dissertation, University of Minnesota. Available at http://purl.umn.edu/92005.

Gould, D.M. and Gruben, W.C. (1996) The role of intellectual property rights in economic growth. Journal of Economic Development, 48: 323–350.

Grossman, G.M. and Helpman, E. (1991) Innovation and Growth in the Global Economy, MIT Press, Cambridge. ICAR (Indian Council of Agricultural Research) (2006) ICAR Guidelines for Intellectual Property Management and Technology Transfer/ Commercialization. Available at: http://www.icar.org.in/ files/reports/other-reports/ icar-ipmttcguide.pdf.

ICAR (Indian Council of Agricultural Research) (2008) Research Achievements of AICRPS on Crop Sciences (2002-07). Available at: http://www.icar.org.in/files/ aicrp-report-2002-07/AICRPs CropScience.pdf.

Kanwar, S. and Evenson, R.E. (2003) Does intellectual property protection spur technological change? Oxford Economic Papers, 55(2): 235–264.

Kolady, D.E and Lesser, W. (2009) Does plant variety protection contribute to crop productivity? Lessons for developing countries from US wheat breeding. The Journal of World Intellectual Property, 12 (2):137–152.

Kumar, A. (2011) Indian seed industry- A banker's perspective, presented at Indian Seed Congress held at Hyderabad.

Leger, A. (2005) Intellectual property rights in Mexico: Do they play a role?. World Development, 33 (11):1865–1879.

Naseem, A., Oehmke, J.F. and Schimmelpfennig, D.E. (2005) Does plant variety intellectual property protection improve farm productivity? Evidence from cotton varieties.

AgBioForum, 8(2&3): 100–107.

NBPGR (National Bureau of Plant Genetic Resources) Annual Report (various years), New Delhi.

NSAI (National Seed Association of India) (various years) National Seeds Directory, New Delhi.

NSAI (National Seed Association of India) (various years) NSAI Magazine (April-June). New Delhi

FERTILIZERS

Arovuori, A. and H. Karikallio (2009), "Consumption Patterns and Competition in the World Fertilizer Markets", Paper presented at the 19th Symposium of the International Food and Agribusiness Management Association, Budapest, Hungary, June 20–21, 2009.

FAI (2008), "Fertilizer Statistics 2007-08 and earlier issues", Fertilizer Association of India, New Delhi

Government of India (2007), "All India Report on Input Survey 1996–97" Agriculture Census Division, Department of Agriculture & Cooperation, Ministry of Agriculture, Govt. of India, New Delhi.

Government of India (2007a), "Report of the Working Group on Fertilizers for Eleventh Five Year Plan (2007–12)", Planning Commission, Govt. of India, New Delhi, p. 127.

Government of India (2008), "All India Report on Input Survey 2001–02" Agriculture Census Division, Department of Agriculture & Cooperation, Ministry of Agriculture, Govt. of India, New Delhi.

Government of India (2009), "Union Budget, various Issues from 1991–92 to 2009–10" Ministry of Finance, Government of India, New Delhi.

Government of India (2009a), "National Accounts Statistics, various Issues from 1991 to 2009", Central Statistical Organization, Ministry of Statistics & Programme Implementation, Government of India, New Delhi.

Government of India (2009b), "Import Parity Price of Urea for the Quarter July 2008 to September 2008 & Earlier Quarters" Department of Fertilizers, Ministry of Chemicals and Fertilizers, Govt. of India, New Delhi.

Gulati Ashok and Sudha Narayanan (2003), "The Subsidy Syndrome in Indian Agriculture" Oxford University Press, New Delhi.

Gulati, Ashok (1990), "Fertilizer Subsidy: Is the Cultivator 'Net Subsidized'? Indian Journal of Agricultural Economics, Vol. 45, No. 1, Jan.-Mar. 1990, pp. 1–11.

B C. Biswas, D.S. Yadav and Satish Maheshwari, "Role of Calcium and Magnesium in Indian Agriculture", Fertilizer News, Vol. 30, Nc. o, July 1985.

Gunvant M. Desai: Growth of Fertilizer Use in Indian Agriculture: Past Trends and Future Demand, New York State College and Life Sciences, Cornell University, Ithaca, New York, 1969.

Gunvant, Desai and Gurdev Singh: Grcwth of Fertiiiser Use in Districts of Inoia; Performance and Policy Implications, Cvntre for Management in Agriculture, Indian Institute of Management, Ahmedabad, 1973.

Gunvant M Desai, "Fertilizer in India's Agricultural Development", in C H. Shah (Ed.): Agricultural Development of India-Policy and Problems, Orient Longman Ltd., Bombay, 1979 a, pp. 379–426.

Gunvant M. Desai, "Impact of the New Rice Technolopy on Fertilizer Consumption", in Economic Consequences of the Development and Diffusion of Modern Rice Varietie, International Rice Research Institute, Los Banos, Phihppines, 1979 b.

Gunvant M. Desai: Sustaining Rapid Grcwth in India's Fertilizer Consumption: A: Perspective Based on Composition of Use, International Food Policy Research Institute, Washington, D.C., 1982.

Bala, B. Sharma, R. K. and Sharma, S. D. (2005), Factors Influencing Fertilizer Production and Consumption in India. Indian Journal of Agricultural Research, 39(2): 146–149.

Bezbaruah, M. P. and Roy, N. (2002), Factors Affecting Cropping Intensity and Use of Fertilizers and High-Yielding Variety Seeds in Barak Valley. Indian Journal of Agricultural Economics, 57(2): 169–170.

Bhaskaran, M. N. (2011), Marketing Strategies for Specialty Fertilizers. FAI Annual Seminar, 2(1): 1–3.

Center for Monitoring Indian Economy, (1997), Profiles of States. CMIE, Mumbai, pp. 5–6.

Center for Monitoring Indian Economy, (2009), Monthly Review of the Indian Economy, CMIE, Mumbai, pp: 12–15.

Chand, R. (2010), State of Imbalance, India's NPK Application. Farmer's Forum, 10(7): 47–54.

Chand, R. and Pandey, L. M. (2008), Fertilizer Growth, Imbalance and Subsidies: Trends and Implications, National Centre for Agricultural Economics and Policy Research.

Chauhan, K. K. S. (1997), Input Demand and Supply Scenario in Indian Agriculture. Agriculture Economics Research Review, 10(2):143–150.

Cuddy, J. D. A. and Della-Valle, P. A. (1978), Measuring the Instability in Time Series Data. Oxford Bulletin of Economics and Statistics, 41(3): 247–248.

Devi, P. I, Radhakrishnan, V. and Thomas, E. K. (1991), Fertilizer Consumption and Agricultural Productivity in Kerala. Agricultural Economics Research Review, 4(2): 119–120.

Dholakia, R. H. and Majumdar, J. (1995), Estimation of Pricing Elasticity of Fertilizer Demand at Micro Level in India. Indian Journal of Agricultural Economics, 50(1): 36–46.

FAI. (2010), Handbook on Fertilizer Marketing. Fertilizer Association of India, New Delhi, pp. 24–36.

FAI. (2012), Fertilizer Policy – 1944 to 2012 Highlights, Fertilizer Statistics 2011-12, Fertilizer Association of India, New Delhi: 1.24.

FAI. (2012), Fertilizer Association of India, Annual Review, Fertilizer Production and Consumption, pp. 130–133.

FAI. (2012), Fertilizer Statistics 2011–12, Fertilizer Association of India, New Delhi. Ghosh, A. Ravichandran, K. and Malik, A. (2011), Indian Fertilizer Industry: Subsidy Policy.

Gupta, S. G. and Kapoor, V. K. (2001), Fundamental of Applied Statistics. Third Edition, Sultan Chand and Sons, New Delhi.

Gupta, U. (1989), Fertilizer Pricing and Subsidy – Need for a Pragmatic Approach. Fertilizer News, 38(8): 11–18.

Gupta, V. K. (2011), Strategy for Maximisation of Fertilizer Sale. Indian Journal of Fertilizer Sales, 7(9): 62–67.

Jaga, P. K. and Patel, Y. (2012), An Overview of Fertilizers Consumption in India: Determinants and Outlook for 2020- A Review. International Journal of Scientific Engineering and Technology, 1(6): 285–286.

Schumacher, K. and Sathaye, J. (1999), India's Fertilizer Industry: Productivity and Energy Efficiency, Working paper

LBNL – 41846, Environmental Energy Technologies Division, Ernest Orlando Lawrence Berkeley Laboratory, USA.

Krishna, P. G. and Sireesha, M. (2010), Single Window System for all Agri-Inputs. Indian Journal of Fertilizers, 6(8): 48.

Malik, P. (2011), 4 Ps of Fertilizer Marketing. Indian Journal of Fertilizers, 8(9):76.

Mathur, V. C. (1992). Factors Influencing the Spread of Fertilizer Retail Outlets in India – An Econometric Analysis. Indian Journal of Agricultural Marketing, 6(2): 18–24.

Minocha, N. (2010), Direct Fertilizer Subsidy, Farmers s' Forum, 10(7): 54. Mishra, B. P. and Singbal, V. (2011), Policies and Reforms in Fertilizer Sector. India Journal of Fertilizers, 4(9): 78–83.

Motsara, A. (2012), Managing Distribution Channels in Present Environment. Indian Journal of Fertilizers. 8(9): 62–67.

Mukherjee, S. (2010) Nutrient-based Fertilizer Subsidy: Will Farmers Adopt Agricultural Best Management Practices? Economic and Political Weekly, 4(49): 71.

Philip, L. M. (2004), Fertilizer Policy and Farm Consumption Implication. Journal of Agricultural Development and Policy, 16(1):18–19.

Prameela, S. and Devaraj, K. (2012), Performance of Fertilizer Industry in India. International Journal of Multidisciplinary Management Studies, 2(3): 233.

Prasad, R. (2011), Nitrogen and Foodgrain Production in India. Indain Journal of Fertilizers, 7(12): 66–65

http://money.livemint.com/news/sector/outlook/government-policy-measures-to-provide-fillip-to-fertilizer-sector-411780.aspx

http://www.livemint.com/Opinion/XCCJwEzbzwiyWFYfK1wRdO/Indias-flawed-fertilizer-policy.html

http://indiabudget.nic.in/es2015-16/echapvol1-09.pdf

http://indianexpress.com/article/opinion/editorials/farm-error/

http://www.gktoday.in/blog/reforming-the-fertilizer-sector-in-india/

http://www.krishijagran.com/corporate-watch/Industry-Profile/2014/12/Indian-Fertilizer-Sector-at-A-Glance

http://www.fao.org/docrep/009/
a0257e/A0257E02.htm

http://iari.res.in/files/News-In-Media/
New_urea_policy-16052015.pdf

http://www.igidr.ac.in/pdf/
publication/WP-2012-014.pdf

http://www.newindianexpress.com/states/
odisha/Fertilizer-Crisis-Casts-Shadow-on-Kharif-
Prospects/2014/09/09/article2422349.ece

http://www.wsj.com/articles/SB10001424
05274870361590457505292161272384

http://www.civilsdaily.com/blog/economic-survey-
for-ias-chapter-08-reforming-the-fertilizer-sector/

http://www.business-standard.com/article/
opinion/soil-imbalance-112062700008_1.html

http://www.business-standard.com/article/
economy-policy/neem-coated-truth-urea-policy-
isn-t-a-game-changer-116021601168_1.html

http://timesofindia.indiatimes.com/india/
New-urea-policy-could-lead-to-its-excessive-use-
impact-human-health/articleshow/47291207.cms

http://indianexpress.com/article/
opinion/columns/from-plate-to-
plough-the-fertilizer-challenge/

http://www.gktoday.in/blog/key-facts-
about-fertilizer-subsidy-policy-in-india/

http://agrariancrisis.in/tag/fertilizer-policy/

http://www.thehindubusinessline.com/
economy/nutrientbased-fertilizer-subsidy-policy-
is-flawed-needs-review/article6193855.ece

http://agrariancrisis.in/tag/soil-fertility/

http://www.faidelhi.org/Frank%20
notes/IJF-April-16.pdf

https://www.researchgate.net/post/How_does_
chemical_fertilizer_use_affect_the_soil_pH_in_
acid_and_neutral_and_slightly_alkaline_soils

http://www.faidelhi.org/reports.htm

http://www.business-standard.com/
article/economy-policy/india-s-n-k-
ratio-has-dropped-to-an-alarming-level-
potash-corp-112092703036_1.html

http://www.ipni.net/publication/bci.nsf/0/
B4EEDC01C4FCACD585257BBA006868BD
/$FILE/Better%20Crops%20International%
202001-2%20p24.pdf

http://www.greenwavefertilizer.com/npk.html

http://www.im4change.previewdns.com/
siteadmin/tinymce/uploaded/Fertilizer_
Use_and_Imbalance_in_India.pdf

http://www.thehindubusinessline.com/
opinion/columns/free-urea-prices-to-
balance-fertilizer-use/article4034933.ece

http://www.livemint.com/Politics/
Z9b38eoxfJYhrRDMpRPqcI/Saving-the-soil.html

http://www.livemint.com/
Politics/1xM0dNr7g9BLYw5Rx45tvK/
A-soil-health-card-not-enough-for-
balanced-fertilizer-use.html

CROP PROTECTION

Birch, A.N.E.; Begg, G.S.; Squire, G.R. How
agro-ecological research helps to address food
security issues under new IPM and pesticide
reduction policies for global crop production
systems. J. Exp. Biol. 2011, 62, 3251–3261.

Pretty, J.; Toulmin, C.; Williams S. Sustainable
intensification in African agriculture. Int.
J. Agric. Sustain. 2011, 9, 5–24.

Pretty, J.; Bharucha, Z. The sustainable
intensification of agriculture. Ann. Bot.
2014, doi:10.1093/aob/mcu205.

Carson, R. Silent Spring; Houghton
Mifflin: Boston, MA, USA, 1962.

Conway, G.R.; Pretty, J. Unwelcome
Harvest: Agriculture and Pollution;
Earthscan: London, UK, 1991.

The Pesticide Detox: Towards a More
Sustainable Agriculture; Pretty, J., Ed.;
Earthscan: London, UK, 2005.

Zhang, W.J.; Jiang, F.B.; Ou, J.F. Global
pesticide consumption and pollution:
With China as a focus. Proc. Int. Acad.
Ecol. Environ. Sci. 2011, 1, 125–144.

OECD. Dataset: 2013 Edition of the
OECD Environmental Database;
OECD: Paris, France, 2013.

China Rural Statistic Yearbook; China
Statistic Press: Beijing, China, 2013.

Science. Smarter Pest Control.
Science 2001, 341, 730–731.

Report Buyer. Global Pesticide and

Agrochemical Market to 2018—Market Size, Growth, and Forecasts in Over 50 Countries; MarketSizeInfo.com: Charing, UK, 2014.

Lamberth, C.; Jeanmart, S.; Luksch, T.; Plant, A. Current challenges and trends in the discovery of agrochemicals. Science 2013, 341, 742–746.

Grovermann, C.; Schreinemachers, P.; Berger, T. Quantifying pesticide overuse from farmer and societal points of view: An application to Thailand. Crop Prot. 2013, 53, 161–168.

EPA. Pesticides Industry Sales and Usage: 2006 and 2007 Market Estimates; Environmental Protection Agency: Washington, DC, USA, 2007.

Brouder, S.M.; Gomez-MacPherson, H. The impact of conservation agriculture on smallholder agricultural yields: A scoping review of the evidence. Agric. Ecosyst. Environ. 2014, 187, 11–32.

Kassam, A.; Friedrich, T.; Shaxson, F.; Bartz, H.; Mello, I.; Kienzle, J.; Pretty, J. The spread of conservation agriculture: Policy and institutional support for adoption and uptake. Field actions Science reports 2014, 7. Available online: http://factsreports.revues.org/3720

Frisvold, G.B.; Reeves, J.M. Resistance management and sustainable use of agricultural biotechnology. AgBioForum 2014, 13, 343–359.

Benbrook, C. Impacts of genetically engineered crops on pesticide use in the U.S.—The first sixteen years. Environ. Sci. Eur. 2013, doi:10.1186/2190-4715-24-24.

Fantke, P.; Friedrich, R.; Jolliet, O. Health impact and damage cost assessment of pesticides in Europe. Environ. Int. 2012, 49, 9–17.

Knutson, R.; Penn, J.; Flinchbaugh, B. Agricultural and Food Policy, 4th ed.; Prentice Hall: Upper Saddle River, NJ, USA, 1998.

Schmitz, P.M. Overview of cost-benefit assessment. In Proceedings of the OECD workshop on the Economics of Pesticide Risk Reduction in Agriculture, Copenhagen, Denmark, 28–30 November 2001; OECD: Paris, France, 2001.

Pearce, D.; Tinch, R. The true price of pesticides. In Bugs in the System: Redesigning the Pesticide Industry for Sustainable Agriculture; Earthscan: London, UK, 1998; pp. 50–93.

Pretty, J.; Waibel, H. Paying the price: The full cost of pesticides. In the Pesticide Detox: Towards a More Sustainable Agriculture; Pretty, J., Ed.; Earthscan: London, UK, 2005.

Leach, A.W.; Mumford, J.D. Pesticide environmental accounting: A decision-making tool estimating external costs of pesticides. Journal für Verbraucherschutz und Lebensmittelsicherheit 2011, 6, S21–S26.

Pretty, J.; Brett, C.; Gee, D.; Hine, R.; Mason, C.F.; Morison, J.I.L.; Raven, H.; Rayment, M.; van der Bijl, G. An assessment of the total external costs of UK agriculture. Agric. Syst. 2000, 65, 113–136.

Waibel, H.; Fleischer, G. Kosten und Nutzen des chemischen Pflanzenschutzes in der Deutsen Landwirtschaft aus Gesamtwirtschaftlicher Sicht (In German); Vauk-Verlag: Kiel, Germany, 1998.

Norse, D.; Li, J.; Leshan, J.; Zheng, Z. Environmental Costs of Rice Production in China; Aileen Press: Bethesda, MD, USA, 2001.

Tegtmeier, E.M.; Duffy, M.D. External costs of agricultural production in the United States. Int. J. Agric. Sustain. 2004, 2, 155–175.

Leach, A.W.; Mumford, J.D. Pesticide Environmental Accounting: A method for assessing the external costs of individual pesticide applications. Environ. Pollut. 2008, 151, 139–147.

Koleva, N.G.; Schneider, U.A. The impact of climate change on the external cost of pesticide application in US agriculture. Int. J. Agric. Sustain. 2009, 7, 203–216.

Kartaatmadja, S.; Pane, H.; Wirajaswadi, L.; Sembiring, H.; Simatupang, S.; Bachrein, S.; Ismadi, D.; Fagi, A.M. Optimising use of natural resources and increasing rice productivity. In Conserving Soil and Water for Society: Sharing Solutions, Proceedings of the ISCO 2004— 13th International Soil Conservation Organization Conference, Brisbane, Australia, 4–9 July 2004.

Popp, J.; Petó, K.; Nagy, J. Pesticide productivity and food security. A review. Agron. Sustain. Dev. 2013, 33, 243–255.

Jepson, P.C.; Guzy, M.; Blaustein, K.; Sow, M.; Sarr, M.; Mineau, P.; Kegley, S. Measuring pesticide ecological and health risks in West African agriculture to establish an enabling environment for sustainable intensification. Philos. Trans. R. Soc. B 2014, doi:10.1098/rstb.2013.0491.

Williamson, S.; Ball, A.S.; Pretty, J. Trends for pesticide use and safer pest management in four African countries. Crop Prot. 2008, 27, 1327–1334.

Praneetvatakul, S.; Waibel, H. Impact Assessment of Farmer Field Schools using A Multi-Period Panel Data Model. In Proceedings of the International Association of Agricultural Economist Conference,

Gold Coast, Australia, 12–18 August 2006.

Praneetvatakul, S.; Schreinemachers, P.; Pananurak, P.; Tipraqsa, P. Pesticides, external costs and policy options for Thai agriculture. Environ. Sci. Policy 2013, 27, 103–113.

Andersson, H.; Tago, D.; Treich, N. Pesticides and Health: A Review of Evidence on Health Effects, Valuation of Risks, and Benefit-Cost Analysis; Working Paper TSE-477; Toulouse School of Economics: Toulouse, France, 2014.

Athukorala, W.; Wilson, C.; Robinson, T. Determinants of health costs due to farmers' exposure to pesticides: An empirical analysis. In Proceedings of the 85th Annual Conference of Western Economic Association, Hilton Portland and Executive Tower, Portland, OR, USA, 29 June–3 July 2010.

Pingali, P.L.; Roger P.A. Impact of Pesticides on Farmers' Health and the Rice Environment; Kluwer Academic Press: Dordrecht, The Netherlands, 1995.

Royal Society. Reaping the Benefits: Science and the Sustainable Intensification of Global Agriculture; The Royal Society: London, UK, 2009.

Royal Society. People and the Planet; The Royal Society: London, UK, 2012.

Godfray, C.; Beddington, J.R.; Crute, I.R.; Haddad, L.; Lawrence, D.; Muir, J.F.; Pretty, J.; Robinson, S.; Thomas, S.M.; Toulmin, C. Food security: The challenge of feeding 9 billion people. Science 2010, 327, 812–818.

Tilman, D.; Balzer, C.; Hill, J.; Befort, B.L. Global food demand and the sustainable intensification of agriculture. Proc. Natl. Acad. Sci. USA 2011, 108, 20260–20264.

Conway, G.R. The Doubly Green Revolution; Penguin: London, UK, 1997.

NRC. Alternative Agriculture; National Academies Press: Washington, DC, USA, 1989.

NRC. Towards Sustainable Agricultural Systems in the 21st Century; Committee on Twenty-First Century Systems Agriculture, National Academies Press: Washington, DC, USA, 2010.

Swaminathan, M.S. An Evergreen Revolution. Biologist 2000, 47, 85–89.

Abhilash, P.C.; Singh, N.; Pesticide use and application. Journal of Hazardous Materials. 2011; 165(3); 1-3

Forget, G. Balancing the need for pesticides with the risk to human health. In: Forget G, Goodman T, de Villiers A, Impact of Pesticide Use on Health in Developing countries. 1993. IDRC, Ottawa: 2.

Mathur, S.C. Future of Indian pesticides industry in next millennium. Pesticide Information. 2010; 24 (4):9–23.

Pier, A.B., Consonni D., Bachetti S., Rubagotti, M., Baccarelli, A., Zocchetti, C. and Pesatori, A.C. (2001). "Health Effects of Dioxin Exposure: A 20-Year Mortality Study.". American J Epidem 153 (11): 1031–1044.

Menon, R.; Pesticide Poisoning in Punjab; India Together; 11 Jan 2006.

Altenbach J.S., Geluso K.N. and Wilson D.E. (1979). Population size of Tadaria brasiliensis at Carlsbad Caverns in 1973. In: Grnoways HH and Baker RJ (eds) Biological investigations in Guadelupe Mountains National Park, Texas. Natl Park Service Proc Trans Ser No 4: 341.

Ambrosi D., Isensee A. and Macchia J. (1978). Distribution of oxadiazon and phoslone in an aquatic model ecosystem. American Chem Soci 26(1): 50–53.

Andreu V., Pico' Y. (2004). Determination of pesticides and their degradation products in soil: critical review and comparison of methods. Trends Anal Chemistry 23(10–11): 772–789.

Arias R.N. and Fabra P.A. (1993). Effects of 2,4-dichlorophenoxyacetic acid on Rhizobium sp. growth and characterization of its transport. Toxicol Lett 68: 267–273.

Asteraki E.J., Hanks C.B. and Clements R.O. (1992). The impact of the chemical removal of the hedge-based flora on the community structure of carabid beetles (Col. Carabidae) and spiders (Araneae) of the field and hedge bottom. J Appl Ent 113: 398–406.

Barcelo D., Porte C., Cid J., Albaiges J. (1990). Determination of organophosphorus compounds in Mediterranean coastal waters and biota samples using gas chromatography with nitrogen–phosphorus and chemical ionization mass spectrometric detection. Int J Environ A Chem 38: 199–209.

Barcelo' D., Hennion M.C. (1997). Trace Determination of Pesticides and Their Degradation Products in Water, Elsevier, Amsterdam, The Netherlands: 3.

Barron M.G., Galbraith H. and Beltman D. (1995): Comparative reproduction and developmental toxicology of birds. Comp. Biochem Physiol 112c: 1–14.

Becker P.H. (1989). Seabirds as monitor organisms of contaminants along the German North Sea coast. Hel Meerr 43: 395–403.

Behera B. and Singh S.G. (1999). Studies on Weed Management in Monsoon Season Crop of Tomato. Indian J Weed Sci 31(1–2): 67.

Belzer W., Evans C. and Poon A. (1998). Atmospheric concentrations of agricultural chemicals in the Lower Fraser Valley.

FRAP study report, 1998, Aquatic and Atmospheric Science Division, Environment Canada, Vancouver, BC.

Bernardz J.C., Klem D., Goodrich L.J., Senner SE. (1990). Migration counts of raptors at Hawk Mountain, Pennsylvania, as indicators of population trends, 1934–1986. Auk 107: 96–109.

Bevans H.E., Lico M.S. and Lawrence S.J. (1998). Water quality in the Las Vegas Valley area and the Carson and Truckee Riverbasins, Nevada and California, 1992–96. Reston, VA: USGS.U.S. Geological Survey Circular 1170.

Bhatia M.R., Fox-Rushby J. and Mills M. (2004). Cost-eff ectiveness of malaria control interventions when malaria mortality is low: insecticide-treated nets versus in-house residual spraying in India. Soil Sci Med 59: 525.

Bortleson G. and Davis D. 1987–1995. U.S. Geological Survey & Washington State Department of Ecology. Pesticides in selected small streams in the Puget Sound Basin: 1–4.

Brammall R.A. and Higgins V.J. (1988). The effect of glyphosate on resistance of tomato to Fusarium crown and root rot disease and on the formation of host structural defensive barriers. Can J Bot 66: 1547–1555.

Brouwer A., Longnecker M.P., Birnbaum L.S., Cogliano J., Kostyniak P., Moore J., Schantz S. and Winneke G. (1999). Characterization of potential endocrine related health eff ects at lowdose levels of exposure to PCBs. Environ Health Perspect 107: 639.

Cade T.J., Lincer J.L., White C.M., Rosenau D.G. and Swartz L.G. (1989). DDE residues and eggshell changes in Alaskan falcons and hawks. Science 172, 955–957.

Castillo L., Thybaud E., Caquet T. and Ramade F. (1994). Organochlorine contaminants in common tern (Sterna hirundo) eggs and young

from the Rhine River area (France). Bull. Environ Contam Toxicol 53: 759–764.

Chakravarty P. and Sidhu S.S. (1987). Effects of glyphosate, hexazinone and triclopyr on in vitro growth of five species of ectomycorrhizal fungi. Euro J For Path 17: 204–210.

Cheney M.A., Fiorillo R. and Criddle R.S. (1997). Herbicide and estrogen eff ects on the metabolic activity of Elliptiocomplanata measured by calorespirometry. Comp. iochem. Physiol. 118C: 159–164.

Clark D.R. and Krynitsky A.J. (1983). DDT: Recent contamination in New Mexico and Arizona. Environment 25: 27–31.

Clark D.R. and Lamont T.G. (1976). Organochlorine residues in females and nursing young of the big brown bats. Bull Environ Contam Toxicol 15: 1–8 (1976).

Clark D.R. (1981). Death of bats from DDE, DDT or dieldrin diagnosis via residues in carcass fat. Bull Environ Contam Toxicol 26: 367–371.

Colborn T. and Smolen M.J. (1996). Epidemiological analysis of persistent organochlorine contaminants in cetaceans. Rev Environ Contam Toxicol 146: 91–172.

Cooke A.S. (1979): Egg shell characteristic of gannets Sula bassana, shags Phalacrocorax aristotelis and great backed gulls Larusmarianus exposed to DDE and other environmental pollutants. Environ Pollut 19: 47–65.

Crisp T.M., Clegg E.D., Cooper R.L., Wood W.P., Anderson D.G., Baeteke K.P., Hoffmann J.L., Morrow M.S., Rodier D.J., Schaeffer J.E., Touart L.W., Zeeman M.G. and Patel Y.M. (1998). Environmental endocrine disruption: An effects assessment and analysis. Environ Health Perspect 106: 11.

Dietary guidelines for Americans. (2005). U.S. Department of Health and Human Services U.S. Department of Agriculture.

Dosman J.A. and Cockcraft D.W. (1989). Principle of Health and Safety in Agriculture. CRC press, Boca Raton, USA 222–225.

Dreistadt S.H., Clark J.K. and Flint M.L. (1994). Pests of landscape trees and shrubs. An integrated pest management guide. University of California Division of Agriculture and Natural Resources. Publication 3359.

Duffard R., Traini L. and Evangelista de Duffard A. (1981). Embryotoxic and teratogenic effects of phenoxy herbicides. Acta Physiol Latinoam 31: 39–42.

Eddleston M. (2000). Patterns and problems of deliberate self-poisoning in the developing world.

Agnihotri, N. (2000), "Pesticide Consumption in India", Pesticide Research Journal, 12(1):150-151.

Arora, P. (2007), "Pesticide and Human Health", A Resource for Health Professionals, 4 (1 – 2): 7-9.

Bag, D. (2000), "Pesticides and Health Risks", Economic and Political Weekly, 6 (16): 20- 21.

Barua, B. (1999), "Review of Agricultural Progress: Trends, Development and Outlook for Future", Journal of Agricultural Finance, 7(4): 6- 9.

Shetty, P. (2004), "Socio-Ecological Implications of Pesticide Use in India", Economic and Political Weekly, 39 (49): 5261–5262.

MISCELLANEOUS

Gopalaswamy, T.P., (2008) Rural Marketing Environment, Problems and Strategies, Vikas Publishing house, New Delhi

Badi, R.V. and Badi, N.V. (2006), Rural Marketing, Hhimalaya Publishing House, New Delhi

Dogra, B. and Shuman, K., (2008) Rural Marketing: Concepts and practices, TATA McGraw- Hill Publishing house, New Delhi.

Singh, S. Rural Marketing: Focus on Agricultural inputs, (2008) Vikas Publishing House, New Delhi.

Kashyap, P. and Raut, S. (2007), The Rural Marketing Book, Biztantra, New Delhi.

Velayudhan, S.K. (2007), Rural Marketing: targeting the noon urban consumer, Sage Publication, New Delhi.

Krishnamoorty, R. (2008), Introduction to Rural Marketing, Himalaya Publishing House.

Lamba, A.J., The Art of Retailing, Tata McGraw Hill Publishing Companies, New Delhi

Marketing of Agricultural inputs by Manohar Lal Jalan., Published by Himalaya Publishing House (Delhi). 1988.

Jha, M. (1998), Rural marketing: some conceptual issues, Economic and political weekly, Vol.13(9),1998

Varshney, J.C. (1997), Rural marketing-A study with refrence to Farm inputs, National publishing House, Jaipur, pp.251-255

Agricultural Price Policy in India by Raj Kumar Singh., Published by Print well Publishers – (Jaipur). 1990.

Communication and Rural Development by J.B. Ambekar Yadav. Published by Mittal Publications (New Delhi). 1992.

Development of Agricultural Marketing in India by Dr. Rajagopal Published by Print well (Jaipur).

Marketing Management by Philip Kotlar. 1992. 8th edition

Singh, A.K., Pandey, S. Rural marketing, New Age International, 2007

CHAPTER II

ON WATER AVAILABILITY

Water is a commodity that resists commodification—a recipe for market failure. States have often cited the Harmon Doctrine, ignoring externalities and past investments, to support the idea of absolute sovereignty over water flowing through a state's territories. More successfully, the Social Contract (Thomas Hobbs, et al) approach has focused on deciding on an initial allocation of property rights and creating a mechanism to trade such rights. The Interstate River Water Disputes Act (1956) was enacted to deal with conflicts, creating adjudication tribunals where direct negotiations failed. However, such tribunal decisions have often not been accepted by disputing parties, leaving arbitration a non-binding mechanism. Interventions by the Centre, as in the Ravi-Beas dispute, have also been unsuccessful.

In recent years, the non-availability of water in rural India has had significant consequences. With Haryana's fields increasingly running dry, the recent Jat agitation obscures an agrarian crisis. The passage of the Punjab Sutlej-Yamuna Link Canal (Rehabilitation and Re-vesting of Proprietary Rights) Bill 2016 by Punjab's state assembly on a non-partisan basis has unilaterally sparked a crisis in riparian management. Over the last few years, water availability in India's ninety-one reservoirs has now reached its lowest level in a decade, touching 29 per cent of storage capacity in 2017.[1] Over 85 per cent of the country's water needs are now supplied by rapidly declining aquifers. With increasing tank er dependence, water conflict is arising—prohibitory orders have been imposed in villages in Latur district while local swimming pools have been cut off from water supply. Short-sighted political tactics, combined with irrigation inefficiency, have served to make water disputes intractable.[2]

---

1   Central Water Commission
2   Khurana, I., 2006

India's water disputes continue to remain in flux.[3] As rivers generally cross state boundaries, the construction of equitable mechanisms for allocating river flows has been a constitutional legacy. With a plethora of stakeholders—state governments, the parliament, courts, water tribunals, central ministries and civil society—water disputes have remained a persistent phenomenon across India. With growing consensus that many such disputes are increasingly intractable, existing institutional arrangements have clearly failed to generate outcomes that focus on growth and the national interest. The Cauvery dispute, long prolonged, led to twenty-six meetings between 1968 and 1990 at the ministerial level, between Tamil Nadu and Karnataka, with no consensus reached. Tamil Nadu argued that Karnataka's construction of the Kabini, Hemavathi and Swarnavathi dams on the Cauvery, along with a unilateral expansion of its irrigation works, led to a diminishing water supply to Tamil Nadu, while leaving the 1924 agreement between the Madras Presidency and the Mysore state unimplemented. With the dispute increasingly politicized, the Cauvery Water Disputes Tribunal (1990) has found resolution a distant mirage.[4]

Similarly, India's agricultural policies have led to water scarcity. India's water tables are dropping by 0.3 m annually (NASA)—a consequence of a system that 'encourages using more inputs such as fertilizer, water and power.'[5] Water management is regulated by multiple central, state and municipal bodies, along with the Central Water Commission—bad coordination exacerbates localized pollution. We encourage sugar cane planting in arid regions, and advise farmers on cropping decisions without consideration of local surface water availability.

Our systemic focus on rice and wheat production, over dry land agriculture, needs to be reversed, while drip feed agriculture can help with declining water tables. A central regulatory agency, focused on the design, control and coordination of national programmes for water conservation needs to be instituted. Water allocation decisions need an operational mechanism for sectoral allocation, based on logic, need and social equity. The government should undertake regional and basin level water planning, enabling communities, industries and civil society to negotiate allocation. Regulatory protection for riverine ecosystems need to be strengthened, with illegal sand mining curbed. We must institute legal protection for minimum water flow in our rivers while political interference in water allocation needs to be curbed.

India's villages have borne an unending cycle of droughts and floods for eons, as is their wont in a tropical deciduous country with varying soil and climatic

---

3   Richards, A. & Singh, N., 2001
4   Ibid
5   Economic Survey, 2016

conditions. To alleviate the worst of these climatic events, India's government has been on a dam building and groundwater extraction spree since independence. Where river waters could not be diverted for irrigation, tube wells were dug. Increasingly, such attempts have limited marginal value, with the effects of over-silting, eutrophication, water pollution, groundwater depletion and an overarching disruption of the embedded hydrological cycle. While river interlinking is proposed as another grand plan to solve this impending water availability crisis, the cost of clean, usable, water for the ordinary villager continues to rise.

ACCESS TO WATER

Pramod Kumar, a farmer in Darbhanga district in Bihar, has seen the torrential Kosi river and its tributaries wash away his crop, year after year, in addition to wiping out a large amount of his topsoil. With alluvium being displaced by sand, yield rates have dropped. While flood-borne silt could have been a saviour, the river, of late, has stopped providing much, courtesy of a range of hydropower dams and embankments upstream.

Meanwhile, Parvez Khan, a farmer engaged in millet farming on 4 acres of land, in Jhansi district in Uttar Pradesh's Bundelkhand region, faces annual rainfall worries. For the last two years, his region has received rainfall that has been 60 per cent deficient, impacting his sowing plans. With little water, Bundelkhand's sandy soil has been unable to provide sustenance to his seeds. There is little scope for groundwater as rain simply runs off. When asked about alternatives, he simply laughs, pointing that soyabean itself could not survive this weather vagary.

Hoshiar Singh, an enterprising farmer, roars a laugh, when asked about challenges in farming in Pantnagar district in Uttarakhand. His forefathers had been allocated 10 bighas of land near the Tanda jungle, post-partition—a pittance compared to the hundreds of acres they had near Lahore. The land was once bountiful, he says, despite having to pull out weeds and conduct significant levelling to turn the land productive. The problem, however, is the land's geology—the slight elevation in the substructure ensures that no running water, pouring off Himalayan streams, stays still to form aquifers. It all moves southwards to the giant Terai region. To sustain his paddy crop, he has installed a range of pumps, which have decreased the local water table. However, some have now started drying up, inducing concern.

For India's farmers, access to water, through rivers, irrigation canals, groundwater, or just variable rain, is a key priority before any cultivation. Cultivating crops in India's dry deciduous and tropical landscape can be challenging, despite fertile soils. With rainfall varying by region, season, quantity and timing, crop growth can be significantly constrained. India's rainfall patterns offer a complex mosaic—parts of Rajasthan witnessing an average of 2–4 inches only, while Tamil Nadu can receive 40–60 inches of rain in a year, usually in short periods. Irrigation, therefore, assumes a critical importance, even in rain-heavy areas in the Himalayas (average of 50–100 inches of rain in a year). Such irrigation, conducted primarily through surface canals, tanks and wells, has been a historical fact in India's farms for generations.

India receives about 1,127 mm average rainfall annually (of which 846 mm is during the monsoon), with a high spatial and seasonal variability. Most of this precipitation occurs during the south-west and north-east monsoons, through rain, storms, hail, snow and cyclones, particularly during the months from June to September.[6] India's long-term average annual rainfall remains over 1,160 mm, significantly high for a country of this size. As is well known, most of our annual rainfall is recorded between June and September, a period of over 120 days. Such precipitation is highly variable, with 21 per cent of the landscape receiving less than 750 mm of rain annually, while around 15 per cent receives over 1,500 mm. Peninsular India receives around 600 mm while parts of Rajasthan and Gujarat receive less than 500 mm.

Despite this bounty, India's demographics ensure that it is classified as a water-stressed country, with a per capita water availability of 1,123 m³ (water stressed defined below 1,170 m³), dropping from 3,000 m³ in the '60s. India supports nearly one-sixth of the global population, along with 20 per cent of the world's livestock population, on 1/50th of the world's land, with just 1/25th of the world's fresh water resources.

India's current consumption of water, particularly in rural areas, is heavily segmented amongst household community usage, irrigation, hydroelectricity and industrial production. Community water supply can consume 5 per cent of total water utilizable (7 km³ in urban areas, 18 km³ in rural areas in 2005). Given such a significant rise in population, India is likely to find it hard to meet rural demand—rural areas are projected to have a 70 litres per capita per day (lpcd) requirement in 2025 and 150 lpcd in 2050.[7]

---

6   Kumar, R., Singh, R.D, Sharma, K.D., Water resources of India, Current Science, Vol. 89, No. 5, 10 September 2005, Sourced from: http://www.iisc.ernet.in/currsci/sep102005/794.pdf

7   Ibid

TABLE 22: ALL-INDIA AREA WEIGHTED MONTHLY SEASONAL AND ANNUAL RAINFALL[8]
(IN MM)

YEAR	JAN–FEB	MARCH–MAY	JUNE–SEPT	OCT–DEC
1901	73.2	107.3	751	99.3
1910	23.8	83.5	928.5	148.2
1920	45.2	145.7	774.1	74
1930	46.7	135.8	856.1	160
1940	38.8	155.4	885.8	121.3
1950	60.8	114.8	905.5	93.1
1960	16.5	112.8	914.9	110.5
1970	50.5	124.8	987.1	92.6
1980	35.1	122.5	932.4	92.4
1990	60.3	210.7	965.2	165.3
2000	46.6	124.3	798.1	66.4
2010	24.5	126.8	911.1	153.2
2011	32.6	116.6	901.3	65.8
2012	39.2	90.5	823.9	101.1
2013	51.4	103.8	937.2	150.1
2014	46.6	131.2	782.1	85.3

TABLE 23: PER CAPITA WATER AVAILABILITY[9]

NO.	YEAR	POPULATION (MILLIONS)	PER CAPITA SURFACE WATER AVAILABILITY (M³)	PER CAPITA UTILIZABLE SURFACE WATER (M³)
1	1951	361	5410	1911
2	1955	395	4944	1746
3	1991	846	2309	816
4	2001	1027	1902	672
5	2025 - LOW CASE	1286	1519	495
	2025 - HIGH CASE	1333	1465	
6	2050 - LOW CASE	1346	1451	421
	2050 - HIGH CASE	1581	1235	

8   Ministry of Earth Sciences. India Meteorological Department (IMD). Sourced from: https://data.gov.in/catalog/all-india-area-weighted-monthly-seasonal-and-annual-rainfall-mm

9   Kumar, R., Singh, R.D, Sharma, K.D, Water resources of India, Current Science, Vol. 89, No. 5, 10 September 2005, Sourced from: http://www.iisc.ernet.in/currsci/sep102005/794.pdf

TABLE 24: PROJECTED WATER DEMAND (BY DIFFERENT USES) IN INDIA[10]

SECTOR	WATER DEMAND IN BILLION CUBIC METRE (BCM)			TOTAL WATER REQUIREMENT FOR DIFFERENT USES (IN BCM)					
	2010	2025	2050	2010		2025		2050	
				LOW	HIGH	LOW	HIGH	LOW	HIGH
IRRIGATION	688	910	1072	543	557	561	611	628	807
DOMESTIC	-	-	-	42	43	55	62	90	111
DRINKING WATER	56	73	102						
INDUSTRY	12	23	63	37	37	67	67	81	81
POWER	5	15	130	18	19	31	33	63	70
INLAND NAVIGATION	-	-	-	7	7	10	10	15	15
FLOOD CONTROL	-	-	-	0	0	0	0	0	0
AFFORESTATION	-	-	-	0	0	0	0	0	
ENVIRONMENT ECOLOGY	-	-	-	5	5	10	10	20	20
EVAPORATION LOSSES	-	-	-	42	42	50	50	76	76
OTHER	52	72	80	-	-	-	-	-	-
TOTAL	813	1093	1447	694	710	784	843	973	1180

INDIA'S RIVERS

India remains gifted with a bouquet of twenty perennial and non-perennial river systems, with several tributaries. Our rivers, mostly originating from the Himalayas, the Chotanagpur Plateau and the Western Ghats, receive a significant run-off, from glaciers and precipitation, accumulating an average annual flow of 1,953 km³, while replenishing groundwater resources of around 432 km³.[11] This enables the formation of a perennial utilizable water resource, expressed in surface water (690 km³) and groundwater (396 km³). Himalayan snow and ice melt offers a significant boon in particular, with water yield in such river basins nearly double that of the peninsular rivers. Groundwater, wherever available, remains a significant source of water, particularly for domestic consumption, contributing 80 per cent of the household requirement and over half of the irrigation requirement.

---

10   Ministry of Environment Statistics, Govt. of India. (ON591); Central Water Commission, Govt. of India. (ON502); IndiaStat Data

11   Kumar, R., Singh, R.D, Sharma, K.D, Water resources of India, Current Science, Vol. 89, No. 5, 10 September 2005, Sourced from: http://www.iisc.ernet.in/currsci/sep102005/794.pdf

TABLE 25: WATER AVAILABILITY—BASINWISE[12]

NO	RIVER BASIN	AVERAGE ANNUAL AVAILABILITY (CUBIC KM/YEAR)	UTILIZABLE FLOW
1	INDUS (UP TO BORDER)	73.31	46
2	A) GANGA	525.02	250
	B) BRAHMAPUTRA, BARAK AND OTHERS	585.6	24
3	GODAVARI	110.54	76.3
4	KRISHNA	78.12	58
5	CAUVERY	21.36	19
6	PENNAR	6.32	6.32
7	EAST-FLOWING RIVERS BETWEEN MAHANADAND PENNAR	22.52	
8	EAST FLOWING RIVERS BETWEEN PENNAR AND KANYAKUMARI	16.46	16.46
9	MAHANADI	66.88	49.99
10	BRAHMANI & BAITARNI	28.48	18.3
11	SUBARNAREKHA	12.37	6.81
12	SABARMATI	3.81	1.93
13	MAHI	11.02	3.1
14	WEST-FLOWING RIVERS OF KUTCH, SABARMATI INCLUDING LUNI	15.1	14.98
15	NARMADA	45.64	34.5
16	TAPI	14.88	14.5
17	WEST-FLOWING RIVERS FROM TAPI TO TADRI	87.41	36.21
18	WEST-FLOWING RIVERS FROM TADRI TO KANYAKUMARI	113.53	
19	AREA OF INLAND DRAINAGE IN RAJASTHAN DESERT	-	
20	MINOR RIVER BASINS DRAINING INTO BANGLADESH & BURMA	31	NA

12   Ministry of Water Resources, River Development & Ganga Rejuvenation. Sourced from: http://wrmin. nic.in/forms/list.aspx?lid=295

TABLE 26: RIVER BASIN-WISE ESTIMATED POPULATION AND PER CAPITA AVERAGE ANNUAL WATER AVAILABILITY IN INDIA (2010, 2025 AND 2050)[13]

RIVER BASIN	AVERAGE ANNUAL WATER RESOURCES POTENTIAL (BCM)$	ESTIMATED POPULATION (MILLION) NO.			ESTIMATED PER CAPITA AVERAGE ANNUAL WATER AVAILABILITY (M³)		
		2010	2025	2050	2010	2025	2050
INDUS (UP TO BORDER)	73.3	57.69	69.2	81.41	1270.58	1059.25	900.38
GANGA-BRAHMAPUTRA-MEGHNA							
A) GANGA	525	494.47	593.04	697.69	1061.74	885.27	752.48
B) BRAHMAPUTRA	537.2	40.07	48.06	56.54	13406.54	11177.69	9501.24
C) BARAK & OTHERS	48.4	8.54	10.24	12.05	5667.45	4726.56	4016.59
GODAVARI	110.5	74.36	89.18	104.92	1486.01	1239.07	1053.18
KRISHNA	78.1	83.72	100.41	118.13	932.87	777.81	661.14
CAUVERY	21.4	40.34	48.39	56.93	530.49	442.24	375.9
SUBARNAREKHA	12.4	12.94	15.52	18.26	958.27	798.97	679.08
BRAHMANI AND BAITARNI	28.5	13.49	16.18	19.04	2112.68	1761.43	1496.85
MAHANADI	66.9	36.63	43.93	51.68	1826.37	1522.88	1294.51
PENNAR	6.3	13.36	16.02	18.85	471.56	393.26	334.22
MAHI	11	14.46	17.34	20.4	760.72	634.37	539.22
SABARMATI	3.8	14.46	17.34	20.4	262.79	219.15	186.27
NARMADA	45.6	20.24	24.28	28.56	2252.96	1878.09	1596.64
TAPI	14.9	20.38	24.44	28.75	731.11	609.66	518.26
WEST FLOWING RIVERS FROM TAPI TO TADRI	87.4	35.53	42.61	50.13	2459.89	2051.16	1743.47
WEST FLOWING RIVERS FROM TADRI TO KANYAKUMARI	113.5	44.89	53.84	63.34	2528.4	2108.09	1791.92
EAST FLOWING RIVERS BETWEEN MAHANADI AND PENNAR	22.5	32.5	38.97	45.85	692.31	577.37	490.73
EAST FLOWING RIVERS BETWEEN PENNAR AND KANYAKUMARI	16.5	61.96	74.32	87.43	266.3	222.01	188.72
WEST FLOWING RIVERS OF KUTCH AND SAURASHTRA INCLUDING LUNI	15.1	30.43	36.5	42.94	496.22	413.69	351.65
AREA OF INLAND DRAINAGE IN RAJASTHAN	NEGL.	9.78	11.73	13.79	-	-	-
MINOR RIVER DRAINING INTO MYANMAR (BURMA) AND BANGLADESH	31	2.07	2.48	2.91	14975.85	12500	10652.92
TOTAL	1869.3	1162.3	1394.02	1640	1608.26	1340.94	1139.82

---

13   Water Resources Information System Directorate, Govt. of India. (ON502), IndiaStat Data

SURVIVING WATER DISASTERS

India's rivers undergo a series of changes across their route and through seasons—turning into a slack pool during winter, raging as a voracious torrent during the monsoon, aweing us with destructive potential. While rivers are often described in a feminine sense, as nadi, beautifully trailing across Jambudvip, as dividers of solid land, they can also be dangerous.[14] After all, the Ganga descended from heaven, bringing with it fertile soil for good crops, but also destruction in its wake. Sustainably managing such mercurial rivers to meet the challenges of rural India can hence be a tough ask.

In 1867, southern Bihar faced excessive rains, 50 per cent over the long-term average, leading to the Ganga and Sone rivers rising above the danger mark and destroying the standing bhadoi crop.[15] Back then, such events were taken as part of a natural cycle. As highlighted by H.W. Alexander, collector of the then Gaya district, 'The lands near the river sown with this crop were always liable to be flooded and were sown with full knowledge of this risk.' If the crops escaped flood damage, it was a bonus; else the floods brought alluvium to the land, replenishing it and making it ideally fertile for the rabi crop. Excessive flooding leads to short-term damage but long-term benefits.

Such natural events have a habit of repeating. The Kosi river, often termed the 'Sorrow of Bihar', is one of the largest tributaries of the Ganga. Emerging in northern Bihar from Nepal, the river has shifted its course over 120 km through more than twelve distinct channels from east to west in the last 250 years, primarily due to heavy silting (a silt yield of 19 m^3/hectare annually; one of the highest in the world) across its route—the river used to flow near Purnea in the eighteenth century and now flows west of Saharsa. Its annual floods affect about 21,000 km^2 of agricultural lands, with a monsoonal flow typically recorded at eighteen times the normal flow (2,166 m^3). In 2008, the Kosi picked an old abandoned channel that it had not used for a century near the Indo-Nepal border.[16,17,18] When the river damaged its embankment at Kusaha (Nepal), over 2.7 million people were affected across 650 km^2 by heavy flooding, particularly in Supaul, Araria, Saharsa, Madhepura, Purnia and Katihar districts.

---

14   Aitken, B., Seven Sacred Rivers, Chapter 1, Penguin.

15   Sheel, A., Floodplains and flash floods, Live Mint, 11 August 2016. Sourced from: http://www.livemint. com/Opinion/a8herzL1neqG1YQ35Yj6RI/Floodplains-and-flash-floods.html

16   http://www.ibnlive.com/news/bihar-flood-catastrophe-cm-seeks-govts-help/72143-3.html?from=rssfeed

17   http://news.bbc.co.uk/2/hi/south_asia/7580587.stm

18   http://www.ndtv.com/convergence/ndtv/story.aspx?id=NEWEN20080062979&ch=8/26/2008%20 12:36:00%20PM

The magnitude of death still remains hard to estimate, with 150 people washed away in a single incident. Consider the litany of water-related disasters that have swept the lay of the land annually.

TABLE 27: MAJOR WATER RELATED DISASTERS IN INDIA[19]

NO.	STATE & AREA	TYPE	YEAR	FATALITIES
1	LARGE PART OF THE COUNTRY	DROUGHT	1972	200 MILLION PEOPLE AFFECTED
2	ANDHRA PRADESH	CYCLONE	1977	10,000 DEATHS, HUNDREDS OF THOUSANDS HOMELESS, 40,000 CATTLE DEATHS
3	15 STATES	DROUGHT	1987	300 MILLION PEOPLE AFFECTED
4	ANDHRA PRADESH	CYCLONE	1990	967 PEOPLE DIED, 435,000 ACRES OF LAND AFFECTED
5	ANDHRA PRADESH	CYCLONE	1996	1,000 PEOPLE DIED, 5,80,000 HOUSE DESTROYED, ₹20.26 BILLION ESTIMATED DAMAGE
6	ORISSA	ORISSA SUPER CYCLONE	1999	OVER 10,000 DEATHS
7	NORTH BIHAR	KOSI FLOODS	2008	527 DEATHS, 19,323 LIVESTOCK PERISHED, 2,23,000 HOUSES DAMAGED, 3.3 MILLION PEOPLE AFFECTED
8	TAMIL NADU	CYCLONE NISHA	2008	204 DEATHS
9	252 DISTRICTS IN 10 STATES	DROUGHT	2009	NA
10	ANDHRA PRADESH, KARNATAKA	KRISHNA FLOODS	2009	300 PEOPLE DIED
11	LADAKH IN J&K	CLOUDBURST	2010	257 PEOPLE DIED
12	MAHARASHTRA STATE	MAHARASHTRA FLOODS	JULY 05	1,094 DEATHS, 167 INJURED, 54 MISSING
13	19 DISTRICTS OF ODISHA	ODISHA FLOODS	SEPT 11	45
14	TAMIL NADU, PUDUCHERRY	CYCLONE THANE	DEC 11	47
15	ASSAM	ASSAM FLOODS	AUG 12	NA
16	UTTARKASHI, RUDRAPRAYAG AND BAGESHWAR	UTTARAKHAND FLOODS	SEPT 12	52
17	TAMIL NADU	CYCLONE NILAM	OCT 12	65
18	TAMIL NADU	CYCLONE MAHASEN	MAY 13	8
19	UTTARAKHAND AND HIMACHAL PRADESH	FLOODS/LANDSLIDES	JUN 13	4,094
20	ODISHA	ODISHA FLOODS	OCT 13	21
21	ANDHRA PRADESH	ANDHRA FLOODS	OCT 13	53
22	ODISHA AND ANDHRA PRADESH	CYCLONE PHAILIN	OCT 13	23
23	ANDHRA PRADESH & ODISHA	CYCLONE HUD HUD	SEP 14	NA
24	JAMMU & KASHMIR	FLOODS	OCT 14	NA

19   http://www.ndma.gov.in/en/disaster-data-statistics.html

More recently, consider the bountiful monsoon in 2016 which led to the Ganga eking ever closer to its all-time high flood levels, last recorded nearly thirty years ago. Hundreds of villages were inundated while over 2 lakh people were affected. Even Bundelkhand, struck with drought in the summer, saw its major rivers flowing nearly 8 m above the danger mark in the Banda area, while 150 villages were submerged.

DAM BUILDING

During summer, Sumati Pokhriyal, from a village near Suratgarh in Ganganagar district in Rajasthan, finds her daily existence prone to the vagaries of the Ghaggar river. In summer, when the river channel tends to dry up, she is often found soliciting local mendicants for tips on the nearest aquifer. It's a game of chance—most wells dry up quickly, given the shallow aquifers, so getting a bucket of drinkable water requires women to go hunting. When asked about provisions for bathing, she laughs, pointing to the sky.

To combat this risk, and to provide irrigation to millions of marginal farmers, modern India has sought to build dams. Starting from 1947, when there were just 300 large dams across India, the government has built around 4,900, with the majority built between 1971 and 1989. The primary purpose of these dams has been to further irrigation, in addition to control floods, ensure water supply and generate hydroelectricity. Large dams, termed as 'temples of Modern India' by Jawaharlal Nehru in 1955, were encouraged post-Independence to jumpstart industrialization and establish a scientific outlook.

TABLE 28: CUMULATIVE PUBLIC SECTOR PLAN OUTLAY
IN IRRIGATION AND FLOOD CONTROL, 1951–97[20, 21]

TYPE	TOTAL (₹ BILLION AT 2015 PRICES)
MAJOR & MEDIUM PROJECTS	526.1
MINOR IRRIGATION	291.6 (INCLUDING ₹134.7 OF INSTITUTIONAL INVESTMENT)
COMMAND AREA DEVELOPMENT	54.2
FLOOD CONTROL	48.6
TOTAL	919.4 (INCLUDING 134.7 OF INSTITUTIONAL INVESTMENT)

20   GOI, 10th Five Year Plan, Chapter 8.1;
21   Vaidyanathan, A., India's Water Resources, Chapter 1, Pg 11, Oxford

TABLE 29: LARGE DAMS, STATEWISE[22]

NO.	STATE	UPTO 1900	1901 TO 1950	1951 TO 1960	1961 TO 1970	1971 TO 1980	1981 TO 1990	1991 TO 2000	2001 & BEYOND	UNKNOWN YEAR	TOTAL COMPLETED DAMS	UNDER CONSTRUCTION	TOTAL
1	ANDAMAN & NICOBAR ISLANDS					1		1	2				2
2	ANDHRA PRADESH	1	6	9	11	24	15	9	21	46	142	25	167
3	ARUNACHAL PRADESH								1		1	3	4
4	ASSAM					2			1		3	1	4
5	BIHAR	1		1	8	5	5	1	3		24	2	26
6	CHHATTISGARH		11	1	18	51	99	37	30	1	248	10	258
7	GOA						3	2			5		5
8	GUJARAT	6	57	59	85	151	155	57	44	5	619	13	632
9	HIMACHAL PRADESH				1	2	1	1	12	2	19	1	20
10	HARYANA								1		1		1
11	JAMMU & KASHMIR					2	2	1	6	3	14	3	17
12	JHARKHAND			9	5	11	22			3	50	29	79
13	KARNATAKA	6	24	11	39	49	54	17	14	16	230	1	231
14	KERALA	1	1	9	15	11	10	10	4	0	61	1	62
15	MADHYA	3	86	35	66	220	301	93	66	28	898	8	906
16	MAHARASHTRA	20	40	23	152	622	416	304	113	3	1693	152	1845
17	MANIPUR				1			1	1		3	1	4
18	MEGHALAYA			1	2	2		1	2		8		8
19	MIZORAM											1	1
20	NAGALAND								1		1		1
21	ODISHA	2	2	4	8	54	77	35	13	4	199	5	204
22	PUNJAB			1			4	6	3		14	2	16
23	RAJASTHAN	17	14	33	23	29	36	26	15	8	201	10	211
24	SIKKIM							1	1		2		2
25	TAMIL NADU	0	10	10	26	26	17	8	19		116	0	116
26	TELANGANA	6	29	6	12	8	13	6	3	79	162	20	182
27	TRIPURA					1					1		1
28	UTTAR PRADESH	4	24	21	22	16	14	11	3		115	15	130
29	UTTARAKHAND			5	4	2	1		4		16	9	25
30	WEST BENGAL			1	1	4	16	2	5		29	1	30
	TOTAL	67	304	234	499	1294	1264	631	386	198	4877	313	5190

---

22   http://www.cwc.nic.in/main/downloads/new%20nrld.pdf

However, this love affair with big dams didn't last long. As Nehru termed, it within three years of the previous speech, in 'Social Aspects of Small and Big Projects':

> For some time past, however, I have been beginning to think that we are suffering from what we may call, 'disease of gigantism'. We want to show that we can build big dams and do big things. This is a dangerous outlook developing in India. The idea of having big undertakings and doing big tasks for the sake of showing that we can do big things is not a good outlook at all... We have to realize that we can also meet our problems much more rapidly and efficiently by taking up a large number of small schemes, especially when the time involved in a small scheme is much less and the results obtained are rapid. Further, in those small schemes, you can get a good deal of what is called public cooperation, and therefore, there is social value in associating people with such small schemes.[23]

The economic gains associated with dams can accrue to different population segments. Most of India's irrigation dams are actually embankments in nature, with a wall built across a valley to impound water, creating a reservoir upstream and in many cases, displacing villagers and livestock; a large dam can easily displace up to 10 per cent of an average Indian district (dam construction submerged 4.5 million hectares of forest land between 1980 and 2000).[24,25] While dams can provide large productivity benefits in aggregate, particularly for irrigation and recharging the water table, they also incur significant social costs, with the economic benefits accruing disproportionately to people living in the command areas; the average dam displaces 31,340 people while submerging 8,748 hectares; Scheduled Tribes typically are amongst those most affected, constituting 47 per cent of those displaced. For those whose agricultural and grazing land is flooded, the government's compensation is often significantly delayed and a pittance at that; such compensation is typically insufficient for replacing lost land by equivalent land with similar quality elsewhere.[26]

Cost-benefit analysis studies have highlighted that dams are mostly marginally effective, offering a rise in agricultural productivity of just 9 per cent (the World Commission of Dams estimates a 10 per cent average).[27] A dam can increase net irrigated area by 0.7 per cent in its own district and around 1 per cent downstream, when accounting for displaced agricultural areas and a ban on upstream canals to maintain flow downstream.[28] A Planning Commission estimate highlighted

---

23   Thakkar, 2000
24   http://www.econ.yale.edu/~rp269/website/papers/dams_OUP_Nov30.pdf
25   World Commission on Dams (2000b)
26   Dreze J., Samson M., and Singh S. 1997
27   Duflo, E., Pande, R., Dams, July 2005. Sourced from: http://economics.mit.edu/files/796
28   Duflo, E., Pande,R., Dams, July 2005. Sourced from: http://economics.mit.edu/files/796

that the development cost per hectare of dam irrigation was ₹16,129 in 1985 (incorporating capital costs, maintenance costs; ₹18,807 per hectare if fertilizer costs are added in). As highlighted in E. Duflo & R. Pande's seminal analysis (2005), comparing this with a purported present discount value of net increase in irrigated area of ₹13,686 and an overall lower irrigation cost (vs groundwater irrigation) gives a marginal net present value; a return of just ~1 per cent. In addition, dams can induce waterlogging and raise soil salinity—by 1991, around 2.46 million hectares of land associated with the command area of dams was suffering from waterlogging, while 3.30 million hectares was suffering from salinity; 10 per cent of the total area actually irrigated back then.[29] Maharashtra has over 40 per cent of India's large dams; even so, over 82 per cent of the state continues to be rainfed; Maharashtra pushed large dams, not irrigation (Devendra Fadnavis, 21 July 2015).[30]

In comparison, other forms of water harvesting (e.g. dykes, groundwater) can prove to be more cost-effective, if given due attention.[31] Maharashtra has over 70,000 small irrigation projects (each with potential to irrigate at least 250 hectares), costing over ₹4,600 crore, but just 12 per cent of their total irrigation potential is actually utilized (2 lakh hectares of 16.25 lakh hectares).[32] While such small bunds and percolation tanks could make a significant difference to drought-stricken villages, most of them have fallen into disrepair, choking with silt or simply vandalized. They have simply been built and forgotten, with no manpower or budget allocated for maintenance and management. Osmanabad district had hundreds of KT weirs built to block river water, but most have fallen into disrepair.

The threat of dam collapse also looms. The 118-year-old, 43.38-metre, Jaswant Sagar dam's collapse on the Luni river in Jodhpur district in Rajasthan flooded nearly forty villages in July 2007.[33, 34] India has 115 century-old dams in various states of decay, which can collapse at a moment's notice—e.g. the 52-metre Mullaperiyar dam in Tamil Nadu and the Thonnur Tank (24.38 m) in Karnataka which date back to AD 1,000. India remains curiously apathetic about decommissioning dams, despite the development of cracks in several dams in seismically active regions. Rajasthan has over twenty-seven large dams that are a century old, while there are an additional 381 dams in India between the age of fifty and hundred years. Our

---

29   World Commission on Dams 2000b; Duflo, E., Pande,R., Dams, July 2005. Sourced from: http://economics.mit.edu/files/796

30   Shah, M., Push irrigation, not dams, Indian Express, 14 August 2015. Sourced from: http://indianexpress.com/article/opinion/columns/push-irrigation-not-dams/

31   Biswas and Tortajada (2001); Dhawan (1989)

32   Kakodari, P., Only 12% potential of Maharashtra's 70,000 small dams used, Times of India, 17 April 2015, http://timesofindia.indiatimes.com/city/mumbai/Only-12-potential-of-states-70000-small-dams-used/articleshow/46951498.cms?intenttarget=no

33   http://www.andhranews.net/India/2007/July/7-Rajasthan-Jaswant-7252.asp

34   Jaswant Sagar Dam Collapse: A Wake up call, SANDRP, July 2007

approach to dam safety is notoriously lax. As a World Bank report notes, 'States generally do not have adequate hydrological capability to estimate design floods and review flood operating strategies' and that the Central Water Commission (CWC) is 'not playing a proactive role' on safety issues associated with dams.[35] Dams also create a natural breeding ground for vector-borne diseases, inducing malaria, filariasis and schistosomiasis.[36]

RIVERINE FISHERIES

Beyond this, dams can have a significant impact on riverine fisheries. While blessed with a rich bounty of riverine fish species, along with a network of hundreds of rivers and over 1.2 million hectares of floodplain lakes and wetlands, India's riverine fisheries are increasingly collapsing, surviving on just subsistence levels (an average yield of 0.3 tonne per km; 15 per cent of their actual potential), impacting the poorest of the poor in rural India (a small river like the Wainganga can play host to over 400,000 fishermen).[37,38] The natural flow of all major rivers in India has been regulated for irrigation and power, while dealing a blow to riverine communities that subsist on fishing. According to the Central Inland Fisheries Research Institute (CIFRI), rivers are increasingly losing their character, disembowelled as they are of fishes by hydrological modification, a near absence of water in rivers, migration obstacles, salinity changes, sediment changes, a decline in riparian areas and stoppage of flowing water.[39] Riverine fishing has been tragically ignored, with the Twelfth Five Plan allocating the majority of a ₹6,000 crore investment in fishing to marine fisheries, along with ₹1,000 crore to the National Fisheries Development Board. A CIFRI study, conducted between 2005 and 2007, on the Krishna stretch between Srikakulam and Hamsala, highlighted that dam construction had led to the diversion of all water towards irrigation, industrial and urban uses, leaving the estuary area dry in summer and increasingly hyper saline.[40] This has led to a disappearance of

---

35 Menon, S., The real truth about our dam problem, Business Standard, 13 December 2011. Sourced from: http://www.business-standard.com/article/economy-policy/the-real-truth-about-our-dam-problem-111121300092_1.html

36 Sharma, 1991.

37 Dandakar, P., Damaged Rivers, Collapsing Fisheries: Impacts of Dams on riverine fisheries in India, South Asia Network on Dams, Rivers and People, September 2012. Sourced from: http://sandrp.in/dams/Impacts_of_Dams_on_Riverine_Fisheries_in_India_ParineetaDandekar_Sept2012.pdf

38 12th Five Year Plan, Working Group on Development and Management of Aquaculture.

39 Central Inland Fisheries Research Institute.

40 Dandakar, P., Damaged Rivers, Collapsing Fisheries: Impacts of Dams on riverine fisheries in India, South Asia Network on Dams, Rivers and People, September 2012. Sourced from: http://sandrp.in/dams/Impacts_of_Dams_on_Riverine_Fisheries_in_India_ParineetaDandekar_Sept2012.pdf

a plethora of fish species (carp, catfish, murrel, feather back, etc.). While CIFRI recommended the discharge of 1,300–1,500 TMC of water from the Prakassam Barrage annually during summer, and the Krishna Water Disputes Tribunal has ordered the respective state governments to release water for environmental purposes, nothing has yet been done.[41]

Fish stocks in rivers such as the Krishna, Godavari, Mahanadi, Narmada, Tapi, Sabarmati and Cauvery are collapsing because of a decline in freshwater in their estuaries and a decline in mangrove forests. Hilsa fish stocks in the Cauvery collapsed after the Mettur Dam was constructed, while mahseer, a once abundant fish found across major Indian rivers, is now an extremely endangered species, wiped out by dams on the Narmada and large dams such as Tehri in the Himalayan states.[42,43] Such a decrease in water flow has also led to an increase in silt, raising river beds and affecting future flow (the Ganga's silt load increased by twenty times near Allahabad and thirty times near Varanasi in 1995–2000, compared to 1980–85).[44] This reduction in fish stocks has been accompanied by an increase in the presence of exotic fishes, which prefer decreased flows through dams. The Farakka Barrage has helped destroy rich hilsa fisheries on the Ganges in areas near Allahabad and Varanasi—the average yield of major carp in the Ganga declined from 26.62 kg/hectare annually to 2.55 kg/hectare over the last four decades (Tenth Five Year Plan).

RIVER FLOW

The unfortunate impact of this spate of dam construction on river flow is slowly coming to light. The Chambal is one of the few unspoiled rivers remaining, offering a pristine habitat to the endangered Gangetic River Dolphin, the critically endangered gharial, and the red-crowned roof turtle, along with a host of birds and fishes. It offers a critical linkage in a fragment forested landscape, providing a vital corridor to Ranthambore, Kuno-Palpur, Madhav, Darrah-Mukundra and Keladevi. However, since Independence, its isolation was disrupted, with a cluster of dams built to provide solace to arid districts in Madhya Pradesh and Rajasthan. Over six major irrigation projects, twelve medium and 134 minor projects came

41   Krishna Estuary: Ecology and Fisheries, CIFRI, 2009; Krishna Water Disputes Tribunal Award, 2010
42   Cumulative Impacts of Hydropower Dams on Alaknanda & Bhagirathi Rivers on Aquatic and Terrstrial Ecosystems, Wildlife Institute of India, 2012
43   Davendra, S. and Kamal Singh Negi, Mahseer Fish Bionomics and Population: Barrage Impact on Fish Biology
44   Pathak et al, Riverine Ecology and Fisheries, vis a vis hydrodynamic alterations: Impacts and Remedial measures, CIFRI, 2010

up across its basin, leading to a steep decline in its pre-monsoon water flow—only 10–15 per cent of the Chambal's length now has the minimum depth required for gharial and dolphins to survive during summer.[45] The Chambal, a serene and yet isolated river, cursed in Hindu mythology, has been disrupted, with its famed ravines (where the dacoits used to roam) being flattened by sand mining and industrial water usage, leaving the river high and dry.

While the Central Water Commission issued a guideline in 1992 outlining that a dammed river must contain a minimum flow of an average of ten days of minimum flow in its natural state, the Chambal has been stripped of its natural sheen. This has had consequences, even for agriculture—the average quantity of Chambal water used for irrigation in Rajasthan and Madhya Pradesh from the Gandhi Sagar dam and the Kota Barrage declined by 22.6 per cent and 41.4 per cent, respectively, between 1990 and 2007; all while industrial usage increased by over 300 per cent. Villages are increasingly running short of water in irrigation canals—at Bhakto ka Ghat, near Kherli village in Rajasthan, the Chambal's depth is usually just knee-deep during the winter months; nonagenarians in the village recall the days when the river could only be crossed on boats.[46] Chambal has witnessed its overall flow decline by 3.4 per cent annually since the '90s, with the gharials losing over half their existing habitat, leading to potential starvation.[47] This river, once cursed, is likely to remain so.

The Ganga has suffered in a similar manner. While over 60 per cent of the Ganga's water is diverted for irrigation, a majority of that diversion is lost to evaporation.[48] The Farakka Barrage has helped reduce the Ganga's average monthly discharge from 2,213 $m^{3/s}$ to 316 $m^{3/s}$. Most of the river currently does not have enough flow to dilute the treated water that is discharged from sewage treatment plants; raw sewage, instead, continues to concentrate.[49]

The Krishna river used to discharge 57 BCM per year into the ocean in the '60s, but has, since 1965, suffered a steady decline of 0.8 BCM per year, reaching 10.8 BCM in 2000 (>15 per cent of its historical run-off), and almost nil (0.4 BCM) in 2004.[50,51]

45   Mazoomdar, J., Bleeding the Chambal Dry, 11 March 2013, Tehelka. Sourced from: http://www.tehelka.com/2013/03/bleeding-the-chambal-dry/

46   Ibid

47   Ibid

48   Depraz, M., Threat of water extraction on the Ganges, WWF. Sourced from: http://wwf.panda.org/about_our_earth/about_freshwater/freshwater_problems/river_decline/10_rivers_risk/ganges/ganges_threats/

49   Saraswati, S. A., Towards a revitalised River Ganga, Global Water Forum, 25 September 2015. Sourced from: http://www.globalwaterforum.org/2015/09/25/towards-a-revitalised-river-ganga/

50   Venot et al, 2003

51   Dandekar, P., Thakkar, H., Ecological Management of Rivers in India: A Long road ahead, South Asia Network on Dams, Rivers and People, Jan 2012. Sourced from: http://sandrp.in/rivers/Ecological_Management_of_Rivers_in_India_Jan_2012.PDF

Indian rivers are unfortunately viewed by policymakers only as providers of water and receivers of effluents, while any ecosystem links between rivers, their upstream areas, floodplains, riparian areas and estuaries are mostly ignored. While the National Water Policy speaks about ensuring minimum flow in perennial rivers in order to maintain ecology and social considerations, it also allocates fourth priority to ecology while asking for transfer of water to water-short areas through transfers from one river basin to another—a paradoxical approach.[52] We don't even have an agreed definition on minimum flow as yet—tribunals like the Cauvery Award have defined minimum flow as a specific figure (10 bcft), without a detailed scientific justification; High Courts like that of Himachal Pradesh have asked that all dams must have 15 per cent of the minimum flow downstream of the dam always.[53] Meanwhile, arbitrary dam construction continues, covering the Ganga basin; some of these, termed run of the river projects, have sought to divert the rivers through tunnels for up to 40 km, leaving earlier channels bereft of any water. Other hydroelectric projects hold back water for up to twenty to twenty two hours, while releasing it for generation over just two to three hours.[54] Dams being constructed on the Dibang, Lohit and Siang, which combine to form the Brahmaputra, are likely to cause water level shifts of 7 feet in a single day in the Dibru Saikhowa National Park. An ecosystem approach for an integrated management of land, water and living resources in a river basin is urgently needed.

RIVER INTERLINKING

Given this limited water flow and the general water deficit in southern and western India, the National Water Development Agency (NWDA) is seeking to implement an interlinking of rivers in the country: the Inter-River Linking Project (IRL). This mega project seeks to ease water shortage by linking over thirty major rivers, at a potential cost of $123 billion (as of 2002)—the largest water development project in the world. The idea, while not new (Sir Arthur Cotton proposed the original idea a century back), has been a backburner issue for the Indian government for decades; Dr K.L. Rao sought to implement the proposal for expansion of irrigation and power. The project itself has two components—Himalayan and Peninsular. The project would build over thirty links (canals, 50–100-m wide, 6-m deep) and around 3,000 storage tanks,

---

52 Ibid
53 Ibid
54 Ibid

connecting thirty-seven Himalayan and Peninsular rivers to create a giant water grid and facilitate navigation, while facilitating 178 km of inter-basin water transfer annually. It would build 12,500 km of new canals, irrigating an additional 35 million hectares and add a 35 GW hydropower capacity (of which 3.7 GW would be needed to lift water across major watersheds and the Vindhyas). This could potentially double agricultural production over the next five years, while providing employment to over 10 lakh people in building canals and tanks over the next few decades, and potentially limit damage due to extreme drought or flood conditions.

However, the initiative has significant demerits. The project would have large environmental costs, destroying a significant chunk of India's limited remaining high-density forests, while leaving millions in need of rehabilitation. It could potentially strain our relationships with our riparian neighbours (Bangladesh, Pakistan, Nepal and Bhutan), while causing untold social unrest due to forced resettlement of people (just the construction of canals and reservoirs in South India could displace half a million people while submerging fertile land and forests). Since the '80s, major irrigation projects have faced significant civil backlash, along with cost inflation, as Iyer (2003) notes, 'we have had great difficulty in completing even a single project successfully and we want to embark on thirty massive projects at the same time.' Bangladesh would be plunged into an ecological disaster, if the Brahmaputra and Ganga's waters are diverted down south. The ecological impact of digging hundreds of canals would be significant, affecting the ecological balance of land, freshwater, oceans and sea water (Shiva, 2003). In addition to the huge initial capital outlay, subsequent maintenance costs associated with canals, dams, tunnels and tanks would be a significant annual burden for central and state budgets. Inter-state cooperation on water has historically been hard (consider the Cauvery dispute), with no state ready to give water to another state—state assemblies in Kerala, Assam and Sikkim have already announced their opposition to ILR. Until recently, the Ministry of Environment too voiced its stringent opposition to the project.

The potential environmental damage that would be caused by this project is inestimable. Simply linking rivers with pipelines and canals can bring about significant hydro-morphological changes, changing the physical and chemical composition of sediments and the delta.[55] Waterlogging, salinity and desertification, as seen with canals in northern India, could spread. The last five decades have seen over 50 million people displaced by the construction of dams, power plants and other development activities, with fewer than 12 million actually regaining their

---

55   Shiva, 2003

livelihood[56]—a project like this would exacerbate social injustice. Treating rivers as bundles of pipelines that can be moulded, cut and re-joined at will, is a mark of technological hubris and conducts violence on our erstwhile considered sacred rivers. While every ILR project has its own local requirements and impact, rushing through on this giant undertaking would be deleterious to our country and its social and environmental fabric.[57]

RIVERINE POLLUTION

In addition, riverine water quality is increasingly toxic. The quality of water in a river is a direct product of our waste management policies. While India's urban sewage treatment capacity stands at ~23,277 million litres per day (MLD), it generates ~62,000 MLD, almost thrice in excess.[58] Of the 816 sewage treatment plants (STPs), ~522 (STPs) actually work; shrinking our treatment capacity to 30 per cent; the remaining 70 per cent of raw sewage is dumped directly into 80 per cent of our surface water resources. [59,60]

Despite the recent Swachh Bharat programme, our past record at cleaning rivers is dismal—the Ganga Action Plan (GAP) launched in 1985 failed largely on account of bad planning (misaligned gravity sewers, lack of electricity and generators), poor execution (cost overruns in U.P., Bihar and West Bengal), extensive corruption (fund diversions) and a general absence of coordination between central and state organizations (disagreement in jurisdiction for O&M of treatment plants) as well as between the states themselves.[61] The project ignored the tributaries and the river basin of the Ganga, focusing solely on the main stem in isolation, spending ₹901.71 crore over fifteen years; [62] failure soon arrived—of sixty-six test sites

---

56 Roy, 1999

57 Iyer, 2003

58 Lok Sabha questions, Unstarred Question No. 1478 answered on 8-Dec'2015, Capacity of Sewage Treatment Plants; Sourced from: http://164.100.47.192/Loksabha/Questions/QResult15aspx?qref=25748&lsno=16

59 Central Pollution Control Board, Mar'2015, Inventorization of Sewage Treatment Plants; Sourced from: http://cpcb.nic.in/upload/NewItems/NewItem_210_Inventorization_of_Sewage-Treatment_Plant.pdf

60 An Assessment of Faecal Sludge Management Policies and Programmes at the National and select State Levels, Water Aid India; Sourced from: http://wateraidindia.in/publication/faecal-sludge-management-report/

61 Mukherjee & BIswas, Lee Kuan Yew School of Public Policy, 2014; Sourced from: http://lkyspp.nus.edu.sg/iwp/wp-content/uploads/sites/3/2014/09/Ganga-cleanup-BT.pdf

62 Dayal, R., India Water Portal, Dirty Flows the Ganga; Sourced from: http://www.indiawaterportal.org/sites/indiawaterportal.org/files/dirty_flows_the_ganga_0.pdf

along the length of the Ganga, only thirty-eight (57.6 per cent) had acceptable water quality in terms of Biochemical Oxygen Demand (BOD) and twenty-four (36.4 per cent) in terms of total-coliform counts.[63]

TABLE 30: WASTEWATER GENERATION IN CLASS 1 CITIES IN THE GANGA BASIN[64]

WASTEWATER GENERATION IN CLASS I CITIES/TOWNS IN GANGA BASIN		
NO. OF CITIES	WASTE WATER VOLUME (MLD)	DISPOSAL STRATEGY
36	2637.7	GANGA RIVER
113	7841.5	TRIBUTARIES
30	907.4	LAND
TOTAL – 179	11386.6	

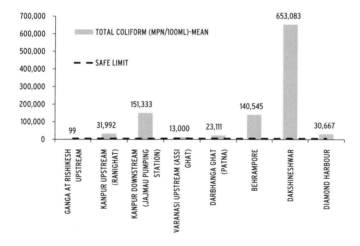

FIGURE 29: TOTAL COLIFORM COUNT (MPN/100 ML) ACROSS GANGA (SOURCE: DATA.GOV.IN)

63   Sharma, A., June 2015; Sourced from: http://www.indiaspend.com/cover-story/rs-986-cr-30-years-ganga-water-quality-plunges-67807

64   CPCB (2010a:31); Iyer, Ramaswamy, Living Rivers, Dying Rivers, Chapter 5, Pg 86, Oxford

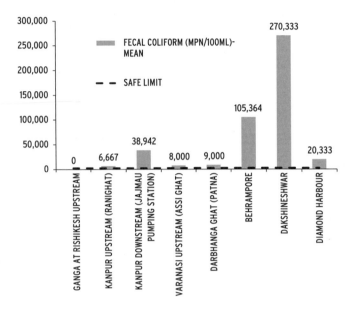

FIGURE 30: FECAL COLIFORM COUNT (MPN/100 ML) ACROSS GANGA (SOURCE: DATA.GOV.IN)

While Kanpur amplifies the total and fecal coliform five times, West Bengal (Dakshineshwar) is the largest outlier—it dumps almost 51 per cent of its waste into the river without any treatment.[65] In addition, a significant amount of pollution goes 'undetected'.

The state of our rivers is dismal—most of them exhibit higher than safe BOD levels (safe limit at 3 mg/l), while more than 50 per cent of them have a deteriorating trend, made worse by increased sewage disposal into the rivers of the sewage generated across Tier-1 and Tier-2 cities.[66] In most cases, we tend to drink this polluted water, particularly so in rural areas downstream of major cities; access to tap water, often treated, stands at ~71 per cent in urban areas and ~31 per cent in rural areas, with total combined at ~43.5 per cent. The remaining 56.5 per cent of the population remains excluded, encouraging water-borne diseases.[67]

65 Central Pollution Control Board, Jul'2013, Pollution Assessment: River Ganga; Sourced from: http://cpcb.nic.in/upload/NewItems/NewItem_203_Ganga_report.pdf

66 Tewari, S., Jul'2014; Sourced from: http://www.indiaspend.com/cover-story/the-environmental-departmental-challenges-to-a-clean-ganga-76624

67 Lok Sabha Questions, Sourced from: http://164.100.47.132/Annexture_New/lsq15/14/au1778.htm

TABLE 31: WATER BORNE DISEASE INCIDENCE[68]

DISEASE	2010		2011		2012	
	CASES	DEATHS	CASES	DEATHS	CASES	DEATHS
ACUTE ENCEPHALITIS SYNDROME (AES)	5,167	679	8,249	1,169	8,344	1,256
CHOLERA	5,004	9	2,341	10	1,583	1
VIRAL HEPATITIS	89,150	430	94,402	520	118,880	551
TYPHOID	1,084,885	440	1,062,446	346	1,477,699	428
ACUTE DIARRHOEAL DISEASE	10,742,327	1,526	10,231,049	1,269	11,701,755	1,647
TOTAL	11,926,533	3,084	11,398,487	3,314	13,308,261	3,883

Rivers remain the key—their clean health and rejuvenation will ensure access to clean water to our populace. The Indo-Gangetic plains account for ~80 per cent of the Indian population, yet today the Ganga remains the fifth most polluted river.[69] When considering the number of river stretches considered 'polluted' across India and the number of towns that lie beside them, the situation becomes stark. There are ~302 polluted river stretches in India (thirty-four in Priority Class – I, seventeen in Priority Class – II, thirty-six in Priority Class – III, fifty-seven in Priority Class – IV and 158 in Priority Class – V) across 275 rivers with a polluted riverine length of 12,363 km.

TABLE 32: REGION-WISE DISTRIBUTION OF POLLUTED RIVER STRETCHES IN INDIA

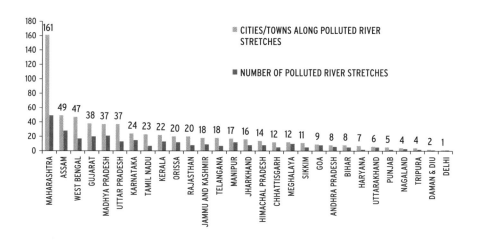

111

The economic benefits of treating riverine pollution are significant—reduced water-borne diseases, reduced cost of supplying treated water for household and industrial use, control of soil quality and fisheries development (tangible in nature) and improved aquatic life and biodiversity (intangible in nature). Environmental degradation contributes sixty years of ill-health per 1,000 population in India, as compared to thirty-four in China and thirty-seven in Brazil. Almost 15 lakh children die annually due to water-borne diseases while nearly 200 million people lose their lives each year (₹366 billion, ~3.95 per cent of GDP, 1995; Parikh, 2004). However, prevention of such pollution (better sanitation, water pollution control) would have comparably cost the government 1.7–2.5 per cent of the GDP (Murty & Kumar, 2004).

RIVERINE PROTECTION

India's rivers have long been without protection amidst a haze of laws, commissions and judicial announcements. The Wildlife (Protection) Act, 1972, prohibits anyone from stopping or enhancing the flow of water into or out of a National Park, except without permission from the Chief Wildlife Warden.[70] This provision, while ideal, has rarely been invoked for the protection of rivers, with a few exceptions; the Bhagirathi's upstream stretch above Uttarkashi was declared an ecological zone, disbarring hydropower projects, in 2010. Other relevant acts at the central (e.g., The Forest Conservation Act, 1980, the Environment Protection Act, 1986) and state (e.g., Maharashtra Water Resources Regulatory Authority Act, 2005) levels do not explicitly seek to protect rivers or their minimum flows from an environmental perspective.

Judicial pronouncements have usually left river channels and their flows to eminent domain decisions,[71,72] with a few exceptions (the Span Motels case, where the Supreme Court admonished the Central Government for 'validating' the actions of a private entrepreneur who had diverted a river to protect his hotel property).[73] The Public Trust doctrine has been cited by the Supreme Court to protect two

---

70 Thakkar, H., Rivers: Legal and Institutional Issues in India, South Asia Network on Dams, Rivers & People, May 2012. Sourced from: http://sandrp.in/rivers/Rivers_Legal_and_Institutional_Issues_in_India.pdf

71 Parambikulam Aliyar Project Assn. v. State of Tamil Nadu AIR 1999 SC 3092.

72 Legal Aspects of Water Resource Management , A.Vaidyanathan and Bharath Jairaj, updated from "Role of Law in Water Resource Management", Indian Jurid. Rev., Vol 1, National University of Juridical Sciences, 2004

73 M.C. Mehta v. Kamal Nath 1997 (1) SCC 388

lakes in Andhra Pradesh which the state government had sought to close and fill, in order to construct public housing—the Supreme Court instead took the view that the tanks were a communal property that the State was a trustee to, and the State could not commit any act or omission that infringed on the community's rights. The struggle of the people of Plachimada (South Kerala) against excessive exploitation of groundwater and improper generation and disposal of toxic waste by the Coca-Cola bottling plant reflects upon the rights of the people vis-à-vis attempts to privatize state property by corporations. Increasingly, urban water needs are winning out over rural requirements—a 23-kilometre stretch of the Sheonath river in Chhattisgarh was privatized in 2001, with a concession given to Radius Water to build a dam and own the subsequent reservoir.[74] The firm asserted its rights by banning local villagers from using the waters for fishing, bathing or agriculture. While the Chhattisgarh Assembly subsequently sought to tear up the concession, such examples of water privatization are bound to raise concerns.

There remain a plethora of central institutions theoretically influencing the fate of rivers—the Ministry of Environment, Forests and Climate Change, the Central Pollution Control Board, the Water Quality Assessment Authority, the Central Water Commission, Central Electricity Authority, the government hydropower development organization and river basin-specific Organizations.[75] At the state level, a similar smorgasbord prevails—the various environment, power and irrigation departments, water resource regulatory authorities and state pollution control boards. But at a fundamental level, India has no law that requires a perennial river to have freshwater flow throughout the year. Cost-benefit analysis associated with dam and irrigation projects rarely accounts for a river's ecosystem benefits. Rivers are considered a resource to be exploited, with water reaching the sea classified as wasteful. When Himachal Pradesh, in September 2005, announced a notification asking for a 15 per cent minimum observed flow in rivers at all times, it was challenged by the Government of India, NHPC and the Punjab State Power Corporation while the Ministry of Environment and Forests supported NHPC.[76] This mindset can cause irreparable damage to rivers and consequently to their historical users, our villages.

There remains cause for optimism. The Tirthan river, a tributary of the Beas River in Himachal Pradesh, has been declared a protected river by the state government,

---

74 Controversial plan to sell water from Sheonath river, Down to Earth, 14 Feb 20013. Sourced from: http://www.indiaenvironmentportal.org.in/content/39490/controversial-plan-to-sell-water-from-sheonath-river/

75 Thakkar, H., Rivers: Legal and Institutional Issues in India, South Asia Network on Dams, Rivers & People, May 2012. Sourced from: http://sandrp.in/rivers/Rivers_Legal_and_Institutional_Issues_in_India.pdf

76 Thakkar, H., Rivers: Legal and Institutional Issues in India, South Asia Network on Dams, Rivers & People, May 2012. Sourced from: http://sandrp.in/rivers/Rivers_Legal_and_Institutional_Issues_in_India.pdf

in order to protect the river basin for the brown trout fish.[77] International norms on river protection provide an ideal example—the Ramsar Convention on the Management of Wetlands (signed and notified by India) seeks to protect biodiversity and ensure wise usage of rivers and their wetlands—India's current definition of wetlands excludes river channels; this needs to be changed. Sweden actively prohibits the construction or expansion of any dams on protected rivers, with the protection applying to all tributaries.[78] We need to identify and protect at least some of our rivers in their natural undammed state, allowing them to flow unhindered to the ocean, particularly in the Western Ghats and the Himalayan and Northeastern states. Active decommissioning of dams, particularly those that are old, uneconomic or structurally weak, should be undertaken—the US, with over 75,000 dams, has increasingly taken to this practice, restoring lush ecosystems as a consequence.

A new National Rivers Policy needs to be promulgated, outlining river zone regulation, floodplain protection, catchment management and the protection of wetlands and forests, while ensuring that perennial rivers have a minimum flow.[79] We need a strong national policy on the conservation of fish, fisheries and associated ecosystems, at the national level—the existing Fisheries Law (1897) and the Wildlife Protection Act need to be amended to include specific rules on the release and maintenance of environmental flow and sediments in rivers. Each such timing of water release will have to be river-specific, catering to local rural needs and requirements, and in active compliance with environmental norms. All our existing or planned dams need to have fish ladders, passes, locks and lifts included, while excluding turbines along the environmental flow passageways.[80] The EIA Notification, 2006, which excludes dams built for drinking and industrial water from an environmental impact assessment (EIA), needs to be modified—such dams, while small, have had a significant impact on Karnataka's riverine biodiversity.[81] The National Rehabilitation and Resettlement Bill, now lapsed, should be revived, with compensatory mechanisms for riverine fishermen affected by development projects explicitly defined. Community fish sanctuaries require extended protection from polluting industries and dam projects.

We also need to improve our institutional knowledge about rivers. Basic information

---

77   http://himachalpr.gov.in/cabinetdes1.htm; http://www.tribuneindia.com/2007/20070415/himachal.htm

78   Dams as Aid: A political anatomy of Nordic development Thinking, Routledge, 1997, p 29

79   Thakkar, H., Rivers: Legal and Institutional Issues in India, South Asia Network on Dams, Rivers & People, May 2012. Sourced from: http://sandrp.in/rivers/Rivers_Legal_and_Institutional_Issues_in_India.pdf

80   Dandakar, P., Damaged Rivers, Collapsing Fisheries: Impact of Dams on riverine fisheries in India, South Asia Network on Dams, Rivers & People, Sep 2012. Sourced from: http://sandrp.in/dams/Impacts_of_Dams_on_Riverine_Fisheries_in_India_ParineetaDandekar_Sept2012.pdf

81   Ibid

on the state of our rivers and their tributaries, and their health, should be regularly collected, in addition to information on the status of riverine fisheries, the population of dependent fishermen and the impact of local dams on rural livelihood.[82] The National Fisheries Development Board's mandate needs to be tweaked to incorporate greater importance of riverine fisheries, along with maintaining fish biodiversity. Such data, along with reports from government institutions like CIFRI, needs to be made publicly available. Research gaps must be addressed through studies on the efficacy of fish ladders, and the mitigating impacts of dams on riverine health. As a policy, new dams, thermal plants or ports should not be built in heavily-forested regions, or those with outstanding biodiversity (avian or piscine).[83] Each state should identify at least one river for protection in its free-flowing condition. We need better monitoring and awareness as well, instead of awaiting a dam developer's discretion. The Ministry of Environment and Forests must set up a rigorous dam project-specific monitoring mechanism that focuses on ensuring compliance with environmental norms.

Restoring rivers to health is hard, with many interlinked components—Europe took over two decades to clean the Thames, Rhine and Danube. Even the central government envisages a time period of eighteen years (from the start of the 'Namami Gange' programme) to clean up the Ganga, with visible improvements only in the medium term (five to ten years).[84] The Singapore river's clean-up highlights the importance of synchronizing urban development with riverfronts while the halting efforts to rejuvenate the Matanza-Riachuelo river (in Argentina) showcase the real costs of corruption and fund diversions. Proper research prior to implementation is also necessary—consider the failure to revive Lake Karachay (Russia). A holistic view of the river basin remains necessary—the rejuvenation of the Rhine focused on regional clean-up combined with a focused target-setting, while the Danube's rejuvenation shows that the benefits of a participatory approach led by awareness campaigns and driven through scientific research can be immense.[85]

Such a project would need significant attention—both in terms of budget allocations and implementation of works. Capital and technical expertise for rejuvenation, particularly for the construction and operation of sewage treatment plants and instituting waste water management, should be sought from other countries. For a long time, bad planning and poor execution have been the bane of cleaning

---

82   Dandakar, P., Damaged Rivers, Collapsing Fisheries: Impact of Dams on riverine fisheries in India, South Asia Network on Dams, Rivers & People, Sep 2012. Sourced from: http://sandrp.in/dams/Impacts_of_Dams_on_Riverine_Fisheries_in_India_ParineetaDandekar_Sept2012.pdf

83   Ibid

84   Indian Express, Sep 2013; Sourced from: http://indianexpress.com/article/india/india-others/ganga-clean-up-to-take-18-years-says-centre/

85   Sinha, U., Daily Pioneer, March 2015; Sourced from: http://www.dailypioneer.com/sunday-edition/agenda/cover-story/cleaning-rivers-cleansing-policies.html

the Ganga—the 'command and control' method of the Indian bureaucracy has alienated local bodies and discouraged a participative approach (through 'command' methods), whereas its 'control' aspect has failed miserably. A quick turnaround time for research, decision-making, implementation and monitoring supported by proper monitoring, training and public awakening will be critical. Instead of pursuing rampant exploitation of our rivers, it would be far better to fix our existing issues with our irrigation and groundwater systems.

CANAL IRRIGATION

Villagers from Kondhane village have been waiting for two decades for the completion of a dam nearby, potentially providing enough water to irrigate 1,000 hectares.[86] Such a dam, costing nearly $65 million, would lessen their dependence on rain-fed water and potentially double their annual income. The dam has taken twenty-seven years to gain the necessary clearances, while environmental concerns and graft charges prevented further progress. Meanwhile, the cost of the dam has increased from ₹8 crore in 1984 to ₹435 crore now. Around 200 irrigation projects, costing $36 billion, have been stuck for decades, with some in Uttar Pradesh languishing for over forty years (increasing the cost of one, the Durgawati Project, to ₹800 crore, an eight-fold jump).

COLONIAL IRRIGATION

The idea of diverting water from streams and rivers through canals to irrigate fallow adjacent land through flooding is a primitive idea, found often in undivided India, especially in the Indus Valley. Most of India's cultivated soils are suitable for irrigation, with the great Indo-Gangetic Plain offering extraordinary fertility. Primarily composed of alluvial formation, ranging from the Vindhyas to the Himalayas, the substrata have significant variance, from the rich loam of the doab, to the deltas in Bengal and the parched sands of the Thar. In comparison, basaltic soil, found in the Deccan Plateau, is spread across Andhra Pradesh, Maharashtra, Karnataka and Madhya Pradesh.

---

86 Jadhav, Rajendra, Bharadwaj, Mayank, Narendra Modi's new growth recipe: just add water, Live Mint, Mar 16 2016, Sourced from: http://www.livemint.com/Politics/ZcpW6gJv5Bt8cktQ2aqV1J/PM-Narendra-Modis-new-growth-recipe-just-add-water.html

Historically, public works in India meant irrigation. The Rig Veda speaks of a kūpa, an artificial hollow in the earth, and an avata, an artificial well, both of which are described as aksita, unfailing and full of water.[87] Raising water from such structures was conducted through a cakra (wheel), which had a varatra (strap) tied to it, along with a kośa (pail)—with water drawn into sūrmī susira (broad channels). Such khanitrima (artificial channels) were often used to irrigate fields in times of poor rain. Panini refers to irrigation from various rivers (the Sindhu, the Suvāstu, Varnu, Sarayu, Vipāś and Candrabhāgā).[88] He refers to the river, Devikā, as especially suitable for the cultivation of Dāvikākūlāh Sālayah (paddy). As drought was common (vigatāh secakā asmād grāmād visecako), fields were often supplied through canals (sālyartham kulyāh praniyante[89]). Megasthenes' Indica refers to the Agronomoi, the district officials overseeing land measurement and irrigation, in Mauryan India while Kautilya highlights the importance of setubandha (irrigation works) for crop cultivation. Land assessment was conducted according soil type and the type of irrigation available, with three distinct rates abounding, along with a uniform 1/4 of produce rate for all lands that were irrigated by rivers, lakes, wells and tanks. Dams were often constructed—the Vaisya governor Pusyamitra constructed one in Junagadh district near the pilgrimage town of Girnar. Lasting for over 800 years, this dam was continually repaired by India's lieges—Aśoka, Rudradaman, and Skandagupta.

The Satavahana period led to the development of paniyakas (cisterns) dug near caves for Buddhist monks. The ancient city of Amaravati, under the reign of Siri-Sivamakasada, witnessed the appointment of pāniyagharika (Superintendent of water-houses), overseeing the distribution of water and regulation for irrigation purposes. The Guptas were conscious about the importance of irrigation works— the *Sukraniti* recommends tax benefits for those individuals who help construct tanks, artificial water bodies, or those bringing fresh land under cultivation, until they have earned twice their investment.

From the erstwhile Shahabad district in Bihar to the temple towns of Tamil Nadu, surface tanks, often measuring a few acres to 9–10 square miles, formed of earthen embankments across local drains, are commonly found, feeding millions of acres of wheat and rice crops.[90] In the erstwhile Madras Presidency, over 550

87   Puri, B.N., Irrigation and Agricultural Economy in Ancient India, Annals of the Bhandarkar
      Oriental Research Institute, Vol. 48/49, Golden Jubilee Volume 1917-1967 (1968), pp. 383-390,
      Published by: Bhandarkar Oriental Research Institute, Sourced from: http://www.jstor.org/
      stable/41694262?seq=1#page_scan_tab_contents

88   Agrawala. India as known to Panini, p. 204, 2nd Edition

89   Puri, Indian in the time of Patanjali, p.122

90   Bucksley, R. B., C.S.I, The Irrigation Works of India, 2nd Edition, E&F. N. Spon, Ltd, 1905. Sourced
      from: https://ia801408.us.archive.org/11/items/irrigationworks00buckgoog/irrigationworks00buckgoog.
      pdf

weirs existed around rivers and streams, connected through a series of tanks, irrigating over 3.5 million acres. The Cumbam tank in colonial Kurnool district, over 80–90-feet high and 100-yards long, covered a water surface area of 8 square miles. Around two-thirds of the irrigation in Gujarat depended on small storage works, while most provinces of India were familiar with tank irrigation (with the due exception of Sind and Punjab). Governments, native and colonial, played an active part in maintaining such irrigation works—387 tanks were maintained by the colonial government in the erstwhile districts of Ajmer and Merwara, while Jaipur's Maharajas constructed over 200 small irrigation works, costing over 60 lakh rupees, ₹124 per acre on average.

As rivers flowing through Punjab descend through the Shivalik Hills, they cut through an arid landscape, with limited rainfall. This landscape is particularly evocative—its higher parts, termed bhangar, form the doabs, the land between the rivers, fertile and yet dependent on flooding and rain; the lower parts, termed khadir, are naturally fertile, but covered with grass. Such inundation canals covered over 2,500 miles in length, irrigating over a million acres across undivided Punjab. But such inundation canals can offer a precarious existence—an irregular flood, with low water, would not allow for passage of sufficient volume to all the fields.

Solace was often provided by perennial canals from large rivers. The Tungabhadra river's various channels saw weirs constructed on them by the Vijayanagara Empire's Krishnadevaraya. The Kallanai dam, popularly called the Grand Anicut, near Thanjavur, is an ancient dam that was built in running water across the Kaveri river in Trichy district in Tamil Nadu by the Chola king, Karikalan, in the second century.[91,92] The dam diverted the river into the delta districts, boosting irrigation across 69,000 acres, by splitting the Kaveri into four streams (Kollidam Aru, Kaviri, Vennaru, and Puthu Aru). Similarly, the Western Yamuna Canal, built during the Prithviraj Chauhan era, was renovated by Firuz Shah Tuqhlaq in AD 1335. Excessive silting caused it to stop flowing in AD 1750, with the British conducting a three-year renovation under Captain G.R. Blane of the Bengal Engineers Group in 1832.[93] The Yamuna canal feeds the Agra canal, built in 1874, near the Okhla barrage after the Nizamuddin bridge.

Canal irrigation underwent rapid expansion in the nineteenth century, with the

---

91   Balaganessin, M., Flowing waters for fertile fields, The Hindu, August 29, 2011. Sourced from: http://www.thehindu.com/features/kids/article2408778.ece

92   Singh, V. P., Yadava, R. N., Water Resources System Operation: Proceedings of the International Conference on water and environment (WE-2003), December 15-18, 2003, Bhopal, India. Sourced from: https://books.google.co.in/books?id=Bge-0XX6ip8C&pg=PA508&dq=kallanai&sig=_bvXlOQqAftum2T7p_6McQJHgUk&redir_esc=y&hl=en#v=onepage&q&f=false

93   Western Yamuna Canal Major Irrigation Project JI01653. Sourced from: http://india-wris.nrsc.gov.in/wrpinfo/index.php?title=Western_Yamuna_Canal_Major_Irrigation_Project_JI01653

British Raj seeking to revive, rehabilitate and expand irrigation channels. Such investments led to a handsome return (8–10 per cent until 1945[94]) for the Raj.[95] It is estimated that irrigation investment returns increased rapidly between 1912 and 1945, rising from 8.3 per cent on productive works to 12.8 per cent, in addition to a higher revenue assessment on the irrigated land. Undivided India had over 12 million hectares of irrigated land in the early twentieth century (compared to ~3 million hectares in the United States, 1.5 million hectares in Italy and just 2 million hectares in Egypt).[96, 97] Even so, less than 20 per cent of pre-Independence India's crops were irrigated in any way.

As Robert Burton Bucksley quotes, 'Of the 44 million hectares that were irrigated in undivided British India, 13 million were from wells, 17 million from canals, 8 million from tanks and 6 million from other ways.'[98]

TABLE 33: IRRIGATION ACROSS BRITISH INDIA (1903)[99]

PROVINCES	AREA IN SQUARE MILES	POPULATION IN MILLIONS	AVERAGE AREA IN MILLIONS OF ACRES ANNUALLY SOWN	AREA ORDINARILY IRRIGATED IN MILLIONS OF ACRES	PERCENTAGE OF THE AREA SOWN WHICH IS IRRIGATED
UPPER BURMAH	87000	3.84	4.66	0.82	17.7
BENGAL	151000	73.04	63.66	6.35	10
UNITED PROVINCES	107000	47.69	41.09	11.06	26.9
PUNJAB	114000	22.36	28.21	10.43	37
MADRAS	142000	37.69	36.57	10.53	28.8
SIND	47000	3.21	3.32	2.92	88
BOMBAY	76000	14.53	24.33	1.09	4.4
FIVE SMALLER PROVINCES	132000	13.6	24.22	0.9	3.7
TOTAL BRITISH INDIA	856000	215.96	226.06	44.1	19.5
NATIVE STATES	438000	51.32	71.07	7.76	10.9

Even now, India's agricultural sector is characterized by irrigation surplus and irrigation deprived regions—48 per cent of India's farm holdings do not have irrigation from any source (Agricultural Census, 2011). Such irrigation deprived districts primarily fall in hill farming states (Uttarakhand, Himachal Pradesh, Kashmir, the Northeastern states, along with districts like Darjeeling, Wayanad,

---

94 Whitcombe, E. (2005), 'Irrigation', in D. Kumar and M. Desai (eds) The Cambridge Economic History of India, c. 1757–1970, Vol. 2, Orient Longman, Hyderabad, India, pp. 677–737.

95 Shah, T., Past, Present and the Future of Canal Irrigation in India, International Water Management Institute, Colombo,2010

96 Deakin, A., The Age, 1891

97 Shah, Tushaar, Past, Present and the Future of Canal Irrigation in India, International Water Management Institute, Colombo,2010

98 Bucksley, R.B., C.S.I, The Irrigation Works of India, 2nd Edition, E&F. N. Spon, Ltd, 1905. Sourced from: https://ia801408.us.archive.org/11/items/irrigationworks00buckgoog/irrigationworks00buckgoog.pdf

99 Bucksley, R.B., C.S.I, The Irrigation Works of India, 2nd Edition, E&F. N. Spon, Ltd, 1905. Sourced from: https://ia801408.us.archive.org/11/items/irrigationworks00buckgoog/irrigationworks00buckgoog.pdf

Coorg, etc.) and semi-arid/arid districts in Rajasthan, Maharashtra, Andhra Pradesh, Telangana, Karnataka, Gujarat, Jharkhand, Odisha and Chhattisgarh. Such districts have limited agricultural productivity (~average of ₹17,837 per hectare vs average of ₹47,142 per hectare in irrigation rich districts).[100] In addition, of these irrigation poor districts, a significant number are adivasi-owned (~12 million holdings). Such districts face significant challenges in the expansion of their irrigation systems—insufficient groundwater recharge during the dry season; a general energy scarcity preventing them from operating pumps and artificial lifts, and high-energy costs (irrigation based on diesel can cost ₹8–10/kWh in eastern India compared to ₹0–1/kWh in western India).[101]

IRRIGATION MANAGEMENT

Canal irrigation management is in for a crisis. As farmers increasingly clamour for on-demand irrigation, the relevance of traditional canal irrigation is declining. Meanwhile, India's canal irrigation systems are in a parlous state, in terms of productivity, financial returns and maintenance costs, even when compared to colonial times.

Colonial irrigation management was an elaborate, albeit low-cost, administration system, which focused on outsourcing water distribution to large zamindars who received such water through public systems into their own private canals.[102] This was supplemented through a large, yet sparsely paid, colonial bureaucracy—the lambardar (patrol), usually paid just ₹5–10 per month, was delegated the task of collecting irrigation fees and managing water distribution in villages. He was overseen by the ameen, with a salary of ₹25–30 per month, overseeing 7,000–10,000 acres of farms. The latter was managed by the ziladar, paid ₹50–100 per month, overseeing 30,000 to 50,000 acres of land. This entire local system was overseen by the Deputy Collector, typically an overseas representative, paid around ₹200–300 per month.[103,104] And this system was profitable to boot—absorbing

100 Shah, T., Verma, S., Durga, N., Rajan, A., Goswami, A., Palrecha, A., Rethinking Pradhan Mantri Krishi Sinchai Yojana, IWMI, June 2016. Sourced from: http://www.iwmi.cgiar.org/iwmi-tata/PDFs/iwmi_tata_pmksy_policy_paper_june_2016.pdf

101 Ibid

102 Shah, T., Past, Present and the Future of Canal Irrigation in India, International Water Management Institute, Colombo, 2010.

103 Ibid

104 Bucksley, R.B., C.S.I, The Irrigation Works of India, 2nd Edition, E&F. N. Spon, Ltd, 1905. Sourced from: https://ia801408.us.archive.org/11/items/irrigationworks00buckgoog/irrigationworks00buckgoog.pdf

employee remuneration and maintenance costs, and yet leaving a substantial surplus (average water fee recovery in 1902–03 was ₹3.15 per acre, of which working expenses were 32 per cent and additional expenses 11 per cent.[105,106] By 1900, the capital cost of construction of an irrigation canal was equal to the value of crops irrigated in a single year, with the fee collected at 10–12 per cent of the value of the output; about two to three times the working expenses.

By 1943, private canals owned by zamindars irrigated ~500,000 acres of land in undivided Punjab. Such large landholdings, in addition to ordinary private irrigators (holding 50–540 acres), made the task of irrigation management simple. All lands that were deemed to be irrigated (regardless of whether they used such water) were exposed to a high water fee, enforced by vast bureaucracy, which expanded this canal network through forced labour.[107] Such ruthless fees encouraged the substitution of staples by cash crops. By 1930, the Punjab province earned far more irrigation fees than even income tax.[108]

India's irrigation finances, post-Independence, have suffered a steep decline, with water fees for major and medium irrigation projects reaching 6.2 per cent of working expenses in 1998–2002 (compared to 8.8 per cent in 1993–97; compared to 200–300 per cent of water expenses in 1900).[109] Water fees recovered were less than 10 per cent of the incurred 'working expenses' of ₹8,250 crore.[110] By 1960, Bihar's irrigation fees were minuscule, covering little of the revenue collector's costs.[111] Capital investment on major and medium irrigation schemes incurred during 1961–2001 was ~₹295,000 crore[112] while offering low returns of 4–12 per cent.[113] Such investments have entailed significant maintenance costs—₹19,000 crore in 2005 (World Bank), with just ₹2,820 crore allocated instead.

This situation has been exacerbated by a litany of scams afflicting the irrigation sector. Andhra Pradesh launched a ₹1.86 lakh crore Jala Yagnam for irrigating 12 million acres in 2004—a CAG audit eight years later highlighted sheer wastage of ₹72,000 crore with little to show.

105 Shah, T., Past, Present and the Future of Canal Irrigation in India, International Water Management Institute, Colombo, 2010

106 Bucksley, R.B., C.S.I, The Irrigation Works of India, 2nd Edition, E&F. N. Spon, Ltd, 1905. Sourced from: https://ia801408.us.archive.org/11/items/irrigationworks00buckgoog/irrigationworks00buckgoog.pdf

107 Hardiman 2002: 114

108 Mufakharul Islam, M., Irrigation, agriculture, and the Raj: Punjab, 1887-1947, Manohar, 1997

109 CWC 2006

110 CWC 2006: Table A1

111 Bhatia, B. M., Famines in India: a study in some aspects of the economic history of India with special reference to food problem, 1860-1990, Konark Publishers, 1991

112 Amarasinghe and Xenarios 2009

113 Daines, S. R. and Pawar, J. R. (1987). Economic Returns to Irrigation in India, SDR Research Groups Inc. & Development Group Inc

TABLE 34: INDIAN CANAL IRRIGATION FINANCES[114, 115]

CRITERIA	UNITS	MAJOR & MEDIUM SYSTEMS IN BRITISH INDIA, 1902-03	MAJOR, MEDIUM AND MULTI-PURPOSE IRRIGATION PROJECTS IN INDIA		MAJOR AND MEDIUM IRRIGATION SYSTEMS IN INDIA, 2001
		1902-03	1977-78	1986-87	
CAPITAL INVESTMENT IN MAJOR AND MEDIUM PROJECTS (NOMINAL)	₹ CRORE	£30 MILLION	3004	26014	295000
AREA IRRIGATED BY ALL GOVERNMENT SCHEMES (M HA)	M HA	7.4	18.75	25.33	18
WATER FEES COLLECTED AS PER CENT OF CAPITAL INVESTMENT	PER CENT	10 PER CENT	1.43 PER CENT	0.30 PER CENT	0.20 PER CENT
VALUE OF CROPS IRRIGATED AS PER CENT OF CAPITAL INVESTMENT	PER CENT	87 PER CENT	-	-	18.30 PER CENT
MAINTENANCE EXPENDITURE AS PER CENT OF WORKING EXPENDITURE	PER CENT	53 PER CENT	42 PER CENT	38 PER CENT	34 PER CENT
MAINTENANCE EXPENDITURE AS PER CENT OF CAPITAL INVESTMENT	PER CENT	2.60 PER CENT	-	-	0.95 PER CENT
WATER FEES COLLECTED AS PER CENT OF VALUE OF CROPS IRRIGATED	PER CENT	11 PER CENT	-	2 PER CENT	1.20 PER CENT
WATER FEE COLLECTED AS PER CENT OF WORKING EXPENSES	PER CENT	280 PER CENT	45 PER CENT	20 PER CENT	7.90 PER CENT

TABLE 35: TARGET VS IMPLEMENTATION IN IRRIGATION[116]

PROJECT	XI PLAN TARGET	ACHIEVEMENT		TARGET FOR 2009-10	PERCENTAGE ACHIEVEMENT
		2007-08	2008-09		
MAJOR & MEDIUM IRRIGATION	9	0.84	1.02	0.9	31
MINOR IRRIGATION	7	0.89	0.9	0.9	38
TOTAL	16	1.73	1.92	1.8	34

114 Shah, T., Past, Present and the Future of Canal Irrigation in India, International Water Management Institute, Colombo, 2010

115 GoI (1992: 2.25)

116 Planning Commission, Govt. of India. (12547); Indiastat Data

POOR IRRIGATION MANAGEMENT

Every day, after school, Ramesh Bisht, a fifteen-year-old living near the town of Tarikhet in Almora district, heads downwards. Jumping across terraces, in which children often play a terraced version of cricket (6s are the third terrace down, 4s the second), he heads for the local well—a journey of thirty minutes from his house. He holds jerry cans, formerly containing vegetable oil, obtained from the local ration shop, over his head, dipping them into the well and filling them up. Times are harder in such alpine towns, despite modernity and tourism. With rivers far away, and piped water still a dream, water is precious.

Surface irrigation underutilization and its subsequent poor performance have had a consequential impact, with limited acreage irrigated.[117] While new facilities were continuously constructed, poor maintenance and bad facility management led to limited realization.[118] Instead of building, maintaining and collecting a hefty surplus, our irrigation management encourages building, then continual neglect and then a costly rebuilding of facilities.

Such irrigation schemes are bedevilled by unauthorized appropriation of water by farmers near the headwater. Irrigation schemes designed to supplement the water supply of substance farmers have instead encouraged farmers to focus on water-fed staple and cash crops—consider the Tungabhadra canal irrigation scheme, constructed for dry crop irrigation, now utilized for rice irrigation.[119] The idea of providing irrigation as insurance in dry seasons has been dismantled.[120] The warabandi system found in rural Haryana, which was ideal for providing a rotational water supply and minimizing inequity between farmers at the head and tail of an irrigation system, has been relinquished—instead of each farmer getting an equal number of turns, per unit of land and time, tail-end farmers suffer from high deprivation across all seasons.[121,122] Instead, irrigation systems now routinely fulfil the needs of just the initial headwater wetland, while the long tail suffices with groundwater.

This decline in irrigation performance has been a consequence of political influence on irrigation allocation, while an irrigation bureaucracy focuses on construction over efficacy. A pump irrigation economy has instead arisen over the hinterland.

---

117 Daines and Pawar 1987
118 Wade 1984, 286
119 Jurriens et al 1996
120 Mollinga 2003
121 Jurriens et al. 1996; van Halsema 2002
122 Shah, A., 2003

TABLE 36: IRRIGATION SCHEME DEPRIVATION AMONGST TAIL-END FARMERS[123]

STATE	IRRIGATION SYSTEM	FLOW IRRIGATION DEPRIVATION PREVALENT
GUJARAT	DHAROI, MAHI	7–37 PER CENT
HARYANA	BHAKRA, WESTERN YAMUNA	56–84 PER CENT
KARNATAKA	TUNGABHADRA	40–91 PER CENT
MAHARASHTRA	MULA	29–70 PER CENT
ORISSA	HIRAKUD	35–72 PER CENT
TAMIL NADU	PARAMBIKULAM ALIYAR	24–55 PER CENT

SILTAGE

Silt remains a key constraint for irrigation works. Often found as suspension in river waters, when floods occur, it can be deposited on fallow fields, providing replenishment, albeit while impeding channels and choking the overall discharge. Silt composition can vary regionally, depending on river velocity and the catchment area character. Seasonal variance can be significant as well, the dry season can have near clear water flowing, while monsoonal floods can have a solid matter to liquid ratio of 1:30; tidal rivers in Bengal can face significant extremes of silt deposition, ranging from 1x to 10x across seasons. Such silt deposition has troubled administrators historically.

TABLE 37: PROPORTION OF SILT TO WATER WEIGHT IN THE SUTLEJ RIVER
NEAR ROPAR IN PRE-INDEPENDENCE PUNJAB[124]

CATEGORY	JULY 7, 1894	JULY 29, 1894	JUNE 13, 1895	AUGUST 14, 1895	JULY 30, 1896	JULY 6, 1897
VELOCITY OF THE RIVER, FEET PER SECOND	7.7	10.81	6.33	9.62	4.1	4.3
PROPORTION OF SILT TO WATER BY WEIGHT AT THE SURFACE	1/89	1/127	1/59	1/82	1/555	1/900
WEIGHT OF SILT AT SURFACE TAKEN AS UNITY	1	1	1	1	1	1
WEIGHT AT DEPTH OF 1.5 FEET	1.015	1.127	1.217	1.036	1.042	1.067
WEIGHT AT DEPTH OF 3.0 FEET	1.038	1.245	1.26	1.047	1.132	1.145
WEIGHT AT DEPTH OF 4.5 FEET	1.038	1.358	1.329	1.056	1.202	1.152
WEIGHT AT DEPTH OF 6.0 FEET	1.066	1.395	1.427	1.078	1.207	1.254
WEIGHT AT DEPTH OF 7.5 FEET	1.084	1.581	1.496	1.088	1.395	1.383
WEIGHT AT DEPTH OF 9.0 FEET	1.164	1.731		1.104	1.689	
WEIGHT AT DEPTH OF 10.5 FEET	2.024			1.144	1.932	
WEIGHT AT DEPTH OF 12.0 FEET				1.154		

---

123 Shah, T., Past, Present and the Future of Canal Irrigation in India, International Water Management Institute, Colombo, 2010.

124 Bucksley, R.B., C.S.I, The Irrigation Works of India, 2nd Edition, E&F. N. Spon, Ltd, 1905. Sourced from: https://ia801408.us.archive.org/11/items/irrigationworks00buckgoog/irrigationworks00buckgoog.pdf

TABLE 38: SIRHIND CANAL —VOLUME OF SILT DEPOSITION[125]

YEAR	VOLUME OF SILT DEPOSIT IN THE FIRST 57,000 FEET IN THE CANAL		VOLUME OF SILT SCOURED AWAY FROM THE BED OF THE CANAL EACH YEAR
	MAXIMUM	MINIMUM	
	CUBIC FEET	CUBIC FEET	CUBIC FEET
1893	2,02,53,000	1,13,36,000	
1894	1,87,19,000	1,00,00,000	1,02,53,000
1895	2,18,34,000	68,23,000	1,18,96,000
1896	2,10,83,000	79,03,000	1,39,31,000
1897	2,49,04,000	73,78,000	1,37,95,000
1898	NA	67,06,000	1,81,98,000
1899	NA	NA	NA
1900	2,08,54,000	70,11,000	NA
1901	82,17,000	23,82,000	1,84,72,000
1902	56,41,000	24,00,000	58,17,000
1903	67,37,000	15,84,000	51,53,000
1904	NA	14,22,000	53,15,000

Large quantities of silt were excavated annually in the inundation canals of Punjab and Sindh, with a new canal head cut sometimes wherever it was relatively cheaper to do so.

SHRINKING CANAL IRRIGATION

Instead of gravity flow irrigation, irrigation wells have taken precedence. Normally, worldwide, irrigation schemes lead to the abandonment of pre-existing irrigation wells or water lift schemes, a substitution, in effect.[126] Tank-based irrigation has declined significantly—particularly in southern India (60 per cent declining to 37 per cent from 1965 to 2000).[127] Irrigation wells have proliferated, leaving irrigation canals functioning purely as recharge schemes, reconfiguring existing irrigation systems. Gujarat has seen significant changes—the Guhai irrigation system typically releases water three to four times a year; instead, farmers have drilled wells to irrigate thirty-five to forty-five times a year; the irrigation system

---

125 Bucksley, R.B., C.S.I, The Irrigation Works of India, 2nd Edition, E&F. N. Spon, Ltd, 1905. Sourced from: https://ia801408.us.archive.org/11/items/irrigationworks00buckgoog/irrigationworks00buckgoog.pdf

126 Dhawan, 1996; Burt & Styles, 1999

127 Selvarajan 2002

simply recharges those wells.[128] Over 75 per cent of Punjab's irrigated areas in 2006 were dependent on tube well irrigation despite the construction of multiple irrigation schemes (Bhakra, et al).[129] India's area under canal irrigation declined by 2.4 million hectares between 1996 and 2002, while groundwater wells increased their share by 2.8 million hectares. Wells have started cannibalizing irrigation canals, let alone water tanks.

The government has sought to reverse this trend—the Accelerated Irrigation Benefits Program (AIBP) has sought to increase investment in tail-end projects, with $7.5 billion invested between 1997 and 2010. However, such investments have offered diminishing returns—an investment of ₹130,000 crore on 210 major and medium irrigation projects led to 2.4 million hectares less of an increase between 1990 to 2006, compared to earlier periods. India's irrigation policies have reached a farcical stage, with governments investing to keep the network size nearly the same.[130] Our dams and canals now exist primarily as monuments to an ancient age, instead of modern water distribution systems that can meet their purported irrigation catchment area's demand.

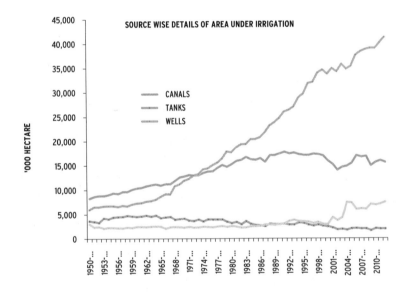

FIGURE 31: SOURCE-WISE DISTRIBUTION OF IRRIGATED AREAS (SOURCE: INDIASTAT)

---

128 Shah 2010; Shah, T., Past, Present and the Future of Canal Irrigation in India, International Water Management Institute, Colombo, 2010.

129 Selvarajan 2002; Thakkar 1999:19

130 Shah 2009

This has had a concomitant impact on agricultural productivity—Ramesh Chand's seminal work on drivers of inter-district productivity variation (2003–04) has highlighted how on-demand water supply from artificial lift can help improve agricultural productivity by a significant quantum over and above canal irrigation. Politicians find such groundwater wells and artificial lift systems an easier give to meet farmer expectations on irrigation—consider Gujarat's irrigation budget for FY17, which is spending ₹9,050 crore on piped distribution and ₹5,244 crore on canal maintenance and lift irrigation schemes.

Certain state governments have sought to reverse this trend. Odisha has sought to implement a variety of projects and initiatives as part of the Integrated Rural Piped Water Supply (IRPWS) project, covering eleven water-deficient villages in Rengali and Dhankauda blocks in Sambalpur district.[131] The project seeks to build a water treatment plant (with 5 MLD capacity), along with overhead tanks at Pradhanpali and Kilsama Hillock, with the former routing water to seven Dhankauda block villages and the latter channeling water to four villages in the Rengali block. Phase 1 of this project will likely lead to over 30,000 villagers gaining access to safe drinking water. The state is also seeking to revive 55,000 hectares of irrigation canal systems, with a budget of ₹635 crore allocated in 2017 for the three-year-long project. The project will seek to rehabilitate and renovate fourteen large and 284 small irrigation projects, covering an area of 46,296 hectares.

GROUNDWATER

THE RISE OF GROUNDWATER

Understanding this switch towards groundwater necessitates understanding farmer behaviour. The Indian farmer faced complex choices on sourcing water for agriculture and livelihood needs—the source, amount, quality and cost of water, all matter. His preference increasingly leans towards on-demand water, free from the vagaries of rainfall or dam sluice timing—as such, depending on this location, he can enjoy abundant safe water at a low cost by digging a borehole, or wait for the canal to provide it (depending on his location from the headwaters). If he lives downstream from a major urban centre, or in an arid region, he could struggle for a few litres of water, which if available, could be polluted and unfit for any use.

---

131 Priya S, L., '30,000 Villagers in Odisha to Now Get Safe Drinking Water, Through New Pipelines', Better India, November 2017. Sourced from: https://www.thebetterindia.com/122068/30000-villagers-in-odisha-to-now-get-safe-drinking-water-through-new-pipelines/

As such, their utilization of groundwater aquifers can vary significantly, given local geology. India possesses a diverse set of geological formations, which, combined with variances in local climate and hydrology, can make the water availability in any district rather unique—aquifers in unconsolidated rock formations carrying alluvial soils are common in the Indo-Gangetic and Brahmaputra plains, offering deep reservoirs which can support large wells with healthy rainfall recharge. In comparison, coastal areas have extensive aquifers but risk saline water intrusion while aquifers in Rajasthan and Gujarat offer high salinity risk combined with low rainfall and negligible recharge. The famed volcanic rocks of the Deccan plateau offer little in water due to poor rock permeability, while the Vindhyas and the Cuddapah region register vastly different permeability in carbonate rocks due to the presence of solution cavities. The Himalayan regions have aquifers with a low storage capacity due to quick run-off gradient. Factors like these make aquifer management a challenging job, and for a majority of farmers access to water remains a struggle.

Maize farmers in Aurangabad and Latur districts in the Vidarbha region of Maharashtra, speak woefully about their water-associated travails. Having cultivated sugar cane, the local water tables have dipped, courtesy of numerous tube wells that sought to quench sugar cane's thirst. While rules permit five borewells per square km, not exceeding a depth of 200 feet, unofficial estimates peg the number at 90,000 (official estimate ~35,000 wells; the number of wells for 715 square km of Latur ideally should not have been more than 3,575 wells)—about ten to twenty-seven times the permissible limit, with borewells reaching a depth of up to 1,300 feet. This causes irreversible damage to deep aquifers and groundwater levels.

Pump irrigation has arisen anew—rural India no longer has a headwater versus tail-end divide in water availability—and with a rise in privately owned irrigation facilities, primarily pumpsets, the age-old disparity has shrunk. The bulk of India's 40 million hectares of new irrigation has come primarily from tube wells, in addition to private lift irrigation (often termed Type II irrigation). Most villages now have a predominance of tube wells, with an NSSO (2003) survey finding 76 per cent of 4,646 villages in such a scenario. Farmers prefer irrigation from such sources, given the short gestation period (irrigation canals can take up to thirty to forty years in some areas while a groundwater well can be commissioned within a week), cost-effectiveness (irrigation canals can cost up to ₹5–7 lakh/hectare in certain districts), and the ability to provide water on an annual basis, across seasons, with a demand focused outlook. Such irrigation is also easily supported by government investment and subsidies for groundwater recharge through community structures like irrigation tanks.

India tops the list of countries with maximum freshwater withdrawals—standing at 761 BCM for 2015 which is more than that of China (554 BCM) and the US (478.4 BCM).[132] Our neighbour, Pakistan, draws only a quarter of India's freshwater withdrawals.[133] Our withdrawals are larger than the most populous country in the world—putting the argument of high population to rest. Such large withdrawals have resulted in reduced per capita availability. India's per capita water availability has declined from 5,000 cubic metre (CM) in 1947 to 1,500 CM in 2011, a drop of 70 per cent in sixty-four years since Independence and below the normal level at which a society is considered to be a water-stressed society (~1700 CM).[134] The main areas which suffer badly from groundwater extraction can be extrapolated from the Figure 32.

Of particular interest are Punjab, Rajasthan and Haryana. Punjab and Haryana are considered the 'wheat bowl of India', however, the chances for continuation of this revered status risks being undone by a brewing groundwater crisis. Other big states like Uttar Pradesh and Tamil Nadu register groundwater development at 74 per cent and 77 per cent, respectively, whereas the national average stands at 62 per cent. Hilly areas register low groundwater exploitation as water run-off in hills caters to majority demand. We are on the verge of emptying our groundwater aquifers.

Groundwater stress remains at an all-time high. In Punjab, 80 per cent of the blocks (talukas) are over-exploited when it comes to groundwater. Rajasthan follows close with 71 per cent of its blocks being over-exploited whereas Haryana registers the metric at 61 per cent. Thus, aquifers in a majority of the areas in these states are subjected to a physically unsustainable situation wherein withdrawal is more than the recharge, leading to long-term declines in the water table. Critical blocks are also on the rise—which have groundwater development between 90 per cent and 100 per cent and are witness to long-term decline in water levels, in both pre- and post-monsoon seasons. The 2011 national assessment indicates 30 per cent blocks to be in semi-critical, critical or over-exploited categories with the situation deteriorating rapidly. Such numbers cannot be passed by as mere statistics, the sheer complexity and impact of environment, socio-economic and cultural factors is humongous.

Even funeral rites have been affected. Mourners in Mota Agariya village in Amreli district of Gujarat have changed their cremation rites—dipping their hands and

---

132 World Development Report, 2011, The World Bank. Sourced from: http://siteresources.worldbank.org/INTWDRS/Resources/WDR2011_Full_Text.pdf

133 Annual freshwater withdrawals, total (billion cubic meters), Food and Agriculture Organization, AQUASTAT data. Accessed on 23 August 2016 from http://data.worldbank.org/indicator/ER.H2O.FWTL.K3

134 Draft Water Policy for Delhi. Executive Engineer (EDP) Delhi Jal Board, Government of NCT of Delhi. Sourced from: http://www.delhi.gov.in/wps/wcm/connect/f91b008046c5ef03bddbfd7d994b04ce/Draft_Water_Policy_for_Delhi.pdf?MOD=AJPERES&lmod=-311071680

feet in a havada (a small pond for bathing cattle), given dry wells.[135] They can't bathe fully as the water has to be saved for the cattle. The 1,800 residents have no direct recourse to water, with the wells dry (the deepest well at 1,005 feet is also dry), and bring in 17,000 litres of water every day through tankers from nearby Rajula town.

Besides high groundwater development stage and increasing water stress, it is observed that it is becoming increasingly difficult to access and afford groundwater. This can be seen from the depths at which water is found across different assessment blocks over time, in pre- and post-monsoon seasons.

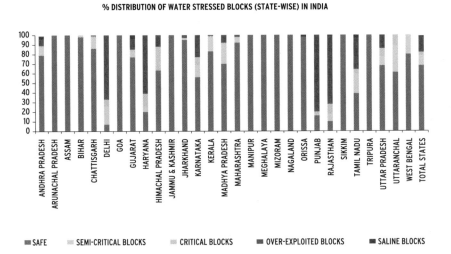

FIGURE 32: PERCENTAGE DISTRIBUTION OF WATER STRESS IN INDIA
(SOURCE: CENTRAL GROUND WATER BOARD, 2011)

---

135 Kateshiya, G., Departure From Tradition: 200 mourners, but no water for ritual bath… they turned to tank for cattle, Indian Express, 16 May 2016. Sourced from: http://indianexpress.com/article/cities/ahmedabad/gujarat-departure-from-tradition-200-mourners-but-no-water-for-ritual-bath-they-turned-to-tank-for-cattle-2802636/

ENERGY SUBSIDIES FOR TUBE WELL-BASED IRRIGATION

Our tube well subsidy culture, entrenched through political patronage, has also contributed to unsustainable extraction and misuse of our groundwater resources. Subsidies have hurt our groundwater levels—the interplay between farmer crop choices (cultivating improper crops i.e. water-intensive crops in water-scarce and water-sensitive regions) and our energy subsidies for irrigation needs has catalyzed an unexpected boom across the landscape.

It is not that groundwater irrigation was unknown to India until recently. But over the past five decades the situation has changed dramatically, particularly after policies associated with the Green Revolution were introduced.[136] Such steps led to an increased usage of high-yielding water-intensive cereal crops, powered by flood requiring low levels of technology and labour. Tube wells became the norm—5-inch pipes were dug and bored into the ground to extract groundwater through pumps powered by electricity or diesel gensets. The subsequent rise of electric tube wells was exponential—from 1 million in 1980 to 12 million in 2001 to more than 15 million in 2010, all compounded by a flat rate tariff and power subsidy regime. There are now ~25 million groundwater wells—~15 million electric wells consuming ~120–150 thousand gWh and ~10 million diesel wells consuming ~5–8 billion litres of diesel pumping ~230–250 billion m^3 annually.[137] This installation led to an increase in the area under groundwater irrigation, which rose from 5 million hectares in 1950–51 to more than 40 million hectares in 2007–08.

Until the advent of the Green Revolution, rural electrification policy sought to incentivize agricultural power use—meters were installed with tube wells that tracked water usage and electricity companies charged fees on the basis of water consumption. Local State Electricity Boards offered subsidies on this tariff, with regional discrepancies. Despite this, tube well uptake remained slow, given high initial tube well capital costs, compared to the farm incomes. Meanwhile, transaction costs (installation, monitoring and maintenance of meters, billing) and operational risks (collusion between consumer and electricity company employee, meter tampering) arose. Central and state governments sought to eliminate such transaction costs and risks by pushing state electricity companies to switch to flat tariffs—charging consumers at a flat rate associated with the pump specification (usually horsepower), irrespective of water use or electricity consumption. The disassociation of tariffs from usage soon degenerated into a free power subsidy, a political freebie, while incentivizing a lack of accountability for consumers and

---

136 Mukherjee, Shah & Giordano, Managing Energy-irrigation Nexus in India, IWMI-Tata Water Policy Program 2012. Sourced from: http://www.iwmi.cgiar.org/iwmi-tata/PDFs/2012_Highlight-36.pdf

137 Shah, T., IWMI, India's Groundwater-Energy nexus. Sourced from: http://programme.worldwaterweek.org/sites/default/files/tuschaar_-_stockholm-e-i_nexus-tushaar.pdf

suppliers. Farmers were perversely incentivized to exploit groundwater while state electricity suppliers had to effectively hide their production and transmission inefficiencies. Average aggregate technical and commercial (AT&C) losses were soon estimated to be at 40 per cent, with nearly 80 per cent of the AT&C losses occurring during distribution stage—theft and pilferage alone are estimated to the tune of ₹20,000 crore—all hidden mostly under the garb of agricultural power. Farmers now have no incentive to preserve groundwater levels, while minimum support prices encourage farmers to stick to water-intensive cereals rather than switching to other less water-intensive crops (oilseeds, pulses).

Such subsidies have placed a massive burden on state exchequers—the associated fiscal deficit between 2008 and 2009 was $6 billion in the energy sector. Most State Electricity Boards operate at a loss, leaving nothing for investments in new infrastructure for generation and transmission purposes. Energy subsidies, such as these, are increasingly crowding out investments on higher education or healthcare, while farmers still wait for quality power supply. Any removal of subsidies would be detrimental to farmers' incomes, given that they are already exposed to falling commodity prices and a rising cost of agricultural inputs. Many policy interventions on the energy supply side have attempted to battle this nexus. While Andhra Pradesh has sought to legislate sustainable use of groundwater, Punjab has sought to regulate the dates of paddy transplantation.

Tackling this menace will require listening to farmer concerns. Poor power quality is a big concern—single-phase power is unable to efficiently run three-phase pumps/engines—farmers hence keep the pumps running longer than planned or required.[138] West Bengal has been able to remove agricultural subsidy (PFC 2010) by providing metered tube wells—a solution possible in areas with low electric tube well concentration, high flat rate tariffs and water available at shallower depths. The Jyotigram Yojana (JGY) in Gujarat has also provided a successful solution model—it delinked rural feeders and provided separate feeders for power for electric tube wells through an investment of ₹1,167 crore,[139] with farmers across 18,000 villages getting an uninterrupted supply of quality power, in a pre-announced schedule which was adequate to efficiently run the pumps while flattening the total electricity demand curve. Andhra Pradesh and Punjab have also experienced success with separate feeders and by utilizing a high voltage distribution system. Such schemes can lead to reduced subsidies while capping groundwater withdrawals, without adversely impacting production. Legislative momentum towards such schemes is building up—the Draft National Water Framework Bill's (2013) Clause 12 stipulates

138 Shah, T., IWMI, India's Groundwater-Energy nexus. Sourced from: http://programme.worldwaterweek. org/sites/default/files/tuschaar_-_stockholm-e-i_nexus-tushaar.pdf

139 Bhatt, S. (2008). Impact of Jyoti Gram Scheme on rural life and economy in Gujarat: A case study of four villages in Anand District. 27. 501-522.

curtailing over-extraction of groundwater through electricity usage regulation. Similar sentiment is found in the National Water Policy (2012) which recommends that electricity for groundwater extraction be regulated. The Commission on Price Policy for Kharif Crops (2015–16) has recommended quantitative ceilings on per hectare use of water.

Technological innovation can also be utilized—tube wells can be powered through solar pumps replacing diesel. They can provide ~3,000 hours per year of reliable, high-quality power, while saving continual subsidy outflows, insulate farmers from diesel price rise and provide a green alternative (by replacing diesel burning/power from coal plants). To guard against over-usage, policies offering an assured buyback of surplus solar power (e.g. as with the Solar Pump Irrigators' Cooperative Enterprise in Dhundi, Gujarat) should be utilized to provide the farmer an alternative for secondary revenue streams while boosting rural income and economy, besides ushering in transformational solar energy usage at the national level.

We need to improve our poor track record for agricultural water utilization. Agriculture accounts for almost 90 per cent of India's water usage—India also has the highest consumption and accounts for ~24 per cent of the total global blue water consumption (surface and groundwater). Our water efficiency, i.e. units of water required to grow one unit of crop, remains poor—for wheat, India uses 1.15 times more total water per unit crop than the global average (3.4 if blue water consumption is considered). Similarly, for rice, India's blue water consumption per unit crop is 1.3 times the global average (at the state level, UP and AP consume 1.9 and 1.8 times). For maize, sugar cane and cotton, India uses 1.3, 2.5 and 1.4 times the global average blue water consumption per unit crop, respectively.

Our state patronage and procurement policies exacerbate this situation. Punjab, with 80 per cent of its blocks considered 'over-exploited' in groundwater, has the highest share of water-intensive rice procurement in the country (Ministry of Finance, Working Paper No. 04/2014-DEA). Madhya Pradesh, with a similarly high water footprint, is increasingly dominating the production of wheat. Maharashtra's average share of national sugar cane production increased from 14.6 per cent (1990–93) to 23.4 per cent (2008–11), despite a high level of groundwater exploitation. Despite continuing aridity, the western and northern states, despite their limited groundwater availability, have seen free or cheap power promoting the use of water-intensive crops. We essentially seek to export water, virtually. This troika of groundwater availability, crop selection and energy supply has been grossly mismanaged.

GROUNDWATER POLLUTION

Even groundwater quality doesn't offer any solace—fluoride and arsenic contamination predominate.[140] High concentration of iron (>1.0 mg/l) in groundwater has been observed in more than 1.1 lakh habitations in the country.[141] Our apathy has made this worse. Chemical contaminants in India's groundwater had been identified as early as 1937 with fluorosis-afflicted individuals in Andhra Pradesh.[142] Furthermore, groundwater arsenic (As) contamination and the health effects resulting from chronic exposure were discovered as early as 1976 in North India.[143]

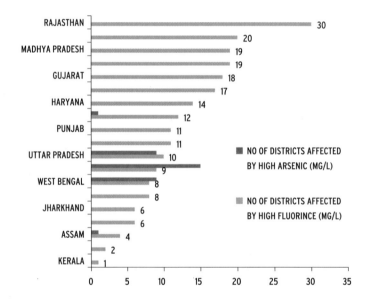

FIGURE 33: DISTRICTS AFFECTED BY FLUORIDE AND ARSENIC
(SOURCE: MINISTRY OF WATER RESOURCES, RIVER DEVELOPMENT & GANGA REJUVENATION)

---

140 Kumar, M.D. and Shah, T., Groundwater Pollution & Contamination in India; Sourced from: http://www.iwmi.cgiar.org/iwmi-tata/files/pdf/ground-pollute4_FULL_.pdf

141 Ministry of Water Resources, River Development & Ganga Rejuvenation; Sourced from: http://wrmin.nic.in/forms/list.aspx?lid=327

142 Shortt, H. E.; McRobert, G. R.; Bernard, T. W.; Mannadinayar, A. S. Endemic fluorosis in the Madras Presidency. Ind. J. Med. Res. 1937, 25, 553–561

143 Datta, D. V. Arsenic and non-cirrhotic portal hypertension; Lancet 1976, (Feb 21), 433

Consider Nalgonda district in Andhra Pradesh, where fluoride contamination in more than 1,100 hamlets,[144] has left at least 10,000 people crippled[145]—prevalent fluoride levels are seven to ten times the safe limit. Water treatment plants failed on account of lack of maintenance, and the $600 million sanctioned pipeline to bring healthy drinking water from the Krishna river (43.5 km away) is still under construction (~3 kms in five years).[146] Water filters were distributed but remain broken and the concept of rainwater harvesting fails when 40 per cent of houses have thatched roofs. The tragedy has reached farcical proportions—even the National Human Rights Commission (NHRC) attributing this to government apathy.

REGULATION AND ENFORCEMENT

Groundwater has been highly under-regulated for decades—individual ownership of groundwater rights are still governed by the Easement Act, 1882 (Chapter 1, Clause 7), allowing the landowner to 'collect and dispose within his own limits of all water under the land which does not pass in a defined channel and all water on its surface which does not pass in a defined channel.' The Indian Constitution puts water under the State List, enabling state assemblies to make their own laws with the central government providing critical inputs with framework laws and model bills. The National Water Framework Bill (2013)—an outcome of the National Water Policy (2012)—prioritized public and secondary water usage while empowering communities to regulate groundwater at aquifer level.

144 Times Of India, Jan 2015; Sourced from: http://timesofindia.indiatimes.com/city/hyderabad/Nalgonda-worst-hit-by-fluorosis-says-report/articleshow/45724239.cms

145 Prabhakar Rao, V, Oct 2011; New Indian Express; Sourced from: http://www.newindianexpress.com/nation/article252739.ece

146 Suravajjula, R., OneWater; Sourced from: http://www.onewater.org/stories/story/india_an_enduring_plague

TABLE 39: REGULATION OF GROUNDWATER

NO.	STATE/UT	STATE ACT / REGULATION
1	ANDHRA PRADESH (ERSTWHILE)	ANDHRA PRADESH GROUND WATER (REGULATION FOR DRINKING WATER PURPOSES) ACT, 1996 ANDHRA PRADESH WATER, LAND AND TREES ACT AND RULES, 2002
2	ASSAM	ASSAM GROUND WATER CONTROL AND REGULATION ACT, 2012
3	BIHAR	BIHAR GROUNDWATER (REGULATION AND CONTROL OF DEVELOPMENT AND MANAGEMENT) ACT, 2006
4	DELHI	DELHI NCT GROUNDWATER REGULATION DIRECTIONS, 2010
5	GOA	GOA GROUND WATER REGULATION ACT, 2002
6	HIMACHAL PRADESH	HIMACHAL PRADESH GROUND WATER (REGULATION AND CONTROL OF DEVELOPMENT AND MANAGEMENT) ACT, 2005
7	JAMMU & KASHMIR	JAMMU AND KASHMIR WATER RESOURCES (REGULATION & MANAGEMENT) ACT, 2010 J&K STATE WATER RESOURCES REGULATORY AUTHORITY REGULATIONS, 2013
8	KARNATAKA	KARNATAKA GROUND WATER (REGULATION FOR PROTECTION OF SOURCES OF DRINKING WATER) ACT, 1999; KARNATAKA GROUND WATER (REGULATION AND CONTROL OF DEVELOPMENT AND MANAGEMENT) ACT, 2011
9	KERALA	KERALA GROUND WATER (CONTROL AND REGULATION) ACT, 2002
10	LAKSHADWEEP	LAKSHADWEEP GROUND WATER (DEVELOPMENT AND CONTROL) REGULATION, 2001
11	MAHARASHTRA	MAHARASHTRA GROUNDWATER (REGULATION FOR DRINKING WATER PURPOSES) ACT, 1993 WATER RESOURCES REGULATORY AUTHORITY ACT, 2005 MAHARASHTRA GROUND WATER (DEVELOPMENT AND MANAGEMENT) BILL, 2009 MAHARASHTRA MANAGEMENT OF IRRIGATION SYSTEMS BY FARMERS ACT, 2005
12	PUDUCHERRY	PUDUCHERRY GROUND WATER (CONTROL AND REGULATION) ACT, 2002
13	BENGAL (BANGA)	WEST BENGAL GROUND WATER RESOURCES (MANAGEMENT, CONTROL AND REGULATION) ACT, 2005
14	GUJARAT	GUJARAT IRRIGATION AND DRAINAGE ACT, 2013
15	PUNJAB	PRESERVATION OF SUBSOIL WATER ACT, 2009
16	MADHYA PRADESH	MADHYA PRADESH IRRIGATION ACT, 1931
17	UTTAR PRADESH	UTTAR PRADESH GROUNDWATER CONSERVATION, PROTECTION AND DEVELOPMENT (MANAGEMENT, CONTROL AND REGULATION) BILL, 2010
18	ODISHA	ODISHA GROUNDWATER (REGULATION, DEVELOPMENT AND MANAGEMENT) BILL, 2011
19	HARYANA	PRESERVATION OF SUBSOIL WATER ACT, 2009 HARYANA GROUNDWATER MANAGEMENT & REGULATION BILL, 2011
20	CHHATTISGARH	CHHATTISGARH GROUND WATER (REGULATION AND CONTROL OF DEVELOPMENT AND MANAGEMENT) BILL, 2012

Groundwater rights continue to remain formally vested with the individual, instead of the State, leading states to adopt a non-confrontational, passive approach towards existing groundwater overuse (Cullet, 2009). The sheer multiplicity of regulatory bodies has added to the complexity, the centre provides direction through the Central Ground Water Authority (CGWA) and the Central Ground Water Authority (CGWB); however, as many as eleven other central bodies, various important state level bodies and the panchayats at district level hold responsibilities for regulation of water services and groundwater management. The CGWA notifies critical groundwater level areas, along with issuing directives for various measures of regulation and registration (drilling agencies, groundwater extraction structures, etc.). Meanwhile, the local District Magistrate (DM) or District Commissioner (DC), being the hub of administrative activities, often beset with other priorities, is tasked with the implementation of such directives. Limited financial, technical and administrative capacities act as a significant barrier to implementing groundwater regulation provisions—most state bodies remain poorly staffed with limited budgets; their focus is usually on surveys and incremental developments, without focus on mitigation.

IMPROVING IRRIGATION MANAGEMENT

DEFINING PERFORMANCE

It remains difficult to assess the performance of an irrigation project. While colonial periods saw the revenue collection and overall financial returns as proxies for irrigation performance, such measures have increasingly become less effective. Farmers routinely underreport the land under canal irrigation to irrigation managers conducting land surveys in order to limit their water-paying charges. While satellites can conduct remote sensing to determine the irrigated area, the allocation by source remains difficult and politically charged. The irrigation potential, as determined at the onset of an irrigation project, for an idealized cropping pattern, is detached from the ground reality of Indian farming's evolution, with realized irrigation often significantly lower than what was initially promised. On an ideal basis, performance should be measured by the amount of water control offered, defined as the ability to apply the right quantity of water at the appropriate time to crops in order to meet their growth and soil replenishment requirements. This can be impacted by the differences between the designed area for irrigation command versus the ultimate users of the irrigation schemes, along with changes in individual farmer demand (volume, timing and quality). Illegal activities (theft of water, unauthorized lifting of waters by head-reach farmers, and a general violation of water distribution agreements), in addition to a general farmer unwillingness to pay the actual cost of maintenance and repair, along with irrigation charges, can have a significant impact on the performance of the irrigation scheme and the size of the catchment area.[147] Guidelines for water release from dams and reservoirs can have little linkage with actual irrigation needs, leading to physical deterioration of irrigation facilities and re-engineering by aggrieved farmers.[148] Crop diversification

---

147   Burt and Styles 1999; Pradhan 1989,18; Oorthuizen 2003,207
148   Oorthuizen 2003

has also contributed to reduction in the efficacy of irrigation systems (rice irrigation systems in Thailand were significantly affected by crop diversification, with other crops reducing the need for continuous irrigation).[149]

To resolve this, governments, both at the state and central levels, have attempted to conduct physical rehabilitation—such projects have led to an enlarged irrigation catchment area, along with higher farmer satisfaction and lower water inequity; however, a few years later, overarching factors would again combine to reduce the new system to degradation, with water fee collection and maintenance languishing. In certain parts of South India, state governments have started planning for rehabilitation the moment a new tank scheme is implemented.

TABLE 40: HISTORICAL IRRIGATED CROP PATTERN[150, 151]

AS A PER CENT OF GROSS IRRIGATED AREA			
CROP	1960-1962	1970-1972	1987-89
COTTON	3.6	4.1	4.1
FRUITS & VEGETABLES	1.7	2.8	4.1
OTHER CROPS	8.3	6.7	2.7
RICE	45.3	37	27.7
SUGAR CANE	5.6	4.7	5.2
TOTAL CEREALS & MILLETS	72	73.6	73
TOTAL OILSEEDS	1.6	2.9	7.3
TOTAL PULSES	7	5	3.6
WHEAT	15.3	26.9	31.7

Other schemes have sought to provide a greater stake to existing farmers in the region through the implementation of participatory irrigation management (PIM). Such schemes have sought to convert existing irrigation relationships into a water use association within the current irrigation system—Uttar Pradesh launched Sinchai Samitis in the '60s to manage irrigation tanks, while Gujarat launched Pani Panchayats in the '80s.[152] However, such schemes have failed to provide accountability through the creation of water property rights, limiting social action. Gujarat's Joint Irrigation Programme, launched in 1983, with seventeen irrigation cooperatives, led to the disbandment of all cooperatives within a few years.

---

149 Plusquellec and Wikham 1985
150 GOI, Ministry of Agriculture, Indian Agriculture Statistics (various issues)
151 Vaidyanathan, A., Water Resource Management, Pg 68, Chapter 2, Oxford
152 Hunt 1989; Narain 2004

BUILDING CAPACITY

However, where due investments are made in building up organizational and social capacity, dividends have paid off. The Ozar on Waghad project in Nashik, the Pingot Project, the Dharoi project in Gujarat are examples of successful farmer-focused irrigation management schemes. The Aga Khan Rural Support Program invested in thirty professional staff over ten to fifteen years to organize 20,000–30,000 farmers into water associations. Kerala, a land with a history of effective governance and local self-empowerment groups, launched thousands of beneficiary farmer associations in 1986, most of which turned dark soon enough—farmers simply refused to pay the ₹5 membership fee. In the Malampuzha Project, only fifty-seven meetings were held by the canal committees over a decade, of which forty-three did not even meet their quorum. Awareness, as always the key arbitrator, remained relatively low. [153]

States like Gujarat have targeted the provision of over 500,000 connections for tube wells to SC/ST farmers, while boosting farm electricity supply, investing in groundwater recharge by desilting over 25,000 reservoirs and irrigation tanks, and constructing 166,000 check dams, 261,785 farm ponds and 122,035 bori bunds, along with boosting micro-irrigation to over 13 lakh hectares in 2015 (from just 50,000 hectares in 2002).[154] Gross cropped area increased by 30 per cent in just seven years, with rising cropping intensity. Saurashtra has sought to accelerate its groundwater recharge investments, with a focus on constructing new check dams, percolation ponds and building rainwater harvesting structures.

Madhya Pradesh has implemented similar measures over the past decade with an investment of ₹36,689 crore (far less than either Maharashtra or Andhra Pradesh)—subsidizing farm ponds, reviving over 4,000 irrigation projects (which doubled their irrigation reach from 367,000 hectares to 760,000 hectares), restructuring canal irrigation management and issuing over a million temporary electricity connections to farmers growing wheat. It also reformed its irrigation management with performance-linked demands and incentives, along with operational autonomy free from political interference, offered to a sclerotic bureaucracy. Canal management protocols were re-established, utilizing rationalized irrigation schedules, operating canals at full supply levels and operating them through osarabandi (a rotation schedule); all to ensure that tail-to-head irrigation was carried out. Water allowances were updated to reflect new cropping patterns on a regular basis, while enforcement of the updated regime was conducted in an orderly manner—tail-end farmers were

153 Joseph, 2001

154 Shah, Tushaar, Verma, Shilp, Durga, Neha, Rajan, Abhishek, Goswami, Alankrita, Palrecha, Alka, Rethinking Pradhan Mantri Krishi Sinchai Yojana, IWMI, June 2016. Sourced from: http://www.iwmi.cgiar.org/iwmi-tata/PDFs/iwmi_tata_pmksy_policy_paper_june_2016.pdf

regularly asked to prepare land earlier than head-end farmers, receiving water in a timely fashion. Maintenance was conducted on a regular basis—with adequate budgeting and accountability; water use associations were charged with clean-up of field channels, while the irrigation department desilted main canals. Engineers were regularly charged with going out on field visits to conduct monitoring of irrigation operations, while regular meetings checked for milestones met. Tail-end farmers were given special attention, particularly in metrics, and personal meetings by government staff. Defunct farmer organizations were revived and embedded in decision-making for irrigation scheduling, maintenance operations and water distribution. Subsequently, irrigated area in Madhya Pradesh's canal catchment areas increased from 0.8 million hectares in 2006 to 1.56 million hectares in 2011 and 2.83 million hectares in 2014—all under a period of significant rainfall volatility and drought-like conditions. This net increase in irrigation-fed farms was observed across a variety of river basins, and not just the Narmada.

Such schemes have succeeded because of their multidimensional focus on alleviating irrigation-based distress by getting canal-based water closer to the farmer, adding on artificial lifts and groundwater wells and providing uninterrupted farm power supply—instead of building large-scale dams that offered intermittent flow, they have sought to fulfil farmer requirement year-round. The central and state governments have often stepped in as well. The Million Wells Scheme, first launched in the '80s, offered subsidies and loans to small farmers to develop groundwater-focused irrigation. Similarly, Uttar Pradesh's 'Free Boring Scheme', during the '80s, led to the proliferation of shallow tube wells across eastern and Central Uttar Pradesh More recently, Jharkhand has sought to dig nearly 100,000 wells in adivasi areas through the MGNREGA scheme. The Pradhan Mantri Krishi Sinchayee Yojana (PMKSY), offering a funding of ₹50,000 crore between 2015 and 2020, on irrigation schemes, along with an additional funding of ₹20,000 crore from NABARD, is part of a long sequence of irrigation schemes that have come and gone.[155] This scheme, in particular, seeks to increase irrigation productivity (Per Drop, More Crop, ₹16,300 crore); encourage watershed programmes (₹13,590 crore); construct one water harvesting structure per village (Har Khet Ko Pani, ₹9050 crore); and launch an Accelerated Irrigation Benefits Program (₹11,060 crore). It seeks to incorporate a variety of pre-existing schemes (micro-irrigation subsidies, etc.) with water harvesting mechanisms. While PMKSY follows in the steps of the successful irrigation programmes launched in Gujarat and Madhya Pradesh, it seeks to adhere to the traditional canal building outlook—an approach that has its pitfalls.

---

155 Shah, T., Verma, S., Durga, N., Rajan, A., Goswami, A., Palrecha, A., Rethinking Pradhan Mantri Krishi Sinchai Yojana, IWMI, June 2016. Sourced from: http://www.iwmi.cgiar.org/iwmi-tata/PDFs/iwmi_tata_pmksy_policy_paper_june_2016.pdf

TABLE 41: PMKSY COMPONENTS[156]

NO.	SCHEME COMPONENT	BUDGET	
		2015-16	2015-20
1	ACCELERATED IRRIGATION BENEFITS PROGRAM (AIBP)	1.2	7.5
2	WATER HARVESTING (HAR KHET KO PANI)	2.8	21
3	IRRIGATION PRODUCTIVITY (PER DROP, MORE DROP)	5	100
4	WATERSHED DEVELOPMENT	4.4	11.5

However, as Tushaar Shah (2010) notes, the conditions that made colonial India's irrigation systems so effective and revenue accretive are no longer present. Irrigation required a centralizing authority to build and maintain canals to provide water; strong local authority (zamindars and local rulers) were able to enforce the writ of irrigation schemes, while enabling the recovery of land revenues; well irrigation was difficult and time-consuming while an exit from farming was non-existent. The colonial state had a significant stake in agriculture, given its potential for high land revenues and the authority's inherent interest in maximizing its recovery of agricultural surplus—this created conditions conducive to boosting irrigation efficacy. Modern India's government has a limited stake in agriculture, with a focus on moving rural Indians out of agriculture, while irrigation investments are driven by food security and poverty reduction needs; marginal farmers are increasingly able to drill their own wells and grow cash crops, instead of relying on a rules-based irrigation regime. The mass availability of pumps, pipes and boring technology, subsidized by the government, has made canal irrigation, in some places, completely redundant.

However, individual action can still accomplish a lot. Rajesh Pravakar Patil, an IAS officer, and a former Collector of Mayurbhanj district in Odisha, sought to alleviate the water scarcity faced by the village of Kendhujhar, in the Simlipal Biosphere in the district, by seeking to preserve spring water, filter it and route it to the households and farms.[157] The village was in a remote location, with scarce water supply leading to villagers having to fetch water from a small non-perennial stream located over 5 km away. Meanwhile, electricity access was non-existent, limiting construction timelines. Patil formed a team of engineers and contractors and built a water allocation system alongside that collected water from the spring,

156 Shah, T., Verma, S., Durga, N., Rajan, A., Goswami, A., Palrecha, A., Rethinking Pradhan Mantri Krishi Sinchai Yojana, IWMI, June 2016. Sourced from: http://www.iwmi.cgiar.org/iwmi-tata/PDFs/iwmi_tata_pmksy_policy_paper_june_2016.pdf

157 Mukherjee, Subhashree, "Water Supply Without Electricity? IAS Officer Makes It Happen in a Remote Village", Better India, December 2017. Sourced from: https://www.thebetterindia.com/125392/odisha-kendujhari-water-supply-ias-rajesh-pravakar-patil/

and stored it within an impounded area, while seeking to block out dry leaves and forest waste. Such water was then channelled through a variety of pipes to reach a select distribution point from where the water was allocated to cultivable land for irrigation.

ADAPTING TO SOCIO-ECONOMIC CHANGE

India's irrigation schemes need to adapt to this changing socio-economic pattern. Given the inherently monopolistic nature of irrigation provision and management, unbundling seems likely to be the way forward. A holding company, offering a transparent management information system that evaluates the performance of each irrigation system in a state, can be established. The irrigation departments, meanwhile, can be broken up into independent companies for each irrigation system, separated by basin, which are offered operational autonomy, free from political interference, with the ability to charge cost plus prices, and a performance-based incentive system. Such systems can be mutated into public-private partnerships, which can help alleviate water scavenging.

Consider Maharashtra—it sought to involve farmers through cooperative lift schemes in its effort to maximize its utilization of its share of Krishna waters, through a capital cost subsidy scheme and a series of weirs across the Krishna's tributaries that would help store water for lift in the dry seasons. Each such irrigation scheme was required to pay irrigation charges for the amount of area actually irrigated, in addition to electricity charges for operating the lift systems.

Canal irrigation also needs to move closer to matching groundwater's flexibility and just-in-time nature. Private players can increasingly be entrusted with providing an irrigation service to lift bulk water from pre-designated points (where water has been provided by the irrigation agency). There remain numerous examples of such systems—the Indira Gandhi Canal has been modified in certain parts of Rajasthan to deliver water to diggis (farm ponds) on a fortnightly basis.[158] Farmer groups lift and irrigate water from canals to fields in the Mahi and Upper Krishna basin.[159] Chinese villages appoint a village contractor, to whom the state delivers water on a gross volumetric basis; he then allocates water to farmers based on

---

158 Amarasinghe, 2008
159 Patil et al. 2006; Birari et al. 2003; Choudhury and Kher 2006; Padhiyari 2006; Choudhury and Shah 2005.

need, with water fee subsequently collected.[160] In other parts of Tamil Nadu and Rayalaseema in Andhra Pradesh, irrigation tanks have increasingly been converted into percolation tanks.[161]

Such arrangements have inherent advantages, offloading capital investment for distribution systems to local private operators, while piped distribution inherently prevents significant amounts of evaporation and waterlogging and enables land used for canals to instead be used for agriculture. The productivity of irrigation water rises, while its distribution across the catchment area spreads significantly. Farmer participation, usually difficult on a post-facto basis, can be encouraged at the construction stage itself for an irrigation scheme. The government can help promote this reform by legalizing the lifting and piped distribution of water from canal systems, while encouraging existing tube well owners to convert their systems to a canal lift. Financial support can be provided by institutions through farmer cooperatives, while the government can offer a 20–30 per cent capital subsidy on the approved projects. A top-down command and control irrigation system can be replaced by one that is a hybrid partnership between farmers and the state.

PROMOTING MICRO-IRRIGATION

Tying this to micro and drip irrigation schemes can prove beneficial as well—just 7.73 million hectares of land in India (located primarily in Rajasthan, Maharashtra, Andhra Pradesh, Karnataka, Gujarat and Haryana) is currently under micro-irrigation, compared to an overall potential of 69.5 million hectares, as of March 2015.[162] They can offer significant benefits as well, about 20–48 per cent savings on water usage, leading to a 28.5 per cent less fertilizer usage and a reduction of 30.5 per cent in energy usage.

While micro-irrigation has been encouraged through dedicated schemes for decades, current micro-irrigation schemes are focused on just a net increase of 0.5 million hectares per year, with a budget of just ₹1,000 crore annually—it would take a

---

160 Shah et al. 2005; Wang et al 2003.
161 Palanisami 1995; Palanisami 2005.
162 Bera, S., Micro-irrigation lags far behind potential, shows study, Live Mint, 23 May 2016. Sourced from: http://www.livemint.com/Politics/BkgERIIfG77UzWZRC3HsAM/Microirrigation-lags-far-behind-potential-shows-study.html

hundred years to cover India's agricultural acreage at this rate.[163] Between 2013 and 2016, budgetary allocations declined by 31 per cent while subsidies to farmers were cut from 50 per cent to 35 per cent of the sprinkler system, leading to a drop in adoption rates. A move towards direct benefit subsidy transfer schemes for promoting micro-irrigation, along with making micro-irrigation mandatory for water guzzling crops, will help encourage adoption. Categorizing micro-irrigation equipment and services under priority lending would also allow farmers to avail of interest subsidies.

TABLE 42: INDIA—DRIP IRRIGATION[164, 165]

AREA IN HECTARES		
STATE	1995	2000
KARNATAKA	11412	40000
TAMIL NADU	5357	34000
ANDHRA PRADESH	11585	31600
RAJASTHAN	304	30000
GUJARAT	3560	8000
KERALA	3035	6000
MADHYA PRADESH	1415	3000
ODISHA		2800
UTTAR PRADESH	111	2000
OTHERS	756	2000
HARYANA	120	1900
PUNJAB		1500
ASSAM	180	200
WEST BENGAL	100	200

Encouraging solar irrigation would also help reduce operating costs, while improving reliability. Farmers in Dhundi village of Gujarat's Anand district have formed a solar irrigation cooperative, termed the Dhundi Saur Urja Utpadak Sahakari Mandali (DSUUSM), utilizing solar power to run their irrigation pumps in their fields while selling surplus energy to the Madhya Gujarat Vij Company Ltd (MGVCL).[166] Farmers typically have to spend ₹500 per day on fuel to irrigate a 12-bigha plot—going solar, which requires a farmer to set aside 80 square m of land for an 8 kWh grid tied solar power generation system, can help bring down

---

163 Bera, S., Micro-irrigation lags far behind potential, shows study, Live Mint, 23 May 2016. Sourced from: http://www.livemint.com/Politics/BkgERIIfG77UzWZRC3HsAM/Microirrigation-lags-far-behind-potential-shows-study.html

164 Alam, A., Kumar, A. (2000)

165 Biswas, R. K., Drip & Sprinkler Irrigation, Pg3, Chapter 1, New India Publishing Agency

166 Singha, T., 'Farmers in This Gujarat Village Have Formed the World's First Solar Irrigation Cooperative', Better India, August 2016. Sourced from: https://www.thebetterindia.com/63211/solar-irrigation-cooperative-gujarat/

operating costs while generating revenue by the sale of surplus solar power (typically ₹200–250 per day, at ₹4.63 per kWh). To go solar, farmers have to collectively fund the solar panels (54.6 kWh capacity of cost ₹6.5 lakh in August 2016) along with new solar pumps (₹4–7 lakh in August 2016). Installing such a system can also help incentivize farmers to increase the productivity of their utilized water, using less of it and selling extra power.

IMPROVING CANAL IRRIGATION MANAGEMENT

In addition, government schemes like PMKSY need to be reconfigured towards India's unirrigated landscape, with a focus on irrigation deprived districts (112 districts where less than 30 per cent of all farms have access to irrigation from any source).[167] Such programmes need to focus on stabilizing the kharif crop in dry regions by investment in groundwater recharge (pipes, tanks, pumps), with a long-term focus on providing sustenance to the rabi crop as well through micro-irrigation; freeing farmers from the vagaries of rain-fed agriculture. Within such irrigation deprived districts, special attention must be given to adivasi districts (typically 10 per cent of adivasi farms have access to irrigation in such districts). Such marginal farmers need to be provided financing to construct a groundwater well, with a solar-based pump (~3.5–5 kWh), along with an optimum distribution pipeline (an overall typical cost of ₹4–5 lakh; providing irrigation to over 3–5 hectares).[168] Such districts need further investment in solar-powered groundwater wells, with recharge provided through canal irrigation—Tushaar Shah (2016) speculates that 1–1.5 million subsidized solar-based irrigation wells can add 5–5.7 million hectares of private lift irrigation by 2020. Farms located near cities can utilize treated urban waste water that typically contains a high urban content (typically India's urban areas release 15 BCM of waste water in a year). Such waste water will need to be treated at special facilities which can be funded under PMKSY.

In addition, special focus must be given to management, operation and maintenance of existing irrigation assets. Current central government funding of such activities is typically 15 per cent of their total budget, leaving little influence to motivate them to prevent degradation. With free or subsidized irrigation schemes operating in most states, state irrigation departments have little to no incentive or

167 Shah, T., Verma, S., Durga, N., Rajan, A., Goswami, A., Palrecha, A., Rethinking Pradhan Mantri Krishi Sinchai Yojana, IWMI, June 2016. Sourced from: http://www.iwmi.cgiar.org/iwmi-tata/PDFs/iwmi_tata_pmksy_policy_paper_june_2016.pdf

168 Ibid

accountability in conducting appropriate maintenance of current irrigation assets. As suggested by the Twelfth Five Year Plan, a National Irrigation Maintenance Fund (NIMF) can be utilized to incentivize state governments to improve irrigation asset maintenance and the quality of irrigation service provided.

IMPROVING GROUNDWATER MANAGEMENT

Satish Madaan, a stout farmer with acreage near Hisar district, has taken to selling his livestock and bovine stock during drought-filled summers—his pair of bullocks can fetch a price of ₹35,000 (a haircut of 20 per cent) but feeding and sheltering them would cost 40 per cent more in water and fodder costs. As groundwater wells dry up, his lifestyle is changing. Groundwater recharge remains a significant priority. Our dependence on borewells needs to be reduced by reviving traditional water harvesting structures, while water extraction has to be reduced.

More recently, Chewang Norphel, a retired civil engineer, fondly called the 'Ice Man of India', created artificial glacier dams in Ladakh, in a cost-effective manner, using local community help and local materials. The johad, a modest structure dating back to 1500 BC, was successfully reinvigorated by Dr Rajendra Singh (noted as the 'Water Man of India') and the Tarun Bharat Sangh (TBS). Farm income has increased, and cost-benefit analysis suggests a per capita income of ₹100/johad results in annual per capita benefit of ₹400. Fisheries have developed and area under forest cover increased from 7 per cent to 40 per cent, through agro-forestry. The Arvari and Ruparel rivers, long dead, have been recharged through judicious and efficient johad use.

Artificial recharge should also be considered. The 2002 Master Plan for Artificial Recharge to Ground Water envisaged construction of 39 lakh structures for artificial recharge; its last version (formalized in 2013) identified an area of 941,541 square km where artificial recharge of groundwater is possible, with an estimated 85,565 MCM of surface run-off. This seeks to construct 1.11 crore structures, along with 88 lakh roof-top rainwater harvesting structures, 2.90 lakh check dams, 1.55 lakh gabion structures, 6.26 lakh gully plugs, 4.09 lakh nala bunds/cement plugs, 84,925 percolation tanks, 8,281 sub-surface dykes, 5.91 lakh recharge shafts, 1.08 lakh contour bunds, 16,235 injection wells and 23,172 other structures at a total outlay of ₹80,000 crore (2011 costs). Such a massive plan can easily be tied up with MGNREGA to provide short-term rural livelihood and long-term water sustainability.

Finally, community-based groundwater management programmes should be encouraged. The Andhra Pradesh Farmer-Managed Groundwater Systems (APFAMGS) Project has adopted a collaborative, participative approach which involves farmers in data collection and analysis purposes, leading to capacity building and promotion of a culture of empowerment through participation. Similarly, the Swadhyaya movement of Gujarat, which led to the construction of 957 nirmal neers (percolation tanks), saw over 100,000 wells being recharged and villagers having access to water even in the drought in 2000.

Our overall irrigation strategy merits a change from the current regimented approach. With a diverse geographic and demographic landscape, our rural areas face different kinds of irrigation challenges, which will require a cluster of policies to fix. Instead of building, neglecting and then rebuilding, we should have our institutions (AIBP, the National Irrigation Management Fund etc.) and state governments focused on management and maintenance of current major, medium and minor irrigation systems.

—

RENOVATING TANKS AND IRRIGATION SYSTEMS

Traditional wisdom can play its part. Our forts had adequate arrangements for drinking water, while our temples were equipped with water tanks, with water sourced from underground springs or harvested rainwater. There remain countless such structures in existence, dilapidated as they might be. The British sought their revival with gusto—Thomas Munro (Governor of Madras, 1820) noted that 'to attempt the construction of new tanks is perhaps a more hopeless experiment than the repair of those which have been filled up through siltation, for there is scarcely a place where a tank can be made to advantage that has not been applied to this purpose by the inhabitants'. Arthur Cotton highlighted the multitudes of old native works in various parts of India which had stood for hundreds of years. Such systems lasted centuries—they ought to be feasible for the current age to alleviate water stress.

Bamboo drip irrigation with four to five distribution stages was often practised in the Khasi and Jaintia Hills in Northeast India. The zabo or ruza systems in Nagaland combined water conservation with forestry, agriculture and animal care. The Apatani system in Arunachal Pradesh combined water conservation with rice cultivation and fish farming. Stepwells called Dighis were quite common in the

Indo-Gangetic plains while ahar and pyne made floodwater irrigation possible in Bihar and saved Gaya district from two great droughts in the 1880s. Bengal's inundation channels utilized floods in the Ganges and Damodar, making overflow irrigation possible. The northern hills (Spiti valley, hilly areas of Uttarakhand, Jammu & Kashmir Valley) employed kul/kuhl structures to collect glacial water or divert run-off water from natural streams. Zings divert and collect glacial water through guiding channels in the Ladakh region. The Chandela tanks and Bundela tanks of Madhya Pradesh were basically massive earthern embankments. The eris of Tamil Nadu, mostly built under Pallava rule, acted as flood control systems, preventing soil erosion and water wastage during times of heavy rainfall, leading to groundwater replenishment. Rice cultivation was made possible through eris, which, until the British arrival, were managed by local communities spending as much as 4.5 per cent of their gross produce on their maintenance. The virdas, first established by the Maldharis in the Kutch region, provided drinking water to the populace in areas containing Banni grass cover. The khadin system, developed by the Paliwal Brahmins in the fifteenth century, extensively found in Jodhpur, Jaisalmer, Bikaner and Barmer regions, enabled rainwater harvesting and use of water enriched land for better crop yields. The vavs of Gujarat and the jhalar of Rajasthan were stepwells which, besides providing water, also served as a place for religious ceremonies and social gatherings.

British rule swept away age-old rights and responsibilities—the East India Company sought to introduce a village revenue management system that saw tank management responsibilities taken over by Company officials, making tank water a property of the government.[169] Community participation was discouraged while irrigation structures were designed, executed, operated and maintained by the Irrigation Department. The abolition of the Proprietary Rights Act in 1950 further transferred such rights to the local irrigation department and the Zilla Parishads. Now, government departments were required to maintain and expand such tanks, something they were not equipped for. The passage of the Malguzari Abolition Act in Maharashtra led to Malguzars stepping away from their age-old responsibilities of supervising the repairs and maintenance of such structures.

---

169 Paranjpye, V., 'Bhandara the Lake District', Seeds of Hope, India Water Portal, 2004. Sourced from: http://www.indiawaterportal.org/sites/indiawaterportal.org/files/Seeds%20of%20hope_Case%20 studies_Lokayan_Planning%20Commission_2004.pdf

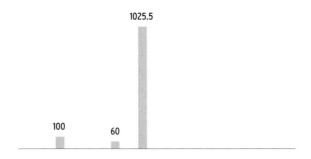

FIGURE 34: TANK-SOURCED NET IRRIGATED AREA AS PER CENT OF TOTAL IRRIGATED AREA
IN TAMIL NADU, 1960–1961 TO 2002–2003 AT FIVE-YEAR INTERVALS[170]

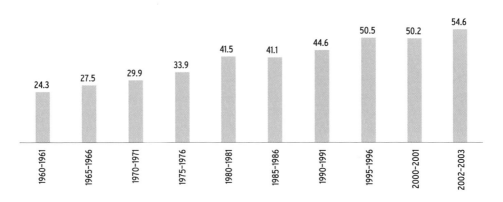

FIGURE 35: WELL SOURCED NET IRRIGATED AREA AS PER CENT OF TOTAL IRRIGATED AREA IN
TAMIL NADU, 1960–1961 TO 2002–2003 AT FIVE-YEAR INTERVALS[171]

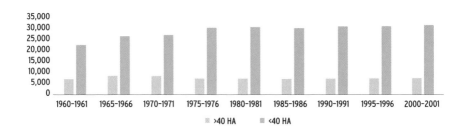

FIGURE 36: NUMBER OF TANKS IN TAMIL NADU, 1960/61–2001 AT FIVE-YEAR INTERVALS[172]

170 Department of Statistics, Government of Tamil Nadu
171 Ibid
172 Ibid

Encouraging the renovation of such tanks and irrigation systems can help improve the resilience of the village economy. A focus on restoring such age-old infrastructure is hence necessary. The Kolar district of Karnataka lies in the Eastern Dry Agro Climatic Zone in the Deccan plateau—this means that it is typically rainfall deficient (average rainfall of 750 mm), while being bereft of any perennial rivers. The district is heavily dependent on 4,488 ancient irrigation water bodies or tanks, which were built to catch and store rainfall run-off from catchment slopes. The advent of the Raj led to a change in authority for maintaining such tanks, with the British Raj administration's Irrigation Department seeking to maintain such tanks for their own interests. This led to a decline in collective ownership for the upkeep of such tanks. When independence was gained, such tanks soon became derelict, with the local administration seeking mega projects for irrigation and large-scale agriculture. Such tanks now suffer from significant siltation, with up to 60 per cent of the capacity silted in some cases. They are also in a state of extensive disrepair, with sluices, spillways and crest gates all in poor condition. This has an impact—such tanks used to support the cultivation of two crops in a year in their catchment area; now they can barely support one. With percolation from such tanks reduced, local aquifers have shrunk, leading to a reduced green cover, and an erosion of the soil (increasingly loamy and sandy). Such tanks have increasingly been encroached upon by local rich landlords, who utilize them to dig borewells to grow cash crops. Meanwhile, the local cropping pattern has changed, with traditional cereals like ragi replaced by wheat and rice, along with mulberry farming.

Gram Vikas, an NGO, has sought to arrest this decline in local water tables by evolving its self-help groups into a movement focused on restoring traditional tanks.[173] This evolution was particularly prominent in the village of Minjenahalli, in rural Mughabal. The village traditionally had two tanks—Mavinakere and Badavankere. Caste conflict was rife, with the latter tank being used only by the lower castes traditionally. Over time, the latter tank silted over, leading to the village's self-help groups seeking the Zilla Panchayat's help for carrying out desiltation work. Such help was not forthcoming for several years, until lobbying and protests led to the disbursement of the necessary funds.

Similarly, the Kohali community in Bhandara district in Maharashtra has sought to store run-off water within small hillocks for use on plains in the region.[174] The district falls within the drainage region of the Wainganga river, with a rolling plain occupied by a range of low hills. It contains a varied soil type, which has arisen

---

173 Acharya, K., The Water Women: A Case Study of Tank Restoration, Seeds of Hope, India Water Portal, 2004. Sourced from: http://www.indiawaterportal.org/sites/indiawaterportal.org/files/Seeds%20of%20 hope_Case%20studies_Lokayan_Planning%20Commission_2004.pdf

174 Paranjpye, V., 'Bhandara the Lake District', Seeds of Hope, India Water Portal, 2004. Sourced from: http://www.indiawaterportal.org/sites/indiawaterportal.org/files/Seeds%20of%20hope_Case%20 studies_Lokayan_Planning%20Commission_2004.pdf

from weathering of crystalline, metamorphic and igneous rocks. The community built up these tanks over 400 years ago, and they still serve as the largest source of irrigation in the region, helping to sustain a diverse crop pattern in Bhandara compared to nearby districts. Even now, the district is termed a 'lake district' with over 238 large tanks (> 10 hectares), 3,007 medium tanks (4–10 hectares) and 7,534 small tanks (2–4 hectares), along with other smaller tanks—such tanks can irrigate 10–15 acres on average, with significant variance. This traditional tank irrigation system had helped create significant intergenerational equity, surviving an indifferent government administration and yet helping to sustain agriculture. Any damage to the tanks, canals and outlets was repaired by the local villagers and supervisors (malguzars), while distribution of water and conflict resolution was carried out by a committee of malguzars.

This helped incorporate inter-generation equity, while ensuring an average of eight tanks' availability for every inhabited village, contributing to well over 88 per cent of food production. Now, however, the wear and tear is showing—sugar cane used to be a primary crop in the region, but very few pockets (areas near Tumsar) cultivate it now. A village in Tumsar region, Aashti, has helped buck this trend—its seventy-six traditional tanks (all spread over 987 hectares, cultivating 413 hectares of land) were previously managed by the local Irrigation Department but poor management goaded villagers to take over management while charging user fees.

Between 2010 and 2015, Madhya Pradesh renovated 229 old irrigation projects (all constructed before 1986), across thirty districts, boosting agricultural productivity, with the construction work costing ₹2,498 crore and funded by the World Bank.[175] These renovated irrigation systems have helped improve irrigation through the Chambal canal, with the canal irrigating over 3 lakh hectares, compared to the 78,000 hectares it was irrigating in 2010.

Similarly, Telangana launched Mission Kakatiya, seeking to restore 9,306 tanks annually over a period of five years. Telangana is a mostly arid state, with the Godavari and Krishna rivers flowing at a lower level than the Deccan plateau, limiting the potential for irrigation. The project essentially plans to rebuild over 5,000 tanks, seeking to increase soil moisture, increase fertility, and yield and limit the need for fertilizers. The tanks were originally constructed under the Kakatiya dynasty, with the Qutub Shahis and Asaf Jahis adding incrementally. Such tanks were typically maintained by rich landlords, who continued to dig, expand and maintain tanks. However, post-Independence, such tanks fell into neglect, with governments doing little to revive them. The tanks were sources of water, particularly during years of lean monsoons, while serving as cultural centres

---

175 Pareek, S., 'Madhya Pradesh Renovates 229 Old Irrigation Projects', Better India, June 2015. Sourced from: https://www.thebetterindia.com/24868/madhya-pradesh-renovates-229-old-irrigation-projects/

for communities, with festivals like Ganga jataraas and Teez typically organized around them. The project aims to create a storage capacity of 265 TMC across ten districts of Telangana.[176]

A dilapidated tank typically undergoes silt removal at first, with repairs to the bund, weir and sluices carried out, while irrigation channels are re-sectioned. Cross masonry and cross drainage works are then repaired, with the feeder channel to the tank restored, and any weed/vegetation cleared from the tank bed. The tank level is raised to the maximum level possible and any encroachment on tank land is removed. Such restoration is relatively simple, albeit requiring hard manual labour, and can be scaled up across states.

Restoring tanks will help store rainwater, raising groundwater levels, and ensuring that borewells and hand pumps work without interruption. The silt extracted from dilapidated tanks can also be used on farms, as it usually contains all the micro-nutrients required, limiting the need for fertilizers and other chemicals. But replication of such traditional practices in other regions is limited by our current water resource development governance. Private participation remains limited to wells, tube wells and private lands, while the Central Water Commission regulates the choice of technology used.[177] Ensuring successful replication will require a new institutional mechanism that encourages a participatory approach amongst local villagers and limits their dependence on an external agency for O&M.

---

176 Janyala, S., 'Desilting Irrigation Tanks', Indian Express, June 2016. Sourced from: http://indianexpress.com/article/india/india-news-india/desilting-irrigation-tanks-restoring-reservoirs-before-monsoon-arrival-2842176/
177 Paranjpye, V., 'Bhandara the Lake District', Seeds of Hope, India Water Portal, 2004. Sourced from: http://www.indiawaterportal.org/sites/indiawaterportal.org/files/Seeds%20of%20hope_Case%20studies_Lokayan_Planning%20Commission_2004.pdf

ADAPTING TO WATER SCARCITY

Many farmers have sought to change their cropping patterns, in response to water shortages. Farmers in Nimbhahera block in south Rajasthan have sought to cultivate strawberries.[178] Local climatic conditions, soil and water availability have proved to be sufficient to enable the cultivation of strawberries, while increasing per acre profit. Farmers are increasingly tapping into local networks to sell such produce in markets like Delhi and Mumbai. The input costs for switching to strawberries can vary between ₹2–4 lakh for one bigha of land, but such strawberries can be sold in 2-kg packs, at ₹200 per box. To farm strawberries, farmers have had to master techniques like drip irrigation, employing a plastic mulching sheet bed and fertigation, relying on training and technical support from the state government.

Sikander Meeranayak, founder of Sankalpa Rural Development Society, an NGO based in Hubli, in rural Karnataka, has sought to help local farmers revive and upgrade traditional water harvesting structures, combining them with modern techniques to improve water availability.[179] His NGO has helped implement over 1,130 rainwater harvesting structures, seeking to channel monsoon rains into underground aquifers, via borewells, recharging them and storing water for future use. A single decent monsoon can help recharge local aquifers through this method, enabling water availability for local agricultural use. Farmers in Sira district in rural Karnataka have benefitted from the utilization of such methods—such farmers have had to face declining output from borewells, limiting their multi-crop output to a single crop in a year. The NGO provides a subsidy of ₹15,000 of a total ₹30,000, helping to fund an initial feeder pond, and implementing a rainwater harvesting system within the existing borewell (the work is carried out on a shared cost basis—the farmers provide the labour and part of the initial capital). Such farmers have been able to go back to multicropping, while local aquifers get recharged. The influx of rainwater has also helped improve the quality of the local water, with a decrease in solids and toxins, making hard water increasingly usable. Topsoil erosion has been contained by directing the run-off to the borewell.

In Mizoram, rainwater harvesting holds sway.[180] The state, with an area of 21,000 square km, is completely mountainous and heavily forested, with towns and villages being located on hilltops. This leads to challenges in water availability as

---

178 Aranha, J., 'This Chittorgarh Farmer Has Cultivated Over 12,000 Strawberry Plants in Rajasthan!', Better India, October 2017. Sourced from: https://www.thebetterindia.com/118527/strawberry-cultivation-rajasthan/

179 Qazi, M., Better India, December 2017. Sourced from: https://www.thebetterindia.com/125025/irrigation-solution-water-scarcity-entrepreneur-sikandar-meeranayak/

180 Dunglena, 'Rain Water Harvesting: Mizoram', Seeds of Hope, India Water Portal, 2004. Sourced from: http://www.indiawaterportal.org/sites/indiawaterportal.org/files/Seeds%20of%20hope_Case%20studies_Lokayan_Planning%20Commission_2004.pdf

most rivers are below habitation areas, necessitating long journeys to collect water, particularly during summer. Springs on hill slopes, along with rivers in valleys, are the main sources of water, but rainwater harvesting has been adopted state-wide. The state receives an average of 250 cm per annum of rainfall—most houses in the state are built with sloping roofs, made of corrugated iron sheets. Such sheets help channel water to semi-circular rain gutters made of plain galvanized sheets, along with masonry ground tanks and reinforced cement concrete tanks. Schemes like the Accelerated Rural Water Supply Programme (ARWSP) and the State Plan of Mizoram have helped build rainwater harvesting tanks across 200 villages in Mizoram, while private tanks may number above 50,000.

Greater community stewardship of water resources would go a long way too.[181] Hiware Bazaar, a drought-prone village in Maharashtra's Ahmednagar district, has faced years without a normal monsoon, with an average of 250 mm of rainfall annually in the district. The local soil strata have limited ability to retain moisture, resulting in low water tables, leading to little, if any, water to drink in the summer months. Overgrazing had prevailed in common lands in the village as villagers sought to supplement poor agricultural income with investments in dairy. Ever since 1972, when the first major drought in living memory occurred, the degradation of the natural ecosystem affected local society, leading to extensive migration to nearby towns. Increasingly, the law and order situation deteriorated significantly, while alcohol offered solace and yet ravaged local society. State bureaucrats saw the village as a punishment posting, with even schoolteachers not willing to teach there. In 1989, the local sarpanch sought to plant imli trees in the middle of the village, but these were soon destroyed by villagers seeking to exploit them.

The villagers learnt the value of building consensus and shramdaan, the voluntary contribution of labour, and sought to revive their gram sabha tradition—utilizing it to make major development decisions, according to agreed priority lists, and revive local trust. The degraded ecology around the village was restored by a ban on unlimited grazing, with user fees attached for procuring fodder from local hills. Outsiders were banned from accessing community grasslands, while fodder collected was capped. With such steps, the grasslands were soon restored, with fodder production rising fourfold between 1994 and 2000. Farmers increasingly shifted towards feeding their cattle in stalls, instead of grazing them on nearby land, with milk becoming the village's biggest export. The gram sabha also banned tree felling and started reforesting the hillsides, planting over 10 lakh trees over a decade, under the state's employment guarantee scheme. A water-harvesting project was created in nearby hills, with villagers building a number of bunds,

---

181 Anand, N., 'Hiware Bazaar: Community Stewardship of Water Resources', Seeds of Hope, India Water Portal, 2004. Sourced from: http://www.indiawaterportal.org/sites/indiawaterportal.org/files/Seeds%20 of%20hope_Case%20studies_Lokayan_Planning%20Commission_2004.pdf

percolation tanks and nullahs; all while using locally available materials. In addition, the gram sabha sought to limit water consumption—water-intensive crops like sugar cane and bananas were prohibited, drip irrigation was made mandatory for horticulture, borewells were banned, while traditional crops like jowar and bajra were encouraged. The village was recognized for its efforts as an 'Adarsh Gaon' by the state of Maharashtra in 1993. This assertion of democratic principles for the cause of adapting to water scarcity gives us hope for the future of Indian villages.

————

THE COST OF WATER

While water as an agricultural resource in India is virtually free of cost, access to it is not. Even colonial-era documents cite the charged use of primitive hydraulic tools, the likes of which continue to abound.[182] The Persian wheel consists of a set of pots that revolve on a wheel with a horizontal axis, each pot delivering water to a trough and then descending again. Such wheels are often moved around by bullocks, camels or even horses, with water lifted from depths of 50–60 feet for irrigation of crops. Another system seen often is the mote, where a pair of bullocks raise a leather bag through a pulley-based rope. A lat, typically a bucket (leather, clay or iron), often used for lifts of 4–10 feet, is hung on a pole which oscillates vertically, counterbalanced by a grindstone, which is operated by a lone man at the edge of a well. A basket scoop is used for lift of 1–4 feet, and the doon, an oscillating trough, typically seen in Bengal, for lifts of 2–3 feet.

TABLE 43: COST OF IRRIGATION IN PRE-INDEPENDENCE INDIA[183]

TECHNIQUE	₹	ANNAS	PAISE
COST OF IRRIGATING ONE ACRE, PER CROP, USING A MOTE	9	0	0
COST OF IRRIGATING ONE ACRE, PER CROP, USING A LAT	13	0	0
COST OF IRRIGATING ONE ACRE, PER CROP, USING A BASKET	6	8	6
COST OF IRRIGATING ONE ACRE, PER CROP, USING A DOON	3	14	0

---

182 Bucksley, R. B., C.S.I, The Irrigation Works of India, 2nd Edition, E&F. N. Spon, Ltd, 1905. Sourced from: https://ia801408.us.archive.org/11/items/irrigationworks00buckgoog/irrigationworks00buckgoog.pdf

183 Ibid

In modern-day India, water pricing, particularly for irrigation, needs a rethink.[184] Irrigation comprises 78 per cent of total water usage in India currently. Given this, and to promote irrigation water efficiency, it is imperative that canal irrigation and groundwater irrigation water are priced appropriately, either on a cost plus or a proxy basis. Such a policy will require additional support from the Deen Dayal Upadhyaya Gram Jyoti Yojana to separate electric feeders for agricultural and non-agricultural purposes. Such pricing should also be cognizant of the socio-economic status of marginal farmers. Pricing water should no longer be a taboo topic.

TABLE 44: DUTIES IN ACRES FOR VARIOUS CROPS FOR CANAL DESIGN[185]

NO.	CROP	KHARIF	RABI	HOT WEATHER
1	SUGAR CANE	60	50	40
2	SORGHUM	200	150	
3	BAJRA	200		
4	WHEAT		100	
5	VEGETABLE	200	200	7.5
6	PULSES	200	200	100

The cost of providing clean water to rural India remains significantly high. Controlled experiments along the Bhima River in Karnataka have estimated the impact of polluted water on sugar cane crop—a difference in yield of 2.5–4.0 tonnes/hectare, contributing to an economic loss of ₹4,400–7,200 with productivity depressed by 0.9 per cent.[186] The loss in water polluted villages along the Musi river (near Hyderabad) due to decline in agricultural income is 23.6 per cent more than in non-water polluted villages. Revenue loss and expenses for employment, human health and livestock health were 37.7 per cent, 16.3 per cent and 34.4 per cent higher, respectively, in polluted villages as compared to non-polluted villages. Similar South Asian studies (Ashraf, Yusoff, Mahmood, 2010, Pakistan) have shown that up to ~76 per cent of rural population can be affected by nail, skin and fever issues when their lands were irrigated with polluted water, while a Nigerian study showcased deteriorating health among rural dwellers with ~37 per cent females experiencing miscarriages. This reduction in income, coupled with a rising cost in medical care, is a primary factor in eroding the economic sustainability of villages.

---

184 Opinion, Moving towards a water pricing regime, Live Mint, 24 May 2016. Sourced from: http://www.livemint.com/Opinion/3TO6p9MTaxiPtioFxWe4eJ/Moving-towards-a-water-pricing-regime.html

185 Roth, D., Vincent, L., Narain, V., Controlling the Water, Chapter 2, pg 69, Oxford.

186 Poddar, R.S. and Byahatti, S. Economic Costs of Water Pollution on Rural Livelihood.

TABLE 45: WATER RATES FOR FLOW IRRIGATION IN INDIA

STATES/UTs	RATE (₹/HECTARE)
ANDHRA PRADESH	148.20 TO 1235
ARUNACHAL PRADESH	NO WATER RATES
ASSAM	150 TO 751
BIHAR	74.10 TO 370.50
CHHATTISGARH	123.50 TO 741
DELHI	34.03 TO 1067.04
GOA	60 TO 300
GUJARAT	160 TO 300
HARYANA	24.7 TO 197.6
HIMACHAL PRADESH	28.17
JAMMU AND KASHMIR	29.65 TO 74.13
JHARKHAND	74.10 TO 370.5
KARNATAKA	37.05 TO 988.5
KERALA	37 TO 99
MADHYA PRADESH	50 TO 960
MAHARASHTRA	238 TO 6297
MANIPUR	45 TO 150
MEGHALAYA	NO WATER RATES
MIZORAM	NO WATER RATES
NAGALAND	NO WATER RATES
ODISHA	28 TO 930
PUNJAB	375
RAJASTHAN	29.64 TO 607.62
SIKKIM	10 TO 250
TAMIL NADU	2.77 TO 61.78
TRIPURA	312.5
UTTARAKHAND	35 TO 474
UTTAR PRADESH	30 TO 474
WEST BENGAL	37.06 TO 123.5
ANDAMAN AND NICOBAR ISLANDS	NO WATER RATES
CHANDIGARH	NO WATER RATES
DADRA AND NAGAR HAVELI	110 TO 830
DAMAN AND DIU	200
LAKSHADWEEP	NO WATER RATES
PUDUCHERRY	NO WATER RATES

REFERENCES

Agarwal, P.K.; Talukdar, K.K.; Mall R.K. 2000. Potential yields of rice-wheat systems in the Indo-Gangetic plains of India. Rice-Wheat Consortium Paper Series 10. New Delhi, India: Rice-Wheat Consortium for the Indo-Gangetic Plains.

Allan, J.A. 1998. Virtual water: Strategic resources. global solutions to regional deficits. Groundwater 36: 545–546.

Amarasinghe, U.A.; Sharma, B.R.; Aloysius, N.; Scott, C.; Smakhtin, V.; de Fraiture, C. 2005. Spatial variation of water supply and demand across river basins of India. Research Report 83. Colombo, Sri Lanka: International Water Management Institute.

Amarasinghe, U. A.; Shah, T.; Singh, O. 2006. Changing consumption patterns: Implications for food and water demand in India. Draft prepared for the IWMI-CPWF project on 'Strategic Analysis of National River Linking Project of India'. Bhaduri, A.

Amarasinghe, U.A.; Shah, T. 2006. Groundwater irrigation India: Ananlysis and prognostics. Draft prepared for the IWMI-CPWF project on 'Strategic Analysis of National River Linking Project of India'.

Bhalla, G. S.; Hazell, P.; Kerr, J. 1999. Prospects of India's cereal supply and demand to 2020. Food, Agriculture and the Environment Discussion Paper 29. Washington, D.C., USA: International Food Policy Research Institute (IFPRI).

CWC (Central Water Commission). 2004. Water and related statistics. New Delhi, India: Water Planning and Projects Wing, Central Water Commission.

de Fraiture, C.; Molden D.; Rosegrant, M.; Cai, X.; Amarasinghe, U. 2004. Does international cereal trade save water? The Impact of Virtual Water Trade on Global Water Use. Comprehensive Assessment Research Report No 5. Colombo, Sri Lanka: International Water Management Institute.

Dyson, T.; Hanchate, A. 2000. India's demographic and food prospects: State level analysis. Economic and Political Weekly 11: 4021-4036 (November).

Falkenmark, M.; Lundquvist, J.; Widstrand, C. 1989. Macro-scale water scarcity requires micro-scale approaches: Aspect of vulnerability in semi-arid development. Natural Resources Forum 13 (4): 258–267.

FAO (Food and Agriculture Organization). 1998. Crop evaporation guidelines for computing crop water requirements. FAO Irrigation and Drainage Paper No. 56. Rome, Italy: Food and Agriculture Organization.

FAO. 2003. Review of world water resources by country. Water Reports No. 23. Rome, Italy: Food and Agriculture Organization.

Gardener-Outlaw, T.; Engleman, R. 1997. Sustaining Water, Erasing Scarcity. A Second Update. Washington, D.C., USA: Population Action International.

GOI (Government of India) 1999. Integrated water resources development. A plan for action. Report of the Commission for Integrated Water Resource Development Volume I. New Delhi, India: Ministry of Water Resources.

GOI. 2002. Consolidated results of crop estimation survey on principal crops 2001-2002. New Delhi, India: National Sample Survey Organization, Ministry of Statistics, Government of India.

GOI (Government of India) 2003. Final Population Totals – India (India, State, District, Sub-district, Town, Ward-in-town & Village). New Delhi, India: Office of the Registrar General & Census Commissioner, India.

GOI. 2004. Agricultural statistics at a glance 2004. New Delhi, India: Ministry of Agriculture, Government of India.

Hargraves, G. H.; Samani, Z. A. 1986. World water for agriculture. Logon, Utah, USA: International Irrigation Center, Department of Agricultural and Irrigation Engineering, Utah State University.

Hemme, T. Garcia, O.; Saha, A. 2003. Review of milk production in with a particular emphasis on smallscale producers. PPLPI Working Paper No. 2. Rome, Italy: FAO.

INCID (Indian Committee on Irrigation and Drainage) 1998. Sprinkler irrigation in India. New Delhi, India: Indian Committee on Irrigation and Drainage.

IWMI (International Water Management Institute). 2000. World water supply and demand 1995 to 2025 (draft). www.cgiar.org/iwmi/pubs/WWVison/WWSDOpen.htm IWMI. 2001.

IWMI climate and water atlas. Colombo, Sri Lanka: IWMI CD-ROM.

IWMI. 2005. Land use land cover (LUCL-MODIS 500m, 2000), www.iwmidsp.org

Joshi, P.K.; Birthal, P.S.; Minot, N. 2006.

Sources of agriculture growth in India. Role of diversification towards high-value crops. MTID Discussion Paper No. 98. Washington, D.C., USA: International Food Policy Research Institute.

Kumar, D.; Singh, O.P. 2005. Virtual water in global food and water policy making: Is there a need for rethinking? IWMI-Tata Water Policy Research Highlights, Kumar, M.D.;

Samad, M.; Amarasinghe, U.A.; Singh, O.P. 2006. Water saving technologies: How far can they contribute to water productivity enhancement in Indian agriculture? Draft prepared for the IWMICPWF project on 'Strategic Analysis of National River Linking Project of India'.

Kumar, M.D.; Singhe, O.P.; Samad, M.; Purihit, C.; Didyla, D. 2006. Water productivity of irrigated agriculture in India. Potential areas of improvement. Draft prepared for the IWMI-CPWF project on 'Strategic Analysis of National River Linking Project of India'.

Mahmood, A.; Kundu, A. 2006. Demographic projections for India 2006-2051: Regional variations. Draft prepared for the IWMI-CPWF project on 'Strategic Analysis of National River Linking Project of India'.

Molden, D.J. 1997. Accounting for water use and productivity. SWIM Paper 1. Colombo, Sri Lanka: International Water Management Institute.

Narayanamoorthy, A. 2006. Potential for drip and sprinkler irrigation in India. Draft prepared for the IWMI-CPWF project on 'Strategic Analysis of National River Linking Project of India'.

Palanisami, K.P.; Senthivel, K.; Ranganathan, C.R.; Ramesh, T. 2006. Water productivity at different scales under canal, tank and tubewell irrigation systems. Draft prepared for the IWMI-CPWF project on 'Strategic Analysis of National River Linking Project of India'.

Pandey, U.K. 1995. The Livestock Economy of India: A Profile. Journal of Indian Agricultural Economics. 50. (3): 264–282. Rao, H.C.H. 2005. Agriculture, food security, poverty and environment. New Delhi, India: Oxford University Press.

Rosegrant, M. W.; Paisner, M.S.; Meger, S.; Witcover, J. 2001. Global food projections to 2020. Washington, D.C., USA: International Food Policy Research Institute.

Rosegrant, M.W.; Cai, X.; Cline, S.A. 2002. World water and food 2025. Dealing with scarcity. Washington, D.C., USA: International Food Policy Research Institute.

Rijsberman, F.R. 2000. World water scenarios:

Analysis. London, UK: Earthscan Publications.

Seckler, D.; Amarasinghe, U.A.; Molden, D.; de Silva, R.; Barker, R. 1998. World water demand and supply to 2025: Scenarios and issues. Research Report No. 19. Colombo, Sri Lanka: International Water Management Institute.

Shah, T.; Roy, A.D.; Qureshi, A.S.; Wang, J. 2001. Sustaining Asia's groundwater boom: An overview of issues and evidence. Draft paper prepared for the International Conference on Freshwater in Bonn.

Sharma, B. 2006. The 'tipping point' in Indian agriculture. Understanding the withdrawal of Indian rural youth. Draft prepared for the IWMI-CPWF project on 'Strategic Analysis of National River Linking Project of India'.

Sharma, B.; Rao, K.V.; Vittal, K.P.R. 2006. Realizing the rain-fed agriculture potential in India. Draft prepared for the IWMI-CPWF project on 'Strategic Analysis of National River Linking Project of India'.

Smakhtin, V.; Anputhas, M. 2006. An assessment of environmental flow requirements of Indian river basins. Research Report 107. Colombo, Sri Lanka: International Water Management Institute.

UN (The United Nations). 2004. World population prospects, the 2004 revision. New York, USA: UN Department for Policy Coordination and Sustainable Development.

WRI (World Resources Institute). 2005. Earth trends. Searchable database http://earthtrends.wri.org. Washington, D.C

INDIA'S RIVERS

Amarasinghe U. A., Shah T., Singh O.P., (2007a), Changing consumption patterns: Implications on food and water demand in India. Research Report 119. Colombo, Sri Lanka: International Water Management Institute (IWMI).

Amarasinghe U. A., Shah T., Turral H., Anand B. K., (2007b), India's water future to 2025-2050: Business as-usual scenario and deviations. Research Report 123. Colombo, Sri Lanka: International Water Management Institute.

Bandyopadhyay, J. (2003), And Quiet Flows the River Project. The Hindu Business Line (Chennai) 14 March.

Bandyopadhyay, J., Perveen S., (2003), The Interlinking of Indian Rivers: Some Questions on the Scientific, Economic and Environmental Dimensions of the Proposal.

Paper presented at Seminar on Interlinking Indian Rivers: Bane or Boon? At IISWBM, Kolkata 17 June 2003, SOAS Water Issues Study Group, Occasional Paper No. 60

Hazarika., S. (2003), Climb-down on River Linking. The Statesman, 28 May. Iyer., R. (2002), Linking of Rivers: Judicial Activism or Error?. Economic and Political Weekly. November 16

Iyer., R. (2003), Water: Perspectives, Issues, and Concerns. New Delhi: Sage Publications

IWMI (International Water Management Institute) (2000), World water supply and demand 1995 to 2025. Draft report prepared for World Water Vision. Colombo, Sri Lanka: IWMI

Krueger K., Segovia F., Toubia M., (2007), Assessment of the India River linking Plan: A closer look at the Ken-Betwa Pilot Linking Plan, Natural Resources and Environment, University of Michigan.

Ministry of Water Resources, Government of India. (1980), The National Perspective. New Delhi. http://wrmin.nic.in/interbasin/perspective.htm.

Ministry of Water Resources, Government of India, (2002), Resolution No.2/21/2002 – BM. 13 (December). New Delhi.

Martin, C. (2003), Dams, Rivers and People. 1(2-3) March - April; also in Hindustan Times (New Delhi)10 February. Available at: (http://www.narmada.org/sandrp/apr2003_1.doc)

Rath, N. (2003), Linking of rivers: Some elementary arithmetic. Economic and Political Weekly, Vol 38(29): 3032–3033

Reddy, V. R., (2008), Water Pricing as a Demand Management Option: Potentials, Problems, and Prospects. Colombo, Sri Lanka: International Water Management Institute (computer script).

Roy, A. (1999), The Greater Common Good, Bombay: India Book.

Shah, T., Raju, K.V. (1986), Working of Groundwater Markets in Andhra Pradesh and Gujarat: Results of Two Village Studies. Mimeo, Institute of Rural Management. Anand, India: Institute of Rural Management.

Shah T., Singhe U. A., McCornick P. G., (2007), India's River-Linking Project: The State of the Debate" Draft. IWMI-CPWF Project on Strategic Analyses of India's National River-Linking Project, Colombo, Sri Lanka: International Water Management Institute.

Shukla A. C., Asthana V., (2005) Anatomy of

Interlinking Rivers in India: A Decision in Doubt ACDIS Publication Series: ACDIS Swords and Ploughshares, University of Illinois.

Shiva V., (2003), River Linking: False Assumptions. Flawed Recipes. New Delhi, Navdanya. http://www.navdanya.org/articles/false_ assumptions.htm

Shiva V., Jalees K., (2003), The Impact of the River Linking Project. New Delhi, Navdanya

Verghese B. G., (1990), Waters of hope: Himalayan-Ganga development and cooperation for a billion people. New Delhi: Oxford and IBH Publishing House.

Verghese B. G., (2003), Exaggerated Fears on Linking Rivers. September 2003. http://www.himalmag.com/2003/

Verma S., Kampman D. A., van der Zaag P., Hoekstra A. Y., (2008), Going against the flow a critical analysis of virtual water trade in the context of India's National River Linking Programme. Value of Water Research Report Series No.31 UNESCO-IHE Institute for Water Education, Delft, the Netherlands.

Vombatkere S. G., (2003), Interlinking: Salvation or folly? – II. India Together, January, www.indiatogether.org.

Wolfensohn J. D., (1995), Address at the Annual Meeting of the World Bank and IMF, World Bank, Washington.

CANAL IRRIGATION

Amarasinghe, U., S. Bhaduri, O.P. Singh, and B.K. Anand (2008), 'Managing Unreliability of Canal Water: Case Study of Diggis in Rajasthan', International Water Management Institute, Colombo, Sri Lanka.

Amarasinghe, U. and S. Xenarios (2009), 'Strategic Issues in Indian Irrigation: Overview of the Proceedings', in International Water Management Institute (IWMI), Strategic Analyses of the National River Linking Project (NRLP) of India Series 5, Proceedings of the Second National Workshop on Strategic Issues in Indian Irrigation, New Delhi, India, 8–9 April 2009. Colombo, Sri Lanka: International Water Management Institute.

Banerjee, A. and L. Iyer (2002), 'History, Institutions and Economic Performance: Th e Legacy of Colonial Land Tenure Systems in India', Working Paper 02–27, MIT, Boston. Bhatia, R. (1991), 'Irrigation Financing and Cost Recovery Policy in India: Case Studies from Bihar and Haryana', in R. Meinzen and M. Svendsen (eds)

Future Directions for Indian Irrigation: Research and Policy Issues International Food Policy Research Institute, Washington, DC., pp. 168–213.

Biggs, T.W., A. Gaur, C.A. Scott, P. Thenkabail, P.G. Rao, M. Krishna Gumma, S.K. Acharya, and H. Turral, (2007), 'Closing of the Krishna Basin: Irrigation, Streamfl ow Depletion and Macroscale Hydrology', Research Report 111, IWMI, Colombo.

Birari, K.S., D.S. Navadkar, D.V. Kasar, and M.S. Yadav (2003), 'Cooperative Lift Irrigation Schemes for Sustainable Use of Water', Indian Journal of Agricultural Economics, July, Vol. 56, No. 3.

Boyce, J.K. (1988), 'Technological and Institutional Alternatives in Asian Rice Irrigation', Economic and Political Weekly, Vol. 23, No. 13, pp. A6–A22.

Buckley, R.B. (1905), The Irrigation Works of India. E. & F.N. Spon Ltd., London.

Burt, C. and S. Styles (1999), 'Modern Water Control and Management Practices in Irrigation: Impact on Performance', in D. Renault (ed.), Modernization of Irrigation System Operations, Proceedings of the Fifth International ITIS Network Meeting, Aurangabad, India, 28–30 October 1998, Food and Agriculture Organization, Bangkok, RAP Publication: 99/43 pp. 93–114.

Chandra, A. and C. Sudhir (2010), 'A Study of Kolhapur Lift Irrigation Cooperatives', MTS Report, Institute of Rural Management, Anand.

Choudhury, N. and V. Kher, (2006), 'Public Private Partnership in Surface Water Irrigation: A Case of Kolhapur', IWMI–Tata Water Policy Program (unpublished report), Anand, India.

Choudhury, N. and Z. Shah (2005), 'Long Term Socio Economic Impacts of Displacement: Case Study of Mahi Bajaj Sagar Dam', IWMI–Tata Water Policy Program (unpublished report), Anand, India.

Coward, E.W. (1983), 'Property in Action: Alternatives for Irrigation Investment', Paper presented at Workshop on Water Management and Policy at Khon Kaen University, Khon Kaen, Thailand, September.

Daines, S.R. and J.R. Pawar (1987), 'Economic Returns to Irrigation in India', SDR Research Groups Inc. & Development Group Inc. Report prepared for US Agency for International Development Mission to India, New Delhi.

Dharmadhikari, S. (2005), Unravelling Bhakra: Assessing the Temple of Resurgent India, Manthan Adhyayan Kendra, Bhopal, India.

Dhawan, B.D. (1996), 'Trends and Determinants of Capital Investments in Agriculture', Indian Journal of Agricultural Economics, Vol. 541, No. 4, pp. 529–42. Down to Earth (2005), 'The Lie of the Land', 31 May, pp. 36–38.

Freeman, D.M., V. Bhandarkar, E. Shinn, J. Wilkins-Wells, and P. Wilkins-Wells (1989), Local Organizations for Social Development: Concepts and Cases of Irrigation Organizations, Westview Press, Boulder, Colorado.

Government of India (1992), Report of the Committee on Pricing of Irrigation Water, Planning Commission of India, New Delhi. (2005), Report on Third Census of Minor Irrigation Schemes (2000–1), Ministry of Water Resources, Minor Irrigation Division, New Delhi.

Hardiman, D. (2002), 'The Politics of Water in Colonial India, in South Asia', Journal of South Asian Studies, Vol. 25, No. 2, pp. 111–120.

Hirschman, A. (1965), Exit, Voice and Loyalty: Responses to Decline in Firms, Organizations and States, Harvard University Press, Boston.

Hunt, R.C. (1989), 'Appropriate Social Organization? Water User Associations in Bureaucratic Canal Irrigation Systems', Human Organization, Vol. 48, No. 1 (Spring), pp. 79–89.

International Water Management Institute [IWMI] (2009), Strategic Analyses of the National River Linking Project (NRLP) of India Series 5. Proceedings of the Second National Workshop on Strategic Issues in Indian Irrigation, New Delhi, India, 8–9, April 2009. Colombo, Sri Lanka: International Water Management Institute, p. 359.

Islam, M.M. (1997), Irrigation Agriculture and the Raj, Punjab, 1887–1947, Manohar Books, New Delhi. Jairath, J. (2001), Water User Associations in Andhra Pradesh: Initial Feedback, Concept Publishing Co., New Delhi.

Janakarajan, S. and M. Moench (2006), 'Are Wells a Potential Threat to Farmers' Well-Being? Case of Deteriorating Groundwater Irrigation in Tamil Nadu', Economic and Political Weekly, Vol. 41, No. 37, pp. 3977–3987.

Joseph, C.J. (2001), 'Beneficiary Participation in Irrigation Water Management: The Kerala Experience', Discussion Paper 36, Centre for Development Studies, Thiruvananthapuram, India.

Jurriens, M., P. Mollinga, and P. Wester (1996), 'Scarcity by Design: Protective Irrigation in India and Pakistan', Liquid Gold 1996, Paper 1, Wageningen University, Netherlands.

Kloezen, W.H. (2002), 'Accounting

for Water: Institutional Viability and Impacts of Market- Oriented Irrigation Interventions in Central Mexico', PhD Thesis, Rural Development Sociology Group, Wageningen University, Netherlands.

Kolavalli, S. (1986), 'Economic Analysis of Conjunctive Use of Water: Th e Case of Mahi–Kadana Irrigation Project in Gujarat India', PhD Thesis, University of Illinois, Urbana, IL, Chapter 6, pp. 100–24.

Lohar, N.S., R.R. Mane, S.N. Patil, and M.B. Nichit (2006), 'Comparative Economics of Lift Irrigation Schemes Operated in Kolhapur District of Western Maharashtra', Indian Journal of Agricultural Economics, 1 July.

Madhav, R. (2007), 'Irrigation Reforms in Andhra Pradesh: Whither the Trajectory of Legal Changes?', International Water Law Research Centre, Working Paper 2007–04, Geneva, available at http://www.ielrc.org/content/ w0704.pdf

Mohanty, N. (2005), 'Moving to Scale', Background Paper for India's Water Economy: Bracing for a Turbulent Future, Report 34750-IN, Agriculture and Rural Development Unit, South Asia Region, World Bank, Washington DC.

Mollinga, P. (2003), On the Water Front: Water Distribution, Technology and Agrarian Change in a South Indian Canal Irrigation System, Orient Longman, New Delhi.

Mukherji, A., T. Facon, J. Burke, C. de Fraiture, J.M. Faures, B. Fuleki, M. Giordano, D. Molden, and T. Shah (2009), Revitalizing Asia's Irrigation to Sustainably Meet Tomorrow's Food Needs, IWMI, Colombo, Sri Lanka and FAO, Rome, Italy, p. 39.

Narain, V. (2004), 'Crafting Institutions for Collective Action in Canal Irrigation: Can We Break the Deadlocks?', Paper presented at Silver Jubilee Symposium on Governance Issues in Water Institute of Rural Management, Anand, India, December.

National Sample Survey Organization [NSSO] (2005), Seasonal Variation in the Operational Landholdings in India, 2002–03, 59th Round, January–December 2003, Report 494(59/18.1/2). Department of Statistics, Government of India, New Delhi.

(2003), Report on Village Facilities, NSS 58th round, July–December 2002, Report 487(58/3.1/1), Department of Statistics, Government of India, New Delhi.

(1999), Cultivation Practices in India, NSS 54th Round, January–June 1998,

Report 451, Department of Statistics, Government of India, New Delhi.

(2005), Situation Assessment Survey of Farmers: Some Aspects of Farming. 59th Round, January–December 2003, Report 496(59/33/3), Department of Statistics, Government of India, New Delhi. Oorthuizen, J.

(2003), Water, Works and Wages: The Everyday Politics of Irrigation Management Reform in the Philippines, Orient Longman, New Delhi. Padhiari, H.K.

(2006), 'Water Service Markets in Surface Irrigation Systems: Institutions and Socio-Economic Impact', Paper presented at the IWMI–Tata Annual Partners' Meet, February 2005.

Palanisami, K. (1995), 'Hydro-economic Integration and Conversion of Tanks into Percolation Ponds', CGWB Project Report, Tamil Nadu Agricultural University, Coimbatore.

(2005), 'Sustainable Management of Tank Irrigation Systems in South India', Working Paper Series No. 2, Afrasian Centre for Peace and Development Studies, Kyoto, Japan.

Palanisami, K. and K.W. Easter (1991), 'Hydro-economic Interaction in Tank Irrigation Systems', Indian Journal of Agricultural Economics, Vol. 46, No. 2 (April–June).

Palanisami, K. and R. Balasubramanian (1998), 'Common property and Private Prosperity: Tanks vs. Private Wells in Tamil Nadu', Indian Journal of Agricultural Economics, Vol. 53, No. 4 (October–December).

Paranjapye, S., K.J. Joy, and C. Scott (2003), 'The Ozar Water User Societies: Impact of Society Formation and Co-management of Surface Water and Groundwater', Paper presented at the National Seminar on Water, Pune, India, July, available at http://www.cess. ac.in/cesshome/ wp/VUMURHJ1.pdf

Pradhan, P. (1989), Patterns of Irrigation Organization in Nepal: A Comparative Study of 21 Farmer Managed Irrigation Systems, International Irrigation Management Institute, Colombo.

Randhawa, M.S. (1983), A History of Agriculture in India, Vol. III, Indian Council of Agricultural Research, New Delhi.

Rao, G.B. (2003), 'Oases of Rayalaseema: SPWD's Tank Restoration Program in Southern Andhra Pradesh', Wastelands News, Vol. 19, No. 1, pp. 64–72.

Rap, E.R. (2004), 'The Success of a Policy Model:

Irrigation Management Transfer in Mexico', PhD Thesis, Rural Development Sociology Group, Wageningen University, Netherlands.

Reddy, V.R. (2003), 'Irrigation: Development and Reforms', Economic and Political Weekly, Vol. 38, Nos. 12–13, pp. 1178–1189.

Renault, D. (1998), 'Modernization of Irrigation Systems: A Continuing Process', in D. Renault (ed.) Modernization of Irrigation System Operations, Proceedings of the Fifth International IT IS Network Meeting, Aurangabad, India, 28–30 October, FAO, RAP Publication, Bangkok, Vol. 99, No. 43, pp. 7–12.

Repetto, R. (1986), 'Skimming the Water: Rent, Seeking and the Performance of Public Irrigation Systems', Research Report 4, World Resources Institute, Washington, DC.

Rice, E.B. (1996), Paddy Irrigation and Water Management in Southeast Asia, World Bank, Washington, DC. Selvarajan, S. (2002), Sustaining India's Irrigation Infrastructure, Policy Brief 15, National Centre for Agricultural Economics and Policy Research, New Delhi.

Shah, A. (2003), 'Tail-Enders and Other Deprived in Canal Irrigation Systems: Gujarat', Paper presented at National Workshop on Tail-Enders and Other Deprived in Canal Irrigation Systems, Ahmedabad, India, November.

Shah, T. (1993), Groundwater Markets and Irrigation Development: Political Economy and Practical Policy, Oxford University Press, Bombay. (2010), 'Guhai, Sabarkantha: Changing Reality of an Irrigation System', Field Note.

Shah, T., M. Giordano, and J. Wang (2004), 'Irrigation Institutions in a Dynamic Economy: What Is China Doing Diff erently from India?', Economic and Political Weekly, Vol. 39, No. 31, pp. 3452–3461. (2009), Taming the Anarchy? Groundwater Governance in South Asia, RFF Press, Washington DC.

Shah, T. and K.V. Raju (2001), 'Rethinking Rehabilitation: Socio-ecology of Tanks in Rajasthan, India', Water Policy, Vol. 3, No. 6, pp. 521–536.

Shukla, P. (2004), 'Exposure cum Training Visit to Participatory Irrigation Management (PIM) Project Ahmedabad, Gujarat', Letters, Vol. 1, No. 3, pp. 12–14. Singh, S. (2006), 'Credit, Indebtedness and Farmer Suicides in Punjab: Some Missing Links', Economic and Political Weekly, Vol. 41, No. 3, pp. 3330–3331.

Singhal, N. and V. Patwari (2009), Evolving

Arrangements for Local Water Diversion-Delivery in SSP, MTS Report, Institute of Rural Management, Anand.

Sivasubramaniyan, K. (2008), 'Irrigation Management and its Effect on Productivity under Parambikulam Aliyar Project in Tamil Nadu', in Managing Water in the Face of Growing Scarcity, Inequity and Declining Returns: Exploring Fresh Approaches, Proceedings of the Seventh Annual Partners Meet, IWMI-Tata Water Policy Research Program, Vol. 2, International Water Management Institute, Hyderabad, India, pp. 819–849.

Talati, J. and D. Pandya (2007), 'Issues in Canal Infrastructure: Development and Canal Irrigation Management', Economic and Political Weekly, Vol. 42, No. 33, pp. 3422–3429.

Talati, J. and T. Shah (2004), 'Institutional Vacuum in Sardar Sarovar Project: Framing "Rules-of-the-Game"', Economic and Political Weekly, Vol. 39, No. 31, pp. 3504–3509.

Thenkabail, P.S., C.M. Biradar, H. Turral, P. Noojipady, Y.J. Li, J. Vithanage, V. Dheeravath, M. Velpuri, M. Schull, X.L. Cai, and R. Dutta (2006), 'An Irrigated Area Map of the World (1999) derived from Remote Sensing', Research Report No. 105, International Water Management Institute, p. 74.

van Halsema, G.E. (2002), 'Trial and Retrial: The Evolution of Irrigation Modernization in NWFP, Pakistan', PhD Thesis, Wageningen University, Netherlands.

Venot, J.P. (2008), 'Why and Where are the Krishna Waters Disappearing?', Economic and Political Weekly, Vol. 43, No. 6, pp. 15–17.

Vermillion, D. (1996), The Privatization and Self-Management of Irrigation: Final Report, International Irrigation Management Institute, Colombo.

Von Oppen, M. and S.K.V. Rao (1987), Tank Irrigation in Semi-Arid Tropical India: Economic Evaluation and Alternatives for Improvement, Research Bulletin 10, ICRISAT, Hyderabad, India.

Wade, R. (1984), 'Irrigation Reform in Conditions of Populist Anarchy: An Indian Case', Journal of Development Studies, Vol. 14, No. 2, pp. 285–303.

Wade, R. and R. Chambers (1980), 'Managing the Main System: Canal Irrigation's Blind Spot', Economic and Political Weekly, Vol. 15, No. 39, pp. A107–A112.

Wang, J., Z. Xu, J. Huang, and S. Rozelle (2003), 'Incentives in Water Management Reform: Assessing the Effect on Water Use, Production and Poverty in the Yellow River Basin', Chinese Council for Agricultural Policy (draft paper), Beijing.

Whitcombe, E. (2005), 'Irrigation', in D. Kumar and M. Desai (eds) The Cambridge Economic History of India, c. 1757–1970, Vol. 2, Orient Longman, Hyderabad, India, pp. 677–737.

Chand, R., Raju, S.S., Garg, S. and Pandey, L.M. 2011. Instability and regional variation in Indian agriculture. New Delhi: National Centre for Agricultural Economics and Policy Research (NCAEPR).

CPCB. 2009. Status of water supply, wastewater generation and treatment in Class-I cities and Class-II towns of India. Central for Pollution Control Board (CPCB), Ministry of Environment and Forests, Government of India.

GoI. 2014. Fourth Census of Minor Irrigation Schemes Report. November, 411p. New Delhi: Minor Irrigation (Statistics) Wing, Ministry of Water Resources, River Development and Ganga Rejuvenation, Government of India (GoI).

Gupta, M., Ravindra, V. and Palrecha, A. 2016. Wastewater irrigation in Karnataka: An exploration. IWMI-Tata Water Policy Research Highlight, 4.

IARI. nd. Engineered wetland technology based eco-friendly wastewater treatment and re-use. Water Technology Center, Indian Agricultural Research Institute (IARI).

Jagadeesan, S. and Kumar, M.D. 2015. The Sardar Sarovar Project: Assessing Economic and Social Impacts. New Delhi: SAGE Publications.

Palrecha, A., Kapoor, D. and Maladi, T. 2012. Wastewater irrigation in Gujarat: An exploration. IWMI-Tata Water Policy Research Highlight No. 30, Anand: IWMI-Tata Water Policy Program.

Strauss, M. and Blumenthal, U. J. 1990. Human waste use in agriculture and aquaculture: Utilization practices and health perspectives. International Reference Centre for Waste Disposal, Duebendorf, Switzerland.

Wade, R. 1984. Irrigation Reform in Conditions of Populist Anarchy: An Indian Case. Journal of Development Studies 14(2): pp. 285–303.

GROUNDWATER

Aarnoudse. E., Bluemling, B., Wester, P. and Qu, W. (2012) The role of collective groundwater institutions in the implementation of direct groundwater regulation measures in Minqin county, China. Hydrogeology Journal, 20(7): pp. 1213–1221.

Abderrahman, W. A. (2001) Water demand management in Saudi Arabia, pp. 68–78. In Water management in Islam (Faruqui, N.I., Biswas, A.K., and Bino, M. Eds). United Nations University, Tokyo, Japan.

Badiani, R. and Jessoe, K.K. (2010) Electricity subsidies, elections, groundwater extraction and industrial growth in India. Paper submitted to the Pacific Development Conference 2010, Berkeley, University of California. Available at: http://mitsloan.mit.edu/neudc/ papers/paper_194.pdf

Barker, R. and Molle, F. (2002) Perspectives on Asian irrigation. Paper presented at the Conference on Asian Irrigation in Transition – Responding to the Challenges Ahead, Asian Institute of Technology, Bangkok, Thailand, 22–23 April 2002.

Bitran, E., Rivera, P., and Villena, M. (2014) Water management problems in the Copiapó Basin Chile: markets, severe scarcity and the regulator.

Brozovic, N. and Islam, S. (2010) Estimating the value of groundwater in irrigation. Paper submitted to the Agricultural and Applied Economics Association Annual Meeting, at Denver, Colorado, 25–27 July 2010. Available at: http://ageconsearch. umn.edu/bitstream/61337/2/10819. pdf

Burke, J.J. and Moench, M. (2000) Groundwater and Society. Resources, Tensions and Opportunities. United Nations, New York, USA.

Evans, W.R. and Evans, E. (2011) Conjunctive use and management of groundwater and surface water. Groundwater governance, thematic paper 2. Available at: http://www. groundwatergovernance.org/ fileadmin/ user_upload/groundwatergovernance/docs/ Thematic_ papers/GWG_Thematic_Paper_2_01. pdf Food and Agriculture Organization of the United Nations (FAO) (2009a)

Groundwater Management in Morocco: Synthesis Report. FAO, Rome, Italy. Food and Agriculture Organization of the United Nations (FAO) (2009b)

Groundwater Management in Iran. Draft Synthesis Report. FAO, Rome, Italy.

Foster, S. and van Steenbergen, F. (2011) Conjunctive use of groundwater: a 'lost opportunity' for water management in the developing world? Hydrogeology Journal, 19(5): pp. 959–962.

Garrido, A., Martínez-Santos, P. and Llamas, M.R. (2006) Groundwater irrigation and its implications for water policy in semiarid countries: the Spanish experience. Hydrogeology Journal, 14(3): 340–349.

Giordano, M. (2006) Agricultural groundwater use and rural livelihoods in sub-Saharan Africa: a first-cut assessment. Hydrogeology Journal, 14(3): pp. 310–318.

He, L. and Perret, S. (2012) Water rights system for sustainable groundwater use in irrigation: government-led and farmer selffinancing case study from Qingxu county, China. College of Humanities and Development Studies, China Agricultural University, Beijing, Peoples Republic of China.

Hernández-Mora, N., Martinez, L., Llamas, R.M., and Custodio, E. (2010) Groundwater in the southern member states of the European Union: an assessment of current knowledge and future prospects. Country Report, European Academies Science Advisory Council. Available at: http://www.easac. eu/fileadmin/PDF_s/reports_statements/ Spain_ Groundwater_country_report.pdf

Hernandez-Mora, N., Martinez, C.L., and Fornes, J. (2003) Intensive groundwater use in Spain, pp. 387–414. In Intensive Use of Groundwater: Challenges and Opportunities, (Llamas, M.R. and Custodio, E. Eds). A.A. Balkema Publishers, Rotterdam, Netherlands.

Hornbeck, R. and Keskin, P. (2011) The evolving impact of the Ogallala Aquifer: Agricultural adaptation to groundwater and climate. National Bureau of Economic Research, Working Paper 17625. Available at: http://www.nber.org/papers/w17625.pdf

Kalf, F.R.P and Wooley, D.R. (2005) Applicability and methodology of determining sustainable yield in groundwater systems. Hydrogeology Journal, 13(1): pp. 295–312.

Konikow, L.F. (2011) Contribution of global groundwater depletion since 1900 to sea-level rise. Geophysical Research Letters, 38: pp. 1–5.

Lee, S.H. and Bagley, E.S. (1973) Ground water and land values in Southwestern Kansas. Groundwater, 10(6): 27-36.

Lopez-Gunn, E. (2003) The role of collective action water governance: a comparative study of groundwater user associations in La Mancha aquifers in Spain. Water International, 28(3): pp. 367–378.

Martinez, C.L. and Hernandez-Mora, N. (2003) The role of groundwater in Spain's water policy. Water International, 28(3): pp. 313–320.

Pahuja, S., Tovey, C., Foster, S., and Garduano, H. (2010) Deep Wells and Prudence: Towards Pragmatic Action for Addressing Groundwater

Overexploitation in India. Report No. 51676. The World Bank, Washington, DC, USA.

Palmer-Jones, R.W. (1999) Slowdown in agricultural growth in Bangladesh: neither a good description nor a description good to give, pp. 92–136. In Sonar Bangla? Agricultural Growth and Agrarian Change in West Bengal and Bangladesh (Rogaly, B., Harris-White, B., and Bose. S. Eds). Sage Publications, New Delhi, India.

Pfeiffer, L. and Lin, C-Y.C. (2013) Does efficient irrigation technology lead to reduced groundwater extraction?: empirical evidence. Journal of Environmental Economics and Management, http://dx.doi.org/10.1016/j. jeem.2013.12.002

Phansalkar, S. and Vivek Kher. (2003) A decade of Maharashtra groundwater legislation: analysis of implementation process in Vidarbha, pp. 148. In Issues in Water Use in Agriculture in Vidarbha, Nagpur (Phansalkar, S. Ed.). Amol Management Consultants, Pune, India. Planning Commission. (2007) Ground Water Management and Ownership – Report of the Expert Group. Government of India, New Delhi, India.

Plummer, J. and Slaymaker, T. (2007) Rethinking governance in water services. Working Paper 284, Overseas Development Institute, London, UK. Postel, S. (1992) Last Oasis: Facing Water Scarcity. W.W. Norton, New York, NY, USA.

Revelle, R. and Lakshminarayana, V. (1975) The Ganges water machine. Science, 188(4188): 611–616.

Rodell, M., Velicogna, I., and Famiglietti, J.S. (2009) Satellite-based estimates of groundwater depletion in India. Letter. Nature, 460: pp. 999–1002.

Rogers, P. and Hall, A. (2003) Effective Water Governance. Technical Committee Background Paper No. 7. Global Water Partnership (GWP), Stockholm, Sweden.

Rosegrant, M.W., and Binswanger, H.P. (1994) Markets in tradable water rights: potential for efficiency gains in developing country water resource allocation. World development, 22(11): 1613–1625.

Rosegrant, M.W. and Gazmuri S.R. (1995) Reforming water allocation policy through markets in tradable water rights: lessons from Chile, Mexico, and California. Cuadernos de Economía, 291–315.

Sandoval, R. (2004) A participatory approach to integrated aquifer management: the case of Guanajuato State, Mexico, Hydrogeology Journal, 12: pp. 6–13.

Scott, C. (2013) Electricity for groundwater

use: constraints and opportunities for adaptive response to climate change. Environmental Research Letters 8(2013).

Shah, T. (2000) Mobilizing social energy against environmental challenge: understanding the groundwater recharge movement in western India. Natural Resource Forum, 24(3): pp. 197–209.

Shah, T. (2003) Governing the groundwater economy: comparative analysis of national institutions and policies in South Asia, China and Mexico. Water Perspectives, 1(1): pp. 2–27.

Shah, T. (2006) Institutional groundwater management in the United States: lessons for South Asia and north China. Kansas Journal of Law & Public Policy, 15(3): pp. 567–571

Shah, T. (2009) Taming the Anarchy: Groundwater Governance in South Asia. RFF Press, Washington DC, USA.

Shah, T. and Verma, S. (2008) Co-management of electricity and groundwater: an assessment of Gujarat's Jyotirgram Scheme. Economic and Political Weekly, 43(7): pp. 59–66

Shah, T., Verma, S., and Pavelic, P. (2013) Understanding smallholder irrigation in sub-Saharan Africa: results of a sample survey from nine countries. Water International, 38(6): pp. 809–826.

Shah, T., Giordano, M., and Wang, J. (2004a) Irrigation institutions in a dynamic economy: what is China doing differently from India? Economic and Political Weekly, 39(31): pp. 3452–3461.

Shah, T., Scott, C., and Buechler, S. (2004b) Water sector reforms in Mexico: lessons for India's New Water Policy. Economic and Political Weekly, 39(4): pp. 361–370.

Shah, T., Burke, J., Villholth, K., Angelica, M., Custodio, E., Daibes, F., Hoogesteger, J., Giordano, M., Girman, J., van der Gun, J., Kendy, E., Kijne, J., Llamas, R., Masiyandama, M., Margat, J., Marin, L., Peck, J., Rozelle, S., Sharma, B., Vincent, L., and Wang, J. (2007) Groundwater: a global assessment of scale and significance, pp. 395-423. In Water for Food, Water for Life: A Comprehensive Assessment of Water Management in Agriculture (Molden, D. Ed.). Earthscan, London, UK, and Colombo, Sri Lanka.

Siebert, S., Burke, J., Faures, J.M., Frenken, K., Hoogeveen, J., Doll, P. and Portmann, F.T. (2010) Groundwater use for irrigation – a global inventory. Hydrology and Earth System Sciences, 14: 1863–1880.

Singh, K. (2009) Act to save groundwater in

Punjab: its impact on water table, electricity subsidy and environment. Agricultural Economics Research Review, 01/2009: 22(2009).

Tsur, Y. (1990) The stabilization role of groundwater when surface water supplies are uncertain: the implications for groundwater development. Water Resources Research, 26(5): pp. 811–818.

van der Gun, J. (2007) Sharing groundwater knowledge and experience on a world-wide scale, pp. 362–392. In The Agricultural Groundwater Revolution: Opportunities and Threats to Development (Giordano, M. and Villholth, K.G. Eds). CAB International, Wallingford, U.K.

van Steenbergen, F. (2006) Promoting local groundwater management. Hydrogeology Journal, 14(3): pp. 380–391.

van Steenbergen, F. (2010) Community-based ground water management in Andhra Pradesh: moving towards proven models. Mimeograph. World Bank GW Mate: Washington, DC, USA.

Venot, J.P. and Molle, F. (2008) Groundwater depletion in the Jordan highlands: can pricing policies regulate irrigation water use? Water Resources Management, 22(12): pp. 1925–1941.

Verma, S., Krishnan, S., Reddy, V.A., and Reddy, K.R. (2012) Andhra Pradesh Farmer Managed Groundwater Systems (APFAMGS): A Reality Check, Highlight 37, IWMI-Tata Water Policy Program, Gujarat, India.

Wang, J., Huang, J., Huang, Q., Rozelle, S.C., and Walker, H.F. (2009) The evolution of China's groundwater governance: productivity, equity and the environment. Quarterly Journal of Engineering Geology and Hydrogeology, 25(1): pp. 141–158.

Wang, J., Huang, J., Blanke, A., Huang, Q., and Rozelle, S. (2007) The development, challenges and management of groundwater in rural China, pp. 37–62. In The Agricultural Groundwater Revolution: Opportunities and Threats to Development (Giordano, M. and Villholth, K.G. Eds). CAB International, Wallingford, U.K.

Young, M. and McColl, J.C. (2009) Double trouble: the importance of defining and accounting for water entitlements consistent with hydrological realities. Australian Journal of Agricultural and Resource Economics, 53(1): pp. 19–35.

Zhu, T., C. Ringler C., and Cai X. (2007) Energy price and groundwater extraction for agriculture: exploring the energy-waterfood nexus at the global and basin levels. Paper presented at the International conference on Linkages Between

Energy and Water Management for Agriculture in Developing Countries. Hyderabad, India, 29–31 January 2007. Available at: http://www.iwmi.cgiar. org/ EWMA/files/papers/Energyprice_GW.pdf

Zhimin, W. and Baojun, C. (no date.) Development and Management of Groundwater Irrigation in Hengshui. Water Resources Bureau of Taocheng District, Hengshui City, People's Republic of China.

IMPROVING IRRIGATION
MANAGEMENT

IMPROVING GROUNDWATER
MANAGEMENT

Water and land management research institute by walamtari (government of India)

Muralidharan, D. and Venugopalan Nair, R., 1998. Percolation tank efficiency and temporal influence analysis-A Hardrock area case stud-Proc.of seminar on "Artificil Recharge of groundwater", New Delhi, IV, pp: 89-97

Muralidharan, D. et al, 2009. Baseline Geohydrological Studies For Developing Strategies On Revival of Defunct Minor Irrigation Tank, NGRI Technical Report No.NGRI-2009-GW-677.

Reddy, P.R., 2013. Relevance of minor irrigation and its restoration to sustain agriculture in Andhra Pradesh-An Overview, J.Ind. Geophys.Union, v. 17, no.3, pp: 259-279

Sakthivadivel, R., P. Gomathinayagam, and Tushaar Shah. 2004. Rejuvenating Irrigation Tanks through Local Institutions. Economic and Political Weekly, v. 39, no. 31, 31 July.

Sakthivadivel, R. and P. Gomathinayagam. 2004. Institutional Analysis of Best Performing Locally Managed Tanks in India. Third IWMI-Tata Annual Partners Meet. Anand, February

Sakthivadivel, R., P. Gomathinayagam, and Tushaar Shah. 2004. Rejuvenating Irrigation Tanks through Local Institutions. Economic and Political Weekly, v. 39, no. 31, 31 July

Shanmugham, C.R, A. Gurunathan and K.T. Ramappa, 2007. Irrigation Tanks and their traditional local management: A Remarkable ancient history of India. Seminar volume of National Seminar on Water and Culture, Hampi (Karnataka): JUNE 25–27, 2007 Batra, S. 2004. A Comparative Study on Tanks in Western, Central and South India. Third IWMITata Annual Partners Meet. Anand, February.

Behera, P.C. 2004. Study of Physical and

Institutional Aspects of Best Performing Tanks: A Case Study from Orissa. Third IWMI-Tata Annual Partners Meet. Anand, February.

Centre for Water Resources. 2002. Baseline Survey of Select Irrigation Systems. Chennai: Anna University.

2000. Monitoring and Evaluation: Phase II Tank Modernization Project with EEC Assistance. Final Report. Chennai: Anna University.

2000. Monitoring and Evaluation: Extension Tank Modernization Project with EEC Assistance. Final Report. Chennai: Anna University.

Centre for Water Resources and Ocean Management. 1996. Farmers' Participation in Tank Rehabilitation and Management: A Case Study of Kedar Tank. Chennai: Anna University.

Datye, K.R. and R.K. Patil. 1987. Farmers Managed Irrigation Systems: Indian Experiences. Bombay: Centre for Applied Systems Analysis in Development.

Deshpande, Pradumna. 2004. Study of Physical and Institutional Aspects of Best Performing Tanks: A Case Study from Maharashtra. Third IWMI-Tata Annual Partners Meet. Anand, February.

Doraiswamy, R. 2004. A Comparative Study of a Traditional and Government Sponsored WUAs in Karnataka. Third IWMI-Tata Annual Partners Meet. Anand, February.

Ford Foundation and Centre for Water Resources. 2001. Participatory Rehabilitation and Management in Pagadaikulam. New Delhi and Chennai.

Ford Foundation and Centre for Water Resources. 2001. Participatory Rehabilitation and Management in Vengal. New Delhi and Chennai.

Gomathinayagam, P. 2005. Two Decades of Tank Rehabilitation in India: Evaluating Sustainability of Rehabilitation. Fourth IWMI-Tata Annual Partners Meet. Anand, February.

2004. Study of Physical and Institutional Aspects of Best Performing Tanks: A Case Study from Tamil Nadu. Third IWMI-Tata Annual Partners Meet. Anand, February.

Gomathinayagam, P., R. Sakthivadivel, D. Sundaresan, and J.D. Sophia. 2005. Land and Water Productivity Potential in Tank Irrigation: A Comparative Analysis. Fourth IWMI-Tata Annual Partners Meet. Anand, February.

Jain, Hitesh and Vanya Sinha. 2004. A Comparative Study of Local Tank Management

Institutions in Gujarat, Madhya Pradesh and Rajasthan. Third IWMI-Tata Annual Partners Meet. Anand, February.

Janakarajan, S. 1996. Note on Irrigation Experience of Tamil Nadu. Proceedings of the Seminar on Conservation and Development of Tank Irrigation for Livelihood Promotion. Madurai: Conservation and Development Forum. July

Kumar, A. 2004. Study of Physical and Institutional Aspects of Best Performing Tanks: A Case Study from Andhra Pradesh. Third IWMI-Tata Annual Partners Meet. Anand, February.

Mosse. David. 2003. The Rule of Water: Statecraft, Ecology, and Collective Action in South India. New Delhi: Oxford University Press.

Murugesan, S. 2004. Study of Physical and Institutional Aspects of Best Performing Tanks: A Case Study from Karnataka. Third IWMI-Tata Annual Partners Meet. Anand, February.

Narayanamoorthi, A. 2004. Status of Tank Irrigation in India: Analysis Across States, 1950-1998. Unpublished. Pant, Niranjan. 2004. Tanks in Eastern India. Unpublished.

Pant, Niranjan and R.K. Verma. 1983. Farmers' Organization and Irrigation Management. New Delhi: Ashish Publishing House.

Raj, A.B.S. and Sundaresan D. 2005. Declining Trend in Tank-irrigated Area: Is There A Way To Arrest? Fourth IWMI-Tata Annual Partners Meet. Anand, February.

Sakthivadivel, R. 2005. Two Decades of Tank Rehabilitation in India: Investment, Institutional, and Policy Issues. Fourth IWMI-Tata Annual Partners Meet. Anand, February.

Improving the Productivity of India's Tanks: Study of Local Tank Management Institutions: A Synthesis. Third IWMI-Tata Annual Partners Meet. Anand, February, 2004.

A Study on Tanks and Ponds. NOVIB and DHAN Foundation. March, 2004.

Sakthivadivel, R. and P. Gomathinayagam. 2004. Institutional Analysis of Best Performing Locally Managed Tanks in India. Third IWMI-Tata Annual Partners Meet. Anand, February.

Sakthivadivel, R., P. Gomathinayagam, and Tushaar Shah. 2004. Rejuvenating Irrigation Tanks through Local Institutions. Economic and Political Weekly, vol. 39, no. 31, 31 July.

Sengupta, Nirmal. 1985. Irrigation: Traditional vs Modern, Economic and Political Weekly, special number, vol. 20, nos 45, 46, and 47, November.

Shah, Tushar and K.V. Raju. 1999. Rajasthan Minor Irrigation Tank Rehabilitation Project: Socio-Ecological and Organizational Assessment. New Delhi: Swedish International Development Agency.

Singh, K.K., Syed Turab-ul-Hasan, C. Sithapathi Rao, and George Kemuel. 1994. Promoting Farmers' Participation: Action Research in Sreeramsagar Project. In M.V.K. Sivamohan and Christopher A. Scott (ed.), India: Irrigation Management Partnerships. pp. 91–106. Hyderabad: Booklinks Corporation.

Sivasubramaniyan, K. 1997. Irrigation Institutions under Two Major System Tanks in Tamil Nadu. Review of Development and Change. Chennai: Madras Institute of Development Studies.

Sivasubramaniyan, K., R. Sakthivadivel, and A. Vaidyanathan. 2005. Farm Level Land and Water Productivity in Tank Irrigation: Some Methodological Issues. Fourth IWMI-Tata Annual Partners Meet. Anand, February.

Sophia, J.D. and B. Anuradha. 2005. Two Decades of Tank Rehabilitation in India: Livelihood Options and Gender Related Issues. Fourth IWMI-Tata Annual Partners Meet. Anand, February.

Tang, Shui Yan. 1992. Institutions and Collective Action: Self-Governance in Irrigation. San Francisco: ICS Press.

Vaidyanathan, A (ed.) 2001. Tanks of South India. New Delhi: Centre for Science and Environment.

CHAPTER **III**

ON ENERGY ACCESS

'Electricity is perhaps the most necessary and the most revolutionary thing which you can take into the rural areas. The moment you take electricity, all kinds of things begin to move. Petty industries grow up, agriculture is affected; everything is in fact affected. The whole life of the people is changed.'—Jawaharlal Nehru

Energy remains a critical input for transforming our rural landscape, with its scope ranging from lighting to cooking to irrigating our farms. Despite decades of focus, a plethora of policies and spending billions of taxpayers' money, adequate energy access for all countrymen remains a dream.

Our increasing rate of electrification has come at a huge environmental cost—India has the highest greenhouse gas GHG emissions for similar electrification rates, globally. Renewable power generation has grown exponentially, yet dependence on coal remains unchanged. Despite the historic announcement of complete electrification of India, as many as 32 million households remain in darkness without electricity.

While we have provided LPG connections to 2.5 crore households, nearly 12 crore households still use firewood for cooking, exposing the women and children to carcinogenic smoke. Access and affordability remain a challenge when it comes to clean cooking.

POWERING IRRIGATION PUMPS

Hari Yadav, a farmer in Azamgarh district in Uttar pradesh has a problem. His farm, a full 2 bighas of it, needs irrigation but the irrigation pump he has (a twelve-year-old standard 5 hp electric motor pump set) needs at least seven units of electricity and the electricity connection he has is erratic, offering electricity just a few times a month, through highly fluctuating and irregular voltage. His pump has burnt out a few times, but he has managed to rewind it locally, using poor-quality copper wires; that however has led to lower motor efficiency and even higher energy requirements. With the season approaching and canals mostly empty, his crops are in peril.

India has over 22 million agricultural connections for irrigation through electric pumps,[1] consuming over 22 per cent of total power generated in the country.[2] While electricity provided for agriculture remains heavily subsidized, encouraging wasteful consumption and reddening state electricity board balance sheets, such connections remain unreliable and offer limited supply. Given such a state, the large number of Indian farmers with agricultural connections tend to rely on diesel pumps, a significantly expensive proposition (9 million diesel irrigation pumps and 19 million electric irrigation pumps in 2010).[3] India's state governments typically incur ₹70,000—₹150,000 for every agricultural connection, all while farmers are charged ₹12,000 on average.[4] When providing grid-based connections to unelectrified villages, we tend not to consider the true cost of such connections. The discovery of this true cost can enable us to make the right decisions about which localized business models will work for electrifying our villages.

---

1   CEA, 2015
2   Planning Commission of India, 2014
3   Raghavan et al 2010
4   (Gopal B. Kateshiya, 2014; Iyer, 2013)

GATHERING FIREWOOD

Meena Kumari, from Jodhpur district, in Rajasthan, finds any reference to her daily work sourcing firewood as drudgery, whimsical. She and fellow women villagers, go off, outside village boundaries, into an arid landscape filled with shrubs and some trees, in a medley of song and banter, speaking about their mothers-in-law, deconstructing their husbands, and laughing about the local panchayat's antics. She makes aside references to lifting over 30–40 kg of firewood, gathering from the Aravallis, while walking in rubber slippers over rocky pathways and dirt-prone streets. Her work, she insists, is traditional and lets her escape the drudgery of her marriage and her status as a housewife, while enabling her to bond with fellow sufferers. When questioned about why her husband cannot gather wood, she laughs and insists that it's a woman's work; tradition has writ it so. It's the only income, in kind, she has—she barters some for food, some for toys; why give it up to the men?

Rajasthan relies heavily on firewood for cooking, with over 67.5 per cent of its energy coming from firewood.[5] Crop residue, as used in other states, is limited, so hiking the Aravalis is a must. Most traditional villages in Rajasthan use three stone hearths for cooking, leaving women prone to smoke and soot. High-efficiency stoves, while offering better health advantages, have mostly failed to meet the demands of local women—they can't accept the wide variety of wood fuel types that are available in Rajasthan while every piece of wood has to whittled down so that the improved stoves can accept it; an arduous task adding to an even more arduous one. Such improved stoves have ended up heating the tawa (griddle) inadequately—raising the temperature too much in the middle but not enough on the sides, leaving rotis inadequately baked. Most commercial stoves found in Rajasthan's local markets have ended up costing over three to four times that of the local traditional chula, leaving women bemused at the intentions of multilaterals and government officials talking of changing cooking habits.

---

5   http://timesofindia.indiatimes.com/city/jaipur/Raj-mostly-relies-on-firewood-for-cooking/article-show/52709810.cms

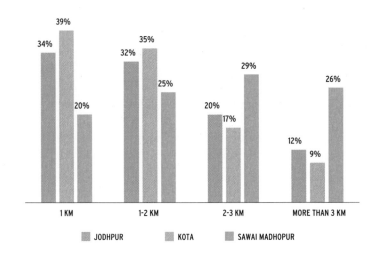

FIGURE 37: DISTANCE TRAVELLED WHEN COLLECTING FIREWOOD IN RAJASTHAN'S
HINTERLAND DISTRICTS (2003). NOT MUCH HAS CHANGED SINCE THEN[6]

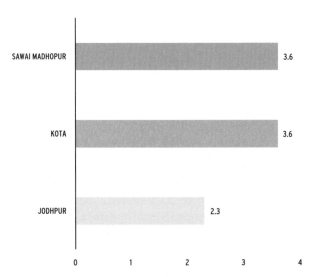

FIGURE 38: TIME TAKEN (IN HOURS) TO COLLECT FIREWOOD IN
RAJASTHAN'S HINTERLAND DISTRICTS (2003) [7]

---

6   Laxmi, V., Parikh, J., Karmakar, S., Dabrase, P., 'Household energy, women's hardship and health impacts
     in rural Rajasthan, India: need for sustainable energy solutions', Energy for Sustainable Development,
     Volume VII No. 1,, March 2003. Sourced from: http://citeseerx.ist.psu.edu/viewdoc/download;jsession-
     id=6B92D55182462E98041F8ACAECB90A38?doi=10.1.1.587.9603&rep=rep1&type=pdf

7   Ibid

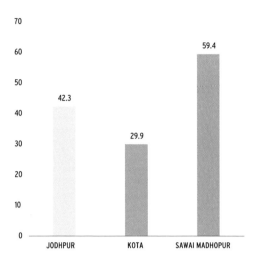

FIGURE 39: TIME SPENT, ON A MONTHLY BASIS, TO COLLECT FIREWOOD, IN RAJASTHAN (2003)[8]

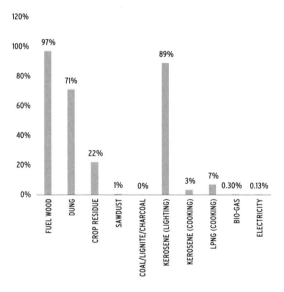

FIGURE 40: DISTRICT-WISE DISTRIBUTION USING DIFFERENT ENERGY SOURCES (2003)
IN JODHPUR DISTRICT. NOT MUCH HAS CHANGED SINCE THEN[9]

---

8   Laxmi, V., Parikh, J., Karmakar, S., Dabrase, P., 'Household energy, women's hardship and health impacts in rural Rajasthan, India: need for sustainable energy solutions', Energy for Sustainable Development, Volume VII No. 1,, March 2003. Sourced from: http://citeseerx.ist.psu.edu/viewdoc/download;jsession-id=6B92D55182462E98041F8ACAECB90A38?doi=10.1.1.587.9603&rep=rep1&type=pdf

9   Ibid

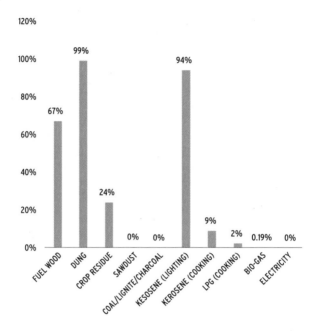

FIGURE 41: DISTRICT-WISE DISTRIBUTION USING DIFFERENT ENERGY SOURCES (2003)
IN KOTA DISTRICT. NOT MUCH HAS CHANGED SINCE THEN[10]

SOURCING COAL

Jauna Lugun wipes her brow while lifting about 8 kg of coal onto her head. The newly mined coal, found amidst mud and sand, in the coal mines in Godda, Jharkhand, was abandoned in waste dumps. When the coal mine was allocated, her family was one of the first to be evicted. Bereft of support and in poverty, she found an opportunity, scouring through the pocket mined landscape for poor quality coal that could be sold in rural markets as household fuel. Blasting in the mines is often a risk, with poisonous gases and rock dust around. She's heard of other threats—dumper trucks can come by suddenly on the edge of the mine, overthrowing tons of 'waste' topsoil, on to the artificial valley—some of her friends have ended up trapped. Her work is not regulated, and it definitely does not come under the Minimum Wage

---

10 Laxmi, V., Parikh, J., Karmakar, S., Dabrase, P., 'Household energy, women's hardship and health impacts in rural Rajasthan, India: need for sustainable energy solutions', Energy for Sustainable Development, Volume VII No. 1,, March 2003. Sourced from: http://citeseerx.ist.psu.edu/viewdoc/download;jsessionid=6B92D55182462E98041F8ACAECB90A38?doi=10.1.1.587.9603&rep=rep1&type=pdf

Act. The mining contractors chase her away sometimes, but she hasn't yet faced the threats that other women often do. If caught, she could be vulnerable to criminal prosecution—it usually ends up being sexual harassment, though. Her income is usually a pittance, about ₹50, if she's lucky—a testament to the rural hinterland she lives in. But it suffices to help feed her three kids sometimes. And if nothing sells, atleast she has coal to burn in her angithi.

Such pallid stories of rural displacement and consequentially, unregularized unemployment, have become uncommonly routine, in India's quest towards improving energy access. Officially, the Ministry of Tribal Affairs states that over 665,131 people (mostly tribals) across India were displaced by such industrial projects between 1999 and 2013 (IndiaSpend says the official data for just eleven states is 840,703[11]). The true number is probably far higher.

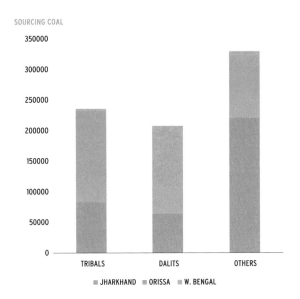

FIGURE 42: WALTER FERNANDES (2007) ESTIMATES THAT THE NUMBER OF INDIANS WHO HAVE BEEN DISPLACED BY MINING HAS BEEN 5 MILLION (1947—2000)[12,13]

---

11 http://www.indiaspend.com/investigations/state/anger-in-coal-rich-orissa-district-reflects-indias-flawed-mining-policies-99723

12 http://www.indiaspend.com/wp-content/uploads/MINES.doc

13 Fernandes, W., Mines, Mining and Displacement in India, Paper presented at the First International Mining Conference organized by Australian National University, New Delhi, November 19-21, 2007

VILLAGES AND HOUSEHOLDS
THAT NEVER GOT ELECTRICITY

A survey in 1974 in Odisha found that thirteen 'electrified' villages, notified as such by the state's public utility, had not a single household with access to electricity. The villages had had transmission wires and poles installed, but only up to the outside areas of the village boundaries. They lived in darkness, as they always had.[14] The village of Kusumasila, in Rayagada district, in Odisha, contains over sixty-five families below the poverty line. While they automatically come under the Rajiv Gandhi Grameen Vidyutikaran Yojana, their households continue to remain without electricity, given transformer issues that have been pending for years.

Despite the historic announcement of complete electrification of India, as many as 32 million households remain in darkness without electricity.[15]

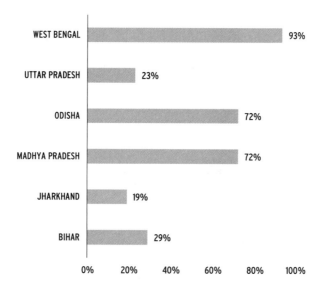

FIGURE 43: HOUSEHOLDS GETTING FOUR OR MORE HOURS OF EVENING SUPPLY (IN PER CENT) CONTINUES TO BE LOW IN UTTAR PRADESH AND BIHAR (2015)[16,17]

14   Report on the Evaluation of Rural Electrification Programme in Orissa, Government of Orissa, 1982

15   Mallapur, C., '96 per cent Villages Electrified. Yet (In 6 States) 31 per cent Homes Lack Electricity', IndiaSpend, Oct 1 2015. Soruced from: http://www.indiaspend.com/cover-story/96-villages-electrified-yet-in-6-states-31-homes-lack-electricity-85393

16   http://ceew.in/pdf/CEEW-ACCESS-Report-29Sep15.pdf

17   http://www.indiaspend.com/cover-story/96-villages-electrified-yet-in-6-states-31-homes-lack-electricity-85393

ENERGY POVERTY AND INEQUALITY

Over 32 million households living mostly in rural India have no access to electricity, the largest population segment in the world.[18] Most of these people live completely off the grid, while others persist with just token access to electricity. Many others have nominal connections, with power availability erratic.[19]

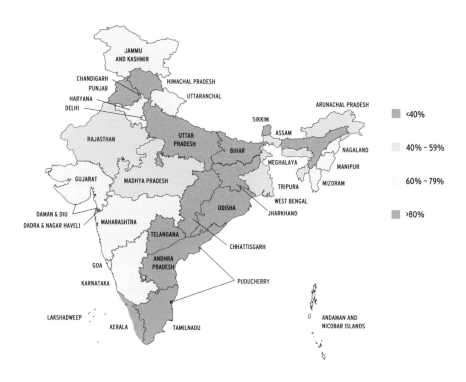

FIGURE 44: A SIGNIFICANT PROPORTION OF INDIA'S CITIZENS,
PARTICULARLY IN RURAL INDIA, LACK ACCESS TO ELECTRICITY[20]

---

18   World Bank Development Indicators, 2015; International Energy Agency, 2015.

19   Achieving universal electrification in India, Institute for Transformative Technologies, April 2016. Sourced from: https://assets.rockefellerfoundation.org/app/uploads/20160503122350/Achieving-Universal-Elec-trification-in-India.ITTReport.April2016.pdf

20   Census, Government of India, 2011.

It is not that progress has not been made. India's electricity production has jumped significantly over the last few decades. Since the economic reforms in 1991, India's electrification rate has jumped significantly, from 50 per cent in 1990 to nearly 80 per cent in 2015 (while the government seeks to close out the gap through the ongoing Deendayal Upadhyaya Gram Jyoti Yojana).

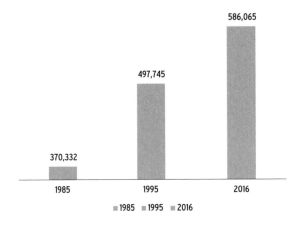

FIGURE 45: NUMBER OF VILLAGES ELECTRIFIED[21, 22]

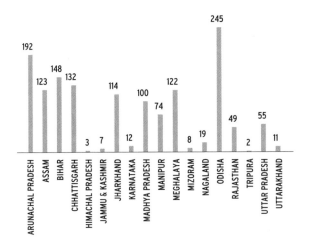

FIGURE 46: THE NUMBER OF VILLAGES WITH 100 PER CENT HOUSEHOLD ELECTRIFICATION CONTINUES TO REMAIN LIMITED EVEN AMONG RECENTLY ELECTRIFIED VILLAGES.[23]

---

21 Tamil Nadu Electricity Board & Ministry of Power, Govt. of India.

22 Indiastat Data.

23 Garv.gov.in; Accessed on 02-Jun-2018

This electrification, conducted through highly polluting coal power plants and environmental displacing hydro power plants, has raised India's environmental footprint and fostered health issues (India's coal power plants are supposed to cause the premature death of atleast 100,000 Indian citizens annually[24]). We are left facing a paradoxical challenge of improving access to electricity without raising our pollution levels.[25]

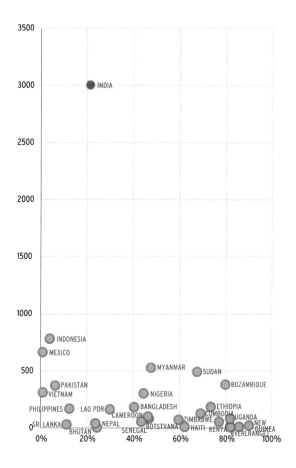

FIGURE 47: ELECTRIFICATION VS GREENHOUSE GAS EMISSIONS, WORLD BANK (2012)[26]

24   L. Friedman, Scientific American, 'Coal power in India may cause more than 100,000 premature deaths annually', 11 March 2013.

25   Achieving universal electrification in India, Institute for Transformative Technologies, April 2016. Sourced from: https://assets.rockefellerfoundation.org/app/uploads/20160503122350/Achieving-Universal-Electrification-in-India.ITTReport.April2016.pdf

26   World Bank, 2012.

This inexorable challenge—and it is one that the Republic has never managed to overcome—has had policymakers in a fix. The Government of India has established ambitious targets (175 GW of clean energy by 2022[27]) but coal still remains the primary source of our baseload energy. Rural electrification, particularly in the past, has often come to mean simply putting up poles and links to irrigation pumps, with the hope that household level electrification happens organically.[28] The provision of electricity, to rural India in particular, has for the past few decades been a subsidy focused affair, with little interest from the private sector. Even India's burgeoning clean tech sector seems likely to be focused on providing energy to urban areas, given better economics. With no major reforms, India looks to be aiming at a future when rural areas are provisioned by micro-grids and erratic supplies of electricity.

BETWEEN CENTRE AND STATE; PUBLIC AND PRIVATE

Prior to Independence, India's access to electricity was dismal, mostly prevalent only in certain major cities (a total of 1.7 GW; less than 1-2 per cent of India's current capacity). Bombay and Bengal dominated installed capacity in British India, while Mysore led the princely states.

This relatively privatized system was criticized by Constituent Assembly members as being irrelevant and inadequate to the task of powering development and provisioning electricity access for the vast rural masses. The 1948 Electricity Supply Act sought to rebalance the sector to 'provide for the rationalisation of the production and supply of electricity and generally for taking measures conductive to electrical development.'[29] The Act created institutional capacity, setting up the Central Electrical Authority and the State Electricity Boards (SEBs) that would help channel the case of electricity access. The Industrial Policy Resolution (1956) subsequently reserved electricity as a completely public domain. Various concerns were raised, particularly with respect to resolving electrification inequality—it was taken as the gospel that the state, unlike the private sector, with its varying motivations, had to be significantly involved in the development of electricity infrastructure, at least until sufficient demand had arisen for private sector interest. The private sector was deemed to focus on the cream of urban areas only— 'charging at the rate of 4 annas per unit, while under the terms of licence they

---

27   NDTV, 'PM Modi Stresses India's Commitment for 175 GigaWatts Clean Energy Goal', 28 September 2015.

28   The Hindu, 'Electrified, but without electricity', 7 October 2014.

29   Electricity Supply Act of 1948, Act No. 54 of 1948

could charge only 9 pies per unit.'[30],[31] Ultimately, as with most such debates in India, a compromise was reached—the existing systems would stay, while the state would take on a greater role. By 1951, over 300 private utilities, and a further 270 state and municipal utilities were generating electricity across India. Subsequent years of nationalization managed to alter this ratio significantly, with only forty-nine private and twenty-one municipality utilities generating electricity by 1976. The question of sustainability of SEB-focused expansion was often questioned. Many eminent legatees argued for greater autonomy to SEBs, in order to help break the link between the supply of electricity and the usage of electricity as a form of political patronage.

Post-colonial India considered the spread of electricity a civilizing mission. Electricity spending was usually a significant chunk of the budget, powered by a nationalist myth that it would bind the nation together while promoting development. Policy debates soon arose over the governance mechanism for such spending—state vs centre, public vs private, city vs rural, etc. Such issues still merit resolution—India has moved from British-era private utility companies to state-led management and expansion of electricity to a push again towards privatization in power generation and distribution. Regulation however has been kept with the centre, despite electricity being a subject in the Concurrent List of the Constitution.

Electricity exerted its own fascination on the body politic. While Nehru waxed eloquently about 'the peasants, whose villages were lighted up by electricity and much of whose farm work was done by electric power, began to get out of the old ruts and superstitions and to think on new lines', Mahatma Gandhi worried about the consequences of electricity expansion on local autonomy. B.R. Ambedkar thought that electricity was 'the surest means to rescue the people from the eternal cycle of poverty in which they are caught.'[32] Visions of railway like planning soon emerged, with Ambedkar further suggested that electricity should be considered like a 'strategic Railway' whose undertaking should be started without consideration of immediate profit. Engineers were soon predominant in policymaking. M. Visvesvaraya, the Dewan of Mysore State until 1919 and the author of its electricity expansion, laid out an economic plan for India in 1936, highlighting electricity as vital for industrialization.

The central government, in colonial times, was primarily in charge of laying out the broad regulation, while the various provinces actually constructed generation and distribution grids, in addition to granting licences and collecting relevant taxes. The 1935 Government of India Act restricted India's central government

30   Ayyanger, A. Constituent Assembly
31   Kale, S. S., Electrifying India, Stanford University Press, 2014
32   Rao, A., Caste Question

in regulating the electricity sector, while giving operational control to the states. Central planning soon met state execution and faltered. Different models were soon sought—the Tennessee Valley Authority project, created in 1933, to provide navigation, flood control, electricity generation, fertilizer manufacturing and economic development to the Tennessee Valley, was looked upon as a harbinger of things to come. The Damodar Valley Corporation was set up, with similar objectives, in West Bengal's Damodar River Valley. Central government intervention was deemed critical in solving collective action problems in the electricity generation and transmission sector.

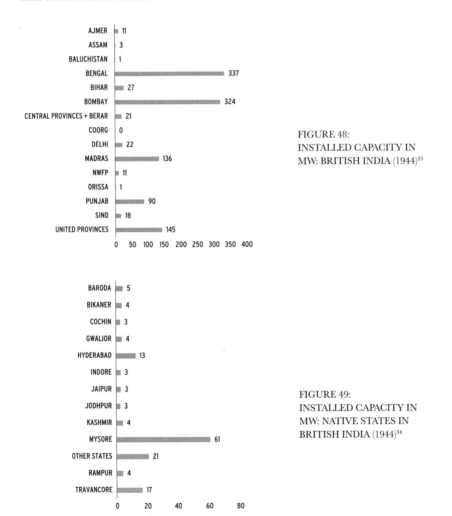

FIGURE 48:
INSTALLED CAPACITY IN
MW: BRITISH INDIA (1944)[33]

FIGURE 49:
INSTALLED CAPACITY IN
MW: NATIVE STATES IN
BRITISH INDIA (1944)[34]

33   Public Electricity Supply, All India Statistics (1944), Government of India Press, 1947
34   Ibid

A PLETHORA OF POLICIES

India's electricity policies, post-Independence, focused on creating a power infrastructure, with significant generation capacity added in the central and state public sector, giving priority to industries. Villages were increasingly left behind, with electrified villages rising from 3,000 in 1951 to just 22,000 in a decade.[35] Given the need for food self-sufficiency, rural household electrification received even less attention, with policymakers focused on increasing access to irrigation works and groundwater pumps. Soon enough, we started measuring rural electrification in terms of transmission line extensions, instead of the number of actual households electrified and receiving electricity regularly. With the share of subsidized agriculture increasing, while rural household electrification stayed mostly stagnant, state electricity boards soon faced rising fiscal deficits.[36] The Rural Electrification Corporation was established in 1969 to focus on financing and promoting rural electrification projects across the country, with partnerships with state electricity departments and state power corporations. Meanwhile, the power sector as a whole was challenged by multiple factors—inadequate investments in power generation, a high level of AT&C losses, provision of below-cost electricity rates, theft and a general deterioration in the balance sheets of state electricity boards. The provision of energy access to rural households was left behind—policymakers often considered the problem a case of simply financing power generation and transmission infrastructure.

A range of well-meaning schemes were launched. A Minimum Needs Programme, launched under the Fifth Five Year Plan, in 1974, sought to fund state electricity boards with grants and loans for rural electrification programmes in remote and geographically distanced villages.[37] Over the next few decades, the interest rate charged for these loans increased markedly, leading to SEBs shirking the option. The scheme was eventually merged with the RGGVY in 2005.

The Kutir Jyoti Scheme, launched in 1988–89, sought to provide single-point light connections to over 60 lakh below poverty line (BPL) households at a total cost of ₹450 crore (till 2004).[38] The scheme sought to offer outlays to state governments for providing target connections. The outlay was allocated on the basis of rural population below the poverty line and the level of rural electrification in villages. An additional one-time cost of service connection (including internal wiring) was

---

35 Maithani, P.C., Gupta, Deepak, 'Achieving Universal Energy Access in India', Challenges and the Way Forward, SAGE, Chapter 4, Page 43, 2015

36 Khandker, S., Barnes, D., Samad, H., 'Energy Poverty in Rural and Urban India', Policy Research Working Paper, 5463, World Bank, November 2010

37 Maithani, P.C., Gupta, Deepak, 'Achieving Universal Energy Access in India', Challenges and the Way Forward, SAGE, Chapter 4, 2015

38 Ibid

also offered. Given apathy in maintenance and unreliable electricity supply, rural beneficiaries were soon refraining from paying their electricity bills. The tariff was usually a flat rate, with connections not metered. The scheme was merged into the Accelerated Rural Electrification Programme in 2004.[39]

The Rural Electricity Supply Technology Mission was announced in 2001, with a focus on providing power to everyone by 2012.[40] It was soon rolled into the Pradhan Mantri Gramoday Yojana in 2002. States were offered additional central assistance (for special states—90 per cent grant, 10 per cent loan; for other states, 30 per cent grant, 70 per cent loan) and also discretion in utilizing the funds (as long as a Dalit/tribal basti was included in each un-electrified village being electrified). Even villages that were defined as electrified were, in reality, barely so. As highlighted by the Gokak Committee (2002),[41] SEBs were increasingly reluctant to take on additional rural electrification tasks, given that such additions were unsustainable for their balance sheets. State utilities, tasked with the maintenance of rural electricity infrastructure, had limited manpower to undertake this—new infrastructure rapidly corroded.

The Accelerated Rural Electrification Programme sought to encompass all previously launched schemes in 2004, while providing an interest subsidy of 4 per cent on loans that were taken by state governments/power utilities from various institutions (National Agricultural Bank and Rural Development, Power Finance Corporation, Rural Electrification Corporation etc).[42] The scheme sought to provide 40 per cent capital subsidy for rural electrification projects, with a focus on grid-based and standalone projects. The capital subsidy was linked to actual delivery of electricity to the targeted beneficiaries over a fifteen year period, with projects needing to demonstrate actual revenue stream.

In 2003, the Electricity Act was enacted, mandating the Universal Service Obligation, requiring the government to provide electricity to all areas, including remote villages (Section 6). It also sought the creation of a National Policy on Rural Electrification, with a focus on local distribution networks. The reforms also sought to enable distributed generation by freeing up standalone generation for generating and distributing power in any manner in off-grid areas. The Act effectively offered a framework for the provision of rural electricity, while enabling any person to set up, maintain and operate a generating plant along with transmission lines.

---

39   Sreekumar, S., 2011

40   Maithani, P.C., Gupta, D., 'Achieving Universal Energy Access in India', Challenges and the Way Forward, SAGE, Chapter 4, 2015

41   Gokak Committee Report on Distributed Generation, Ministry of Power, 2002. Sourced from: http://111.93.33.222/RRCD/oDoc/33_gokak.pdf

42   Maithani, P.C., Gupta, D., 'Achieving Universal Energy Access in India', Challenges and the Way Forward, SAGE, Chapter 4, 2015

Soon enough, by 2005, the National Electricity Policy was announced. It again sought to provide access to electricity for all households within five years, while ensuring that demand was fully met by 2012 by overcoming shortages and maintaining spinning reserves. It also aimed to increase the per capita availability of electricity above 1,000 units by 2012, with every household consuming a minimum of 1 unit per day by 2012. It sought to build an institutional framework for the provision of rural electricity, while making local utilities in partnership with local authorities, panchayats, NGOs, etc., responsible for the operation and maintenance of electricity infrastructure. It provided a pathway for captive power plants to gain access to licences and grid-interconnections for open-access consumers.

The Ministry of Power launched the Rajiv Gandhi Grameen Vidyutikaran Yojana (RGGVY) in 2005, with a focus on providing universal electricity access to all rural households by 2009, while again subsuming all previous programmes.[43] It appointed the Rural Electrification Corporation (REC) as the nodal agency for the programme's implementation. The programme sought to provide grid extension to 125,000 unlit villages, with a focus on connecting over 23.4 million BPL households. It also sought to remove discrimination against rural households vs urban households (a notification that was honoured only in abeyance). It sought to offer capital subsidies only if projects were implemented satisfactorily, with the subsidies converted into interest-bearing loans if the implementation lagged severely (again, a promise ignored). It strived to push the responsibility of regular electricity provision to such households on the state governments—their apathy soon led to a change in its requirements; by 2005, state governments were required to only provide a minimum daily supply of six to eight hours of electricity to the RGGVY network (the timing and continuity of six to eight hours was kept flexible; hence, most states were easily able to meet this).

Evaluations of the impact of the RGGVY on 1,000 villages in 150 districts in twenty states conducted by the REC through commissioned studies in 2011, highlighted that major states (Bihar, Maharashtra, Uttar Pradesh & even Haryana) failed to provide significant supply during peak hours. While many BPL households had gained connections, there remained significant gaps—a Greenpeace study in 2011[44] found that only 48 per cent of all BPL households surveyed in Uttar Pradesh who were entitled to a free electricity connection, actually received one, with supply provided only during the evening for about six to eight hours, essentially when not required. The purported franchisee system had failed to take off, with

---

43   Maithani, P.C., Gupta, D., 'Achieving Universal Energy Access in India', Challenges and the Way Forward, SAGE, Chapter 4, 2015

44   'Rajiv Gandhi Grameen Vidyutikaran Yojana Social Survey Report', Greenpeace India, April 2011. Sourced from: http://www.greenpeace.org/india/Global/india/report/AP%20RGGVY%20social%20 audit%20report%20FINAL.pdf

most ill-trained and focused only on collecting revenue. Above poverty line (APL) households were consistently ignored—with just 2.4 per cent in Bihar, and 3.4 per cent of APL households in Assam covered. According to the Integrated Research and Action for Development Report, Uttar Pradesh's situation was equally dismal, with just two of 1,536 APL households surveyed having a connection, while most APL households had had to pay ₹5,000 to ₹12,000 just get a connection. Any infrastructure set up in such villages was typically found to serve just 10 per cent of targets, with transformer and voltage burnouts having a concomitant impact. The vast majority of households (97 per cent) that the RGGVY targeted were found by Greenpeace to be buying kerosene for lighting, while a similar number had decided not to avail of an electricity connection for irrigation. A similar survey by Greenpeace[45] in 2011 in Madhubani district in Bihar had highlighted that at least 95 per cent of all covered BPL houses reported erratic electricity supply, with limited voltage, that too available mostly at night.

By 2006, the Rural Electrification Policy was notified. It sought to provide grid connectivity for rural households through the development of transmission systems, off-grid solutions for areas where grid connectivity was not feasible and adoption of solar photovoltaic lighting systems in places where offgrid systems and grid connectivity, were both not feasible. State governments were required to prepare and implement Rural Electrification Plans for providing access to all households. It also sought to change the definition of an electrified village—defining it as one where transmission infrastructure was available, and electricity was supplied to the locality along with any Dalit hamlets (atleast 10 per cent of all households have to be electrified in the village). Local distribution was to be managed by franchisees (the local cooperative, entrepreneurs or even an NGO) who could collect bills and provide customer service. More recently, the central government launched the Deendayal Upadhyaya Gram Jyoti Yojana (DDUGJY), aimed at separating agriculture and non-agriculture feeders, while augmenting rural transmission and distribution infrastructure.

---

45   Rajiv Gandhi Grameen Vidyutikaran Yojana Social Survey Report, April 2011. Sourced from: http://www.greenpeace.org/india/Global/india/report/RGGVY-_Madhubani_Report%20FINAL.pdf

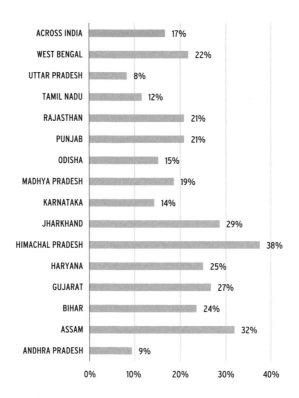

FIGURE 50: PERCENTAGE OF TRANSFORMERS BURNT OUT/DEFECTIVE
AND REPLACED IN SAMPLE SET OVER TWO YEARS (DATA AS OF 2013)[46]

---

46   Evaluation Report on Rajiv Gandhi Grameen Vidyutikaran Yojana (RGGVY)—May, 2014. Sourced
      from: https://data.gov.in/resources/replacement-burntdefective-transformers-sample-villages-du-
      ring-last-two-years-2013/download

PROGRESS OF VILLAGE ELECTRIFICATION

This set of well-meaning policies has mostly failed in meeting its targets. If we counted the number of villages purportedly electrified by the RGGVY and added them to villages electrified by previous policies, we would not have so many un-electrified villages left by now! The RGGVY, having failed to meet its targets by 2008, was quietly extended to 2012, with a focus on providing supply of reliable power to all BPL households. Hours of supply have never been strictly defined—the RGGVY considered six to eight hours of supply as ideal, but without specifying when they should be provided; consequentially, most states that could provide such supply did so during evening time hours; others provided it intermittently. While many villages have been electrified, this does not seemingly mean that all or even the majority of households in those villages have electricity. By 2011, over 91 per cent of all villages were declared electrified, with over 68 per cent of all rural BPL households connected; but this barely raised overall household electrification levels to 56 per cent.[47]

By 2018, while all villages were electrified, using the same definition, the overall household electrification level stood at 82 per cent, with state variations from 47 per cent to 100 per cent.[48] The provision of free electricity has helped raise connection levels among BPL households, although availability remains a significant ask. APL households, however, given the requirement to pay for a connection, and the erratic availability of power and effective voltage, have consistently chosen not to avail of electricity connections, perceiving them as an expensive, and unreliable, public good. Just 3 per cent of the total unconnected APL households (~54.6 million households) were connected between 2005 and 2011.

Our demographics make this a difficult ask. With our population rising, our electricity connection targets are a moving one (rural households rose by 29.5 million between 2001 and 2011; the number of rural household connections rose by ~32 million), keeping progress relatively stagnant. Most of our expected population increase is likely to happen in rural areas with limited government footprint, which happen to be precisely the areas where electricity connections remain the fewest.

Geographical remoteness plays its part as well. Most of India's unelectrified households remain clustered in rural pockets of Uttar Pradesh, Odisha, Bihar, Assam and Madhya Pradesh. In many of these areas, it might not be physically or economically feasible to provide grid access. Offgrid solutions will need to be explored as well.

---

47   Sreekumar, S., 2011

48   Hindustan Times, 30-Apr'18 Sourced from https://www.hindustantimes.com/india-news/household-elec-trification-level-in-rural-areas-is-more-than-82-centre/story-p9WwQbWzDFL4PfRoNVvTuO.html

Our definition of electrified villages needs to change as well. Our original, post-Independence, definition of an electrified village was one with any presence of electricity (say, for irrigation) in its revenue area. By 1997, the definition had been changed to one where electricity was being used in any of the inhabited localities. By 2004, a village was defined as electrified if it had basic electrical infrastructure (transformers, transmission lines, etc), with that electricity being provided to public places like schools and government offices and with atleast 10 per cent of the households electrified. This needed to be certified by the local panchayat as well. P. C. Maithini and Deepak Gupta (Achieving Universal Energy Access in India, Challenges and the Way Forward, SAGE, Chapter 4, 2015), note that an ideal definition would require atleast '50 per cent of the households and public places to have an actual connection' with electricity supplied for at least twelve hours, the majority of it during the night, when most needed. This should ideally be supported by a robust transformer with adequate capacity to manage the potential load of providing atleast 50–75 per cent of the population with 1 kWh per household per day. This arrangement would need to be sustained by monthly billing of the majority of the households, with some subsidies provided to BPL households.

We need to move away from simply erecting poles and installing transformers—we need to monitor whether actual supply is reaching households (Parliamentary Standing Committee on Energy, 41st Report, December 2013). The focus on the erection of poles and installation of transformers, instead of actually focussing on providing electricity, has caused some discrepancy in official declarations and ground reality in the past. For real-time dissemination of village electrification, the GARV app was made available, which would use inputs from Gram Vidyut Abhiyantas (GVAs) besides officials.

While claims of officials would reflect in the claims, the comments by GVAs would reflect ground reality. In some villages, power lines were installed but they were stolen before they could be charged. In others, no work was done on account of remote location, absent roads and Naxalite presence. In some cases, villages were declared electrified without any visit by the GVA, and if found otherwise, there was no way to reflect an electrified village as unelectrified. While these villages were electrified in official books, the ground reality was that people in these villages still suffered in darkness. In addition, data on electrification of some villages didn't make sense—as they were completely uninhabited or in forest areas.[49]

Our capacity utilization estimates need to be improved. Even the type of transformers we use remain prone to burnout. In Bihar, the use of low-capacity power transformers of the 16 and 25 KVA variety has been limited by its low

---

49   Samarth Bansal, The Hindu, 27th Feb 2017 Sourced from: http://www.thehindu.com/opinion/op-ed/On-paper-electrified-villages-%E2%80%94-in-reality-darkness/article14176223.ece

capacity (even irrigation needs are not met) and its tendency to burn out when power drawn (with or without theft) is way above expected load.[50]

By focusing on improving household connectivity, our planning ignored the requirements for local socio-economic development, stifling the prospects of any significant urbanization in these areas. We've aimed to provide energy access so that the poor can continue to subsist in their existence in a pre-industrial era; we should have instead aimed for building energy capacity for livelihood generation.[51,52]

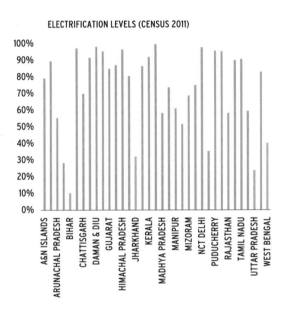

FIGURE 51: RURAL HOUSEHOLD ELECTRIFICATION LEVELS (SOURCE: CENSUS OF INDIA, 2011)[53]

Our focus remained on improving supply, instead of improving distribution, with a complete neglect of the demand side of energy access. Our policies assumed that household electrification would just happen—a consequence of increasingly electrified irrigation. SEBs and state utilities, while mandated to build infrastructure were not incentivized correctly to take up some uneconomic projects—the cost of implementing rural electrification was much higher than the revenues they could generate from such access; their balance sheets would eventually pay the price. Given their inherent, market-based preference for profitable consumers (mostly urban), applications for APL connections in the rural hinterland were continually delayed.

---

50   De, 2013
51   Sreekumar, S., 2011
52   Shankar, 2013
53   Census of India 2011

Once connected, maintenance of newly set up infrastructure was poor, leading to the cost of energy procurement rising. Soon enough, rural consumers, inured by decades of poor or no supply, started either avoiding the availing of connections or started stealing them. For state utilities, this proved a greater disincentive. The franchisee model, the great hope of operating last-mile connections, turned into a revenue collection mechanism, with limited focus on customer service. Franchisees have mostly failed to develop a sustainable revenue model.

Our central missions remained focused on solving the problem of funding of power generation projects, instead of actually monitoring service delivery and real-time sufficiency of power. Our rural electrification projects have been run mostly in a symbolic fashion, aiming to hit vague statistics, instead of aiming to reach revenue sustainability. Our one size-fits-all approach, across the entire country has failed to deliver energy access.

ELECTIONS AND ELECTRICITY

India's cabinet reshuffles can have unusual and rather far-reaching effects. Naresh Agarwal defected from the Congress party to the BJP in the UP assembly in 1997. He was soon appointed the state's Energy Minister—with his rural constituency, Hardoi, benefitting the most. His department was diligent enough to provide free power to his constituency, with even the most remote areas benefitting.[54] When he was removed from his cabinet post in August 2001, Hardoi experienced a steep decline in power supply, with electricity provision dropping back to pre-1997 levels.

Mulayam Singh Yadav's election as MLA from Gunnaur, in Uttar Pradesh, in a by-election in 2004, provided dividends to the rural constituency. Rural villages soon got electricity for over twenty hours a day, compared to not even having electricity poles in 2004. When Mulayam Singh was deposed as Chief Minister of Uttar Pradesh by Mayawati, the constituency was again plunged into darkness.

India's energy access stems from various factors—but public representatives have had the ability to distort this access at the local level for decades. Electrification is typically a coordinated activity, requiring approvals and actions at different levels across the state and rural governments. As such, opportunistic legislators and parties can easily manipulate and shape electricity access. As distribution is politicized,

---

54 'Caste adrift in India', The Economist, 7 February 2002. Sourced from: http://www.economist.com/node/976546

access can be provided and taken away easily given political considerations and priorities. Simply building electricity related infrastructure (transmission lines, transformers, etc.) is not a panacea and does not imply the actual delivery of services.[55]

Uttar Pradesh has historically been a state with regular power deficits. Its governments, whatever their political hue, have routinely sought to focus on redistribution and reallocation of electricity, instead of investments in increasing generation capacity. The result—Uttar Pradesh, which usually reports a significant power deficit (11.6 per cent in May 2015), regularly imports heavily from the central grid (typically two-third of its total power), despite the higher cost. Such decision-making is what enables Uttar Pradesh governments to routinely increase electricity provision on a temporary basis, particularly during elections.[56] A study on village electricity supply in 2002, prior to and after elections, in Uttar Pradesh (with a sample treatment set of 2,679 villages in twenty-nine constituencies which had switched to BSP support from BJP, compared to a control set of 3,223 villages in twenty-nine constituencies that retained BJP support) highlighted that Mayawati's ascendancy to the chief ministership led to 10 per cent of unlit villages that switched loyalties to BSP being lit by 2003 itself. This sudden bonanza highlights how BSP legislators were successful in improving their constituency village electrification.

CHALLENGES AND CONSTRAINTS

A number of challenges and constraints present themselves in scaling up sustainable electrification programmes. Energy access initiatives remain focused on meeting specific electrification targets, instead of a robust strategy that seeks to drive down costs—the initiatives are linked to subsidies that focus on capital costs; higher the capital cost, the higher the subsidy provided. Given a low initial level of demand from rural areas, most projects typically incur a high upfront capex and significant operational costs. Investors and entrepreneurs seeking opportunities in such arrangements are hence focused on ensuring cost recovery first and scale later. Providing them with greater assurance on cost recovery, in addition to providing a beneficial local ecosystem and effective on-ground facilitation is what the government should really be focusing on.

---

55   Chaudhary, et al (2006)

56   Min, Brian, 'Power and the Vote', Elections and Electricity in the Development World Cambridge University Press, 2015.

Uncertainty remains rife in such prospects. Every investor is likely to be concerned about payment issues associated with customer price points and delayed payments from government utilities; the prospect of default raises the need for security through high initial connection fees. The frequency of such payments raises further logistical challenges—a daily fee mechanism requires a larger on-ground presence than a monthly fee model. Another way to solve this conundrum would be to consider the incorporation of a feed-in tariff. In 2012, MNRE issued draft guidelines that sought to regulate off-grid power, with tariff collected from end-consumers, while the local Discom provides an additional feed-in tariff to the developer.[57] The Discom itself would be subsidized by the government for this feed-in tariff. MNRE sought to have this model applied to villages where less than six hours of electricity was provided (a questionable metric given that the hours are not defined) with a tariff set by the state utility. The local state government was asked to take on the responsibility of replacing batteries while subsidies covering 90 per cent of the total cost were proposed. Given this high subsidy driven mechanism, progress has been halting and slow. While power generation investors are already plagued with doubts about the ability of the government to provide a capital subsidy, asking them to await feed-in tariff on a regular basis from the local state utility would be a step too far. In addition, expecting the local state utility to realistically determine an appropriate consumer tariff could prove challenging, given variance in rural income, the cost of different energy sources and the availability of electricity. Until true scale is established in this sector, market prices and consumer willingness to pay should be allowed to prevail. Instead of fixed tariffs, let the market prevail.

Customer service can prove another key constraint—the high probability of breakdown of the transformers or other ancillary infrastructure needs a trained technician. The availability of local technical manpower, especially for photovoltaic systems, can be challenging.

---

57   13/14/2011-12/RVE, Government of India, Ministry of New and Renewable Energy, Remote Village Electrification Programme. Sourced from: http://www.indiaenvironmentportal.org.in/files/file/village_lighting_programme_scheme_2012_13_for_comments_feedback.pdf

COOKING FUELS

GATHERING FIREWOOD

Jhabua district in Madhya Pradesh is a rain-fed region. With an area of over 6,793 sq. km., hosting 1.3 million people, the district, compared to average Indian standards, seems sparsely populated. The villagers in this 90 per cent rural district are tribals, who live mostly below the poverty line.[58] Bhils like Ramesh Meena and his wife, Geeta, hailing from formerly pastoral adivasi tribes, chase clouds regularly. When the rains come, they engage in agriculture. About 20 per cent of the district is host to mostly degraded forests. When it comes to cooking, Geeta often sources firewood from the barren wastelands nearby. However, with tree cover going down, firewood is increasingly sparse (an average family like this typically uses 3.5 tonnes of firewood per year). To compensate, they must burn their crop waste instead.

UTILIZING GOBAR GAS

Soundarya Gundappa from Mulabagal Talu in Kolar district of Karnataka wipes her brow as she speaks. Crouched down to her knees, her repeated coughs highlight years of cooking using firewood, inhaling smoke and soot. Her house, surrounded by an arid landscape, has heaps of dung set in the corner, a reflection of her household's bovine wealth. Her days are better now, she says, as gas, piped in from a nearby community gobar gas plant, is available up for cooking. She had always thought it was normal for women to cough when cooking, a habit set by tradition.

India remains a pioneer in utilizing gobar-based gas plants, helping villagers use local resources in improving their cooking habits. Biogas systems take organic material like cow dung and kitchen waste, and utilize bacteria to help break it down and release biogas (a combustible mix of methane and carbon dioxide). A typical 3 m³ plant can cost ₹16,340, with the government providing 60 per cent of the subsidy while end-users usually contribute the remaining 40 per cent by providing in-kind raw materials (sand, gravel, stones and bricks) and labour.[59] An average gobar gas plant can also help save the environment—a typical plant can save 4 tonnes/year of equivalent CO2.

---

58   HDR, 1998
59   https://www.ashden.org/files/SKG%20full.pdf

STOVES

India's poverty is eminently highlighted in its stoves. The poorest typically use stones and firewood fires for cooking, with those slightly above the ladder utilizing mud stoves; with greater prosperity, comes access to metal and brick kilns, chimneys, and finally gas and electricity. Combusting biomass in such primitive stoves is a recipe for indoor air pollution (IAP)—with inherently high moisture content and long gestation period for cooking, most of the fuel is wasted as smoke or soot. Such pollution created especially fine particles and high levels of smoke (>30 times recommended health limits) and given repeated exposure especially for housewives, can have a deleterious impact on their health (a greater propensity for acute lower respiratory infection in children and pulmonary diseases in women).[60] Indoor air pollution can also raise the risk of cardiovascular diseases, perinatal mortality and even cataract.[61] The World Health Organization (WHO) states that indoor air pollution from solid fuel combustion is the fourth major health risk in developing countries.[62] IAP is estimated to lead to 2 million premature deaths annually and remains the leading health hazard in India, far more than tobacco use, malaria or tuberculosis.[63,64] Such traditional stoves, while being difficult and time consuming to use, can leave one worse in health over the long term.

60 'Lung health consequences of exposure to smoke from domestic use of solid fuels', International Union against Tuberculosis and Lung Disease, 2009. Sourced from: http://www.theunion.org/what-we-do/publications/english/pub_indoor-air-pollution_eng.pdf

61 Ekouevi, K.; Tuntivate, V. 2012. Household Energy Access for Cooking and Heating: Lessons Learned and the Way Forward. A World Bank Study. Washington, DC: World Bank. © World Bank. Sourced from: https://openknowledge.worldbank.org/handle/10986/9372 License: CC BY 3.0 IGO

62 World Health Report, WHO, 2002. Sourced from: http://www.who.int/entity/whr/2002/en/whr02_en.pdf?ua=1

63 Mathers C. D., Loncar D, Projections of global mortality and burden of disease from 2002 to 2030, 2006

64 http://www.iiasa.ac.at/web/home/research/Flagship-Projects/Global-Energy-Assessment/GEA-Summary-web.pdf

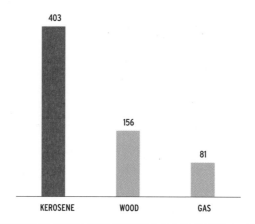

FIGURE 52: AVERAGE PARTICULATE CONCENTRATION
EXPOSURE ACROSS FUEL TYPES FOR COOKS[65,66,67]

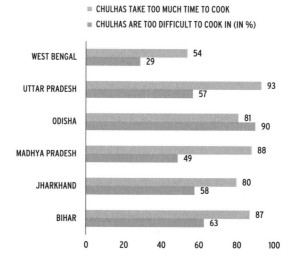

FIGURE 53: A LARGE NUMBER OF RURAL USERS FIND USING
TRADITIONAL STOVES DIFFICULT AND TIME-CONSUMING[68]

65   Barnes, D., Kumar, P., Openshaw, K., 'Cleaner Hearths, Better Homes', New Stoves for India and the developing World, Oxford, 2012

66   Balakrishanan et al, 2004

67   World Bank, 2012

68   Mallapur, C., 95% Rural Homes Use Wood, Dung For Cooking In 6 States, Indiaspend, October 2, 2015. Sourced from: http://www.indiaspend.com/cover-story/95-rural-homes-use-wood-dung-for-cooking-in-6-states-67095

SOURCING FIREWOOD

Wood fuel continues to be consumed in several forms—logs, twigs, wood shavings, sawdust[69]—with forest areas contributing 46 per cent of India's total firewood but we cut down our forests to cook. Estimates suggest that we remove over 400 million m^3 worth of fuelwood annually, while the annual allowable cut from government forests is just 66.7million m^3;[70] fuelwood regularly meets at least 40 per cent of the total energy needs of the country.

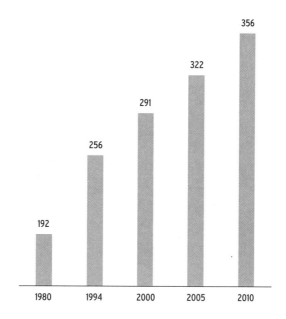

FIGURE 54: CONSUMPTION OF FUELWOOD (MILLION TONNES)[71]

Collecting this biomass can require significant effort and consumes the greater part of the day for women in remote hilly areas. Meanwhile, just the preparation of dung cakes can leave women vulnerable to faecal and skin infections; those producing charcoal are susceptible to smoke poisoning.[72]

69   Ahmed, 1997, Asia-Pacific Forestry towards 2010. Rome: Forestry Policy and Planning Division

70   Forest Survey of India, 1988

71   FAO,1999

72   Batliwala, S., and Reddy. A.K.N. 1996. 'Energy for Women and Women for Energy (Engendering Energy and Empowering Women)'

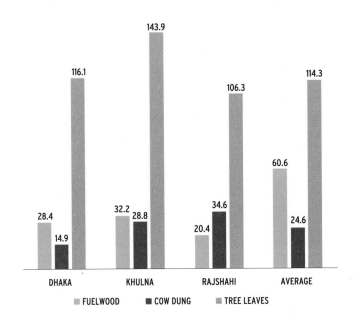

FIGURE 55: ANNUAL BIOMASS COLLECTION TIME (HOURS PER HOUSEHOLD)[73]

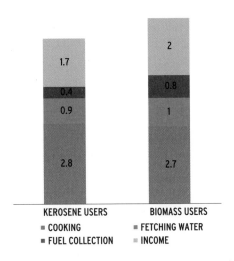

FIGURE 56: MEAN HOURS PER DAY FOR WOMEN'S TIME ALLOCATION IN RURAL INDIA (1996)[74,75]

73   Asaduzzaman, M., Barnes, D., Khandker, S., Restoring Balance: Bangladesh's Rural Energy Realities, International Bank for Reconstruction, 2009
74   World Bank, 2004
75   Barnes, D., Kumar, P., Openshaw, K., 'Cleaner Hearths, Better Homes', New Stoves for India and the developing World, Oxford, 2012

Over 90.5 per cent of all rural households used solid fuels for cooking in 1994, a fact that barely changed by 2000, despite economic growth.[76] Even by 2010, 87 per cent of all rural households were still using firewood and wood chips, in addition to cow dung cakes.[77] Only the richest 20 per cent of all rural Indians have managed to gain access to LPG. Others who were lucky to own cattle also had the chance to use biogas. The indoor air pollution issue remains one that troubles the forgotten majority of India.

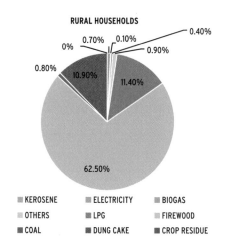

FIGURE 57: RURAL HOUSEHOLDS—
PRIMARY COOKING FUEL (2011)[78]

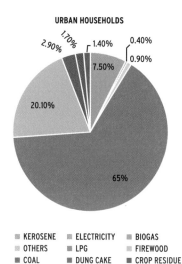

FIGURE 58: URBAN HOUSEHOLDS—
PRIMARY COOKING FUEL (2011)[79]

---

76   50th NSS round
77   NSSO Report on Household Consumption, 66th Round, 2009-10
78   Census of India, 2011
79   Ibid

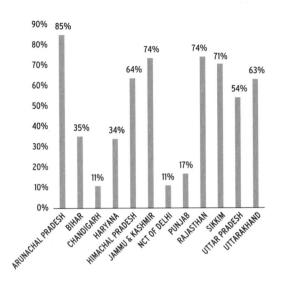

FIGURE 59: FIREWOOD CONSUMPTION AS A COOKING FUEL CONTINUES TO REMAIN
HIGH IN HILLY AND BACKWARD STATES[80]

TABLE 46: COOKING FUEL SOURCES CONTINUE TO VARY SIGNIFICANTLY ACROSS STATES[81]

STATE	FIRE-WOOD	CROP RESIDUE	COW DUNG CAKE	COAL, LIGNITE, CHARCOAL	KEROSENE	LPG/PNG	ELECTRICITY	BIOGAS	ANY OTHER
ARUNACHAL PRADESH	85%	1%	0%	0%	0%	13%	0%	0%	0%
BIHAR	35%	35%	23%	0%	0%	3%	0%	0%	1%
CHANDIGARH	11%	0%	1%	0%	18%	67%	0%	0%	0%
HARYANA	34%	21%	20%	0%	0%	24%	0%	0%	0%
HIMACHAL PRADESH	64%	1%	0%	0%	2%	33%	0%	0%	0%
JAMMU & KASHMIR	74%	3%	5%	0%	0%	16%	0%	1%	0%
NCT OF DELHI	11%	2%	4%	0%	8%	75%	0%	0%	0%
PUNJAB	17%	10%	30%	0%	2%	39%	0%	2%	0%
RAJASTHAN	74%	14%	3%	0%	0%	8%	0%	0%	0%
SIKKIM	71%	1%	0%	0%	3%	24%	0%	0%	0%
UTTAR PRADESH	54%	10%	28%	0%	0%	6%	0%	0%	0%
UTTARAKHAND	63%	2%	4%	0%	1%	29%	0%	1%	0%

Given the deleterious impact of using traditional stoves, significant research has
been conducted for improving stove options (biomass, charcoal, LPG and electric
ones), with a significant number approaching economic parity. A study published
in January 2016 showed that from an individual perspective, there were significant
time and health benefits from using improved stoves after deducting fuel costs.

80   Census of India, 2011. Sourced from: https://data.gov.in/resources/households-availability-sepa-
      rate-kitchen-and-type-fuel-used-cooking-2011/download
81   Ibid

At a program level, after deducting costs for stove design and promotion, such options were attractive, given societal losses from black carbon (organic carbon, CO) emissions from traditional stoves. Biomass stoves, given their limited energy savings, offer the most limited set of benefits. Estimates suggest that global net benefits of shifting from traditional to various improved stoves could be between $18—54 billion per year.[82]

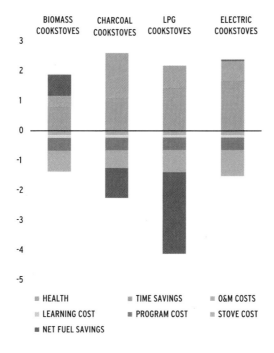

FIGURE 60: COST/BENEFIT, AT AN INDIVIDUAL LEVEL, PER MONTH,
ACROSS DIFFERENT IMPROVED STOVES ($/HH-MONTH)[83]

India's public policy has mostly neglected the potential for improvement of rural stoves, with the IAP problem remaining mostly unnoticed by policymakers for decades.[84] While the technology for improving stoves has existed for decades, its economics were open to question. India launched the National Project on Biogas Development (renamed in 2003 as National Biogas and Manure Management Programme) in 1981, with a focus on building capacity to meet cooking energy needs and providing high quality manure for farming. The Integrated Energy Policy,

82   Larson, 2014
83   Jeuland, M., Soo, Jie-Sheng Tan, 'Analyzing the costs and benefits of clean and improved cooking solutions', Clean Cookstoves, January 2016. Sourced from: https://cleancookstoves.org/binary-data/RE-SOURCE/file/000/000/459-1.pdf
84   Barnes, et al, 2012

in 2006, considered the matter but sought to have a larger number of fuel wood plantations, while assuming that subsidized LPG would be provided to a significant proportion of the rural population. The National Improved Cookstove Initiative was launched in 2009 but dithered soon enough. India's policies have considered the issue low-priority, one that could eventually be solved by the expansion of the LPG network.

The National Programme for Improved Cookstoves (NPIC) was launched in 1983 to help promote wood conservation, reducing smoke emission and limiting the drudgery that women and children put themselves through in rural India to gather firewood. The programme sought to increase fuel efficiency, through the Ministry of Non-Conventional Energy Sources and state-level agencies. By 2002, the programme had distributed over 35 million improved stoves (mostly mud and steel based), against a potential target of 120 million. Usage crept up over the years, with 60 per cent of the handed out stoves in use by 1996. Facing slow growth, the programme soon shifted towards focusing on fixed-type improved cookstoves that came with chimneys and able to last five years. By 2003, the programme was shifted towards the states, with subsequent dissolution. For all its effort, by 2006, only 5 per cent of all households had improved stoves.[85] The majority of such adopted cookstoves had poor quality, with little maintenance, lasting a lifetime of less than two years. While stove production with inexpensive local materials kept costs low, their performance offered only a rudimentary improvement over existing devices. The commercialization of such devices, along with after-sales support, was considered irrelevant, while the provision of large subsidies tragically prevented the development of markets in improved stoves while discouraging users from maintaining them well. Most designs were not created after interaction with rural households, and had very few in-field user trials before release. Chimney covers, in particular, proved to be difficult to manage for most users, with the majority of the consumers shifting back to their old stoves. Instead of improving health, the programme created dependency. However, this programme also proved to be the genesis of a range of private, NGO and state programmes.

Even Arvind Panagariya, formally Vice Chairman, NITI Aayog, highlights the failure of India's clean cooking strategy—'What has held back the country from including electricity in the national strategy? Perhaps, we chose to go for a two-pronged strategy—LPG for urban India, and biomass for rural India. To be sure, we tried to usher in efficiency in biomass cooking by promoting improved cook-stoves (normal one and forced-draft type) but until the recent decision to take LPG to rural India, our strategy remained confined to looking for stoves that would minimize the emission of smoke indoors. Hence, it may be stated that for rural

---

85   Zhang, et al, 2006

India, which comprises 69 per cent of the nation's population as per 2011 census, we have had no 'clean cooking fuel' strategy until recently. Instead, we only had an 'efficient-cook-stove' strategy.' The number of households without clean cooking today is more than twice that without electricity.[86] This state of affairs highlights the paradox of policymaking in this arena—despite clear benefits of using improved stoves; a range of such programmes has suffered from low adoption rate and a lack of eventual usage.[87]

In comparison, China launched the world's largest improved stove programme in the early '80s, covering 186 million of its 236 million rural households by 1998.[88] The programme offers a 26 per cent subsidy and sought to cover the entire population. Its success was primarily due to significant decentralization, with quality control kept through central production of critical components (e.g. combustion parts), while keeping the product reliable and innovative through regular design competitions. Designs were regularly improved, upwards with technical work done at national design centres with high engineering standards and a number of user trials, while standardization prevailed. Central government funding was limited, while payments were provided to local governments only when independent reviews of their achievements were conducted. Assembly and maintenance was allowed only by specialized and certified artisans (compared to a free for all in India), leading to longer stove life.

For India, improving the basic design of stoves to increase combustion efficiency, ventilation and overall heat transfer can have a significant impact on IAP, with reported reductions in child pneumonia.[89] Replacing inefficient and primitive stoves with well-designed ventilated ones could have significant environmental impact as well, annually saving 196 MT of solid fuel (95 MT wood; 6 MT coal) for the replacement of 150 million stoves; India's total estimated greenhouse emissions could fall by 4 per cent through this simple shift.[90]

---

86 http://niti.gov.in/writereaddata/files/document_publication/NITIBlog28_VC-AnilJain.pdf

87 Barnes et al. 1994, Ruiz-Mercado et al. 2011, Hanna et al. 2012, Gall et al. 2013

88 Maithani, P.C., Gupta, Deepak, 'Achieving Universal Energy Access in India', Challenges and the Way Forward, SAGE, 2015

89 Smith K. R., McCracken J. P., Weber M. W., Hubbard A., Jenny A., Thompson L. M., Balmes J., Diaz A., Arana B., Bruce N., Effect of reduction in household air pollution on childhood pneumonia in Guatemala (RESPIRE): a randomised controlled trial, Lancet, 2011. Sourced from: https://www.ncbi.nlm.nih.gov/pubmed/22078686

90 Venkataraman, C. Sagar, A.D. Habib, G. Lam, N. Smith, K.R. The Indian National Initiative for Advanced Biomass Cookstoves: The benefits of clean combustion, Energy for Sustainable Development Volume 14, Issue 2, June 2010, Pages 63—72. Sourced from: http://www.sciencedirect.com/science/article/pii/S0973082610000219

BIOGAS

Meanwhile, biogas (60–65 per cent methane, 35–40 per cent carbon dioxide, 0.5–1 per cent hydrogen sulphide) has proven popular. Biogas is the product of anaerobic digestion by methanogenic bacteria of fermentable organic materials (cattle dung, kitchen waste, night soil waste, poultry droppings and agricultural waste). This combination of gases has an average calorific value of 20 MJ/m^3 while being 20 per cent lighter than air. Biogas is similar in composition to CNG and can be used for all the latter's applications. In addition to biogas, this process also produces a digested slurry from biogas plants that can be utilized as manure in agriculture.

The National Project on Biogas Development was launched in 1981, with a successful track record of designing biogas plants that were suitable across geographies and met local needs. Models were standardized regularly, for individuals and communities alike, while extensive infrastructure was created to help conduct construction and maintenance. Over 4.5 million family-type biogas plants were set up by 2013, reaching ~40 per cent of the country's potential. By 2011, over 1.1 million households had their cooking needs met through biogas plants.[91] Larger subsidies (₹8,000 per plant) have helped boost numbers, with annual targets regularly above 1.5 lakh plants. The programme is a successful example of a top down central government-driven project that has led to results and considered maintenance.[92]

However, it did have some issues. The Planning Commission's study (2002) on the project found that a majority of biogas-using households were well-to-do farmers (the average size of cattle holding for owners was 5.23), while just 45 per cent of all the plants were working properly.[93] Despite considerable effort, only 7 per cent of the total number of households in the sample villages were found to be using biogas, that too mostly as a supplementary fuel. Plant maintenance issues, along with non-availability of cattle dung, pipeline leakage & corrosion and the easy availability of substitutes meant that a number of plants were increasingly non-functional. While state-level biogas cells were significantly overstaffed, on-ground maintenance faced staffing deficiency, which led to inadequate supervision during construction and maintenance. The programme was spending ₹3,000 (in 2002) on installing every new plant (a sum on which at least three non-functional plants could be revived). While family-type biogas plants were highly favoured, promotion of community biogas plants was increasingly discontinued due to a lack of uptake. With a larger number of member stakeholders, non-contribution of

---

91   National Census, 2011

92   Public Accounts Committee, 96th Report, 30th April 1987

93   Planning Commission, Evaluation Study On National Project on Biogas Development, May, 2002.
      Sourced from: http://planningcommission.nic.in/reports/peoreport/peoevalu/peo_npbd.pdf

dung, monthly maintenance charges and labour availability, in addition to disputes over gas availability led to non-cooperation amongst members. The further scale-up of biogas plant programmes thus remains limited.

Large-scale usage of biogas plants remains constrained by this preference for family-type biogas plants, in addition to easy substitutability by alternative fuels (biomass, firewood, etc.). The social and economic viability of community-based biogas plants need to be significantly improved.

LPG DISTRIBUTION

The government has sought to roll out LPG as an alternative to kerosene. The preference for LPG led the government to launch the Rajiv Gandhi Gramin LPG Vitaran Yojana (RGGLVY) in 2009, with a focus on setting up small-size, low-cost LPG dealerships in rural areas. The programme sought to increase the population covered to 75 per cent by 2015, through the distribution of 55 million LPG connections in rural areas (by early 2015, 4,183 agencies were commissioned to focus on the initiative). Each distributor was expected to recover their initial capital expenditure within 1,800 connections, while earning a monthly income approximating ₹7,500. LPG cylinders weighing just 5 kg were launched in hilly areas. The initiative has been mostly a failure, with just 7 per cent of the rural population using LPG by February 2015[94] (the Global Alliance for Clean Cookstoves estimates it at 12 per cent in 2013;[95] Indian Oil says there are 9.5 million rural consumers).[96] The government has tried to improve the subsidy schemes for kerosene—the Direct Benefit Transfer (DBT) Kerosene Scheme has been proposed (Jharkhand launched it at a state level in October 2016), which combined with improved biometrics has been significantly successful.

Even for cooking, subsidized LPG provides a healthier and cheaper (at consumer level) option as fuel.[97]Assuming an average of 9.9 cylinders per household per year (equivalent of 197 litres of kerosene annually), a household spends ~₹256/month to ₹382/month on cooking fuel for subsidized and unsubsidized LPG, respectively,

94   Padmanabham, D., 'Rural India's LPG Failure Kills People, Changes Weather', IndiaSpend, 20 February 2015. Sourced from: http://www.indiaspend.com/cover-story/rural-indias-lpg-failure-kills-people-changes-weather-29044

95   http://cleancookstoves.org/resources_files/india-cookstove-and-fuels-market-assessment.pdf

96   Maithani, P.C., Gupta, D., 'Achieving Universal Energy Access in India', Challenges and the Way Forward, SAGE, 2015

97   Jain. & Ramji., Reforming Kerosene Subsidies in India: Towards Better Alternatives, CEEW, 2016

on NPV basis, whereas it spends as much as ~₹588/month if it uses kerosene on an NPV basis. The transition of such households to subsidized cylinders shall reduce their monthly cooking fuel spend substantially and increase the government's LPG subsidy outgo—which may be reduced further through the Give it Up campaign. As of March 2016, as per official estimates, the number of consumers who have given up LPG subsidy stand at 8.22 million, helping the government save as much as ~4,166 crore in subsidy outgo. The official estimates remain challenged by the Comptroller & Auditor General (CAG) of India saying that the total savings on account of direct bank transfers and voluntary forsaking of LPG subsidy were less than ₹2,000 crore, not even 10 per cent of the savings claimed by the government over 2014–15 and 2015–16 through these two initiatives.[98]

The main issues in converting people to LPG from kerosene as a cooking fuel are administrative and economic. The urban poor, majority of times migrated labour from other states, do not have proof of residence or even recognized residence, and this lack of address proof acts as a hindrance in getting an LPG connection. With DBT of subsidy in case of LPG connections, OMCs can take proactive measures to reduce administrative hurdles in getting LPG connections. An important contention comes from unauthorized slums—recognition of such addresses shall risk providing legal sanctity to unauthorized occupation, yet some steps need to be taken to ensure that this particular strata of society does not get left out. We can also look at smaller cylinder sizes, with existing kerosene dealers being asked to stock smaller cylinders, which, even unsubsidized cost less than the expense of cooking with non-PDS kerosene. This ensures that those dealers who might lose their livelihood on removal of kerosene have an alternative means of livelihood. Smaller cylinder sizes will also prove to be a synergistic option economically for economically weaker sections of society. The government's decision to provide a boost to sales of 5 kg mini gas cylinders at petrol pumps and even grocery stores with minimal paperwork can hike LPG usage and eventually help in complete phasing out of kerosene for cooking purposes.

---

98   TCA Sharad Raghavan, The Hindu, Sep 2016 Sourced from: http://www.thehindu.com/news/national/
      CAG-audit-nails-Centre%E2%80%99s-claim-on-LPG-subsidy-saving/article14499201.ece

SUBSIDIES

Subsidies remain a powerful tool, which can help achieve a broad set of pre-defined social, financial and environmental objectives—as long as prudent and efficient fiscal management and resource allocation are conducted. However, in India, subsidy management has become an opaque process, one that has degenerated into a complex maze, with various doorkeepers, while efficiency and clarity are lost for the needy villager.

SUBSIDIZING ELECTRICITY

Free electricity aside, India's electricity regime is a complex mix of subsidies and regulations. All states have different policies and different tariff rates—even within the same state, tariff rates are different for different types of consumers. Addition of capital subsidies to state utilities alongside consumer subsidies further complicates matters. Even within a state and with one particular type of consumer—be it residential, commercial, industry, agriculture or railways—various sub-categories are defined, based on consumption levels. The lack of symmetry in the definition of sub-categories among various states is further complicated by different tariffs for urban and rural areas. While a subsidy definition based on classification is complex, its administration impacts state utilities. With the aim of meeting social objectives, tariffs are kept low and subsidy is announced to state utilities as compensation, better called 'subsidy booked'. While Section 65 of the Electricity Act, 2003, clearly calls for advance payments for a party affected by subsidy grants in a manner directed by the state commission, the rule is commonly flouted by states themselves. The payments or 'subsidy released' is often delayed and less than 'subsidy booked'. All this has one major consequence—state electricity boards (SEBs) end up reddening their balance sheets.

The poor financial health of SEB is not a new thing. In 1964, the Venkatraman Committee was instituted to improve the financial health of SEBs. The amendments in 1956 to the Electricity Supply Act of 1948 provided the states with more power in electricity policy (eroding autonomy of SEBs), and in order to attract industries, despite calls for equitable power pricing, industries were provided power cheaper than the marginal cost of production, whereas tariffs in residential and rural areas offset the losses. SEBs ran into losses, given huge losses on industry supply (not fully offset from rural and residential areas) which hindered their capacity to invest further in a capital intensive sector (fact: In the mid '60s, households consumed 8 per cent of electricity and contributed 22 per cent of revenues). So, while SEBs paid a high cost for connecting to the hinterland, it disincentivized proper usage of electricity and bled itself through subsidies to industries. Moreover, with states being all-powerful in guiding utilities, the evolution of electrification has varied across states and been heavily influenced by politically powerful agrarian interests.

The 'power for all' scheme envisions power for all Indians and all regions by 2019—the goal remains a challenging one. The supply scenario remains robust, with muted coal prices, coal field auctions and the government's target to mine 1 billion tonnes of coal by 2019 presenting factors for stability in power generation. Mounting financial losses, operational inefficiencies and grid indiscipline mean that SEBs continue to sink deeper into losses, while end-consumers get no respite.

Rising debt, sinking net worth and accumulated losses just form the symptoms of a fiscally profligate power tariff policy adhering to populism.

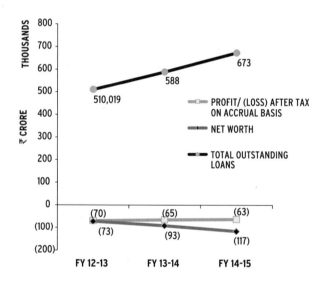

FIGURE 61: STATE ELECTRICITY BOARD HEALTH CONTINUES TO REMAIN POOR (2015)[99]

99   Ministry of Power, 2016

The main challenge faced by SEBs is their poor financial health. The aggregate book losses (on accrual basis) of all the state power utilities decreased from ₹65,286 crore in 2013–14 to ₹63,355 crore in 2014–15, with Maharashtra, Gujarat and Delhi being the few states that earned a profit. On the other hand, Uttar Pradesh, Rajasthan and Tamil Nadu suffered huge losses, to the tune of ₹44,839 crore combined, representing as much as 71 per cent of the entire losses by SEBs across the nation. The northern and southern states represent the highest share in losses—accounting for as much as 80–87 per cent of the losses (after tax) on accrual basis, for FY12–13 to FY14–15.

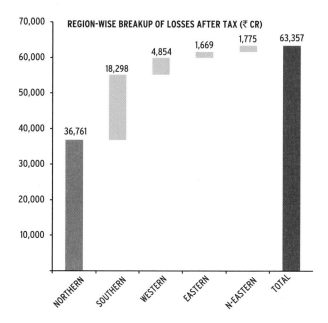

FIGURE 62: STATE ELECTRICITY BOARD LOSSES, ACROSS REGIONS (2015)[100]

Consider the debt scenario—for the year ending March '20, as many as thirty-five utilities out of ninety-nine had negative debt to equity ratio—meaning that the net worth of the company is negative or simply, the cumulative loss is more than the equity itself. Most banks would not even lend to such companies/utilities unless there are special circumstances or they have assets to pledge. Similarly, forty-four companies have debt-to-equity ratio greater than one, which underscores their dependence on using debt to fund their operations. Only twenty companies have their debt-to-equity ratio less than one.

100 Ministry of Power, 2016

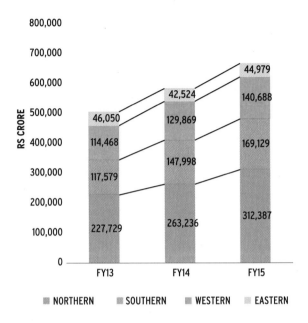

FIGURE 63: GROWTH IN SEB DEBT, ACROSS REGIONS (FY15)[101]

The figure above demonstrates the growth in SEB debt from FY12–13 to FY14–15, registering a CAGR of 15 per cent. Consider Uttar Pradesh Power Corporation Limited—the utility had its total debt increase by ₹20,403 crore in two years, with state loans growing by ₹22,827 crore in the same time. The interest payment itself assuming 9 per cent interest rate on incremental debt, would amount to ~₹1,836 crore. During the same time, its financial performance has deteriorated—while revenue has increased by 36 per cent (from ₹26,630 crore to ₹36,140 crore) its expenditure has increased by 50 per cent in two years (from ₹30,109 crore to 45,050 crore) leaving its losses to multiply ~2.6 times (from ₹3,479 crore to ₹8,910 crore). Similar is the case with other utilities. Deteriorating financial performance with increasing debt remains the norm. An interesting aspect is that while the cause of such debt is mostly the fiscally profligate power policy by the state, a majority of the loans do not come from the state government, but from other banks and financial institutions.

Approximately 90 per cent of all outstanding debt is from banks—even the increase in outstanding debt from FY12–13 to FY14–15 of ₹163,038 crore is financed mostly from bank debt—banks paid ~₹152,747 crore of the incremental debt.

101   Ministry of Power, 2016

Such loans have proved to be a bane for the banking sector NPAs—while power sector accounts for 8.3 per cent share in advances for all Scheduled Commercial Banks (SCBs), it accounts for 16.1 per cent share in stressed assets (Financial Stability Report, Issue 11, June 2015). For public sector banks, the power sector accounts for the highest stressed advances at 17.3 per cent of their total stressed advances. The probability of these stressed advances slipping into Non-Performing Assets (NPAs) is high—with restructured loans for ₹53,000 crore and non-payment of principal amount for matured loans worth ₹43,000 crore for more than a quarter (March—June 2015), the banks continue to treat them as stressed advances. The Ministry of Finance report acknowledges the weak financial position of public utilities and throws caution to the wind by asking banks to 'exercise adequate caution while dealing with the sector.'

One apparent issue is the constant operational losses for power utilities—the gap between the Average Cost of Supply (ACS) and average revenue realized (ARR) remains constant. The table below provides us with the difference between ACS and ARR—the gap for each unit of power supplied.

TABLE 47: CONSTANT OPERATIONAL LOSSES FOR POWER UTILITIES[102]

REGION	GAP WITHOUT SUBSIDY			GAP ON SUBSIDY BOOKED BASIS			GAP ON SUBSIDY RECEIVED BASIS		
	12-13	13-14	14-15	12-13	13-14	14-15	12-13	13-14	14-15
EAST	1.01	1.03	0.76	0.52	0.54	0.22	0.52	0.54	0.24
NORTH EAST	1.69	1.68	1.64	1.52	1.50	1.16	1.65	1.64	1.18
NORTH	1.65	1.80	1.56	1.02	1.25	0.84	1.03	1.25	0.88
SOUTH	1.88	1.18	1.27	1.34	0.65	0.70	1.36	0.66	0.73
WEST	0.36	0.46	0.42	0.23	0.32	0.25	0.23	0.32	0.25
NATIONAL AVG.	1.27	1.18	1.08	0.84	0.76	0.58	0.84	0.77	0.60

Another significant challenge faced are Transmission & Distribution (T&D) losses—corresponding to electricity produced, but not sold or saved. While popular perception holds that T&D losses are caused by improper billing and theft, a significant proportion of losses are caused by energy sold at low voltages, inadequate investments in distribution infrastructure and low loads over large areas.

Meanwhile, Aggregate Transmission and Commercial (AT&C) losses remain unmoved at ~22 per cent levels. The national average of AT&C losses for FY14–15 stood at 24.62 per cent—an increase over the 22.58 per cent registered two years back.

---

102 Ministry of Power, 2016

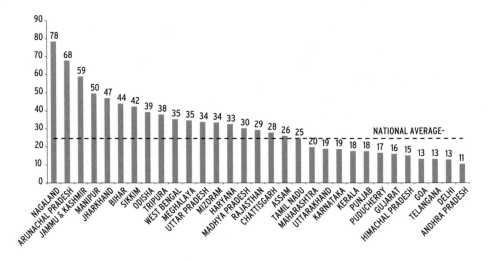

FIGURE 64: AT&C LOSSES ACROSS STATES (FY15)[103]

The Power Distribution Franchisee (PDF) model could be utilized to bring down AT&C losses in the beginning. Bhiwandi faced AT&C losses of 58 per cent (2006), mandatory six hours of load shedding, 40 per cent transformer failure, outdated transmission infrastructure, inadequate high voltage capacity network, besides huge thefts, faulty meters and unsatisfied customers, before enrolling a third party for managing its capex and operations. Within seven years, AT&C losses were reduced to 19.5 per cent.[104] Realizing that each region shall have its own set of challenges to reduce AT&C losses, each discom should devise their own customized solution for catering to the challenge. Administrative interventions like setting up special/ dedicated courts and police cells, governance solutions like loss monitoring and comprehensive energy auditing, nomination of feeder managers, incentivizing theft reporting and encouraging employees through incentives and training can be explored. Existing policies can be modified to incorporate loss reduction-based multi-year tariffs, and loss level based-tariff designing. Competition can be increased through distribution franchisees with pre-defined loss reduction targets, third party monitoring and local community engagement. Separation of agricultural and rural feeders can help, and focussing on improved metering (pre-paid metering reduces need for billing and improves working capital cycle), implementation of High Voltage Distribution System and improving government capital infusion in the sector can also help in improving the financial health of discoms.

---

103   Ministry of Power, 2016

104   CUTS Institute for Regulation & Competition, Case Study 12, Dec 2013 Sourced from: https://www.circ. in/pdf/ER_Case_Study_12.pdf

SUBSIDIZING KEROSENE

Kerosene was included in the list of the Public Distribution System (PDS) from the Second Five Year Plan onwards. However, identifying beneficiaries remained challenging—it is estimated that 41 per cent of PDS kerosene is lost as leakage[105] while just 27.1 per cent of poor households actually benefit. The vast majority of beneficiaries are non-poor households.

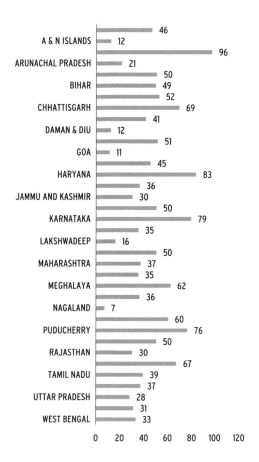

FIGURE 65: KEROSENE CONSUMPTION BY POOR HOUSEHOLDS (PER CENT) (2015)[106]

---

105 Economic Survey of India, 2014–15
106 Ibid

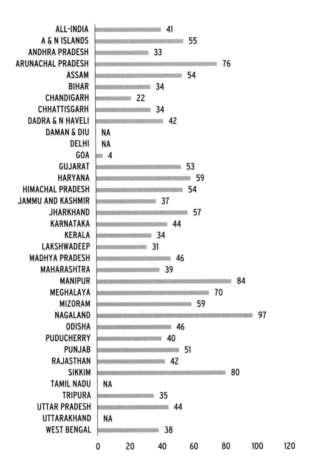

ALL-INDIA 41
A & N ISLANDS 55
ANDHRA PRADESH 33
ARUNACHAL PRADESH 76
ASSAM 54
BIHAR 34
CHANDIGARH 22
CHHATTISGARH 34
DADRA & N HAVELI 42
DAMAN & DIU NA
DELHI NA
GOA 4
GUJARAT 53
HARYANA 59
HIMACHAL PRADESH 54
JAMMU AND KASHMIR 37
JHARKHAND 57
KARNATAKA 44
KERALA 34
LAKSHWADEEP 31
MADHYA PRADESH 46
MAHARASHTRA 39
MANIPUR 84
MEGHALAYA 70
MIZORAM 59
NAGALAND 97
ODISHA 46
PUDUCHERRY 40
PUNJAB 51
RAJASTHAN 42
SIKKIM 80
TAMIL NADU NA
TRIPURA 35
UTTAR PRADESH 44
UTTARAKHAND NA
WEST BENGAL 38

FIGURE 66: ESTIMATED LEAKAGE (PER CENT) IN KEROSENE PDS DISTRIBUTION (2015)[107]

PDS kerosene leakages have now become universally common, happening across states and union territories. In particular, West Bengal and Uttar Pradesh remain the highest in the amount lost, while North-eastern states have a high level of leakage in percentage terms (Nagaland loses 97 per cent of its PDS kerosene!). The idea that keeping kerosene subsidized is useful for the poor remains a controversial, given the state of our PDS system.

To understand the need for subsidies, one must understand spending and affordability patterns. A rural household can typically spend between ₹36 and

---

107 Economic Survey of India, 2014-15

₹130 per month on kerosene requirements. Where kerosene is heavily consumed, NSS data highlights that spending can average ₹100–180 per month. Rural consumers can theoretically seek an LPG connection, which would be cheaper than kerosene, but on-ground area serviceability and onerous requirements of documentation prevent take-up. So India's rural markets have taken over the job— one increasingly sees small cylinders (2, 3 and 5 kg cylinders) of LPG being sold illegally with unsafe handling and refilling.

Kerosene is an inefficient fuel, used primarily for basic lighting. To improve subsidy delivery, we must consider taking the politically brave call of limiting kerosene subsidies and retargeting them to make off-grid renewable alternatives cheaper. The savings that can accrue to the government if kerosene subsidies are reduced and off-grid renewable alternatives are implemented can be significant (₹8,160 crore to ₹12,630 crore).

Consumer willingness to pay remains significant, even with consumers from poor rural households,[108] as long as there is reliable access to electricity and far fewer outages. When access is poor, such consumers have regularly substituted kerosene, diesel, batteries or coal for their lighting needs, at higher lifecycle costs. Instead of bemoaning the rural consumer's apparent propensity for electricity subsidies, we should instead consider whether regular supply of electricity could induce demand for connections. If and when subsidies on kerosene are dropped, the uptake for renewables and off-grid power could rise significantly. Asking such consumers to wait for grid connections and make do with kerosene and its resulting indoor air pollution would be immoral.

108 Dossani, R., Ranganathan, V., 'Farmers' willingness to pay for power in India: conceptual issues, survey results and implications for pricing', Energy Economics 26 (2004) 359–369. Sourced from: http://aoatools. aua.gr/pilotec/files/bibliography/pricing_dossani-1017744384/pricing_dossani.pdf

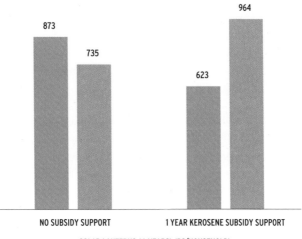

FIGURE 67: ANNUAL SAVINGS PER HOUSEHOLD TO THE GOVERNMENT IF KEROSENE
SUBSIDIES ARE LIMITED AND DIVERTED TO OFF-GRID ALTERNATIVES[109]

IMPROVING ENERGY ACCESS

DRILLING FOR SALT

Consider the case of salt pan farmers in the Little Rann of Kutch, an arid landscape
where farmers used diesel irrigation pumps (mostly burnout) to extract brine to
conduct salt harvesting. Diesel can typically account for as much as 40–50 per cent
of their total seasonal revenue.[110] Pilot projects utilizing solar irrigation pumps
have highlighted a potential for reducing irrigation costs significantly, with annual
savings rising to ₹70,000–₹90,000, a 150 per cent increase compared to diesel-
powered pumps. When the season is done, the solar pumps are often used to power
local households.

---

109 CEEW, 2015
110 SEWA and NRDC (2015)

A NEW STRATEGY

We must realize that our historical approach to rural electrification has had a limited impact, and is likely to provide limited gains over the next few decades—a grid-focused approach with subsidies provided to consumers will continue to impact the balance sheets of State Electricity Boards while providing irregular and pricey electricity to the vast majority of consumers. Our policymakers have experimented with renewables, and are seeking to scale them up in off-grid areas, considering them as interim solutions that can help bridge the gap until grid connections are achieved. However, we must realize the potential of such off-grid technologies, which are increasingly reaching price parity with coal power generation. Instead of simply considering them as niche options, we must consider them to be the primary solution for solving our energy access deficit issues in rural India—our institutions and policies must reflect this change in mindset.

Solving India's energy access conundrum will require initiatives along three directions—an extension of the grid (as has been conducted in the RGGVY scheme), with franchisees incorporated for last-mile connectivity; an entrepreneur driven small-scale decentralized distributed generation (DDG); and a household generation-driven initiative (rooftop solar, anyone). Instead of a supply-focused policy landscape, which depends on annual budgets and multilateral funding, we need to encourage the growth of renewables. Choosing which option is relevant to a particular village should be determined on existing infrastructure available and the government's institutional presence. Such considerations would need to be cognizant of the availability of power supply, the remoteness of the village and affordability. The governments needs to focus its efforts on organizing a market around these three options, helping entrepreneurs develop a sustainable model and scale up.

MAPPING ENERGY ACCESS

A detailed mapping on India's energy access needs should be conducted with areas classified according to whether they have satisfactory power supplies and adequate household electrification levels. A village by village search identifying electrical infrastructure previously set up and not maintained should also be conducted to determine what could be activated again and who would be obligated to do so. A similar exercise would be needed to replace CFL and old batteries previously given out and now redundant. Awareness about the proper maintenance of power generation equipment needs to be raised significantly.

PROVIDING BASIC LIGHTING

Numerous policy-driven examples that highlight this shift and can be scaled up exist. The erstwhile Ministry of New & Renewable Energy launched the Remote Village Electrification Programme (RVEP) in 2001, with a focus on providing basic lighting in all un-electrified villages by 2012. Under RGGVY, RVEP was revamped with a focus on deploying home lighting systems (solar photovoltaic), biomass gasification systems, biogas engines, small hydropower plants, etc. The programme sought to provide each household two CFL (later LED) lights, enabling them to gain lighting during the night in an interim form. By the time RVEP was replaced with a new scheme, it had reached 10,000 villages and hamlets, while providing lighting systems to 750,000 households. This success had some pitfalls. Some villages had the wrong beneficiaries provided with lighting systems; some batteries had early discharge issues. Maintenance of the lighting systems proved to be a significant constraint for the private sector, with public sector firms stepping into the gap. Furthermore, this success led to newly connected households, particularly in Uttarakhand (in villages near Almora and Pithoragarh), preferring to stick with the interim lighting systems, instead of migrating, when feasible, to a more expensive grid connected system.[111] Success had bred its own constraints.

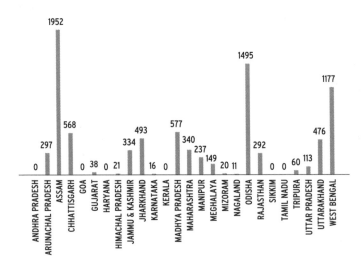

FIGURE 68: STATE-WISE NUMBER OF VILLAGES/HAMLETS SANCTIONED
AND COMPLETED UNDER RVEP (2014)[112,113]

---

111 Centre for Science & Environment, 2012

112 Indiastat data

113 Rajya Sabha Unstarred Question No. 52, dated on 07.07.2014.

ENCOURAGING FRANCHISEES

Improving the viability of the franchisee model remains key. Current economics remain significantly skewed—a World Bank study highlighted that the current average retail tariff is usually ₹3–4/kWh for rural households while the cost of supply can usually stretch beyond ₹7/kWh. While consumer willingness to pay can stretch significantly, there remains a significant deficit which requires either state utility subsidies or a significant viability gap funding to address.

There remain significant uncertainties to address. Franchisees remain significantly dependent on utilities, with payments usually delayed significantly. This model requires a grid with adequate capacity, a utility that supports franchisees with viability gap funding, a tariff that reflects market rates enabling price discrimination and an infrastructure that supplies regular electricity. India's current rural electricity scenario rarely has this conflation.

REVAMPING COOKSTOVES

Shifting the behaviour of millions of rural households with regards to cookstoves is not an easy task. Instead of piecemeal stove distribution policies, we should ideally focus on building a holistic approach that focuses on poverty reduction and the creation of a secondary market.[114] We need to ramp up public awareness through information campaigns that can highlight the health, economic and social benefits of such products, while detailing the risks of using current primitive stoves. Our rural consumers need to be convinced of the need to substitute their cookstoves while being assured of the reliability of the replacements and the presence of an on-ground maintenance network.

Other countries have successfully changed behaviour patterns.[115] In Bangladesh, potential users saw door-to-door visits from promotional campaigns which helped create awareness about improved cookstoves, conducting live demonstrations and helping enunciate government subsidies.[116] Community leaders were lobbied for endorsements, while change agents (teachers, doctors and people with influence)

---

114 IEA, 2010

115 Matin, N., 'What boosts cookstove uptake? A review of behaviour change approaches and techniques', Stockholm Environment Institute, 2015. Sourced from: https://www.sei-international.org/mediamanager/documents/Publications/SEI-2016-DiscussionBrief-WhatBoostsCookstoveUptake.pdf

116 www.cleanenergy-bd.org www.idcol.org; and www.ecostoriesbd.com

were encouraged to share their experiences of using improved cookstoves. Regular after sales services were instituted, serving as a monitoring function, which helped to support existing customers and build word of mouth for potential customers. Co-design of cookstoves with users was regularly carried out. Kenya saw campaigns to highlight the energy-saving potential of improved cookstoves, along with bolstering cultural acceptance. Cheap and locally available material was regularly used to build such stoves, while local microfinance institutions were tied in to help offer micro-credit to potential users.[117] Uganda saw a long-lasting campaign to 'keep my kitchen clean', with improved cookstoves promoted through radio talk shows, text messages, street art exhibitions and toll-free lines.[118] Unemployed youth were trained in the construction and maintenance of improved cookstoves, while local households were encouraged to gather and contribute onsite materials for construction. Benefits of the improved cookstoves were heavily enunciated to differentiate from traditional three-stone fires. Such efforts showcase that focusing simply on rewards (fuel costs, subsidies from the government and tax benefits) is not enough—one has to mobilize public opinion through change agents and the use of comparative strategies.

To ensure this, we need to build local community participation (including self-help groups) in such programmes from the very beginning, involving them in designs and utilizing their entrepreneurial spirit in setting up maintenance networks. To improve reliability, careful consideration needs to be given to the quality of materials used in the production of the stoves and the suitability of designs to the target geographies and climates (we should ideally be aiming for a stove life of atleast five years). Our focus on subsidized programmes hampers our awareness campaigns and deters the expansion of quality control and supply infrastructure. Central and state government input should ideally be limited to providing initial seed funding, along with stove component standardization and certification programmes. It would make sense to tie in microfinance programmes with funding for these improved stoves. This strategy has to scale up—the coverage of efficient cookstoves in sample areas has lately been highlighted at 1 per cent.[119] India's policies have recently shifted towards provisioning LPG access to rural India, but this could be constrained by gas availability, rural reach (given the need to set up a large LPG distribution infrastructure) and household economics. The Ujjwala scheme has made it easier to get an LPG connection—the cost of getting a connection reduced from ₹4,000–5,000 to ₹3,200, of which half the amount was waived, with an option to convert the balance amount into a loan

---

117 www.wisdomstoves.org; www.endev.info/content/Kenya; www.visionfund.
     org; scode.co.ke/energy-saving-cookstoves; and www.co2balance.com

118 www.krcuganda.org

119 Council of Energy, Environment and Water (CEEW). Sourced from: ceew.in/pdf/CEEW-ACCESS-Re-port-29Sep15.pdf

from oil marketing companies. Yet, refilling hits affordability. Once a connection is obtained, market rates have to be paid, with subsidy either deposited in Aadhaar-linked bank accounts or used up to pay EMI to the oil marketing company (in case of loan taken at the time of getting a connection). Refilling costs anywhere between ₹500—₹800, and with inter-state subsidy variations, it would take approximately eight refills to pay the loan amount and subsidy to reflect in the bank account. As price of refilling increases, households find it attractive to switch to alternative fuels like firewood, crop residue or cow dung cakes.[120] Assuming a BPL family of five with all members having daily income of ₹33, and approximate effective cost of refilling a cylinder at ₹500 (Odisha), a BPL family spends almost 10 per cent of their monthly income on energy for cooking, leading them to ration LPG use and continue using unhealthy alternative energy sources.

Even access is an issue—despite enrolling additional 5,000 LPG distributors in the country, many people have to cycle or take three-wheelers for as long as anywhere between 3–50 km for refilling. In such scenarios, the access is ensured through middlemen who charge additional money from the end-consumer, thereby further worsening the economic attractiveness of LPG for individual households. The market-based, 'one size fits all' approach fails to ensure LPG access at affordable rates. In comparison, electric cookstoves (usually 1 kWh), widely adopted in the West, remain convenient and yet out of reach in India. Utilizing electricity for cooking could help solve the indoor air pollution issue at a faster rate and could be financially feasible, if electricity is regularly available at an affordable cost. Assuming a long-term oil price of $50/barrel, using electricity for cooking should be on a par with utilizing kerosene.[121] Of course, personal preferences for using electric cookstoves versus traditional stoves will matter as well (the impact of using such cookstoves on the taste of food will have to be tested).

We need to revive and revamp our improved cookstoves programmes while pushing for an expansion of the biogas programme. To ensure scalability, we must focus on finalizing technical standards (combustion efficiency, particulate matter production, etc.) from the beginning, while following this with extensive testing and user trials. Institutional support matters—national and state-level testing and technical support centres will have to be set up, while pilot projects should be launched to familiarize and test new designs. Any programme should be gender-sensitive, helping to highlight women's empowerment while attaching a premium status to having an improved cookstove. A voucher-based programme should be utilized to initially launch new cookstoves, with subsidies reducing gradually over the long term. Such launches should be tied in with local self-help groups. We

---

120 Pandey K., Sahu P., Thakur P. & Jitendra, Downtoearth, Aug 2017 Sourced from: http://www.down-toearth.org.in/coverage/india-steps-on-the-gas-58502

121 http://niti.gov.in/writereaddata/files/document_publication/NITIBlog28_VC-AnilJain.pdf

should focus on realistic goals, aiming to reach a few million people at first, before expanding to the larger population. This will be a decadal journey.

———

REVAMPING ELECTRIC PUMPS

The vast majority of India's electric irrigation pumps (>22 million pumpsets) were distributed a decade ago and farmers rarely tend to replace them.[122] The consequence, after multiple burnouts, is that a standard 5 hp electric motor pump, which ideally should not consume more than 3.7 kWh of energy, under a 440V three phase supply, tends to consume 7–8 kWh of energy. This reflects in agriculture's share of the power budget—consuming 21.69 per cent of all electricity consumption in 2014 and yet contributing just 8 per cent of the discom revenues (agriculture's average revenue per unit sale was just ₹1.75; industry provided ₹ 6.66 in 2014). Meanwhile, farmers are charged at a fixed rate per hp basis, delinked completely from the actual units consumed; farmers are effectively not incentivized to purchase a more efficient pump while seeking to overdraw groundwater.

If farmers were incentivized to using modernized Bureau of Energy Efficiency (BEE)-rated electric pumps, they could cut electricity consumption by about 25 per cent, which would have a significant impact on overall consumption from agriculture. They would also save on maintenance and burnout repair costs (each burnout repair requires the pump to be taken out from 100–300 feet of soil and then put back again after the motor is replaced). Another option would be to explore solar pumps, which can offer similar savings with low maintenance requirements, all while addressing concerns associated with power availability, access and regularity. The government has recognized this value proposition, with the MNRE seeking to incentivize 100,000 solar pumps (mostly through capital subsidies on upfront cost and long-term loans), while the states of Maharashtra and Gujarat set limited targets.[123] By August 2015, India had over 35,000 solar pumps, insignificant in number compared to the vast majority of India's diesel and electric pumps. Incentivizing such pumps would require tinkering with current incentive schemes (up the upfront subsidy to at least 50–70 per cent of costs) and rebalancing India's current allocations towards electric irrigation pumps towards solar.[124]

---

122 http://indianexpress.com/article/india/india-news-india/cutting-power-subsidies-by-giving-new-pumps-free/

123 Kulkarni, 2015

124 Agrawal, S., Jain, A., Solar Pumps for Sustainable Irrigation, CEEW Policy Brief, August 2015. Sourced from: http://ceew.in/pdf/CEEW-Solar-Pumps-Policy-Brief-1Sep15.pdf

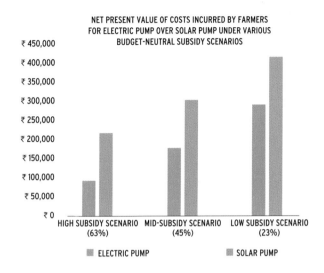

FIGURE 69: THE DISCOUNTED LIFETIME COST (7 YEARS) OF A 5 HP SOLAR PUMP
(WITH SUBSIDY) IS STILL SIGNIFICANTLY HIGHER THAN THE COST OF AN
ELECTRIC PUMP (WITH SUBSIDY) (2015)[125]

LEAPING FORWARD WITH RENEWABLES

Renewables, and solar in particular, offers a way out. The combination of decentralized mini-grids, with solar, can provide the requisite combination of access, economies of scale and affordability. There remain significant constraints, of course—despite a significant reduction in cost, solar still remains more expensive than coal, while the cost of installing solar-focused mini-grids can be too much for the local rural consumer to bear. In addition, demand for electricity in rural India is suppressed by the lack of affordable appliances (fridges, television sets, irrigation pumps, etc.), impacting demand that could make a rural electrification project economically feasible. Cost reduction can be hard to pursue, particularly on the infrastructure side, given the large number of components used to make solar panels or mini-grids, leading to high capex. Economical energy storage, particularly at a mini-grid level, through lead acid batteries, remains a distant frontier. Meanwhile, smart meters, which could have curbed the theft of power and overuse of subsidized power, are ruinously expensive. Pursuing economies of

125 Ibid

scale at the mini-grid level can be a tough ask, given its affinity for functioning as a loose collection of various systems. Financing rural electrification projects, mini-grids in particular, can be difficult given the lack of significant 'anchor customers' in such villages. India's regulatory scene, on off-grid electrification, is still evolving, with significant risk to investors remaining.

BOLSTERING SOLAR POWER

FIGURE 70: ANNUAL GLOBAL HORIZONTAL IRRADIANCE (GHI)[126]

---

126   NREL. Sourced from: http://mnre.gov.in/sec/GHI_Annual.jpg

Solar's share in India's power mix has grown significantly over the last few years, rising to 4 per cent in 2015[127]—a reflection of the trend towards solar globally; a consequence of the dramatic decrease in cost of photovoltaic panels. For India, solar remains an ideal resource, available in plenty, regularly and costing (gradually) little. Over 60 per cent of India's landmass receives an annual average global insolation of 5 kWh/m²/day; so much that even decentralized power could be feasible.[128]

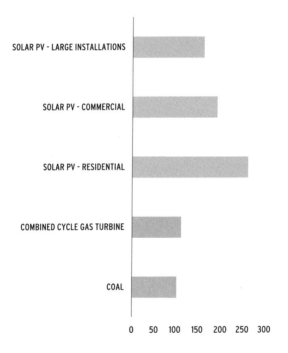

FIGURE 71: LEVELIZED COST OF ENERGY COMPARISON (2015)[129]

Solar systems, by virtue of being modular and low maintenance, also enable distributed installation, reducing the need for large initial capital investments; in contrast, coal-fired plants required significant initial capex, while any incremental ramp-up or distributed generation is, in most cases, not feasible.[130] With no fuel

---

127 India Central Electricity Authority, March 2015.

128 Achieving universal electrification in India, Institute for Transformative Technologies, April 2016. Sourced from: https://assets.rockefellerfoundation.org/app/uploads/20160503122350/Achieving-Universal-Electrification-in-India.ITTReport.April2016.pdf

129 International Energy Agency, 'Projected costs of generating electricity', 2015

130 Achieving universal electrification in India, Institute for Transformative Technologies, April 2016. Sourced from: https://assets.rockefellerfoundation.org/app/uploads/20160503122350/Achieving-Universal-Electrification-in-India.ITTReport.April2016.pdf

costs, operational costs tend to be low. The levelized cost of electricity (LCOE), a ratio of discounted lifetime system costs with lifetime electricity generation, for solar is still higher than baseload coal, but is inching downwards rapidly. With the domestic manufacturing market maturing and government policies being encouraging, solar has room to grow.

Solar systems, in India, are being deployed in five different formats, depending on need and affordability. Small solar systems help provide power for recharging mobile phones and lamps, while home systems can power a full home (a few fans and appliances, excluding air-conditioning).[131] Nano micro-grids can help power a cluster of homes, while a micro-grid (varying in size from 5—100 kW), can power a full village. Finally grid-connected solar farms can help power urban agglomerations. The current trend in India's solar industry is towards this segment, which offers exposure to the majority of India's commercially lucrative urban power consumers.

The latter, with its need for scale and grid connections, remains a poor solution for providing electricity access to rural areas (unless they are close to urban islands). Remote community electrification projects, with poor infrastructure, will incur a higher capex to help connect such farms to the grid through long transmission lines (which are likely to be prone to breakage). Such systems are relevant only to rural areas that are adjacent to large urban cities, enabling grid extension. For those completely off grid low density areas, micro or nano-grid solar systems remain ideal. The majority of the un-electrified population, living in medium to high-density off-grid areas, are the ones that require creative policymaking.

---

131 Achieving universal electrification in India, Institute for Transformative Technologies, April 2016. Sourced from: https://assets.rockcfellerfoundation.org/app/uploads/20160503122350/Achieving-Universal-Elec-trification-in-India.ITTReport.April2016.pdf

INCREASING SOLAR CAPACITY

India has been ramping up its solar capacity, reaching 5 GW by end-2015, with a push towards increasing this to 100 GW by 2022. Government policy has been overarching, seeking to set targets, mandating discoms to fulfil their renewable obligation purchases. A National Solar Mission has been set up, to help set up green corridors while NTPC has been pushed to engage in trading in solar power, all while encouraging states to pursue rooftop solar.

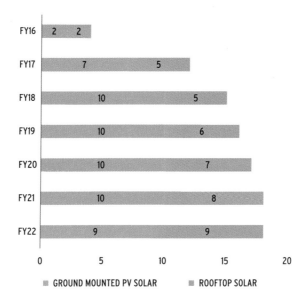

FIGURE 72: ANNUAL CAPACITY ADDITION TARGETS (IN GW) UNTIL 2022[132]

The government has also sought to institute two bidding mechanisms (reverse bidding and viability gap funding) for awarding tenders. Renewable purchase obligations (RPOs) have been utilized to help boost demand for renewable power from SEBs (the SEBs can choose to either generate it or purchase renewable energy certifications, REC). However, state non-compliance with RPOs has constrained growth, particularly in the REC market. The rooftop solar policy, along with net-metering, could further encourage growth. Given such efforts, nationally and globally, solar is increasingly inching towards grid parity with coal. By 2013, solar prices reached ₹5.5/kWh in bids conducted by certain states. This saw a further decline to ₹4.63/kWh in 2015.

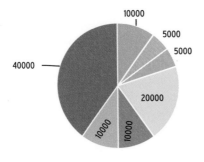

♦ NTPC
♦ SOLAR ENERGY CORPORATION
♦ LARGE PRIVATE SECTOR IPPS
♦ STATE POLICIES
♦ ONGOING PROGRAMS INCL PAST ADDITIONS
♦ DECENTRALIZED CAPACITY FOR UNEMPLOYED
♦ ROOFTOP

FIGURE 73: SOLAR
CAPACITY INCREASE:
BREAKUP IN MW[133]

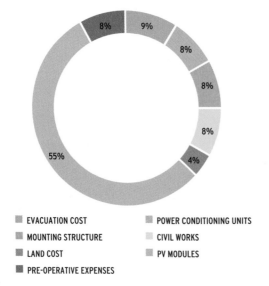

EVACUATION COST   POWER CONDITIONING UNITS
MOUNTING STRUCTURE   CIVIL WORKS
LAND COST   PV MODULES
PRE-OPERATIVE EXPENSES

FIGURE 74: SOLAR POWER
PLANT COST BREAKUP
(2016)[134]

---

133 MNRE, 2016
134 Ministry of Power, 2016

Further price declines are expected. Solar panels (comprising most of the cost of a solar power system) have declined steeply in price over the last decade, from $1.31 to $0.5 per watt, driven by a combination of overcapacity amongst Chinese suppliers and decline in the price of solar panels and base of system costs.

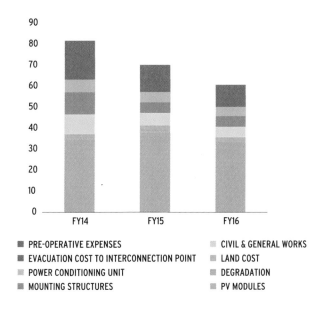

FIGURE 75: CERC-AUTHORIZED BENCHMARK CAPITAL COSTS FOR SOLAR PANEL PLANTS[135]

UTILIZING MINI-GRIDS

Mini-grids, defined as standalone power generators that can provide electricity to consumers on a localized grid, can offer a promising way for off-grid generation. They can serve medium to high-density populations (100–1,000 people per square km), through a combination of low wattage systems (<15kW), three-phase AC systems (15–100 kW) and infrastructure sharing with the main grid, where possible. Mini-grids, in their varying sizes and configurations, remain an ideal fit for the majority of India's un-electrified populations living in high-density

135 CERC, 2016

rural agglomerations. When such agglomerations urbanize, their mini grids will automatically be absorbed into the main grid. The government remains encouraging, launching well-funded schemes like the Deendayal Scheme. However, there remain few, if any, examples of mini-grids being utilized to power rural villages (<1 per cent of total solar output).[136] Part of the reason remains the cost of installing a mini-grid (typically $2.5–3/W; about $70,000 to $100,000 for a 30kW system). This cost, with PV panels the most expensive (30 per cent of cost), has no single component that can be targeted for drastic cost reductions. Batteries remain another significant constraint—the currently used lead acid batteries perform poorly in Indian conditions with a shorter life, but lithium ion batteries remain far too expensive.

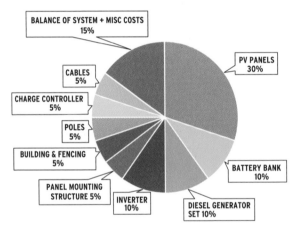

FIGURE 76: COST BREAK-UP–30 KW MINI-GRID (ROCKEFELLER FOUNDATION)[137]

At the same time, limited demand, given a lack of affordable appliances, in rural villages means that economies of scale do not arise and without economies of scale, rural electrification stagnates, limiting the market for affordable appliances.[138] Jumpstarting the scale-up of mini-grids will require either the break-even cost of mini-grids to come down or demand from villages to go up (through the introduction of affordable appliances that consume electricity). A study by the Institute for Transformative Technologies has highlighted that a majority of India's rural consumers would not be able to afford a mini-grid charging more than $7.5 per month (the current break even is $30 per month for an 80 kWh package that could power multiple appliances). Meanwhile, most villages will fail to have 'anchor

---

136 Achieving universal electrification in India, Institute for Transformative Technologies, April 2016. Sourced from: https://assets.rockefellerfoundation.org/app/uploads/20160503122350/Achieving-Universal-Electrification-in-India.ITTReport.April2016.pdf

137 The Rockefeller Foundation—Smart Power for Rural Development initiative

138 Global Leap, Dalberg Global Development Advisors, and the Clean Energy Ministerial, 'The State of the Off-grid Appliance Market', March 2016

users' that can help consume electricity in a reliable manner to guarantee financial viability.

There are some models that can be considered. Chhattisgarh's government launched a solar mini-grid model, with a focus on establishing a village-level mini-grid powered by a solar power plant that could serve two lighting points for six hours a day for each household, along with some additional street lights.[139,140] The state backed this initiative with significant resources, with a focus on subsidizing both initial installation as well as later maintenance costs. Villager participation was encouraged by asking them to conduct site selection and work as paid labourers during the installation phase. Payments to contractors for installation and distribution were provided when the majority of the work was completed, with the remaining 10 per cent provided after five years. Maintenance of a cluster of villages was outsourced to a contractor for a period of ten years. Each BPL household was charged a connection fee of ₹100 (₹200–500 for each APL household), while monthly maintenance charges were usually ₹30 per household (subsidized to the tune of ₹25 by the state government). While this initiative was unlikely to be sustainable in the long run, it was successfully utilized in scaling up the usage of renewable energy in off-grid areas in Chhattisgarh.

West Bengal's Renewable Energy Development Agency (WBREDA) has helped electrify Sagardeep Island, in the Ganges delta, through the installation of individual solar lighting systems and ten solar photovoltaic plants with a capacity of 300 kW, powering over 3,600 families daily.[141,142] WBREDA has innovated significantly, launching a wind-diesel hybrid programme in 2002 with four 55 kW wind turbines connected to two 180 kW diesel gensets—sufficient for the energy needs of 700 households. The entire system is managed by the Sagar Rural Energy Development Cooperative, with each power plant having a beneficiary committee and local representation consumers themselves responsible for tariff collection and maintenance. MNRE provided 50 per cent capital funding for the solar mini-grids, with an additional 20 per cent provided by the state government and 30 per cent from the Indian Renewable Energy Development Agency (IREDA). As of now, the system is sustainable, with operating costs covered by customer revenue (each consumer pays ₹85/month for three lighting points; ₹135/month for five lighting points).

---

139 Millinger, M., 2010

140 Maithani, P.C., Gupta, D., 'Achieving Universal Energy Access in India', Challenges and the Way Forward, SAGE, Chapter 5, 2015

141 Shrank, S., 'Another Look at Renewables on India's Sagar Island', Working Paper 77, July 2008. Sourced from: https://pesd.fsi.stanford.edu/sites/default/files/WP_77,_Shrank,_Sagar_Island,_07_July_2008.pdf

142 Maithani, P.C., Gupta, D., 'Achieving Universal Energy Access in India', Challenges and the Way Forward, SAGE, Chapter 5, 2015

The private sector offers other examples. The Omnigrid Micropower Company (OMC), founded in 2010, has helped provide reliable and cheap renewable electricity in Uttar Pradesh's Hardoi district. The firm's business model involves setting up 10 kW solar power plants which can charge solar lanterns and batteries (a single charged battery can power most household equipment such as a fan, a bulb and even a TV) which are rented through dealers to local villagers at affordable prices (₹120 per lantern; ₹250–₹350 for a battery). This model is easy to scale up, and could power tens of thousands of villages across the country.

Such initiatives typically require a cluster of factors to succeed.[143] Any village-level local grid should have enough power capacity installed to reduce maintenance costs and prevent local allocation issues. Maintenance of wiring and batteries can be significant overheads, along with a need for robust inverters that can last for the long term (10 per cent of the installed inverters in the Chhattisgarh model were found to be damaged every month, given overload from changing from CFL to incandescent bulbs). A remote monitoring system would be ideal, with local officials trained as operators. A combination of a solar system with a pumped hydro or diesel generation system would help drive down operational costs. Investment support, particularly at the upfront capital stage, remains critical while off-take guarantees are much needed. Dynamic tariffs can help with energy allocation (charging higher tariffs towards the evening), while price discrimination should be utilized wherever economically bearable.

We also need a suite of product innovations to help take the next leap forward. The government should incentivize solar manufacturers to push for building an integrated suite of mini-grid configurations, one that incorporates billing systems, batteries, inverters, etc., with the potential for reducing capex costs. It will also have to incentivize the production of affordable appliances (e.g. through DC motors for fans, irrigation pumps, etc.) that can be used by impoverished customers in rural, off-grid areas.[144]

In addition, government policy needs to be clarified on off-grid power (particularly the interaction between mini-grids and grid power, whenever it reaches a village). We should encourage public-private partnerships for rural electrification, while allowing such firms access to existing infrastructure, however defunct. Similar to the Swachh Bharat Abhiyan, we must incentivize communities and households for getting connected to mini-girds (subsidies, in vouchers or in kind).

---

143 Indo-Norwegian Pilot 'The 30 Village Project' Key Learning's, Scatec Solar, July 2012. Sourced from: http://haritika.in/Presentation,solar%20(1).pdf

144 Phadke A., Jacobson A., Park W. Y., Lee G. R., Alstone P., and Khare A., 'Powering a Home with Just 25 Watts of Solar PV: Super-Efficient Appliances Can Enable Expanded Off-Grid Energy Service Using Small Solar Power Systems', April 2015

The draft version of the National Policy on RE-based mini/micro grids is a welcome step in this direction.[145] However, the policy still leaves the question of grid interconnection unanswered: 'Mini-grids may want to connect with the DISCOM grid in the future to sell excess power. The existing CEA regulation of 2013— Technical Standards for Connectivity of the Distributed Generation Resources— can guide the interconnection of a mini grid with the DISCOM grid. However, the incumbent regulations require the mini grid generator to cease in case the DISCOM grid supply fails, disallowing the mini-grid to supply to its consumers. From a mini grid standpoint, these regulations will need to be followed unless proper controls can be installed to ensure islanding/isolation to the satisfaction of discom.' This paradox between enabling grid interconnection and yet meeting the needs of a mini-grid's local consumers needs resolution.

INSTITUTING MAINTENANCE

Another challenge faced with off-grid solutions is proper maintenance of installed systems. The uptime for such systems is critical in case of discontinuation of kerosene subsidies and to encourage people to migrate from kerosene lamps. Proper operation and maintenance are hindered by lack of consumer awareness, frequent breakdown of cheap products (which penetrate the market on account of low upfront prices), high after-sales service cost on account of low volumes and geographically dispersed consumers, and low incentives for after-sales service as most metrics measure only installed capacities which places focus on products sold. For raising awareness, mass communication programmes can be undertaken promoting awareness and information as well as decision-making support in local languages. The channels could be decided (radio/SMS/pamphlets, etc.), depending on their suitability in a local context and focus has to be placed on providing information in a consistent manner and formats. With respect to avoiding cheap quality products, stringent product quality restrictions could be imposed that not only focus on product design but also on end-user in-use performance. Such initiatives can improve the quality and reliability of these products. We need to incorporate the lessons learnt from implementation of such solutions in the North-east.

Another solution is to include significant incentives for off-grid players to improve after-sales service to in turn improve system reliability in the long term. Ease of registering complaint has to be improved, with consumers being able to register

---

145 http://mnre.gov.in/file-manager/UserFiles/draft-national-Mini_Micro-Grid-Policy.pdf

complaints through SMS or call toll-free numbers and such complaints being tracked on a daily basis by a central grievance redressal system that can then direct the solution provider to hasten repairs. Significant penal provisions may be introduced, but that may stifle participation. A simple solution would be to provide financing through the off-grid solution provider itself, wherein regular complaints and non-functioning lanterns could be offset against the regular loan repayments. The off-grid solutions provider can also be eligible for a 'sunset payment' wherein, subject to meeting stringent service criteria, the solutions provider shall be rewarded with a pre-decided bonus, thereby aligning his incentive to improving system reliability. The providers need to recognize that it's a service package they sell, not just the product design.

IMPROVING ACCESS

Improving access is another critical part in the puzzle—in cases where government provides one time subsidy for upfront cost financing, very poor households can opt for a smaller number of lanterns and if the government does not provide any upfront subsidy, it can look forward to creating a subsidy fund for very poor households to ensure access. The question of access can lead to innovative models. The success story of Rajasthan's Gramin Aajeevika Vikas Parishad and its collaboration with the Indian Institute of Technology, Mumbai (IIT-M), has provided employment opportunities to over 200 tribal women from various self-help groups in Dungarpur, Rajasthan. The women are trained in making solar lanterns and they in turn train other women, making the initiative self-sustaining. IIT-M provides the raw materials and technical know-how while the women make, pack and market the solar lanterns in remote villages with no electricity. While a solar lantern in the open market costs ~₹60–700, the lanterns made by the women cost as little as ₹120—a big difference, especially for very poor rural households. They also turn women into green energy entrepreneurs, thereby improving their lives. Such initiatives have also been tried in other places—'Solar Sahelis' explored the said concept with peer-to-peer marketing. Besides reducing the manufacturing cost, rentals of solar lanterns is also an interesting idea. The success of such concepts is visible in the village of Bairi Dariyaon and its ten neighbouring villages in Uttar Pradesh, wherein solar lanterns are rented out at just ₹2–3/day for basic lighting purposes, benefitting as many as 500 homes, inspiring the Prime Minister to praise the initiative in 'Mann ki Baat'.

REVAMPING BIOMASS POWER

India's yearly wooden outgrowth is estimated to be 307.4 million tonnes, while we have an estimated 280 million livestock.[146] This amounts to a significant amount of reusable biomass content, one that can be recycled into biogas too. Each individual cattle can be estimated to provide 5–10 kg of dung daily; totalling 500 million to a billion tonnes of wet dung every year, enough to supply 30 million biogas plants (with about 1–2 m³ capacity) yearly (even accounting for environmental and infrastructural limitations, like cattle sheds and water availability, this would allow for 15 million biogas plants, helping at least 50–80 million people with cooking gas daily).

The MNRE's Village Energy Security Programme (VESP) sought to address total energy needs in remote villages by using local biomass gasifiers. The programme was soon foreclosed, given a lack of interest by state governments, and difficulties in providing maintenance of such generators. While revenues paid by local users were inadequate in covering system costs, such plants could not be run on the cheap with ill-trained personnel.

Since 2008, the Ministry of New and Renewable Resources has been conducting pilot plants to bottle biogas (which is similar in composition to CNG).[147] The initiative seeks to install medium-sized mixed-feed biogas plants for generating, purifying and then bottling biogas. A range of biogas bottling projects across varying capacities and demonstrating different technologies, has been commissioned. Such purified biogas is now routinely bottled in CNG cylinders and used in hotels, industries and mid-day meal scheme schools.

Husk Power, led by Gyanesh Pandey, has scaled up a well-tested biomass gasification technology that utilizes a fixed bed for processing rice husk; one that can easily offer a 25–80 kW system.[148] Even accounting for transmission losses (~1–2 kW) and theft (~1–2 kW), the system can easily provide enough electricity to an entire village. Such a system is economical as well, with a household monthly charge of ₹45 per 15 W CFL, in addition to an installation charge of ₹100 (the MNRE has helped subsidize projects to the tune of 50 per cent of total cost). Gasifiers are usually procured locally, and then modified to operate on producer gas. Most households that replace their kerosene lanterns have ended up saving at least 30–40 per cent. The system has proven economically feasible, offering significant returns

---

146 NSS estimates

147 http://mnre.gov.in/file-manager/UserFiles/case-study-Biogas-Generation_Purification_and_Bottling-Development-In-India.pdf

148 Maithani, P.C., Gupta, Deepak, 'Achieving Universal Energy Access in India', Challenges and the Way Forward, SAGE, Chapter 5, 2015

on a regular basis. The entire system is significantly decentralized, requiring local personnel, suitably trained, to operate it, with husk bought and used locally. By building an integrated operation across the value chain, Husk Power has managed to solve issues related to local power generation, inadequate maintenance and irregular revenue collection, all while establishing local partnerships to keep operating costs low and to benefit from distribution efficiency. To establish scale, Husk Power adopted the franchisee model, with local entrepreneurs purchasing plant machinery and building a local distribution network. Funding for such entrepreneurs is the only way to resolve our energy access issues.

PROVISIONING OFF-GRID POWER

When providing grid-based connections to un-electrified villages, we tend not to consider the true cost of such connections. The true cost of energy should be reflected in our pricing (whether or not it includes a feed-in tariff). While our state electricity boards typically assume that providing grid-based electricity to rural areas averages ₹3–5/kWh, the true cost could be upwards of ₹9/kWh, with additional charges if the village is quite remote or un-electrified. The discovery of this true cost can enable us to make the right decisions about which localized business models will work for electrifying our villages.

Consider another model. For farmers like Kishanbhai Manharlal, from Sidhpur tehsil in Patan district of Gujarat, biogas continues to remain a relevant proposition. They have started investing in communitarian biogas plants—taking inspiration from a local village called Methan which has been saving over 500 MT of firewood for the last three decades.[149] Its secret—a biogas plant that has been running since 25 April 1987. The plant has eight digesters with a capacity of 630 m^3—each of which is filled, on a rotational basis, with cow dung mixed with groundwater. When sealed, the digester stays shut at an ambient 35°C temperature, perfect for anaerobic bacteria to work. Given Methan's predilection for livestock, its digesters are never short of dung. The digester converts a daily trolley of cow dung (about 2.5 tonnes) into biogas and slurry (in high demand by local farmers; usually sold at a premium to the cow dung). The biogas is supplied through underground pipelines to local houses, with supply provided in the early morning and evening. Each such house pays a fixed contribution of ₹50–100 per month, in addition to a one-time charge for a connection and maintenance. The biogas plant itself is profitable,

149 Jamwal, N., 'What's cooking in India's largest biogas plant', 15 March 2003, http://www.downtoearth.org.in/coverage/whats-cooking-in-indias-largest-biogas-plant-12615

with cow dung cheap and plenty and the plant itself requiring just two people to run and maintain it. This idyllic village has figured out how to run a biogas plant in a communitarian environment—local cow dung is fed to a locally owned biogas plant which produces gas that is locally used and slurry that is sloshed on local farms. The plant and pipelines are maintained locally, keeping costs low and providing employment. Aside from initial seed funding, the government has no role to play here. These are the kind of models that we need to work towards. Ensuring that our farmers have access to affordable electricity and their households should continue to remain our primary policy focus.

REFERENCES

Office of Registrar-General and Census Commissioner (ORGCC), 2001. Census of India 2001, Office of Registrar-General and Census Commissioner, India.

Cecelski, E., 1995. 'From Rio to Beijing, engendering the energy debate', Energy Policy, 23(6), pp. 561-575.

Barnes, D.F., and Sen, M., 2000. Energy Strategies for Rural India: Evidence from Six States, UNDP/World Bank Energy Sector Management Assistance Program. UNDP/World Bank Energy Sector Management Assistance Program (ESMAP), 2001.

'Energy and health for the poor', Indoor Air Pollution Newsletter.

Leach, G., 1992. 'The energy transition', Energy Policy 20, pp. 116-123, February.

Natarajan, I., 1985. Domestic Fuel Survey with Special Reference to Kerosene, Volume I & II, National Council of Applied Economic Research, New Delhi.

Natarajan, I., 1995. 'Trends in firewood consumption in rural India', Margin, Vol. 28, No. 1, pp. 41-47.

Neudoerffer, R.C., Malhotra, P., and Ramana, P.V., 2001. 'Participatory rural energy planning in India -- a policy context', Energy Policy, 29(5), pp. 371-381.

Parikh, J., 1995. 'Gender issues in energy policy', Energy Policy, 23, p. 745.

Parikh, J., Smith, K., and Laxmi V., 1999. 'Indoor air pollution: a reflection on gender bias', Economic and Political Weekly, 34(9) pp. 539-544.

Parikh, J., 2000. 'Rural energy and health impacts', IGIDR Project Report No. 048.

Parikh, J., and Laxmi, V., 2000a. 'Gender and health considerations for petroleum product policy in India', Energia News, 3(2), pp. 11-13.

Parikh, J., and Laxmi, V., 2000b. 'Biofuels, pollution and health linkages: a survey of rural Tamil Nadu', Economic and Political Weekly, 35(47), pp. 4125-4138.

Parikh, J., Laxmi, V., Parikh, K.S., and Karmakar, S., 2000. 'Rural pollution and health impacts: three states of North India, Vol I & II' (unpublished).

Parikh, J., Balakrishna, K., Laxmi, V., and Biswas,

H., 2001. 'Exposure from cooking with biofuels: pollution monitoring, and analysis from rural Tamil Nadu, India', Energy, 26, pp. 949-962.

Parikh, J., 2002. 'Mainstreaming gender and energy in South Asia', Energia, International Network on Gender and Sustainable Energy, regional paper prepared for the World Summit on Sustainable Development, August.

Raiyani, C.V., Shah, S.H., Desai, N.M., Venkaiah, K., Patel, J.S., Parikh, D.J., and Kashyap, S.K., 1993. 'Characterization and problems of indoor air pollution due to cooking stove smoke', Atmospheric Environment, 27(A) (11), pp. 1643-1655.

Ravindranath, N.H., and Ramakrishna, J., 1997. 'Energy options for cooking in India', Energy Policy, 25(10) pp. 63-75.

Sarmah, R., Bora, M.C., and Bhattacharjee, D.J., 2002. 'Energy profiles of rural domestic sector in six un-electrified villages of Jorhat district of Assam', Energy, 27(1), pp. 17-24.

Saxena, N.C., 1997. The Woodfuel Scenario and Policy Issues in India, Field Document No. 49, Regional Wood Energy Development Programme in Asia, GCP/RAS/154/NET, pp. 1-70.

Saxena, N.C., 1999. 'Fuelwood -- issues for the Ninth Plan', Wood Energy News, 14(2) p. 3-4.

Sinha, C.S., Venkata, R.P., and Joshi, V., 1994. 'Rural energy planning in India: defining effective intervention strategies', Energy Policy, 22(5), pp. 403-414.

Smith, K.R., 1987. Biofuels, Air Pollution and Health, Plenum Press, New York.
Smith, K.R., 1993. 'Fuel combustion, air pollution exposure, and health: the situation in developing countries', Annual Review Energy and Environment, 18, pp. 529-566.

Smith, K.R., 1996. 'Indoor air pollution in India', National Medical Journal of India, 9(3), pp. 103-104.

Wickramsinghe, A., 2001. 'Gender sights and health issues in the paradigm of biofuel in Sri Lanka', Energia News, 4(4).

Areeparampil, Mathew. 1996. Tribals of Jharkhand: Victims of Development. New Delhi: Indian Social Institute.

Bharali, Gita. 2007. 'Development-Induced Displacement: A History of Transition to Impoverishment and Environmental Degradation,' Paper presented at the

Seminar on Ecology, Department of History, Dibrugarh University, March 27-28.

BJA & NBJK. 1993. Social Impact: Piparwar and the North Karanpura Coal Fields. Hunterganj and Chauparan: Bharat Jan Andolan and Nav Bharat Jagruti Kendra.

Cernea, M. M. 2000. 'Risks, Safeguards and Reconstruction: A Model for Population Displacement and Resettlement,' in Michael M. Cernea and Christopher Mc Dowell (eds). Risks and Reconstruction: Experiences of Resettlers and Refugees. Washington D. C.: The World Bank, pp. 11-55.

CMIE. 1986. Basic Statistics Relating to the Indian Economy, Vol. I & II. Bombay: Centre for Monitoring Indian Economy.

Department of Mines.1998. Mining Leases in Goa. Panaji: Directorate of Industries and Mines.

Deputy Commissioner, Sivasagar1987. LA File No 35/86-87,dt NA, Bensali Coal India LTD Project, LAQ office, District Collectorate.

Directorate of Mining and Geology. 1996. Mineral Statistics of Orissa 1994-95. Bhubaneshwar: Department of Steel and Mines.

Downing, T. 2002. Avoiding New Poverty: Mining-Induced Displacement and Resettlement. International Institute of Environment and Development.

Ecoforum. 1993. Fish, Curry and Rice: A Citizens' Report on the Goan Environment. Mapuca: The Other India Press.

Ekka, A. and Asif M. 2000. Development-Induced Displacement and Rehabilitation in Jharkhand: A Database on its Extent and Nature. New Delhi: Indian Social Institute (mimeo).

Fernandes, W. 1998. 'Development-Induced Displacement in Eastern India,' in S.C.Dube (ed). Antiquity and Modernity in Tribal India: Vol. I: Continuity and Change Among the Tribals. New Delih: Inter-India Publishers, pp. 217-301.

Fernandes, W. 2007. 'Singur and the Displacement Scenario,' Economic and Political Weekly, 42 (n. 3, Jan. 20-26, pp. 203-206.

Fernandes, W. and Raj, S.A. 1992. Development, Displacement and Rehabilitation in the Tribal Areas of Orissa. New Delhi: Indian Social Institute (mimeo).

Fernandes, W. and Asif M. 1997. Development-Induced Displacement in Orissa 1951 to

1995: A Database on Its Extent and Nature. New Delhi: Indian Social Institute.

Fernandes, W. and Naik, N. 2001. Development-Induced Displacement in Goa 1965-1995: A Database on Its Extent and Nature. Guwahati: North Eastern Social Research Centre and Panjim: INSAF (mimeo).

Fernandes, W., D'Souza N.G., Choudhury A.R. and Asif M. 2001. Development-Induced Displacement, Deprival and Rehabilitation in Andhra Pradesh 1951-1995: A Quantitative and Quantitative Study of Its Extent and Nature. New Delhi: Indian Social Institute and Guwahati: North Eastern Social Research Centre.

Fernandes, W., Chhetri S., Joseph S. and Lama S. 2006. Development-Induced Displacement and Deprivation in West Bengal 1947-2000: A Quantitative and Qualitative Database on Its Extent and Impact. Guwahati: North Eastern Social Research Centre (mimeo).

Fernandes, W. and Bharali G. 2006. Development-Induced Displacement in Assam 1947-2000: A Quantitative and Qualitative Study of Its Extent and Nature. Guwahati: North Eastern Social Research Centre (mimeo).

George, S.S. 2002. 'Women and Mining in the Singhbhum Districts of Jharkhand,' in Anon (ed). Women and Mining: A Resource Kit. New Delhi: Delhi Forum, pp. 16-21.

Govt. of India. 1985. Report of the Committee on Rehabilitation of Displaced Tribals due to Development Projects. New Delhi: Ministry of Home Affairs.

IBM. 1991. Mining Leases in India 1991. Nagpur: Indian Bureau of Mines.

IBM. 1994. Indian Mineral Yearbook 1994. Nagpur: Indian Bureau of Mines.

IBM. 1997a. Indian Mineral Yearbook 1997. Nagpur: Indian Bureau of Mines.

IBM. 1997b. Mineral Facts and Problems No. 17: Iron Ore. Nagpur: Indian Bureau of Mines.

IBM. 1998. Indian Mineral Yearbook 1998. Nagpur: Indian Bureau of Mines.

IWGIA. 2004. The Indigenous World 2004. Copenhagen: International Work Group for Indigenous Affairs.

Kalshian, R. 2007. 'Preface,' in Rakesh Kalshian (ed). Caterpillar and the Mahua Flower: Tremors in India's Mining Fields.

New Delhi: Panos South Asia, pp. 4-10.

Kamat G.V. 1995a. 'The Goan Economy 1961-1992,' in GCCI (ed). Industrial and Commercial Directory Goa. 1995. Panjim: Goa Chamber of Commerce and Industry, pp. 15-21.

Kamath, U.D. 1995b. 'Tourism Profile in Goa,' in GCCI (ed). Op. Cit. pp. 31-33.

Lobo, L. and Kumar S. 2007. Development-Induced Displacement in Gujarat 1947-2004. Vadodara: Centre for Culture and Development.

MCL. 1995. Status of Land Acquisition in 1995. Sambalpur: RR and LA Department, Mahanadi Coalfields Limited.

Menon, G. 1995. 'The Impact of Migration on the Work and Tribal Women's Status,' in Loes Schenken-Sandbergen (ed). Women and Seasonal Labour Migration. New Delhi: Sage, pp. 79-154.

MRD. 1993. National Policy for Development-Induced Displacement and Rehabilitation of Persons Displaced as a Consequence of Acquisition of Land. New Delhi: Ministry of Rural Development, Government of India (First draft).

Murickan, J. et al 2003. Development Induced Displacement: The Case of Kerala. Jaipur and New Delhi: Rawat Publications.

Pandey, B. 1995. 'Impoverishing Effects of Coal Mining Projects: A Case Study of five Villages in Orissa,' in Hari Mohan Mathur and David Marsden (eds). Development Projects & Impoverishment Risks: Resettling Project-Affected People in India. Delhi: Oxford Unversity Press, pp. 174-192.

Padel, F. and Das S. 2007. 'Agya, What Do You Mean by Development?' in Rakesh Kalshian (ed). Op. cit. pp. 24-46.

Pandey, B. 1998a. Displaced Development: Impact of Open Cast Mining on Women. New Delhi: Fiiedrich Ebert Stiftung.

Pandey, B. 1998b. Depriving the Underprivileged for Development. Bhubaneshwar: Institute of Socio-Economic Development.

Patnaik, G. and Panda D. 1992. 'The New Economic Policy and the Poor,' Social Action, 42 (n.2, AprJune), pp. 201212.

Ramanathan, U. 1999. 'Public Purpose: Points for Discussion,' in Walter Fernandes (ed). The Land Acquisition (Amendment) Bill 1998: For Liberalisation or for the Poor? New Delhi: Indian Social Institute, pp. 19-24.

Rau, G. A.V. 1990. 'Sardar Sarovar Project in Gujarat State: The Project and Rehabilitation Policy,' in Aloysius P. Fernandez (ed). Workshop on Persons Displaced by Development Projects. Bangalore: ISECS and MYRADA, pp. 60-67.

Sen, I. 1992. 'Mechanisation and the Working Class Women,' Social Action 42 (n. 4, Oct.Dec.), pp. 391400.

Sherman, C. 1993. The Peoples' Story: A Report on the Social Impact of the Australian-Financed Piparwar Coal Mine, Bihar, India. Melbourne: AID/WATCH.

Singh, C. 1989. 'Rehabilitation and the Right to Property,' in Walter Fernandes and Enakshi Ganguly Thukral (eds). Development, Displacement and Rehabilitation: Issues for a National Debate. New Delhi: Indian Social Institute, pp. 91-103.

TERI. 1997. Final Draft Report of Areawide Environmental Quality Management (AEQM) Plan for the Mining Belt of Goa State. New Delhi: Tata Energy Research Institute.

Thukral, E.G. 1999. 'Bottom-Up' Humanscape 6 (n. 11, November), pp.10-12.

Thukral, E.G. and Singh. M. 1995. 'Dams and the Displaced in India,' in Hari Mohan Mathur (ed). Development, Displacement and Resettlement: Focus on Asia. New Delhi: Vikas Publishing Company, pp. 93-121.

VAK. 1997. 'The New Economic Path Trends and Impact,' in Ajit Muricken (ed). Globalisation and SAP: Trends and Impact, An Overview. Mumbai: Vikas Adhyayan Kendra. pp. 151180.

Anand, R. (2013), The Fiscal and Welfare Impacts of Reforming Fuel Subsidies in India, International Monetary Fund, Washington, DC.

CEA (Central Electricity Authority) (2014a), General Review 2014, CEA, New Delhi.—(2014b), Monthly Generation Report, www.cea.nic.in/reports/monthly/generation_rep/actual/dec14/actual-dec14.html

Chaturvedi, V., et al. (2014), State of Environmental Clearances in India: Procedures, Timelines and Delays across Sectors and States, Council on Energy, Environment and Water, New Delhi.

CSO (Central Statistics Office) (2015), Energy Statistics 2015, CSO, New Delhi. DAE (Department of Atomic Energy) (2015), Annual Report 2014-15, DAE, Mumbai.

FICCI (Federation of Indian Chambers of Commerce & Industry) (2012), Lack of Affordable & Quality Power: Shackling

India's Growth Story, FICCI, New Delhi.

IEA (International Energy Agency) (2012), Understanding Energy Challenges in India: Policies, Players and Issues, OECD/IEA, Paris.—(2015), World Energy Outlook 2015, OECD/IEA, Paris.

IMF (International Monetary Fund) (2015), 2015 Article IV Consultation—Staff Report, IMF, Washington, DC. Jain, A., et al. (2015), Access to Clean Cooking Energy and Electricity—Survey of States, Council on Energy, Environment and Water, New Dehli.

MNRE (Ministry of New and Renewable Energy) (2015), Small Hydro, http://mnre.gov.in/ schemes/grid-connected/small-hydro/,

Ministry of Statistics and Programme Implementation (2012), National Sample Survey Office, Household Consumption of Various Goods and Services in India, Government of India, New Delhi.

National Sample Survey Office (2014a), Household Consumption of Various Goods and Services in India 2011-2012, Government of India, New Delhi.—(2014b), Urban Slums in India, 2012, Government of India, New Delhi.

OECD (Organization for Economic Co-operation and Development) (2014), Economic Survey of India, OECD, Paris.

Pargal, S. and Banerjee S.G. (2014), More Power to India: The Challenge of Electricity Distribution, World Bank, Washington, DC

Petroleum Planning and Analysis Cell (2015), http://ppac.org.in/content/212_1_Import Export.aspx,

Power Finance Corporation (2014), The Performance of State Power Utilities for the years 2010/11 to 2012/13, Power Finance Corporation, Mumbai.

TERI (The Energy Research Institute) (2015), Policy Brief. Crisis in India's Electricity Distribution Sector: Time to Reboot for a Viable Future, TERI, New Delhi.

UNICEF (United Nations Children's Fund) (2012), The State of the World's Children 2012, UNICEF, New York.

UNCTAD (United Nations Conference on Trade and Development) (2015), World Investment Report, UNCTAD, Geneva. United Nations Population Division (UNPD) (2015), World Population Prospects: The 2015 Revision, United Nations, New York. World Bank (2014), Brief: The Transport Sector in India,

http://go.worldbank.org/ FUE8JM6E40

World Health Organization (WHO) (2014), Ambient Air Pollution Database, WHO, Geneva. WRI (World Resources Institute) (2014), 'Identifying the Global Coal Industry's Water Risks', WRI, Washington, DC.

Airbus (2015), Market Forecast, www.airbus.com/company/market/forecast/

BP (2015), BP Statistical Review of World Energy 2015, BP, London. CDKN (Climate & Development Knowledge Network) (2013), Creating Market Support for Energy Efficiency: India's Perform, Achieve and Trade Scheme, CDKN, London.

Chaturvedi, V. and Sharma M. (2015), 'Modelling Long-term HFC Emissions from India's Residential Air-Conditioning Sector: Exploring Implications of Alternative Refrigerants, Best Practices, and A Sustainable Lifestyle within an Integrated Assessment Modelling Framework', Climate Policy, Vol. 9.

Department of Fertilizers (2014), India Fertilizer Scenario 2013, Government of India, Ministry of Chemicals and Fertilizers, Department of Fertilizers, New Delhi.

Department of Fertilizers (2015), Annual Report 2014-15 Towards Sustainable and Shared Prosperity, Government of India, Ministry of Chemicals and Fertilizers, Department of Fertilizers, New Delhi.

Ghosh, A., & Agrawal, S. (2015, August 17), 'Sustainable solar irrigation', Business Standard, www.business-standard.com/article/opinion/arunabha-ghosh-shalu-agrawal-sustainablesolar-irrigation-115081701282_1.html

Government of India, GEF, UNDP (2012), GEF-UNDP-MoEF Project 3465—Energy Efficiency Improvements in Indian Brick Industry Project, United Nations Development Programme.

Gulati, A. and Banerjee P. (2015), Rationalising Fertiliser Subsidy in India: Key Issues and Policy Options, Indian Council for Research on International Economic Relations, New Delhi.

IEA (International Energy Agency) (2007), Tracking Industrial Energy Efficiency and CO2 Emissions, OECD/IEA, Paris.—(2015), World Energy Outlook 2015, OECD/IEA, Paris.

JPC (Joint Plant Committee) (2014), Annual Statistics 2013/14, JPC, Kolkata, India.

Lalchandani, D. and Maithel S. (2013), Towards Cleaner Brick Kilns in India, Greentech Knowledge

Solutions Private Limited, Chennai, India.

Maithel, S. (2013), Evaluating Energy Conservation Potential of Brick Production in India, SAARC (South Asian Association for Regional Cooperation), New Delhi.

Ministry of Agriculture (2013), State of Indian Agriculture 2012-13, Government of India. Department of Agriculture and Cooperation, New Delhi.

Ministry of Petroleum & Natural Gas (2014), Indian Petroleum and Natural Gas Statistics, Government of India, Ministry of Petroleum & Natural Gas, Economics and Statistics Division, New Delhi.

Nand, S. and Goswami M. (2008), 'Recent Efforts in Energy Conservation in Ammonia and Urea Plants', Indian Journal of Fertilisers, Vol. 4(12), pp.17-20.

Phadke, A., Abhyankar, N., & Shahh, N. (2014), Avoiding 100 New Power Plants by Increasing Efficiency of Room Air Conditioners in India: Opportunities and Challenges, Berkeley, Lawrence Berkeley National Laboratory.

Palit, B. (2014), 'Indian Approaches to Energy Access' in Energy Poverty, Oxford University Press, Oxford.

Practical Action (2015), Gender and Livelihoods Impacts of Clean Cookstoves in South Asia, Global Alliance for Clean Cookstoves (GACC).

SME Chamber of India (Small and Medium Business Development Chamber of India) (2015), 'About MSMEs in India', www. smechamberofindia.com/about_msmes.aspx,

Shrimali, G., Slaski, X., Thurber, M., & Zerriffi, H. (2011), Improved stoves in India: A study of sustainable business models, Energy Policy, 7543-7566.

TERI (The Energy and Resources Institute) (2015), Energy Security Outlook: Defining a Secure and Sustainable Energy Future for India, TERI, New Delhi.

USGS (United States Geological Survey) (2012a), 'Assessment of Potential Additions to Conventional Oil and Gas Resources of the World (Outside the United States) from Reserve Growth', Fact Sheet 2012-3052, USGS, Boulder, Colorado

(2012b) 'An Estimate of Undiscovered Conventional Oil and Gas Resources of the World', Fact Sheet 2012-3042, USGS, Boulder, Colorado

BGR (German Federal Institute for Geosciences and Natural Resources) (2014), Energiestudie

2014, Reserven, Ressourcen und Verfügbarkeit von Energierohstoffen (Energy Resources 2014, Reserves, Resources and Availability of Energy Resources), BGR, Hannover, Germany.

CEA (Central Electricity Authority) (2014), Status of Hydro Electric Projects under Execution for 12th Plan & Beyond, http://cea.nic.in/ reports/proj_mon/status_he_execution.pdf

Coal Directory of India (2014), Coal Statistics 2013-14, Government of India, Ministry of Coal, Coal Controller's Organization, Kolkata http://coal.nic.in/sites/upload_files/ coal/files/coalupload/coaldir13-14.pdf

IAEA/OECD (International Atomic Energy Agency and Organization for Economic Co-operation and Development) (2014), Uranium 2014: Resources, Production and Demand (The Red Book), OECD, Paris.

IEA (International Energy Agency) (2013), World Energy Outlook 2013, OECD/ IEA, Paris.—(2014), World Energy Outlook 2014, OECD/IEA, Paris.—(2015), World Energy Outlook 2015, OECD/IEA, Paris.

Inventory of Coal Resources of India (2015), www.cmpdi.co.in/coalinventory.php

National Institute of Solar Energy (2014), State-wise Estimated Solar Power Potential in the Country, http://mnre.gov.in/file-manager/UserFiles/Statewise-Solar-Potential-NISE.pdf, accessed 9 October 2015.

National Institute of Wind Energy (2015), Wind Resource Assessment, http:// niwe.res.in/ department_wra.php

Beinhocker, E. (2007), Tracking the Growth of India's Middle Class, McKinsey&Company.

Climate Policy Initiative, 'Reaching India's Renewable Energy Targets Cost-Effectively: A Foreign Exchange Hedging Facility; Climate Policy Initiative'

Council on Energy, Environment and Water and Natural Resources Defense Council (2014), Creating Green Jobs: Employment Generation by Gamesa-Renew Power's 85 megawatt wind project in Jath, Maharashtra, New York and New Delhi.

Didier, T., and Schmukler, S. (2013), 'The Financing and Growth of Firms in China and India: Evidence from Capital Markets', Journal of International Money and Finance, Elsevier, Vol. 39.

Dubash, N., et al. (2015), Informing India's Energy and Climate Debate: Policy Lessons from Modelling Studies, Centre for Policy Research, New Delhi.

Government of India (2012), Census of India 2011: Houses, Households Amenities and Assets, New Delhi.

Group of Thirty (2013), Long-term Finance and Economic Growth, Group of Thirty, Washington, DC.

Hijoka, Y., et al. (2014), Climate Change 2014: Impacts Adaptation, and Vulnerability, Cambridge University Press, Cambridge.

IEA (International Energy Agency) (2012), World Energy Outlook 2012, OECD/IEA, Paris.—(2014a) World Energy Outlook 2014, OECD/IEA, Paris.—(2014b), World Energy Investment Outlook, OECD/IEA, Paris.—(2015) Energy and Climate Change: World Energy Outlook Special Report, OECD/IEA, Paris. India Department of Industrial Policy and Promotion (2015), 'Fact Sheet on Foreign Direct Investment (FDI): From April, 2000 to June, 2015', www.dipp.nic.in/English/publications/FDI_statistics/2015/india_FDI_June2015.pdf

Ministry of Labour and Employment (2013), Pocket Book of Labour Statistics 2013, Government of India, Shimla/Chandigarh OECD (Organization for Economic Co-operation and Development) (2014), Economic Survey of India, OECD, Paris.

REN21 (2015), Renewables 2015 Global Status Report, REN21 Secretariat, Paris. Rutovitz (2012), Calculating Global Energy Sector Jobs: 2012 Methodology, Institute of Sustainable Futures, University of Technology Sydney, Australia. World Bank (2014), Enterprise Surveys, World Bank Enterprise Surveys, www.enterprisesurveys.org/data/exploreeconomies/2014/india

WWAP (United Nations World Water Assessment Programme) (2014), The United Nations World Water Development Report 2014: Water and Energy, UNESCO, Paris.

Ashok, S. (2007) Optimized model for community-based hybrid energy system. Renewable energy 32(7): P.1155.

Banerjee, R. (2006) Comparison of options for distributed generation in India. Energy Policy 34(1): P.101-111.

Barnes, D. F., Fitzgerald K. B. and Peskin H. M. (2002) The Benefits of Rural Electrification in India: Implications for Education, Household Lighting, and Irrigation. Draft manuscript, July.

Barnes, D. F. and Sen M. (2002) Energy Strategies for Rural India: Evidence from Six States. ESMAP, Washington, DC Available at http://imagebank.worldbank.org/servlet/WDS_IBank_Servlet.

Bharadwaj, A. and Tongia R. (2003). Distributed Power Generation: Rural India-A Case Study. 34

Bose, R. K. and Shukla M. (2001) Electricity tariffs in India: an assessment of consumers' ability and willingness to pay in Gujarat. Energy Policy 29(6): P.465-478.

Chakrabarti, S. and Chakrabarti S. (2002) Rural electrification programme with solar energy in remote region—a case study in an island. Energy Policy 30(1): P.33-42.

Choynowski, P. (2002). Measuring willingness to pay for electricity.

Deshmukh and Bilolikar (2006) Optimisation of rural electrification methods. Advances in Energy Research.

Duke, R. D., A. Jacobson and D. M. Kammen (2002) Photovoltaic module quality in the Kenyan solar home systems market. Energy Policy 30(6): P.477-499.

Ghosh, D., Shukla P. R., Garg A. and Ramana P. V. (2002). Renewable energy technologies for the Indian power sector: mitigation potential and operational strategies, Elsevier. 6: 481-512.

Ghosh, S., Das T. K. and Jash T. (2004) Sustainability of decentralized woodfuel-based power plant: an experience in India. Energy 29(1): P.155-166.

GoI (2005). National Electricity Policy. M. o. Power, Government of India.

GoI (2006). Integrated Energy Policy: Report of the Expert Committee. P. Commission, Government of India, New Delhi,. Gokak Committee (2003). Gokak Committee Report on Distributed Generation. M. o. Power, Government of India. available at powermin.nic.in.

Gunaratne, L. (2002). Rural Energy Services Best Practices. USAID, USAID.

Hansen, C. J. and Bower J. (2003). An Economic Evaluation of Small-scale Distributed Electricity Generation Technologies, Oxford Institute for Energy Studies. IEA (2002). World Energy Outlook. World Energy Outlook. IEA.

Karekezi, S. (1994) Disseminating Renewable Energy Technologies in Sub-Saharan Africa. Annual Review of Energy and the Environment 19(1): P.387-421.

Kishore, V. V. N., Bhandari P. M. and Gupta P. (2004). Biomass energy technologies for rural infrastructure and village power—opportunities and challenges in the context of global climate change concerns, Elsevier. 32: 801-810.

Miller, D. (1998). Agents of sustainable technological change; the case of solar electrification. Judge Business School. Cambridge, Cambridge University. Doctoral Thesis.

Miller, D. and Hope C. (2000) Learning to lend for off-grid solar power: policy lessons from World Bank loans to India, Indonesia, and Sri Lanka.

Energy Policy 28(2): P.87-105. Ministry of Power (2003). The Electricity Act, 2003. M. o. Power, Government of India, New Delhi. MOSPI (2006). Level and pattern of consumer expenditure 2004-5 NSS 61st. N. S. S. Organization. Delhi.

Mukhopadhyay, K. (2004) An assessment of a Biomass Gasification based Power Plant in the Sunderbans. Biomass and Bioenergy 27(3): P.253-264.

Nouni, M. R., Mullick S. C. and Kandpal T. C. (2005) Techno-economics of micro-hydro power plants for remote villages in Uttaranchal in India. International Journal of Global Energy Issues 24(1): P.59-75.

Nouni, M. R., Mullick S. C. and Kandpal T. C. (2006) Photovoltaic projects for decentralized power supply in India: A financial evaluation. Energy Policy 34(18): P.3727-3738.

Nouni, M. R., S. C. Mullick and T. C. Kandpal (2007) Biomass gasifier projects for decentralized power supply in India: A financial evaluation. Energy Policy 35(2): P.1373-1385.

NSSO (2001). Consumption of Some Important Commodities in India: 1999-2000.

G. o. I. Ministry of Statistics and Programme Implementation, New Delhi, National Sample Survey Organization.

Powerline (2007). Average grid tariffs by state. Powerline. Radulovic, V. (2005) Are new institutional economics enough? Promoting photovoltaics in India's agricultural sector. Energy Policy 33(14): P.1883-1899.

Ravindranath, N. H. (2004) Sustainable biomass power for rural India: Case study of biomass gasifier for village electrification. Current science 87(7): P.932.

Ravindranath, N. H., Somashekar H. I., Nagaraja M. S., Sudha P., Sangeetha G., Bhattacharya S. C. and Salam P. A. (2005) Assessment of sustainable non-plantation biomass resources potential for energy in India. Biomass and Bioenergy 29: P.178- 190.

Tongia, R. (2003). Stanford-CMU Indian Power Sector Reform Studies.

Tongia, R. (2006). The Political Economy of Indian Power Sector Reforms. The Political Economy of Power Sector Reform: The Experiences of Five Major Developing Countries. D. G. Victor and T. C. Heller, Cambridge University Press.

Tripathi, A. K., Iyer P. V. R. and Kandpal T. C. (1997) A financial evaluation of biomassgasifier-based power generation in India. Bioresource Technology 61(1): P.53-59. UREDA (2006). Determination of Tariff for Ramgarh Small Hydro Plant for FY 2005-06 for sale of energy to State Distribution Licensee. UREDA, http://uerc.org/PetitionRamgad.pdf.

Velayudhan, S. K. (2003) Dissemination of solar photovoltaics: a study on the government programme to promote solar lantern in India. Energy Policy 31(14): P.1509-1518.

COOKING FUELS

Beltramo, T., Levine, D., Blalock, G. (2014). The Effect of Marketing Messages, Liquidity Constraints, and Household Bargaining on Willingness to Pay For a Non-traditional Cook Stove. The Center for Effective Global Action, University of California, Berkeley. https://escholarship.org/uc/item/4vj3w941

Clark, M. L., Heiderscheidt, J.M. and Peel, J.L. (2015). Integrating behavior change theory and measures into health-based cookstove interventions: a proposed epidemiologic research agenda. Journal of Health Communication. 20(sup1): 94-97. doi: 10.1080/10810730.2014.989346

Goodwin, N.J., O'Farrell, S.E., Jagoe, K., Rouse, J., Roma, E., Biran, A. and Finkelstein, E.A. (2014). Use of behaviour change techniques in clean cooking interventions: a review of the evidence and scorecard of effectiveness. Journal of Health Communication: International Perspectives. 20(sup1).

Michie, S., et al. (2013) The behavior change technique taxonomy (v1) of 93 hierarchically clustered techniques: building an international consensus for the reporting of behavior change interventions. Annals of Behavioral Medicine. 46(1): p. 81-95. doi: 10.1007/s12160-013- 9486-6

Namagembe A., Muller N., Scott, L.M., Zwisler, G., Johnson, M., Arney, J., Charron, D., and Mugisha E. (2015). Factors influencing the acquisition and correct and consistent use of the top-lit updraft cookstove in Uganda.

Journal of Health Communication. 20(sup1): 76-83. doi: 10.1080/10810730.2014.994245.

Puzzolo, E., Stanistreet, D., Pope, D., Bruce, N. and Rehfuess, E. (2013). Factors Influencing the Large-scale Uptake by Households of Cleaner and More Efficient Household Energy Technologies. EPPI-Centre, Social Science Research Unit, Institute of Education, University of London. London, England.

Rosenbaum, J., Derby E. and Dutta, K. (2015). Understanding consumer preference and willingness to pay for improved cookstoves in Bangladesh. Journal of Health Communication. 20(sup1): 20—27. doi: 10.1080/10810730.2014.989345.

Rosenthal, J. and Borazzo, J. (Eds). (2015) Special issue. Advancing communication and behavior change strategies for cleaner cooking. Journal of Health Communication. 20(sup1).

Shankar, A. V., Onyura, M.A. and Alderman, J. (2015). Agency-based empowerment training enhances sales capacity of female energy entrepreneurs in Kenya. Journal of Health Communication. 20(sup1): 67—75. doi:10.1080/10810730.2014.1002959

Treiber, M.U., Grimsby, L.K., and Aune, J.B. (2015). Reducing energy poverty through increasing choice of fuels and stoves in Kenya: Complementing the multiple fuel model. Energy for Sustainable Development. 27. 54—62. doi:10.1016/j.esd.2015.04.004

van der Kroon, B., et al. (2014). The impact of the household decision environment on fuel choice behavior. Energy Economics. 44(0). 236—247.

Kammila, S, Kappen, J.F., Rysankova, D., Hyseni, B. and Putti, V. R. (2014). Clean and Improved Cooking in Sub-Saharan Africa: A Landscape Report. Washington, D.C., World Bank Group. http:// documents.worldbank.org/curated/en/2015/07/24853349/cleanimproved-cooking-sub-saharan-africa-landscape-report

Adler, T. (2010). 'Better burning, better breathing: Improving health with cleaner cook stoves.' Environmental Health Perspectives 118(3): 124-129.

Anenberg, S. C., K. Balakrishnan, J. Jetter, O. Masera, S. Mehta, J. Moss and V. Ramanathan (2013). 'Cleaner cooking solutions to achieve health, climate, and economic cobenefits.' Environmental science & technology 47(9): 3944-3952.

Bailis, R., Drigo R., Ghilardi A. and Masera O. (2015). 'The carbon footprint of traditional woodfuels.' Nature Climate Change 5(3): 266-272.

Barnes, D. F., Openshaw, K., Smith, K. R., Van der Plas, R. and Mundial B. (1994). What Makes People Cook with Improved Biomas Stoves? Washington, DC, World Bank.

Beltramo, T., Blalock, G., Levine, D. I. and Simons, A. M. (2015). 'Does peer use influence adoption of efficient cookstoves? Evidence from a randomized controlled trial in Uganda.' Journal of health communication 20(sup1): 55-66.

Beltramo, T., Blalock, G., Levine, D. I. and Simons, A. M. (2015). 'The effect of marketing messages and payment over time on willingness to pay for fuel-efficient cookstoves.' Journal of Economic Behavior & Organization.

Bensch, G. and Peters, J. (2015). 'The intensive margin of technology adoption—Experimental evidence on improved cooking stoves in rural Senegal.' Journal of health economics 42: 44-63.

Boardman, A. E., Greenberg, D., Vining, A. and Weimer, D. (2005). Cost-benefit analysis: concepts and practice, Prentice Hall.

Bond, T. C., Doherty, S. J., Fahey, D., Forster, P., Berntsen, T., DeAngelo, B., Flanner, M., Ghan S., Kärcher, B. and Koch, D. (2013). 'Bounding the role of black carbon in the climate system: A scientific assessment.' Journal of Geophysical Research: Atmospheres 118(11): 5380-5552.

Bond, T. C., Streets, D. G., Yarber, K. F., Nelson, S. M., Woo, J. H. and Klimont, Z. (2004). 'A technologybased global inventory of black and organic carbon emissions from combustion.' Journal of Geophysical Research: Atmospheres (1984—2012) 109(D14).

Bond, T. C. and Sun, H. (2005). 'Can reducing black carbon emissions counteract global warming?' Environmental Science & Technology 39(16): 5921-5926.

Brooks, N., Bhojvaid, V., Jeuland M., Lewis, J. J., Patange, O. and Pattanayak, S. K. (2014). How much do clean cookstoves reduce biomass fuel use? Evidence from North India. Duke University Working Paper.

Durham, N. C. Bruce, N., McCracken, J., Albalak, R., Schei, M., Smith, K. R., Lopez, V. and West, C. (2004). 'Impact of improved stoves, house construction and child location on levels of indoor air pollution exposure in young Guatemalan children.' Journal of Exposure Science and Environmental Epidemiology 14: S26- S33. 35

Burnett, R. T., Pope, C. A., Ezzati M., Olives, C., Lim, S. S., Mehta, S., Shin, H. H., Singh G., Hubbell, B. and Brauer, M. (2014). 'An integrated risk function for estimating the global burden of disease attributable to ambient fine particulate matter exposure.'

Chowdhury, Z., Campanella, L., Gray, C., Al Masud, A., Marter-Kenyon, J., Pennise D., Charron, D. and Zuzhang, X. (2013). 'Measurement and modeling of indoor air pollution in rural households with multiple stove interventions in Yunnan, China.' Atmospheric Environment 67: 161-169.

Ezzati, M. and Kammen, D. M. (2001). 'Indoor air pollution from biomass combustion and acute respiratory infections in Kenya: an exposure-response study.' The Lancet 358(9282): 619-624.

Ezzati, M. and Kammen, D. M. (2002). 'Household energy, indoor air pollution, and health in developing countries: knowledge base for effective interventions.' Annual review of energy and the environment 27(1): 233-270.

Ferraro, P. J., Lawlor, K., Mullan, K. L. and Pattanayak, S. K. (2011). 'Forest figures: ecosystem services valuation and policy evaluation in developing countries.' Review of Environmental Economics and Policy: rer019.

Fitzgerald, C., Aguilar-Villalobos, M., Eppler, A. R., Dorner, S. C., Rathbun, S. L. and Naeher, L. P. (2012). 'Testing the effectiveness of two improved cookstove interventions in the Santiago de Chuco Province of Peru.' Science of the total environment 420: 54-64.

Gall, E. T., Carter, E. M., Matt Earnest, C. and Stephens, B. (2013). 'Indoor air pollution in developing countries: research and implementation needs for improvements in global public health.' American journal of public health 103(4): e67-e72.

Hanna, R., Duflo, E. and Greenstone, M. (2012). Up in smoke: the influence of household behavior on the long-run impact of improved cooking stoves, National Bureau of Economic Research.

Hutton, G., Rehfuess, E. and Tediosi, F. (2007). 'Evaluation of the costs and benefits of interventions to reduce indoor air pollution.' Energy for Sustainable Development 11(4): 34-43.

Interagency Working Group on Social Cost of Carbon (2015). Technical Support Document: Technical Update of the Social Cost of Carbon for Regulatory Impact Analysis Under Executive Order 12866. Washington, USA, United States Government

IPCC (2013). 'Climate change 2013: The physical science basis. Contribution of working group I to the fifth assessment report of the intergovernmental panel on climate change.'

Jagger, P. and Shively, G. (2014). 'Land use change, fuel use and respiratory health in Uganda.' Energy policy 67: 713-726.

Jeuland, M., Bhojvaid, V. , Kar, A., Lewis, J. J., Patange, O. , Pattanayak, S. K., Ramanathan, N., Rehman, H., Tan Soo, J. S. and Ramanathan, V. (2014). 'Preferences for improved cook stoves: Evidence from North Indian villages.' Duke Environmental and Energy Economics Working Paper Series No. EE: 14-07. 36

Jeuland, M., Lucas, M., Clemens, J. and Whittington, D. (2010). 'Estimating the private benefits of vaccination against cholera in Beira, Mozambique: A travel cost approach.' Journal of Development Economics 91(2): 310-322.

Jeuland, M., Pattanayak, S. and Bluffstone, R. (2014). 'The Economics of Household Air Pollution.' Annual review of resource economics (forthcoming).

Jeuland, M., Pattanayak, S. K. and Soo, J. T. (2014). Preference heterogeneity and adoption of environmental health improvements: Evidence from a cookstove promotion experiment. Duke Environmental and Energy Economics Working Paper Series EE-14-10. Durham, USA.

Jeuland, M. A. and Pattanayak, S. K. (2012). 'Benefits and costs of improved cookstoves: assessing the implications of variability in health, forest and climate impacts.' PloS one 7(2): e30338.

Johnson, M. A., Pilco, V., Torres, R., Joshi, S., Shrestha, R. M., Yagnaraman, M., Lam, N. L., Doroski, B., Mitchell, J. and Canuz, E. (2013). 'Impacts on household fuel consumption from biomass stove programs in India, Nepal, and Peru.' Energy for Sustainable Development 17(5): 403-411.

Lam, N. L., Smith, K. R., Gauthier, A. and Bates, M. N. (2012). 'Kerosene: a review of household uses and their hazards in low-and middle-income countries.' Journal of Toxicology and Environmental Health, Part B 15(6): 396-432.

Larsen, B. (2014). Air Pollution Assessment Paper: Benefits and costs of the air pollution targets for the post 2015 development agenda: Post 2015 Consensus. Copenhagen, Denmark, Copenhagen Consensus Center.

Lim, S. S., Vos, T. , Flaxman, A. D., Danaei, G., Shibuya, K., Adair-Rohani, H., AlMazroa, M. A., Amann, M., Anderson, H. R. and Andrews, K. G. (2013). 'A comparative risk assessment of burden of disease and injury attributable to 67 risk factors and risk factor clusters in 21 regions, 1990—2010: a systematic analysis for the Global Burden of Disease Study 2010.' The lancet 380(9859): 2224-2260.

MacCarty, N., Still D. and Ogle D. (2010). 'Fuel use and emissions performance of fifty cooking stoves in the laboratory and related benchmarks of performance.' Energy for Sustainable Development 14(3): 161-171.

Mackie, P., Jara-Diaz S. and Fowkes A. (2001). 'The value of travel time savings in evaluation.' Transportation Research Part E: Logistics and Transportation Review 37(2): 91-106.

Mehta, S. and Shahpar C. (2004). 'The health benefits of interventions to reduce indoor air pollution from solid fuel use: a cost- effectiveness analysis.' Energy for Sustainable Development 8(3): 53-59.

Naeher, L., Leaderer B. and Smith K. (2000). 'Particulate matter and carbon monoxide in highland Guatemala: indoor and outdoor levels from traditional and improved wood stoves and gas stoves.' Indoor air 10(3): 200-205.

Pennise, D., Brant S., S. Agbeve M., Quaye W., Mengesha F., Tadele W. and Wofchuck T. (2009). 'Indoor air quality impacts of an improved wood stove in Ghana and an ethanol stove in Ethiopia.' Energy for Sustainable Development 13(2): 71-76. 37

Ramanathan, V. and Carmichael G. (2008). 'Global and regional climate changes due to black carbon.' Nature geoscience 1(4): 221-227.

Robinson, L. A. (2007). 'How US Government Agencies Value Mortality Risk Reductions.' Review of Environmental Economics and Policy 1(2): 283-299.

Ruiz-Mercado, I., Masera O., Zamora H. and Smith K. R. (2011). 'Adoption and sustained use of improved cookstoves.' Energy Policy 39(12): 7557-7566.

Shindell, D. T. (2015). 'The social cost of atmospheric release.' Climatic Change: 1-14.
Smith, K. R. (2000). 'National burden of disease in India from indoor air pollution.' Proceedings of the National Academy of Sciences 97(24): 13286-13293.

Smith, K. R., Dutta K., Chengappa C., Gusain P., Masera O., Berrueta V., Edwards R., Bailis R. and Shields K. N. (2007). 'Monitoring and evaluation of improved biomass cookstove programs for indoor air quality and stove performance: conclusions from the Household Energy and Health Project.'

Energy for Sustainable Development 11(2): 5-18.

Smith, K. R., Frumkin H., Balakrishnan K., Butler C. D., Chafe Z. A., Fairlie I., Kinney P., Kjellstrom T., Mauzerall D. L. and McKone T. E. (2013). 'Energy and human health.' Annual review of public health 34: 159-188.

Smith, K. R., J. P. McCracken, Weber M. W., A. Hubbard, A. Jenny, L. M. Thompson, J. Balmes, A. Diaz, B. Arana and N. Bruce (2011). 'Effect of reduction in household air pollution on childhood pneumonia in Guatemala (RESPIRE): a randomised controlled trial.' The Lancet 378(9804): 1717-1726.

van der Plas, R. J. and Abdel-Hamid M. A. (2005). 'Can the woodfuel supply in sub-Saharan Africa be sustainable? The case of N'Djamena, Chad.' Energy Policy 33(3): 297-306.

Viscusi, W. and Aldy J. (2003). 'The Value of a Statistical Life: A Critical Review of Market Estimates Throughout the World.' The Journal of Risk and Uncertainty 27(1): 5-76.

Vose, D. (1996). Risk Analysis, A Quantitative Guide. New York, John Wiley & Sons.
Whittington, D., W. M. Hanemann, C. Sadoff and M. Jeuland (2009). 'The challenge of improving water and sanitation services in less developed countries.' Foundations and Trends in Microeconomics 4(6): 469—609.

Whittington, D., Jeuland M., Barker K. and Yuen Y. (2012). 'Setting priorities, targeting subsidies among water, sanitation, and preventive health interventions in developing countries.' World Development 40(8): 1546-1568.

SUBSIDIES

Cabinet extends UDAY scheme deadline. (2016). The Hindu. Retrieved from http://www.thehindu.com/business/Economy/cabinet-extends-udayscheme-deadline/article8760873.ece

Govt may leave excise duty on petrol, diesel unchanged till oil prices touch $65. (2016). Daily News and Analysis. Retrieved from http://www.dnaindia.com/money/report-govt-may-not-cutexcise-duty-on-petrol-diesel-for-now-2230720

Govt mulling ways to bring petroleum products under GST: Dharmendra Pradhan (2016). Daily News and Analysis. Retrieved from http://www.dnaindia.com/money/report-govt-mulling-ways-tobring-petroleum-products-under-gst-dharmendrapradhan-2237960

Government of India. (2016, April 22). 1 crore Consumers join the 'GiveitUp' Movement. Press Information Bureau. Retrieved from http://pib. nic. in/newsite/pmreleases.aspx?mincode=20

GoI. (2016, April 25). DBT for kerosene subsidy. Press Information Bureau. Retrieved from http:// pib.nic.in/newsite/pmreleases.aspx?mincode=20

GoI. (2016, May 11). Gas connections in villages. Press Information Bureau. Retrieved from http:// pib.nic.in/newsite/pmreleases.aspx?mincode=20

GoI. (2016, April 1). Kerosene free Chandigarh from April 1, 2016. Press Information Bureau. Retrieved from http://pib.nic.in/ newsite/pmreleases. aspx?mincode=20

GoI. (2016, June 3). Unified guidelines for LPG distributorships issued. Press Information Bureau. Retrieved from http://pib.nic.in/ newsite/pmreleases. aspx?mincode=20

GoI. (2016, July 18). India's gas share is 6.5 per cent country's fuel basket. Press Information Bureau. Retrieved from http://pib.nic.in/ newsite/pmreleases. aspx?mincode=20

GoI. (2016, July 25). 17.66 Lakh LPG Connections given under Pradhan Mantri Ujjwala Yojana. Press Information Bureau. Retrieved from http://pib. nic. in/newsite/pmreleases.aspx?mincode=20

Joseph, J. (2016, July 20). CAG audit nails Centre's claim on LPG subsidy saving. The Hindu. Retrieved from http://www.thehindu. com/news/national/cagaudit-nails-centres-claim-on-lpg-subsidy-saving/ article8871994.ece

Mahamalkari, S. (2016, June 29). Govt nod for power subsidy to backward area industries. Times of India. Retrieved from http:// timesofindia.indiatimes. com/city/mumbai/ Govt-nod-for-power-subsidy-tobackward-area-industries/articleshow/52980025. cms

Nalinakanthi, V. (2016). All you wanted to know about Aadhaar Bill. Hindu Business Line. Retrieved from http://www.thehindubusinessline. com/opinion/ columns/all-you-wanted-to-know-about-aadhaarbill/article8381808.ece

Press Trust of India (PTI). (2016). Delhi government approves proposal to continue 50 per cent subsidy on power bills. News18.com. Retrieved from http://www.news18.com/news/ india/delhigovernment-approves-proposal-to-continue-50- subsidy-on-power-bills-1268492.html

Shyam, J., & Vyas, A. (2016). Oil companies get nod to increase kerosene price by 25 paise every month till April 2017. Economic Times. Retrieved from http://economictimes.indiatimes. com/ industry/energy/oil-gas/oil-companies-get-nodto-increase-kerosene-price-by-25-paise-everymonth-till-april-2017/articleshow/53182201. cms?utm_source=contentofinterest&utm_ medium=text&utm_campaign=cppst

Singh, S. (2016). PFC, REC will drop interest rates to double lending in three years. Economic Times. Retrieved from http://economictimes. indiatimes. com/industry/energy/power/pfc-rec-will-dropinterest-rates-to-double-lending-in-three-years/ articleshow/53371276.cms

Anand, R., Coady, D., Mohommad, A., Thakoor, V., & Walsh, J.P. (2013). The fiscal and welfare impacts of reforming fuel subsidies in India (IMF Working Paper WP/13/128). Asia and Pacific Department, International Monetary Fund. Retrieved from https://www.imf.org/ external/pubs/ft/wp/2013/ wp13128.pdf Asian Development Bank (ADB). (2013). Affordable pay-as-you-go solar power for India's energy poor homes. Knowledge Showcases, Asian Development Bank. Retrieved from http://www.adb.org/ sites/ default/files/publication/30383/affordable-solar-power-india-energy-poor-homes.pdf

Awasthi, S., Glick, H. A., & Fletcher, R.H. (1996). Effect of cooking fuels on respiratory diseases in preschool children in Lucknow, India. American Journal of Tropical Medicine and Hygiene, 55(1), 48—51.

Azizi, B.H., & Henry, R.L. (1994). Ethnic differences in normal spirometric lung function of Malaysian children. Journal of Respiratory Medicine, 88(5), 349—56.

A.T. Kearney & Global Off-Grid Lighting Association (GOGLA). (2014). Investment and Finance Study for Off-Grid Lighting. A.T. Kearney and Global Off-Grid Lighting Association. Retrieved from http://global-off-grid-lighting-association.org/wp-content/ uploads/2013/09/A-T-Kearney-GOGLA.pdf

Balani, S. (2013). Functioning of the Public Distribution System: An analytical report. PRS Legislative Research. Retrieved from http://www.prsindia.org/administrator/ uploads/ general/1388728622~~TPDS per cent20Thematic per cent20Note.pdf

Behera, D., Sood, P., & Singh, S. (1998). Passive smoking, domestic fuels and lung function in north Indian children. Indian Journal of Chest Disease and Allied Sciences, 40(2), 89—98.

Bhanumurthy, N.R., Das, S., & Bose, S. (2012). Oil price shock, pass-through policy and its impact on India (National Institute of Public Finance and

Policy Working Paper No. 2012-99). Retrieved from https://ideas.repec.org/p/npf/wpaper/12-99.html

Central Electricity Authority. (2015). Power Sector—Executive Summary. Ministry of Power, Government of India. Retrieved from http://www.cea.nic.in/reports/monthly/executivesummary/2015/ exe_summary-12.pdf

Chaurey, A., Ranganathan, M., & Mohanty, P. (2004). Electricity access for geographically disadvantaged rural communities—technology and policy insights. Energy Policy, 32(15), 1693—1705. Climate Group. (2015).

The business case for off-grid energy in India. The Climate Group. Retrieved from http://www.theclimategroup.org/_assets/files/The-business-case-for-offgrid-energy-in-India.pdf

Department of Food and Public Distribution, Ministry of Consumer Affairs, Food and Public Distribution, Government of India. (n.d.). Targeted public distribution system. Retrieved from http://dfpd.nic.in/public-distribution.htm Department of Food and Public Distribution. (2015).

Annual Report 2014—15. Ministry of Consumer Affairs, Food and Public Distribution, Government of India.

Eapen, M, & Varghese, G. (2016). Power sector in India: Recent challenges and measures undertaken. Asian Journal of Research in Business Economics and Management, 6(1), 33—46.

Economic Survey of India, 2014—15. (2015). Public Finance & 'Wiping every tear from every eye': The JAM Number Trinity Solution.

Ministry of Finance, Government of India. Retrieved from http:// indiabudget.nic.in/es2014-15/echapvol2-02.pdf Food and Agriculture Organization of the United Nations (FAO). (2006). Public distribution system in India-evolution, efficacy and need for reforms.

Regional Office for Asia and the Pacific, Food and Agriculture Organization. Retrieved from http://www.fao.org/docrep/x0172e/x0172e06.htm Integrated Research and Action for Development (IRADe). (2014).

Evaluation on the scheme for kerosene free Delhi. Retrieved from http://irade.org/KFD per cent20Report_final.pdf Jain, A., Agrawal, S., & Ganesan, K. (2014).

Rationalising subsidies, reaching the underserved: Improving effectiveness of domestic LPG subsidy and distribution in India. Council on Energy,

Environment and Water (CEEW). Retrieved from http://ceew.in/pdf/CEEW-Rationalising-LPG-Subsidies-Reachingthe-Underserved-5Dec14.pdf

Jain, A., Ray, S., Ganesan, K., Aklin, M., Cheng, C., & Urpelainen, J. (2015). Access to clean cooking energy and electricity—Survey of states. Council on Energy, Environment and Water and Columbia University. Retrieved from http://ceew.in/pdf/CEEW-ACCESS-Report-29Sep15.pdf

Jain, R., & Raghuram, G. (2009). Role of universal service obligation fund in rural telecom services: Lessons from the Indian experience (IIMA Working Papers). Retrieved from https://ideas.repec.org/p/iim/ iimawp/8326.html

Jain, A., Ray, S., Ganesan, K., Aklin, M., Cheng, C., Urpelainen, J. (2015). Access to clean cooking energy and electricity—Survey of states. Council on Energy, Environment and Water and Columbia University. Retrieved from http://ceew.in/pdf/CEEW-ACCESS-Report-29Sep15.pdf

Jolly, S., Raven, R., & Romijn, H. (2012). Upscaling of business model experiments in off-grid PV solar energy in India. Sustainability Science, 7(2), 199—212. Retrieved from http://link.springer.com/ article/10.1007/s11625-012-0163-7

Kelkar Committee Report. (2012). Report of the Committee on Roadmap for Fiscal Consolidation. Ministry of Finance, Government of India. Retrieved from http://finmin.nic.in/reports/Kelkar_ Committee_Report.pdf

Lam, L.N., Smith, K.R., Gauthier, A., & Bates, M.N. (2012). Kerosene: A review of household uses and their hazards in low and middle income countries. Journal of Toxicology and Environmental Health Part B, 15(6), 396—432. Retrieved from http://www.ncbi.nlm.nih.gov/pubmed/22934567 Martinot, E., Cabraal, A., & Mathur, S. (2001).

World Bank/GEF solar home system projects: experiences and lessons learned 1993—2000. Renewable and Sustainable Energy Reviews, 5(1), 39—57. Retrieved from http://www.sciencedirect.com/science/article/pii/S1364032100000071

Mills, E. (2003). Technical and economic performance analysis of kerosene lamps and alternative approaches to illumination in developing countries. Lawrence Berkeley National Laboratory, University of California. Retrieved from http://evanmills.lbl.gov/pubs/pdf/offgrid-lighting.pdf Mills, E. (2012). Health impacts of fuel-based lighting. Lawrence Berkeley National Laboratory, University of California. Retrieved from http://light.lbl.gov/pubs/tr/lumina-TR10-health-impacts.pdf Ministry of

New and Renewable Energy (MNRE). (2016).

Physical Progress (Achievements)—As of January 2016. Ministry of New and Renewable Energy, Government of India. Retrieved from http:// mnre.gov.in/mission-and-vision-2/achievements/

Ministry of Petroleum and Natural Gas (MoPNG). (n.d.). Distribution—List of policies and guidelines formulated.

Ministry of Petroleum and Natural Gas, Government of India. Retrieved from http:// www. petroleum.nic.in/poldist1. htm MoPNG. (1993).

The Gazette of India: Extraordinary—Part II. Ministry of Petroleum and Natural Gas, Government of India. Retrieved from http:// petroleum.nic.in/docs/newgazette/GN per cent20 No.300 per cent20dtd per cent2002-09-93.pdf Ministry of Power. (2014).

Deen Dayal Upadhyay Gram Jyoti Yojana—F. No. 44/44/2014-RE. Ministry of Power, Government of India. Retrieved from http://powermin.nic. in/upload/pdf/Deendayal_ Upadhyaya_Gram_ Jyoti_Yojana.pdf Ministry of Power. (2015).

24x7 Power For All. Ministry of Power, Government of India. Retrieved from http:// www.powerforall.co.in/DASHBOARDLogin. aspx?ReturnUrl= per cent2f National Council for Applied Economic Research (NCAER). (2005).

Comprehensive study to assess the genuine demand and requirement of SKO (Special Kerosene Oil). National Council for Applied Economic Research.

National Sample Survey Organization. (2013). Key indicators of household consumer expenditure in India, 2011—12.

Ministry of Statistics and Programme Implementation, Government of India. Retrieved from http://mospi.nic.in/Mospi_ New/upload/press-release-68th-HCE.pdf

Nilekani Committee Report. (2011). Interim Report of the Task Force on Direct Transfer of Subsidies on Kerosene, LPG and Fertiliser. Ministry of Finance, Government of India. Retrieved from http://finmin. nic.in/reports/ Interim_report_Task_Force_DTS.pdf Overseas Private Investment Corporation (OPIC). (2014).

Simpa Networks: Making solar power affordable in India. Overseas Private Investment Corporation. Retrieved from https://www.opic.gov/ opic-action/ featured-projects/south-asia/simpa-networks-making-solar-power-affordable-rural-india

Palit, D. (2013). Solar energy programs for rural electrification: Experiences and lessons from South Asia. Energy for Sustainable Development, 17(3), 270—279.

Palit, D., & Chaurey, A. (2011). Off-grid rural electrification experiences from South Asia: Status and best practices. Energy for Sustainable Development, 15(3), 266—276.

Parikh Committee Report. (2010). Report of the Expert Group on a Viable and Sustainable System of Pricing of Petroleum Products. Government of India. Retrieved from http:// petroleum.nic.in/docs/ reports/reportprice.pdf

Petroleum Planning and Analysis Cell (PPAC). (2016). Subsidy on petroleum products. Petroleum Planning and Analysis Cell, Ministry of Petroleum and Natural Gas, Government of India.

Press Information Bureau (PIB). (2015). Petroleum Minister reviews LPG availability and infrastructure in Odisha. Ministry of Petroleum and Natural Gas, Government of India.

Rangarajan Committee Report. (2006). Report of the Committee on Pricing and Taxation of Petroleum Products. Government of India. Retrieved from http://petroleum. nic.in/docs/reports/Report1.pdf

Reiche, K., Covarrubias, A., & Martinot, E. (2000). Expanding electricity access to remote areas: Offgrid rural electrification in developing countries. World Power. Retrieved from http:// www.martinot.info/ Reiche_et_al_WP2000.pdf

Tapsoba, S. J. A. (2013). Options and strategies for fiscal consolidation in India. International Monetary Fund. Retrieved from http:// www.imf.org/external/pubs/ft/wp/2013/ wp13127.pdf Tata Power Solar (2016).

Solar microgrids. Retrieved from http://www. tatapowersolar.com/SolarMicrogrid UPA hikes subsidized LPG cap to 12 cylinders. (2014). Hindustan Times. Retrieved from http://www.hindustantimes.com/india/ upa-hikes-subsidized-lpg-cap-to-12-cylinders/ storyk9pdi4ZWOeEUXhkzjvMOTP.html

Upadhyay, A. (2014). Optimization and mapping of the process of tariff determination by the electricity regulator's in context of Indian power sector. International Journal of Scientific Research and Engineering Studies, 1(3), 11—20. Retrieved from http://www. ijsres.com/2014/vol-1_issue-3/paper_4.pdf

IMPROVING ENERGY ACCESS

Amazonas Energia (2009, September). (M. Obermaier, Interviewer).

Andrade, C.S. (2009a). Photovoltaic system for electrical power generation in remote rural areas of the Brazilian Amazon.

ANEEL (2009). Resolução Normativa No 365 de 19.05.2009. Asian Development Bank (2008). Proposed Loan Rural Electrification Corporation of India, India. Philippines: Asian Development Bank. Asian Development Bank (2009).

Key Indicators for Asia and the Pacific 2009. Philippines: ADB.

Assocham (2008). Assocham Eco Pulse Study: Free electricity @ what cost? New Delhi: Assocham.

Avert (2009). The Scale of South Africa's Aids Crisis. from Averting HIV and AIDS: http://www.avert.org/aidssouthafrica.htm

Baker and McKenzie (2008). Identifying Optimal Legal Frameworks for Renewable Energy in India,APP Project REDG-06-09. Sydney: Baker and McKenzie.

Barnes, D. F. (2007). The challenge of rural electrification: strategies for developing countries. Washington: Resources for the Future.

Barnes, D. & Foley, G. (2004). Rural Electrification in the Developing World: A Summary of Lessons from Successful Programs. Washington: World Bank.

Bhattacharyya, S. C. (2006). Energy access problem of the poor in India: Is rural electrification a remedy?. Energy Policy, 3387-3397.

Cabraal, A. R., Barnes, D. F., & Agarwal, S. G. (2005). Productive Uses of Energy for Rural Development. Annual Review of Environment and Resources, 30:117-144.

Camargo, E., Ribeiro, F.S., Guerra, S.M.G. (2008). O programa Luz para Todos: metas e resultados. Espaço Energia 9, pp. 21-24. Central Electricity Authority (2008).

CO2 Baseline Database for the Indian Power Sector. New Dehli: Government of India, Ministry of Power. Central Electricity Authority (2009a).

Power Sector Reports. New Delhi: Central Electricty Authority, Ministry of Power. Central Electricity Authority (2009b).

Monthly Power Sector Reports. New Dehli: Central Electricity Authority. CIA (2009).

The World Factbook India. from Central Intelligence Authority, https://www.cia.gov/library/publications/the-world-factbook/geos/in.html

Chen Lei, Minister of Water Resources (2009). Developing the small hydropower actively with a focus on people's well-being, protection and improvement. The 5th Hydropower for Today Forum. Hangzhou. Comparative Study on Rural Electrification Policies in Emerging Economies—© OECD/IEA 2010 Page | 108 China Daily (2009). http://5.http//www.chinadaily.com.cn/bizchina/2009-08/27/content_8622023.htm China Southern Grid Corporation.(2009).

China Southern Grid Corporation. http://www.csg.cn/ Chinese Academy of Science (2003). Survey, Institute of Electrical Engineering, JKD Renewable Energy Development Center.

Cortez, L. and Rosillo-Calle, F. (2001). A report on the Third Conference on Energy in Rural Areas in Brazil. Energy for Sustainable Development 5, pp. 5-7.

Costa, C.d.V., La Rovere, E.L., Assmann, D. (2008). Technological innovation policies to promote renewable energies: lessons from the European experience for the Brazilian case.

Renewable and Sustainable Energy Reviews 12, pp. 65-90. Department of Energy (2009a).

Electrification Records 2009. Pretoria: DoE. Department of Energy (2009b, May).

Interview Electricity Supply Directorate. (H. R. Gron, Interviewer). Department of Energy (2009c).

Policy guideline on non-grid-electrification. Pretoria: DoE. Department of Energy (2009d).

Guidelines for electrification of un-proclaimed land. Pretoria: DoE. Department of Energy (2009e).

Medium-term expenditure forecast 2007-2012. Pretoria: DoE. Department of Energy (2009f). Reported data from Eskom to the DoE. Pretoria: DoE. Department of Energy (2009g).

Socio-economic impact of electrification 2008 and 2009. Pretoria: DoE. Department of Energy (2009h).

Guidelines on electrification of farm dwelling houses. Pretoria: DoE. Department of Energy (2009i).

Facts and figures of electrification. Pretoria: DoE. Department of Energy (2009j).

Electrification Status—Fact Sheet Pretoria: DoE. Department of Minerals and Energy (2006).

Energy key documents—Aggregate energy balances. from Department of Energy: http://www.dme.gov.za/ energy/documents.stm#6 Department of Minerals and Energy (2008a).

Socio-economic impact of electrification: household perspective 2008. Pretoria: DoE. Department of Minerals and Energy (2008b). Socio-economic impact of national electrification programme—2008. Pretoria: DoE. Downs, E. S. (2008). China's 'New' Energy Administration. Chinabusinessreview.com, 42-45.

Eletrobras (2008). Agentes do Programa e Atribuições. Accessible via http://www.eletrobras.gov.br

Eletrobrás, MME (2005).

Programa Nacional de Universalização do Acesso e Uso da Energia Elétrica—Manual de Operacionalização. Version 2.0, Eletrobrás/ Ministry of Mines and Energy, Brasília. Eletrobrás, MME (2009).

Programa Nacional de Universalização do Acesso e Uso da Energia Elétrica—Manual de Operacionalização. Revision No. 6., Eletrobrás/ Ministry of Mines and Energy, Brasília. Comparative Study on Rural Electrification Policies in Emerging Economies—© OECD/IEA 2010 Page | 109

Energy Research Institute (ERI) (2009). Han, Wenke,. Credit Suisse, Beijing Clean Energy Conference. Beijing. EPE (2008).

Balanço Energético Nacional 2008: Ano Base 2007. EPE, Rio de Janeiro. Erickson, J. D., & Chapman, D. (1995).

Photovoltaic technology: markets, economics and rural development. World Development, 1129-1141. ESMAP (2005).

Brazil Background Study for a National Rural Electrification Strategy—Aiming for Universal Access. World Bank, Washington, D.C. EU-China (2009).

EU-China Energy & Environment Programme, Development Support for Sustainable Rural and Renewable Energy Training in China. In Teachers Training Book (p. page 5). Source: ISBN 978-7-122-06001-3.

FinMark Trust (2009). South African in Black and White—Press Release. FinMark Trust and TNS Research Surveys.

Fugimoto, S.K. (2005). A Universalização de Energia Elétrica—Acesso e Uso Continuo. M.Sc. thesis, Escola Politécnica da Universidade de São Paulo, São Paulo.

Gendenhuys, H., & McLaren, B. (2007). Eskom's experience with SWER—single wire earth return. Paper presented at PIESA-IERE Africa Forum. Zambia.

Girardi, E.P. (2008). Proposição Teórico-Metodológica de uma Cartografia Geográfica Crítica e sua Aplicação no Desenvolvimento do Atlas da Questão Agrária Brasileira. Ph.D. thesis, Universidade Estadual Paulista, Presidente Prudente.

GNESD (2006). Energy access, Making power sector reform work for the poor, Summary for Policy Makers, Global Network on Energy for Sustainable Development.

Goldemberg, J., La Rovere, E.L. and Coelho, S.T. (2004). Expanding electricity access to Brazil.

Energy for Sustainable Development 8, pp. 86-94. Government of India (2001). Census of India. from Census of India: http://censusindia.gov.in/ Habitat for Humanity (2009, May). (H. R. Gron, Interviewer).

Human Sciences Research Council (2009). South African National HIV Prevalence, Incidence, Behaviour and Communication Survey, 2008. Cape Town: Human Sciences Research Council Press. Holland, R., Perera, L., Sanchez, T., & Wilkinson, R. (2001). Decentralized rural electrification—Critical success factors and experiences of an NGO.

Elsevier, Volume 2, Number 6, July 2001, pp. 28-31(4). IBGE (2002). Censo Demográfico 2000. IBGE, Rio de Janeiro. IBGE (2007a). Contas Regionais do Brasil—2002-2005.

Volume 21, IBGE, Rio de Janeiro. IBGE (2007b). Pesquisa Nacional por Amostra de Domicílios.

Volume 28, IBGE, Rio de Janeiro. IEA (2002a). World Energy Outlook. Paris: International Energy Agency. IEA (2002b).

Electricity in India. Paris: International Energy Agency. IEA (2006). World Energy Outlook 2006. Paris: International Energy Agency. IEA (2007).

World Energy Outlook. Paris: International Energy Agency. Comparative Study on Rural Electrification Policies in Emerging Economies—© OECD/IEA 2010 Page | 110 IEA (2008).

Key World Energy Statistics. Paris: IEA. IEA (2009a). IEA—South Africa Country Page.

from IEA website: http://www.iea.org/ Textbase/stats/indicators.asp?COUNTRY_ CODE=ZA IEA (2009b). World Energy Outlook. Paris: International Energy Agency.

IEA (2009c). Key World Energy Statistics 2009. Paris: International Energy Agency. IEA (2009d).

Luz para Todos (Light for All) electrification programme. from IEA website: http:// www.iea.org IEA (2009e).

Key World Energy Statistics. Paris: International Energy Agency. International Finance Corporation (2007).

Selling Solar: Lessons from more than a decade of IFC'S experience. Washington: International Finance Corporation. International Monetary Fund (2009). International GDP statistic. Washington: IMF.

Instituto Acende Brasil (2007a). A universalização dos serviços de distribuição de energia elétrica. Cadernos de Política Tarifária No. 2, Instituto Acende Brasil, São Paulo, Brasília. Instituto Acende Brasil (2007b). Tarifa de baixa renda. Cadernos de Política Tarifária No. 6, Instituto Acende Brasil, São Paulo, Brasília.

Khandker, S. R., Barnes, D. F., & Samad, H. A. (2009). Welfare Impacts of Rural Electrification: A Case Study from Bangladesh. Policy Research Working Paper no. WPS 4859.

Loureiro de Azeredo, L.C. (2004). Investimento em infra-estrutura no plano pluranual (PPA) 2004-2007 —uma visão geral. Texto Para Discussão No. 1024, IPEA, Brasília. Luo, G. (2007). The Analysis on Current Situation, Difficulties and Strategies on Power Universal Service in China Rural Areas. Journal of North China Electric Power University (Social Sciences).

Madzhie, L. (2009, May). Data Modelling Manager. (H. R. Gron, Interviewer). Martinot, E., Cabraal, A. and Mathur, S. (2000). World Bank Solar Home System Projects: Experiences and Lessons Learned 1993-2000. Washington, D.C.: World Bank, Rural and Renewable Energy Thematic Group Asia Alternative Energy Program.

Ministry of Finance (2009). Economic Survey 2008-2009. New Delhi: Ministry of Finance. MME (2003). Luz para Todos. from Ministry of Mines and Energy. website: http://www. mme.gov.br MME (2009a, September).

Ministry of Mines and Energy (M. Obermaier, Interviewer). MME (2009b). Pesquisa Quantitativa Domiciliar de Avaliação da Satisfação e de Impacto do Programa Luz para Todos. Ministry

of Mines and Energy, Brasília. MME (2009c).

Luz para Todos. from Ministry of Mines and Energy website: http://www.mme.gov.br MME (2009d). Programa Nacional de Universalização do Acesso e Uso da Energia Elétrica—Manual de Projetos Especiais. Anexo à Portaria N° 60, de 12 de fevereiro de 2009. Eletrobrás/Ministry of Mines and Energy, Brasília. Ministry of New and Renewable Energies (2003-2004).

Remote Village Electrification Programme. New Delhi: MNRE. Comparative Study on Rural Electrification Policies in Emerging Economies—© OECD/IEA 2010 Page | 111 Ministry of New and Renewable Energies (2007).

Remote Village Electrification Programme. from Remote Village Electrification Programme: http://mnes.nic.in/prog-rvlp.htm Ministry of New and Renewable Energies (2009).

Annual Report 2008-2009. New Delhi: MNRE. Ministry of Power (2005). Resolution, No.44/26/05-RE (Vol-II). New Delhi: Ministry of Power.

Ministry of Power (2005-2006). Standing Committee on Energy (2004-2005) Fourteenth Lok Sabha. New Delhi: Ministry of Power.

Ministry of Power (2008). Order: Continuation of Rajiv Gandhi Grameen Vidyutikaran Yojana in the XI Plan—Scheme of Rural Electricity Infrastructure and Household Electrification. New Delhi, India: Ministry of Power.

Ministry of Power (2009a). Agenda. Conference of Power Ministers. New Delhi. Ministry of Power (2009b). Power Sector at a Glance 'ALL INDIA'. from Ministry of Power: http://www.powermin. nic.in/JSP_SERVLETS/internal.jsp Ministry of Power (2009c). Power for All by 2012. from Power for All by 2012: http://www.powermin. nic.in/indian_electricity_scenario/power_for_ all_target.htm Ministry of Power (2009d).

Rajiv Gandhi Grameen Vidyutikaran Yojana, Franchisee. from Rajiv Gandhi Grameen Vidyutikaran Yojana: http:// www.rggvy.gov.in/rggvy/rggvyportal/ index.html Ministry of Power (2009e).

Order: Guidelines for Village Electrification through Decentralized Distributed Generation (DDG) under Rajiv Gandhi Grameen Vidyutikaran Yojana in the XI Plan—Scheme of Rural Electricity Infrastructure and Household Electrification. New Delhi: Ministry of Power.

Mketsi, M. (2009, May). Director Electricity Supply, Department of Energy. (H. R. Gron, Interviewer).

Molefe, P. (2008). South Africa: Electricity Pricing Considerations. Presentation at the National Electricity Summit, May 16. National Bureau of Statistics of China (2008).

China Statistical Yearbook. Beijing: China Statistics Press. National Bureau of Statistics of China (2009). Statistical Communiqué of the People's Republic of China on the 2008 National Economic and Social Development from National Bureau of Statistics of China: http://www.stats.gov.cn/english/ newsandcomingevents/ t20090226_402540784.hm NBS and NDRC (2008).

China Energy Statistical Yearbook 2008. Beijing: China Statistics Press. NDRC (2008).

The China Renewable Energy Development Plan. National Development and Reform Commission. National Energy Regulator South Africa (2006a).

Electricity Statistics and Annual Report. Pretoria: NERSA. National Energy Regulator South Africa (2006b). Annual Report 2006. Pretoria: NERSA.

National Energy Regulator South Africa. (2009, May). (H. R. Gron, Interviewer).

National Energy Regulator South Africa. (2009b). South Africa Renewable Energy Feed-in-Tariff (REFIT)—Regulatory Guidelines 26 March 2009. Pretoria: NERSA. Comparative Study on Rural Electrification Policies in Emerging Economies—© OECD/IEA 2010 Page | 112

Obermaier, M. (2005). Rural Electrification in Brazil—Lessons from Recent Experience. M.Sc. Thesis, Freie Universität Berlin, Berlin.

Obermaier, M. (2009). An analysis of energy and income trends following rural electrification in the state of Bahia, Brazil. 32 IAEE conference, 21-24 June, San Francisco. OECD (2009).

OECD Economic Surveys: Brazil. Organization for Economic Co-operation and Development, Paris. ONS (2009).

Mapa de Transmissão. from MME website: http://www.mme.gov.br Pan, J., Li, M., Wu, X., Wan, L., Elias, R. J., Victor, D. G. et al. (2006).

Rural Electrification in China 1950-2004: Historical processes and key driving forces— working paper. Program on Energy and Sustainable Development Working Paper #60.

Peng, W. and Pan, J. (2006). Rural Electrification in China: History and Institution. China and World Economy, Vol. 14, 71— 84. Pertusier, F.L.R. (2004). O programa Luz para Todos e as fontes renováveis de energia. Primeiro Seminário sobre a Utilização

de Fontes Renováveis de Energia no Contexto de Eletrificação Rural no Norte e Nordeste do Brasil, December 2004, Rio de Janeiro.

Planning Commission (2005). Draft Report of the Expert Committee on Integrated Energy Policy.

New Delhi: Planning Commission, Government of India. Planning Commission (2006). Towards Faster and More Inclusive growth, An Approach to the 11th Five Year Plan.

New Delhi: Planning Commission, Government of India. Planning Commission (2007). Poverty Estimates for 2004-2005. from Planning Commission, Government of India: http://www.planningcommission.gov.in /news/prmar07.pdf Planning Commission—Government of India. (2008). Eleventh Five Year Plan (2007-2012). New Delhi: Oxford University Press. Platts (2008).

UDI World Electric Power Plants Data Base. March 2008 Edition. Poppe, M.K. (2002). Universalizacao do acesso a energia elétrica no Brasil: características, oportunidades e desafios. MME, Brasilia.

Poppe, M.K. (2009, August). (M. Obermaier, Interviewer). Presidency of the Republic (2007).

Objetivos e Desenvolvimento do Milenio. Relatorio Nacional de Acompanhamento. IPEA, SPI/MP, Brasilia. Presidency of the Republic (2009). Destaques: Ações e Programas do Governo Federal. Presidência da República/ Secretaria de Comunicação Social, Brasília.

Press Information Bureau (2009, August 13). Press Release. from Press Information Bureau, Government of India: http:// www.pib.nic.in/release/release.asp? relid=51835 Reiche, K., Tenenbaum, B. and de Mästle, C.T. (2006). Electrification and regulation: principles and a model law. E

SMAP Discussion Paper No. 18, World Bank, Washington, D.C. Comparative Study on Rural Electrification Policies in Emerging Economies—© OECD/IEA 2010 Page | 113

Rosa, L.P., Ribeiro, S.K., da Silva, N.F. et al. (2006). Primeiro Seminário de Construção de Cenários do Projeto de Construção de Consenso para Eletrificação de Comunidades Rurais Localizadas em Áreas Remotas e Isoladas. IVIG/IIE/COPPE, Rio de Janeiro.

Rural Electrification Corporation (2009). Rajiv Ghandi Grameen Vidyutikaran Yojana—Progress Reports. from REC: http:// powermin.gov.in/bharatnirman/pdf/

Progress_on_electrification_of_villages_households. pdf Silveira, F.G., Carvalho, A.X.Y., Azzoni, C.R., Campolina, B. and Ibarra, A. (2007).

Dimensão, magnitude e localização das populações pobres no Brasil. Texto Para Discussão No. 1278, IPEA, Brasília. Silveira, R.M. and Fernandes, F.C. (2007). Pobreza e indigencia no Brasil, 2001-2005. Boletim 2 da Rede de Laboratorios Acadêmicos para Acompanhamento dos Objetivos de Desenvolvimento de Milênio.

from: http://ead01.virtual.pucminas. br/idhs/milenio Seshotlho, B. (2009, May). Director, Supply National Energy Regulator. (H. R. Gron, Interviewer).

Smuts, W. (2007). Cell Phone Vending of Prepaid Electricity: Lessons Learnt in South Africa. Paper Presented at PIESA-IERE Africa Forum, September 2007. South Africa Info (2008). South Africa: Fast Facts. from SouthAfrica.info: http:// www.southafrica.info/about/facts.htm State Electricity Regulatory Commission (2009).

Survey on basic status of no power villages and families in the whole country. SERC. State Grid Corp. of China (2009).

Credit Suisse/Power Economic Research Institute, Jiang Liping, September 18, 2009, Beijing Clean Energy Conference. Beijing.

State Grid Corporation (2009). General Situation of China's Rural Electricity. from State Grid Corporation: http://www.rpsg.com.cn/ndjj. asp State Power Information Network (2009).

State Power Information Network. from http://www.sp.com.cn/zgdl/ Statistics South Africa (2008a).

Mid-year 2007 population count esimates. Pretoria: Statistics South Africa. Statistics South Africa (2008b).

Labour Force Survey—historical revisions, march series 2001-2007. Pretoria: Statistics South Africa. Statistics South Africa (2009). from Population Statistics: http://www.statssa. gov.za/publications/populationstats.asp

Strazzi, P.E., Betiol Jr. G., Marques, F., Ribeiro, F.S. and Guerra, S.M.G. (2008). Programa 'Luz para Todos': a necessidade do aporte de recursos subsidiados—estudo de caso Elektro. Congresso Internacional sobre Geração Distribuída e Energia no Meio Rural (AGRENER), 23-25 August 2008, Fortaleza.

Taniguchi, M. and Kaneko, S. (2009). Operational performance of the Bangladesh rural electrification programme and its determinants with a focus on political interference. Energy Policy, Volume 37, Issue 6, pp. 2433-2439. Tang, A. (2009). Window of China. from China View: http://news.xinhuanet. com/english/2009-10/02/content_12173548. htm Comparative Study on Rural Electrification Policies in Emerging Economies—© OECD/ IEA 2010 Page | 114 UNDP China. (2008).

Capacity Building for the Rapid Commercialization of Renewable Energy in China, Renewable Energy Based Chinese Un-Electrified Region Electrification. Beijing: United Nations Development Programme China. United Nations Population Division (2008). An overview of urbanization, internal migration, population distribution and development in the world. New York: United Nations Population Division.

Vidyasagar, K. (2007, July 15). Presentation: Universal Service Obligation in Rural Electrification—Rajiv Gandhi Grameen Vidyutikaran Yojana (RGGVY).

14th Steering Committee Meeting, South Asia Forum for Infrastructure Regulation. New Delhi. WCMC (1992).

Global Biodiversity: Status of the Earth's Living Resources. Chapman & Hall, London. Wikipedia (2009a). Brazil. Accessible at http://en.wikipedia. org/wiki/Brazil,. Wikipedia (2009b). Wikipedia. from List of countries and dependencies by population density: http://en.wikipedia.org/ wiki/List_of_countries_and_dependencies_ by_population_density World Bank (1975). Rural Electrification. Washington D.C.: The World Bank.

World Bank (2000). Energy Services for the World's Poor. Washington DC: The World Bank. World Bank (2004). Reforming the Power Sector, Controlling Electricity Theft and Improving Revenue.

Public Policy for the Private Sector. World Bank (2008). India at a Glance. from http://devdata. worldbank.org/AAG/ind_aag.pdf World Bank (2009a). Brazil Country Brief. http:// www.worldbank.org World Bank. (2009b).

Gross domestic product 2008, PPP. from Data Statistics World Bank: http://siteresources. worldbank.org/DATASTATISTICS /Resources/ GDP_PPP.pdf World Bank. (2009c). Population 2008. from World Bank Data Statistics: http:// siteresources.worldbank.org/DATASTATISTICS/ Resources/POP.pdf World Bank. (2009d).

World Bank. from Gross national income per capita 2008, Atlas method and PPP: http:// siteresources.worldbank.org/DATASTATISTICS/ Resources/GNIPC.pdf World Bank. (2009e).

World Bank Indicators Database. from The World Bank: http://siteresources.worldbank.org/DATASTATISTICS/Resources/POP.pdf Yao, X. and Barnes, D. F. (2007). 'National Support for Decentralized Electricity Growth in Rural China'. In: The Challenge of Rural Electrification: Strategies for Developing Countries. Washington D.C.: Resources for the Future.

Zerriffi, H. (2007). From çaí to access: distributed electrification in rural Brazil. International Journal of Energy Sector Management 2, pp. 90-117.

CEA. (2014). Power Sector: Executive Summary for the month of February. Sourced from www.cea.nic.in/reports/monthly/executive_rep/feb14.pdf

Central Electricity Authority. (2014). Tariff and Duty of electricity supply in India.

Department of Agriculture and Cooperation. (2014). Annual Report 2013-2014. Sourced from http://www.agriculture.gov.au/about/annualreport/2013-14

Kateshiya G.B. (2014). 5,000 farmers in Saurashtra, Kutch to get power connections this year | The Indian Express. Sourced from http://indianexpress.com/article/cities/ahmedabad/5000- farmers-in-saurashtra-kutch-to-get-power-connections-this-year/ IASRI. (2014).

Agriculture Research Data Book. Sourced from iasri.res.in/agridata/14data/chapter1/db2014tb1_19.pdf

Iyer, P. V. (2013). 'Power tariff in Maharashtra will remain higher than other states.' Indian Express. http://indianexpress.com/article/cities/mumbai/power-tariff-in-maharashtra-will-remain-higher-than-other-states/

Jin, S., Yu, W., Jansen, H. G. P., & Lansing, E. (2012). The impact of Irrigation on Agricultural Productivity : Evidence from India, 18—24.

Joshi, V., & Acharya, A. (2005). Addressing Agricultural Power Subsidy: A Case Study of North Gujarat. Working Papers. Sourced from http://ideas.repec.org/p/ess/wpaper/id2533.html

Kannan, E. (2013). Do Farmers Need Free Electricity? Implications for Groundwater Use in South India. Journal of Social and Economic Development, 13. Sourced from https://www.academia.edu/7710263/Do_Farmers_Need_Free_Electricity_Implications_for_Groundwater_Use_in_ South_India

Kulkarni, D. (2015). Maharashtra government plans to give 5 lakh solar pumps to farmers. dna Analysis. http://www.dnaindia.com/mumbai/report-maharashtragovernment-plans-to-give-5-lakh-solar-pumps-to-farmers-2049952

Mcneil, M., & Sathaye, J. (2009). India Energy Outlook : End Use Demand in India to 2020. Energy, (January), 1—62. Sourced from http://ies.lbl.gov/iespubs/india_energy_outlook.pdf MNRE. (2014).

Installation of Solar Water Pumps. Sourced from http://pib.nic.in/newsite/erelease. aspx?relid=107379

Murthy, K. V. S. R., & Raju, M. R. (2009). Analysis on Electrical Energy Consumption of Agricultural Sector in Indian Context. ARPN Journal of Engineering and Applied Sciences, 4(2), 6—9. Sourced from http://www.arpnjournals.com/jeas/research_papers/rp_2009/jeas_0409_165.pdf

Planning Commission. (2014). Annual Report (2013-14) on The Working of State Power Utilities & Electricity Departments.

Pullenkav, T. (GIZ). (2013). Solar Water Pumping for Irrigation—Opportunities in Bihar.

Raghavan, S. V, Bharadwaj, A., Thatte, A. a, Harish, S., Iychettira, K. K., Perumal, R., & Nayak, G. (2010). Harnessing Solar Energy: Options for India, 122.

Saini, S. S. (2011). Mitigation Initiatives Through Agriculture DSM.

Sharma, M., & Kaur, R. (2012). Agricultural Subsidies in India : Case Study of Electricity Subsidy in Punjab State : An Analysis. International Jounral of Scientifi c and Research Publications, 2(10), 1—7.

Swain, A., & Charnoz, O. (2012). In Pursuit of Energy Effi ciency in India's Agriculture: Fighting 'Free Power' or Working with it?, (August).

LEAPING FORWARD WITH RENEWABLES

ABPS Infrastructure Advisory Private Ltd (ABPS Infra). Report on Policy and Regulatory Interventions to Support Community Level Off-Grid Projects, available at http://www.forumofregulators.gov.in

Yadoo A. Delivery Models for Decentralized Rural Electrification: Case Studies in Nepal, Peru and Kenya. International Institute for Environment and Development, London (2012).

Yadoo A. & Cruickshank H. The Value

of Cooperatives in Rural Electrification. Elsevier, Energy Policy. DOI:10.1016/ j.enpol.2010.01.031 (2010).

Christian Matyelele Msyani, C. M. Current Status of Energy Sector in Tanzania: Executive Exchange on Developing an Ancillary Service Market, available at http://www.usea.org

Debajit Palit & Akanksha Chaurey. Off-grid Rural Electrification Experiences from South Asia: Status and Best Practices, 2011, Elsevier, ESD-00124, doi:10.1016/j.esd.2011.07.004.

Palit D. & Sarangi G.K. Renewable Energy based Mini-grids for Enhancing Electricity Access: Experiences and Lessons from India, International Conference and Utility Exhibition 2014 on Green Energy for Sustainable Development (ICUE 2014)

Jomtien Palm Beach Hotel and Resort, Pattaya City, Thailand, 19-21 March 2014 (2014).

Shaw D. Securing India's Energy Needs: The Regional Dimension, Center for Strategic and International Studies (CSIS), Washington D. C. (2005).

Shanghvi I. Operative Environment of Microfinance: A Call for a Holistic Research Approach— The Case of Rural and Urban Tanzania.

Inter Press Service. Mothers Light Up Homes in Rural Tanzania, available at http://www.ipsnews.net/2014/06/mothers-light-up-homes-in-ruraltanzania/ (

Cust J., Singh A. & Neuhoff K. Rural Electrification in India: Economic and Institutional aspects of Renewables. Available at http://www.eprg.group.cam.ac.uk

Ulsrud K, et al. The Solar Transitions Research on Solar Mini-grids in India: Learning from Local Cases of Innovative Socio-technical Systems. Elsevier, ESD-00117, doi:10.1016/j.esd.2011.06.004 (2011).

Swai M. Energy Sector, Opportunities and Challenges to Attain Sustainable Energy. Tanzania Traditional Energy Development Organization (TaTEDO), Dar es Salaam (2014).

Ministry of Energy and Minerals (MEM) (of the United Republic of Tanzania). Scaling-Up Renewable Energy Programme: Investment Plan for Tanzania, available at https://mem.go.tz/

Ministry of Energy and Minerals (of the United Republic of Tanzania). Tanzania Electricity Supply Industry Reform Strategy and Roadmap

2014/ 15, available at https://mem.go.tz/wp-content/uploads/2014/02/ 0001_17022013_ National_Energy_Policy_2003.pdf

Ministry of Energy and Minerals (of the United Republic of Tanzania). The National Energy Policy, available at https://mem.go.tz/

Ishengoma R. Biomass Energy in Tanzania. Faculty of Forestry and Nature Conservation, Sokoine University of Agriculture—Morogoro (2013)

Rocha S. Democratising Energy Supply: Sundarbans and Purulia, India, available at http://www.mlinda.org

Sridhar, G. et al. Case Studies on Small Scale Biomass Gasifier Based Decentralized Energy Generation Systems. Indian Institute of Science, Mahatma Gandhi Institute of Rural Energy and Development, Bangalore (2012).

Alex Z., Kimber H.M., & Komp R. Renewable Energy Village Power Systems for Remote and Impoverished Himalayan Villages in Nepal. Proceedings of the International Conference on Renewable Energy for Developing Countries (2006).

Addison, D.M., and Stewart B.P. 2015. 'Nighttime lights revisited: the use of nighttime lights data as a proxy for economic variables.' World Bank Working Paper, no. 7496.

Allcott, H., Collard-Wexler A., and O'Connell S.D. 2016. 'How Do Electricity Shortages Affect Industry? Evidence from India.' American Economic Review 106 (3): 587—624.

Asher, S., and Novosad P. 2016. 'Market Access and Structural Transformation: Evidence from Rural Roads in India.' Working Paper.

Banerjee, A., Duflo E., and Qian N. 2012. 'On the Road: Access to Transportation Infrastructure and Economic Growth in China.' NBER Working Paper, no. 17897.

Barron, Manuel, and Maximo Torero. 2016. 'Household Electrification and Indoor Air Pollution.' Working Paper.

Bickenbach, F., Bode E., Nunnenkamp P., and Söder M. 2016. 'Night lights and regional GDP.' Review of World Economics 152 (1): 1—23.

Blumenstock, J., Cadamuro G., and On R. 2015. 'Predicting poverty and wealth from mobile phone metadata.' Science 350 (6264): 1073—1076. Central Electricity Authority. 2015. Progress report of village electrification as on 31-03-2015 as per 2011.

Chakravorty, U. Emerick K., and Ravago M. 2016. 'Lighting up the last mile: The benefits and costs of extending electricity to the rural poor.' Working Paper.

Chand, T. R. Kiran, K. V. Badarinath S., Christopher D. E., and Tuttle B. T. 2009. 'Spatial characterization of electrical power consumption patterns over India using temporal DMSP—OLS night—time satellite data.' International Journal of Remote Sensing 30 (3): 647—661.

Chen, Xi., and Nordhaus W.D. 2011. 'Using luminosity data as a proxy for economic statistics.' Proceedings of the National Academy of Sciences 108 (21): 8589—8594.

Cook, T. D. 2008. 'Waiting for Life to Arrive: A history of the regression-discontinuity design in Psychology, Statistics and Economics.' Journal of Econometrics, The regression discontinuity design: Theory and applications, 142 (2): 636—654.

Dinkelman, T. 2011. 'The Effects of Rural Electrification on Employment: New Evidence from South Africa.' American Economic Review 101 (7): 3078—3108.

Donaldson, D. Forthcoming. 'Railroads of the Raj: Estimating the Impact of Transportation Infrastructure.' American Economic Review.

Duflo, E., and Pande R. 2007. 'Dams.' The Quarterly Journal of Economics 122 (2): 601— 646. Faber, Benjamin. 2014. 'Trade Integration, Market Size, and Industrialization: Evidence from China's National Trunk Highway System.' The Review of Economic Studies.

Gertler, P., Shelef O., Wolfram C., and Fuchs A. Forthcoming. 'The Demand for Energy-Using Assets among the World's Rising Middle Classes.' American Economic Review.

Harish, S. M., Morgan G. M., and Subrahmanian E. 2014. 'When does unreliable grid supply become unacceptable policy? Costs of power supply and outages in rural India.' Energy Policy 68:158—169.

Henderson, Vernon J., Storeygard A., and Weil D. N. 2011. 'A Bright Idea for Measuring Economic Growth.' American Economic Review 101 (3): 194—99. . 2012. 'Measuring Economic Growth from Outer Space.' American Economic Review 102 (2): 994—1028.

Imbens, G. W., and Lemieux T. 2008. 'Regression discontinuity designs: A guide to practice.' Journal of Econometrics 142 (2): 615—635.

Imbens, G., and Kalyanaraman K. 2012. 'Optimal Bandwidth Choice for the

Regression Discontinuity Estimator.' Review of Economic Studies 79 (3): 933—959.

International Energy Agency. 2011. World Energy Outlook 2011: Energy for All. 2015. 'Energy Poverty.' http://www.iea.org/topics/energypoverty/.

Jayachandran, S., de Laat J., Lambin E., and Stanton C. 2016. 'Cash for Carbon: A Randomized Controlled Trial of Payments for Ecosystem Services to Reduce Deforestation.' Working Paper.

Lee, D. S., and Lemieux T. 2010. 'Regression Discontinuity Designs in Economics.' Journal of Economic Literature 48 (2): 281—355.

Lee, K., Brewer E., Christiano C., Meyo F., Miguel E., Podolsky M., Rosa J., and Wolfram C. Forthcoming. 'Barriers to Electrification for 'Under-Grid' Households in Rural Kenya.' Development Engineering.

Lee, K., Miguel E., and Wolfram C. 2016. 'Experimental Evidence on the Demands for and Costs of Rural Electrification.'

Mimeo. L., Molly, Mobarak A.M., and Barham T. 2013. 'Development Effects of Electrification: Evidence from the Topographic Placement of Hydropower Plants in Brazil.' American Economic Journal: Applied Economics 5 (2): 200—231.

McRae, S. 2015. 'Efficiency and Equity Effects of Electricity Metering: Evidence from Colombia.' Working Paper.

Miguel, E., Wolfram C., Brewer E., and Lee K. 2014. 'Evaluation of Mass Electricity Connections in Kenya.' AEA RCT Registry Pre-Analysis Plan. Min, Brian. 2011. 'Electrifying the Poor: Distributing Power in India.' Working Paper.

Min, B., and Gaba K.M. 2014. 'Tracking Electrification in Vietnam Using Nighttime Lights.' Remote Sensing 6 (10): 9511—9529.

Min, B., Gaba K.M., Sarr O.F., and Agalassou A. 2013. 'Detection of rural electrification in Africa using DMSP-OLS night lights imagery.' International Journal of Remote Sensing 34 (22): 8118—8141.

Rosenzweig, M., and Udry C.R. 2013. 'Forecasting Profitability.' NBER Working Paper, no. 19334.

Rud, J.P. 2012. 'Electricity provision and industrial development: Evidence from India.' Journal of Development Economics 97 (2): 352—367.

Ryan, N. 2014. 'The Competitive Effects of Transmission Infrastructure in the Indian Electricity Market.'

Mimeo. Ryan, Nicholas, Sudarshan A., Burgess R., and Greenstone M. 2014. 'Welfare benefits of decentralized Solar energy for the rural poor.' AEA RCT Registry Pre-Analysis Plan. The World Bank. 2008. The Welfare Impact of Rural Electrification: A Reassessment of the Costs and Benefits. Independent Evaluation Group Impact Evaluation.

Tsujita, Y. 2014. Inclusive Growth and Development in India: Challenges for Underdeveloped Regions and the Underclass. Palgrave Macmillan.

UNDP. 2015. 'Energy access.' Energy Access. http://www.undp.org/content/undp/en/home/ ourwork/climate-and-disaster-resilience/ sustainable-energy/energy-access.html.

Usami, Y. 2014. 'The NSSO/Labour Bureau Series on Wage Rates in Rural India, 1998-99 to 2012-13, Statistics on Indian Economy and Society.' http://www.indianstatistics.org/ wrri.html.

Van de Walle, D., Ravallion M., Mendiratta V., and Koolwal G. 2013. 'Longterm impacts of household electrification in rural India.'

World Bank Working Paper, no. 6527. World Bank. 2015. 'Energy Overview.' http://www.worldbank.org/en/topic/energy/overview.

CHAPTER IV

ON AGRICULTURAL MARKETING

In the past, India's policymakers focused primarily on raising agricultural output while pursuing food security. They achieved this successfully by raising per acre productivity, using better seed varieties and technologies, increasing the usage of fertilizers, agrochemicals and irrigation, and establishing a floor for remunerative prices for some crops. These were supported by additional public investments in agriculture and in rural India, along with a network of relevant institutions. The success of such initiatives was significant, with India's food production rising by 3.7 times at the same time that the population rose by 2.5 times, effectively resulting in a 45 per cent increase in per person food production. India's self-sufficiency in food, at an aggregate level, is due to the wisdom of such policymakers.

However, such policies did not explicitly seek to raise farmer income—so increase in output in agriculture was increasingly delinked from farmer income growth, as is visible in the incidence of poverty that still stalks farmer households (~20 per cent of all rural households with self-employment in agriculture in 2011 were below the poverty line, with poverty rates acute especially in states like Jharkhand and Odisha).[1] When compared with a non-agricultural worker, the farmer income per cultivator shows a significant disparity, with a typical non-agriculture worker earning three to four times more than a cultivator annually.[2] This disparity is one of the primary causes of the agrarian distress that prevails in our country, leading to low agricultural income and farmer suicides.[3] And for India's policymakers, changing this paradigm is necessary to usher in an age of rural prosperity.

It's not that there has been no attention on increasing agricultural income in the past. NITI Aayog's push to double farmer income by 2022, while dubbed impossible

1   NSSO, 2012
2   Doubling Farmer's Income, Niti Aayog, NITI Policy Paper No.1/2017, 2017
3   Chand, Parappurathu, 2012

by some experts[4], given that it would require raising agricultural revenue by 10–14 per cent annually, is notable in its ambition.

Now, raising farmer income can be accomplished from two ends—the use of better technology, lower input prices and labour usage can lead to lower cost in cultivating agricultural produce, or the prices of farm products compared to other commodities can increase substantially. The impact of increasing farm product prices can be substantial, although the past record of farmer income increasing substantially is slim—nominal prices have doubled over a period of five years only twice in the last three decades.

When we consider the period between 1994 and 2005, the value added in agriculture increased by 2.52 per cent CAGR annually, while the price index for agricultural commodities rose by 5.65 per cent annually and farmer income rose by 8.45 per cent annually at nominal prices. Converting this to real income after stripping the impact of inflation, the growth rate annually in income was 3.3 per cent. During the same time period, cultivators rose from 143.9 million to 166.1 million, highlighting increasing fragmentation in India's farms. Therefore, the impact of the overall increase in per farmer income was diminished, effectively leading to a sub-2 per cent CAGR annually in farmer income.[5] Since then, up till 2012, farmer income has increased by 5.52 per cent annually, while the number of cultivators has declined, leading to an overall higher growth in per farmer income of ~7.46 per cent. Crop output declined slightly in 2013, and two below-normal monsoons in 2015 and 2016 had a deleterious impact, decelerating the growth rate in value add in agriculture to 1.6 per cent for those two years. Meanwhile, agricultural prices received by farmers stagnated, leading to a decline in real farmer income between 2012 and 2016.[6]

How do farmers make money in agriculture—what are the true sources of growth in farmer income? One of the very first is increasing agricultural productivity by using better savings and better agricultural inputs, while another is utilizing resources efficiently, leading to an overall saving in the cost of production. Increasing cropping intensification, along with diversification towards high-value crops can also lead to significant growth. And beyond this, simply lowering the number of cultivators in agriculture, shifting them to non-farm occupations and raising the real prices received by farmers can have a powerful impact on farmer income.

Let's first consider agricultural productivity. Raising agricultural output can only be done by either substantially increasing the agricultural land bank (unlikely, given

---

4   Gulati, 2016
5   Doubling Farmer's Income, Niti Aayog, NITI Policy Paper No. 1/2017, 2017
6   Ibid

the high share of arable land in India's geographical area currently; there could actually be a significant decline, given urbanization) or by seeking improvement in agricultural productivity per unit of land. India's per-crop productivity, as noted earlier, is relatively low, with significant scope for improvement in most crops (excluding wheat), along with variations in yield across states. Aggregate productivity of all crops in India has risen by 3.1 per cent annually between 2000 and 2014. Some of this rise is due to increasing application of irrigation and technological advancement. Some of this is also due to increasing income from livestock (~30 per cent of the total agricultural income), which has seen a growth rate of 4.5 per cent annually between 2001 and 2014.[7]

For a dramatic shift in the rate of farmer income growth annually, there will instead have to be a focus on improving total factor productivity (i.e. the rate of adoption of technology, skills and infrastructure in rural India), along with a diversification push towards high-value crops. Currently, staple crops like wheat, rice, pulses and oilseeds occupy more than 77 per cent of India's total cropped area but contribute only 41 per cent of the total agricultural output by value.[8] Most of the output is actually contributed by fruits, vegetables, fibres, condiments, spices and sugar cane, all of which are grown on just 19 per cent of India's gross cropped area (as of 2014). In value terms, once cropping intensity variation is taken into account, staple crops mentioned above will give an average productivity of ₹41,169 per hectare (in 2014) versus ₹141,777 per hectare from more high-value crops, as mentioned above.[9] Ergo, shifting away from staple crops to such high-value crops would increase returns by ~₹1 lakh per hectare (2014 figures). The current ongoing shift away from staple crops to such high-value crops (growth in area covered by such crops was at 3.31 per cent annually between 2005 and 2014) can lead to an increase in agricultural output, by value, of ~1 per cent annually.[10]

Now India itself has been gifted with two main crop-growing seasons, rabi and kharif, allowing its farmers to cultivate two crops—and in some cases, three— annually on the same piece of land.[11] However, cropping intensity continues to remain low, with land-use statistics highlighting that the second crop is grown only on 38.9 per cent of India's net sown area, leaving over 60 per cent fallow during that season—this limited crop intensity is constrained primarily due to a lack of access to water, even in irrigated areas. While crop intensity is increasing annually by 0.7 per cent, there is significant scope to raise this further, with resultant consequences for farmer income.

---

7   Doubling Farmer's Income, Niti Aayog, NITI Policy Paper No. 1/2017, 2017
8   Ibid
9   Ibid
10   Ibid
11   Ibid

In the near term, however, increasing farmer income will require a step change in the terms of trade for farmers. Some of this is a consequence of marketing channel efficiency and will be alleviated only by undertaking reform to reduce middlemen, investing in technology to modernize the value chain, and a push towards agro-processing, all to improve the terms of trade for farmers. Consider the Rashtriya e-Market Services Pvt Ltd (ReMS) initiative, a joint venture between the government of Karnataka and NCDEX e-Markets Limited, which led to the Unified Market Platform (UMP) being utilized—the introduction of online trading and UMP-driven prices have led to an increase in wholesale commodity prices, with a variation of 1–43 per cent across crops between 2014 and 2016.[12] Such small reforms, even in agricultural marketing, can lead to a significant difference in the prices received by farmers. A greater implementation of reforms in agricultural marketing would lead to a significant increase in farmer income in the near term.

INDIA'S AGRICULTURAL MARKETS

Indian agriculture, despite massively subsidized inputs and price floors, along with supporting infrastructure, does not realize economies of scale, offers marginal farmers few, if any, profits, and has limited scope of growth. Despite the bounty that India offers to farmers—rich farmland, growing seasons, comprising a few—government policies have led to a marketing system that is increasingly skewed against farmers.

THE GREAT ONION ROBBERY

In December 2010, India's newspapers ran out of print reporting on the 'Great Indian Onion Robbery'.[13] Newspapers highlighted that speculative traders had corned the onion markets, with wholesale traders in Delhi purchasing onion at ₹34/kg, while it was retailed at ₹80/kg, a markup of 135 per cent. Typically, 45 per cent of India's onions come from the states of Maharashtra and Karnataka. However,

---

12   Doubling Farmer's Income, Niti Aayog, NITI Policy Paper No. 1/2017, 2017
13   Varmal, Subodh, The Great Indian Onion Robbery, (Times of India), (10 December 2016). Sourced from: http://timesofindia.indiatimes.com/india/The-great-onion-robbery-135-mark-up-from-mandi-to-retail/articleshow/7147837.cms

November had seen excessive rainfall in and around Nashik, the hub of India's onion trade, which delayed the arrival of onions in major markets. The centre responded immediately to the domestic crisis, banning onion exports, lowering import taxes and even importing from Pakistan, where onions were retailing at PKR 40/kg. Even after deducting for transport and storage costs, the markup for intermediaries had clearly shot up. The farmers, however, profited much, much less. Even when wholesale prices started declining, the retail price for onions stayed sticky for a few weeks.

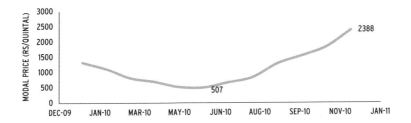

FIGURE 77: MODAL ONION PRICES IN DELHI IN 2010[14]

Government policies were partly to blame. With unseasonal rains in September and October 2010 affecting the onion crop (35 per cent–40 per cent of the crop by acreage was damaged), traders were still allowed to export 1.03 lakh tonnes of onions in October 2010.[15]

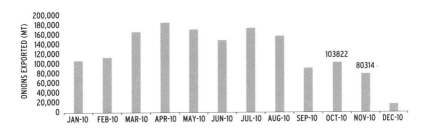

FIGURE 78: ONIONS EXPORTED IN 2010[16]

But more so, the marketing structure for onions remains a key factor. Most onion farmers have small landholdings, face unpredictable weather conditions and have little say in the determination of the final price of their produce. Different regions

---

14   NHRDF data, 2010

15   Chengappa, P.G., Manjunatha, A.V., Dimble, Vikas, Shah, Khalil, Competitive Assessment of Onion Markets in India, Competition Commission of India, 2012

16   NHRDF data, 2010

of India seek different kinds of onions—the eastern parts prefer small-sized ones, while north and west Indian consumers prefer large, bulbous ones. Most traders buy small lots, from various farmers across markets, while pooling the produce together at their warehouses. Once the onions are sorted and graded, they are sent to markets offering the best prices. While the farmer only has his local market as a reference for onion prices, the traders track regional and national markets, along with potential export avenues, before sending produce where it fetches the most handsome profits. While the obvious answer to this information disparity would be the formation of a cooperative association of onion farmers, the short growing season and the disparate areas of onion production across India prevent collectivization. The traders hold leverage—through large storage areas that can mostly protect onions from rotting, and through a domination of the commission agent trade and membership of marketing committees of various Agricultural Produce Market Committee (APMC) markets. Many also are store owners, transport agents and wholesalers. Meanwhile, government regulations that require licencing of such marketing roles constrict competition amongst intermediaries—most onion traders have been established in the trade for over two decades.

REGULATED MARKETS

Vikram Yadav shouts himself hoarse, seeking a price for his sacks of onions at the local APMC market in Sultanpur. Sweat beads his face—with the sun up high, the rot will soon set in. Price discovery is a grinding process in such markets. Often, customers come by, check a sample of his produce and walk past, or negotiate. Others use the traditional 'hada' method—a complex system of verbal tics and gestures to highlight prices, while maintaining confidentiality on them. Sometimes, the 'dara' method is followed, with fixed prices for different varieties. And if Yadav is lucky, an open auction will help him recover true value. The ways of APMC markets are strange, indeed.

When grains are in surplus, any farmer seeks to sell them to a nearby profitable market. While it sounds simple, such an arrangement is usually hard to find—most farmers are disadvantaged, seeking the most optimum price, while their produce rots away in open markets.

Such disadvantages were enforced by the colonial economic system. The Berar Cotton & Grain Market Act (1887) sought to empower the British Regent to declare any place in the assigned district a market for sale and purchase of agricultural produce, while setting up a committee to oversee the said regulated market. This market was necessary to ensure that cotton was available at reasonable prices to the textile mills of Manchester. The Royal Commission on Agriculture (1928) spoke about 'there being a great absence of information with regard to marketing conditions in India. In all provinces markets vary greatly in character and importance. Some are privately owned; some are directly under the control of the district board or municipality. It is only in Berar that the constitution of markets is regulated by special legislation and that the management is in the hands of elected committees.'[17]

The commission recommended 'the establishment of regulated markets, and we recommend for the consideration of other provinces the establishment of regulated markets on the Berar system as modified by the Bombay legislation. The establishment of regulated markets must form an essential part of any ordered plan of agricultural development in this country. The Bombay Act is, however, definitely limited to cotton markets and the bulk of the transactions in Berar markets are also in that crop. We consider that the system can conveniently be extended to other crops and, with a view to avoiding difficulties, would suggest that regulated markets should only be established under provincial legislation. Local governments should also take the initiative and such markets should immediately be established in a few principal centres. This way, the public opinion can be refined to realize the advantages of markets of this character and a demand for them be created. The relationship of a regulated market to the council of any municipality or to the local board in the area in which the market is being established will require careful consideration in drafting legislation.'

By 1937, the Agricultural Produce Act established statutory powers with state governments over agricultural markets, allowing them to make rules 'fixing grade designations to indicate the quality of any scheduled article, defining the quality indicated by every grade designation, specifying grade designation marks to represent particular grade designations'. [18]

By the time Independence came, India's agricultural sector, by modern standards, was severely underdeveloped. Wherever villages had surplus, a 'haat' or a 'mandi' would spring up, catering to wholesale markets within a few km. Traders, often termed 'arathdars', and retailers operated in long supply chains to bring produce to the urban end consumer. The same traders and retailers acted as agents and moneylenders too, and in some cases as landlords, enveloping farmers in a viciously disadvantaged trade cycle. Most farmers had limited freedom in which crops they

---

17   Royal Commission On Agriculture In India Report, 1928
18   The Agricultural Produce (Grading and Marking) Act, 1937

could grow, what inputs they could use and how they could sell their produce. Most sale contracts were unwritten, with little regulatory oversight, and committed to by individual farmers with no legal support or price discovery overview.

Post-Independence, the Green Revolution was launched, while state regulation of agricultural marketing continued, with states passing regulation to build up the regulatory environment around the traditional marketing system.[19]

The Agricultural Produce Marketing (APMC) Act, enacted by state governments, sought to bring the range of State-defined regulatory regimes under one umbrella, while seeking to empower farmers against traders and retailers, all while narrowing the price quoted by the farmer and that received by the end consumer. Now, all agricultural transactions were legally required to be conducted in 'mandis', regulated markets, if you will, which were democratically run through elected committees— all while prices were discovered in open auctions. Such committees, made up of representatives of all stakeholders, helped provide the infrastructure and facilities for trading, while charging fees from the respective parties to cover operational expenses. The passage of the Act led to a significant increase in regulated markets, which grew from just 286 in 1947 to more than 7,521 in 2005.[20]

Other institutions were soon set up—the Agricultural Prices Commission (later termed the Commission for Agricultural Costs and Prices) focused on price intervention. Other product-specific institutions were set up—the Tea Board of India, the Jute Corporation of India, the Coir Board of India, etc., along with the National Agricultural Cooperative Marketing Federation of India Ltd (NAFED), the National Cooperative Development Corporation and the National Dairy Development Board.

Other states tried to directly intervene in agricultural markets through Market Intervention Schemes (MIS). In 1974, Himachal Pradesh launched the Himachal Pradesh Horticultural Produce Marketing and Processing Corporation (HPMC), with a focus on processing and marketing fresh fruits.

---

19   Ghosh, N., India's Agricultural Marketing: Market Reforms and Emergence of New Channels, India Studies in Business and Economics, Springer India, 2013
20   Ibid

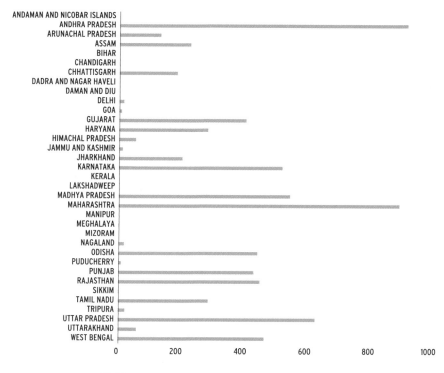

FIGURE 79: WHOLESALE MARKETS IN INDIA (2014)[21, 22]

Until the 1990s, most processors in India were primarily small firms running rice mills, flour mills and oilseed 'ghanis'. But with a dramatic change in consumer taste, demand shifted, with a greater need for an established market for perishable fruits and vegetables. The transit between farmers and consumers was interspersed with too many intermediaries, who had their eyes on rent-seeking, and had few resources to contribute to significant infrastructure buildup. Even now, it is estimated that just 2.25–4 per cent of India's fruits are processed.[23]

The Guru Committee (2001) on agricultural marketing reviewed India's marketing system, which led to the recommendation of a new model APMC Act (finalized in 2003), which sought to increase competition in India's agricultural markets, while allowing for the development of innovative marketing channels. State governments were pushed to amend their existing APMC Acts in order to align with this Act. The new Act offered significant central assistance for developing storage infrastructure, while fashioning a warehouse receipt-based system for grain storage. Future trading in cereals was allowed through a modification of the Forward Market Act (1952).

21   Lok Sabha Unstarred Question No. 3525, dated 11 August 2015
22   India Stat data
23   GOI, 2007

However, this regulated marketing system, despite its optimistic intentions, has also induced significant downsides. Consider post-harvest losses—about 15–50 per cent of India's fruits are lost during marketing.[24,25] Roads inside such regulated markets are usually unpaved, with auctions conducted in open spaces, and hence, prone to congestion. As the APMC Acts usually forbid purchases from farmers outside the market, the onus lies on farmers to bring their produce inside the market, subjecting them to long queues. Most farmers are prevented from selling their produce in bulk, while exporters and retailers are prevented from accessing such farmers directly. Given such constraints, farmers have increasingly resorted to contract farming, leasing out fruit trees in advance for a fixed price, reducing their risk. Many others simply sell fruit produce in the local market, avoiding the APMC markets completely.

In addition, structural factors prevent them from fulfilling their mandate. Moral hazards, faced by organizers on a daily basis, ensured that price discovery was not completely debiased, while rent-seeking behaviour soon became common. Collusion amongst traders and market officials during the bidding process usually ensures that price discovery does not happen, netting the farmer lower prices than due to him. In addition, most traders and agents end up collectivizing, while farmers bargain in an individual capacity. While licencing of such traders ought to have been a barrier to such behaviour, it ends up creating a cartel within the market, preventing new traders from breaking the monopsony. The State Agricultural Marketing Board (SAMB), set up to monitor such behaviour, ends up usually having an advisory role. Such regulated markets are reduced to being checkposts that collect maintenance fees from farmers, while traders run amok with unfair pricing. Instead of having open democratic elections and being run by farmers, such markets usually postpone their elections while being run by conniving bureaucrats. Regulated market coverage can be a significant issue—an average regulated market in Punjab can cover around 115 sq km, serving farmers in that hinterland. In contrast, Meghalaya has to make do with one every 11,215 sq km.[26]

Finally, the price spread between what the farmer earns and what the end user is charged remains stark. A study in 1972 in Kolkata found that just 2 per cent of the end-user price of an orange reached the farmer[27]—such marketing channels have taken to consuming the majority of the value. Meanwhile, in more robust regulatory environments, where the marketing channel lengths are shorter, the price spread can be far smaller—a farmer in Madurai would on average receive 95 per cent of the end user's price.

---

24   FAO, 1981
25   Roy, 1989
26   Acharya, Aggarwal, 2004
27   Mahalanobis, 1972

India's agricultural system is undergoing a significant transition—the front of the value chain, namely, the retailers, are rapidly modernizing along with their supply chain, while the backend, the marginal farmers themselves, continue to fragment their holdings across their patrimony. Should this continue, we will end up with a natural monopsony, with corporates buying directly from the farmers, with maximum leverage enforced.[28] It's not that marginal farmers are without advantages—they offer significant low cost, given an abundance of related populations, along with traditional knowledge, on how best to till and grow from the land. Where they fail, usually, is on providing standardized products to their markets that meet customer expectations regularly. Without activities like grading, cleaning, sorting and packaging, India's farmers will always have a small share of the overall pie (typically, 35 per cent of the wholesale price), remaining price-takers, with limited contacts or market intelligence. Without a reformation of our existing marketing system, the gap between farmers being unable to find the right price and the appropriate market, and the produce quality issues faced by retailers will not be bridged.

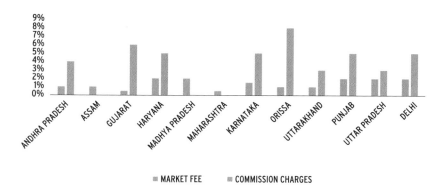

FIGURE 80: APMC MARKET CHARGES (2012)[29]

28   Gopalakrishnan, Sreenivasa, 2009

29   Kumar, R. Reddy, B. Framework for One National Market for Agricultural Produce, India Commodity Year Book, 2012. Sourced from: http://www.ncml.com/pdf/agri-market/framework-for-one-national-market-for-agricultural-produce.pdf

PRICE POLICY

Let's consider how commodity prices have behaved in the last few years. The weighted average wholesale prices of wheat were above the minimum support price (MSP) from April 2015 to May 2017. However, the onset of the peak arrival season between May and June 2017 saw prices drop below the MSP in Madhya Pradesh. In particular, in the Sehore and Raisen markets in the state, market prices for wheat were below MSP for fifteen to nineteen days between March and May 2017.[30] Similarly, for barley, the wholesale price was above the MSP in the same period—however, prices declined to ₹1,463 per quintal by June 2017, given an increase in the area under cultivation. The gap between market prices of barley and the minimum support prices narrowed significantly in 2017.[31] For lentils, market prices were significantly above the MSP in 2017, albeit showing a declining trend, partially because of the prevalence of low prices in Madhya Pradesh in May and June 2017.[32] Meanwhile, in Madhya Pradesh's Mandsaur district, the wholesale market for garlic crashed, with garlic selling for as low as ₹1 per kg.

REFORMING APMC

While agriculture is considered the third rail of Indian politics, reforming agricultural marketing can often be and is construed as playing with the economic well-being of marginal farmers and the urban poor. Most Indian consumers still prefer non-processed, farm-fresh and traditional farm produce.[33] Concerns about food price inflation, along with any potential adverse impact on the vast intermediary population of traders led the government to go slow on reform. Food retail chains, embodied by multibrand retail, finally saw FDI limits raised in 2012, with the hope that such a measure would draw in greater investment in cold-chain infrastructure and promote greater domestic sourcing. With agriculture a state subject, reform of marketing channels has been an ad hoc process across India's states, with contract farming in particular mistrusted, given its similarity to the old zamindari days.

Ideally, there should be an agricultural market in every 5-km-radius (~80 sq km) area of agricultural land (National Commission on Farmers), which should be regulated by APMC committees that offer competitive prices. Given significant

---

30   Ministry of Agriculture, 2017
31   Ibid
32   Ibid
33   Shah, 1997

regulatory constraints, dreams of the APMC Act ushering in a new era of cold chains, with storage and processing facilities, and the active writ of market institutions, all resulting in Indian agriculture becoming globally competitive, have come to naught. Around 30–40 per cent of India's farm produce (typically worth $10–$15 billion) annually is lost prior to reaching consumers[34]—all due to a significant lack of processing of fruits and vegetables (~1.7 per cent of production vs the US' 60–70 per cent).[35]

West Bengal, in particular, no matter the government, has considered the model APMC Act as riven with 'anti-poor' and 'anti-farmer' provisions, while considering contract farming as patently unfair. Farmers and corporations have found their ways around it—Pepsi has sought to collaborate with farmers in Bamanpara village in Burdwan district of West Bengal, for the cultivation of the Atlanta variety of potato—a source for its eponymous Lay's chips.[36,37] The company guarantees its demand for the entire year's production, while offering an assured price of ₹305 for a 50-kg bag (as of 2012), potentially leading to profits of over ₹15,000 per acre farmed—a 50 per cent jump over normal conditions.[38] Farmer profit is assured, while price risk is mitigated.

Bihar repealed its APMC Act in 2006, but has failed to replace it with another Act till date.[39] With the abolishment of APMC-regulated markets, an unregulated private wholesale market ecosystem has grown. Now, farmers come and sell in nearby markets with unpaved roads and little to no infrastructure. There are no restrictions on what or how much a farmer can bring into a market, and none whatsoever on whom he can sell it to. Many farmers prefer such arrangements, allowing them to sell and monetize their produce on a daily or monthly basis, instead of having to wait in queues for entering the market in the first place. The cost—a typical 1–2 per cent charge by mandi organizers from the farmers. However, price discovery is unlikely—this is no competitive open auction, and there is no recourse for farmers to any institutional authority if wholesale traders press their claim.

Punjab has implemented significant reforms to its APMC Act, allowing for direct

---

34   Dagar, 2007

35   Blatt, 2008

36   Acharya, N., Bengal farmers reap benefits of collaborative farming, Business Standard, 20 December 2012. Sourced from: http://www.business-standard.com/article/economy-policy/bengal-farmers-reap-benefits-of-collaborative-farming-112122002041_1.html

37   Roy, S., Contract farming lures Bengal potato growers, The Hindu, 7 January 2012. Sourced from: http://www.thehindubusinessline.com/economy/agri-business/contract-farming-lures-bengal-potato-growers/article2783433.ece

38   Dutta, A., Dutta, A., Sengupta, S., A Case Study of Pepsico Contract Farming For Potatoes, IOSR Journal of Business and Management, 2016

39   Singh, S., Reforming markets, lessons from Bihar, 5 February 2015. Sourced from: http://www.tribuneindia.com/news/comment/reforming-markets-lessons-from-bihar/37892.html

purchase of perishable crops, including fruits and vegetables, by retail chains, but further reforms are significantly opposed by commission agents and artyas. Any private players seeking access to Punjab's farmers are required to seek permission from the Mandi Board to set up any direct purchase points, keeping such markets limited.

Other states, like Andhra Pradesh, Himachal Pradesh, Jharkhand and Maharashtra, have fewer qualms about amending their APMC Acts to allow contract farming and direct marketing.

The advent of e-trading has also enabled existing APMC markets to be in tune with customer requirements. States like Gujarat, Andhra Pradesh, Uttar Pradesh and Delhi have accepted e-trading in agricultural produce, with the famed apple market of Himachal Pradesh and the Azadpur mandi in Delhi already placing online orders. The AGMARKNET initiative, which seeks to transform the current system into one that responds on a real-time basis, should deliver a fair market price to farmers, while being at scale with other private channels. The initiative seeks to establish a nationwide market information network that will collect and disseminate information on a timely basis across all regulated markets. Instead of seeking out prices written with chalk on a board, farmers will seek digital ledgers.

MARKETING STAPLE CROPS

WHEAT

Amongst staple crops, wheat and paddy occupy the heights. Despite the volumes grown, the marketing channels remain noted for the limited margins that they offer farmers. A study in Chhattisgarh's Durg district highlighted that farmers utilize two channels—one focused on direct selling and the other on utilizing a village trader as intermediary.

When comparing the distribution of marketing costs, Channel 1 has the wholesaler and village trader taking on the majority of transportation and loading/unloading costs, while Channel 2 sees these distributed between the farmer and the wholesaler.

FIGURE 81: MARKETING CHANNELS FOR WHEAT IN DURG DISTRICT, CHHATTISGARH (2014)[40]

FIGURE 82: MARKETING COST BREAKUP FOR CHANNEL 1 (PRODUCER - VILLAGE TRADER - WHOLESALER) FOR WHEAT IN DURG DISTRICT, CHHATTISGARH (2014)[41]

FIGURE 83: MARKETING COST BREAKUP FOR CHANNEL 2 (PRODUCER - WHOLESALER) FOR WHEAT IN DURG DISTRICT, CHHATTISGARH (2014)[42]

---

40   Pallewar, S., Shrey, R., Bante, R., Marketing cost and marketing margin of wheat in Durg district of Chhattisgarh, International Journal of Agricultural Sciences, Volume 10 | Issue 2 | June 2014 | 681-684. Sourced from: http://www.researchjournal.co.in/upload/assignments/10_681-684.pdf

41   Ibid

42   Ibid

When comparing marketing margins, net margins are better in Channel 2 than in Channel 1, given the lack of an intermediary.

FIGURE 84: MARKETING MARGIN FOR CHANNEL 1
FOR WHEAT IN DURG DISTRICT, CHHATTISGARH (2014)[43]

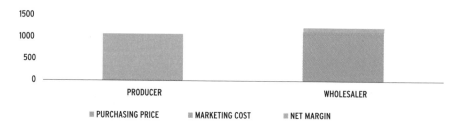

FIGURE 85: MARKETING MARGIN FOR CHANNEL 2
FOR WHEAT IN DURG DISTRICT, CHHATTISGARH (2014)[44]

---

43 Pallewar, S., Shrey, R., Bante, R., Marketing cost and marketing margin of wheat in Durg district of Chhattisgarh, International Journal of Agricultural Sciences, Volume 10 | Issue 2 | June 2014 | 681-684. Sourced from: http://www.researchjournal.co.in/upload/assignments/10_681-684.pdf

44 Ibid

PADDY

For paddy, a study of cultivators in Tamil Nadu highlighted the usage of three marketing channels—one focused on wholesalers, another on local brokers and the third on direct procurement. The first channel had farmers selling their produce directly to wholesalers, at a gross price of ₹933 per quintal in 2015. The second channel had the farmers selling their produce to a broker, with the farmer's share of the consumer's rupee working out to be 50.53 per cent. The third channel had farmers selling paddy to the direct purchase centres of Tamil Nadu Civil Supplies Corporation (TNCSC), which adopted the government price support initiative of ₹1,050 per quintal.

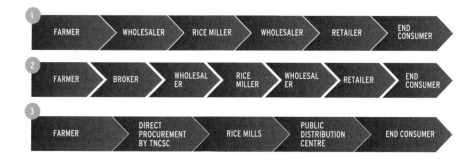

FIGURE 86: MARKETING CHANNELS FOR PADDY IN TAMIL NADU (2014)[45]

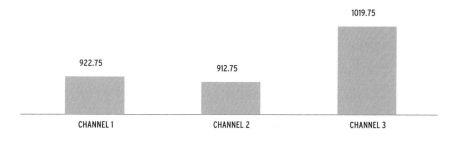

FIGURE 87: NET PRICE RECEIVED BY PADDY FARMERS IN TAMIL NADU (2015)[46]

45   Saravanakumar, V., Kiruthika, N., Economic analysis of production and marketing of paddy in Tamil Nadu, International Research Journal of Agricultural Economics and Statistics, Volume 6 | Issue 2 | September 2015 | 249-255, e ISSN-2231-6434
46   Ibid

MARKETING FRUITS AND VEGETABLES

The marketing of fruits and vegetables can vary heavily, depending on the nature of the produce, the existence of local infrastructure and consumer demand. Marketing potatoes in the Nilgiris district of Tamil Nadu is typically done through two channels—one focused on cooperative societies and the other on local mandis, with the first channel typically more efficient.[47,48]

Marketing channels can vary across fruits and vegetables. In the early '60s, grape produce in Punjab was typically sold through commission agents and local retailers, with grading and packing typically forming more than 70 per cent of the total marketing costs in such markets.[49] For sweet oranges in Punjab, about 77 per cent of farmers typically sold their produce to pre-harvest contractors, with an additional 20 per cent sold to terminal markets far away.[50] Farmers in Himachal Pradesh sold 86 per cent of their marketable produce to commission agents, while pre-harvest contractors took the rest.[51] Commissioning agents typically accounted for 41 per cent of the marketing margins in the market of Jammu, Amritsar and Delhi.[52] A study in 1978 highlighted that farmers selling mandarin oranges in Karnataka typically ended with a profit of ₹57.89 per thousand fruits, while commissioning agents made a net profit of ₹25.06 per thousand fruits.[53] Alphonso mangoes in Maharashtra are typically sold through four channels, focusing on direct sales, cooperative sales, sales via middlemen and pre-harvest contracted sales.

Meanwhile, mangoes in the Dharwad district of Karnataka are sold through four channels that focus on commissioning agents, pre-harvest contractors, processing unit agents and a combination of pre-harvest contractors and commissioning agents.[54]

Cashew in Karnataka is typically sold through six marketing channels. While going via a local merchant would typically net a farmer a high share of the end-consumer price, going through a commissioning agent would slash that significantly.[55]

---

47 Selvaraj, K., 1991

48 Kumar, R., N.S., Marketing of Tender Coconut in Madhur APMC of Mandya District, 2012

49 Singh, Kahlon, 1968

50 George, Singla, 1969

51 Kochha, Thakur, 1971

52 Dhar, 1976

53 Krishnamurty, et al, 1978

54 Gummangolmath, 1994

55 Raikat, 1990

FIGURE 88: MARKETING CHANNELS FOR POTATOES IN NILGIRIS DISTRICT IN TAMIL NADU

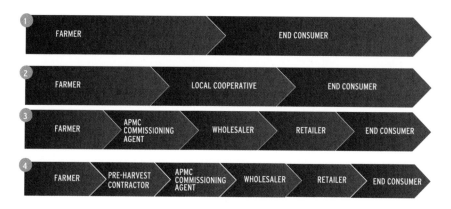

FIGURE 89: MARKETING CHANNELS FOR ALPHONSO MANGOES IN MAHARASHTRA

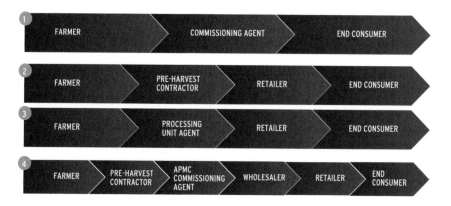

FIGURE 90: MARKETING CHANNELS FOR MANGOES IN DHARWAD DISTRICT IN KARNATAKA[56]

---

56   Gummangolmath, 1994

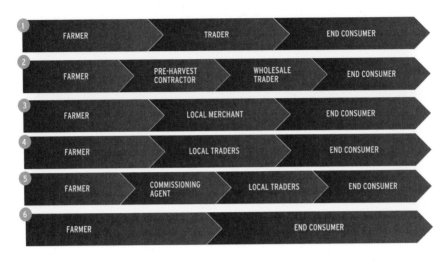

FIGURE 91: MARKETING CHANNELS FOR CASHEW IN KARNATAKA[57]

FIGURE 92: MARKETING CHANNELS FOR POMEGRANATES IN BIJAPUR DISTRICT[58]

FIGURE 93: MARKETING CHANNELS FOR BANANAS
IN TIRUCHIRAPPALLI DISTRICT IN TAMIL NADU[59]

---

57   Raikat, 1990

58   Koujalagi, Kunnal, 1991

59   Senthilnathan and Srinivasan, 1994

Pomegranates in Bijapur district are typically sold through either a pre-harvest contractor or through a commissioning agent.

Bananas are marketed in the Tiruchirappalli district of Tamil Nadu through a combination of pre-harvest contractors, wholesalers, commissioning agents and regulated markets. Meanwhile, cultivators in Karnataka sought to market their produce through two channels—focused on commissioning agent and village traders.[60]

Producer share in such marketing channels can vary significantly as well. Citrus fruit growers in Kashmir have a producer share of just 35.71 per cent of the consumer's price through a pre-harvest contracting marketing channel, which improves to 81.25 per cent with the retailer marketing channel.[61] Banana cultivators in Maharashtra have an average of 58.44 per cent share of the consumer's rupee, through two marketing channels—one focused on a wholesaler route, the other on a commissioning agent.[62] Meanwhile, formerly mentioned banana cultivators from Tiruchirappalli gained a 71.6 per cent and 61.27 per cent producer share in the consumer price through the commissioning agent and the APMC market wholesaler channels, respectively.

The eventual wholesale prices can vary, depending on seasons, local warehousing and cold-storage facilities, and supply from alternative sources as well.[63] Given the perishable nature of potatoes, prices tend to remain high after the post-harvest period.[64] Spice crops in Rajasthan are typically priced high in February, starting to decline when the first lots of the new batch of spices arrive in the market, and then rising again in September.[65] Grape prices in Pune's markets typically declined from January to March, as seasonal arrivals started coming in, with prices rising again from April onwards.[66]

There can be significant constraints in the marketing of such produce as well. Mango cultivators in the Dharwad district of Karnataka have been cited as facing issues with non-availability of farm labour, price volatility and market collusion between wholesalers and commissioning agents.[67] Meanwhile, mango growers in the Srinivaspur region Karnataka highlighted the lack of nearby processing

---

60   Gangal, 2002
61   Singh, 1996
62   More, 1999
63   Balakrishnan, et al, 1981
64   Singh, et al, 1993
65   Agarwal, Dhaka, 1998
66   Pagire, 1998
67   Gummagolmath, 1994

facilities, storage facilities, middlemen exploitation and grading issues as significant constraints.[68] Tomato growers in the Belgaum district of Karnataka speak about facing significant price volatility, along with high transportation to the market cost.[69]

Let's consider a specific fruit. Coconut growers typically tend to sell their produce to local traders who operate in such remote locations—such traders typically provide advance payments and are locally known, helping them collect the produce for sale to wholesale producers. Wholesalers typically dispatch coconuts by the truckload, depositing them in warehouses of commission agents, who pay an advance of approximately 60–80 per cent of the market value to the wholesalers. The commission agents finally sell the produce to local buyers, who can be exporters or secondary wholesalers, while gaining a commission for their services. Usually, there are four channels through which coconut marketing is conducted—1) from the producer directly to a local consumer 2) from the producer to a wholesaler to a retailer to an end consumer 3) from the producer to a local retailer to a local consumer 4) from the producer to a middleman to a wholesaler to a retailer to an end consumer. A study in Kerala (1992)[70] highlighted that 81 per cent of farmers sold their coconuts to middlemen directly at the farm gate, while just 1.5 per cent utilized local cooperative networks. As a consequence, this resulted in extortion from middlemen, price volatility and lack of facilities for copra-making and processing. While the first channel allowed the producer to gain maximum producer share of the consumer price, other channels naturally showcased smaller shares. Government intervention or the formation of local cooperatives is typically necessary for reducing the price spread between the producer price and the local consumer price.[71]

Another study in the Maddur APMC in the Mandya district of Karnataka highlighted that coconuts were sold through three channels—one focused on the local APMC trader, another on the village trader and the third on a different APMC trader in the Mumbai market. For a grower, the primary costs are typically the commission paid to the local APMC trader and his transportation costs. In comparison, the village trader is focused on limiting his loading/unloading costs, along with any commission paid out. APMC traders are most concerned about wastage of produce during transportation post-purchase.

---

68   Govinda, Reddy, 1997
69   Kumar, S., 2004
70   Das, Prafulla K., 1992
71   Ratha Krishnan L, 1989

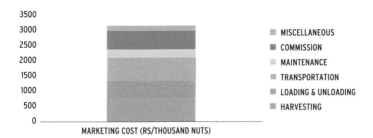

FIGURE 94: COST BREAKUP FOR COCONUT GROWERS
IN MANDYA DISTRICT OF KARNATAKA (2012)[72]

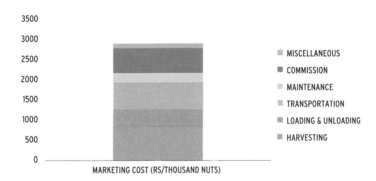

FIGURE 95: COST BREAKUP FOR VILLAGE-LEVEL COCONUT TRADERS
OF MANDYA DISTRICT IN KARNATAKA (2012)[73]

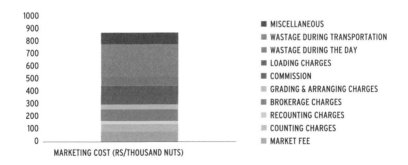

FIGURE 96: COST BREAKUP FOR APMC COCONUT TRADERS
IN MANDYA DISTRICT OF KARNATAKA (2012)[74]

72   Kumar, R., N.S., Marketing of Tender Coconut in Madhur APMC of Mandya District, 2012
73   Ibid
74   Ibid

Across all three channels, the third channel, selling to a wholesale trader in the Mumbai market, provided the lowest share of the consumer's rupee, while offering the highest value.[75] The first channel, where the farmer sold to the local APMC trader, had the APMC trader charging a typical commission of five nuts for every hundred nuts, along with ₹150 for every 1,000 tender coconuts. Such traders sold Grade II (medium-sized nuts, with low tenderness) to wholesale traders in Bengaluru.

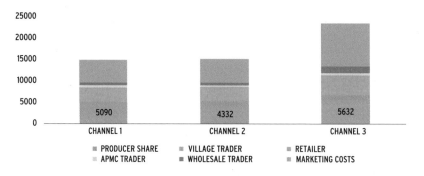

FIGURE 97: BREAKUP OF CONSUMER RUPEE (₹/THOUSAND NUTS)[76]

Increasingly, for marginal farmers, the way to survive seems to lie in horticulture—an agricultural segment that is people-intensive and heavily supported by both government and private players. It can be profitable too—farmers are reported to have increased their incomes by 30–40 per cent, when compared with staple crops like rice and wheat.[77] Shifting to such produce—which is low-volume and yet relatively high-value, and requires manpower intensity that plays to marginal farmers' strengths—is something that hilly states like Himachal Pradesh have particularly specialized in. Given their remote accessibility, climatic variability and limited employment options, farmers in such regions, with mostly fragmented holdings, tend to place a high premium on growing a variety of temperate and tropical fruits and vegetables.

When considering agricultural marketing in hilly states like Himachal Pradesh, one must understand their unique geographical and socio-economic conditions. Farming typically provides employment to a majority of the labour force (70 per cent for Himachal Pradesh), with the average farm size declining over time. Large-scale agricultural commercialization is simply not possible here. In addition, climatic conditions ensure that such mountainous states are best suited only for the production of temperate and tropical fruits and vegetables, driving inherent preference towards them.

---

75   Kumar, R., N.S., Marketing of Tender Coconut in Madhur APMC of Mandya District, 2012
76   Ibid
77   Viswanadham, 2006

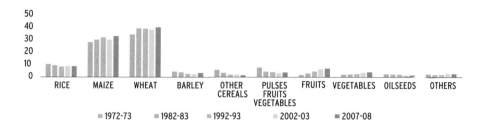

FIGURE 98: CROPPING PATTERN CHANGES (PER CENT OF TOTAL CROPPED AREA)
IN HIMACHAL PRADESH FROM 1972 TO 2007[78]

As can be seen, the area under fruits has risen substantially over the last few decades, driven by an expansion of apple cultivation. That under vegetables has increased similarly, rising to 6.69 per cent by 2009. Given the constraints of mountain agriculture, many farmers are increasingly adopting new technologies, such as drip farming. For Himachali horticulture farmers like Jayant Negi, from a hamlet near Shimla, easy proximity to prime markets in Chandigarh, Amritsar and Delhi also plays a role. It has been a long story—most Himachali farmers grew potatoes in the early 1970s, with most vegetables and fruits grown in home gardens for residents' consumption. However, the state's horticulture initiatives bore fruit, literally, with cultivation of apples, tomatoes, green peas, cabbages and cauliflowers. While a significant proportion of production is still retained for local consumption, a long distribution channel has arisen for the sale of such fresh produce.

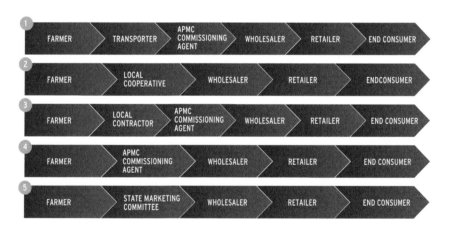

FIGURE 99: CHANNELS FOR TRADITIONAL MARKETING[79]

---

78 Directorate of Land Records, Government of Himachal Pradesh, Shimla
79 Bhat, A., Singh, S.P., Prasher, R.S., Chandel, S., Sharma, S., Chapter 2, Agricultural Marketing: Perspectives & Potentials, Nipa, 2016

Even with horticulture's added advantages, the traditional marketing channels structurally ensure that the producer share of the end retail price is limited, ranging from 53 per cent for oranges to 42 per cent for plums, while apples can garner 48.49 per cent.[80] Intermediaries consumed a significant proportion of marketing costs, with such traditional marketing systems beset with inefficiency,[81,82] trader collusion[83] and a significant amount of produce wastage.[84,85]

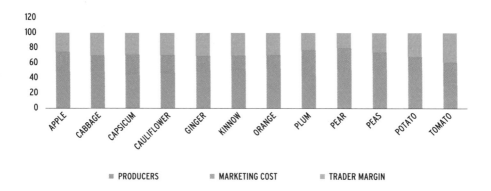

FIGURE 100: PRODUCER SHARE IN FRUITS AND VEGETABLES IN HIMACHAL PRADESH[86]

The repeal of the Himachal Pradesh Agricultural Produce Markets Act, 1969, and its replacement by the Himachal Pradesh Agricultural and Horticultural Produce Marketing Act (2005) helped improve the regulatory environment in agricultural marketing, allowing private players to participate in agricultural markets, while removing compulsions on farmers to sell only in regulated markets. Thus, the farmers were free to sell their produce directly to retailers, corporates and supermarkets. With contract farming allowed, state monopolies were dismantled, and price discovery enabled.

This led to aggregation amongst farmers across the state. The Karsog Valley Farmers Society, a cooperative between over 500 farmers from 40 villages in the Karsog valley of Mandi district, has sought to market its produce under a brand termed North Harvest, achieving better rates than through individual sale.

80   Negi, et al, 1997
81   Ramaswami, Balakrishnan, 2002
82   Singla, 2011
83   Banerji, M., 2004
84   Prasher, 2000
85   Matoo, 2007
86   Singh, et al, 2004

Increasingly, commission agents from wholesale markets are directly linking with farmers and farmer cooperatives, seeking to remove local intermediaries.

Jain Irrigation, in particular, has sought to establish itself in the contract farming business for onions—they provide seeds to farmers, while committing to purchasing the crop upon harvest at rates that are 5–10 per cent higher than APMC rates.

But there have been pitfalls as well. Supermarket chains sought to link up directly with farmers in Himachal Pradesh to procure vegetables like tomatoes, cabbage and cauliflower, while insisting on the highest quality requirements. Such an approach was unsustainable, as farmers, after selling their best produce at higher rates to supermarkets, found that they had lower bargaining power for the rest of the produce in the local markets.

The current marketing channel in Himachal Pradesh utilizes the state's investments in mechanized grading and packing houses, to grade fruits and vegetables in hygienic conditions. Such fruits and vegetables are then usually packed in corrugated cartons, often supplied on subsidy by the state government, or in gunny bags (usually for vegetables). Once packed, the fruits are usually sent to Delhi via trucks, a route that can take more than twelve hours to reach the Azadpur mandi. Once sold, the commissioning agent takes his cut (usually 5–6 per cent), and the farmer receives the balance, after deducting for transportation and labour costs. Farmers are usually paid either in person or through draft/cheques. Cold-storage facilities, established by the state government in Kullu, Solan and Shimla districts, help prolong the longevity of the produce. Other produce is often sold to the processing industry for conversion into jams and juices. The establishment of this network of processing plants, transhipment centres, sales offices, grading/packing houses and cold-storage areas has helped cut the cost of post-harvest facilities for the farmer. The market intervention scheme, launched in 1981, for apples, mangoes and citrus fruits, has helped ensure that unmarketable fruits are procured and processed by the HPMC, for conversion under hygienic conditions.

Himachal Pradesh continues to double down on its focus on horticulture. With the advent of global warming, alpine areas are increasingly facing a decline of chilling hours, affecting the apple crop. As a consequence, the state government has sought to encourage farmers to switch to plums, pears and peaches, while importing hardier varieties of apples that can survive warmer conditions. The export potential of other fruits, like kiwi, hazelnut, litchi and walnuts, is being explored, while the state's agricultural research organization is increasingly focusing on high-density planning, water management, greenhouse cultivation and micro-irrigation.

For states to pursue horticulture, a number of lessons can be drawn from Himachal

Pradesh's experience. The state, early on, sought to establish standardization of grades of fruits and vegetables, along with investing in packing material. Ensuring the timely availability of transport in harvest season was critical for remote areas, while substantial investment was provided for provision of marketing facilities and market yards in local producing hubs. The establishment of a cold chain, along with digitization of APMC markets provided a critical boost to farmer income. Reforming onerous regulation and allowing greater freedom to both farmers and end consumers to purchase produce have helped form a positive feedback loop.

SPECIALITY CROPS

JUTE

Jute, produced primarily from plants of the Corchorus genus, is essentially a shiny vegetable fibre which is spun into coarse, strong threads. This affordable fibre helped propel Bengal's economy in the colonial era and filled the coffers of imperial rulers, with the British East India Company and Dundee Jute Barons establishing jute mills across the landscape, producing more than a billion jute sandbags for European trenches in the First World War. Extracting jute requires retting, bundling jute stems together in slow-running water, after which non-fibrous matter is stripped off and the fibres are extracted, in a laborious process, typically given to women and children. This combination of retting with weeding, can typically take up to 70 per cent of the total cost of cultivation.[87]

Most farmers follow age-old agricultural practices, despite encouragement from Central Research Institute for Jute and Allied Fibres (CRIJAF) to adopt new technologies and fertilizers, resulting in an actual yield of 2.1 tonnes per hectare, versus a potential yield of 2.7 tonnes per hectare using the most basic modern technologies, let alone comparisons with China and nearby Bangladesh.

Despite the Indian Council of Agricultural Research's efforts to improve seed quality, there remains little incentive for farmers to upgrade, as the current MSP mechanism does not consider the quality of the fibre produced—sale of jute at such auctions is usually unassorted and ungraded. Most farmers barely care about the quality of the fibre or its suppository grading. The lack of awareness and the absence of institutional support have also kept coverage limited to just one-third of the jute-bearing areas.

---

87   Kumar, S., Shamna, A., Pandey, S.K., Marketing of Jute: Problems and Remedies, Rashtriya Krishi, Volume 9, Issue 2, December 2014, 1-5

Post-harvest, jute is typically sold by farmers as a raw material, with limited processing, to jute mills, with prices ideally allocated according to grades. Given its long life, jute can be stored in warehouses for a long period—however, most farmers seek to monetize their produce as quickly as possible. Barpeta district in Assam, on the northern bank of the Brahmaputra, is a major jute-producing area, with its jute made famous by the Tara Bari brand for its quality and high tensile strength.[88] Given the lack of availability of jute mills and factories in Assam, most of the district's jute produce is sold, via middlemen, to mills in West Bengal, Nepal and Madhya Pradesh.[89] Such middlemen are typically noted for reducing producer share to the bare minimum.[90] There are typically two main marketing channels utilized by jute farmers. The first has the farmers selling to small traders (colloquially known as faria), who sell to traders in regulated markets, from whom jute mills finally purchase. Another channel has commission agents purchasing from traders in regulated markets and selling to jute mills. The producer share in the consumer price, during peak seasons, can vary between 70 per cent of unregulated local village markets and 83 per cent in regulated markets. Deducting cost of production leaves the farmer with ~15–30 per cent of the end-consumer price.

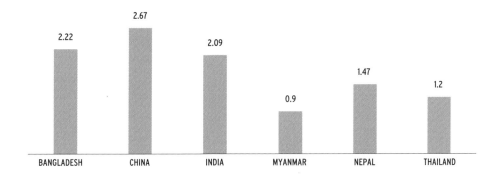

FIGURE 101: YIELD OF JUTE ACROSS ASIAN COUNTRIES (2010)[91]

88 Das, Manashree, Chanu, Dr. A. Ibemcha, Farmer's Share in Consumers' Price in Jute Marketing With Reference To Jute Farmers of Barpeta District of Assam, Indian Journal of Applied Research, Volume 6 | Issue 4 | April 2016 | ISSN - 2249-555X | IF : 3.919 | IC Value : 74.50

89 Das, 2015

90 Ahmed, 1979

91 Planning Commission Working Group on Textiles and the Jute Industry

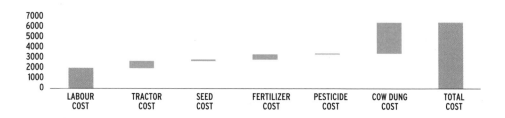

FIGURE 102: JUTE CULTIVATION COST IN BARPETA DISTRICT IN ASSAM (₹/BIGHA) (2015)[92]

The Jute Corporation of India (JCI) typically procures less than 5 per cent of the total raw jute[93], with most farmers selling their produce via intermediaries. In FY15, the total jute production was estimated to be 72 lakh bales (about 180 kg each), while the JCI was able to procure just 28,000 quintals.

FIGURE 103: JCI PROCUREMENT OF JUTE[94]

Despite the government-mandated MSP (₹2,400 per quintal in FY15), most farmers typically sell at prices ~20 per cent lower than the JCI rate. This is reflective of an inefficient procurement mechanism, while highlighting the utter inefficacy of the MSP.

The jute industry's challenges itself are numerous—with limited modernization, most jute mills are underutilized, unable to meet global quality standards. The capacity utilization of most of the 66 jute mills in India was found to be 50–83 per cent, a result of the obsolete technology they have.[95] The Jute Packaging Materials Act (1987) has helped cosset the industry, reducing incentives to innovate and

---

92 Das, Manashree, Chanu, Dr. A. Ibemcha, Farmer's Share in Consumers' Price in Jute Marketing With Reference To Jute Farmers of Barpeta District of Assam, Indian Journal of Applied Research, Volume 6 | Issue 4 | April 2016 | ISSN - 2249-555X | IF : 3.919 | IC Value : 74.50

93 National Fibre Policy, Ministry of Textiles

94 Swaniti Initiative, A Value Chain Study of the Jute Industry. Sourced from: http://www.sparc.swaniti.com/wp-content/uploads/2016/09/Growth-Roadmap-for-Jute-Industry_Barrackpore_Mr.-Trivedi.pdf

95 Standing Committee on Jute

improve productivity, keeping jute products limited with little to no diversification.[96] The industry, as a result, works mostly in silos, with no industry-wide marketing efforts to raise product awareness and boost demand. There is limited to no marketing infrastructure for jute in the country.[97] Frequent strikes in jute mills have not helped—jute workers in West Bengal have apparently gone on strike every year in the last half-decade, with 18 million man-days lost to strikes in 2010. They have their just grievances—non-payment of wages, working conditions that range from dismal to poor, and the increasing employment of contract labour, to name some. With limited focus on upskilling and training of such labour, worker satisfaction and productivity remain stagnant, constraining production.

COTTON

A study of cotton growers in the Khargone district of Madhya Pradesh highlighted that cotton growers utilized five marketing channels for selling their produce.

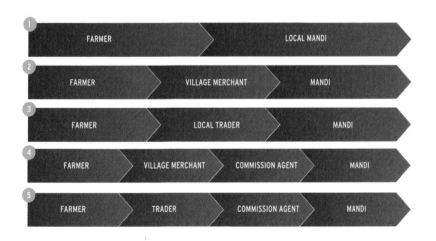

FIGURE 104: MARKETING CHANNELS FOR COTTON GROWERS
IN KHARGONE DISTRICT OF MADHYA PRADESH (2014)[98]

---

96   Swanitri Initiative, A Value Chain Study of the Jute Industry. Sourced from: http://www.sparc.swaniti. com/wp-content/uploads/2016/09/Growth-Roadmap-for-Jute-Industry_Barrackpore_Mr.-Trivedi.pdf

97   Parliamentary Questions, July 2014

98   Birla, H., Meena, L.K., Lakra, K., Bairwa, S.L., Beohar, B.B., Study on Marketing of Cotton in Khargone District of Madhya Pradesh; India, J Recent Adv Agr, 2014, 2(6): 244-25

Across marketing channels, Channel 1, direct to the local mandi, has the highest producer expense, given high transportation costs that are borne individually, while offering the lowest net price received.

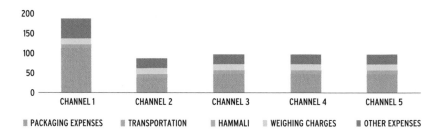

PACKAGING EXPENSES ▪ TRANSPORTATION ▪ HAMMALI ▪ WEIGHING CHARGES ▪ OTHER EXPENSES

FIGURE 105: PRODUCER EXPENSES FOR COTTON GROWERS IN KHARGONE DISTRICT OF MADHYA PRADESH (2014) (₹/QUINTAL)[99]

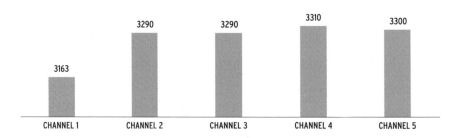

FIGURE 106: PRODUCER NET PRICE RECEIVED (₹/QUINTAL)[100]

99   Birla, H., Meena, L.K., Lakra, K., Bairwa, S.L., Beohar, B.B., Study on Marketing of Cotton in Khargone District of Madhya Pradesh; India, J Recent Adv Agr, 2014, 2(6): 244-251
100 Ibid

FLORICULTURE

Most Indian towns have a marigold flower seller around a corner, patiently stringing flowers together. Flowers, as such, have long held a symbolic and aesthetic value in Indian society, used for a variety of religious and social settings.[101] More recently, India has played host to a floriculture industry that focuses on commercial cultivation of roses, anthuriums, carnations, orchids and lilies. While traditional farms have seen slow growth, cut flower production has seen a significant rise.[102] Loose flower production has risen from 233,000 MT to 1,754,000 MT between 1993 and 2014, with Maharashtra, Karnataka, Tamil Nadu, West Bengal and, surprisingly, Mizoram dominating.[103,104] Gujarat and Maharashtra are conducive to the production of the Dutch rose and the Gerbera, while other flowers like anthuriums and orchids, which require high investment and colder climates, are spread across northern states. The Northeast in particular has specialized in anthurium cut flower production, with 97 per cent of India's production sourced from Nagaland (15.99 per cent), Mizoram (44.11 per cent), Arunachal Pradesh (36.22 per cent), Karnataka (2.28 per cent) and Sikkim (1.41 per cent).

In Mizoram, marketing channels for anthurium cut flowers tend to vary—one popular channel sees cultivators relying on private marketing agencies to move produce to retailers in cities.[105] Another channel sees a cooperative, Anthurium Growers Society of Kolasib, sourcing flowers from growers and selling them to wholesale agencies based in Guwahati, which subsequently sell them to retailers. The third channel is far more traditional, with growers selling their produce to retailers in the local market. Local demand is influenced by the wedding season, decorations for religious festivals and daily domestic use. A field survey conducted in June 2014 found that nearly two-third of cultivators sold their produce through the first channel, while an additional 25 per cent utilized the traditional third channel. Private marketing agencies dominated the total monthly market arrival (actual quantity of flowers sold in the market), contributing over 50 per cent. Marketing cost share for the producer varied across channels—while the private agency channel sought to sell such flowers in metropolitan markets, incurring airfare and packaging costs, the local cooperative channel sought to sell such flowers in regional markets like Guwahati, leaving the packaging costs to the cultivators themselves. More than 74.35 per cent of flowers were spoilt prior to reaching their end customer.

---

101 Gajanana, Sudha, 2006

102 Reddy, 2006

103 National Horticulture Board data, 2015

104 Mohan, V., Times of India, 14 February 2016. Sourced from: http://timesofindia.indiatimes.com/india/ Flower-fascination-India-set-to-be-floriculture-trade-leader/articleshow/50979808.cms

105 Rohmingliani, Thanja, James, L.T., Marketing Efficiency of Anthurium Cut Flowers in India: An Analysis, Management Convergence, Volume 5, No 1&2, January and June 2014. Sourced from: www. inflibnet.ac.in/ojs/index.php/MC/article/download/3169/2453

Producer share in the end consumer's price was the highest in the local retailer channel (75.65 per cent) and lowest in the private marketing agency channels.

FIGURE 107: MARKETING COST SHARE FOR ANTHURIUM FLOWERS
SOURCED FROM MIZORAM IN 2014 (₹/STEM)[106]

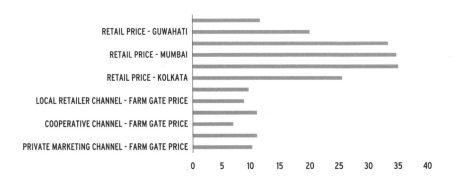

FIGURE 108: ANTHURIUM PRICES IN DIFFERENT MARKETS (2014) (₹/STEM)[107]

106 Rohmingliani, Thanja, James, L.T., Marketing Efficiency of Anthurium Cut Flowers in India: An Analysis, Management Convergence, Volume 5, No 1&2, January and June 2014. Sourced from: www.inflibnet.ac.in/ojs/index.php/MC/article/download/3169/2453

107 Ibid

FIGURE 109: ANTHURIUM PRODUCER SHARE IN END-CONSUMER PRICE (PER CENT) AS OF 2014[108]

However, the private marketing agency channel offered better value to the producer, compared to the other two channels.

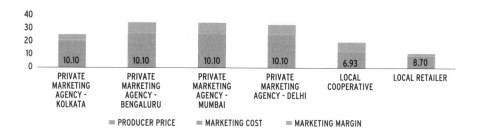

FIGURE 110: PRODUCER PRICE AS PER CENT OF END RETAILER PRICE FOR
ANTHURIUM CUT FLOWERS FROM MIZORAM IN 2014 (₹/STEM)[109]

Similarly, a study conducted in Uttar Pradesh highlighted that marigold flower cultivators survived on limited margins, with fertilizer, weeding and transplanting costs being prominent. What is highlighted across such cases is that improving access to markets, either through air transport or good roads, ensures that producers can gain access to market prices.

108 Rohmingliani, Thanja, James, L.T., Marketing Efficiency of Anthurium Cut Flowers in India: An
    Analysis, Management Convergence, Volume 5, No 1&2, January and June 2014. Sourced from: www.
    inflibnet.ac.in/ojs/index.php/MC/article/download/3169/2453
109 Ibid

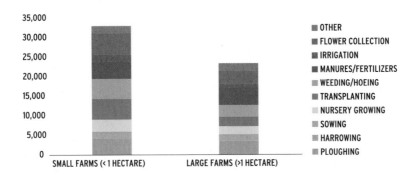

FIGURE 111: COST BREAKUP: FLORICULTURE IN UTTAR PRADESH[110]

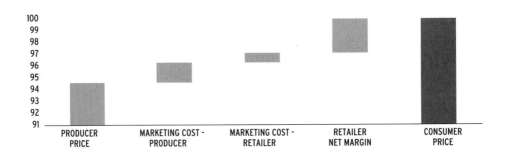

FIGURE 112: MARGIN SPREAD: MARIGOLD FLOWERS IN UTTAR PRADESH[111]

The central government provides varying levels of subsidies for floriculture through the National Horticulture Board, typically at 20 per cent of the project cost, given post-project implementation by the financing agency.

---

110 Singh, A.K., Singh, H.L., Singh, D.V., Production and Marketing of Marigold Flowers in Uttar Pradesh (2014)
111 Ibid

EVALUATING MARKETING CHANNELS

DIRECT MARKETING

The simplest marketing channel is to go direct—removing any middlemen, commission agents or aratiyas, thus benefitting the farmer on account of higher realizations and the consumer on account of lower purchase prices. The middleman gets eliminated, thus benefitting the supply chain by removing mechanisms which lead to artificially reduced prices for farmers, artificially increased retail prices for consumers and the commission fee. The origins of modern-day direct marketing have been traced back to 'Kal Ghoj', Russian farmer markets which were set up in 1975 to sell vegetables to the local populace. The concept was replicated in Haryana and Punjab, with the establishment of 'Apna Mandis'. The old Rythu bazaars of Andhra Pradesh, which originated as a social initiative to connect the farmer with the consumer, is a step in the right direction.[112] At present, there are 96 Rythu bazaars in the state, with each Rythu bazaar covering ten to fifteen villages, and at least 250 farmers, who are then rearranged into self-help groups selected by agricultural and horticultural officers. The Rythu bazaars also help in providing the farmers remunerative prices for eggs and mushrooms, which typically have limited storage options in India's crumbling supply chain infrastructure, while consumers like them fresh for consumption.

Such a channel can be improved upon, by tying it up with facilities for cleaning, grading, weighing and packaging, along with associated infrastructure like sheds and logistics.

PRICING

Pricing of products in such markets is subject to significant factors. The prices in the Rythu markets are higher than wholesale markets by 20–25 per cent on an average. Alongside, farmers don't have to pay any 'participation fee' in Rythu markets, as opposed to a 10 per cent commission in wholesale markets, taking their net realization in terms of unit price up by 30–35 per cent. Meanwhile, the same price is 15–20 per cent less than retail prices—thereby passing the value to the end consumer. The wholesale market players influence the prices by fixing their own prices at levels closer to those prevailing in the farmer markets away from

---

112 Dey, Subhendu, A Direct Study of Rythu Bazaars, 2012, Asian Journal of Research in Business Economics and Management 2 (6), 90-109

the collectively run farmer markets, and then closing at unrealistic price levels. As price finalization in such markets happens in the morning, it may turn out that the wholesale market rates may even be higher than the farmer market prices on account of such manipulation, sometimes making it unsustainable economically for the farmer to sell at the rates in farmer markets. Besides higher price realization, there are other factors at play as well—most important being the ready availability of cash or immediate cash realization in case of sales in farmer markets.

MARKETING BENEFITS

Such a channel offers numerous benefits. As per a primary survey conducted among the participating farmers, almost 52 per cent indicated 'fixed monthly income' as the biggest benefit, followed by 36 per cent who suggested that Rythu markets offered better income, while 7 per cent said that proximity/easy accessibility to Rythu markets was a critical factor for them to sell there.[113] While farmers do not have a direct say in promoting such markets, they have a direct say in price fixation at Rythu markets. A committee comprised of farmers and supervisors receives prices of commodities by fax from wholesale markets early in the morning and it then fixes the prices of the produce. The farmer on the committee is also rotated periodically to prevent any chance of misdeeds.

The prime perceived benefit for farmers is the proximity of markets for selling their agricultural produce—as many as 99 per cent of the farmers were satisfied with their location. Besides location, 87 per cent were satisfied that they did not have to deal with middlemen. Almost 92 per cent farmers believed that the markets offered them better remuneration, leading to better earnings. A similar number of farmers (90 per cent) felt that immediate cash realization was an incentive to operate in Rythu markets. However, the survey also showed that a majority of farmers were dissatisfied with the stall space offered to them or the storage facilities present at the markets. This reflects a clear need for the government to improve its efficiency as a facilitator for direct marketing of farm produce.

---

113 Dey, S., A Direct Study of Rythu Bazaars, 2012, Asian Journal of Research in Business Economics and Management 2 (6), 90-109

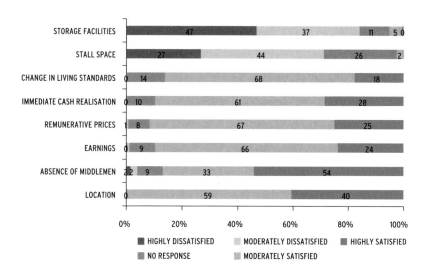

FIGURE 113: SATISFACTION INDEX FOR VARIOUS PERCEIVED BENEFITS UNDER
DIRECT AGRICULTURAL MARKETING IN A RYTHU BAZAAR[114]

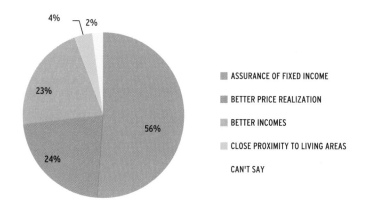

FIGURE 114: MOST IMPORTANT FACTOR FOR PARTICIPATION IN RYTHU MARKETS[115]

While we have discussed the beneficial aspects, it is equally important to focus on factors that are not satisfactory for the farmers—which are mostly infrastructural or procedural in nature.

---

114 Dey, S., A Direct Study of Rythu Bazaars, 2012, Asian Journal of Research in Business Economics and Management 2 (6), 90-109

115 Ibid

The experience with Uzhavar Sandhai markets in Tamil Nadu has been similar. Nearly 99 per cent of the farmers who were surveyed believed that the Sandhai was beneficial to them. The prices in the Sandhais are fixed by linkages to prices in the wholesale markets.

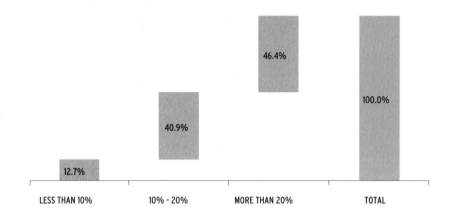

FIGURE 115: PERCENTAGE OF FARMERS AND THEIR INCREMENTAL PROFIT MARGIN IN SANDHAIS COMPARED TO WHOLESALE MARKETS[116]

MARKETING CONSTRAINTS

Infrastructure matters a lot—storage facilities, along with proper shops/stalls, can encourage farmers to repeatedly engage with the farmer markets. While farmers are highly satisfied with the location of the markets, it is important that the designated spaces are on raised land to ensure they are not subject to floods or inundation, alongside having proper facilities for drainage and sewage. Additionally, the markets should have sufficient space for vehicles. The stalls, at present 12–80 sq. ft. in area, can be enlarged and should face the internal walkway to properly display their wares. Additionally, each such market can be equipped with facilities for cleaning, grading and sorting, weighing, packing, a market office, parking space and firefighting. Lack of storage is a critical aspect for the farmers when it comes to direct marketing.

---

116 Kallummal, M., Srinivasan, K. Sakthi, The Dynamics of Farmers' Market, 2007

Price volatility is another significant concern; ~79 per cent of farmers utilizing Rythu markets feel that they never get the same rate in the evening for their vegetables and fresh produce as they do in the morning. From the same user group, ~58 per cent respondents believed that inadequate storage facilities were the main reason for the variance in rates. Provision of small godowns of capacity 50/100 MT can be made by the Department of Agricultural Marketing for sellers to store their goods for short durations. This would prevent last-moment distress sales by farmers. Additionally, a cold-storage facility can also be considered.

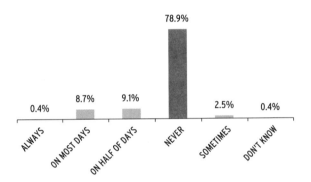

FIGURE 116: PERCENTAGE OF FARMERS WHO BELIEVE THEY GET
THE SAME SELLING RATES IRRESPECTIVE OF TIME OF DAY[117]

Given such constraints, profit margins are often unpredictable. The profit margin defined above is highly dependent on the cost incurred by the farmers in bringing their produce to the Sandhais, as compared to wholesale markets. The success of programmes like Rythu bazaars or the Sandhais depends on the ease of bringing the produce to the market—thus location, access and cost gain importance. While the state government provides dedicated buses for the farmers and their produce, some farmers may also use their own private vehicles—either in search of better flexibility or because the state buses prove inadequate. Rythu markets earlier provided dedicated buses for farmers and stipulated that they bring their produce only via the state buses—while farmers' travel was free, the produce was charged at nominal rates. However, such buses are infrequent—as estimated from the fact that despite such stipulations, many farmers use their own private vehicles. In terms of access, a majority of farmers come to Rythu markets from distances of 25–50 km. In terms of mode of transport, 66 per cent preferred buses, 14 per cent preferred trains and 20 per cent used both.

---

117 Kallummal, M., Srinivasan, K. Sakthi, The Dynamics of Farmers' Market, 2007

Additionally, ~79 per cent of farmers responded that there were no dedicated trains, whereas 27 per cent said there were no dedicated buses; ~74 per cent were moderately happy with the services provided. Clearly, our farmers don't demand much—yet an efficient transportation system is due, which can contribute to the success of such direct markets.

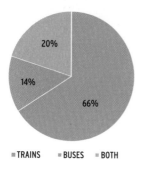

FIGURE 117: TRANSPORTATION TO/ FROM RYTHU MARKETS[118]

Similar insights can be derived from the Sandhais—as many as 90 per cent of farmers travel a distance of less than 30 km, with most farmers preferring the bus (~56 per cent). A significant fraction of farmers—~42 per cent—prefer to use vehicles to transport their produce, with 28 per cent using their own vehicles and 14 per cent using rented vehicles. Mode of transportation and distance travelled also has a strong correlation—for distances greater than 50 km, farmers prefer to use their own vehicles, as government services are not available at such early hours.

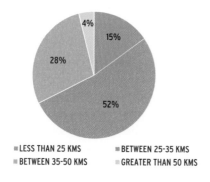

FIGURE 118: DISTANCE TRAVELLED TO SANDHAI MARKETS[119]

118 Kallummal, M., Srinivasan, K. Sakthi, The Dynamics of Farmers' Market, 2007
119 Ibid

STORAGE

Storage is another significant constraint. India stores over 3 million tonnes of grain in the open, enough to feed Italy, exposed to rain and pests, with plastic sheets, offering minimal protection. While the food security law entitles ~65 per cent of Indians to low-cost grains, the challenge remains in getting the grains to the poor, with wastage and corruption rampant. Despite the ongoing revival of the PDS system, beneficiary households are regularly deprived of over 44 per cent of wheat and rice.[120]

The Food Corporation of India (FCI) was set up in 1965, under PL-480, to meet major shortfalls and stabilize food markets. Given rising food inflation, and increasing volatility in other crops like onions (concentrated in Maharashtra, Madhya Pradesh, Karnataka and Andhra Pradesh), the FCI's procurement policy must be changed to include the twenty-three items under the MSP policy, including pulses and oilseeds. Onions, produced in four months, can be stored for the entirety of the political calendar.

The FCI stored 68.7 MT of wheat, rice and coarse grains in FY15, double its requirement of 31.9 MT , and nearly double its capacity of 39 MT (3.3 MT under open sheets)—all at a cost of ₹1 lakh crore annually. Its warehouses have not expanded over the last decade, restricting themselves to just 13 MT. Only 6 per cent of farmers benefit from selling rice and wheat directly to the FCI, while a majority remain unaware of its procurement activities. Leakages—caused by poor-quality wagons, inadequate security, multiple handling, etc.—can run up to 90 per cent.

As recommended by the High Level Committee (August 2014), the FCI should be encouraged to outsource its stocking operations to the private sector, while following a proactive liquidation policy to offload excess stocks in the market. It should also consider moving to states like Assam, Bihar and Uttar Pradesh, areas of hunger discontent and distress sales for farmers, moving out of Punjab, Haryana and Andhra Pradesh. A break-up of the FCI into its constituent parts could be explored, decentralizing procurement and encouraging local storage.

Ultimately, direct marketing will always be tied to the local market, with pricing at local terms, until a national agricultural market is evolved. While providing the highest producer share of the consumer's rupee, the actual value earned can vary, depending on the farmer's location.

---

120 Khera R., IIT Delhi, 2011

CONTRACT FARMING

Amalendu Guha, a resident of Bamunia village on the banks of the Damodar river, in the Burdwan district of West Bengal, sits in a pensive mood, like many other farmers from his village. He has been growing potatoes every year on his parcel of 10 acres. The region has witnessed a bumper crop of almost 10 million tonnes in 2010. While crop failure can lead to mounting debts and penury, bumper crops can cause price crashes, leading to losses—it's a fine balance that has been left at nature's mercy. Mandi prices have crashed to ₹300 per quintal—all the arthia commissions, transportation fees, market fees and levies, and illegal bribes aside, a farmer can expect a wafer-thin margin if lucky. The farmer also has the choice to take a truck to Kolkata, about 100 km away, where he can realize ₹ 600 per quintal, but he will have to sell directly to retail or consumer. Most of them have sold at ₹300– ₹350 per quintal at local markets, half the price they got the previous year. Amalendu, however, has realized ₹600– ₹800 per quintal without travelling to the nearby cities. He was one among 6,000-odd farmers who did contract farming for a food and beverages company. His foray into contract farming and assured returns have helped him procure a tractor and potato harvester. He thinks of renting it to nearby farms to supplement his income. Technical expertize and extension services have helped him increase his income by as much as ₹20,000/acre. His neighbour, meanwhile, has renovated his home after his realizations went from ₹7,000/acre to ₹18,000/acre. Both of them have also bought weather insurance from a leading private bank in India with support from the contract processor.[121]

The experience of Amalendu is not a singular one; there are multiple companies engaged in contract farming with local farming communities across the country. Farmers in Karnataka, Tamil Nadu, Maharashtra and Punjab have also experienced gains accruing from contract farming. Despite the prevalence of this farm partnership model from pre-Independence days, it is yet to realize its full potential.[122]

---

121 http://www.business-standard.com/article/companies/buoyant-pepsi-to-take-contract-farming-to-troubled-states-110061100004_1.html

122 Food & Agriculture Organization (FAO) of the United Nations (Sourced from : http://www.fao.org/docrep/004/y0937e/y0937e05.htm)

BEING HISTORICALLY UNJUST

Farming for a non-state entity has a grim history in India. Peasants in Bihar and Bengal, particularly in and around Champaran, Burdwan, Bankura, Birbhum and Murshidabad, were encouraged and forced by the East India Company's planters to grow indigo instead of other crops, with the promise of loans, then termed 'dadon', to fund their initial expenses (usually at usurious rates). When harvest time came, the planters usually purchased the crop at just 2.5 per cent of market rates, with farmers required, by an institutional system termed tinkathia, to sell two-third of their crop at such rates. Farmers who protested against the compensation arrangements were liable to face property destruction or expropriation. D.N. Mitra's *Nildarpan* evocatively describes the plight of peasants under the 'neel sahibs':

On the day the Saheb said, 'If you don't hear the Amin, and don't plant the Indigo within the ground marked off, then shall we throw your houses into the river Betraboti, and shall make you eat your rice in the factory godown.' The eldest Babu replied, 'As long as we shall not get the price for the fifty bigahs of land sown with Indigo last year, we will not give one bigah this year for Indigo. What do we care for our house? We shall even risk (pawn) our lives.'[123]

Contract farming has had a distasteful historical origin. Impressed by successful Indian cotton exports, the British settlers took to plantation crops—tea, coffee and rubber in the hilly climates of southern India and the Northeast, while the Gangetic plain witnessed the introduction of poppy and indigo. Lured by ready purchases and seemingly attractive prices, farmers took to crops which had no other market and no intrinsic value to their daily lives. With agri-inputs also coming from the British government, the farmer was exploited in a system which was perhaps worse than the 'rentier' system prevalent earlier. Mahatma Gandhi's fight for indigo farmers in Champaran is an important intersection between India's agri-marketing and its Independence struggle. However, its colonial-era, exploitative image notwithstanding, contract farming is seen as an agri-marketing solution in its own right. Though it started and metamorphosed into an instrument of exploitation of the small farmer in the colonial era, it holds the promise of correcting the market imperfections of the traditional mandi system of agri-marketing.

Formalized contract farming in India traces its origins back to the '20s, when the Indian Tobacco Company (ITC) established the first documented large-scale contract-farming operation in coastal Andhra Pradesh. The early years after Independence witnessed the emergence of sugar cooperatives in Maharashtra and dairy cooperatives in Gujarat with many features similar to contract farming. The '80s saw the emergence of popular contract farming by associations of farmers in

---

123   Mitra, D.N., Nildarpan. Sourced from: https://archive.org/stream/nildarpanorindig00mitriala/
nildarpanorindig00mitriala_djvu.txt

north India and Wimco, a leading match company. However, tomato procurement from farmers in Punjab by PepsiCo heralded the true emergence of contract farming in its modern form in India—yields grew threefold, from 7.5 MT/hectare to 20 MT/hectare while costs for transplantation were reduced, leading to higher net realization for the farmers.[124]

APPLE CULTIVATION

Apples cultivated in Himachal Pradesh (about 93 per cent of the total fruit production in the state) usually undergo a long journey to reach urban consumers. A range of traders, pre-harvest contractors and commission agents, big and small, licenced through the local mandi, purchase apples without due regard for quality or variety. With limited infrastructure in the regulated markets, long delays are often expected during the sale process, rotting away supply, while operating costs, borne by the farmer, can be steep. Many farmers prefer simply to sell their produce in the local markets, instead of approaching such intermediaries.

The state's Himachal Pradesh Horticultural Produce Marketing and Processing Corporation Ltd (HPMC), has built a wide network of post-harvest facilities, incorporating cold storage, warehousing and food processing.[125] Collection centres have been set up every 3–4 km in major apple-bearing areas, while cold–storage facilities have enabled the produce to last longer. Farmers are required to deposit their produce at such collection centres, while collecting receipts, which are later exchanged for payments. However, given the social charter and bureaucratic DNA, payments to farmers can be a bit slow.

In comparison, corporate groups like Adani Enterprises have set up integrated storage, handling and transportation infrastructure for apples across the state. Sale agreements, with multiyear contracts, have been signed with thousands of farmers for direct procurement, through agents. Such farmers, now members of its sourcing network, are supplied with free plastic crates for the collection of apples. While such firms gain access to high-quality, high-elevation apple-growing areas, cultivators get income security. Given populist pressure, such firms are required to purchase all apples from such members, and not just the 'A' grade ones which are ideal for faraway markets—the remaining apples are typically

---

124   Boston Consulting Group, Indian Agri Business, July 2012
125   Brara, S., From the Tree to the Table, The Hindu, 17 June 2016. Sourced from: http://www.
     thehindubusinessline.com/specials/india-interior/from-the-tree-to-the-table/article8742019.ece

sold off in local markets through intermediaries. And such firms pay on time to cultivators too.

———

IMPLEMENTATION MODELS

Contract farming as a concept has multiple implementation models—some corporations may adopt the *centralized model*, wherein the firm typically engages directly with a large number of farmers. In most cases, the contract processor determines the farmer quotas at the beginning of the season, with quality control regularly tracked. The number of partner farmers can vary—it can be reduced to an elite club of large-landholding farmers or thousands of farmers for a single venture. In case of fruits and vegetables, grading, sorting, packing and storage facilities can also be provided by the contract processor. Sugar cane production in Thailand mainly adopts the same model—wherein the mills procure directly from farmers' quotas fixed at the start of the season, with large farmers also getting produce from other farmers through intermediaries, with the government monitoring quotas and regulating prices, besides fixing revenue sharing modalities between the millers and the producers.

The *nucleus estate model* is a variant of the centralized model, wherein the contract processors/sponsors manage an estate of their own, mostly for research or breeding purposes or to ensure common minimum plant throughput. The model requires significant allocation of the firm's financial and non-financial resources.

Multipartite models are also popular, usually existent in the form of joint ventures, which enter into a direct agreement with farmers, while each member of the joint venture provides a separate essential extension service. The model is effective to counter extra-contractual marketing by organizing farmers into cooperatives and public institutions providing credit and extension services. This reduces extra-contractual marketing and makes transaction costs cheaper for the contract processor.

Informal model is also practised, where processing is minimal—mostly in the case of tropical fruits, fresh vegetables and watermelons. The small companies enter into direct informal contracts with farmers on a seasonal basis, with the produce most likely repackaged and sold. Material inputs are limited to basic seeds and fertilizers, with technical advice on quality control following suit. With minimal investment by the processor and informal/seasonal contracts, it has a high level of risk for both producer and processor. However, the model is preferable for starting up in contract farming. Sri Lanka in the '90s saw gherkin production rise from almost nothing to 12,000 tonnes within a decade, as many companies under 'production contracts' supplied material and agri-inputs, besides advice on packing and harvest management. A similar example is seen in chrysanthemum farming in Thailand, with most flowers ending up in Bangkok markets.

TABLE 48: CONTRACT FARMING COMBINATIONS ACROSS INDIA

STATE	CROP	COMPANY	MODEL USED
KARNATAKA	ASHVAGANDHA	HIMALAYA HEALTH CARE LTD	CENTRALIZED
KARNATAKA	DHAVANA	MYSORE SNC OIL COMPANY	CENTRALIZED
KARNATAKA	MARIGOLD CAPRICA CHILLI	AVT NATURAL PRODUCTS PVT LTD	CENTRALIZED
KARNATAKA	COLEUS	NATURAL REMEDIES PVT LTD	CENTRALIZED
KARNATAKA	GHERKIN	SEVERAL PRIVATE COMPANIES	INTERMEDIARY
MAHARASHTRA	SOYABEAN	TINNA OILS AND CHEMICALS	CENTRALIZED
MAHARASHTRA	FRUITS AND VEGETABLES, CEREALS, SPICES, PULSES	ION EXCHANGE ENVIRO FARMS LTD	MULTI-PARTITE
MAHARASHTRA	SAFFLOWER, OILSEEDS	MARICO INDUSTRIES	CENTRALIZED
MADHYA PRADESH	WHEAT, MAIZE, SOYABEAN	CARGILL INDIA LTD	INTERMEDIARY
MADHYA PRADESH	WHEAT	HINDUSTAN LEVER LTD	
MADHYA PRADESH	FRUITS AND VEGETABLES, CEREALS, SPICES, PULSES	ION EXCHANGE ENVIRO FARMS LTD	
MADHYA PRADESH	SOYABEAN	ITC_IBD	MULTI-PARTITE
PUNJAB	TOMATO, CHILLI	NIJJER AGRO FOODS	CENTRALIZED
PUNJAB	BARLEY	UNITED BREWERIES LTD	MULTI-PARTITE
PUNJAB	BASMATI, MAIZE	SATNAME OVERSEAS, MAHINDRA SHUBHLABH	INTERMEDIARY
PUNJAB	BASMATI	ESCORTS	INTERMEDIARY
PUNJAB	BASMATI, GROUNDNUT, POTATO, TOMATO, CHILLI	PEPSICO INDIA	CENTRALIZED
PUNJAB	MILK	NESTLE INDIA	
TAMIL NADU	COTTON	SUPER SPINNING MILLS	INTERMEDIARY
TAMIL NADU	MAIZE	BHUVI CARE PVT LTD	
TAMIL NADU	PADDY	BHUVI CARE PVT LTD	
TAMIL NADU	COTTON	APPACHI COTTON COMPANY	INTERMEDIARY

The intermediary model is basically the formal subcontracting of crops from intermediaries—a processor purchases crops from individual collectors, who in turn have informal arrangements with farmers. While this model reduces transaction costs, it carries a greater risk of having the intermediary gain more power—thus the processor faces risk to his supplies and the farmer faces risks to his produce realizations, and by diluting the link between the farmer and the processor, the model can lead to lower farm income, poor quality and irregular production if not managed properly.

In some ways, the biggest contract-farming model was run by the Government of India itself—wherein the farmer was required to plant the crops suggested by the government on his own lands, and sell the harvest back to the government at pre-agreed prices. The Green Revolution was a resounding success—on the input side, the government ensured controlled fertilizer prices, and assured availability of inputs in times of improved varieties of hybrids; on the output side, it ensured guaranteed procurement at steadily increasing MSPs. It gifted food security and employment to the rural landless, while doubling farm incomes and securing the public distribution system. However, it came with its own costs—controlled fertilizer prices led to misaligned incentives and encouraged farmers to overfertilize in most cases. The MSP became a benchmark reference price, instead of acting as a safety net, and centrally driven agriculture with high emphasis on cereals and sugar cane led to agriculture not being adequately diversified. Mono-crop culture also encouraged excessive water usage, with an adverse impact on soil and reservoir quality.[126]

BENEFITS AND CONSTRAINTS

Such a contracting model on a centralized basis has particular issues in India—where agriculture is dominated by marginal farmers. Out of 101 million households, ~86 per cent have landholdings less than 2 hectares, with their average size being 0.53 hectares. The true objective should be to utilize contract farming for the benefit of the marginal and poor farmers, and not remain limited to large farmers, as seen elsewhere globally. With the food basket of the Indian consumer changing fast, diversification seems to be a possible option. Economic growth and a fast-growing urban population are fuelling rapid demand growth for high-value products (milk, fish, eggs, fruits, vegetables, meat)—demand for high-value products grew in the last decade by registering increases in food expenditure. Besides domestic markets, export also presents a potential opportunity—the share of horticultural and animal food products in total agricultural exports from India increased from 24 per cent in 1981 to 35 per cent in 2003. However, market access remains an issue. Their inability to access big markets is one of the major limitations—trading in such high-value commodities is thin in rural markets, and trading in distant markets becomes difficult on account of logistics and transaction costs. Apart from markets, they are also constrained by lack of access to credit, technology and other input services.

126 Birthal, Pratap S., Making Contract Farming Work in Smallholder Agriculture, 2005

The main advantage of contract farming is the presence of an assured market at an assured price, within pre-specified quality and quantity parameters. Under the open-market pricing system, farmers can have their margins swing wildly, depending on a host of factors, weakened by their limited ability to negotiate prices. Contract farming can offer them a fixed pre-specified price and mitigate price risk. Contract farming provides a guaranteed market—an assurance to cultivate a particular crop at a particular time and place, which then enables the processor to invest in ventures which can reliably supply input commodities. The contract can also enable the farmer to access and avail of a host of managerial, technical and financial extension services that may have been beyond their reach earlier.

Many contracts provide for considerable production support, besides help in basic inputs such as seeds and fertilizer—and may extend to land preparation, cultivation and harvesting, as well as free technical training and inputs. They also come in handy when the small farmer goes out looking for agricultural credit to finance the production cost. In many cases, the contract serves as the collateral and the commercial banks and government agencies provide loans guaranteed by the contract farming processor. Besides agri-inputs, services and financial credit, contract farming sponsors also provide better technical inputs to lead to higher yield. However, some of these new techniques come with their own risk profile in terms of cost and demand, thus making the small and marginal farmer averse to trying out a new concept. However, with direct partnership in the success of the small farmer, the extension services can be better targeted for risk mitigation and techno-commercial success. Constant engagement with the processor and access to technical advice also improve the farmer's skill level, which may range from efficient land usage, optimal usage of chemicals (fertilizers/pesticides/insecticides), and the realization of the importance of quality and consumer requirements, be it domestic or export. The knowledge could lead to resource deployment in buying improved equipment, which can improve realizations further. Such skills, once learnt, can be applied to other non-contract crops as well.

For the contract processor, it is a politically acceptable solution—involving a large number of small and marginal farmers to gain from the model, rather than engaging in estate plantations. Additionally, it also helps overcome barriers of land acquisition—the processor should be interested in the crop produced by the farmers, not their lands, which are their means of sustenance and livelihood. The processor also reduces its risk in this partnership model, as the farmer can take the risk of production failure (if any) and be compensated through insurance. It allows them to obtain raw materials more consistently, rather than making ad hoc open-market purchases.

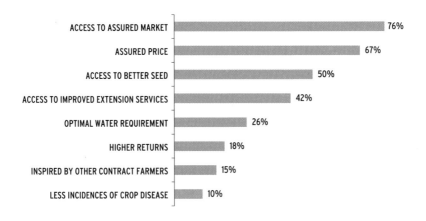

FIGURE 119: TOP PERCEIVED BENEFITS OF CONTRACT FARMING[127]

The success of contract farming can be measured by the economic gain accruing to the farmer within the said model.

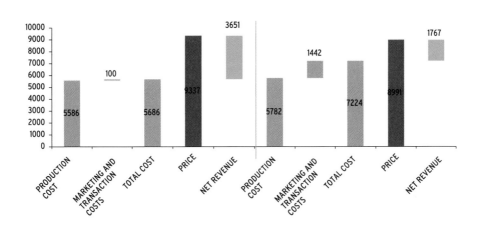

FIGURE 120: ECONOMICS FOR MILK PRODUCTION (₹/TON) UNDER
CONTRACT & NON-CONTRACT FARMING[128]

127   Sharma, V.P., International Food and Agribusiness Management Review, 2008
128   Birthal, 2005

The cost of production under contract farming is less than that compared to non-contract farming, primarily on account of improved technical advice and extension services, which may be financial credit or seeds and fertilizers. However, the most important aspect is the reduction in marketing cost for the farmer—while the farmer under contract farming spends ~₹100/MT for non-production costs, his counterpart doing non-contract farming spends ~14.5 times more—~₹1,442/ MT, which eats considerably into this profit margins. This leads to the total cost of production under the contract farming model to be ~21 per cent less than the cost in traditional, non-contract farming. Contract farming demonstrates improved performance on the final sale price as well, with sale prices being higher by a modest 3 per cent than non-contract farming prices. In terms of net margin, the farmers under contract farming earn 2.1 times more—almost double of what they expect to earn in traditional non-contract farming.

In cases where the difference in transaction and marketing costs is similar across contract and non-contract farming models, contract farming provides banking and insurance services—an essential input if the farming type is capital-intensive and price-sensitive. Besides credit services, the firms in case of poultry farming also provide fixed growing charges and mortality allowance, allowing farmers to manage their price-realization risks—as per studies[129] poultry farmers can transfer as much as 88 per cent of their market risks to the contracting firms. With a majority of farmers being small and marginal, they lack the capacity to make any capital investment for high-value agriculture. While informal and formal rural credit mechanisms are fairly present, management of risk is mostly absent—with a minuscule percentage of Indian farming households insuring their farming activity (GoI). The firms, thus, have a critical role to play, as success is largely driven by the firms' capability to manage the market risk for the farmer.

Besides pure margins, non-price factors also play an important role in determining the success of contract farming. Regular output purchase, along with timely payments and provision for incremental profit-sharing in case of higher-than-stipulated quality produce, also incentivizes the farmers to adhere to the contract farming model. A study of milk marketing options in Tamil Nadu in the open-market scenario suggested that 57.3 per cent of dairy farmers had shifted from one marketing option to another, primarily driven by factors like stoppage of procurement and irregularity in payments by contractor firms.[130]

In terms of participation, it is important that small and marginal farmers, who face a Hobbesian life, have access to the benefits of contract farming. As per sample

---

129 Ramaswamy, 2006
130 http://www.lrrd.org/lrrd17/8/thir17092.htm

surveys conducted, the participation of such farmers across various contract farming initiatives is shown in the chart below:

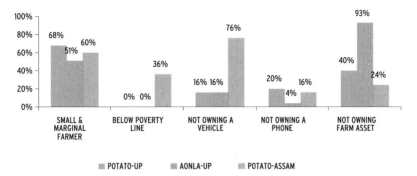

FIGURE 121: SOCIO-ECONOMIC CHARACTERISTICS OF PARTICIPATING FARMER PARTNERS IN VARIOUS CONTRACT FARMING INITIATIVES IN INDIA[131]

The involvement of our small and marginal farmers has been mixed across different models of contract farming in India. A comparison between potato farmers in Uttar Pradesh, potato farmers in Assam and aonla farmers in Uttar Pradesh reveals that while contract farming plays a good role in enrolling small and marginal farmers across models, the enrolment of Below Poverty Line (BPL) farmers in Uttar Pradesh can only improve with time, as no BPL farmers have availed of the benefits of contract farming—pointing to access issues in the first place. It is pertinent to keep in mind that while a majority of farmers in Uttar Pradesh under contract farming have ownership of a vehicle and a phone, they don't have ownership of farm assets, indicating that the spillover effect into farm equipment investment at the local level needs to improve and that in some cases, a rental model for farm equipment seems to make greater sense.

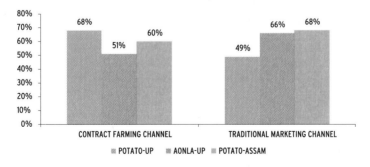

FIGURE 122: PARTICIPATION OF FARMERS IN EMERGING CONTRACT MARKETING CHANNEL VIS-À-VIS TRADITIONAL MARKETING CHANNEL[132]

131 Ghosh N., India's Agricultural Marketing, 2012
132 Ibid

This comparison shows the participation of small and marginal farmers in the emerging contract farming model vis-à-vis the traditional marketing model. While contract farming firms may prefer large farmers in order to reduce transaction and monitoring costs, small and marginal farmers allow them to diversify their procurement risks. Firms can also reduce their transaction costs by procurement through direct agents, self-help groups or growers' associations. Nestlé, for one, sources milk through a local intermediary, who, in turn, procures milk from small farmers to reduce cost. This enables the firm to enlist a large number of small farmers—nearly 56 per cent of its suppliers were farmers who had fewer than or equal to five milch animals. Similarly, Mother Dairy Fruit and Vegetables Limited (MDFVL) employs growers' associations to reduce transaction costs—consequently resulting in 50 per cent supplies coming from small and marginal farmers (less than 2-hectare landholdings). This creates a mutually beneficial relationship between the farmers and the firms—whereas firms gain by reduced transaction cost and procurement risk, a higher number of small and marginal farmers can be empanelled to reap the benefits of contract farming. The firms, while starting small, can scale out and scale up, which leads, to a higher number of empanelled farmers and more produce per farmer—it can enable the company to earn returns on capital investments made and enable the farmers to earn more, thereby allowing the beneficiaries to climb up the income ladder.

FORMALIZING CONTRACT FARMING

It is an anomaly that a majority of contract farming is conducted without any proper contracts in the first place. In many Indian states, the incumbent APMC Act prohibits the contractor/processor from entering into a direct contract with the farmer, as the produced goods are compulsorily required to be canalized through the regulated markets[133]—which in turn reflects a failure on the part of the state government to incorporate provisions in the APMC Act (as recommended in the model APMC Act of 2003) to allow for contract farming by processing firms. It goes against the basic idea that the produce can move freely from the farmers' fields to any destination in India or abroad without passing through agents or regulated markets, provided it is covered under a legally valid and enforceable contract.

Firstly, the practice of formalizing contracts is not common. Agricultural contracts can be of various types—production management contracts foresee large-scale

---

133 Prasad, V., CCS Working Paper No. 293, 2013

involvement of the contractor/processor in farm practices—especially in the deployment of farm inputs. The farmer is thus able to pass on the risk of crop failure to the contractor/processor but also forgoes independence in farm management and production practices. At the opposite end, the market specification contract entails agreements that describe the conditions for sale, along with the quantity and quality specifications upon which the sale shall take place. The farmer in this contracting model has fairly independent control over farm practices, but also bears a large part of the risk of production failure. The resource providing contract is a mix of both models—wherein the contractor is involved in the production practices and the farmer has minor freedom to decide on utility of provided inputs. Agricultural contracts, especially in India, remain simple—they are essentially informal, oral agreements that do not contain dispute resolution and contract-risk mechanisms. A study shows that out of a random sample of 438 contract farmers drawn from various contract farming initiatives across India, only 54 per cent had written contracts.[134] Out of those with written contracts, only 49 per cent believed that the contracts were enforceable, only 13 per cent believed that the contracts had legal implications and about 37 per cent believed that the contracts had no validity in courts of law. In the entire sample, only 28 per cent had a copy of their contract and only 24 per cent had read the agreement or had it read to them by someone else. Contract signing is also taken up in a casual manner. Farmers sign the contract in the name of someone else from the family who has brought them luck in the past—mostly toddlers. The contract is usually signed by someone else in the family (cousins or someone who knows how to sign) and then the farmer carries out the contractual obligations.[135]

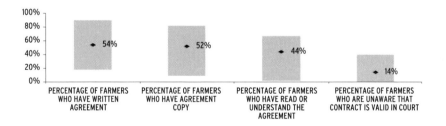

FIGURE 123: MEASUREMENT OF FARMER AWARENESS OF LEGAL
SANCTITY OF CONTRACTS IN CONTRACT FARMING[136]

134 Narayanan, 2012

135 Narayanan, S., – September 2012 Indira Gandhi Institute of Development Research (IGIDR) – Working Paper – (Sourced from: http://www.igidr.ac.in/pdf/publication/WP-2012-020.pdf)

136 Narayanan, S., IGIDR, WP-2012-020-Sep'12

Low awareness levels about the legal sanctity of agricultural contracts in contract farming makes effective enforcement of contracts more difficult. The situation is not very different when it comes to farmers dealing with large corporations/ processors in states which are success stories in contract farming. A study done in 2007 reveals the following statistic:

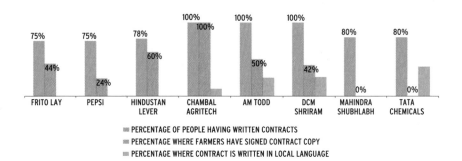

PERCENTAGE OF PEOPLE HAVING WRITTEN CONTRACTS
PERCENTAGE WHERE FARMERS HAVE SIGNED CONTRACT COPY
PERCENTAGE WHERE CONTRACT IS WRITTEN IN LOCAL LANGUAGE

FIGURE 124: COMPARISON OF VARIOUS COMPANIES IN TERMS OF TRANSPARENCY IN EXECUTION OF FARMING CONTRACTS[137]

Even multinational corporations like Frito Lay, Pepsi and Hindustan Lever do not enforce a strict, zero-tolerance and fully compliant policy of ensuring written contracts with farmers. Even for Punjab, which pioneered contract farming in India, we see that farmers do not have their written copies of signed contracts, which makes enforcement of these contracts legally challenging in cases of dispute.

Thus, we see that despite the absence of formalized and institutionalized contracts in India, contract farming still works—loosely bound by the moral alignment to agreed terms. Contracting firms do not find adequate incentive in pursuing legal remediation for contract violation by farmers—a farmer usually contributes a small percentage of the firm's entire offtake—as per studies[138], it is estimated that the average value of a default is ₹ 3,750, hardly worth the amount of time and money for pursuing legal recourse. Additionally, it will take at least a few years for the firm to train a new farmer to replace the errant farmer. A similar situation exists for the farmer, where he has to condone any defection by the contract processor due to lack of access to legal remediation. If we are to expand the concept of contract farming for mutual benefits on a national priority, the system of written contracts will need legal justification and power.

137   Prasad, V., CCS Working Paper No. 293, July 2013
138   Narayanan, 2012

Farmer Producer Organizations (FPOs) can be the way forward to mitigate the contract risks in contract farming. FPOs are created and controlled by farmers who democratically have a final say on the organizational activities. They can be harnessed to contract with corporations to supply crop to them. Non-compliance by farmers can be dealt with by the FPO, wherein any disciplinary issue can be referred to a committee of members, who in turn can decide the punishment on the basis of the provisions of the FPO previously laid down. The FPO is responsible for two important functions—information management and coordinated community response (McMillan and Woodruff, 2000). In case of non-compliance, the FPO can refer to the farmer database and refer it to the disciplinary committee, which then takes the role of coordinated community response to the deviation.

Farmers, on the other hand, have better bargaining power. No more can the processor turn them down on quality parameters on re-engage on quantity promises. It enables the farmer to negotiate terms of contract before they are written. Being members of an FPO, farmers also get additional access to resources through participating resource organizations. The issue of individual farmers being unable to pursue legal recourse against organized large contract processors becomes less of an issue, simply because of the financial capacity and legal powers of the FPO. FPOs also serve to effectively enforce quality standards for the companies—consequently, farmers adapt to improved technologies and processes in due time. There are high implementation costs to forming an FPO, mainly in terms of time and resources from participating organizations, and cycle time from incorporation to self-sustaining operations needs to be reduced. Additionally, discipline among the FPO members remains critical for the FPO-contract processor partnership to remain fruitful. Additionally, it is the farmers who decide the activities of the FPO, and failure of an FPO due to lack of motivation after months of hand-holding and guidance from the resource organization can be an impediment in the long run. Besides FPOs, the panchayats and the gram sabhas should be connected in the process.

The government's National Agricultural Policy recognizes contract farming as an important activity of agri-business and envisages increased private participation through contract farming to allow transfer of technology, assured market and capital inflows. Institutional credit remains critical to contract farming initiatives. NABARD has already taken steps, and a special refinance package for contract farming arrangements remains an appreciable move. Besides providing refinance to farmers, strengthening the rural credit network should be a priority. Full refinancing of reimbursements made by commercial banks, rural banks and agricultural cooperative banks with controlled NPAs should be implemented. The terms for repayment should be relaxed in the initial stages (from three to five years) and thus can also be examined. Besides financial interventions, development interventions are also necessary—the bankers at rural level need to be sensitized to the potential benefits and requirements of contract farming projects. The scope of contract farming itself can be extended to include medicinal plants. The contract processor can collaborate in a partnership with a scheduled commercial bank or cooperative banks to provide weather insurance to all farmers. The contract processor can examine paying the farmer's share of insurance premium under the Pradhan Mantri Fasal Bima Yojana (PMFBY) for each season, which can go a long way in improving credibility and creating goodwill among the farmers. Besides managing the premium outgo, what would be more important is that the contract processor also manages the documentation part of insurance claims, with strict guidelines and penalties in any usurping of the insurance benefit due to the farmer.

Selection of inputs is also of considerable importance—unless the seed has high yield and the plant is disease-resistant, the contract farmers may lose their confidence and discontinue with contract farming. Let us consider the example of Parthibhai Chaudhary and his potato farm in Palanpur—the Lady Rosetta variety grown by him is known to be high in solids, low in sugar and very high when it comes to plant yield. Such potato is highly desirable for wafer companies, with Shree Balaji Wafers and PepsiCo vying for it. He is lucky to have access to cold storage, 1,400 tonnes of it and stock is valued at ₹1.96 crore at applicable prices of ₹ 14/kg[139]. Such results are spillover effects of McCain's contract farming of potato in Banaskantha district of Gujarat. Farmers start under contract farming and then, like Parthibhai, move on within a few years once they get a hang of it. Such is the case with Manjibhai Chaudhary, who finds potato, farming under contract farming to be 'majedaar', as can be seen from his allotment of 35 acres to potato, as against 1.5 acres earlier. The farmer-contractor partnership that the region has witnessed is one potential way of ushering in rural prosperity.

Assured markets for processed products of the company should also exist, as they ensure that the farmers get an assured market to sell their produce, which again ensures investment in equipment and provision of extension services. The success of the contract processor plays a huge role in determining the success of the contract farming model. The government should formulate policies to encourage more players into the contract farming fold, which will lead to lower costs and increased choice for the farmer. Yet, balances need to be maintained. Contract farming is generally commodity-specific and promotes monoculture (as seen in the case of Manjibhai), and thus can cause risks to regional biodiversity and agricultural ecology. In terms of infrastructure, the Central Warehousing Corporation and State Warehousing Corporation should develop quality standards and processes for storage and maintenance of various commodities over a sufficiently long period. The

139 http://www.smartindianagriculture.in/240/

state agricultural universities, in collaboration with the contract processor-farmer partnership, can provide assistance in development of storage processes, which can then be standardized across the country. For it to succeed, the government's role in ensuring supporting infrastructure like roads, public transport, power and water supplies, market yards and cold-storage facilities remains a starting point.

TENANCY ISSUES

Legally, agricultural tenancy is banned, yet concealed tenancy exists. Tenants who do not enjoy any security in terms of tenure are not likely to participate in contract farming. Their will to participate further dissipates once legally enforceable formal contracts are put in place. It is important to devise a method so that share croppers can also participate in contract farming. In case legal issues pertain, wastelands can be looked at to bring landless share croppers into the picture.

WASTELAND DEVELOPMENT

Partnership with corporates can be explored to achieve high rates of agricultural growth. A Wasteland Development Programme, similar to the one implemented in Tamil Nadu, could be implemented, wherein the government lends out fallow and degraded land to corporate houses and cooperative societies for development into agricultural use while acting as a facilitator between the corporate and the farmer. The crops under focus could be cash crops, fruits and vegetables, besides spices and plantation crops. Leasing for a longer term of twenty-five to thirty years could attract private investment into the supply chain of agri-business, cold storage, processing and marketing. The model can be taken up as a revenue-sharing model. Contract farming in lands recognized under the Forest Rights Act needs special attention, as they are violative of the spirit of the contract and the Act itself. The government needs to take special protective measures in this context.

ORGANIZED RETAILER SOURCING

Arvind Jhajaria, a small farmer in the village of Chanan Khera, in Fazilka district of Punjab, sits happy in his 3-acre farm today—he has figured out a relatively easy way of selling his produce. In the process, he has bypassed the mandatory visit to the local mandi. He has also avoided sourcing of transport vehicles for his produce, negotiating with and paying unloading and weighing agents, or 'paldaars'. He has avoided dealing with commission agents and the subsequent harassment of paying legal fees, taxes and illegal bribes. Yet, he has realized the rates prevalent in the Azadpur mandi in Delhi—the final market for his produce. This had happened as MDVF—Safal, directly purchased the produce from him, at the nearest collection centre. He is happy, as he knows his produce has an assured market—with this in mind, he can focus on growing products with higher margins. He has successfully changed from supplying bottle gourd to kinnow, as the latter has better profit margins. Besides kinnow, he has also commenced sales of carrots and radish to the retail chain.

Jhajaria's fellow villagers dread going to the mandi to sell their produce—in Punjab, a farmer pays a 4 per cent market fee and 5.5 per cent VAT on his produce, apart from commissions paid to the arthiyas. Sometimes, the arthiyas impose arbitrary conditions, which include giving 2 kg of produce for free per quintal of produce sold. Moreover, if they want to bring their final produce to the Azadpur mandi in Delhi, they have to pay taxes and octroi for each state they pass through. The entire experience is painful and time-consuming—the prime reason why many villagers are adopting the new way of selling to organized retail, and this receives a boost after witnessing success cases like Jhajharia.

Jhajaria also gains in terms of reduced input cost—Safal also offers him agriculture extension services, mainly pertaining to the use of fertilizers, besides seed usage and crop planning. Without advice, Jhajaria would have resorted to extensive use of pesticides for his produce, which reduced significantly post Safal's advice. This enables Jhajaria to reduce his input cost, meanwhile allowing Safal to reduce its turnaround time. With the advent of newer private entrants, opportunity knocks on their doors.

Fresh supply of vegetables in an efficient manner remains a major challenge in the farm-to-fork agri-supply chain. This challenge served as an inspiration behind Safal, a successful agri-retail supply chain. Ultimately, the aim is to provide an assured market to the farmer with competitive prices on a cooperative basis in a sustainable manner.

The success of Safal (or Mother Dairy) lies in the supply chain itself—it connects the producers with the consumers directly. These intermediaries have the financial and non-financial resources to purchase materials from producers, and collect, sort, grade, transport and distribute to retail shops in destination markets. Mostly, the retail stores are owned (or franchised) by the company itself, thus enabling the produce to cater to a larger geographic market.

GREATER SCOPE

Organized retail reaches out to a far bigger market, with the role and nature of the facilitator changed.[140] Unlike direct marketing, where mostly the government acts as a facilitator for transactions between the producer and the consumer, in organized retail it is the firm (public or private) which purchases directly from the farmer—thus having one intermediary in-between. This also leads to prices being higher in organized retail stores, as opposed to farmer markets, where rates are higher than wholesale markets but less than prices in organized retail stores. In terms of consumer profile, while direct farmer markets cater to the middle class and people living in fringe areas of metro cities, organized retail also reaches out to people in metros, which have higher per capita spending capacity. The facilitating organization is mostly private, whereas for direct marketing it is mostly the government which acts as a facilitating agency—which, in turn, also governs the profit motives. The organized retail marketing channels with private agencies as facilitators would have certain profit motives, whereas direct marketing channels with the government as facilitator would operate on a no-profit, no-loss basis. Additionally, the consumer has the choice of buying graded produce in organized retail, as opposed to buying it directly from the farmers' markets. The most glaring difference is in terms of participants in the marketing channel—while farmers, unemployed youth, women and self-help groups (SHGs) participate in the market facilitated by government agencies and cooperative societies, it is usually a private company in organized retail.

---

140 http://crida.in/agrl_martng/ISAM/PDF%20FILES/T-II/Dastagiri.pdf

CHANNEL OVERVIEW

Horticultural crops can add substantial commercial value to a farmer's income, yet remain highly dependent on marketing methodology on account of its perishable nature. In case access to market is available, further challenges lie in terms of peak and lean seasons, which may affect a farmer's margins. Sometimes even the timing of sale (day or night) can play a big role in determining the farmer's income. In traditional marketing, the *'kuccha arthiya'* is the most important intermediary to buy vegetables from the farmer. At times and places when the regulated market is found unsuitable, the transaction can even occur in the rural periodic markets, where the farmer has a weak hand in pricing and other terms of sale on account of lack of requisite infrastructure (of transport and storage) and lack of enforcement of regulation. Some producers in small towns can act as retailers or as direct sellers to wholesalers; the most common model would involve the commission agent besides the wholesaler and the retailer in the supply chain. The trader, for instance, would dispose of the vegetables with short shelf lives (e.g. cauliflower) to the retail markets to avoid spoilage, while taking some time for leafy vegetables—as the same can be preserved with appropriate temperature and humidity before being transported into trucks in nets.

We will now contrast this with the organized retail model. Take Reliance Fresh, for instance, which owns and operates through small and medium stores in metro cities, offering high-quality vegetables at affordable prices—vegetables can be pre-packed with specific labelling about expiry dates or can be loose. It manages procurement of vegetables through collection centres, wherein the produce is measured and recorded, along with the name of the supplier (farmer/producer). Each collection centre is then linked with agencies that undertake grading and ensure standardization, before being transported to stores in urban areas, wherein they are available fresh for nine to ten hours on a daily basis.

MARGIN ANALYSIS

In organized retail, the involvement of small and marginal farmers in vegetable/ horticultural crops is higher due to relatively easy availability of family labour and expected higher returns, as compared to traditional foodgrains. Typically, the margin realized in organized retail can be as much as 40 per cent higher than in traditional marketing. This usually happens on account of higher unit-price realization and lower marketing cost.

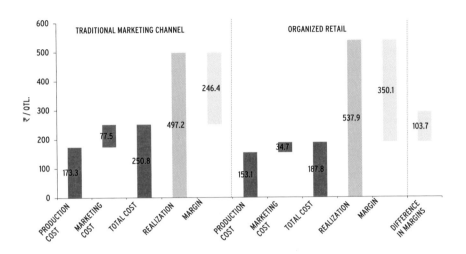

FIGURE 125: MARGIN ANALYSIS FOR TOMATO MARKETING UNDER ORGANIZED RETAIL
AND TRADITIONAL MARKETING IN HARYANA[141]

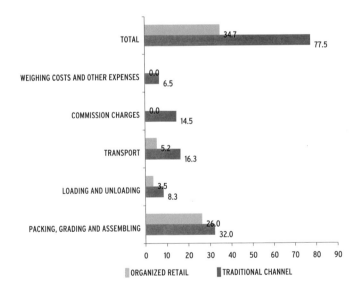

FIGURE 126: BREAKUP OF MARKETING COST (₹/QUINTAL)
UNDER DIFFERENT MARKETING CHANNELS[142]

141 Usha, T., Subhash, C., Agricultural Economics Research Centre, 2012
142 Ibid

Marketing costs are less in organized retail as compared to traditional marketing, despite the presence of well-defined operations and working capital terms that are favourable to farmers. The collection centres in organized retail purchase farm produce directly from the farmers after grading and sorting. Electronic weights are used to maintain transparency in the weighing process and payments are made within one or two days, as compared with a couple of weeks at times in traditional markets. The purchased produce after weighing is further distributed, using temperature-controlled vans or trucks. Thus, the marketing costs should be higher than the traditional channels—yet the marketing cost borne by the farmer is half of that borne in the traditional channel, as most of it is shared or incurred by the retail partner chain. Lack of market intermediaries also makes the supply chain efficient in terms of marketing cost.

In order to improve marketing channel efficiency, it is critical to ensure a barrier-free movement of goods across different states by lifting various restrictions and fiscal charges. Additionally, market levies and mandi taxes need to be minimized in order to lend a competitive edge to the traditional marketing channel.

Market infrastructure has a pivotal role in determining efficiency of the marketing channel. Infrastructure would comprise multiple cogs in the supply chain—ranging from proximity to the market, road condition, availability of cold storage and godowns, to auction arrangements, loading, sorting, weighing and packing facilities.[143]

Under organized retail, a majority of farmers reported favourable proximity to the market (in this case, distribution centre) as compared with traditional marketing, where a majority reported travel of more than 50 km to the nearest market. The availability of cold storage and godowns in traditional marketing remains a considerable improvement. Internet and modernization facilities need to be improved, if modernizing agri-chains remains a goal.

Considering pricing margins, the producer's share of the consumer's rupee is higher in organized retail than in the traditional channel, and most of the margin is realized by the organized retailer. In terms of value, the channel takes more than 50 per cent of consumer value, whereas the farmer realizes ~40 per cent of the consumer price. This is contradictory to the traditional channel, where the farmer realizes ~50 per cent and the channel takes about 45 per cent. The plus point is reduction in marketing cost, which stands at ~8 per cent for traditional marketing and gets reduced to almost half (~4 per cent) in organized retail. The farmer gets a 6 per cent higher price, but that is much less, considering it is procured directly

---

143   Usha, T., Subhash, C., Agricultural Economics Research Centre, 2012

from the farmer and bypassing all intermediaries, implying that the majority gains of shorting the supply chain are being enjoyed by organized retail. Increasing market depth—having an increasing number of buyers with participation across multiple varying marketing arrangements—will offer better choice to farmers and will have wider impact on the marketing scenario. Additionally, farmers can also be offered marketing assistance if the produce is perishable. Establishing processors/cold storage and godowns remains imperative to ensure farmers do not sell their produce in a harried and hurried manner, especially with the production and marketing cost incurred. The need for a mechanism to pass on a greater share of consumer price to the farmer is felt here, while ensuring sustainability of the marketing chain.

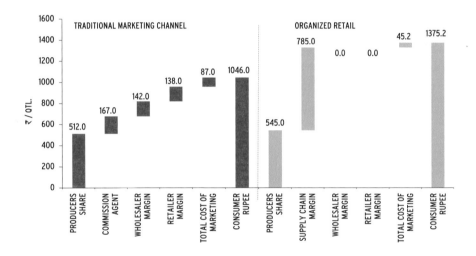

FIGURE 127: PRICE BUILD-UP FROM PRODUCER SHARE TO CONSUMER RUPEES
IN TRADITIONAL AND EMERGING CHANNELS[144]

144 Usha, T., Subhash, C., Agricultural Economics Research Centre, 2012

COMPARING MARKETING CHANNELS

Marketing cost traditionally is a function of crop type, besides a host of factors like state and central laws, regional geography, associated infrastructure and the power of the trader lobby. The figure below shows the cost of marketing in the traditional channel per farmer's rupee and the associated savings when we move to the alternative emerging channel. Gains are usually seen when we move from the traditional channel to contract farming. Similarly, reductions in marketing costs are observed in direct marketing. However, that does not free the farmer of marketing hassles, as he needs to get the produce to the consumer without any middlemen. Corporate marketing also offers an interesting insight. Within the same state, different crops have varying outcomes for the same buyer company—the channel is value-accretive for pomegranate but increases marketing cost as compared to the traditional channel in the case of onion. This indicates the presence of a well-functioning traditional channel for onion, which is true, as Maharashtra has a large, developed and well-functioning onion market. The average savings are almost the same for fruits and vegetables, yet vegetables have a wider margin range.

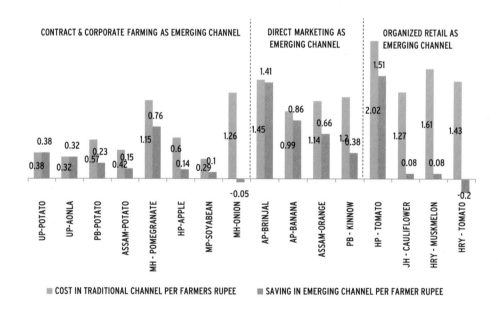

FIGURE 128: MARKETING COST AND SAVINGS AS SHARE OF FARMER RUPEE
IN TRADITIONAL AND EMERGING CHANNELS[145]

---

145 Ghosh, N., India's Agricultural Marketing, 2012

In terms of channel performance, the following table illustrates the average gross marketing cost reduction in emerging channels per farmer's rupee.

TABLE 49: AVERAGE GROSS MARKETING COST REDUCTION IN EMERGING CHANNELS[146]

	PER FARMER'S RUPEE		PER CONSUMER RUPEE	
	QUANTUM (₹)	RELATIVE TO TRADITIONAL CHANNEL (PER CENT)	QUANTUM (₹)	RELATIVE TO TRADITIONAL CHANNEL (PER CENT)
DIRECT MARKETING	0.83	69 PER CENT	0.33	59 PER CENT
CORPORATE MARKETING	0.24	28 PER CENT	0.09	21 PER CENT
CONTRACT FARMING	0.27	64 PER CENT	0.18	72 PER CENT
ORGANIZED RETAIL	0.37	23 PER CENT	0.08	14 PER CENT

OVERHAULING AGRICULTURAL MARKETING

The transitions that have been witnessed from the emergence and acceptance of emerging channels suggest that the traditional system desperately needs an overhaul. Besides economic considerations, farmers also seek alternative channels to dispose of produce that is found unsuitable by other existing/alternative channels. The existence of multiple channels not only offers greater choice to the farmer, but also reduces wastage and transportation effort, and provides an option to farmers when regulated mandis fail and farmers are forced to sell in local markets outside mandated precincts. As the channel is shortened, gains are bound to accrue, which, when shared with the farmer, translate into better quality of life for farm-dependent households. It is important to understand that increased efficiency in one channel doesn't mean that we abandon the other alternative or existing channels, but it signals that the regulated markets respond to competition and traders should be encouraged to modernize the operations as demonstrated by emerging channels. This needs policy support and financial resources to sustain the traditional channel based on regulated markets and upgrade it to compete with the emerging channel.

Any policy reform in this sector, considering its size, reach and impact, risks its own share of misinterpretations.[147] In the new system, the large number of intermediaries with limited functions will be replaced by a single entity that combines multiple functions, which will come as an onslaught on the existing chains or even obliterate

---

146   Ghosh, N., India's Agricultural Marketing, 2012
147   Ibid

them, which in turn will hurt the roadside vendor and pushcart vendor the most. Additionally, the single large entity will have greater experience, larger resources and legal firepower to take on farmers, and this can cause large-scale permanent damage to rural entrepreneurs. Discrimination against farmers is a real fear, as evidenced from high regulation of private bodies and greater public participation. With relaxing norms, a minuscule opportunity arises for farmer exploitation. Our policies need to be designed to encourage private participation, yet ensure the safety and prosperity of the farmer.

Emerging channels can also bring about inequality, as channel partners will only be interested in buying high-margin-yielding, high-quality products, which to a certain extent will be a result of technology adopted by the farmer and geographical advantages and not of the farmer's efforts. Keeping in mind transaction costs for small and marginal farmers, the channels may prefer only large farmers and thus drive many marginal farmers out of farming, which will have far-reaching socio-economic consequences. Policies should be designed and programme implementation monitored closely to ensure that small and marginal farmers are empowered to participate and reap the benefits of the emerging channels and not left behind.

If the objective of such channels, especially corporate/contract farming, deteriorates to just making short-term high profits from land, then with a monoculture focus and pre-described cultivation techniques, the Indian farmer will just become an implementation agent, with no freedom to think or innovate or act for the betterment of his land, his soil and his crop, with holistic farm-management practices being taken for a ride. The capability of a farmer for traditional foodgrain farming and long-term food security may be compromised, as farmers move en masse to lucrative cash crops. Our policies need to ensure that the farmer does not sacrifice recommended farm-management practices and become a pawn in the partnership whose fate rests solely with the channel partner.

RAISING FARMER INCOME

India has a long history of initiatives seeking to raise farmer income. More recently, the government has focused on enhancing agricultural output and reduce input costs through initiatives like the Pradhan Mantri Krishi Sinchai Yojana, Paramparagat Krishi Vikas Yojana and soil health cards. However, overall public investment in agriculture continues to remain low (~2.8 per cent of agricultural GDP in 2013).

We have discussed multiple sources of potential growth in farmer income—combined reforms in all of these sources could raise farmer income by ~75 per cent in seven years and 107.5 per cent in a decade.

TABLE 50: RAISING FARMER INCOME—SOURCES OF GROWTH[148]

NO	SOURCES OF GROWTH	POTENTIAL CONTRIBUTION TO FARMER INCOME (PER CENT)	
		OVER 7 YEARS	OVER 10 YEARS
1	RAISING CROP PRODUCTIVITY	16.7	25
2	INCREASING LIVESTOCK VALUE ADD	10.8	16.6
3	INPUT RESOURCE EFFICIENCY	16.7	25
4	CROP INTENSITY	3.4	4.9
5	CROP DIVERSIFICATION	5	7.3
6	AGRICULTURAL MARKETING REFORMS	9.1	9.1
7	SHIFT TO NON-FARM INCOME	13.4	19.6
	TOTAL	75.1	107.5

Ensuring that the latter scenario comes through requires there to be a step change in growth rates in current sources. Making this happen will require a significant reform of the current way agriculture is managed in India.

TABLE 51: RAISING FARMER INCOME—SOURCES OF GROWTH[149]

NO	SOURCES OF GROWTH	POTENTIAL CONTRIBUTION TO FARMER INCOME (PER CENT)	
		CURRENT GROWTH RATE	REQUIRED GROWTH RATE
1	RAISING CROP PRODUCTIVITY	3.1 PER CENT	4.1 PER CENT
2	INCREASING LIVESTOCK VALUE ADD	4.5 PER CENT	6.0 PER CENT
3	INPUT RESOURCE EFFICIENCY	2.26 PER CENT	3.0 PER CENT
4	CROP INTENSITY	1 PER CENT	1.3 PER CENT
5	CROP DIVERSIFICATION	3.89 PER CENT	5.17 PER CENT
6	AGRICULTURAL MARKETING REFORMS	13 PER CENT	17 PER CENT
7	SHIFT TO NON-FARM INCOME	1.81 PER CENT	2.4 PER CENT

148 Doubling Farmer's Income, Niti Aayog, NITI Policy Paper No. 1/2017, 2017
149 Ibid

Increasing agricultural productivity will require increasing the coverage of high-yielding varieties, particularly on cereal crops (eg: for rice, high-yielding varieties cover 62 per cent of the total rice-growing area). Secondly, the provision of institutional credit can help improve credit supply in rural areas, leading to higher uptake of agricultural inputs.

Greater collectivization, for lack of a better word, is also needed. India's agriculture, as mentioned earlier, is dominated by marginal and small farmers—small farm size is a significant deterrent for farmers to diversify towards fruits and vegetables, given the uneconomic size of the lot for agricultural marketing, along with price risk. Organizing farmers in an institutional mechanism like an FPO can help increase the benefits for farmers from the agricultural value chain.[150] There are numerous stories of how FPOs have been successful, albeit on a small scale.[151] SFAC itself has promoted over 510 FPOs, with a membership of over 5.71 lakh farmers.[152] However, FPOs are still quite small in size and need to be expanded significantly in order to reduce transaction costs for farmers and improve access to technology, raising their bargaining power. But beyond this, India's policymakers also need to consider avenues for diversifying sources of income for marginal farmers.

---

150 Singh, 2008
151 SFAC, 2013
152 SFAC, 2016

REFERENCES

INDIA'S AGRICULTURAL MARKETS

Acharya, S.S. and N. L. Agrawal (1994). Agricultural Prices: Analysis and Policy, New Delhi: Oxford and IBH Publishing Co. Pvt. Ltd.

Acharya, S.S. and N. L. Agrawal (2004). Agricultural Marketing in India, New Delhi: Oxford and IBH Publishing Co. Pvt. Ltd.

Anderson, Kym (2010). The Political Economy of Agricultural Price Distortions, New York: Cambridge University Press.

Bansal, P.C. (2002). Agricultural Marketing and Marketing Institutions: Economic Problems of Indian Agriculture, New Delhi: CBS Publishers and Distributors.

Banerji A (2004), 'Buyer Collusion and Efficiency of Government Intervention in Wheat Markets in Northern India: An Asymmetric Structural Auctions Analysis', American Journal of Agricultural Economics, 86(1): 236-253

Banerji, A and J. V. Meenakshi (2002). 'Buyer Collusion and Efficiency of Government Intervention in Wheat Markets in Northern India: A Symmetric Structural Auction Analysis', Working Paper No. 104, Centre for Development Economics, Delhi School of Economics.

Basu, Kaushik (2011). 'Understanding Inflation and Controlling It', Working paper No.5, New Delhi: Ministry of Finance, Government of India.

Boeninger, Edardo (1991). Governance and Development: Issues and Constraints, in Proceedings of the World Bank Annual Conference on Development Economics, Washington D. C.: The World Bank.

Byres, Terence J. (1997). The State Development and Liberalisation in India. New Delhi: Oxford University Press.

Chenery, Hollis and T.N. Srinivasan (1989). Handbook of Development Economics, New York: Elsevier Science Publishers.

CMIE (1993). Profile of Districts, Mumbai: Centre for Monitoring Indian Economy Pvt. Ltd.

CMIE (2000). Infrastructure, Mumbai: Centre for Monitoring Indian Economy Pvt. Ltd. Mumbai.

Dantwala. M.L. (1937). Marketing of Raw Cotton in India, Bombay: Longmans, Green and Co. Ltd.

Dasgupta, Dubey and Sathish (2011). 'Domestic Wheat Price Formation and Food Inflation in India', Working Paper No.2, New Delhi: Department of Economic Affairs, Ministry of Finance. Government of India.

Datta-Chaudhuri, Mrinal (1990). 'Market failure and Government Failure', Journal of Economic Perspectives, Vol. 4 (3): 25-39.

Deshpande, R.S., Prachitha J (2004). Marketing System To Obviate the Need for Large Scale State Intervention In Karnataka, Research Report: IX/ADRT/104, Bangalore: Institute for Social and Economic Change.

Deshpande, R.S., Khalil Shah and P. Pandhari (2008). Market Imperfections and Farmers' Distress, Research Report: IX/ADRT/122, Bangalore: Institute for Social and Economic Change.

Elenchezhian, T. and S. Kombairaju (2003). 'Comparing Marketing Efficiency of Farmer Market with Central Vegetable Market', Indian Journal of Agricultural Marketing, Vol.17 (1), pp.45-51.

GOI (2002). Report of Inter-Ministerial Task Force on Agricultural Marketing Reforms, New Delhi: Directorate of Agriculture and Cooperation, Ministry of Agriculture.

GOI (2011). Agricultural Statistics at a Glance 2010, New Delhi: Directorate of Economics and Statistics, Ministry of Agriculture, Government of India.

GOI (2012). Economic Survey 2011-12, New Delhi: Department of Economic Affairs, Economic Division, Ministry of Finance, Government of India.

GOM (1991). Report of the Committee to Study the Agri-Marketing and Setting-up of Cooperative Agro-Processing Units for Fruits, Vegetables and Other Agricultural Products (S.B. Kolhe Committee), Mumbai: Government of Maharashtra.

GOM (1996). Agricultural Policy (Draft), Mumbai: Government of Maharashtra.

GOM (2005). Seventeenth All India Livestock and Farm Equipment Census 2003, Maharashtra State, Pune: Department of Animal Husbandry, Maharashtra State.

GOM (2007). The Maharashtra Agricultural Produce Marketing (Development and Regulation) Rules, 1963 (as amended by Notification dated 02.11.2007), Nagpur: Nagpur Law House.

GOM (2008). The Maharashtra Agricultural

Produce Marketing (Development and Regulation) Act, 1963 (Maharashtra Act XX of 1964), as Amended by Maharashtra Act X of 2008, Nagpur: Nagpur Law House.

Acharya, S.S. and N. L. Agrawal (1994). Agricultural Prices: Analysis and Policy, New Delhi: Oxford and IBH Publishing Co. Pvt. Ltd.

Acharya, S.S. and N. L. Agrawal (2004). Agricultural Marketing in India, New Delhi: Oxford and IBH Publishing Co. Pvt. Ltd.

Anderson, Kym (2010). The Political Economy of Agricultural Price Distortions, New York: Cambridge University Press.

Bansal, P.C. (2002). Agricultural Marketing and Marketing Institutions: Economic Problems of Indian Agriculture, New Delhi: CBS Publishers and Distributors.

Banerji A (2004), 'Buyer Collusion and Efficiency of Government Intervention in Wheat Markets in Northern India: An Asymmetric Structural Auctions Analysis', American Journal of Agricultural Economics, 86(1): 236-253

Banerji, A and J. V. Meenakshi (2002). 'Buyer Collusion and Efficiency of Government Intervention in Wheat Markets in Northern India: A Symmetric Structural Auction Analysis', Working Paper No. 104, Centre for Development Economics, Delhi School of Economics.

Basu, Kaushik (2011). 'Understanding Inflation and Controlling It', Working paper No.5, New Delhi: Ministry of Finance, Government of India.

Boeninger, Edardo (1991). Governance and Development: Issues and Constraints, in Proceedings of the World Bank Annual Conference on Development Economics, Washington D. C.: The World Bank.

Byres, Terence J. (1997). The State Development and Liberalisation in India. New Delhi: Oxford University Press.

Chenery, Hollis and T.N. Srinivasan (1989). Handbook of Development Economics, New York: Elsevier Science Publishers.

CMIE (1993). Profile of Districts, Mumbai: Centre for Monitoring Indian Economy Pvt. Ltd.

CMIE (2000). Infrastructure, Mumbai: Centre for Monitoring Indian Economy Pvt. Ltd. Mumbai.

Dantwala. M.L. (1937). Marketing of Raw Cotton in India, Bombay: Longmans, Green and Co. Ltd.

Dasgupta, Dubey and Sathish (2011). 'Domestic Wheat Price Formation and Food Inflation in India', Working Paper No.2, New Delhi: Department of Economic Affairs, Ministry of Finance. Government of India.

Datta-Chaudhuri, Mrinal (1990). 'Market failure and Government Failure', Journal of Economic Perspectives, Vol. 4 (3): 25-39.

Deshpande, R.S., Prachitha J (2004). Marketing System To Obviate the Need for Large Scale State Intervention In Karnataka, Research Report: IX/ADRT/104, Bangalore: Institute for Social and Economic Change.

Deshpande, R.S., Khalil Shah and P. Pandhari (2008). Market Imperfections and Farmers' Distress, Research Report: IX/ADRT/122, Bangalore: Institute for Social and Economic Change.

Elenchezhian, T. and S. Kombairaju (2003). 'Comparing Marketing Efficiency of Farmer Market with Central Vegetable Market', Indian Journal of Agricultural Marketing, Vol.17 (1), pp.45-51.

GOI (2002). Report of Inter-Ministerial Task Force on Agricultural Marketing Reforms, New Delhi: Directorate of Agriculture and Cooperation, Ministry of Agriculture.

GOI (2011). Agricultural Statistics at a Glance 2010, New Delhi: Directorate of Economics and Statistics, Ministry of Agriculture, Government of India.

GOI (2012). Economic Survey 2011-12, New Delhi: Department of Economic Affairs, Economic Division, Ministry of Finance, Government of India.

GOM (1991). Report of the Committee to Study the Agri-Marketing and Setting-up of Cooperative Agro-Processing Units for Fruits, Vegetables and Other Agricultural Products (S.B. Kolhe Committee), Mumbai: Government of Maharashtra.

GOM (1996). Agricultural Policy (Draft), Mumbai: Government of Maharashtra.

GOM (2005). Seventeenth All India Livestock and Farm Equipment Census 2003, Maharashtra State, Pune: Department of Animal Husbandry, Maharashtra State.

GOM (2007). The Maharashtra Agricultural Produce Marketing (Development and Regulation) Rules, 1963 (as amended by Notification dated 02.11.2007), Nagpur: Nagpur Law House.

GOM (2008). The Maharashtra Agricultural Produce Marketing (Development and

Regulation) Act, 1963 (Maharashtra Act XX of 1964), as Amended by Maharashtra Act X of 2008, Nagpur: Nagpur Law House.

Agarwal, Bina. Mechanisation of Indian Agriculture, An Analytical Study based on Punjab, (Allied Publishers, New Delhi 1983).

A Field of One's Own: Gender and Land Rights in South Asia, (Cambridge University Press, Cambridge 1994a).

'Gender, Resistance and Land: Interlinked Struggles over Resources and Meanings in South Asia'. Journal of Peasant Studies, Vol. 22, No. 1 (1994b.)

'Gender and Land Rights Revisited: Exploring New Prospects via the State, Family and Market'. Journal of Agrarian Change, 3(1 and 2): 184-224 Jan to April (2003).

Banerjee, Nirmala. 'How Real is the Bogey of Feminisation'. in Gender and Employment in India, (eds) Papola T.S. and Alakh N Sharma, (New Delhi, Vikas Publishing House Pvt Limited, 1999), pp. 299-317.

Bardhan, Kalpana. 'Rural Employment, Wages and Labour Markets in India: A Survey of Research'. Economic and Political Weekly, 12(26): A34–A48; 12(27) 1062-74; Vol. 12, No. 28. (1977).

Baneria, Lourdes and Shelly Feldman (eds.). Unequal Burden: Economic Crisis, Persistent Poverty and Women's Work, Boulder: (Westview Press 1992).

Bhalla, Sheila. 'Casual Labourers in Rural Areas'. Paper prepared for IIPA-CPRC Seminar on 'Chronic Poverty and Development Policy in India, 4th and 5th November (New Delhi 2003).

Cagatay, Nilufer. Engendering Macroeconomics and Macroeconomic Policies. United Nations Development Programme (1998).

Chadha, G.K and P.P. Sahu. Post -- 'Reform Setbacks in Rural Employment—Issues That Need Further Scrutiny'. Economic and Political Weekly, 37(21): 1998-2026 (2002).

Chopra, R. 'Voices From the Earth: World and Food Production in a Punjabi Village'. Sociological Bulletin, Vol.43, No 1 (1994).

Chowdhry, Prem. The Veiled Women: Shifting Gender Equations in Rural Haryana. (New Delhi, Oxford University Press, 1994).

Desai, B.M and M. V. Namboodiri. Developing Agriculture in Gujarat: A Strategic Perspective for Ninth Plan. Economic and Political Weekly, Vol 32, No 13. (1997)

Duvvury, Nata. 'Women and Agriculture in the New Economic Regime'. Gender, Population and Development (ed.) Maithreyi Krishnaraj, Ratna Sudarshan and Abusaleh Shariff, (New Delhi, Oxford University Press, 1998).

Fan, Sheggen and Peter Hazell. 'Should Developing Countries Invest More in Less Favoured Areas? An Empirical Analysis of Rural India'. Economic and Political Weekly, Vol. 35, No. 17 (2000).

Government of India. National Agricultural Policy. (New Delhi, Ministry of Agriculture, July 2000).

Iyengar, Sudarshan. 'Women's Initiatives in Development and Management of Sustainable Drinking Water Sources in Gujarat Villages: Issues and Case Studies, Paper presented at the workshop on Empowering Rural Women? Policies'.

Institutions and Gendered Outcomes in Natural Resources Management, Abstracts and Papers, IRMA, September 7-9 (2000).

Krishnaraj, Maithreyi. 'Women's Work in the Indian Census: Beginnings of Change'. (Economic and Political Weekly) Vol. 25, Nos. 48 & 49 (1990).

Krishnaraj, Maithreyi and Amita Shah. 'Women Farmers in India—Declining Options—Future Possibilities', (mimeo), (Gujarat Institute of Development Research, Ahmedabad 2003).

Nair, K. 'Impact of New Technologies in South Asia'. The Changing Division of Labour in South Asia, (ed.) James Warner Bjorkamn, (New Delhi 1987).

Oza, Apoorva. 'Role of Women in Management of Drinking Water Programme AKRSP(I)'s Experiences in Sundernagar District, Paper presented at the workshop on Empowering Rural Women? Policies, Institutions and Gendered Outcomes in Natural Resources Management'. Abstracts and Papers, IRMA, September 7-9 (2000).

Patnaik, Utsa. Rural India in Ruins, Frontline, March (2004), pp. 16-27

Pangare, Vasudha. 'Incorporating Gender Perspectives in Watershed Projects'.

Participatory Watershed Development: Challenges for Twenty First Century, (eds.) Farrington, John, Cathryn Turton and A. J. James, (New Delhi, Oxford University Press, 1999).

Rao, C.H. Hanumantha. 'Sustainable Development of Agriculture'. Paper presented at the First Biennial Conference of the Indian Society of Ecological Economics, ISEC, Bangalore, December 20-22 (1999).

'Reform Agenda for Agriculture'. Economic and Political Weekly, 38(7): 1089-1093 (2003).

Satheesan, P.V. 'An Innovative PDS Experiment Comes Under Fire, Exchanges'. (Hyderabad, Deccan Development Society, 1997).

Sen, A.K. 'Gender and Cooperative Conflicts' in Tinker (ed)' (1990).

Sen, Abhijit and Praveen Jha. 'Rural Employment: Patterns and Trends from the National Sample Survey, paper presented at the seminar on Rural Transformation in India: The Role of Non-Farm Sector, Institute of Human Development'. (New Delhi 2001).

Shah, Amita. 'Natural Resource Management and Gender: Reflections from Watershed Programmes in India'. Indian Journal of Gender Studies, Vol. 7; No.1. (2000).

'Strategies for Main streaming Women in the Emerging Process of Globalisation'. Paper presented in the National Level Workshop on Strategies for Economic Empowerment of Women, September 22nd and 23rd (2003).

'Poverty and Agricultural Growth: Implications for Women'. Paper presented at International Gender Poverty Summit, Nov 9-11 (New Delhi 2003).

Shah, Amita and D. C. Sah. 'Chronic Poverty in a Remote Rural District in South West Madhya Pradesh: An Multidimensional Analysis of its Extent and Causes' in Chronic Poverty in India'. (eds)

Mehta, Aasha Kapur, Sourabh Gosh, DeepaChatterjee, (New Delhi, Indian Institute of Public Administration, 2003).

Sharma, A. N. 'Rural Transformation in India: The Role of Non-Farm Sector'. (New Delhi, Institute of Human Development, 2004).

Singh, Jaivir and J.V. Meenakshi. 'Understanding the Feminisation of Agriculture Labour (mimeo), Centre for the Study of Law and Governance'. (New Delhi, JNU and Delhi School of Economics, 2003).

Singh, Ram D. 'Female Agricultural Worker's Wages, Male-Female Wage Differentials, and Agricultural Growth in Developing Country, India'. Economic Development and Cultural Exchange, 45(1): 89–119 (1996).

Singha, Debal K Roy. Women, New Technology and Development: Changing Nature of Gender Relations in Rural India. (New Delhi, Manohar Publishers, 1995).

Srivastava, Ravi. 'Changes in Contractual Relations in Land and Labour in India'. Indian Journal of Agricultural Economics, 55(3): 253-282 July-September. (2000).

Sundaram, K. 'Employment—Unemployment Situation in the Nineties Some Results from NSS 55th round survey'. Economic and Political Weekly, 36(11): 931-940 (2001).

Unni, Jeemol. 'Globalisation and Securing Worker Rights for Women in Developing Countries'. Working Paper No 132, (Gujarat Institute of Development Research, Ahmedabad 2002).

Vasavada, Shilpa. 'Women Irrigators and Participatory Irrigation Management: Policy and Approaches for Mainstream Gender Concerns: Lessons from Aga Khan Rural Support Programme, Paper presented in the workshop on Empowering Natural Resources Management'. Abstract and Papers, IRMA, September 7-9 (2000).

Visaria, Praveen. 'Level and Pattern of Female Employment' in T S Papola and Alakh N Sharma (eds.)', op.cit, (1999), pp.23-51.

Wadhwa, Sneha (undated). 'Working with women Groups: Indian Experience' ' downloaded from www.worldbank.org: World Bank/Sustainable Development/RuralPoverty/Agriculture Extension.

MARKETING STAPLE CROPS

WHEAT

Goel, Veena (2000). A study of market arrivals and procurement pattern of wheat by public and private agencies in Punjab. Indian J. Regional Sci., 32(2) : 94-102.

Gupta, V.K. and Mathur, D.P. (1976).Wheat production, marketing and procurement- a study in selected surplus and deficit areas. Center for management in agricultural, Indian Institute of Management, Ahmedabad, Gujarat, India, 42(11) : 292.

Jain, K.K. (1993). An appraisal of costs and prices on different farms in Punjab. Agric. Situ. India, 47(10) : 763-773.

Jairath, M.S. and Bob Baukh (1992). Trading costs and margins—A case of wheat crop. Agric. Marketing, Issues & Challenge, 47 :387.

Kumar, S., Gaur, Rajesh Kumar and Anil Kumar, B. (2008). A study on marketing of wheat and mustard in Allahabad district of Uttar Pradesh. Agric. Econ. Res. Rev., 21 : 461.

Mishra,G.P., Uddin, F. and Bajpai, B.K. (1988).Wheat marketing in eastern Uttar Pradesh: Evidences and implications. Agric. Situ. India, 42(11) : 975-980.

Rangi, P.S. and Sindhu, M.S. (2001). Production and marketing of wheat in Punjab. The Indian J. Econ., 325 : 209-223.

PADDY

Abbot, J.C. and Makeham, J.P. (1981). Agricultural economics and marketing in the tropics. Wing Tai Cheung Printing Co. Ltd., ROME, ITALY.

Acharya, S.S. and Agarwal, N.L. (2004). Agricultural marketing in India. Oxford and IBH Publishing Co. Pvt. Ltd., NEW DELHI, INDIA.

Baba, S.H., Wani, M.H., Wani, S.A. and Shahid, Y. (2010). Marketed surplus and price spread of vegetables in Kashmir valley. Agric. Econ. Res. Rev., 23(1) : 221.

Basavaraja, H., Mahajanashetti, S.B. and Naveen, C.U. (2007). Economic analysis of post harvest losses in food grains in India: A case study of Karnataka. Agric. Econ. Res. Rev., 20 : 117-126.

Basavaraja, H. Mahajanashetti, S.B. and Sivanagaraju, P. (2008). Technological change in paddy production: A comparative analysis of traditional and SRI methods of cultivation. Indian J. Agric. Econ., 63(4) : 629-640.

Bhatia, G.R. (1996). Marketing cost and margins of agricultural commodities. Agric. Mktg., 39(1) : 8-11.

Dewasish, G. (2011). Value chain analysis of paddy in Andhra Pradesh, Post Graduate Diplomo in Management (Agriculture) Thesis, National Academy of Agricultural Research Management, Hyderabad, A.P. (INDIA).

Economic Survey (2013-14). Ministry of Finance, Government of India.

Garrett, H.E. and Woodworth, R.S. (1969). Statistics in psychology and education, Bombay, Vakils, Feffer and Simons Pvt. Ltd., p. 329.

Government of India (1990). Report of the expert committee for review of methodology of cost of production of crops, Ministry of Agriculture. p. 31.

Government of India (2002). Marketable surplus and post harvest losses of paddy in India. Directorate of Marketing and Inspection, Department of Agriculture and Cooperation, Ministry of Agriculture, Faridabad,HARYANA, (INDIA).

Hile, R.B., Kamble, B.T., Darekar, A.S. and Dattarkar, S.B. (2014). Economic analysis and impact assessment of production technology of paddy of Marathwada region in Maharashtra. Adv. Res. J. Soc. Sci., 5 (2) : 153-161.

Kohls, R.L. and Uhl, J.N. (1980). Marketing of agricultural products. (5th Ed.). Macmillan Publishing Co., Inc, NEW YORK, U.S.A.

Mahendra Dev, S. and Sharma, Alakh N. (2010). Food security in India: Performance, challenges and policies, Working Paper Series, September, Oxfam, INDIA.

Prasanna, P.H.S.N., Gunaratne, L.H.P. and Withana, W.D.R.S. (2004). Economic analysis of paddy threshing methods.

Sri Lankan J. Agric. Econ., 6(1) : 57-66. Rahman, S.M, Takeda, J. and Shiratake, Y. (2005). The role of marketing in standard of living: A case study of rice farmers in Bangladesh. J. Appl. Sci., 5 : 195-201.

Ramesh, C. and Vijayan, S. (2012). Marketing cost of paddy in Cuddalore district of Tamil Nadu. Language India, 12: 553-564.

Shelke, R.D., Nagure, D.V. and Patil, S.N. (2009). Marketing of paddy in Konkan region of Maharashtra state. Agric. Update, 4 (3&4): 439-442.

Shergill, H.S. (2007). Sustainability of wheat-rice production in Punjab: A Re-examination. Econ. & Political Weekly., 45 (52) : 81-85.

Sita Devi, K. and Ponnarasi, T. (2009). An economic analysis of modern rice production technology and its adoption behaviour in Tamil Nadu. Agric. Econ. Res. Rev., 22 : 341-347.

Stern Louis, W., Adel, I. Ansary and Anne T. Coughlan (1998). Marketing channels. Prentice Hall of India, NEW DELHI, INDIA.

Virdia, H.M. and Mehta, H.D. (2010). Economics of paddy based cropping system under south Gujarat condition . Agric. Update, 5 (1&2): 64- 68.

William, L.W. and Elizabeth, S.M. (1999). Marketing constraints to society. J. Mktg., 63 : 198-218.

MARKETING FRUITS & VEGETABLES

Geoffrey Bastin., 'Coconut Marketing: Issues for a Threatened Industry', Cord, July 1986, p.20.

Raveendran .P., 'Demand, Consumption Pattern and Consumer Acceptability of Desiccated

Coconut' Processing and Marketing of Desiccated Coconut, Coconut Development Board, Cochin, April 1987 p.25.

'Marketing of Coconut Products in Andaman and Nicobar Islands', Indian Coconut Journal, December 1989, p.14

Ratha Krishnan 'Price Spread in Coconut Marketing', Indian Coconut Journal, March 1989, p.20.

Hameed Khan .H and others., 'Improving The Coconut Production', Indian Coconut Journal, April 1990, p.2.

Punchihewa . P.G., 'Coconut Industry - Current Situation and Prospects', Indian Coconut Journal, November 1990, p.2.

Anitha Sharma., 'Villagers can do well with better marketing', Indian Farmer Times, December 1990, p.9

George.M.V and others., 'Trend in Area, Production and Productivity of Coconut in India', Indian Coconut Journal, November 1991, p.45.

Thomas Mathew., 'A Study on the Consumption of Tender Coconuts in Tamil Nadu', Indian Coconut Journal, September 1990, p.5.

Jaganathan. N., 'An Economic Analysis of Coconut Farming in Anamalai Block of Coimbatore District, Tamil Nadu', 1991, p.10.

Ron Harris., 'The Coconut Industry Utilization and Marketing', The Planter, April 1991, p. 161.

Jos.C.A, 'Cooperativization of Marketing and Processing of Coconuts - Problems and Prospects', Processing and Marketing of Coconuts in India., Cochin: Coconut Development Board, 1992, p. 93.

Profulla Das., 'Coconut Marketing Problems, Prospects and Challenges in Kerala', Processing and Marketing of Coconuts in India., Cochin: Coconut Development Board, 1992, p. 134.

Ramakrishna Pillai.K., 'Role of Cooperatives in Processing and Marketing of Coconuts in Kerala with special reference to MARKETFED' , Processing and Marketing of Coconuts in India., Cochin: Coconut Development Board, 1992, p. 90.

Markose. V.T and Sree kumar., 'Coconut Based Rural Industries—An Overall Perspective', Indian Coconut Journal, December 1993, P-2.

'Coconut Development in the Last Decade', Indian Coconut Journal, November 1994, p. 12.

Chengappa.P.G and others., 'Methods of

Disposal of Coconut and Economics of Processing Coconut at Farm Level', Indian Coconut Journal, April 1993, p.5.

Marapandiyan .P., 'Role of KERAFED in Coconut Processing and Marketing', Processing and Marketing of Coconuts in India', 1995, p. 92.

Narasimhappa., 'Processing and Marketing of Coconut and its Products' Processing and Marketing of Coconuts in India., Cochin: Coconut Development Board, 1995, p. 129.

Haridas.R and Chandran.C., 'Marketing systems, costs, margin, price spread and marketing problems of coconut - A case study of coconut growers and traders in Tamil Nadu', Indian Coconut Jouranl, May 1996, p. 13

Aravindakshna.M., 'Challenges of the Coconut Industry in India and Strategy for Making it Competitive', Paper presented in the COCOTECH Meeting held at Kochi, July 1995, p.1.

Thampan.P.K., 'Coconut Diversification, a Must', The Survey of Indian Agriculture, Chennai: The Hindu, 1996, p. 99.

Venkitachalam.V., 'Global Coconut Situation and Strategy for Development', Coconut for Prosperity, cochin : 1996, p.109.

Thomas.P.T and Venkitachalam.V., 'Investment Opportunities in Coconut in Tamil Nadu', Indian Coconut Journal, June 199T7, p.4.

Subburaj.B., 'Marketing of Coconuts', Research Monograph, Gandhigram Rural Institute, January 2000, p.67.

Dr.P. Rethinam and others., 'a study on problems and prospects of coconut industry in Andaman Nicobar Islands', Indian Coconut Journal, June 2001, p.2.

M.K. Nair and M.K. Rajesh, 'a study on coconut production and productivity', Indian Coconut Journal, June 2001, p.13.

Dr. P. Rethinam and P.K Thampan,, 'a study on Reviving coconut based economy of Kerala state' Indian Coconut Journal, December 2001, p.2

NABARD., 'Coconut Development in Tamil Nadu - An Ex-Post Evaluation Study in Coimbatore District', Evaluation Study Series No:11, NABARD, February 2002, p.9.

Thomas Mathew. M., 'a study on Trade in Tender coconut - A future vista of Indian coconut industry'.Indian Coconut Journal, July 2002,p.1.

Dr. R.K. Singh and Dr. B. Subburaj., 'a study on

Pricing the coconut in Tamil Nadu - An Analysis', Indian Coconut Journal, December 2002, p.1.

Dr. B. Subburaj and Dr. R.K. Singh., 'a study on Marketing Mix for Coconut Products - Consumers' Perception with the help of empirical study', Indian Coconut Journal, March 2003, p.6

Dr. R.K. Singh and Dr. B. Subburaj., 'a study on Highways- The potential markets for tender nut sale in Tamil Nadu', Indian Coconut Journal, August 2003. p.6.

Anitha Kumari .P and Jissy Geroge., 'a study on Gender Perspectives In Coconut Product Diversification - An Analysis', Indian Coconut Journal, October 2003. p.17.

H.P.Singh., 'Augmentation of Coconut Marketing', Indian Coconut Journal, October 2003, p.3.

Thomas Mathew, Hameed Khan and Shivapuje., 'a study on Coconut in Konkan', Indian Coconut Journal, November 2003. p.9.

Thomas Mathew.M., 'Coconut Products in Support of Health and the importance of coconut in Maharashtra', Indian Coconut Journal, November 2003. p.25.

Dr. R. Haridass and M. Muthuraj., 'A study on Economics of Coconut Cultivation in Tamil Nadu - A comparative Analysis of Tall and Dwarf Variety', Indian Coconut Journal, May 2004. p.3.

Subburaj B., 'Markets of Non-Conventional Coconut Products', Research Monograph, Gandhigram Rural Institute, January 2004, p.34.

'Research study on Coconuts in Regulated Markets', Research Monograph, Gandhigram Rural Institute, January 2004, p.37.

SPECIALITY CROPS

JUTE

Acharya, S.S. and Agarwal, N. L. (1994), Agricultural Marketing in India, New Delhi: Oxford & IBH Publishing Co.

Das, Manashree, (2015) Entrepreneurship Development in Agricultural Sector in Conflict Areas in A. Ibemcha Chanu (ed) Entrepreneurship Development in Conflict Regions Vishakhapatnam: Global publishing House Pp 173-182.

Goyal, H.D. (1990), Indian Jute Industry, Problems and Prospects, New Delhi: Commonwealth publishers.

Jaffer, A.M. (2005), Marketing Efficiency of Banana in Theni District, Tamilnadu, Indian J. Agricultural Marketing, vol XLVII no-4

Khatkar, R.K. et. al. (2005), 'Marketing of Fresh Mushroom in Haryana'. Marketing Agricultural (April- June).

Sudha et.al (2005), Price spread and Market Margin of Gingerly in Visakhapatnam district of Andhra Pradesh, Agricultural Marketing, vol- XLVII, NO-4

FLORICULTURE

Boran, S (2008), 'Overview to Cut Flower Sector', Izmir Chamber of Commerce AR&GE Bulletin, Turkey.

Chadha, K.L., A.K. Singh and V.B. Patel (2011), Horticulture to Horti-business, Westville Publishing House, New Delhi.

Chattopadhyay, S.K (2007), Commercial floriculture, Gene-Tech Books, New Delhi.

Ganjana, T.M and M. Sudha (2006), 'Production and Marketing Research on Traditional Flowers', Advances in Ornamental Horticulture, Vol.6, Pointer Publishers, Jaipur.

Jyothi, S.H and V.T. Raju (2003), 'Study on marketing of crossandra, jasmine and rose flowers in East Godavari District of Andhra Pradesh', Agriculture Marketing Journal, XLVI (2), pp.2-4.

Khushk, A.M and M.I. Lashari (2003), 'Marketing margin analysis of flowers in Sindh', Finance and Market, Aug.27-Sept.02.

Majumdar, Sujata and Debabrata Lahiri (2012), 'Cost-Benefit and Sensitivity Analysis of Cut Flower Roses and Comparision with Other Floriculture Crops', Agriculture Situation in India, February. pp.609-624.

National Horticulture Board (2013), Indian Horticulture Database 2013. Ministry of Agriculture, Government of India.

National Centre for Agricultural Economics and Policy Research (2010), Estimation of Marketing Efficiency of Horticultural Commodities under different Supply Chains in India. Research Project Report.

Omar, Md Imran, et.al (2014), 'Marketing Efficiency and Post Harvest Loss of Flower in Banladesh', IOSR Journal of Business and Management, Vo. 1, pp.45-51.

Ozkan, B., et.al (1997), 'Production, Structure and

Main marketing problems of export oriented cut flower industry in Turkey', Acta, 491, pp.481-487.

Taj, Sajida, et. al (2013), 'Price Spread and Marketing of Cut Rose in Punjab, Pakistan', Pakistan J. Agric. Res., Vol.26, No.1, pp16-23.

EVALUATING MARKETING CHANNELS

DIRECT MARKETING

Krishnamoorthy R., February 23, 2006,'Cultivators' plea to streamline jasmine procurement', The Hindu {http:// www.thehindu.com}.

The Hindu, November 09, 2005, 'An informative experience',

Sundar S., September 23, 2005, 'Uzhavar Sandhais getting a raw deal now?', The Hindu

Kavitha S.S., September 21, 2005, 'Barnala bowled over by `Uzhavar Sandhai'', The Hindu, http://www.thehindubusinessline.com} 2005092111400100.htm.

The Hindu, June 2, 2005 'Uzhavar Sandhai, a picture of neglect'

The Hindu, 10 June, 2004, 'Govt. ignoring Uzhavar Sandhais: Cuddalore MLA',

Revathy L.N., May 6, 2004, 'Dharapuram riots hit by poor quality onion seeds, Hindu Business Line, http://www.thehindubusinessline.com/2004050701821900.htm.

Sivakumar R, 2003, 'A study on Working of Uzhavar Sandhai in Erode District', dissertation submitted in December.

Subramanian Karthik, August 10, 2002, 'Govt. apathy keeps farmers away from market', The Hindu,

The Hindu, May 30, 2001, 'Plug loopholes, revamp Uzhavar Sandhai scheme'

Krishnamoorthy R., May 30, 2001, 'Vegetable cultivators in a soup', The Hindu

Shanker S., Wednesday, May 29, 2001,'Farmers launch campaign for continuing Ambattur Uzhavar Sandhai', The Hindu,

Monday, June 26, 2000, 'Farmers' market runaway success in Madurai', Hindu Business Line

Subhendu Dey, Rythu Bazaar: A Study of the Supply Chain of the Farmers'

Markets of Andhra Pradesh

Subhendu Dey, Rythu bazaars—A study of the benefits received by farmer , ASIAN JOURNAL OF MANAGEMENT RESEARCH 220, Volume 3 Issue 1, 2012

Murali Kallummal & K Sakthi Srinivasan, The Dynamics of Farmers' Market: A Case Analysis of 'Uzhavar Sandhai' of Tamil Nadu

CONTRACT FARMING

Rahul Chaturvedi, 'Contract Farming and Fritolay's Model of Contract Farming for Potato', Potato J. 34 (1-2) : 16-19, 2007,Gneral Manager-Agro (R&D), PepsiCo India Hodlings Pvt. Ltd. (FritoLay Division) Global Business Park, M.G. Road, Gurgaon-122 002, Haryana, India.

Preetinder Kaur, 'Contract Farming of Potatoes: A Case Study of PEPSICO Plant' , International Journal of Scientific and Research Publications, Volume 4, Issue 6, June 2014 1 ISSN 2250-3153, Research Scholar, Department, of Geography, Panjab University Chandigarh.

Meeta Punjabi,'The potato supply chain to PepsiCo's Frito Lay', Food and Agriculture Organization of the United Nations (FAO).

'Potato Contract Farming –Win-Win Model for Agro Processing', http://www.fmpcci. com/pdf/Contract per cent20Farming.pdf

Parthapratim Pal ,'Contract farming in India: A Case study of potato cultivation', Indian Institute of Management, Calcutta,www.networkideas.org/ideasact/jan15/ppt/PARTHAPRATIM_PAL.pptx

http://www.fao.org/ag/ags/contract-farming/faq/en/

http://www.ijsrp.org/research-paper-0614/ijsrp-p3040.pdf

https://en.wikipedia.org/wiki/Contract_farming

http://www.pepsicoindia.co.in/purpose/environmental-sustainability/partnership-with-farmers.html

https://www.nabard.org/english/contract_farm.aspx

http://www.fao.org/ag/ags/contract-farming/faq/en/

http://www.ibnlive.com/news/india/contract-farming-the-key-to-raising-productivity-1107108.html

http://timesofindia.indiatimes.com/city/
kolkata/Contract-farming-way-out-for-potato-
growers/articleshow/11370291.cms

http://www.thehindubusinessline.com/
todays-paper/tp-agri-biz-and-commodity/
pepsico-engages-contract-farmers-
for-potatoes/article987370.ece

http://www.slideshare.
netprincesahilkhannacontract-farming-pepsico

http://www.csrworld.netpepsico per centE2 per
cent80 per cent93corporate-social-responsibility.asp

http://www.business-standard.com/article/
companies/pepsico-aims-to-increase-contract-
farming-of-potato-112120600164_1.html

http://swapsushias.blogspot.
in/2014/02/contract-farming-in-india-
oppurtunities.html#.VqHh4Pl97IU

http://www.fao.org/fileadmin/user_
upload/contract_farming/presentations/
Contract_farming_in_India_2.pdf

http://www.fmpcci.com/pdf/
Contract per cent20Farming.pdf

Aghion, B., and J. Morduch. 2005. The economics
of microfinance. Cambridge, MA: MIT Press.

Banerjee, A., T. Besley, and T. Guinnane. 1993.
Thy neighbor's keeper: The design of a credit
cooperative with theory and a test. Quarterly
Journal of Economics 109: 491—515.

Besley, T., and S. Coate. 1995. Group lending,
repayment incentives and social collateral.
Journal of Development Economics 46: 1—18.

Chayanov, A.V. 1992. The theory of peasant
cooperatives. Columbus: University of Ohio Press.

Dr Venkatesh Tagat, Financing for
Farmer Producer Organizations (FPOs),
National Bank for Agriculture and Rural
Development (NABARD), 2016

Economic and Political Weekly. 2006.
Suicides by farmers. April 22.

Food and Agricultural Organization. 2002.
Comprehensive Africa agricultural development
programme. Available at http://www.fao.
org/docrep/005/y6831e/y6831e00.htm

Grossman, L. 1998. The political ecology
of bananas: Contract farming, peasants and
agrarian change in the eastern Caribbean. Chapel

Hill : University of North Carolina Press.

Guinnane, T. 1994. A failed institutional
transplant: Raiffesein's credit cooperatives
in Ireland, 1894-1914. Explorations in
Economic History 31: 38—61.

Little, P., and M. Watts , eds. 1994. Living
under contract: Contract farming and agrarian
transformation in sub-Saharan Africa.
Madison: University of Wisconsin Press.

Moore, B. 1967. Social origins of dictatorship
and democracy: Lord and peasant in the making
of the modern world. Boston: Beacon.

Motiram, S., and V. Vakulabharanam . 2006.
Alternative futures for smallholder agriculture:
A theoretical comparison of cooperative,
corporate and traditional solutions. Mimeo,
Dalhousie University and Queens College.

N Vishwanadham, Achieving Rural & Global
Supply Chain Excellence—The Indian Way

Ramachandran, V.K., and M. Swaminathan. 2002.
Rural banking and landless labour households:
Institutional reform and rural credit markets in
India. Journal of Agrarian Change 2: 502—44.

Rao, J.M., and S. Storm. 2003. Agricultural
globalization in developing countries:
Rules, rationale and results. In Work and
well being in the age of finance, ed. J.
Ghosh and C. P. Chandrasekhar, 212—55.
New Delhi, India: Tulika Publishers.

Rao, J.M., and V. Vakulabharanam . 2006.
Immiserizing growth and anomalous supply
response: A South Indian economy during
globalization. Mimeo, Queens College.

The Boston Consulting Group, Indian
Agribusiness—Cultivating Future
Opportunities, Ashish Iyer & Abheek Singhi

Thorner, D. 1964. Agricultural
cooperatives in India: A field report.
London: Asia Publishing House.

Youngjohns, B.J. 1983. Cooperatives and credit:
A reexamination. In Rural financial markets in
developing countries: Their use and abuse, ed. J. D.
Von Pischke, D.W. Adams, and G. Donald, 346—
63. Baltimore: Johns Hopkins University Press.

World Bank. 2005. Shocks and social
protection: Lessons from the Central
American coffee crisis, Report no. 31857-
CA. Washington, DC: World Bank.

Agrawal, R C (2000): 'Perspectives for Small

Farmers in Developing Countries: Do They have a Future?', Forum zur Gartenkonferenz 2000 http://userpage.fu.berlin/~garten/ Buch/Agrawal(englisch).htm. (April 6, 2005.)

Bayes, A and M. S Ahmed (2003):'Agricultural diversification and self-help group initiatives in Bangladesh', Paper presented at the IFPRI-FICCI Workshop on Vertical Integration in Agriculture in South Asia, Nov.3, New Delhi.

Benziger, V (1996):'Small Fields, Big Money: Two Successful Programs in Helping Small Farmers Make the Transition to High Value-Added Crops', World Development, 24 (11), 1681-1693.

Bharwada, C and V Mahajan (2006): 'Gujarat: Quiet Transfer of Commons', Economic and Political Weekly, 41(4), January 28, 313-315.

Bose, P R (2006): 'Reliance Ind plans to enter agri sector', The Hindu Business Line, Mumbai, March 19, p.2.

Chadha, G K (1996): Wastelands in Rural India: Policy initiatives and programmes for their development, National bank for Agricultural and Rural Development (NABARD) Occasional Paper No. 2, NABARD, Mumbai.

Dash, M (2004): 'Political Economy of Contract Farming', Mainstream, 42(52), December.

Deshingkar, P, U Kulkarni, L Rao and S Rao (2003):'Changing Food Systems in India: Resource Sharing and Marketing Arrangements for Vegetable Production in Andhra Pradesh,' Development Policy Review, 21(5-6): 627-639.

Dev, S M and N C Rao (2004): 'Food Processing in Andhra Pradesh—Opportunities and Challenges', CESS Working Paper No. 57, Centre for Economic and Social Studies (CESS), Hyderabad, June.

Dhaliwal, S (2005): ''Political, farmers' bodies propose agri policy to Centre', The Tribune, March 13, Chandigarh.

Dhall, Y (2006): 'Punjab govt. picks up Ambani's Agri Bill,' The Economic Times, Ahmedabad, p.7.

Dileep, B K, R K Grover, and K N Rai (2002): Contract Farming in Tomato: An Economic Analysis', Indian Journal of Agricultural Economics, 57(2), 197-210.

Dogra, B (2002): 'Land Reforms, Productivity and Farm Size', Economic and Political Weekly, 37(6), 532-533.

Eaton, C and A W Shepherd (2001): Contract Farming: Partnerships for Growth, FAO, Rome.

FES (Foundation for Ecological Security) (n.d.): Spaces for the Poor- Working with Communities and Commonlands in Central Aravalis, Rajasthan, FES, Anand.

Glover, D. and K. Kusterer (eds.) (1990): Small Farmers, Big Business - Contract Farming and Rural Development, Macmillan, London.

Goldsmith, A (1985): 'The private sector and rural development: Can agribusiness help the small farmer?', World Development, 13(11/12), 1125-1138.

Jha, D (2001): 'Agricultural Research and Small Farms', Presidential Address at the 60th Annual Convocation of the Indian Society of Agricultural Economics, Kalyani (WB), January 22-24.

Johl, S S (1995):'Agricultural Sector and New Economic Policy', Indian Journal of Agricultural Economics, 50(3), 473-487.

Johnson, D A (1985):'Sabritas' backward integration into agricultural production', in J Freivalds (ed.): Successful Agribusiness Management, Gower, Vermont, 108-115.

Johnson, N L and V W Ruttan (1994): 'Why Are Farms So Small?', World Development, 22(5), 691-706.

Joshi, S (2006): 'Give Farmers a real way out', The Hindu Business Line, March 22, p.10.

Lipton, M (1993):'Land Reform as Commenced Business -The Evidence Against Stopping', World Development, 21 (4), 641-657.

Mani G and V K Pandey (1995): 'Agrarian Structure under the New Economic Policy', Indian Journal of Agricultural Economics, 50(3), 524-530.

Mishra, S N (1997):'Agricultural Liberalisation and Development Strategy in Ninth Plan', Economic and Political Weekly, 32 (13), March 29, A19-A25.

Morvaridi, B (1995): 'Contract Farming and Environmental Risk - The Case of Cyprus', The Journal of Peasant Studies, 23 (1), 30-45, October.

Muller A R and R Patel (2004): Shining India? Economic Liberalisaiton and Rural Poverty in the 1990s, Food First Policy Brief No. 10, Food First/Institute for Food and Development Policy, Oakland, May.

Parikh, K and H K Nagarajan (2004): How Important is Land Consolidation? Land Fragmentation and Implications for Productivity: Case Study of Village Nelpathur in Tamil Nadu, National Bank for Agricultural and Rural Development (NABARD) Occasional Paper No. 31, NABARD, Mumbai.

Patel, A (2006): 'Gujarat's first 'Contract cattle farm'', Divya Bhaskar, May 6, Ahmedabad (in Gujarati).

Patnaik, U (1996): 'Export-Oriented Agriculture and Food Security in Developing Countries and India', Economic and Political Weekly, Special Number, September.

PSFC (Punjab State Farmers' Commission) (2006): Agricultural and Rural Development of Punjab- Transforming From Crisis to Growth, PSFC, Govt. of Punjab, Chandigarh, May.

Rangswamy, G (1993):'Corporate Agriculture: The key to poverty eradication', Guide on Food Products (GFP) Year Book, 114-116.

Rao, C H H (1995):'Liberalisation of Agriculture in India - Some Major Issues' Indian Journal of Agricultural Economics, 50 (3), 468-472.

Rao, V M and H G Hanumappa (1999): 'Marginalisation Process in Agriculture— Indicators, Outlook and Policy Implications', Economic and Political Weekly, 34(52), A133-A138.

Raynolds, L T, D Myhre, P McMichael, V Carro-Figueroa and F Buttel (1993):'The 'New' Internationalisation of Agriculture - A Reformulation', World Development, 21 (7), 1101-1121.

Shome, P (2006): 'At the threshold of 10 per cent economic growth?', Economic and Political weekly, 41(11), March 18, 943-946.

Singh, R B, P Kumar and T Woodhead (2002): Smallholder Farmers in India: Food Security and Agricultural Policy, FAO, ROAP, Bangkok, March.

Singh, R V (2002): Forests and Wastelands: Participation and Management, The Ford Foundation, New Delhi.

Singh, S (1994): 'Corporate farming: Risky step?' Financial Express, February 16, Mumbai.

Singh, S (2002): 'Contracting Out Solutions: Political Economy of Contract Farming in the Indian Punjab', World Development, 30(9), 1621-1638.

Singh, J P (2005): 'Changing Agrarian Relations in Rural India', a Keynote Paper presented at the 65th Annual Conference of the ISAE held at PAU, Ludhiana, November 24-26.

Singh, S (2006): Organic Produce Supply Chains in India, a research report, Centre for Management in Agriculture (CMA), Indian Institute of Management (IIM), Ahmedabad.

Singh, S (2006a): Leveraging Contract Farming for Agricultural Development in India: Status, Issues, and Strategies, a draft paper prepared for the Working Group (of the NDC, Govt. of India) on Agricultural Marketing Reforms, Centre for Management in Agriculture (CMA), Indian Institute of Management (IIM), Ahmedabad.

Strohl, R J (1985):'Farming failures: the fate of large-scale agribusiness in Iran', in J Freivalds (ed.): Successful Agribusiness Management, Gower, Vermont, 133-146.

Toulmin, C and B Gueye (2003): Transformations in West African agriculture and the role of family farms, IIED Issue paper No. 123, IIED, London, December.

Vyas, V S (2001):'Agriculture: Second Round of Economic Reforms', Economic and Political Weekly, 36 (10), 829-836.

Warning, M, N Key and W S Hoo (2003): Small Farmer Participation in Contract Farming, a draft paper.

Winson, A (1990): 'Capitalist Coordination of Agriculture: Food Processing Firms and Farming in Central Canada', Rural Sociology, 55(3), 376-394, Fall.

Varun Prasad, CCS Working Paper #293, Contract Farming through Farmer Producer Organizations (FPOs) in India

Vijay Paul Sharma, India's Agrarian Crisis and Corporate-Led Contract Farming: Socio-economic Implications for Smallholder Producers, International Food and Agribusiness Management Review Volume 11, Issue 4, 2008

Ashok Gulati, P.K. Joshi, Maurice Landes, Contract Farming in India—An introduction

Pranaya Kumar Swain, Chandan Kumar, C. Prudhvi Raj Kumar, Corporate Farming vis-a-vis Contract Farming in India: A Critical Perspective, International Journal of Management and Social Sciences Research (IJMSSR), ISSN 2319-4421, Volume 1, No. 3, December 2012

Contract Farming Ventures in India: A Few Successful Cases, National Institute of Agricultural Extension Management (MANAGE)

Dr Manas Chakrabarti, An Empirical Study On Contract Farming In India, International Journal

of Informative & Futuristic Research, ISSN
2347-1697, Volume 2, Issue 5, January 2015

Pratap S Birthal, Making Contract Farming
Work in Smallholder Agriculture

S Erappa, Contract Farming In
Karnataka: A Boon Or A Bane?

R.C.A. Jain, Regulation and Dispute
Settlement in Contract Farming in India

Dr C S Deshpande, Contracting Farming
As Means Of Value-Added Agriculture,
National Bank for Agriculture and Rural
Development (NABARD), 2005

Sudha Narayanan, Notional Contracts:
The Moral Economy of Contract Farming
Arrangements in India, WP-2012-020

Maximo Toreto, A framework for Linking
Small Farmers to Markets, January 2011

ORGANIZED RETAILER SOURCING

National Bank for Agriculture and Rural
Development (NABARD), Organized Agri-
food retailing in India, January 2011

Impact Of Organized Retail Chains On
Revenue Of Farmer, Jitender Singh, Department
of Industrial Policy & Promotion (DIPP),
Ministry of Commerce & Industry, 2011

Impact of Emerging Marketing Channels in
Agricultural Marketing—Benefits to Producer-
Seller and Marketing Costs and Margins of
Agricultural Commodities in Haryana, Usha
Tuteja & Subhasah Chandra, Agricultural
Economics Research Centre, July 2012

Modern Organized Retail and Its Impact
on Agriculture, C. Rangarajan, 2012

The Case For Organized Agri-Retail—The Indian
Imperative, Umashankar Venkatesh, Journal of
Services Research, Volume 8, Number 1, 2008

National Bank for Agriculture and
Rural Development (NABARD),
Doubling Farmers Income by 2022

CHAPTER V

ON NON-FARM INCOME

The traditional image of farm households in India is one of farms and farmers, with some livestock available, and a local potter, blacksmith and weaver to boot. Most rural policy debates in India tend to equate farming income with rural income, and assume any non-farm activities are in urban areas. However, there is significant evidence that rural non-farm income is often an important source of income and self-employment for rural households, with the promotion of rural non-farm activity being a key tool for policymakers.

Let's consider the alternatives—the promised holy grail of mass urban employment in India may not materialize, given existing challenges associated with India's infrastructure and competitiveness, at least in the near to medium term. As such, opportunities for unskilled and semi-skilled labourers from rural India will remain limited, leading to a constraint on the rural to urban migration pattern. Meanwhile, while economies of scale would dictate that mechanization would lead to a consolidation of farmland, it is likely that rural India will see further fragmentation of farm sizes, as farmers seek to pass down appropriate parcels to their progeny and others seek to hold on to farmland in order to benefit from higher real estate prices and to save for a rainy day or entrepreneurial opportunities (farm sizes have risen only modestly even in Punjab). Land renting, as a concept, has seen limited application. Agriculture will continue to be dominated by a set of small part-time farm households, along with a large majority of marginal farmers, increasingly focusing on horticulture, poultry, eggs and milk. Farms will become more capital-intensive and with the rise of organic farming, the traceability of agricultural output will become important.

For agriculture to prove sufficient to provide a regular income, agricultural markets need to work. However, given that output costs rarely reflect the real cost of production, while input prices are subsidized and distorted; and at the same time, the government wants to keep food prices low, effectively impoverishing farmers. Raising non-farm income is the primary policy option to come out of this conundrum. Theoretically, there is an inverse relationship between farm and non-farm employment[1]—wherever agriculture is unable to provide sufficient income, rural non-farm income is utilized to pick up the slack, if feasible. However, there are significant studies that showcase that the Green Revolution led to an increased demand for locally produced labour-intensive goods and services, thereby raising non-farm income.[2] This is reflected in employment growth in non-farm areas in rural India—while the '80s had four out of ten jobs in the non-farm sector, the 2010s saw this proportion rise to six out of ten.[3] Effectively, the rural non-farm sector is now the largest source of new jobs in India, with gains seen particularly in states like Kerala, West Bengal and Tamil Nadu, while low growth was seen in Chhattisgarh, Madhya Pradesh and Karnataka.[4] The majority of such non-farm jobs were associated with the services, transport and construction sectors, unlike the '80s, when the growth was in rural manufacturing. However, the greatest boom has been in the construction space, generating over 19 per cent of all rural non-farm jobs since 2010; this is visible in the high level of rural construction that is transforming Indian villages. Between 1999 and 2007, the proportion of rural households that were engaged in non-farm self-employment doubled from 10 per cent to 20 per cent.

With farming having increasingly marginal economics, it becomes imperative for farmers to supplement their income through non-farm means to escape from the trappings of rural poverty. Non-farm diversification is typically an important pathway for empowering especially landless labourers and marginal farmers, helping them overcome the land constraint for growth while offering sustainable income that can provide capacity to absorb external farm shocks and provide capital for agricultural investment. Most of rural non-farm income is associated with urban migration, with most village youth working as labourers in nearby towns and cities. However, the diversification of income source is mostly seen in richer rural households, with poor and marginal farmers relying more on their marginal farm holdings and the dependence level declining with household assets. Among non-farm income sources, livestock and construction incomes are a broad-based critical component.

Studies have indicated a strong negative correlation between livestock sector growth and rural poverty reduction. We have typically followed a two-track approach to livestock since Independence, with some states performing well while others continue

---

1   Bhaumik, 2002
2   Mellor, 1976
3   Himanshu, 2010
4   World Bank, 2010

to have limited contribution from the livestock sector to their overall agricultural output. Our support for livestock is driven by a top-down strategy—technology is typically transferred to progressive farmers, while large ruminants are mostly ignored; instead, milk production is prioritized, with support services concentrated in more urbanized areas, with inherent gender biases ignored. Research on livestock continues to be relatively limited. Input factors like feed, cross-breeding, and most importantly, credit have yet to see impactful reforms. Various models for livestock development exist, but the success of any model depends on its ability to address local/ground-level issues.

Meanwhile, construction remains the mainstay for employment generation in the non-farm sector in India, with its employment share rising from 14.4 per cent in 1999–2000 to 30.1 per cent in 2011–12. Construction remains a preferred destination, primarily due to lack of needed skills and optionality of seasonal employment. However, construction labour, consisting mainly of migrants (inter-state and inter-district) in the 18–45 age group, work in dismal safety conditions, as exploitative practices by private contractors continue unabated. The existing legislation to improve their condition—The Building and Other Construction Workers (Regulation of Employment and Conditions of Service) Act, 1996, and The Building and Other Construction Workers Welfare Cess Act (1996)—should be enforced in a stringent manner with special focus on targeted utilization of cess collected under the Act.

The provision of such rural non-farm income will help provide farmers with the cash to invest in enhancing their productivity. Creating sustainable employment opportunities in the rural non-farm sector will go a long way in helping India's rural poor to overcome barriers to economic prosperity, while preventing rapid or excessive urbanization and natural resource degradation.

NON-FARM DIVERSIFICATION

Dharamveer Singh looks forlornly at his burnt-out landscape in Tikamgarh district. His farms, along with those of his relatives, have faced one of the most vicious drought cycles to have hit India in 2016, with his wheat crop parched out. With a debt of over a ₹100,000, and the pressure of paying for his daughter's dowry, life has brought him to a fork in the road. He has few options to diversify.

In 2001, the suicide mortality rate for farmers in India was 14 per 100,000 for males in India. In comparison, the suicide mortality rate for male farmers in Maharashtra was 17 in 1995 and had increased to 53 in 2004.[5] Farmers with small holdings are typically under pressure to raise production from their limited landholdings. The average size of landholdings in India has shrunk from 1.84 hectares in 1980–81 to 1.16 hectares in 2010–11. With such a steep decline, how could farmer households possibly enrich themselves? If agriculture were to remain their sole source of income, farmers would be permanently wedded to a life of poverty.[6] This battle for subsistence usually ends in the farmer entering a vicious cycle of debt with a dismal end, or seeking avenues to bolster his non-farm income. Whenever non-agricultural rural income increases, rural poverty declines.[7] The problem of marginal farming can only be solved with the trifecta of limiting agricultural costs, raising agricultural income (particularly through ancillary activities) and pursuing non-farm income avenues.

Typically, agriculture forms the basis of any non-industrialized economy. When industrialization does occur, the higher productivity of the non-agricultural sector leads to the share of agriculture declining in the economy. Labour typically moves away from agriculture towards industry and services, while a boost in machine-led agricultural productivity helps narrow the wage gap. When countries develop, their agricultural sector approaches a 'tipping point'[8], one where agricultural income rises but most of the agricultural labour heads out of the fields and into towns and cities. Therein, an inverse relationship is observed between non-farm income and land ownership, along with household income.[9,10] Diversification towards non-farm income has led to a reduction in rural poverty and localized inequality in China.[11] Similar studies in Rwanda,[12] Burkina Faso,[13] Tanzania[14] and Jordan[15] have highlighted opposite trends, with non-farm income boosting inequality.

Non-farm diversification is typically an important pathway for empowering

---

5   Mishra, S., Suicides of Farmers in Maharashtra, Indira Gandhi Institute of Development Research, Mumbai, 2006

6   Chand, et al, 2011

7   Sen, Amartya, 1999

8   Sharma, Amrita, Bhaduri, Anik, The Tipping Point in Indian Agriculture, Understanding the Withdrawal of Indian Rural Youth

9   Adams & He, 1995

10   Adams, 2001

11   De Janvry et al., 2005

12   Dabalen et al., 2004

13   Reardon and Taylor, 1996

14   Collier et al., 1986

15   Adams, 2001

landless labourers and marginal farmers.[16] Diversification, away from marginal farming, is typically the answer[17,18,19,20]—helping to overcome the land constraint to income growth, while allowing farmers to cope with exogenous shocks through additional income; in some cases, this even allows them to reinvest in productivity-enhancing agricultural technologies.[21,22] Growth in expanding rural non-farm sectors can even absorb excess labour leaching from agriculture, helping to reduce rural to urban migration while linking farming to the wider industrial economy. India's rural economy has been gradually shifting towards non-farm activities (their share in rural income rising from 35 per cent in 1980–81 to 62 per cent in 2004–05[23]), with a similar trend in rural employment (rising from 22.3 per cent of rural employment to 31.5 per cent in 2004–05).[24]

In India, what is increasingly seen is that ~30 per cent of village youth commute to nearby towns and villages for work, working as agricultural labour, construction workers and contractual workers. Such jobs are typically low-paying and irregular. The issue remains that very few of them have the skill sets to succeed in a non-farm economy—most of them can drive, conduct electrical or mechanical work, conduct masonry or work as pure labourers.

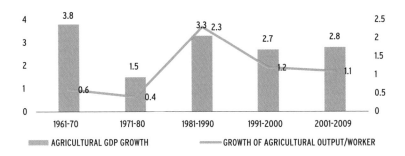

FIGURE 129: INDIA AGRICULTURE GDP GROWTH FROM 1960 TO 2010;
GROWTH OF AGRICULTURAL OUTPUT PER WORKER[25]

16   Coppard, 2001
17   Adams and He, 1995
18   Lanjouw, 1999
19   Janvry et al., 2005
20   Reardon et al., 1998
21   Collier et al., 1986
22   Reardon and Taylor, 1996
23   GoI, 2010
24   Lanjouw and Murgai, 2008
25   Binswanger-Mkhize and d'Souza, 2011

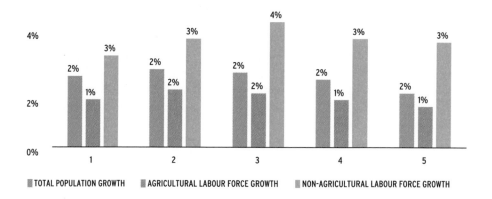

■ TOTAL POPULATION GROWTH ■ AGRICULTURAL LABOUR FORCE GROWTH ■ NON-AGRICULTURAL LABOUR FORCE GROWTH

FIGURE 130: GROWTH RATES FOR TOTAL POPULATION VS AGRICULTURAL LABOUR FORCE VS NON-AGRICULTURAL LABOUR GROWTH[26]

INCOME CONTRIBUTIONS

Marginal gains feasible from agriculture are not the sole reason for such trends—such diversification into non-farm activities is increasingly pursued by the rich and the poor, with richer households benefitting far more.[27] The causes for such patterns vary—in some places, genuine agricultural distress has led to farmers shifting to non-agricultural sources of income, while in others an agricultural surplus has boosted demand for ancillary products and services.

Consider it in terms of income contributions—agriculture is the dominant source of income for the lowest quintile of households, contributing 50 per cent of their household income in 2014, while wages, salaries and livestock contribute the majority of the remaining. For the top quintile, however, non-farm business activities and agriculture are the major income sources, comprising almost 75 per cent of their income in 2014. What this implies is that the lowest on the inequality scale rely the most on agriculture, with dependence reducing as one goes up.

26   Ibid
27   Hazel & Ramasamy, 1990

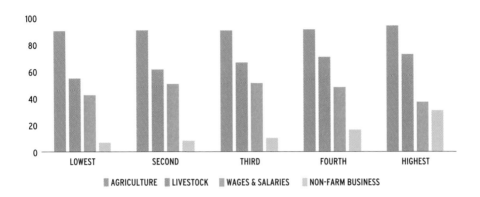

FIGURE 131: PARTICIPATION RATE, BY TYPE, ACROSS INCOME QUINTILES (PER CENT) (2014)[28]

FIGURE 132: SHARE OF INCOME, BY TYPE, ACROSS INCOME QUINTILES (PER CENT) (2014)[29]

If you consider this in landholding sizes, those with marginal or lower landholdings have non-farm income comprising over 69 per cent of their total income in 2014. As one's landholdings increase, the contribution of non-farm business income to one's total income rises.

---

28 Birthala, Pratap S., Negia, Digvijay S., Jhab, Awadesh K., Singh, Dhiraj, Income Sources of Farm Households in India: Determinants, Distributional Consequences and Policy Implications, Agricultural Economics Research Review Vol. 27 (No.1) January-June 2014, pp 37-48

29 Ibid

FIGURE 133: PARTICIPATION RATE, BY TYPE, ACROSS LANDHOLDING SIZES (PER CENT) (2014)[30]

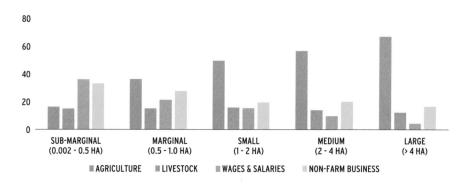

FIGURE 134: INCOME SOURCES, BY TYPE, ACROSS LANDHOLDING SIZES (PER CENT) (2014)[31]

NON-FARM INCOME OPPORTUNITIES

One might wonder—where is the excess labour going? What we term as non-farm includes both non-farm wage employment and non-farm self-employment (although excluding any agricultural wage employment)—this comprises a wide range of activities, including trading, agro-processing, construction, manufacturing and other service activities. Accessing such opportunities is a matter of education and networks.

---

30   Ibid
31   Ibid

Weaving apparel has surged significantly—rising from 1.3 per cent of non-farm employment in FY2000 to 3.2 per cent in FY12.[32] Meanwhile, wood and ancillary industries saw a significant decline in their share of employment, falling from 4.4 per cent to 0.4 per cent. Despite concerns of an oversprawling bureaucracy, public administration declined from 5.5 per cent to just 2.4 per cent, highlighting the withdrawal of the state from a variety of public services. Textile, surprisingly, has shrunk, with employment shrinking by 1.82 per cent annually. Meanwhile, construction has boomed, with its share rising from 14.4 per cent to 30.1 per cent, partly given significant infrastructure investment and the fact that construction jobs have few requirements, apart from being able-bodied. Many rural workers typically undertake construction work as non-seasonal employment, while conducting agricultural activities during peak season.[33]

However, such figures mask the type of employment. Manufacturing employment is increasingly shifting towards wage employment, while construction is focusing more on casual employment only (72 per cent of all casual workers were employed in the construction sector in FY12).[34] Meanwhile, non-farm employment has seen PSUs maintain their share (18.4 per cent in FY2000 and 19.2 per cent in FY12). There has been a definite shift towards larger enterprises—the proportion of labour working in enterprises with less than six employees declined from 60 per cent in 2000 to 41 per cent in 2012.[35] Meanwhile, the proportion of labour working for enterprises with more than ten employees grew from 32.8 per cent to 38.4 per cent.[36] However, construction saw the opposite trend, with the proportion of labour working for enterprises with more than ten employees declining from 37.7 per cent to 30.3 per cent. Most rural workers continue to work primarily in rural areas—with 86 per cent working in rural areas in 2000, which rose to 87.2 per cent in 2012.

The selection of non-farm activity is dependent on a number of factors—geographical proximity to the existing village would draw more labourers, with the cost of transport a key deterrent. Seasonality also plays a part—labourers possessing land would be 'tied' to them, unable to migrate between the sowing and the harvesting seasons, unlike landless labourers. The capital requirement associated with picking up a trade can be a significant deterrent, along with prerequisite skill sets. In this chapter, we will focus on two key sectors—livestock and construction.

---

32   National Sample Survey Organization, 2003; National Sample Survey Organization, 2013
33   Ranjan, 2009
34   NSSO, 1999-2000 and 2011-12
35   Ibid
36   Ibid

LIVESTOCK

LIVESTOCK DEMAND

Livestock production has been intrinsically linked to agricultural production for centuries. As of 2012, India had 16.4 million workers engaged in the farming of animals, conducting fishing and aquaculture.[37] As a result, India had over 300 million bovines, 65 million sheep, 135 million goats, 10 million pigs and 729 million poultry, with buffaloes, mithuns and poultry exhibiting positive growth between 2007 and 2012.[38] The livestock sector had a total output of ₹591,691 crore in 2015–16, contributing 28.5 per cent of the agricultural and allied sectors.[39] In particular, India remains the largest milk producer in the world,[40] with milk production rising from 102.6 MT at the end of the Tenth Five Year Plan (2006–07) to 155.5 MT in 2015–16, a growth rate of 6.27 per cent. Produced in over 75 million dairy farms, milk is one of India's primary agricultural commodities.[41] The performance of the livestock sector varies across states. Milk production can vary significantly—ranging from just 2 kg per cow per day in Assam to as high as 7.8 kg in Punjab.[42] Even milk yields of indigenous cows vary—from 1.1 kg per day in Odisha to 4.6 kg per day in Haryana.

Income from milk is an important constituent of livestock income. While many Union Territories registered reduction in milk production, Arunachal Pradesh and Mizoram recorded the highest growth rates in milk production, albeit helped by the low base effect. Among states of considerable size, Madhya Pradesh, Rajasthan and Andhra Pradesh, accounting for almost 28 per cent of indigenous production, grew at a CAGR of more than 8 per cent, and Haryana, Bihar and Gujarat, comprising ~18 per cent of production volumes, grew at a CAGR of 4–5 per cent.

---

37   NSSO 68th Round Survey (July 2011–June 2012)

38   19th Livestock Census

39   Annual Report, 2016–17, Department of Animal Husbandry, Dairying & Fisheries, Ministry of Agriculture & Farmers Welfare. Sourced from: http://dahd.nic.in/sites/default/files/Annual%20 Report%202016–17.pdf

40   Gandhi and Zhou, 2008

41   Delgado, Rosegrant and Meijer, 2001

42   Basic Animal Husbandry Statistics, 2008

TABLE 52: ESTIMATES OF MILK PRODUCTION DURING 2012–13 TO 2016–17 (IN '000 TONNES)
(BASIC ANIMAL HUSBANDRY & FISHERIES STATISTICS, 2017)

NO	STATE / UT	2012-13	2013-14	2014-15	2015-16	2016-17	CAGR	% SHARE OF TOTAL (2016-17)
1	ARUNACHAL PRADESH	22.72	43.35	46.07	50.13	52.53	18.2%	0.03%
2	MIZORAM	13.63	15.30	20.49	22.00	24.16	12.1%	0.01%
3	MADHYA PRADESH	8837.79	9599.20	10779.07	12148.37	13445.32	8.8%	8.13%
4	RAJASTHAN	13945.92	14573.05	16934.31	18500.08	20849.59	8.4%	12.61%
5	ANDHRA PRADESH	12761.65	13007.08	9656.15	10816.99	12177.94	8.0%	7.36%
6	LAKSHADWEEP	2.21	6.07	4.19	3.25	3.24	8.0%	0.00%
7	JAMMU & KASHMIR	1630.56	1614.67	1950.93	2273.35	2376.09	7.8%	1.44%
8	TRIPURA	118.04	129.70	141.23	152.23	159.59	6.2%	0.10%
9	SIKKIM	42.24	45.99	49.99	66.74	54.35	5.2%	0.03%
10	HARYANA	7040.24	7441.67	7901.35	8381.33	8974.75	5.0%	5.43%
11	BIHAR	6844.84	7197.06	7774.89	8288.42	8711.07	4.9%	5.27%
12	GUJARAT	10314.63	11112.18	11690.57	12262.35	12784.12	4.4%	7.73%
13	TELANGANA	-	-	4207.26	4442.45	4681.09	3.6%	2.83%
14	MAHARASHTRA	8733.69	9089.03	9542.29	10152.61	10402.15	3.6%	6.29%
15	UTTAR PRADESH	23329.55	24193.90	25198.36	26386.81	27769.74	3.5%	16.79%
16	CHHATTISGARH	1164.05	1208.61	1231.57	1277.32	1373.55	3.4%	0.83%
17	HIMACHAL PRADESH	1138.60	1150.81	1172.16	1282.86	1329.11	3.1%	0.80%
18	ODISHA	1724.40	1861.19	1903.14	1930.47	2003.42	3.0%	1.21%
19	PUNJAB	9724.34	10011.10	10351.41	10774.20	11282.06	3.0%	6.82%
20	KARNATAKA	5718.22	5997.03	6120.93	6344.01	6562.15	2.8%	3.97%
21	UTTARAKHAND	1478.38	1550.15	1565.35	1655.81	1692.42	2.7%	1.02%
22	JHARKHAND	1679.00	1699.83	1733.72	1812.38	1893.80	2.4%	1.14%
23	TAMIL NADU	7004.73	7049.19	7132.47	7243.53	7556.35	1.5%	4.57%
24	ASSAM	799.67	814.52	829.47	843.46	861.27	1.5%	0.52%
25	WEST BENGAL	4859.23	4906.21	4961.00	5038.47	5182.60	1.3%	3.13%
26	MEGHALAYA	80.52	82.16	82.96	83.95	83.96	0.8%	0.05%
27	PUDUCHERRY	47.17	47.25	47.64	48.04	48.31	0.5%	0.03%
28	NAGALAND	78.66	80.61	75.69	77.00	79.37	0.2%	0.05%
29	MANIPUR	80.03	81.70	82.17	78.97	78.82	-0.3%	0.05%
30	DELHI*	286.58	284.31	280.06	280.83	279.11	-0.5%	0.17%
31	KERALA	2790.58	2654.70	2711.13	2649.82	2520.34	-2.0%	1.52%
32	GOA	61.24	67.81	66.60	54.34	51.36	-3.5%	0.03%
33	CHANDIGARH	44.03	44.43	44.00	43.18	36.39	-3.7%	0.02%
34	A&N ISLANDS	21.45	14.21	15.56	15.43	16.14	-5.5%	0.01%
35	DADRA & NAGAR HAVELI	11.00	11.00	8.52	8.52	7.50	-7.4%	0.00%
36	DAMAN & DIU	1.00	0.82	0.82	0.80	0.62	-9.1%	0.00%
	TOTAL INDIA	132430.59	137685.89	146313.55	155490.51	165404.38	4.5%	

TABLE 53: AVERAGE YIELD PER IN- MILK ANIMAL OF EXOTIC/CROSSBRED COWS DURING 2012–13
TO 2016–17 (IN KG/DAY) (BASIC ANIMAL HUSBANDRY & FISHERIES STATISTICS 2017)
* - (INCLUDES TELANGANA FOR 2012–13 & 2013–14)

NO	STATE / UT	2012-13	2013-14	2014-15	2015-16	2016-17	CAGR
1	ANDHRA PRADESH*	7.45	7.42	7.43	7.66	7.78	0.9%
2	ARUNACHAL PRADESH	7.28	6.60	6.52	6.54	6.27	-2.9%
3	ASSAM	4.05	3.99	4.18	4.30	4.66	2.8%
4	BIHAR	6.05	6.11	6.49	6.40	6.53	1.5%
5	CHHATTISGARH	4.79	5.41	6.09	5.65	5.96	4.5%
6	GOA	6.54	6.93	7.47	7.77	7.97	4.0%
7	GUJARAT	8.81	8.94	9.08	9.00	8.96	0.3%
8	HARYANA	8.17	8.37	8.75	8.16	8.26	0.2%
9	HIMACHAL PRADESH	4.68	4.68	4.71	4.76	4.70	0.1%
10	JAMMU & KASHMIR	5.66	5.65	6.31	7.60	7.64	6.2%
11	JHARKHAND	5.94	5.99	5.82	9.00	7.29	4.2%
12	KARNATAKA	6.03	6.11	6.09	6.02	6.25	0.7%
13	KERALA	9.11	8.55	8.62	10.18 - 10.25	10.25	2.4%
14	MADHYA PRADESH	6.99	7.38	7.99	8.31	8.35	3.6%
15	MAHARASHTRA	6.89	7.18	7.38	8.31	8.62	4.6%
16	MANIPUR	7.31	7.31	7.33	7.17	7.03	-0.8%
17	MEGHALAYA	8.98	8.96	8.92	8.92	8.91	-0.2%
18	MIZORAM	6.52	6.53	6.75	7.17	7.40	2.6%
19	NAGALAND	5.30	5.40	5.33	5.50	5.45	0.6%
20	ODISHA	6.15	6.18	6.20	6.23	6.21	0.2%
21	PUNJAB	11.00	11.04	11.21	11.82	12.72	2.9%
22	RAJASTHAN*	7.67	7.75	7.93	7.80	7.74	0.2%
23	SIKKIM	5.74	5.74	5.62	5.59	5.05	-2.5%
24	TAMIL NADU	6.81	6.87	6.87	6.99	6.79	-0.1%
25	TELANGANA	-	-	7.20	7.43	7.47	0.7%
26	TRIPURA	4.93	5.40	5.58	5.64	5.69	2.9%
27	UTTAR PRADESH	7.08	7.09	7.10	7.07	7.15	0.2%
28	UTTARAKHAND	6.82	6.88	6.96	7.13	7.13	0.9%
29	WEST BENGAL	5.56	3.58	5.29	5.74	5.83	1.0%
30	A&N ISLANDS	5.88	4.54	6.13	5.77	5.72	-0.6%
31	CHANDIGARH	9.00	9.03	9.10	9.74	10.38	2.9%
32	D & N HAVELI	8.65	9.28	-	0.00-		
33	DAMAN & DIU	8.65	8.65	0.00	8.40	7.26	-3.4%
34	DELHI	5.94	5.91	-	5.92-	-	
35	LAKSHADWEEP	5.00	5.00	5.00	5.02	5.00	0.0%
36	PUDUCHERRY	5.65	5.83	5.85	6.00	5.94	1.0%
	ALL INDIA	7.02	6.78	7.15	7.45	7.51	1.4%

While milk production grew steadily, average yields from crossbred cows have remained fairly constant.

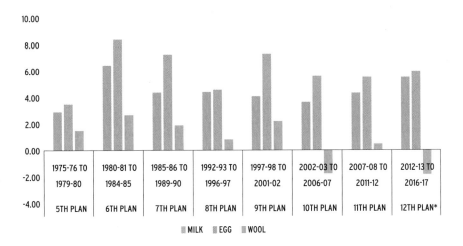

FIGURE 135: PLAN-WISE ANNUAL GROWTH RATE OF MILK, EGG, WOOL IN INDIA[43,44]

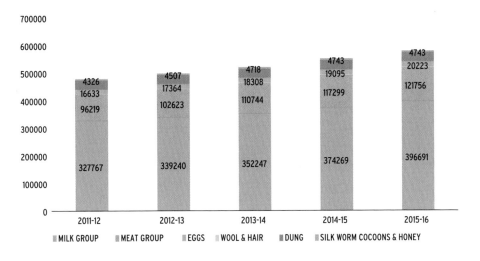

FIGURE 136: VALUE OF OUTPUT FROM LIVESTOCK SECTOR IN INDIA
(₹ CRORE IN CONSTANT 2012 PRICES)[45,46]

43   Ministry of Agriculture, Government of India, 2016
44   Indiastat, 2017
45   Central Statistical Organization, 2016
46   Indiastat, 2016

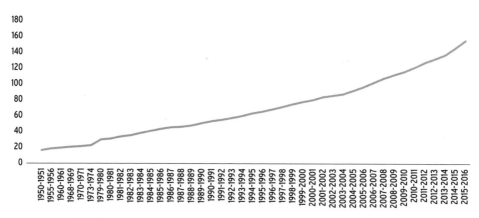

FIGURE 137: MILK PRODUCTION—INDIA (IN MILLION TONNES)[47]

TABLE 54: INDIA DEMAND PROJECTION—LIVESTOCK
(IN MILLION TONNES, EXCEPT FOR EGGS, WHICH ARE IN BILLION)[48, 49]

PRODUCT	1993	2000	2010	2020
MILK	46.18	60.77	94.3	147.21
MUTTON AND GOAT MEAT	0.83	1.36	3.81	12.72
BEEF AND BUFFALO MEAT	0.49	0.61	0.84	1.15
CHICKEN	0.25	0.33	0.52	0.81
EGGS	9.62	13.88	24.9	44.06

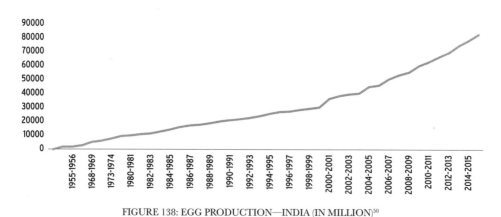

FIGURE 138: EGG PRODUCTION—INDIA (IN MILLION)[50]

---

47   Ministry of Agriculture, Government of India (16363) & Ministry of Agriculture & Farmers Welfare, Government of India (ON1353)

48   Indiastat 2017

49   Annual Report, Department of Agriculture, 2002

50   Ministry of Agriculture, Government of India (16363) & Ministry of Agriculture & Farmers Welfare, Governmen of India (ON1353)

Egg production has risen similarly, from 50.7 billion at the end of Tenth Plan (2006–07) to 66.45 at the end of the Eleventh Plan (2011–12) and 82.93 in 2015–16, with a significant concentration in southern India (~60 per cent of all eggs in India are produced in Andhra Pradesh and Tamil Nadu).[51] Poultry production is significant in coastal and urban areas, given the proximity to local demand and feed supply sources. Commercial poultry production has now shifted from 500 birds per cycle per farm to flocks approaching 3,000–50,000 birds on average.[52,53]

Sheep and goats account for about 10 per cent of the value of the livestock sector, with concentrations in certain states—goats are typically found more in Bihar, West Bengal, Uttar Pradesh and Odisha, along with more arid areas like Rajasthan, Maharashtra, Madhya Pradesh and Gujarat. Meanwhile, sheep are found more in the arid regions of Rajasthan, Maharashtra and Gujarat, along with the Himalayan states and plateaus of Andhra Pradesh, Karnataka and Tamil Nadu. The challenges in rearing sheep or goats, however, are different. In arid regions, seasonal migration is a necessity, particularly during the summer months when grazing resources are scarce. Such animals are fed on common grazing lands in states like Rajasthan, Gujarat and Maharashtra (which typically have one-fifth to one-third of their land under the 'common category'). However, in summer, herders typically migrate away from Rajasthan and Gujarat, towards irrigated areas in Haryana, Punjab, Uttar Pradesh and Madhya Pradesh. Unlike the West, where intensive feed lots are common, India's goat and sheep rearing is dependent on migration systems.

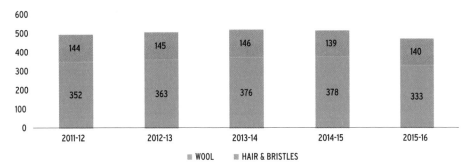

FIGURE 139: VALUE OF OUTPUT FROM LIVESTOCK WOOL SECTOR IN INDIA
(₹CRORE IN CONSTANT 2012 PRICES) [54,55]

51 Karaky, R., Jabbar, M., Shrivastava, A., Delgado, C., Borwa, S., Mghenyi, E., 'Demand-led transformation of the livestock sector in India – Achievements, Challenges & Opportunities', June 2011, The World Bank Group. Sourced from: http://documents.worldbank.org/curated/en/668321468041641776/pdf/689010ESW0P0990the0Livestock0setcor.pdf

52 Mehta, Nambiar, et al

53 Broiler, Egg, 2003

54 Central Statistical Organization, 2016

55 IndiaStat, 2016

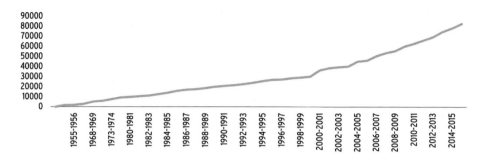

FIGURE 140: WOOL PRODUCTION – INDIA (IN MT) [56]

This is a demand-led growth, with changing tastes in the urban and rural populations. The share of animal products in rural household expenditures has risen from 21.8 per cent in 1983 to 25 per cent in 2005–06 in urban areas, while rural India saw an increase from 16.1 per cent in 1983 to 22.6 per cent in 2005–06. Between 1983 and 2000, the per capita consumption of livestock products increased sharply, with milk consumption nearly doubling from 43 kg per capita to 73.5 kg per capita.[57] Similarly, poultry-meat consumption rose by 122 per cent between 1983 and 2000, while similar increases were observed in bovine meat consumption and pork consumption. Both poor and rich households increasingly consumed animal products, with per capita animal-product consumption doubling in poor households between 1983 and 2000.

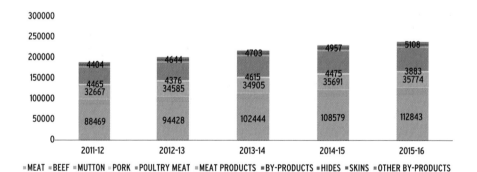

FIGURE 141: VALUE OF OUTPUT FROM LIVESTOCK MEAT SECTOR IN INDIA
(₹CRORE IN CONSTANT 2012 PRICES)[58,59]

56   Ministry of Agriculture, Government of India (16363) & Ministry of Agriculture & Farmers Welfare, Government of India (ON1353)

57   Kumar, Mruthyunjaya and Birthal, Changing Consumption Pattern in South Asia (2007)

58   Central Statistical Organization, 2016

59   Indiastat, 2016

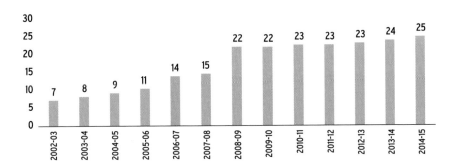

FIGURE 142: PER CAPITA AVAILABILITY OF EGGS IN GUJARAT (NOS./YEAR)[60]

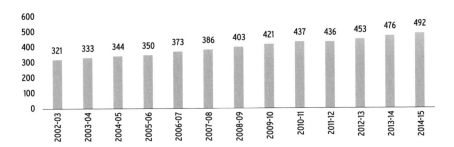

FIGURE 143: PER CAPITA AVAILABILITY OF MILK IN GUJARAT (GM/DAY)[61]

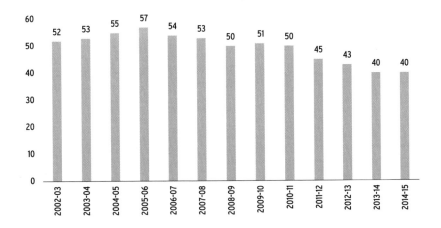

FIGURE 144: PER CAPITA AVAILABILITY OF WOOL IN GUJARAT (GM/DAY)[62]

60   Directorate of Animal Husbandry, Government of Gujarat, 2016
61   Ibid
62   Ibid

And yet, the proportion of landless households holding livestock has declined—landless households owned 9.3 per cent of all poultry and pigs in 1982; by 2003, this had declined to less than 1 per cent for cattle or buffalo, 2.8 per cent for small ruminants and 4.7 per cent for poultry.[63] Meanwhile, common grazing resources decreased by 35 per cent between the same period, as a consequence of privatization, government land redistribution and encroachment by farmers for expanding crop production, along with overexploitation and improper management. This is a cruel irony; those agricultural labourers in need of greater non-farm income are unable to afford the upkeep of livestock which could give them one.

Consider the example of the Rajasthan Microfinance Initiative—launched in March 2003 to conduct livelihood development in three districts of Rajasthan (Dholpur, Dausa and Tonk). The Trust has been supporting a range of organizations that seek to provide subsidies to the poor for undertaking income-enhancement activities. In Tonk, 1,250 women have been provided with 1,613 buffaloes, while support clusters have been organized to provide veterinary services, collect milk and provide feed. Women deciding to become members are given a credit facility, with the amount adjusted against the milk collected from them. The NGOs have also sought to establish marketing linkages with a private dairy company, leading to an increase in return of ₹3–₹4 per litre for each member.[64]

The sector has historically provided significant employment to the rural population, engaging 6.8 per cent of the labour force in 1994, and 8.8 per cent in 2005. Regional variation amongst India's states highlights the sector's contribution—~40–48 per cent of all agricultural employment in Punjab and Haryana in 2005 was provided by livestock. Beyond statistics, the role of women in the care of livestock lies mostly unnoticed, given their traditional responsibility of feeding, breeding and managing livestock. This ingrained preference is why women, even now, utilize micro-credit schemes to purchase livestock—it can serve as a source of credit, nutrition, draft power and even natural fertilizer. Employment in this sector, however informal, empowers women in the larger rural society.

In addition, it can, in certain regions, be the primary source of income. Arid zones in India have seen livestock's share of the household income in rural areas average 36 per cent, increasing to 39 per cent among those with less than 0.5 hectares of land.[65] Typically, the higher the share of livestock in agricultural income, the lower the chances of that household being in poverty. Studies have indicated a strong negative correlation between livestock sector growth and rural poverty reduction.[66]

---

63   Jha, Birthal, Joseph, Livestock Production and the Poor in India, 2006
64   Sirohi, 2008
65   Jha, Birthal, Joseph, Livestock Production and the Poor in India, 2006; Birthal, 2008
66   Birthal, Taneja, 2006

Dairying provided ~12.5 per cent of family income in 2015 for landless households, which remain constrained only by funding to expand the scope of their business.[67]

TABLE 55: EXPORT OF LIVESTOCK AND LIVESTOCK PRODUCTS FROM INDIA
(2013–14, 2014–15 AND 2015–16—UP TO OCTOBER 2016) (₹CR) [68,69]

LIVESTOCK	EXPORT (PROGRESSIVE)		
	2013-2014	2014-2015*	2015-2016#
AQUATIC ANIMALS (PRAWN, SHRIMP, CRAB, ETC.)	12,674	24,34,614	00
BIRDS (WILD, DOMESTIC)	-	7	4
BUFFALOES	-	-	00
CATS	379	298	268
CATTLE	-	-	-
DOGS	1,335	1,191	996
EARTHWORMS	80,000	-	-
FISH	7,25,772	39,7760	00
G.P. CHICKS, INCLUDING DUCKLINGS	3,47,503	1,94,774	3,090
HORSES/OTHER EQUIDAE	59	41	65
LAB. ANIMALS (GUINEA PIGS, RATS, MICE, RABBITS, FROGS, HAMSTERS, ETC.)	204	2	268
LLAMAS	-	-	-
REPTILES/SQUIRRELS (CROCODILES, TORTOISES, LIZARDS, SNAKES, ETC.)	10	-	-
SHEEP/GOATS	600	790	-
ZOO ANIMALS (TIGERS, GIRAFFES, WOLVES, CHIMPANZEES, ETC.)	29	-	0
LIVESTOCK PRODUCTS (KG, SPECIFY OTHERS, E.G. LITRES, NOS., DOSES, ETC.)	-	-	-
ANIMAL BYPRODUCTS (CASEIN GLUE, OX GALL, BILE ACID, OX BILE POWDER SUTURES,GOAT BEZOUR, ACID LAC, CHOLECALCIFEROL, CHOLIC ACID, CHONDROITIN SULFATE, ETC.)	3,58,780	7,74,621.85	59,932.725
ANIMAL FEED (POULTRY, MICE, HORSES, CATTLE, ETC.)	5345698	535940	3546981.715
AQUATIC BYPRODUCTS (CORAL, SHELLS, POWDER WASTE, ETC.)	75	860408	28.5
BACTERIAL CULTURE (LACTOBACILLUS, PROBIOTICS)	-	-	00
BONE & BONE PRODUCTS (INCLUDING CRUSHED BONES, GRIST, BUTTONS, PEARLS, HANDICRAFT ITEMS, ETC.)	22625523	5875706.2	958737.5
CASINGS (BOVINE, SHEEP)	51004	9653	224190
EGGS/EGG POWDER	6994199	955267	-
EGGS/SEEDS OF AQUATIC ANIMALS (INCLUDING FISH)	-	-	-

67   Karaky, R., Jabbar, M., Shrivastava, A., Delgado, C., Borwa, S., Mghenyi, E., 'Demand-Led Transformation of the Livestock Sector in India – Achievements, Challenges & Opportunities', June 2011, The World Bank Group. Sourced from: http://documents.worldbank.org/curated/en/668321468041641776/pdf/689010ESW0P0990the0Livestock0setcor.pdf
68   Ministry of Agriculture, Government of India, 2016
69   Indiastat, 2017

EMBRYOS (BOVINE)	-	-	-
EMBRYOS (OVINE, CAPRINE)	-	-	-
FEATHER (INCLUDING PROCESSED, SHUTTLE COCKS, BRUSHES, PILLOWS, ETC.)	26827.13	14821.185	49024.25
FERTILIZERS	-	-	0.00
FISH FEED/OIL/PASTE (INCLUDING PRAWN FEED, SHRIMP FEED, ARTEMIA CYSTS, ETC.)	21353657	13075494	10241157
FISH & FISH MEAT PRODUCTS (RAW, CHILLED, FROZEN, SMOKED, ETC.)	18796761	13528854	3186657.7
FUR SKIN (TANNED/DRESSED) (INCLUDING HEADS, TAILS, PAWS AND OTHER PIECES)	-	-	-
GELATIN/OSSEIN/GLUES (PRODUCTS, CAPSULES, SHEETS, DERIVATIVES)	4807751	9568197.586	2133927.23
HATCHING EGGS (DUCK, POULTRY)	400830	24844704	10913824
HOOVES, HORNS, NAILS, CLAWS, BEAK & HORN CORES (PRODUCTS, DRIED MEAL, CORES, GRIST, BUTTONS, HANDICRAFT ITEMS, ETC.)	67514873	2052929.5	1528518.55
LEATHER OF BOVINE, EQUINE, SHEEP, GOAT, SWINE, REPTILE, ETC. (WETBLUE, FINISHED, TANNED CRUST, POWDER, FLOUR, LAMINATED, ETC.)	7140606	5399991.59	9394755
MEAT & MEAT PRODUCTS (PORK)	-	-	00
MEAT & MEAT PRODUCTS (POULTRY)	2365706	1607187.4	25200
MEAT & MEAT PRODUCTS (LAMB, GOAT)	-	-	265405
MEDICAMENTS AND DIAGNOSTICS (INCLUDING ALBUMIN, IN-VITRO USE BLOOD/ SERUM FRACTION, DRUG OF ANIMAL ORIGIN, HEPARIN, ETC.)	249.99	3485.274	2169.99
MILK & MILK PRODUCTS (CHEESE, GHEE, WHEY POWDER, CASEIN, ICE-CREAM, BUTTER, YOGURT, LACTOSE OIL, ETC.)	18082059	6586557.34	80244744
MISCELLANEOUS (SILK, HONEY, CANDY, CHOCOLATE, ETC.)	1613649	2070395.45	8345918
PET FOOD/DOG CHEWS	11241512	4305532.628	3279924.48
PIG/HOG/BOAR BRISTLES/HAIR (BADGES, BRUSHES)	1300	1760	9934
RAW FUR SKIN (INCLUDING HEADS, TAILS, PAWS AND OTHER PIECES)	-	-	-
RAW SKIN/HIDES OF BOVINE, EQUINE, SHEEP, GOAT, SWINE (FRESH, PICKLED, LIMED, SALTED, DRIED, PRESERVED BUT NOT TANNED)	5079149	136184	189000
RAW SKIN/OTHER PARTS OF BIRDS (WITH/WITHOUT FEATHERS)	90366	-	0
READY-TO EAT-ITEMS (BISCUITS, SNACKS, PROCESSED FOOD, ETC.)	7599041	357007479.8	7435345.6
SEMEN (DOSES) (BOVINE)	6000	300	57
SEMEN (DOSES) (SWINE)	-	-	0
SERUM (LTR.) (BOVINE)	-	981.23	00
SERUM (LTR.) (OTHER ANIMALS—SPECIFY)	-	-	23609.854
SPF EGGS (NOS.)	-	-	720
SWEETS	-	2696421.48	3183684
VACCINES	-	185000	00
WOOL/HAIR/YARN (SHEEP, GOAT, RABBIT, HORSE)	-	654345.1	344624.4

Livestock helps address problems of rural poverty, mainly caused by low level of assets and an uncertain and low return on those assets. Land and livestock are two major types of assets for a rural household, especially for small and marginal households. As the average farm size shrinks with time, livestock remains a potent potential option for households to support their income on a sustained basis.

TABLE 56: RURAL POVERTY ACROSS MAJOR STATES (IN PER CENT)

STATES	1983	1987-88	1993-94	1999-2000
ANDHRA PRADESH	26.5	20.9	15.9	11.1
ASSAM	42.6	39.4	45	40
BIHAR	64.4	52.6	58.2	44.3
GUJARAT	29.8	28.7	22.2	13.2
HARYANA	20.6	16.2	28	8.3
KARNATAKA	36.3	32.8	29.9	17.4
KERALA	39	27.1	25.8	9.4
MADHYA PRADESH	48.9	41.9	40.6	37.1
MAHARASHTRA	45.2	40.8	37.9	23.7
ODISHA	67.5	57.6	49.7	48
PUNJAB	13.2	12.6	12	6.4
RAJASTHAN	33.5	33.2	26.5	13.7
TAMIL NADU	54	45.8	32.5	20.6
UTTAR PRADESH	46.5	41.1	42.3	31.2
WEST BENGAL	63.1	48.3	40.8	31.9
ALL INDIA	45.6	39.1	37.3	27.1

SOURCE: PLANNING COMMISSION OF INDIA

The table above illustrates rural poverty across major states—a faster decline is witnessed in states that experience faster growth in either agriculture or livestock—mainly Punjab, Haryana, Andhra Pradesh, Gujarat, Karnataka, Kerala, Maharashtra and Tamil Nadu. Usually, livestock share in agricultural output demonstrates an inverse relation with rural poverty.

Livestock as a business remains highly concentrated amongst small farmers, who own ~78 per cent of the total ruminant population in India.[70] Forty-four per cent of all farm households are currently associated with dairy. Rajasthan and Maharashtra's arid regions see a greater level of consolidation, with large farmers (with over 4 hectares of land each) controlling 35–40 per cent of the ruminant

70 Birthal, Overview, 2008

population. Meanwhile, in Bihar, Odisha and West Bengal, small landholders (with less than 4 hectares of land each) own over 78 per cent of the ruminant population.[71] Marginal farmers typically consider such small ruminants a significant source of income—marginal farmers and landless labourers in Bihar usually rear goats with a holding size of one to three per family. Similarly, poultry is reared by such farmers, albeit in a more disorganized manner, with flocks ranging from two to as many as thirty birds.[72] Business on this scale is challenged by rather mundane issues—limited skill sets associated with rearing and management of livestock, disease prevention, limited marketability and poor genetic stock. Livestock share of contribution to Gross Value Added (GVA) at current basic prices has been on an increase, as witnessed from the table below:

TABLE 57: PERCENTAGE CONTRIBUTION OF LIVESTOCK IN TOTAL AGRICULTURE GVA

	GVA AT CONSTANT (2011-12) BASIC PRICES					GVA AT CURRENT BASIC PRICES				
	GVA AGRICULTURE		GVA LIVESTOCK			GVA AGRICULTURE		GVA LIVESTOCK		
	(₹ CR)	(% TO GVA)	(₹ CR)	(% TO GVA)	(% TO AGRICULTURE)	(₹ CR)	(% TO GVA)	(₹ CR)	(% TO GVA)	(% TO AGRICULTURE)
2011-12	982,151	12.1	327,334	4.0	21.8	982,151	12.1	327,334	4.0	21.8
2012-13	983,809	11.5	344,375	4.0	22.6	1,088,814	11.8	368,823	4.0	22.0
2013-14	1,037,060	11.4	363,558	4.0	22.6	1,248,776	12.1	422,733	4.1	21.9
2014-15	997,959	10.3	390,436	4.0	24.3	1,277,590	11.1	510,020	4.4	24.7
2015-16	975,739	9.3	415,949	4.0	25.7	1,312,189	10.5	560,613	4.5	25.8

SOURCE: BASIC ANIMAL HUSBANDRY & FISHERIES STATISTICS, 2017

SECTORAL ISSUES

India has followed a two-track approach to livestock since Independence. In one, the dairy revolution occurred, via Operation Flood (launched in 1970), seeking to replicate a farmer-based cooperative model in livestock rearing. The programme scaled up dairy development across India, while enabling private participation, leading to 12.4 million farmer members by 2005–06, of whom 3.4 million were women, all belonging to over 117,575 cooperative societies across 346 districts.[73]

---

71 Birthal, Overview, 2008

72 Karaky, Rabih, Jabbar, Mohammed, Shrivastava, Animesh, Delgado, Christopher, Borwa, Saswati, Mghenyi, Elliot, Demand-Led Transformation of the Livestock Sector in India – Achievements, Challenges & Opportunities, June 2011, The World Bank Group. Sourced from: http://documents. worldbank.org/curated/en/668321468041641776/pdf/689010ESW0P0990the0Livestock0setcor.pdf

73 Ibid

The states that received this largesse, primarily in western and southern India, gained the majority of cooperative dairy-processing plants. By 2005–06, Punjab had thirteen cooperative dairy plants and Gujarat sixteen, while Bihar had just seven and West Bengal merely two.[74] States with a history of milk consumption benefitted the most—Punjab, Haryana, Kerala, Tamil Nadu, Gujarat, Rajasthan and Andhra Pradesh while those that were backward (e.g. Bihar, Madhya Pradesh, West Bengal and Odisha) remained so. A majority of the total processing capacity (private and government) in 2005–06 was established in the former set. States that already had a relatively low rate of poverty incidence have done well in livestock rearing. In Punjab and Haryana,[75] the livestock sector produces a third of the agricultural output by value; meanwhile, rural poverty rates in these states are below 10 per cent. Such successful states have not just pursued higher dairy production but have used institutions and processes established in dairy production to improve the quality and productivity of other stock animals and poultry. Similarly, poultry production in the southern states was raised through improved layering, greater private investment in modernization across the process (i.e. breeding, hatching, feeding) and investments in marketing and processing.[76] Success stories remain few and far—consider Kegg Farms, which has bred an improved backyard chicken (termed Kuroiler), which can lay 100–150 eggs a year, growing to 2.5 kg in the same time a local chicken would reach 1 kg. The firm now produces over 16 million day-old chicks that are distributed down branches to pheriwallas, who sell them to female customers in villages, with sales made to ~1 million farmers. The business has scaled up significantly, while creating thousands of jobs in rural business selling chicks.[77, 78]

In summary, support for livestock is driven by a top-down strategy—technology is typically transferred to progressive farmers, while large ruminants are mostly ignored; instead, milk production is prioritized, with support services concentrated in more urbanized areas, with inherent gender biases ignored.

---

74 NDDB Annual Report, 2006-2007

75 Planning Commission, 2008

76 Landes, Persaud, Dyck, India's Poultry Sector: Development and Prospects, 2004

77 Dixie, 2008

78 Subrahmanyam, Murthy, 2006

SUPPORT SERVICES

Research on livestock continues to be relatively limited, with expenditure on animal science research as a percentage of overall spending on livestock barely exceeding 3 per cent in the period 1990–91 and 2004–05. This is despite the inclusion of research by (ICAR)—the share of animal science in research staff at ICAR has hovered around 17 per cent over the last few decades.[79] Much of this research continues to be disciplinary-focused, while issues that need solutions remain multidimensional, with limited coordination between agencies collecting statistics and discipline-focused research staff. The linkage between research and market scale-up remains poor, with few extensions in livestock—The Agricultural Technology Management Agency (ATMA) approach to coordinating agricultural extensions was piloted and has now been adopted, with the model seeking to have the public-sector research staff operate at the block level, in conjunction with private players like farmer organizations, agri businesses and agro-clinics.[80] Instead, many NGOs like Bharatiya Agro Industries Foundation (BAIF), Pradan, Basix and Anthra conduct dissemination activities.

TABLE 58: TARGETS AND ACHIEVEMENTS UNDER NATIONAL LIVESTOCK MISSION (NLM) IN INDIA (2015, 2016)[81,82]

QUANTIFIABLE DELIVERABLE	2014–15		2015–16	
	TARGET	ACHIEVEMENT	TARGET	ACHIEVEMENT
ENTREPRENEURSHIP DEVELOPMENT AND EMPLOYMENT GENERATION (EDEG)- NUMBER OF UNITS TO BE COVERED	1700	14488	1360	12051
RAM DISTRIBUTION BY CENTRAL SHEEP BREEDING FARM (IN NUMBERS)	900	783	360	521
BUCK DISTRIBUTION BY CENTRAL SHEEP BREEDING FARM (IN NUMBERS)	300	131	72	22
INDIGENOUS THREATENED BREEDS TO BE CONSERVED (NUMBER OF BREEDS)	10	2	2	-
PARENT STOCK OF LOW INPUT TECHNOLOGY VARIETY SUPPLIED BY CENTRAL POULTRY DEVELOPMENT ORGANIZATION (NUMBER IN THOUSANDS)	100	135	40	68.13
ANIMALS TO BE PROVIDED WITH INSURANCE COVER (NUMBER IN THOUSANDS)	1500	1650	660	652
PRODUCTION OF HIGH-YIELDING FODDER SEED VARIETIES (IN QUINTALS)	70000	40573.43	26000	43690
GRASSLAND TO BE DEVELOPED	1400	535	560	77.5

---

79 Birthal, 2008
80 Saha 2001, Conroy, 2004
81 Lok Sabha Unstarred Question No. 68, dated 21 July 2015, & Lok Sabha Unstarred Question No. 1770 dated on 8 March 2016
82 Indiastat, 2017

ARTIFICIAL INSEMINATION

Raising productivity in livestock continues to be a hard ask. Despite significant interbreeding, India's cow-milk yield is about half of the world's average, and about one-fifth that of developed countries. A study indicates that most bovine species only reach 26–54 per cent of their purported yields, given feed and fodder scarcity, poor animal health and insufficient veterinary and breeding services.

Similarly, with small ruminants, like sheep, genetic stock becomes an issue. Less than 10 per cent of all sheep are improved breeds, while the rest suffer from high mortality rates.[83] The upkeep of such animals draws little institutional attention, with greater preference given to dairy animals. There is little marketing support to speak of, while credit and insurance products remain in their infancy.

Supporting the rearing and upkeep of livestock requires a range of services—production services that assist breeding and feeding, along with providing credit and insurance; health services that focus on both prevention and cure, along with disease surveillance; and, finally, market-linked services that provide price information and marketing of the output.[84] India's strategy for improving breeds has focused primarily on cross-breeding, with little to no attention paid to appropriately selecting and grading from local breeds. The problem, however, is that many cross-bred foreign breeds fail to adapt to Indian climatic conditions, while being affected by feed shortages and disease. A few states, like Andhra Pradesh and Tamil Nadu, have taken the lead in utilizing artificial insemination to conduct breed improvement in state animal husbandry department centres. India's National Dairy Plan has sought to raise artificial insemination of 35 per cent of all fertile cattle by 2018.[85]

The usage of artificial insemination in India lags primarily because of its stationary nature, with the farmer required to bring his cattle to their doorstep for insemination—there is no concept of door-to-door service delivery, reducing their utilization rate. Such artificial insemination services have limited monitoring and performance appraisal, while there is limited regulatory oversight of the breeding activity (including semen production and delivery).[86] Most supporting infrastructure continues to remain inadequate, with few semen centres and stations, liquid nitrogen plants and semen banks, while inseminators remain poorly trained.

---

83   Subrahmanyam, Murthy, 2006
84   Redmond, Ahuja, 2004
85   Rao, Smitha, Srinivasan, Krithika, Kasturirangan, Rajesh, 'Dark and dairy: the sorry tale of the milch animals'
86   Singh, Chauhan, 2006; Singh, 2006

While pricing for artificial insemination by government providers is heavily subsidized (~₹20–₹40 per insemination vs an actual cost of ₹200), transaction charges (e.g. bribing the insemination staff to conduct the insemination on time) can be a constraint. In comparison, private players charge higher fees but provide service at the farmer's doorstep, leading to a lower effective cost per calf, with farmers turning repeat buyers.[87]

Meanwhile, buffaloes, which provide over half the milk production in India, get limited attention in government-breeding programmes, while small ruminants like pigs get limited and ineffective breeding support. The All India Coordinated Research Projects (AICRP) (under the ICAR), along with state agricultural universities, have sought to set up breeding farms and breeding centres to promote and finance cross-breeding programmes for sheep and goats. However, scale-up remains a necessity for the implementation of their mandate.

The private sector has taken the lead in breeding commercial poultry, linked to contract farming. In comparison, backyard poultry remains heavily neglected, with 95 per cent of India's poultry-breeding farms and hatcheries under non-government institutions. Studies have found that ~25–30 per cent of all backyard poultry eggs fail to produce chicks, given egg sterility, bacterial contamination and improper storage.

---

87   Sirohi, 2008

PROVISIONING FEED

North India typically sees plain rice straw and wheat straw produced and utilized as animal feed. Post-harvesting, shredded wheat straw and rice straw are typically burnt, leading to extensive air pollution in the winter months in Delhi. Some of this straw is pulverized and palletized in a feed mill, with enrichment using molasses or urea, allowing it to be stored, transported and consumed easily. The provisioning of feed varies widely, with ~44 per cent of the 890 MT of feed produced in 2005 estimated to come from crop residue and ~34 per cent from planted fodder, while the remaining was sourced from forests, fallow land, wastelands and common property.[88] This feed can vary across ecological zones, with irrigated areas offering more than arid zones. Public and private sector support, when available, is usually focused on developing high-yielding varieties of fodder and fodder seeds, while training field officers, demonstrating modernized agronomy practices to farmers and distributing fodder seed mini-kits. New varieties of high-yielding fodder seeds have remained far from commercialization. The degradation of common property resources will eventually have an impact on the supply of feed for landless labourers and small holders—for them livestock is valued for their monetary value as well as non-monetary benefits (as food or as risk management). Permanent pastures and grazing lands have been reduced by 25 per cent between 1960–61 and 2004–05.[89]

The Karnataka Watershed Development Project (Sujala), supported by the World Bank, has shown the way forward for managing common lands—the programme commissioned an exhaustive study to define benefit-sharing rules, roles and responsibilities, with MoUs being signed between local government agencies and NGOs on the usage of common lands. Such benefit-sharing mechanisms have evolved into common land-management mechanisms, with participation motivated by the prospect of regular employment.[90]

In addition, the cost of raw materials and products remains a major concern for feed manufacturers, impacting the demand for feed—a sharp increase in wholesale prices for major feed ingredients (maize, rapeseed and mustard cake) since the '90s has led to further increases in feed prices. The rapid rise in cattle-feed prices has come despite slower increases in fodder and milk. Addressing feed availability will require greater attention to feed scarcity in flood-prone areas like Bihar and Assam; while food security is often addressed in the event of floods, feed scarcity is rarely considered.

---

88   National Institute of Animal Nutrition and Physiology, 2005
89   Directorate of Economics and Statistics, Ministry of Agriculture, Government of India, 2011
90   Milne, 2009

TABLE 59: STATE-WISE FUNDS RELEASED FOR FEED AND FODDER DEVELOPMENT UNDER NATIONAL LIVESTOCK MISSION IN INDIA (2011–12 TO 2016–17 UP TO 21 MARCH 2016)[91]

STATES/UT	2011-2012	2012-2013	2013-2014	2014-2015	2015-2016	2016-2017*
ANDAMAN AND NICOBAR ISLANDS	-	-	-	-	-	2.25
ANDHRA PRADESH	0.00	473.70	1234.10	-	-	558.00
ARUNACHAL PRADESH	55.00	-	255.50	-	-	-
ASSAM	218.20	-	209.00	-	-	-
BIHAR	0.00	-	-	343.00	0.00	-
CHHATTISGARH	65.20	65.20	234.20	0.00	212.61	41.57
GOA	-	-	9.80	-	-	-
GUJARAT	1368.40	1163.70	896.30	1500.00	0.00	937.22
HARYANA	120.00	32.30	220.00	490.00	0.00	-
HIMACHAL PRADESH	0.00	-	525.00	74.99	0.00	-
JAMMU & KASHMIR	213.40	361.00	866.20	-	-	-
JHARKHAND	0.00	415.40	864.70	500.00	0.00	200.00
KARNATAKA	0.00	894.20	-	0.00	422.00	1.04
KERALA	130.30	-	-	-	-	-
MADHYA PRADESH	199.00	34.60	44.50	-	-	-
MAHARASHTRA	376.30	1825.40	2643.40	157.14	500.00	1338.21
MANIPUR	0.00	-	-	-	-	-
MEGHALAYA	0.00	-	12.10	-	-	-
MIZORAM	0.00	278.00	213.00	-	-	-
NAGALAND	127.80	56.00	-	39.94	23.25	-
ODISHA	0.00	45.00	-	178.50	72.60	131.40
PUNJAB	0.00	845.50	-	-	-	-
RAJASTHAN	0.00	270.80	-	0.00	338.82	177.45
SIKKIM	124.00	128.50	150.00	7.65	15.11	-
TAMIL NADU	0.00	20.60	77.00	600.00	0.00	-
TRIPURA	0.00	36.50	10.40	5.70	0.00	-
UTTAR PRADESH	0.00	152.00	267.80	321.00	0.00	-
UTTARAKHAND	247.40	122.50	174.30	0.00	101.55	-
WEST BENGAL	0.00	228.40	5.20	550.35	0.00	27.72
INDIA	3251.00	7449.00	8912.20	4768.27	1685.94	3414.85

91   Lok Sabha Unstarred Question No. 3319, dated 17 March 2015, Lok Sabha Unstarred Question No. 1400, dated 08 December 2015, Lok Sabha Unstarred Question No. 4212, dated 28 March 2017 and Lok Sabha Unstarred Question No. 3183, dated 21 March 2017

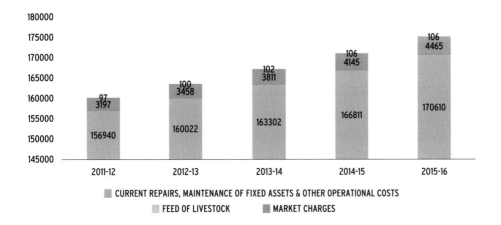

FIGURE 145: VALUE OF INPUT FOR LIVESTOCK SECTOR IN INDIA
(₹CRORE IN CONSTANT 2012 PRICES)[92,93]

ACCESS TO CREDIT

Livestock requirements typically gain 10 per cent of total agricultural term loans, with allocation rates varying (e.g., between 1998 and 2006, the allocation ranged from 2.5–5.5 per cent).[94,95] Formal credit is still limited, with livestock owners typically turning to local moneylenders and non-governmental organizations for funding. Typically most banks only finance the purchase of two or more animals, in small units, with the amount disbursed less than the cost of the animal, while 10–11 per cent of the loan is utilized for meeting non-interest credit costs.[96,97,98] Most banks typically require a detailed financial projection report highlighting projected revenues for financing any commercial project, but there is limited institutional support for creating such techno-commercial feasibility reports. Even now, under NABARD, the primary credit assistance to dairy farmers is provided by cooperative banks.[99]

---

92   Central Statistical Organization, 2016
93   IndiaStat, 2016
94   Birthal, Overview, 2008
95   National Bank for Agriculture and Rural Development, 2008
96   Krishnan, Krishnan, 1989
97   Singh, Nanda, Dahiya, 1995
98   Sinha, 1999
99   NABARD, 2007

It's not that the sector has been completely ignored—the Kisan Credit Card Scheme launched in 1998 sought to simplify procedures to obtain institutional credit—a number of microcredit institutions have also emerged, but there remains no integrated sector-wide strategy to promote microfinance in the livestock sector. A number of state governments have launched schemes to protect livestock—Rajasthan has launched the Avikavach scheme for sheep flock owners. Livestock insurance has existed, but outreach has been limited; insurance typically covers less than 10 per cent of all livestock (excluding poultry)—in comparison, most commercial poultry farmers typically seek insurance coverage to reduce the exposure to the high risk of mass mortality.[100] Low coverage continues due to low awareness, limited affordability, issues in loan settlement and high transaction costs.[101] Private players are increasingly entering the market, with BASIX seeking to distribute livestock insurance products. However, addressing moral hazards and adverse selection remains a hard ask.

Access to finance remains limited by a multitude of factors. Primarily, interest charged in rural areas remains higher than in urban areas because of higher transaction costs, driven by demand-side constraints like highly dispersed, hard-to-reach communities, low levels of economic activity, and supply-side constraints like weak infrastructure, financial service providers with limited capacity and a narrow range of financial products. Yet, despite higher interest charges, the formal loan system rates are usually less than the rates charged by local moneylenders. This results in credit from financial institutions to flow to households that are better off financially and meeting the financial requirements for taking a loan from financial institutions.

Understanding local conditions and customizing solutions catering to the local community matters—without an insightful understanding of a household's cash flow and local demand for types of financial services, such steps can misfire by burdening people, especially the poor, with additional loans. In areas where credit has been extended through non-customized means by government-owned financial channels, we have witnessed low repayment rates, low customer service, poor monitoring and limited prospects for sustainability. Strengthening local infrastructure and reducing transaction costs to reach the marginalized communities, alongside increasing competition in the livestock credit space, can improve the situation for marginalized farmers.[102] To counter the limitations of the conventional credit system, the Provincial Development Programme of Central Java province offers a solution. It provides a 'credit-in-kind' arrangement for loan repayment. Under the system, beneficiaries are divided into groups of ten, with

---

100 Chawla, Kurup and Sharma, Animal Husbandry: State of the Indian Farmer, 2004
101 Raju, Chand, 2008
102 Livestock & Rural Finance, IFAD

each member receiving two female goats or sheep and the leader being trained in ruminant management and a good-quality buck/ram. The repayment is in 'kind'—with each member having to provide four eight-month-old lambs or kids over a three-year period. Such a programme could be replicated, which could lead to an increase in farmer income, improve group dynamics among farmers and production of existing livestock, and introduce new technologies into livestock management.

Such a 'credit-in-kind' model also negates the adverse impact of subsidized credit, which doesn't even cover the cost of service provision. Credit provision on unreal terms, if not successful, will end up making farmers indebted and hurt the ability of financial institutions through low revenues and low repayment rates, thereby impacting their ability and intent of making additional loans for livestock development.

The factors behind the establishment of a formal bank, the Mahila Shakti Gramkosh, also provides valuable insights. The Maldhari Rural Action Group (MARAG) provided financial assistance to local livestock owners, primarily with a view to creating sustenance and development opportunities among the marginalized communities in the Kutch region, severely affected by the earthquake of 2001. The World Initiative for Sustainable Pastoralism (WISP) provided small loans to pastoralist women, initially with the aim of helping them in their daily activities. The women were to develop a group strategy to initiate and promote income generation activities and repay the loan through resulting income-generation. With a view to paying back the principal amount, the women started local savings groups to collect and save money for repayment. Within just two years, the loan was repaid and the bank established, linked with national banks for access to additional capital for lending. All bank activities, including general management, loan processing and recoveries, and governance are carried out by pastoral women, with MARAG acting as a facilitator.

Other countries also offer insightful solutions. Mongolia has launched an index-based livestock-insurance scheme, seeking to share risks amongst herders—the scheme has elements of self-insurance, market linkage and social obligations, with herders retaining small losses that don't affect the viability of their insurance, while larger losses are held by the private insurance industry and catastrophic losses covered by the government. Herders are asked to pay premiums for the base insurance, with individual herders paid whenever mortality rates exceed local regional thresholds (reflecting the climate, whether hot or cold, and historical mortality rates). Moral hazards and the risk of adverse selection are hence reduced, thereby reducing costs. Adopting this would require maintaining data for a livestock mortality index—Mongolia looks at a 33-year series on adult animal mortality, broken up into regions, and across animal species (whether cattle, yak, horse, sheep or goat).[103]

Once access to financial services for rural households is granted, the farmers can be assisted by cooperatives and SHGs, as witnessed under the Income-Generating Project for Marginal Farmers and the Landless (P4K) in Indonesia. The success of programmes in the Niger delta illustrates that both formal and informal rural financial institutions, including commercial banks, development banks, credit NGOs and cooperatives, need to adapt to the user's requirements and local conditions. For example, in marginal areas—characterized by low production inputs and low returns small cooperatives, local herder associations and SHGs have proved to be more useful.

On the other hand, formal institutions (e.g., commercial banks) may be more suitable in high potential areas for commercial growth. In the Maradi region of Niger, the farmers (much like in other areas across poor/developing countries) sold their livestock to generate cash, used mostly for food and purchasing seeds. Under such conditions, a project was initiated that established 'lean-period cereal banks'. The amount allocated was repaid during harvest time, along with a maximum 25 per cent interest rate to replenish stock and cover the working capital needs of the bank. Under such a system, the villagers provided the 'storage facility' for cereals, and the project committee was responsible for creating awareness among the villages about the existence and functions of such a bank. Beneficiaries from each village were identified on the basis of their vulnerability, depending on land availability, livestock availability and level of food security. A management committee at the village level was formed, with women in key roles like president, treasurer and secretary. While purchase of cereal was done at a project level, the Management Committee would oversee foodstuff being made available to the beneficiaries and replenishing being done during harvest time. Besides improving food security for most vulnerable groups, the project ensured that household capital in the form of livestock did not.

In terms of designing the viable financing model for livestock development, a few factors need to be kept in mind. A study conducted on a sample of sixty members of dairy SHGs formed under the Swarnajayanti Gram Swarozgar Yojana (SGSY) programme, implemented by the government, provides some interesting insights into policy formulation and credit delivery, especially to poor/marginalized livestock keepers. The study revealed that both the frequency of obtaining loan and the ticket size per loan increased as the wealth status of livestock keepers declined. Even for the same level of debt, poor livestock keepers took more

---

103   World Bank, 2008

time to repay their loans than their richer counterparts. Among the factors of critical importance, four factors were preferred—a shorter time from approval to disbursal, a lower interest rate compared to market-prevalent rates, provision to get full credit, and credit for production purposes. While poorer livestock feeders gave more importance to lower interest rates and provision to obtain credit for full amount, richer participants gave more importance to purposes of taking a loan. In order to adapt better to the needs of livestock feeders, banks and other financial institutions should develop credit packages incorporating the components of lower interest rates, shorter loan disbursal periods and incorporating provision for credit up to 100 per cent of the required amount. Thus, various models exist, apart from conventional means to provide capital for livestock rearing, which serves as a storage of value for rural households. The success of any model depends on its ability to address local/ground-level issues.

ANIMAL HEALTH

Animal diseases (like foot-and-mouth, black quarter, hemorrhagic septicemia, blue tongue, etc.) continue to inflict significant losses on livestock owners, with losses arising through a combination of declining production levels, reduced fertility and higher mortality. While data on the financial and economic losses due to diseases remains limited, it is estimated that the losses are between ₹50 billion and 132 billion annually.[104,105] India has an established preventative healthcare programme, seeking to conduct disease diagnosis and surveillance, along with immunization and, if required, control, against endemic diseases. However, under-reporting and absence of reporting of diseases are quite common, with most disease reports based on subjective assessments, but with limited laboratory confirmation. Typically, disease-outbreak reports are compiled manually, block by block, district by district, all the way up to the state, with information diluted at each level, when consolidated and transmitted. Most disease-reporting formats remain quite complicated,[106] while disease diagnosis is usually inaccurate, as few samples undergo laboratory testing.

The animal health service delivery system faces a number of issues—most of the budgetary allocation is towards supporting staff salaries, with little left for drugs and veterinary supplies. As a consequence, farmer satisfaction with government veterinary services is lower than with private vets and cooperative vets.[107]

---

104 Chawla, Kurup, Sharma, 2004
105 Rajashekhar, Raju, 2008
106 Ahuja, Rajasekhar and Raju, Poverty Alleviation (2008)
107 Ahuja, McConnell, et al, 2003

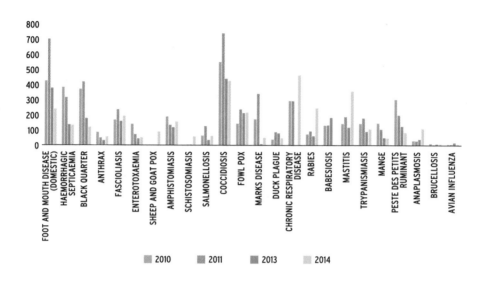

FIGURE 146: SPECIES-WISE INCIDENCE OF LIVESTOCK DISEASES IN INDIA
(JANUARY-DECEMBER 2010, 2011, 2013 AND 2014)[108,109]

Private business models are increasingly fostering reforms in animal health provision. Vishaka Livestock Development Association recruits local youth from Below Poverty Line (BPL) families, training them in veterinary first aid and innoculation, giving them the title of 'Gopal Mitra' (literally, a livestock health assistant) and having them work in their own localities providing veterinary services for a fee. Such workers are trained and compensation is at above-average salaries too.[110] The Tamil Nadu Livestock Development Project has been training couples in basic skills associated with veterinary work, with such couples providing services in vaccinating poultry, deworming and de-ticking.

The government needs to consider the devolvement of responsibility for delivering curative veterinary services to the private sector, while instead focusing on providing disease surveillance and monitoring, regulation and the creation of an encouraging environment for the private sector to contribute. Livestock producers are willing to pay for quality services—it remains up to the government to encourage such delivery

---

108 Ministry of Agriculture, Government of India, 2015
109 Indiastat, 2017
110 Pradhan, Ahuja and Venkatramaiah, 2003

provision.[111] We need to enact legislation to regulate the control of infectious and contagious diseases of animals, following up on the Livestock Importation Act (1898) and the Livestock Importation Act Amendment (1953). Existing statutes remain ineffective, with necessary quarantine processes required at the ports of embarkation and rules for inspection, detention, disinfection and destruction of imported animals needing clarification. The government should seek to entrust the provision of such inspection to state laboratories, with budgetary support provided on a cost-reimbursement basis.

VALUE CHAIN

The livestock value chain, particularly for dairy, typically has the milk producers (whether commercial, traditional or contractual) operating through three channels. One channel is focused on sale to/through informal and semi-formal chains, selling forward to small milk product manufacturing units, creameries and small sweet shops, which provide processed milk and milk products (like ice-cream, sweets, etc.) and fresh milk to the local market, where local consumers purchase from. Another channel, usually the most common, sees milk producers directly sell milk to local consumers. A third has the milk producers sell to increasingly formalized chains, which, through cooperative societies (with chilling plants and collection centres), sell further to large private government and cooperative plants, which eventually sell processed products in local retail outlets.

Such chains also provided members with feed inputs, veterinary services and breeding services, helping to improve productivity and raise marketable surplus, while incentivizing members through profit-sharing. The channeling of dairy imports through the NDDB helped to shield the sector from competition, while allowing imports to be utilized only as food aid. Such dairy cooperatives eventually standardized the sector and adopted branding, while creating a platform for private players to enter.

Dairy marketing institutions evolved in a similar manner in Andhra Pradesh, with the AHD introducing a pilot scheme to organize milk marketing in 1961 and an integrated milk project in 1964, while a Dairy Development Department was created to expand marketing activities in 1970 (this was eventually converted into the Andhra Pradesh Dairy Development Cooperation). By the '90s, steps were

---

111   Ahuja, McConnell, et al, 2003

being taken to integrate modern technologies across districts, with outlays provided by the National Cooperative Development Corporation (NCDC). Eventually, private dairy processing plants were established by 2006, following the delicencing of the dairy sector.[112]

However, much need for reform in cooperatives remains. Lack of competition in the industry, along with limited transparency in decision-making due to apathetic member participation, has led to prices being set arbitrarily, with limited quality testing and rather poor delivery of input services (like veterinary care and feed provision). Reforms are much needed—especially to force cooperatives to hold free and fair elections regularly, while creating a set criterion for board membership. The provision of autonomy in deciding milk-procurement prices and sale prices, along with staff recruitment, would help boost efficiency. Periodic audits by independent and certified auditors would help keep such cooperatives on the right path.

Across the value chain, a number of issues remain—there is no coherent livestock development policy, with ineffective implementation of policy and projects, and there is a lack of clarity about the roles of different projects. From a disease-control perspective, there is inadequate coverage of health and breeding services, with significant scope to expand the activities of NGOs in backward areas, especially in Bihar. The quality and cost of the feed are significant concerns, while an ineffective approach to managing the common property resources leaves little fodder for marginal farmers. There is poor access to formal credit at the farm level, while informal loans offer a very high rate of interest, with the farmer typically selling milk at a low price to the very trader he has taken a loan from. Production is meanwhile impacted by poor management and feeding practices, while marketing and processing are affected by a lack of coverage of villages, lack of transparency in milk testing and pricing.

Mutually aided cooperative societies provide a template. The Mulukanoor Women's Mutually Aided Milk Producers Cooperative Union Limited in Andhra Pradesh was set up in August 2002, with the area of operation limited to 25 km. The organization had two tiers—a village level and a union level, with no government control in administration, and democracy at the two tiers. There was freedom in setting prices, along with accountability and ownership at the village and union levels. A strong governance mechanism, along with an internal audit system, enabled the organization to pursue long-term goals while devolving more freedom to village- level societies.[113]

---

112 Raju, S., 2008
113 Ibid

Encouraging private-sector growth would also boost competition, while improving hygiene and sanitary standards across the value chain. The current value chain leaves low margins for unorganized dairy producers. Most of the milk continues to be sold through informal channels, through private traders, and through direct sale to farmers. Dairy cooperatives in backward states like Bihar and Odisha continue to face issues, with limited share of the marketable surplus going to cooperatives, low prices received by farmers, limited transparency in pricing and low quality of management provided by the state federation.

The poultry sector offers a template towards transforming the value chain. Backyard scavenging (with birds and eggs marketed through traditional value chains with a range of intermediaries) was dominant in poultry farming until the '80s, when the introduction of contract farming in broiler production transformed the industry.[114] By 2004–05, ~37 per cent of total broiler production was under contract arrangements–contracting, across different types of arrangements, enabled the inclusion of sharing of disease risk, and the contractor provided a range of inputs and services, usually on credit.

LIVESTOCK SECTOR STRATEGY

India's livestock-development strategy has led to uneven development across regions and states. State governments need to create incentive structures to attract the private sector and other sources of investment, while considering providing support to cooperatives to facilitate the commercialization of small holders.

The current breeding policy, based on exotic blood and artificial insemination, is clearly insufficient and needs to be revamped. A national breeding policy is needed to upgrade the best performing indigenous breeds, via selection and grading—this needs to run alongside current artificial-insemination programmes, with a view towards long-term convergence. Buffalo breeding ought to be given greater attention, while poultry breeding should be focused on conservation. State governments need to be encouraged to participate in national breeding policy implementation, creating an environment for competition amongst alternative suppliers of artificial insemination. Consensus needs to be built among breeders to develop indigenous breeds.

---

114 Landes, Persaud and Dyck, India's Poultry Sector: Development and Prospects, 2004

The currently inadequate feed supply needs to be mitigated through greater imports, with feed technology packages developed for extension dissemination, while taking into account potential demand for feeds. GIS-based analysis should be utilized to map production systems and recommendation domains for a range of feed technology options, while encouraging private investment.

Animal healthcare should be given its rightful priority by the government, with greater investment in preventative healthcare. State governments need to increase coordination with the government and neighbouring states in designing strategies for disease control. Loss-making vaccine production units should be disinvested from, with collaboration fostered with neighbouring states for inter-state trading of vaccines. Sound epidemiological and economic analysis on various important diseases needs to be conducted by the government to help promote rational decision-making in this segment.

The government needs to create better incentive structures for investment in livestock in lagging states, while harmonizing rules, regulations and regulatory authorities across states. State governments should sponsor research and assessment of the market, along with highlighting investment potentials to potential investors, private and foreign.

—

CONSTRUCTION

Construction remains the mainstay for employment generation in the non-farm sector in India. The table below illustrates that in the non-farm sector, all spheres except construction have witnessed a decline in their respective shares of employment generation. As a matter of fact, the employment in the construction sector doubled in a decade, from 1999–2000 to 2011–12.

TABLE 60: NON-FARM SECTOR ALLOCATION (PER CENT), FY2000–FY 2012

	1999-2000		2011-12	
SECTOR	INDUSTRY	% OF WORKERS	INDUSTRY	% OF WORKERS
MANUFACTURING	TEXTILE	5.2	TEXTILE	2.5
	FOOD PRODUCTS & BEVERAGES	4.7	FOOD PRODUCTS & BEVERAGES	2.7
	WOOD & ALLIED PRODUCTS	4.4	WEARING APPAREL	3.2
	OTHER NON-METALLIC MINERAL PRODUCTS	3.7	OTHER NON-METALLIC MINERAL PRODUCTS	3.1
TOTAL MANUFACTURING (A)		29.2		22.7
CONSTRUCTION		14.4		30.1
OTHER NON-MANUFACTURING		2.8		2.1
TOTAL NON-MANUFACTURING (B)		17.2		32.2
SERVICES	RETAIL TRADE	17.1	RETAIL TRADE	14.1
	LAND TRANSPORT	8.1	LAND TRANSPORT	7.9
	PUBLIC ADMINISTRATION	5.5	PUBLIC ADMINISTRATION	2.4
	EDUCATION	5.9	EDUCATION	6
TOTAL SERVICES (C)		53.6		45.1
TOTAL NON-FARM SECTOR (A+B+C)		100		100

SOURCE: INTERNATIONAL LABOUR ORGANIZATION

The non-farm sector, besides construction, also includes manufacturing and services. Within manufacturing, apparel and textiles remain the main industry for employment generation, followed by food products and other non-metallic minerals.

EMPLOYMENT SHARE

The construction industry has witnessed a massive rise in its employment share—from 14.4 per cent in 1999–2000 to 30.1 per cent in 2011–12. Increased spend on infrastructure, along with non-requirement of any specialized skills for participation and the option of seasonal participation have allowed farmers to take up jobs in the construction sector. During this period, employment in construction grew at 19.9 per cent per annum—a rate higher than the average growth in the construction sector as a part of the GDP. Overall, it alone accounted for more than half of the overall increase in non-farm employment.

Among services, retail trade remains the mainstay industry, followed by road transport—with many in the rural workforce preferring to ply trucks and buses. Public administration has dipped from 5.5 per cent in 1999–2000 to 2.4 per cent in 2011–12, signifying withdrawal of the government from public services.

TABLE 61: EMPLOYMENT GROWTH IN CONSTRUCTION SECTOR IN INDIA
HAS FAR OUTSTRIPPED GROWTH IN OTHER SECTORS

INDUSTRY	GROWTH % PER ANNUM FROM 1999-2000 TILL 2011-12
TEXTILE	-1.8
MANUFACTURING	2.1
CONSTRUCTION	19.8
RETAIL TRADE	2.7
LAND TRANSPORT	4.8
SERVICES	3
NON-FARM	5.1

SOURCE: INTERNATIONAL LABOUR ORGANIZATION

For the said duration, we also witness a decline in self-employment and dependence on casual-wage employment. The tables below illustrate the percentage of rural workers in non-farm employment, depending on employment type and sector.

TABLE 62: SOURCE: INTERNATIONAL LABOUR ORGANIZATION

SECTOR	SELF-EMPLOYMENT		SALARIED EMPLOYMENT		CASUAL EMPLOYMENT	
	1999-2000	2011-2012	1999-2000	2011-2012	1999-2000	2011-2012
MANUFACTURING	55.6	51.2	23.1	26.3	21.3	22.5
CONSTRUCTION	20.8	8.9	3.3	2.3	75.9	88.7
OTHER NON-MANUFACTURING	9.8	6.2	34.3	38.4	55.9	55.4
SERVICES	50.4	53.8	33.4	37.5	16.2	8.7
ALL NON-FARM	46.5	38.7	24.6	24.4	28.9	36.9

TABLE 63: SOURCE: INTERNATIONAL LABOUR ORGANIZATION

SECTOR	SELF-EMPLOYMENT		SALARIED EMPLOYMENT		CASUAL EMPLOYMENT	
	1999-2000	2011-2012	1999-2000	2011-2012	1999-2000	2011-2012
MANUFACTURING	35.9	30.0	22.0	2 4.4	24.1	13.9
CONSTRUCTION	4.9	7.0	1.9	2.8	43.5	72.3
OTHER NON-MANUFACTURING	0.5	0.3	3.7	3.2	6.0	3.1
SERVICES	58.7	62.7	72.4	69.5	26.4	10.7
ALL NON-FARM	100	100	100	100	100	100

Thus, we see that for manufacturing, the general trend has been a shift from self-employment to salaried and casual-wage employment. The 'other non-manufacturing sector' has shrunk overall, with maximum decline in the numbers for casual employment. Construction witnessed the maximum gain, with the trend moving towards casual-wage employment from salaried and self-employment.

The shift in employment pattern is also reflected in the shift towards employment in larger enterprises. Enterprises that employed six or fewer employees accounted for 60 per cent employment in 1999–2000, which declined by almost 50 per cent from its base levels in a decade to 41 per cent in 2011–12. This offsets an increase in employment share of enterprises employing more than six employees, with maximum increase witnessed in enterprises of a six to nine employee size. Thus, for non-farm employment, the general trend has been a move away from small enterprises (fewer than six employees). However, the same is not witnessed in the construction sector. While 62.3 per cent of people employed in construction in 1999–2000 were working in enterprises employing fewer than nine employees, the number has risen to 68.5 per cent of employees. Our medium-scale enterprises have a disproportionately lower share of employment—partly explained by stringent labour laws that apply once a firm grows in size. As the number of workers increases, the firm comes under the purview of almost forty central and state labour laws, and in order to avoid the implications, most firms offer casual employment or sub-contract to multiple vendors. Studies have exposed the fundamental disadvantage of working in small enterprises (fewer than nine employees) with productivity at such firms being one-eighth the productivity in medium and large enterprises (Mazumdar, Sarkar, 2008)

TABLE 64: EMPLOYMENT, BY SIZE OF COMPANY

SECTOR	FEWER THAN 6		6 TO 9		10 OR MORE	
	1999-2000	2011-2012	1999-2000	2011-2012	1999-2000	2011-2012
MANUFACTURING	32.7	24.4	7.1	11.7	60.2	63.6
CONSTRUCTION	49.9	42.5	12.4	26	37.7	30.3
OTHER NON-MANUFACTURING	18.1	14.1	11.8	11.3	70.1	74.4
SERVICES	65.1	49.9	5.2	16.9	29.7	32.3
ALL NON-FARM	60.2	40.8	7	19.8	32.8	38.4

SOURCE: INTERNATIONAL LABOUR ORGANIZATION

The wage rates offered in the construction sector compare well with the wage rates offered by other sectors, considering that most men do not need any special skill for working as project construction labour and they also have the optionality of seasonal employment. The following table presents the average wages earned by various construction workers over the years.

TABLE 65: WAGE RATES FOR CONSTRUCTION WORKERS, 2013–14 ONWARDS

AVERAGE WAGES OF PROJECT CONSTRUCTION WORKERS (IN ₹/DAY) IN RURAL INDIA												
YEAR	NOV	DEC	JAN	FEB	MAR	APR	MAY	JUNE	JULY	AUG	SEPT	OCT
2013-14	247	268	268	269	266	268	272	270	274	275	274	275
2014-15	277	276	279	279	280	281	280	282	284	286	287	288
2015-16	291	293	294	295	295	296	296	297	299	301	302	305
2016-17	307	308	311	312	312	314						
AVERAGE WAGES OF ELECTRICIANS (IN ₹/DAY) IN RURAL INDIA												
YEAR	NOV	DEC	JAN	FEB	MAR	APR	MAY	JUNE	JULY	AUG	SEPT	OCT
2013-14	365	367	366	365	366	364	366	365	365	366	367	370
2014-15	372	372	373	372	372	372	372	374	376	379	381	382
2015-16	385	385	386	387	388	387	388	389	388	389	394	395
2016-17	399	400	402	402	403	405						
AVERAGE WAGES OF MASONS (IN ₹/DAY) IN RURAL INDIA												
YEAR	NOV	DEC	JAN	FEB	MAR	APR	MAY	JUNE	JULY	AUG	SEPT	OCT
2013-14	351	351	354	357	361	365	366	366	373	374	379	373
2014-15	384	385	387	388	391	392	393	395	399	402	405	407
2015-16	408	409	412	413	414	416	418	421	423	425	427	431
2016-17	433	433	436	437	438	439						
AVERAGE WAGES OF PLUMBERS (IN ₹/DAY) IN RURAL INDIA												
YEAR	NOV	DEC	JAN	FEB	MAR	APR	MAY	JUNE	JULY	AUG	SEPT	OCT
2013-14	398	395	393	390	386	383	386	383	380	381	383	385
2014-15	385	388	387	388	389	385	385	388	390	391	393	394

2015-16	396	395	397	398	400	400	401	402	403	404	407	414
2016-17	417	419	421	421	423	427						
AVERAGE WAGES OF SWEEPERS (IN ₹/DAY) IN RURAL INDIA												
YEAR	NOV	DEC	JAN	FEB	MAR	APR	MAY	JUNE	JULY	AUG.	SEPT	OCT
2013-14	183	172	168	177	178	182	183	185	186	187	192	194
2014-15	193	195	195	197	198	199	199	200	202	206	206	206
2015-16	208	209	210	211	212	212	213	213	214	212	211	214
2016-17	217	217	219	220	220	220						

SOURCE: INDIASTAT, MINISTRY OF LABOUR & EMPLOYMENT

Given the average daily wage rates are approximately in line with the rates under Mahatma Gandhi National Rural Employment Gurantee Act. (MGNREGA), the construction sector offers a higher minimum number of employed days—making it attractive to move into the sector on a seasonal basis.

Most migrants work in poor conditions in urban centres to save money. A sample survey of migrant workers shows that purchase of consumer durables, improving living conditions at the originating village and increased consumption during the lean season, occupy top priority. However, this may not happen for sure, as 33 per cent of workers report that the remittances are used to settle loans taken from various sources, mostly informal in nature. This presents a question on the reason for migration itself—as migration fuelled by debt pressures may not add to the welfare of the worker family.

Such remittances are found to have a positive effect on education in the source village—with fewer children dropping out of school in the five- to fourteen-years age group. The percentage of children enrolled in school is also found to be higher in migrant families at source villages, as compared to non-migrant workers. Migration also impacts the choice of schooling, with a higher proportion of migrant workers opting to look for private schools for their wards, as compared to non-migrant workers. The NSSO data (64th Round) confirms these findings of increased remittances being used to meet the education and health requirements of the children in source villages.

Remittances are also used for building up farm assets, with migrant families reporting a higher consumption expenditure on farm, livestock and transport equipment, which can help them set up passive revenue streams, as compared to non-migrant families.

TABLE 66: MONTHLY PER-CAPITA EXPENDITURE FOR
NON-MIGRANTS AND CONSTRUCTION WORKERS

	NON-MIGRANT	CONSTRUCTION MIGRANT	OTHER MIGRANT
FOOD EXPENSES	582	1074	803
EDUCATION EXPENSES	8	42	36
HEALTH EXPENSES	30	27	8
OTHER (NON-FOOD) EXPENSES	160	322	279
OVERALL MONTHLY EXPENSE	742	1396	1082

SOURCE: RAVI SRIVASTAVA AND RAJIB SUTRADHAR, SAGE PUBLICATIONS, 2016

However, their improved condition rurally, if at all it happens, comes at a great cost. Despite the burgeoning employment in the construction sector, exploitative practices continue unabated. India's citizens are treated as unequals in their own country, if they happen to be construction workers.

Shankar Yadav, a thin thirty-year-old man, came to Delhi from his village Gorauli (Tehsil: Baikunthpur, District: Gopalganj), in Bihar, looking for work in 2009. Since he came to Delhi, he shares his daily morning routine with hundreds of other men and women in similar situations. Every day, Yadav walks to the nearest labour chowk—where labourers, carpenters and masons looking for work are recruited by middlemen or thekedaars on a daily basis. Such labour chowks have become commonplace—an undesired byproduct of immigration of millions from rural areas to urban centres. He considers himself lucky if he gets work. If he doesn't get work and feels that the day shall slip by without any income, he reduces his daily rate by as much as 50 per cent to ensure that he doesn't go home empty-handed and sleep on an empty stomach. His friend, Sushil Yadav, witnessing the drudgery of such labour chowks in the National Capital Region (NCR), took another decision—to migrate to Kerala, almost 2,500 km away. While he says the initial period was good, primarily due to continued employment (although on a daily basis) by the thekedaar, the situation is deteriorating due to inflow of labour from Tamil Nadu. The middleman also has incentives to bring cheap labour from another corner of the country—while a native mason may charge ₹600–₹800 per day, the migrant labour will do the same job at ₹400 per day, almost half the prevalent rate. Unskilled workers, not qualified to become masons, earn about ₹300–₹350 per day.

Abid Khan, a twenty-year-old from West Bengal, faces the same condition. He works as a construction helper and plans to become a 'mason' to get higher daily wages. Back home, his education till Class 8 did not yield any employment opportunities and his aversion to continue his father's work as agricultural labour meant that employment options in his hometown were slim. If one stays longer, they can even learn the local language and make attempts to earn a little more, most of which is stashed away for savings and remittance homet.

The working conditions are deplorable—most migrant workers end up living in makeshift tents at the construction site or in one-room apartments, rented by the contractor, with ten or more other workers with just one toilet. A heavy breakfast ensures that they can skip lunch and save money and time. Language barriers also prevent migrant workers from joining welfare unions, which is compounded by the fear of loss of jobs.

Most migrant workers lack identification papers, and thus are deprived of any local government schemes or benefits that require identity proof. This also leads to harassment at the hands of police officials at times. Though workers are provided ID cards, their sole purpose remains limited to providing better security to the construction-site area.

In a bid for cost-cutting by reducing construction costs, worker safety is the first aspect to be sacrificed. Take the example of Pramod Kumar, a 37-year-old labourer who succumbed to his injuries after falling from the scaffolding on the third floor of a high-rise apartment complex in Gurgaon. While he did not have any safety harness when working at such heights, it is common for the contractor to claim that the worker's inebriated state was the cause of the accident, overlooking the fact that drunkenness should not have been tolerated by the contractor in the first place. Absence of ID cards and formal documentation at the workplace ensure that later, the contractor can completely shrug off any responsibility. In such cases, the family of the migrant worker is forced to forgive and forget for minor compensation, just enough to take care of funeral expenses. Kumar's death certificate was collected by the contractor from the hospital, on the pretext that he needed the certificate to process the compensation payment. His widow now has limited options—even a legal-claim case will be weakened in the absence of any documents.

Such incidents are not isolated. However, most go unreported.[115] While a reply to a Lok Sabha question puts the number of fatalities at 77 across the country for the period 2012–15, the actual figure could be far higher. RTI applications filed with the Labour Ministry and various police departments revealed that between 2013 and 2016, 452 workers died, while 212 were injured. The RTI number is six times the official figure stated in the Lok Sabha, an anomaly difficult to reconcile, despite just a year's difference in time period. NGO estimates were even higher—pegging the number of deaths at 1,092 for the said duration, along with 377 injured workers. The

---

115 Jain, S., and Matharu, S., 5 August 2017, NDTV India. Sourced from: https://www.ndtv.com/india-news/fatal-heights-the-untold-deaths-of-indias-construction-workers-1733974

gap in data quality, depending on data source, is huge—while the RTI information showed twelve construction-related deaths in Mumbai, the Police Commissioner's office pegged the number at 235 in the same time period. In Gujarat, RTIs pegged it at thirty-six, whereas data from the Bandhkam Mazdoor Sangathan, an NGO, pegged it at 231 in a similar period. Such poor record-keeping is convenient for everyone involved—except the policymakers and construction workers. The RTI information reveals that about 60 per cent of deaths occur due to a fall, about 25 per cent from the collapse of a wall or a building, and the remaining 15 per cent from electrocution. Most workers are migrants from different states and districts (if the same state), and in the productive age group of eighteen to forty-five, with parents or children depending on them for survival.

Usually, the workers are paid anywhere between ₹300 and ₹450 for a gruelling day's work—frequently extending up to ten hours without any breaks. Assuming a worker is lucky to find employment all days in a month, he earns ₹9,000 to ₹13,000 a month in an urban centre, where he spends about ₹2,000 on room rent (if he doesn't get a makeshift tent at the construction site). If lucky, he is able to send his kids to school. When asked about childhood ambitions, one says he wanted to become a teacher, but shortage of money meant that he had to quit school and contribute to the family's budget by working as a labourer. He dreams of making his only son a teacher, but has extremely limited resources for his training and education. He ironically states that the very building he is constructing would be beyond his access, once finished. He has no idea about the existence and functioning of the Building and Construction Workers' Welfare Board, the only government support for workers like him.

Sunita, wife of Yadav, looked forward to her life in the city after marriage, hoping to make a better start after escaping prolonged economic challenges caused by failing agriculture in her village. She got a reality check when, on her first day in her new life, she was pushed on to a truck and taken to her new home—a makeshift tent on the side of a pavement. Women are usually assigned the roles of carrying bricks, breaking stones, shovelling gravel or cleaning the site. While they make up about 20 per cent of the construction workforce, they are more prone to harassment and abuse, with most men complaining that they are 'weak' and do not work 'hard enough'.

Sunita might put in the same effort as Yadav, but she would be paid just half the daily rate as him (₹250, compared to ₹450). Research shows that most women complain of intensive labour, lack of childcare and sexual harassment by contractors. Social stigma causes them to downplay any incident, fearing punishment from their husbands for behaving in an improper manner and attracting the contractor's undesired attention, besides losing employment.

Her children, too, end up suffering. With both parents working at the construction site, toddlers are left unattended at the construction site, playing amidst dust and gravel, exposed to various health hazards from a very early age. Their migrant status and lack of identity proof also act as a deterrent in the availing of Anganwadi facilities and proper education, thereby restricting their proper development.

At times, the exploitation becomes too much to bear, as witnessed at the construction site of the Army Welfare Housing Organization in Bengaluru, in 2012. The contractor was found paying workers ₹50/week, as opposed to ₹150/day, promised to them when they were brought to Bengaluru from their village. Several workers were not even paid and threatened when they demanded money. Attempts to quit and leave were met with workplace violence. Besides being inhuman, the contractor was found openly violating the provisions of various other laws—namely, the Inter-State Migrant Workmen Act (1979), Building and Other Construction Workers Act and the Minimum Wages Act (1948). However, the penalties for violation—₹500–₹2,000—are minor and do not act as a deterrent. Under the provisions of the Inter-State Migrant Workmen Act, any establishment looking to employ five or more migrant workers needs to register itself. However, the Act is openly flouted. Standing Committee on Labour reports show that compliance is low, witnessed from the low number of licenced contractors (only 285) and registered firms (only 240) for 22 Indian states. Exploitation by the contractor is not a new phenomenon—it was the preferred mode of labour recruitment during the colonial era. In 1929, the Royal Commission on Labour recommended the abolition of the contractor, while independent India passed the Contract Labour (Regulation and Abolition) Act in 1970. However, not only has the labour contractor survived, but he has flourished in recent times—fuelled by the growth in construction.

One of the primary initiatives undertaken to improve work conditions and benefit migrant workers, particularly in construction, were the two pieces of umbrella legislations passed by Parliament—The Building and Other Construction Workers (Regulation of Employment and Conditions of Service) Act, 1996, and The Building and Other Construction Workers' Welfare Cess Act, 1996. These two Acts form the basis on which the states are expected to enact state-level legislation. The Acts are applicable to any establishment that employs ten or a greater number of workers with project value equal to ₹10 lakh or more. The Acts have provisions to implement a welfare fund financed through cess on construction (~1–2 per cent of construction cost), contributions by beneficiaries and non-mandatory grants by central and state governments. Kerala was one of the first state governments which introduced legislation pertaining to welfare and security of construction workers, in a manner acting as a precursor to the central government legislation. The Kerala Construction Workers' Welfare Act was passed in 1990, about eight years before the central legislation.

EMPLOYMENT SCHEMES

The details of the schemes of various states in this regard are presented in the tables below. Low registration levels and poor collection of employees' contribution in a timely manner remain a risk to their success.

TAMIL NADU

Name of Scheme: Welfare Board for Construction Workers (1995)

Target Beneficiary: Construction workers in the age group of fifteen to sixty years

Benefits: ₹1 lakh in case of death, loss of limbs, eyes, etc. ₹1,000–₹10,000 as education assistance, ₹2,000 as marriage assistance, ₹2,000 as maternity assistance, ₹2,000 as funeral assistance and ₹10,000 as natural death assistance. Old-age pension of ₹200 per month.

Financing: Government. Departments and local authority to pay 0.3 per cent of cost of construction. Registration for workers at ₹25/worker and renewal at ₹10/worker.

WEST BENGAL

Name of Scheme: West Bengal Building and Other Construction Workers' Welfare Board

Target Beneficiary: Building and construction workers

Benefits: Upon reaching sixty years of age, a pension of ₹150/month. Medical expenses—₹2,000/annum for a set of ailments, which can be increased to ₹10,000/annum when an operation is required. Accident assistance—₹200 for first five days and ₹20/day thereafter, subject to a maximum of ₹1,000/annum. In case of disability, the amount is increased to ₹10,000. Death benefit of ₹10,000, which can be extended to ₹30,000, if death happens during the course of employment.

GOA

Name of Scheme: Goa Employment (Conditions of Service) and Retirement Benefit Act

Target Beneficiary: Workers in all establishments in every industrial activity, including services and construction, and plantations

Benefits: Retirement benefits to the unorganized-sector workers who have completed 240 days of continuous employment. Contribution made by the employer in the workers' account, along with the interest accrued at 6 per cent or as fixed by the government, will be paid to the worker when he reaches the age of fifty years, or to his dependents/heirs in case of death of the worker before the age of fifty years.

Financing: 5 per cent of the gross wages of the workers made by the employer.

KERALA

Name of Scheme: Kerala Construction Workers Welfare Funds (KCONWWF, 1990)

Target Beneficiary: Construction workers (employed in any construction work, such as masons, carpenters, bricklayers, excluding supervisory functionaries like engineers, etc.), and quarry workers excluding supervisors

Benefits: Pension ₹200 per month. Natural death: ₹1,500. Accidental death: ₹1 lakh. Marriage benefit: ₹3,000 for daughter and ₹2,000 for son. Medical benefit: up to ₹5,000 and ₹10,000 for permanent disability. Housing allowance: ₹50,000. Educational allowance: ₹5,000.

Financing: From all stakeholders—government: 10 per cent of initial member's contribution per annum.

Employer: 1 per cent of the construction cost and yearly contribution made by the contractors (₹100 to ₹1,000).

Employee: Monthly contribution per member—slabs ₹10, ₹15 and ₹25.

Labour Department & Board of Directors to be the implementing agency.

Thus, we see that a majority of schemes do not include any provision for illnesses—a major source of insecurity among the workers, especially when frequent instances of work-related illness occur, causing loss of employment and expenses towards medical care and possible hospitalization.

WELFARE FUND UTILIZATION

In terms of collection of funds for welfare of construction workers, most states have performed decently. The big gap lies in utilization.

TABLE 67: DETAIL OF CESS COLLECTED UNDER THE BUILDING AND OTHER CONSTRUCTION WORKERS' WELFARE CESS ACT, 1996 & THE AMOUNT SPENT (TILL 31 MARCH 2014) UNSTARRED QUESTION NO: 2719, RAISED BY FEROZE VARUN GANDHI, ANSWERED ON 28.07.2014

NO.	STATE / UT	AMOUNT OF CESS COLLECTED (₹ CR)	AMOUNT SPENT (₹ CR)	AMOUNT AVAILABLE (₹ CR)	UTILIZATION (%)
1	ANDHRA PRADESH	993.94	73.42	920.52	7%
2	ARUNACHAL PRADESH	22.96	4.56	18.40	20%
3	ASSAM	205.09	1.82	203.27	1%
4	BIHAR	374.33	4.04	370.29	1%
5	CHHATTISGARH	324.45	177.94	146.51	55%
6	GOA	27.62	0.00	27.62	0%
7	GUJARAT	190.22	0.41	189.81	0%
8	HARYANA	1,047.16	32.67	1,014.49	3%
9	HIMACHAL PRADESH	51.22	0.00	51.22	0%
10	J&K	282.44	93.60	188.84	33%
11	JHARKHAND	21.09	0.11	20.98	1%
12	KARNATAKA	1,741.13	34.49	1,706.64	2%
13	KERALA	954.50	888.10	66.40	93%
14	MADHYA PRADESH	931.53	370.01	561.52	40%
15	MAHARASHTRA	2,092.15	62.93	2,029.22	3%
16	MANIPUR	0.00	0.00	0.00	-
17	MEGHALAYA	34.12	0.11	34.01	0%
18	MIZORAM	16.14	8.93	7.21	55%
19	NAGALAND	3.49	0.05	3.44	1%
20	ODISHA	312.32	0.34	311.98	0%
21	PUNJAB	455.56	10.24	445.32	2%
22	RAJASTHAN	203.40	22.30	181.10	11%
23	SIKKIM	18.64	2.44	16.20	13%
24	TAMIL NADU	755.68	330.99	424.69	44%
25	TRIPURA	69.24	3.01	66.23	4%
26	UTTAR PRADESH	1,169.08	99.52	1,069.56	9%
27	UTTARAKHAND	39.17	0.16	39.01	0%
28	WEST BENGAL	290.62	4.59	286.03	2%
29	DELHI	1,362.95	149.10	1,213.85	11%
30	A&N ISLAND	20.91	0.35	20.56	2%
31	CHANDIGARH	45.94	1.28	44.66	3%
32	DADRA & NAGAR HAVELI	3.08	0.00	3.08	0%
33	DAMAN AND DIU	16.63	0.02	16.61	0%
34	LAKSHADWEEP	1.71	0.00	1.71	0%
35	PUDUCHERRY	20.65	4.62	16.03	22%
	TOTAL	14,099.16	2,382.15	11,717.01	17%

As per the Ministry of Labour statistics, till 31 March 2014, a sum of ₹14,099 crore had been collected by various states and Union Territories as construction cess under the said Act. The utilization stood at a meagre ₹2,382 crore—indicating a utilization rate of only 16.9 per cent. If, by the above example, the reader thinks that the situation in Kerala is bad, other states fare worse. Overall, till March 2014, Kerala spent ₹888 crore out of a total of ₹954 crore collected. This compares with a meagre ₹34 crore spent by Karnaraka out of a collected amount of ₹1,741 crore or only ₹64 crores spent by Maharashtra out of a collected amount of ₹2,092 crore. The utilization rates for Karnataka and Maharashtra stand abysmally low, at 2 per cent and 3 per cent, respectively.

Delhi collected ₹484 crore in three years under the scheme and utilized only ₹38.6 crore (utilization rate of less than 10 per cent) under the eighteen schemes announced by the Welfare Board. Rajasthan also spent a similar amount on workers' welfare—₹38 crore out of a total collection of ₹579 crore over 2011–14. Overall, eight states—Maharashtra, Meghalaya, Delhi, Rajasthan, Tamil Nadu, Haryana, Jharkhand and Himachal Pradesh—collected ₹4,179 crore over 2011–14 but utilized only 8.6 per cent of the collected fund: ₹361 crore during the said duration. Money collected by the state government has to pass from the state government to the welfare boards and from the boards to the collective welfare of the workers.

Consider the Kerala experience—one of the only states to have an old-age home for retired construction workers, Snehasadanam in Thiruvananthapuram. The home has a capacity for thirty workers across an entire state, but it operates under-capacity with ~66 per cent utilization rates. In order to secure admission into the home, a worker needs to get a recommendation from either an MP, an MLA or a registered trade union.

The success of Kerala can be attributed to the trade unions—which helped organize the workers, increase their numbers and ensured access of workers to such schemes. The Board, as of 2014, has about 18 lakh registered workers, out of which 2 lakh are pensioners. In terms of pension amounts, the 2 lakh pensioners account for about ₹100 crore expenditure out of a total expenditure spend of ₹150 crore. Apart from pension at the old-age home, the residents also get free medical care (free medicines and free doctor visits once every ten days) and an annual day-long leisure trip. Kerala still has lower collection than the true potential—while other states collect cess during project-approval stage, Kerala collects it at the project commissioning stage, thus exposing them to the risk of collection risks and arrears. To correct such dismal utilization records, The Building and Other Construction Workers Related Laws (Amendment) Bill, 2013, was introduced. Yet, even after four years of its introduction, it remains pending. The observations of the Parliamentary Standing Committee were harsh but true when it questioned the seriousness of the government's intent regarding welfare of construction workers as it had accepted only nine out of the twenty recommendations made by a task force under the Ministry of Labour.

IMPROVING CONSTRUCTION CONDITIONS

Improving the conditions of migrant workers in the construction sector requires a multipronged approach. Firstly, we have to enable migrant workers to get deserved access to various government (both central and state) schemes, despite the lack of identity proof. Access to Anganwadi facilities should be provided, regardless of thier identity proofs. While multiple laws exist for welfare of construction workers, compliance with them is abysmal.

The penalties for the non-compliance have to be increased to a significant fraction of the construction cost, payable by the builder, instead of the maximum penalty of ₹2,000 applicable. Registration of workers with the Welfare Board should be made mandatory and be the responsibility of the contractor and the builder. If the contractor is found to engage any worker without a registration card/ID, both monetary and non-monetary penalties should be imposed, which would then be used for improving awareness and penetration of registration cards and their benefits. The registration cards should be linked to their Jan Dhan accounts and transfer of payments on a periodic basis must be made directly to their accounts. In order to improve the condition of women, strict anti-harassment laws should be implemented. Creche facilities at construction sites should be provided to ensure that children do not remain abandoned all day, playing with gravel and dust, which can threaten their health.

Utilization of construction cess has to be improved, if we have to make any difference to the condition of our construction workers. They should also be provided training and skilling in their areas of interest, as it can lead to higher earnings and credit-worthiness, thereby playing a major role in lifting them out of poverty. Such opportunities should also be provided to women, who are usually left to continue with unskilled tasks and remain at the lowest rung of the construction ladder their entire lives. Organizations like SEWA (Self Employed Women's Association)—India's oldest and largest female trade union—have played an important role in skilling and training of women, besides educating them about their rights and providing work insurance. However, its implementation will remain critical. We need to actively ensure that the cost of non-compliance with the law is higher than the cost of compliance, and that the chances of getting caught for non-compliance will be next to certain. When such conditions are ensured, welfare of construction workers will become an economic priority for the builders.

MINING

Mining is another source of non-farm income, albeit in certain geographies. India is a major minerals producer, across chromite, coal, iron ore, bauxite and zinc production. India's mining sector comprises large and small mines, with public players dominating (~72 per cent by value produced, 92 per cent in coal, 31 per cent in iron ore; PwC 2012). The industry remains significantly fragmented—there are over 573 coal, 553 metallic and 1,523 non-metallic mines—with fuel minerals like coal dominating (67 per cent). India's resources remain substantial on paper—over 26 billion tonnes of iron, at a grade cut-off of 55 per cent, while India ranks as the fourth largest producer in the world. Much coal remains to be mined (more than 280 billion tonnes), while the demand-supply gap continues to rise (demand growing over 6 per cent per annum), driven primarily by power generation (70 per cent of total demand).

The National Mineral Policy (2008), the Mines Act (1952) and the Mines and Minerals Act (1957), and a slew of state laws have led to a situation where the enforcement of regulations is lax, with poor coordination amidst bureaucratic circles leading to illegal mining. Political interference and institutional corruption are rife, keeping production low and accountability limited, leaving local community and environmental needs unmet.

However, mineral resource extraction is bedevilled by a duality of control.[116] Constitutional arrangements restrict the proprietary title of onshore minerals to the states, while keeping regulatory powers with the centre. Multiple state and central agencies overlap across enforcement duties, while being poorly funded. This results in production shortfalls and industrial logjam.

Consider illegal mining in Odisha—in 2011, the state government complained to the centre over the Indian Bureau of Mines (IBM)'s inadequacy in preventing illegal iron ore mining (through overproduction) in the state. IBM contended that

---

116 Planning Commission, 2012

checking illegal mining was a state responsibility under the Odisha Minerals Rules (2007). The centre, meanwhile, asserted that 20 per cent overproduction was permissible, with modifications allowed. Meanwhile, illegal mining continues, with over 15,534 cases in Andhra Pradesh alone in 2010 (Indian Bureau of Mines).

To bolster coal production, capacity should be improved through technology upgradation, utilizing underground mining over open cast techniques. A significant portion of India's coal reserves lies at depths below 300 m—despite this, the share of coal derived from underground mining has dropped to ~9.6 per cent since FY12. Underground mining, resilient to monsoonal rain, with a lower land and environmental footprint and decreased need for last-mile connectivity, should be encouraged. Such practices could be bolstered by utilizing underground and open cast safety technologies.

While the government's robust new auction process should disincentivize illegal mining, data aggregation is a must to auction these resources in the right quantities at sustainable prices. It remains necessary to invest in information systems and radio frequency identification (RFID) systems, all while enforcing sustainability reporting. Environmental governance is rife with overlaps—IBM is required to monitor environmental protection measures, while the State Pollution Control Board (SPCB) provides consent to establish and operate post a due diligence process.

Our mining regulations need to be effective and enforceable, empowering state administration supported by adequate budget allocations. The mining regulations also need to account for a region's biodiversity, its sustainable mining rates and any tribal/cultural concerns (e.g., Niyamgiri). Mine closure should be legislated, requiring community consultations, legal obligations and rehabilitation requirements.

Mining is always an inherently 'dirty' industry, ravaging landscapes and aggregating pollution, amenable to kickbacks and illegal operations. Strip mining, widely practised, destroys local habitats, damages productive top soil and wipes out villages. Its usage of vast areas of land raises further issues of adequate compensation and resettlement, despite potential for economic and infrastructural development. The Joda Block, in Odisha, witnessed a 110 per cent increase in wasteland (18,540 hectares in 2004 vs 8,294 hectares in 1989).[117] During the monsoon, the river waters often turn red, due to iron oxide particles, with total suspended solids reaching 1,000 mg/litre. This calls for deployment of improved technologies on sustainable development and the 'precautionary principle'.

---

117 Vasundhara (2008)

The idea of sustainable development in mining seems paradoxical.[118] While large and medium mines ideally should utilize scientific mining methods and adopt comprehensive environmental conservation measures, most players prefer to conform to regulatory norms in form rather than substance. Local stakeholder consultation remains highly neglected, with little interaction with local communities (aside from an initial public hearing). While mining firms have set up CSR funds, their spending is mostly determined by the mine owner's interests.

We need to look at sustainable development in mining in a new light. South Africa's Social and Labour Plan, Papua New Guinea's Mineral Development Fund and Canada's Impact Benefit Agreement offer pathways to environmentally conscious local development. By including provisions for mine closure, reclamation and rehabilitation that are strictly enforced, such countries work towards lessening the deleterious impact of mining. A mandatory obligation for local development should replace voluntary CSR projects, with funds being spent on works being determined by local bodies and execution conducted by mining enterprises, instead of semi-government agencies. Without social consensus, mining can be easily disrupted (Bougainville, Papua New Guinea [1986]; Bellary, Karnataka [2011]). Simply offering money to villagers will no longer do.

IMPROVING RURAL LIVELIHOOD

While agriculture remains the dominant source of income for rural households, non-farm sources are increasingly contributing a larger share of the pie. While this share does decline with landholding size, diversification towards it can serve as a mechanism to making villages economical and stemming urban migration. Encouraging farmers and landless labourers to diversify towards non-farm activities, which they already are doing to a certain extent, will be influenced by the landholding size, further decline in profits associated with marginal farming and rising educational levels, along with access to credit. Increasing the share of income from regular or casual wages (associated with construction) and livestock (mostly associated with marginal farmers and landless labourers) could help reduce inequality and transform the village economy. Livestock will lead to a regular source of income, helping to boost household incomes during times of drought and famine, while performing an informal banking role, considering how livestock can be stores of value. Our policies should help create sustainable long-term rural non-

---

118 Brundtland Commission, 1987

farm employment options, which can aid the rural poor in overcoming barriers to economic prosperity. India's rural development policies should increasingly focus on developing markets, infrastructure and institutions that can help sectors like livestock and construction grow, while allowing migration, across states and nations, to occur.

APPENDIX

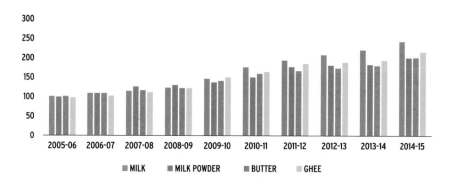

FIGURE 147: INDEX NUMBERS OF WHOLESALE PRICES FOR MILK PRODUCTS IN INDIA[119,120]

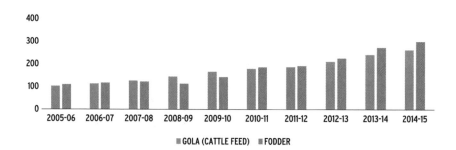

FIGURE 148: INDEX NUMBERS OF WHOLESALE PRICES FOR CATTLE FEED IN INDIA[121,122]

---

119 Ministry of Agriculture, Government of India, 2015
120 Indiastat, 2017
121 Ministry of Agriculture, Government of India, 2015
122 Indiastat, 2017

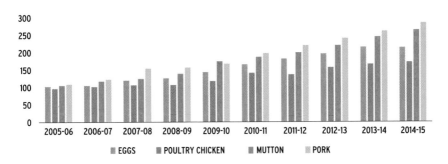

FIGURE 149: INDEX NUMBERS OF WHOLESALE PRICES FOR EGGS & MEAT PRODUCTS IN INDIA[123,124]

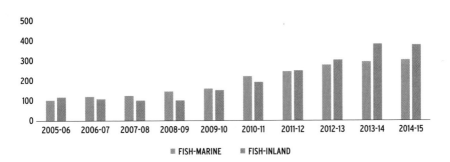

FIGURE 150: INDEX NUMBERS OF WHOLESALE PRICES FOR FISH PRODUCTS IN INDIA[125,126]

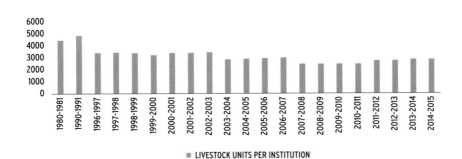

FIGURE 151: AVERAGE NUMBER OF LIVESTOCK UNITS SERVED
PER HEALTH INSTITUTION IN PUNJAB[127,128]

123 Ministry of Agriculture, Government of India, 2015

124 Indiastat, 2017

125 Ministry of Agriculture, Government of India, 2015

126 Indiastat, 2017

127 Economic Adviser, Government of Punjab, 2015

128 Indiastat, 2017

REFERENCES

NON-FARM INCOME

Christiaensen, Luc; Introduction: Rural Diversification, Secondary Towns and Poverty Reduction: Do Not Miss the Middle, Agricultural Economics 44 (2013) 433-434

Christiaensen, Luc, Joachim De Weerdt, Yasuyuki Todoc; Urbanization and Poverty Reduction: the Role of Rural Diversification and Secondary Towns, Agricultural Economics 44 (2013) 447-459

Davis, J. (2006). Rural non-farm livelihoods in transition economies: Emerging issues and policies. Journal of Agricultural and Development Economics 3(2):180-224

Nagler, P. and W. Naude. (2014). Patterns and Determinants of Non-Farm Entrepreneurship in Rural Africa: New Empirical Evidence

Davis, Junior R., and Dirk J. Bezemer Non-Farm Economies in Developing Countries and Transforming Countries (2004) by published by DfID

Dorosh, Paul, James Thurlow; Agriculture and small towns in Africa, Agricultural Economics 44 (2013) 449-459

Dudwick, Nora at al. From Farm to Firm: Rural Urban Transition in Developing Countries. Directions in Development. The World Bank. Washington DC

Fox, Louise and Thomas Pave Sohnesen, Household Enterprises in Sub Saharan Africa: Why the Matter for Growth, Jobs and Livelihoods, Policy Research Working Paper 6184

Giné X., Mansuri. 2011. Money or ideas? A field experiment on constraints to entrepreneurship in rural Pakistan. Unpublished manuscript, World Bank, Washington, DC

Haggblade, Steven, Peter Hazell and Thomas Reardon. (2007). Transforming the Rural Non-farm Economy. IFPRI

Washington DC. Hazell, S. W. (2008). Access to rural non-farm employment and enterprise development

Haussmann, R., et al. The Atlas of Economic Complexity: Mapping Paths to Prosperity. IFAD. (2010). Rural Poverty Report 2011. Rome, Italy: Quintily. ILO. (2008)

Livestock Thematic Papers Tools for project design, Livestock and rural finance, IFAD

Report V: Skills for improved productivity, employment growth and development. Geneva. IEG (Independent Evaluation Group). 2014. The Big Business of Small Enterprises: Evaluation of the World Bank Group Experience with Targeted Support to Small and Medium-Size Enterprises, 2006-12. Washington, DC: World Bank. 2011. Assessing IFC's Poverty Focus and Results. Washington, DC: World Bank

Jonasson, E., and Helfand, S. (2008). Locational Determinants of Rural Non-agricultural Employment: Evidence from Brazil. Working Paper 2008/02. University of California.

Lampetti et al. The Changing Face of Rural Space: Agriculture and Rural Development in the Western Balkans. Directions in Development. Agriculture and Rural Development. World Bank. Washington DC

Lanjouw, P. (2001). Non-Farm Employment and Poverty in Rural El Salvador. Great Britain: Pergamon

Lanjouw, Jean O. and Peter Lanjouw. (2001). The Rural Non-Farm Sector: Issues and Evidence from Developing Countries

Losch, Bruno; Sandrine Fréguin-Gresh, Eric Thomas White. 2012. Structural Transformation and Rural Change Revisited: Challenges for Late Developing Countries in a Globalizing World. African development Forum Series. Washington DC: World Bank

Nagler, P. and W. Naude. (2014). Patterns and Determinants of Non-Farm Entrepreneurship in Rural Africa: New Empirical Evidence

Reardon, Thomas, J. Edward Taylor, Kostas Stamoulis, Peter Lanjouw and Arsenio Balisacan, Effects of Non-Farm Employment on Rural Income Inequality in Developing Countries: An Investment Perspective (2000)

Reka Sundaram-Stukel, K. D. (2006). Fostering growth of the rural non-farm sector in Africa: The case of Tanzania. Sawada, Naotaka. Improving the Rural Investment Climate for Income generation. A Background Paper for the World Development Report 2013

Start, D. (2011). The Rise and Fall of the Rural Non-farm Economy: Poverty Impacts and Policy Options. Development Policy Review 19 (4): 491-505. World Bank. (2008)

World Development Report: Agriculture for Development. Washington D.C World Bank. (2009)

World Development Report 2009: Reshaping Economic Geography. Washington D.C. World Bank, IMF. (2013)

Global Monitoring Report 2013: Rural-Urban Dynamics and the Millennium Development Goals. Washington D.C. World Bank (2013)

Growing Africa: Unlocking the Potential of Agribusiness. World Bank (2015)

Zhu, N., X. Luo (2006), "Non-farm activity and rural income inequality: a case study of two provinces in China", Policy Research Working Paper No. 3811, The World Bank

Acharya, S. (1989), Agricultural Wages in India: A Disaggregated Analysis, Indian Journal of Agricultural Economics, Vol.44, pp. 121–139

Acharya, S. and Mitra, A. (2000), The Potential of Rural Industries and Trade to provide Decent Work Conditions: A Data Reconnaissance in India, SAAT Working Paper, South Asia Multidisciplinary Advisory Team, New Delhi: International Labour Organization

Banerjee, A. (1996), Notes Towards a Theory of Industrialization in the Developing World mimeo, M.I.T., Cambridge, Massachussets, USA

Banerjee, A. and Munshi, K. (2000), Networks, Migration and Investment: Insiders and Outsiders in Tirupur's Production Cluster, mimeo, M.I.T. Cambridge, Massachussets, USA

Bliss, C., P. Lanjouw, and N. Stern (1998), Population Growth, Employment Expansion and Technological Change, in Economic Development in Palanpur Over Five Decades (ed. P. Lanjouw and N. Stern), Oxford: Oxford University Press

Datt, G. (1997), Bargaining Power, Wages and Employment: An Analysis of Agricultural Labor Markets in India, New Delhi: Sage

Datt, G. and M. Ravallion (1998), Farm Productivity and Rural Poverty In India, FCND Discussion Paper No. 42, Washington DC: IFPRI

Datt, G. and M. Ravallion (1996b), India's Checkered History in the Fight Against Poverty: Are There Lessons for the Future?, Economic and Political Weekly, 31(35–37)

Deaton, A. (1997), The Analysis of Household Surveys, World Bank: Johns Hopkins Press

Deaton., A. and A. Tarozzi (2000), Prices and Poverty in India, mimeo, Research Program in Development Studies, Princeton University, Princeton, New Jersey, USA

Drèze, J.P. and A.K. Sen (1995), India: Economic Development and Social Opportunity, New Delhi: Oxford University Press

Drèze, J.P., P. Lanjouw, and N. Sharma (1998), Economic Development 1957-93 in Economic Development in Palanpur Over Five Decades (eds. Lanjouw, P. and N.H. Stern), New Delhi and Oxford: Oxford University Press

Drèze, J.P. and A. Mukherjee (1989), Labour Contracts in Rural India, in The Balance Between Industry and Agriculture in Economic Development, 3 (ed. S. Chakravarty), London: Macmillan

Epstein, S. (1973), South India: Yesterday, Today, and Tomorrow. Mysore Villages Revisited, London: Macmillan

Fisher, T., V. Mahajan, and A. Singha (1997), The Forgotten Sector: Non-Farm Employment and Enterprises in Rural India, London: Intermediate Technology Publications

Government of India (1993), Report of the Expert Group on Estimation of Proportion and Number of Poor, Planning Commission, Government of India, New Delhi, India

Greene, W. (1993), Econometric Analysis, Fourth Edition, New Jersey: Prentice-Hall Inc

Guhan, S. and Joan P. Mencher (1983), Iruvelpattu Revisited, Economic and Political Weekly, 17(23): 1013–1022

Haggblade, S., C. Liedholm, and D. Mead (1986), The Effect of Policy and Policy Reforms on Non-Agricultural Enterprises and Employment in Developing Countries. A Review of Past Experiences, International Development Working Paper No. 27, Michigan State University, East Lansing, Michigan, USA

Harriss, B. (1987a), Regional Growth Linkages from Agriculture, Journal of Development Studies, 23 (2): 275–289

Harriss, B. (1987b), Regional Growth Linkages from Agriculture and Resource Flows in Non-Farm Economy, Economic and Political Weekly, 22 (1 – 2): 31–46

Harriss, B. and J. Harriss (1984), Generative or Parasitic Urbanism? Some Observations from the Recent History of a South Indian Market Town, in Development and the Rural Urban Divide, (eds. J. Harriss and M. Moore), London: Frank Cass, pp.82–101

Harriss, J. (1977), The Limitations of HYV Technology in North Arcot District: The View from a Village, in The Green Revolution? Technology and Change in Rice Growing Areas of Tamil Nadu and Sri Lanka (ed. B. H. Farmer), London: Macmillan

Harriss, J. (1989), Knowing About Rural Economic Change in Conversations Between Economists and Anthropologists (ed. P. Bardhan), Oxford: Oxford University Press

Hazell, P. and S. Haggblade (1990), Rural-Urban Growth Linkages in India, PRE Working Paper Series No. 430. Agriculture and Rural Development Department, Washington DC: World Bank

Hazell, P., C. Ramasamy and V. Rajagopalan (1991b), An Analysis of the Indirect Effects of Agricultural Growth on the Regional Economy, The Green Revolution Reconsidered: The Impact of High-Yielding Rice Varieties in South India (eds. P. Hazzell and C. Ramasamy), Baltimore: Johns Hopkins University Press

Hazell, P. and C. Ramasamy (1991), The Green Revolution Reconsidered: The Impact of HighYielding Rice Varieties in South India, Baltimore: Johns Hopkins

Hossain, M. (1984), Productivity and Profitability in Bangladesh Rural Industries, Bangladesh Development Studies (Special issue on Rural Industrialization in Bangladesh), 2 (March/June): 127–162. IFPRI (1985), International Food Policy Research Institute Report, 1984, Washington: IFPRI

Jayaraman and Lanjouw (1999), The Evolution of Poverty and Inequality in Indian Villages, World Bank Research Observer, 14(1): 1–30

Jolliffe, D. (1998), Skills, Schooling and Household Income in Ghana, World Bank Economic Review, 12(1): 81–104

Kurien, C. T. (1980), Dynamics of Rural Transformation: A Case Study of Tamil Nadu, Economic and Political Weekly, Annual Number (February)

Lanjouw, J. and P. Lanjouw (forthcoming), Rural Non-Farm Employment: A Survey, Agricultural Economics

Leaf, M.J. (1983), The Green Revolution and Cultural Change in a Punjab Village, 1965-1978, Economic Development and Cultural Change,31(2): 227–270

Little, I.M.D., D. Mazumdar and J. Pager Jr. (1987), Small Manufacturing Enterprises: a Comparative analysis of India and Other Economies, New York: Oxford University Press for the World Bank

Ramachandran, V. K. (1990), Wage Labour and Unfreedom in Agriculture, London: Claredon

Ranjan, S. (1994), Rural Non-farm Employment in Uttar Pradesh: 1971–1991: A Regional Analysis, M. Phil. Thesis, Trivandrum: Centre for Development Studies

Ravallion, M. and Datt, G. (1996), How Important to India's Poor is the Sectoral Composition of Economic Growth?, World Bank Economic Review 10(1): 1–25

Ravallion, M. and Datt. G. (1999), When is Growth Pro-Poor? Evidence from the Diverse Experiences of India's States, Policy Research Working Paper 2263, Washington DC: World Bank

Saith, A. and A. Tankha (1992), Longitudinal Analysis of Structural Change in a North Indian Village: 1970–1987, Working Paper Series No. 128, The Hague: Institute of Social Studies

Sen, A. (1996), Economic Reforms, Employment and Poverty: Trends and Options, Economic and Political Weekly, Vol.31, No.35–37

Shariff, A. (1999), India Human Development Report: A Profile of Indian States in the 1990s, New Delhi: Oxford University Press

Sharma, Rita, and Thomas Poleman (1993), The New Economics of India's Green Revolution: Income and Employment Diffusion in Uttar Pradesh, Ithaca: Cornell University Press

Sipahimalani (1999), Education in Rural Indian Household – A Gender-based Perspective, Working Paper No.68, p.56, New Delhi: National Council of Applied Economic Research

Srinivas, M.N. (1976), The Remembered Village, New Delhi: Oxford University Press. Unni, J. (1996), Non-Agricultural Employment and Rural Livelihoods: Macro Vis-a-Vis Micro View, The Indian Journal of Labour Economics, 39(4): 795–808

Unni, J. (1997), Non-Agricultural Employment, Livelihoods and Poverty in Rural India, Working Paper No. 88, Ahmedabad: Gujarat Institute of Development Research

Vaidyanathan, A. (1983), Labor Use in Rural India, Economic and Political Weekly, Vol.21, No.52

Vijverberg, W. (1988), Profits from Self-Employment, LSMS Working Paper No. 43, Washington DC: World Bank

Visaria, P. and R. Basant (1994), Non-Agricultural Employment in India: Trends and Prospects, New Delhi: Sage

Wadley, S.S. and B.W. Derr (1990), Karimpur 1925–1984: Understanding Rural India Through Restudies, in Conversations Between Economists and Anthropologists (ed. P.Bardhan), New Delhi: Oxford University Press

Walker, T.S. and J.G. Ryan (1990), Village and Household Economies in India's Semi-Arid Tropics, Baltimore: Johns Hopkins

Wiser, W. and C. Wiser (1971), Behind Mud Walls, Berkeley: California

Adams (Jr), R.H. (2001) Non-farm Income, Inequality and Poverty in Rural Egypt and Jordan

Policy Research Working Paper 2572. World Bank, Washington, D.C. Adams (Jr), R.H. and He, Jane J. (1995) Sources of Income Inequality and Poverty in Rural Pakistan. Research Report No. 102. International Food Policy Research Institute, Washington, D.C

Barrett, C.B., Reardon, T. and Webb, P. (2001) Non-farm income diversification and household livelihood strategies in rural Africa: Concepts, dynamics and policy implications, Food Policy, 26(4): 315-332

Birthal, P.S. and Singh, M.K. (1995) Structure of rural income inequality: A study in western Uttar Pradesh. Indian Journal of Agricultural Economics, 50(2): 168- 175

Chand, R., Prasanna, P.A.L. and Singh, A. (2011) Farm size and productivity: Understanding the strengths of smallholders and their livelihoods. Economic and Political Weekly, 54 (26/27): 5-11

Collier, P., Radwan, S. and Wangwe, S. (1986) Labor and Poverty in Rural Tanzania. Calarendon Press, Oxford, U.K

Coppard, D. (2001) The Rural Non-farm Economy of India: A Review of the Literature. NRI Report No. 2662. Natural Resources Institute, London, U.K

Cowell, F.A. (1995) Measuring Inequality. Harvester Wheatsheaf, Hemel Hempstead

Dabalen. A., Paternostro, S. and Pierre, G. (2004) The Returns to Participation in Non-farm Sector in Rwanda. Policy Research Working Paper 3462. World Bank, Washington, D.C

Datt, G. and Ravallion, M. (1996) Why Have Some Indian States Done Better than Others at Reducing Poverty. Policy Research Working Paper 1594. World Bank, Washington, D.C

Davis, B., Winters, P., Carletto, G., Covarrubias, K., Quinones, E., Zezza, A., Stamoulis, K.,

Bonomi, G. and DiGiuseppe, S. (2007) Rural Income Generating Activities: A Cross Country Comparison. ESA Working Paper No. 07-16. Agricultural Development Economics Division, Food and Agriculture Organization, Rome

de Janvry, A., Sadoulet, E. and Zhu, N. (2005) The Role of Non-farm Incomes in Reducing Rural Poverty and Inequality in China. Working Paper 1001. Department of Agricultural & Resource Economics, University of California, Berkley. Available at http:// repositories.cdlib.org/are_ucb

Foster, A.D. and Rosenzweig, M.R. (2004) Agricultural productivity growth, rural economic diversity and economic reforms: India, 1970-2000. Economic Development and Cultural Change, 52(3): 509-542

Greene, W. (1993) Econometric Analysis, Prentice-Hall Inc, New Jersey. GoI (Government of India) (2005) Income, Expenditure and Productive Assets of Farmer Households

NSS Report No. 497 (59/33/5). National Sample Survey Organization, Ministry of Statistics and Program Implementation, New Delhi

GoI (2006) Provisional Results of the Fifth Economic Census. Central Statistical Organization, Ministry of Statistics and Program Implementation, New Delhi

GoI (2010) National Accounts Statistics, 2007

Central Statistical Organization, Ministry of Statistics and Program Implementation, New Delhi

Lanjouw, P. (1999) Rural non-agricultural employment and poverty in Ecuador. Economic Development and Cultural Change, 48(1): 91-122

Lanjouw, P. and Stern, N. (1993) Agricultural change and inequality in Palanpur. In: The Economics of Rural Organization: Theory, Practice and Policy, Eds: A

Braverman, K. Hoff, and J. Stglitz. Oxford University Press, New York. Lanjouw, P. and Shariff, A. (2002) Rural Non-farm Employment in India: Access, Income and Poverty Impact. Working Paper 81. National Council of Applied Economic Research, New Delhi. 48 Agricultural Economics Research Review Vol. 27 (No.1) January-June 2014

Lanjouw, P. and Murgai, R. (2008) Poverty Decline, Agricultural Wages and Non-Farm Employment in Rural India: 1983-2004. Working Paper 437. Stanford Centre for International Development, Stanford University, Stanford

Lerman, R. and Yitzhaki, S. (1985) Income inequality effects by income source: a new approach and application to the U.S. Review of Economics and Statistics, 67(1): 151- 156

Micevska, M. and Rahut, D.B. (2008) Rural non-farm employment in the Himalayas. Economic Development and Cultural Change, 57(1): 163-193

Paul, S. (2004) Income sources effects on inequality. Journal of Development Economics, 73: 435-451

Reardon, T. and Taylor, J.E. (1996) Agro-climatic shock, income inequality and poverty: Evidence from Burkina Faso. World Development, 24(4): 901-914

Reardon, T., Stamoulis, K., Cruz, M.E., Balaiscan, A., Berdegue, J. and Banks, B. (1998) Rural non-farm income in developing countries. The State of Food and Agriculture 1998 (Part III). Food and Agriculture Organization, Rome

Reardon, T., Berdegue, J., Barrett, C.B. and Stamoulis, K. (2007) Household income diversification into rural nonfarm activities. In: Transforming the Rural Non-farm Economy: Opportunities and Threats in the Developing World, Eds: S

Haggblade, P. Hazell, T. Reardon. Johns Hopkins University Press, Baltimore. Sen, A. (1994) Rural labour markets and poverty. Indian Journal of Labour Economics, 37(4): 575-607

Shorrocks, A.F. (1982) Inequality decomposition by factor components. Econometrica, 50: 193-211

Warr, P. (2003) Poverty and economic growth in India. In: Economic Reform and the Liberalization of the Indian Economy, Eds: K. Kalirajan and U. Shankar. Edward Elgar, Cheltenham, UK and Northampton, MA, USA.

Acharya, S. and A. Mitra (2000). "The Potential of Rural Industries and Trade to Provide Decent Work Conditions: A Data Reconnaissance in India", SAAT Working Papers, International Labour Organization, New Delhi. Ahluwalia, M. S. (1978). "Rural Poverty and Agricultural Performances in India" Journal of Development Studies, Vol. 14, No. 3, April

Basant, R., B. L. Kumar and R. Parthasarathy (1998). (edited). Non-Agricultural Employment in Rural India: The Case of Gujarat, Rawat Publications, Jaipur, India

Bhalla, G.S. and G. Singh (1997). "Recent Developments in Indian Agriculture-A State level Analysis" Economic and Political Weekly, Vol. 32, No. 13 (March 29)

Bhattacharya, B. B., N.R. Bhanumurthy and S. Sakthivel (2004). "Economic Reforms and Structural Changes in Employment: A Comparative Analysis of Gender- Specific Employment Behaviour in Organized and Informal Sector in India", an unpublished report, Institute of Economic Growth, Delhi

Central Statistical Organization (CSO). Annual Series of Income – various issues, New Delhi. (2001)

Economic Census 1998- All India Report, New Delhi. Centre for Monitoring Indian Economy, CMIE (2002)

Profiles of Districts, October issue, Centre for Monitoring Indian Economy (CMIE), Mumbai

Chadha, G.K. (2001). "Impact of Economic Reforms on Rural Employment: No Smooth Sailing Anticipated." Indian Jl. of Agricultural Economics, Vol. 56, No.3, pp. 491-97

Chandrasekhar, CP and Jayati Ghosh (2004). "How Feasible is a Rural Employment Guarantee?" Social Scientist, No.4 (July-August): 374-375

Chinna, Rao B. (2004). "Rural Non-farm Employment in Andhra Pradesh", Unpublished report submitted by Agro-Economic Research Centre (AERC), Waltair to the Ministry of Agriculture, GoI, New Delhi

Dreze, J. (2004). "Financial Implications of an Employment Guarantee Act: Preliminary Estimates", A note prepared on behalf of the National Advisory Council, Government of India, New Delhi

Dutta, R.A. and S.L. Bhaiya (2004). "Rural Non-farm Employment in Gujarat", Unpublished report submitted by Agro-Economic Research Centre (AERC), Vallabh Vidyanagar, Gujarat, to the Ministry of Agriculture, GoI, New Delhi

Fisher, T. and V. Mahajan (1998). The Forgotten Sector: Non-farm Employment and Enterprises in Rural India, London: Intermediate Technology Publications

Ghosh, J.K., V. Datta and A. Sinha (2004). "Rural Non-farm Employment in West Bengal". Unpublished report submitted by Agro-Economic Research Centre (AERC), Shantiniketan, West Bengal to the Ministry of Agriculture, GoI, New Delhi

Gogoi Bharati (2004). "Rural Non-farm Employment in Assam", Unpublished report submitted by AgroEconomic Research Centre (AERC), Jorhat to the Ministry of Agriculture, GoI, New Delhi

Gopalappa, D. V. (2004). "Rural Non-farm

Employment in Karnataka", Unpublished report submitted by Agriculture Development and Rural Transformation Unit of the Institute of Economic and Social Change, Bangalore to the Ministry of Agriculture, GoI, New Delhi. Government of India (1994)

Report of the Technical Committee on DPAP and DDP, Ministry of Rural Development, New Delhi. (2001)

Report of the Task Force on Employment Opportunities, Planning Commission, July 2001 (2002)

Special Group on Targeting Ten Million Employment Opportunities Per Year, Planning Commission, May 2002 (2004)

Economic Survey 2003-04, Economics Division, Ministry of Finance, GOI, New Delhi

Grover, D.K. and Sanjay Kumar (2004). "Rural Non-farm Employment in Punjab", Unpublished report submitted by Agro-Economic Research Centre (AERC), Ludhiana, to the Ministry of Agriculture, GOI, New Delhi

Harriss, B. and J. Harris (1984). "Generative or Parasitic Urbanism? Some Observations from the Recent History of a South Indian Market Town", in J. Harris and M. Moore (eds), Development and the Rural Urban Divide, London: Frank Cass, pp. 82-101

Hazell, P.B.R. and S. Haggblade (1991). "Rural-Urban Growth Linkages in India", Indian Jl. of Agricultural Economics, Vol. 46, No.4, pp. 515-529

Hossain, M. (1988). "Nature and Impact of the Green Revolution in Bangladesh," Research Report no. 67, International Food Policy Research Institute, Washington, D.C. USA

Islam Nurul (1997). The Non-farm Sector and Rural Development: Review of Issues and Evidences, FAED paper no. 22, IFPRI, Washington DC

Jha, B. (2005). Rural Non-farm Employment in India, A coordinated and consolidated unpublished report, submitted to Ministry of Agriculture, GOI, New Delhi (2006)

"Employment, Wages and Productivity in Indian Agriculture", IEG Working Paper Series No. E/266/2006

Kajale, Jayanti (2004). "Rural Non-farm Employment in Maharashtra", Unpublished report submitted by Agro-Economic Research Centre (AERC), Pune to the Ministry of Agriculture, GOI, New Delhi

Kumar, Amalendu (2004). "Rural Non-farm Employment in Bihar", Unpublished report submitted by AgroEconomic Research Centre (AERC), Bhagalpur to the Ministry of Agriculture, GoI, New Delhi

Lanjouw, P. and A. Shariff (2002). "Rural Non-farm Employment in India: Access Impact and Poverty Impact", Working Paper Series N. 81, National Council of Applied Economic Research (NCAER), New Delhi

Lewis, W. A., (1954). "Economic Development with Unlimited Supplies of Labour", The Manchester School, Vol. 22, No. 2, pp. 242-258

Lipton, M. (1983) "Poverty, Undernutrition and Hunger", World Bank Staff Working Paper No. 597, Washington: World Bank

Mahendra Dev, S (2000). "Economic Reforms, Poverty, Income Distribution and Employment", Economic and Political Weekly, Vol. 35, No. 10 (March 4)

Mellor, John W. (1978) The New Economics of Growth – A Strategy for India and the Developing World, A Twentieth Century Fund Study, Ithaca : Cornell University Press

Mishra, B. K. (2003). "Rural Non-farm Employment in Uttar Pradesh", Unpublished reports submitted by Agro-Economic Research Centre (AERC), Allahabad to the Ministry of Agriculture, GOI, New Delhi

NABARD (1992). Refinance Assistance for Non-Farm Sector Activities, NABARD, Mumbai

Nayyar, Rohini (1998). "An Assessment of Wage Employment Programmes", in R. Radhakrishna and A. N. Sharma (ed.), Empowering Rural Labour in India: Market, State and Mobilisation published by, Institute for Human Development, New Delhi

National Sample Survey Organization (NSSO, 1990). Results of the Fourth Quinquennial Survey on Employment and Unemployment (All India), NSS Forty third Round (July 1987-June 1988), NSS Report no. 409, New Delhi

(NSSO, 1997) Employment and Unemployment in India, 1993-94, NSS Fiftieth Round (July 1993-June 1994), NSS Report no. 409, New Delhi

(NSSO 2001). Employment and Unemployment Situation in India, 1999-2000, NSS Fifty-fifth Round (July 1999-June 2000), NSS Report no. 458, Key Results, Part-I, Part-II, New Delhi

Papola, T.S. (1987). "Rural Industrialisation and Agricultural Growth: A Case Study in India", in Islam Rizwanul, (eds.) Rural

Industrialisation and Employment in Asia,
ILO / ARTEP, New Delhi (2005)

"A Universal Programme is Feasible",
Economic and Political Weekly, Vol.
(40), No.7 (February 12): 594-599

Patnaik, P. (2005). "On the Need for Providing
Employment Guarantee", Economic and Political
Weekly,Vol.40, No. 2 (January 15): pp. 203-207

Rajiv Gandhi Foundation (2000). Panchayati
Raj in India Status Report 1999, Rajiv Gandhi
Task Force on Panchayati Raj, New Delhi

Saith, A. (1991). "Development
Strategies and the Rural Poor", Journal
of Peasant Studies 17(2): 171-243

Saleth, R.M. (1999). Strategic Linkages in Rural
Diversification: Empirical Analysis and Policy
Issues. New Delhi: Commonwealth Publishers

Sen, Abhijit (2003). "Globalisation Growth
and Inequality in South Asia- The Evidence
from Rural India", in Jayati Ghosh and C. P.
Chandrasekhar (eds), Work and Well being in
the Age of Finance, New Delhi : Tulika Books

Shah, Mihir (2004). "National Rural
Employment Guarantee Act: A Historic
Opportunity", Economic and Political Weekly,
Vol. 39, No.49 (December 11): 5287-5290

Sidhu, R. S. and Sukhpal Singh (2004).
"Agricultural Wages and Employment in
Punjab," Economic and Political Weekly,
Vol.39, (September 11): 4132-4135

Srivastava, A. (2004). "Rural Non-farm
Employment in Madhya Pradesh", Unpublished
reports submitted by Agro-Economic
Research Centre (AERC), Jabalpur to the
Ministry of Agriculture, GOI, New Delhi

Srivastava, Ravi (1997). "Poverty Reduction in
India: Economic Growth, Human Development
and Antipoverty Programme", a background paper
for the World Bank. Swaminathan, R. (2004).
"Rural Non-farm Employment in Tamilnadu",
Unpublished report submitted by Agro-Economic
Research Centre (AERC), Chennai to the
Ministry of Agriculture, GOI, New Delhi

Tuteja, U. (2004). "Rural Non-farm Employment
in Haryana", Unpublished report submitted by
AgroEconomic Research Centre (AERC), Delhi
to the Ministry of Agriculture, GOI, New Delhi

Uma Rani and Jeemol Unni (2004).
"Unorganized and Organized Manufacturing
in India- Potential for Employment Generating
Growth" Economic and Political Weekly,

Vol. 49, (October 9): 4568-4580

Unni, J. (1997). 'Non-Agricultural Employment,
Livelihoods and Poverty in Rural India",
Working Paper No. 88, Ahmedabad: Gujarat
Institute of Development Research

Unni, Jeemol, N. Lalitha, and Uma Rani (2001).
"Economic Reforms and Productivity Trends
in Indian Manufacturing", Economic and
Political Weekly,Vol..36, No. 41, pp. 3915-3922

Vaidya, C.S, M.L. Sharma and N.K. Sharma
(2004). "Rural Non-farm Employment in Himachal
Pradesh", An unpublished reports submitted by
Agro-Economic Research Centre (AERC), Shimla
to the Ministry of Agriculture, GoI, New Delhi

Vaidyanathan, A. (1986). "Labour Use in
Rural India: A Study of Spatial and Temporal
Variations", Economic and Political Weekly, Vol.21,
No. 52 (December 27): A130-A146 (1994).

"Employment Situation: Some Emerging
Perspectives," Economic and Political Weekly,
Vol.29, No. 50 (December 10): 3147-3156

Visaria, P. and R. Basant (1994). "Non
Agricultural Employment in India:
Problems and Perspective", in P

Visaria and R. Basant (ed.) Non Agricultural
Employment in India, New Delhi: Sage
Publications Vyas, V. S. and G. Mathai (1978)
"Farm and Non-Farm Employment in Rural
Areas: A Perspective for Planning" Economic
and Political Weekly, Vol.13, No. 6 and 7,
(February annual number): 333-347.

LIVESTOCK

[CLMFA] Compound Livestock Feed
Manufacturers Association

CLFMA Of India. http://www.clfmaofindia.org/

Ahuja, V, and E. Redmond. "Economic
and Policy Issues in the Livestock Service
Delivery to the Poor." In Tropical and
Animal Health and Production. 2004

Ahuja, V, J Morrenhof, and A Sen. "The Delivery
of Veterinary Services to Poorer Communities:
The Case of Rural Orissa, India." Scientific and
Technical Review (OIE) 22, no. 3 (2003): 931-948

Ahuja, V, K.E. McConnell, D Umali, and
C de Haan. "Are the Poor Willing to Pay for
Livestock Services? Evidence from Rural
India." Indian Journal of Agricultural
Economics 58, no. 1 (2003): 84-100

Ahuja, V, M Rajasekhar, and R Raju. Animal Health for Poverty Alleviation: a Review of Key Issues for India. Background Paper, Washington, DC: mimeo, 2008

Ahuja, V., et al. Agricultural Services and the Poor: Case of Livestock Health and Breeding Services in India. IIM, Ahmedabad, The World Bank, Washington DC and SDC, Bern

Akter, S, et al. Drought and Vulnerability of Livestock in India. Vol. ILRI Targeting and Innovation Discussion Paper 9. London and Nairobi: Overseas Development Institute, 2008

Bhasin, N.R. "Livestock and Pro-poor in Bihar and Orissa". Background paper prepared for a World Bank study. Washington DC

Bhatia, J., K. Pandey, and K.S. Suhag. "Economic Analysis of Sheep and Goat Rearing in Rainfed Region of Haryana." Indian Journal of Animal Sciences 75, no. 12 (2005): 1423-1432

Birthal, P.S. India's Livestock Sector: an Overview. Background Paper prepared for a World Bank study, Washington, DC:

"Linking Smallholder Livestock Producers to Markets: Issues and Approaches." 67th Annual Conference of the Indian Society of Agricultural Economics, November 5-7, 2007. Lucknow: Indian Society of Agricultural Economics

Birthal, P.S. "Linking Smallholder Livestock Producers to Markets: Issues and Approaches." Indian Journal of Agricultural Economics 63, no. 1 (2008): 19-37

Birthal, P.S., A.K. Jha, and A.K. Joseph. Livestock Production and the Poor in India. New Delhi

Birthal, P.S., and A.K. Jha. "Economic Losses Due to Various Constraints in Dairy Production in India." Indian Journal of Animal Sciences (75) 12 (2005): 1470-1475

Birthal, P.S., and V.K. Taneja. Livestock Sector in India: Opportunities and Challenges for Smallholders. Vol. Workshop proceedings 14, in Smallholder Livestock Production in India: Opportunities and Challenges, edited by P.S. Birthal, V.K. Taneja and W. Thorpe. New Delhi and Kenya: National Centre for Agricultural economics and Policy Research (NCAP); The International Livestock Research Institute (ILRI), 2006

Birthal, P.S., P.K. Joshi, and A. Gulati. Vertical Coordination in High-value Food Commodities: Implications for Smallholders. Markets, Trade and Institutions Division Discussion Paper No. 85, Washington, DC: International

food Policy Research Institute, 2005

Birthal, P.S., P.R. Deoghare, S. Kumar, Riyazuddin, J. Jayshankar, and A. Kumar. Development of Small Ruminant Sector in India. Project Report, New Delhi: NCAP, 2003

Blümmel, M., and P. Parthasarathy Rao. "Fodder Market in Hyderabad in India and Stover Value Chain Evaluation from Farmer to Trader in One Selected Supply Area: a Rapid Assessment." Draft report prepared for the International Livestock Research Institute, Nairobi, 2008. Central Statistical Organization. Central Statistical Organization. http://mospi.nic.in/cso_test1.htm

Central Statistical Organization. National Accounts Statistics Back Series 2007. Government of India report, New Delhi: Ministry of Statistics & Programme Implementation, 2007

Chand, S. An Economic Analysis of Production and Marketed Surplus of Milk on Rural Farms in Kurukshetra District. PhD Thesis, Karnal: Division of Dairy Economics, Statistics and Management, National Dairy Research Institute, 1997

Chandel, B.S., D.K. Jain, and J.P. Dhaka. Dairy Value Chain Analysis in Dynamic Regions of India. Background paper to the India Livestock Sector Review, Washington, DC: World Bank

Chawla, N.K., M.G.P. Kurup, and V.P. Sharma. Animal Husbandry: State of the Indian Farmer. Vols. A Millennium Study, Vol. XII. New Delhi: Academic Foundation, 2004. —. Animal Husbandry: State of the Indian Farmer. Vols. A Millennium Study, Vol. XII. New Delhi: Academic Foundation, 2004. Comptroller and Auditor General of India. Comptroller and Auditor General of India. 2009. http://www.cag.gov.in/

Conroy, C. Livestock Sector Growth and Poverty, with Particular Reference to India. Chatham: National Resources Institute, 2004

Conroy, C., et al. "Improving Backyard Poultry Keeping: A case study from India." Agricultural Research and Extension Network. 2005. http://dfid-agricultureconsultation.nri.org/theme1/keypapers/livestockrevolution.pdf.

Punjabi, M., K.M. Singh, R.K.P.Singh, Sujitav Dash, N.R. Bhasin. Dairy Value Chains in Bihar and Orissa. Background paper for the India Livestock Sector Review, Washington, DC: Worldbank

Punjabi, M., K.M. Singh, R.K.P.Singh, Sujitav Dash, N.R. Bhasin. Goat Value Chain Analysis in Bihar and Orissa. Background Paper for the India Livestock Sector

Review, Washington, DC: World Bank

Punjabi, M., K.M. Singh, R.K.P.Singh, Sujitav Dash. Poultry Value Chains in Bihar and Orissa. Background paper prepared for the India Livestock Sector Review, Washington, DC: World Bank

Punjabi, M., B.S. Sathe. Poultry Value Chains in Andhra Pradesh. Background paper prepared for India Livestock Sector Review, Washington, DC: World Bank

Dairy India Yearbook. Dairy India 2007. 2007. http://www.dairyindia.com/

Datanet India Pvt. Ltd. Indiastat.com. http://www.indiastat.com/default.aspx

Delgado, C, M.W. Rosegrant, and S. Meijer. "Livestock to 2020: The Revolution Continues." International Food Policy Research Institute. 2001. http://www.ilri.org/ILRI_Dev/misc-pdf/delgado.pdf

Delgado, C., M.W. Rosegrant, H. Steinfeld, S. Ehui, and C. Courbois. Livestock to 2020: The Next Food Revolution. Vol. Agriculture & Environment Discussion Paper 28. Washington, DC: International Food Policy Research Institute, 1999. Department of Animal Husbandry, Dairying, & Fisheries. 17th Indian Livestock Census 2003-District Wise. 2003

Dhaka, J.P., D.K. Jain, V.K. Kesavan, and L. Singh. A Study of Production and Marketed Surplus Functions for Milk in India. Indo-Swiss Project Report, Karnal: Division of Dairy Economics, Statistics and Management, National Dairy Research Institute, 1998

Dixie, Grahame. "Personal communication." 2008. Erenstein, O., W. Thorpe, J. Singh, and A. Varma. Crop-Livestock Interactions and Livelihoods in the IndoGangetic Plains, India: A Regional Synthesis . Mexico City: CIMMYT., 2007

Fairoze, M.N., et al. "Equitable intensification of smallholder market-oriented poultry production in India through contract farming." In Contract Farming of Milk and Poultry in India: Partnerships to Promote the Environmentally Friendly and Equitable Intensification of Smallholder Livestock Production, by IFPRI-FAO. Washington, DC: International food Policy Research Institute, 2006

FAO. FAOSTAT. Rome: Food and Agriculture Organization of the United Nations, 2009. Gandhi, V., and Z. Zhou. Marketing Of Livestock And Livestock Products. background paper to the India Livestock Sector Review, Washington, DC

GOI. Department of Consumer Affairs. 2002-2008. http://wbconsumers.nic.in/

Government of India. Basic Animal Husbandry Statistics. AHS Series 10, New Delhi: Ministry of Agriculture, 2006. —. Census of India. Registrar General and Census Commissioner. 2001. http://www.censusindia.net/

Government of India. Employment and Unemployment Situation in India: 2004-05

NSS Report No. 515, New Delhi: National Sample Survey Organization, Government of India, 2006

Government of India. Report of the Working Group on Animal Husbandry and Dairying for the Eleventh Five Year Plan (2007-2012). New Delhi: Planning Commission, Government of India, 2007

Government of India. "Report of the Working Group on Animal Husbandry and Dairying for the Tenth Five Year Plan (2002-2007)." Planning Commission Report, New Delhi, 2002

Gupta, J.N., C.B. Singh, and R.K. Patel. "Creditworthiness of Landless Farm Labours, Marginal and Small Farmers for Dairy Loans." Asian Journal of Dairy Research 2, no. 3 (1983): 153-156

Kalra, K.K., S.B. Agarwal, and R. Malhotra. Milk Pricing for Dairy Farms in Milk Shed Area of a Dairy Federation. Research Project Report, Karnal: National Dairy Research Institute (Deemed University), 2008

Krishnan, C., and B. Krishnan. "Role of RRB's in Dairy Financing- A Case Study." Agricultural Banker 12, no. 3 (1989): 10

Kulkarni, S.D. "Agricultural Mechanization: Present Scenario and Perspective." Paper presented at the meeting of the Governing Council of the Asia and the Pacific Center for Agricultural Engineering and Machinery of the UNESCAP, New Delhi, 2005

Kumar, P., and P.S. Birthal. "Changes in Consumption and Demand for Livestock and Poultry Products in India." Indian Journal of Agricultural Marketing 18, no. 3 (2004): 110-123

Kumar, P., Mruthyunjaya, and M.M. Dey. "Long Term Changes in India Food Basket and Nutrition." Economic and Political Weekly, 2007

Kumar, P., Mruthyunjaya, and P.S. Birthal. "Changing cosumption Pattern in South Asia." In Agricultural Diversification and Smallholders in South Asia, edited by P.K. Joshi, A. Gulati and Jr., R. Cummings. New Delhi: Academic Foundation, 2007

Kumar, S. Commercialization of Goat Farming and Marketing of Goats in India. Mathura:

Central Institute for Research on Goats, 2007

Kurup, M.P.G. Livestock Sector: Punjab. Background paper for the India Livestock Sector Review, Washington, DC: World Bank

Kurup, M.P.G., ed. Livestock: the Socio-economic Perspective in Orissa. New Delhi: Manohar Publishers and Distributors, 2003

Kurup, M.P.G. Study of the Livestock Sector in Selected States of East India: Orissa. Background paper for the World Bank review of the India livestock sector

Kurup, M.P.G. Study of the Livestock Sector in Selected States of East India: Punjab. Background paper for the World Bank review of the Livestock Sector

Landes, M., S. Persaud, and J. Dyck. "India's Poultry Sector: Development and Prospects." Agriculture and Trade Reprot WRS04-03, 2004

Landes, M., S. Persaud, and J. Dyck. India's Poultry Sector: Development and Prospects. USDA Agriculture and Trade Report WTS -04-03, Washington, DC: USDA, 2004

Mehta, R. India's Livestock Trade Review. Background paper for the India Livestock Sector Review, Washington, DC: World Bank

Mehta, R., R.G. Nambiar, C. Delgado, and S. Subrahmanyam. Policy, Technical, and Environmental Determinants and Implications of the Scaling-Up of Broiler and Egg Production in India. Annex II, Final Report of IFPRI-FAO Livestock Industrialization Project: Phase II, Washington, DC: International Food Policy Research Institute, 2003

Mehta, R., R.G. Nambiar, C. Delgado, and S. Subramanyam. "Policy, Technical and Environmental Determinants and Implications of the Scaling-up of Broiler and Egg Production in India." In Livestock Industrialization, Trade and Social-Health-Environmental Impacts in Developing Countries, Phase II, by IFPRI-FAO. Washington, DC: International Food Policy Research Institute, 2003

Mehta, Rajesh. India's Livestock Trade Review. Background paper for the World Bank review of India's livestock sector

Milne, Grant. "Personal communication." Washington, DC, June 9, 2009

NABARD. National Bank for Agriculture and Rural Development. 2007. http://www.nabard. org/ NDDB [National Dairy Development Board]

Annual Report 2007/07. Anand: National Dairy Development Board, 2007. NDDB. National Dairy Development Board. 1999-2009. http://www.nddb.org/

NSSO [National Sample Survey Organization]. Access to Modern Technology for Farming: Situation Assessment Survey of Farmers. NSS Report No. 499, New Delhi: Government of India, 2005

NSSO [National Sample Survey Organization]. Livestock Ownership Across Operational Landholding Classes. Report of the Ministry of Statistics and Programme Implementation Report No. 493 (59/18.1/1), New Delhi: Government of India, 2006

Pathak, N.N., and A.K. Garg. "Role and Expectations from Indian Livestock Feed Industry in the Next Millennium." In Proceedings of the 41st National Symposium on Animal Production in the Next Millennium. Mumbai: Compound Livestock Feed Manufacturers Association of India, 1999. Planning Commission. Planning Commission, Government of India. 2008. http://planningcommission.nic.in/

Pradhan, P., V. Ahuja, and P. Venkatramaiah. Livestock Services and the Poor in Orissa – a Case Study. Copenhagen: DANIDA, 2003

Punjabi, M. Private Sector Initiative in Dairy Development in India: Case Study of Nestlé India in Punjab Region of India. Background paper for the World Bank, Washington, DC

Raju, S.R. Dairy Value Chain in Andhra Pradesh. Background paper prepared for the World Bank, Washington, DC

Raju, S.S., and R. Chand. Agricultural Insurance in India: Problems and Prospects. New Delhi: National Centre for Agricultural Economics and Policy Research, 2008

Ramachandra, K.V., V.K. Taneja, K.T. Sampath, S. Anandan, and U.B. Angadi. Livestock Feed Resources in Different Agro-ecosystems of India: Availability, Requirement and Their Management. Bangalore: National Institute of Animal Nutrition and Physiology

Ramaswami, B., P.S. Birthal, and P.K. Joshi. Efficiency and distribution in contract farming: The case of Indian Poultry Growers. Markets, Trade and Institutions Discussion Paper No. 91, Washington, DC: International Food Policy Research Institute, 2006

Rao, Viroji S.T. "Research Priorities and Policy Options for Backyard Poultry Development to 2020." In Poultry Research Priorities to 2020, edited by P.V.K. Sasidhar. Izatnagar: Central Avian Research Institute, 2006

Reddy, Y V R Chandra Mohan. "A Study of Livestock Markets and Marketing of Livestock in Rangareddy District of Andhra Pradesh." Hyderabad: MSc Dissertation, Department of Agricultural Economics, Acharya N.G. Ranga Agricultural University, 2000

Saha, A. "An Analysis of the Dairy Knowledge and Information System in Birbhum West Bengal." Karnal: National Dairy Research Institute (unpublished M.Sc. Thesis), 2001

Sathe, B.S. "Personal communication." January 2008. Sharma, R., and A. Sharma. "Cytokines: Novel immunoregulatory molecules." In Advance in Immunology and Immunopathology, edited by R.S. Chauhan, G.K. Singh and D.K. Agrawal, 19-25. Patnagar: SIIP, 2001

Sharma, V.P., A. Nin Pratt, A. Kumar, R.V. Singh, and S. Staal. Dairy Development in India. Vol. Pakistan and India Dairy Development Case Studies, in Dairy Development for the Resource Poor, edited by S. Staal, A. Nin Pratt and M.A. Jabbar. Rome and Nairobi: FAO and ILRI, 2008

Singh, C.B., S.B. Agarwal, N. Chandra, S.K. Jha, and R.A. Dey. Cross-breeding Technology Adoption and Constraints Identification in Different Regions of India. Karnal: Dairy Economics, Statistics and Management Division, National Dairy Research Institute

Singh, M., and A. Chauhan. "Constraints Faced By Dairy Owners In Adoption Of Scientific Dairy Farming Practices." Indian Journal of Dairy Science 59, no. 1 (2006): 49-51

Singh, N., K.B. Singh, H.K. Verma, and J. Singh. "Adoption Pattern of Artificial Insemination in Punjab." Indian Journal of Animal Reproduction 27, no. 1 (2006): 23-26

Singh, R., A.L. Nanda, and P.S. Dahiya. "Agricultural Credit Overdues." Financing Agriculture 27, no. 1 (1995): 4-7

Singh, Surjit, and Radheyshyam Sharma. Impact Assessment of the District Poverty Initiative Project, Rajasthan. Impact Assessment, Institute of Development Studies, Jaipur: Institute of Development Studies, 2008

Sinha, M.K. "Economic Analysis of Institutional Dairy in Tribal Area of Bihar." Karnal: Ph.D. Thesis, National Dairy Research Institute

Sirohi, S., A. Kumar, S. Gokhale, K. Elumalai, G. Sinha, and I. Wright. Livestock Support Services in India. Washington, DC:

Skees, J. R., and A. Enkh-Amgalan. "Examining the Feasibility of Livestock Insurance in Mongolia." Working Paper 2886, Washington, DC, 2002

Staal, S., A. Nin Pratt, and M.A. Jabbar. Dairy Development for the Resource Poor: a Comparison of Dairy Policies in South Asia and East Africa. Vol. 2. Rome and Nairobi: FAO and ILRI, 2008

Subrahmanyam, S., and C.S. Murthy. "Economics of Small Ruminant, Pigs, and Backyard Poultry Production in Orissa." ISNRMPO Programme Series 5, 2006

Thornton, P.K., et al. "Mapping Poverty and Livestock in the Developing World." International Livestock Research Institute. International Livestock Research Institute. 2002. http://www.ilri.org/InfoServ/Webpub/Fulldocs/Mappoverty/index.htm

Vaidya, S.V. "Presidential Address." In Proceedings of 41st National Symposium on Animal Production in the Next Millennium. Mumbai: Compound Livestock Feed Manufacturers Association of India, 1999

World Bank. India Livestock Sector Review: Enhancing Growth and Development. Economic and Sector Work, Washington, DC: The World Bank, 1996. —. World Development Report: Agriculture for Development. Washington, DC: The World Bank, 2008.

CONSTRUCTION

http://www.caravanmagazine.in/vantage/welfare-construction-workers-why-has-kerala-succeeded-where-other-states-have-failed

https://www.youthkiawaaz.com/2017/02/conditions-of-construction-workers/

http://nceuis.nic.in/Final_Edited_Social_Security_Repor.htm

http://www.rediff.com/business/special/special-why-indias-construction-slowdown-threatens-to-increase-poverty/20160510.htm

http://journals.sagepub.com/doi/pdf/10.1177/0973703016648028

http://timesofindia.indiatimes.com/india/Minimal-use-of-building-cess-for-workers-shocks-Supreme-Court/articleshow/46248891.cms

https://www.equaltimes.org/indias-inner-migrants-find-work-but-not-rights?lang=en#.WWJZ04SGPIU

http://www.thehindu.com/news/cities/bangalore/labourers-at-army-housing-project-illtreated/article3278237.ece

https://www.equaltimes.org/indias-inner-migrants-find-work-but-not-rights?lang=en#.WWJZ04SGPIU

http://www.firstpost.com/business/underpaid-vulnerable-overworked-indias-unseen-women-labourers-2041003.html

http://www.thehindu.com/opinion/op-ed/india-has-no-room-for-its-wandering-builders/article3371330.ece

https://www.youthkiawaaz.com/2017/02/conditions-of-construction-workers/

http://www.indiatogether.org/law-and-welfare-benefits-for-construction-workers-human-rights

http://www.rediff.com/business/special/special-why-indias-construction-slowdown-threatens-to-increase-poverty/20160510.htm

http://www.aajeevika.org/labour-and-migration.php

http://www.eldis.org/vfile/upload/1/document/0903/Dhaka_CP_2.pdf

https://cafedissensus.com/2014/08/01/the-invisible-city-makers-of-migration-and-migrant-workers-in-india/

http://www.ijaiem.org/Volume4Issue5/IJAIEM-2015-05-22-61.pdf

http://data.conferenceworld.in/MIMT/P143-149.pdf

CHAPTER VI

ON HANDICRAFTS

What we call handicrafts and handlooms now are innovations of yesterday, providing economic sustenance while strengthening cultural moorings. Like our diversity in cuisines, our great aesthetic traditions are reflected in our crafts and arts, across a variety of colours and shapes, highlighting a country with eighteen major and 1,600 minor languages, cutting across six major religions, fifty-two major tribes, over 6,400 castes, twenty-nine major festivals—all this produced by over 23 million craftsmen, from 360 craft clusters. This patchwork quilt of utility products and sacred objects for daily and ritualistic use across a range of refinement levels is one that provides sustenance to a range of craftsmen (an overused word that can define a simple labourer or a highly skilled artist). The diversity of India's handicrafts remains staggering—a reflection of the numerous historical processes that have shaped the transformation of our society over centuries. Such artefacts showcase prolific variety, highlighting the range of regional and sub-regional group identities across our country—whether it's an implement, an ornament, a headgear, a body decoration or even clothing, this innate need to distinguish tribal identity and conserve its historicity is what has led to this cornucopia of variety.

Consider the impact of our vast geography on local solutions for geo-climatic needs. The bamboo rain shields (termed, 'japi' in Assam), utilized in Assam, Tripura and Meghalaya, are used by farmers as headgear, while similar palm-leaf sunshades are utilized by shepherds as umbrellas in Andhra Pradesh. Such rain shields are often decorated by red appliqued forms, effectively transforming them into votive offerings for a good harvest. The preservation of historicity is another attribute of our handicrafts. When you witness the wielding of tools, and the application of age-old manufacturing techniques, you can hear our ancestors at work, a culture frozen in wood, clay, stone and metal. Whether it's birth or death, marriage or childbearing, all such occasions for joy and sorrow are celebrated through the application of craft—consider the use of terracotta, 'ayyanar' horses as village guardians in Tamil Nadu; many have decorative motifs and ornamentation, others simply showcase subtlety in their proportions. Ordinary functional artefacts are turned into items that hold significant meaning, forming part of life's tribulations and successes—a simple container is utilized by Jains (wooden 'paatra') for alms collecting, while the ornate 'meenakari' is utilized for offering gifts to guests of honour. Our diversity has also been transplanted and modified across distant lands—the 'bandhani' textiles of Gujarat have found transformation in the 'sungadi' of Madurai. Solitary ordinary objects can also turn out to be repositories of differential shades of meaning and symbolism—a 'lota' is equally at home in the kitchen, the bathroom and the prayer room. Similarly, the humble chappal, in its Kolhapuri form, can have multiple variations, of design, structure and texture, with simple and complex methods of assembly, across regions.

The idea of deploying craft regularly is one that has been baked into our body politic—Tamil women utilize kolam as a daily ritual to clean and decorate the entrances of their houses. While we castigate our villages for being dens of ignorance, creativity continues to sprout—with our village youth routinely exposed to techniques of making and transforming materials. While our formal education systems have deprioritized the teaching of craft experiences, there remains significant potential for the rediscovery of our rich heritage of fine craftsmanship.

This synthesis of meaning, function and material, highlights the ingenuity of our tribes and cultures—banana-leaf plates are routinely cut or trimmed as containers; a bamboo can also be processed to create a durable fibre for conversion into bags and pouches. It's not as such about the form or function: the preservation of such motifs and versatile patterns, many of which have evolved through intra-India and external trade-related interactions, have been disseminated across styles—from wood to metal to cloth to stone, with each material and technique providing its own unique amalgamation. Meanwhile, the arrival of foreign immigrants, traders, refugees and conquerors alike has influenced Indian culture—the Mughals brought Iranian influences in metalwork, carpet and silk weaving, while the British and Portuguese introduced wooden carvings of the West in Indianized churches and coastal houses. Showcasing such craft heritage was traditionally done through local bazaars and temple festivals. More recently, exhibitions and trade fairs, government and private alike, have provided additional channels.

STATE OF HANDLOOMS

Cotton is a rather unremarkable plant. Coming in many hues, shapes and sizes, it was historically cultivated across continents, with farmers in India choosing to grow G. Arboreum, a plant about 6 feet in height, which bore yellow or purple flowers and yielded a short-staple fibre. For millennia, peasants in India have cultivated small quantities of cotton, weaving it for their own use and sale in local and regional markets. The crop was typically harvested by hand, with a roller gin employed to remove seeds, a bow used to remove dirt and knots, and the fibre itself spun on a distaff. A spindle was subsequently used to thread it, which was then converted into fabric using looms hung between trees. Such fabric was typically manufactured within rural households, with in-house family labour spending time in non-agricultural seasons spinning cotton on an intermittent basis. Such archaic and laborious methods led to the creation of fabrics whose quality was legendary— the European traveller Marco Polo confirmed Herodotus's observations, terming the fabrics found on the coast of Coromandel as 'the finest and the most beautiful cottons that were found in any part of the world'.[1] The Indian cloth was termed a work of 'incredible perfection', 'a work of fairies or insects, rather than that of men' by Edward Baines, a newspaper proprietor and cotton expert from Leeds in the late eighteenth century.

The town of Khambat, in Anand district, Gujarat, is a nondescript town sitting on alluvial plain deposited by the Mahi River at the north end of the Gulf of Cambay (a moniker for Khambat). A sleepy little town, with a historical tradition for agate bead making that has survived since the Harappan age, the locality was once India's grandest port—its houses were built of stone, despite stone quarries being at least 200 km away, a fact reflective of its grandeur and wealth. Its harbour is now dilapidated and silted, with spring tides rising up more than 30 ft. The city supplied cotton and silk fabrics to merchants from Persia, Tartary, Turkey, Syria, Barbary, Ethiopia and Malacca. The Gujarati cotton cloth has been a significant export item across the Middle East, East Africa and the African hinterland, criss-crossing the landscape on bullock carts, camels, junks and dhows since the fourth century BC. Indian cotton was traded to Egypt via the Red Sea and Persian Gulf ports, and subsequently sold to Greek and Roman merchants.

The net benefit was one of continued affluence, with Roman emperors and Ottoman bureaucrats complaining of the world's treasury accumulating in India. India's exports to Malacca filled the holds of fifteen ships annually in the sixteenth century. As India supplied Europe with clothing, 'the Europeans were themselves submerged in barbarism, ignorance and a state of wilderness' (Mahatma Gandhi).

---

1   Beckert, Sven, Empire of Cotton, 1st Edition, Page 1-15, Penguin Books

The Europeans concocted legends about the origin of cotton, imagining it to be an amalgam of a plant and an animal, pursuing trees where little sheep grew and bent down at night to drink water.

With demand growing, production in cotton workshops became more common by AD 1000, with professional weavers emerging, who focused on the long-distance caravan trade; clusters emerged—Bengal was known for its muslins, the Coromandel coast for its calicoes and Surat for its common fabric.[2] The Mughals contracted weavers in and around Dhaka to produce muslins for the court. New technology was introduced—the roller gin to remove seeds, the treadle loom for silk manufacturing, the upright warper and the spinning wheel. As India's exports grew, so did its influence. India's fabric and subsequently its cotton technology had a wide audience, seeping into Southeast Asia via Buddhist monks, who took it to Java in the fourth century. The Sanskrit word for cotton goods (karpasi) entered the parlance of Hebrew, Greek, Latin, Persian, Arabic, Uigur, Mongolian and Mandarin.

However, things changed soon. The landing of Vasco da Gama at the port of Calicut, pioneering a sea route from Europe to India around the Cape of Good Hope, provided direct access to Indian weavers, cutting out the varied middlemen who were transporting Indian cloth by ship across the Indian Ocean or through the Thar, and the deserts in Persia and Arabia. Da Gama obtained permission from local rulers to trade in Calicut in 1498, which subsequently evolved into the Portuguese establishing a series of trading outposts on India's west coast. The entrance of joint stock companies from the Netherlands and Great Britain saw further expansion of Western interest.[3] The Europeans began expanding their role in the trans-Atlantic trade of Indian cloth, and that between Gujarat and the Arabian Peninsula and eastern Africa, cutting out Gujarati merchants in between.

By the seventeenth century, the British and Dutch were seizing Gujarati ships, regulating the trade in Gujarati textiles on their muskets and bayonets. Such European trading companies purchased cotton textiles in India, trading it for spices in Southeast Asia and exporting it to Europe, or shipping them to Africa to pay for slaves, who were subsequently put to work in the New World. By 1621, the East India Company was importing an estimated 50,000 pieces of cotton goods in Britain annually; within forty years, the number had increased by five times, becoming the firm's most important trading goods (75 per cent of the company's exports in 1766 was Indian cloth). Cotton cloth (now termed calicoes) was now being used in England's bed chambers, curtains, cushions, chairs and closets. The company set up warehouses, terming them factories, in Indian cities like Madras,

2   Beckert, Sven, Empire of Cotton, 1st Edition, Page 20-45, Penguin Books
3   Beckert, Sven, Empire of Cotton, 1st Edition, Page 30-55, Penguin Books

Surat, Dhaka and Calicut, with their agents spanning out far and wide to place orders with banias for cloth and handloom wares.

The process was rather simple—the English merchants contracted a number of banias about eight to ten months before the ships were due to arrive, asking them to secure cloth with particular qualities, designs, prices and delivery dates. Such banias advanced cash to a variety of middlemen, who went from village to village, advancing funds for finished cloth to individual weavers. The cloth came back through the same intermediaries to warehouses in Dhaka, Madras and Calcutta, where merchants graded and prepared them for shipment. The weavers had control over the timing and organization of their work, with access to their own tools and the right to sell their wares to whoever they wanted to. Most were still poor, but could increase production and raise prices. This warehousing-bania system lasted for over two centuries, until the advance of trading networks on the power of a bayonet became unstoppable, squeezing out Indian and Arab traders. The decline of Surat was reflected in the rise of Bombay.

The company and its agents went even further, seeking to replace local moneylenders with their own currency fiat. Weavers, who had already lost the ability to set prices for cloth, were now in hock for loans to the company as well. Coercive power was deployed directly against the weavers, seeking to convert them into wage workers, who were regulated and prevented from selling their own cloth on the open market. Taxation sought to penalize those workers who produced for others, while corporal punishment and violence were administered through a local force. The value of a product that an Indian weaver gained, subsequently fell from 33 per cent in the seventeenth century to just 6 per cent by the late eighteenth century. Meanwhile, European cloth imports from India rose from 30 million yards in 1727 to 80 million yards by the 1790s.

With Indian cloth becoming more accessible, demand rose and so did the means of production to substitute imports in countries like England.[4] European linen and woollen manufacturers sought protection from their governments from Indian imports. The British parliament debated Indian textile imports in 1623, terming them as injurious to national interest. England imposed a 10 per cent duty on all calicoes and Indian linen and silks imported in 1685, which was doubled to 20 per cent by 1690. Printed cottons were banned for import in England in 1701, leading to importation of plain calicoes for further processing in England. By 1774, the parliament had decreed that cotton cloth sold in England had to be spun and woven in England. European manufacturers sought to copy Indian techniques and designs, with the French East India Company paying specific attention to

---

4   Beckert, Sven, Empire of Cotton, 1st Edition, Page 40-65, Penguin Books

India's woodblock printing techniques. Over two centuries, English cotton printers sought to collect and copy Indian designs. Eventually, the impact of this technology transfer and the subsequent Industrial Revolution led to a reversal, under arms, of the traditional trading pattern. The British now sought to purchase cotton, ship it to factories in Manchester and then ship back textiles to the vast unprotected Indian market. Where once they sought to disintermediate Indian merchants, they now did the same to Indian weavers.

In modern times, we've seen a recovery of sorts. The handloom segment contributes over 11 per cent of the total cloth produced in the country, along with a significant proportion of export earnings (US$360.02 million in FY2015–16).[5] India has the highest handloom capacity in the world, while possessing the lowest average cotton-spinning cost. We also remain the largest exporter of yarn in the international market, the biggest producer of jute in the world, second in silk production (producing all four commercial varieties of silk) and second in cotton production, while being fifth in synthetic fibre production as of 2015.[6] With over 4.3 million people directly involved in production, India's handloom industry is the second largest provider of employment for rural India, with about 2.4 million handlooms of varying designs and age in existence. About 84 per cent of all weavers live in rural India, with 60.5 per cent living in North-east India and West Bengal (Assam accounts for 44.6 per cent, West Bengal 14.6 per cent and Andhra Pradesh 6.4 per cent); 78 per cent of all weavers are female, who account for the labourious pre-loom and post-loom activities.

CASE STUDY: DANKE KA KAAM

Danke Ka Kaam is a surface ornamentation technique often practised in Udaipur and the Mewar region of Rajasthan.[7] The technique uses diamond concave relief (typically made of sheet metals like gold, silver and plated metals), all of which is stitched on to a fabric using zardozi embroidery. The technique is often utilized to build flower and border motifs on textile garments. This craft was originally pioneered by Bohra Muslims, who migrated to the area in the sixteenth century. The four-sided concave metal pieces offer versatility in shape, with combinations with zardozi, coloured threads and beads offering extra variety. Such work is

---

5   Handloom Industry in India, IBEF. Sourced from: https://www.ibef.org/exports/handloom-industry-india.aspx
6   Ministry of Textiles, Ministry of Chemicals, 2015
7   Languishing Craft, Danke Ka Kaam, Craft Revival Trust, Ministry of Textiles

typically practised in karkhanas, with four to five embroiderers, who all work with a senior artisan (who severally deals with patrons). They use antiquated tools like an ari (a long instrument that has a hook-shaped needle to ply vertically through the fabric), Mewari Rajput women were traditionally customers for such craft, commissioning embroidery on their customized attire (typically called paushaks). However, there have been very limited measures taken to diversify customers and expand the craft geographically. Even now, patrons remain few, with most danka work not available off the shelf—many women from Rajput families continue to take their fabrics and panels to the local kaarkhana and then choose the patterns and commission embroidery work. A typical commission requires the customer to pay half up front, given the high cost of materials. Meanwhile, the actual making, material sourcing and trading of danka-related materials continue to be related to the Bohra communities.[8] This remains a craft that cannot be reproduced by mass production.

The craft is languishing of late, with the rising cost of materials leading to fewer patrons being available to put up the initial deposit for the materials.[9] With patronage declining, practitioners are moving into other forms of embroidery or seeking alternative professions. As the community remains quite close-knit, availability of materials to non-Bohra practitioners remains difficult. While state handicraft centres have been established, their guidelines do not include danka work, which can require a different approach. There have been few large-scale commissions to showcase the work and increase visibility of the craft, say, in the form of state or national awards. There needs to be linkage of such craft with couture designers, which will lead to changes in design that are necessary to keep the craft alive. Heritage status should be bestowed on the work, particularly from state or national-level bodies. Pensions and scholarships to surviving practitioners should be provided in order to help them support their families better.[10]

---

8   Languishing Craft, Danke Ka Kaam, Craft Revival Trust, Ministry of Textiles
9   Ibid
10   Ibid

CASE STUDY: NANDANA HAND BLOCK PRINTING

Deep in the hinterland of Madhya Pradesh, the Chippa community has developed a wax resist dye process of hand-block printing termed Nandana.[11] The technique is complex, with over eighteen steps, which can result in a rich colour palette on durable textiles. A patron community of Bhils and Bhilai tribals, clustered around places like Ummedpura and Tarapur, has helped the craft grow and take root. The primary product of this craft is full-length skirts or ghaghras worn by tribal women, with finer counts of cotton introduced for the urban markets. However, in a more modern age, design interventions have been rather limited, with the focus primarily on mixing the placement of motifs within the fabric. The craft is considered to be over 500 years old, with a clientele spread over the Dhar and Jhabua districts of Madhya Pradesh, along with the Panchmahal district of Gujarat and some parts of Rajasthan. Such prints were once popular in export markets as varied as Singapore and Rangoon, along with the Middle East, but industrialization proved to be too much of a competition.[12]

In the '60s, Tarapur and Ummedpura had over 1,000 people working in the hand-block printing industry. The craft continues to be handed down through generations, but the younger generation has different aspirations. Most printers continue to be employed at marginal rates, with a cup of chai provided in the karkhana and two days off annually (during Basant Panchami and Sitla Panchami). Salary increments are relatively low—there are cases where a block printer who earned ₹70 per day over fourteen years back currently earns ₹120 per day. A typical block printer can print six to seven saris per day, earning ₹15–20 per sari. Most artisans don't have a bank account and remain unaware of the concept of artisan cards. In comparison, working in agriculture as a daily labourer can bring in ₹150–₹200 per day, while working at a local factory can lead to an earning of ₹165/day.[13] As a result, most artisans are increasingly shifting to setting up shops in local villages and small towns or working in local cement factories.

Historically, Nandana prints were sold primarily in local markets in Madhya Pradesh's tribal belts, including places like Jhabua and Panchmahal. The wholesale business in local markets can often account for 75 per cent of total sales, while direct sales are typically done through exhibitions. Profit margins can vary, with 20–40 per cent observed in the wholesale business—most business relationships are informal, with no written contracts and payments received within a month from the buyer.[14] Such Nandana prints require adequate marketing support from the

---

11 Languishing Craft, Nandana Hand Block Printing, Craft Revival Trust, Ministry of Textiles
12 Ibid
13 Ibid
14 Ibid

state, with a focus on reasonable pricing and promotion through newer marketing channels. The positioning of the craft remains towards the lower end, with limited support for raising awareness from government marketing channels. In particular, artisan selection for exhibitions remains significantly non-transparent, with limited linkage with merit.

There are some positive moves. The Madhya Pradesh Hastshilp Evam Hathkargha Vikas Nigam Ltd has helped develop a textile cluster near Tarapur, which provides fabrics like mulberry silk to printers. In addition, such a cluster also sources products from nearby artisans for its retail chain. The institution also organizes exhibitions on a regular basis, along with training to young boys and girls in the craft. Health insurance has also been provided to the craftsmen. The primary issue, however, remains—there is simply not enough demand for Nandana prints.

Additional focus on tying design interventions with the overall marketing strategy, in order to make the finished product in line with modern sensibilities, is needed. Price points and customer targeting should be appropriately determined as well. There needs to be well-developed partnerships with craft support organizations, along with branded retail stores that can help provide access to customers. Government craft shops need to push awareness campaigns for such products, along with promoting forums where craftsmen and entrepreneurs in this space can share learnings. Given that poor wages remain a key barrier for expanding talent available for this craft, perhaps MGNREGA can consider such activities under its ambit as well. There is a need for greater monitoring and assessment of existing schemes and programmes, along with accountability for fund usage.

SARIS

India's handloom segment clusters around particular states, with each bringing its own niche and design directory to the fore.

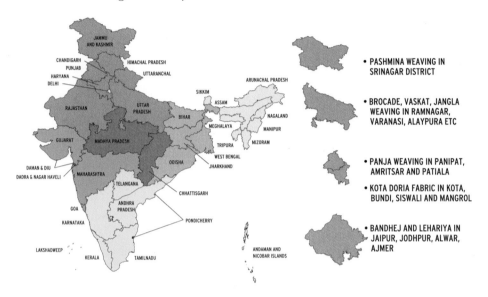

FIGURE 152: HANDLOOM PRODUCTION CLUSTERS IN INDIA (1/4)[15]

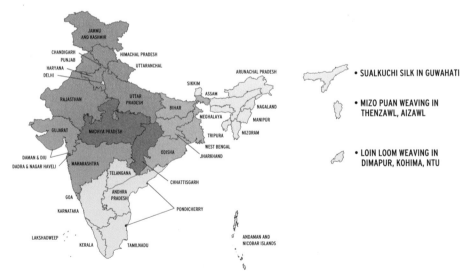

FIGURE 153: HANDLOOM PRODUCTION CLUSTERS IN INDIA (2/4)[16]

15   Export Promotion Councils of Handloom and Handicrafts; NSDC, KPMG, Human Resource and Skill
     Requirements in the Handlooms and Handicrafts Sector (2013-17, 2017-22)
16   Ibid

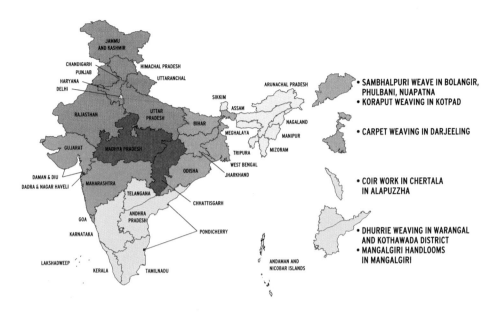

FIGURE 154: HANDLOOM PRODUCTION CLUSTERS IN INDIA (3/4)[17]

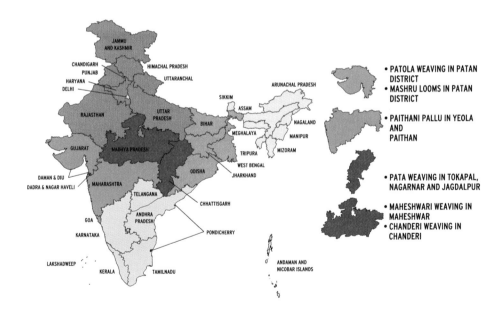

FIGURE 155: HANDLOOM PRODUCTION CLUSTERS IN INDIA (4/4)[18]

17 Export Promotion Councils of Handloom and Handicrafts; NSDC, KPMG, Human Resource and Skill
    Requirements in the Handlooms and Handicrafts Sector (2013-17, 2017-22)
18 Ibid

427

Maharashtra, while culturally divided into three zones, Vidarbha, Marathwada and coastal Maharashtra, has had a great tradition of handloom woven saris, with significant homogeneity across distances—a limited set of patterns and designs have been reworked for local requirements and discretionary spending power, with Nagpur's bugdi katari and Saoner's rahva neel reshami dhadi representative of this trend.[19] Segmentation by material type is linked to the local crop variety—with coarse and medium-count cotton-based saris found in and around Marathwada and Vidarbha, with medium and fine-count cotton/silk saris predominate in and around Vidarbha and coastal Maharashtra. The utilization of iconography and colour, and pertinence to seasons and festivals, can be seen in the use of the chandrakala, typically indigo-dyed, with a printed ground, which is worn by Marathi women on their first Makar Sankranti after marriage; the bride's mother, on the other hand, typically wears the mae sari.

The rise of power looms in the early twentieth century carried grim portents for handloom weavers, spreading in access from Mumbai to Bhiwandi, Malegaon, Ichalkaranji and other outlying villages.[20] Even villages without electricity saw handloom weavers adopting shuttle looms in order to raise productivity. Studies highlight that weavers were seemingly more financially secure pre-Independence, with enough clients, while decreasing patronage led to a decline in Paithani saris and the shalu. With the introduction of Indo-Western outfits, rural production has lost ground to a proliferation of mill-made prints and power loom-based imitations of traditional patterns. Mumbai has witnessed a trend reversal, with handlooms reviving, courtesy of a demand for better quality and the use of vintage colours. The Handloom Directorate and the Handloom Corporation of Maharashtra have helped in these efforts by seeking to subsidize non-common (non-janta) varieties of saris. The Maharashtra government has sought to bolster efforts to raise demand by initiating Visvakarma exhibitions in the '80s and supporting a Paithani production centre in Paithan.

Meanwhile, to the West, Gujarat has had long-established links and patronage for its cottons, silks and embroideries in markets across Persia, East Africa, China and South-east Asia.[21] Its bandhani (fabric resistant) saris, available in cotton, silk and wool, along with a historical tradition of embroidery and prints, have led to significant scale and diversity in areas ranging from Saurashtra to Vadodara, Mehsana and the Kutch.[22] You can find coarse cotton-based textiles in shepherd communities in and around Dwarka, along with the finely embroidered asawali saris and double ikat saris in Patan. The daily usage of saris in Gujarat

19   Sanyal, Amba, Chishti, Rta Kapur, Saris: Tradition and Beyond, Roli Books
20   Ibid
21   Journal of Indian Art, 1886
22   Mehra, Priya Ravish, Kumar, Tushar, Saris: Tradition and Beyond, Roli Books

is predominantly by the merchant class (the Jains, the Parsees, the Patels), while tribals in the Panchmahal and Chota Udaipur areas, along with the Dang district, also see use of the printed sadlo. Maratha communities, long established, tend to prefer the single-piece draped sari, garnished with a stitched aabha (tunic) and ejhaar (loose trousers).

The rise of mills in and around Ahmedabad has had a significant impact, especially on hand-block printing, although weavers who upgraded to rotor printing have survived.[23] When considering weaving, the lugda sari, found in and around Mandvi, Bardolia, Vyara and Valod, near Surat, has suffered a steep decline, with a survey in 1990 finding it to be woven on just thirty of the 400 looms in existence pre-Independence. While coarse in texture, they traditionally utilized natural dyes—which is no longer the case, given a lack of scale. Similarly, Harijan weavers in and around Wadhawan, in Surendranagar district, have been found to be using coarse-count cotton as a substitue for wool for making the Ahmedabadi pania. The usage of silk in such saris, particularly for the Parsi agara, brocades and yarn-resist saris, has also risen significantly. Gujarat has a rich tradition of silk weaving, with weavers found from Surendranagar to Ahmedabad and down to Surat, along with a number of plain silk-weaving centres that produce base fabrics for bandhani saris and Parsee gara prints. An embargo on silk imports, particularly during the two World Wars, along with the freedom movement in India, led to significant growth for silk production in Gujarat.

In comparison, bandhani saris have seen a significant expansion, especially since the '60s, with mill prints unable to match the quality and variety of hand-resist patterns associated with it. The usage of bandhani saris has expanded beyond Jamnagar, Porbandar and Kachchh to Surendranagar, Bhavnagar, Ahmedabad and other parts of Gujarat. The bandhanis associated with Kutch, especially popat vel bandhani sadlo (typically going up to 40,000 kandis per square metre; a kandi is about 4 bindhis or tied spots). Such intricate density of patterns, along with the usage of stark colours, has allowed the bandhani saris to withstand the expansion of mill-based printing. Gujarat's weavers play host to a strong tradition of handspinning and hand-block printing, which when combined with the traditional flair for entrepreneurship, could expand beyond its current state of neglect to significant growth.

In Kerala, the white mundu, a lower white drape, was popular amongst both men and women in the '30s, with the upper half kept bare or covered by a torte for women; it evolved by the '40s into the two-piece mundu veshti. This lower garment was typically worn in single or double cloth terms, while combined with an onnare

---

23   Mehra, Priya Ravish, Kumar, Tushar, Saris: Tradition and Beyond, Roli Books

(a 2-metre underwrap), along with a veshti. Travancore's royal family played a critical role in settling weavers from Mysore and Tamil Nadu in Kerala over a thousand years ago, sustaining them through patronage, helping them evolve their craft into products like the sett mundu and the one-piece sari. The white sett mundu, mostly used even now for special occasions like marriages and religious festivals, was typically undyed, reflective of an ideal compromise between form and function, the heat and the necessity to appear dignified, in an era when dyed clothing was rare. As a consequence, the white unbleached drape was perceived to be pure and auspicious, and often tinged with turmeric or saffron-tinted water, to reflect an auspicious occasion like a marriage or a festival. Typically, colour, when used, was sparse and rare, utilized on the outer edges, borders and end-pieces of a garment, with class barriers reflected in the quality of the cotton cloth (coarse to fine) and the handspun silk. Historically, exports to European destinations were streaked with colour and patterning, earning India its well-earned reputation for having the finest-quality textiles, in both fabric and patterns. Indigo was cultivated in Chernamangalam in Alapuzzha district, for creating dyes.

Given a rise in living costs, a sense of greater aspiration and increasing politicization of weavers' cooperative societies, Kerala's handloom-weaving culture has been subject to gradual erosion. Rising competition from power looms from Tamil Nadu's Coimbatore, Salem and Erode districts has also had a significant impact. The lack of a quality brand, or trademark, associated with Kerala's handloom fabrics, has prevented them from creating a perception of a quality standard and associated marketing. Strengthening the buyer base and patronage will require expanding their range of designs and engendering a sense of refinement amongst buyers.

Madhya Pradesh, expressing the vast diversity of India, across its 2,000-km length, has had a historic cluster of textile production across centres like Chanderi, Maheshwar, Burhanpur and Balaghat. Each major region has its own distinct homogeneity in textile patterns and materials, with the sendri (a wedding sari) worn only in the Balaghat region of Madhya Pradesh, across social ranges—a Gond tribal, a Kumbhar and a Pandit can all be seen patronizing it.

Madhya Pradesh's weavers relied on an age-old supply system, one reflected in its Chanderi cluster till date. Historically, the yarn for fine-count pure-cotton sari in Chanderi was sized using a koli kanda (a local root), which was sourced by traders from the local forests. With the root becoming a rarity, and weavers becoming reticent about sizing a fine-count cotton sari, they prefer silk warp, cotton weft saris instead. More recently, the silk supply by itself broke down, with few weaving a cotton body silk order sari, as cheap substitutes from other states swept in. This historically evolved chain of inter-relationships, which provided a set of raw materials and sale outlets for Chanderi sari weavers, has broken down. In some cases, the introduction of modern innovations has led to an improvement in output, raising productivity, but has grievously impacted quality. Weavers in Chhindwara district have given up on brushsizing the cotton yarn, as it becomes inconvenient in producing thirty to forty saris on a regular basis annually. Weavers in Jabhua, Dhar and Nimach districts in western Madhya Pradesh have increasingly lost out to mill-made substitutes, given their higher productivity for printing and fabric-resist demand.

Traditional support structures, which were connected intimately with the local feudal order, have collapsed, with a concomitant impact on demand. Typically, Devangan weavers used to sell a significant proportion of their bhanwarai saris, typically used for family weddings, to the farmers of Rajnandgaon (now in Chhattisgarh)—such inherent assumptions are no longer true. As cheaper imitations of traditional saris and substitutes like salwar kameez rise, traditional saris are increasingly becoming irrelevant, with pockets of excellence still maintained purely due to the continued purchases of large, rich buyers. Despite an extensive network of state and central government outlets for handloom products, weavers have failed to keep up with modern trends in taste and material, with no long-term planning for to meet demands for private retail outlets. With margins shrinking, the traditional weaver no longer has the wherewithal to invest in his product, while his distance and time from his market grow. Traditional cooperatives, set up once, to reduce this distance in margins and market access, have failed to serve their purpose, despite access to cooperative bank loans and national and state retail outlets. Without the development of a wide production base, the continuing variety of Madhya Pradesh's textiles will be hard to sustain. In the midst of a decline in demand for handloom saris, as power-loom-based saris sweep in, weavers in Madhya Pradesh have aligned themselves along caste/community lines, along with finding solace in traditional spiritual movements. The Koshta Samaj has sought to hold socio-economic gatherings to bring together weaving clans like the Devangans, Koshtas, Mehers, Gadhewals, Halbas, Mehras, Pankas, Maharas and Mirgans. Meanwhile, other weavers have found solace in Kabir Panths, seeking spiritual illumination in a time of economic turmoil.

Uttar Pradesh, the heartland of northern India, with its Ganga-Jamuna tehzeeb, has had a distinct and influential tradition of handicrafts, particularly textiles, for eons. The Doab, the area between the Ganga and the Yamuna, along with the increasingly arid Bundelkhand, once grew cotton in significant numbers, along with silk. Historically, Uttar Pradesh was a vast sari-producing area, with focus on coarse cottons, along with a strong base of spinning and weaving, creating significant economies of scale in khadi production. Access to chemical dyes in the late nineteath century led to such saris becoming more striking in their colour combinations, particularly in the case of motia saris.

When considering finer ranges, the fine cotton loom embroidery (often termed jamdani) of Tanda, in Ambedkarnagar district, still maintains its niche—the maintenance of a curvilinear edge in its patterning and a dense clarity within it has created a well-defined motif appealing across niche buyers. Promoted heavily by the royal houses of Varanasi, Awadh and Rampur, along with the Mughals, their constant exhortation for greater refinement provided significant support and inspiration to the printing, embroidery and weaving communities.

Chikan embroidery, found in various ranges in and around Rampur, Agra, Varanasi and Lucknow, was inspired by the effect and delicacy of the famed jamdani. The nawabs of Avadh promoted chikan embroidery extensively, enabling expansion of production to Malihabad, Kakori, Kushalganj, Alamnagar, Sitapur, Godhi and Kannauj. It is estimated that Lucknow played host to at least 70,000 chikan embroiderers in Lucknow in 1989, with over 50 per cent of their output constituting saris. Such weavers have benefitted by a significant rise in demand for such embroidery, along with zardozi (metallic yarn) embroidery.

Dyed and printed saris have also seen an upsurge in demand, with clusters like Farrukhabad, with exposure to printing curtain drapes and international products, providing increasing variety for printing on base fabrics like coarse gara and gazi, along with the finest muslins. Printing is commonly done for the Mathura and Pahari saris, along with tent coverings, hangings, curtains, floor cloths, prayer cloths, table covers and bedcovers. Historically, printing was prevalent in major clusters like Mathura, Varanasi and Farrukhabad, along with smaller areas like Kashipur, Kanpur and Bijnor. However, such centres, unlike those in, say, Rajasthan, have failed to keep up with changing consumer preferences in the export and urban markets. Many weavers have migrated instead to Gujarat and Maharastra, making furniture and home accessories to survive.

Varanasi and its adjoining areas have historically been producers of warp/weft patterned fine-count cotton and silk. Its absorption of weaving skills and techniques from across India has created a unique capability to cater to all kinds of customer preferences. As mill yarns and imported printed fabrics spread across India in the colonial era, many capable coarse sari and fabric weavers migrated towards Varanasi, boosting its expertise and expanding its influence—even today, regional patterns in Tamil Nadu and West Bengal are significantly influenced by fabrics from Varanasi.

However, on an overall scale, grim tidings have stalked Uttar Pradesh's weavers. Recent surveys have highlighted that most weavers in rural areas are landless, while facing starvation-like conditions. Most traders in Tier 2 and Tier 3 cities, who would traditionally have helped such weavers hawk their wares, have left the profession, becoming street vendors or rickshaw drivers instead. The dumping of plain Chinese silks (estimated at 25,000 m per day) has skewed the market, with such silks being easily sold post-dyeing or embellishment with embroidery. The rise in raw material prices, along with irregular supply, continuing low wages and inadequate market support, has led to a significant decline in weaving. The advent of power looms in the '80s has led to weaver after weaver giving up coarse count weaving, and signing up for power looms, given the latter's ability to offer them a rupee more per metre. Those with access to a finer clientele have maintained a range of finer counts, with refined border and pallu patterning.

Andhra Pradesh's weaving communities are divided into three major segments—the Devangas, the Sales and Togatas, who are regionally clustered. The Sales, the largest community, are linked to the Saliyas of Tamil Nadu and the Padmasalis of Karnataka and Maharashtra; their community names are derived from the Sanskrit name, shalika (a weaver). The Devangas, on the other hand, share a common history with the Devanganas of Maharasthra and Madhya Pradesh. The Togatas live primarily in the Rayalaseema region, with a focus on weaving coarse-cotton cloths. With a rich and varied heritage of textiles, Andhra Pradesh has benefited from centuries of royal patronage. In modern times, its fine-count weaves of mangalgiri and printed kalamkari have found significant market demand, while other items like coarse cloth and fine-count saris have faced potential extinction. Specialized woven products like Gadwal and Narayanpet, along with Uppada, remain in a vestigial condition. The Chirala cluster, located in Prakasam district of Andhra Pradesh, contains ~60,000 weavers, who focus mostly on saris (60 per cent), dress materials (20 per cent), handkerchiefs (10 per cent) and lungis and shirts.[24]

The historical silk-weaving areas are in terminal decline, with limited, if any, production in traditional centres like Peddapuram, Narayanpet, Armoor and Dharmavaram. The growth of larger and more accessible silk-production centres in Tamil Nadu, along with changing modern tastes and preferences, have had a significant impact.

Tamil Nadu has historically been a centre for weaving, with an extensive repertoire of designs and expertise across fabrics. Along with its large residential population of weavers, it has attracted and often settled, through royal patronage, weavers from Karnataka, Andhra Pradesh and even as far as Gujarat (the famed King Thirmalai Nayak settled weavers from Saurashtra in Madurai in the sixteenth century). Even now, the heritage remains—the Kaikolars and the Saliyas hold a significant monopoly of the production of coarse-count cottons, while the Kannada Devangas

---

24   NIFT, Handlooms of India, Part 1. Sourced from: http://www.nift.ac.in/mumbai/downloads/handloom. pdf

have focused on fine-count cottons, and the Padma Sele and Pattu Sele on silk weaving in centres like Kanchipuram, Tiruchchirappalli, Thanjavur, Madurai and Ramanathapuram. Despite this rich heritage, and passion for traditional clothing, the handloom sector in Tamil Nadu faces significant decline, both in the private and the cooperative sectors. The lessening of handweaving skills, along with a focus on volume production instead of quality, has led to a decline in demand, while power looms have compensated.

As illustrated by this regional dipstick, the sector remains significantly unorganized, and beset by numerous challenges. Raw material costs, especially for cotton, are rising due to high local prices and transport costs, especially in the southern states. Individual weavers lack significant economies of scale, despite an en masse diversification away from cotton to silk and other materials. Most weavers lack financial literacy, and operate outside the formal banking system, increasing their financing challenges. The business model dependence on a singular master weaver or trader in a region remains high, with significant bottlenecking on raw material, design and customer orders. Weavers are also seemingly unaware of government schemes and policies.

CARPETS AND RUGS

India's weavers diversified beyond clothing to carpets and rugs as well. The famed Kaleen carpets are typically made on vertical looms, wrapping silk or wool fibre on successive warps, which ends up creating short fabric. While inspired by the Persian carpet tradition (as showcased in depictions of the Chahar Bagh, the erstwhile Garden of Eden), and the historic rule of Emperor Zain-ul-Abadin, indigenous flora and fauna are typically utilized to give a local sheen. Akbar's historic legacy is reflected in elaborate hunting scenes, while Jehangir has inspired depictions of vines, plants and animals. In addition, mythological elements prevail, the gaja-simha, the half-lion elephant being prominent. The skill for fashioning such intricate carpets has been passed down through generations of carpet weavers, through the ustaad-shagird system, with apprentices typically allocated at the age of six. Such carpets were used historically as prayer rugs (denoted by a mihrab, an arch motif), or to cover Mughal tents.

The Namda rugs are typically used in Kashmiri houses as floor coverings and mattresses. Made by meshing wool fibre with water and soap, and subsequent embroidering, the rugs are typically white in colour, with floral patterns or animal figurines. Similarly, the Gabba rugs, are used as mattresses in colder areas. They are typically recycled woollen blankets, which are washed, milled and dyed in different colours and patterns, with backing from waste cotton cloth. Traditionally, carpet weavers from Srinagar were routinely given orders for gabba for applications in shamianas, quanat (tent hangings) and for home flooring.

In Punjab, the rule of Maharaja Ranjit Singh in the early nineteenth century in both Punjab and Kashmir had a marked influence on the carpet designs associated with Amritsar and its hinterland. The Bokhara patterns (geometrical patterns typically found in black and cream colours) stuck, drawn by weavers on a colour-coded pattern on a graph. The craft remains in significant decline, with Delhi-based exporters and the Punjab Crafts Emporium some of their few clients.

Despite a significant volume of production, some of which is exported, India's carpets and rugs have limited branding. The use of GI certification to highlight the unique techniques and motifs used in such carpets and rugs would go a long way in preserving their niche, instead of having them subsumed under the machine-made bracket.

SHAWLS AND VEILS

Barabanki district (once known as Jasnaul) is one of four districts of Faizabad division, and lies at the heart of Awadh in Uttar Pradesh, confined by the Ghaghara and Gomti rivers.[25] The district is famed for its weavers, who specialize in shawls, scarves, stoles and handkerchiefs, along with zardozi embroidery. The handloom cluster of Barabanki produces about ₹150 crore worth of wares, of which ~95 per cent is exported. Weavers tend to specialize along two lines—those who produce higher-end products like stoles, scarves and shawls for export markets; and those who produce low-quality products like Gamcha for the local market. On average, a weaver will earn ₹12,000–₹15,000 annually, with an average wage of ₹50–₹60 per day.

Other examples abound. Handspinning, an ancient craft practised across households, from Ladakh to Varanasi, usually starts with a spindle (termed a phang in Ladakh), made of willow, which is used to spin soft yarn-like wool and pashmina (the famed pashmina wool is obtained from the inner coat of the Changra goats

---

25   NIFT, Handlooms of India, Part 1. Sourced from: http://www.nift.ac.in/mumbai/downloads/handloom. pdf

found in the Changtang region of Ladakh). In Ladakh, men typically use a drop spindle (termed haa), which allows them to spin while walking. Another spindle type (termed the phang) is usually used by women in a resting position, allowing them to congregate and talk about daily happenings.

The famed Kullu shawls (often made in the brown, grey or white shades of natural wool, with a multicoloured geometrical tapestry), are made from pashmina and three varieties of wool—the byangi (from Kinnaur), the imboo (made from the first shearing of a lamb) and the deshkar (a wool made in Kullu). This is often combined with merino wool, imported from Ludhiana and other areas in Punjab. Such shawls are often used as garments for men (termed chandru) and women (termed pattu). This technique of combining a twill-weave base with vegetable-dyed wool bears close resemblance to that found in Kashmir and other parts of Himachal Pradesh, with the migration of the Bhushahra community of Kinnaur to the Kullu valley having a significant impact.

The Panja Dhurries of Punjab are intimately connected with marital gifting, with the bride typically bringing a collection of eleven auspicious beddings, all embroidered and woven by her. The bedding typically consists of a dhurrie, a tallai (a thin, padded mattress), a chatai (a mat), quilt covers and khes. The dhurrie can typically be intricately embroidered, highlighting vegetable crops in fields, the mother goddess, Sanjhi Devi, or wished-for possessions. Such bridal dhurries continue to be woven in villages in and around Jalandhar and the Malwa region. Dhurries are also woven for the gurudwara, made on horizontal looms with a plain weave that is encrusted with multiple forms and colours, using a panja (a metal beater). Villages in and around Nakodar specialize in two types of cotton dhurries—one woven in a pit loom in multicoloured stripes and the other in a floor loom in contrasting colours, both encrusted with motifs of birds, beasts, plants and abstract patterns.

In a similar manner, across Punjab, women embroider odhni (veils) or chaddar (wraps), which are bedecked with phulkari (flower work) and bagh (garden patterned embroidery). Such textiles are usually based on khaddar (heavy cotton, typically 45–60 cm in width), which is supported by an auspicious dark red, indigo blue or white fabric. The embroidery itself is made on untwisted floss silk (termed pat) which is sourced from West Bengal or Kashmir and then dyed. The reverse of the fabric is embroidered with darning stitch, allowing for large, densely embroidered surfaces on the fabric. The phulkari is typically used across ceremonies, whether for birth, death or marriage. The birth of a girl child sees the child's grandmother typically crafting a chope (a reversible phulkari) and a suber phulkari (made of eight-petalled lotuses, usually worn by the bride when walking around the sacred fire).

The desi cotton, or rooi as it is termed, is used often for creating the thin Jaipuri Razai. The cotton is typically enhanced by application of herbal substances, along with the addition of block-printed fabrics, which enable each side of the quilt to possess a distinctive pattern. The filling of the patterns, termed bharai, involves the separation of the cotton fibres, distribution over the base sheet of the quilt and its repeated beating to give it shape. Such quilting can often use motifs like shakarpari (diamond), paan ki patti (a spade) and thaali (a circular plate).

GOVERNMENT INITIATIVES

Immediately after Independence, there was an urgency to stabilize the handloom sector. Parliament passed the Khadi and Other Handloom Industries Development (Additional Excise Duty on Cloth) Act in 1953 to raise funds for the sector and organize weaver cooperatives. The All India Handloom Fabrics Marketing Cooperative Society Ltd was set up to facilitate handloom ware marketing in 1955. The Handloom Export Promotion Council was established in 1958 to help cooperative societies reach significant scale and quality through a focus on export promotion. Its interventions have sought to introduce designers to handloom weavers, exposing them to international fairs and assisting with brand development via the Handloom Mark. The government has sought to pay attention to this segment—common facility centres have been established to help make small handicraft operators sustainable, providing them with infrastructure like warping machines, subsidized raw materials and sizing plants.

IMPROVING VALUE

Typically, raw materials in the handloom segment are sourced by the master weaver, who hires workers and takes orders from the customer. The weavers working under him finish the product, with regular weavers getting access to gainful employment. Rising wages and falling handloom ware prices have led to a decline of the master weaver system, with master weavers cutting back their scale and employing fewer weavers. As a substitute, the cooperative society system has emerged, along with private companies, for organizing weavers for purchase orders. Weavers are sold good-quality raw material products at subsidized prices, with the finished ware bought back at guaranteed rates, which are typically higher than private traders. Such products are then sold by the cooperative societies in the wider market, both in the domestic and the export segments.

In this value chain, weavers face multiple challenges—in addition to rising input costs and sparse credit coverage, there are significant marketing bottlenecks. There remains a significant lack of innovation, with most weavers drawing on historical patterns associated with master weavers and ancestral knowledge; the ability to adopt new patterns remains lacking. Power looms have increasingly been selling their products as handloom fabric, despite regulatory safeguards to prevent this [e.g. The Handloom (Reservation of Articles For Production) Act of 1985]. The Handloom Mark remains relatively unknown and offers little credibility to handloom wares to differentiate them from the general market. Job orders remain relatively sparse— master weavers typically hire weavers on a daily-wage basis. Most institutions that ought to provide monetary and institutional support are heavily centralized, with little on-ground presence to reach India's heterogeneous population of weavers. The North-eastern region, which hosts a significant proportion (more than 60.5 per cent) of India's weavers, faces significant infrastructural bottlenecks, with poor road and rail connectivity limiting access to urban markets. The lack of adequate data on the handloom segment is another significant constraint—the last few significant surveys on the segment were held in 1988, 1996 and 2010. India's formal education system has bypassed the handloom segment, with limited options for teaching, training and skill development for it. Introducing new products and process innovations is a responsibility that has been left traditionally to the master weaver. The fact that handloom is a state subject has meant that central schemes face coordination issues with local state governments, reducing efficacy.

STATE OF HANDICRAFTS

India's handicrafts segment clusters around particular states, with each bringing its own niche and design directory to the fore.

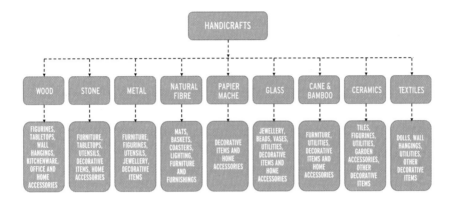

FIGURE 156: HANDICRAFTS CLASSIFICATION[26]

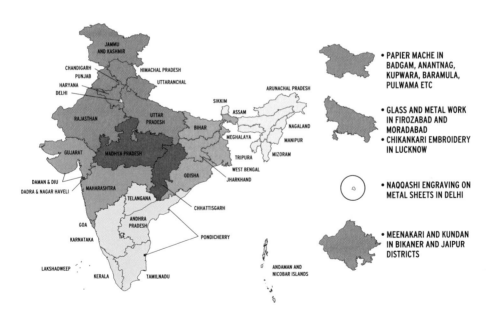

- PAPIER MACHE IN BADGAM, ANANTNAG, KUPWARA, BARAMULA, PULWAMA ETC

- GLASS AND METAL WORK IN FIROZABAD AND MORADABAD
- CHIKANKARI EMBROIDERY IN LUCKNOW

- NAQQASHI ENGRAVING ON METAL SHEETS IN DELHI

- MEENAKARI AND KUNDAN IN BIKANER AND JAIPUR DISTRICTS

FIGURE 157: HANDICRAFTS PRODUCTION CLUSTERS IN INDIA (1/5)[27]

---

26   Export Promotion Councils of Handloom and Handicrafts; NSDC, KPMG, Human Resource and Skill Requirements in the Handlooms and Handicrafts Sector (2013-17, 2017-22)
27   Ibid

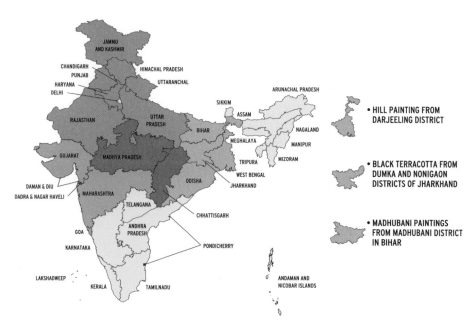

FIGURE 158: HANDICRAFTS PRODUCTION CLUSTERS IN INDIA (2/5)[28]

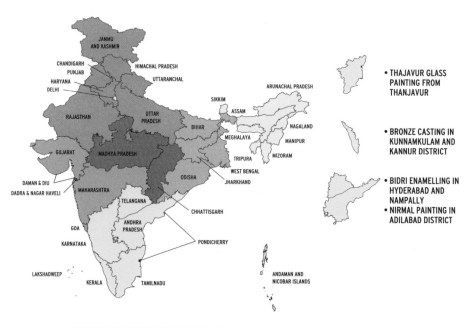

FIGURE 159: HANDICRAFTS PRODUCTION CLUSTERS IN INDIA (3/5)[29]

---

28   Export Promotion Councils of Handloom and Handicrafts; NSDC, KPMG, Human Resource and Skill Requirements in the Handlooms and Handicrafts Sector (2013-17, 2017-22)

29   Ibid

FIGURE 160: HANDICRAFTS PRODUCTION CLUSTERS IN INDIA (4/5)[30]

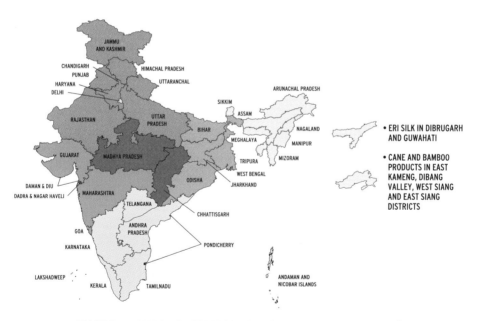

FIGURE 161: HANDICRAFTS PRODUCTION CLUSTERS IN INDIA (5/5)[31]

---

30 Export Promotion Councils of Handloom and Handicrafts; NSDC, KPMG, Human Resource and Skill
    Requirements in the Handlooms and Handicrafts Sector (2013-17, 2017-22)
31 Ibid

CASE STUDY: KAAVAD

A mobile temple shrine, the Kaavad is a 400-year-old tradition practised by Kaavadia Bhat, who used it to recite holy stories and highlight family genealogies. Originally made of mango-tree wood, the Kaavad is typically detailed with illustrations for multiple stories, with the panels, doors and corners of the object all decorated, all 12- inches of it. Usually painted in bright colours, the Kaavad consists of multiple panels, each opening up and revealing a story inside. The object was typically displayed with great respect, accompanied by singing (colloquially known as Kaavad Banchna) by the Bhats. The craft is currently practised by the artisans of the Bassi village in Chittorgarh district, with over twenty-five families engaged in manufacturing the wooden items. The artisans typically belong to the Suthar caste (carpenter caste) but are Jangid Brahmins, with origins in Nagaur. Raw material sourcing and trading of the finished object is typically done by local Bhils and Muslims. Artisans are paid labour per piece that they actually produce, with differential rates across products—a 10- inch Kaavad piece can result in an artisan earning between ₹120 and ₹150.

Given modern sensibilities, Kaavad are increasingly being used as teaching devices in certain schools, finding usage as a storytelling device. They have become popular as gift items, with production across many size varieties. However, product marketing remains a significant constraint.

CASE STUDY: SPLIT PLY BRAIDING

Jaisalmer, situated in the extreme west of Rajasthan, was once known as Marusthali in ancient literature. It is also known for the practice of split ply braiding. A camel belt is typically created by using goat's hair—the camel girth is often used as a trapping to keep the saddle in place. A camel is also decorated with a garbandh during ceremonies and important festivals in Jaisalmer, with such activities celebrated in traditional songs are 'garbandh nakharalo'. The origins of the craft are shrouded in myth—there is a tale of a woman awaiting her husband and making a gift of a garbandh; she found it quite alluring and decided to hang it up on the house wall. However, the garbandh was stolen before the husband returned. There are other stories told about six brothers, of whom a Mota Bhai went to a Muslim wedding near Sindh, where he saw camels wearing a belt to hold the saddle in place—his eagerness to learn the craft led to a profusion of the craft in the region.[32]

The Bhattis of Jaisalmer, who trace their lineage to Yadu, were famed for the practice, with the craft often pursued as a hobby by young males who owned their own camels.[33] Most braiders now exchange such braided camel belts for consumables like oil, chillies and spices, amongst other things. The craft is a dying one—known only to two to three people per village in the Jaisalmer district. Meanwhile, the next generation is looking for government jobs. The craft continues to prevail in regions of Barmer (e.g. Sundra, Aapia, Chindania and Dagari villages in Shiv tehsil) and in Jaisalmer (e.g. Khuri, Fatehgarh and Kutchdi villages).

Studies done on the craft by the Craft Revival Trust have showcased that most artisans do not have an artisan card, and rarely avail of any government schemes.[34] Most artisans ask for a subsidy on the raw materials (mostly ready-made cotton cords), along with a large-scale customer for the product. A camel belt can have a geometric design, decorated with figures inspired from the desert ecosystem, with the belt itself being 6 feet long and ~5–6- inches wide. The craft has existed in pastoral communities in small villages in the region for centuries and has never turned commercial.

The process for crafting such camel girths was rather simple—they were usually made of black and white goat hair, with the yarn made from goats used in their original colour, with no dyeing.[35] The material properties of goat hair ensure that any dirt is easily washed away, while the colour does not fade over time. When insects do attack, the braid is typically kept in the sun for disinfection. This entire process—harvesting, cleaning and spinning of such goat hair into a yarn—is completely manual, with goats sheared annually at the beginning of summer. Once collected, the hair is typically cleaned with clumps separated into individual strands, which are then collected and twisted into a long and thick rope (a roving). The goat hair is then spun into a single ply thread, using a locally available spindle termed dhera. Finally, the thread is spun off the spindle, and twisted into a two-ply yarn. Once the yarn is ready, the camel belt is made by an oblique interfacing of a cord which is untwisted and separated into two plys, using a special tool termed gunthani.

Where the trade falters is in the lack of viable commerciality.[36] There is need for greater research in terms of mechanization of the process, along with creating new designs and training existing craftsmen to create new products that are suitable for modern tastes. The technique is easily adaptable to other products and can be

---

32   Camel girth belts of split ply braiding, Languishing Craft, Craft Revival Trust, Ministry of Textiles
33   Ibid
34   Ibid
35   Ibid
36   Ibid

utilized for creating accessories like handbags, belts, wall hangings, wallets, etc. A raw material bank is also necessary in order to help craftsmen gain access to cords and other materials. However, diversification is also necessary in terms of raw materials, with a focus on silk and jute. Branding such products at a national level remains necessary. The craft remains heavily dependent on manual intervention and antiquated tools, with significant need for a mechanical tool to twist multiple yarns together.

Jaisalmer itself typically shuts down during the summer months, providing time for craftsmen to pursue this profession—the occupation itself is gender neutral.[37] While this craft is effectively a hobby, it has significant potential—there remains the question of awareness, both for customers and budding craftsmen. There is currently no listing of any braider in the local Udyog Vibhag office, with significant need for carrying out a survey to determine the total number of weavers in the area. There must be a push for promoting the craft at the national level in fairs and festivals.

WOOD WORK

Given the ubiquitous concentration of walnut trees in Kashmir, walnut wood carvings have arisen as a rather intricate art form. The master carver, the naqqash, typically etched the basic pattern on the wood, with the unwanted areas removed via chisels and mallets, with embossment carried out towards the end. Deep carvings, about 2 inches deep, are usually utilized for flower and dragon motifs, while shallow carvings, about half an inch deep, are typically done over flat surfaces. Open, latticework, depicting chinar motifs, along with semi-carving techniques which create ornamental semi-panels are often depicted in a range of historically intricate buildings—the shrine of Noor-ud-din-Wali at Chrar-e-Sharif and that of Nund Rishi being prime examples.

The Kharadi community found in villages in and around Hoshiarpur, in Punjab, specializes in wood furniture decorated with motifs on a lac coating. Such furniture pieces are rotated on power lathes, and coated with lac layers, usually in white, black and red colours, along with yellow and purple. A sharp metal stylus is then used to etch motifs on the lac, highlighting underlying colours. Such techniques are often used to make singhardaani (containers) and peedi (low stools).

---

37   Camel girth belts of split ply braiding, Languishing Craft, Craft Revival Trust, Ministry of Textiles

The fine art of Tarkashi, inlaying metal in wood, is practised by the Jangid community in Rajasthan, who are believed to have migrated from Mainpuri in Uttar Pradesh. Typically, seasoned sheesham wood is used, as its high oil content enables the metal to be fastened securely. Meanwhile, the geometric or floral patterns, often Mughal-inspired, are drawn on the wood and engraved to a depth of 1 mm. Metal strips are then heated in flames, straightened and then beaten into the created grooves with hammers. Coiled dot-like forms, typically termed bhiriyan, are also added to the wood in an ancillary manner. Once fastened, the wood piece is sanded and given a fine polish.

The arid regions of Barmer and Jodhpur are famous for their wooden handicrafts, with it constituting 75 per cent of the total handicraft industry in the Jodhpur region. Initially starting out for furniture production, it has diversified into gift articles, toys, utility items and other wood-based products. There are about 500 manufacturing units in Jodhpur itself, providing employment to more than one lakh people. About 50 per cent of the units are export-focused, generating annual revenues of ₹400 crore, with other handicrafts consisting of textiles and jewellery. Some exporters are trading firms who purchase wooden items from artisans and export with an added margin.

In terms of wood procurement, a third of manufacturers/exporters use reclaimed wood—mostly sourced from Indian Railways who use wood for track support—through open-market auctions. The method is preferred, as it is cheaper to procure than imports and has a degree of price stability and transparency. A majority of wood procurement (~61 per cent) happens through the wood agent/merchant, who in turn procures from wood contractors, with permission and licences from the government for cutting trees, mostly in forest areas. For artisans requiring huge quantities of wood, direct procurement from contractors makes a difference, as it cuts out the middlemen's margins. Artisans requiring small quantities of wood (~6 per cent) may procure it from local depots. Besides handicrafts, many artisans also carry out wood-reclamation works, remaking old furniture items with reclaimed wood.

In terms of type, almost 90 per cent of the wood procured is indigenous, with the balance being met with imports. Sheesham remains the most commonly used wood, with its heartwood being stable and termite-resistant, and brought mostly from UP, Punjab and Rajasthan. The price varies between ₹400 and ₹750 per cubic feet, depending on quality and logistics cost. Mango wood from Gujarat, UP and MP, and babool wood from Rajasthan and Gujarat account for further 34 per cent and 21 per cent wood procurement, respectively.

The source and method of wood procurement have emerged as an impediment in the export growth of wood-based handicrafts from Jodhpur.[38] The future of tropical forests has been a constant point of concern among the developed nations and a simplistic interpretation of the 1992 United Nations Conference on Environment and Development (UNCED) guidelines led to such wood contractors being key people responsible for deforestation. The focus has since moved to sourcing of food from sustainably managed forests, with proper certification established that help consumers identify whether the products have been sourced from the environmentally responsible value chain. Timber Certifications, for instance, focuses on the origin of wood and its status, allowing for validation of any environmental claims made by the producer. This helps in connecting the environmentally conscious consumer with the environmentally responsible producer, besides generating premium through product differentiation on the basis of social/environmental attributes.

Such certification has its own set of cost increases, thereby potentially squeezing the margins realized by the producer and the value chain.[39] To maintain sustainability, deforestation rates may be revised each year to match growth rate in forest areas. While this may lead to better planning and increased utilization over years, the immediate concern remains of income foregone through reduced yields. Certification assessments have been estimated to cost ~₹60/per hectare on an annual basis, while identification of origin through tracing of custody chain can add a further 1 per cent of the border prices (Baharuddin and Simula, 1994). Not all buyer segments will have the willingness to pay the premium for green practices; however, the environmentally conscious buyer segments are projected to increase. The cost of certification, in terms of money, time and additional processes, has led to a larger part of the producer value chain being unwelcoming of such measures. The producers claim that while benefits would be realized by society at large, the cost should be borne by all stakeholders equally and not be limited to the producers alone. Further, false certification and undetected fraud may end up disincentivizing compliant producers. Most consumers/importers strongly support certification, as it leads to opening up of market segments and creates product differentiation, yet the impact of such costs on the distribution chain and attractiveness of substitutes raises genuine concerns.

However, the certification system suffers from the lack of an internationally accepted certification system with uniform principles on forest sustainability, leading to multiple parallel systems trying to achieve the same objective. Many countries are focusing on uniform guidelines, which may not be designed for certification uses.

---

38 Wood-Based Handicraft Industry, Report on Survey of Woodbased Handicraft Industry: Jodhpur, (Rajasthan), Traffic India, WWF. Sourced from: http://awsassets.wwfindia.org/downloads/report_on_survey_of_woodbased_handicraft_industry_jodhpur___rajasthan_.pdf

39 Ibid

In Europe, the International Tropical Timber Organization (ITTO) has developed guidelines under the Helsinki process, Brazil has defined certification criteria under the Cerflor certification system and the Swedish Society for Nature Conservation has finalized national-level criteria in association with the World Wide Fund for Nature, with a potential to be interconnected with the Forest Stewardship Council (FSC). The UK has its own Wordmark system, which attests more to the origin of the wood and not the status of the forest per se. Germany's system is mostly a product of private-sector initiative, Tropenwald, whereas the Netherlands has its own separate system for certification of imported timber. Meanwhile, Canada is working on a system upon which an ISO system can be fashioned. Thus, we see that much of the work is fragmented and parallel in nature, which can lead to many systems, often conflicting.

The practical implication for our artisans could be the requirement to adhere to multiple systems for the same product and same process, in order to export to a particular market, given the applicable certification regime. Any certification scheme will need to have objective and measurable criteria and should be independent and credible. It is also imperative that such systems do not impose a high price in terms of money and time on the already struggling handicraft producers. Even today, the exporter artisans of Jodhpur are getting familiar with the Lacey Act, the FSC provisions, the EU Forest Law Enforcement, Governance and Trade (FLEGT) provisions and the CODE certificates, which are required/applicable on exports to developed nations. The certification systems at a regional level (particularly EU) add another layer of complexity when connected with the bilateral trade agreements with various constituent countries. For artisans, almost 61 per cent have no certificates, while 24 per cent follow ISO requirements. Among the one-fourth with ISO, many have not even renewed. Only 2 per cent of the exporters have the required CODE certification, 3 per cent have their credit ratings in place and 2 per cent have Star Exporter certification. There is immediate need at a regional level for enabling more artisans to obtain the required certifications for exports to the US and EU, leading to higher craft incomes.

The private sector and NGOs may be enrolled for better coordination between the artisans and the trade bodies of the respective countries, with provisions for time-bound resolution.[40] Adherence to such certification needs to be worked upon as well—at present, the wood agent/broker supplying wood to artisans acts as an aggregator of wood from various sources and thus, one cannot differentiate the products based on origin. At yards, even segregation of wood from sources is

---

40   Dr Nuruzzaman Kasemi, Problems Of Pottery Industry And Policies For Development: Case Study Of Koch Bihar District In West Bengal, India, ISSN: 2278-6236, International Journal of Advanced Research in Management and Social Sciences, Vol. 3 | No. 7 | July 2014. Sourced from: http://www.garph.co.uk/IJARMSS/July2014/20.pdf#

difficult to implement. A cost-effective batch system needs to be formulated, which can trace each log/batch of wood to its origin and the processes involved.

METAL WORK

Copperware in Kashmir has been traditionally created by shaping, decorating (naqqashi) and tinning (kalai), with the surface usually highly decorated with floral and leaf forms, calligraphic patterns, religious symbols and hunting scenes. The patterns are usually formed on a metal sheet using repousse, piercing and chasing techniques, with the depressed surface subsequently oxidized. Such copperware can be available in a range of forms—incense burners, hookah bases, kettles (samovars), wine jugs (surahi) and rosewater sprinklers. Many are used for rituals like ablutions and henna-holding during pre-wedding ceremonies. A typical Kashmiri bride is gifted a range of copper vessels.

The antique craft of lost wax bronze casting is believed to have been brought to the Chamba Valley in Himachal Pradesh by Kashmiri craftsmen who were sponsored by the local Pahari kings. Over centuries, the craftsmen specialized in idols, with a number of metalware products crafted to serve local and royal needs. Many popular versions of this typically have the idols standing in a tribhanga mudra, decked with ornaments and large crowns, with the background covered with Pahari patterns. Typically, the casting is an alloy of brass, with a hint of silver.

In terms of employment generation, the brass and bell metal crafts remain the most important in Odisha. With their numbers not precisely known, in the absence of a craft-specific census, it is estimated that 20 per cent of the state's craft workforce is employed in brass and bell metal craft work. The employment-generation potential remains significant with each artisan unit requiring about four to five working hands for production, and additional members for ancillary services and supplies. Despite its importance, the craft and its practitioners remain mired in various issues. The craftsmen mostly comprise the Kansari community (deriving their name from the Sanskrit word for brass, or kansu), and most of them are tribal in origin. The Tambera community, deriving its name from the word tamra (Sanskrit for copper), remains engaged in production of copper utensils and craft items. The production and marketing efforts remain family-based, with hardly any external improvements. Thus, production has remained traditional in nature, with no technological improvements. Other functional areas, especially in finance and marketing, suffer in the wake of lack of education among the artisans. With most artisans being tribal, with limited exposure to the outside world, the success of the craft assumes even more importance.

The craft faces tough competition from emerging metals and the manufacturing scenario, which utilizes better technology, compared to the traditional methods employed by the artisans. Upgradation needs remain unmet, with almost no training facilities for the craftsmen. R&D institutes, quality laboratories and design institutions remain absent.

The traditional methods have also not served the artisans well, by posing significant health risks.[41] The most common ailment is the metal fume fever, accompanied by irritation in the nose, eyes and respiratory tracts, which can lead to pneumonitis and pulmonary oedema. Lung diseases are most common and artisans risk increased chances of lung cancer in the long run. Finance and raw materials remain the biggest problem with a common root. Owing to illiteracy and lack of knowledge, the artisans work for the village mahajans on a job-work basis. The artisans refuse to resort to formal sources of credit, despite multiple schemes and various channels of credit applicable. A key attraction of job-work is that the mahajan supplies them with the required raw materials; thus, the artisans do not have to buy them separately. However, this also creates a dependency on the mahajan for their livelihoods. With rising raw material prices, the mahajans stopped procuring the raw materials, leading to loss of income and jobs. The mahajans' monopolistic nature of supply also implies the inability of the artisans to bypass them for their survival needs.

The finished products are all sold within India, mostly to neighbouring West Bengal through agents/traders and dealers. Despite its rich history and quality products, the region doesn't witness any export income. At present, there are about fourteen government departments with stakes in the development of the brass and bell metal crafts, each with its own set of schemes and benefits, yet the ground reality remains untouched and unchanged, signifying lack of communication and trust between the artisans and the government. Thus, we see that despite a rich cultural history and provision of benefits, the sector faces risks ranging from lack of design innovation, lack of product diversification, lack of formal credit, obsolete production technology and rising raw material cost to inefficient marketing—non-existent exports and nil common infrastructural support.

The production processes need to be re-fashioned and re-engineered in order to remove redundancies and reduce health risks. The products need diversification;

---

41   Mukherjee, Meera, Metal Craftsmen of India, Anthropological Survey of India, Memoir No 44, Published in August 1978. Sourced from: http://sandhi.hss.iitb.ac.in/Sandhi/Books/Indian%20 Technology/Metal%20Craftsmen%20of%20India%20-%20Mukherjee%20(1978).pdf

from the existing portfolio of bells, thalis, buckets, etc., it can be diversified to include various other household utensils and decorative items. This can also improve chances of export, as the success of Moradabad cluster illustrates.[42] Common infrastructure needs to be established, which can undertake the tedious job of sheet-cutting, rolling, pressing, pattern-making and packaging through machines, thereby reducing operating cost. Besides upgrading infrastructure and installation of common machines, the artisans also need to be trained in the use and features of the common infrastructure. Availing of formal credit should be proactively encouraged. Marketing channels need to be rethought—elimination of middlemen will lead to improved margins for the artisan. Besides these, the artisans need to be taken into confidence and awareness campaigns undertaken that will inform them of the benefits available and assist them in availing of the benefits without hassles.

Granting of a Geographical Indication (GI) tag would help the craft in the long run.[43] Consider the metalwork in Moradabad—the goods manufactured are lighter than the same goods produced elsewhere, on account of the goods being 'finished' from the inside, which is usually not visible. In terms of scale, the region has ~5,250 small-scale metal craft units, engaging about 2.8 lakh workers, leading to an annual turnover of ~₹3,800 crore (Export Promotion Bureau), with exports alone clocking ~₹2,200 crore. It has a distinguished history, being the chief centre of lac-coloured metal craft (George Watt, Indian Art in Delhi, 1903). Even in 1946, Moradabad brassware was sent to 226 destinations from Kolkata to Karachi. The artisans are mostly illiterate, but have mastered the brassware work, with skills being passed from one generation to another orally. The only distinguishing factor between brassware from Moradabad and other places, besides the fine-grained Ram Ganga sand found on the river banks, remains the mastery of the skills, including the designing and production process, by the artisans. The products from Moradabad are likely unmatched anywhere in the world, and the GI tag would assist in providing a strong marketing value chain. The GI tag shall also require the formation of an inspection body or upgradation of an existing one to ensure that the products meet the stipulated quality parameters.

---

42 Application for the Registration of a Geographical Indication in Part A of the Register, Moradabad Metal Craft. Sourced from: http://ipindiaservices.gov.in/GI_DOC/161/161%20-%20GI%20-%20Reply%20 to%20ER%20-%20Form%20GI-1%20-%2024-07-2013.pdf
43 Ibid

POTTERY AND SCULPTURE

Potters from Jhajjar and its surrounding environs in Haryana specialize in slim-necked pitchers (termed surahi), which are made from a combination of crafted clay rolled into an upturned pot with engraved patterns. Spouts, necks and handles are attached separately, after dipping them with red (banni) and yellow (sunaihri) clay. Pots made from such clay are said to give water stored within a unique taste.

The forests of Rajasthan possess an insect that produces a resinous substance, lac, which can be formed into a variety of jewellery items, including chudis (bangles). The bangles are manufactured in a range of colours, and studded with glass pieces, stones and beads, along with motifs associated with leheriya (diagonal line patterns), patta (straight lines) and phooldar (floral) designs marked on to the lac coats.

The Kumbhar community of Sawai Madhopur and the surrounding villages typically creates a range of decorative figurines, pots and sculptures of animals and deities. Often made of clay taken from the nearby Banas River, the terracotta is often made on traditional wheel, which is turned until a desired shape is formed. The object is typically dried in the sun for at least two hours, and then fired.

Pottery remains one of the most ancient craft professions, with most archaeological discoveries containing shards of pottery across all locations. Potters are known by various names across India—kumhar in central, western and northern India, kumor in Bengal, and kusavan and kummara in the south, all derived from the Sanskrit word for potmaker, the kumbhkar. Even within the same state, the same craft will have different practising communities with different products. Consider the pottery artisans of Gujarat—the Variya community (distributed over Kalol, Kheda, Ahmedabad, Bhavnagar and Jamnagar), Gurjar and Maru community (spread across the state) are actually the potmakers, whereas the Vataliya community (spread across Ahmedabad, Bhavnagar and Dholka region) made hookahs and the Dalwadi potters were famous for their brick-making skills.

One of the most important inputs for pottery lies in its basic raw materials—the soil, colours and the fuel for firing the clay. It is preferred to procure soil from the nearby areas; however, it has to be fine in nature and considered fit for pottery-making. The artisans have the misfortune of paying extra money to middlemen and transporters in case the preferred soil is not available locally. The colours can be procured from the local markets. While earlier the colours were more pigment-based and dependent on local support, increasingly, potters prefer oil-based colours or chemical colours today, considering their durability, ease of application and no further requirement for processing before application. Firing fuel usually consists of dried wood and bushes from nearby areas, with grain husk and straw from agricultural fields used as substitutes. In case of the absence of any fuel, the potters arrange for waste wood from the local carpenters, traditionally in exchange for pots in a barter system. However, many villages do not get access to even the basic raw material of soil and have to pool with various artisans in the region to pay for a tractor-load of clay, estimated at ₹20,000 per tractor (2013 prices) in Basantpur village on the outskirts of Bhubaneswar. Considering the fragmented nature of pottery-making and small-unit requirements for raw materials, raw material depots should be set up in suitable places to ensure that raw materials are available to artisans at reasonable rates. Studies (International Journal of Advanced Research in Management and Social Sciences) reveal that the average distance travelled for procuring raw materials for potters is ~22 km, which needs improvement.

Capital constraints faced by potters reduce their ability to invest in fixed assets. Over 40 lakh rural potters still use conventional pottery wheels. Despite the know-how for operating better tools and improving productivity, potters remain constricted to using outdated technology, due to lack of investments. Consider the filtering process of pottery-making—the impurities are first removed by hand, then the remaining clay is battered with a wooden mallet and filtered using a chhalni, then saturated with water and the same process is followed the next day. The clay is then again tempered with sawdust, which provides strength to the pot. On the other hand, capital investment can transform the process—the ball mill can grind the clay to extremely fine particles, the blunger can be used to mix the resultant clay with water and the pug mill can be utilized for the tempering process. With the use of advanced equipment/tools, the artisan can take bigger orders, thus achieving economies of scale and improving his revenues and profit margins.

This can be more helpful in the Indian context, especially during Diwali, when most artisans operate at full capacity to produce earthern lamps, yet the production process is entirely manual. Potters reported that sales can fall to as low as 20 per cent of peak period sales—with the peak period lasting just a few weeks in a year. Considering the seasonality of the work, the machines could be a common pool resource among a group of artisans. The government can further subsidize the cost of machines under the existing schemes, or provide an impetus to existing schemes, disbursing loans at lower interest rates for such investments. With most artisans facing issues of broken or spoilt inventory due to poor work sheds, infrastructure development remains as important as upgrading tools and machinery.

Lack of product diversification also riddles pottery-making, with artisans usually focusing on traditional utilitarian items. Cheap machine-made goods have worsened the situation further, with synthetic products replacing almost all products of the decentralized pottery sector through price advantages. Consider the traditional diyas sold during Diwali—the potters of Malkaganj in north Delhi price the diyas at ~₹50 per dozen, the Chinese alternatives are priced almost 20–30 per cent lower (₹35–₹40 per dozen), with the price-conscious consumer opting for the latter. Almost 95 per cent of India's traditionally skilled potters are engaged in the conventional red-soil pottery. The product set thus needs to be augmented through examination of consumer preferences. Some innovations made have also been commercialized—Neer Patra are handmade earthen water bottles, which have self-cooling properties and are equivalent in function (if not better) to prevalent plastic bottles. Some innovators, like Mr Mansukhbhai Prajapati, have gone a step ahead and even made refrigerators using clay and locally available materials. The product, Mitticool, has features equivalent to a refrigerator, is much cheaper and hence, easily affordable and doesn't consume any electricity. Starting with a seed capital of ₹1.8 lakh, the product registered revenues of ₹45 lakh in 2012–13, with growth rates of ~15–20 per cent each year. Similar innovations in other kitchen utilities demonstrate that pottery-making has the potential to innovate and make better, high-utility, items rather than remaining limited to being craft products. This requires adequate research and development efforts, to increase value of existing products and to increase the product set itself to higher-margin, high-utility products. Historical neglect of pottery research has stymied the development and growth of the sector.

Like all craft sectors, marketing remains an issue in the pottery sector. In the absence of any cooperative organization or government agency capable of purchasing and centralizing the products, the selling of products is primarily achieved through middlemen. Besides, the traditional products have seasonal demand and may be geographically limited in nature. In the absence of any centralized negotiation with the buyer/middlemen, the singular pottery workers are forced to sell at prices dictated to them, which are usually not remunerative in nature. Going directly to the consumer may help, but more often, the potters fail to increase the price of their products, with consumers unaware of the laborious production process and thinking the pot to be just a combination of soil and water. Considering the sale channel limitations, marketing support through institutional support or department intervention needs urgent attention. Private-sector development enterprises and NGOs need to be tapped for marketing support to ensure value creation and value redistribution in the value chain. India is dotted with various pottery firms, yet artisans struggle to make ends meet. India exports pottery products to almost all developed nations, yet our share of the global market in pottery is estimated to be about 1 per cent. The new generation needs to be interested in pursuing the skill—while some may take it up considering it to be a family heirloom, most young potters look for other sources of primary income. Thus, the potter could be having his primary job as a carpenter, or be employed in the service industry.

Most pottery artisans are standalone in nature—the artisan is responsible for the procurement of materials, production, arranging the finances, sales and marketing, and design improvements as well. The artisans need to be assisted through various duties, with skilling in the production process being critical. Managerial training can help in widening the artisans' outlook regarding various processes and functions. The slack periods (considering seasonal demand of the sector) can be utilized for such training. Besides, such periods can also be used by government emporia and cooperatives to engage artisans for production of decorative items, which can address peak-season demands and also provide regular employment to artisans.

Establishment of cooperative organizations for pottery remains an urgent need. The cooperative can provide inputs on quality improvements and product diversification, besides centralizing raw material purchase and storage, credit provisions and purchase of finished goods from artisans.

ANCILLARY CRAFTS

Kashmir's kar-e-kalamdani, otherwise known as papier mâche, has routinely been practised as a decoration on wooden panels of walls and furniture. Ingenious techniques, associated with naqqashi (painting), are utilized to create intricate floral patterns depicting apples (bumchuthposh), pomegrantes (dainposh), saffron (kongposh) and narcissi (yambarzal), or scenes depicting long-forgotten hunts or battles. Such production is usually found in craft clusters in Anantnag, Kupwara, Baramulla and Srinagar districts.

The famed thangka paintings in Ladakh are essentially scrolls that depict Buddhist deities in a range of stories—such scrolls are often used as a talisman against evil and as navigational aids for the spirit. Such thangka paintings are typically not signed by the artist but given to a lama for blessings. When finished, the painting is then mounted on a frame of silk brocade panels (gyasser), backed by plain cloth and secured at the top and bottom with wooden rods, finally topped off with silver or brass knobs.

The Chamba painting style, a style of miniature paintings that emerged in the seventeenth to the nineteenth centuries in the hill states in the Himalayas, was originally a folk-art form in Basohli, with the painting styles gradually spreading across regions and gaining royal patronage, especially after the attack on Delhi by Nadir Shah in 1739. The paintings were often made with mineral or stone-based colours, and painted on handmade paper, and finished by rubbing the painting's back with an agate stone. The paintings soon acquired fame for their elegant use of colours, their picturization and their idealization of the Radha-Krishna dichotomy. Apart from painting mythological and religious scenes, the painters also sought to reflect daily life and everyday activities in the erstwhile Pahari landscape. Aesthetically similar, the Chamba rumals (often termed paintings in embroidery) were embroidered fine cloths of silk, which were used to cover utensils, given as gifts to noted people or used to provide offerings to a praised deity. The dorukha technique was often used to conduct the embroidery in a double satin stitch technique, allowing for a replication of the image on both sides of the cloth. The styles usually depicted popular themes like Raaslila, Rasmandal, Ashtanayika and various noblemen hunting and playing choupad.

The Kullu Valley, situated in central Himachal Pradesh, by the river Beas, has a long historicity—it was termed kulanthapith (the end of the habitable world) in Sanskrit texts, a reference to the barren lands lying in Lahaul and Spiti beyond the orchards of Kullu. In this bountiful land, its craftsmen have come up with a famed array of traditionally attired dolls. Typically made of a metal-wire skeleton, they are generally stuffed with local grass, which is then attired in miniature garments depicting the local fabric and embroidery, with a papier mâché face and a wooden base affixed. The typical attire comprises of a pattu (a checkered dress, which is often worn like a short sari) combined with a dhatu (a headscarf) and a keelta (a cane basket). On dolls that depict the traditional attire of Lahaul and Spiti districts, a full-sleeved jacket made of velvet and a Kullu cap can often be seen.

Traditional accounting books seen in North India, especially Rajasthan, often termed Bahi, were once created manually; their yellow and white pages manually creased at specific intervals to create columns, while the binding cover was kept in the auspicious red colour, representing shubh labh (i.e. good luck). Such a cover is typically bordered with green, yellow or blue threads (niwar), preventing the edges from fraying. Increasingly, such books cater to urban consumers and tourists, with a range of materials used for covers (silk, zari fabric, leather, etc.).

The art of making *katputlis* (puppets) is typically practised by a community of Putli Bhats found in Rajasthan. Such puppets often potray representations of allegorical or historical rulers, members of the court and spouses. Typically, such puppets have their head, neck and face carved out of a single piece of wood, while the torso and hands are made of coloured rags. Footwear is usually added for male puppets. The puppet is typically coated with chalk and painted, allowing for the creation of strikingly elongated eyes.

In Ajmer district, Kishangarh, once a centre of an eponymous Rajput kingdom, is now a defined centre for miniature paintings, famed for the creation of stylized paintings, with arched eyebrows, elongated faces and overall refined aesthetics. The colour combinations are often striking, utilizing ganguli (yellow), neelbat (blue) and harabata (green). Such paintings have increasingly been extended to furniture and wooden items, highlighting parables associated with Radha-Krishna, local folklore and mythological tales.

The kangri, a wicker basket, is often used to carry clay pots containing heated coal. Made of willow, the fibre is typically boiled till the outer skin comes off, leaving the inner skin exposed, which is then cleaned and cut into 5-mm-wide strips, and then woven into a basket, which can be dyed in a range of colours and geometric patterns. Further embellishment using foil, mirrors and metal pieces is often added by the shaksaz, the local basket-maker. These baskets are also used by the Kashmiri pandit community during Shushur Sankrant.

Chipkiang, a local grass that grows across the wilderness in Ladakh, is usually used as raw material for baskets and mats. The typical basket comes in two sizes—a small one, which is used for carrying groceries, while the larger one (a tsepo) is used for heavy loads. Each basket is typically made of two branches of willow (termed salchang), while chipkiang is utilized for the body of the basket, woven using the weft twinning technique. The grass is typically soaked in water for at least two weeks, following which branches are selected and placed at right angles in a circular fashion. The basket is typically dried in the sun for at least a month prior to first use.

Haryana's palm-leaf baskets are inspired by migrants associated with the Audh community from Multan. Made from locally grown date palm, wild grass (termed phoos), and thin leaves of the sarkanda plant, such raw materials were crafted into round-bottomed baskets and lids. Such leaves are also converted into strips, which are then transformed into bags and mats. The sarkanda plant's stalk, when dried, is usually used to make stools (termed mooda), while its leafy covering (termed moonj) is converted into fibre and mashed into rope (termed jeverdi). Traditional shallow baskets, known as changeri, and larger bread baskets with the moniker boiya are utilized to keep rotis dry and fresh, while bound with coloured threads (gota).

A STORY OF DECLINE

Official statistics say that India's handicrafts sector offers employment to ~7 million artisans, 56 per cent of whom are women, while 20.8 per cent are SCs. However, despite our historical crafts tradition, India's share of the global crafts market is less than 2 per cent.[44] The decline in India's handicrafts production is reflected in the handloom censuses carried out over the decades—the number of handloom weavers and ancillary workers decreased by 2.2 million between the second (1995) and third handloom censuses (2009–10).[45] This steep decline, similar to that seen in agriculture, is indicative of how our natural advantage in such trades has been frittered away.

Let's consider the historicity. This historicity of Indian handicrafts stretches back centuries. Verses in the *Mahabharata* praise the skill of Lord Viswakarma, the master of a thousand handicrafts, while the *Arthashastra* speaks highly of the aesthetic sense of Bharatvarsha.

Post-Independence, the national government sought to develop traditional occupations (Jalal, 1991). The Industries Conference (1947) highlighted that cottage industries faced issues associated with a lack of finance, outdated techniques of manufacturing, defective marketing, non-availability of raw materials and competition from mechanized goods, whether imported or locally made. The government sought to set up the Cottage Industries Board (1948), but the board soon recommended that it was insufficient to revive the sector, with sub-groups needed urgently, given the peculiarities of various kinds of handicrafts.

Even now, not much has changed for the handicrafts sector. Consider the word, artisan—we still don't have a precise definition of the word from an institutional standpoint.[46] Most of our artisans lack modern technological skills and education, while their production is irregular, leading to low quality of work, which, combined with the lack of a vocational training system in this field, means that consumers often find products that are inconsistent in quality, made by artisans shrinking in number.[47]

Comparing this to China, the Chinese handicraft industry has evolved to become machine-focused, allowing for increasing standardization and mass production. Indian artisans, in comparison to Chinese ones, conspicuously lack access to credit facilities, raising issues in procurement of raw materials and limited access to larger

---

44   Madhavan, V. K., India's forgotten handicrafts, Live Mint, 29 October 2012. Sourced from: http://www.livemint.com/Opinion/vIrLcNMj0otqEeAxXgijmJ/Indias-forgotten-handicrafts.html
45   Ibid
46   Craft Economics and Impact Study, 2011
47   Sarvamangala, 2012

markets, while they possess little to no knowledge about trade incentives/subsidies that can encourage growth. As trade barriers fell, the import of cheap, mass-made artefacts flooding the country choked domestic producers.[48]

IMPROVING VALUE

Historically, artisans used whatever raw materials were available locally, with the barter system sufficient to serve local commercial needs. However, the advent of plastic and other substitutes has broken down this informal system. Given the labour intensity of the segment, and its decentralized nature, most handicrafts businesses live a hand-to-mouth existence, with limited economies of scale to serve urban markets. Most artisans typically sell their produce at local fairs, with the state handloom emporia providing a potential market. In addition, trade fairs organized by the Handlooms and Handicrafts Exports Corporation, along with state-themed events, have an important role in promoting the handicrafts of rural artisans. The government has also been seeking to encourage the development of a variety of e-marketing platforms similar to the Central Cottage Industries Corporation and the Handicrafts and Handloom Export Corporation.

The segment suffers from issues similar to those faced by weavers. There is limited data on handicrafts, with significant data gaps about the socio-economic status and livelihood conditions associated with artisans, impacting policymaking and planning for the sector. Most artisans are relatively poor, to limited access to capital and low economies of scale, leaving them in hock to moneylenders. Raw material quality is hence a significant issue, while a lack of local infrastructure locks them out of urban markets. There is limited downstream flow of technical innovations, with few, if any, links between designers and artisans, while most artisans are unaware of the transferable skills associated with their craft.

---

48 Jena, 2010

LEATHER WORK

JUTTIS AND CHAPPALS

In comparison, in Himachal Pradesh, bhang (cannabis) grass is used to make traditional footwear (the pula chappal). Such shoes are often worn during religious ceremonies, mostly used to walk within temples and on snow. Typically, buckwheat or cannabis stems are dried and converted into rope-like strips, which are then strengthened by twisting and stretching processes. A T-shaped tool is used to tighten around a junction. The chappal's body is made by combining grass thread spun on a spindle (termed takli). An upper portion of the shoe is often attached; decorative in function, it is often embroidered with wool of different colours. The craft is currently practised in Chad, a village near Banjar.

The famed footwear of Punjab, the jutti, is typically hand-stitched with tilla (gold and silver wire), without using a single nail. The embroidery on the jutti is related to the region it is produced in—Fazilka's villages see juttis embroidered in checkered patterns, while those from Muktsar are multicoloured. Malerkotla's embroiderers are famed for their use of dense embroidery with sunahare (golden), laharai (waves), jalil (trellis) and shakarpara (rhombus) motifs. The Patiala jutti, termed khussa jutti, usually has an upturned toe that resembles a coloured moustache. Making juttis is equal opportunity—the women typically craft the shoe uppers, embroidering them with an ari, while the men construct the shoe using cow and buffalo hides for the uppers and soles.

Rajasthan's traditional leather footwear, the mojari, is typically made of goat or buffalo leather, with sole and heel constructed of differing layers of leather, which are then stitched together with a cotton thread. Such leather work is typically embellished with studding and ornamental work, while embroidery is sometimes done directly on the leather using wool, cotton or silk threads. Responding to modern trends, the traditional unidirectional mojari is increasingly being made with a left-right foot distinction, along with an open-toed development. The usage of sequins, as part of European needs for greater comfort, is also increasing.

INDUSTRY EVALUATION

Jajmau, a small industrial suburb of Kanpur, one of the oldest inhabited places in the region, has been witness to human struggles for survival for almost 3,000[49] years. The town offers glimpses of life in the times of the Maurya, Singha, Kushana and Gupta kings. Once known as Siddhapuri, owing to the temples of Siddhanath and Siddha Devi, the town was believed to be the kingdom of Yayati, the Pandava ancestor, with references to the place also found in the Puranas and Khands.

However, today the focus is on a particular government structure, the Common Treatment Plan (CTP) and its mismanagement is turning into a cause for misery and penury for about 400 tanneries in the area and their employees—a generous mix of local and migrant labourers. Most of the small tanneries evacuating their effluents to the Jajmau CTP were closed down between 2011 and 2015 as they were unable to keep up with the environmental regulations governing the quality of wastewater dumped into the Ganga River, mostly on account of the obsolete treatment plant, with decade-old and improperly maintained equipment. The dark results can be seen at Dabka Ghat, where effluents from ~hundred tanneries are dumped into the Ganga. This impacts the local ecosystem—disappearance of riverine fishes, local fauna and worsening drinking-water quality due to rising water salinity. While plans to upgrade the Jajmau CTP remain stuck on paper, the local tannery owners and labourers face actual loss of employment—signifying continual human struggle for survival.

Ashraf Qureshi, a resident of Kanpur with business interests in the hide godowns of Pech Bagh, is distraught by the economic challenges he faces. He is unaffected by the mess at the Jajmau CTP but business is at an all-time low, with the decline mostly caused by the mechanized slaughterhouses. His tannery employs manual labour to prepare the hides and a direct consequence is a quality differential to machines—manual tanning sometimes leads to a few holes in the hide offered, whereas the ones offered by large mechanized slaughterhouses ensure uniform thickness. Despite the lower price offered by Ashraf, customers are few and far between. He contemplates shutting the hide godown and leasing it to ready-made garments businessmen. His employees do not have the luxury of substitute income and keep thinking about alternative professions, when (and not if) Ashraf decides to close down.

Similar people associated with the business may not be as fortunate as Ashraf. Moin Hussein, an auto driver in Kanpur, has another story to share. He dropped out of school in Class VI to work as labour in a leather factory. Till a few years back,

---

49   http://www.newsgram.com/jajamau-this-is-indias-2700-year-old-city-which-is-still-evolving/

he remained illiterate but learnt to create proper and comfortable shoes. Moin recalled that he used to create designer shoes after just having a look at photos. However, poor working conditions, and lack of salary hikes and other benefits that formal employment usually provide being absent, he decided to be his own master. He now drives an autorickshaw in Kanpur. His skill remains lost.

Indian leather exports have been a classic case of rising up the value chain to attain higher margin business, from being known as a raw material supplier in the '60s and '70s to being a supplier of high-quality leather products. Furthermore, with the leather industry being in focus under the 'Make in India' scheme, and given a target of 50 per cent growth in exports from 2016–20, the future looks promising for the world's second largest exporter of footwear and leather garments.

While environmental challenges and mechanization have caused decline of business in recent years, lack of infrastructural support, coupled with misaligned and ill-executed policies, has been a historical construct.[50] Consider India's Foreign Trade Policy (FTP) 2015–20 and its impact on the leather sector. Under the previous policy, the duty credit scrip available to leather exporters for leather products and footwear under the Merchandise Exports from India Scheme (MEIS) was 4 per cent, independent of the destination country. While the leather industry lobbied for increasing the duty credit scrip to 5–6 per cent, the FTP actually reduced the duty credit scrip to 3 per cent for notified leather products and footwear, and 2 per cent for finished leather products to a specific group of countries.[51] Moreover, the duty credit scrip was made dependent on the destination country, thus making exports lucrative to a select group of countries at the cost of global expansion. Thus, while an exporter would get 4 per cent duty credit scrip earlier, it would not be eligible for any duty credit scrip if exported to Australia or Hong Kong. Similarly, 2 per cent duty credit scrip was revoked on the export of finished leather to Europe.

The change in Duty Free Import Authorization (DFIA) norms for the 'actual user' condition also makes things worse. The FTP states that no DFIA shall be issued for export products where standard input-output norms (SION), as specified by the Directorate General of Foreign Trade (DGFT), states 'actual user' condition for any input. For a leather exporter producing and exporting ~1,000 sq ft of finished leather, as per SION specified by DGFT, a host of more than fourty inputs are required, out of which only one input, the tanning agent/chemical, has the actual user condition attached. Thus, under the applicable FTP, no DFIA shall be issued for finished leather products, which could push small finished-leather exporters into losses.

---

50 https://www.thedollarbusiness.com/magazine/meis-simple-is-always-rational-really/20109
51 http://dipp.nic.in/English/Investor/Make_in_India/sector_achievement/Make_in_India_Leather_
    Sector_Achievement_Report_22122016.pdf

Such reduction of benefits acts as impediments for exporters, especially at a time when the target for export growth is steep, yet achievable. The policy misalignments do not cease with the FTP, but extend beyond.[52] The Union Budget is expected to be in line with the views of the Economic Survey, more so when they are released on consecutive days. While the Economic Survey mentioned the importance of the leather sector for employment generation and export potential, the Union Budget allocated a measly ₹10 lakh for FY2017–18, reducing from ~₹110 crore in 2015–16 and ₹25 crore in 2016–17, for Footwear Design & Development Institute, which is responsible for providing skilled labour and technology for the leather industry. Meanwhile, the Indian Leather Development Programme (ILDP), responsible for improving raw material supply to leather units, witnessed an allocation of ₹500 crore for FY2017–18.

COMPETITION

The scenario for the leather industry becomes more difficult at the global stage due to the presence of country-specific tariffs. India's major competitors, by virtue of being less developed countries (LDCs), enjoy better market access by way of zero/negligible tariffs for exports to major importing markets, the US and the European Union (EU).

Figures 162 and 163 illustrate how, while India continues to face significant tariff barriers for market access in the EU and the US, emerging competitors like Bangladesh and Ethiopia, on account of being LDCs, enjoy minimal tariffs. Tariff barriers faced by India are similar to its competitors, thus trade agreements would prove effective in giving the exporters a competitive edge. This, too, may be lost if competitors like Vietnam race ahead to actualize the Vietnam-EU Free Trade Agreement.

While tariff barriers exist, the increased cost of logistics makes it all the more difficult for Indian leather exporters. Indian leather faces the highest logistics cost (US$/km) from factory to port amongst its competitors, along with Vietnam. It also takes a long time for customs clearance and, again, a long time for shipping to the biggest market (US), along with competitor Sri Lanka.

---

52   http://www.livemint.com/Opinion/7dxD9ny6qTxBTpCSrmQltJ/The-budget-sidesteps-geostrategic-risks.html

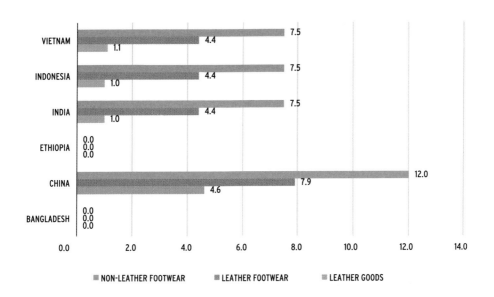

FIGURE 162: TARIFF (PER CENT) ON EXPORTS FROM LISTED COUNTRIES TO EU
(SOURCE: ECONOMIC SURVEY OF INDIA, 2016–17)

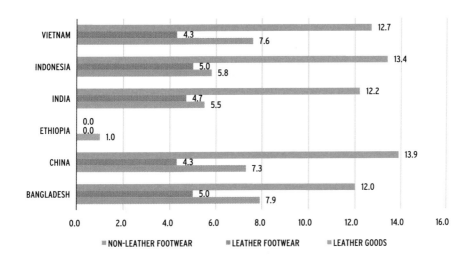

FIGURE 163: TARIFF (PER CENT) ON EXPORTS FROM LISTED COUNTRIES TO US
(SOURCE: ECONOMIC SURVEY OF INDIA, 2016–17)

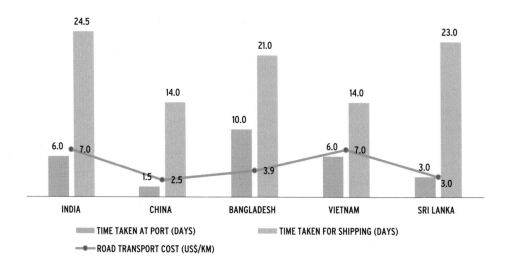

FIGURE 164: SOURCE (ECONOMIC SURVEY OF INDIA, 2016–17)

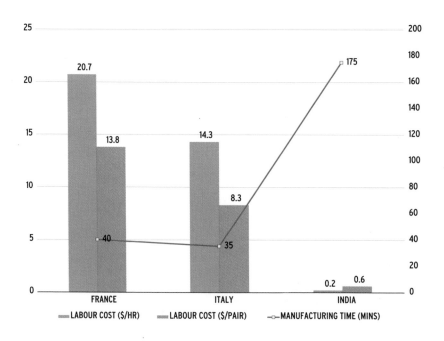

FIGURE 165: LABOUR INTENSITY OF VARIOUS SECTORS, ALONG WITH THE INVESTMENT ACROSS
SECTORS (SOURCE: ECONOMIC SURVEY OF INDIA, 2016–17)

Leather can mitigate India's unemployment woes—most countries in east Asia that experienced successful economic growth take-off have done so by registering a multiplied growth in the leather sector. The leather sector offers high chances of employment creation, given its high labour intensity to investment (measured by number of jobs generated per unit investment), and is as much as thirty-three times more labour-intensive than the auto sector and hundred times the corresponding numbers in the steel industry.

Thus, it can be seen that the leather sector (including tanning and dressing, leather goods manufacturing and footwear production) have about twice the employmen-generation potential per unit investment when compared to the food industries, ten times greater than the auto industry and about twenty to sixty times when compared to the steel industry.

An economic view that has usually persisted around boosting export of leather and leather products to our main export markets, viz., the US and the EU, is that it should take place through large corporations and multinational organizations. However, a majority of the leather industry is unorganized and small-scale in nature; consequently, the potential of exports through small-scale firms remains high. One can view it as a challenge to further increase exports through small enterprises, or as an opportunity for further employment generation and development of SMEs.

The chart below illustrates the demographic of leather firms in India:

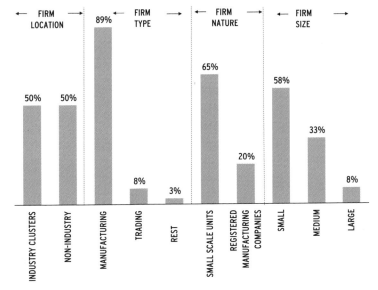

FIGURE 166: DEMOGRAPHICS OF INDIAN LEATHER FIRMS (SOURCE: PRODUCTIVITY COMPETITIVENESS OF INDIAN MANUFACTURING SECTOR, SIDBI) (2010)

Even among the disorganized nature of the industry, dominated by small firms, 63 per cent of manufacturing firms agreed that quality accreditation improved their business prospects, yet only 45 per cent were able to obtain it.

The same phenomenon is observed for other non-farm means of rural income, wherein certain places have evolved as clusters for a particular skill set, be it the textiles of Varanasi in the north and Tirupur in the south, locks in Aligarh, brassware in Moradabad or glassware in Faizabad. The small-scale clusters have emerged for reasons organic to the locations, hence can survive even under difficult situations, as the present case reflects. Consider leather production around the Kanpur region, long believed to be a 'dead city',—the city has survived constant deindustrialization and remains the largest Indian city on the Delhi-Kolkata corridor. The leather production, which originated 200 years ago, survives and thrives in challenging conditions. An important centre of industrial production since the nineteenth century, Kanpur saw its leather production declining after Independence, yet the revival and growth was in large parts due to the flexibility of the industry to adapt to domestic and global requirements. While the '70s saw Kanpur being the central supplier for wet blue leather (intermediate stage of leather/hide), the '80s saw it being the leading supplier for shoe uppers. It changed to supplying whole shoes in the '90s, from industrial safety shoes to footwear for ladies and children. Thus, despite the disadvantages of deindustrialization and information asymmetry, the leather industry has been able to adapt and grow successfully through time.

Such adaptability would not be possible without a continuous supply of a highly skilled workforce associated with various aspects of the leather supply chain—be it selection of hides, skinning, tanning, designing, leather-cutting, leather-stitching and finishing, besides production and maintenance of the large varieties of machines and tools required for these processes. Leather, despite being a natural product, undergoes a metamorphosis through various artificial processes, thus each step requires a particular skillset. Historically, the development of such skillsets has been achieved through informal means, passed on from one generation to the next, without much formal training by institutions or factories who employ them for production, with most manual and hide-processing work being taken up by Dalits and Muslims.

Despite the fact that the region has adapted to new challenges and grown from strength to strength on the basis of a high-quality workforce and cooperation among the industry players, the set-up itself brings misery to the skilled workers, with working conditions being substandard and below par. In most tanneries around the Jajmau area of Kanpur, peak demand season witnesses all-day operations, with workers working informally in two shifts of ten to twelve hours each, despite laws suggesting eight hour work shifts, in order to reduce costs. Cost-cutting through poor employment terms can be witnessed from the fact that a majority of the workers are employed as temporary employees. For a firm, about 75 per cent–80 per cent workers would be temporary, depriving them of paid leave, sick leave, higher wages, weekly holidays and legal benefits like provident fund and gratuity, with wages being less than those of permanent employees by about 20 per cent. Companies also skirt labour laws by registering 'temporary' employees as contract workers; thus, while a firm may employ hundreds of workers, it divides and further subdivides them into groups, with each group managed and supervised by a contractor, to evade labour laws and the providing of benefits to workers. Besides lower pay and the absence of any social security, the working conditions are abysmal. Consider a reputed tannery near Unnao. Except for those workers working with hides in acid or lime mixtures, no workers were given adequate footwear or gloves. The gloves fit poorly and are small, not even covering the wrist properly as opposed to the stipulation of being elbow-length for those working in hazardous areas. Those involved in scudding the hides are bare-bodied, bare-handed, bare-headed and barefoot. Those buffing the hides are covered in dust from the buffed leather, a leading cause of respiratory problems. The work area has a corrugated roof, with inadequate lighting and no provision for fans or coolers.

Ahmed Hussein, a cousin of Moin Hussein, has a similar story to tell. He has been working for an export unit for more than five years and conditions even in semi-organized firms do not offer any encouragement. For the days that he misses work, he doesn't get paid. For times when he goes to work but the factory doesn't have an order or is in a lean season, he gets turned away from the factory gate itself, without any compensatory pay. In bad times, he may be turned away from the gate as many as fifteen days in a month. In peak season, he does overtime, hoping to compensate for the lost days, but gets paid at normal rates, as opposed to the stipulated double of normal rates during overtime. Getting 'promoted' to be a 'permanent' worker requires about a decade of continuous work, yet even a permanent worker may not get any pay for days he reports sick. Ahmed works for a contractor, along with seventeen other workers. His work is supervised by a contractor who is responsible for his pay hikes, which are discretionary. Introduction of machinery has considerably changed working conditions for worse, at times. While quality has improved, the pace of production means workers are not provided adequate breaks. At times, he also cites instances when the factory owner locked them inside the premises during the shift to prevent any chance of theft of machinery or inventory.

Such abysmal labour costs and reduced machinery are reflected in lower production cost, despite higher manufacturing standard time in minutes (STM) as compared to developed countries. A study in 2000 by Schmel presents the results in the following figure.

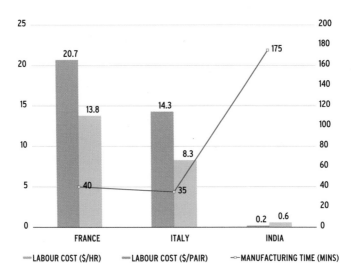

FIGURE 167: WAGES AND PRODUCTION COSTS IN INDIA VS DEVELOPED COUNTRIES
(SOURCE: LABOUR IN GLOBAL VALUE CHAINS, MANALI C. & RAHUL V., 2009)

The chart below illustrates the comparative hourly wage of a leather industry worker across various countries—with India paying the least to its leather workers. The much praised competitive price advantage comes alongside deplorable working conditions and abysmal wages for the workforce.

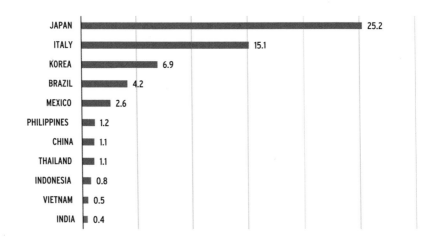

FIGURE 168: SOURCE: NATIONAL SKILL DEVELOPMENT CORPORATION, GOI

Thus, we see that the main reason for the growth of Kanpur's leather industry, its skilled workers, have been traditionally squeezed into pauperization with time.

We witness that India's leather industry traditionally lacks in mechanization and makes up for it in terms of low-cost skilled labour, a pertinent reason being that most of the leather hubs had their origins in the unorganized sector being developed with private sector initiative. With most firms being small in nature, large-scale investments are difficult to come by on a standalone basis, without being supported by government or industry level initiatives. A cluster development approach has been proposed in order to overcome the difficulties, yet effective implementation remains an issue.

SKILL TRAINING

The skill gap faced by the leather industry is immense and across all levels of employment. When it comes to entry-level jobs, like operator, cutter, stitcher and finisher, it has been noted that they have limited knowledge of handling machines and troubleshooting when needed. Lack of awareness of hygiene implies training needs, which may eat into the productive time. Experienced professionals are scarce, thus hands-on training to new workers is lacking. Designers face problems, with a lack of knowledge on global customer standards and trends; with focus solely on apparels, sector specific designers are scarce. Quality assurance and control officials often lack the understanding and ability to undertake advanced due diligence processes and audit checks. Supervisors, in most cases labour lords, have no experience of working with leather-factory machines and hence cannot understand the workers' needs and skills—thereby usually ending up misallocating people and work. The Production In-Charge (PIC) usually lacks planning skills and, like contractors, has no experience of working with machines. Communication skills are also at a premium, as most of the workforce comes from rural areas, having limited customer interaction. Considering the acute skill gap on shop floors and designers, there is need for product-specific trainings, including machine experience of factory workers. Low margins effect low investment, if any, in terms of time and money, in training workers—leading to higher attrition. Considering the demanding nature of the work, it is imperative that expectations of entry-level staff are managed and they are made aware of working conditions and benefits, leading to lower attrition.

While there are about six key skill-training institutes for the leather sector, there is no single body that provides accreditation to the courses leading to variation in curricula and quality of training received by the workforce. This also leads to variation in job role and pay offered by firms to qualified students. Greater coordination between the academia and industry bodies would bring about standardized courses, job roles and salaries.

The sector employs mostly rural people with limited reading and writing skills, with a majority of them unaware of the schemes and benefits provided by the government. Thus, awareness needs to be created among students about the benefits of training.

While the leather sector is projected to require a workforce of 4.66 million people, the Placement Linked Skill Development Programme (PLSDP) can provide shop-floor operational skills to unemployed youth, besides upgrading the skills of workers in unorganized units, leading to better quality and higher chances of employment in the organized sector. PLSDP envisages setting up new training centres (which are expected to be self-sufficient within a few years), similar to an ITI, and imparting training linked to placement. The 12th Five Year Plan (FYP) increased allocation to the scheme from ₹50 crore to ₹250 crore for creation of more centres and targeting one lakh youth for employment generation. PLSDP can leverage the support from various stakeholders—NGOs, private firms, technical training institutes and the government—to effectively cater to the demands of a particular leather-processing region.

The skill levels of Indian workers can be further augmented through secondary training programmes, which can be provided at the shop floor by reputed/certified trainers, in coordination with state governments/ITIs. Trainers should also be provided training at various national and international institutions to keep in line with industry-best practices and trends. However, the funding of the trainer-training proposal under the 12th FYP (₹10 crore) remains inadequate.

Our leather artisan clusters remain unorganized, and lack of awareness on design and market realities remain their weakness—enabling middlemen to corner a greater part of the consumer price. Creation of and support to SHGs, enabling transfer technology to smaller firms and artisans, could lead to improved work conditions and augmented incomes. Functional advice on product diversification and design improvement could enable them to create better products and reduce costs, thereby increasing cost efficiency. Besides technical inputs, SHGs should also be provided financial support through cheaper means of credit from microfinance institutions or banks. Marketing support would ensure that producers (artisans) get a higher share of the consumer price, as opposed to the middlemen getting the bigger share without any apparent value-add. Sometimes, the cluster workers seek nothing more than a chance at fair trade or a remunerative price for their produce. Consider the case of the Jodhpuri chappals produced by the artisans in the 'chappalon wali gali' in the Sardar Market, wherein the family takes collective responsibility for making the chappals. While the men treat the leather and give it shape, the women embroider the piece, making each pair of chappals unique in its own respect. On an average, a woman embroider three to four chappals each day. While traders buy them and supply to bigger cities, the cost to consumer is in the range of ₹300–₹600. However, the work that truly sets them apart— the embroidery done by the women—gets remunerated at just ₹30/piece. Even assuming 365 days of work, the income generated by women from the work is just 66 per cent of the average per capita income of Rajasthan in 2013–14.[53] Yet, the pride they take in their work makes one ponder that appreciation of their 'art' is what an artist truly seeks, with economic support being the secondary motivation.

REVIVING HANDICRAFTS AND HANDLOOMS

India's handicrafts received royal patronage before the advent of the British and acted as a tool in our freedom struggle, yet are today treated as a 'sunset' industry with peripheral and decorative use, made worse by lack of well-implemented policies and schemes to bolster artisans. With the advent of technology enabling mass production, the artisan-consumer relation has been replaced with traders, and lack of economies of scale reduces an artisan's chances of competing with cheap, mass-produced ware. Efforts to mass-produce goods often lead to declining quality, leading to skill loss over a few generations.

Productivity remains a big challenge for India's handmade handicrafts industries. With most production being family-governed, there is a lack of economies of scale. Thus, there are problems of economic production, warehousing, work space, storage sheds, and packing and shipping inefficiencies. The unorganized nature of the sector translates to little or no investments in tools and technologies, while competitors, mostly China, use updated manufacturing technologies for mass production, bringing down production costs both in terms of time and money.

For a majority of crafts, production is a family-wide effort, with skills getting passed from one generation to the other. Estimates reveal that ~71 per cent of artisans work as family units, while almost 76 per cent attribute their learning

---

53   http://trak.in/2012/average-per-capita-income-indian-states/

of family skills leading to their current profession. For most weaving families, women warp the yarn, wind threads and help men during starching of threads. Even for leather work, while men prepare the juttis, the women stitch colourful embroidery on them. Such efforts have led to children missing schools and losing out on education. Studies reveal that in 2003, as many as 50 per cent of heads of households producing crafts had no education, and ~90 per cent of women in such households were illiterate.

Inputs of various kinds are also a problem for most craft skills, raw material being the most important of all. The unorganized nature of the industry means most craftsmen have low volume requirements and thus have limited negotiating leverage, if at all the raw material is provided to them. Historically, raw materials were available due to close linkages of the crafts industry with the locally available materials. The 'jajmani' system of trade between the artisans and the village assisted the artisans further with procurement of raw materials. Deterioration of the jajmani system with advancements in technology has led suppliers to provide material to the organized industry (mostly in search of better prices), thus making it challenging for artisans and making them procure raw materials at higher prices through middlemen or switching to other non-traditional inputs.

Consider the bell metal utensils of Assam made since the reign of King Kumar Bhaskar Burman. The tradition of producing bell metal utensils has been popular in and around the regions of Namshala village, in the Barpeta district of Assam.[54] Swaponil Bharali, an artisan in the village, is happy that he supplies his products to various districts of Assam, neighbouring Arunachal Pradesh and, if lucky, even to Bhutan. However, he rues the availability of soft metal, which remains in the hands of a few monopolistic traders, making it difficult to obtain, thereby raising its price. Even the coal used in melting the metal has become expensive. While his family has been in the profession for generations, declining profit margins on account of high raw material costs has left his sons and nephews wondering if they should consider alternative professions. Low productivity further hampers their prospects. Even bigger industry clusters are not spared—the brassware industry of 'peetal-nagari' of Moradabad relies on constant supply of aluminium and copper sheets, mostly recovered from scrap. Demonetization led to an adverse impact on production on account of the cash-driven nature of the business, leading to work getting reduced by ~66 per cent and raw material prices rising by as much as 25 per cent within a week's span. Even bigger exporters faced issues because, despite making payments to artisans by cheque, the artisans did not get money on account of non-functioning/dormant bank accounts.[55]

---

54 http://timesofindia.indiatimes.com/city/guwahati/Bell-metal-utensil-makers-hopeful-despite-funds-crunch/articleshow/27589517.cms
55 http://www.thehindubusinessline.com/economy/brasswaremakers-woes/article9436648.ece

A fragmented marketing value chain has evolved as the bane of today's craftsmen. While craftsmen remain limited to the rural/semi-urban areas, they have limited means to approach the malls/retail stores to reach clientele, which is increasingly becoming urbanized. Lack of education makes it more difficult to access means and technology to supply products to online sale channels. There is a big gap in the aggregation systems that obtain goods from craftsmen, perform quality-assurance checks, warehousing, and supply to traders for sale to retail channels in urban areas. Given the fragmented nature of production, such aggregation systems that provide marketing support assume more significance. While some producers may be fortunate enough to have direct linkages to urban retailers, many artisans lose out. Middlemen come in handy in such situations. However, more often than not, they exploit the artisans, given the latter's lack of education and lack of awareness about markets and prices. Though this may also be due to lack of knowledge of input costs, the plausible impact remains that lack of bargaining power, education and information further squeeze the artisans' margins.

On the policy front, there are innumerable schemes for improving the conditions of artisans and the handicrafts industry at large. However, they remain on paper. A significant proportion of the government's crafts budget remains allocated to export development, with focus on other development aspects lacking. This has been reflected in the historical rise of handicraft exports, as shown in the following table.

TABLE 68: EXPORTS, DOMESTIC CONSUMPTION, AND PRODUCTION OF
HANDICRAFTS AND CARPETS (IN ₹ CRORE)
DURING THE ELEVENTH FIVE YEAR PLAN AND PROJECTION FOR 2016-17[56,57]

	2008	2009	2010	2011	2012	2017
HANDICRAFTS						
EXPORT	14,012	8,183	8,719	10,534	12,975	28,368
DOMESTIC CONSUMPTION	14,012	8,183	8,719	10,534	12,975	18,912
PRODUCTION	28,024	16,366	17,438	21,068	25,951	47,280
CARPETS						
EXPORT	3,255	2,709	2,505	2,993	3,876	8,079
DOMESTIC CONSUMPTION	622	271	251	299	431	898
PRODUCTION	3,877	2,980	2,756	3,292	4,307	8,977
HANDICRAFTS & CARPETS						
EXPORT	17,267	10,892	11,224	13,527	16,851	36,447
DOMESTIC CONSUMPTION	14,634	8,454	8,970	10,833	13,406	19,810
PRODUCTION	31,901	19,346	20,194	24,360	30,257	56,257

56 Report of the Steering Committee on Handlooms and Handicrafts Constituted for the 12th Five Year Plan (2012- 2017), Planning Commission, Government of India
57 Working Group Report on Handicrafts for 12th Five Year Plan, Ministry of Textiles, Government of India

TABLE 69: GROWTH RATE OF HANDICRAFT CATEGORIES EXPORTED[58]

HANDICRAFT	2014-15	2015-16	2016-17
ART METALWARE	35%	-28%	26%
WOOD WARES	1%	16%	-3%
HAND-PRINTED TEXTILES & SCARVES	181%	50%	13%
EMBROIDERED AND CROCHETED GOODS	-32%	20%	12%
SHAWLS & ARTWARE	233%	-68%	12%
ZARI GOODS	40%	32%	-11%
IMITATION JEWELLERY	-10%	8%	-12%
MISC. HANDICRAFTS	-7%	17%	22%

It is interesting to note that the handicrafts sector comes under the purview of seventeen ministries, ranging from Ministry of Textiles and Ministry of Micro, Small & Medium Enterprises to Ministry of Women & Child Development, leading to confusion and eventually lack of action. At the same time, there are significant funds allocated by the centre for activities like handloom development, as illustrated in the following table.

---

58   Office of the Development Commissioner, Handicrafts, Ministry of Textiles, Government of India

TABLE 70: FUNDS ALLOCATED/RELEASED AND SPENT TO VARIOUS STATES FOR
HANDLOOM DEVELOPMENT DURING 2012–13 TO 2015–16[59]

NO.	NAME OF STATE(S)	2012-13		2013-14		2014-15		2015-16	
		FUND ALLOCATED	FUND SPENT	FUND ALLOCATED	FUND SPENT	FUND ALLOCATED	FUND SPENT	FUND ALLOCATED	FUND SPENT
1	ANDHRA PRADESH	9.8	9.8	5.6	5.6	1.5	1.5	1.5	0.4
2	ARUNACHAL PRADESH	1.3	1.3	1.3	1.3	0.4	0.4	1.0	1.0
3	ASSAM	15.3	15.3	20.1	20.1	5.0	5.0	1.1	1.1
4	BIHAR	0.4	0.4	0.0	0.0	0.2	0.2	0.2	0.2
5	CHHATTISGARH	2.3	2.3	1.8	1.8	0.5	0.5	0.2	0.0
6	DELHI	0.3	0.3	0.0	0.0	0.0	0.0	0.0	0.0
7	GOA	0.0	0.0	0.0	0.0	0.0	0.0	0.0	0.0
8	GUJARAT	1.4	1.4	0.5	0.5	0.5	0.5	0.0	0.0
9	HARYANA	0.1	0.1	0.1	0.1	0.3	0.3	0.0	0.0
10	HIMACHAL PRADESH	2.2	2.2	0.6	0.6	0.2	0.2	0.2	0.2
11	J&K	1.4	1.4	0.6	0.6	1.5	1.5	0.1	0.1
12	JHARKHAND	0.1	0.1	0.8	0.8	2.5	2.0	1.1	0.1
13	KARNATAKA	1.8	1.8	2.7	2.7	1.7	1.7	0.2	0.2
14	KERALA	2.3	2.3	1.6	1.6	0.2	0.2	0.0	0.0
15	MADHYA PRADESH	4.8	4.8	0.9	0.9	0.8	0.8	0.2	0.2
16	MAHARASHTRA	2.7	2.7	2.2	2.2	1.7	1.7	0.4	0.4
17	MANIPUR	5.1	5.1	10.8	10.8	2.4	2.4	0.0	0.0
18	MEGHALAYA	0.9	0.9	1.2	1.2	0.4	0.4	0.0	0.0
19	MIZORAM	0.7	0.7	0.3	0.3	0.3	0.3	0.1	0.1
20	NAGALAND	6.4	6.4	3.9	3.9	2.7	2.7	0.1	0.1
21	ODISHA	7.5	7.5	2.9	2.9	0.7	0.7	0.3	0.3
22	PUDUCHERRY	0.0	0.0	0.0	0.0	0.0	0.0	0.0	0.0
23	PUNJAB	0.0	0.0	0.0	0.0	0.0	0.0	0.0	0.0
24	RAJASTHAN	0.6	0.6	0.9	0.9	0.6	0.6	0.0	0.0
25	SIKKIM	0.7	0.7	0.7	0.7	0.6	0.6	0.6	0.6
26	TAMIL NADU	32.9	32.9	32.6	32.6	10.2	10.2	47.1	47.1
27	TELANGANA	0.0	0.0	0.0	0.0	0.8	0.8	0.4	0.4
28	TRIPURA	4.9	4.9	2.6	2.6	3.5	3.5	0.0	0.0
29	UTTAR PRADESH	18.7	18.7	13.5	13.5	28.2	28.2	6.7	3.2
30	UTTARAKHAND	0.9	0.9	0.6	0.6	0.7	0.7	0.2	0.2
31	WEST BENGAL	4.7	4.7	4.7	4.7	5.8	5.4	1.0	0.0

Let us consider the central schemes that aim to provide assistance to handloom artisans. The Integrated Handlooms Development Scheme (IHDS) encourages Cluster Development Programmes, with a focus on forming SHGs, central yarn depots, design inputs, skill upgradation, marketing support and access to credit. The Institutional Credit for Handloom Sector has provisions for credit access similar to those described above for the HACWA scheme. The Comprehensive Handloom Cluster Development Scheme (CHCDS) covers issues of raw material,

---

59   Figures are in Rs. Crore; In response to RAJYA SABHA SESSION - 237 UNSTARRED QUESTION NO.2399

credit, skill upgradation and marketing across 25,000 handlooms across multiple clusters—Varanasi in the north and Sivakasi in the south being the most prominent. The Marketing & Export Promotion Scheme comprises of marketing promotion through haats, exhibitions and marketing complexes and specializes in branding initiatives (Handloom Mark). The Mahatma Gandhi Bunkar Bima Yojana (MGBBY) and Health Insurance Scheme (HIS) integrate with the Handloom Workers Comprehensive Welfare Scheme and are both well-funded.

The Diversified Handloom Weavers Development Scheme focuses on handloom R&D and technology upgradation. Credit access is made easier with the Revival, Reform and Restructuring Package, which opens up choked credit lines by offering one-time loan write-off through NABARD. To protect artisan livelihoods against competition from machines, the The Handlooms (Reservation of Articles for Production) Act of 1985, has also been passed. In order to provide special assistance to artisans from the North east, the North-East Region Textile Promotion Scheme (NER-TPS) has been initiated, which aims to address issues of low productivity due to poor infrastructure, design and technology issues through increasing cluster count and technical assistance. In order to ensure price-competitive procurement of yarn, the Mill Gate Price Scheme is in place, enabling handloom agencies to obtain raw material yarn at mill gate prices, as well as creation of yarn depots which facilitates supply of raw material to individual weavers.

From a governance perspective, the handicrafts sector comes at the intersection of various ministries. The Ministry of Textiles (MoT) remains the main ministry handling affairs relating to the crafts and handlooms sector through bodies like Association of Corporations and Apex Societies of Handlooms (ACASH), National Handicrafts and Handlooms Museum (NHHM), National Centre for Textile Design (NCTD), National Handloom Development Corporation Ltd (NHDC) and Handloom Export Promotion Council (HEPC) which are responsible for advocacy, policy formulation and scheme implementation at the national level. At the state level, the sector is governed by state-level bodies, with marketing and production being handled by the State Handloom Development Corporations. When it comes to handicrafts, the central office remains the office of the Development Commissioner (Handicrafts), which has six regional offices, five research and development centres, twenty-three cane and bamboo centres, the Handicrafts Export Promotion Council and the Carpet Export Promotion Council, IICTs and other associated autonomous bodies.

TABLE 71: STATE/ UT-WISE WEAVERS BENEFITED/ ENROLMENT UNDER THE HANDLOOM
WEAVERS COMPREHENSIVE WELFARE SCHEME DURING 2014–2016
(FROM: MINISTRY OF TEXTILES)[60]

STATE/ UT NAME	HEALTH INSURANCE SCHEME		MAHATMA GANDHI BUNKAR BIMA YOJANA	
	2014-15	2015-16	2014-15	2015-16
ANDHRA PRADESH	140043	-	87704	62234
ARUNACHAL PRADESH	6000	-	-	-
ASSAM	387563	-	54627	61021
BIHAR	46300	-	309	-
CHHATTISGARH	4953	-	5148	488
DELHI	-	-	-	-
GUJARAT	5018	-	6381	7637
GOA	-	-	-	-
HARYANA	23000	-	378	110
HIMACHAL PRADESH	12030	-	6161	4940
J&K	16265	-	563	515
JHARKHAND	15002	-	745	745
KARNATAKA	45000	-	41263	53628
KERALA	13084	-	5233	8446
MADHYA PRADESH	15720	-	1010	434
MAHARASHTRA	1687	-	2714	135
MANIPUR	51135	-	5368	3579
MEGHALAYA	30919	-	15837	165
MIZORAM	1386	-	-	-
NAGALAND	39501	-	-	-
ODISHA	46531	-	5418	26488
PUDUCHERRY	-	-	1027	990
PUNJAB	-	-	-	-
RAJASTHAN	4983	-	2220	2698
SIKKIM	342	-	129	87
TAMIL NADU	270296	194294	232739	226677
TELANGANA	NA	-	19503	16385
TRIPURA	9367	-	1266	970
UTTAR PRADESH	178316	-	15959	1353
UTTARAKHAND	3297	-	1588	955
WEST BENGAL	381714	-	61500	91447
TOTAL	1749452	194294	574790	583853

TABLE 72: STATE/ UT-WISE FUNDS RELEASED UNDER HANDICRAFTS SCHEMES DURING 2015–16
(FROM: MINISTRY OF TEXTILES)[61]

NO.	STATE	AHVY	DESIGN	MSS	R&D	HRD	WELFARE	INFRA	MEGA CLUSTER	TOTAL
1	ANDHRA PRADESH	23	8	90	11	66	-	91	1140	1427
2	A&N ISLANDS	-	-	-	-	1	-	-	-	1
3	ARUNACHAL PRADESH	-	6	-	5	13	-	-	-	24
4	ASSAM	81	95	229	16	146	-	62	-	629
5	BIHAR	-	-	-	12	23	-	-	-	35
6	CHANDIGARH	-	5	26	-	2	-	-	-	33
7	CHHATTISGARH	4	88	160	17	40	-	-	-	309
8	DELHI	27	823	1430	155	74	-	3112	-	5621
9	GOA	-	-	8	3	-	-	-	-	11
10	GUJARAT	649	36	32	9	170	-	-	300	1195
11	HARYANA	82	3	20	13	26	-	-	-	144
12	HIMACHAL PRADESH	14	23	24	5	7	-	-	-	73
13	JHARKHAND	51	5	-	-	26	-	-	1500	1582
14	JAMMU & KASHMIR	57	19	9	18	90	-	20	470	682
15	KARNATAKA	29	18	19	-	40	-	6	-	112
16	KERALA	7	6	19	15	25	-	-	909	981
17	MADHYA PRADESH	265	34	38	27	65	-	28	573	1030
18	MAHARASHTRA	18	26	31	14	34	-	-	-	124
19	MANIPUR	33	5	79	7	23	-	114	-	262
20	MEGHALAYA	-	4	-	14	30	-	-	-	48
21	MIZORAM	-	2	-	-	19	-	-	-	21
22	NAGALAND	17	13	36	3	18	-	-	-	87
23	ODISHA	35	10	18	2	87	-	300	-	451
24	PUNJAB	60	42	44	29	192	-	-	-	366
25	PUDUCHERRY	-	-	8	-	-	-	-	-	8
26	RAJASTHAN	52	14	21	3	43	-	18	1068	1219
27	SIKKIM	-	7	-	10	15	-	-	-	32
28	TELANGANA	-	-	28	7	10	-	-	-	44
29	TAMIL NADU	22	6	67	-	40	-	120	1019	1273
30	TRIPURA	-	29	-	10	12	-	-	-	51
31	UTTAR PRADESH	257	280	177	165	473	-	547	1876	3775
32	UTTARAKHAND	16	33	7	14	40	-	-	1013	1123
33	WEST BENGAL	84	49	18	19	98	-	-	-	269
34	DAMAN & DIU	-	-	-	-	3	-	-	-	3
35	ALL STATES	-	-	-	-	-	245	-	-	245
	TOTAL	1883	1687	2639	602	1948	245	4417	9869	23290

TABLE 73: STATE/UT-WISE FUNDS RELEASED UNDER VARIOUS SCHEMES IMPLEMENTED BY DC (HANDICRAFTS) DURING 2016–17 UP TO JANUARY 2017 (FROM: MINISTRY OF TEXTILES)[62]

NO.	STATE/ UT NAME	AHVY	DESIGN	MSS	R&D	HRD	WELFARE	INFRA	MEGA CLUSTER	TOTAL
1	ANDHRA PRADESH	8	33	0	8	53	-	79	765	946
2	A&N ISLANDS	0	-	0	0	0	-	0	0	0
3	ARUNACHAL PRADESH	12	7	3	3	2	-	0	0	26
4	ASSAM	90	22	167	15	50	-	0	0	345
5	BIHAR	42	2	21	0	15	-	0	1130	1210
6	CHANDIGARH	0	-	22	0	0	-	0	0	22
7	CHHATTISGARH	29	3	41	0	27	-	0	0	100
8	DELHI	6	153	2775	136	8	-	0	0	3078
9	GOA	0	1	10	0	0	-	0	0	12
10	GUJARAT	72	148	36	37	70	-	0	0	363
11	HARYANA	28	7	57	25	9	-	0	0	126
12	HIMACHAL PRADESH	60	56	28	1	3	-	0	0	149
13	JHARKHAND	34	5	23	0	4	-	0	0	66
14	JAMMU & KASHMIR	104	7	0	6	21	-	78	870	1086
15	KARNATAKA	1	8	38	1	49	-	19	173	289
16	KERALA	25	21	23	0	15	-	24	0	107
17	MADHYA PRADESH	152	37	70	11	65	-	0	0	335
18	MAHARASHTRA	18	2	8	0	26	-	0	0	53
19	MANIPUR	98	31	22	4	26	-	70	0	251
20	MEGHALAYA	0	-	2	4	9	-	0	0	15
21	MIZORAM	0	-	0	8	14	-	0	0	22
22	NAGALAND	25	-	5	2	14	-	0	0	46
23	ODISHA	17	14	66	5	51	-	0	0	154
24	PUNJAB	23	44	13	3	63	-	0	0	147
25	PUDUCHERRY	0	-	9	0	0	-	0	0	9
6	RAJASTHAN	8	30	64	5	12	-	3018	0	3138
27	SIKKIM	0	12	7	2	11	-	0	0	31
28	TELANGANA	4	10	70	0	10	-	0	72	165
29	TAMIL NADU	6	12	69	7	74	-	0	2141	2308
30	TRIPURA	1	8	20	2	28	-	0	0	59
31	UTTAR PRADESH	250	155	126	38	290	-	139	0	998
32	UTTARAKHAND	29	12	13	3	12	-	5	0	75
33	WEST BENGAL	58	36	38	1	12	-	109	0	253
34	DAMAN & DIU	0	-	0	0	0	-	0	0	0
35	ALL STATES	-	-	-	-	-	53	-	-	53
	TOTAL	1198	876	3844	329	1044	53	3541	5152	16038

TABLE 74: BLOCK-LEVEL HANDLOOM CLUSTERS SECTIONED FOR TAMIL NADU UNDER NATIONAL HANDLOOM DEVELOPMENT PROGRAMME DURING 2015–16 (MINISTRY OF TEXTILES)[63]

NO.	NAME OF BLOCK / DISTRICT	TOTAL PROJECT COST	GOI SHARE	AMOUNT RELEASED AS 1ST INSTT.	EXPENDITURE INCURRED SO FAR
1	WEST ARNI, THIRUVANNAMALAI	147	142	63	43
2	PALLADAM, TIRUPUR	182	175	67	19
3	KANCHEEPURAM, KANCHEEPURAM	162	158	55	39
4	KARAMADAI–I, METTUPALAYAM	181	174	66	41
5	AYOTHIYAPPATINAM, SALEM	171	167	63	26
6	CHENNIMALAI, ERODE	171	166	62	65
7	TIRRUPUR, TIRUPUR	182	175	67	21
8	PARAMAKUDI, RAMANATHAPURAM	123	116	58	53
9	KURUNTHANCODE, KANYAKUMARI	79	74	37	13
10	POLLACHI NORTH, COIMBATORE	181	174	66	24
	TOTAL	1579	1523	605	342

Ministry of Micro, Small & Medium Enterprises (MoMSME) facilitates the development of MSMEs in the handicrafts sector, with greater focus on operations, technological advancement, employment generation and financial flows for the firm, yet remaining very similar in aspects of legal and regulatory framework, marketing, skill and infrastructure development. With the crafts sector providing employment to ~70 lakh artisans, with many struggling with marginal economics, the National Rural Livelihoods Mission (NRLM) of the Ministry of Rural Development also comes into the picture. Yet, whereas NRLM focuses solely on providing the beneficiaries with a hybrid social security net, seeking to stabilize their incomes and provide basic sustenance, it doesn't focus on design, technology improvements and improved market access. For firms employing artisans, health and safety remain critical and important to attract and retain the talent pool, and thus the Ministry of Labour & Employment also comes into the picture. The ministry, through its associated bodies like National Safety Council and National Institute of Occupational Health, prescribes best industry practices regarding child labour, hazard protection and mitigation, minimum wages and so on through laws and guidelines. The Ministry of Skills Development and Entrepreneurship contributes by addressing the major need of skill upgradation and development of ancillary business support services. The National Skill Development Corporation (NSDC) under the ministry has set up three Sector Skills Councils (SSCs) in the field of textiles and handicrafts, consisting of industry experts for addressing the skilling needs and incubating craft clusters for revenue generation and achieving self-sufficiency. The Ministry of Environment, Forests & Climate Change (MoEFCC) also has linkages to the sector, especially when it comes to adoption of clean technologies, waste minimization, environmental contribution and minimizing

---

63   Rajya Sabha Session - 240 Unstarred Question No. 2301; Data are in Rs in lakh

environmental damage. Yet, despite the crafts sector being the focus area for so many prominent ministries, there has been no attempt to create a comprehensive handicrafts census, reflecting that while it may be on the list and domain of many ministries, policy implementation remains ineffective.

Artisans in most cases suffer from working capital limitations due to lack of credit access, many times unable to take on bulk orders, as they lack financial resources to purchase the requisite raw materials. While NABARD and SIDBI do provide credit access schemes, lack of awareness among workers makes it difficult for them to avail of the benefits. On the other hand, banks cite poor recovery rates and siphoning off of funds for non-core usages as primary reasons for reduced lending to small-scale artisans, forcing them to borrow from local moneylenders at usurious interest rates.

Various schemes have been introduced by various ministries to tackle the issue. The Ministry of Textiles extends benefits to artisans under the Ambedkar Hastshilp Vikas Yojana (AHVY), which provides one-time financial assistance as margin money to facilitate artisans to avail of loans from financial institutions.[64] Besides margin money, AHVY also calls for minimum wages to be provided to each the during the training period.[65] The Handicrafts Artisans Comprehensive Welfare Scheme (HACWA) provides collateral-free credit guarantee cover of 75 per cent credit facility (subject to a maximum loan disbursal of ₹25 lakh) for loan and working capital. In addition, HACWA also provides for interest subvention up to 3 per cent from scheduled commercial banks. Methods for disbursal of funds under the Credit Guarantee Scheme have also been improved, so that banks receive funds in a timely manner and consequently pass them on to the artisans. In addition, the CHCDS, also provides for margin money capped at ₹4,000 per artisan. Furthermore, the Amended Technology Upgradation Fund Scheme (ATUFS) is again implemented by the Ministry of Textiles in coordination with SIDBI. The scheme, through its sub-scheme, Scheme for Production & Employment Linked Support for Garmenting Units (SPELSGU), approved through a resolution dated 25 July 2016,[66] provides incentive for modernization of equipment. Under this scheme, eligible garment units which have earlier availed of 15 per cent benefit under the ATUFS will be provided with an additional 10 per cent Capital Investment Subsidy (CIS), subject to an additional maximum cap of ₹20 crore, thereby increasing the CIS under the scheme from ₹30 crore to ₹50 crore, with CIS to be paid after three years post-verification of production volumes, turnover and employment generated. The scheme helps artisans to modernize their tools, more so in the high-employment-generating garment segment. Besides Ministry

---

64   http://handicrafts.nic.in/pdf/Office%20of%20Development%20Commissioner%20(Handicrafts).html
65   http://www.indianyojana.com/vikas-yojana/ambedkar-hastshilp-vikas-yojna.htm
66   http://texmin.nic.in/sites/default/files/special_package_under_ATUFS_250716.pdf

of Textiles, other ministries have also taken initiatives to improve credit flow to artisans—with the Shilp Sampada[67] scheme initiated by the Ministry of Social Justice & Empowerment provisioning for loans up to ₹10 lakh to craftsmen and artisans from backward classes to upgrade their entrepreneurial skills.

TABLE 75: STATEMENT SHOWING FUNDS ALLOCATED, FUNDS UTILIZED AND
FUNDS LAPSED UNDER DEVELOPMENT OF HANDLOOM/HANDLOOM WEAVERS
FOR THE YEARS 2014–15 TO 2015–16 (MINISTRY OF TEXTILES)[68]

NO	NAME OF SCHEMES - PLAN	2014-15 - BE	2014-15 - RE	2014-15 - FUNDS UTILIZED	2014-15 - FUNDS LAPSED	2015-16 - BE	2015-16 - RE	2015-16 - FUNDS UTILIZED	2015-16 - FUNDS LAPSED
1	HANDLOOM WEAVERS COMPREHENSIVE WELFARE SCHEME	85	58	42	15	20	19	19	0
2	MILL GATE PRICE SCHEME/ YARN SUPPLY SCHEME	130	130	128	2	150	322	322	0
3	REVIVAL REFORM AND RESTRUCTURING PACKAGE FOR THE HANDLOOM SECTOR	MERGED WITH NHDP		-	-	-	-		0
4	COMPREHENSIVE HANDLOOM DEVELOPMENT SCHEME	MERGED WITH NHDP		-	-	-	-		0
5	NATIONAL HANDLOOM DEVELOPMENT PROGRAMME	362	285	221	65	150	136	134	2
6	TRADE FACILITATION CENTRE AND CRAFT MUSEUM	-	7	7	0	80	81	80	1
7	CHCDS-HANDLOOM MEGA CLUSTER	20	18	14	4	95	37	37	0
	TOTAL (PLAN)	597	498	412	86	495	595	592	3

Considering the gamut of financial assistance on offer, it would seem that artisans have quality access to cheap capital without any collateral requirements, which they can use for capital purchases or working capital. However, with no special milestone-linked loan disbursal and no checks and balances to ensure if funds have been utilized for the right cause, in most cases the artisans end up spending the money for domestic needs and personal purposes. Lack of financial education and fiscal discipline makes them prone to spending huge amounts up front, leaving them vulnerable to seeking private-moneylender financing for completion of the said work. At times, the chief artisan can also be lured away from his core art to double as a moneylender or a middleman, considering that such services could add another income stream for him at the expense of fellow artisans. Lack of access to scheduled banks, on account of low banking penetration, doesn't help matters either.

At a macro level, inclusion of Non-Banking Finance Companies (NBFCs) in the fold of schemes supported by NABARD and SIDBI can help in improving access

---

67   http://theindianiris.com/loan-for-artisans-and-handicrafts-persons/
68   Rajya Sabha Session - 240 Unstarred Question No. 2295; Rs in crores; BE: Budget Estimates; RE: Revised Estimates

for India's millions of artisans, with loan disbursal remaining a core area where such skills and reach could be capitalized. Efficient and timely loan disbursal of loans would enable artisans to undertake bigger orders and provide timely products to the market. For providing relief under the AHVY scheme, NGOs, NBFCs (including microfinance companies) and social sector firms could also be empanelled, thereby improving funds circulation.

The Credit Guarantee Scheme could further be extended to the entire banking and financing (NBFC) sector, helping build confidence at the national level. Provision of electronic cards linked to the schemes and artisans' accounts would facilitate access of funds to artisans. Additionally, private equity funding for small-scale artisan organizations or artisan clusters can also be explored, where private equity players can provide technical and marketing assistance for the organization to scale up, besides equity funds. Besides improving credit access, a few measures that could improve demand could be sub-reservation in FDI in the furnishings sector. Additionally, checks and balances need to be put in place to ensure that artisans do not divert the funds earmarked for production/capital purchases for domestic needs. This would improve recovery rates, encouraging more players to provide capital, thereby reducing capital cost and improving service delivery.

Development of craft-based entrepreneurship remains the need of the hour. Craft-based income has historically been a significant supplement to farm incomes for most rural households, yet in current times, we witness craft suffering from declining skills, disinterest in hand-crafted products and general lack of interest in skills handed down from one generation to the other. Firstly, having seen their parents barely manage their finances despite being skilled in crafts dissuades the new generation, as they fail to see any point in picking up the profession/skills. The present-day school system fails to integrate any knowledge about local crafts in school curricula even on an optional basis, thus the children of artisans are pushed towards potentially lower-skilled, low-paying jobs. Youth employment should be a key focus area for any government and revival of interest of the next generation in handicrafts as a profession remains key to achieving the employment targets.

A key scheme for development of craft-based entrepreneurship, initiated by the MoMSME, is the Scheme of Fund for Regeneration of Traditional Industries (SFURTI), which aims to introduce economies of scale by organizing artisans into clusters, thereby making traditional industries competitive and productive at a macro level. The scheme outlines development of artisan clusters of three major types, each with its own set of financial assistance—mini clusters (>500 artisans) with assistance limit at ₹1.5 crore, major clusters (between 500 and 1,000 artisans) with cluster assistance limit at ₹3 crore, and heritage clusters (<1,000 artisans) with cluster assistance limit at ₹8 crore.[69] The scheme targets about 44,500 artisans across seventy-one artisan clusters involving a financial outlay of ~₹150 crore in the first phase. The assistance would vary from soft intervention (design development, skill training, etc.) to hard interventions (common raw material resource pools, training centres).[70]

In tandem with SFURTI, the Integrated Skills Development Scheme (ISDS) initiated in 2010 by the Ministry of Textiles also aims to train artisans, with training type ranging from basic training to entrepreneurship development. As of April 17, about 10.23 lakh people were trained, 9.32 lakh people had their skills assessed and 7.17 lakh placed with the help of ninety active implementation agencies. Yet, SHGs lack the support to scale up and achieve self-sufficiency, with artisans lacking financial, marketing and entrepreneurial skills, compounded with lack of exposure to global markets, technologies and design development. The scope of ISDS may be expanded to include social enterprises, private sector firms and producer organizations. Funding for the skill development and training programme could be further augmented through the National Skills Development Corporation (NSDC). Private participation should be encouraged to incubate small enterprises, whereas the tax regime applicable for products manufactured under artisan clusters should be made liberal. Entire value chain training needs to be incorporated, covering manufacturing, finance, marketing and product/design development. The visibility of a stable craft income can encourage youth to take it up as a viable livelihood option.

When it comes to artisan welfare, health and occupational safety, a gamut of schemes has been in place theoretically. For insurance coverage, the Rajiv Gandhi Shilpi Swasthya Bima Yojana (RGSSBY) aims to financially enable handicraft artisans to avail of the best healthcare facilities in the country, yet the annual assistance remains quite low, limited to ₹30,000 for in-patient treatment and ₹7,500 for out-patient treatment. The annual premium of ₹700–₹800 is financed with the government paying a larger share and the artisan paying ~₹100–₹200 per annum. The Aam Aadmi Bima Yojana (AABY) also aims to provide insurance coverage to artisans between eighteen and fifty-nine years of age, with economic status near the poverty line. Like the RGSSBY, the AABY premia are also financed mostly by the government, with the artisan having to pay ~₹80 out of the ₹480 annual premium. The same scheme is implemented for handloom weavers under the name Mahatma Gandhi Bunkar Bima Yojana (MGBBY) with similar eligibility, premium and benefit provisions. The Handloom Workers Comprehensive Welfare Scheme also provides insurance benefits to artisans. The Ministry of Labour & Employment provides its own set of rules and guidelines on occupational health

---

69   http://www.msme.nic.in/WriteReadData/DocumentFile/GuidelinesSFURTI.pdf
70   http://www.msme.nic.in/Web/Portal/Scheme-Msme-Sfurti.aspx

& safety, insurance schemes and housing schemes, and the NRLM has its own distinctive set of policies for the benefit of artisans. The table below shows a few insurance schemes applicable for Indian handicrafts and handloom artisans.

TABLE 76: INSURANCE SCHEMES FOR HANDICRAFTS AND HANDLOOM ARTISANS

MINISTRY	SUB-SECTOR	SCHEME
MINISTRY OF TEXTILES	HANDLOOM WEAVERS COMPREHENSIVE WELFARE SCHEME	1. MAHATMA GANDHI BUNKAR BIMA YOJANA
		2. HEALTH INSURANCE SCHEME
	HANDICRAFTS ARTISANS COMPREHENSIVE WELFARE SCHEME	1. BIMA YOJANA FOR HANDICRAFTS ARTISANS
		2. RAJIV GANDHI SHILPI SWASTHYA YOJANA
	WOOL SECTOR	1. SHEEP BREEDERS INSURANCE SCHEME
		2. SHEEP INSURANCE SCHEME
	POWER LOOMS	1. GROUP INSURANCE SCHEME FOR POWER LOOM WORKERS
MINISTRY OF MICRO SMALL & MEDIUM ENTERPRISES	KHADI	1. KHADI KARIGAR JANASHREE BIMA YOJANA
	COIR INDUSTRY	1. COIR WORKERS GROUP PERSONAL ACCIDENT INSURANCE SCHEME
MINISTRY OF HEALTH AND FAMILY WELFARE	ALL	1. FAMILY WELFARE LINKED HEALTH INSURANCE PLAN
MINISTRY OF LABOUR AND EMPLOYMENT	ALL	1. RASHTRIYA SWASTHYA BIMA YOJANA
MINISTRY OF FINANCE		1. AAM AADMI BIMA YOJANA
		2. UNIVERSAL HEALTH INSURANCE SCHEME
		3. JANASHREE BIMA YOJANA

Despite the large number of schemes available, a majority of artisans are unaware of the benefits of the various schemes they can avail of in times of need. This also stems from the fact that for a majority of these schemes, ground-level implementation remains poor. The Rashtriya Swasthya Bima Yojana (RSBY) aims to provide social security and healthcare insurance to BPL families. Now, with the advent of RSBY, it was proposed to remove insurance schemes for artisans below the poverty line (as they would be covered under RSBY) and implement it only for APL families, disregarding the fact that benefits extended under the two schemes are vastly different. The health insurance schemes for handloom weavers and handicraft artisans include expenses for out-patient treatment; and in a country where a majority of medical expenses are out-of-pocket expenses and one illness in the family is capable of sending millions of families back below the poverty line, such benefits are crucial. Consolidation of various schemes offered to various beneficiary groups with varying features into one universal life insurance and health insurance scheme remains the answer.

Firstly, the pooling of individuals under various schemes under one common umbrella will achieve derisking of the scheme. Secondly, it will considerably reduce identification, target and implementation times. With such schemes under one designated ministry, implementation could be made more effective, leading to better results. For health insurance schemes, a separate trust should be formed which would actively look to pre-authorize medications/procedures and delist hospitals misusing the scheme. Insurance services should be made broad-based and invite more interest from service players, thereby maximizing the returns for a given premium. Outreach campaigns need to be undertaken with the local trade associations and NGOs among the artisan communities to ensure that deserving beneficiaries get enrolled into the system. Artisans should be equipped with special artisan ID cards that could be utilized for effective healthcare insurance delivery. The current process of issuing ID cards remains tedious, and most artisans, being uneducated, are unable to avail of benefits provided under the said schemes. This needs to be streamlined if ID cards are to be a success at the national level.

A pilot done by an NGO in Jaipur has shown that given the right environment and efforts, within two years, ~11,500 people can get access cards, with ~25,000 members gaining access to healthcare. The role of the private sector and NGOs in bridging the gap between the policy offered and the benefit availed of cannot be ignored. Furthermore, pension and distress relief should also be provided to artisans. One-time pension benefits have been provided to artisans during their old age, however, the requirements are stringent and the benefits not commensurate with needs and skills.

Despite the presence of various policies and institutional support, crafts have tended to be a 'sunset' industry. An integrated approach is needed, wherein each craft can be encouraged and developed in clusters, thus benefiting from common infrastructure and resource pooling. The crafts sector has to evolve into a creative and cultural industry, which integrates various aspects—diverse markets for growth, industry sustainability, intellectual property rights (IPR) and efficient production and value-add across the value chain.

Certain pre-conditions need to be met in order for craft clusters to develop into creative industries—cluster development approach needs to be strengthened, focusing on creation of common assets, infrastructure and capability building of the artisans. Various social-sector enterprises and NGOs need to be enrolled with the aim of achieving timely results. Crafts have to be provided with certain quality standard marks, signifying that it meets a basic set of quality practices and complete adherence to existing laws, especially pertaining to artisan welfare and zero tolerance of child labour. While such standards are set, backward production standard linkages and forward market linkages (including setting up urban haats and expos) for each cluster should be designed appropriately. Cluster management needs to be professionalized, with set goals and targets for the short, medium and long terms. The cluster should also seek to introduce training programmes in universities, and artisans should be given the option of design internship/ mentorship (as applicable) in reputed national and international design institutes and craft enterprises. Lending to the crafts sector could be made priority sector lending. Infrastructure and benefits under various government schemes, viz, AHVY, DTUS and MSS, need to be consolidated and optimized. The NSDC needs to be leveraged for skill development of cluster artisans. The tax regime for crafts sector could be liberalized to provide higher margins during initial stages of cluster development.

During the next stage, linkages between various dependent clusters need to be established, with a focus on the entire value chain. Craft clusters could be utilized to promote craft/heritage tourism, which can further boost local trade and income. Credit scope should be enlarged to include MFIs/NBFCs at competitive rates. Once aligned with NSDC, artisans should be trained in design innovations, production and inventory management, market linkages and financial matters. Common resource pools (raw material/facility centres/testing labs) and shared workspaces would provide requisite infrastructure at effective cost. Adherence to environmental norms (viz., waste disposal) and use of renewable energy should be emphasized. Linkages between private sector and crafts industry should be encouraged for business orientation of clusters, along with empanelling designers for each craft.

This can ultimately lead to realizing stated goals of social entrepreneurship with artisan/producer-owned organizations in clusters, which have gradually emerged as cultural tourism/craft tourism hubs. Craft education could be taught in schools to create awareness among the youth and give them chances to pursue their studies in crafts through specialized courses on craft design and craft businesses. Gradual rise in incomes among the cluster members in a geographic area, besides adding stability to their lives, will usher in ground-level, broad-based economic growth. Success will also provide villagers with a sustainable and successful means of livelihood and thus reduce migration to urban areas. Success in handicrafts would augment rural incomes and can potentially make the craft-rich village a lively, self-sustaining economic entity.

REFERENCES

STATE OF HANDLOOMS

Planning Commission, 'Report of the Steering Committee on Handlooms and Handicrafts Constituted for the Twelfth Five Year Plan (2012–2017)', VSE Division, Govt. of India, 2012.

Strategic Plan (2011-2016) of the Ministry of Textiles, Govt.of India, 2011. (http://texmin.nic.in/aboutus/rfd/strategic_plan_2011_2016.pdf) Outcome Budget - 2013-2014;

Ministry of Textiles, Govt. of India. (http://texmin.nic.in/budget/outcome_budget/Outcome_Budget_13_14_b_and_a_section_20130909.pdf)

Expenditure Budget, Vol. I, 2015-2016, p 35, Ministry of Finance Department of Economic Affairs, New Delhi. (www.finmin.nic.in)

Planning Commission, 'Report of the Working Group on Handlooms for the 12th Five Year Plan 2012-17'. (http://planningcommission.gov.n/aboutus/committee/wrkgrp12/wg_handloom1101.pdf)

N.V.Shaha, 'Problems and Prospects of Handloom Industry in India', Tactful Management Research Journal, Vol. 1, Issue. 11, 2013.

Bhagavatula, Suresh, 'The Working of Entrepreneurs in a Competitive Low Technology Industry: The Case of Master Weavers in the Handloom Industry',Research Paper No. 321,IIM Bangalore, 2010.

R. Raveendra Nadh, P.Venkata Rao, B.M. Harsha Vardhan, 'Handloom Market - Need For Market Assessment, Problems & Marketing Strategy', International Journal of Emerging Research in Management & Technology, Volume - 2, Issue - 5,2013.

Philip R. Kotler; Marketing Management, 11th edition, Prentice Hall,2002.

Peter Drucker, The Practice of Management, Harper & Brothers, New York,1954. Philip R. Kotler, 'Dr. Philip Kotler Answers Your Questions on Marketing', Kotler Marketing Group, (http://www.kotlermarketing.com/phil_questions.shtml)

George S. Day, David B. Montgomery,'Fundamental Issues & Directions for Marketing', Research Paper No. 1562, Graduate School of Business, Stanford University, 1999.

Bradley T. Gale, Donald J. Swire, 'Value-Based Marketing & Pricing', Customer Value, Inc. 217 Lewis Wharf, Boston, USA, 2006. (http://ifcongress.cval.com/pdfs/VBMarketingAndPricing.pdf)

Mike Easey, 'Fashion Marketing', 3rd Ed.John Willy & Sons Ltd., UK,2009.

Mukund, K. and Syamasundari, B, Traditional industry in the new market economy: The cotton handlooms of Andhra Pradesh, Sage Publications, New Delhi, 2001.

Miranda Moss, '18 Views on the Definition of Design Management', Design Management Journal, Vol. 9, Issue 3, 1998

Arasaratnam, S (1990) 'Weavers Merchants and Company: The Handloom Industry in South Eastern India, 1750–1790' in S.Subramanyam (Ed.) Merchants, Markets and the State in Early Modern India, Delhi: Oxford University Press

Arasaratnam, S (1986) Merchants, Companies and Commerce in the Coromandel Coast, 1650–1740, Delhi: Oxford University Press

Baker, C.J. (1984) An Indian Rural Economy, 1880–1955: The Tamil Nadu Countryside, Oxford: Oxford University Press

Brennig, J.J. (1990) 'Textile Producers and Production in late 17th Century Coromandel', in S.Subramanyam (Ed.) Merchants, Markets and the State in Early Modern India, Delhi: Oxford University Press

Buchanan (1966) The Development of Capitalistic Enterprise in India, London: Frankess and Company Limited

Census of India (1931) Vol. XXIII, H.E.H. The Nizam's Dominions (Hyderabad State), Part I–Report

Chakraborty, K et al (1999) An Overview of the Cotton and Textile Industries in India, Mimeo

Chandrasekhar, C.P. (2001) 'Handlooms: In Survival Mode', Paper presented in the seminar on 'Growth and Prospects of the Handloom Industry', Centre for Economic and Social Studies, Hyderabad, September 23–24

Chaudhuri, K.N. (1974) 'The Structure of Indian Textile Industry in the 17th and 18th Centuries', Indian Economic and Social History Review, XI, 2-3: 127-82

Dastkar (1988) A Plea for Perspective. Memorandum on Behalf of Handlooms to the Review Committee, New Delhi

Das, S.K. (2001) The Warp and the Woof: An

Enquiry into the Handloom Industry in West Bengal, Kolkata: K.P.Bagchi and Company

Eapen, M (1984) 'And Now Legislation for Handloom Protection', Economic and Political Weekly, 17 April: 19 (14)

EXIM Bank (2000) Indian Handloom: A Sector Study, Occasional Paper No.79, August

Francis (1904) Madras District Gazetteer: Bellary, Cited in District Gazetteer (1916), Bellary, Vol. A, 207–208

Government of Andhra Pradesh (GOAP) (2000-01) Note on Handlooms and Textiles, Hyderabad: Directorate of Handlooms and Textiles

GOAP, State Administrative Reports, 1995-96, 1996-97, 1997-98, Hyderabad: Directorate of Handlooms and Textiles

GOAP (1992) Reprint of 1886 Manual of Kurnool District, Andhra Pradesh District Gazetteers

GOAP (1978) Nalgonda District, Andhra Pradesh District Gazetteer

Government of India (GOI) (2000) National Textile Policy 2000, New Delhi: Ministry of Textiles

GOI (1999) Report of the Expert Committee on Textile Policy, New Delhi: Ministry of Textiles

GOI (1996) Report of High Powered Committee on Handlooms, New Delhi: Ministry of Textiles

GOI (1990) 'The Textile Industry in 1990s: Restructuring with a Human Face'.

Report of the Committee to Review the Programme of Implementation of Textile Policy of June 1985, New Delhi: Ministry of Textiles

GOI (1988) Report on the Working and Living Conditions of Workers in the Power loom Industry in India, New Delhi: Ministry of Labour

GOI (1986-87) Report of the Working and Living Conditions of Workers in the Handloom Industry in India, New Delhi: Ministry of Labour

GOI (1985) Report of the Expert Committee on Textiles, New Delhi: Ministry of Textiles

GOI (1974) Report of the High Powered Study Team on the Problems of Handloom Industry, New Delhi: Ministry of Commerce

GOI (1964) Report of the Power looms Enquiry Committee, New Delhi: Ministry of Industry

GOI (1955) Report of the Village and Small Industries Committee, New Delhi: Planning Commission

GOI (1954) Report of the Textile Enquiry Commission, New Delhi: Ministry of Commerce

GOI (1942) Report of the Fact Finding Committee (Handlooms & Mills), Calcutta Government of Tamil Nadu, Directorate of Handlooms and Textiles, Note on Weavers

Welfare and Development Schemes, n.d.

Harnetty, P (1991) ' 'De-industrialization' revisited: The Handloom Weavers of the Central Provinces of India, c.1800–1947', Modern Asian Studies, XXV: 445-510

Haynes, D (1996) 'The logic of the artisan firm in a capitalist economy: Handloom weavers and technological change in Western India, 1880–1947', in Stein and Subrahmanyam (Ed) Institutions and Economic Change in South Asia, Delhi: Oxford University Press

Independent Handloom Research Group (IHRG) (1997) 'Koyyalagudem Handloom Weavers and their Problems', Textiles Working Group Newsletter, 9, January: 2 –3

ILO (1960) Handloom Weaving Industry in India with specific reference to Madras State, New Delhi: Indian Branch

Leadbeater, S.R.B. (1993) The Politics of Textiles–The Indian Cotton Mill Industry and the Legacy of Swadeshi, 1900–1985, New Delhi: Sage Publications

Marx, K (1979) Collected Works, Vol. 12, Moscow: Progress Publishers

Mahammad, P.H. (2000) Entrepreneurship and Structural Dynamic among Handloom Weavers in Andhra Pradesh, Unpublished Ph.D. thesis, University of Hyderabad

Morris, S. et al (2001) The Growth and Transformation of Small Firms in India, Delhi: Oxford University Press

Mukund, K and B.Syamasundari (2001) Traditional Industry in the New Market Economy–The Cotton Handlooms of Andhra Pradesh, New Delhi: Sage Publications

Ramaswamy, V (1985) Textiles and Weavers in Medieval South India, Delhi: Oxford University Press

Ranga, N.G. (1930) The Handloom Weaving Industry, Bombay Raoot, S.G. (n.d.) Strategies for the Development and

Growth of Handloom Sector, Mimeo

Roy, T (1999) Traditional Industry in the Economy of Colonial India, Cambridge: Cambridge University Press

Roy, T (1998) 'Economic Reforms and Textile Industry in India', Economic and Political Weekly, August 8: 2173–2182

Roy, T (1998) 'Development or Distortion? 'Power looms' in India, 1950 –1997', Economic and Political Weekly, April 18: 897–910

Roy, T (1993) Artisans and Industrialization. Weaving in the Twentieth Century, Delhi: Oxford University Press

Roy, T (1989) 'Relations of Production in Handloom Weaving in the mid-thirties', Economic and Political Weekly, XXIV: PE 21–24

Sahai, R (1933) Report on the Survey of the Handloom Weaving and Dyeing Industries in the Nizam's Dominions

Satya, L.D. (1997) Cotton and Famine in Berar, 1850–1900, New Delhi: Manohar Publishers

Sekhsaria, P (2000) 'Killing the Handloom Industry', The Hindu, 14 May Specker, K (1989) 'Madras Handlooms in the Nineteenth Century', Indian Economic and Social History Review, XXVI: 131–66

Srinivasulu, K (1996), '1985 Textile Policy and Handloom Industry: Policy, Promises and Performance', Economic and Political Weekly, 7 December: 31 (49)

Srinivasulu,K (1997) 'High Powered Committee, Low Voltage Report : Mira Seth Report on Handlooms', Economic and Political Weekly, 14 June: 32 (24)

SRUTI (1995) India's Artisans–A Status Report

Subrahmanyam, S (Ed) (1990) Merchants, Markets and the State in Early Modern India, Delhi: Oxford University Press

Sudhir, P and P. Swarnalatha (1992) 'Textile traders and Territorial imperatives: Masulipatnam, 1750–1850', Indian Economic and Social History Review, 29 (2): 145–169

Uzramma (1996) Field Notes, Dastkar Andhra

Yadagiri, T (1998) 'Chitkipotunna Koyyalagudem Chitukuparishrama', Netana, July: 14–16

Yanagisawa (1996) 'The Handloom Industry and its Market Structure: The Case of the

Madras Presidency in the First Half of the 20th century', in T.Roy (Ed) Cloth and Commerce, Reprint, New Delhi: Sage Publications

Arterburn, Y.J. (1982) Loom of Interdependence: Silk Weaving Cooperatives of Kanchipuram, New Delhi: Hindustan Publishing Corporation Press

Bharathan, K (1988) The Handloom Industry in Tamil Nadu: A Study of Organizational Structure, University of Madras

Chandra, P (Ed) (1998) Technology, Practices and Competitiveness; The Primary Textile Industry in Canada, China and India, Mumbai: Himalayan Publishing House

Dash, S (1995) Handloom Industry in India, New Delhi: Mittal Publications

Datta, A.K. & Hein Streflkeak (1985) 'Weavers, Traders and the State: Handloom

Weaving in Bangladesh', Economic and Political Weekly, 14 September:

Debroy, B (1996) Beyond the Uruguay Round: The Indian Perspective on GATT,

New Delhi: Response Books, A Division of Sage Publications

Eapen, M (1985) 'The New Textile Policy', Economic and Political Weekly, 22 June:

IRMA (1995) A study on the Problems of Weavers' Cooperative Societies in

Andhra Pradesh. Report submitted to NABARD

Iyengar, S.K. (1951) Rural Labour Enquiries in the Hyderabad State, 1949–51, Government of Hyderabad

Jain, L.C. (1983) 'Handlooms Face Liquidation: Power looms Mock at Yojana Bhawan', Economic and Political Weekly, 27 August: 18 (35)

Latif, M.A (1997) Handloom Industry in Bangladesh, Dhaka: University Press Limited

Laxmi Narsaiah, M & C.H.Thandavakrishna (1999) Crisis of Handloom Industry, New Delhi: Discovery Publishing House

Loksabha Secretariat (1989) Factual Study on 'National Textile Policy, Third Edition, New Delhi

Mahapatro, P.C. (1986) Economics of Cotton Handloom Industry in India, New Delhi: Mittal Publications

Meher, R (n.d.) The Handloom Industry and the

socio-economic conditions of weavers in Orissa, Working Paper No.8, Bhubaneswar: Vabakrushna Choudhury Centre for Development Studies

Mines, Mattison (1984) The Warrior Merchants: Textiles, Trade and Territory in South India, Cambridge: Cambridge University Press

Misra, Sanjiv (1993) India's Textile Sector: A Policy Analysis, New Delhi: Sage Publications

Nath, Pradosh et al (2001) 'National Textile Policy and Textile Research', Economic and Political Weekly, February: 36 (5 & 6)

Noorbasha, A (1996) 'Handlooms in Distress', Economic and Political Weekly, 6 June: 31 (23)

Rajyalakshmi, P (1994) Handloom Industry in Andhra Pradesh–The Case of Venkatagiri Handlooms, M.Phil Dissertation, B.R.Ambedkar Open University

Rama Mohana Rao, K (1990) Development of Handloom Industry, New Delhi: Discovery Publishing House

Uchikawa, S (1998) Indian Textile Industry: State Policy, Liberalization and Growth, New Delhi: Manohar Publishers and Distributors

Venkatraman, K.S. (1940) Handloom Industry in South India, Madras: The Dieceson Press

Venkateswara Rao, A (1991) A Directory of Hand weaving Industry of India, Hyderabad: Shuttle Craft Publications

Weiner, Annette.B & Jane Scheneider (Ed) (1991) Cloth and Human Experience, Washington: Smithsonian Institution Press

Annual Report of Ministry of Textile. Retrieved from http://texmin.nic.in/annualrep/ar_10_11_english.pdf. (2010-11)

Niranjana S., Thinking with Handlooms: Perspectives from Andhra Pradesh, Economic and Political Weekly, 39(6), 553-563 (2004)

Ganguly-Scrase R., Paradoxes of Globalization, Liberalization, and Gender Equality: The Worldviews of the Lower Middle Class in West Bengal, India, Gender and Society, Sage Publications, 17(4), 544-566 (2003)

Roy T., Acceptance of Innovations in Early Twentieth Century Indian Weaving, The Economic History Review New Series, 55(3), 507-532 (2002)

Khanna S., Technical Change and Competitiveness in Indian Textile Industry, Economic and Political Weekly, 24 (34), M103-M111 (1989)

Goswami O., Sickness and Growth of India's Textile Industry: Analysis and Policy Option, Economic and Political Weekly, 25(44), 2429-2439 (1990)

Harnetty P., Deindustrialization' Revisited: The Handloom Weavers of the Central Provinces of India, 1800-1947. Modern Asian Studies, Cambridge University Press, 25(3), 455-510 (1991)

Mizuno K., Rural Industrialization in Indonesia: A Case Study of Community-based Weaving Industry in West Java, Occasional Paper Series, Tokyo: Institute of Development Economies, 31,114 (1996)

Roy T., Development or Distortion? Power looms in India 1950-97, Economic and Political Weekly, 33(16) (1998a)

Roy T., Growth and Recession in Small-Scale Industry: A Study of Tamil Nadu Power looms, Economic and Political Weekly, 34(44), 3137-3145 (1999)

Haynes E.D., Artisan Cloth-Producers and the Emergence of Power loom Manufacture in Western India 1920 -1950, Past and Present. Published by: Oxford University Press on behalf of The Past and Present Society, 172, 170-198 (2001)

Srinivasulu K., Handloom Weavers' Struggle for Survival, Economic and Political Weekly, 29(36), 2331-2333 (1994)

Mukund K., Indian Textile Industry in 17th and 18th Centuries: Structure, Organization and Responses, Economic and Political Weekly, 27(38), 2057-2065 (1992)

Narasaiah L. and Krishna T., Crisis of Handloom Industry. New Delhi: Discovery Publishing House, (1999)

Gurumoorthy T.R. and Rengachary R.T., Problems of Handloom Sector, In Soundarapandian. M (Eds.), Small Scale Industries: Problems. New Delhi: Concept Publishing House, 1, 168-178 (2002)

Mathiraj S.P. and Raj Kumar P., Analytical study on Handloom products production and marketing, Tamil Nadu, Journal of Cooperation, 69-73 (2008)

Tripathy S.G., Odisha Handlooms: Problems and Perspectives, Orissa Review, 54-56 (2009)

Mukherjee S., Looms of Doom, Outlook India, (2004, September 27)

V Leeladhar (2005) 'Beyond agriculture: is there a big market out there?' Vikalpa, Volume 30, No 2, April - June 2005, p-92.

Dr. Amit K. Chatterjee (2005) ': FAIDA -
Newsletter on Business Opportunities from India
and Abroad', Vol. 6, Issue 5 ; July 29' 2005

M. Sivakkannan (2005) 'The handloom
industry has not prepared itself to face
the post-WTO dispensation', The Hindu
Business Line, 13 November 2005.

Jayaswal Rajeev (2005), 'Now, Foreign Investors
Have Designs on Handloom Sector', The
Economic Times, 10thSept2005, http://articles.
economictimes.indiatimes.com/2005-09-10/
news/27473214_1_handloom-showrooms-epch

Ramanurjan (2005) 'The number of
skilled master weavers is dwindling', The
Hindu Business Line, 22 March 2005.

M. Sivakkannan (2005) 'The handloom industry
will never receive the same support as the organized
sector from the Central and State governments',
The Hindu Business Line, 9 Oct 2005.

Shingi P M (2006) 'Vinchur Handloom
Weavers Cooperative Society: A Case Study',
http://www.iimahd.ernet.in/publications/
public/FullText.jsp?wp_no=00000000544

LEATHER WORK

http://dipp.nic.in/English/Investor/
Make_in_India/sector_achievement/
Make_in_India_Leather_Sector_
Achievement_Report_22122016.pdf

https://www.thedollarbusiness.com/magazine
/meis-simple-is-always-rational-really/20109

https://www.thedollarbusiness.com/
magazine/leather-industry---yet-to-
put-the-best-foot-forward/32843

https://smallb.sidbi.in/sites/default/files/
knowledge_base/Productivity
CompetitivenessofIndianManufacturing
Sector.pdf

https://smallb.sidbi.in/sites/default/files/
knowledge_base/

TheIndianLeatherIndustry.pdf

http://pulitzercenter.org/reporting/
india-toxic-price-leather-0

http://www.tntdpc.com/technoblaze/
may/casestudy.pdf

http://indianexpress.com/article/india/
demonetization-on-a-shoestring-how-up-leather-
industry-is-hit-by-cash-crunch-4443645/

http://rupe-india.org/47/leather.html

http://www.indiaspend.com/cover-story/
the-slow-death-of-kanpurs-leather-
economy-and-ups-job-crisis-69555

http://www.indiaenvironmentportal.org.in/
content/176/artisans-the-untold-story/

http://www.businesstoday.in/magazine/
features/hell-for-leather/story/551.html

https://thewire.in/25567/the-unmaking-
of-kanpurs-leather-industry/

https://scroll.in/article/828173/an-unholy-
mess-at-kanpur-how-all-plans-to-clean-up-
the-ganga-have-totally-failed-so-far

http://www.historydiscussion.net/
history-of-india/economic-history/de-
industrialization-in-india-process-causes-and-
effects-indian-economic-history/5970

http://www.economicsdiscussion.net/
india/industries-india/cottage-industries-
of-india-decline-and-effects/21211

http://www.thecitizen.in/index.php/
NewsDetail/index/9/8244/Kanpur-The-
Slow-Decline-of-a-Historic-Legacy

http://shodhganga.inflibnet.ac.in/
bitstream/10603/92643/12/12_chapter3.pdf

CHAPTER **VII**

ON RURAL LABOUR

'The hungry millions ask for one poem—invigorating food. They cannot be given it. They must earn it. And they can earn only by the sweat of their brow.' —Mahatma Gandhi, Young India, 13 October 1921, p. 326

The ample supply of peasants in India's agricultural economy has been a consistent theme for centuries. While there are few historical sources that highlight real rural wages, it is estimated that rural wages declined by 50 per cent between the time of Akbar (1600) and the Second World War (1939).[1,2] Scattered reports showcase that real wages remained stagnant between 1850 and 1873.[3] The khudkhast system, in the late eighteenth century, in Delhi and its environs, saw farmers utilizing peasant labour for cultivating their holdings.

Meanwhile, the caste ban on touching the plough by Brahmin landowners in South India meant the utilization of a large corpus of hired labour.[4] The hali labour system found in south Gujarat in the early sixteenth century saw Anavil Brahmins utilizing attached bonded labour given ongoing debts.[5] The inter-caste exchange of labour services was skewed one way—from the halis to the Brahmins, with wages paid to the halis typically lower than prevailing market rates.[6] Equality, between the landowner and the labourer, was non-existent. This coercive utilization of such peasants, in the form of bonded labour or with a pittance of a wage, has been the hallmark of India's agricultural society for centuries. The chamars (leather workers)

---

1   Mukherjee, R., 1939

2   Lal, D., Trends in Real Wages in Rural India, Report No. DRD103, World Bank, June 1984. Sourced from: http://documents.worldbank.org/curated/en/202581468042563759/pdf/DRD1030WP00Tre000Public00Box374341B.pdf

3   Mukherjee, M. 1969

4   Kumar, D., Land and Caste in South India

5   Breman, J., Labour Bondage in West India, Oxford University Press, 2007

6   Chaudhuri, B.B., Peasant History of Late Pre-colonial and Colonial India, Volume 8, Pearson Education

and the dhanuks (paddy huskers) were often forced to supplement their meagre income through work as agricultural labourers, with the caste system helping to create a fixed labour reserve for agricultural production.[7] Since Independence, India's rural labour market has been marked by significant changes over the last few decades. In 1951, India was estimated to have 58 million rural households, of which 17.7 million were agricultural labour households (segmented almost equally into those with land and those without).[8] By 1957, the number of rural households had gone up to 64.5 million, of which 15.8 million were agricultural labour households (of which 9.2 million had no land).

Indian agriculture was marked by an ample supply of labour, which was usually under-utilized, given the seasonal nature of agricultural work. As labour supply grew, wages in farming declined, with labour absorption increasing further to compensate. Even now, India's agricultural labourers remain a neglected class, with low income and irregular employment, while possessing little to no skills or training. Their fate has rarely been in their hands, while the government's attention to their plight sometimes seems to exist primarily in platitudes.

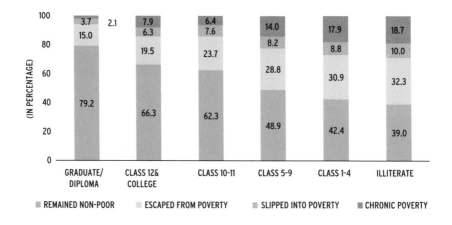

FIGURE 169: EDUCATION LEVELS IN RURAL INDIA[9]

---

7   Habib, I., The Agrarian System of Mughal India, 1556-1707, 2014, Oxford University Press

8   For ALE 1950-51: 'Agricultural Labour Enquiry, Vol. 1 — All India' Government of India; for ALE 1956-57, NSS Draft No 31,

9   Desai, S., Vashishtha P. and Joshi. O. 2015. Mahatma Gandhi National Rural Employment Guarantee Act: A Catalyst for Rural Transformation. New Delhi: National Council of Applied Economic Research

Tamil Nadu's Kolappan Committee Report on Agricultural Labourers in Tamil Nadu (1998) vividly describes the working conditions faced by them. As agricultural operations are seasonal, most agricultural workers face unemployment during the lean months, which can range from three to six months—such workers tend to migrate to urban areas in search of jobs during such periods. A typical male agricultural worker in Tamil Nadu's hinterland gets ~150 days of work in a year, while a female worker could get ~100 days of work per year. Being dispersed and unorganized, such workers typically have minimal bargaining power, leaving their wage structures at the mercy of local landlords. Such labourers are often socially vulnerable, depending mainly on seasonal agricultural work for their livelihood—47 per cent of such workers are landless, while 38.56 per cent were marginal landowners in 2015; 19 per cent are chronically poor, while a further 9.5 per cent have recently slipped back into poverty. Most agricultural labourers have limited education (being either illiterate or at most having studied up to Class 3 or Class 4).

SHIFTING FROM AGRICULTURE

And yet, reports over the last decade have highlighted agricultural labour shortages. Currently, of India's 1.3 billion population, we possess a workforce of around 467 million, of which, a bit above 230 million works in the agriculture sector.[10] This agricultural workforce has seen substantial reduction in the last two decades, falling from 259 million in 2004–05 to around 230 million currently; however, agricultural labour still constitutes a significant portion of our labour force. The greatest reduction has been in surprising areas, with Uttar Pradesh seeing 8.47 million labourers shifting away from agriculture between 2005 and 2012, while Karnataka saw 4.69 million and West Bengal 3.71 million. This has resulted in localized shortages—Andhra Pradesh has notably seen ~5 per cent of its rural workforce migrate to other sectors between 2005 and 2012, leading to significant shortage in labour for rice cultivation. This has been reflected across its districts—West Godavari district, with over 0.25 million hectares under paddy cultivation, has been facing labour shortage, with the local administration responding through encouragement of farm mechanization.[11] In Surat district, in Gujarat, labour shortage (with fewer able-bodied men seasonally migrating from Maharashtra's

---

10   NSSO 55th Round, NSSO 61st Round, NSSO 66th Round, NSSO 68th Round

11   '150 paddy transplanters for W.Godavari to combat labour shortage', The Hindu, 12 June 2011. Sourced from: http://www.thehindu.com/news/cities/Vijayawada/150-paddy-transplanters-for-w-godavari-to-combat-labour-shortage/article2098517.ece

Dhulia and Jalgaon districts) for harvesting 0.14 million tonnes of sugar cane has led to farmers utilizing tractors for harvesting or, failing that, burning the crop down to clear the field for fresh sowing.[12] About 15 per cent of the rural workforce shifted out of agriculture in Tamil Nadu and Haryana between 2004–05 and 2011–12, resulting in a sharp increase in wages. Effectively, about 30.5 million peasants quit farming between 2004–05 and 2010–11, looking for employment in other non-farm sectors.[13] We face a paradoxical situation where the rural labour market is tightening, despite sub-optimal growth in measured employment.

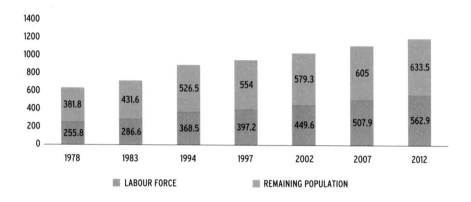

FIGURE 170: INDIA LABOUR FORCE GROWTH[14]

Statistics paint a wider picture. In 1993–94, 58 per cent of all able-bodied rural men and women were self-employed, while 35.6 per cent served as casual labour. By 1999–2000, those serving as casual labourers had inched up to 37.4 per cent, which by 2009–10 had reached 38.6 per cent.[15] When considering gender, the picture changes slightly—rural males working as casual labour have jumped from 33.8 per cent in 1993–94 to 38 per cent in 2009–10, while rural females, initially at 38.7 per cent, have inched up to 39.9 per cent. This shift away from agriculture is also reflected in rural migration patterns. NSSO's 64th round data indicates that households belonging to the migrant category in urban areas increased to

---

12   Saiyed, K., 'Labour pains have sugar cane farmers in a bitter soup', Indian Express, June 24, 2011. Sourced from: http://indianexpress.com/article/cities/ahmedabad/labour-pains-have-sugar cane-farmers-in-a-bitter-soup/lite/

13   Planning Commission, 2011

14   Rural Development Statistics, National Institute of Rural Development, Government of India, 2012

15   Various NSSO rounds. Alha, Akhil, Yonzon, Bijoyata, 'Recent Developments in Farm Labour Availability in India and Reasons behind its Short Supply', Agricultural Economics Research Review, Vol 24 (Conference Number) 2011 pp 381-390. Sourced from: http://ageconsearch.umn.edu/bitstream/119388/2/3-Akhil-Alha.pdf

~3 per cent in 2007, compared to 2 per cent in 1993–94. Meanwhile, rural to urban migration accounted for ~20 per cent of all internal migration in 2007–08, with rural to rural migration accounting for 62 per cent. Rural to urban migration among males increased from 34 per cent in 1999–2000 to 39 per cent in 2007–08. Such outflow is typically from backward states like Uttar Pradesh and Bihar (albeit declining) to more urbanized states like Delhi, Maharashtra, Gujarat, Punjab and Madhya Pradesh.[16] Labour has instead withdrawn from the local labour market and temporarily migrated to other parts of India and, in some cases, even abroad, especially to the Gulf.

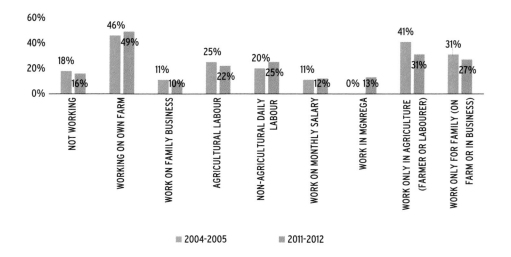

FIGURE 171: CHANGES IN LABOUR FORCE BEHAVIOUR FOR POPULATION AGED 15–59
(PARTICIPATING WORKFORCE PER CENT)[17]

16   Bhagat, M., 2009
17   Desai, S., Vashishtha P. and Joshi. O. 2015. Mahatma Gandhi National Rural Employment Guarantee
      Act: A Catalyst for Rural Transformation. New Delhi: National Council of Applied Economic Research

DETERMINANTS OF LABOUR MIGRATION

This shift away from agriculture has been driven by a range of factors—greater urbanization has led to better opportunities in manufacturing and services, while the impact of government schemes like MGNREGA has boosted rural incomes and wages (rural wages have been growing by 17 per cent annually since 2006–07). Labourers increasingly cite the higher wages in jobs available locally, the preference for a permanent job (agricultural work remains primarily seasonal) and lack of social esteem attached to agricultural jobs as reasons for shifting out.[18] While overall rural employment grew by ~1 per cent between FY00 and FY12, rural non-farm employment increased at a whopping pace of 5.1 per cent.[19] Non-farm income, on average, now accounts for one-third of all household income.[20] National-level studies, conducted by the National Sample Survey Organization (NSSO), along with various regional studies have also indicated that non-farm activities like running a tea stall, a cycle repairing workshop, cane crushing, rice milling and local transportation are growing in number.[21] Rural non-farm employment jumped by 1 per cent CAGR between 2000 and 2012, which, given the size of India's current rural workforce, is a large shift. Rural non-farm employment jumped by 33 per cent in Jammu & Kashmir, 21 per cent in Goa and 20 per cent in Punjab during this period, while the proportion of agricultural households who are principally dependent on agriculture declined from 63 per cent in FY03 to 58 per cent in FY13. The poorer the household, the more pronounced the shift—the 10th percentile of rural households dependent primarily on agriculture went down from 42.1 per cent in FY03 to 34.8 per cent in FY13. As labour shortages widen, India's farmers will face a productivity challenge.

Consider Odisha: The state saw over 849,000 hectares of fertile land remain uncultivated in 2012–13, while 722,000 hectares were uncultivated in 2014–15.[22] With a changing climate, a lack of adequate marketing facilities in the state and the high cost of agricultural labour, farming has few, if any, margins left as an occupation. The scheme offering cheap rice (at ₹1/kg up to 25 kgs to six million families) introduced in the state has helped reduce malnutrition, but has disincentivized villagers from working, leading to a dearth of agricultural labour. The number of small, medium and large-scale farmers has dropped by 460,000 between 2005–06 and 2010–11, while the number of marginal farmers rose by 771,000 to reach 3,368,296 in 2011.

---

18   Prabakar C., Sita Devia K. and Selvamb S., Labour Scarcity—Its Immensity and Impact on Agriculture
19   Saha, P., Verick, S., State of Labour Markets in India, May 2016, ILO Asia-Pacific Working Paper Series
20   Lanjouw and Shariff, 2004
21   Epstein, 1973; Srinivas, 1976; Wiser & Wiser; 1971
22   'Agriculture as an occupation losing lure in Odisha', Business Standard, IANS, 10 September 2015. Sourced from: http://www.business-standard.com/article/news-ians/agriculture-as-an-occupation-losing-lure-in-odisha-115091000562_1.html

The reasons for such migration vary, with the search for better employment opportunities emerging as a primary driver. With landless labourers facing economic deprivation, while marginal farmers face up to low fertility and lower margins, rural India is migrating en masse.[23] With the introduction of labour savings methods in agriculture, rural labour, already oversupplied, has been rendered mostly surplus. Even those with a parcel of land, face a declining land-to-labour ratio, forcing them to move out from backward areas to regions with more non-farm opportunities. Sometimes the migration is seasonal, with such migrants returning every cropping season or for cultural/personal festivities. For lower caste agricultural labourers, migration provides an avenue to escape hardships and social ostracism imposed by the caste system.[24] While such migration used to occur in the past as well, the availability of better communication (via mobile phones) and inter-state transport facilities have raised the rate of migration.[25] Large farmers in Punjab are now directly linked to casual labourers in Purnea district in Bihar through mobile phones, reducing the lag and the transaction cost associated with using intermediaries, while raising the velocity of migration.[26]

RISING AGRICULTURAL GROWTH, INCREASING MECHANIZATION

Agricultural growth is typically tightly coupled with non-farm income. Higher productivity, along with higher output, in agriculture, typically leads to an increase in ancillary activities in the rural economy. Agricultural growth implies a higher demand for agricultural inputs like seeds and fertilizers, while increasing growth in the non-farm sector.[27] A study has calculated that an increase in agricultural income by ₹100 typically boosts non-farm income by ₹64 (split between villages and towns).[28] Meanwhile, when agricultural incomes decline, given pests, drought, floods or change in market prices, the non-farm sector is critical to absorbing surplus labour.[29]

---

23 Jetley 1987, Korra, 2011, Rodgers, Rodgers, 2011

24 Sharma, 2005

25 Rodgers, Rodgers, 2011

26 Alha, Akhil, Yonzon, Bijoyta, 'Recent Developments in Farm Labour Availbility in India and Reasons behind its short supply', Agricultural Economics Research Review, Vol. 24 (Conference Number) 2011, pp 381-390. Sourced from: http://ageconsearch.umn.edu/bitstream/119388/2/3-Akhil-Alha.pdf

27 Mellor, 1976

28 Hazell and Haggblade, 1990

29 Vaidyanathan, 1983

In addition, the increasing mechanization prevalent in Indian agriculture since 1991 has led to displacement of workers from the farm sector by making the peak period of farming activities shorter, resulting in lower demand and wages for casual labourers. Typically, such labourers were offered minimal wages for two to three months of farm work; naturally, when given the option for non-farm employment, many took up the chance.

ACCESS TO LAND OR CAPITAL

Access to land usually determines whether a rural household will seek to serve as casual labour in the non-farm sector or seek to eke out a living using agricultural productivity.[30] Non-farm employment has been found to be higher in villages with a larger proportion of landless households in five districts of Gujarat.[31] Studies in Punjab have also showcased that non-farm employment of agricultural households is usually 50 per cent of households with a non-agricultural background. Most such rural folks are joining non-farm jobs because they are unable to find year-round employment or because of the limited capacity of their lands to support their household needs.[32] As landholdings have fragmented, the proportion of rural households not cultivating any land has increased from 35.4 per cent in 1988 to 48.5 per cent in 2012.[33] Typically, states and districts with higher proportion of rural households without access to land to cultivate have also had a higher proportion of non-farm workers.[34]

In addition, one's financial ability to lock up personal effects and migrate plays a role. As one moves up social decile classes, the largest migration is seen by those at the highest levels.[35] Migration, in effect, is a coping mechanism for those who can afford it—the very poor cannot migrate away given the need for initial financial security for food and lodging. The inception of MGNREGA, along with increased spending on public works in rural areas, has helped stem their rise somewhat, by providing them an option compared to agricultural work.

---

30   De Janvry et al (2005)
31   Basant, 1993
32   Ghuman, 2005
33   Rawal, 2013
34   Saha, P., Verick, S., State of rural labour markets in India, May 2016, ILO Asia-Pacific Working Paper Series
35   NSSO, 64th Round: Migration Particulars of India

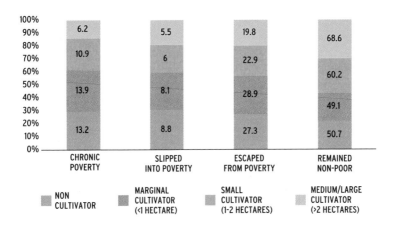

FIGURE 172: LAND OWNERSHIP IN RURAL INDIA[36]

WAGE DIFFERENTIALS

As agricultural labourers are withdrawing from agriculture, wages offered to them in agriculture are rising, the real wages have increased by 3.17 per cent annually for females and by 2.69 per cent annually for males between 1995–96 and 2011–12. Reports from the Commission for Agricultural Costs & Prices highlight that nominal farm wages grew at 11.6 per cent CAGR in the '90s, while slowing to 8.9 per cent between 2000 and 2011.[37] There has been inter-state variation—states like Kerala, Rajasthan, Karnataka and Tamil Nadu saw a downtick in their growth rate in the 2000s compared to the '90s, while Gujarat and Haryana had low growth in real farm wages during the entire period.[38] Meanwhile, labour costs now account for a greater proportion of cultivation costs—53 per cent for paddy, 34 per cent for wheat and 59 per cent for cotton in 2011,[39] a consequence of rising agriculture labour costs.

---

36   Desai, S., Vashishtha P. and Joshi. O. 2015. Mahatma Gandhi National Rural Employment Guarantee Act: A Catalyst for Rural Transformation. New Delhi: National Council of Applied Economic Research

37   Gulati, A., Jain, S., Satija, N., 'Rising Farm Wages in India—The Pull and Push Factors', Discussion Paper No. 5, Commission for Agricultural Costs and Prices, Ministry of Agriculture, April 2013. Sourced from: http://cacp.dacnet.nic.in/ViewQuestionare.aspx?Input=2&DocId=1&PageId=42&KeyId=475

38   Gulati, 2013

39   Department of Agriculture, 2011

With the average landholding size decreasing (from 2.3 hectares in 1971 to 1.16 hectares in 2011) and average input prices rising, the cost of cultivation has increased; hence margins associated with farming have reduced. Media reports highlight that a farmer now on average earns ₹2,400 per month per hectare of paddy and about ₹2,600 per month per hectare of wheat, while farm labourers earn less than ₹5,000 per month.[40, 41] Average daily wage rates in agricultural occupations continue to remain significantly low—ploughing would earn ₹280.50 in daily wages in 2016, while a woman would earn just ₹183.56.[42] Similarly, weeding would earn a labourer ₹246.89 while a woman would earn just ₹202.64. Other promising segments of agriculture offer similar wages; female picking workers in tea, coffee or tobacco plantations earned an average of ₹218.37 per day while male horticulture workers could earn ₹239.47. Shockingly, the rates for children were much lower at ₹178.97 per day for picking. Meanwhile, loggers and wood-cutters earn about ₹323.85, while animal husbandry workers make do with just ₹198.45 per day.

TABLE 77: AVERAGE DAILY WAGES FOR NON-AGRICULTURAL LABOURERS IN RURAL INDIA[43,44]

STATE-WISE AVERAGE DAILY WAGE RATES FOR NON-AGRICULTURAL LABOURERS IN RURAL INDIA (APRIL 2017; IN ₹/DAY)			
STATES	MEN	WOMEN	CHILDREN
ANDHRA PRADESH	239.3	168.8	-
ASSAM	237.5	242.1	-
BIHAR	232.1	191.8	-
GUJARAT	213.4	227.5	-
HARYANA	353.8	-	-
HIMACHAL PRADESH	323.3	-	-
JAMMU AND KASHMIR	413.2	-	-
KARNATAKA	240.0	190.0	-
KERALA	615.0	-	-
MADHYA PRADESH	196.0	178.6	131.3
MAHARASHTRA	223.3	148.1	-
MANIPUR	-	-	-
MEGHALAYA	221.4	-	-
ODISHA	216.4	188.9	-
PUNJAB	313.1	-	-
RAJASTHAN	304.3	-	-
TAMIL NADU	394.3	272.9	-
TRIPURA	250.0	-	-
UTTAR PRADESH	232.1	202.7	-
WEST BENGAL	270.8	224.3	-
INDIA	268.9	203.2	121.8

40   IndiaStat, 2016

41   'Labour in Indian Agriculture: A Growing Challenge', FICCI, KPMG. Sourced from: http://ficci.in/
     spdocument/20550/FICCI-agri-Report per cent2009-03-2015.pdf

42   Wage Rates in Rural India, 2015-2016, Ministry of Labour & Employment. Sourced from: http://
     labourbureaunew.gov.in/UserContent/WRRI_Report_2015_16.pdf?pr_id=9Q3iaK86AA0 per cent3d

43   IndiaStat, 2017

44   Ministry of Labour and Employment, Govt. of India, 2017

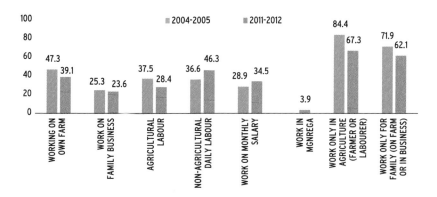

FIGURE 173: CHANGES IN LABOUR FORCE BEHAVIOUR FOR POPULATION AGES 15–59
(DAYS WORKED ON AVERAGE)[45]

TABLE 78: AVERAGE DAILY WAGE RATES FOR NON-AGRICULTURAL LABOURERS
(NOVEMBER 2013 TO APRIL 2017) (₹/DAY)[46,47]

MONTH-WISE AVERAGE DAILY WAGE RATES FOR NON-AGRICULTURAL LABOURERS (INCLUDING PORTERS/LOADERS) BY SEX IN RURAL INDIA (NOVEMBER 2013 TO APRIL 2017) (₹/DAY)											
YEAR/SEX	NOV	DEC	JAN	FEB	MARCH	APRIL	MAY	JUNE	JULY	AUG	SEPT	OCT
2013-14												
MEN	238.0	232.5	234.1	234.4	232.7	233.2	232.4	233.6	234.5	236.3	237.2	238.7
WOMEN	173.8	166.3	171.0	168.3	172.2	172.5	172.0	173.0	171.2	174.9	173.5	172.6
CHILDREN	86.8	103.0	105.3	103.8	105.3	107.3	107.3	105.6	106.9	106.9	101.3	101.3
2014-15												
MEN	238.4	240.7	241.3	242.8	243.5	243.8	245.3	245.7	248.3	249.6	250.7	249.3
WOMEN	169.4	176.7	175.5	177.6	177.9	179.5	179.3	179.9	183.1	182.5	181.9	180.0
CHILDREN	96.4	94.2	94.2	94.2	94.2	93.3	96.4	96.4	105.0	103.1	103.1	103.1
2015-16												
MEN	250.2	251.6	253.8	253.5	254.5	254.8	254.8	255.7	256.8	258.3	261.9	263.2
WOMEN	180.6	182.5	185.8	188.2	187.8	186.7	187.3	187.0	188.4	192.0	196.5	196.8
CHILDREN	105.4	105.4	117.5	108.5	109.2	105.8	116.7	117.5	117.5	120.8	116.4	130.0
2016-17												
MEN	263.7	264.5	266.4	267.7	268.2	268.9						
WOMEN	200.1	200.8	201.1	200.8	202.2	203.2						
CHILDREN	129.1	129.1	129.1	129.1	121.8	121.8						

45   Desai, S., Vashishtha P. and Joshi. O. 2015. Mahatma Gandhi National Rural Employment Guarantee
     Act: A Catalyst for Rural Transformation. New Delhi: National Council of Applied Economic Research

46   Ministry of Labour and Employment, Govt. of India, 2017

47   IndiaStat, 2017

TABLE 79: AVERAGE ANNUAL RATE OF GROWTH OF WAGE RATES FOR MAJOR OCCUPATIONS IN RURAL INDIA IN PER CENT; NOTE: *, **, AND *** STAND FOR SIGNIFICANCE LEVEL AT 10, 5, AND 1 PER CENT, RESPECTIVELY[48,49]

STATE	PLOUGHING (MALE)		STW (MALE)		STW (FEMALE)		HTW (MALE)	
	1998-99 TO 2006-07	2006-07 TO 2014-15	1998-99 TO 2006-07	2006-07 TO 2014-15	1998-99 TO 2006-07	2006-07 TO 2014-15	1998-99 TO 2006-07	2006-07 TO 2014-15
	GROWTH RATE	GROWTH RATE	GROWTH RATE	GROWTH RATE	GROWTH RATE	GROWTH RATE	GROWTH RATE	GROWTH RATE
ANDHRA PRADESH	1.16*	7.1**	2.4***	6.2***	1.0*	7.3***	1.1	5.6***
ASSAM	-1**	6.1***	3.0***	4.1***	-0.3	4.9***	2.5***	5.7***
BIHAR	3***	8.2***	1.6	10.0***	1.8	9.4***	3.1**	9.1***
GUJARAT	2***	2.7**	0.7	4.0**	0.5	4.9***	-0.5**	4.0***
HARYANA	0.3	7.7***	0.7	5.1***	2.2**	5.4***	1.2*	4.7***
HIMACHAL PRADESH	3.3***	4.3***	2.3**	4.7***			1.9**	5.9***
JAMMU AND KASHMIR	1.3	6.2***	3.7**	6.8***			3.2*	7.4***
KARNATAKA	1.3	9.2***	4.1**	7.4***	0.2	7.3***	0.7	8.0***
KERALA	0.7	4.0***	0.7	5.0***	0.3	8.6***		8.9***
MADHYA PRADESH	0.1	6.7***	-0.5	7.7***	-1.4**	9.1***	-0.6	8.9***
MAHARASHTRA	0.1	6.9***	-0.5	6.1***	-0.9	7.0***	1.2	6.8***
MANIPUR	2.2**	6.0***	1.3	9.2***	1.5	9.3***	0.1	10.7***
MEGHALAYA	4.1***	4.4**	3.7***	2.8	3.2**	3.3*	4.9***	3.5*
ODISHA	3.2**	7.5***	3.3**	6.4***	2.9**	7.8***	2.5**	8.8***
PUNJAB	3.5**	6.6***	0.4	6.4***			1.6*	6.0***
RAJASTHAN	-1.3	4.6***	-2.1	6.9***	-2.8**	6.6***	-4.3***	8.5***
TAMIL NADU	-0.7	8.5***	0.6	8.8***	-0.2	9.6***	-1	10.5***
TRIPURA	6.2***	2.7*	6.0***	2.6*			6.2***	2.7*
UTTAR PRADESH	0.3	6.3***	0	6.9***	0.4	6.9***	0.1	7.4***
WEST BENGAL	3.3***	4.9***	2.6***	5.8***	2.7***	6.8***	3.2**	6.4***
INDIA	-0.6*	6.4***	-0.1	6.5***	-1.1**	7.6***	-0.40 PER CENT	7.3**

TABLE 80: MONTH-WISE CONSUMER PRICE INDEX FOR AGRICULTURAL LABOURERS IN INDIA {(BASE: 1960–61/1986–87/=100) (APRIL 1966 TO APRIL 2017)}[50,51]

YEAR	JAN	FEB	MAR	APR	MAY	JUN	JUL	AUG	SEPT	OCT	NOV	DEC	AVG
BASE : 1960-61=100													
1966	-	-	-	159	164	170	176	181	182	183	187	189	177
1967	189	195	195	195	199	207	222	224	221	220	215	206	207
1968	200	199	193	190	189	191	190	192	195	195	189	182	192
1969	178	177	178	180	181	186	192	194	196	194	191	189	186
1970	191	192	193	193	193	196	198	198	197	196	194	190	194
1971	188	188	187	187	187	189	193	197	201	201	201	199	193
1972	200	200	200	200	200	204	212	221	223	223	222	221	211

48   Computed from Wage Rates in Rural India, various issues
49   Wage Rates in Rural India, 1998–99 to 2016–17, Arindam Das and Yoshifumi Usami
50   Ministry of Labour and Employment, Govt. of India, 2016
51   IndiaStat, 2017

1973	221	223	229	230	237	242	249	265	263	266	272	272	247
1974	279	286	297	307	314	321	337	351	370	385	378	365	333
1975	369	375	373	367	372	375	374	365	360	344	332	316	360
1976	302	292	279	278	281	280	289	295	295	294	296	297	290
1977	298	302	311	310	314	319	325	330	332	334	329	330	320
1978	325	318	318	313	310	312	318	320	321	325	325	318	319
1979	315	312	310	313	314	318	330	342	350	360	364	370	333
1980	370	361	364	362	366	376	388	398	399	402	407	408	383
1981	404	414	419	420	425	429	439	451	457	460	460	454	436
1982	451	445	440	440	439	443	453	470	477	476	480	478	458
1983	475	482	488	489	500	509	521	535	542	537	529	521	511
1984	523	519	514	510	508	511	524	530	530	530	530	522	521
1985	523	522	517	518	524	530	540	551	555	559	561	557	538
1986	553	552	556	555	555	561	570	576	579	586	585	579	567
1987	573	573	573	572	579	588	604	621	649	653	655	654	608
1988	657	655	658	651	667	671	691	705	710	724	737	741	689
1989	739	726	729	721	727	736	746	756	772	777	760	753	745
1990	740	734	736	744	751	759	780	791	792	804	824	828	774
1991	843	861	858	853	854	876	904	936	975	990	999	1008	913
1992	1015	1038	1046	1046	1058	1068	1090	1114	1112	1099	1085	1067	1070
1993	1066	1058	1053	1039	1038	1057	1068	1088	1113	1134	1156	1166	1086
1994	1166	1166	1175	1165	1175	1189	1211	1231	1251	1265	1285	1297	1215
1995	1292	1301	1300	1306	1316	1337	1387	1405	1413	1411	-	-	1347
BASE : 1986-87=100													
1995											240	238	239
1996	236	236	237	240	243	247	252	256	259	260	262	263	249
1997	262	263	262	261	258	259	261	262	263	263	262	265	262
1998	274	273	272	273	276	282	289	293	297	304	310	305	287
1999	299	297	296	295	298	301	304	308	310	315	316	311	304
2000	307	306	306	307	310	310	310	308	306	305	306	303	308
2001	301	299	300	301	303	306	309	312	311	313	313	312	302
2002	308	308	309	309	311	314	316	319	321	322	323	321	310
2003	320	322	324	326	327	330	331	331	332	333	333	332	328
2004	332	332	332	331	333	336	338	341	343	345	344	342	337
2005	341	340	340	341	343	345	350	352	354	356	360	358	348
2006	357	357	358	360	365	370	372	375	380	386	390	390	372
2007	391	392	392	394	395	399	404	408	410	413	414	413	402
2008	413	417	423	429	431	434	442	450	455	459	460	459	439
2009	461	462	463	468	475	484	499	508	515	522	532	538	494
2010	542	538	536	538	540	547	554	557	562	566	570	581	553
2011	589	584	585	587	592	598	604	610	615	619	621	618	601
2012	618	621	625	633	638	646	656	666	673	680	685	688	652
2013	694	700	704	711	719	729	740	754	759	766	777	765	735
2014	757	757	763	771	777	785	799	808	811	813	813	807	788
2015	804	803	803	805	811	820	822	832	839	849	853	853	825
2016	849	843	843	848	860	869	877	876	873	876	878	876	864
2017	870	869	866	870									

While wage rates remain low, agricultural labourers have historically faced rising consumer prices—since 1966, the monthly-wise consumer price index for agricultural labourers has risen from 159 in April 1961 (on a base of 100 for 1960), to 1347 in 1995. When rebasing in April 1987 as 100, the index has risen from 239 in December 1987 to 870 in April 2017.

TABLE 81: MONTHLY CONSUMER PRICES OF SELECTED ARTICLES OF AGRICULTURAL LABOURERS IN HARYANA {(BASE: 1986–87=100) (MARCH 2016)}[52,53]

ITEMS	UNIT	HARYANA
RICE	KG	24.47
WHEAT		
(A) WHEAT WHOLE	KG	-
(B) WHEAT ATTA	KG	19.07
JOWAR	KG	-
BAJRA		
(A) BAJRA WHOLE	KG	-
(B) BAJRA ATTA	KG	17.43
MAIZE		
(A) MAIZE WHOLE	KG	18.67
(B) MAIZE ATTA	KG	-
RAGI	KG	-
ARHAR DAL	KG	148.37
GROUNDNUT OIL	LITRE	-
MUSTARD OIL	LITRE	91.52
GOAT MEAT/MUTTON	KG	339.54
FISH FRESH	KG	130.00
MILK	LITRE	46.79
ONION	KG	17.90
CHILLIES DRY	100 GM	19.75
POTATO	KG	10.76
SUGAR	KG	31.79
GUR	KG	33.87
TEA LEAF	100 GM	22.78
FIREWOOD	40 KG	294.70
KEROSENE OIL	LITRE	14.11

52   Ministry of Labour and Employment, Govt. of India, 2016
53   IndiaStat, 2017

CHANGING AVAILABILITY OF FAMILY LABOUR

The rise in local employment opportunities, courtesy of programmes like MGNREGA, has helped reduce the out-migration of female labourers, who typically prefer working in the same village—the wage rate for female casual labourers in 2009–10 for activities 'other than public works' was higher in urban areas (at ₹77) compared to rural areas (at ₹69). However, under MGNREGA, the wage rates for female casual labourers in rural areas are higher than urban rates.[54] Under such conditions, rural families are increasingly withdrawing women from farm work, as evidenced by the decline in female workforce in agriculture by 8.02 per cent between 1993–94 and 2009–10.[55]

IMPACT OF EDUCATION

Finally, the impact of rising education levels has led to an improvement in skills, particularly amongst females (female literacy rates jumped from 32.1 per cent in 1993–94 to 53.3 per cent in 2009–10).[56] This changing distribution of skill-sets in the rural market has shifted bargaining powers in the rural labour market, while job preferences are increasingly changing. The stigma associated with agricultural labour has meant that non-farm income is increasingly preferred. It's the illiterate who continue to be the most unemployed and hence the most prone to being used as agricultural labourers.

54 Hirway, 2010

55 Chand, R., Srivastava, S.K., Changes in the Rural Labour Market and Their Implications for Agriculture, EPW, Vol XLIX No 10, March 8, 2014. Sourced from: http://www.im4change.org/siteadmin/tinymce/uploaded/Changes_in_the_Rural_Labour_Market_and_Their_Implications_for_Agriculture.pdf

56 Chand, R., Srivastava, S.K., Changes in the Rural Labour Market and Their Implications for Agriculture, EPW, Vol XLIX No 10, March 8, 2014. Sourced from: http://www.im4change.org/siteadmin/tinymce/uploaded/Changes_in_the_Rural_Labour_Market_and_Their_Implications_for_Agriculture.pdf

MIGRATION ABROAD

India's labour migration to Gulf Cooperation Council (GCC) countries is not a new phenomenon. International migration of labour, over time, has evolved as a critical feature of the Indian economy and its employment scenario. For instance, India receives the largest amount of foreign exchange remittances in the world; estimated at US$71 billion in 2014, with nearly 50 per cent of the remittances originating in the GCC countries (World Bank, 2014). Additionally, there are strong linkages between international labour migration and development at the state and household levels—recent evidence from Kerala and Andhra Pradesh, having higher migration rates, indicate positive correlation between migration and health, educational attainments, especially in low to lower and middle-income households.[57] In terms of policy, international labour migration is a critical tool which can balance the vagaries of supply and demand in the domestic labour market by offering an alternative employment option.

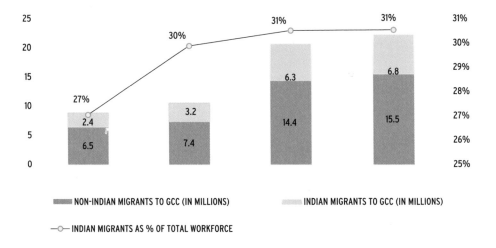

NON-INDIAN MIGRANTS TO GCC (IN MILLIONS)   INDIAN MIGRANTS TO GCC (IN MILLIONS)

—o— INDIAN MIGRANTS AS % OF TOTAL WORKFORCE

FIGURE 174: TREND OF INDIAN MIGRANT WORKERS IN GCC COUNTRIES[58]

57   Rajan, 2013; Thimothy and Sasikumar, 2012
58   UNDESA, 2013

In terms of the gender distribution, we have high growth for female migration, as evident from the following table below. Migration of women from South Asia to the Gulf region has more than doubled in the past two decades, from 2.4 million in 1990 to 6.8 million in 2013 (UNDESA, 2013).

TABLE 82: GENDER-WISE GROWTH IN INDIAN MIGRATION TO GCC COUNTRIES[59]

	1990			2013			GROWTH %		
	MALE	FEMALE	TOTAL	MALE	FEMALE	TOTAL	MALE	FEMALE	TOTAL
BAHRAIN	46,828	13,665	60,493	199,767	63,088	262,855	327%	362%	335%
KUWAIT	380,458	173,123	553,581	541,143	189,415	730,558	42%	9%	32%
OMAN	180,878	31,678	212,556	551,885	92,819	644,704	205%	193%	203%
QATAR	101,233	27,914	129,147	473,069	103,707	576,776	367%	272%	347%
SAUDI ARABIA	652,957	328,665	981,622	1,223,552	538,335	1,761,887	87%	64%	79%
UAE	353,659	104,635	458,294	2,224,781	627,426	2,852,207	529%	500%	522%
TOTAL	1,716,013	679,680	2,395,693	5,214,197	1,614,790	6,828,987	204%	138%	185%

In terms of state-wise distribution of such migration, it is interesting to note that migration from relatively poorer states, like Uttar Pradesh and Bihar, has increased substantially, whereas the proportion from relatively prosperous states like Kerala has reduced. The difference can be explained by difference in wage rates whereby low-skilled and low-educated workforce in some states consider the option of migrating overseas for higher income.

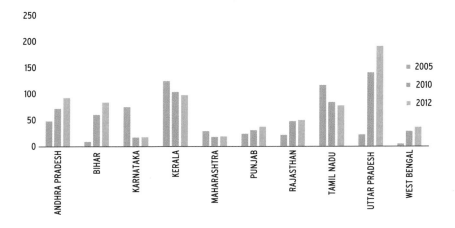

FIGURE 175: YEAR-WISE STATE-WISE NUMBER OF MIGRANTS
(IN THOUSANDS) TO GCC COUNTRIES[60]

59   UNDESA, 2013
60   Ibid

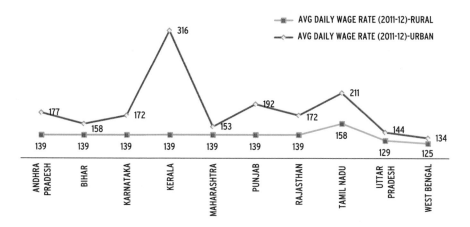

FIGURE 176: AVERAGE DAILY WAGE IN URBAN AND RURAL AREAS IN DIFFERENT STATES[61]

The above two charts tell us that states that have higher daily wages in rural areas have seen a decline in number of workers migrating to GCC countries whereas states with low average daily incomes have witnessed a phenomenal growth in number of workers seeking foreign shores for their economic upliftment.

It is widely acknowledged that lack of relevant and systematic data, particularly pertaining to skills, is a major impediment in evolving efficient short-term as well as long-term policies on international labour mobility in India. Considering that the India–GCC corridor is one of the densest migration routes, there is an immediate need to evolve robust mechanisms to continuously monitor and forecast the emerging labour and skill requirements in all GCC countries. Although forecasting forms a critical component of the labour market information system, it is equally important to institute mechanisms that facilitate the link between foreign employers and Indian job-seekers. The examples of Kerala and Andhra Pradesh are worth emulating for expansion at a national level as well as other states.

As a major labour-sending country, it is equally imperative that India develops a comprehensive database to capture the trends and characteristics of labour outflows that encompass all categories of migrant workers. This data can be integrated with the data from the Ministry of Labour & Employment for job creation and matching within India, thereby servicing a larger number of employers and potential employees on a national scale.

While the number of migrants as a proportion of India's total workforce is meagre now, keeping in mind the long-term demographic changes and persisting demand

61 NSSO, 2012

for migrant labour in the Gulf countries, international migration and the soft power of the migrants can be an important instrument for leveraging India's demographic dividend.

Private recruitment agencies play an instrumental role in arranging for migration of semi-skilled and unskilled workers, while highly-skilled workers take a proactive role in arranging their own overseas employment. A better policy framework is needed to regulate the functioning of private recruitment agencies as unskilled and semi-skilled labourers have a higher chance of ending up in vulnerable employment, leading to their abuse and negatively affecting the migration outcome. It is also pertinent to assess the emerging demand for particular skills in destination countries.

International labour migration gets covered under the Emigration Act, 1983, which provides for facilitating the recruitment of Indian workers on best terms of employment. However, adherence to the provisions and process under the relevant clauses remains low. Consider the process for recruitment and migration of an Indian worker—the recruiting agent (1,439 registered agents in 2013) needs a job letter, contract copy and a Power of Attorney from the prospective employer before even advertising for the job requirement. The advertisement, besides mentioning the job details, also has to contain the registration number of the recruiting agent. The selected worker needs to have the employment contract attested by a Protector of Emigrants, thereby avoiding any unscrupulous activity by agents and protecting the workers and their rights. The Act also seeks to limit the recruitment fees, ₹2,000 for unskilled workers, ₹3,000 for semi-skilled workers, ₹5,000 for skilled workers and ₹10,000 for other categories. Despite provisions which prevent the agent from making excessive profits leading to abuse of workers' rights, the labour market dynamics alter the on-ground reality. The prospective migrants in some cases outstrip the formal labour demand expressed, and in some cases, agents make payments to employers for obtaining placement orders, thereby increasing the agents' expenditure which ultimately gets transferred to and borne by the migrant labour. In India, the responsibility of managing international labour flows primarily rests with the Ministry of Overseas Indian Affairs (MOIA). Recognizing the increasing importance of skill acquisition within the framework of international migration, the MOIA recently launched innovative schemes to link skill development with the international labour outflows.

An important scheme implemented by the government is the Swarna Prawas Yojana which aims to position India as the preferred source of skilled workers in skill-sets in which India has competitive advantage and such skill-sets face international shortage. The scheme also looks to widen the destination country base anticipated to face skill shortage and improve the chances of employability for

Indian migrants by providing internationally recognized training and certification, thereby enabling them to move to better jobs.

The MOIA has also been active in educating the masses on the pitfalls of migration through illegal channels, while providing them assistance through different mediums on the available help and how to avail of such assistance offered. Besides conventional mediums of advertisement, the MOIA also runs a twenty-four-hour helpline and walk-in counselling facilities operated by Overseas Workers Resource Centres, in Kochi, Hyderabad and Kerala. Besides skill identification and skill matching, pre-departure orientation also assumes significance. In such cases, the initiatives undertaken by the governments of Kerala and Andhra Pradesh have had a positive influence on migration outcomes.

Data collection and assimilation, particularly pertaining to skills, remains an important piece to create and enhance short-term and long-term policies on international mobility of labour, to and from India. The India–GCC route remains one of the world's densest migration routes, thus robust forecast of the quality and quantity of labour requirements along with emergent skills becomes critical. Besides forecasting, it is important to forge links between the potential employers and the migrant workers. The examples of Kerala and Andhra Pradesh are worth emulating for expansion at a national level as well as other states.

India remains a major source for migrant labour and should have a detailed database of migrant flows in order to capture the emerging trends and prevailing characteristics of outflows encapsulating all categories of migrant workers. This data on migrant workers can be merged with the data from Ministry of Labour and Employment for job-skill matching within India, thereby benefitting a multitude of employees and employers at a national level.

There is also a need for collecting information on returning migrants, as implemented in Sri Lanka and Bangladesh on a national scale, which can help them reintegrate within our workforce besides offering insights on skills acquired during their overseas stay, their financial resources and entrepreneurial skill gaps.

Greater linkages need to be developed between our skill development systems (through the National Skill Development Corporation) and skills in demand in the international markets, which will eventually improve migration outcomes for Indian workers. Short-term certificate courses aiming at skilling workers in emerging skills in international markets should be set up in quick time. Our existing certificate courses also need to be altered to cater to the emerging skills requirement. Besides courses, new and existing, we also need to align our course quality and standards in line with international standards, thereby providing employers in destination countries with greater confidence to recruit, and providing migrant workers a high degree of acceptance. The National Skill Qualification Framework needs to be strengthened in order to achieve these objectives. Our vocational training courses need to be benchmarked to standards developed by international skill certifiers, which will help India emerge as a leading supplier of skilled labour. Skill acquisition through formal channels is equally important. A majority of our workforce labour acquires skills through informal methods, which needs certification in the present and correction in the future. While it is important to identify skill gaps and train workers in skills having an emerging demand in destination countries, this currently remains limited to a handful of private institutions within a small sector set, especially healthcare and hospitality. The government needs to identify the top rung of Industrial Training Institutes (ITIs) and facilitate their links with employers in destination countries. Such linkages will also serve as an incentive to ITIs to improve their efficiency and delivery. Such initiatives have already been taken in other countries which have emerged as a supplier of skilled labour internationally. In Sri Lanka, the Ministry of Youth Affairs and Skill Development has links with State and private technical training institutes helping different migrant workers by developing national vocational qualification and providing resources to equip training centres, besides setting up a marketing desk to promote employment by skill identification and demand in destination countries.

Reintegration of returned migrants also needs to be revamped, especially in the wake of temporary immigration policies. Most workers, when migrating, are semi-skilled or unskilled and develop their skills through work in the destination country. In order to improve migration outcomes for workers, it is imperative to develop a process to certify such acquired skills, with proper assessment of a migrant's pre-migration and post-migration skill-set. Such certification shall help them get access to financial and technical resources, which, in turn, help them find employment or initiate self-employment enterprises. Assistance could be provided to migrants in destination countries which include free business training and career guidance to help workers find a job or start a business in the source country. This could be supplemented with free training at training centres near their workplaces and facilitating their job applications in both destination and source countries in order to enable them to make better career decisions. Counselling services that help the migrants settle during their resettlement phase can also be considered.

Collaboration between labour-sending and labour-receiving countries, based on skill certification would further improve migration outcomes for all stakeholders. The MoUs should, besides covering social security, working conditions and mobility, also include recognition of prior learning and improve a migrant's employability. Such collaboration would help expand the qualified labour pool and human capital.

Private recruitment agencies are an indispensable part of the recruitment and migration process in India, especially to GCC countries. Considering their sizeable role, they should be encouraged to improve skill matching and facilitating migration of skilled labour. State encouragement can come in the form of providing them with improved and relevant training, and providing them permission to conduct programmes and set up common standards and certified curriculum.

For semi-skilled and unskilled labour, pre-migration skill development can cause vastly different outcomes. For vulnerable migrants, pre-employment training can provide higher wages and improved working conditions.

Any encouragement for migration has to be matched in efforts and outcomes to protect the rights and well-being of the potential migrants. The government needs to work closely with its counterparts in GCC countries to ensure that the rights of migrant workers are protected. This would include collaboration with the local government to abolish systems that enable exploitation of workers' rights. The support to Indian diplomatic missions in GCC countries needs to be ramped up to support the migrant workers in case of abuse, with the help extending to financial and legal aid. Bilateral agreements with GCC countries should be effected that aim to standardize working conditions and formalize migrant worker rights. The government can also request and assist countries in ratifying and implementing the international treaties and conventions pertaining to migrant labour, especially the ILO conventions and the UN Convention on the Protection of the Rights of All Migrant Workers and their family members. The government can also agree upon an independent inspector who would ensure that the workers get the benefits of labour protections, in reality and in theory. Additionally, training migrants about their rights and ways to seek help in any country should be mandatory.

GENDER DIVERSITY

Meanwhile, the feminization of the rural labour force continues apace. Theoretically, declining fertility rates (2.6 in 2011 as compared to 3.9 in 1990) would lead to increased female participation in the workforce. The implementation of MGNREGA would also mean increased female participation. Yet, as of 2012, India ranked 84th out of eighty-seven countries in terms of female participation in the national workforce. NSSO data indicates that labour force participation rate for women fell by 10.1 percentage points, corresponding to a decline of 2.26 crore women in the workforce in 2010 as compared to 2005. Female participation fell by another 2 per cent from 2010 till 2013.

TABLE 83: CHANGES IN FEMALE-MALE RATIO OF WAGE RATES FOR
SOWING/TRANSPLANTING/WEEDING[62,63]

STATE	FEMALE-MALE RATIO (STW)		
	1998–99 TO 2000–01	2006–07 TO 2008–09	2014–15 TO 2016–17
ANDHRA PRADESH	0.76	0.74	0.75
ASSAM	1.06	0.87	0.87
BIHAR	0.9	0.91	0.85
GUJARAT	0.91	0.89	0.95
HARYANA	0.86	0.95	0.96
HIMACHAL PRADESH			
JAMMU AND KASHMIR			
KARNATAKA	0.73	0.72	0.71
KERALA	0.68	0.55	0.73
MADHYA PRADESH	0.87	0.85	0.94
MAHARASHTRA	0.7	0.65	0.67
MANIPUR	0.95	0.9	0.86
MEGHALAYA	0.73	0.71	0.73
ODISHA	0.86	0.78	0.82
PUNJAB			
RAJASTHAN	0.79	0.8	0.81
TAMIL NADU	0.64	0.63	0.63
TRIPURA			
UTTAR PRADESH	0.84	0.86	0.88
WEST BENGAL	0.91	0.89	0.91
INDIA	0.83	0.79	0.82

---

62   Computed from Wage Rates in Rural India, various issues
63   Wage Rates in Rural India, 1998–99 to 2016–17, Arindam Das and Yoshifumi Usami

TABLE 84: CHANGES IN FEMALE-MALE RATIO OF WAGE RATES FOR
HARVESTING/THRESHING/WINNOWING (HTW) [64,65]

STATE	FEMALE-MALE RATIO (HTW)		
	1998-99 TO 2000-01	2006-07 TO 2008-09	2014-15 TO 2016-17
ANDHRA PRADESH	0.8	0.75	0.77
ASSAM	1.03	0.9	0.85
BIHAR	0.85	0.92	0.91
GUJARAT	0.93	0.97	0.98
HARYANA	0.96	0.98	0.99
HIMACHAL PRADESH	0.9	1	0.5
JAMMU AND KASHMIR	1.49		0.59
KARNATAKA	0.76	0.76	0.69
KERALA	0.74	0.86	0.77
MADHYA PRADESH	0.88	0.85	0.92
MAHARASHTRA	0.71	0.64	0.69
MANIPUR	0.87	0.9	0.9
MEGHALAYA	0.81	0.69	0.62
ODISHA	0.85	0.76	0.84
PUNJAB	0.81		0.82
RAJASTHAN	0.9	0.9	0.83
TAMIL NADU	0.66	0.7	0.61
TRIPURA	0.79		
UTTAR PRADESH	0.86	0.89	0.85
WEST BENGAL	0.91	0.9	0.9
INDIA	0.82	0.8	0.84

Reduced female participation in the workforce can have negative economic effects, thereby impacting growth rates. ILO studies have estimated that global GDP could grow by US$1.6 trillion (in PPPs) compared to the business-as-usual scenario, if global gender gaps between male and female participation progresses towards those witnessed in the EU and North America in 2012. A study in 2008 (Lawson) estimated that India's per capita income can increase by 10 per cent in 2020 and 20 per cent in 2030 if India can reduce its gender participation gap by 50 per cent. Given the huge socio-economic benefits of increasing female participation in the workforce, it is important that we determine the reasons for such gaps and provide policy solutions for remediation.

---

64   Computed from Wage Rates in Rural India, various issues
65   Wage Rates in Rural India, 1998–99 to 2016–17, Arindam Das and Yoshifumi Usami

TABLE 85: CHANGES IN FEMALE-MALE RATIO OF WAGE RATES FOR UNSKILLED LABOURERS[66,67]

STATE	FEMALE-MALE RATIO (UNSKILLED LABOURER)		
	1998-99 TO 2000-01	2006-07 TO 2008-09	2014-15 TO 2016-17
ANDHRA PRADESH	0.71	0.72	0.67
ASSAM	0.88	0.73	0.98
BIHAR	0.87	0.89	0.85
GUJARAT	0.93	0.97	1.02
HARYANA			
HIMACHAL PRADESH			
JAMMU AND KASHMIR			
KARNATAKA	0.75	0.74	0.75
KERALA			
MADHYA PRADESH	0.88	0.86	0.81
MAHARASHTRA	0.68	0.64	0.63
MANIPUR			
MEGHALAYA			
ODISHA	0.89	0.83	0.92
PUNJAB			
RAJASTHAN			
TAMIL NADU	0.67	0.73	0.69
TRIPURA			
UTTAR PRADESH	0.81	0.83	0.86
WEST BENGAL	0.88	0.89	0.85
INDIA	0.78	0.76	0.74

India's majority labour workforce (~70 per cent) resides in its rural areas where most households are engaged in farm activity, directly or indirectly. With agriculture being seasonal in patterns, the labour supply itself is influenced by seasonality of crops, which leads to large unpredictable swings in economic activity each year. Absence of popular insurance schemes in case of crop damage due to weather conditions has led to most households working simultaneously as agricultural labour to generate a parallel revenue stream for the household (Behrman, 1999).

Social norms also play a big part in gender roles and workforce participation. Under such social norms, men are expected to be the primary bread-earners in the family and thus, more needy of employment than women, everything else remaining constant, whereby women are expected to devote their time to taking care of their family and the household. Such social norms lead to differences in

---

66   Computed from Wage Rates in Rural India, various issues
67   Wage Rates in Rural India, 1998–99 to 2016–17, Arindam Das and Yoshifumi Usami

employment outcomes, mostly in the form of sectoral and occupational segregation. Additionally, women have historically had unequal access to land and financial resources, thereby restricting their ability to participate and rise up the value chain in the Indian workforce.

One reason for decreased female participation could be the increase in the number of young adults attending educational institutions. This is corroborated by the decrease in male participation as well (Planning Commission, 2011). This would translate to improved job prospects and an increase in the quality and quantity of participation in the labour workforce.

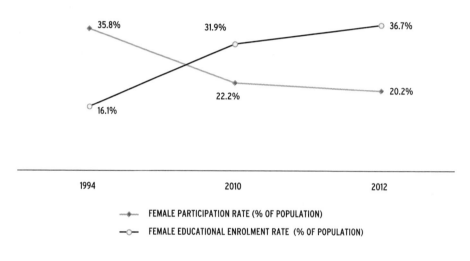

FIGURE 177: FEMALE WORKFORCE PARTICIPATION RATE VS. FEMALE EDUCATIONAL ENROLMENT RATE[68]

The above chart illustrates the proportion of young women (age ranging from fifteen to twenty-four years) attending educational institutes and the decline in overall female youth participation in the labour workforce. There emerges a clear inverse ratio, within the selected timeframe. It is estimated that from 1994 to 2012, an increase in female enrolment rate in educational institutes resulted in an additional 21 million young women in education. A direct consequence of higher enrolment rate has been a decline in female participation in the agricultural workforce, estimated to stand at 6.4 million fewer young women in 2012 as compared to 1994 (negating population impact).

Within the fifteen to twenty-four age group, the percentage of women receiving education and not participating in labour market has grown considerably—from

68   Planning Commission, 2011

16.1 per cent of the population in 1994 to 36.7 per cent in 2012. This also gets reflected in declining overall female youth labour participation rate, which reduced from 35.8 per cent in 1994 to 20.2 per cent in 2012.

Another reason for declining female participation could be the U-shaped relationship between national income and female labour force participation (Mammen & Paxson, 2000)—as a household becomes prosperous, increasing number of women move out of sustenance/subsistence jobs. More often than not, this is accompanied by increased female enrolment in educational institutions, as households are encouraged and incentivized to educate their children. Later, when jobs that are acceptable to women on the basis of their education and work preferences, become available, female participation in the workforce is witnessed, thereby creating a U-shaped curve.

The third hypothesis that is drawn up to explain the 10 per cent drop in female participation in 2009–10 lies in the data collection methodology, wherein NSSO used more contract workers to carry out the surveys whereby data quality is questioned. The monsoon failure in 2009 and the global financial crisis would have also led to one-off shocks, which need to be segregated from the long-term trend of female participation in the workforce. Another reason could be simply that job growth has not kept up with increase in the numbers in the workforce, thereby having an increasing number of women take up informal and poorly-remunerated jobs. Additionally, industrial and occupational segregation may also play its part— if industries/occupations that are experiencing job growth are male-dominated, then the positive effects of the job growth may not percolate in an equal proportion between the genders.

	1994-2000	2000-05	2005-10	2010-12	1994-05	1994-10	1994-12	2000-10	2000-12	2005-12
TOTAL CHANGE IN FEMALE PARTICIPATION	-3.8	3.9	-10.1	-1.3	0.1	-10.1	-11.4	-6.3	-7.6	-11.5
INCREASED ENROLMENT (PER CENT)	-0.5	-0.4	-0.9	-0.5	-0.9	-1.4	-1.7	-1.1	-1.4	-1.2
INCREASED HOUSEHOLD PROSPERITY (PER CENT)	-0.8	-1.0	-0.9	-	-1.6	-2.4	-	-2.0	-	-
MEASUREMENT BIAS (PER CENT)	1.2	4.3	-4.1	2.5	5.5	1.4	4.0	0.2	2.7	-1.6
CHANGES IN EMPLOYMENT OPPORTUNITIES (PER CENT)	-3.7	1.0	-4.2	-	-2.9	-7.7	-	-3.5	-	-

FIGURE 178: IMPACT ON FEMALE LABOUR PARTICIPATION

The table illustrates the findings of a study (ILO, 2014) indicating the impact on female labour participation due to each of these factors. From 2005–10, the increased attendance rates accounted for 0.9 per cent of the 10.1 per cent drop in overall participation rates or just about 9 per cent of the overall decline. Thus, increased attendance only has a limited impact on the female participation in the workforce.

Similar modest impact of 9 per cent contribution to overall decline is visible for the duration of 2005–10 due to increased household prosperity levels (consumption levels used as proxy). Together, increased female enrolment in educational institutes and increased household prosperity levels contributed to 18 per cent fall in women's participation in the labour workforce during 2005–10. We also see that measurement bias accounts for a 4.1 per cent fall in labour participation, or 40 per cent of the total decline in the female participation during 2005–10, meaning that ~42 per cent of the decline in female participation in the labour force was due to lack of employment opportunities.

A possible explanation for declining female participation in the workforce is that women benefit less than men given a particular increase in the number and quality of jobs. This is made particularly acute by occupational and sectoral segregation caused by social norms which would socially pressurize women to remain confined to a particular set of sectors and professions.

Figure 179 (following page) illustrates the actual female employment growth vis-à-vis the hypothetical share of women's participation in the labour force if opportunities were distributed among women in the same ratio as men. Thus, it is indicative of the impact of occupational segregation on the overall female participation in the workforce.

The calculations suggest that the female workforce participation in India should have grown by 29.3 million, instead of the actual witnessed growth of 8.7 million— in other words, the actual workforce participation is just 30 per cent of its potential. For India's ten fastest-growing professions, women took up less than 19 per cent of the incremental job opportunities created. Women's share of employment increased in only three occupation types out of ten, which again were not exhibiting rapid growth.

DIVISION	SUBDIVISION	TOTAL EMPLOYED (2010)	CHANGE IN TOTAL EMPLOYED ('000) 1994-2010	CHANGE IN TOTAL EMPLOYED (%) 1994-2010	FEMALE SHARE IN TOTAL EMPLOYMENT, 1994 (%)	FEMALE SHARE IN TOTAL EMPLOYMENT, 2010 (%)	FEMALE SHARE OF EMPLOYMENT GROWTH (%) 1994-2010
LEGISLATORS, SR OFFICIALS & MANAGERS	CUSTOMER SERVICE	469	73	18.4	13.5	12.9	9.3
	MANAGERS	20644	12384	149.9	25.3	13.9	6.3
PROFESSIONALS	PHY, MATHS & ENGG SC PROFESSIONALS	1990	1160	139.8	9.1	10.3	11.1
	LIFE SCIENCE PROFESSIONALS	1181	359	43.7	30.5	29.6	27.5
	TEACHING	3825	1671	77.6	28.6	38.7	51.8
	OTHERS	7283	5604	333.8	8	10.7	11.5
TECHNICIANS/ ASSOCIATE PROFESSIONALS	PHY, MATHS & ENGG SC PROFESSIONALS	1365	-459	-25.2	14.7	10.7	26.7
	LIFE SCIENCE PROFESSIONALS	1270	773	155.5	38.1	46.5	52
	TEACHING	4825	4525	1508.3	71.5	45.7	44
	OTHERS	3992	-1730	-30.2	14.3	12.1	19.2
CLERKS	OFFICE	6415	1784	40.9	14.5	15	16.3
	CUSTOMER SERVICE	1213	593	95.6	11.9	22.6	33.8
SERVICE WORKERS/ MARKET SALES/ SHOP SALES	PERSONAL & PROTECTIVE SERVICES WORKERS	9310	3852	70.6	17.5	19.9	23.2
	MODELS/ SALESPERSONS/ DEMONSTRATORS	18316	2133	13.2	14.2	12	-4.1
SKILLED AGRICULTURE & FISHERIES	MARKET ORIENTED SKILLED AGRI & FISHERIES WORKERS	126656	-17860	-12.4	36.2	35.1	44.1
CRAFTS & RELATED TRADES	BUILDING TRADE WORKERS	17391	8004	85.3	11	8.1	4.7
	METAL & MACHINERY RELATED	7135	2361	49.5	2.4	4.5	8.6
	PRECISION, HANDICRAFT AND PAINTING	3432	-408	-10.6	22.9	22.4	27.6
	OTHER CRAFTS AND RELATED TRADES	16347	7742	90.0	48.1	42.1	35.5
PLANT & MACHINE OPERATORS	STATIONARY PLANT & RELATED OPERATORS	1177	235	24.9	7.3	8	10.9
	MACHINE OPERATORS & ASSEMBLERS	4248	-4915	-53.6	34.1	15.5	50.2
	DRIVERS & MOBILE PLANT OPERATORS	9142	5923	184.0	1.8	1.0	0.5
ELEMENTARY OCCUPATIONS	SALES & SERVICES	10951	7040	180.0	45.8	34.3	27.9
	AGRICULTURE & FISHERY-RELATED	84225	20143	31.4	42.6	37.2	20.2
	LABOUR-MINING, CONSTRUCTION, MANUFACTURING & TRANSPORT	31615	20835	193.3	13.4	19.2	22.3
UNCLASSIFIED WORKERS		1506	-1094	-42.1	40.6	22.6	65.5

FIGURE 179: FEMALE EMPLOYMENT, ACROSS SECTORS

Simply put, the largest impediment to increasing gender equality in workforce participation is the lack of employment opportunities. Persistent informality in terms of nature of work and low growth in salaried professionals limited prospects further. Indian women have further disadvantages which take root in social norms, made worse by occupational segregation. Thus, reducing occupational segregation by challenging gender stereotypes and promotion of skills development in women in industries with high growth rates is an area of policy improvement.

MGNREGA

'We should be ashamed of resting, or having a square meal, so long as there is one able-bodied man or woman without work or food.'[69] —Mahatma Gandhi

Jagriti Pokhriyal smiles while wiping her brow of sweat. She lifts a basket of bricks, following the teamster who directs them to pile them into a bundle on the other side of the railway track in Haldwani, Uttarakhand. It has been a long hot day, while the Gola river glistens in the background. Married at the age of sixteen, she finds herself hunting for employment to help feed her two young sons, while her husband remains afflicted by the age-old problem associated with hill people—alcoholism. Last year, in 2016, there was little to no MGNREGA work, leaving her to beg for work in the sugar cane fields. This year, the availability of work, and that too, in the short daytime period, has allowed her to utilize the rest of the day working as a common labourer, supplementing her income.

The utility of tying social benefits to work requirements has had a long albeit heavily questioned history. In pre-revolutionary France, there existed 'charity workshops' allowing the poor to exchange menial labour for food and lodging. The English Poor Law (1834) had the poor required to be housed in a workhouse in order to be eligible to receive welfare.[70] Public welfare was often used in colonial India as a mechanism to deliver famine relief.[71] Even Adolf Hitler used unemployed youth to build his famed autobahns in Germany. Other countries like Argentina, Chile, Egypt and Mexico have tried different versions of such mechanisms. The constant tussle between welfare and workfare reflects a reality between social inequality and fiscal probity.

---

69   Mahatma Gandhi, Young India, 6th October, 1921, p. 314
70   Himmelfarb, 1984
71   Dreze, J., 1990

HISTORICAL PUBLIC WORKS

India has a long history of using such programmes—the Drought-Prone Areas Programme in the '70s, the National Rural Employment Programme in 1980, the Rural Landless Employment Guarantee in 1983, the Jawahar Rozagar Yojana in the '90s, along with the Sampoorna Grameen Rozgar Yojana in 2001.[72] The Maharashtra Employment Guarantee Scheme (EGS) began as a drought relief scheme in the '70s but was soon transformed into an anti-poverty programme, eventually serving as a model for the advocacy of rural employment. The Supreme Court weighed in by linking the right to food to the right to work, while asking for speedier implementation of the Sampoorna Gramin Rozgar Yojana (a precursor to MGNREGA). Such programmes, however, failed to generate enough employment for rural labour on a large enough scale, leaving unemployment and rural poverty mostly untouched. Given the declining level of employment in agriculture, along with a rising population, the utilization of such programmes has become a political necessity in India.

Such public works are typically cited as offering certain key benefits—a monetary and social impact on those working under it, a change in the local labour market as a reaction to changing labour demand and a rise in productivity associated with the public goods being created.

---

72   Berg, E., Bhattacharya, S., Durgam, R., Ramachandra, M., 'Can Rural Public Works Affect Agricultural Wages? Evidence from India', CSAE Working Paper (WPS/2012-05), May 2012. Sourced from: http://www.csae.ox.ac.uk/workingpapers/pdfs/csae-wps-2012-05.pdf

MGNREGA'S MANDATE

The National Rural Employment Guarantee (NREGA) Act was passed by Parliament in 2005, coming into force in 2006, with eventual renaming as the Mahatma Gandhi National Rural Employment Guarantee (MGNREGA) Act in 2009. The programme continues to draw praise and opprobrium in its impact—it remains the world's largest social programme, benefitting 50 million rural households annually since 2008, with its budget increased annually. The budget has risen from ₹39,100 crore in 2010 to ₹47,749 crore in 2017.

YEARS	BUDGET ESTIMATES (₹CR)	REVISED ESTIMATES (₹CR)
2009-2010	39,100	39,100
2010-2011	40,100	40,100
2011-2012	40,000	31,000
2013-2014	33,000	33,000
2014-2015	34,000	33,000
2015-2016	34,699	37,346
2016-2017	38,500	47,749
2017-2018	48,000	-

FIGURE 180: BUDGET ESTIMATE AND REVISED ESTIMATE UNDER THE
MGNREGA IN INDIA,
(2009–10 TO 2011–12 AND 2013–14 TO 2017–18)[73, 74]

The Act sought to provide employment guarantee for at least hundred days in a financial year for rural households with adult members volunteering to do unskilled manual work. The programme sought to extend social protection and create local assets (through activities promoting water and soil conservation, and flood/drought protection) as shown in the following table.

---

73 Rajya Sabha Starred Question No. 186, dated on 27.03.2012 &Lok Sabha Unstarred Question No. 4779, dated on 30.03.2017
74 IndiaStat, 2017

TABLE 86: NUMBER OF WATER CONSERVATION AND WATER HARVESTING STRUCTURES CONSTRUCTED UNDER MGNREGA FROM 2012–13 TO 2015–16 (FROM: MINISTRY OF WATER RESOURCES, RIVER DEVELOPMENT AND GANGA REJUVENATION)[75]

NO.	STATES	WATER CONSERVATION AND WATER HARVESTING			
		2012-13	2013-14	2014-15	2015-16
1	ANDAMAN AND NICOBAR	188	195	147	137
2	ANDHRA PRADESH	1400195	314563	94041	167545
3	ARUNACHAL PRADESH	94	131	139	178
4	ASSAM	3215	2401	2827	3582
5	BIHAR	19836	18040	12037	14955
6	CHHATTISGARH	24559	22811	20606	33325
7	GOA	21	35	41	40
8	GUJARAT	16846	10803	10238	11940
9	HARYANA	2504	2067	1550	971
10	HIMACHAL PRADESH	24165	24201	18800	14852
11	JAMMU AND KASHMIR	10795	10858	9983	12224
12	JHARKHAND	117210	70786	55983	45601
13	KARNATAKA	55336	66694	46153	56722
14	KERALA	35624	55064	65008	62032
15	LAKSHADWEEP	49	40	42	39
16	MADHYA PRADESH	162200	96225	65350	52189
17	MAHARASHTRA	96070	74227	72482	77607
18	MANIPUR	1672	1333	1586	1835
19	MEGHALAYA	2339	2577	2533	2932
20	MIZORAM	467	382	535	497
21	NAGALAND	818	638	425	880
22	ODISHA	40952	34923	23896	21751
23	PUDUCHERRY	NR	2	26	26
24	PUNJAB	230	250	273	343
25	RAJASTHAN	56931	40211	38439	40097
26	SIKKIM	347	391	480	517
27	TAMIL NADU	24612	20369	19782	14440
28	TELANGANA	NA	NA	179261	196450
29	TRIPURA	13683	16684	22798	12930
30	UTTAR PRADESH	64605	54499	50499	88122
31	UTTARAKHAND	8203	4186	3992	5574
32	WEST BENGAL	82860	86950	92873	103268
	TOTAL	2266626	1032536	912825	1043601

75   Rajya Sabha Session - 238 Unstarred Question No.1915

TABLE 87: STATE-WISE TARGET FOR CONSTRUCTION OF FARM PONDS UNDER
MGNREGA DURING 2016–17 (FROM: MINISTRY OF RURAL DEVELOPMENT)[76]

NO.	STATE/UT	NO. OF FARM PONDS
1	ANDAMAN AND NICOBAR ISLANDS	307
2	ANDHRA PRADESH	250000
3	ARUNACHAL PRADESH	1108
4	ASSAM	13239
5	BIHAR	15000
6	CHHATTISGARH	55000
9	GOA	25
10	GUJARAT	27516
11	HARYANA	61
12	HIMACHAL PRADESH	10361
13	JAMMU AND KASHMIR	1885
14	JHARKHAND	128132
15	KARNATAKA	111340
16	KERALA	5000
17	MADHYA PRADESH	50000
18	MAHARASHTRA	1000
19	MANIPUR	2724
20	MEGHALAYA	300
21	MIZORAM	2131
22	NAGALAND	603
23	ODISHA	20340
24	PUDUCHERRY	5
25	PUNJAB	1581
26	RAJASTHAN	25000
27	TAMIL NADU	17500
28	TELANGANA	25000
29	TRIPURA	18700
30	UTTAR PRADESH	5705
31	UTTARAKHAND	3814
32	WEST BENGAL	88948
	TOTAL	882325

Every household was entitled to hundred days of employment in a financial year, with work possibly split up between adult household members or, failing that, providing unemployment allowances if work was not available. The programme has helped bring in some level of economic security for a large number of households.

76   Rajya Sabha Session - 239 Unstarred Question No.1707

TABLE 88: DETAILS OF HOUSEHOLDS PROVIDED MORE THAN HUNDRED DAYS' EMPLOYMENT
IN TEN DROUGHT-AFFECTED STATES UNDER THE MGNREGA DURING 2015–16
(MINISTRY OF RURAL DEVELOPMENT)[77]

NO.	STATE	HOUSEHOLDS EMPLOYED MORE THAN 100 DAYS (IN NOS.)
1	ANDHRA PRADESH	418822
2	CHHATTISGARH	236574
3	JHARKHAND	160652
4	KARNATAKA	126281
5	MADHYA PRADESH	204648
6	MAHARASHTRA	215447
7	ODISHA	180497
8	RAJASTHAN	211742
9	TELANGANA	374976
10	UTTAR PRADESH	154723
	TOTAL	2284362

The Act offers a rights-based approach, instead of simply focusing on a market-based opportunity. Wherever possible, manual unskilled jobs are offered at minimum wages, limiting labour exploitation and putting a floor on rural wages. The programme utilizes a bottom-up approach, with significant involvement from the Panchayati Raj Institutions as stakeholders. The Act also envisaged the creation of sustainable assets in rural areas, which would contribute towards the natural resource base (in the form of drought-proofing, renovating water bodies, water conservation, etc.), while furthering sustainable development. Theoretically, review and strict vigilance over projects was an integral part of the programme.

The scheme operates like any major central scheme, with incentives to encourage states to implement it—the majority of the cost (~75 per cent) is covered by the centre, with the state putting up the remaining, shifting the public works parlance from relief-works mode to an integrated national resource management strategy. The programme represented a significant paradigm shift in India's development strategy, utilizing a rights-based approach, with bottom-up feedback, along with a focus on creating sustainable assets. The three-phase programme started in February 2006 with the 200 most backward districts, and ramped up towards the remaining by end-2007.

---

77   Rajya Sabha Session - 240 Unstarred Question No.826

TABLE 89: PHYSICAL AND FINANCIAL PERFORMANCE OF MGNREGA FROM 2006–07 TO 2011–12[78]

CATEGORY	2006–07 : (200 DISTRICTS)	2007–08: (330 DISTRICTS)	2008–09: (ALL DISTRICTS)	2009–10	2010–11	2011–12
HOUSEHOLDS EMPLOYED (CRORE)	2.1	3.39	4.51	5.26	5.49	4.99
PERSON-DAYS OF EMPLOYMENT GENERATED (CRORE)	90.5	143.59	216.32	283.59	257.15	211.41
WORK PROVIDED PER YEAR TO HOUSEHOLDS WHO WORKED (DAYS)	43	42	48	54	47	42
CENTRAL RELEASE (₹ CRORE)	8640.85	12610.39	30000.19	33506.61	35768.95	29184.85
TOTAL FUNDS AVAILABLE (INCLUDING OPENING BALANCE) (₹ CRORE)	12073.55	19305.81	37397.06	49579.19	54172.14	43273.58
BUDGET OUTLAY (₹ CRORE)	11300	12000	30000	39100	40100	40100
EXPENDITURE (₹ CRORE)	8823.35	15856.89	27250.1	37905.23	39377.27	37548.79
AVERAGE WAGE PER DAY (₹)	65	75	84	90	100	117
TOTAL WORKS TAKEN UP (LAKH)	8.35	17.88	27.75	46.17	50.99	74.13
WORKS COMPLETED (LAKH)	3.87	8.22	12.14	22.59	25.9	15.01

As part of its annual planning, public meetings of village communities are held, with individuals and households interested in obtaining work registering their interest. The gram panchayat consolidates the list of works required, which are then provided to the intermediate panchayat at the block level to gain sanction. Once approved, at least 50 per cent of the works are implemented by the gram panchayat. Typically, 60 per cent of the expenditure is allocated as wages, with catchment area of 5 km of the village. For workers travelling from farther than 5 km, a 10 per cent wage increment is provided to cover transportation costs.

PARTICIPATION

Narain Singh bellows with laughter when asked if he will have another cup of tea to slake his thirst. 'I have miles of digging to undertake, Sahib, and one must earn one's keep,' he says. He coughs, grievously, amidst the sandy landscape surrounding Pushkar in Rajasthan. He hardly remembers his age, except to say that he became a grandfather decades back. But with his offsprings migrating away or turning into beggars, he must continue to earn the family keep.

While stereotypes about MGNREGA associate participation in it with the extremely poor, this is not always true. MGNREGA does attract workers who have low education levels and come from rather poor backgrounds but three-fourths

---

78   Ministry of Rural Development, Government of India

of the households participating in MGNREGA are non-poor. Given declining poverty rates, only 21 per cent of all households are now classified as poor, with 75 per cent of all households in 2012–13 having a per capita income of ₹1,900 per month. In fact, MGNREGA tends to appeal most to households with very small farms (less than 1 hectare)—such farmers typically have little work throughout the year, except during the peak cultivation and peak harvesting periods. Of course, it is possible that higher income households have asked for the job cards simply as insurance, and never actually applied for work; 31 per cent of the poor and 23 per cent of the non-poor participated in MGNREGA in 2011–12, with the remaining unable to, given lack of work or lack of time.

Participation is also limited by the kind of local conditions—for example, in Rajasthan, the overall participation rate is high (~48 per cent in 2012) but about 11 per cent of villages do not contain a single MGNREGA participating household. Effective wage rates can be lower, given the nature of the soil and the requirement that a certain minimum amount of work must be performed per day.

HOUSEHOLD CHARACTERISTICS	PER CENT OF HOUSEHOLDS IN SAMPLE	HOUSEHOLD PARTICIPATION IN MGNREGA (PER CENT)	
		NO	YES
ALL INDIA	100	75.6	24.4
J&K, HIMACHAL PRADESH & UTTARAKHAND	3.8	72.5	27.5
PUNJAB, HARYANA	4	92.1	8
UTTAR PRADESH, BIHAR, JHARKHAND	28.5	84.1	15.9
RAJASTHAN, CHHATTISGARH, MADHYA PRADESH	14.5	61.3	·38.7
WEST BENGAL, ODISHA, ASSAM, NORTHEAST REGION	16.4	68.1	31.9
GUJARAT, MAHARASHTRA, GOA,	11.4	96.9	3.1
ANDHRA PRADESH, KERALA, KARNATAKA, TAMIL NADU	21.4	66.1	33.9

FIGURE 181: HOUSEHOLD-LEVEL MGNREGA PARTICIPATION, BY REGION[79]

In addition, access to land determines the need for participation in a program like MGNREGA—the proportion of landless, marginal and small landowners is relatively higher in MGNREGA at 31 per cent, 33 per cent and 29.4 per cent, respectively, in 2015.[80]

---

79   Desai, S., Vashishtha P. and Joshi. O. 2015. Mahatma Gandhi National Rural Employment Guarantee Act: A Catalyst for Rural Transformation. New Delhi: National Council of Applied Economic Research
80   Ibid

TABLE 90: ALL-INDIA LEVEL IMPLEMENTATION REPORT UNDER
MGNREGA FROM 2006–07 TO 2015–16[81]

YEAR	CUMULATIVE NUMBER OF HOUSEHOLDS ISSUED JOB CARDS	NO. OF HOUSEHOLDS WHO HAVE DEMANDED EMPLOYMENT	NO. OF HOUSEHOLDS PROVIDED EMPLOYMENT	PERSON DAYS IN LAKHS - TOTAL	PERSON DAYS IN LAKHS - SCS	PERSON DAYS IN LAKHS - STS	PERSON DAYS IN LAKHS - OTHERS	PERSON DAYS IN LAKHS - WOMEN	AVERAGE PERSON DAYS PER HOUSE-HOLD	NUMBER OF HOUSEHOLDS WHO AVAILED OF 100 DAYS OF EMPLOYMENT
2006-07	37850390	21188894	21016099	9051	2295	3299	3457	3679	NA	NA
2007-08	64740595	34326563	33909132	14368	3942	4206	6220	6109	NA	NA
2008-09	100145950	45516341	45112792	21632	6336	5502	9795	10357	48	6521268
2009-10	112548976	52920154	52585999	28359	8645	5874	13840	13640	54	7083663
2010-11	119824434	55756087	54947068	25715	7876	5362	12478	12274	47	5561812
2011-12	125025265	51128994	50645132	21876	4847	4092	12938	10527	43	4166070
2012-13	166991184	41965919	41570020	14066	3142	2214	8710	7474	34	1365649
2013-14	128162177	51797601	47930454	22036	5027	3862	13147	11640	46	4658234
2014-15	127753390	46482783	41376652	16620	3723	2820	10077	9121	40	2492415
2015-16	128944639	53482541	48131429	23521	5239	4175	14106	12995	49	4848020

81   Ministry of Rural Development and also published in statistical year book 2017 by MOSPI

TABLE 91: STATE/UT-WISE ACTUAL EXPENDITURE AS A PERCENTAGE OF
TOTAL OUTLAY UNDER MGNREGA FROM 2010–11 TO 2015–16

STATE/ UT	% OF EXPENDITURE AGAINST TOTAL AVAILABLE FUND					
	2010–11	2011–12	2012–13	2013–14	2014–15	2015–16
ANDHRA PRADESH	60%	72%	103%	99%	93%	147%
ARUNACHAL PRADESH	25%	2%	36%	63%	52%	63%
ASSAM	72%	86%	94%	91%	85%	60%
BIHAR	75%	87%	77%	90%	70%	100%
CHHATTISGARH	72%	85%	83%	92%	98%	100%
GOA	59%	87%	26%	45%	81%	69%
GUJARAT	62%	72%	76%	102%	131%	106%
HARYANA	94%	94%	94%	87%	100%	99%
HIMACHAL PRADESH	61%	76%	86%	95%	97%	88%
JAMMU & KASHMIR	82%	59%	82%	95%	67%	96%
JHARKHAND	78%	67%	78%	92%	115%	127%
KARNATAKA	89%	95%	78%	101%	85%	139%
KERALA	80%	88%	95%	98%	98%	92%
MADHYA PRADESH	66%	66%	80%	105%	104%	86%
MAHARASHTRA	60%	109%	93%	82%	99%	99%
MANIPUR	99%	49%	64%	84%	93%	79%
MEGHALAYA	101%	85%	89%	103%	96%	102%
MIZORAM	96%	62%	95%	99%	100%	100%
NAGALAND	95%	70%	88%	91%	91%	59%
ODISHA	83%	77%	87%	94%	96%	100%
PUNJAB	72%	80%	91%	99%	99%	93%
RAJASTHAN	52%	72%	81%	89%	96%	102%
SIKKIM	100%	69%	99%	92%	94%	99%
TAMIL NADU	79%	79%	90%	73%	81%	90%
TELANGANA	-	-	-	-	99%	119%
TRIPURA	99%	94%	71%	96%	114%	92%
UTTAR PRADESH	78%	76%	85%	87%	106%	95%
UTTARAKHAND	94%	94%	96%	94%	97%	96%
WEST BENGAL	91%	93%	93%	97%	101%	90%
ANDAMAN & NICOBAR	65%	85%	75%	88%	68%	31%
CHANDIGARH	-	-	-	-	-	-
DADRA & NAGAR HAVELI	-	-	-	-	-	-
DAMAN & DIU	-	-	-	-	-	-
LAKSHADWEEP	43%	70%	57%	65%	72%	66%
PUDUCHERRY	21%	49%	54%	61%	67%	64%

MARKET INTERVENTION

While socially equitable, this has meant a significant intervention by the government in the local labour supply market.[82] In 2009–10, the programme provided employment to 36.3 per cent of all rural labour households, with each household provided an average thirty-six to thirty-seven days of employment annually. MGNREGA was found to provide employment for 2 per cent of the total rural labour supply. Raising this to hundred days of employment would have provided employment for 5.2 per cent of all rural households. Real wages have also been rapidly increased, with a study indicating that the scheme raised the real daily wage rate by 5.3 per cent, with a lag time of six to eleven months.[83] MGNREGA has helped set a higher benchmark for wage rates, while changing work ethics (MGNREGA work is typically less strenuous than agricultural activities).[84]

When viewed closely, the MGNREGA-induced shift from agriculture throws up curious trends. Tamil Nadu is increasingly seeing an influx of Bihari agricultural labourers, who despite the language challenge, are being employed in paddy, jasmine, sugar cane and banana fields. The daily wage for local workers in Tamil Nadu has shot up to ₹250 per day for male workers and ₹150 per day for female workers, making labour scarce for agriculture, with even districts like Ariyalur and Perambular, which were typically known for migratory labour, facing a labour shortage. While MGNREGA stipulations require that such work is typically undertaken post the agricultural season, such guidelines are observed primarily in abeyance by the Collectors. The programme has helped transform Tamil Nadu's agricultural labour market.[85]

---

82   Chand, R., Srivastava, S.K., Changes in the Rural Labour Market and Their Implications for Agriculture, EPW, Vol XLIX No 10, March 8, 2014. Sourced from: http://www.im4change.org/siteadmin/tinymce/uploaded/Changes_in_the_Rural_Labour_Market_and_Their_Implications_for_Agriculture.pdf

83   Berg, E., Bhattacharyya, S., Durgam, R., Ramachandra, M., 'Can Rural Public Works affect Agricultural Wages? Evidence from India', CSAE Working Paper WPS/2012-05, May 2012. Sourced from: http://www.csae.ox.ac.uk/workingpapers/pdfs/csae-wps-2012-05.pdf

84   Chand, R., Srivastava, S.K., Changes in the Rural Labour Market and Their Implications for Agriculture, EPW, Vol XLIX No 10, March 8, 2014. Sourced from: http://www.im4change.org/siteadmin/tinymce/uploaded/Changes_in_the_Rural_Labour_Market_and_Their_Implications_for_Agriculture.pdf

85   Sathyamoorthy, G., 'Agriculture Operations in the grip of labour shortage', The Hindu, 13 July 2012. Sourced from: http://www.thehindu.com/news/cities/Tiruchirapalli/agriculture-operations-in-the-grip-of-labour-shortage/article3634664.ece

POLICY SOLUTIONS

One must remember that MGNREGA constitutes a relatively small part of the rural labour market—this shift out of agricultural work has been accompanied by a rise in non-farm wage labour. Non-farm casual labour (excluding work associated with MGNREGA) has grown by ten days a year, while work associated with salaried jobs has risen by six days per year. Such significant transformation of the rural labour market has been accompanied by greater accessibility, transportation within and between villages and towns is now easier, allowing labourers to find jobs in nearby areas and even allowing them to migrate. Government employment has risen sharply, as witnessed in the growth of anganwadis and community health workers.

More well-off areas typically don't see workers hankering for work from MGNREGA—their wages from other agricultural or manufacturing work are typically higher, while payments from the latter are far more regular and less prone to the whims and fancies of the local revenue secretary. MGNREGA work can also be back-breaking and paid in line with project completion milestones, whereas casual labour or manufacturing work or even farming work would end up paying at the end of the day. So, while MGNREGA has a significant contribution to the household income of the chronic poor, it plays a limited role in the overall rural economy.

MGNREGA'S IMPACT

Despite significant shortfalls in its implementation, the programme has had a positive impact on the provision of livelihood security, with migration reduced significantly in a number of villages in Andhra Pradesh, Chhattisgarh, Odisha and Rajasthan during the second year of the programme. Since its inception, ~51 per cent of its works until 2014 have been focused on water, with a focus on water conservation, irrigation and flood control, while an additional 19 per cent focus on improving rural connectivity.[86] Such activities have helped reduce rural vulnerability to exogenous shocks, improving livelihood in areas with uncertain rainfall and poor soil fertility.[87] The programme has helped increase the employment capacity of the rural economy with a focus on expanding activities like the construction of ponds and wells.

---

86   Gulati, 2013
87   Tiwari, 2013; Verma 2011

TABLE 92: EMPLOYMENT UNDER MGNREGA DURING 2013–14 TO 2016–17 (FROM: MINISTRY OF RURAL DEVELOPMENT)[88]

NO.	STATE	PERSON DAYS GENERATED				NO. OF HH PROVIDED EMPLOYMENT			
		2013-14	2014-15	2015-16	2016-17	2013-14	2014-15	2015-16	2016-17
1	ANDHRA PRADESH	2995	1556	1991	1470	60	33	36	36
2	ARUNACHAL PRADESH	37	19	50	33	1	1	2	2
3	ASSAM	298	211	486	254	13	10	15	10
4	BIHAR	862	353	671	350	21	10	15	12
5	CHHATTISGARH	1299	556	1014	650	25	17	22	18
6	GUJARAT	230	182	225	205	6	5	6	5
7	HARYANA	118	62	48	54	3	2	2	2
8	HIMACHAL PRADESH	283	191	177	109	5	5	4	4
9	JAMMU AND KASHMIR	338	121	316	62	7	3	7	2
10	JHARKHAND	436	453	586	492	11	11	11	14
11	KARNATAKA	719	434	599	521	15	11	12	13
12	KERALA	866	589	742	329	15	14	15	13
13	MADHYA PRADESH	1229	1172	1238	562	29	28	27	17
14	MAHARASHTRA	517	614	764	511	11	12	13	12
15	MANIPUR	113	101	75	89	5	5	5	5
16	MEGHALAYA	216	167	200	107	4	4	4	3
17	MIZORAM	134	44	131	60	2	2	2	2
18	NAGALAND	184	90	219	179	4	4	4	4
19	ODISHA	712	535	894	512	17	15	20	16
20	PUNJAB	135	65	144	109	4	3	5	5
21	RAJASTHAN	1839	1685	2341	1729	36	37	42	39
22	SIKKIM	44	24	44	22	1	1	1	1
23	TAMIL NADU	3677	2680	3687	2441	63	57	61	59
24	TELANGANA	-	1047	1417	795	-	25	26	23
25	TRIPURA	522	512	539	315	6	6	6	6
26	UTTAR PRADESH	1754	1313	1822	1237	50	39	54	44
27	UTTARAKHAND	166	148	224	140	4	5	5	4
28	WEST BENGAL	2296	1697	2865	1301	61	51	61	45
29	ANDAMAN AND NICOBAR	8	5	3	1	0	0	0	0
30	DADRA & NAGAR HAVELI	-	-	-	-	-	-	-	-
31	DAMAN & DIU	-	-	-	-	-	-	-	-
32	GOA	1	2	1	1	0	0	0	0
33	LAKSHADWEEP	0	0	0	-	0	-	-	-
34	PUDUCHERRY	8	4	6	5	0	0	0	0
TOTAL	TOTAL	22036	16629	23521	14645	479	414	481	416

TABLE 93: AVERAGE PERSON-DAYS' EMPLOYMENT PROVIDED PER HOUSEHOLD IN MGNREGA DURING 2012–2015 (FROM: MINISTRY OF RURAL DEVELOPMENT)[89]

NO.	STATE/ UTS	2012-13	2013-14	2014-15
1	ANDHRA PRADESH	56	50	47
2	ARUNACHAL PRADESH	34	26	14
3	ASSAM	25	24	22
4	BIHAR	45	42	34
5	CHHATTISGARH	45	52	32
6	GUJARAT	41	40	35
7	HARYANA	44	36	28
8	HIMACHAL PRADESH	51	52	42
9	JAMMU & KASHMIR	57	51	36
10	JHARKHAND	40	38	41
11	KARNATAKA	46	50	40
12	KERALA	55	57	43
13	MADHYA PRADESH	40	42	42
14	MAHARASHTRA	54	45	53
15	MANIPUR	62	25	22
16	MEGHALAYA	52	59	48
17	MIZORAM	88	75	22
18	NAGALAND	63	45	22
19	ODISHA	34	42	36
20	PUNJAB	27	33	22
21	RAJASTHAN	52	51	46
22	SIKKIM	64	70	43
23	TAMIL NADU	58	59	47
24	TELANGANA	-	-	43
25	TRIPURA	87	88	88
26	UTTAR PRADESH	29	35	34
27	UTTARAKHAND	44	42	32
28	WEST BENGAL	35	37	33
29	ANDAMAN & NICOBAR	52	48	38
30	DADRA & NAGAR HAVELI	-	-	-
31	DAMAN & DIU	-	-	-
32	GOA	14	23	24
33	LAKSHADWEEP	26	24	26
34	PUDUCHERRY	21	21	13
	TOTAL	46	46	40

89   In Response To Rajya Sabha Session - 237 Unstarred Question No.1738

It has effectively created a labour wage floor in the rural labour market, raising minimum wages and increasing women's participation in the labour force.[90] This has led to the rural poor feeling empowered, and in some cases even renegotiating with private employers.[91] A brief snapshot of the outlay of the programme on wages as illustrated below.

TABLE 94: STATE/UT-WISE CENTRAL RELEASE OF FUNDS
UNDER MGNREGA FROM 2010–11 TO 2015–16[92]

STATE/ UT	CENTRAL RELEASE (IN LAKH)					
	2010-11	2011-12	2012-13	2013-14	2014-15	2015-16
ANDHRA PRADESH	741807	147758	321674	475049	290314	307380
ARUNACHAL PRADESH	3529	6079	6834	13853	2704	4395
ASSAM	60929	42686	53446	57350	50023	87830
BIHAR	210366	130073	122781	158071	95968	102412
CHHATTISGARH	168505	163856	203136	144602	150570	106341
GOA	508	260	241	206	138	247
GUJARAT	89486	32429	47441	33530	35443	30599
HARYANA	13100	27512	34936	37688	16715	12471
HIMACHAL PRADESH	63625	31138	36130	47797	35543	39610
JAMMU & KASHMIR	31360	78131	76276	60316	52171	55802
JHARKHAND	96287	123733	80917	62143	72433	97880
KARNATAKA	157305	66257	123194	159607	171687	99155
KERALA	70423	95105	131118	127711	158758	152634
MADHYA PRADESH	256577	296851	161015	183982	245163	236732
MAHARASHTRA	20471	104044	157324	115292	79952	123835
MANIPUR	34299	62497	59023	23100	21997	25532
MEGHALAYA	20981	28498	22611	27106	27786	22183
MIZORAM	21603	32957	25229	24474	11141	28517
NAGALAND	51157	67347	46012	29215	11305	26666
ODISHA	156186	97822	84798	75753	103530	147941
PUNJAB	12879	11429	11421	22615	18948	24533
RAJASTHAN	278882	161970	258534	205943	297610	269583
SIKKIM	4449	10080	7407	10684	7386	8623
TAMIL NADU	202490	281552	354605	469021	378180	547037
TELANGANA	-	-	-	-	191996	182485
TRIPURA	38261	95933	76890	94366	63662	135894
UTTAR PRADESH	526659	424048	129202	289639	251341	269569
UTTARAKHAND	28981	37351	26827	33001	28636	45077
WEST BENGAL	211761	259703	339548	289438	374495	471174
ANDAMAN & NICOBAR	769	1644	1381	1918	1302	1036
CHANDIGARH	-	-	-	-	-	-
DADRA & NAGAR HAVELI	48	100	40	-	-	-
DAMAN & DIU	-	-	-	-	-	-
LAKSHADWEEP	234	35	118	17	45	12
PUDUCHERRY	2982	100	886	880	740	1293

90   Chand, R., Srivastava, S.K., Changes in the Rural Labour Market and Their Implications for Agriculture, EPW, Vol XLIX No 10, March 8, 2014. Sourced from: http://www.im4change.org/siteadmin/tinymce/uploaded/Changes_in_the_Rural_Labour_Market_and_Their_Implications_for_Agriculture.pdf

91   Mathur, 2007

92   Ministry of Rural Development and also published in statistical year book 2017 by MOSPI

TABLE 95: STATE/UT-WISE SPEND ON WAGES UNDER MGNREGA FROM 2010–11 TO 2015–16[93]

STATE/UT	EXPENDITURE ON (IN LAKHS) -WAGES					
	2010-11	2011-12	2012-13	2013-14	2014-15	2015-16
ANDHRA PRADESH	335056	281808	346093	331450	171552	261022
ARUNACHAL PRADESH	642	48	1740	5949	1949	3936
ASSAM	50240	45953	40101	45386	33314	38279
BIHAR	138910	92711	116964	108773	52969	102653
CHHATTISGARH	114622	148240	155756	147203	124318	86415
GOA	464	493	101	205	339	215
GUJARAT	47886	34914	32918	28982	27849	30565
HARYANA	14217	19379	23713	24729	15999	10500
HIMACHAL PRADESH	27617	32455	31878	37689	28653	28627
JAMMU & KASHMIR	22200	24847	40694	39585	17866	34130
JHARKHAND	85711	73359	68673	58001	70184	88303
KARNATAKA	159185	108505	87281	142392	98902	112066
KERALA	61141	92055	131651	120293	149778	140220
MADHYA PRADESH	215283	193393	164001	165695	181062	145947
MAHARASHTRA	26732	112112	151740	80894	104641	130908
MANIPUR	26001	28058	31497	17442	17412	14425
MEGHALAYA	17342	19358	16453	24567	21025	18616
MIZORAM	17733	16206	20753	20430	7411	24325
NAGALAND	34392	30636	25555	20101	8820	12780
ODISHA	91512	55922	66686	92605	71411	157727
PUNJAB	9789	9143	9935	17081	15248	22715
RAJASTHAN	227203	189206	217035	181722	210421	249959
SIKKIM	4813	3841	4605	5850	3485	5693
TAMIL NADU	215280	278643	394076	364088	312138	463337
TELANGANA	-	-	-	4687	114479	183374
TRIPURA	39359	57884	64089	69715	69410	91949
UTTAR PRADESH	352294	320704	167038	222756	196601	232436
UTTARAKHAND	23468	24979	19341	23116	19245	32453
WEST BENGAL	165658	188322	253595	249380	271235	364339
ANDAMAN & NICOBAR	617	1425	1002	1610	815	161
CHANDIGARH	-	-	-	-	-	-
DADRA & NAGAR HAVELI	-	-	-	-	-	-
DAMAN & DIU	-	-	-	-	-	-
LAKSHADWEEP	185	238	96	34	22	8
PUDUCHERRY	786	1252	1133	1041	530	825

While the average employment generated per household remains less than hundred, about 3.5 per cent of households gained such employment in 2013–14, with the mean level of employment per household hovering around forty-one days between FY12 and FY14. While administrative data highlights that almost all households got work when sounded, NSSO data does not bear this out, showcasing that 20 per cent of the households were regularly left out.

---

93   Ministry of Rural Development and also published in statistical year book 2017 by MOSPI

STATES/UTS	2007-2008	2008-2009	2009-2010	2010-2011	2011-2012	2012-2013	2013-2014	2014-2015	2015-2016	2016-2017
ANDAMAN & NICOBAR ISLANDS	-	1	6	4	8	7	8	5	3	2
ANDHRA PRADESH	2010	2735	4044	3352	2939	3273	2995	1556	1991	1852
ARUNACHAL PRADESH	3	35	17	31	1	44	37	19	50	74
ASSAM	488	751	733	471	353	314	298	211	486	415
BIHAR	843	992	1137	1603	682	942	862	353	671	779
CHANDIGARH	-	0	0	NR	NR	0	NR	NR	-	-
CHHATTISGARH	1316	1243	1042	1110	1207	1194	1299	556	1014	814
DADRA & NAGAR HAVELI	-	0	1	0	NR	0	NR	NR	-	-
DAMAN AND DIU	-	0	0	NR	NR	0	NR	NR	-	-
GOA	-	0	2	4	3	1	1	2	1	1
GUJARAT	90	213	585	492	313	282	230	182	225	258
HARYANA	36	69	59	84	109	129	118	62	48	77
HIMACHAL PRADESH	98	205	285	219	270	262	283	191	177	215
JAMMU AND KASHMIR	37	79	129	211	209	366	338	121	316	239
JHARKHAND	748	750	842	831	610	567	436	453	586	669
KARNATAKA	198	288	2003	1098	701	618	719	434	599	844
KERALA	61	154	340	480	633	838	866	589	742	638
LAKSHADWEEP	-	2	1	1	2	0	0	0	0	0
MADHYA PRADESH	2753	2947	2624	2198	1689	1399	1229	1172	1238	1023
MAHARASHTRA	185	420	274	200	772	872	517	614	764	663
MANIPUR	48	286	306	296	224	285	113	101	75	99
MEGHALAYA	41	86	148	200	168	174	216	167	200	244
MIZORAM	32	126	170	166	131	154	134	44	131	166
NAGALAND	24	203	284	334	297	245	184	90	219	252
ODISHA	405	433	554	977	454	546	712	535	894	681
PUDUCHERRY	-	2	9	11	11	9	8	4	6	5
PUNJAB	19	40	77	75	65	66	135	65	144	148
RAJASTHAN	1678	4830	4498	3026	2121	2203	1839	1685	2341	2447
SIKKIM	9	26	43	48	33	36	44	24	44	41
TAMIL NADU	645	1204	2391	2686	3016	4081	3677	2680	3687	3563
TELANGANA	-	-	-	-	-	-	0	1047	1417	916
TRIPURA	181	351	460	375	490	519	522	512	539	442
UTTAR PRADESH	1363	2272	3559	3349	2673	1412	1754	1313	1822	1472
UTTARAKHAND	80	104	182	230	199	192	166	148	224	215
WEST BENGAL	969	787	1552	1553	1496	2018	2296	1697	2865	2077
INDIA	14359	21633	28360	25715	21876	23048	22036	16629	23521	21334

FIGURE 182: STATE-WISE PERSON-DAYS GENERATED UNDER MGNREGA
IN INDIA (2007–08 TO 2016–17 UP TO 22.03.2017)[94,95]

---

94   Ministry of Labour and Employment, Govt. of India, 2017

95   Desai, S., Vashishtha P. and Joshi. O. 2015. Mahatma Gandhi National Rural Employment Guarantee
     Act: A Catalyst for Rural Transformation. New Delhi: National Council of Applied Economic Research

The issue of person-days generated hasn't remained unnoticed with the question being raised and discussed several times in the Lok Sabha over many years. MGNREGA guidelines have sought to ensure that the programme benefits vulnerable groups, seeking to organize them into labour groups to demand work, such groups are also granted job cards of a distinct colour. Typically, such activities have helped benefit a variety of different kinds of rural households, with over 50 per cent of associated households coming from agricultural labourer or other labour household backgrounds. For the poorest of the poor, typically SCs and STs, the programme has been heaven-sent with SCs and STs accounting for 30 per cent and 25 per cent, respectively, of the total person-days worked, much higher than their population share.[96] Meanwhile, ST households had the highest proportion of job cards (a document highlighting the days of employment and payment received) at 57.2 per cent, followed closely by SC households at 50 per cent in FY12.[97] However, given the fact that the programme is self-selecting, i.e. those in need apply for it, the large number of SC and ST households on the job card rolls indicates that the program has been successful in reaching the marginalized poor in India. Indeed, the programme has a near perfect record on this front with almost all who applied for a job card receiving one.[98]

Fund utilization, especially after 2009–10, has been significantly high, but physical performance (actual number of projects completed) has not improved in a concomitant manner, with the ratio of works completed to the total number of public works reaching a peak of 51 per cent in 2010–11 and falling ever since.

YEAR	TOTAL FUNDS AVAILABLE (₹ CR)	EXPENDITURE (₹ CR)	TOTAL FUNDS AVAILABLE AT CONSTANT PRICES (₹ CR)	ANNUAL GROWTH OF FUNDS AVAILABLE AT 2011-12 PRICES (%)	EXPENDITURE AS PER CENT OF AVAILABLE FUNDS	TOTAL WORKS TAKEN UP (100,000)	WORKS COMPLETED	WORKS COMPLETED AS A PER CENT OF TOTAL WORKS TAKEN UP
2006–07	12,074	8,823	17,655	73.1	8.4	3.9	46.4	
2007–08	19,306	15,857	26,578	50.5	82.1	17.9	8.2	46 PER CENT
2008–09	37,397	27,250	47,352	78.2	72.9	27.8	12.1	44 PER CENT
2009–10	49,579	37,905	59,092	24.8	76.5	46.2	22.6	49 PER CENT
2010–11	54,172	39,377	59,029	-0.1	72.7	51	25.9	51 PER CENT
2011–12	48,806	37,073	48,806	-17.3	76	80.8	27.6	34 PER CENT
2012–13	45,631	39,778	42,485	-13.0	87.2	104.6	25.5	24 PER CENT
2013–14	42,216	38,672	36,820	-13.3	91.6	94.1	24.1	26 PER CENT

FIGURE 183: USE OF AVAILABLE FUNDS AND PERCENTAGE OF WORKS COMPLETED[99,100]

96   Census, 2011
97   66th Round and 68th Round Employment and Unemployment Survey, 2009-10
98   Ministry of Rural Development, 2016
99   Ministry of Rural Development 2013
100 Desai, S., Vashishtha P. and Joshi. O. 2015. Mahatma Gandhi National Rural Employment Guarantee Act: A Catalyst for Rural Transformation. New Delhi: National Council of Applied Economic Research

STATES/UTS	2013-14		2014-15		2015-16		2016-17	
	SCS	STS	SCS	STS	SCS	STS	SCS	STS
ANDAMAN AND NICOBAR ISLANDS	0.00	0.02	0.00	0.01	0.00	0.00	0.00	0.01
ANDHRA PRADESH	14.97	7.73	8.30	3.32	8.99	3.64	9.51	3.80
ARUNACHAL PRADESH	0.00	1.31	0.00	1.28	0.00	1.66	0.00	1.79
ASSAM	0.79	2.27	0.62	1.76	0.85	2.96	0.75	2.97
BIHAR	5.88	0.43	2.80	0.18	3.68	0.26	5.00	0.38
CHANDIGARH	-	-	-	-	-	-	-	-
CHHATTISGARH	2.45	9.26	1.81	5.86	2.09	8.08	2.00	7.35
DADRA AND NAGAR HAVELI	-	-	-	-	-	-	-	-
DAMAN AND DIU	-	-	-	-	-	-	-	-
GOA	0.00	0.02	0.00	0.02	0.00	0.01	0.00	0.02
GUJARAT	0.41	2.54	0.33	2.28	0.36	2.62	0.44	2.76
HARYANA	1.56	0.00	1.01	0.00	0.91	0.00	1.41	0.00
HIMACHAL PRADESH	1.53	0.37	1.26	0.33	1.17	0.32	1.40	0.37
JAMMU AND KASHMIR	0.44	1.02	0.18	0.67	0.41	1.05	0.33	0.92
JHARKHAND	1.40	4.53	1.39	4.30	1.34	4.45	2.01	5.83
KARNATAKA	2.35	1.09	1.74	0.84	2.10	1.08	2.94	1.58
KERALA	2.25	0.42	2.25	0.44	2.39	0.49	2.29	0.50
LAKSHADWEEP	0.00	0.01	0.00	0.01	0.00	0.00	0.00	0.00
MADHYA PRADESH	5.01	9.66	4.55	8.76	4.38	9.15	4.37	10.01
MAHARASHTRA	1.11	2.31	1.16	2.17	1.21	2.49	1.27	2.76
MANIPUR	0.13	2.30	0.13	2.32	0.14	2.36	0.14	2.36
MEGHALAYA	0.03	3.30	0.03	3.23	0.03	3.38	0.03	3.73
MIZORAM	0.00	1.77	0.00	1.93	0.00	1.93	0.00	1.88
NAGALAND	0.04	3.82	0.03	3.81	0.04	3.92	0.04	4.01
ODISHA	2.93	6.34	2.41	5.63	3.39	7.39	3.14	6.55
PUDUCHERRY	0.12	0.00	0.10	0.00	0.11	0.00	0.11	0.00
PUNJAB	3.19	0.00	2.28	0.00	3.69	0.00	4.04	0.00
RAJASTHAN	7.22	8.57	7.38	8.86	8.56	9.78	9.27	9.96
SIKKIM	0.03	0.24	0.02	0.22	0.03	0.25	0.03	0.25
TAMIL NADU	18.33	0.90	16.34	0.68	17.11	0.81	17.26	0.82
TELANGANA	-	-	5.79	3.95	6.03	4.15	5.66	4.05
TRIPURA	1.08	2.41	1.03	2.40	1.02	2.33	1.02	2.38
UTTAR PRADESH	17.59	0.50	13.89	0.35	19.01	0.55	15.98	0.47
UTTARAKHAND	0.71	0.11	0.78	0.14	0.93	0.22	0.90	0.21
WEST BENGAL	19.50	5.72	16.21	4.58	19.45	5.34	17.39	4.76
INDIA	111.04	78.93	93.82	70.31	109.40	80.66	108.73	82.47

FIGURE 184: STATE-WISE NUMBER OF HOUSEHOLDS PROVIDED EMPLOYMENT (SC/ST) UNDER MGNREGA IN INDIA (2013–14 TO 2016–17 UP TO 24.03.2017) (₹ IN LAKH)[101,102,103]

---

101   Lok Sabha Unstarred Question No. 3734, dated on 19.03.2015 & Lok Sabha Starred Question No. 406, dated on 30.03.2017

102   Ministry of Labour and Employment, Govt. of India, 2017

103   Desai, S., Vashishtha P. and Joshi. O. 2015. Mahatma Gandhi National Rural Employment Guarantee Act: A Catalyst for Rural Transformation. New Delhi: National Council of Applied Economic Research

Most states seem to adhere to the requirement of ensuring that at least 60 per cent of the expenditure of the programme is on wages, with Andhra Pradesh and Kerala spending the majority of their expenses on wages.

STATE	2013-14	2012-13	2011-12
ANDHRA PRADESH	85%	83%	76%
ARUNACHAL PRADESH	67%	91%	100%
ASSAM	69%	66%	62%
BIHAR	60%	68%	60%
CHHATTISGARH	77%	75%	75%
GUJARAT	61%	81%	67%
HARYANA	71%	60%	76%
HIMACHAL PRADESH	71%	73%	71%
JAMMU AND KASHMIR	48%	72%	52%
JHARKHAND	68%	49%	69%
KARNATAKA	68%	61%	66%
KERALA	98%	63%	98%
MADHYA PRADESH	73%	98%	62%
MAHARASHTRA	70%	64%	82%
MANIPUR	79%	80%	100%
MEGHALAYA	77%	81%	70%
MIZORAM	88%	72%	82%
NAGALAND	79%	85%	36%
ODISHA	74%	67%	63%
PUNJAB	73%	63%	62%
RAJASTHAN	72%	68%	70%
SIKKIM	62%	73%	68%
TAMIL NADU	99%	61%	100%
TRIPURA	77%	99%	62%
UTTAR PRADESH	68%	77%	70%
UTTARAKHAND	65%	74%	63%
WEST BENGAL	67%	64%	61%
ANDAMAN	98%	74%	100%
DADRA	..	100%	..
DAMAN	..	0%	..
GOA	79%	..	80%
LAKSHADWEEP	79%	0%	98%
PUDUCHERRY	100%	82%	100%
CHANDIGARH	..	100%	..
TOTAL	76%	76%	72%

FIGURE 185: SHARE (PER CENT) OF WAGE IN TOTAL EXPENDITURE, BY STATE[104,105]

---

104 Ministry of Rural Development 2012, 2013, 2014

105 Desai, S., Vashishtha P. and Joshi. O. 2015. Mahatma Gandhi National Rural Employment Guarantee Act: A Catalyst for Rural Transformation. New Delhi: National Council of Applied Economic Research

Similarly, most states and union territories have sought to keep administrative expenses around the 6 per cent mark, with Andhra Pradesh and Arunachal Pradesh being large outliers.

STATE	2013-14	2012-13	2011-12
ANDHRA PRADESH	9.4	10.5	4.9
ARUNACHAL PRADESH	5.1	2.5	82.6
ASSAM	5.4	5.2	5.8
BIHAR	2	2.4	3.5
CHHATTISGARH	5	3.7	3.3
GUJARAT	8.5	6.7	8.5
HARYANA	2.6	2.9	3.3
HIMACHAL PRADESH	4.3	4.7	4.5
JAMMU AND KASHMIR	4.5	3.1	5.6
JHARKHAND	4.7	4.4	4.8
KARNATAKA	2.2	3.8	3.5
KERALA	4.2	3.7	3.7
MADHYA PRADESH	8.4	4.7	4.3
MAHARASHTRA	5	3.2	2.7
MANIPUR	7	1.5	2.2
MEGHALAYA	5.6	3.8	2.6
MIZORAM	5.1	5.2	6.8
NAGALAND	3.1	0	0
ODISHA	3.3	4	5.2
PUNJAB	3.9	5.8	5.3
RAJASTHAN	6.7	5	5.7
SIKKIM	6	6.1	6.5
TAMIL NADU	3.9	1.5	2.5
TRIPURA	4.9	3.4	3.4
UTTAR PRADESH	3.7	6.5	4
UTTARAKHAND	2.3	3.8	3.5
WEST BENGAL	3.9	2.6	5.5
ANDAMAN	17.3	15.1	10.9
DADRA	..	..	..
DAMAN	..	0	..
GOA	2.7	8.2	9
LAKSHADWEEP	32.7	20.1	11
PUDUCHERRY	5.6	5.4	1.4
CHANDIGARH	..	0	..
TOTAL	5	4.6	4.3

FIGURE186: SHARE (PER CENT) OF WAGE IN TOTAL EXPENDITURE, BY STATE

The programme has had inter-state variations, with Rajasthan and Madhya Pradesh, leading in the number of households having job cards, while Maharashtra and Karnataka hosted a low proportion (~12 per cent in FY12). Such variances are partly due to lack of awareness, along with local governance issues. Even intra-state variations remain significant—northern Madhya Pradesh, covering Bundelkhand, had just 55 per cent of all rural households holding job cards, while the Vindhya region had 90 per cent coverage.[106] In addition, participation rates vary across states, with Union Territories and the Northeastern states generally showcasing higher participation rates. Chhattisgarh, Himachal Pradesh, Rajasthan and Tamil Nadu generally see above average participation rates.

STATE	PARTICIPATION RATE (PER CENT) (2012)	POVERTY ESTIMATE (PER CENT) (2011–12)
ANDHRA PRADESH	35.1	9.2
ARUNACHAL PRADESH	2.2	34.7
ASSAM	24.9	32
BIHAR	10.5	33.7
CHHATTISGARH	62.4	39.9
GUJARAT	12.1	16.6
HARYANA	9.1	11.2
HIMACHAL PRADESH	38.5	8.1
JAMMU & KASHMIR	27.8	10.4
JHARKHAND	33.3	37
KARNATAKA	20.8	20.9
KERALA	34.1	7.1
MADHYA PRADESH	35	31.7
MAHARASHTRA	11.4	17.4
MEGHALAYA	77.9	11.9
ODISHA	17	32.6
PUNJAB	7.3	8.3
RAJASTHAN	47.6	14.7
SIKKIM	58.6	8.2
TAMIL NADU	66.6	11.3
TRIPURA	91.9	14.1
UTTAR PRADESH	28.5	29.4
UTTARAKHAND	32.9	11.3
WEST BENGAL	39.9	20
GOA	8.7	5.1
TOTAL	31.2	21.9

FIGURE 187: PARTICIPATION RATE AND POVERTY RATIO, BY STATE[107,108]

106 Nss 59Th Round, All India Debt And Investment Survey
107 Planning Commission poverty estimates in 2013, MoRD 2013
108 Desai, S., Vashishtha P. and Joshi. O. 2015. Mahatma Gandhi National Rural Employment Guarantee Act: A Catalyst for Rural Transformation. New Delhi: National Council of Applied Economic Research

STATES/UTS	DELETED JOB CARDS IN CURRENT FINANCIAL YEAR (IN NOS.)	ACTIVE WORKERS (IN ₹ CR)	% OF PAYMENT GENERATED (MORE THAN 15 DAYS	
			2015-2016	2016-2017*
ANDAMAN AND NICOBAR ISLANDS	0	0.00	83	54
ANDHRA PRADESH	238857	0.78	19	10
ARUNACHAL PRADESH	5845	0.02	91	70
ASSAM	508766	0.35	80	32
BIHAR	118843	0.53	85	60
CHHATTISGARH	476135	0.56	92	83
GOA	20	0.00	69	40
GUJARAT	333854	0.19	66	61
HARYANA	22831	0.07	70	45
HIMACHAL PRADESH	34518	0.10	70	65
JAMMU AND KASHMIR	106898	0.15	88	87
JHARKHAND	110349	0.29	28	23
KARNATAKA	667561	0.65	69	56
KERALA	55296	0.23	80	25
LAKSHADWEEP	0	0.00	38	0
MADHYA PRADESH	2158434	0.80	72	53
MAHARASHTRA	75034	0.44	65	55
MANIPUR	4653	0.06	18	14
MEGHALAYA	13032	0.07	99	92
MIZORAM	2668	0.03	21	31
NAGALAND	0	0.06	96	92
ODISHA	394595	0.49	63	66
PUDUCHERRY	1596	0.01	80	100
PUNJAB	6174	0.10	86	54
RAJASTHAN	614282	0.92	55	24
SIKKIM	9540	0.01	58	27
TAMIL NADU	936999	0.89	68	91
TELANGANA	0	0.56	32	15
TRIPURA	19190	0.11	44	29
UTTAR PRADESH	1679318	1.00	80	78
UTTARAKHAND	127825	0.09	76	31
WEST BENGAL	60464	1.47	83	77
TOTAL	8783577	11.03	63	54

FIGURE 188: STATE-WISE PERCENTAGE OF DELAYED PAYMENT TO WORKERS UNDER MGNREGA IN INDIA (2015–16 AND 2016–17 UP TO 10.03.2017)[109,110,111]

109   Lok Sabha Unstarred Question No. 2319, dated on 16.03.2017

110   Ministry of Labour and Employment, Govt. of India, 2017

111   Desai, S., Vashishtha P. and Joshi O. 2015. Mahatma Gandhi National Rural Employment Guarantee Act: A Catalyst for Rural Transformation. New Delhi: National Council of Applied Economic Research

Despite significant delays in payments (63 per cent of all payments were delayed in FY16 and 54 per cent of all payments in FY17), the programme continues to enjoy broad support.

YEAR	NUMBER OF HOUSEHOLDS PROVIDED EMPLOYMENT (CR)	TOTAL EMPLOYMENT DAYS GENERATED (100,000)	AVERAGE EMPLOYMENT DAYS PER HOUSEHOLD	SHARE OF SCHEDULED CASTES & TRIBES IN EMPLOYMENT (%)	SHARE OF WOMEN IN EMPLOYMENT (%)
2006-07	2.1	90.5	43	61%	40%
2007-08	3.39	143.59	42	56%	43%
2008-09	4.51	216.32	48	54%	48%
2009-10	5.26	283.59	54	51%	48%
2010-11	5.49	257.15	47	52%	48%
2011-12	5.06	218.76	43	41%	48%
2012-13	4.99	230.48	46	40%	51%
2013-14	4.79	220.22	46	40%	53%

FIGURE 189: TOTAL EMPLOYMENT GENERATED AND SHARES OF WOMEN, SCHEDULED CASTES AND SCHEDULED TRIBES[112,113]

The impact that this can have on household income can be considerable. The mean annual per capita income associated with MGNREGA households in 2011–12 was ₹13,800, which was lower than other households by ~31 per cent. Farm income typically contributed 24.4 per cent of the total household income for MGNREGA households, with other income sources including casual wages, non-agricultural wages and business income. MGNREGA income was the fifth-largest component for such households (~8 per cent). Households participating in MGNREGA typically have 25 per cent lower levels of per capita income, with a much greater dependence on wage income than salary income. They are generally less entrepreneurial, with few having their own businesses, while they possess a strong dependence on MGNREGA income.

---

112 Ministry of Rural Development 2010, 2015

113 Desai, S., Vashishtha P. and Joshi O. 2015. Mahatma Gandhi National Rural Employment Guarantee Act: A Catalyst for Rural Transformation. New Delhi: National Council of Applied Economic Research

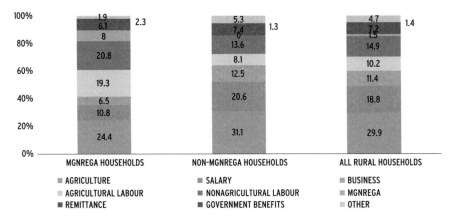

FIGURE 190: INCOME SOURCE, BY HOUSEHOLD TYPE[114]

Hence, it follows that **MGNREGA** has a significant impact on poverty, reducing it by 32 per cent for the entire group in sample studies. MGNREGA seems to have a greater impact in reducing poverty in less developed regions than in more developed regions, cutting it by 33.8 per cent in less developed areas compared to 27.1 per cent in more developed areas.

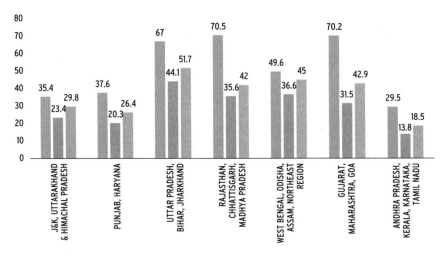

FIGURE 191: IMPACT OF MGNREGA ON POVERTY REDUCTION BETWEEN 2005 AND 2012[115]

---

114 Desai, S., Vashishtha P. and Joshi O. 2015. Mahatma Gandhi National Rural Employment Guarantee Act: A Catalyst for Rural Transformation. New Delhi: National Council of Applied Economic Research

115 Ibid

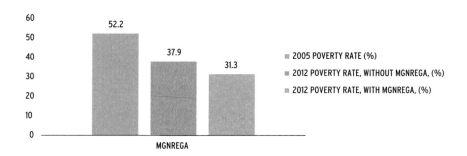

FIGURE 192: IMPACT OF MGNREGA ON POVERTY REDUCTION FOR PARTICIPANTS (PER CENT)[116]

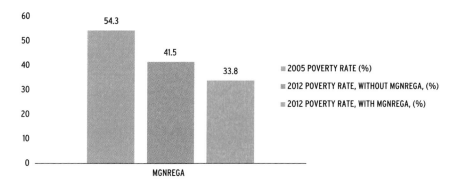

FIGURE 193: IMPACT OF MGNREGA ON POVERTY REDUCTION FOR
DALIT/SCHEDULED CASTE PARTICIPANTS (PER CENT)[117]

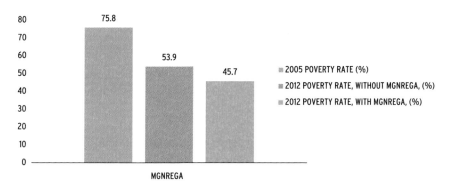

FIGURE 194: IMPACT OF MGNREGA ON POVERTY REDUCTION FOR
DALIT/SCHEDULED TRIBE PARTICIPANTS (PER CENT)[118]

116 Desai, S., Vashishtha P. and Joshi O. 2015. Mahatma Gandhi National Rural Employment Guarantee Act:
     A Catalyst for Rural Transformation. New Delhi: National Council of Applied Economic Research
117 Ibid
118 Ibid

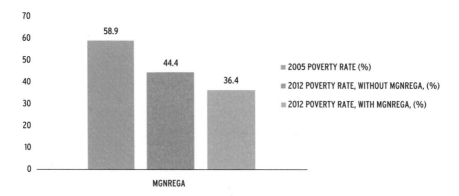

FIGURE 195: IMPACT OF MGNREGA ON POVERTY REDUCTION FOR
PARTICIPANTS FROM LESS DEVELOPED REGIONS (PER CENT)[119]

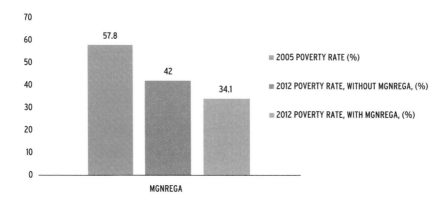

FIGURE 196: IMPACT OF MGNREGA ON POVERTY REDUCTION FOR
PARTICIPANTS FROM MORE DEVELOPED REGIONS (PER CENT)[120]

Pushing those who are chronically poor above the poverty line will require raising their work allocation beyond the current forty-two days, to at least 140–150 days. The magnitude of this change highlights how MGNREGA can be a policy tool to reduce poverty, albeit with real policy reform required to solve livelihood issues associated with agricultural labourers.

In addition, resolution of a range of implementation challenges associated with MGNREGA remains pending, as illustrated in the following table.

---

119 Desai, S., Vashishtha P. and Joshi O. 2015. Mahatma Gandhi National Rural Employment Guarantee Act: A Catalyst for Rural Transformation. New Delhi: National Council of Applied Economic Research
120 Ibid

TABLE 96: DETAILS OF COMPLAINTS RECEIVED UNDER MGNREGA IN 2015 (FROM :MINISTRY OF RURAL DEVELOPMENT)[121]

NO.	STATE	MISAPPROPRIATION OF FUNDS	UNDER PAYMENT	WAGES NOT PAID	CORRUPTION UNDER NREGA	IRREGULARITIES (NOT SPECIFIC)	TOTAL
1	ANDHRA PRADESH	1	0	0	2	5	8
2	ARUNACHAL PRADESH	0	0	0	0	0	0
3	ASSAM	23	0	2	12	3	40
4	BIHAR	17	74	16	123	19	249
5	CHHATTISGARH	9	23	18	38	6	94
6	GOA	0	0	0	0	0	0
7	GUJARAT	1	0	0	2	12	15
8	HARYANA	55	3	14	16	20	112
9	HIMACHAL PRADESH	20	3	5	3	6	37
10	JAMMU & KASHMIR	0	0	1	0	0	1
11	JHARKHAND	45	6	13	36	40	140
12	KARNATAKA	8	0	6	0	4	18
13	KERALA	4	1	3	4	7	19
14	LAKSHADWEEP	0	0	0	0	0	0
15	MADHYA PRADESH	220	7	44	109	38	418
16	MAHARASHTRA	2	4	1	4	3	14
17	MANIPUR	1	1	2	0	8	12
18	MEGHALAYA	0	0	0	0	0	0
19	MIZORAM	0	0	0	0	0	0
20	NAGALAND	3	0	0	0	0	3
21	ODISHA	34	1	20	19	22	95
22	PUNJAB	8	0	1	1	3	13
23	PUDUCHERRY	0	0	0	0	1	1
24	RAJASTHAN	6	1	3	1	8	19
25	TAMIL NADU	7	1	2	4	4	18
26	TELANGANA	3	2	0	0	0	5
27	TRIPURA	3	0	0	1	0	4
28	UTTAR PRADESH	400	26	92	301	362	1181
29	UTTARAKHAND	3	2	5	7	4	21
30	WEST BENGAL	3	5	2	6	1	17
31	SIKKIM	0	0	0	0	1	1
	TOTAL	875	160	250	689	577	2555

MGNREGA suffers from low budgetary allocations—with allocation for FY18–19 being ₹55,000 crore, not a paisa more than the revised estimate for FY17–18. In 2016–17, an allocation of ₹48,000 crore was made, which, when examined, reveals that it contained accumulated arrears of ₹11,644 crore—thereby making it a net allocation of ₹36,356 crore. With the centre having to meet as much as[122] 96 per cent of the total cost of implementation, the allocations for MGNREGA remain pretty much stagnant, despite state government action. The Mahatma Gandhi

---

121 Rajya Sabha Session - 237 Unstarred Question No. 2529

122 http://nrega.nic.in/netnrega/writereaddata/Circulars/1756NEFMS_Upscaling.pdf

National Rural Employment Guarantee Act, 2005 Section 22(1), stipulates, that the central government will meet the cost of unskilled manual labour up to 75 per cent of material cost for works undertaken (including wage payment to skilled and semi-skilled workers) and administrative costs, with the state government meeting the cost of unemployment allowances and 25 per cent of material costs.

USEFULNESS OF ASSETS

The main objective of the scheme, to provide employment assurance for creation of durable assets in rural areas, remains impacted due to inadequate allocations and payment delays. With works under the scheme having a high requirement of unskilled labour, rural workers are mostly employed in digging-related works. Out of a range of 153 kinds of projects that can be undertaken under the scheme, almost hundred fall under the Natural Resource Management (NRM) component, with seventy-one of them being related to water, ranging from[123] creation of recharge wells/pits, desilting and embankment strengthening, canal lining, check dams and farm ponds. While some groups have made unsubstantiated claims that MGNREGA involves digging trenches and then filling them up, without any usefulness, the reality has been different.[124] A survey of 4,100 works created under MGNREGA revealed that 87 per cent of them were functional (with 75 per cent of works being related to agriculture, directly or indirectly) and a majority of the remaining connecting habitations, farms and markets. With people's involvement in deciding the types of works, almost 90 per cent participants felt that the works were useful, especially with works on private lands scoring better in terms of usefulness and maintenance.[125] Studies conducted across 2,057 households in forty villages across four districts in four different states (by Indian Institute of Science in collaboration with MoRD), have shown that implementation of MGNREGS works have contributed to increased groundwater levels, improved water availability for irrigation and, consequently, increased the net area under cultivation. Meanwhile, land development works have increased soil fertility (higher soil organic content) and reduced top soil erosion. This positively impacts crop production through improved crop diversity and crop yields, furthered by positive impact on plantations and fruit orchards. Besides these benefits, the core benefit of employment generation and reduced migration cannot be forgotten.[126] For MGNREGA water assets, the best

---

123 http://nrega.nic.in/netnrega/writereaddata/Circulars/1816Water_Conservation_Mission.pdf
124 Mgnrega Works And Their Impacts, Sudha Narayanan, Krushna Ranaware, Upasak Das and Ashwini Kulkarni, Indira Gandhi Institute of Development Research (IGIDR)
125 http://fes.org.in/studies/report-env-benefits-vulnerability-reduction.pdf
126 https://www.livemint.com/Opinion/hz2CLtVBL7q45SrIfg1BfL/Saving-peoples-livelihoods.html

performing 143 MGNREGA water works reported a savings in budget—completed at ₹5.9 crore, against the budgeted ₹ 6.67 crore[127] (for 140 out of 143 assets), with each work creating greater than 2,000 person-days in terms of employment, translating into 700 days of labour per ₹ 1 lakh worth of investment. For 117 assets out of 143 water assets studies, the investment was recovered within a year of usage.

TABLE 97: GROSS RETURNS FROM ONE YEAR OF USE AS A
PROPORTION OF THE INVESTMENT MADE IN DIFFERENT STATES

STATE	ASSET TYPE	PERCENTAGE OF COST RECOVERY IN 1 YEAR
BIHAR	MICRO CANALS	206%
	PONDS	92%
	PRIVATE WELLS	4%
	RIVER WORKS	54%
	ALL ASSETS (BIHAR)	121%
GUJARAT	VILLAGE PONDS	155%
	PRIVATE WELLS	44%
	CHECK DAMS	53%
	ALL ASSETS (GUJARAT)	126%
RAJASTHAN	ANICUTS	61%
	PRIVATE WELLS	23%
	FARM PONDS	24%
	CANAL WORKS	125%
	ALL ASSETS (RAJASTHAN)	61%
KERALA	VILLAGE PONDS	167%
	PRIVATE PONDS	40%
	TEMPLE PONDS	69%
	ALL ASSETS (KERALA)	101%

SOURCE: BEYOND DIGGING AND FILLING HOLES, SHILP VERMA & TUSHAAR SHAH, IWMI-TATA, 2012

TABLE 98: BENEFITS FROM ONE YEAR OF USE AS A
PROPORTION OF THE INVESTMENT MADE IN DIFFERENT ASSET TYPES

ASSET TYPE	PERCENTAGE OF COST RECOVERY IN 1 YEAR
ASSETS ON PUBLIC LAND	116%
ASSETS ON PRIVATE LAND	35%
NEW ASSETS CREATED	65%
EXISTING ASSETS RENOVATED	136%
ALL ASSETS	98%

SOURCE: BEYOND DIGGING AND FILLING HOLES, SHILP VERMA & TUSHAAR SHAH, IWMI-TATA, 2012

127 http://www.iwmi.cgiar.org/iwmi-tata/PDFs/2012_Highlight-42.pdf

Thus, looking at the data only from an economic returns perspective, the government should focus on enhancement and renovation of existing water assets, especially those which have deteriorated with time due to changing scenarios. Additionally, while the economic return on private land is lesser compared to other work asset types, it mostly benefits the poorest and marginalized households. The results of both studies prove that as water availability increases, farmers realize savings in diesel costs.[128]

PAYMENT DELAYS

While assets created under MGNREGA have a positive impact on rural economy, with the additional gain of ensuring employment to the rural workforce, the scheme remains severely hampered by payment delays.[129]

Laxmi, a thirteen-year-old girl in Titli village of Buldhana district in Maharashtra, spends her day with her mother in a field plucking cotton, a workfront that will feed them for three months since the start of the plucking season in October. She dropped out of school a few months before her thirteenth birthday, in order to ensure that her three younger siblings don't suffer the same fate. Her days in school were cut short after her father committed suicide, mainly troubled by the ₹1.1 lakh loan he had taken. He is no more, but the loan burden continues. He used to work under the MGNREGA scheme, but was not paid for more than three years, with his receivables exceeding ₹1 lakh. When working for MGNREGA, all he got was ₹150 per week for his family, in the name of 'bazaar kharcha'.

Meanwhile, farmers in Miragpur village of Lalitpur district of Uttar Pradesh had all their hopes pinned on the nullah work being undertaken in their village under MGNREGS, since the wider Bundelkhand region suffered from acute drought. The workers were mostly landless labourers and small/marginal farmers, and these hard days increased risk of pauperization, hunger and malnutrition. The work gave them hope of ensuring their sustenance, for they would be paid promptly for their labour, but that money never came. In the initial days, they complained and when nothing happened for a few months, they got on with their lives and even stopped complaining.

128   https://www.tribuneindia.com/news/jammu-kashmir/mgnrega-wages-delayed-in-72-villages/563483. html

129   https://www.hindustantimes.com/india/delayed-nrega-payments-drive-workers-to-suicide/story-MlLZGwzDHkWE1ifOykxcrM.html

While the MGNREGA payments are meant to provide sustenance to rural workforce, delays can even cause deaths. In some cases, farmers prefer to work as bonded labour for private contractors as at least food is ensured. Jaggu Bhuiyan, a fifty-year-old villager in Palamau district of Jharkhand, was full of hope when MGNREGA was launched in his village. Work was hard to come by and it was difficult for him to seek, with the nearest pucca road being 10 km away. He was hired to construct a well, but with only 8 per cent of the allocated money being released for payments, it became increasingly difficult to continue construction. He started to spend less time on construction, and more time making trips to the Block Office for release of funds, and after countless futile trips to get money released alongside allegations by workers holding him responsible for payments, he ended his life by hanging himself from a tree on the outskirts of the village.

Delay in payment of MGNREGA wages is not a localized phenomenon, with almost 72 per cent of our villages witnessing such cases. Despite MGNREGS being the world's largest jobs programme, payment delays are routine, sometimes even for several months.[130]

Under the MGNREGA provisions, a worker should receive wages within fifteen days of completion of work, failing which a delay compensation per day of delay shall be paid, in addition to base wages. In order to understand the delays, it is required to examine the process following completion of work up to wages being credited in bank accounts.[131]

In order to improve the payment mechanism under MGNREGS, the National Electronic Fund Management System (Ne-FMS) was implemented in April 2016, which is supposed to expedite payments by reducing the number of days taken to credit the payments into bank accounts. Prior to Ne-FMS, the state governments maintained a contingency fund, which could be utilized in case of delays by the centre, but with the Ne-FMS being centralized, the state government's powers to credit payments got stymied. Under the current system, at first the muster roll is closed, which records the attendance of workers at the work location. Post-finalization of muster roll, the data is finalized alongside a measurement book, which together records the details of attendance and the quantum of work done under the Management Information System (MIS). Using this data, the wage list is prepared (which stipulates the wages due to each worker) and an electronic Fund Transfer Order (FTO) is generated. The FTO is then verified using the Maker-Checker principle—thus, the 'maker' of the FTO, responsible for generating it, first signs which is then forwarded to a second signatory, or the 'checker', who verifies the

---

130 https://www.tribuneindia.com/news/jammu-kashmir/mgnrega-wages-delayed-in-72-villages/563483.html

131 http://azimpremjiuniversity.edu.in/SitePages/pdf/PaymentDelayAnalysisWorkingPaper-2018.pdf

veracity of the FTO. Post-signatures, this gets recorded in the MGNREGA server as an e-pay order (FTO). The state government is responsible for carrying out all the above mentioned steps. These files are then pulled into the Public Finance Management System (PFMS), a central government online application responsible for making payments under various social security schemes. Post-processing these files through its payment systems, the PFMS notionally sends it to the State Employment Guarantee Fund, in other words, the bank account under Ne-FMS responsible for making wage payments. This is then sent to the post office or bank, which then deposits the money into workers' accounts. Thus, the entire payment mechanism remains under central government control. Now, one would think that the workers would get compensation within fifteen days, and be compensated for each day of delay. Unfortunately, that is not the reality. The existing method doesn't acknowledge any delay post the second signature on the FTO, thereby any delays from signatures to final payments remains unaccounted, leading to significant underestimation of the actual delay experienced by the worker. A study of 3,446 and 3,603 gram panchayats across ten states in FY16–17 and 17–18, respectively, found that almost ₹26 crore of compensation due to workers is not reflected because of the nature of definition of 'delay'. An analysis of ten states revealed the following statistics:

TABLE 99: STATE-WISE STATISTICS (IN PERCENTAGE) ON MGNREGS PAYMENTS

	PAYMENTS MADE ON TIME	PAYMENTS UNDER NO COMPENSATION	PAYMENTS UNDER PARTIAL COMPENSATION
UTTAR PRADESH	20	30	50
CHHATTISGARH	28	64	9
MADHYA PRADESH	63	17	19
JHARKHAND	68	25	7
RAJASTHAN	36	56	8
BIHAR	20	26	54
KARNATAKA	31	44	24
KERALA	33	62	5
ODISHA	19	56	25
WEST BENGAL	17	64	19
OVERALL	32	45	23

SOURCE: RAJENDRAN NARAYANAN, SAKINA DHORAJIWALA, AND RAJESH GOLANI)

The state-wise unaccounted compensation for FY17–18 due to the ineffective definition of 'delay' is illustrated below.

TABLE 100: STATE-WISE ESTIMATES OF UNACCOUNTED COMPENSATION IN FY17–18

STATES	DELAY COMPENSATION CALCULATED IN THE MIS	DELAY COMPENSATION NOT CALCULATED IN THE MIS (IN ₹)	TOTAL COMPENSATION DUE (IN ₹)	PER CENT OF TRUE DELAY COMPENSATION NOT CALCULATED
	(A)	(B)	(C=A+B)	D=B/C
UTTAR PRADESH	759,674	3,286,032	4,045,706	81
CHHATTISGARH	251,947	2,940,104	3,192,051	92
MADHYA PRADESH	579,517	855,195	1,434,712	60
JHARKHAND	136,026	857,912	993,938	86
RAJASTHAN	608,411	3,078,106	3,686,517	83
BIHAR	2,900,271	3,308,440	6,208,711	53
KARNATAKA	1,293,535	5,899,298	7,192,833	82
KERALA	138,373	6,179,941	6,318,314	98
ODISHA	1,101,796	3,860,618	4,962,414	78
WEST BENGAL	2,538,610	34,674,719	37,213,329	93
OVERALL	10,308,160	64,940,365	75,248,525	86

SOURCE: RAJENDRAN NARAYANAN, SAKINA DHORAJIWALA, AND RAJESH GOLANI[132]

At the beginning of FY18–19, about 99 per cent of FTOs were delayed which reduced to 42 per cent by month end, still translating to about 57 per cent of payments yet to be paid to rightful beneficiaries. In the six months from April 2017 to September 2017, less than a third of payments were made on time, and instead of improving on that front, payments were frozen in nineteen states in October 17. Grassroots organizations like NREGA Sangharsh Morcha estimated that over 9.2 crore workers may not be getting their dues on time, with delayed wage payments estimated at ₹3,066 crore. Under stipulated guidelines, states are mandated to provide audited reports of the previous financial year after six months for release of second tranche of funds by the centre, through the Ministry of Rural Development (MoRD). Excluding the provision of submission of audited reports, the centre didn't have enough budget for eight states.[132,133]

In cases when FTOs are generated within fifteen days, but money is not credited within the stipulated duration, compensation is not calculated for an average of 59 per cent transactions (across a survey of ten states), with wide inter-state variability—ranging

---

132 http://www.indiaspend.com/cover-story/despite-record-allocation-57-mgnregs-wages-due-remained-unpaid-in-april-2018-2018

133 http://mnregaweb4.nic.in/netnrega/Citizen_html/financialstatement.aspx?lflag=eng&fin_year=2017-2018&source=national&labels=labels&Digest=cT/J7ChEq5LOfEr0AmsuAQ

from 20 per cent in Madhya Pradesh to 79 per cent in West Bengal. This also gets reflected in the number of days taken to credit payments into accounts (when FTO is generated within fifteen days), ranging from ten days in Madhya Pradesh to fifty-three days in West Bengal. However, not all fault lies with the state—for crediting payments, the centre takes one day for Madhya Pradesh but fifty-one days for West Bengal.

TABLE 101: STATE-WISE AVERAGE DELAY WHEN FTO IS
GENERATED WITHIN FIFTEEN DAYS IN FY17–18

STATES	NUMBER OF TRANSACTIONS FOR WHICH FTO IS GENERATED WITHIN 15 DAYS	TRANSACTIONS FOR WHICH FTO IS GENERATED WITHIN 15 DAYS BUT CREDITING TO WORKERS' ACCOUNTS EXCEEDS 15 DAYS	PERCENTAGE OF TRANSACTIONS FOR WHICH DELAYS ARE NOT CALCULATED	AVERAGE DAYS TAKEN TO CREDIT INTO ACCOUNTS WHEN FTO IS GENERATED WITHIN 15 DAYS	DELAY COMPENSATION NOT CALCULATED (IN ₹)
UTTAR PRADESH	64,470	38,133	59	24	555,069
CHHATTISGARH	249,817	173,058	69	32	2,493,858
MADHYA PRADESH	375,955	75,996	20	10	356,316
JHARKHAND	313,996	81,423	26	16	658,949
RAJASTHAN	449,809	271,726	60	11	2,418,020
BIHAR	133,223	73,318	55	14	952,823
KARNATAKA	295,264	170,462	58	17	2,706,125
KERALA	496,675	321,981	65	31	5,473,559
ODISHA	325,884	240,543	74	25	2,569,123
WEST BENGAL	735,259	580,564	79	53	25,866,079
OVERALL	3,440,352	2,027,204	59	25	44,049,921

SOURCE: RAJENDRAN NARAYANAN, SAKINA DHORAJIWALA, AND RAJESH GOLANI

TABLE 102: STATE-WISE DETAILS OF CREDITED PAYMENTS
WHEN FTO GENERATION EXCEEDS FIFTEEN DAYS

STATES	NO. OF TRANSACTIONS	AVERAGE DAYS TO FTO 2ND SIGNATURE	AVERAGE DAYS TAKEN TO CREDIT AFTER FTO 2ND SIGNATURE	DELAY COMPENSATION CALCULATED IN THE MIS (IN ₹)	TOTAL UNACCOUNTED DELAY COMPENSATION (IN ₹)	TOTAL DELAY COMPENSATION TRULY PAYABLE (IN ₹)
UTTAR PRADESH	37,153	31	19	397,330	453,988	851,318
CHHATTISGARH	21,745	35	27	189,707	266,198	455,905
MADHYA PRADESH	86,496	27	1	478,484	46,022	524,506
JHARKHAND	24,284	26	9	132,066	112,414	244,480
RAJASTHAN	39,555	35	10	579,994	319,242	899,236
BIHAR	154,112	35	14	2,555,099	1,761,064	4,316,163
KARNATAKA	64,545	26	16	673,595	987,867	1,661,462
KERALA	16,225	24	31	81,059	297,747	378,806
ODISHA	106,577	34	16	1,050,191	901,867	1,952,058
WEST BENGAL	149,673	30	51	1,956,569	6,468,938	8,425,507
OVERALL	700,365	31	21	8,094,094	11,615,347	19,709,441

SOURCE: RAJENDRAN NARAYANAN, SAKINA DHORAJIWALA, AND RAJESH GOLANI

Thus, we see that a misplaced definition of 'delay' and the meagre amount of delay compensation are discouraging workers to enrol for the MGNREGS work, despite the provisions in the MGNREGA disincentivizing payment delays. Overall, the percentage of delayed compensation paid (for delayed wages) has been declining—total delayed compensation paid stood at 93 per cent of approved amount of delayed compensation in 2014–15, declined to 85 per cent in FY16–17, and to 72 per cent (till Jan 18) for FY17–18.[134] Studies reveal that payment-related delays were responsible for almost 71 per cent of abandoned works, while technical difficulties accounted for 15 per cent.[135] No matter where the responsibility for delay lies, it's always the common man who pays with his own coin—in an era of instant payments, we cannot make our countrymen wait months for their due wages.

Besides payments, other aspects of the MGNREGS needs reform as well. For one, MGNREGS needs to be demand-driven instead of being directed by 'supply' or targets from higher levels. The block and district administrations remain straitjacketed within their defined budgets, which may be delinked from the demanded quantum of work programme, while few sarpanches look at MGNREGS work as a means to improve their social clout. Such outlook results in inferior quality assets. This is mostly true in pockets where rural market wages are higher than those under MGNREGS—with villagers showing minimal interest in MGNREGS in such cases, the local administration can succumb to dubious methods to create demand for employment. Overzealous local administration can also distort asset quality—the construction of 250,000 boribunds in Gujarat, post announcement by the CM in 2009–10, under less than ideal conditions, led to 85 per cent of assets rendered useless within a short span of time (Shah & Mistry, 2012). In terms of creating demand, awareness levels play a critical role. The large enrolment of women in the MGNREGA programme in Kerala owes a lot to the involvement of Kudumbashree, a women's empowerment and poverty eradication scheme. When a work programme is demand-driven, i.e., demanded by the local village communities, instead of the Sarpanch and the local administration, the asset quality is found to be better. Most of the best-performing MGNREGA assets were demand-driven. One of the factors of demand-driven assets is that their importance is felt, recognized and acknowledged.

Demand-driven programmes can also address farmer complaints about farm labour. The impact of MGNREGA on agricultural labour cannot be ignored, as farmers in many places complain of further tightening of the farm labour market,

---

134 Mahatma Gandhi National Rural Employment Guarantee Scheme (MGNREGS) GOI 2018-19, Budget Briefs, Vol 10, Issue 9, Accountability Initiative, Centre for Policy Research,

135 All's Well that ends in a well, An economic evaluation of MNREGA wells in Jharkhand, Anjor bhaskar 7 Pankaj Yadav, Institute for Human Development

alongside rising farm labour wages, reduced timings and improved working conditions. While farmers in Kerala and Andhra have demanded that MGNREGA works also include labour-intensive farm activities, it has also led to rifts between farmers and labourers, with the latter complaining that sarpanches along with gram panchayats and local administration get MGNREGA work blocked during peak agricultural season. If the programme is more demand-driven, then the distortion created by MGNREGA in already tight labour markets could be reduced, while increasing awareness about utility of MGNREGA works will make farmers realize the importance of assets created and its supplementary benefit to their farms—be it water security through water assets like dams, better linkages to markets through roads and so on. A concerted effort is required in analysis of issued job cards to understand if the same households are getting unskilled work year-on-year, and if true, efforts are needed to ensure that additional job cards that do not get work have work in coming years, and those who get unskilled work get trained and are employed in semi-skilled or skilled jobs.

In order to transform the nature of the programme into being more demand-driven, a committee at the village level should be adequately trained to evaluate projects and recommend the selected works to the gram sabha, which would then rank projects in priority order, based on consensus/vote on recommended projects (post-establishing technical feasibility) and post-selection/ranking, accord them greater priority over 'top-driven' projects.

While MGNREGS is quite focussed on reporting the quantum of work, almost no measurement metric focussing on asset quality, sustainability and potential benefits is tracked regularly in the MGNREGA implementation Management Information System (MIS)—tracking a work stops with completion. Thus, most manpower focusses on initiating new works or completing initiated works. This creates undue pressure on field engineers, who may be looking after as many as hundred projects across a few gram panchayats, besides possibly managing some other non-MGNREGA works. In such a scenario, the MGNREGA mate may be provided basic technical training which can ultimately provide relief to site engineers, besides raising a cadre of grassroots workers with experience in civil works. Often affected by high work load and low pay, the talented engineers are always at risk of moving away to the private sector—this often leads to poor technical supervision which in turn lead to deterioration in asset quality. In such cases, a smart system of balanced work load and aligning incentives with asset quality can provide new impetus.[136]

Lack of focus on asset quality requires increased maintenance, a critical aspect which remains largely overlooked, thereby affecting sustainability of benefits.

---

136 Gaur & Chandel, 2010

When assets are built on public land, it is felt that the onus of maintenance lies on MGNREGA or gram panchayats, leaving the structure to deteriorate. It is a common phenomenon—when benefits accrue to a larger group, individual users do not have significant incentive to take up the entire cause. Even in cases when villagers were aligned to taking up the maintenance responsibility, it was found that they were either incapable or financially inadequate. In such cases, special provisions can be made to enable gram panchayats to undertake maintenance work. In cases where assets were created and handed over to groups for maintenance, the users were found reluctant to take up the responsibility; one potential way to overcome it would be to identify the group of villagers prior to the designing and implementation stage, instead of enrolling them post-commissioning.[137] This idea gains credibility as assets built on private land, with clearly defined roles and responsibility, witness improved maintenance. This can be done by making the MGNREGA programme flexible for accommodating maintenance through local institutional arrangements, inclusion of asset quality metrics in the MGNREGA MIS and regular inspections of post-completion assets.

This would require increased technical inputs by engineers during construction and post-completion, along with special teams for monitoring completed works. Training can also be provided to gram panchayats which can prove beneficial in peak-work times. The ratio of materials to labour prescribed for works could be made range-bound, providing more flexibility for various work types. For maintenance, a contingency fund with the gram panchayat could be maintained, alongside mandatory village committee for maintenance of high-impact, high-maintenance works. Periodic reviews of completed assets could be incorporated into the programme. Complementary projects should be explored and encouraged—e.g. in case of water assets, plantation projects can also be implemented simultaneously.

We need to strengthen the local MGNREGA administration, especially in poor areas/blocks. The poor areas would typically have a larger unmet MGNREGA demand whereas richer states might be better-off, with the local administration sometimes resorting to supply-push even amidst less than expected demand. A strong gram panchayat, alongside effective local administration, can create positive impact in poor areas.

---

137 Verma and Schwan 2012

TENANCY REFORMS

A fundamental challenge for the success of Indian agriculture remains the small and fragmented landholding pattern of our farmers. The average landholding size is 1.13 hectares, a far cry from the global average of 3.7 hectares. The size of landholding has decreased marginally from 1.41 hectares in 2000.[138] Nearly 72 per cent of our farmers are small and marginal, owning just 6 per cent of agricultural land. If semi-medium farmers are also included, we witness that 80 per cent of our farmers own just 11 per cent of India's agricultural land. The maximum number of these small and marginal landholdings are in populated states of Uttar Pradesh, Bihar, Maharashtra and Andhra Pradesh.

On the other hand, large landholdings account for 8 per cent of the total number of landholdings but a staggering 80 per cent of total land. By 2030, it is expected that small and marginal landholdings would account for 91 per cent of the total farm holdings. Small and marginal farmers face imperfect markets for purchase of inputs and sale of produce, low access to credit leading to overdependence on informal sources—causing sub-optimal investment decisions and reduced access to extension services and technical know-how, besides poor access to public infrastructure like irrigation and electricity. Research suggests that only 14 per cent of marginal and 27 per cent of small farmers were able to avail of credit from formal institutional sources, whereas 33 per cent of medium farmers were able to get formal credit. Getting the smaller agricultural produce from the fragmented landholdings to the markets increases their dependence on middlemen, thereby reducing their net incomes. Small landholdings also face issues of obtaining extension services and infrastructural facilities, like on-farm pack houses, grading services and machinery utilization. The problem gets acute with time as population increase only further reduces the average size of landholdings. To ensure economies of scale for small and marginal farm holdings, consolidation of landholdings needs to be undertaken.

Simply put, land consolidation is the process of converting a number of small fragmented landholdings into one big continuous farm and then re-allotting them in a manner so that each farmer gets a single farm of equal size as his earlier landholding. It could also be implemented for convincing farmers to get one or two compact farms in place of their fragmented landholdings. Land consolidation, as an idea, dates back to the 1750s when Denmark implemented the concept. Voluntary land consolidation was introduced in Punjab in 1921—implemented by local cooperative societies, it ensured no disputes as no coercion was exerted on any participant, with participation being voluntary in nature. However, such

---

138 http://agcensus.dacnet.nic.in/nationalholdingtype.aspx

a process is usually very slow and can be manipulated by the powerful zamindars or stubborn farmers opposing the scheme. Besides Punjab, other states like Gujarat, Maharashtra and West Bengal have also passed legislation for voluntary consolidation. However, with time, the nature of consolidation has also varied. In 1923, Madhya Pradesh passed the first Act for partial compulsory consolidation, which in spirit meant that if a majority of farmers in a village agree to consolidation, then the remaining minority will also have to agree to have their fragmented landholdings consolidated. In 1936, Punjab passed a similar Act which provisioned that if 66 per cent of farmers holding 75 per cent of land agree to consolidation, then the remaining farmers have to compulsorily agree also. In 1948, Punjab followed this with overriding compulsion on consolidation of landholdings, with the state government directing the consolidation irrespective of the number of farmers in favour of such consolidation. This drew inspiration from the Act passed in 1947 in erstwhile Bombay State.

The main benefits of consolidation accrue in the form of efficient farming— better methods of cultivation, improved access to irrigation and power, utilizing economies of scale for labour and agricultural machinery, thereby reducing the cost of farming. It also saves the farmer's time, money and energy from moving between different tracts of land. Additionally, it saves land earlier used up in making farm boundaries. However, consolidation comes with its own set of challenges, with most farmers having land as their sole security, they are unable to give away the land of their ancestors.

Soil fertility adds another layer of complexity. A farmer owning a fertile piece of land will not be amenable to it being exchanged for another piece of land, inferior in fertility. Land price and land quality within a tehsil can vary significantly— thereby creating a scenario wherein farmers will have to exchange money, besides exchanging land, which is still manageable provided the price determination is fair and correct. However, lack of land surveys, agricultural surveys and officials inept in handling such price determination makes it a daunting task. Under British rule, land revenue was a significant source of revenue collection, so having updated and accurate land records was imperative. Post-Independence, revenue administration fell under 'non-Plan' expenditure, thereby limiting its budget which ultimately led to deterioration in quality of land records.

The National Land Records Modernization Programme (NLRMP) introduced in 2008 by the Department of Land Resources under the Ministry of Rural Development is a potential solution. The NLRMP aims for computerization of all land records, with states being encouraged to legalize such computerized records through digital imprints and signatures. It also calls for digitalizing the registration process through linking of the revenue office with the registrar's office. Thirdly, it provides for surveys and preparation of maps using advanced technology including aerial surveys, Global Positioning Systems (GPS) and High Resolution Satellite Imagery (HRSI) and boosting technical and administrative capability under the NLRMP. The funding patterns are illustrated below.

TABLE 103: FUNDING PATTERN FOR NRLMP

ITEM	FUNDING PATTERN (%)	
	CENTRE	STATE
COMPUTERIZE LAND RECORDS	100	0
SURVEY	90	10% (NE STATES)
	50	50% (OTHERS)
COMPUTERIZE REGISTRATION PROCESS, LINK SUB-REGISTRAR'S OFFICE WITH REVENUE OFFICES	90	10% (NE STATES)
	25	75% (OTHERS)
MODERN RECORD ROOMS IN TEHSIL OFFICES	90	10% (NE STATES)
	50	50% (OTHERS)
TRAINING, CAPACITY BUILDING	100	0
CORE GIS	100	0

While the NLRMP cannot take away the emotional attachment of a farmer to his piece of land, it can provide valuable insights into price determination, which will come into play once consolidation of landholding takes place.

Consolidation of landholdings can also come in the form of implementation of land lease reforms. While the first wave of legislation in tenancy reforms to overcome inequity in land distribution was introduced post-Independence, the time for the next step of reforms adjusting to the reality and the need of the day is in order. The existing land tenancy reforms have ended the monopoly of a few landlords who end up exploiting the landless and the agricultural labour. With each state having varying land tenancy laws, the results have been mixed. Under these laws, about 10 per cent of tenant farmers have received owner rights to the land they had leased, since the introduction of such laws. However, such gains are limited to only a few states and the number of new tenant farmers obtaining owner-rights has dropped sharply.

With tenants having legal rights to the land they lease, most landlords ended up evicting tenants, mostly through finding loopholes in the legislation—as much as 33 per cent of India's agricultural land had tenants being evicted as an adverse consequence of land lease reforms (Land Reforms in India, P.S. Appu, 1996). The laws have also incentivized informal tenancy, wherein owners typically get into oral agreement with the tenant farmers, bereft of any legal status, leaving them disfranchised in availing of cheaper formal credit, input subsidies, crop insurance, market access and minimum price support, and other public benefits. Our agricultural profile has changed since Independence. While earlier, most land was in the clutches of a few zamindars, today large farmers account for only 12 per cent of total land, a far cry from the monopolistic nature witnessed at the time of Independence. On the other hand, 80 per cent of our farmers on average live on less than 1 hectare of land. Restrictions on land leasing also has a broad-based impact on agriculture—most land owners underuse their land, due to unexpected side effects of tenancy reforms amidst a changed agricultural profile. Even when they use their land, informal tenancy agreements mean that tenants do not invest in the overall, long-term health of soil. Due to such changes in agricultural profile, it is imperative to reform land tenancy laws—although land ownership still remains the primary goal, access to land via leasing reforms will promote an alternative to ownership and provide legal validity to the work of millions of informally working agricultural tenants. This assumes greater significance with many farmers ageing and the youth migrating in search of better opportunities, mostly to cities rather than towns. For 2016–26, studies estimate 200 million citizens will migrate from rural India to urban areas in search of better livelihoods. Reforms in land lease laws would provide these 200 million with a cushion of rental income, and improving access to land and enhance its economic usage for citizens in rural areas.

The success of other countries, most importantly China, in this respect deserves mention. Land market reforms would facilitate the migrants to urban areas and provide economic security, thereby increasing economic opportunities for those who lease out and those who rent. The Model Agricultural Land Leasing Act will provide ownership security over their land to multiple land owners, especially small and marginal farmers, and enable them to work in the non-farm sector without fear of losing their land.

Such rented land could provide a big fillip for new-age agricultural start-ups. A case in point is the Argentina experience, wherein many Argentinians continue to hold rural land and specialist agricultural startups like Los Grobos have emerged that take care of farming operations on small and marginal landholdings. Such examples are already present at a micro level. Consider the Bengaluru-based agricultural asset management company, Hosachiguru, which has evolved a distinct agri-investment model. It takes management of the land from the land owner and follows up with design and development of the land, depending on the crop to be sown, which again is a function of various other input factors.

The preparation of land for cultivation includes soil preparation, setting up irrigation systems (mostly drip irrigation or borewell), hiring labour and obtaining power for running the operations. Post preparation, it executes a pilot for farm management for three months, which, on the land owner's decision, could be extended further.

Using precision farming techniques, the firm aims to produce more crops using less resources (thereby reducing the production cost), giving meaning to the adage, More Crop Per Drop. In order to improve quality and efficiency, it ropes in experts and scientists, leaders in their fields, for various domains, be it irrigation, soil preparation, and even crop specialists. Farm data is made accessible to land owners on a real-time basis, enabling the owner to keep track of the progress of their crops and the value of their investments. Similar start-ups could be encouraged to take up farm management as their domain area. The firms can recruit agricultural labour or explore partnership models as well, in line with the tenets of contract farming.

Various other revenue-sharing or profit-sharing mechanisms could be devised between the firms and the land owners, with each land owner receiving periodic payments proportionate to the share of landholding. The owners would also be free to choose the type of crop sown on their land, short-term crops or long-term crops, depending on their future financial requirements. Multiple agri-preneurial startups would lead to competition, thereby improving the entire ecosystem of service delivery to the agricultural asset management model, and creating value for all stakeholders—the agricultural labour employed by the firm and the landowners. Such partnership models would also provide a fillip to other agri-based startups, and would receive mentoring from other agri-entrepreneurs. Consider the products of Santepp Systems, a high-growth company in the agricultural technology production area. The company is supported by NABARD and NIF and has multiple products to make agriculture easier and convenient. It makes borewell scanners, which can check inflow and outflow of water and click downhole pictures, thereby helping the farmer with the decision to dig the borewell further or abandon—a big help for citizens facing challenges similar to Mt Harishchandra Yerme (Jagalpur village, Latur, Maharashtra) who dug sixty-three borewells, as deep as 800 ft–1,000 ft deep, in search of water on his 40-acre mosambi farm.

Other products also include an irrigation controller which enables users to operate pumps and valves from remote places using sensors. While individual marginal and small farmers may not have the financial wherewithal to buy such products, a margin-sensitive agri-asset management company may surely be interested, especially if it utilizes economies of scale. Focus on margins and scaling up would allow firms to enter into symbiotic partnerships. Consider agricultural waste disposal, at present, most agricultural waste stubble gets burnt, especially in northern India, as farmers do not have adequate resources (especially labour) for proper disposal. However, a company, BIO-LUTIONS, arranges for such cleanup and also pays the farmer for such waste supply, which can then be used to make biodegradable packaging material (replacing plastic packaging) and disposable tableware. Such partnerships among agricultural entrepreneurs will diversify incomes and monetize unused waste resources.

To mitigate the impact of ongoing labour migration away from agriculture, it is necessary to push through structural reforms in rural India. The average landholding size has been reducing, reaching 1.13 hectares in 2011, with tenancy regulations preventing consolidation of landholdings. If such tenancy regulations were relaxed, the viability of mechanization would improve, along with improving farmer access to credit and raising net returns per farmer. Most states currently either ban all agricultural tenancies (e.g. Jammu and Kashmir), apply certain exemptions for widows, minors or army personnel (e.g. Karnataka, Himachal Pradesh, Madhya Pradesh, Uttar Pradesh, Odisha), or discourage tenancies by empowering tenants with protected rights on the land or the right to purchase in a specified period (e.g. West Bengal, Punjab, Haryana, Gujarat) or finally, operate a few restrictions on tenancies (e.g., Rajasthan, Tamil Nadu). Pursuing tenancy reform would enable rural households that are better suited for non-farm jobs to lease out their land for productive use, allowing a market-determined optimal farm holding size to develop, while allowing for rational utilization of labour and capital. Such reforms could include ensuring that the land owner is not dispossessed of his/her land during the leasing process, while prolonging the lease period to ten to fifteen years and removing any ceiling on the size of lease, enabling private players to invest in making farms more productive. These reforms would ensure that such farms revert automatically to the owners at the end of the lease period.

ANNEXURES

Trends in Wage Rates in Rural India

TABLE 104: STATE-WISE REAL WAGE RATES FOR PLOUGHING
OCCUPATIONS IN RURAL INDIA, 1998–2017, IN ₹[139,140]

PLOUGHING (MALE)	1998–99	1999–2000	2000–1	2001–2	2002–3	2003–4	2004–5	2005–6	2006–7	2007–8
ANDHRA PRADESH	94.5	89.81	97.26	97.47	100.26	95.35	93.02	100.9	105.96	114.89
ASSAM	104.46	104.21	106.86	108.57	101.24	105.62	100.72	97.39	98.62	100.95
BIHAR	71.56	75.73	85.18	91.14	92.4	93.67	92.41	91.56	91.69	93.34
GUJARAT	95.15	94.93	101.83	109.42	107.58	109.8	112.77	112.44	106.53	111.28
HARYANA	135.04	145.09	155.29	144.75	149	145.39	147.35	145.29	145.26	150.26
HIMACHAL PRADESH	143.07	139.54	153.75	156.9	151.81	172.07	178.71	168.82	182.26	206.74
JAMMU AND KASHMIR	154.62	151.19	180.66	188.29	184.25	183.33	184.24	182.92	162.75	164.42
KARNATAKA	80.12	83.38	98.02	99.05	95.8	92.98	90.35	95.81	92.96	96.56
KERALA	292.89	281.79	294.42	368.2	365.16	347.99	300.8	293.53	314.8	337.3
MADHYA PRADESH	76.98	76.37	75.93	82.29	81	84.13	81.36	77.06	74.76	78.17
MAHARASHTRA	94.38	100.05	111.21	107.51	109.71	105.64	99.64	99.19	102.91	107.58
MANIPUR	82.46	85.82	95.08	92.61	91.85	103.21	104.3	98.71	95.01	117.46
MEGHALAYA	93.45	91.2	90.33	91.48	107.14	124.97	121.68	117.63	112.33	107.56
ODISHA	67.78	63.18	78.88	88.38	91.24	84.84	88.64	87.35	81.08	78.08
PUNJAB	124.35	125.85	113.73	138.47	145.39		134.17	141.48	173.97	126.18
RAJASTHAN	145.47	136	156.54	167.95	153.71	148.09	148.12	135.26	127.06	153.49
TAMIL NADU	156.24	181.71	192.83	190.87	176.82	172.52	165.71	163.65	168.91	176.71
TRIPURA	69.45	74.87	78.05	86.27	88.12	105.24	97.95	108.62	109.5	103.05
UTTAR PRADESH	84.09	91.58	98.4	97.47	95.91	97.88	95.98	92	88.4	92.47
WEST BENGAL	101.23	117.74	120.19	120.58	129.76	132.52	124.5	138.94	140.15	136.78
INDIA	115.79	118.66	113.96	119.04	117.37	117.84	112.01	112.98	111.72	116.14

139 Note: CPI-AL (2009–10=100) is used as a deflator.
140 Wage Rates in Rural India, 1998–99 to 2016–17, Arindam Das and Yoshifumi Usami

TABLE 105: STATE-WISE REAL- WAGE RATES FOR PLOUGHING
OCCUPATIONS IN RURAL INDIA, 1998–2017, IN ₹[141,142]

PLOUGHING (MALE)	2008-9	2009-10	2010-11	2011-12	2012-13	2013-14	2014-15	2015-16	2016-17
ANDHRA PRADESH	129.25	140.01	166.42	171.85	184.8	172.74	173.02	178.34	178.28
ASSAM	98.6	97.48	108.43	115.22	120.98	141.11	162.51	164.68	170.73
BIHAR	96.17	107.09	114.4	126.44	144.85	151.88	162.79	178	181.24
GUJARAT	114.47	102.18	100.79	119.17	121.57	121.76	138.39	140.02	151.01
HARYANA	155.75	163.62	180.43	188.94	220.34	251.84	242.13	252	228.44
HIMACHAL PRADESH	219.95	202.4	205.4	224.04	233.39	263.25	269.89	284.11	291.75
JAMMU AND KASHMIR	162.26	173.15	193.32	197.45	215.05	239.72	255.02	260.33	263.68
KARNATAKA	101.14	98.22	113.41	126.62	149.87	171.68	174.35	171.95	168.2
KERALA	320.08	321.12	350.73	393.94	418.39	415.77	405.48	412.81	389.47
MADHYA PRADESH	82.03	77.58	82.98	91.76	98.8	116.02	127.73	130.66	138.1
MAHARASHTRA	108.92	108.57	120.74	138.64	152.37	168.22	158.29	154.6	161.19
MANIPUR	121.83	114.63	118.39	126.26	145.96	156.08	164.84	173.4	170.49
MEGHALAYA	98.11	99.25	103.76	101.7	113.73	140.96	162.13	160.19	173.23
ODISHA	85.12	98.38	120.75	131.58	116.92	120.4	137.81	143.3	155.97
PUNJAB	163.52	141.53	179.8	187.51	196.86	246.77	232.71	214.89	215.65
RAJASTHAN	149.18	138.77	131.75	168.72	177.49	190.55	186.15	170.28	161.71
TAMIL NADU	169.77	194.85	217.08	236.26	253.24	272.29	323.7	266.74	259.27
TRIPURA	112.5	109.82	99.39	97.63	116.21	135.77	134.05	101.51	145.63
UTTAR PRADESH	98.54	100.17	110.88	116.43	128.81	136.85	139.2	144.35	155.53
WEST BENGAL	134.98	133.17	140.33	161.84	166.25	189.59	192.73	207.79	206.51
INDIA	118.05	120.85	133.66	145.25	156.33	171.83	176.61	175.56	179.68

141 Note: CPI-AL (2009–10=100) is used as a deflator.
142 Wage Rates in Rural India, 1998–99 to 2016–17, Arindam Das and Yoshifumi Usami

REFERENCES

Anonymous (2011) Don't shoot the messenger, Economic and Political Weekly, XLIV (28):7-8

Bhagat, R.B. and Mohanty, S. (2009) Emerging pattern of urbanization and the contribution of migration in urban growth in India, Asian Population Studies, 5(1)

Dupont, V. (1992) Impact of In-Migration on Industrial Development, Economic and Political Weekly, XXVII(45): 2423-36

GoI (Government of India) (2008) (NREGA)-Report of the Second Year April 2006—March 2007, Ministry of Rural Development, New Delhi

Hirway, I. (2010) NREGA after four years: Building on experiences to move ahead, The Indian Journal of Labour Weekly, 53(1)

Jetley, S. (1987) Impact of male migration on rural females, Economic and Political Weekly, XXII(44):WS- 47-WS-54

Korra, V. (2011) Labour migration in mahabubnagar: Nature and characteristics, Economic and Political Weekly,XLVI(2): 67-70

Kundu, A. and Gupta, S. (1996) Migration, urbanisation and regional inequality, Economic and Political Weekly, XXI(46): 2005-08

Kundu, A. (2009) Exclusionary urbanisation in Asia: A macro overview, Economic and Political Weekly, 44(48):48-58

Kundu, Amitabh and Sarangi, Niranjan (2007) Migration, employment status and poverty, Economic and Political Weekly, 42(4): 299-306

Manocha, A.C. (1993) Pattern of urbanisation in Madhya Pradesh, Economic and Political Weekly, XXVIII(37): 1950-51

Paris, T., Singh, A., Luis, J., and Hossain, M. (2005) Labour outmigration, livelihood of rice farming households and women left behind, Economic and Political Weekly, 40(25): 2522-29

Rodgers, G. and Rodgers, J. (2011) Inclusive development? Migration, governance and social change in rural Bihar, Economic and Political Weekly,XLVI(23): 43-50

Sharan, V. (2009) Report on National Rural Employment Gurantee Scheme, SUPAUL, Under GOI –UN Joint Programme on Convergence, Source: http:// supaul. bih.nic.in/Report per cent20on per cent20NREGA, per cent20Supaul.pdf

Sharma, A. N. (2005) Agrarian relations and socioeconomic change in Bihar, Economic and Political Weekly, 40(10): 960-72

MGNREGA

Acharya, S. 2004. 'Guaranteeing Jobs or a Fiscal Crisis.' Business Standard November 30. http://www.business-standard. com/article/opinion/shankar-acharya -guaranteeing-jobs-or-fiscal-crisis -104113001072_1.html

Afridi, F., Mukhopadhyay A., and Sahoo S. 2012. 'Female Labour Force Participation and Child Education in India: The Effect of the National Rural Employment Guarantee Scheme.' In Institute for the Study of Labor (IZA) Discussion Paper No. 6593, IZA, Bonn

Afridi, F., Iversen V., and Sharan M.R. 2013. 'Women Political Leaders, Corruption and Learning.' In Institute for the Study of Labor (IZA) Working Paper No. 7212, IZA, Bonn

Afridi, F., and Iversen V. 2014. 'Social Audits and MGNREGA Delivery: Lessons from Andhra Pradesh.'

In India Policy Forum 2013-14, vol. 10, edited by Shekhar Shah, Barry Bosworth and Arvind Panagariya, 297-331. New Delhi: Sage Publications India

Agarwal, B. 1997. ''Bargaining' and Gender Relations: Within and Beyond the Household.' Feminist Economics 3(1):1-51

Ambas ta, P. 2012. 'MGNREGA and Rural Governance Reform: Growth with Inclusion through Panchayats.' In Right to Work and Rural India, edited by Ashok Pankaj, 335-368. New Delhi: Sage Publications India

ASER Centre. 2015. ASER 2014: Annual Status of Education Report. New Delhi: ASER Centre

Azam, M. 2012. 'The Impact of Indian Job Guarantee Scheme on Labor Market Outcomes: Evidence from a Natural Experiment.' In Institute for the Study of Labor (IZA) Discussion Paper Series No. 6548, IZA, Bonn

Bardhan, P., and Rudra A. 1978. 'Interlinkage of Land, Labour and Credit Relations: An Analysis of Village Survey Data in East India.' Economic and Political Weekly 13(6/7):367-384

Basu, K. 1984. 'Implicit Interest Rates, Usury and Isolation in Backward Agriculture.'

Cambridge Journal of Economics 8(2):145–159

Berg, E., Bhattacharyya S.S., Rajasekhar D., and Manjula R. 2012.'Can Rural Public Works Affect Agricultural Wages? Evidence from India.' Oxford: University of Oxford, Department of Economics

Besley, T. and Coate, S. 1989. 'Workfare vs welfare: incentive arguments for work requirements in poverty alleviation programs.' Warwick Economics Research Paper 314, University of Warwick Department of Economics, Coventry, England

Bhaduri, A. 1973. 'A Study in Agricultural Backwardness under Semi-Feudalism.' The Economic Journal 83(329):120–137

Bhagwati, J. N., and Chakravarty S. 1969. 'Contributions to Indian Economic Analysis: A Survey.' American Economic Review 59(4):1–73. Bhandari, Laveesh, and Mridusmita Bordoloi. 2006. 'Income Differentials and Returns to Education.' Economic and Political Weekly 41(36):3893–3900

Bhargava, A. K. 2014. 'The Impact of India's Rural Employment Guarantee on Demand for Agricultural Technology.' In International Food Policy Research Institute (IFPRI) Discussion Paper 01318, IFPRI, Washington, DC

Bhattarai, M., Ponnamaneni P., and Bantilan C. 2015. 'Has NREGA Helped in Reducing Debt Burden in Rural India?' Hyderabad, India: International Crops Research Institute for the Semi-Arid Tropics

Carswell, G., and De Neve G. 2014. 'MGNREGA in Tamil Nadu: A Story of Success and Transformation?' Journal of Agrarian Change 14(4):564–585

Chand, R. 2014. 'From Slowdown to Fast Track: Indian Agriculture Since 1995.' National Centre for Agricultural Economics and Policy Research Working Paper 01/2014, Indian Council of Agricultural Research, New Delhi. http://www. ncap.res.in/upload_files/Slowdown_final per cent20for per cent20printing.pdf

Chandrasekhar, S . 2011. 'Workers Commuting between the Rural and Urban: Estimates from NSSO Data.' Economic and Political Weekly 46(46):22–25

Chaudhuri, S. 2003. Assessing Vulnerability to Poverty: Concepts, Empirical Methods and Illustrative Examples. New York: Columbia University

Chopra, D. 2011. 'Interactions of 'Power' in the Making and Shaping of Social Policy.' Contemporary South Asia 19(2):153–171

Christiaensen, L., and Subbarao K. 2005. 'Toward an Understanding of Household Vulnerability in Rural Kenya.' Journal of African Economies 14(4):520–558.

Christiaensen, L. J.M., and Boisvert R.N. 2000. 'On Measuring Household Food Vulnerability: Case Evidence from Northern Mali.' In Applied Economics and Management Working Paper No. 2000-05, Cornell University, Ithaca, NY

Das, S., and Singh A. 2014. 'The Impact of Temporary Work Guarantee Programs on Children's Education: Evidence from the Mahatma Gandhi National Rural Employment Guarantee Act from India.' Working Paper 13-03, University of Wisconsin, Whitewater, WI

Das, U. 2014. 'Can the Rural Employment Guarantee Scheme Reduce Short-Term Migration: Evidence from West Bengal, India.' Mumbai: Indira Gandhi Institute of Development Research, 2015. 'Rationing and Accuracy of Targeting in India: The Case of the Rural Employment Guarantee Act.' Oxford Development Studies. DOI: 10.1080/13600818.2015.1042445

Datar, C. 2007. 'Failure of National Rural Employment Guarantee Scheme in Maharashtra' Economic and Political Weekly 42 (34):3454–3457

Datt, G., and Ravallion M. 1994. 'Transfer Benefits from Public–Works Employment: Evidence for Rural India.' Economic Journal 104(427):1346–1369.

Deininger, K., and Liu Y. 2013. 'Welfare and Poverty Impacts of India's National Rural Employment Guarantee Scheme: Evidence from Andhra Pradesh.' In International Food Policy Research Institute (IFPRI) Discussion Paper 1289, IFPRI, Washington, DC

Desai, S., and Dubey A. 2011. 'Caste in 21st Century India: Appendix II: MGNREGA's governance structure 181 Competing Narratives.' Economic and Political Weekly 46(11):40–49

Desai, S., Dubey A., Joshi B. L., Sen M., Shariff A., and Vanneman R., 2010. Human Development in India: Challenges for a Society in Transition. New Delhi: Oxford University Press

Dev, S. M. 2011. 'NREGS and Child Well Being.' In Indira Gandhi Institute of Development Research (IGIDR) Working Paper No. 2011-004, IGIDR, Mumbai

Dreze, J. 2011. 'Dantewada: Guarantee Withdrawn.' In The Battle for Employment Guarantee, edited by Reetika Khera, 220–232. New Delhi: Oxford University Press

Dreze, J., and Reetika Khera R. 2011. 'The Battle for Employment Guarantee.' In The Battle for Employment Guarantee, edited by Reetika Khera, 43–80. New Delhi: Oxford University Press, 2012.

'Regional Patterns of Human and Child Deprivation in India.' Economic and Political Weekly 47(39):42–49

Dreze, J., and Sen A. 2013b. An Uncertain Glory: India and Its Contradictions. Princeton: Princeton University Press

Dutta, P., Murgai R., Ravallion M., and De Valle D.W. 2012. 'Does India's Employment Guarantee Scheme Guarantee Employment?' Economic and Political Weekly 47(16):55–64. Right to Work?, 2014.

Assessing India's Employment Guarantee Scheme in Bihar. Washington, DC: World Bank. Economic and Political Weekly. 2014. 'Why This Attack on MGNREGA?' Economic and Political Weekly 49(43–44):2

Emad, A. 2013. 'Effects of Mahatma Gandhi National Rural Employment Guarantee Scheme on Expenditure in Rural Households.' Dissertation, Master of Arts, Department of Economics, Colgate University, Hamilton, NY

Foster, J., Greer J., and Erik Thorbecke. E. 1984. 'A Class of Decomposable Poverty Measures.' Econometrica 52(3):761–766

Gehrke, E. 2014. 'An Employment Guarantee as Risk Insurance? Assessing the Effects of the NREGS on Agricultural Production Decisions.' Bavarian Graduate Program in Economics Discussion Paper Series No. 152, German Development Institute, Bonn

Gertler, P. J., Martinez S., Premand P., Rawlings L.B., and Vermeersch. C. M. J. 2011. Impact Evaluation in Practice. Washington, DC: World Bank

Ghosh, J. 2009. 'Equity and Inclusion through Public Expenditure: The Potential of the NREGA.' Ministry of Rural Development/Indian Council of Agricultural Research International Conference on NREGA, New Delhi, January 21–22.

Government of India. 2001. Census of India 2001

Office of the Registrar General and Census Commissioner. New Delhi: Ministry of Home Affairs, 2005

'National Rural Employment Guarantee Act, 2005.' Gazette of India, Extraordinary, Part II. New Delhi: Ministry of Law and Justice, 2011

Census of India 2011. Office of the Registrar General and Census Commissioner. New Delhi: Ministry of Home Affairs, 2015

Socio-Economic and Caste Census 2011 for Rural India. New Delhi: Press Information Bureau, Ministry of Finance

Goyal, A., and Baikar A. K. 2015. Psychology, Cyclicality or Social Programmes: Rural Wages and Inflation Dynamics in India.' Economic and Political Weekly, 50(23): 116–125

Gulati, A., Jain S., and Satija N. 2013. 'Rising Farm Wages in India: The 'Pull' and 'Push' Factors.' In Commission for Agricultural Costs and Prices Discussion Paper No. 5, Commission for Agricultural Costs and Prices, New Delhi

Hill, Z. 2004. 'Reducing Attrition in Panel Studies in Developing Countries.' International Journal of Epidemiology 33:393–498

Himanshu, Mukhopadhyay A., and Sharan M R. 2015. 'NREGS in Rajasthan: Rationed Funds and Their Allocation across Villages.' Economic and Political Weekly 50(6):52–60

Imbert, C., and Papp. J. 2011a. 'Estimating Leakages in India's Employment Guarantee Using Household Survey Data.' New Delhi: RICE Institute. http://catalog.ihsn.org/ index. php/citations/9422. 2011b.

'Government Hiring and Labor Market Equilibrium: Evidence from India's Employment Guarantee.' Seventh Annual Conference on Economic Growth and Development, New Delhi, December 15–17, 2012.

'Equilibrium Distributional Impacts of Government. Employment Programs: Evidence from India's Employment Guarantee.' ParisJourdan Sciences Economiques Working Papers n2012-14, HAL. https://halshs.archives-ouvertes. fr/ halshs-00680451/document, 2013.

'Labor Market Effects of Social Programs: Evidence from India's Employment Guarantee.' Centre for the Study of African Economies WPS/2013-03, 2014.

'Short-Term Migration, Rural Workfare Programs and Urban Labor Markets: Evidence from India.' Oxford, England: Oxford University. http://www.cepr.org/sites/ default/files/Imbert. pdf. International Labour Office. 2009.

Bolsa Familia in Brazil: Context, Concept and Impacts. Geneva: International Labour Office Social Security Department

Jacoby, H. G. 2013. 'Food Prices, Wages, and

Welfare in Rural India.' Policy Research Working Paper WPS6412, World Bank, Washington, DC

Jha, R., Bhattacharyya S. , Gaiha R., and Shankar S. 2009. 'Capture of Anti-Poverty Programs: An Analysis of the National Rural Employment Guarantee Program in India.' Journal of Asian Economics 20(4):456–464

Jha, R., Gaiha R., and Pandey. M. K. 2011. 'Net Transfer Benefits under India's Rural Employment Guarantee Scheme.' Journal of Policy Modeling 34(2):296–311

Joshi, O., Desai S., Vanneman R., and Amaresh. D. 2015. 'MGNREGA: Employer of Last Resort?' India Human Development Surveys Working Paper 2015- 01. College Park, MD: University of Maryland

Kabeer, N. 1999. 'Resources, Agency, Achievements: Reflections on the Measurement of Women's Empowerment.' Development and Change 30(3):435–464

Kashyap, A. 2014. 'Aadhaar Linked MGNREGA: Looking Back on the Way Forward. A study on Implementational Challenges in Linking of Aadhaar to MGNREGA.' Paper presented at Conference on MGNREGA in India: Taking Stock, Looking Ahead, Mumbai, March 26–28

Khera, R., ed. 2011. The Battle for Employment Guarantee. New Delhi, India: Oxford University Press, 2011. 'Wage Payments: Live without Pay?' In The Battle for Employment Guarantee, edited by Reetika Khera, 250–256. New Delhi, India: Oxford University Press

Khera, R., and Nayak. N. 2009. 'Women workers and Appendix II: MGNREGA's governance structure 183 perceptions of the National Rural Employment Guarantee Act in India.' Paper presented at the FAO-IFAD-ILO Workshop on Gaps, Trends and Current Research in Gender Dimensions of Agricultural and Rural Employment: Differentiated Pathways Out of Poverty, Rome, April 2

Klonner, S., and Oldiges C. 2014. 'Can an Employment Guarantee Alleviate Poverty? Evidence from India's National Rural Employment Guarantee Act.' Heidelberg, Germany: University of Heidelberg. Krishnamurty, J. 2008. 'Indian Antecedents to Disguised Unemployment and Surplus Labour.' Indian Journal of Labour Economics 51(1):53–61

Kumar, P. 2010. Targeted Public Distribution System: Performance and Inefficiencies. New Delhi: Academic Foundation

Lanjouw, P., and Murgai R. 2009. 'Poverty Decline, Agricultural Wages, and Non-Farm Employment in Rural India, 1983–2004.' Policy Research Working Paper No. 4858, World Bank, Washington, DC

Ligon, E., and Schechter L. 2003. 'Measuring Vulnerability.' Economic Journal 113(486):c95–c102

Liu, Y., and Barrett C. B. 2013. 'Heterogeneous Pro-Poor Targeting in the National Rural Employment Guarantee Scheme.' Economic and Political Weekly 48(10):8

Mahajan, K. 2015. 'Farm Wages and Public Works: How Robust Are the Impacts of the National Rural Employment Guarantee Scheme?' Indian Growth and Development Review 8(1):19–72

Malla, M. A. 2014. 'NREGA in Kashmir: Opportunity for Social Protection Derailed.' Economic and Political Weekly 49(52):109–114

Mansuri, G., and Rao V. 2013. Localizing Development: Does Participation Work? Washington, DC: World Bank

Mathew, G. 1995. Status of Panchayati Raj in India, 1994. New Delhi: Institute of Social Sciences. Ministry of Rural Development, 2010.

Mahatma Gandhi National Rural Employment Guarantee Act, 2005—Report to the People. New Delhi: Government of India. 2nd February, 2006 through 2nd February, 2010, 2012.

Mahatma Gandhi National Rural Employment Guarantee Act, 2005—Report to the People. New Delhi: Government of India, 2012.

MGNREGA Sameeksha: An Anthology of Research Studies on the Mahatma Gandhi National Rural Employment Guarantee Act, 2005. New Delhi: Orient Black Swan, 2013.

Mahatma Gandhi National Rural Employment Guarantee Act, 2005—Report to the People. New Delhi: Government of India, 2013.

Mahatma Gandhi National Rural Employment Guarantee Act, 2005—Operational Guidelines. New Delhi: Government of India, 2014.

Mahatma Gandhi National Rural Employment Guarantee Act, 2005—Report to the People. New Delhi: Government of India, 2015.

Mahatma Gandhi National Rural Employment Guarantee Act, 2005—Report to the People. New Delhi: Government of India

Mukherjee, D., and Sinha U. B. 2011. 'Understanding NREGA: A Simple Theory and Some Facts.' In Centre for Development Economics

Working Paper 196, University of Delhi, New Delhi

Muralidharan, K., Paul Niehaus P., and Sandip Sukhtankar S. 2014. 'Building State Capacity Evidence from Biometric Smartcards in India.' In National Bureau of Economic Research

Working Paper No. 19999, NBER, Cambridge, MA. Nagarajan, Hari K., Hans BinswangerMkhize, and S. S. Meenakshisundaram, eds. 2014. Decentralization and Empowerment in Rural Development. New Delhi: Cambridge University Press

Narayan, D., ed. 2006. Measuring Empowerment: Cross-Disciplinary Perspectives. New Delhi: Oxford University Press

Narayanan, S. 2008. 'Employment Guarantee, Women's Work and Childcare.' Economic and Political Weekly 43(9):10–13

Narayanan, S., and Das U. 2014. 'Women Participation and Rationing in the Employment Guarantee Scheme.' Economic and Political Weekly 49(46):8

Niehaus, P., and Sukhtankar S. 2013. 'Corruption Dynamics: The Golden Goose Effect.'

American Economic Journal: Economic Policy 5(4): 230-269. NSSO (National Sample Survey Organization). 2006a

Employment and Unemployment Situation in India, 2004–05 (Part I). National Sample Survey Report 515.

New Delhi: Government of India. 2006b. Household Assets Holding, Indebtedness, Current Borrowings and Repayments of Social Groups in India, National Sample Survey Report 503.

New Delhi: Ministry of Statistics and Programme Implementation. 2011. Employment and Unemployment Situation in India, 2009–10, NSS 66th Round.

New Delhi: Government of India. 2013a. Key Indicators of Employment and Unemployment in India, 2011–12, NSS 68th Round.

New Delhi: Government of India. 2013b. Key Indicators of Consumption Expenditure in India 2011–12, NSS 68th Round. New Delhi: Government of India

Pankaj, A. K. 2008. Processes, Institutions and Mechanisms of Implementation of NREGA: Impact Assessment of Bihar and Jharkhand. Institute for Human Development. Delhi: Ministry of Rural Development and United Nations Development Programme.

ed. 2012. Right to Work and Rural India. New Delhi: Sage Publications India

Pankaj, A., and Tankha R. 2010. 'Empowerment Effects of NREGS on Women Workers: A Study in Four States.' Economic and Political Weekly 45(30):45–55

Raabe, K., Birner R., Sekher M., Gayathridevi K.G., Shilpi A., and Schiffer E. 2010. 'How to Overcome the Governance Challenges of Implementing NREGA: Insights from Bihar Using Process-Influence Mapping.' In International Food Policy Research Institute (IFPRI) Discussion Paper 00963, IFPRI, Washington, DC

Raghunathan, K., and Fields G. 2013. 'For Better or For Worse? The Effects of an Employment Guarantee in a Seasonal Agricultural Market.' Eighth Institute for the Study of Labor/ World Bank Conference on Employment and Development, Bonn, August 22–23, 2013

Rajan, R. 2014. 'Fighting Inflation.' Inaugural speech by Raghuram Rajan, Governor, Reserve Bank of India at FIMMDA-PDAI Annual Conference 2014, Mumbai, February 26, 2014

Ravallion, M. 2008. 'Evaluating AntiPoverty Programs.' In Handbook of Development Economics, vol. 4, edited by T. Paul Schultz and John Strauss, 3847–3894. Amsterdam: North Holland. 2013. 'The Idea of Antipoverty Policy.' In National Bureau of Appendix II: MGNREGA's governance structure 185 Economic Research (NBER) Working Paper Series, NBER, Cambridge, MA

Ravallion, M., and Wodon Q. 1999. 'Poor Areas, or Only Poor People?' Journal of Regional Science 39(4):689–711

Ravi, S., and Engler. M. 2014. 'Workfare as an Effective Way to Fight Poverty: The Case of India's NREGS.' World Development 67:57–71

Raychaudhuri, T, and Habib I. 1982. The Cambridge Economic History of India, vol. I. New York: Cambridge University Press

Rockwell, K., and Bennett. C. 2004. 'Targeting Outcomes of Programs: A Hierarchy for Targeting Outcomes and Evaluating Their Achievement.' Paper 48, Agricultural Leadership, Education and Communication Department, University of Nebraska, Lincoln

Rodgers, G. 2012. 'Interpreting the Right to Work: What Relevance for Poverty Reduction?' In Right to Work and Rural India, edited by Ashok Pankaj, 72–80. New Delhi: Sage Publications India

Roy, A., and Dey. N. 2011. 'The Wages of

Discontent.' In The Battle for Employment, edited by Reetika Khera, 250–256. New Delhi: Oxford University Press

Sahu, G. B., and Mahamallik M. 2011. 'Identification of the Poor: Errors of Exclusion and Inclusion.' Economic and Political Weekly 46(9):71–77

Saith, A. 2005. 'Poverty Lines versus the Poor, Method versus Meaning.' Economic and Political Weekly 40(43):4601–4610

Sarap, K. 1990. 'Interest Rates in Backward Agriculture: The Role of Economic and Extra-Economic Control.' Cambridge Journal of Economics 14(1):93–108

Sarris, A., and Karfakis P. 2006. 'Household Vulnerability in Rural Tanzania.' Centre for the Study of African Economies Conference on Reducing Poverty and Inequality: How Can Africa Be Included? Oxford, England, March 19–21

Schultz, T. W. 1967. 'Significance of India's 1918–19 Losses of Agricultural Labour—A Reply.' Economic Journal 77(305):161–163

Sen, A. 1981. Poverty and Famines: An Essay on Entitlement and Deprivation. Oxford: Clarendon Press

Shah, A. 2012. 'Assets Creation and Local Economy under MGNREGS: Scope and Challenges.' In Right to Work and Rural India, edited by Ashok Pankaj, 197–225. New Delhi: Sage Publications India

Shankar, S. Gaiha R., and Jha R. 2011. 'Information, Access and Targeting: The National Rural Employment Guarantee Scheme in India.' Oxford Development Studies 39(1):29

Subbarao, K., del Ninno C., Andrews C., and Rodriguez-Alas C. 2013. Public Works as a Safety Net: Design, Evidence and Implementation. Washington, DC: World Bank

Sudarshan, R. 2011. 'India's National Rural Employment Guarantee Act: Women's Participation and Impacts in Himachal Pradesh, Kerala and Rajasthan.' CSP Research Report 06, Institute of Development Studies, Sussex, England.

The Planning Commission. 1979. Report of the Task Force on Projections of Minimum Needs and Effective Consumption Demand. New Delhi:

Government of India. 2003. Identification of Districts for Wage and Self Employment Programmes. New Delhi: Government of India.

2009. Report of the Expert Group to Review the Methodology for Estimation of Poverty. New Delhi: Government of India.

2013. 'Press Note on Poverty Estimates, 2011 12.' New Delhi: Government of India

Thomas, D., Frankenberg E., and Smith J.P. 2001. 'Lost but Not Forgotten: Attrition and Follow-up in the Indonesia Family Life Survey.' Journal of Human Resources 36:556–592

Todd, P. E. 2008. 'Evaluation of Social Programs with Endogenous Program Placement and Selection of the Treated.' In Handbook of Development Economics, vol. 4, edited by T. Paul Schultz and John Strauss, 3847– 3894. Amsterdam: North Holland

Uppal, V. 2009. 'Is the NREGS a Safety Net for Children? Studying Access to the National Rural Employment Guarantee Scheme for Young Lives Families and Its Impact on Child Outcomes in Andhra Pradesh.' Dissertation, Master of Science in Economics for Development, University of Oxford

Wiseman, M. 1986. 'Welfare and Welfare Policy.' Focus 9(3):1–8. World Bank. 2001. World Development Report 2000: Attacking Poverty. New York: Oxford University Press. 2011. Social Protection for a Changing India. Washington, DC: World Bank

Zimmermann, L. 2012. 'Labor Market Impacts of a Large-Scale Public Works Program: Evidence from the Indian Employment Guarantee Scheme.'

Institute for the Study of Labor (IZA) Working Paper DP No. 6858, IZA, Bonn. http:// ftp.iza.org/ dp6858.pdf. 2013.

'Why Guarantee Employment? Evidence from a Large Indian Public-Works Program.' Ann Arbor, Michigan: University of Michigan. 2014.

'Public works programs in developing countries have the potential to reduce poverty.' IZA World of Labor (25):10.

CHAPTER VIII

ON RURAL EDUCATION

Sending a child to school is typically an expensive proposition, even in rural India. Firstly, there is the fees (if attending a private school). Then comes the requirement for stationery, uniforms and other costs for school participation. Then come indirect costs, like transportation, particularly for those living far from the school (those who can't afford a vehicular transport, rented or owned, have to send their children on a long jaunt to school every day). Even the time taken by a parent to walk their children to school in a village is an opportunity cost, albeit one that is difficult to quantify. There can be other discretionary costs as well—the poor teaching quality in many government schools can also force parents to pay for private tuition. In an ideal scenario, many of these costs are borne by the State, through direct or indirect mechanisms.

Furthermore, such costs rise even further as the child moves up in grades in school (the cost of schooling a lower secondary child is about 50 per cent more than a primary student).[1] Should such parents make a choice to send their children to private schools, the cost differential with a government school can be between six to nine times.[2] Surprisingly enough, the cost of schooling (including such things as examination fees, books, stationery, uniform and private tuition) can often be much higher than the cost of the school tuition.[3]

For a long time, in post-Independence India, politics at the grassroots level in rural districts was driven by the provision of irrigation and access to water. The mobilization of communities, based on common strands of ethnicity, caste or religion, manifested itself in a demand for greater subsidies for expanding irrigation or improving access to water through canals or groundwater. However,

---

1   NSS, 64th Round
2   NSSO, 2010
3   NSSO, 2008

as agriculture became increasingly unprofitable, particularly for marginal farmers, migration away from rural districts started. The demands of mobilized communities changed towards seeking better education and better access to jobs through reservation and budgetary allocations. Consider what happened in Karnataka—a district like Dakshin Kannada has had 53.1 per cent of its workers in agriculture in 2001 leaving the sector by 2011. Similar tales have been heard from Udupi (48.8 per cent), Tumakuru (23.4 per cent), Mandya (18.2 per cent) and Hassan (14.4 per cent). Meanwhile, the educational infrastructure in such districts has historically lagged behind those of coastal Karnataka. Aspiring politicians like C.P. Yogeshwar, from Channapatna in Ramanagara district, have positioned themselves as champions of rural education.[4]

In the most dismal area of Bundelkhand, the Dalit community's fight for access to education continues. Sometimes the lack of access is due to physical unavailability—the nearest school may be across a river, with no bridge in sight. The apathy of teachers can be a factor too—many teachers come for an hour or two and then leave when lunch is in sight, once the mid-day meal scheme has been administered. Caste is a key determinant there of how much someone can study. A schoolteacher can often refer to a Dalit child as a 'chamar' in the class environment; even Dalits officially working in such schools as cooks are often told to clean the toilets.[5] Given the extreme poverty, Dalit parents are often forced to stop the studies of their children and have them work in back-breaking tasks on the marginal fields, along with ragpicking. In 2014, 51 per cent of all Dalit children dropped out of elementary schools, compared to 37 per cent of children from non-adivasi or non-Dalit backgrounds.[6]

In 1920, the total number of primary schools in India was 1,42,203, with the majority in cities.[7] Adult illiteracy was quoted as 89 per cent for males and as much as 99 per cent for females. Only 2.8 per cent of the population underwent elementary education, with 4.5 per cent for boys and 0.95 per cent for girls. The majority of those being educated were in the lowest primary classes, with significant leakage between the first and the fourth classes.

In Punjab, the aggregate attendance in the first two classes was significantly higher than half the total attendance in institutions. The quality of these institutions was generally poor, with students considered to be badly educated. As the Director of

---

4   Pani, Narender; Bajari, Sumedha, Times of India, April 16, 2108

5   Khabhar Lahariya, Firstpost April 2018. Sourced from: https://www.firstpost.com/india/dalit-history-month-in-rural-bundelkhand-education-remains-a-dismal-scenario-for-dalit-children-4437809.html

6   Global Initiative on Out-of-School Children, Unicef, Jan 2014. Sourced from: http://idsn.org/wp-content/uploads/user_folder/pdf/New_files/India/2014/Unicef_Report_on_Out_of_School_Children_in_South_Asia_-_2014.pdf

7   The Progress of Education in India, Seventh Quinquennial Review

Public Instruction in Punjab noted: 'Is it a matter of wonder that habits of apathy and mental inertia are engendered, and that boys whose early education has begun on such lines should show a lack of keenness and originality when they reach the stage when such qualities are expected in their work?'[8]

The condition was far worse in the United Provinces (now Uttar Pradesh)—'out of thirteen and a half million adult males, only one million were shown by the Census as literate, and the test of literacy was so low that only a small proportion of this million could be assumed to possess even the lowest educational qualification for an intelligent electorate.' Infrastructure in such schools was woeful, as cited by the report of Progress of Education in India (1920), 'there was a real village school in session four hours a day for three full weeks. There were fourteen pupils, four of whom were very irregular in attendance. The materials used for all the improved and interesting methods were strictly limited to those obtainable in the villages. The teachers learned to prepare their own materials for handwork, arithmetic, reading, nature study etc.' Somehow, today's rural schools carry a faint echo of 1920.

It is not that we haven't made significant progress. According to the 2001 Census, ~26 per cent of all 18-year-olds in rural localities were enrolled in some educational programme. This had increased to 44 per cent by the 2011 Census; by 2017, this is estimated to have reached 70 per cent.[9] Even in village districts in Rajasthan, change has come through. While, in 2006, 30 per cent of all 14-year-old girls in rural Rajasthan were out of school, the picture now is different; nearly 15 per cent of girls are out of school. Literacy rates have seen a significant leap as well, while only 53.7 per cent of all females in Udaipur district were counted as literate in the Census in 2001, this had risen to above 65 per cent by 2011.

However, we have to go deeper into the details. Over 86 per cent of youth in the 14–18 age group are still educated within the formal education system (school or college).[10] Of this age group, more than half are enrolled in Class 10 or below, while a further 25 per cent are in Class 11 or 12, and just 6 per cent are enrolled in any undergraduate or degree courses. There is significant gender inequity within this cohort; by the age of 18, over 32 per cent of all girls are not enrolled in the formal education system compared to 28 per cent of all males. In addition, only 5 per cent of youth are taking some type of vocational training, typically undergoing three to six month courses. And the cruel fact is that over 42 per cent of all youth in the age group of 14–18 years are working, irrespective of their education enrolment status; amongst these, 79 per cent work primarily in agriculture, seeking to feed their families. Given this, the percentage of students enrolled in agricultural or veterinary

---

8   Village Education in India, 1920, The Report of a Commission of Inquiry, University of Calcutta
9   Beyond Basics, ASER, 2017
10   Beyond Basics, ASER, 2017

courses in India is less than 0.5 per cent of all the undergraduates—despite the need for significant productivity improvements in this arena.

And finally, over 77 per cent of all males and 89 per cent of all females do household chores, leaving them limited time to focus on education. Even excluding household work, there are plenty who have to do odd jobs to help supplement family income—over 38.5 per cent of all youth enrolled in a college or a school worked for more than half a month. Of these, 75.8 per cent worked in their own family's agricultural tasks. And 60.2 per cent of those who were not enrolled in any college or school whiled away their time working in odd jobs. Of these, 56.1 per cent worked on their own family's agricultural tasks.

Over 25 per cent of rural youth can't read a simple textbook while over 57 per cent of them are unable to solve basic mathematics problems.[11] Over half of rural males and nearly 3/4th of all rural females have never used the internet. Even among those who have had the good fortune of studying beyond Class 12, over half can't read a Class 2 text, while fewer than two-third would be able to do routine financial calculations. The quality of education, particularly in rural India, remains a matter of significant concern. Lack of accountability is one of the primary constraints for this poor quality. And this low quality is caused by systemic factors instead of managerial failures, necessitating the requirement for an institutional solution.

On the current growth path, India is likely to achieve universal primary education only in 2050, with lower secondary education coverage reaching 100 per cent by 2060 and universal upper secondary education finally reached in 2085. By then, our demographic dividend would be long gone and ageing.[12]

RURAL EDUCATION SYSTEM

Sangita Kashyap, a 46-year-old schoolteacher from Madhya Pradesh, who taught at the Government Ahilya Ashram School, is rather famous in and around Indore. She has been absent from work for the last 23 years of her 24-year-old career, working as a teacher in Dewas' Government Maharani Radhabai Kanya Vidyalaya. She was transferred to Ahilya in 1994, but she went on 'maternity leave' and has never reported for duty since then.[13] Such are the travails of our education system.

---

11 Beyond Basics, ASER, 2017

12 Sanghera, Tish, IndiaSpend, Business Standard, 14 March 2018

13 PTI, School teacher sets record for missing 23 of 24-year teaching career, Firstpost. Sourced from: http://

For anyone taking a walk in the countryside or in the village, the various public facilities are often descriptors of the state of development in the region. The local public school is often a set of rectangular rooms, filled with some ageing chairs, benches and blackboards, with books and other teaching apparatus conspicuous in their absence. Any such primary school can also be bereft of windows or even doors, with the walls crumbling, and the roof leaking. Classes, especially at the primary stage, are often overcrowded, with children crammed in, preventing teachers from offering any individual attention. As one goes up the classes, the size of the class grows smaller, as older children are often utilized by their parents in household and farming tasks, while other children often drop out because of boredom or unaffordability. The teachers themselves are no subject matter experts, often having just a bachelor's degree, and if lucky, some teacher training experience. Those who are the intellectual cream of their generation are unlikely to join this profession. Such teachers often have many grievances, ranging from low pay scales (despite regular revisions) to limited prestige. This lack of institutional infrastructure can create barriers to social mobility, a ceiling preventing those in rural areas from having access to information and opportunities that would better their lot. The statistics are dismal enough; only 56 per cent of schools in rural India have functional electricity and just 12 per cent have any functional computers to speak of.[14] While we speak of launching digital blackboards, only Delhi, Chandigarh, Lakshadweep and Daman & Diu have 100 per cent functional electricity in schools. This is despite the progress gained under centrally sponsored schemes like the Sarva Shiksha Abhiyan and the Rashtriya Madhyamik Shiksha Abhiyan.

There are of course, exceptions to such a situation—sometimes a progressive panchayat or group of parents seek quality in the education offered to their children, while sometimes proactive bureaucrats seek to improve education infrastructure. However, the arc of social progress is often elongated, with change coming slowly; many villagers would rather wait out an overbearing bureaucrat who wishes to change age-old social practices that prevent children (especially young girls) from seeking education. After all, the purpose of a modern school is antithetical in some ways to the rural economy—the school, as introduced by the colonial state and later by the government, sought to indoctrinate the young and have the brightest of them leave the village and seek their fortunes elsewhere. This purpose and its consequence will not change until the village economy becomes sustainable and offers better financial returns, stability and ease of work compared to urban jobs.

The challenge is also one of perception—rural education schools can seek to

---

www.firstpost.com/india/school-teacher-sets-record-for-missing-23-of-24-year-teaching-career-1652493.html

14   HRD Ministry, Indian Parliament, March 6, 2018

educate local children in skill sets necessary to survive in the rural economy, but as long as farming is considered to be a brutish existence, with marginal returns, such children will continue to migrate away. Until there is a shift away from unproductive subsistence farming to one where young adults can seek just rewards for their manual labour, education will continue to be seen as an avenue to escape the village economy.

All these factors highlight that our education system, particularly in rural areas, is broken. We need to attack this problem across the process, instituting a greater number of school inspections while improving school infrastructure and motivating teachers.

PROVISIONING EDUCATION

It's not that education has not been given its due since Independence. India enshrined universal education as a national policy goal in 1947, with legal sanction provided in the Constitution in Article 45 in 1950. The State was obligated to 'provide, within a period of ten years from the commencement of this constitution, for free and compulsory education for all children until they complete the age of fourteen years.' National leaders considered this a key priority with major debates focused on the intended aims and curriculum content. An urgent national need to improve educational infrastructure, in order to encourage economic development and establish constitutional values, was acknowledged.[15] The Five Year Plans sought to operationalize this mandate, with the First Five Year Plan focusing mostly on creation of more schools in order to assure universal provision. By the 1960s, this focus was aided by investments in additional arrangements (for schooling children who drop out for work). But the scale of the problem still remained.

By the mid-1960s, it was clear that opening more schools and programmes had not reduced dropout or repetition rates, leading to alternative measures being proposed, for example, a no-detention policy;[16] 1968 saw the first National Policy on Education passed, which led to the establishment of a common structure for formal education, along with a National Curriculum Framework. A National Survey of Education was conducted in 1971, leading to a full counting of habitations with schools, and the establishment of distance norms; a school was mandated within

---

15   Dyer, 2000
16   Govinda & Varghese, 1993: 2-3

1 km for any habitation with a population of 300 or more.[17] While the National Policy was supposed to be revised every five years, the next reassessment happened in 1986. Incremental progress was made; 94 per cent of the national population had access to a primary school within 1 km of their habitation.[18] However, with the government's focus on building new facilities, limited focus was available on ensuring appropriate maintenance and enhancement of existing facilities, leading to schools in increasingly poor conditions. While the austerity of school buildings was initially due to budgetary limitations, the lack of national standards for schools (defined teacher pay rate, pupil-teacher ratios, and building construction standards) also played a role.[19] By the 5th All India Educational Survey (AIES), serious overcrowding was prevalent across two-third of government primary schools. Meanwhile, at the same time, over 50 per cent of children enrolling in primary schools were failing to complete five years in school.[20]

In 1986, the National Policy on Education was modified, leading to a greater focus on improving school environments, instruction materials and teacher training. The Policy also sought to establish minimum learning levels through a combination of expected learning results and minimum competencies for each grade.[21] The Tenth Five Year Plan sought to achieve universal enrollment of all children (in schools or equivalent centres) by 2003, besides earmarking universal completion of minimum number of years in school—first five years of schooling by 2007 & the first eight years by 2010.[22] Needless to say, it didn't work out like that.

Currently, governance on education is shared by the centre and various states, along with regional and local administrative authorities (as a consequence of the reassignment of elementary education in 1976 in the Constituion as a concurrent subject).[23] This brings with it additional coordination problems; central government intervention is often construed as unnecessary, but offers national oversight to provide a system which is equitable across all states. The centre provides the policy and the funding but relies on the states for the implementation, and how the funding is utilized. Consequently, the education system infrastructure is distributed across all levels; the national level has institutions like the National University for Educational Planning & Administration (NUEPA), along with the National Council for Educational Research and Training (NCERT), the National Council for Teacher Education, the National Institute for Open Schooling, the Central

---

17 NCERT, 1965
18 NCERT, 1990
19 Dyer, 2000, 22
20 NCERT, 1990
21 Raina, 2002, 177
22 GOI, 2002, 30
23 Dyer, 2000, 18

Board of Secondary Education (CBSE), the All India Council for Technical Education (AICTE) and the University Grants Commission (UGC). Meanwhile, the states have their own State Council for Educational Research & Training, State Institute for Education Management & Training and various state universities. At lower levels, we have the District Institute of Education & Training (DIET) which focuses on primary teacher training. Such state, district and block level institutions were established under the District Primary Education Programme (DPEP), seeking to encourage local self-government and limit central government influence in education administration and teacher postings.[24,25]

Specialized projects were also launched to improve the state of education; a few examples are Operation Blackboard (1987-88), District Primary Education Programme (DPEP, 1994) and the Sarva Shiksha Abhiyan (SSA, 2001). The SSA is the most prominent of these, acting as an overarching umbrella under which different aspects of elementary education provision are sought to be improved.[26] There were other, even more tightly focused, national programmes like the Mid-Day Meal Programme (initiated in 1995), which sought to provide primary schoolchildren, living in economically deprived areas, with either a cooked meal or food rations at school each day. At the state level, we have examples of progressive programmes initiated by state governments. In Rajasthan, the Lok Jumbish project, established in 1992, with support from the Swedish International Development Cooperation Agency, spread from a few blocks to over 100 within a decade, while being critically acclaimed for using participatory village mapping techniques, and flexible local planning strategies.[27]

However, large government initiatives, like Operation Blackboard and DPEP, have faced implementation issues, given their large-scale and insufficient attention provided to diverse contexts, circumstances and challenges in different regions and communities.[28,29] Most programmes are finely announced, with their own implementation and monitoring bureaucracy, but end up being absorbed within existing government bureaucracy within a few years. Such projects don't typically last long, leading to little change within the system, while demotivating people working in bureaucratic institutions and stymieing real structural reforms in education.

Currently, India's government spends ~₹12,500 annually per enrolled student (as

---

24 Aggarwal, 1998
25 Dyer, 2005, 140
26 GOI, 2002, 30
27 Raina, 2002, 116
28 Dyer, 2000
29 Aggarwal, 1998

of 2014),[30] spent across 1.5 million schools, with an annual enrolment of over 260 million students. However, despite establishing so many schools (comprising over 75 per cent of the total number of schools in the country), only 57 per cent of students go to government schools.[31] The private sector's share of primary enrolments has in fact increased from 25 per cent in 2006 to 38 per cent in 2016. In comparison, the world average for the private sector's share of such enrolments tends to be around 13.4 per cent in primary schools and 25 per cent in secondary schools. We spend 5.2 per cent of the world's education budget on 20 per cent of the world's population, and then are surprised by our sub-par performance in education. Such spending has consequences. Parents and children increasingly don't rely on the educational system—nearly 40 per cent of students attending government schools go for private tuition.

BARRIERS TO SCHOOL EDUCATION

Rural households tend to weigh a variety of factors in their preference for sending their children to school on a regular basis. Such factors can be categorized in numerous ways—socio-cultural, economic, supply side and systemic. Social mores and aspirations can play a significant role in restricting schooling for students in rural India. A feudalistic outlook, as tends to prevail in Indian villages, can restrict the mobility of girls for religious or social reasons, preventing them from attending school. In a situation where child marriage is prevalent, the possession of education can actually be a negative asset in the marriage market for a girl child. Girls are often married early to much older men, and find themselves in new households with a range of responsibilities, with little to no education.[32] In many areas in northern India, dowry rates increase with age, increasing the incentive to marry off girls early.[33] As a consequence, many rural families, across religious groups, tend to have their girls withdrawn from schooling and married off early.[34,35] In the 1980s, this was especially prevalent—studies in South India have highlighted that over 50 per cent of girls were typically taken out of school for being married off once they reached menarche.[36]

---

30   U-DISE report, 2014; World Bank Database; MHRD Report
31   U-DISE report, 2016
32   Mathur et al, 2003
33   Amin, Huq, 2008
34   Jha, Jhingran, 2005
35   Hasan, Menon, 2004
36   Caldwell, Reddy, 1983

In addition, patriarchy, combined with the purdah system, can lead to young girls being secluded, and barred from schooling.[37] In other areas, conservative mores amongst tribal groups and religious sects may also lead to parents avoiding sending girls to schools, to avert breaking religious taboos.[38] This is especially the case when schools are far away from home, with the resulting journey considered unsafe for girls—partly due to the risk of sexual harassment. Such public sexual harassment can have deleterious consequences, leading to high rates of dropout, particularly for older girls.[39,40] Domestic violence, on the home front, may also impact the cognitive abilities of young children, along with their psychological development, leading to poor concentration and focus in studies.[41] Children suffering undernutrition are more likely to start school later than their peers, and to perform poorly, when they do join.[42,43] In addition, children subject to social neglect and abuse are often excluded from school, their unstable environment removes incentives for attending school, with little support from adults who are concerned about their future prospects.[44,45] Such conditions often lead to low cognitive skills and learning abilities, along with causing lack of concentration in school.[46] Consequently, low learning productivity can lead to lower work productivity and earnings later in life.[47]

Consider the economic factor. Financing education is a significant constraint for parents in rural India, with parents of out-of-school children citing finance as the primary reason for the non-participation of their children in local schools.[48] There are opportunity costs—the cost of losing out on the revenue that a child can generate in labour, on their own field or shop, or in seasonal work, in cash or kind—when sending them to school. For many families, this can be a substantial sum or task. In addition, families in rural India don't necessarily have a lot of liquidity, most of their wealth can often be tied up in fixed assets (land, cattle, etc.), which cannot be easily converted into cash to pay for schooling costs. Such labour market failures can often lead to rural families having to make a trade-off between schooling and consumption or production.[49] In a situation where a rural household cannot hire a local labourer for cheap or substitute the children's efforts by the

---

37   Mandelbaum, 2010
38   Zafar, 2010
39   Action Aid, 1999
40   Bandopadhyay, Subramanian, 2008
41   Bandopadhyay, Subramanian, 2008
42   Alderman et al, 1997
43   Huda et al, 1999
44   Giani, 2006
45   Conticini & Hulme, 2006
46   IFPRI, 2001
47   Glewwe, Jacoby and King, 2001
48   Campe, 2009, 2006
49   OPM, 2010

use of another relative, they may be forced to utilize their children for household labour and withdraw them from school. Such tendencies can be exacerbated by economic shocks (family incidents like death, illness, accidents, disabilities, marriage in the family, etc). Children who hail from families that are associated with seasonal migration for work are particularly susceptible to disrupted education; their families typically have uncertain and fluctuating household incomes, making decisions about schooling difficult. Natural disasters or forced displacement can make this trend worse. In places like Kerala and Sri Lanka, the migration of fathers or even mothers to the Middle East for work can also have an adverse impact on attendance of school.[50]

Such child labour may not simply be due to the usual factors; low wages in the adult labour market, loss of a regular job, crop failure or simply seasonal agricultural work at home. Such work may also help in building up skills for them to serve as alternatives to their parents in regular labour work, or to showcase skill sets suitable for an early marriage. Social mores may also make such child labour more common, especially in situations where a family has taken a loan from a moneylender (the child becomes a bonded labour) or when children are compelled to work as the entire family is a sharecropper for the landlord. Moreover, household wealth can have a significant linkage with child nutrition, with children from poor families more likely to be undernourished, which can eventually have a deleterious impact on learning outcomes. Such children are liable to suffer from a variety of health problems, courtesy of their standard of living (unsafe water, lack of sanitation, etc.), reducing the potential gains from schooling.[51] Labour market aspirations can be shaped by the presence or absence of suitable role models in the local society as well.[52] Formal sector opportunities can also be limited by discriminatory social practices, with high unemployment rates amongst low-caste communities reducing their incentive to send children to schools.[53] Such cost-related barriers may lead to self-selection, with children from low-income backgrounds being sent to low-quality schools—with lower costs, but also far poorer learning outcomes and higher rates of drop-out.

On the supply side, ensuring an adequate ratio between the number of schools available and the size of cohort is a hard ask. India's overall classroom supply is mostly adequate at the primary level (pupil-classroom ratios are in the range of ~32:1) but at a secondary level such ratios worsen, exacerbated by a shortage of land supply.[54] While double shifting of classrooms is often used to overcome

50   Pinto-Jayawardena, 2006
51   Jha, Jinghran, 2005
52   Hossain, Tavakoli, 2008
53   Sachar Committee Report, 2006
54   14th JRM, 2011

crowding, such practices can often eat into lesson time as well. Meanwhile, the distribution of schools can be skewed in certain regions, leaving some communities significantly underserved. Moreover, in remote areas, teachers can often refuse to serve (particularly if they don't hail from the region). Such issues can make teacher deployment inefficient and lead to shortages in key remote districts.[55] In addition, there are few, if any, mechanisms for parents in rural India to hold teachers and school administrators to account for the poor quality of teaching that prevails in most government schools.[56] The lack of school facilities is often another significant barrier. Many girls tend to drop out due to a lack of adequate sanitation in their schools,[57] while others reduce their attendance due to a lack of resources for menstrual hygiene management.[58]

Another study has highlighted that over 50 per cent of girls interviewed did not attend school during menstruation given the lack of private facilities for cleaning and washing.[59] Even simple things like textbook content can have a significant impact. Most class textbooks are crafted without considering the context of rural children, and are not age-appropriate.[60]

The use of non-vernacular language as the medium of instruction in rural schools is also a significant barrier to learning. Such differences in learning style can have a significant impact on student attendance.[61] The teaching process in India is ripe for criticism, with teachers in government schools often putting relatively little effort in helping children who are lagging behind.[62] There is little emphasis on building problem solving skills, with an emphasis instead on rote learning and an engendered reliance on textbooks.[63]

There are other supply side barriers to access as well. The need for official documentation (ration card, birth certificate, etc.), for students can be a significant deterrent, forcing households to limit their school choice given admission policies. Marginalized and displaced families, who may have lost access to crucial documents, are very susceptible to such administrative barriers. In addition, any administrative procedures that require illiterate parents in rural India to fill up forms are a significant barrier.

---

55   FMRP, 2006
56   Hossain, Tavakoli, 2008
57   WaterAid, 2008
58   Ten, 2007
59   Fernandes, 2008
60   Probe, 1999
61   SAFED, 2011
62   Campe, 2005
63   Probe, 1999

Finally, systemic barriers can also prevail. While education budgets vary year to year at the centre and state levels, the composition of such budgets can be skewed towards teacher salaries, leaving little for non-salary related overheads like maintenance of school infrastructure. Meanwhile, strategic planning for education at the centre is often delinked from actual budgetary allocations, with significant educational commitments not reflected in actual budgets. Poor financial management can exacerbate such a situation; delays, due to cash rationing and administrative complexity, can add on. Counterintuitively, this can also lead to underutilization of allocated budgets, as school administrators fail to access funds.

RURAL EDUCATION INFRASTRUCTURE

A typical school in Bikaner district in Rajasthan often has two classes conducted at the same time in a single room; with children sitting in rows, one group facing one way, towards a wall with a blackboard, and another the other way. Sometimes, lessons can be mixed up, making it hard for any student to understand arithmetic over the din of learning history. In Varanasi, news reports highlight schools which have rooms made of brick and mortar, with metal roofs—when summer approaches, the roof can become heated, making the room stifling; when the monsoon comes through, the rain falling on the roof is able to drown out the voices of teachers. When students skip a class, the teacher may not even come to know.

Ratan Singh works in his family's gutka shop on the rural outskirts of Barmer in Rajasthan. He started working there when he was 10 years old, and has grown up as the shop has expanded; now serving tea and samosas too. As desert sand heats up to 48°C, the demand for condiments and chai rises. He has studied at the same time as well in the local government school, while seeking coaching for PSU examinations in a local centre. His life is comfortable in rural Barmer, as he mingles with family, siblings and local cousins. But something remains missing. The lack of facilities in Barmer compares woefully with the dreams shown on the television relating to the large metros. Now that he is in college, he drives his scooter 25 km every day, to get an opportunity for education in his B.Com course. For him, this is his get-out-ticket, but so far, his aspirations remain the same as that for most rural youth: the Army.

An ideal rural education system should have three components: the teacher, the student and the underlying infrastructure. For any rural student, there are significant challenges to education—there is limited transport to schools that are typically situated far away from their villages, while electricity can be a significant constraint to enable them to study (instead of seeking to study under streetlights). Meanwhile, the lack of good educational materials, along with the lack of a full-blown laboratory or library facilities, can limit exposure. Finally, any education should be offered in the learner's local language.

AGRICULTURAL EDUCATION

Let's consider a small, albeit relevant, segment of this rural education infrastructure. India faced food scarcity in the early 1960s, constrained by its Ship to Mouth Situation. India's agricultural education was significantly augmented during the Green Revolution, with the establishment of agricultural universities on the pattern of the Land Grant University pattern.[64] By 1958, the Indian Agricultural Research Institute (IARI) had reorganized its post-graduate school on a similar pattern, qualifying as a Deemed University. A state agricultural university was first established in Pantnagar, now termed the Govind Ballabh Pant University of Agriculture & Technology, with S. Radhakrishnan exhorting India's leaders to not fail its farmers—'We can't blame the farmers, we can't blame the land and we can't blame anything. We, who are leaders of the country, must not fail the farmers. We must try to bring to them the most up-to-date knowledge. If we do that, I have no doubt on the discontinuance of the import of food grains from abroad.'

Agricultural education in India itself has since expanded significantly, particularly in the past two decades, rising from 35 agricultural universities in 2000, to over 75 in 2018 (of this, 15 are focused primarily on veterinary sciences while five focus on horticulture and three on fisheries). These universities have over 159 private agricultural colleges affiliated to them. And yet, just 58 of these universities, as of early 2018, had accreditation from the Indian Council of Agricultural Research (ICAR), while just eight of these universities were considered in the Ministry of Human Resource Development's National Institutional Ranking Framework in 2017. When we consider the quality of the graduates from these universities, about 20 per cent (of the over 30,000) of graduates are able to clear the ICAR's National Eligibility Test (a test that would open doors for them for recruitment as lecturers). Anecdotal evidence suggests that our agricultural science graduates have limited domain knowledge, along with few, if any, transferable skills, which would

---

64   5th Dean's Committee Report, ICAR

be relevant to the market.[65]

Beyond this, the value of agriculture, as an educational subject, has declined, particularly at state levels. This has its impact on gross enrolment levels, with agricultural courses seeing a gross enrolment ratio of only 0.03 per cent, highlighting the limited employability of its graduates. There is significant non-uniformity and dilution of standards, with universities and colleges consistently starved of investment and regulatory review. There are fewer and fewer faculty members, with limited faculty available in emerging areas like informatics and communication. There remains significant disconnect between the type of agricultural education provided, the needs for employment and limited requirement of industries? There is limited inclusion of basic sciences in agricultural curricula, which, combined with outdated curriculum delivery mechanisms, has led to increasing irrelevance of such courses.

The ICAR prescribes a minimum requirement of 75 acres in a plains region and 40 acres in a hilly/island/coastal region for an agricultural college, and yet, many agricultural colleges suffice with just 25–35 acres. The nature of the ICAR's standards being a recommendation and not a mandate, ensure that colleges can easily offer less than the barest minimum and yet offer degrees. New universities are increasingly launched without adequate funding being provided, while other agricultural universities are split to achieve regional diversification—all a case of poor resource planning. There is significant lack of evaluation, monitoring, impact assessment, accountability and incentive systems. ICAR needs to be empowered as the sole body for the regulation of agricultural education, in a manner similar to the Medical, Dental and Bar Councils of India, incorporating it through an Act of Parliament. It needs to be allowed to enforce minimum standards for the colleges and universities, with accreditation made mandatory. The government's initiative to implement the recommendations of the 5th Dean Committee Report in all agricultural universities, with all graduate-level courses in agriculture and related subjects declared as professional courses, is a promising step towards improving the opportunities available for agricultural graduates.[66]

We also need to pair promising agricultural universities with world-class technical institutes. In the 1960s, universities like G.B Pant University of Agriculture, Acharya N. G. Ranga Agricultural University and Orissa University of Agriculture & Technology were paired with leading American land grant universities to help build the quality of teachers and curricula. Steps taken by the Indian Council of Agricultural Research to increase the quality of education in this field, in regard

---

65   Ibid
66   5th Dean's Committee Report, ICAR

to such issues, are quite welcome. Most agricultural faculty currently have little to no exposure to upcoming research areas in agriculture technology, including areas like agri-informatics and nano-technology applications in agriculture. Most state agricultural universities currently remain dependent on government funding, with few if any internal resource generation measures like advisory services or professional courses.[67]

In addition, further reforms are needed to institutionalize transparency and autonomy in such agricultural institutes, with accountable flow of funds, a transparent examination system and judicious allocation of resources. Central and state assistance to such agricultural universities needs to be increased, with a focus on support for new construction. In particular, there needs to be a minimum grant of ₹4 crore for the construction of student hostels, with the quantum rising to ₹5 crore in difficult terrain and the Northeast. As the number of students in agricultural education rises, it is imperative that there be adequate infrastructure built for their residential accommodation. There needs to be additional financing provided for the construction of modernised classrooms and examination halls, along with a provision of atleast ₹10 lakh per university for faculty and student amenities (e.g. healthcare facilities, cultural activities, sports, etc). While most state agricultural universities have access to electricity, they tend to suffer from a serious deficiency in electricity supply due to poor electricity infrastructure. Similarly, many of these universities have poor road connectivity. Such connectivity issues need prompt resolution at the state level.

In addition, there needs to be greater focus on upgrading or replacing facilities, including equipment in such colleges and universities, with annual maintenance contracts requiring audits and renewal. There needs to be significant budgetary allocation provided for curriculum development and delivery, along with strengthening of existing undergraduate and post-graduate teaching (by updating the professional and technical competence of professional and administrative staff).

---

67   Ibid

TEACHERS

Consider teacher absenteeism. A recent World Bank study highlighted that 25 per cent of teachers were absent from school, while only about 50 per cent were actually teaching.[68] And such absence rates can have significant variance, ranging from 25 per cent in Maharashtra to 42 per cent in Jharkhand. Best practice rates internationally for teacher absenteeism are typically between 5 per cent and 10 per cent, India's performance marks it out between Uganda and Bangladesh, a sub-optimal performance for a nation seeking to capitalize on its demographic dividend.

Such absentee rates are usually higher in low-income states, with a two-fold increase in per capita state income corresponding to a 7.2 per cent lower degree of predicted absence.[69] When breaking down absentee statistics, it was also determined that official non-teaching duties accounted for only 4 per cent of total absences, while an estimated 8-10 per cent of absence could be attributed to leaves and official puposes. While dated, a World Bank study from 2004 also highlights that this absentee rate is higher as one goes up the hierarchy. Heads of public schools had an absentee rate of 30.2 per cent, while deputy heads had a rate of 22.2 per cent and contract/informal employees had a rate of 24 per cent in 2004.[70] Effectively, the higher paid teachers are the ones who are absent more. And it's not that paying teachers well is an incentive to improve attendance; the study found that more educated and experienced teachers who were paid more were at fault with the same frequency. Perhaps this is also because of innate conservatism of our education bureaucracy; teachers have little risk of being fired for absence.

The same World Bank study highlights that only 1 head teacher in 3,000 schools surveyed reported firing a teacher for repeated absence. Only poor working conditions and the possibility of receiving an undesirable posting are significant constraints for such behaviour, along with the inherent limitations of the school inspector system. The better the infrastructure of a school, the lower the teacher absenteeism.[71] And the more monitoring of the attendance of teachers, the greater the decline in teacher absence; a study by MIT, conducted in 2004, highlighted that teacher absence reduced by 21 per cent when CCTV cameras were used to

68   Teacher Absence in India, 2004, World Bank. Sourced from: http://siteresources.worldbank.org/DEC/Resources/36660_Teacher_absence_in_India_EEA_9_15_04_-_South_Asia_session_version.pdf

69   Kremer, Michael, Chaudhary, Nazmul, Rogers, F.Halsey, Muralidharan, Karthik, Hammer, Jeffrey, Teacher Absence in India, Journal of the European Economic Association, 2004, World Bank. Sourced from: http://siteresources.worldbank.org/DEC/Resources/36660_Teacher_absence_in_India_EEA_9_15_04_-_South_Asia_session_version.pdf

70   Teacher Absence in India, 2004, World Bank. Sourced from: http://siteresources.worldbank.org/DEC/Resources/36660_Teacher_absence_in_India_EEA_9_15_04_-_South_Asia_session_version.pdf

71   Teacher Absence in India, 2004, World Bank. Sourced from: http://siteresources.worldbank.org/DEC/Resources/36660_Teacher_absence_in_India_EEA_9_15_04_-_South_Asia_session_version.pdf

monitor and pay teachers according to their actual attendance.[72] Such absenteeism has huge fiscal costs, estimated to be ₹7,200 crore to ₹8,400 crore across 19 major states.[73]

The chronic shortage of teachers means that multi-grade teaching is a predominant feature in many primary schools, particularly in areas with low population density. Many states have sought to deal with teacher shortages by appointing untrained individuals or less trained teachers, also termed para-teachers, or shiksha karmis. Such contract workers can have a limited impact, given the limited training provided to such individuals.[74]

Meanwhile teacher recruitment and performance remains dismal particularly at the primary level. This is partly structural, primary schoolteachers receive a different kind of training and qualification than their secondary school equivalents. While secondary schoolteachers are required to have a B.Ed degree, primary teacher training is typically conducted by the State Councils of Educational Research & Training and District Institutes of Education & Training. Such primary teachers, with limited education and general lack of a university degree, also have constraints in future progression; they cannot move up to primary education administration or policymaking, offering them little room for professional advancement. Such administrative posts are typically occupied by secondary education teachers who have limited understanding of the challenges faced by primary schoolteachers.

Inspections have a role to play here—schools that had been inspected within a 3-month period reported a 2 per cent less chance of absenteeism.[75] This absenteeism imposes significant social costs, a study has pegged this cost at more than $1.5 billion annually in wages.[76] But more than that, this has an impact on the quality of education. A 10 per cent increase in teacher absence is typically associated with a 1.8 per cent decline in student attendance. As marginal students drop out of schools due to an absence of teachers, the diversity of classes changes, while other students are spurred to move to private schools. We end up wasting a considerable portion of our education budget, with ~25 per cent of government teachers absent on an average day, and only ~50 per cent actually teaching.

---

72 MIT, 2010. Sourced: http://economics.mit.edu/files/5995

73 The Fiscal Cost of Weak Governance, Evidence from Teacher Absence in India. Muralidharan, K., Das, Jishnu, Holla, Akala, Mohpal, Aakash, Policy Research Working Paper 7579, World Bank

74 Govinda, Josephine, 2004

75 Teacher Absence in India, 2004, World Bank. Sourced from: http://siteresources.worldbank.org/DEC/Resources/36660_Teacher_absence_in_India_EEA_9_15_04_-_South_Asia_session_version.pdf

76 Muralidharan, K., Das, Jishnu, Holla, Akala, Mohpal, Aakash, Fiscal Cost of Weak Governance, Working Paper 20299, National Bureau of Economic Research, July 2014. Sourced from: http://econweb.ucsd.edu/~kamurali/papers/Working%20Papers/Fiscal%20Cost%20of%20Weak%20Governance%20(NBER%20WP%2020299).pdf

The poor quality of teachers is reflected in other metrics too. The performance of applicants in teacher eligibility tests (with pass rates typically between 1–11 per cent) highlights that applicants have inadequate training during their B.Ed and D.Ed courses. Meanwhile, only 55 per cent of contractual teachers have any teaching qualifications, while continuous training to enhance the skills of teachers is practically non-existent. Even more worrying, the number of teachers is still limited, with 8 per cent of existing elementary schools being single-teacher schools, while over 5 lakh sanctioned teaching posts stood vacant in early 2016.[77,78]

QUALITY OF EDUCATION

Ramesh lives in a small village near Jhansi in Uttar Pradesh and is currently pursuing electrician training at an ITI near his village. He didn't choose this course, but simply followed what his peers in the village were doing. A similar paucity of information exists for him with respect to opportunities post obtaining his qualification. He has no idea about potential placements or job opportunities. He is now planning to pursue a B.Com course, while simultaneously seeking to join the Army. When asked about conducting information research on the internet, pat comes the reply: he uses his friend's mobile phone for watching cricket or Bollywood videos. Anything beyond that never really occurred to him. Other than studying at the ITI or working out to join the Army, Ramesh focuses on helping with agricultural tasks at the local family farm. While farming is in his genes, he does not want to be a farmer in the future.

This paucity of information and educational quality is reflected in other ways too. A survey conducted by Annual Status of Education Report (ASER) in 2017 highlighted that only 48.7 per cent of youth can identify their own state on a map. Only 43.1 per cent of all youth can perform division; a reflection of the quality of our education in mathematics. When you take this further, only 37.7 per cent of youth can apply a discount on their purchases; similarly, 46.6 per cent of youth cannot read and understand even 3 out of 4 instructions in their native language. Just 39.7 per cent of all youth can measure the length of a pencil using a ruler, while just 38.6 per cent is able to calculate time in a simple problem. Finally, only 54.6 per cent of those youth who can read words in English are able to explain their meaning.

---

77 'Teaching teachers, the great challenge for India's education system', Hindustan Times, 2016
78 'Restoring dignity to the teaching profession in India', Ideas for India, 2014

This is despite exposure from other information sources. Over 72.6 per cent of youth surveyed had used a mobile phone in the past week; about 28 per cent had used the internet and about 25.5 per cent had used a computer in the past week. Over 85 per cent were exposed to television within the past week surveyed, while 45.8 per cent had access to a radio broadcast over the past week.

This has an impact on their aspirations. Most rural male youth typically aspire to join the Army, the police, or become an engineer; females seek to become teachers, doctors or nurses. A government job was cited as the aspiration to strive for by 12.8 per cent of male youth surveyed, along with 9.3 per cent of female youth surveyed. Only 1.2 per cent of youth wanted to work in agriculture, a stark reminder of the fragility of the rural economy. Very few wanted to work in the same occupation as their parents.

India faces a key challenge in enabling access to and equity in education, particularly in rural villages. While the Sarva Shiksha Abhiyan (2001) and the Right to Education Act (2009) imposed legal obligations on the government at both state and central level to ensure the provision of elementary education to every child between the ages of 6 and 14, equity in educational opportunities remains a concern.

ENROLMENT

Annual Status of Education Report's (ASER's) 2016 survey covering 589 rural districts, across 17,743 villages, including 350,232 households and 562,305 children in the age group of 3–16 years reports halting progress on enrolment rates. While enrolment increased for all age groups between 2014 and 2016, certain states have had a rollback, with the proportion of out-of-school children, between the age of 6 and 14, rising during the same period (e.g. Madhya Pradesh from 3.4 per cent to 4.4 per cent; in Chhattisgarh from 2 per cent to 2.8 per cent; in Uttar Pradesh from 4.9 per cent to 5.3 per cent). At 14 years of age, 5.3 per cent of youth are not enrolled in the public education system; by the age of 15 this rises to 8 per cent, and by the age of 17, this pushes up to 20.7 per cent.

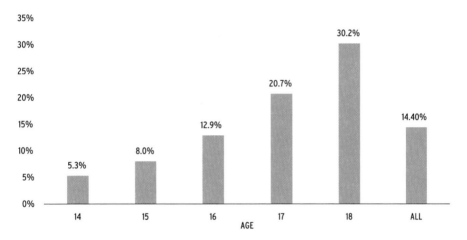

FIGURE 197: PER CENT OF YOUTH NOT ENROLLED IN SCHOOL OR COLLEGE, 2017[79]

When we consider the number of youth with schooling completed, 80.7 per cent of male youth had completed 8 or more years of schooling, while 81.3 per cent of females had done so as well.

When we consider enrolment statistics for private schools, the picture is similarly dismal—with stagnant private school enrolment between 2014 and 2016. The proportion of children between the ages of 6 and 14 who were enrolled in private schools was unchanged in 2016 from the 30.8 per cent in 2014. Kerala and Gujarat, meanwhile, have shown a significant increase in government school enrolment, particularly with regards to 2014 levels. The proportion of children (aged 11–14) increased from 40.6 per cent in 2014 to 49.9 per cent in 2016. Private school enrolment, meanwhile, had three states showcasing substantial improvement;

Uttarakhand (jumping from 37.5 per cent to 41.6 per cent), Arunachal Pradesh (shifting from 24.4 per cent to 29.5 per cent) and Assam (moving from 17.3 per cent to 22 per cent).

This enrolment gap, particularly between primary and secondary levels, matters, as it implies that a large number of students in primary school are not progressing through the educational system to the higher grades, with dropout rates particularly elevated in disadvantaged groups. The primary level dropout rate for girls in Hyderabad district was 7.95 per cent in 2014, but those for ST girls was 57.18 per cent, both significantly higher than the national average. In overall terms, while 97 per cent of targeted children are enrolled in primary schools, this drops to 78.5 per cent for secondary schools and reaches 24.3 per cent by the time they enter the tertiary system.[80,81,82]

Part of the reason for this is the sheer lack of educational infrastructure. For every 100 elementary schools in rural India, covering Classes 1 to 8, there are only 14 offering secondary education in Classes 9 and 10 and just six that offer higher secondary education (Classes 11 and 12). So as a student progresses across classes, they have to journey further to reach their next school.

This has consequences. We top the global list of out-of-school children, more than the entirety of sub-Saharan Africa, with West Bengal, Rajasthan, Uttar Pradesh and Bihar accounting for 70 per cent of out-of-school children. The majority of these children belong to SC, ST and other minorities (76 per cent).[83,84,85,86,87]

———

80   UDISE Report, 2014
81   AISHE report 'Teaching teachers, the great challenge for India's education system', 2014
82   UNESCO-Education For All Monitoring report, 2014
83   UDISE Report, 2014
84   AISHE report 'Teaching teachers, the great challenge for India's education system', 2014
85   UNESCO-Education For All Monitoring report, 2014
86   'Why children drop-out from primary school', The Hindu, 2016
87   'Restoring dignity to the teaching profession in India', Ideas for India

FOUNDATIONAL SKILLS

At the very minimum, India's children in elementary schools should have acquired foundational skills like basic arithmetic and reading, and yet, about 25 per cent of this age group still cannot read basic text fluently in any language, while over 50 per cent struggle with basic multiplication and division problems. Only half have the ability to understand certain sample words in English. When ASER conducted lateral tests to check for intellectual ability, only 56 per cent of the sample set could add weights correctly in kg.[88]

When considering reading abilities, the proportion of children in Class 3 who were able to read the text of two classes lower rose from 40.2 per cent in 2014 to 41.6 per cent in 2016. This rise implies a significant jump in reading abilities of children in government schools, including Punjab, Haryana, Uttarakhand, Chhattisgarh, Gujarat, Maharashtra and Telangana.

When we consider higher grades, a seeming stagnation has set in, three out of every four children enrolled in Class 8 were able to read at least a Class II level text.

There can be significant disparities in the achievement levels of students amongst states on the learning front, 80 per cent of students in Karnataka can perform geometric operations but those in Chhattisgarh have fewer than 50 per cent students with such capabilities.[89] India continues to be ranked low in reading, maths and science abilities, being ranked 71st out of 73 countries surveyed.[90] Meanwhile, an 8th grader Indian is equivalent to a 3rd grader South Korean, lagging behind global toppers by 200 points.

Let's consider this at a district level. In Khordha district in Odisha, only 43.5 per cent of youth can conduct division; and just 68.9 per cent of youth can read a sentence in English;[91] 46.5 per cent of youth cannot read and understand three out of four instructions in their native language; 56.7 per cent of youth can add weights, while only 40.2 per cent can calculate time; only 45.8 per cent can identify their own state on a map.

In Meghalaya's Jaintia Hills, only 12.4 per cent of youth could conduct division; only 29.2 per cent could add weights; and just 66.6 per cent could manage a budget. Just 41.9 per cent could identify their own state on a map.

---

88   Beyond Basics, ASER, 2017
89   NAS, NCERT, 2016
90   PISA, OECD, 2016
91   ASER, 2017

VOCATIONAL SKILLING

By the age of 17, over 20.7 per cent of youth in that age bracket are not in the formal educational system. This rises to 30.2 per cent by the age of 18. For such youth, the great hope has been vocational training and yet pick-up has been limited, even now, only 5.3 per cent of youth aged between 14 and 18, are enrolled in such courses. Delving into this number in detail, only 4.3 per cent of youth enrolled in Class 12 or below partake in such courses; only 6.2 per cent of youth not enrolled in any educational institution are engaging in vocational courses. This is a worrisome statistic.

The shorter the course, the greater the enrolment as well. For vocational courses with less than 3 months' duration, 40.3 per cent of youth enrolled in Class 12 or lower have some exposure to such courses.

FINANCING EDUCATION

About 25 per cent of all youth discontinue their studies due to financial reasons. Affordability is a significant constraint. While at the elementary school stage, ~5 per cent of all schools are private in nature; at the post-elementary stage, ~40 per cent of all schools offering secondary or higher secondary classes are private institutions with no government aid (this varies, of course, across states: private, un-subsidized, schools are 7 per cent of all secondary schools in West Bengal; the ratio is 71 per cent in Uttar Pradesh).

When we consider the cost of education, there are two perspectives: an individual one and a systemic one. From a system perspective, the provision of education will have institutional costs, including teachers' salaries, staff salaries, scholarships, stipends, depreciation and other expenditure, along with other non-recurring costs like buildings, furniture, equipment, etc.

Ideally, if the public education system offered quality education, in an accessible manner, there would be no push from the public to have their children educated in the private sector.

The Indian Constitution places education in the concurrent list, thereby categorizing it as a shared responsibility between the Union and state government, each having its own policy and budgetary allocations. It becomes critical to evaluate necessitated sectoral expenditure for the given set of policies announced, and compare with other global economies. Calls for increasing budgetary allocation to education have been made since the early years after Independence. The Kothari Commission (1964) recommended 6 per cent of Gross National Product (GNP) to be spent on education by 1985-86, with two-third of it (4 per cent of GNP) prioritized for school education. By 1986, the Kothari Commission recommendation, instead of being achieved, was reiterated through the National Policy on Education, 1986. Almost two decades later, the CABE Committee (2005) recommended that an additional 1.2-1.5 per cent of GDP needs to be allocated, incremental to existing allocations for universal education. A similar exercise was carried out after passing the Right to Education (RTE) Act, wherein NUEPA (2009) estimated the resource requirements for universalization of education by 2015. While the need to increase allocation to education sector till 6 per cent at GDP has been repeated, questions have also arisen about the sufficiency of such allocation, given the cumulative resource gap created over decades.

There are three major streams of financing education in India; funds directly disbursed by Union and state governments, devolution of untied funds to local bodies and expenditure financed by own revenue by local bodies. While the first stream disbursal accounts for a majority of school expenditure, the other two streams differ significantly across various regions and are focussed on education at all levels (including tertiary).

In terms of financial resources allocated as percentage of GDP, the allocations have typically remained below 3 per cent, i.e. less than half of the recommended 6 per cent of GDP levels.

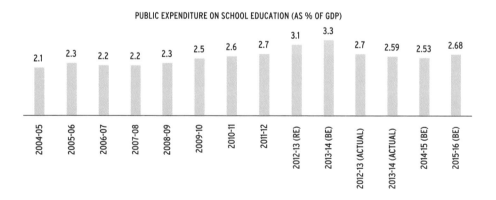

FIGURE 198: PUBLIC FINANCING OF EDUCATION IN INDIA, CRY & CBGA, 2016

Additionally, despite the introduction of RTE in 2010, the financial resources have increased incrementally instead of witnessing a step change. Amidst higher Union government allocations due to RTE, the incremental spend on education implies a lesser corresponding allocation by respective state governments. While the share of elementary education stood at 1.53 per cent (out of 2012-13 actual of 2.7 per cent), it declined to 1.49 per cent in 2014–15 BE for 2014–15.

The figure below illustrates the budgeted expenditure on education by education departments as a percentage of GSDP (2012-13), pointing out that while some states budgeted as much as 8.3 per cent of their GSDP for education, as many as 16 states budgeted 3.0 per cent or less of their GSDP.

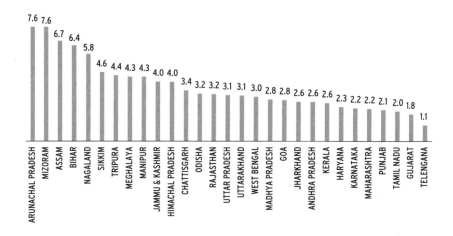

FIGURE 199: RELATIONSHIP BETWEEN BUDGETED EXPENDITURE ON EDUCATION AND GROSS STATE DOMESTIC PRODUCT (GSDP) OF STATES DURING 2014–15 (SOURCE: ANALYSIS OF BUDGETED EXPENDITURE ON EDUCATION: 2012–13 TO 2014–15)

The following table illustrates the school education budget as a percentage of the state budget and as percentage of state GSDP for 2012–13 to 2015–16. We see that economically backward states (Bihar & UP) spend a higher GSDP share on education as compared to economically well-off states (Maharashtra & Tamil Nadu). Additionally, the school education budget, as component of state budget, has reduced for all the below mentioned states from 2012–13 to 2015–16.

TABLE 106: SCHOOL EDUCATION BUDGET AS PERCENTAGE OF GSDP AND STATE BUDGET

	SCHOOL EDUCATION BUDGET AS PER CENT OF STATE BUDGET					
	2012-13	2013-14	2014-15 (BE)	2014-15 (RE)	2015-16 (BE)	2015-16 (BE+SB)
BIHAR	19.3	16.9	20.2	18.1	18.0	17.7
CHHATTISGARH	18.3	18.0	14.8	18.9	17.2	17.0
JHARKHAND	13.7	12.5	15.9	13.4	13.9	13.2
KARNATAKA	13.4	13.8	13.1	14.2	12.6	10.8
MADHYA PRADESH	20.7	22.8	17.7	14.6	14.8	15.9
MAHARASHTRA	19.2	20.3	17.5	17.9	19.0	18.0
ODISHA	15.0	14.1	13.7	13.2	14.2	14.0
RAJASTHAN	16.8	16.1	17.8	16.1	17.1	16.7
TAMIL NADU	13.9	14.4	13.0	13.8	13.3	13.4
UTTAR PRADESH	19.8	17.2	15.3	15.3	16.8	17.2
	SCHOOL EDUCATION BUDGET AS PER CENT OF GSDP					
	2012-13	2013-14	2014-15 (BE)	2014-15 (RE)	2015-16 (BE)	2015-16 (BE+SB)
BIHAR	4.5	4.0	6.2	6.2	4.8	5.6
CHHATTISGARH	3.7	3.3	3.8	4.9	4.6	4.6
JHARKHAND	2.8	2.2	4.1	3.5	3.4	3.6
KARNATAKA	2.4	2.4	2.5	2.7	2.3	2.2
MADHYA PRADESH	4.6	4.3	4.1	3.4	3.3	3.7
MAHARASHTRA	2.3	2.4	2.2	2.3	2.3	2.3
ODISHA	2.8	2.9	3.5	3.3	3.5	3.9
RAJASTHAN	2.9	2.9	4.1	3.5	3.5	3.5
TAMIL NADU	2.1	2.2	2.0	2.3	2.1	2.1
UTTAR PRADESH	4.4	4.0	4.3	4.1	4.6	5.0

SOURCE: CBGA & CRY

However, taking into account the different GSDP levels of individual states and the number of children, the data on percentage spend on education needs to be evaluated alongside the per student expenditure made by various states.

The following table presents the per student spend on education in a few general category states for different years. Despite spending less than 3 per cent of its GSDP on education, Kerala has the highest per student expenditure, whereas despite growth in spend in the recent past, Jharkhand and Bihar have the lowest per student expenditure.

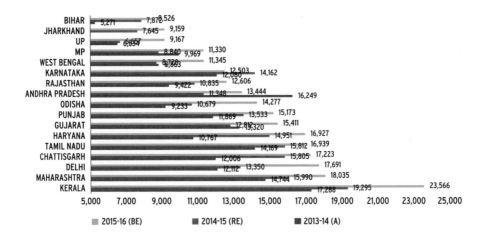

FIGURE 200: PER STUDENT SPEND ON EDUCATION FOR DIFFERENT STATES
(SOURCE: CRY & CBGA, 2016)

SARVA SHIKSHA ABHIYAN

The financing can be further explored under various education programmes aimed to provide easily accessible, quality education at affordable price. Consider the Sarva Shiksha Abhiyan (SSA), the flagship elementary education programme of the Union government aimed at providing universal education to children between 6 and 14 years and selected to be the primary vehicle for implementing RTE. Allocations made to the scheme have fallen short consistently of the estimate of funds required by the Ministry of Human Resource Development (MHRD). For FY2016–17 and 2017–18, the MHRD estimated resource requirements for SSA at ₹55,000 crore each year, whereas the money allocated was only ₹22,500 crore in 2016–17 (45 per cent of required) and ₹23,500 crore (47 per cent of required). For 2018–19, the allocation increased by 11 per cent to ₹26,129 crore.

The administrative process pertaining to funds adds a layer of complexity. The resource requirements are estimated on a school-level, district-level basis, and are then finalized after negotiations between the state government and the MHRD. There are significant budget cuts in the discussion between the state government and the MHRD for 2011–12, the total value of Annual Work Program & Budgets (AWP&Bs) stood at ₹81,886 crore, whereas MHRD approved only 75 per cent, i.e. ₹61,734 crore For FY2015–16, the annual resource requirement was estimated at ₹91,485 crore, whereas the final approved amount stood at ~69 per cent (i.e. 63,413 crore). Final approved budgets are then prepared and individual contributions of the central and state governments determined in accordance with the funding ratio. While funding ratios are fixed, the GoI allocations as a proportion of GoI share approved have also varied, and been declining since 2013–14.

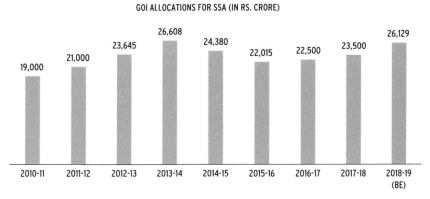

FIGURE 201: GOI ALLOCATIONS FOR SARVA SHIKSHA ABHIYAN (SOURCE: BUDGET BRIEFS, VOL 10, ISSUE 1, ACCOUNTABILITY INITIATIVE, CENTRE FOR POLICY RESEARCH)

In terms of releasing the money, the GoI transfers the money to state treasuries, which is then transferred to State Implementing Societies (SISs), with almost 98–99 per cent of the money allocated being released.[92] The money is released primarily in two instalments, the first instalment in the first quarter and the second instalment at the end of the second quarter of the financial year. While the first instalment depends on the past year's expenditure, the state government matching its share of expenses and provisional utilization certificates for past year expenses, the second instalment depends on expenditures made in the current year, the state government matching its share, audited accounts and provisional utilization certificates of expenses in current year. The pace of release of funds needs to be improved and ensured. For example, in 2015–16, only 35 per cent the funds were released in the 1st quarter, and out of 42 per cent of funds released in the second half of the year, as much as 11 per cent was in March '16, the last month of the financial year.

The situation improved in 2016–17, where 82 per cent of funds were released in the first half of the year, and only 12 per cent of funds were released in the last quarter of the financial year. Delays in releasing money, from central to state treasuries to SIS, impact the opening balances at the start of the year, ranging from ₹10,681 crore (FY 2010–11) to ₹17,282 crore (FY2014–15). Expenditure made demonstrates an increasing trend, rising from 59 per cent in 2011–12 to 79 per cent in FY2015–16. Increasing absolute expenditures on SSA have also resulted in increasing per-student

92   Sarva Shiksha Abhiyaan, 2018–19, Budget Briefs, Volume 10, Issue 1, Accountability Initiative, Centre for Policy Research

expenditure under SSA, rising from ₹2,455 in FY2010–11 to ₹4,385 in FY 2016–17, albeit also, because of decreasing enrolment in public schools.

In FY2011–12, the Project Approval Board (PAB) released ₹42,519 crore against approved budgets of ₹61,722 crore, converting to a release ratio of just 69 per cent. In the prior financial year (FY2010–11), the MHRD had released only 38 per cent, 40 per cent and 46 per cent of its funds for Andhra Pradesh, Himachal Pradesh and Bihar, respectively, by the third quarter of the financial year. Such delays at the central level have amplified negative impact at the local level. Even when money reaches the beneficiaries, bottlenecks for spending exist in the form of paperwork, technical sanctions and approvals to spend at various levels. Vacancies in key positions further complicate matters. Vacancies at the Block Resource Coordinator level (responsible for disbursing funds to schools and primary point of contact for grievance redressal) in Bihar and Odisha stood at 60 per cent and 58 per cent, respectively, in FY2011–12. This leads to expenditure decisions being made with procedural concerns at higher priority, rather than achieving specified planned outcomes. For example, schools may prioritize purchase of construction materials over teacher salaries in the early part of the financial year, as they have higher lead times. Moreover, construction activity needs to receive techno-commercial approvals from various authorities, which, if not present, just makes the money sit in a school's bank account. Absence of junior engineers may also lead the school to postpone construction activities. At times, money meant for training remained unspent as training programmes could not be organized in time. Such discrepancies adversely impact achieving the stated RTE goals.

A major reason for the shortfall could be lengthy approval/sanction process for civil works; other states prove that such challenges could be overcome. Even for other tasks like providing uniforms, Bihar could achieve only 34 per cent of its targets. In Bihar and West Bengal, only 46 per cent and 42 per cent of teachers were recruited against targets, while only 42 per cent of SSA targets for teacher training were met in Jharkhand. Analysis indicates that ₹1,000 increase in per student spend can increase the number of students in Classes 3–5 who can read Class 1 text by 2.2 per cent, and increase the number of students in Classes 3–5 who can perform basic subtraction by 2.5 per cent.

Amidst the finalization between the MHRD and state governments on budgetary allocations, negotiations by the state government, priority of the MHRD and robustness of AWP&B calculations matter substantially.[93] For example, in FY2017–18, Haryana got 89 per cent of the funds proposed, whereas Jharkhand got only 56 per cent of the funds proposed. Within the approved budgets, expenditures vary

---

93 Sarva Shiksha Abhiyaan, 2018–19, Budget Briefs, Volume 10, Issue 1, Accountability Initiative, Centre for Policy Research

significantly among states as well. For example, in 2016–17, the expenditure as a percentage of funds allocated ranged from 84 per cent (Maharashtra) to 37 per cent (West Bengal). The same year also witnessed declining spends in percentage terms from 2015–16, as Gujarat spent only 46 per cent of its allocated funds in FY2016–17 as compared to 92 per cent in FY2015–16. Himachal Pradesh also registered a similar decline from 94 per cent to 72 per cent. Differences in funds allocated and money released change the picture slightly, for FY2015–16, Tamil Nadu spent 99 per cent of the funds available, whereas Jharkhand managed to spend only 53 per cent.

It is also imperative to understand where most of the spend was made—e.g. for FY2016–17, teacher salaries and civil works account for a majority (76 per cent) of the total allocated budget, followed by entitlements (textbooks, uniforms, maintenance grants, fee reimbursement, etc.) at 15 per cent and the remaining 9 per cent for quality improvement initiatives, including library, training material, teacher training, community mobilization and other initiatives. The aim for AWP&B for FY2017–18 was to increase the sum total of allocation for entitlements and quality improvement initiatives to 30 per cent, but the numbers point to a different narrative. Out of the funds allocated for quality improvement initiatives, only 69 per cent was spent, while the teacher salaries and civil works categories witnessed a 75 per cent spend (out of funds allocated) and entitlements reported a higher proportion at 87 per cent. While these are national averages, state-wise variations exist.

The chart below presents the percentage of funds allocated to various categories, and funds spent (as percentage of funds allocated)

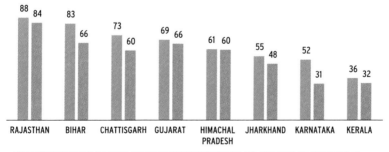

DETAILS OF BUDGET ALLOCATED & SPEND ON TEACHER SALARIES & CIVIL WORKS, FY 2016-17

■ PERCENTAGE SHARE OF APPROVED BUDGET GOING FOR CIVIL WORKS AND TEACHERS' SALARY IN 2016-17

■ PERCENTAGE SPENT OF APPROVED BUDGET GOING FOR CIVIL WORKS AND TEACHERS' SALARY IN 2016-17

DETAILS OF BUDGET ALLOCATED & SPEND ON TEACHER SALARIES & CIVIL WORKS, FY 2016–17 (SOURCE: SSA BUDGET BRIEFS, ACOCUNTABILITY INITIATIVE, CENTRE FOR POLICY RESEARCH)

With a view to improving early grade reading, writing, and maths skills in rural schools, the Union government started a programme Padhe Bharat, Badhe Bharat in 2014. Yet, outcomes far lag our expectations, as even in 2016, 46.1 per cent of students in Class 1 couldn't read letters while 39.9 per cent couldn't recognize numbers (ASER). While spends on higher education increase, the quality and outcomes in elementary education play an important role in higher education as well.

Solution: besides increasing education outlays, allocations and actual expenditure on education, it is important to increase the efficiency of each rupee spent. NITI Aayog has already proposed ranking schools based on their learning outcomes, using the School Education Quality Index (SEQI), a composite index of 34 indicators, among which learning outcomes have significant weightage. Such an index can help shift part of states' focus from inputs and resources to learning outcomes, encourage innovation and continuous yearly improvements. Moreover, learning outcomes have to be monitored regularly , whereas the annual reports by schools contain details of number of students and teachers, no objective measurement of education quality is provided. The Shala Siddhi programme was introduced in 2013, focussing on self-assessment by schools, but till January '17, no proper detailed report was made available to the public.

FINANCING UNDER RTE

Despite rising enrolment in private schools, government schools still dominate the school education system, especially in Bihar, Odisha, Jharkhand, Chhattisgarh and Madhya Pradesh where government schools accounted for at least 80 per cent of total number of schools in the states. Amongst government schools, private-aided schools show a high incidence in Maharashtra (20.8 per cent of total schools), Tamil Nadu (14.6 per cent of total schools) and Karnataka (9.5 per cent of total schools). States with a higher number of private-aided schools are able to reduce their need for capital expenditure, as only recurrent costs need to be allocated. In terms of enrolment, government schools in many states have significantly lower enrolment compared to the number of government schools, e.g. Uttarakhand, with 76 per cent schools being government schools, accounts for only 46.5 per cent of the state's students, whereas the government schools in Tamil Nadu (79 per cent of all schools in the state) only account for 60 per cent of its students. The trend points to a well-known fact—that enrolment in government schools remains less than in their private counterparts.

In terms of financing schools, the table below provides us with total requirement vs actual expenditure for 12 states:

TABLE 107: TOTAL REQUIREMENT VS ACTUAL EXPENDITURE IN 12 STATES FOR 2015–16

STATE	ANNUAL RECURRENT COST	ANNUAL CAPITAL COSTS	TOTAL REQUIREMENT	RECURRENT EXPENDITURE TO TOTAL REQUIREMENT	ACTUAL TOTAL EXPENDITURE	PER STUDENT REQUIRED RECURRENT COST	PER STUDENT REQUIRED TOTAL COST	PER STUDENT ACTUAL EXPENDITURE	ACTUAL TOTAL EXPENDITURE TO TOTAL REQUIRED COST	TOTAL REQUIREMENT TO GSDP	ADDITIONAL REQUIREMENT TO GSDP	REIMBURSEMENT TO GSDP
	(₹ CR)	(₹ CR)	(₹ CR)	(%)	(₹ CR)	(₹)	(₹)	(₹)	(%)	(%)	(%)	(%)
	A	B	C=A+B	D = A/C	E	F	G	H	I=E/C	J	K	L
BIHAR	32,745	10,090	42,835	76.4	12,803	14,348	18,770	5,929	29.9	11.2	7.9	0.006
CHHATTISGARH	7,034	1,276	8,310	84.6	5,341	20,457	24,168	16,099	64.3	3.2	1.1	0.020
JHARKHAND	8,844	1,458	10,302	85.9	4,473	17,067	19,880	8,979	43.4	4.5	2.5	0.001
KARNATAKA	11,940	1,469	13,409	89.0	9,165	22,382	25,136	17,751	68.4	1.3	0.4	0.013
MADHYA PRADESH	18,321	3,811	22,132	82.8	11,502	21,655	26,160	14,384	52.0	4.1	2.0	0.084
MAHARASHTRA	23,668	1,603	25,271	93.7	19,825	19,319	20,627	16,502	78.5	1.3	0.3	0.003
ODISHA	10,877	2,589	13,466	80.8	6,148	19,998	24,758	11,630	45.7	3.9	2.1	0.001
RAJASTHAN	14,658	3,138	17,796	82.4	10,939	21,554	26,168	17,600	61.5	2.6	1.0	0.000
TAMIL NADU	9,594	986	10,580	90.7	11,353	17,211	18,979	20,427	107.3	0.9	0	0.013
UTTAR PRADESH	37,534	5,341	42,875	87.5	35,791	17,141	19,581	18,348	83.5	3.8	0.6	0.001
UTTARAKHAND	2,097	344	2,441	85.9	2,303	25,938	30,197	28,931	94.3	1.4	0.1	0.026
DELHI	2,499	255	2,754	90.8	-	13,998	15,425	-	-	0.5	-	0.007

SOURCE: RESOURCE REQUIREMENTS FOR RIGHT TO EDUCATION (RTE): NORMATIVE AND THE REAL, SUKANYA BOSE, PRIYANTA GHOSH AND ARVIND SARDANA, NATIONAL INSTITUTE OF PUBLIC FINANCE AND POLICY

As observed from the table above, recurrent costs are the major component of the total expenditure requirement for a government school, which can be as high as 93 per cent for schools in Maharashtra. The recurrent cost, on a per capita basis, exhibits significant variation. Variation in teacher salaries, the biggest component of recurrent expenditure for a school, leads to such significant variation in per student recurrent expenditure. Teacher salary variations occur primarily due to difference in teaching experience among teachers in various states, besides varying teacher-pupil ratio. In terms of actual expenditure, we see that Bihar spends only ~30 per cent of its total required cost, while Uttarakhand spends 94 per cent and Tamil Nadu spends even 107 per cent of the total required cost, explained by low enrolment ratio in government schools and comparatively higher teacher salaries— thus indicating that a higher ratio (of actual expenditure to total required cost) may not necessarily lead to better education outcomes.

A deeper analysis of recurrent expenditure for FY2015–16 reveals the following results:

	TEACHER SALARY	TEACHER TRAINING	INFRASTRUCTURE	INSPECTION & MONITORING	INCENTIVES	MID-DAY MEAL	OTHERS
BIHAR	51.6	1.6	7.2	0.6	21.9	8.3	8.8
CHHATTISGARH	61.0	0.6	6.1	0.0	7.7	5.4	19.2
JHARKHAND	54.0	0.4	12.5	0.9	9.6	9.3	13.3
KARNATAKA	71.6	0.5	8.9	0.0	4.2	9.5	5.3
MADHYA PRADESH	63.7	0.2	6.3	0.1	10.1	7.2	12.4
MAHARASHTRA	68.8	0.4	3.8	0.5	1.9	4.0	20.6
ODISHA	54.3	0.3	13.5	1.2	11.7	7.2	11.8
RAJASTHAN	80.4	0.3	5.4	0.8	6.1	2.8	4.2
TAMIL NADU	67.0	0.3	2.6	1.2	7.8	6.2	14.9
UTTAR PRADESH	74.5	0.3	3.2	0.4	12.1	3.2	6.3

FIGURE 202: COMPONENT-WISE DISTRIBUTION OF SCHOOL-EDUCATION BUDGET
(SOURCE: HOW HAVE STATES DESIGNED THEIR SCHOOL BUDGETS, CBGA & CRY, 2016)

For Bihar, the spend of ~52 per cent on teacher salary follows a 10 per cent drop over FY2014–15, when it spent ~62 per cent of its budget on teacher salaries.[94] Even with 1 lakh classrooms built and 3 lakh teachers recruited, Bihar still faces shortage of 1.14 lakh teachers, with student-teacher ratio of 57 and student-classroom ratio at 103 despite having 95 lakh children out of school. Even school infrastructure needs rapid improvement, with 13 per cent schools operating without even a building and 45 per cent with no access to toilets for girls. Various schemes like Mukhyamantri Balak/Balika Cycle Yojana, Mukhyamantri Poshak Yojana, Chief Minister Student Incentive Scheme, and scholarships for marginalized children have been implemented which contribute to a larger incentive share in the school budget. This can pose challenges if the total education budget is itself inadequate as higher incentives may attract students at secondary level, but may not be sustainable in the long run as weak infrastructure and support systems will be unable to retain the students for a longer term. A comparatively higher spend on infrastructure indicates steps to comply with RTE norms, while Mid-Day Meals (MDMs), accounting for 8.3 per cent of the education budget, comprise the Dopahar scheme and other state-level nutritional interventions.

Shortage of teachers is experienced in Chhattisgarh as well, which spent about 61 per cent of its state education budget on teacher salaries.[95] While there is shortage

---

94   How Have States Designed Their School Education Budgets, Source: CBGA & CRY, 2016
95   How Have States Designed Their School Education Budgets, Source: CBGA & CRY, 2016

of 32 per cent of teacher positions in public schools, only 69 per cent of teachers enrolled are professionally qualified. Infrastructure poses a separate challenge, with about 20 per cent schools not having drinking water facility and 47 per cent schools operating without toilets for girls (ASER, 2014). In such times, unspecified spending and administrative costs accounting for 19.2 per cent of the education budget seems an outlier. Incentives were primarily driven by spends on the Saraswati Cycle Yojana, free textbooks, free uniforms and the student accident insurance scheme and can be increased further through scholarships. The increased allocation can come while keeping costs constant through reduction in unspecified expenditure and administrative costs. This would be critical to reduce the dropout rate and increase the gross enrollment rate.

Jharkhand's spend of ~54 per cent on teacher salaries is the lowest among the states listed in the table above, primarily contributed by vacancy in 78 per cent posts of regular teachers in public secondary schools coupled with majority enrolment in schools with higher than stipulated PTR (65.2 per cent of total enrolment at primary level in schools with PTR above 30, and 62.9 per cent enrolment at upper primary level in schools with PTR above 35) (Rustagi & Menon, 2013). The comparatively higher share of infrastructure spend is primarily on account of catching up with RTE-stipulated norms, while teacher training and inspection and monitoring spends remain weak.

Karnataka has relatively better learning outcomes, with two-third of its population literate and 41 per cent of students in schools funded by the department of education. It fares well on the infrastructure front with provisions for drinking water and toilets in almost all schools. Yet, teacher shortage is common; almost 1 per cent of its 74,953 schools have no teachers, with 5 districts having more than 100 schools without a teacher, 7.3 per cent of schools having just 1 teacher and ~19.6 per cent of schools having just two teachers (DISE, 2015–16). The state's expenditure on mid-day meals has risen from 8.2 per cent in 2012–13 to 9.5 per cent in 2015–16, providing nutrition under the Akshara Dasoha scheme.

Shortage of teachers and infrastructure are the key reasons for lagging outcomes in education in Madhya Pradesh. With 19,269 schools being single-teacher schools, only 77 per cent of teachers being professionally trained, 51 per cent of posts for regular teachers and 72 per cent of posts for headmasters remaining vacant, the state witnessed the dropout rate increase to 16.6 per cent in 2015–16.

Financial resources determine a state's spending capacity and thus remain critical to achieving the stated goals of universal education. As seen in Table 107, all states except Chhattisgarh have a declining trend for school education as a percentage of their state budget. Even the Economic Survey 2017–18 pointed out that 'being a developing economy, there is not enough fiscal space to increase the expenditure on critical social infrastructure like education and health in India'.[96] In such case, states need to protect and enhance the fiscal pool available for education. Additionally, states need to increase their expenditure on school education, which can be achieved by efforts to increase allocation as percentage of state budgets. With teacher salaries forming the biggest constituent of education expenditure, some may wrongfully opine that states are overspending on teacher salaries. However, even OECD countries spend ~79 per cent of their education expenditure on teacher salaries. With government schools in most states facing a shortage of qualified teachers, any reduction in teacher salaries or benefits will only discourage qualified teachers from wanting to continue in the teaching profession. A cadre of highly trained teachers needs to be recruited in order to improve the learning quality and outcomes in government schools, followed by prioritizing teachers' training and inspection-monitoring at school level.

PPP MODELS—USAGE, LIMITATIONS, SUCCESS AND GAPS

Besides improving access at elementary levels, increased focus needs to be placed on improving quality of education. While Gross Enrolment Ratio (GER) has increased at both primary and secondary levels, retention remains a cause of concern. Within a decade from 2002–03 till 2012–13, we have increased GER at primary level from 90 to 106, at secondary level from 53 to 66, and at senior secondary level from 29 to 39 respectively. The numbers tell their own story, as GER falls from 106 to 39 as we move from primary to senior secondary education. Quality of teaching remains a concern, with the Annual Status of Education Report (ASER) repeatedly claiming that over 50 per cent of students of Class 5 in public schools failed to read a Class 2 text. At the global[97] Programme for International Student Assessment (PISA) tests, students from states of Himachal Pradesh and Tamil Nadu, faring better than other Indian states, ranked at the bottom of the rankings list, just above Kyrgyzstan. Thus, while we have improved enrolment in recent years, quality improvement of education imparted needs to happen as well. Despite witnessing a rise in enrolment rates in private schools, mostly driven by parents' search for quality education, the government cannot ignore its pivotal role in uplifting education quality. PPPs can serve the purpose, by synchronizing synergies of scale presented by public school infrastructure and innovation and service delivery by the private sector. The PPP

---

96   Chapter 10, Volume II, Economic Survey, 2017–18

97   https://www.thequint.com/news/india/indias-pisa-moment-are-we-turning-into-a-nation-of-nitwits

model also allows the government to test the transition from an 'administrator/executor' role to a 'facilitator/regulator' role. The key value addition that PPP may bring is the creation and administration of service delivery models, which improve quality and can be scaled up at a macro/national level.

Over the last decade, we witness an increasing number of low-to-middle income parents enrolling their children in affordable private schools, mainly driven by quality differentials in imparting education and subsequent outcomes. The 71st-round survey by the National Sample Survey Office (NSSO), conducted across 65,926 households in urban and rural areas, indicates rising expenditures per student in India, primarily driven by expenditure on private education.

AVERAGE EXPENDITURE PER STUDENT IN RURAL INDIA	2007–08	2014	INCREASE (IN %)
PRIMARY LEVEL	826	2,811	240.3
UPPER PRIMARY	1,370	3,242	136.6
HIGHER SECONDARY	3,019	9,031	199.1
AVERAGE PRIVATE EXPENDITURE PER STUDENT	2007–08	2014	INCREASE (IN %)
PRIMARY LEVEL	1,413	4,610	226.3
UPPER PRIMARY	2,088	5,386	158.0
HIGHER SECONDARY	4,351	12,619	190.0

Amidst private expenditure, course fees account for 46 per cent, private coaching for 15 per cent, books and uniforms for 22 per cent and transport for 11 per cent, with almost 81 per cent and 78 per cent of students in Tripura and West Bengal taking private coaching. Besides, expenditure trends and enrolment rates reveal that enrolment in municipal schools has declined by about 25 per cent to 50 per cent in urban areas (Mumbai, Kolkata, Bengaluru, Chennai, Ahmedabad and Pune), while expenditure rose between 50 to 150 per cent, thereby increasing the per student government expenditure substantially. As low-income communities show increasing preference for private schools in search of better education quality, only those municipal schools which teach English have bucked the trend. This situation of under-utilized existing infrastructure due to a search for quality is conducive for growth of PPP in the education sector.

PPP models of various hues can be utilized for different objectives. School management and school adoption remain the most prevalent and earliest adopted PPP models in India, with more than 16 million students being benefitted under such models. Under such models, the school is managed by a private board, which is responsible for infrastructure costs, with the government pay encompassing teacher salaries (~90–95 per cent), utilities and other infrastructural support. All school norms and rules (including fees) are in line with government schools. The grants paid by the government are delinked from any performance metrics like attendance of students, enrolment of students and quality of teaching imparted. While teacher salaries were initially under the purview of private management, malpractices led governments to pass Acts (e.g. Salary Distribution Act (1971) in UP and Direct Payment Agreement (1972) in Kerala, among others) protecting teacher interests. Subsequently, the private partner remains responsible for teacher training. While the model has helped the government to increase access to education, it needs certain policy interventions when it comes to improving quality of education.

The central government's 'Model School Programme' used PPP for infrastructure creation, wherein the private party builds, owns and operates the school infrastructure, the government runs the school (using these facilities) and reimburses the private player over the contract period (20–30 years) with linkages to maintenance metrics. In the other model, the Akansha Foundation schools in Mumbai or the Bharti Foundation schools in Punjab and Rajasthan illustrate employment of private players for school management, wherein private contractors operate/manage schools, which remain public-owned and public-funded. This allows for developing a responsive/updated curriculum and better teachers with the aim of achieving better learning outcomes for each per capita government expense leading to efficiency gains. PPP can also be employed for capacity building initiatives at macro level, wherein the government enrols a private contractor for support in particular areas, e.g. teacher training, curriculum development, pedagogical support, etc. while retaining full ownership and administration of schools.

The Adarsh Model School Scheme, introduced in Punjab in 2007, aimed to provide quality secondary education in rural areas, by setting up one such school in each block and providing quality educational opportunities on a par with urban areas.[98] Under the scheme, the private partner is responsible for building and operating the school, with a state body, the Punjab Educational Development Board (PEDB)— responsible for managing the school. The children are not charged any fees in these schools and admission is merit-based and for under privileged children, barring a 25 per cent reservation for students from the village which has provided land at concessional rates for building the school. The PEDB is responsible for releasing grants, supervising/monitoring the working of each school, determining performance standards for the schools, taking over the school in case of private party default and managing policy-level matters regarding Adarsh schools.

The capital expenditure for such school is shared equally, with government share capped at ₹3.75 crore per school, while the operating expenditure is shared between

---

98   Public-Private Partnerships In School Education, Learning and Insights for India, S Chaudhry & A Uboweja, Working Paper March 2014

the Government and the private party in a 70:30 ratio, with maximum student intake capped at 2,000 students for reimbursement of operating expenses by government. Land is taken on concessional rates from gram panchayats, preferably in a central location in each block. The government is responsible for providing the incentives like books, uniforms and mid-day meals, besides the benefits of other state schemes. Private parties empanelled are usually business or educational groups, evaluated on a set of pre-defined criteria. The 5 Adarsh schools adopted by the Bharti Group recorded a zero dropout rate in 2010–11, with more than 74 per cent of students having more than 90 per cent attendance rates. The schools received applications twice their capacity.

Around the same time, Rajasthan introduced the Rajasthan Education Initiative (REI) wherein under a Memorandum of Understanding (MoU), it gave 49 primary schools in Amer and Neemrana districts for adoption by the Bharti Group.[99] Under this model, the private partner would adopt an already existing government school, and retains both management and operational control ranging from renovation of existing schools, hiring teachers, introducing teaching innovations and managing daily administration and operations of the school. The resource requisition by the government reduces significantly, remaining limited to providing incentives and mid-day meals, in line with applicable state and central government schemes. The Block Resource coordinators monitor the progress of the REI schools on a monthly basis, with third-party evaluations scheduled every alternate year. The private partner, having full autonomy over school affairs, bears the entire operational cost and thus has to end up charging a fee to school students. This creates a few ecosystem issues. While government officials question the motive and capability of the private partner, locals are resistant to paying fees in a school which was earlier a public school. Meanwhile, the private partner has to restart the hiring process for qualified teachers, as most existing government teachers would be transferred out to other schools. Financial challenges also remain, degraded infrastructure adds to capital expense by the private party—which is then passed on to the students in terms of fees, while lack of any opex cost sharing keeps the management focused on ensuring that cash flows from the school are financially viable. Despite the challenges, 20 out of 24 schools in Amer district got grades of A and B during the SSA Quality Assurance Test, as opposed to 7 before adoption, besides having 50 per cent higher enrolment with improved girl-boy ratio and improved infrastructure in all adopted schools.

The Municipal Corporation of Greater Mumbai (MCGM), witnessing decline in enrolment and quality outcomes, alongside increase in budgets, empanelled NGOs and private agencies under the PPP framework in 2013 to impart quality

99   Public-Private Partnerships In School Education, Learning and Insights for India, S Chaudhry & A Uboweja, Working Paper March 2014

education. In terms of the PPP model used, it operationalized both models; firstly, school management (known as Full School Management with Private Teachers or FSMPT) and, secondly, school adoption (known as Full School Management with MCGM Teachers or FSMMT). Under FSMPT, the contract, usually of 10 years duration, provides the private party with school functioning in line with RTE norms, while the government remains responsible for providing space within public schools, financing, and incentives like uniforms and books. With pre-defined performance standards stated in the contract, the private partner (e.g. Muktangan, Akansha) has the flexibility to innovate in terms of content delivery and to have their own teachers (with their own training patterns) to improve outcomes. Under the scheme, no fee is charged from students, and the private partner is entirely responsible for operational expenses in the first year, and eligible for up to 60 percent of public school (MCGM school) opex on a per student basis, depending on the learning outcomes achieved. While financing can be improved, as under the current system, the private partner may provide more focus on raising funds than educational purposes, the system of reimbursement based on outcomes achieved needs to be made robust, so that no unfair assessments are made, leading to either extra benefits or unwanted fiscal damage to the private partner.

Under FSMMT, the private partner has limited autonomy as hiring teachers and managing their performance remains beyond their purview. The private partner, usually an NGO, provides a facilitator in each school who improves on teacher training, provides curriculum support, improves content delivery and supports school operations. Each teacher is also provided an assistant at pre-primary level, to assist in classroom management and group activities. Financing pattern under FSMMT remains similar as under FSMPT, and thus creates dependency on donors. The performance of the NGO faces compromises due to government inefficiencies, as the lack of teachers, which remains under the government, adversely impacts their own performance.

The Gujarat PPP model—the Vidyateerth PPP—aimed to provide high quality education in rural areas by consolidating smaller schools, envisaging a tri-partite arrangement.[100] The government provides the infrastructure, incentives to students, teachers and financing (approximately ₹1,000 per student annually) linked to education outcomes, the private partner provides the curriculum and training, and a PSU provides monitoring support for the programme.

Various PPP models followed around the world also present learning for India in its quest for universal education. Uganda, when faced with inadequate public secondary schools (mostly in urban areas) and poor secondary Gross Enrolment

---

100 Public-Private Partnerships In School Education, Learning and Insights for India, S Chaudhry & A Uboweja, Working Paper March 2014

Ratio (GER, 33 per cent in 2008) started a Universal Secondary Education (USE) policy, contracting private schools to provide education on a fixed per student subsidy (₹1,200 per student) basis. While the private operator has flexibility to run the daily operations of the school, there are strict guidelines for usage of subsidy resources, the grant of which is contingent on finalization of annual plans and submission of previous term's progress report and work programme for the next term. Private schools need to apply to be empanelled under the USE programme, with eligibility criteria designed such that enrolment in private schools does not come at the cost of decreasing enrolment in public schools. The USE programme quickly ramped up from 42,000 students in 363 schools in 2007 to 806,992 students in 879 schools by 2013. Thus, we witness that it is possible to increase secondary GER, while improving access and quality, at fixed per-student costs. This can be done by improving the reimbursement process to avoid any working capital issues, having strict financial controls and audits while providing schools with operational flexibility, and shifting focus to learning outcomes, besides strong contracts enforcing performance standards (staffing, maintenance, etc.) from the private partner.

In terms of strict contract enforcement, the US sets an example, wherein the schools are directly responsible for quality outcomes specified in the contract or 'charter' in return for partial operational funding on a per student basis. Failure to meet specified outcomes can even lead to closure of schools until another school management company takes over, while some states adopt higher discretion and closure is done only if operational funding of a school is financially unviable due to low enrolment. The US charter schools have been found to accelerate learning gains in reading and Maths, compared to public schools (CREDO 2013, National Charter School Study, Stanford University), whereas another study indicates that learning outcomes are better in states that choose to close schools for underperformance. The charter schools receive about 60 per cent of operational funding, with the remaining amount being tackled through philanthropy and efforts to reduce operating cost.

In UK, schools in areas with a long history of student underachievement or focused in specific areas were encouraged to convert to 'academies', independent of control from local government. In addition to being helped in the start up phase to move from a government-dependent entity to an independent provider, the academies are funded on a per student basis, at exactly the same rate as state schools, besides having top-up funding for needy students and schools being free to raise independent philanthropic funding. With more than 600 trusts operating the schools, it has been found that a trust running three or more schools or academies achieves better results than trusts with less schools, due to scaling up innovation gains and better access to an improved teacher pool. Moreover, the number of schools that can be opened by a trust are capped, to ensure that trusts do not compromise quality in search of volume.

Philanthropy can also be channelled effectively into education, wherein large multi-national corporations and MSMEs are encouraged to adopt a school, involving them funding the programme on pre-defined terms leading to reinventing the school and engaging the local community. Such philanthropic efforts are also in line with the mandate of the Companies Act, 2013, which provides for most firms to spend about 2 per cent of their annual profits for Corporate Social Responsibility (CSR) purposes.

CHALLENGES

When we consider the broad range of PPP models described above, we see that besides their success, a few structural challenges persist, across the ecosystem and model implementation. Finance remains a critical issue. Most private partners depend largely on government reimbursements on a per student basis; systemic delays by government in reimbursing these costs lead to working capital issues and issues in proper management of the school. Funding gaps also lead to undesired result. For example, under the Mumbai PPP model, the NGOs selected to run the government schools were reimbursed 60 per cent of the government cost per child, thereby creating the perpetual need for gap funding. This leads the private partner to expend significant energy and attention on raising funds from various sources, at the cost of managing daily operations of the school.

Thus, organizations willing to enter PPPs must have the fund-raising ability to cover expenses that government doesn't reimburse, thereby limiting the participation of NGOs. Further, without proper exit clauses, institutional donors are reluctant to enter into such PPP with funding. Delays and bureaucratic hurdles discourage low-cost private operators and other professional private players. All these issues compound with the fact that there are only a handful of private operators with adequate capacity and willing to operate in a vernacular environment. Due to the limited number of English-medium schools, the government operates when most private partners are managing English-medium schools, scaling up at macro level can be inhibited.

Furthering the challenges of limited and insecure funding status is the lack of a well-defined PPP policy that clearly stipulates the process for selection and evaluation of private partners, ensuring that only reliable partners enter into PPP arrangements. The process of enrolling private partners mostly lacks a formal bidding or tendering process, and is sometimes awarded on a nomination basis. An equal lack of clarity emerges on the operations front, due to lack of objective evaluation of private partners' performance. In the absence of well-defined selection, operation and revenue clauses bound by agreements, institutional donation and help remain stalled.

The primary problem faced by private partners is of stakeholder management; they have to mitigate any government concerns that they have a profit motive in managing the schools, while overcoming perception among parents of poor quality teaching to make them enrol their children. In the absence of any well-formulated PPP policy, the enrolment of PPP has been ad hoc in nature.

In order to impart quality, greater operational flexibility should be provided to the private management. At present, teachers have no accountability to private management, thereby absence or non-performance of teachers remains an issue. With promotions delinked from performance, teachers may feel demotivated from putting in their best. Thus, teacher management can be improved through private boards, while their appointments and salaries continue to be under the government. The school, while being asked to follow the state board curriculum, should be encouraged to innovate in terms of delivery of the curriculum. Such flexibility should be tied into their grant-in-aid funds through performance metrics. The school's grants could then be linked to performance metrics like attendance of students and teachers, examination results, learning outcomes and even maintenance of school infrastructure. Another major challenge is the availability of high-quality and dedicated principals and teachers, as private players face challenges in hiring them and then providing adequate training. Year-long training programmes for aspiring teachers may be planned, in line with the Muktangan programme in Mumbai. The KIPP example in the US also presents a solution, wherein heavy investments are made in teachers and principals and a charter school opened only after finding adequate teachers and principals, who act as the chief positive change catalysts. Limited, if any, teacher accountability to private partners also restricts the private partner to introducing innovation in content delivery. Adoption of existing schools also leads to challenges from existing staff, who face fears of either losing their jobs or being transferred to inconvenient locations.

INSTITUTING REFORM

There are three key policy changes that are required to change the state of education in India. The government needs to increase public spending on basic education. Budgetary policy, at the centre, seems to have stagnated in India, reduced to increasing by a few low percentage points every year. Education sector-wide planning policies should continue to be strengthened, along with a focus on increasing opportunities for alternative pathways to basic education. Such sector-wide planning needs to be focused on explicitly announced objectives, with coordinated action mixed with integrated programming and financing mechanisms. Any sectoral plans need to have adequate resource provision to enable equity and in order to drive a significant scale up in the number of alternative pathways to basic education. We also need to implement more large-scale holistic interventions to address the multiple barriers to schooling that currently prevail. While the past few decades have seen concerted efforts to address economic barriers, there are other systemic barriers that still prevail, preventing children (primarily from minority groups) from being able to access quality education. Any policy responses that address these barriers need to be cross-sectoral in order to improve efficacy.

Improving education has the power to remove social inequalities—as a nation develops, economic inequality increases first and decreases later, in a classic inverted U-shaped curve (Simon Kuznets), thereby causing less inequality in developed countries than developing nations. This is primarily driven by effective education ecosystem, which raises output and productivity alongside wage growth. As we struggle with unequal growth, quality education imparted to our children and skilling our youth in a skill and knowledge-based market economy remains crucial for sustainable growth.

ADDRESSING BARRIERS TO EDUCATION

There are a range of successful interventions that showcase how to tackle socio-cultural demand side barriers. In Bangladesh, the Meena Communication Initiative (MCI), a community mobilization initiative, focused on rights, life skills and practices for girls. It seeks to communicate behavioural development messages through popular entertainment, primarily focused on a nine-year-old girl called Meena. The initiative has changed behaviour at the grassroots level, creating awareness about the importance of ensuring that girls acquire life skills at an early age.[101]

Similarly, in India, the Mahila Samakhya initiative, launched in 1988, seeks to empower women in rural areas, especially those from marginalized backgrounds, to demand education. It seeks to break down traditional female stereotypes that often lead to young girls dropping out of school to do household chores. The initiative seeks to equip women with basic literacy skills, along with the ability to critically analyse, solve problems and build life skills—it does this by organizing such women into local groups (often called sanghas), strengthening their capacity to effectively participate in and support village level educational processes.[102]

TABLE 108: PROGRAMMATIC INTERVENTIONS IN SOUTH ASIA FOR
CHANGING BEHAVIOUR AND ATTITUDES TOWARDS EDUCATION[103]

COUNTRY	CATEGORY	INTERVENTION TYPE
BANGLADESH	CHANGING CULTURAL NORMS FOR GIRLS	COMMUNITY MOBILIZATION (E.G. MEENA CAMPAIGN); STIPEND PROGRAMME CONDITIONS (E.G. SECONDARY SCHOOL GIRLS MUST REMAIN UNMARRIED). LEGISLATION BANNING CHILD MARRIAGE
	PREVENTING CHILD LABOUR	CL PROGRAMMES (E.G. URBAN INFORMAL ECONOMY PROJECT). LEGISLATION: UN CRC; ILO CONVENTION ON WORST FORM OF CHILD LABOUR, 2001; LABOUR LAW ON MINIMUM AGE FOR ADMISSION TO WORK, 2006.
	PREVENTING CHILD ABUSE	CHILD PROTECTION PROGRAMMES (E.G. PROTECTION OF CHILDREN AT RISK -SOCIAL SERVICES FOR CHILDREN LIVING OR WORKING ON THE STREETS; AMADER SHISHU PROJECT (CONDITIONAL FAMILY-BASED CARE TO ORPHANS)
PAKISTAN	RAISING AWARENESS ON BENEFITS OF EDUCATION	COMMUNITY MOBILIZATION (E.G. COMPONENT OF RURAL SUPPORT PROGRAMMES).
	CHANGING CULTURAL NORMS FOR GIRLS	REPRODUCTIVE HEALTH (E.G. LADY HEALTH WORKER PROGRAMME). LEGISLATION: CHILD MARRIAGE RESTRAINT ACT, 1929; INTERNATIONAL CONVENTION ON ELIMINATION OF ALL FORMS OF DISCRIMINATION AGAINST WOMEN
	PREVENTING CHILD LABOUR	CL PROGRAMMES LEGISLATION: UN CRC; ILO CONVENTION ON MINIMUM AGE OF EMPLOYMENT, 2006; ILO CONVENTION ON WORST FORM OF CHILD LABOUR, 2001.
	PREVENTING CHILD ABUSE	LEGISLATION AGAINST TRAFFICKING OF YOUNG CHILDREN
SRI LANKA	RAISING AWARENESS ON BENEFITS OF EDUCATION	COMMUNITY MOBILIZATION (E.G. COMMUNITY AWARENESS PILOT PROGRAMME; PROGRAMMES FOR PARENTS OF CHILDREN WITH DISABILITIES); COMMUNITY BODIES (E.G. COMPULSORY ATTENDANCE COMMITTEES).
	CHANGING CULTURAL NORMS FOR GIRLS	LEGISLATION: AMENDMENT TO MARRIAGE ORDINANCE, 1995, TO RAISE MINIMUM AGE TO 18 YEARS (NOT APPLICABLE TO MUSLIM COMMUNITY).
	PREVENTING CHILD LABOUR	ENFORCEMENT OF LABOUR LEGISLATION (BY LOCAL LABOUR, PROBATION AND CHILD CARE OFFICERS AND POLICE). LEGISLATION: UN CRC; ILO CONVENTION ON MINIMUM AGE OF EMPLOYMENT, 2000; ILO CONVENTION ON WORST FORM OF CHILD LABOUR, 2001; AMENDMENTS TO EMPOWERMENT OF WOMEN, YOUNG PERSONS & CHILDREN ACT, 1956.
	PREVENTING CHILD ABUSE	LEGISLATION ESTABLISHING NATIONAL CHILD PROTECTION AUTHORITY (INCLUDES REMIT ON ENFORCING COMPULSORY EDUCATION), 1998

Bangladesh has a Female Secondary School Stipend Programme that seeks to increase female enrolment and at the same time delay the age of marriage for girls (the stipend is conditioned on the girls remaining unmarried). This stipend has entered into parental decision-making in rural Bangladesh, with a modest

---

101 Unicef, 2004

102 India OOSCI Study, 2011

103 Unicef Report on Out of School Children in South Asia, 2014

decline in early marriage witnessed.[104] The programme has paid off, with female secondary school enrolment jumping from 1 million in 1991 to over 4 million by 2006. Within a year of being implemented, the likelihood of girls enrolling rose by 12 per cent.[105] Sri Lanka, meanwhile, has sought to revive Compulsory Education Committees (CEC) in order to increase the enrolment of children—the school level committees have a mandate to improve enrolment and to continuously monitor the attendance of students.[106]

To reduce costs and help the poorest households overcome economic barriers to schooling, a range of interventions have been utilized in South Asia. In Bangladesh, the BRAC-developed 'Challenging the Frontiers of Poverty Reduction—Targeting the Ultra Poor' programme has sought to provide ultra-poor households with food transfers, health services and technical training, while raising awareness and eventually moving towards asset transfers. The programme seeks to rigorously identify the poorest households and currently covers over a million households. It has had a significant beneficial impact, with positive effects on food security, income and wealth.[107]

The Punjab Education Foundation Education Voucher Schemes (PEF EVS) has benefitted over 31,000 poor households in rural and urban slum areas in Pakistan. The scheme provides vouchers that are redeemed against tuition payments in participating private schools, with parents able to transfer their children if they are not satisfied.[108]

Sri Lanka pursued free education from 1945, reducing the number of non-school going children from 68 per cent in 1940 to 8 per cent in 2004.[109] The measures included free textbooks and uniforms, along with subsidized transport.

Even in India, the cooked mid-day meal scheme, which benefits millions of children, has helped raise enrolment and attendance rates, with the effect found to be far higher for girls and for children from Scheduled Tribes and Scheduled Castes.[110, 111]

---

104 Schurmann, 2009
105 Khandker et al, 2003
106 Sri Lanka Gazette Extra Ordinary Notification No. 1003/5, Nov 1997
107 Das, Shams, 2011
108 Malik, A.B, 2010
109 ESDFP, 2007
110 Pratichi Trust, 2005
111 Jyotsna et al, 2005

TABLE 109: PROGRAMMATIC INTERVENTIONS IN SOUTH ASIA FOR
OVERCOMING ECONOMIC BARRIERS IN SCHOOLING COSTS[112]

COUNTRY	CATEGORY	INTERVENTION TYPE
BANGLADESH	POVERTY ALLEVIATION	CASH TRANSFERS (E.G. EMPLOYMENT GENERATION PROGRAMME FOR HARD-CORE POOR); IN-KIND TRANSFERS (FOOD TRANSFERS E.G. VULNERABLE GROUP DEVELOPMENT; FOOD FOR WORK; ASSET TRANSFERS E.G. CHALLENGING THE FRONTIERS OF POVERTY REDUCTION); MICROCREDIT PROGRAMMES CASH TRANSFERS (E.G. NATIONAL FAMILY BENEFIT SCHEME; NATIONAL RURAL EMPLOYMENT GUARANTEE SCHEME); IN-KIND TRANSFERS (E.G. TARGETED PUBLIC DISTRIBUTION SYSTEM)
	COST OF SCHOOLING	FEE ABOLITION (PRIMARY & FEMALE LOWER SECONDARY STUDENTS); FREE TEXTBOOKS (PRIMARY); STIPEND/CCT PROGRAMMES (E.G. PRIMARY EDUCATION STIPEND PROGRAMME, FEMALE SECONDARY STUDENT STIPEND PROJECTS, REACHING OUT-OF-SCHOOL CHILDREN (ROSC) STIPEND COMPONENT
	CHILD HEALTH AND NUTRITION	SCHOOL FEEDING (E.G. PRIMARY SCHOOL FEEDING PROGRAMME; BEHTRUWC 'SCHOOL' FEEDING COMPONENT (NON-FORMAL CENTRES))
PAKISTAN	POVERTY ALLEVIATION	CASH TRANSFERS (E.G. BENAZIR INCOME SUPPORT PROGRAMME; WATAN CARD SCHEME (FLOOD-AFFECTED AREAS); ZAKAT PROGRAMME; MICROCREDIT PROGRAMMES (E.G. PAKISTAN POVERTY ALLEVIATION FUND); MULTI-INTERVENTION (E.G. RURAL SUPPORT PROGRAMMES)
	COST OF SCHOOLING	FEE ABOLITION (ALL LEVELS OF SCHOOLING); FREE TEXTBOOKS (GOVT SCHOOLS); STIPEND/CCT PROGRAMMES (E.G. PUNJAB CCT (LOWER SECONDARY GIRLS), SINDH STIPEND SCHEME (LOWER SECONDARY GIRLS), SINDH DIFFERENTIAL STIPENDS PROGRAMME, ZAKAT (STIPENDS); EDUCATION VOUCHERS (E.G. PUNJAB EVS (URBAN SLUMS))
	OPPORTUNITY COSTS	COMPENSATION FOR LOST EARNINGS (E.G. BAIT-UL-MAL SCHEME: STIPEND, CLOTHING, FOOTWEAR FOR FORMER CLS ATTENDING NATIONAL CENTRES FOR REHABILITATION OF CHILD LABOUR)
	CHILD HEALTH AND NUTRITION	SCHOOL FEEDING (E.G. FOOD FOR EDUCATION PROGRAMME (GIRLS' SCHOOLS), TAWANA PAKISTAN PROGRAMME (PRIMARY SCHOOL-AGE GIRLS), HIGH-ENERGY BISCUITS (FLOOD-AFFECTED AREAS))
SRI LANKA	POVERTY ALLEVIATION	CASH TRANSFERS (E.G. SAMURDHI POVERTY ALLEVIATION PROGRAMME); IN-KIND TRANSFERS
	COST OF SCHOOLING	FEE ABOLITION (ALL LEVELS OF SCHOOLING); FREE TEXTBOOKS; FREE UNIFORMS; SUBSIDIZED TRANSPORT TO SCHOOLS;
	CHILD HEALTH AND NUTRITION	SCHOOL FEEDING (FREE SCHOOL MEALS FOR POOR CHILDREN); SCHOOL HEALTH SERVICES (E.G. SYSTEM OF REGULAR MEDICAL INSPECTIONS FOR CHILDREN IN VARIOUS GRADES; PROVISION OF IRON FOLIATE TO CHILDREN IN GRADES 7-10 FOR 6 MONTHS IN POOR COMMUNITIES); FREE HEALTHCARE IN EXTENSIVE NETWORK OF PUBLIC CLINICS/HOSPITALS

On the supply side, there have been numerous efforts to expand the supply of formal and informal school places, with a focus on large-scale construction of standardized schools. Bangladesh built over 40,000 classrooms between 2004 and 2011 under the Primary Education Development Programme (PEDP II). A similar scale of construction occurred in India between 1995 and 2005, with the number of primary schools rising by 30 per cent and lower secondary schools rising by 66 per cent, all under the SSA. Under the Seva Mandir scheme in rural Udaipur, a number of randomly selected schools were assigned a monitoring and incentive programme, requiring the schoolteachers to take a daily photograph with

112 Unicef Report on Out of School Children in South Asia, 2014

a student—such teachers were paid only when cameras recorded that they were present. The programme raised teacher attendance significantly, thereby raising test scores.[113]

The example of Kasturba Gandhi Balika Vidyalayas in rural India is promising—these are typically lower secondary schools that are located in rural areas with a record of low school attendance, with a focus on enrolling out-of-school girls. Such schools are single-sex in nature, while possessing residential facilities for some of their students. The schools often have a very diverse curriculum, specialising in music, theatre, dance and the arts. Such schools have been quite successful in getting out-of-school girls to enrol, particularly those from ST and SC communities, with over 200,000 girls in 27 states enrolled in 2,565 KGBVs in 2011.[114]

The Punjab province of Pakistan has instituted a Child-Friendly School (CFS) programme to support over 300 government schools to create a child supportive environment in primary education. The programme's interventions are focused on child health, safety and learning, along with encouraging the professional development of teachers and efficiency improvements in school management and participation.[115]

In Tamil Nadu, an activity-based learning programme has been instituted to focus on improving the quality of learning in classrooms. The programme seeks to change existing learning materials, introduce self-paced learning and ensure frequent assessment by both the student and the teacher. From starting with just 13 schools in 2003, the scheme has now been implemented across the state.[116]

Meanwhile, tribal communities in Andhra Pradesh have been exposed to a Multi-Lingual Education Programme (MLE). The scheme, operating in over 2,500 schools, seeks to expose children to education in four languages—one of which is their mother tongue, another being the state's language, with English and Sanskrit added in. Students have been found to be actively engaged in learning and performing well in achieving various competencies; meanwhile attendance and punctuality have also increased.[117]

---

113 MIT AJPAL, 2008
114 Planning Commission, 2011
115 Unicef, 2008
116 Little, 2010
117 Andhra Pradesh MLE Status, National Multilingual Education Resource Consortium, 2014

TABLE 110: PROGRAMMATIC INTERVENTIONS IN SOUTH ASIA FOR
OVERCOMING SUPPLY SIDE BARRIERS IN SCHOOLING[118]

COUNTRY	CATEGORY	INTERVENTION TYPE
BANGLADESH	SCHOOL CONSTRUCTION	SCHOOL CONSTRUCTION (E.G. PEDP II CIVIL WORKS; SECONDARY SCHOOL CIVIL WORKS); ALTERNATIVE SCHOOL PLACES (E.G. ROSC ANANDA; PRE-PRIMARY PARA CENTRES); NFE PLACES (GOVERNMENT: E.G. BEHTRUWC, MOLE CHILD LABOUR PROGRAMMES; NON-GOVERNMENT: E.G. BRAC, GSS; DAM; FIVDB, UCEP); PPPS (E.G. MAINSTREAMING MADRASAHS).
	SUPPORTING INFRASTRUCTURE	WATER, SANITATION & HYGIENE (E.G. PEDP II; SANITATION, HYGIENE, EDUCATION AND WATER SUPPLY IN BANGLADESH OR SHEWA-B); EDUCATIONAL MATERIALS (E.G. PEDP II TEACHING AIDS; NEW TEXTBOOKS EACH YEAR FOR ALL PRIMARY STUDENTS; MLE MATERIALS; SECONDARY TEXTBOOK REFORM).
	TEACHING AND LEARNING PROCESSES	MEDIUM OF INSTRUCTION (E.G. BILINGUAL INSTRUCTION (BRAC SCHOOLS)); CURRICULUM & ASSESSMENT (E.G. SECONDARY CURRICULUM & ASSESSMENT REFORM).
PAKISTAN	SCHOOL CONSTRUCTION	SCHOOL CONSTRUCTION (E.G. SECONDARY GIRLS' SCHOOLS IN PUNJAB AND SINDH); TEACHER INCENTIVES AND RECRUITMENT (E.G. PROGRAMMES TO ENCOURAGE FEMALES/RURAL POSTING IN BALOCHISTAN, KP, SINDH; CONTRACT TEACHERS);NFE PLACES (GOVERNMENT E.G. CO-ED NCHD FEEDER SCHOOLS; NON-GOVERNMENT PROGRAMMES); PPPS (E.G. PUNJAB AND SINDH EDUCATION FOUNDATIONS; RURAL SUPPORT PROGRAMMES);PRE-SCHOOL PLACES (E.G. SINDH EARLY LEARNING).
	SUPPORTING INFRASTRUCTURE	SCHOOL REHABILITATION (E.G. ESR CIVIL WORKS); WATER, SANITATION & HYGIENE (E.G. WASH IN SCHOOLS); EDUCATIONAL MATERIALS (E.G. GENDER-SENSITIVE MATERIALS).
	TEACHING AND LEARNING PROCESSES	PEDAGOGY (E.G. PUNJAB CHILD-FRIENDLY SCHOOLS); CURRICULUM & ASSESSMENT (E.G. PRE-PRIMARY CURRICULUM; PRIMARY & SECONDARY EDUCATION CURRICULUM REFORM);
SRI LANKA	SCHOOL CONSTRUCTION	SCHOOL CONSTRUCTION (E.G. ISURU SECONDARY SCHOOLS IN 100 POOREST DIVISIONS); MAINSTREAMING CHILDREN WITH DISABILITIES (E.G. ADAPTATION OF INFRASTRUCTURE, PROVISION OF SPECIALIZED EQUIPMENT & EDUCATIONAL MATERIALS); NFE PLACES (E.G. SECOND CHANCE PROGRAMMES FOR OOSC)
	SUPPORTING INFRASTRUCTURE	SCHOOL REHABILITATION (E.G. DEVELOPMENT OF NAVODAYA SCHOOLS AS CENTRES OF EXCELLENCE IN EACH DIVISION)
	TEACHING AND LEARNING PROCESSES	PEDAGOGY (E.G. CHILD-FRIENDLY SCHOOLS); CURRICULUM & ASSESSMENT (E.G. CURRICULUM REFORMS)

INCREASING ACCESS AND EQUITY

Timli Vidyapeeth was started in the hinterland of Dehradun in the colonial era, with the aim of imparting good education in the Garhwal Himalayas.[119] However, a visit by the great-grandson of the school's founder, Ashish Debral, in 2013, highlighted that only three students had remained in the school by then. Migration from the villages, combined with the poor quality of education available in government schools had dis-incentivized enrolment. The village of Timli was

---

118   Unicef Report on Out of School Children in South Asia, 2014

119   Patel, Tanvi, Better India, April 2018. Sourced from: https://www.thebetterindia.com/138486/gurgaon-travels-teach-kids-uttarakhand/

increasingly getting depopulated. Ashish decided to revive the school, setting up a centre of excellence in 2014 and launching the school with modern science and technology. Every weekend, Ashish now travels 700 km to Timli, to oversee the functioning of the school.

Raising enrolment rates requires a focus on increasing investments in education and incentivizing the education of socially challenged students.[120] The government needs to increase its spending on education—our current per capita education spending, on PPP basis, is $500, which is about 25 per cent that of most upper middle income countries. We should seek to adopt models adopted by successful states, with higher GER ratios and a better quality of education, thereby limiting disparity across states. We need to consider a hub and spoke model, with a model school in each district developed to incentivize other low-quality schools to improve their quality of education. We need to also leverage the use of ICT, particularly in remote areas.

Private investment in education needs to be encouraged through a variety of funding channels, with PPP models in particular leveraged for existing low-performing and low enrolment government schools.[121] The government could even consider introducing a voucher-based system allowing students to choose between a government and a private school. Subsidies for the cost of the entire K-12 education should be provisioned for socially challenged groups, who are typically discriminated against on the basis of gender, caste and religion. A 'Heart-Beat' Program has been created for pre-school students who hail from migrant families, in an attempt to improve their language abilities, social skills and cognitive abilities. We need to institute similar measures, in order to ensure that no child is left behind.

We need to support this by better infrastructure, every school should have a certain amount of computing capability, along with the provision of adequate bandwidth, and good quality housing. We should seek to consolidate schools with partially filled capacities. There needs to be progressive investment on excluded children, particularly those from areas with weak schools, and from under-performing areas. Those children who are never likely to enter schools (~9.7 million in India[122]) need to be targeted, alternative models of education that are tailored to attracting such marginalized students must be scaled up to ensure that they are equipped with basic literacy, numeracy and life skills.

We need to increase transition rates between the primary and lower secondary education cycle. This can be done by delivering secondary education on the same site

---

120 Vision for School Education 3.0, EY, April 2017
121 Vision for School Education 3.0, EY, April 2017
122 Unicef, 2017

as primary education (with budgetary allocations for infrastructure improvement). We also need to address dropout rates and repetition rates in primary schooling in order to enable more rural children to transition to lower secondary education.

In order to ensure equity, we need to translate political commitment into detailed objectives for education plans, focusing on specific and equitable results, which seek to overcome disparities between varied backgrounds (e.g. children with disabilities, ethnic minorities, geographic deviations, etc). Budget allocations need to be gender sensitive, equitable and responsive to on-ground local needs, with allocations calculated from ground-up requirements, based on local expenditures, level of schooling and geographic location. Bottlenecks that hinder implementation should be identified and absorption capacity increased significantly. Direct cash grants need to be explored, with school grants provided in a predictable, timely and transparent fashion. If there is a budgetary deficit on the education front, the government should at the very least seek to match statutory requirements under the Right of Children to Free and Compulsory Education Act while providing incentives to private schools to expand enrolment and serve disadvantaged students.

There needs to be push to accelerate efforts in mitigating socio-cultural barriers in schooling. Higher priority should be given to reducing or eliminating discriminatory practices in rural India that impede the schooling of children; examples include child marriage, restrictions on social mobility for older girls, social neglect and caste/religion based abuses for marginalized children.

In addition, further research, in an Indian context, in rural education management is needed. We need to have a system of comprehensive review of early childhood development and the impact of early grades of primary education in rural India. We need to understand the varied reasons at a regional level for late entry to school for young children. Further research is also warranted on the type of multi-lingual education required in early grades of primary education; in order to improve enrolment and retention ratios. Greater understanding is required of alternative pathways to basic education (e.g. flexible learning programmes) for primary and lower secondary age out-of- school children in rural India. Further research is also required on meeting the learning needs of children with disabilities, in an Indian context. Furthermore, we need to solve how to provide education for children who drop in and out of schooling, given seasonal migration by their parents. Such children are typically difficult to track and require special attention given the disruption they face in their schooling.

IMPROVING ACCOUNTABILITY

We need to bring accountability to the student-teacher relationship. For teachers, we need to train them in modern pedagogy, enabling them to deliver quality education outcomes, while existing teachers should be encouraged to upgrade their skills, all while developing an appraisal system to monitor their performance. We need to turn teaching's image around, making it a wanted career profession, with meaningful impact and better pay. In Finland and Japan, being a teacher is a noble and prestigious profession. Only 10 per cent applicants are qualified as teachers, despite teaching not popular as a very high paying job in Finland. Every teacher needs to have a master's degree and highly level teacher training. Meanwhile, the work load of a teacher is kept low, with 600 hours per annum, compared to more than a thousand in the United States. Finally, Finland has built a non-judgemental ecosystem, with limited government control.[123] South Korea offers its teachers incentives like small class sizes and higher salaries along with a choice of location in future teaching positions.[124]

We should announce existing teacher training institutes as institutes of national importance, while encouraging research in education. Location and career mobility should be enabled for teachers, allowing them to grow on merit. Investing in a national registry of teachers would help develop a free market for teaching jobs.

We need a child-centred approach to education, with legal action required to eliminate corporal punishment, transforming schools into child-friendly environments that are actually conducive to learning. While laws limiting corporal punishment are in place, this issue needs further attention in order to eliminate such social norms and practices. Reform efforts need to keep modern teaching and learning processes at their core, with appropriate interventions required in curriculum, assessments, teacher education and school management. In addition, India should be focusing on ensuring age appropriate enrolment, and reducing any age related disparities in existing rural education cohorts. Pre-primary education should be made a part of the basic education cycle, encouraging more children to enrol in Class 1, at the appropriate age, while making them 'school-ready'. Campaigns need to be undertaken at the grassroots level to encourage parents to enrol children at the correct age, all while making them voice their demands for quality education.

To reduce dropout rates, there needs to be greater empowerment of schools, local district education and social welfare authorities, holding them responsible for

---

123 Finnish Teacher Training Schools (FTTS), 2016
124 National Centre on Education and the Economy, USA, 2014

discouraging dropping out. In the areas of class repetition, continuous assessments should be preferred over school examinations, while remedial teaching is explored. Encouraging the practice of multi-lingual teaching (preferably in the local vernacular) in early primary education would go a long way in making school a comfortable learning environment. Students should be encouraged to speak in their mother tongues, instead of adhering to a centre-imposed language constraint. There should be zero tolerance for teacher absenteeism, while encouraging teachers to visit students when in case of prolonged absenteeism.

Teacher management needs to be improved significantly, with teachers provided clear incentives to perform well in classrooms. School management committees should be empowered to reward and sack teachers for performance. Teacher recruitment and deployment ought to be kept free of politics, and instead focused on reducing wide disparities in class sizes. Local decentralization of education should also seek to address urgency situations, actions like granting the right to print books locally, along with providing flexibility on enrolment in schools in host communities would make local education nimbler.

Furthermore, we need additional data to analyse educational outcomes. The existing household survey data should be utilized by the Ministry of Education to complement administrative data in designing policies and interventions. The quality of data gathered on pre-school programmes needs to be improved significantly, with standardized definitions. Standardization is also required in primary and secondary school surveys, with definitions on dropout rates and school types varying across states. Data collection systems should be slated for improvement, with a focus on increasing coverage and reliability of data on non-formal and flexible education programmes.

IMPROVING QUALITY

As much as 25 per cent of our rural youth cannot read or write in their own language. The public provision of education needs to be expanded by targeted infrastructure investments, in areas where the need is greatest. Many primary schools often operate double shifts, with restricted learning hours, given insufficient classrooms. Pre-primary provision of educational facilities in marginalized rural areas is also necessary. Those districts that have schools performing below average, particularly in terms of retention and learning achievements, should be given appropriate support in a needs focused manner. The same set of tools (performance-based incentive schemes, per capita grants, matching grants for community contributions, social audits, cash transfers, etc.) need not be used across under-performing schools.

Our current K-12 education system assumes that all students learn the same concepts in the same manner. However, this may not be true.[125] As demonstrated by Howard Gardner, any batch of students will have different mindsets and cognitive abilities, with a distinctive set of intelligences which are responsive to different learning styles. Our schools continue to be evaluated on their inputs, instead of actual learning outcomes. In particular, the RTE Act laid down norms and standards like the maximum pupil-teacher ratio, pupil-classroom ratio, minimum working days, drinking water facilities, etc., but excludes quality norms (e.g. minimum learning outcomes).[126]

We need to adopt outcome-focused teaching practices, with performance objectives sought to be aligned to learning objectives, while teacher effectiveness is evaluated on the student's success.[127] Any formative assessments of students should be integrated in evaluation and assessment frameworks, while students should be tested on concepts instead of theoretical knowledge. Secondary education needs to be tweaked around, with an increased focus on career readiness. We need greater emphasis on building social skills and emotional quotient, while seeking to provide experiential learning that helps students solve real-life problems. Vocational education should be integrated to enable students to be job-ready, with apprenticeship options available for students to mitigate dropping out. Students need to be allowed to move at their own pace, allowed to pursue learning in a manner that is more exciting and be given responsibility for their own learning outcomes. Germany ensures that most 25 to 64-year-olds are provided vocational training in their secondary or tertiary levels. Meanwhile, Ethiopia is expanding its

---

125 Vision for School Education 3.0, EY, April 2017
126 National Policy on Education
127 Vision for School Education 3.0, EY, April 2017

vocational system, with enrolment rates rising above 30 per cent.[128]

Our regulatory regime needs to undergo significant change. There is significant lack of uniformity in the regulatory regime, with overlapping and ambiguous regulations, which along with the need for multiple licenCes prevent the system from functioning smoothly.[129] Our education policies change with the political pendulum, affecting the outcome of prior reforms. Meanwhile, most of our schools continue to function without a full time head (80 per cent of schools in Bihar, for example). Seniority-based promotions in the system, combined with minimal weightage to capabilities and skill sets, make a teaching career subject to patronizing influence. Finally, the diversion of school staff for election duties along with other non-governmental work can deplete focus and affect motivation. We need regulation to ensure regular training programmes are conducted to upskill teachers and principals, while an education focused IAS-like cadre needs to be instituted to ensure strategic thinking at the policy level. Meanwhile, promotions should be on merit, instead of seniority, all while school ratings are increasingly pushed to be based on student outcomes, with periodic goals broken down into specific targets and enhanced data systems developed to gather data on performance of schools. We need a faster system of approvals to be implemented, for education administration work, while offering increased autonomy to top performing schools and opening up low performing schools to external intervention. The community, along with parents, should be encouraged to mobilize funds for modernizing school infrastructure, with social audits conducted regularly.

We also need to pivot away from formal learning systems. Let's consider another aspect, the Indian government routinely funds large-scale agricultural extension programmes that seek to spread educational information about a variety of agricultural practices and technologies. Such technologies can help farmers raise productivity, by applying fertilizer in appropriate applications along with using modern planting and harvesting techniques. The majority of such agricultural extension programmes have agents visiting farmers individually or in groups, and thereby demonstrating agricultural best practices. However, typically only 5.7 per cent of farmers receive information through such channels[130]—farmer receptiveness to receiving new information on farming depends on regional tastes and preferences.

There are other mechanisms for transmitting such information. Consider the case of Khedut Saathi, a mobile voice service for small-scale farmers in Gujarat,

---

128 International Growth Centre, Ethiopia, 2016

129 Vision for School Education 3.0, EY, April 2017

130 Cole, Shawn and A. Nilesh Fernando, 2016. 'Mobilizing Agricultural Advice', Harvard Business School Working Paper, 13-047

which seeks to provide sustainable agricultural practice lessons in local languages on feature phones.[131] Farmers typically subscribe to the service by leaving a missed call on a local phone number and then pressing the number 9. The subscribers end up receiving three voice messages per week, which talk about the best agricultural practices for locally relevant crops in that season. Farmers are encouraged to put queries and provide comments through a recording feature, with a 1 per cent unsubscription rate, the service has social catchet, with a 75 per cent pick-up rate of broadcasts (indicating that its audience is highly engaged). The addition of a forwarding service, enabling peer-led targeting, allows new information about precision agriculture to be circulated amongst farmers quickly.

Finally, we need to have a vision for education that is diverse and inclusive. We need multiple learning paths: academics oriented schools that focus on delivering formal learning across disciplines for students; vocational schools that seek to enhance employment prospects; globally ranked schools that set the bar for everyone else, and offer knowledge based on global standards. A third party rating framework should be established for all schools. Students need to be encouraged to make diverse subject combinations, enabling a choice-based approach to learning, along with the adoption of an interdisciplinary approach to K-12 and higher education.

---

131 Opoku-Agyemang, Kweku, Shah, Bhaumik, Parikh, S. Tapan, 'Scaling up Peer education with Farmers in India', ICTD 2017

REFERENCES

Chaudhury, Nazmul, Jeffrey Hammer, Michael Kremer, Karthik Muralidharan, and F. Halsey Rogers. 2004. 'Teacher and Health Care Provider Absenteeism: A Multi-Country Study.' World Bank

Glewwe, Paul, Michael Kremer, and Sylvie Moulin. 1999. 'Textbooks and Test Scores: Evidence from a Prospective Evaluation in Kenya.'

Habyarimana, James, Jishnu Das, Stefan Dercon, and Pramila Krishnan. 2004. 'Sense and Absence: Absenteeism and Learning in Zambian Schools.' World Bank

Kremer, Michael, Karthik Muralidharan, Nazmul Chaudhury, Jeffrey Hammer, and F. Halsey Rogers. 2004. 'Teacher Absence in India.' World Bank

Pratichi Trust. 2002. Pratichi Education Report

Probe Team. 1999. Public Report on Basic Education in India. Oxford University Press

World Bank. 2001. Honduras: Public Expenditure Management for Poverty Reduction and Fiscal Sustainability

World Bank. World Bank. 2004. Papua New Guinea: Public Expenditure and Service Delivery (Discussion Draft). World Bank

Aggarwal, Y. (1998) Access and Retention under DPEP: A National Overview. Unpublished research report. New Delhi: National Institute of Educational Planning and Administration [NIEPA]. Available online: http://www.dpepmis.org/downloads/ar98.pdf.

Aggarwal, Y. (1997) Small Schools: Issues in Policy and Planning. NIEPA Occasional Paper 23. New Delhi: NIEPA.

Aikmen, S. and el Haj, H. (2006) EFA for Pastoralists in North Sudan: A mobile multigrade model of schooling. In Little, A. (ed.) Education for All and Multigrade Teaching: Challenges and Opportunities

Dordrect: Springer. Ames, P. (2006) A Multigrade Approach to Literacy in the Amazon, Peru: School and community perspectives

In Little, A. (ed.) Education for All and Multigrade Teaching: Challenges and Opportunities

Dordrect: Springer. André, R. (2005) School Without Walls. Documentary, produced by Mosaic Films.

Bharadway, N.S. and Boda, A. (1998) Multigrade Teaching in Small Schools.

Bray, M. (1987) Are Small Schools the Answer? Cost-Effective Strategies for Rural School Provision. London: Commonwealth Secretariat.

Chickermane, D.V. (1981) Arresting Stagnation in Small One-Teacher Rural Primary Schools in an Indian Experiment in Non-Grading. Paris: UNESCO

Chopra, R. and Jeffery, P. (eds.) (2005) Educational Regimes in Contemporary India. New Delhi: Sage Publications.

Dighe, A. (2002) Social Mobilization and Total Literacy Campaigns. In Govinda, R. (ed.) India Education Report: A Profile of Basic Education. New Delhi, NIEPA.

DISE (2006) Elementary Education in India: Progress towards UEE, Analytical Report 2004–2005. New Delhi: NIEPA.

DISE (2007) Elementary Education in India: Progress towards UEE, Analytical Report 2005–2006. New Delhi: NIEPA.

DISE (2007a) Elementary Education in Rural India: Where do we stand? New Delhi: National University for Educational Planning and Administration [NUEPA].

DISE (2007b) Elementary Education in Urban India: Where do we stand? New Delhi: NUEPA.

Dyer, C. (2000) Operation Blackboard: Policy Implementation in Indian Elementary Education. Oxford: Symposium Books.

Dyer, C. (2005) Decentralization to Improve Teacher Quality? District Institutes of Education and Training in India. Compare 35(2): 139–152.

Freire, P. (1972) Pedagogy of the Oppressed. Middlesex: Penguin Books Ltd.

Forero, C., Escobar-Rodriguez, D. and Molina, D. (2006) Escuela Nueva's Impact on the Peaceful Social Interaction of Children in Colombia.

In Little, A. (ed.) Education for All and Multigrade Teaching: Challenges and Opportunities. Dordrecht: Springer.

GOI [Government of India] (2007) Report of the Working Group on Elementary Education and Literacy for the 11th Five Year Plan. Unpublished draft report, Planning Commission, New Delhi.

GOI (2002) Tenth Five-Year Plan. New Delhi: Government of India.

GOI (1992) National Policy on Education 1992. New Delhi: Government of India.

GOI (1986) National Policy on Education 1986. New Delhi: Government of India.

GOI (1971) Education and National Development: Report of the Education Commission, 1964–1966. New Delhi: NCERT.

Govinda, R. and Bandyopadhyay, M. (2007) Access to Elementary Education in India: Country Analytical Review. CREATE Country Analytic Review. Brighton: University of Sussex.

Govinda, R. (2002) India Education Report: A Profile of Basic Education. New Delhi, NIEPA.

Govinda, R. and Josephine, Y. (2004) Parateachers in India: A Review. Unpublished draft paper for UNESCO/IIEP. Available online: http://www.unesco.org/iiep/eng/research/basic/PDF/teachers5.pdf

Govinda, R. and Varghese, N.V. (1993) Quality of Primary Schooling in India: A Case Study of Madhya Pradesh. Paris: International Institute for Educational Planning, and New Delhi: NIEPA. Gupta, D., Jain, M. and Bala, N. (1996) Multigrade Teaching: Status and implications. Unpublished research paper. New Delhi: National Council of Educational Research and Training. Jain, M. (1997) Initiatives in Multilevel Teaching at the Primary Stage. Unpublished paper. New Delhi: NCERT. Available online: http://ncert.nic.in/sites/publication/ptchap7.htm

Jain, M. (2001) Multiage Classrooms at Primary Stages—Some Initiatives. Primary Teacher Journal, Vol. XVVI, No.1. Also available online: http://ncert.nic.in/sites/publication/ptchap7.htm

Asadullah, Mohammad Niaz, and Nazmul Chaudhury, 'Poisoning the mind: arsenic contamination of drinking water wells and children's educational achievement in rural Bangladesh', Economics of Education Review, vol. 30, no. 5, October 2011, pp. 873-888.

'Madrasas and NGOs: complements or substitutes? Non-state providers and growth in female education in Bangladesh', World Bank Policy Research Working Paper 4511, 2008.

ASER Centre, India Annual Status of Education Report 2011, ASER Centre, New Delhi, 2011 http://images2.asercentre.org/aserreports/ASER_2011/aser_2011_report.pdf

Aturupane, Harsha, 'Equitable Access to Primary and Secondary Education and Enhancing Learning in Sri Lanka', Create Pathways to Access Research Monograph No. 29, March 2009.

Awasthi, Shally, and Siddharth Agarwal, 'Determinants of Child Mortality and Morbidity in urban slums in India', Indian Pediatrics, vol. 40, no. 1, December 2003, pp. 1145-60.

Bandyopadhyay, Madhumita, and Ramya, Subramanian, 'Gender equity in education: A review of trends and factors', CREATE Pathways to Access, Research Monograph No. 18, April 2008.

Banerjee, Rukmini, 'Poverty and primary schooling: fi eld studies from Mumbai and Delhi', Economic and Political Weekly, vol. 35, no. 10, 4 March 2000, pp. 795-802.

Baulch, Bob, 'The medium-term impact of the primary education stipend in rural Bangladesh', Journal of Development Effectiveness, vol. 3, no. 2, 2011.

Behrman, Jere R., Susan W. Parker, and Petra E. Todd, Long-Term Impacts of the Oportunidades Conditional Cash Transfer Program on Rural Youth in Mexico. Ibero-America Insitute for Economic Research, Goettingen, Germany, 2005.

Betcherman, Gordon, 'Child labor, education, and children's rights', Social Protection Discussion Paper Series, World Bank, Washington D.C., 2004.

Bhalotra, Sonia and Zafi ris Tzannatos, 'Child labor: what have we learnt?,' World Bank Social Protection Discussion Papers 27872, September 2003.

Blanco Allais, Federico, and Frank Hagemann, 'Child labour and education: evidence from SIMPOC Surveys', Working Paper, ILO, Geneva, June 2008.

Bruns, Barbara, Alain Mingat, and Ramahatra Rakatomalala, Achieving Universal Primary Education by 2015: A Chance for Every Child, World Bank, Washington D.C., 2003.

Caldwell, John C., P.H. Reddy and Pat Caldwell, 'The causes of marriage change in South India', Population Studies, vol. 37, no. 3, November 1983, pp. 343-361.

Cameron, Laurie, 'Primary Completion Rates', Technical Paper WP-09-01, Education Policy and Data Center, Academy for Educational Development, Washington, D.C., September 2005.

Campaign for Popular Education (CAMPE), Education Watch 2008—State of primary education in Bangladesh: progress made, challenges remained, CAMPE, Dhaka, Bangladesh, 2009.

Education Watch 2006—Financing primary and secondary education in Bangladesh,

CAMPE, Dhaka, Bangladesh, 2007.

Education Watch 2005—The state of secondary education: progress and challenges, CAMPE, Dhaka, Bangladesh, 2006.

Education Watch 2003–2004—Quality with equity: the primary education agenda, CAMPE, Dhaka, Bangladesh, 2005.

Canals-Cerdá, Jose, and Cristobal Ridao-Cano, 'The dynamics of school and work in rural Bangladesh', Policy Research Working Papers 3330, World Bank, Washington D.C., 2004.

Catani, Claudia, et al., 'Tsunami, War, and Cumulative Risk in the Lives of Sri Lankan Schoolchildren', Child Development, vol. 81, issue 4, 15 July 2010, pp. 1176-1191.

Chadhury, Nazmul and Dilip Parajuli, Conditional Cash Transfers and female schooling: the impact of the female school stipend programme on public enrolment in Punjab, Pakistan, World Bank South Asia Human Development Unit, Washington D.C., 2008.

Chaudhury, Nazmul, et al., Roll call: teacher absence in Bangladesh. 2004. Mimeo. http://siteresources.worldbank. org/INTSOUTHASIA/Resources/Roll_ Call_Teacher_Absence_Bangladesh.pdf

Consortium for Research on Education, Access, Transitions & Equity (CREATE), 'Access, age and grade',CREATE Policy Brief No. 2, University of Sussex, Brighton, UK, March 2008.

Conticini, Alessandro, and David Hulme, 'Escaping violence, seeking freedom: why children in Bangladesh migrate to the street', Programme for Research on Chronic Poverty in Bangladesh Working Paper 10, September 2006.

Dang, Hai-Anh, Leopoldo Sarr, and Niaz Asadullah, 'School access, resources, and learning outcomes: evidence from a non-formal school program in Bangladesh,'

Discussion Paper Series IZA DP No. 5659, Institute for the Study of Labor, Bonn, Germany, April 2011 http://ft p.iza.org/dp5659.pdf

Das, Narayan C. and Raniya Shams, 'Asset Transfer Programme for the Ultra Poor: A randomized control trial evaluation.' CFPR/ Working Paper no. 2, BRAC Research and Evaluation Division, July 2011.

Das, Deepa, et al., Early childhood development in fi ve South Asian countries, Working draft, World Bank Institute, Washington, D.C.

De, Anuradha, et al., PROBE Revisited, Oxford University Press, Delhi, 2011.

De Benitez, Sarah Thomas, 'State of World's Street Children: Violence', Street Children Series UK, Consortium for Street Children, 2007.

De Janvry, Alain, et al., 'Can conditional cash transfer programs serve as safety nets in keeping children at school and from working when exposed to shocks?', Journal of Development Economics, vol. 79, Issue, 2, 30 April 2006, pp. 349-373.

De Neubourg, Elise and Chris de Neubourg, 'The Impact of Malnutrition and Post Traumatic Stress Disorder on the Performance of Working Memory in Children', UNU-MERIT Working Papers 2012-005, Directorate of Primary Education, Annual sector performance report, Directorate of Primary Education, Ministry of Primary and Mass Education, Government of Bangladesh, Dhaka, 2011.

Dryden-Peterson, Sarah, Refugee Education: A Global Review, UN High Commissioner for Refugees, Geneva, 2011.

Barriers to Accessing Primary Education in Conflict-Affected Fragile States - Literature Review, Save the Children Alliance International, London, 2010.

Elbert, Thomas, et al., 'Trauma-related impairment in children - A survey in Sri Lankan provinces affected by armed conflict', Child Abuse & Neglect vol. 33, no. 4, 25 March 2009, pp. 238-246.

Emergency Events Database (EM-DAT), The OFDA/CRED International Disaster Database, Centre for Research on the Epidemiology of Disasters (CRED), Université catholique de Louvrain, Brussels, Belgium, 2011 www.emdat.be/

Education Policy Data Center (EPDC), 'The effect of violent conflict on the primary education in Khyber Pakhtunkhwa, Pakistan', Background paper prepared for the Education for All Global Monitoring Report 2011. The hidden crisis: Armed confl ict and education, UNESCO, Paris, 2010.

Edmonds, Eric V., 'Child Labour in South Asia', OECD Social, Employment and Migration Working Papers No 5, 20 May 2003.

Fernandes, Maria and Therese Mahon, 'The Untold Story Menstrual Hygiene: Issues Of Awareness And Practices', Paper presented at the 3rd South Asian Conference on Sanitation, Delhi, India, November 19-21, 2008.

Ferreira, Francisco H.G., Deon Filmer, and Norbert Schady, 'Own and Sibling Effects of Conditional Cash Transfer Programs: Theory and Evidence from Cambodia', Policy Research Working Paper No 5001, World Bank, 1 July 2009.

Ferris, Elizabeth, and Rebecca Winthrop, 'Education and Displacement: Assessing Conditions for Refugees and Internally Displaced Persons affected by Conflict', Background paper for the EFA Global Monitoring Report 2011.

The hidden crisis: Armed conflict and education, UNESCO, Paris, 2010.

Financial Management Reform Programme (FMRP), Bangladesh, Social Sector Performance Surveys: primary education. FMRP, Oxford Policy Management, UK, 2006.

Social Sector Performance Surveys: secondary education, FMRP, Oxford Policy Management, UK, 2005.

Foundation for Research on Educational Planning and Development (FREPD), A baseline survey of street children in Bangladesh - National Child Labour Survey 2002–03, Bangladesh Bureau of Statistics, Dhaka, 2003.

Global Coalition to Protect Education from Attack (GCPEA) http://protectingeducation.org

Ghosh, Shanti and Dheeraj Shah, 'Nutritional problems in urban slum children', Indian Pediatrics, vol. 41, no. 7, July 2004, pp. 682-96.

Giani, Laura, 'Migration and education: child migrants in Bangladesh', Sussex Migration Working Paper 33, 2006.

Glewwe, Paul, Hanan G. Jacoby, and Elisabeth M. King, 'Early childhood nutrition and academic achievement: a longitudinal analysis', Journal of Public Economics, vol. 81, issue 3, September 2001, pp. 345-368.

Global Education Cluster, Short Guide to Education in Rapid Needs Assessments, Global Education Cluster, Geneva, 2009.

Government of Bangladesh, and UNDP, Policy Study on the Probable Impacts of Climate Change on Poverty and Economic Growth and the Options of Coping with Adverse Effect of Climate Change in

Bangladesh, Government of Bangladesh and UNDP Bangladesh, Dhaka, 2009.

Government of India, India and the ILO http://labour.nic.in/ilas/indiaandilo.htm

Guarcello, Lorenzo, Fabrizia Mealli, and Furio C. Rosati, 'Household vulnerability and child labour: the effect of shocks, credit

rationing, and insurance,' Journal of Population Economics, vol. 23, issue 1, 2010, pp. 169-198.

Guarcello, L., et al., 'Children's work in Andhra Pradesh: trends and determinants', Understanding Children's Work (UCW) Programme Working Paper Series, February 2010.

Guarcello, Lorenzo, Scott Lyon, Furio C. Rosati, 'Child labour and education for all: An issue paper', Understanding Children's Work Project Working Paper Series, November 2006, revised 2008.

Guarcello, Lorenzo, and Furio C. Rosati, 'Does school quality matter for working children?', Understanding Children's Work Project Working Paper Series, April 2007.

Guarcello, Lorenzo, Scott Lyon, and Furio C. Rosati, Impact of Children's Work on School Attendance and Performance: A Review of School Survey Evidence from Five Countries, UCW Programme, Rome, 2005.

Gunawardena, C., Inclusive education in Sri Lanka, National Education and Research Evaluation Centre, University of Colombo, and UNICEF Sri Lanka, 2009.

Hasan, Zoya and Raju Menon, Unequal Citizens: A study of Muslim women in India, Oxford University Press, Delhi, 2004.

Heneveld, Ward and Helen Craig, 'Schools Count,' World Bank Technical Paper Number 303, Africa Technical Department Series, January 1996.

Hossain, Altaf, 'Age in grade congruence and progression in basic education in Bangladesh,' CREATE Research Monograph 48, October 2010.

Hossain, Naomi, and Heidi Tavakoli, School choice in Bangladesh, Oxford Policy Management and Institute of Development Studies, UK, December 2008.

Hou, Xiaohui, 'Wealth crucial but not sufficient: Evidence from Pakistan on economic growth, Child Labor, and Schooling,' World Bank Policy Research Working Paper 4831, February 2009.

Huda, S.N., et al., 'Biochemical hypothyroidism secondary to iodine deficiency is associated with poor school achievement and cognition in Bangladeshi children', Journal of Nutrition, vol. 129, issue 5, May 1999.

Human Rights Watch, Sabotaged Schooling, Naxalite Attacks and Police Occupation of Schools in India's Bihar and Jharkhand States, Human Rights Watch, New York, 2009.

Humanitarian Practice Network, Education in

Emergencies in Meeting Reports, Humanitarian Practice Network/ODI, London, 2010.

Internal Displacement Monitoring Centre (IDMC), Displacement due to natural hazard-induced disasters: Global estimates for 2009–2010, IDMC/ Norwegian Refugee Council, Geneva, 2011a.

Internal Displacement Caused by Confl ict and Violence, IDMC/Norwegian Refugee Council, Geneva, 2011b.

Pakistan: Millions of IDPs and returnees face continuing crisis, IDMC/Norwegian Refugee Council, Geneva, 2009.

International Food Policy Research Institute (IFPRI), 'Micronutrient and Gender Study' as cited in Chronic Poverty and Long Term Impact Study in Bangladesh, IFPRI, Chronic Poverty Research Centre, and Data Analysis and Technical Assistance datasets, Washington, D.C., Manchester, UK, and Dhaka, Bangladesh, 2011 www.ifpri.org/dataset/chronic-poverty-and-long-term-impact-study-bangladesh

Institute for Fiscal Studies (IFS), Econometría, and SEI, Evaluació de impacto del programa Familian en Acción, Informe Final, Departamento Nacional de Planeación, Bogotá, 2006.

International Labour Organization (ILO), Child labour and responses in South Asia, ILO, Geneva, 2009

www.ilo.org/legacy/english/regions/asro/ newdelhi/ipec/responses/index.htm#5

Baseline survey on child domestic labour in Bangladesh, ILO, Geneva, 2006.

Combating child labour in Asia and the Pacifi c: Progress and Challenges, ILO, Geneva, 2005.

International Institute for Population Sciences (IIPS) and Macro International, India National Family Health Survey-3, 2005–06, vol. I and II, Mumbai, 2007.

Jamil, Baela Raza, 'Curriculum Reforms in Pakistan –A Glass Half Full or Half Empty?', Paper presented at the Seminar on School Curriculum Policies and Practices in South Asian Countries, NCERT Delhi, India, 10-12 August 2009.

Jayaweera S. and C. Gunawardene, School participation in conflict-affected and selected districts in Sri Lanka, Save the Children, Colombo, 2009, Unpublished.

National Survey on non-schooling and absenteeism, Save the Children, Colombo, 2004, Unpublished.

Jeffery, Patricia, Roger Jeffery and Craig Jeffery, 'Investing in the future: Education in the social and cultural reproduction of Muslims in UP' in Mushirul Hasan (ed.), Living with Secularism: The Destiny of India's Muslims, Manohar Publications, New Delhi, 2007, pp. 63-89.

Jha, Jyotsna and Dhir Jhingran, Elementary education for the poorest and other deprived groups: The real challenge of universalization, Manohar Publishers, New Delhi, 2005.

Jhingran, Dhir, Language disadvantage: The learning challenge in primary education, APH Publishing Corporation, New Delhi, 2005.

Joint Review Mission - India, 14th Joint Review Mission, Aide Memoire, SSA, 2011.

Joint Review Mission - India, 11th Joint Review Mission, Aide Memoire, January 15-29, 2010.

Justino, Patricia, 'Violent Confl ict and Human Capital Accumulation', Institute of Development Studies Working Paper 379, November 2011.

Jyotsna, Jain, and Shah Mihir, 'Antyodaya Anna Yojana and Mid-day Meals in Madhya Pradesh', Economic and Political Weekly, vol. 40, no. 48, November 26 - December 2, 2005.

Kannangara, Nayomi, de Silva Harendra, and Parndigamage Nilakshi, Sri Lanka child domestic labour: A Rapid Assessment, International Programme for the Elimination of Child Labour, ILO, Geneva, September 2003.

Kaul, V., C. Ramachandran, and G.C. Upadhyaya, Impact of early childhood education on retention in primary grades: A longitudinal study, The National Council of Educational Research and Training, Integrated Child Development Services (ICDS), New Delhi, 1993.

Khandker Shahidur, Zaid Bakht and Gayatri B. Koolwal, 'The poverty impact of rural roads: Evidence from Bangladesh', World Bank Policy Research Working Paper 3875, 2006.

Kirk, Jackie (ed.), Certifi cation counts. Recognizing the learning attainments of displaced and refugee students, International Institute of Educational Planning-UNESCO, Paris, 2009.

Building Back Better: Post-Earthquake Responses and Educational Challenges in Pakistan, IIEPUNESCO, Paris, 2008.

Kirk, Jackie, and Rebecca Winthrop, 'Learning for a bright future: Schooling, armed confl ict, and children's well-being', Comparative Education Review, vol. 52, no. 4, November 2008, pp. 639-661.

Kremer, Michael, et al., 'Teacher absence in India: A snapshot', Journal of European Economic Association, vol. 3, no. 2-3, April-May 2005, pp. 658-67.

Krutikova, Sofya, 'Determinants of child labour: The case of Andhra Pradesh', Young Lives Working Paper No. 48, May 2009.

Kurosaki, Takahashi, et al., 'Child labor and school enrollment in rural India: Whose education matters?', Developing Economies, vol. 44, no. 4, December 2006, pp. 440-464.

Lai, Bryan, and Clayton Thyne, 'The effect of civil war on education, 1980–97', Journal of Peace Research, vol. 44, no. 3, 2007, pp. 277-292.

Leach, Fiona, 'Gender violence in schools, Learning and Educational Achievements in Punjab Schools (LEAPS 2003–07): Insights to inform the education policy debate', Education Update, vol. 7, no. 1, 2007.

Leclercq, Francois, 'Child work, schooling, and household resources in rural North India', Background paper for the Consultative Workshop on Child Work and Food Insecurity in Rural India, New Delhi, March 15-17, 2001.

Lewin, Keith M., 'Improving access, equity and transitions in education: Creating a research agenda', CREATE Pathways to Access Research Monograph No. 1, June 2007.

Little, Angela W., 'Access to elementary education in India: Politics, policies and progress', CREATE Pathways to Access Research Monograph No. 44, September 2010.

Luby, Stephen P., et al., 'The effect of handwashing at recommended times with water alone and with soap on child diarrhea in rural Bangladesh: an observational study', Public Library of Science—Medicine vol. 8, no. 6, 28 June 2011.

Mahmud, Simeen, and Sajeda Amin, 'Girls' schooling and marriage in rural Bangladesh', Emily Hannum and Bruce Fuller (eds.) Children's lives and schooling across societies: Research on the sociology of education, vol. 15, pp. 71-99.

Malik, Allah Bakhsh, Public-private partnerships in Education: Lessons learned from the Punjab Education Foundation, Asian Development Bank, Mandaluyong, Philippines, 2010.

Maluccio, John A., et al., 'The Impact of Nutrition during Early Childhood on Education among Guatemalan Adults', PIER Working Paper No. 06-026, 2006.

Maluccio, John, and Rafael Flores, 'Impact

Evaluation of a Conditional Cash Transfer Program. The Nicaraguan Red de Protección Social', Research Report No 141, International Food Policy Research Institute, 2005.

Mandelbaum, David G., Women's seclusion and men's honor: sex roles in north India, Bangladesh and Pakistan, University of Arizona Press, Arizona, 1993.

Massachusetts Institute of Technology (MIT) - Abdul Latif Jamel Poverty Action Lab (AJPAL), 'Solving Absenteeism, raising test scores', MIT-AJPAL Policy Briefcase No. 6, 1 September 2008.

Mathur, Sanyukta, Margaret Greene and Anju Malhotra, Too young to wed: The lives, rights, and health of young married girls, International Council for Research on Women (ICRW), 2003.

Ministry of Education of Sri Lanka/ UNICEF/MG Consultant, Study on children who have dropped out of school with emphasis on schools with high dropout rates, Government of Sri Lanka, Colombo, 2009.

Ministry of Education, Sri Lanka, Education Sector Development Framework and Programme, Government of Sri Lanka, Colombo, 2007.

Ministry of Human Resource Development (MHRD), 7th All India School Education Survey, National Council of Educational Research and Training, MHRD, New Delhi, 2011.

Mooney, Erin, and Colleen French, Barriers and bridges: access to education for internally displaced children, The Brookings-Bern Project on Internal Displacement, The Brookings Institution, Washington D.C., 2005.

Myers, Robert, The twelve who survive: Strengthening programs of early childhood development in the third world, Second edition, High/Scope Press, Michigan, 1995.

Nambissan, Geetha B., 'Dealing with Deprivation', India Seminar, 2000 www. india-seminar. com/2000/493/493%20 geetha%20b.%20nambissan.htm

National Council of Applied Economic Research (NCAER) and University of Maryland, India Human Development Survey (IHDS), India Human Development Report 2010

http://ihds.umd.edu/IHDS_ fi les/02HDinIndia.pdf

National Education Commission (NEC), Envisioning education for human development: Proposals for a National Policy Framework on general education in Sri Lanka, NEC, Colombo, 2003.

National Education Research and Evaluation Centre (NEREC), National assessment of Grade 4 cognitive achievement, National Education Research and Evaluation Centre, University of Colombo, Colombo, 2003.

National Institute of Education (NIE) and UNICEF. Rapid needs assessment survey: education of children in conflict affected areas, NIE, UNICEF Sri Lanka, Colombo, 2003.

National Sample Survey Office (NSSO), 'Education in India: 2007–08 - Participation and Expenditure', National Sample Survey Organization, 64th Round, Report No. 532, NSSO, Ministry of Statistics and Programme Implementation, Government of India, New Delhi, 2010.

Nicolai, Susan, and Carl Triplehorn, The Role of Education in Protecting Children in Conflict, Humanitarian Practice Network (ed.), ODI, London, 2003.

O'Malley, Brendan, 'The Threat of Political and Military Attacks on Schools, Students and Education Staff', Background paper for EFA Global Monitoring Report 2010 : Reaching the marginalized, UNESCO, Paris, 2009.

O'Keefe Philip, People with disabilities in India: from commitments to outcomes, World Bank, Washington D.C., 2007.

Oxford Policy Management (OPM), Formative research to guide strategic communication interventions for children in the cotton growing areas and cotton seed producing states: Final Report, UNICEF India, New Delhi, 2010.

External evaluation of the National Programme for Family Planning and Primary Health Care: Lady Health Worker Programme—Lady Health Worker study of socio-economic benefits and experiences, OPM, UK, August 2009.

Pakistan Bureau of Statistics (PBS), Pakistan Social and Living Standards Measurement Survey—Household Income Expenditure Survey (PSLM-HEIS), 2007-08, PBS, Islamabad, 2009.

Papadopoulos, Nina, 'Achievements and Challenges of the Education Cluster in the occupied Palestinian territory, Somalia and Sri Lanka', Background paper for EFA Global Monitoring Report 2011, UNESCO, Paris, June 2010.

Pinto-Jayawardena, K., Left behind, left out: The impact on children and families of mothers migrating for work abroad, Save the Children in Sri Lanka, Colombo, 2006.

Planning Commission, Government of India, Mid-term appraisal, 11th Five Year Plan 2007–2012, Planning Commission, Government of India, Oxford University Press, Delhi, 2011 http://planningcommission.nic.in/plans/mta/11th_mta/chapterwise/Comp_mta11th.pdf

Planning Commission, Government of Pakistan, Development Amidst Crisis: Millennium Development Goals Report 2010, Planning Commission, Government of Pakistan, 2010.

Pratichi Trust, Mid-day meal scheme and primary education: prospects and challenges in West Bengal, September 2006.

Peace Research Institute Oslo (PRIO), The Battle Deaths Dataset Version 3.0., new version released October 2009, Oslo, Norway. www.prio.no/Data/Armed-Conflict/Battle-Deaths

PROBE Team, Public Report on Basic Education in India, Oxford University Press, New Delhi, 1999.

Ramachandran V., S., Bhattarcharjea and K.M. Sheshagiri, Primary school teachers, the twists and turns of everyday practice, Unpublished Manuscript for Project Supported by Azim Premji Foundation, ERU Consultants, New Delhi, 2008.

Ravallion, Martin, and Quentin Wodon, 'Does child labor displace schooling? Evidence on Behavioral Responses to Enrollment Subsidy', World Bank Policy Research Working Paper No. 2116, 31 May 1999.

Ray, Ranjan, 'Child Labor, child schooling, and their interaction with adult labor: empirical evidence for Peru and Pakistan', World Bank Economic Review, vol. 14, no. 2, May 2000, pp. 347-67.

Ray, Ranjan and Geoffrey Lancaster, The impact of children's work on schooling: Multi-Country evidence based on SIMPOC Data, School of Economics, University of Tasmania, Hobart, Australia, 2004.

Rasmussen, Stephen F., et al., 'Pakistan: Scaling Up Rural Support Programs', Case studies in scaling poverty reduction, World Bank, Washington D.C. May 2004.

Reddy, Anugula N., and Shantha Sinha, 'School dropouts or pushouts? Overcoming barriers for the Right to Education', CREATE Pathways to Access Research Monograph No. 40, July 2010.

Rosati, Furio Camillio, and Maraicristina Rossi, 'Children's working hours and school enrollment: Evidence from Pakistan and Nicaragua', World Bank Economic Review vol. 17, no. 2, 2003, pp. 283-295.

Sachar Committee Report, Social, economic and educational status of the Muslim community of India: A Report, Prime Minister's High Level Committee, Government of India, New Delhi, November, 2006

www.zakatindia.org/Files/Sachar%20 Report%20%28Full%29.pdf

Saddhananda, K.W.S., Analysis of disability statistics in Sri Lanka, Department of Census and Statistics, Government of Sri Lanka, Colombo, 2001.

South Asia Forum for Education Development (SAFED), Pakistan Annual Status of Education Report (ASER) 2010, SAFED, Lahore, Pakistan, 2011.

Saha, K.C., 'Learning from empowerment of Sri Lankan refugees in India', Forced Migration Review May 2004.

South Asia Initiative to End Violence Against Children (SAIEVAC), Prohibition of Corporal Punishment of Children in South Asia: a progress review, SAIVEC, Global Initiative to End All Corporal Punishment of Children, Save the Children Sweden, Kathmandu, 2011.

Sakamoto, Shunsuke, 'Parental attitudes toward children and child labor: Evidence from rural India', Hi- Stat Discussion Paper Series No. 136, Institute of Economic Research Hitotsubashi University, Tokyo, January 2006.

Schurmann, Ann T., 'Review of the Bangladesh female secondary school stipend project using a social exclusion framework', Journal of Health, Population and Nutrition, vol. 4, 27 August 2009, pp. 505-517.

Stockholm International Peace Research Institute (SIPRI), SIPRI Yearbook 2011: Armaments, Disarmament and International Security. SIPRI, Stockholm, 2011a. SIPRI Military Expenditure Database, SIPRI, Stockholm, 2011b.

Tariquzzaman, Sheikh and Naomi Hossain, 'The boys left behind: where public policy has failed to Prevent Child Labour in Bangladesh', IDS Bulletin vol. 40, no. 1, January 2009, pp. 31-37.

Taylor, Nick, et al., 'Seeds of their struggle: The features of under- and over-age enrolment among Grade 4 learners in South Africa', CREATE Pathways to Access Research Monograph No. 47, October 2010.

Ten, Varina Tjon A., Menstrual Hygiene: A Neglected Condition for the Achievement of Several Millennium Development Goals. European External Policy Advisors, Brussels, 2007.

Uppsala Confl ict Data Program (UCDP), UCDP Confl ict Encyclopaedia 2011, Uppsala University, Sweden www.ucdp.uu.se/database

Understanding Children's Work (UCW) Programme, Understanding Children's Work in Bangladesh, UCW Programme, 2011.

'Joining Forces Against Child Labour', Inter-Agency Report for The Hague Global Child Labour Conference of 2010, UCW Programme, Rome, 2010.

United Nations, Annual report of the Special Representative of the Secretary-General for children and armed conflict, Radhika Coomaraswamy, UN, New York, 2011.

Right to Education in Emergency Situations: Report of the Special Rapporteur on the Right to Education, Vernor Munez Villalobos, UN Human Rights Council, UN, New York, 2008.

United Nations Children's Fund (UNICEF), The State of the World's Children 2013: Children with Disabilities, UNICEF, New York, 2013.

South Asia Data Pocketbook. UNICEF Regional Office for South Asia, Kathmandu, 2013.

Global Initiative on Out-of-School Children: Pakistan Country Study, UNICEF Pakistan, Islamabad, 2013.

Global Initiative on Out-of-School Children: Sri Lanka Country Study, UNICEF Sri Lanka, Colombo, 2013.

Global Initiative on Out-of-School Children: Bangladesh Country Study, Working draft, UNICEF Bangladesh, Dhaka, forthcoming.

Global Initiative on Out-of-School Children: India Country Study, Working draft, UNICEF India, New Delhi, forthcoming.

The State of the World's Children 2012: Children in an Urban World. UNICEF, New York, 2012.

The State of the World's Children 2011: Adolescence—an age of opportunity, UNICEF, New York, 2011.

Ensuring education of children during emergency is a priority, UNICEF Bangladesh, Dhaka, 2010a.

Progress Evaluation (PREV) of the UNICEF Education in Emergencies and Post-Crisis Transition Programme (EEPCT), UNICEF, New York, 2010b.

Mainstreaming child-friendly schools in Sri Lanka: a case study, UNICEF Sri Lanka, Colombo, 2009s.

Equity in School Water and Sanitation: Overcoming Exclusion and Discrimination in South Asia, UNICEF Regional Office for South Asia, Kathmandu, 2009b.

Education in Emergencies in South Asia. Reducing the Risks Facing Vulnerable Children, UNICEF Regional Office for South Asia, Kathmandu, 2009c.

Child-friendly schools in Punjab province, Pakistan, UNICEF Pakistan, Islamabad, 2008.

Behind Closed Doors: The Impact of Domestic Violence on Children, UNICEF, Child Protection Section, New York, 2006.

United Nations Children's Fund (UNICEF) and UNESCO Institute for Statistics (UIS), Global Initiative on Out-of-school Children: Conceptual and Methodological Framework (CMF), UNICEF and UIS, New York and Montreal, 2011.

Children out of school: Measuring exclusion from primary education, UNICEF and UIS, New York and Montreal, 2005.

United Nations Department of Economic and Social Affairs, Population Division, World Population Prospects: The 2010 Revision, UNDESA, New York, 2012.

World Economic Situation and Prospects-2011, UNDESA, New York, 2011.

United Nations Development Programme (UNDP), Sustainability and Equity: A better future for all, Human Development Report, UNDP, New York, 2011.

United Nations Economic and Social Commission for Asia and the Pacific (UNESCAP), Disability at a Glance: Strengthening the Evidence Base in Asia and the Pacific, Social Development Division, UNESCAP, Bangkok, 2012.

United Nations Educational, Scientific and Cultural Organization (UNESCO), Education for All Global Monitoring Report 2011: The hidden crisis: armed conflict and education, UNESCO, Paris, 2011.

Education Under Attack, UNESCO, Paris, 2010.

'Four studies of education growth: Inequality by wealth, age effects, sub-national learning differentials, and projections', Background paper prepared for EFA Global Monitoring Report 2009—Overcoming inequality: Why governance matters, UNESCO, Paris, 2008.

EFA Global Monitoring Report 2008, Education for All by 2015: Will we make it?, UNESCO, Paris, 2007.

An assessment of inclusive education in Bangladesh, UNESCO, Dhaka, 2006.

EFA Global Monitoring Report 2005 - Education for All: the Quality Imperative, UNESCO, Paris, 2004.

UNESCO and UNICEF, End of Decade Notes on Education for All Goal 2: Universal Primary Education, UNESCO and UNICEF, Bangkok, 2013.

UNESCO Institute for Statistics (UIS), Global Education Digest: Comparing education statistics around the World, UIS, Montreal, 2011.

United Nations High Commissioner for Refugees, UNHCrore Global Trends 2010, UNHCR, Geneva, 2011.

United Nations Human Settlements Programme (UN-HABITAT), State of the World's Cities Report 2012/2013: Prosperity of Cities, UN-HABITAT, New York, 2013.

United Nations Population Fund (UNFPA), State of the World Population: 2000, UNFPA, New York, 2000.

United Nations Office for the Coordination of Humanitarian Affairs (OCHA), Financial Tracking Service (FTS), OCHA, New York, 2011.

WaterAid, Sanitation and Water Why We Need A Global Framework For Action, WaterAid and Tearfund, 2008.

Williams, J.R.A., 'The Impact of Conflict and Displacement (2006–2010) on Education in Sri Lanka', Background paper for the EFA Global Monitoring Report 2011, UNESCO, Paris, 2010.

Wils, Annababette', Late entrants leave school earlier: Evidence from Mozambique, 'International Review of Education, vol. 50, no. 1, 2004, pp. 17-37.

Women's Commission for Refugee Women and Children, Global Survey on Education in Emergencies, Women's Commission for Refugee Women and Children, New York, 2004.

World Bank, Gender Equality and Development, World Development Report, World Bank, Washington D.C., 2012.

People with disabilities in India: from commitments to outcomes, Human Development Unit, South Asia Region, World Bank, Washington D.C., 2009.

Project appraisal document on a proposed credit to the People's Republic of Bangladesh for a disability and children-at-risk project, World Bank, Washington D.C., 2008 http://tinyurl.com/yhuqa6u

Reshaping the Future, World Bank, Washington, D.C., 2005.

Treasures of the educational system in Sri Lanka: restoring performance, expanding opportunities and enhancing prospects, World Bank, Colombo, 2005.

Project Performance Assessment Report: Bangladesh Female Secondary School Assistance Project, Bangladesh, Operations Evaluation Department, World Bank, Washington D.C., June 2003.

World Health Organization, WHO PCT Databank on schistosomiasis and soil-transmitted helminth infections www.who.int/neglected_diseases/preventive_chemotherapy/databank/en/index.html

Global Database on Child Growth and Malnutrition, WHO <www.who.int/nutgrowthdb/database/ countries/en/index.html#I>

World Report on Disability 2011, WHO, Geneva, 2011.

Zafar, Fareeha, Situation analysis of gender disparities in primary and middle education in the Punjab Case Studies of Khanewal and Rawalpindi Districts, Society for Advancement of Education (SAHE), Lahore, Pakistan, 2010.

How Have States Designed Their School Education Budgets, Source: CBGA & CRY, 2016

Public-Private Partnerships In School Education, Learning and Insights for India, S Chaudhry & A Uboweja, Working Paper March 2014, Central Square Foundation

Rashtriya Madhyamik Shiksha Abhiyan (RMSA), BUDGET BRIEFS, Vol 10/ Issue 2, Accountability Initiative, Centre for Policy Research

Sarva Shiksha Abhiyan (SSA), BUDGET BRIEFS, Vol 10/ Issue 1, Accountability Initiative, Centre for Policy Research

Report of the Comptroller and Auditor General of India on Implementation of Right of Children to Free and Compulsory Education Act, 2009; Report No 23 of 2017

'How Much Does India Spend Per Student on Elementary Education?',PAISA Report Series, Accountability Initiative, Centre for Policy Research

Young Lives School Survey, 2016–17: Evidence from India

Elementary Education & Sarva Shiksha Abhiyaan, Accountability Initiative, Centre for Policy Research

'Between the lines', Accountability Initiative, Centre for Policy Research

Education reforms, bureaucracy and the puzzles of implementation, Yamini Aiyer, Ambarish Dongre, Vincy Davis, International Growth Centre, Sep 2015

'Debating The Role Of India's Frontline Education Bureaucracy'; Yamini Aiyer, Accountability Initiative, Centre for Policy Research

All India Survey on Higher Education, 2015–16, Ministry of Human Resource Development, 2016

Educational Statistics at a Glance; Ministry of Human Resource Development, 2016

'Funding Education With Impact: A Guide For Social Investment In India'; Credit Suisse & Sattva Knowledge Centre & Consulting

'Making The Grade: Improving Mumbai's public schools', Dasra

Selected Socio-Economic Statistics, Ministry of Statistics and Programme Implementation, Central Statistics Office, Social Statistics Division, India Sep 2017,

Private Sector's Role in Indian Higher Education, Anand Sudarshan and Sandhya Subramanian

Not So Elementary - Primary School Teacher Quality in Top-Performing Systems, Centre on International Education benchmarking

The India Early Childhood Education Impact Study, UNICEF, ASER & CEDED

Right to Education Act, Oxfam Policy Brief, March 2015

There's an urgent need for reforms in our education system, Divya S, Indian Express, February 2016

India's schools fail to keep pace with growth, Financial Times, 11-Jun-2016

Report of the Working Group on Private Sector participation including PPP in School Education, 12th Five Year Plan, Department of School Education and Literacy, Ministry of Human Resource Development

Revamping education sector: Is it time for Public-Private Partnership models, Indian Express, 8-February-2016

'Public-private partnership in education',

The Hindu, 11-Jun-2017

'Learning to realize Education's promise', World Bank Group

Twelvth Five Year Plan, Planning Commission

'A renewed model of education', K Muralidharan, Livemint, 21-Jan-2014

'How unequal is access to education', M Chakravarty, Livemint, 9-May-2016

Annual Status of Education Report (Rural) 2016, Provisional, 18-Jan-2017

School Education In India, flash Statistics, U-DISE 2015–16, National University of Educational Planning and Administration

Diverging Pathways: When and Why Children Discontinue Education in India, Renu Singh and Protap Mukherjee, Working Paper No 173, Young Lives

The Fiscal Cost of Weak Governance Evidence from Teacher Absence in India: Karthik Muralidharan, Jishnu Das, Alaka Holla, Aakash Mohpal, World Bank 2016

The Crisis Within: On Knowledge and Education in India, G N Davy

India Education Report: Progress of Basic Education, R. Govinda & Mona Sedwal, Oxford University Press

Village Education in India, 1920: The Report of a Commission of Inquiry

History of Education in India, RN Sharma & RK Sharma

Financing of education in India, Jandhyala B. G. Tilak

The Economics Of Elementary Education In India: The Challenge Of Public Finance, Private Provision And Household Costs, Santosh Mehrotra

Public Expenditure on Education in India by the Union Government and Roadmap for the Future, Anit N. Mukherjee, Satadru Sikdar

Per-child funding model for financing school education in India, Centre for Civil Society

Public Financing of School Education in India: A Fact Sheet 2016, CRY & CBGA

Education Budget: The School Education Crisis And Opportunity, Shreya Shah, Indiaspend, January 25, 2017

Resource requirements for Right to Education (RTE): Normative and the Real, Sukanya Bose, Priyanta Ghosh and Arvind Sardana, NIPFP Working paper series, 09-Dec-2017

'How Much Does India Spend Per Student On Elementary Education', Ambrish Dongre, Avani Kapur, Vibhu Tewary, Accountability Initiative, Centre for Policy Research

Analysis Of Budgeted Expenditure On Education (2010–11 To 2012–13), Ministry of Human Resource Development

Analysis Of Budgeted Expenditure On Education (2012–13 To 2014–15), Ministry of Human Resource Development

'How Have States Designed Their School Education Budgets?', CBGA & CRY, 2016

Times Of India, Arindam Banik, 02-Apr-2018

'Do Schools Get Their Money? Paisa 2012', Accountability Initiative, Centre for Policy Research

'Do Schools Get Their Money? Paisa 2014', Accountability Initiative, Centre for Policy Research

Trends in Public Expenditure on Elementary Education in India, Ambrish Dongre, Avani Kapur, EPW, 24-Sep-2016

❈

CHAPTER IX

ON RURAL HEALTHCARE

India's healthcare delivery remains a troika of the lack of accessibility, affordability and quality. Despite having carved out a name for itself in medical tourism, India's healthcare facilities fail our countrymen with an estimated 39 million people falling below the poverty line trying to avail healthcare in our hospitals and clinics. Despite the presence of a well-defined structure, our inadequate per capita public healthcare remains plagued by crumbling infrastructure and lack of maintenance, while construction of new facilities lags behind national needs. Healthcare facilities face a shortage of doctors, nursing staff and resources like equipment and medicines, while staff amenities present a huge scope for improvement.

The National Rural Health Mission (NRHM) has sought to provide effective healthcare to rural areas by focusing on capacity and infrastructure while seeking to promote policies at the various levels to strengthen healthcare management and service delivery.

India's numerous pieces of legislation for epidemic preparedness are policing in nature, without focusing on consolidated public health outcomes. Our healthcare spending pattern has deviations from desired results—spending on tertiary care is higher than that on secondary care, indicating a proclivity for hospitalization, mostly on account of failure to tackle the disease at primary and secondary care stages. As healthcare spending increases with time, it becomes critical to align policy incentives with improved quality of service delivery and healthcare spends.

Healthcare expenditure management remains shackled in bureaucratic shenanigans and needs reform in order to better respond amidst modern-day changing needs. India's demand side healthcare financing presents a host of complex issues on their own. Given the lack of quality public healthcare initiated by a cycle of chronic underfunding and the rapid emergence of private facilities providing improved medical care on a fee-for-service basis, the rapid rise in healthcare insurance spends is hardly surprising. For health insurance, a multitude of schemes exists (both at the national and state level), yet each one has its own fair share of impact and side-effects.

Many features of India's State-sponsored insurance programmes are consistent with the best global practices and suitable for country's requirements. Improved scale by bringing millions under the insurance net, reducing OOP payments for high-cost tertiary care and providing cashless facilities at point-of-care is laudable. Capitalizing on the inherent strengths of public insurance systems, coupled with design and policy changes to overcome the inherent weaknesses will lead to improved health outcomes for the same levels of demand-side financing.

Generic manufacturing by PSUs for essential drugs can increase competition and employment, steadily reducing the overarching need for ever-increasing price controls. Our public healthcare spends need to focus more on prevention (primary care) than cure (tertiary care).

Keeping in mind the long term mission of universal healthcare, supported by political consensus on hard choices, sustained long-term funding and efficient regulations, consistent and supporting policies at the centre and the state level and integration of healthcare facilities across villages, towns and districts can help in the universal coverage of good quality healthcare.

RURAL HEALTH

Roshni, a seven-year-old girl from Chintamanpur village (East Champaran district) in Bihar often wonders why she is living on the streets of Delhi, beside the AIIMS Metro station, instead of attending her village school and playing with her friends. Meanwhile, her father, Kishore Vijay, a forty-year-old farmer, has been doing the rounds of a reputed doctor with his wife and has finally managed to get an appointment after four months of effort. However, his predicament has no end— the scheduled appointment is thirteen months away and he is confused about whether to keep his child in the same condition, undiagnosed, or go back to his village and find some other line of treatment. Earlier, his efforts to get the medical condition diagnosed in the local and district hospitals have rendered no result, leaving him with no option but to come to AIIMS where he seems to have hit a deadlock. Kishore is not the sole suffererer—he is accompanied by many others huddled outside the AIIMS Metro station, each with their own story reflecting on the limitations and failure of the public healthcare system. Reema and her thirteen-year-old son, Nilesh, came to Delhi from Motihari to seek treatment for Reema's husband, a farm help with no income last year due to an unidentified brain problem. Having exhausted their family savings of ₹2 lakh, saved meticulously for Nilesh's education, they depend solely on their friends and family for donations. Meanwhile, her husband is still undiagnosed and hasn't received proper/desired care. Reema is now considering visiting other private doctors in Delhi, for which she requires a little guidance and more financial help, and is awaiting the latter from her ailing parents. Sita, from Dekpura village (Nalanda District) in Bihar shares a similar story—she has spent ₹1 lakh on the treatment of Ramesh, her ten-year-old son. Her husband continues to toil on the family farm, trying eagerly to generate income and send it to Sita, who, on the other hand, has expressed her desire to sell her kidney, if need be, for Ramesh's treatment.

Kishore, Sita and Reema are among the 200 to 300 families living outside the AIIMS Metro station and striving to get medical care on an urgent basis. Despite the lack of health insurance, they are ready to spend on private healthcare, even after exhausting a bulk (if not all) of their lives' savings. Such families are just a few among India's 86 per cent rural population with no insurance support and each ailment can set them back financially by at least a few months of income. On an average, each time a rural family takes an overnight trip for health reasons; it ends up spending approximately ₹15,336 (NSSO data).[1] In the absence of any shade and food due to the lack of money, they are dependent on public generosity for food, without which they will have to spend about ₹40 for a plate of rice and vegetables. Without any public health support, they would be forced to avail services provided by private healthcare without any insurance, which can likely lead them to being one among the 39 million people that are pushed back into poverty each year due to healthcare expenses (The Lancet, 2011[2]).[3]

The tragic scenes of patients sleeping outside the AIIMS Metro station have found another parallel to those on the footpaths of Mumbai's Jerbai Wadia road, adjoining the Tata Memorial Hospital, where, on an average, each visitor patient has not worked for a year, lost ₹55,000 in potential income and spent ₹76,000 before winding up on the pavement. One in every four patients has exhausted their savings and resorted to loans from friends, family and moneylenders in seeking cancer treatment from the eminent institution. Cancer remains one of the most

---

1   https://scroll.in/pulse/811882/1000-km-journey-and-a-1-5-year-wait-for-a-doctors-appointment-rural-indias-quest-for-healthcare

2   http://www.thelancet.com/journals/lancet/article/PIIS0140-6736%2810%2961894-6/abstract

3   http://www.indiaspend.com/cover-story/bankrupt-poorly-educated-desperate-cancer-patients-on-mumbai-footpath-54419

expensive to treat diseases in India, with an average annual spend of ₹36,812 in a government facility, an amount which is a significant proportion of the average national annual per capita income. The lack of widespread cancer referral centres, especially in rural areas (only twenty-seven government cancer referral centres and 250 cancer centres nationwide with 40 per cent present in metropolitan cities), force, citizens to land up on footpaths outside the hallowed gates of reputed cancer centres.

India has approximately twenty-seven million babies born annually, of which 13 per cent are born pre-term and 28 per cent are considered to be in the low-weight category, both with a higher risk of dying in the neonatal period.[4] Our maternal mortality rate also continues to be high, with ~167 maternal deaths for every 100,000 live births. Structural factors tend to make this worse—vulnerable populations (including Dalits and adivasis), have a higher probability of being excluded from healthcare services, with a subsequent higher risk of mortality. Such maternal healthcare-related expenses (including childbirth, antenatal care and postnatal care expenses) tend to push over 46.6 per cent of all mothers into poverty.[5] Over 63 per cent of all households nationwide face a situation where maternal health expenditure can exceed a critical threshold of 40 per cent of their non-subsistence income (income available after basic needs have been met). Over 65.7 per cent of all households in Telangana were pushed into poverty due to expenses related to childbearing requirements (amongst other expenses), while Chhattisgarh had 53.7 per cent. Between 2004 and 2014, over 50.6 million people were pushed back into poverty due to childcare expenses.[6] Such a situation is especially prevalent amongst illiterate women, with 61 per cent of them pushed into poverty—as a consequence, most of them prefer to rely on public hospitals for delivery, particularly in rural areas (79.2 per cent of rural women prefer to utilize public hospitals for deliveries).

---

4   Tandon, Rajiv, A healthy future for mothers and babies, Live Mint, 30 August, 2017. Sourced from: http://www.livemint.com/Opinion/o2wiuM998gUBmfQyDURT7N/A-healthy-future-for-mothers-and-babies.html

5   Saha, Devanik, IndiaSpend, 'Maternal healthcare expenses push 46.6% mothers in India into poverty: Study', Hindustan Times, 22 May 2017. Sourced from: http://www.hindustantimes.com/india-news/maternal-healthcare-expenses-push-46-6-mothers-in-india-into-poverty-study/story-tIM8Fio6iUn3yKRDzB1AOM.html

6   IndiaSpend, 8 May, 2017

STATE OF RURAL HEALTHCARE INFRASTRUCTURE

POPULATION NORMS

India's rural healthcare infrastructure is defined in a tiered manner, with sub-centres, primary healthcare centres (PHCs) and community health centres (CHCs). A sub-centre is typically the first contact point in the primary healthcare system for the local individual, with responsibilities of dealing with maternal and childcare services, family welfare, nutrition, immunization drives, diarrhoea control, communicable disease control and interpersonal communication for driving behaviour change to improve community healthcare. Typically, each sub-centre is supposed to be manned by at least an auxiliary nurse midwife (ANM) or a female health worker, along with one male health worker (MHW), all monitored by a lady health visitor (LHV). The salary burden for the sub-centre is covered partially by the central government (for the ANM and LHV) and the remaining by the state government (for the male health worker).

A primary health centre supplements the sub-centre, providing integrated, curative and preventative healthcare to individuals, serving as a first point of contact between the medical officer and the village individual. Such PHCs are typically established and maintained by state governments, to serve basic healthcare needs. Each PHC is typically manned by a medical officer who is supported by fourteen paramedical and other staff, along with potentially two additional staff nurses on a contractual basis. The PHC is the referral unit for six sub-centres, with four–six beds for patients.

A community health centre comes under the basic minimum needs programme instituted by state governments. A CHC is typically supported by four medical specialists (a surgeon, physician, gynaecologist and paediatrician), with thirty indoor beds, along with an operating theatre, X-ray, labour room and laboratory facilities. A CHC is typically a referral centre for 4 PHCs, while providing facilities for obstetric care and consultations.

Population norms for healthcare in India are typically defined as 5,000 individuals for a sub-centre located in the plains, while this can go down to 3,000 individuals in a hilly, tribal or difficult area. For primary healthcare centres, the norm is typically considered to be 30,000 individuals in the plains, declining to 20,000 in geographically difficult areas. Similarly, for community health centres, the norm is 120,000, declining to 80,000 in difficult areas. Yet, in 2015, India's national average for sub-centres was touching 5,426,[7] with PHCs serving 32,944 on average and

---

7   Rural Health Statistics, Ministry of Health and Family Welfare Statistics Division, 2014-15. Sourced from: http://www.indiaenvironmentportal.org.in/files/file/Rural%20Health%20Statistics%202014-15.pdf

CHCs serving 154,512, respectively. The average rural area served by a sub-centre was 20.27 sq km, while that by a PHC was 123.09 sq km and that by a CHC was 577.32 km. Each sub-centre typically served four villages, while each PHC served twenty-five; a CHC would serve about 119 villages.

The shortfall is particularly revealing at the state level. In sub-centres, Bihar, Meghalaya and Uttar Pradesh come up short, while for PHCs, Jharkhand and West Bengal are key laggards. The availability of facilities in Rajasthan was considerably less than IPHS norms in tribal areas and much higher in non-tribal areas (13.24 per cent of CHCs, 32.96 per cent of PHCs and 20.65 per cent of SCs).[8] While the Ministry of Health attributed the shortfall in facilities to the shortage of funds in the Twelfth Five Year Plan, with only ₹91,022 crore made available against a requirement of ₹1,93,405 crore. However, states are not always able to spend allocated resources, ending up with unspent funds.

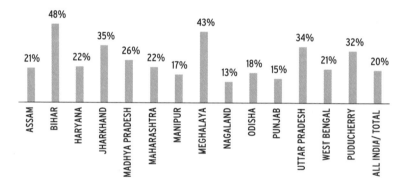

FIGURE 203: SHORTFALL IN HEALTHCARE INFRASTRUCTURE SUB-CENTRES (INCLUDING RURAL & URBAN POPULATIONS), BY STATE[9]

When this viewpoint is flipped and we consider the shortfall in manpower across sub-centres in states, a stark picture emerges. States like Rajasthan, Gujarat and Karnataka have faced a significant shortfall in manpower in sub-centres, impacting patient coverage and quality of services offered.

---

8   CAG, Report No. 25 of 2017. Sourced from: http://cag.gov.in/sites/default/files/audit_report_files/ Report_No.25_of_2017_-_Performance_audit_Union_Government_Reproductive_and_Child_Health_ under_National_Rural_Health_Mission_Reports_of_Ministry_of_Health_and_Family_Welfare.pdf

9   Table 11, Part 2, Section III, Rural Health Statistics, Ministry of Health and Family Welfare Statistics Division, 2015-16

FACILITY LOCATION AND CONNECTIVITY

IPHS norms require SC facilities to be located within the village to provide for easy coverage of the local villagers, through the Auxiliary Nurse and Midwives. An individual should not have to walk more than 3 km to reach the SC, while the SC should be equipped with communication facilities. Each PHC and CHC should be located in an easily accessible area, while each health facility should be located away from unhygienic areas (garbage collection centres, cattle sheds, etc.).

In reality, facilities at sub-centres can suffer from significant shortfalls, including water supply, electricity and an approachable motorable road. Surveys conducted by the CAG highlight that most SCs (73 per cent) across twenty-nine states surveyed were located at a distance of more than 3 km from the remotest village in their catchment area, while 28 per cent were not accessible by public transport, and 17 per cent were located in unhygienic areas.[10] Similarly, 20 per cent of PHCs were not accessible by public transport, and 19 per cent were located in unhygienic areas; meanwhile, 26 per cent of all CHCs were located in unhygienic areas. A survey of 1,443 SCs, 514 PHCs, 300 CHCs and 134 district hospitals in 2017 across 29 states and Union Territories highlighted that only 28 per cent of SCs had their own designated government building. Just 12 per cent of SCs were rated highly on the cleanliness of their premises, while just 36 per cent overall had regular electricity and water supply. Only 34 per cent of SCs had an in-house toilet, while just 20 per cent of Type B SCs had a labour room. Meanwhile, for PHCs, 8 per cent had their own designated government buildings, with 46 per cent having poor condition of plaster on them. Just 33 per cent had proper flooring, only 6 per cent had regular electricity supply, while 68 per cent had a standby electricity generator in place. Just 12 per cent overall had regular water supply while only 43 per cent had a transport facility for referrals. CHCs had a similar scenario—37 per cent had poor condition of plaster on their walls, while 28 per cent had proper flooring. Meanwhile, over 33 per cent had an operation theatre available, which was not in use, and only 19 per cent had separate male and female wards.

The consequence of the non-availability of such connecting infrastructure can have a significant impact.[11] In Jharkhand, essential services like the out-patient departmental services, 24-hour emergency services, referral services and in-patient departmental services were absent in seventeen selected PHCs, given a shortage of beds and, in some cases, the building itself. Even in Kerala only 23 CHCs of

---

10   CAG, Report No. 25 of 2017. Sourced from: http://cag.gov.in/sites/default/files/audit_report_files/Report_No.25_of_2017_-_Performance_audit_Union_Government_Reproductive_and_Child_Health_under_National_Rural_Health_Mission_Reports_of_Ministry_of_Health_and_Family_Welfare.pdf

11   CAG, Report No. 25 of 2017. Sourced from: http://cag.gov.in/sites/default/files/audit_report_files/Report_No.25_of_2017_-_Performance_audit_Union_Government_Reproductive_and_Child_Health_under_National_Rural_Health_Mission_Reports_of_Ministry_of_Health_and_Family_Welfare.pdf

1,158 CHCs and PHCs, provided delivery services with the remaining unable to do so given a lack of prerequisite infrastructure (manpower, equipment, etc.). The CAG report cites that while over 75 per cent of pregnant women utilized antenatal services in government health facilities, most preferred private hospitals for the actual delivery given a perception of safety and better availability of paediatric services. General Hospitals (GH) in Gujarat had similar issues—with a GH in Godhra having only 210 beds against a requirement of 440, while a waiting room was being used as a laboratory at the entrance of a GH in Nandiad.

CHCs in Meghalaya had faulty drainage systems, leading to water overflowing during the rainy season, flooding almost all the rooms in the surveyed CHCs. DHs in Nongpoh, Meghalaya, were noted to have leaking pipes and an overflowing septic tank near the kitchen area. Overcrowding is especially prevalent in rural hospitals in West Bengal (e.g., Krishnapur) and Maharashtra (e.g., Bandara). Rajasthan's newly constructed health facilities were found to have significant structural issues—cracked walls, leaking roofs, blocked drains, broken railings—which are indicators of the sub-standard quality of construction. Tripura was reported to have non-operational labour rooms in three surveyed PHCs, given a lack of prerequisite factors.

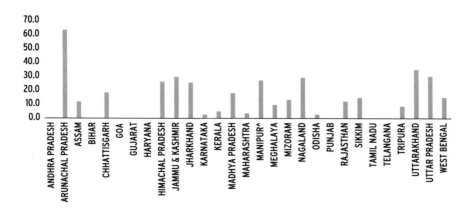

FIGURE 204: ACCESS BY REGULAR ALL-WEATHER MOTORABLE ROAD TO SUB-CENTRES IN FY15[12]

---

12   Table 11, Part 2, Section V, Rural Health Statistics, Ministry of Health and Family Welfare Statistics Division, 2015-16

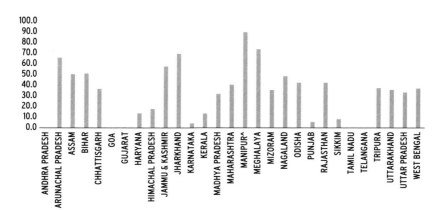

FIGURE 205: ACCESS TO REGULAR WATER SUPPLY IN SUB-CENTRES IN FY15[13]

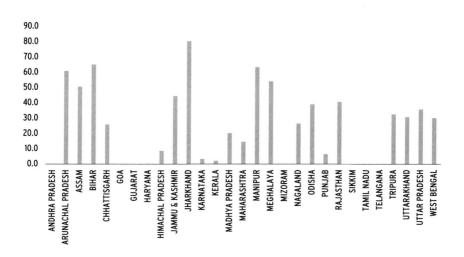

FIGURE 206: ACCESS TO REGULAR ELECTRICITY IN SUB-CENTRES IN FY15[14]

---

13   Table 11, Part 2, Section V, Rural Health Statistics, Ministry of Health and Family Welfare Statistics
     Division, 2015-16
14   Table 11, Part 2, Section V, Rural Health Statistics, Ministry of Health and Family Welfare Statistics
     Division, 2015-16

CONSTRUCTION OF NEW FACILITIES

The cumulative state of rural healthcare infrastructure on a state level gives a varied picture. Kerala had over 4,575 sub-centres, while Maharashtra opened over 10,580 sub-centres as of March 2016.

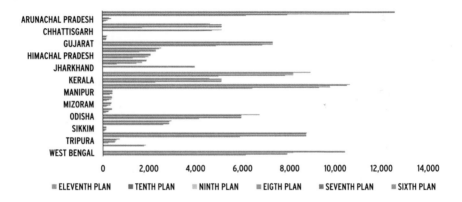

FIGURE 207: NUMBER OF HEALTHCARE SUB-CENTRES DURING FIVE YEAR PLANS[15]

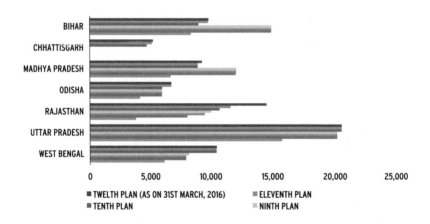

FIGURE 208: NUMBER OF HEALTHCARE SUB-CENTRES (BIMARU STATES)
DURING FIVE YEAR PLANS[16]

---

15 Part 2, Section III, Rural Health Statistics, Ministry of Health and Family Welfare Statistics Division, 2015-16

16 Part 2, Section III, Rural Health Statistics, Ministry of Health and Family Welfare Statistics Division, 2015-16

TABLE 111: NUMBER OF FUNCTIONING SUB-CENTRES, CHCS AND PHCS[17]

STATE/UT	FY15			FY16		
	SUB-CENTRE	PHCS	CHCS	SUB-CENTRE	PHCS	CHCS
ANDHRA PRADESH	7659	1069	179	7659	1075	193
ARUNACHAL PRADESH	286	117	52	304	143	63
ASSAM	4621	1014	151	4621	1014	151
BIHAR	9729	1883	70	9729	1802	148
CHHATTISGARH	5186	792	155	5186	790	155
GOA	209	21	4	212	22	4
GUJARAT	8063	1247	320	8801	1314	322
HARYANA	2569	461	109	2576	474	110
HIMACHAL PRADESH	2065	500	78	2071	518	79
JAMMU & KASHMIR	2265	637	84	2805	637	84
JHARKHAND	3957	327	188	3953	327	188
KARNATAKA	9264	2353	206	9332	2353	206
KERALA	4575	827	222	4575	824	225
MADHYA PRADESH	9192	1171	334	9192	1171	334
MAHARASHTRA	10580	1811	360	10580	1811	360
MANIPUR	421	85	17	421	85	17
MEGHALAYA	428	110	27	431	109	27
MIZORAM	370	57	9	370	57	9
NAGALAND	396	128	21	396	126	21
ODISHA	6688	1305	377	6688	1305	377
PUNJAB	2951	427	150	2951	427	150
RAJASTHAN	14407	2083	568	14408	2080	571
SIKKIM	147	24	2	147	24	2
TAMIL NADU	8706	1372	385	8712	1368	385
TELANGANA	4863	668	114	4863	668	114
TRIPURA	1017	91	20	1033	94	20
UTTARAKHAND	1848	257	59	1847	257	59
UTTAR PRADESH	20521	3497	773	20521	3497	773
WEST BENGAL	10357	909	347	10369	909	349
ANDAMAN & NICOBAR ISLANDS	122	22	4	123	22	4
CHANDIGARH	16	0	2	17	3	2
DADRA & NAGAR HAVELI	56	7	1	56	11	0
DAMAN & DIU	26	3	2	26	4	2
DELHI	27	5	0	26	5	0
LAKSHADWEEP	14	4	3	14	4	3
PUDUCHERRY	54	24	3	54	24	3
ALL INDIA	153655	25308	5396	155069	25354	5510

17   Part 2, Section III, Rural Health Statistics, Ministry of Health and Family Welfare Statistics Division, 2015-16

TABLE 112: NUMBER OF SUB-DIVISIONAL HOSPITALS,
DISTRICT HOSPITALS AND MOBILE MEDICAL UNITS[18]

NO.	STATE/UT	AS ON 31ST MARCH 2015			AS ON 31ST MARCH 2016		
		SUB DIVISIONAL HOSPITAL (SDH)	DISTRICT HOSPITAL (DH)	MOBILE MEDICAL UNITS (MMU)	SUB DIVISIONAL HOSPITAL (SDH)	DISTRICT HOSPITAL (DH)	MOBILE MEDICAL UNITS (MMU)
1	ANDHRA PRADESH	31	8	0	31	8	0
2	ARUNACHAL PRADESH	0	14	16	0	18	16
3	ASSAM	13	25	65	14	25	65
4	BIHAR	45	36	7	55	36	9
5	CHHATTISGARH	10	27	0	13	24	0
6	GOA	1	2	0	1	2	0
7	GUJARAT	31	21	30	33	22	30
8	HARYANA	20	20	9	23	20	9
9	HIMACHAL PRADESH	48	12	0	58	12	0
10	JAMMU & KASHMIR	NA	23	11	NA	23	11
11	JHARKHAND	10	24	101	12	24	95
12	KARNATAKA	146	32	19	146	32	19
13	KERALA	79	16	13	79	18	13
14	MADHYA PRADESH	66	51	84	66	51	80
15	MAHARASHTRA	86	23	40	86	23	40
16	MANIPUR	1	7	9	1	7	9
17	MEGHALAYA	1	12	7	1	12	5
18	MIZORAM	2	8	9	3	8	8
19	NAGALAND	0	11	11	0	11	11
20	ODISHA	27	32	114	27	32	114
21	PUNJAB	41	22	24	41	22	33
22	RAJASTHAN	19	34	52	19	34	52
23	SIKKIM	0	4	4	0	4	4
24	TAMIL NADU	240	31	407	246	31	416
25	TELANGANA	31	7	0	31	7	0
26	TRIPURA	11	6	0	11	6	1
27	UTTARAKHAND	17	19	30	17	19	30
28	UTTAR PRADESH	0	160	133	0	160	133
29	WEST BENGAL	37	22	40	37	22	50
30	ANDAMAN AND NICOBAR ISLANDS	0	3	0	0	3	0
31	CHANDIGARH	0	1	5	1	1	7
32	DADRA AND NAGAR HAVELI	0	1	1	1	1	1
33	DAMAN AND DIU	0	2	2	0	2	2
34	DELHI	7	41	2	10	47	2
35	LAKSHADWEEP	2	1	0	2	1	0
36	PUDUCHERRY	0	5	8	0	5	8
	ALL INDIA/ TOTAL	1022	763	1253	1065	773	1273

18   Part 2, Section III, Rural Health Statistics, Ministry of Health and Family Welfare Statistics Division, 2015-16

While the Ministry of Health and Family Welfare regularly allocates funds to the states for creation of new health facilities and the upgradation of existing ones, there remain significant shortfalls in execution. Between 2011 and 2016, the Ministry had targeted the construction of 9,563 SCs across twenty-five states—34 per cent of the target was not met.[19] Similar numbers prevail for targets for PHCs (44 per cent shortfall across twenty-five states) and CHCs (32 per cent shortfall across seventeen states). Such shortfalls can be due to various causes—a lack of land availability due to non-allotment, delays in tendering and delays in the cost approval.

Typically, construction of such facilities needs to be carried out by government agencies under the General Financial Rules while following guidelines issued by the Central Vigilance Commission and the Public Works Department (PWD) tendering manual. Such construction of healthcare facilities has witnessed significant violations of the rules, with 400 works (costing ₹2,207.67 crore) in four states awarded on a nomination basis—in particular, Uttar Pradesh saw 220 works awarded (costing ₹2,083.37 crore) between 2012 and 2014, in an arbitrary manner on nomination basis, without any diligence on the ability of the nominee to carry out the work in a faithful manner.[20] The UPRNN was awarded projects worth ₹685 crore on a nomination basis in FY13, with the agency completing only three works during the year. The execution of such public works in healthcare is witness to other discrepancies—Kerala, during the same period, was awarded of agreements without any mandatory clauses for timely completion of the public works or any provision for timely inspections.[21] Uttar Pradesh saw many instances of cost escalation, with approvals given by the local departments to favoured suppliers, all while PWD norms were ignored in the preparation of detailed estimates or in conducting quality assurance. Over 1514 works (across the states of Assam, Himachal Pradesh, Karnataka, Kerala, Madhya Pradesh, Odisha, Rajasthan, Sikkim and Tripura) were not even commenced in the same period, given various factors (non-availability of land, delay on the part of the construction agencies, etc.). Meanwhile, 199 works, costing over ₹186.55 crore, faced delays of periods beyond three years, given causes such as site and land disputes, funds paucity and issues in obtaining site clearances.

When we consider rural healthcare facilities that were supposed to be upgraded, the picture is equally dismal. Only 61 per cent of all PHCs targeted for upgradation

---

19   CAG, Report No. 25 of 2017. Sourced from: http://cag.gov.in/sites/default/files/audit_report_files/ Report_No.25_of_2017_-_Performance_audit_Union_Government_Reproductive_and_Child_Health_ under_National_Rural_Health_Mission_Reports_of_Ministry_of_Health_and_Family_Welfare.pdf

20   CAG, Report No. 25 of 2017. Sourced from: http://cag.gov.in/sites/default/files/audit_report_files/ Report_No.25_of_2017_-_Performance_audit_Union_Government_Reproductive_and_Child_Health_ under_National_Rural_Health_Mission_Reports_of_Ministry_of_Health_and_Family_Welfare.pdf

21   Ibid

(for 24x7 delivery facilities) in fifteen states were upgraded.[22] Between 2011 and 2016, over 175 PHCs were nominated for upgradation for the provision of 24x7 emergency services in Kerala, but none was ultimately upgraded. Even where upgrades were carried out, facilities were still non-functional. Over 301 healthcare facilities upgraded during the same period, across states like Assam, Himachal Pradesh, Jammu & Kashmir, Maharashtra, Manipur and Odisha were non-functional for a variety of reasons (including a general lack of manpower, infrastructure, equipment and emergency services).

STAFF AMENITIES

Ideally, quarters for staff working in the healthcare units ought to be at the facility itself. SCs typically require a residential facility for at least two healthcare workers, while PHCs require accommodation for a wider set (consisting of a Medical Officer, nursing staff, a pharmacist, a laboratory technician, etc.).[23] CHCs require even more—provision for at least eight doctors, eight staff nurses or paramedical staff, along with at least two ward boys and one driver. When compared with actual occupancy rates, the contrast is striking—most staff quarters, wherever available, are actually underutilized, given a lack of basic amenities like toilets, electricity and water supply.

AVAILABILITY OF MEDICINES AND EQUIPMENT

Theoretically, the availability of medicines and equipment ought to be a priority for rural health administrators—even the NRHM provides an incentive through a 5 per cent outlay of the total budget to prepare policies and establish systems for free distribution of essential drugs and the development of a stringent procurement system.[24] A standard set of surgical equipment would typically include delivery equipment, along with immunization and contraceptive tools, for SCs. For PHCs, a standard surgical set along with delivery equipment is necessary, while for a

---

22   Ibid
23   Ibid
24   Ibid

CHC, an additional set of imaging equipment is necessary. Such equipment is typically procured by the State Health Society or any State Health Corporation, so established.

However, when considering the actual ground, the reality is stark; 31 per cent of SCs do not have the necessary labour table equipment available, across the ten states surveyed by the CAG in FY17. Meanwhile, 32 per cent of PHCs do not have a normal delivery kit, while 70 per cent of CHCs lack emergency obstetric care equipment. In addition, 63 per cent of all CHCs lack a proper ECG facility, while a similar 47 per cent lack X-ray facilities. District hospitals face similar conditions, with 23 per cent lacking a proper ECG facility, 10 per cent without X-ray facilities and 21 per cent not having a blood storage unit. In fact, Sikkim's DHs were all operational despite not having an ICU, with all critically ill patients referred to the Central Referral Hospital in Gangtok or outside the state. All of Sikkim's CHCs lack essential equipment associated with ECG and ultrasound. This situation is also bedevilled by underutilization of existing equipment—with 428 pieces of equipment across seventeen states reportedly lying idle or underutilized in FY17. Meghalaya, in particular, had blood storage equipment in DHs in Nongstoin and Nongpoh lying idle, given a lack of blood storage facilities in the state.

There are similar issues associated with the procurement of drugs and supplies. Tendering procedures were not followed in instances in Jammu & Kashmir and Uttar Pradesh (absorbent cotton wool was purchased from M/s Om Surgical Ltd., a blacklisted firm in Tamil Nadu, for a cost of ₹5.3 crore). Meanwhile, 35 per cent of all SCs had deficiencies in the number of allopathic drugs available as per Indian Public Health Standards (IPHS). Similarly, over 20 per cent of PHCs and 16 per cent of all CHCs were found to be deficient. Furthermore, medicines were also found to have been issued in particular instances to patients in states as varied as Assam and Haryana, without considering prescribed quality checks and verifying the expiry dates. Meanwhile, the operationalization of Mobile Medical Units (MMUs), quite significantly hyped, remains limited—MMUs had achieved no operationalization in four states (Chhattisgarh, Himachal Pradesh, Mizoram and Uttar Pradesh) while deficient services were provided by MMUs in most other states. Even Accredited Social Health Activist (ASHA) were found to be deficient in their possession of essential medicines—83 per cent of ASHAs surveyed by the CAG in FY17 were found to be deficient in terms of having a disposable delivery kit; similarly, 81 per cent lacked a blood pressure monitor, while 27 per cent did not even have a thermometer!

ANMS, MHWS AND LHVS

While building sub-centres is half the problem, populating them with right personnel is another challenge. Let's consider MHWs—approximately 80 per cent of Indian women have stated that they need permission from their husbands or a senior family member to visit a health centre.[25] There are, of course, regional variations (only 4.76 per cent of women in Mizoram cite the need to ask family members). Given India's feudalistic hinterland, the presence of an MHW can help swing health-related opinions by educating men about maternal issues (e.g., what to do during pregnancy; providing the right care during the postpartum period) and guiding their decisions. MHWs are key in changing the level of involvement of men during pregnancy, childbirth and post-birth, along with removing gender bias. They can also help deliver health services in remote areas and at late hours. However, their availability is sparse—there are no MHWs in 48 per cent of all sub-centres in rural India, while there is a 65 per cent shortage overall.

Given the PHC's function as a critical link between the village community and the Medical Officer, the shortage in manpower, particularly of ANMs, male health assistants and LHVs can have a critical impact.

In PHCs, this problem is amplified by a shortage of doctors, where vacancies can remain unfilled for years (e.g., Uttar Pradesh in FY15 and FY16).

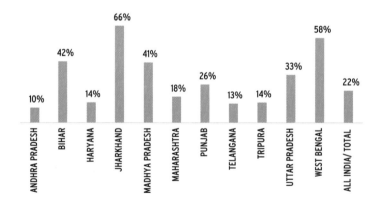

FIGURE 209: SHORTFALL IN RURAL HEALTHCARE INFRASTRUCTURE IN PHCS
(INCLUDING RURAL & URBAN POPULATIONS) BY STATE[26]

---

25   Indian Human Development Survey (IHDS) Survey, 2012
26   Table 11, Part 2, Section III, Rural Health Statistics, Ministry of Health and Family Welfare Statistics Division, 2015-16

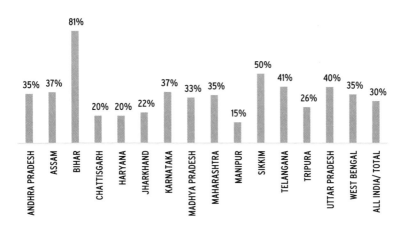

FIGURE 210: SHORTFALL IN RURAL HEALTHCARE INFRASTRUCTURE IN CHCS
(INCLUDING RURAL & URBAN POPULATIONS) BY STATE[27]

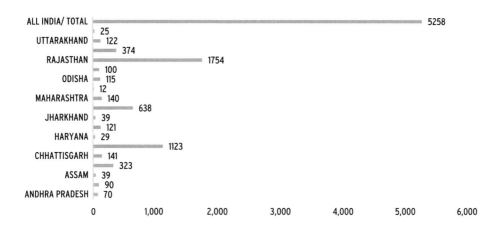

FIGURE 211: NUMBER OF SUB-CENTRES WITHOUT ANMS OR MALE HEALTH WORKERS[28]

---

27   Ibid

28   Part 2, Section IV, Rural Health Statistics, Ministry of Health and Family Welfare Statistics Division,
     2015-16

While newer states like Uttarakhand have a better handle on meeting local vacancies, larger states like Uttar Pradesh, West Bengal and Chhattisgarh fare far worse.

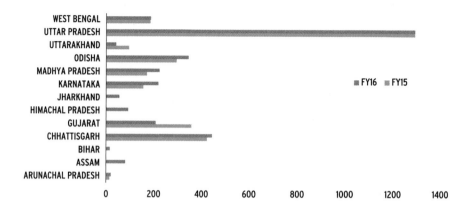

FIGURE 212: NUMBER OF PHCS WITHOUT DOCTORS[29]

This problem is even more widespread when we consider lab technicians—Odisha's vacancies rose between FY15 and FY16, while even Gujarat has jumped from a shortfall of 22 to 367.

TABLE 113: NUMBER OF PHCS WITHOUT LAB TECHNICIANS[30]

NO.	STATE/UT	WITHOUT LAB TECH	WITHOUT LAB TECH
1	ANDHRA PRADESH	347	347
2	ARUNACHAL PRADESH	57	64
3	ASSAM	272	185
4	BIHAR	256	256
5	CHHATTISGARH	290	309
6	GOA	0	0
7	GUJARAT	22	367
8	HARYANA	45	94
9	HIMACHAL PRADESH	119	144
10	JAMMU & KASHMIR	285	318
11	JHARKHAND	204	204
12	KARNATAKA	536	515
13	KERALA	709	710
14	MADHYA PRADESH	557	525
15	MAHARASHTRA	564	564

29 Ibid
30 Part 2, Section IV, Rural Health Statistics, Ministry of Health and Family Welfare Statistics Division, 2015-16

16	MANIPUR	33	33
17	MEGHALAYA	6	6
18	MIZORAM	0	0
19	NAGALAND	88	65
20	ODISHA	1305	1268
21	PUNJAB	165	159
22	RAJASTHAN	690	669
23	SIKKIM	2	3
24	TAMIL NADU	701	636
25	TELANGANA	251	123
26	TRIPURA	22	20
27	UTTARAKHAND	166	191
28	UTTAR PRADESH	1252	1252
29	WEST BENGAL	703	606
30	A & N ISLANDS	1	1
31	CHANDIGARH	0	2
32	D & N HAVELI	0	0
33	DAMAN & DIU	0	0
34	DELHI	1	1
35	LAKSHADWEEP	0	0
36	PUDUCHERRY	0	0
	ALL INDIA/ TOTAL	9649	9637

PHCs face other issues as well—a lack of labour rooms, limited number of operation theatres (OTs) and few, if any, beds.

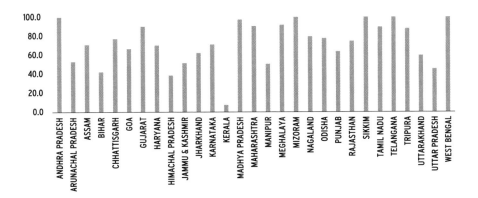

FIGURE 213: PERCENTAGE OF PRIMARY HEALTH CENTRES WITH A LABOUR ROOM[31]

---

31 Table 11, Part 2, Section V, Rural Health Statistics, Ministry of Health and Family Welfare Statistics Division, 2015-16

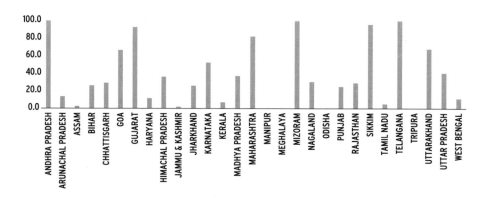

FIGURE 214: PERCENTAGE OF PRIMARY HEALTH CENTRES WITH AN OPERATING THEATRE[32]

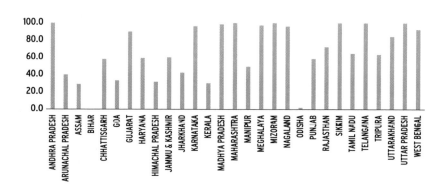

FIGURE 215: PERCENTAGE OF PRIMARY HEALTH CENTRES WITH AT LEAST FOUR BEDS[33]

There are significant shortages in specialist manpower at CHCs, with significant shortfall in the number of obstetricians, gynaecologists, physicians and paediatricians.

---

32   Ibid
33   Table 11, Part 2, Section V, Rural Health Statistics, Ministry of Health and Family Welfare Statistics Division, 2015-16

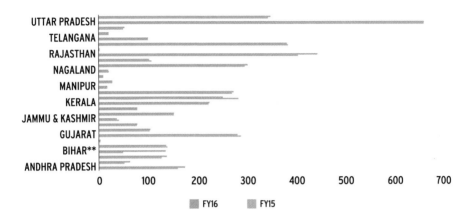

FIGURE 216: SHORTAGE OF SURGEONS AT CHCS[34]

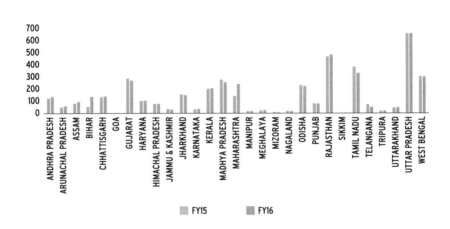

FIGURE 217: SHORTAGE OF OBSTETRICIANS AND GYNAECOLOGISTS AT CHCS[35]

34 Part 2, Section IV, Rural Health Statistics, Ministry of Health and Family Welfare Statistics Division, 2015-16

35 Part 2, Section IV, Rural Health Statistics, Ministry of Health and Family Welfare Statistics Division, 2015-16

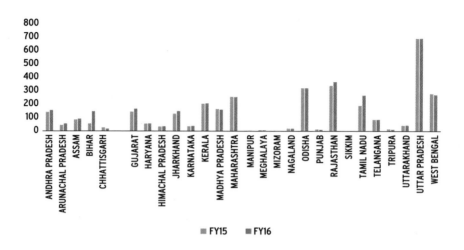

FIGURE 218: SHORTAGE OF RADIOGRAPHERS AT CHCS[36]

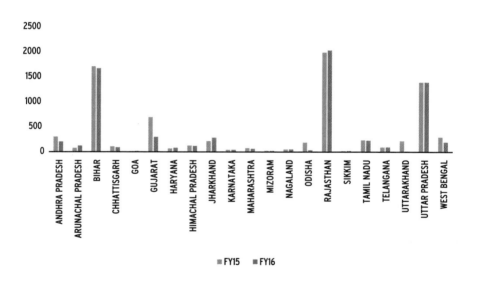

FIGURE 219: SHORTAGE OF PHARMACISTS AT CHCS[37]

---

36   Ibid
37   Part 2, Section IV, Rural Health Statistics, Ministry of Health and Family Welfare Statistics Division, 2015-16

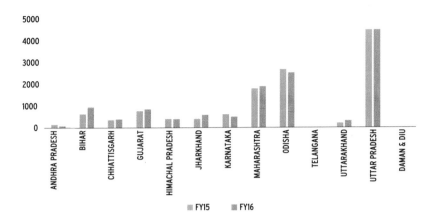

FIGURE 220: SHORTAGE OF NURSING STAFF AT PHCS & CHCS[38]

A survey of CHCs, across twenty-seven states, by the CAG[39] has highlighted that even specialized posts (like general surgeons, obstetricians, gynaecologists, paediatricians, etc.) have an average shortfall of 77 per cent to 87 per cent in FY17. More backward states like Odisha and Tripura have CHCs where not a single doctor has been working in FY17! Furthermore, an audit of over 305 PHCs across thirteen states has highlighted over 67 PHCs where not a single doctor had been posted. In particular, Uttar Pradesh in FY16 had ~50 per cent of its selected PHCs running without a doctor. Over 421 PHCs across the country had 64 per cent shortage of nurses/mid-wives when compared to IPHS norms. Comparing 448 PHCs across twenty-four states, the percentage of PHCs without a laboratory technician, pharmacist, ANM, MHW and LHV ranged between 24 per cent and 75 per cent in FY17.

TRAINING

Even training needs face a significant shortfall.[40] With 29 per cent of ANMs surveyed, across 11 states show a shortfall of 29 per cent in meeting training targets between FY11 and FY16. Similarly, there was a shortfall of 36 per cent in training staff nurses, and a shortfall of 28 per cent in training medical officers in the same period. Despite ANMs requiring mandatory training to conduct deliveries at home or SCs, over 50 per cent of ANMs surveyed in twenty-nine states did not receive any such skilled birth attendant training.

---

38   Ibid

39   CAG, Report No. 25 of 2017. Sourced from: http://cag.gov.in/sites/default/files/audit_report_files/ Report_No.25_of_2017_-_Performance_audit_Union_Government_Reproductive_and_Child_Health_ under_National_Rural_Health_Mission_Reports_of_Ministry_of_Health_and_Family_Welfare.pdf

40   Ibid

NRHM

It's not that rural healthcare has been ignored. The National Rural Health Mission (NRHM) has sought to provide effective healthcare to rural areas by focusing on capacity and infrastructure building in eighteen key states, as varied as Chhattisgarh, Himachal Pradesh and Manipur. The NRHM has sought to transform the architecture of healthcare in India, making it handle allocations more effectively, while seeking to promote policies at the central and state level that strengthen public health management and service delivery. It hopes to empower women, by seeking a female health activist (termed Accredited Social Health Activist, ASHA) in each village, with a village health plan prepared locally, through a Village Health, Sanitation and Nutrition Committee of the panchayat. The ASHA is envisaged as being a bridge between the village council and the ANM, with accountability to the local panchayat. Such an individual would be compensated on performance basis, with targets for promoting universal immunization, construction of household toilets and other healthcare delivery programmes. Such an individual would also be provided training on public health, seeking to build skill-sets that would enable her to facilitate the preparation and implementation of the Village Health Plan, along with other anganwadi workers.

The programme has also sought to strengthen sub-centres by envisaging an untied fund (~₹10,000) with a mandate for local action. This fund would be deposited in a joint bank account of the sarpanch and the ANM. In addition, annual maintenance grant of ₹10,000 is also offered. Other initiatives seek to improve PHCs, encouraging adequate and regular supply of essential quality drugs and equipment, along with an untied grant of ₹25,000 per PHC for local health action.

It also seeks to strengthen rural hospitals by establishment of the Indian Public Health Standards, while seeking an integration of health and family welfare programmes. It has also sought to decentralize programmes associated with district management of health while seeking to improve access.

HEALTHCARE EFFICACY

The quality of healthcare provided is also important, particularly in rural areas. We have a seemingly robust institutional framework for furthering the cause of quality in healthcare—the National Quality Assurance Programme and its underlying guidelines are meant to create a facilitative environment for the sustainable provision of quality public healthcare services. However, monitoring seems to be lacking.

The Ministry of Health's quality assurance team (consisting of representatives from its programme divisions and from the National Health Systems Resource Centre) has had limited meetings, while audits by the CAG have highlighted that the team did not review any of the quarterly reports sent by state-level quality teams. At the state level, while guidelines require each state to set up a State Quality Assurance Committee (SQAC), such SQACs have had limited activity. There have been no review meetings held by the SQACs of seven states between 2013 and 2016 (including states like Assam, Jharkhand, Punjab, Telangana and Tripura) while twelve other SQACs have had a 25–80 per cent shortfall in meetings held.

PANDEMIC POLICY

Human influenza, while causing ordinary sneezes, occurs in three types. Type A can cause pandemics. The 1918 influenza pandemic, involving the H1N1 influenza virus, infected 500 million across the world, including the remote Pacific and the Arctic, and ultimately killed 100 million, 5 per cent of the world's population. Considered the 'greatest medical holocaust in history', this pandemic killed more in twenty-four months than AIDS has killed in the past three decades. In India, 17 million died, 5 per cent of the population. In the Pacific, the flu reached Nauru and Tonga, killing 10 per cent to 15 per cent of the population. The virus tilted the balance against the Central Powers in the First World War, with mortality and morbidity in Germany and Austria far higher than in France and Britain.

More recently, avian influenza virus A/H5N1 affected poultry farmers in Maharashtra, Gujarat and Madhya Pradesh in 2006. By 2008 and 2009, it had affected backyard chickens in West Bengal, Assam and Sikkim. Massive culling within a 3-km radius contained the spread, preventing human infections, but 262 people died worldwide, of 442 infected. In 2009, another virus, A/H1N1, highly transmissible, but with low virulence, spread rapidly across North America. Of late, with nearly 14,000 people affected and 833 dead, the courts and citizenry are rightfully asking questions about the country's preparation.

A pandemic, whether Ebola or influenza, can have a cruel and sudden economic impact. Aside from high body counts, the social and financial damage can be devastating. Public health responses to such events don't come cheap—the outlay for drugs, visits by doctors and hospitalization. The domestic airlines and tourism industry can see revenues plunge suddenly, while indirect costs rise due to risk aversion. People change their behaviour to avoid exposure. Consumer demand decreases suddenly as people stop going to markets or their jobs. The World Bank estimated China's SARS losses at $15 billion in 2003, while the global GDP was reduced by $33 billion. And SARS killed just 916 people. A global pandemic would trigger a major global recession.

An epidemic can lead to economic and political destabilization, a crisis in health resources and sheer panic. Having a sound public health law infrastructure ensures that the powers and duties of the government are well defined during a time of public crisis. Legal frameworks help define the scope of government responses to public health emergencies at local and international levels. Specific trade-offs, prior and during such an event, require policy-based evidence. Should workplace vaccination take place? If so, should it target specific age groups? Does shutting schools down contain viral spread, saving healthcare costs, despite the increased childcare costs? According to the Brookings Institution, closing all American K-12 schools for two weeks would cost between $5.2 and $23.6 billion. Increasing that to four weeks pushes the cost up to $47.6 billion. Can we afford such trade-offs on a frequent basis, with every monsoon and winter season? Evidence-based public healthcare policy-making must be encouraged.

India's existing legislation for epidemic preparedness is numerous—the Epidemic Diseases Act (1897), Livestock Importation Act (1898), Drugs and Cosmetics Acts (1940), etc. The National Health Bill (2009) provides that the central government will review regulations, standards and protocols for port quarantine, seamen's and marine hospitals every five years, along with monitoring maintenance of vaccines and medicines in stock.

The World Health Organization has defined specific public health measures that require policymaking to ensure transparent assessment. They include isolation or quarantining of infected persons, travel or movement restrictions, closure of educational institutions, prohibition of mass gatherings, availability of vaccines and drugs, and usage of privately owned buildings as hospitals.

India's legislation is 'policing' in nature, with little attention to public health focus. The provisions lack a consolidated public health approach in responding to an outbreak. With the local District Collector put in charge of overall coordination during an epidemic and the Chief Medical Officer acting in a supporting role, roles and responsibilities need to be delegated and defined. The true public health legislation focusing on pandemics, the Epidemic Act (1897), is 118 years old and considered archaic. The major public health legislation is over half a century old. The above mentioned legislation allows for action to deal with small outbreaks and emergencies, unable to cater to socio-economic breakdown and epidemic-scale healthcare needs. Human rights, under such conditions, are ignored. At a municipal level, the situation is even starker—while Delhi's Municipal Corporation Act offers reasonable detail on epidemic preparation, Manipur and Karnataka do not.

There is an urgent need to assemble all public health provisions under a single piece of legislation, to ensure that implementation is not hampered. We need a critical mass of public health legislation that offers impact, along with a regulatory agency for implementation of these laws. A 'public health standards agency', akin to the UK's National Institute of Health and Clinical Excellence, which can set standards and build uniformity in control measure implementation. The National Health Bill needs to be expedited, while utilizing the National Development Council for inter-state dialogue.

India needs to implement a five-pronged strategic plan to contain and mitigate epidemic-like situations. It needs to reduce the possibilities of human infection, thereby reducing the chances of the virus/vector to emerge. An early warning system could be strengthened to ensure that affected districts, local health officials and the ministry have all the data and clinical specimens needed for accurate assessments. Rapid containment operations must be planned and intensified when an epidemic is declared, decreasing transmissibility. Local capacity, interlinked with international organizations such as the WHO, should be developed, with pandemic response plans formulated and tested. Local and global scientific research and development should be coordinated, to ensure that vaccines are created, tested and made affordable and available quickly.

Engagement with civil society, instead of demonization of NGOs, needs to be encouraged. The UK's national pandemic framework engages the public and civil society in the development of policies, plans and realistic choices, while sensitizing the public to hard choices that are made. Ensuring that advice and information are readily available during such a situation will help cut down on civil disorder. Full integration of legal frameworks with such intentions will ensure adequate healthcare before, during and after a public health crisis.

HEALTHCARE SPENDING

Healthcare spending on each type of care is an important component to determine the allocative efficiency of public resources.[41] In India, tertiary care accounts for ~14 per cent of public spending, whereas primary and secondary care account for ~75 per cent of total spend. On the other hand, the US spends ~90 per cent of its budget on tertiary care, which by nature benefits a smaller proportion of its population (~1 per cent), and thus, crowds out other types of care which need equal attention and allocation. Thus, spends on each type of care have to be in line with the requirements of our healthcare sector and should aim to maximize the gains to a majority of the population.

It is also critical to note that even within the same type of care, rational allocations to different spend types have to be made to get the desired results—e.g., we may provide for all facilities and equipment in hospitals, but without trained doctors to use them, such spend would only result in limited gains, if any. The balancing of spends achieves greater significance during fiscal stringency, when overall budgets are slashed leading to direct cuts in budgets for drug and equipment procurement, as manpower cost cannot be reduced in such ad hoc manner. Such reduction(s) in drug purchase is detrimental in achieving desired results—the medical condition of the patient deteriorates due to lack of proper dosage, or complete absence of any drug administration. Protecting primary care against constant reductions is an important feature, and the Twelfth Plan Document (2012-17) did provide for earmarking 70 per cent of the health budget for primary care.

The table below provides us with the healthcare spend on different types of care at the start and conclusion of the Eleventh Plan Period for most Indian states. We observe that overall spending in primary healthcare for the states mentioned increased from ₹13,020 crore in 2007–08 to ₹30,594 crore in 2011–12, accompanied by individual increases in each state. While some states increased their spending in absolute terms, their spending as a part of their healthcare budget reduced. All states in South India reduced their spending on primary care on a percentage allocation basis while the absolute spend increased. Bihar's spending on primary care rose by 38 per cent, from ₹1432 crore in 2007–08 to ₹1,982 crore in 2011–12, but in percentage points, fell from 85 per cent of its healthcare budget to 68 per cent in 2011–12. Of particular interest is Andhra Pradesh, where primary care fell from 53 per cent to 46 per cent of the healthcare budget, accompanied by a high rise in spending on tertiary care—from 24 per cent in 2007–08 to 38 per cent in 2011–12. This can be explained by more resources being allocated to the state-sponsored RAS

---

41   Rao, K.S. Do We Care. India's Health System

scheme, which provided cover against low-frequency, high-impact treatments required in patient care.

The healthcare spends reported in Table 112 (following page) include funds transferred by the central government (mostly under the NRHM) and the actual state effort would need to be revisited after omitting the central funding. Including such transfers, the healthcare spend of most states doubled during the period, a testimony to the growing capacity of the states to absorb and utilize funds.

In terms of the composition of spending, West Bengal, Himachal Pradesh, Punjab and Gujarat witnessed a decline in salary costs. All other states witnessed increase in salary costs as a proportion of their healthcare spending, primarily driven by the impact of the Sixth Pay Commission and NRHM support for appointment of contractual manpower. Filling long-pending vacancies also explains such increase, especially in states like Uttar Pradesh (salary component increased from 39 per cent to 60 per cent), Madhya Pradesh (salary component increased from 38 per cent to 51 per cent), Uttarakhand (salary component increased from 42 per cent to 55 per cent) and Karnataka (salary component increased from 40 per cent to 54 per cent).

Spend on drug purchases witnesses a huge variation—while Karnataka, Tamil Nadu and Andhra Pradesh spent more than 10 per cent of their healthcare budgets on drugs, a few states like Chhattisgarh, Haryana, Punjab, Himachal Pradesh, Rajasthan, Uttar Pradesh and Uttarakhand spent a meagre 1 per cent to 3 per cent of their healthcare budgets. Widely accepted norms suggest spending cost at ~50 per cent of healthcare spending and drug procurement at ~10 per cent of healthcare spending.

Capex has also witnessed a decline during the Plan Period—from 9 per cent of healthcare spending in 2007–08 to 6 per cent of healthcare spending in 2011–12. This follows despite expenditure incurred under NRHM budgets for refurbishment of old facilities and construction of new facilities. Thus, the capex spend seems to be driven more by the centre, less by the states.

TABLE 114: STATE-WISE SPENDING ON DIFFERENT TYPES OF CARE DURING
ELEVENTH PLAN PERIOD

	PRIMARY CARE		SECONDARY CARE		TERTIARY + MED EDUCATION		OTHERS		TOTAL	COMPARED TO OTHER STATES
	₹ CR	%	₹ CR	%	₹ CR	%	₹ CR	%	₹ CR	%
EAST REGION										
ODISHA										
2007-08	269	36%	71	9%	153	20%	257	34%	750	3%
2011-12	727	44%	143	9%	305	19%	468	28%	1643	3%
WEST BENGAL										
2007-08	666	40%	798	48%	176	10%	37	2%	1677	7%
2011-12	1827	44%	1713	42%	562	14%	10	0%	4112	7%
SUB-TOTAL (EAST)										
2007-08	935	39%	869	36%	329	14%	294	12%	2427	10%
2011-12	2554	44%	1856	32%	867	15%	478	8%	5755	10%
WEST REGION										
GOA										
2007-08	NA	NA	NA	NA	NA	NA	NA	NA	NA	NA
2011-12	160	39%	137	33%	99	24%	19	5%	415	1%
GUJARAT										
2007-08	922	57%	185	11%	434	27%	76	5%	1617	7%
2011-12	2115	54%	470	12%	1189	31%	124	3%	3898	7%
MAHARASHTRA										
2007-08	NA	NA	NA	NA	NA	NA	NA	NA	NA	NA
2011-12	3883	66%	243	4%	1059	18%	707	12%	5892	11%
SUB-TOTAL (WEST)										
2007-08	922	57%	185	11%	434	27%	76	5%	1617	3%
2011-12	6158	60%	850	8%	2347	23%	850	8%	10205	18%
NORTH REGION										
BIHAR										
2008-09	1432	85%	42	3%	181	11%	20	1%	1675	7%
2011-12	1982	68%	202	7%	660	23%	77	3%	2921	5%
CHHATTISGARH										
2007-08	347	61%	59	10%	76	13%	90	16%	572	2%
2011-12	805	58%	105	8%	178	13%	311	22%	1399	3%
HARYANA										
2007-08	0	0	0	0	0	0	0	0	0	0
2011-12	958	65%	13	1%	288	20%	207	14%	1466	3%
HIMACHAL										
2007-08	226	70%	89	28%	6	2%	0	0%	321	1%

2011-12	509	61%	154	19%	156	19%	10	1%	829	1%
JHARKHAND										
2007-08	391	68%	66	12%	105	18%	11	2%	573	2%
2011-12	826	61%	135	10%	241	18%	163	12%	1365	2%
MADHYA PRADESH										
2007-08	1089	62%	173	10%	309	18%	191	11%	1762	8%
2011-12	1772	51%	445	13%	926	26%	358	10%	3501	6%
PUNJAB										
2007-08	449	54%	150	18%	139	17%	101	12%	839	4%
2011-12	1143	59%	312	16%	288	15%	198	10%	1941	3%
RAJASTHAN										
2007-08	920	50%	103	6%	511	28%	324	17%	1858	8%
2011-12	1768	47%	361	10%	870	23%	754	20%	3753	7%
UTTARAKHAND										
2007-08	215	59%	88	24%	42	12%	19	5%	364	2%
2011-12	558	62%	138	15%	143	16%	64	7%	903	2%
UP										
2007-08	2323	56%	827	20%	952	23%	49	1%	4151	18%
2011-12	3999	60%	1190	18%	1460	22%	49	1%	6698	12%
SUB-TOTAL (NORTH)										
2007-08	7392	61%	1597	13%	2321	19%	805	7%	12115	57%
2011-12	14320	58%	3055	12%	5210	21%	2191	9%	24776	55%
SOUTH REGION										
ANDHRA PRADESH										
2007-08	1509	53%	345	12%	677	24%	328	11%	2859	12%
2011-12	2521	46%	499	9%	2118	38%	364	7%	5502	10%
KARNATAKA										
2007-08	918	47%	354	18%	693	35%	7	0%	1972	8%
2011-12	1419	42%	615	18%	1345	40%	5	0%	3384	6%
KERALA										
2007-08	0	0	0	0	0	0	0	0	0	0
2011-12	766	75%	145	14%	95	9%	13	1%	1019	2%
TAMIL NADU										
2007-08	1344	58%	103	4%	594	26%	262	11%	2303	10%
2011-12	2856	54%	188	4%	1312	25%	906	17%	5262	9%
SUB-TOTAL (SOUTH)										
2007-08	3771	53%	802	11%	1964	28%	597	8%	7134	31%
2011-12	7562	50%	1447	10%	4870	32%	1288	8%	15167	27%
ALL STATES										
2007-08	13020	56%	3453	15%	5048	22%	1772	8%	23293	100%
2011-12	30594	55%	7208	13%	13294	24%	4807	9%	55903	100%

SOURCE: DO WE CARE, INDIA'S HEALTH SYSTEM, K. SUJATHA RAO

TABLE 115: COMPOSITION OF HEALTHCARE SPENDING IN VARIOUS STATES DURING ELEVENTH PLAN PERIOD

	SALARIES		SUPPLIES & DRUGS		MAJOR WORKS		EQUIPMENT		INCENTIVES		MAINTENANCE		GRANTS-IN-AID		OTHERS		TOTAL	COMPARED TO OTHER STATES
	₹ CR	%	₹ CR	%	₹ CR	%	₹ CR	%	₹ CR	%	₹ CR	%	₹ CR	%	₹ CR	%	₹ CR	%
EAST REGION																		
ODISHA																		
2007-08	73	27%	54	20%	17	6%	2	1%	78	29%	2	1%	9	3%	34	13%	269	2%
2011-12	202	31%	93	14%	36	5%	14	2%	23	4%	2	0%	103	16%	183	28%	656	3%
WEST BENGAL																		
2007-08	381	57%	41	6%	5	1%	5	1%	0	0%	4	1%	106	16%	124	19%	666	5%
2011-12	899	50%	83	5%	53	3%	30	2%	0	0%	12	1%	272	15%	436	24%	1785	7%
SUB-TOTAL (EAST)																		
2007-08	454	49%	95	10%	22	2%	7	1%	78	8%	6	1%	115	12%	158	17%	935	7%
2011-12	1101	45%	176	7%	89	4%	44	2%	23	1%	14	1%	375	15%	619	25%	2441	9%
WEST REGION																		
GOA	NA	NA	NA	NA	NA	NA	NA	NA	NA	NA	NA	NA	NA	NA	NA	NA	NA	NA
2007-08	98	62%	14	9%	3	2%	3	2%	1	1%	1	1%	8	5%	30	19%	158	1%
2011-12																		
GUJARAT																		
2007-08	601	65%	54	6%	17	2%	1	0%	0	0%	6	1%	21	2%	222	24%	922	7%
2011-12	1250	58%	107	5%	195	9%	11	1%	3	0%	17	1%	15	1%	564	26%	2162	8%
MAHARASHTRA																		
2007-08	NA	NA	NA	NA	NA	NA	NA	NA	NA	NA	NA	NA	NA	NA	NA	NA	NA	NA
2011-12	NA	NA	NA	NA	NA	NA	NA	NA	NA	NA	NA	NA	NA	NA	NA	NA	NA	NA
SUB-TOTAL (WEST)																		
2007-08	601	65%	54	6%	17	2%	1	0%	0	0%	6	1%	21	2%	222	24%	922	7%
2011-12	1348	58%	121	5%	198	9%	14	1%	4	0%	18	1%	23	1%	594	26%	2320	9%
NORTH REGION																		
BIHAR																		
2008-09	382	27%	44	3%	52	4%	15	1%	5	0%	132	9%	0	0%	802	56%	1432	11%
2011-12	630	31%	118	6%	267	13%	9	0%	22	1%	116	6%	0	0%	859	43%	2021	8%
CHHATTISGARH																		
2007-08	175	50%	42	12%	31	9%	11	3%	44	13%	4	1%	0	0%	40	12%	347	3%
2011-12	455	56%	38	5%	61	8%	21	3%	73	9%	8	1%	0	0%	157	19%	813	3%
HARYANA																		
2007-08	0	0	0	0	0	0	0	0	0	0	0	0	0	0	0	0	0	0
2011-12	591	80%	24	3%	0	0%	10	1%	5	1%	0	0%	3	0%	107	14%	740	3%
HIMACHAL PRADESH																		
2007-08	176	78%	8	4%	15	7%	1	0%	1	0%	0	0%	0	0%	25	11%	226	2%
2011-12	396	66%	6	1%	12	2%	0	0%	1	0%	3	0%	0	0%	185	31%	603	2%
JHARKHAND																		
2007-08	164	42%	20	5%	139	36%	16	4%	15	4%	1	0%	0	0%	36	9%	391	3%

2011-12	449	53%	20	2%	136	16%	4	0%	84	10%	16	2%	1	0%	134	16%	844	3%
MADHYA PRADESH																		
2007-08	409	38%	197	18%	50	5%	12	1%	249	23%	43	4%	0	0%	129	12%	1089	8%
2011-12	944	51%	145	8%	164	9%	29	2%	291	16%	55	3%	1	0%	210	11%	1839	7%
PUNJAB																		
2007-08	373	83%	3	1%	9	2%	0	0%	1	0%	2	0%	0	0%	61	14%	449	3%
2011-12	569	56%	15	1%	10	1%	25	2%	18	2%	0	0%	0	0%	376	37%	1013	4%
RAJASTHAN																		
2007-08	489	53%	24	3%	79	9%	1	0%	0	0%	13	1%	0	0%	314	34%	920	7%
2011-12	1106	63%	58	3%	95	5%	22	1%	20	1%	12	1%	12	1%	443	25%	1768	7%
UP																		
2007-08	906	39%	106	5%	629	27%	5	0%	1	0%	78	3%	0	0%	598	26%	2323	18%
2011-12	2402	60%	166	4%	296	7%	2	0%	145	4%	45	1%	0	0%	952	24%	4008	16%
UTTARAKHAND																		
2007-08	91	42%	7	3%	66	31%	2	1%	3	1%	8	4%	1	0%	37	17%	215	2%
2011-12	305	55%	10	2%	46	8%	5	1%	7	1%	8	1%	0	0%	176	32%	557	2%
SUB-TOTAL (NORTH)																		
2007-08	3165	43%	451	6%	1070	14%	63	1%	319	4%	281	4%	1	0%	2042	28%	7392	57%
2011-12	7847	55%	600	4%	1087	8%	127	1%	666	5%	263	2%	17	0%	3599	25%	14206	55%
SOUTH REGION																		
ANDHRA PRADESH																		
2007-08	845	56%	141	9%	28	2%	2	0%	117	8%	35	2%	66	4%	275	18%	1509	12%
2011-12	1634	65%	368	15%	65	3%	3	0%	105	4%	44	2%	63	2%	239	9%	2521	10%
KARNATAKA																		
2007-08	463	50%	92	10%	27	3%	1	0%	100	11%	14	2%	36	4%	185	20%	918	7%
2011-12	907	64%	201	14%	36	3%	27	2%	50	4%	20	1%	46	3%	126	9%	1413	5%
KERALA																		
2007-08	0	0	0	0	0	0	0	0	0	0	0	0	0	0	0	0	0	0
2011-12	0	0	0	0	0	0	0	0	0	0	0	0	0	0	0	0	0	0
TAMIL NADU																		
2007-08	597	44%	112	8%	16	1%	5	0%	30	2%	47	3%	303	23%	234	17%	1344	10%
2011-12	1301	46%	134	5%	86	3%	82	3%	39	1%	55	2%	559	20%	552	20%	2808	11%
SUB-TOTAL (SOUTH)																		
2007-08	1905	51%	345	9%	71	2%	8	0%	247	7%	96	3%	405	11%	694	18%	3771	29%
2011-12	3842	57%	703	10%	187	3%	112	2%	194	3%	119	2%	668	10%	917	14%	6742	26%
ALL STATES																		
2007-08	6125	47%	945	7%	1180	9%	79	1%	644	5%	389	3%	542	4%	3116	24%	13020	100%
2011-12	14138	55%	1600	6%	1561	6%	297	1%	887	3%	414	2%	1083	4%	5729	22%	25709	100%

SOURCE: DO WE CARE, INDIA'S HEALTH SYSTEM, K. SUJATHA RAO

The healthcare spending clearly shows us that the quantum of funding is increasing, and it becomes critical to align policy incentives with improved quality of spending, thereby realizing the desired outcomes. Our supply side interventions have to be in sync with demand-side needs—e.g., the number of beds in primary hospitals has to increase if we have to introduce the Janani Suraksha Yojana (aimed to promote institutional deliveries alongside incentives) to reduce maternity and neonatal mortality rates.

Sometimes, even the allocated money doesn't get spent. The Comptroller & Auditor General of India's (CAG) performance audit report (Report No. 25 of 2017) on the Reproductive & Child Health under National Rural Health Mission reveals that the amount of allocated yet unspent funds, over twenty-seven states, rose from ₹7,375 crore in 2011–12 to ₹9,509 crore in 2015–16. Out of these twenty-seven states, a minimum of seven states experienced shortfall in expenditure in excess of 40 per cent. Sometimes, the State Health Society, which failed to utilize these allocated funds is not the usual suspect as a considerable chunk of these funds get released by the State treasuries after considerable delays. As per established rules, the funds released are supposed to reach the State Health Societies within 15 days of receipt, failing which penalty in the form of interest remains payable (between 5 to 8 per cent, depending on prevalent bank rates)—yet, funds totalling ₹5,037 crore (released in 2014–15) and ₹4,016 crore (released in 2015–16) were transferred to the State Health societies with delay anwhere between 50 to 271 days, without any interest component. Even the funds released were used for purposes other than the explicitly stated objectives—CAG report observed that in six states (Andhra Pradesh, Gujarat, Jammu & Kashmir, Rajasthan, Telangana and Tripura), an amount of ₹36 crore was utilized for schemes other than NRHM, namely the Mukhyamantri Subh Lakshmi Yojana (MSLY) and the Sukhibhava Scheme.

Thus, while central funds are absorbed and utilized in addition to the states' own funds, it seems that states accorded less preference to health despite increased healthcare spending indicating that unconditional central government transfers have partial impact. Such transfers from the central government to improve primary care and healthcare in rural areas incentivized states to utilize their own funds on demand-side financing despite weak primary healthcare infrastructure.

EXPENDITURE MANAGEMENT

The adverse impact of poor healthcare spending and low efficiency of such spends is further exacerbated by the process of transfer of funds and expenditure management.[42] The process of fund allocation has always been a formal exercise. Before the commencement of any Five Year Plan, working groups consisting of subject-matter experts would be formed for concerned ministries. The recommendations of these working groups from various ministries would be then examined by a Steering Committee under the Planning Commission, which NEXT formed inputs to the sectoral plan that laid out the priorities, targets to be achieved and the resources required for various programmes for each ministry. These sectoral plans would be then approved by the Planning Commission and placed before the National Development Corporation (NDC), which had all Chief Ministers of states as members. The plan approved by the NDC would then become the base plan, on the basis of which resources would be allocated and progress would be tracked for various approved programmes. Despite the approved five-year allocation, uncertainty created by discussions on 'fixing' the plan size meant that departments would be unable to undertake advanced planning of programmes and ordering long-lead items. The annual plans created by departments would thus not be based completely on requirement, but on the persons year, adjusted for inflation.

Appointment of health personnel would be a time-consuming affair. A formal appointment, to be made by the Union Public Service Commission (UPSC), could take as long as three years, by which time the candidate would have chosen other opportunities. Long timelines for recruitment along with low salaries do not attract the best available talent. This directly impacts the government hospitals where many vacancies are not filled or persons with less experience are being recruited. Tight controls on funds and inflexible processes have led departments to increase enlisting of contract workers on annual contracts. Lack of visibility on employment would also mean a constant flux of annual contract workers.

Even while the Plan is finalized and resource planning is complete, resource allocation and funds transfer is a different story. At the beginning of the Plan Period, each health plan has to be approved by the Expenditure Finance Committee (EFC), which makes sure that the expenditure plan is in line with the allocated funds. The EFC finally prepares a Cabinet Note detailing the justification for funds, targets to be achieved after usage of such funds and strategy to be followed, on an annual basis. Such details are insightful and provide clarity but they often take anywhere between three to twelve months. The process remains the same even if departments avail of foreign money through grants and the same cycle is repeated before

42   Rao, K. Sujatha. Do We Care, India's Health System

concluding any agreement with a foreign partner. For small schemes, delegation of authority to the Department Secretary (also a member of the Standing Finance Committee) has helped decision-making. The release of funds to the concerned department is also highly rigid and formal.

For every approved expenditure, a file detailing the scheme has to go to the Finance Advisor (FA) (under the Department Secretary) and the Expenditure Secretary (in the Finance Department). Any variation from the approved details requires financial approval, which may cause further delays. Usually, three quarters into a Financial Year, a revised Budget estimate is prepared based on actual expenditure which may see unexplained budget cuts in the name of fiscal tightening, thereby putting to waste all efforts made to secure the funds approved at the beginning of the year. This severely restricts the programme's ability to procure drugs or equipment.

The problems pertaining to the release of funds is further made complex by imposing difficulties in spending. Annual funds are released in quarterly tranches and insistence on Utilization Certificate (UC) for expenditures in the previous quarter results in the delay in releasing funds. At times, the UC is difficult to obtain in cases where external implementation agencies are involved. Consider drug procurement for thousands of district-level centres—a UC for such cases will not be available unless signed receipts of all consignments are made available. Additionally, funds that remain unspent on the last day of the financial year get transferred back to the treasury, which leads to manipulations to show that funds have been committed/spent for expenditure, even if the funds have actually been released just a few days before owing to various procedural delays. Moreover, for release of funds under the second tranche, audited statements for expenditure of funds released in the previous year have to be released. Thus, a large amount of time and effort is used up in securing approval of funds, release of funds, availing of a UC and preparation of audited statements, which can be devoted to implementation and outcomes. Instead of propagating fiscal tightening by cutting budgets, resource efficiency could be improved and focus can be placed away from funds allocated and funds spent to more meaningful metrics of availability of critical drugs and number of lives taken out of risk. Lack of release of funds by December impacts the funds released in that particular year, and the annual budget prepared on the basis of inflation-adjusted previous year's expenses impact the next year's programme implementation.

Consider the National Rural Health Mission (NRHM)—with a budget of ₹200 billion in 2009, it only had one director, one IAS officer in charge of finance and a team of contract workers/consultants with little experience in public finance.

Proper allocation, efficient utilization and quick, accurate accounting are three important pillars for the success of any approved scheme; yet, much time is spent on accounting for funds. This is a consequence of misaligned incentives—while the finance representative is concerned only with funds, associated UC and accounting, the failure of any scheme falls on the Health Department. Goals and responsibilities have to be shared, and the performance of the Department and the finance official need an integrated evaluation approach, not a segregated one. Public financing needs to be consistent with the requirements of processes—which may be time-consuming, have high procurement times, or have clumpy expense outflows.

Expenditure management in states is much worse. The budget proposals from the Directorate may take as long as 6 months to reach the Secretariat and an equally long time for the District Treasury officials to release the funds. Sometimes, central government grants may get stuck to show better fiscal position of the state. At the district level, the finance officer can again reject the release of funds due to procedural reasons.

Health societies were incorporated as a solution to overcome these hurdles—with funds being allocated to the state and district level health societies, bypassing the State Finance system. Reduction in time spent on ensuring fund allocation, non-expiry of allocated funds at year-end and flexibility in real-time decision-making helped increase absorption of funds, leading to better outcomes. Yet, the same freedom which helps them deliver outcomes also renders it vulnerable to abuse and misuse. Hence, the established method of allocating funds through the state system was reinstated in 2014 for health societies. The need is to plug the potential leaks in fund utilization by health societies, not to subject them to bureaucratic processes which necessitated their existence in the first place.[43]

Consider the predicament faced by the Mizoram Health Society in 2015. Even in May 2015, they hadn't yet obtained the earmarked funds of their final instalment for 2014, amounting to ₹25 crores. The funds are required for treatment of malaria, control of diseases like tuberculosis, family planning, childbirth, immunization and taking care of new mothers. Faced with paucity of funds, the committed health workers raise finance by taking loans in a personal capacity. In Champhai district of Mizoram, the mobile medical unit consisting of minibuses with doctors, nurses, X-ray machines and lab facilities contribute significantly in taking the healthcare facility to people's doorsteps. The lack of funds means no medicines for free clinics, lack of fuel for running mobile units and constraints in dearness allowance for workers. The lack of personnel due to lack of funds means reduced services by such units, if any. The units did not work at all for two to three months, awaiting

---

43   https://scroll.in/article/724629/why-medical-workers-are-taking-personal-loans-to-keep-mizorams-healthcare-system-running

central funds. Constrained funds also forces the local administration to pick and choose its programmes, thereby never achieving the intended objectives. This also means no money for volunteers of the Janani Suraksha Yojana or promised payments to new mothers.

The state's fiscal position also plays a big role in such issues. The chart below illustrates Mizoram's state finances for FY2014–15.

FIGURE 221: STATE OF MIZORAM FINANCES (FY2014–15), ₹ CRORE

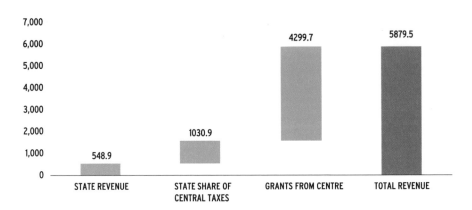

Thus, we see that the State is free to spend ₹1,580 crore as per its needs, while about 73 per cent of total finances (₹4,299.7 crore) come through as grants from the centre. It is pertinent to note that the centre's grants are sporadic/periodic in nature and have their own timelines. Meanwhile, these funds also have pre-defined uses. The State's expenses on salaries and subsidies alone amount to ~₹2,000 crore, which are regular in nature. This creates a cash flow problem, and health services are usually the first to be sacrificed and can be met with working capital loans or prioritizing healthcare services.[44] Consider the case of millions of Accredited Social Health Activists (ASHAs) and Urban Social Health Activists (USHAs) around the country. Usually, the first face of public healthcare delivery for rural India, they are the principal force for reduction of the infant mortality rate and the maternal mortality rate in the country. Collectively, they are present in each village and know each mother–child, take care of mothers by taking them to hospitals, ensure safe delivery, distribute iron tablets and birth control pills and also check on the welfare of village kids. Besides the work, they also contribute in completing the paperwork and undertake surveys on a regular basis. In lieu of this service, they are paid only ₹2,000– ₹2,500 per month. The centre contribution

---

44   http://economictimes.indiatimes.com/news/politics-and-nation/why-are-over-10-lakh-ashas-and-ushas-across-the-country-angry/articleshow/60253826.cms

is just ₹1,000/month and the rest is provided by the state, with Tripura being the only state with mandated minimum pay.

Chhattisgarh, with electricity production of 21,000 MW[45] is a power-surplus state, with 44 lakh consumers and new consumers getting online connections within three to seven days, depending on the location. Yet, nearly 90 per cent of all PHCs in Chhattisgarh reported poor healthcare delivery, be it childbirth, laboratory tests or inpatient services—due to lack of electricity (Council on Energy, Environment and Water [CEEW], 31 August 2017).[46] About 60 per cent of the PHCs reported that the service delivery was 'severely affected'. Not surprisingly, with only 66 per cent of PHCs having regular electricity supply, Chhattisgarh's health indicators are worse than the national average—67 per cent of babies getting delivered in healthcare institutions as opposed to the national average of 75 per cent and an infant mortality rate of 41 deaths per 1000 live births (2015)—among the bottom ten states in India. Infrequent electricity supply has also led to loss of lives—a twenty-minute power outage rendered the haemodialysis machines useless, leading three patients to die as doctors were unable to revive them. The usual practice in such cases is to hold the doctor, nurse and technician accountable leading to their suspension, with the patients' families being provided an ex-gratia compensation.

As per CEEW, severe problems were faced by PHCs in various services; 3.7 per cent of PHC's in outpatient services, 27 per cent of PHCs in outpatient services, 61 per cent in delivery services and 33 per cent in laboratory services. About 90 per cent of PHCs reported power cuts during peak working hours, between 9 am and 4 pm. Even the electricity supplied was of poor quality, with 28 per cent of PHCs reporting fluctuating voltage, resulting in a damage to equipment in 22 per cent of PHCs. However, instead of depending on connecting to the state electricity grid, 147 PHCs across fifteen districts were equipped with off-grid solar systems (2 kW each) in order to improve power conditions, leading to better services. Many emergency services, like childbirth, benefitted from solar units, and eliminating voltage fluctuation reduced consequent equipment damage. Various PHCs reported improved service delivery for various types of care; 59 per cent for outpatient services, 77 per cent for inpatient services and 78 per cent for deliveries. Such improvements led to increase in capacity of solar power using PHCs by as much as 50 per cent in terms of patient intake and a doubling of institutional deliveries within a month, as compared to PHCs without such facility.

---

45   http://www.sundayguardianlive.com/news/6223-power-surplus-chhattisgarh-shining-example-other-states

46   http://www.indiaspend.com/special-reports/how-solar-powered-health-centres-could-transform-indian-healthcare-68778

HEALTHCARE FINANCING

India's demand-side healthcare financing presents a host of complex issues on their own. Given the lack of quality public healthcare initiated by a cycle of chronic underfunding and the rapid emergence of private facilities providing improved medical care on a fee-for-service basis, the rise in healthcare insurance spends is not surprising. Research studies have found that private healthcare expenditure as a percentage of per capita income doubled from the 1960s to 2000. The table below illustrates the growth in share of private healthcare expenditure as a percentage of total per capita income.

TABLE 116: SHARE OF PRIVATE HEALTHCARE EXPENDITURE
AS PERCENTAGE OF PER CAPITA INCOME

PERIOD	AVERAGE PRIVATE HEALTHCARE EXPENDITURE AS A PERCENTAGE OF PER CAPITA INCOME
1961-1970	2.71
1971-1980	3.27
1981-1990	3.72
1991-2000	3.26
2001-2003	5.53

SOURCE: JAIN & BHAT, EPW, 2006.

Thus, while a citizen was spending an average of 2.7 per cent of per capita income on private healthcare, it doubled to 5.53 per cent in 2001–03. The most pronounced increase was over 1991 to 2003, when private healthcare expenditure grew at the rate of 10.9 per cent per annum as compared to the growth of 3.76 per cent in per capita income in real terms.

Such high out-of-pocket (OOP) spend usually resulted in greater financial distress for the average citizen, with many families being pushed below the poverty line due to high costs of medication, mostly financed by the families. The growing network of private medical facilities needed volumes to survive, and medical insurance provided just the right fillip for their growth. This was the period when India's efforts to provide healthcare moved from supply-side interventions to a demand-side policy focus with engagement from the private sector.

By 2015, over 28 crore people were covered under some form of health insurance through a total premium outgo of ₹32,300 crore—financed through private contributions and tax-based contributions. With private healthcare (PrHE) being comparatively more expensive than public healthcare, also a result of their focus on expensive-to-treat medical conditions, most states witnessed a rise in per-capita OOP expenditure. Per capita OOP expenditure in Kerala, for instance, was recorded at ₹2,663—10 times the share of public expenditure.

This was the time when alongside putting in efforts through the National Rural Health Mission (NRHM), the growth of public and private health insurance schemes brought new opportunities for the healthcare sector. The Rajiv Aarogyasri Scheme (RAS) implemented in Andhra Pradesh inspired similar schemes in Karnataka (Yeshaswini), Tamil Nadu and Maharashtra.[47] However, the concept of health insurance in India was implemented way back in 1948, through a Parliamentary Act, when the Employees' State Insurance Scheme (ESIS) was introduced. Launched in 1952, ESIS covered all employees from any firm having more than 10 employees and earning a monthly salary of ₹15,000 or less. While growth in population and formal employment led the number of beneficiaries to rise to 55.4 million by 2009–10, an estimated 8 per cent of eligible beneficiaries were outside the ambit of the scheme due to its launch in notified areas. By limiting itself to formal employment, it fails to capture more than 300 million workers engaged in the unorganized sector.

Its coverage is comprehensive, covering expenses for preventive, primary, secondary and tertiary care, allowance for loss of wages due to sickness, maternity, funeral expense and rehabilitation. The benefit package can be termed liberal, with no maximum limits, or cost sharing in terms of co-insurance, sub-limits or deductibles, leading to nil OOP when using ESIS facilities. The ESIS medical network consists of 121 hospitals managed by state ESI departments and an additional twenty-seven hospitals managed by the Central ESI Corporation. In some areas, ambulatory care providers are utilized where the ESIS network is not present and if the ambulatory care provider and hospital are far, secondary care is provided by empanelled private hospitals (400 networked private hospitals by 2008–09).

Tertiary care is mostly outsourced to private hospitals, with Central Government Health Scheme (CGHS) guidelines deciding the pricing and empanelment criteria. As of 2008–09, ESIS had the second largest healthcare provider network in India, outdone only by the colossal public healthcare network. The ESI is funded by monthly contributions from employee and employer (at 1.75 per cent and 4.75 per cent of monthly wage, respectively), which accounts for 80 per cent of its funds while interest on funds remains the second largest contributor to ESI funds. In terms of expense, ESIC contribution has a ceiling prescribed limit (₹1,200 multiplied by number of people insured in the state under ESIS), while the state goverment pays the remaining bill and one-eighth of costs of all benefit packages through direct subsidy. While some may question the subsidy provided by the state government, especially when the scheme leaves out millions of poor workers engaged in the unorganized sector, it is also to be noted that doing so ensures that these employees do not avail of the benefits under the state's fully subsidized facilities. In terms of

---

47   Government sponsored health insurance in India, GL Forgia & S Nagpal, World Bank, 2012

prevention of moral hazard, the ESIS is a robust scheme since most facilities are captive. The referral system for tertiary care at private hospitals weeds out undesired hospitalization and rates are controlled through pre-agreed prices in line with CGHS guidelines. About 17 per cent of the cost is incurred towards procuring medicines and pharmaceuticals, and is sourced through a central tendering process with two-year price validity. States then procure these drugs directly at contracted prices. However, a decline in utilization rates since the 2000s have led to increasing per unit costs, which remains to be examined as it happened during a time of increased OOP healthcare expenditure in particular and increased spend on healthcare in general. For example, only 17 out of 148 ESIS hospitals had a bed occupancy ratio of greater than 80 per cent, suggesting either low demand or overcapacity or under-utilization of facility. A high average length of stay indicates inefficient use of available bed-days. The cost per bed per day ranged significantly, from ₹138,594 (hospital in Odisha with occupancy rate of 21 per cent) to ₹496 (hospital in Gujarat with occupancy rate of 50 per cent). For hospitals having greater than 80 per cent utilization, the cost per bed per day averaged just ₹660. Thus, proper utilization needs to be achieved to reduce unit costs, which will also help in long-term access and sustainability of the scheme. While ESIS facilities remain better off in terms of infrastructure and equipment, service delivery standards need to be strengthened to ensure higher utilization, besides formulating policy for use of underutilized ESIS facility outside the defined network.

The introduction of the ESIS was followed by the introduction of the Central Government Health Scheme (CGHS) in the '50s for central government employees and their families. Similar to the ESIS, it allowed comprehensive medical coverage and followed traditional mode of financing—contributions from employer and employee, with additional government subsidy, if required. Since the '50s, it took almost five decades for demand-side interventions to be popular for the informal sector, mostly driven by the inadequacy of our public healthcare system. The Universal Health Insurance Scheme (UHIS) was pronounced in 2003, basically catering to inpatient/hospitalization expenses and available from state insurance companies at subsidized rates. It was based on the standardized insurance model in private markets—cashless treatment, service provided by networked hospitals, pre-agreed requirement-based package rates, and use of health insurance company or third-party administrators for risk-sharing and administrative function. The significant difference was only in premia—where the private market would entail end-user paying the entire premium amount, UHIS saw subsidized premium.

The Yeshasvini scheme announced in 2003 by the Karnataka government is a tripartite arrangement of cooperative societies, the state, and private hospitals. The state government finances operates and finances the scheme, the cooperative society encourages membership and acts as the main communication channel between beneficiaries (farmers, casual workers) and the service providers (private hospitals). The scheme is implemented by a Yeshasvini Cooperative Farmers Health Care Trust and engages a third-party administrator for managing empanelment, authorization and payment. Under the scheme, any rural citizen below 75 years of age, who is a member of a participating cooperative society for a minimum of six months, is eligible to enrol along with family. The cooperative society collects the premium, mainly through linking with other financial transactions. Membership of the scheme grew at rapid rates for the first 5 years since inception, reaching 3 million beneficiaries by 2008–09 but remained flat for the subsequent 5 years. Despite its stated target membership of 6 million by 2009–10, the membership till 2016–17 stands at 4.2 million. The flat enrolment rate could be explained by high turnovers. Old members not renewing after fulfilling their anticipated medical needs in a particular year. The table below illustrates the growth in the Yeshasvini scheme since inception:

TABLE 117: RATES OF MEMBERS CONTRIBUTION SINCE INCEPTION OF THE SCHEME

YEAR	MEMBERS ENROLLED (LAKHS)	MEMBERS' CONTRIBUTION (₹ IN CRORE)	GOVT. CONTRIBUTION (₹ IN CRORE)	NO. OF FREE OPD AVAILED	NO. OF SURGERIES AVAILED	SURGERY AMOUNT REIMBURSED TO HOSPITAL (₹ CRORE)
RURAL YESHASVINI SCHEME						
2003-04	16.01	9.49	4.5	35814	9047	10.65
2004-05	21.05	12.87	3.57	50174	15236	18.47
2005-06	14.73	16.94	11	52892	19677	26.16
2006-07	18.54	21.56	19.85	206977	39602	38.51
2007-08	23.18	27.75	25	155572	60668	54.09
2008-09	30.47	36.1	30	191109	75053	61.03
2009-10	30.69	41.36	30	134534	66796	55.08
2010-11	30.47	41.68	30	157480	73963	57.23
2011-12	30.7	45.08	30	116690	77619	60.09
2012-13	30.36	58.88	35	110842	80401	74.12
2013-14	37.97	52.33	45	123205	95715	95.89
2014-15	38.72	69.4	61.95	172442	134792	153.64
2015-16	39.43	70.42	101.15	199549	168591	264.41
2016-17	41.47	91.83	170.43	243318	177045	285.6
URBAN YESHASVINI SCHEME						
2014-15	1.72	12.22	10	16844	6129	9.1
2015-16	1.85	11.86	8.41	19895	11142	20.21
2016-17	2.25	14.44	-	28458	17084	32.21
CAGR (RURAL)	7.0%	17.6%	29.6%	14.7%	23.7%	26.5%
CAGR (URBAN)	9.4%	5.7%	-	19.1%	40.7%	52.4%

(SOURCE: YESHASVINI TRUST[48])

---

48   http://yeshasvini.kar.nic.in/achieve.htm

The scheme offers treatment for more than 1,200 pre-defined procedures at any of the 722 networked hospitals. The scheme does encourage adverse selection behaviour among enrolled members by covering existing conditions and providing for voluntary enrolment. A novel feature of the scheme is ensuring complete cashless treatment with all rates pre-defined on a package basis. Annual medical limits are rarely exceeded, only if a member has multiple high-cost procedures in the same year. However, the benefit package doesn't cover any other treatment apart from defined surgeries, outpatient consulting and discounted diagnostic tests. The long list of exclusions results in balance billing incurred by the consumer. Additionally, procedures requiring follow-up treatment lead to high OOP expenditure.

The scheme also seems to have contributed generously to the private hospital expansion—a study (Aggarwal, 2010) found that 75 per cent of the empanelled hospitals (mostly private) invested in expanding their capacity post-empanelment with the Yeshasvini scheme. The study also found evidence of a 17 per cent increase in utilization rates in private hospitals by better-off members as opposed to no increase for poor beneficiaries, besides a 19 per cent decline in utilization of public facilities. Despite benefitting from Yeshasvini, many private hospitals have been accused of turning down patients, because they were Yeshasvini beneficiaries.[49] Complaints include non-availability of specialist doctors, rationing of consultation hours and payment of differential amount between the actual market rate and the pre-agreed rate for a surgical procedure.

Utilization and spending under the scheme has outpaced the growth in enrolment and member contribution. While, for rural Yeshasvini, CAGR for member enrolment and member contribution stands at 7 per cent and 17 per cent, respectively, the government contribution and surgery amount reimbursed to the hospitals grew at a faster pace—at 29.6 per cent and 26.5 per cent, respectively. Comparable rates for urban areas fare worse. Government contribution stood at 47 per cent of member contribution at the time of inception and has since risen to stand at 186 per cent of member contribution, despite a generous 17.6 per cent CAGR in member contribution. Member contribution was equal to 89 per cent of the surgery amount reimbursed to the hospital in 2003–04, but has since declined to only 32 per cent of the amount reimbursed to the hospitals in 2016-17. Frequency of availing of benefits increased—the frequency rate for OPD benefit availed of has increased from 2.2 per cent in 2003–04 to 5.9 per cent in 2016–17. Similarly, the frequency for surgeries availed of swelled from 0.6 per cent in 2003–04 to 4.3 per cent in 2016–17. Increased utilization may be partially explained due to improved access and awareness. Thus, while the scheme ensured cashless treatment at network hospitals at lower pre-decided package rates, its benefit design

---

49   http://www.deccanchronicle.com/160107/nation-current-affairs/article/private-hospitals-ignoring-us-yashaswini-beneficiaries

has stagnated while other insurance schemes provide the benefit at minimal or nil annual costs.

The entire gamut of schemes could be classified under four buckets: (a) the Central Government Health Scheme (CGHS), wherein government employees obtain health cover in lieu of a nominal premium amount deducted from their salary (b) State government schemes covering state government employees in addition to other tax-based schemes for poor citizens (c) Central government-funded insurance schemes for all citizens e.g. Rashtriya Swasthya Bima Yojana (RSBY) and (d) Private insurance for all citizens, with premia being paid in an individual capacity.

RAS was introduced across three districts in Andhra Pradesh in 2007 and quickly ramped up to cover all twenty-eight districts by 2008, with a view to providing tertiary care for BPL families with quality healthcare through a network of health-care providers for treatment of defined ailments and procedures, earlier covered under the CM Relief Fund. The scheme provides financial protection up to ₹2 lakh for each family for 938 low-frequency, high-impact, pre-defined treatments. The eligibility list was relaxed to include the 'vulnerable poor' with people earning less than ₹75,000/year in urban areas and less than ₹60,000/year in rural areas also being eligible for scheme benefits. The scheme achieved rapid depth and by 2009 covered 20.4 million families, about 85 per cent of the State's population. The package for BPL families covers all inpatient costs, reimbursement of patients' travel costs (lowest cost), medicines for ten days post-discharge and follow-up facilities for treatments that require constant follow-up. RAS was one of the more successful schemes, with coverage being as high as 85 per cent of the population. There was minimal end-user intervention, with the state directly depositing the insurance premium with the Trust on behalf of 'below poverty line' beneficiaries.

However, besides the 'feel-good' factor created by RAS, the policy carried the image that it ensured a steady income stream for large and medium-scale corporate-style private hospitals, without any improvements in health outcomes, particularly for the poor. A survey covering 8,623 households to assess the impact of RAS illustrated an overall reduction in OOP expenditure alongside increased hospitalization, but for the poorest, the results were negative. While OOP for the fourth quintile dropped from ₹1,819 to ₹1,174 (over 2004–12), the OOP for the poorest for the same duration actually trebled from ₹391 to ₹1,083. While the rich faced a reduction in the percentage of people facing catastrophic medical events, the proportion for the poor increased from 1.1–1.2 per cent to 2.8–3.4 per cent over 2004–12. Such differential outcomes based on economic status were attributed to the inequitable geographic distribution of hospitals.

Thus, while richer districts had a concentration of empanelled private and public hospitals, the poor and backward districts had fewer empanelled medical centres, leading to reduced or difficult access for people in such districts who are more likely to be poor or backward. Incongruence between the ailments covered under an insurance policy and the common medical conditions ailing the populace also deteriorates the performance of such schemes. Almost 49 per cent of the reimbursement under RAS was for cancer, cardiac ailments and kidney issues while poor people in backward districts suffered from conditions which were avoidable and treatable with effective primary care (viz. malaria, TB, impoverishment). Since availing of RAS benefits entailed hospitalization, it incentivized people to get admitted in hospitals and risk hospitable-related infections. Thirdly, increased focus on a successful scheme focusing on secondary and tertiary care—at the cost of primary care—was also a reason for muted impact, if any, on the poor. Between 2011 and 2016, Andhra Pradesh spent just 16 per cent of the total central grants on NRHM and disease control programmes, nearly half of the expense proportion registered in Maharashtra (32 per cent). The primary care budget was reduced from 53 per cent to 46 per cent and secondary care reduced from 12 per cent to 7 per cent of its total health spending. Meanwhile, RAS accounted for 23 per cent of the total healthcare spending for hospitalization of 1 per cent of the state population.

Pricing is also a critical point of discussion for an insurance scheme. For RAS, the pre-agreed rates for surgeries and procedures were arrived at through negotiations, instead of a bottom-up unit costing exercise to analyse pricing and enhance value for money proposition. Generous pricing, compared to other similar schemes in other states, would only lead to high bills for the State, which would ultimately be financed through public sources. In the absence of any quality measurement or outcome-linked payments, private compulsions may lead to unnecessary procedures.

GOVERNMENT INSURANCE SCHEMES

Rashtriya Swasthya Bima Yojana (RSBY), a national level publicly funded healthcare insurance scheme, was introduced in 2007 by the Government of India (GOI) to provide BPL families unt. The enrolment process faces c with access to quality care at affordable prices. The scheme provides annual cashless coverage up to ₹30,000 per family for inpatient treatment in more than 8,000 empanelled hospitals. Under this scheme, the insurer would try and maximize the number of beneficiaries within the eligibility criteria in order to enhance premium income, and the service provider would try to maximize the number of treatments in order to extract the maximum amount per patient. This obviously calls for a strong administrative mechanism and a stronger regulatory body.[50]

Under the scheme, insurance providers are responsible for empanelling hospitals and ensuring that their infrastructure meets the parameters set for a healthcare facility within the scheme. Enrolment of beneficiaries is also a responsibility borne by the insurance company—in the presence of a field officer under the district key manager—a district-level government authority responsible for implementation of the scheme in their jurisdiction. Each district has an RSBY helpline call centre managed by the insurance company. For enrolment and issuance of cards, the companies take the help of Third Party Assistants (TPAs) and smart card providers.

Enrolment per BPL family is limited to five members; head of the family, his/her spouse, and three dependents specified in the BPL list, with modifications allowed during the annual renewal to account for deaths and new births. The enrolment is done in RSBY enrolment stations performing a range of functions—collecting/correcting personal information of beneficiaries, taking their pictures, registering biometric information and issuing the smart card at a charge of ₹30/card. The cost for enrolment is borne by the insurance agency, within the quoted premium amount. The enrolment process faces certain supply-side constraints like the cost of transportation to the centre, wages foregone by missing a day's work, absence of the head of household and improper documentation available. Distance from centre and BPL density in a particular area also play an important role in RSBY enrolment, as entities responsible for the enrolment face additional cost for logistics, if the target village is far or has a lesser number of potential enrolments (low BPL density). A study by Sun (2011) conducted over 17,000 villages across twenty-four districts pointed out that 2.5 per cent villages had full enrolment of BPL families while 10 per cent villages had no enrolment. Enrolment also remains impacted by the five-member limit rule, whereby social traditions lead to preference for the male members of the family to be enrolled.

---

50 http://www.iasparliament.com/current-affairs/govt-policies-interventions/rashtriya-swasthya-bima-yojana

The chart below presents the enrolment data for RSBY across fifteen different states (remaining data unavailable):

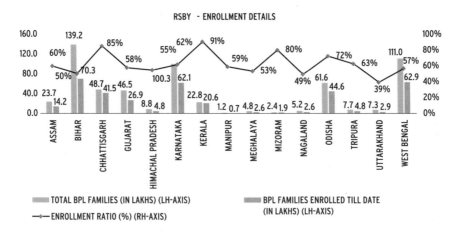

FIGURE 222: RSBY ENROLMENT DETAILS
(SOURCE: HTTP://WWW.RSBY.GOV.IN/OVERVIEW.ASPX)

RSBY provides relief against only in-patient hospitalization claims of up to ₹30,000 per family of five—however, when we consider that approximately 75 per cent of OOP expenditure occurs on outpatient costs—consultations, investigations and medicine, we realize that this in-patient coverage is not enough.

District-level fragmentation requires strong administrative and regulatory control, for lack of it could lead to cost escalation on account of induced demand stimulated by the insurance provider, which may over time lead to higher inflation of healthcare costs and reduced welfare. District-wise differentiation in rates do bring bidding efficiency, but have also witnessed premia ranging from ₹331 in Himachal Pradesh to ₹744 in Arunachal Pradesh (2011 estimates, Dror & Vellakal).

District-level implementation issues range from beneficiaries not receiving their smart cards to submission of false claims. Dang district in Gujarat saw private hospitals submitting false claims and driving claims ration to above 200 per cent before being de-empanelled. On the other hand, some districts have witnessed less than normal utilization rate, leaving the insurance provider to pocket most of the claim amount (Robert Palacios, Centre for Policy Research, 2011).[51] In some cases, even the insurance provider is accused of creating over 11,000 fake beneficiaries in order to gather state-sponsored premia. Such irregularity can enable the

---

51   http://www.thehindu.com/news/national/Government-paid-private-insurer-crores-in-premium-for-ghost-beneficiaries/article11851940.ece

provider to participate in the next year's bidding process due to higher beneficiary enrolment, while leading to direct benefit transfer of crores of rupees from the public exchequer to private coffers.

INEQUALITY IN INSURANCE

Despite a gender bias towards enrolling male members of the family, the female hospitalization ratios have been found to be on the higher side. The rising prevalence of hysterectomy, especially in younger women, have raised many eyebrows in what is considered to be a spree to make money by private medical practitioners. A survey across 2,214 rural and 1,641 urban women in low-income households revealed that 9.8 per cent of insured women in rural areas had undergone hysterectomy compared to 7.0 per cent of uninsured women. For urban areas, 5.3 per cent insured women had hysterectomies compared to 4.0 per cent of uninsured women. Nearly a third of such operations were on women below the age of thirty-five. Similar incidents have also been reported in Chhattisgarh and Bihar, wherein a higher number of hysterectomies have been performed after introduction of RSBY—mostly at private hospitals to avail of private benefit at the expense of the health rights of unaware citizens. In 2010, Andhra Pradesh removed hysterectomy at private hospitals from its list of procedures in order to prevent misuse and exploitation.

The promise of RSBY would weaken considerably if households were to experience the same levels of OOP expenditure irrespective of their enrolment status in RSBY. A survey in Patan district among 3,120 BPL households (17,420 members) throws up a few surprising results[52]—nearly 8 per cent of households never received cards despite enrolment, and 30 per cent of cardholding households were not registered, making them ineligible to avail of the benefits of RSBY. Women were in the majority among the non-insured and 76 per cent of children under five remained uninsured. Among those insured, only 15 per cent had cashless experience; the remaining 85 per cent witnessed OOP expenditure similar to those uninsured (₹7000–₹8000). Among the top three packages—hysterectomy, cataract (55 per cent), deliveries (72 per cent)—83 per cent, 55 per cent and 72 per cent patients faced OOP expenditure to the magnitude of 100–160 per cent of package rates. RSBY needs to address the non-surgical needs for secondary care, as it incentivizes

---

52   https://bmcproc.biomedcentral.com/articles/10.1186/1753-6561-6-S5-O9

surgical treatment for hospitals and beneficiaries, even when it is not required.[53] Thus, we see that each scheme has its own advantages and disadvantages—be it the national level RSBY or the state-level insurance schemes like RAS and Yeshasvini. We need to study the design features of these schemes separately in order to evaluate what features have produced desired results in line with the state objectives, and what features haven't produced desired results, reasons thereof and how we can make them better. This shall form the basis of modifications to our public-funded insurance policies in order to achieve the stated goal of Universal Health Coverage (UHC).

Pro-poor focus and approach have been a constant feature in India's recently introduced public insurance schemes. Countries like Mexico and Argentina started with healthcare for formal workers and civil servants and then moved further to the poor. India had a similar approach, with early insurance schemes like ESIS and CGHS targeting formal sector employees, while the recently introduced schemes are focused on the poor. However, by beneficiary definition itself, such programmes are not universal in nature, whereas UHC demands that people across income levels be brought under the same programme within the same risk pool. This can be achieved by extending the scope of the centrally sponsored schemes to the entire population, with premium payments linked to income levels. For BPL candidates, the premium needs to be minimal, if not completely waived, to ensure greater coverage. For citizens above the poverty line, the premium could be a direct contribution, and for formal sector employees, could be financed through payment deduction at source (like TDS). It is to be noted that many countries achieved UHC through multiple risk pools, but had to consolidate the pools through unified feature benefits at a later stage. Developing broader risk pools through unified features would enable us to avoid large-scale consolidation at a later stage.

Another important feature of public-funded insurance schemes in India is the tax-reliant funding nature and limited point-of-treatment fees for pre-defined treatments and benefits. Tax-based funding, be it in general terms or in payroll terms is a better approach for UHC from an administrative and coverage perspective, as voluntary contributions, no matter how minimal, can discourage poor beneficiaries to drop out of the programme at the initial or later stage. In high-income countries, where most services are exempted from fees, co-payments are introduced as a demand-control measure—e.g., in the US, immunization and child check-ups are exempted from fees whereas minor illnesses require larger user fees. In such a scenario, even small co-payments can reduce utilization among the poor. Voluntary contributions also pose administrative challenges, considering India's population, although a seemingly simple solution would be to deduct the

53 Results for Development Institute, April 2011

premium contributions from the Aadhaar-linked Jan Dhan accounts in a manner similar to the Pradhan Mantri Suraksha Bima Yojana (PMSBY) and the Pradhan Mantri Jeevan Jyoti Bima Yojana (PMJJBY). On the other hand, tax-based funding will ensure greater coverage in line with the objectives of the UHC, resulting in secondary benefits of lower per unit costs. For non-poor households, coverage can be provided on a premium basis, deducted from payroll or included in taxation. As coverage increases, co-payments for high-frequency, non-critical treatments/services may also be explored to reduce over-demand chances.

The common belief behind India's insurance schemes, aiming to reduce OOP expenses, is to provide coverage for high-impact treatments; thus covering mostly secondary and tertiary care. This is correct as well, considering that an illness in a family not covered by insurance pushes 39 million people back into poverty in India. Studies (Hsiao & Yip, China) have demonstrated that over a long period of time, a household may end up spending more on outpatient care than inpatient care on a cumulative basis, which finds resonance in the fact that a large part of OOP expenses in India are on drugs (Selvaraj). Thus, financial protection has to extend beyond inpatient care. One can think that it may be prudent to cover only drugs and outpatient care under UHC; as such care will reduce fatality at a lower cost, thereby delivering more 'bang for buck' for healthcare spends. However, we cannot completely ignore inpatient care when we endeavour for UHC, as it remains a critical component. Thus, what is needed is to widen the coverage from just inpatient care to a broader range of drug purchases, outpatient and inpatient care.

Additional focus on inpatient care covering high-cost, low-frequency treatments in healthcare insurance schemes have skewed the ratio of state healthcare spends away from primary and secondary care towards tertiary care as evidenced by the RAS scheme. The experience in the USA illustrates that lopsided focus on hospital care leads to higher healthcare costs.

An important feature of demand-based financing is that providers have an extra incentive to provide care, for they get paid only after care has been provided. As patients are empowered with provider choice, the providers then have an extra incentive for over-provision services, working as a proxy for high-quality care at times. Thus, it leads to 'supply-induced' demand, resulting in higher costs and potentially lower healthcare service quality, especially when the payment mechanism is on a 'fee-for-service' basis. In countries like the UK and Thailand, providers are paid capitation fees for each registered user. While this takes care of over-provisioning services in a 'fee-for-service' model, the capitation fee-based model wrongly incentivizes providers for under-provision of services. Such conditions can be mitigated using case-based payment methods used in most OECD countries. Thus, the current case-rate system under RSBY may be tweaked to provide for case-based bundled payments.

Another important feature of insurance schemes is the healthcare delivery system, a mix of private and public healthcare providers with different service levels and accreditation. Incorporating private players within the RSBY umbrella makes sense, as it helps provide width and depth to healthcare delivery. The large number of fragmented service providers poses a challenge in terms of misaligned incentives. Fragmented service providers increase chances of an oversupply of services or misrepresentation of services rendered to extract larger payments, apart from false enrolment and faulty billing. Considering that most services are cashless in nature, the incentives are aligned towards increasing consumption, necessitated or not. Varied accreditations and quality levels pose another challenge. Public providers are also a critical component of service delivery under an insurance-based system, and such schemes have also helped public hospitals to build their infrastructure bolstered by demand-side revenues, which act as secondary financing sources apart from the supply-side financing. This helps build public health infrastructure, and improve customer-centric service delivery to standards better than private hospitals. However, in some cases, the hospitals do not have the facilities to capitalize on demand-side benefits, or are not able to utilize the earned insurance-driven spending. Failure to retain such insurance reimbursements may act as a disincentive for public hospitals.

As we embark to operationalize the much promised Ayushman Bharat–National Health Protection System (AB-NHPS) for more than 10 crore poor families across the nation, we need to ensure that demand-side interventions are complemented by supply-side capacity building. The AB-NHPS has two components—firstly, the creation of nationwide network of 150,000 Health & Wellness Centres (HWCs) and secondly, the coverage to members of more than 10 crore households with ₹5 lakh medical insurance coverage.

A budget outlay of ₹1,200 crore was allocated for 1.5 lakh HWC's – yet some experts opine that the allocated budget can support about 10,000 HWC's instead of the promised 150,000 HWC's (A. Shukla, *The Hindu,* 13 April 2018), with the allocation coming out of the existing NRHM budgets (itself facing progressive budget cuts) instead of any dedicated allocations. Assuming annual requirement of ₹20 lakh per HWC, the budget requirements for 1.5 lakh HWC's would be ₹30,000 crore annually (T. Sundararaman, *The Hindu,* 13 April 2018), which needs to be allocated in budget outlays. The Human Resource requirements for HWC's shall be as enormous as the financial one, if not more. Assuming a minimum of three workers per HWC, a total of 4.5 lakh healthcare professionals would be required—which if properly recruited and trained, could provide a huge boost to Indian healthcare service delivery and youth employment, seeming extremely challenging amidst budget cuts and manpower shortage across the existing public healthcare infrastructure.

Regarding the medical insurance coverage, we need to ensure that lessons for the existing gamut of insurance schemes are learned and incorporated – a fact reiterated by the Parliamentary Standing Committee Report (Report No 106 of the Ministry of Health & Family Welfare, tabled on 8 March 2018) which even went on to express that the NHPS is not a 'step forward' for excluding outpatient medical expenditures. While NHPS remains driven by the Centre, its success will be eventually driven by its acceptance and administration by various states, especially with healthcare being a state subject.

The scheme remains fraught with implementation risks. Many states have their own medical insurance system—Rajasthan for example, has the Bhamashah Swasthya Bima Yojana, which provides coverage up to ₹3 lakh to people who are beneficiaries under the National Food Security Act. Subsuming the Bhamashah scheme under the NHPS will require identification of beneficiaries as per the SECC data (as opposed to the already identified beneficiaries), a complicated task given the size and population of the state. Meanwhile, closure of the scheme and switching to other schemes will cause confusion to the thousands of patients who avail healthcare treatment under the scheme at any given point of time. Meanwhile, a continuance of both schemes in parallel might mean different rates for same package/treatment at the same hospital, which will create further imbalanced incentives, which may lead to deteriorated health outcomes in short term. The Centre and States shall need to work together closely to resolve any implementation crises.

Consider overall coverage—the National Food Security Act covers 80 crore people, while the proposed beneficiaries of the AB-NHPS stands at 50 crore as per the SECC data. It sounds puzzling that people who require support for their daily nourishment needs do not require support for medical expenses[54]. Similar to the challenges in merging Bhamashah Swasthya Bima Yojana with AB-NHPS, each state has its own unique set—e.g., the Mahatma Jyotiba Phule Jeevan Dayi Arogya Yojana offers a coverage of ₹1.5 lakh for 971 types of surgeries and 121 packages, Tamil Nadu covers 1,016 types of procedures subject to coverage of ₹1.5 lakh, while Bhamashah scheme discussed above covers 1,715 packages, Some states have a wider coverage net than the SECC data, while some like Karnataka covers every state resident[55], Merging of schemes with only beneficiaries being those recognized by SECC data shall potentially leave out needy citizens already covered, while continuing with parallel schemes might lead to higher financial requirements for

---

54   Shankkar Aiyyar, BloombergQuint, 21-Feb-2018
55   Raajeev Dubey, Business Today, 22-Mar-2018

the State Govt. exchequer. Consider Punjab – the state provides insurance coverage of ₹50,000 to 29.3 lakh families under the Bhagat Puran Singh Sehat Bima Yojna (BPSSBY)[56], and with the proposal to cover ~14 lakh families (as per AB-NHPS) with ₹5 lakh insurance coverage might create a divide, and if state tries to match the insurance coverage under AB-NHPS, it stands to incur an additional burden of ₹200 crore considering the cost-sharing mechanism in 60:40 ratio between the Centre & the State. The merging modalities thus, shall need careful deliberation and meticulous on-ground planning and execution.

Announcing healthcare insurance schemes in budget speech is not a novelty—in 2016, NHPS was announced with a coverage of ₹1 lakh, but suffered from low allocations (₹1,000 crore allocated in FY 2017–18 and disbursal of ₹456 crore in FY 2016–17, primarily driven by the existence of widely popular state insurance schemes). For NHPS to be successful, approximate allocations of ₹25,000 crore (estimated at ₹2500 per family for 5 lakh insurance coverage for 10 crore families) are required—significantly higher than the amount provisioned in FY 2018–19 Budget, calling for further supplementary budgetary support.

While AB-NHPS empanells private hospitals to provide healthcare facilities, it needs effective regulation to ensure that patients are not refused treatment, on some pretext or the other, if the rates for procedures are found uneconomic to the private hospital. [57]Additionally, with ₹1.5 to ₹3 lakh being adequate for most treatments in most states (barring disease-specific exceptions), the insurance coverage of ₹5 lakh should not offer a moral hazard for hospitals—thereby leading to tertiarization of healthcare and increased out-of-pocket expenses, which are not covered under the AB-NHPS.

Besides above-mentioned challenges, one critical aspect should not be forgotten— insurance is of no use if hospitals and clinics remain inaccessible, which remains the case for the majority of citizens in Indian hinterland. Fixing issues of access remain primary to the national delivery of promised healthcare. Besides improving access, reducing OOP expenses for outpatient care and improving confidence in public hospitals needs attention, while eliminating tragic incidents as observed at BRD Hospital in Gorakhpur which erode faith in our healthcare model.

Thus, our healthcare delivery system is highly fragmented, with inadequate integration between different types of care (from primary to secondary to tertiary), leading to suboptimal outcomes at a higher cost compared to a service delivery structure with high levels of integration. Larger integrated systems can pool

---

56   Ravinder Vasudeva, Hindustan Times, 15-Sep-2018
57   T. Sundararaman, The Scroll, 5 February 2018

resources leading to lower per unit costs and provide seamless integration across different care types. The desired UHC should look for an integrated approach leading to better care at lower cost.

While using private insurance companies to manage the funds and pay the service provider has expedited scaling up the programme to millions of beneficiaries, the 'winner takes all' administrative approach raises some concerns. In this model, followed under RSBY, the private insurer collects capitated premium and pays the service provider as per the claim, while bearing the entire financial risk across the supply chain and is hence incentivized to minimize payouts, thereby increasing individual entity profits. Yet, some states witnessed payouts by private insurers exceeding state government allocations, and in other states, the payouts were a minuscule fraction of the government budgets.

Similarly structured administrative models in the US have produced mixed results—while some firms collected money and eloped, others raised questions if private insurers were making super-normal profits. Payments to insurers on a cost-plus basis take away any incentive to reduce cost, besides providing reasons to 'gold-plate' costs and skim profits. 'Care management' remains highly customer-centric but may not be financially prudent for private insurers operating on fixed capitated premiums. We need to think of a suitable administrative model for usage of private insurers as risk-bearing agents for tax-based, fixed premium insurance schemes.[58] We also realize that there may not be a single solution to the provider payment mechanism. Under the capitation system, providers are paid a fixed, pre-defined amount in advance in lieu of a package of services for an enrolled individual for a fixed period of time, when management capacities of providers and purchasers are advanced and competition among providers robust, so that expansion of primary care with controlled cost becomes possible. Capitation improves efficiency because it offers flexibility to the provider to deploy the funds generated in a manner that optimizes service delivery and retains surplus (if any). Capitation systems require strong review, monitoring and redressal mechanisms to be implemented by the purchaser, to prevent quality compromises by the provider, besides having better estimation methods for enrolled populations.

Case-based (diagnosis-related groups) payment mechanisms, under which hospitals are paid a fixed amount per admission, depending on clinical characteristics, work well when there is an oversupply of hospital capacity and improving utilization remains the primary objective, with cost control being secondary. Such systems also allow for cost variations per case, thereby incentivizing the provider to improve efficiency without compromising on quality. Efficiency can further be increased

---

by allowing hospitals to retain part of the surplus revenue. The fee-for-service payment model, under which the provider is paid for each individual service or bundle of services rendered at a pre-defined and agreed rate works well when increasing supply and access are top priorities, with cost control remaining low-priority. Such systems, while ensuring improved quality, introduce high levels of 'moral hazard' into the system. If cost control is the sole priority, line-item budgets could be implemented which account for a fixed amount for a specified period for input expenses, but incentivize the provider towards under-provision services, and over-provision inputs with no efforts to improve quality. Thus, the mix of methods should be selected after a detailed study of how the incentives created by the individual payment methods and their mix will affect the stated healthcare goals.

We see that many features of India's state-sponsored insurance programmes are consistent with global best practices and suitable for India's requirements. Improved scale by bringing millions under the insurance net, reducing OOP payments for high-cost tertiary care and providing cashless facilities at point-of-care are laudable. Some schemes have also shown success by being funded through tax revenues while healthcare spending as a proportion of GDP has remained stagnant. The schemes also provide flexibility to the patient/customer, who is free to choose the service provider and also the service provider may be private or public in nature. On the other hand, some features like targeting only tertiary care at the expense of ignoring primary and secondary care, covering only inpatient care at the expense of drug purchases and outpatient care, and schemes only providing benefits to BPL families need rethinking in order to improve service delivery. The fragmented nature of service delivery and the administrative structure for risk-sharing between State and private stakeholders/insurance providers also need to be revisited.

Capitalizing on the inherent strengths of public insurance systems, coupled with design and policy changes to overcome the inherent weaknesses will lead to improved health outcomes for the same levels of demand-side financing.

CENTRALIZING RISK

From an Indian perspective, one may propose replacing all national and state-level insurance with one big risk pool. However, such a proposal would throw up multiple political challenges without equivalent incremental gain through reduced costs. Even if all states have their own state-level insurance scheme, it would place millions in a single-risk pool which can effectively result in efficiency gains. Additionally, as public health and sanitation remain under the State List of the Constitution, state-level insurance schemes preserve responsibility, increase accountability and maintain the operational consistency of various schemes that have already been working for almost two decades.

The government can thus look forward to combining the centrally-sponsored insurance schemes (ESIS, CGHS and RSBY) into one pan-India scheme, which would form the backbone, while various state-sponsored schemes may act as supplementary additions to the central scheme. This decision itself would entail various challenges, as those having higher service depth (broad coverage of healthcare services) would feel left out with their entitlements being reduced. In such situations, gradual harmonization of processes, benefits and payments should be followed. This should be followed concurrently with increasing membership in central schemes, e.g., RSBY has already been expanded from BPL families to cover a range of professions and can be expanded further to include citizens regardless of economic status. This would be accompanied by increasing the depth of RSBY, and include drug purchases, outpatient services and inpatient benefits in line with efforts to harmonize various aspects of centrally sponsored schemes. Another option that may also be explored is to allow greater enrolment under ESIS by altering the eligibility criteria. Harmonization would entail using the same payment systems by the government and using methods that contain costs. Capitation could be explored for prevention, primary and secondary care, while tertiary care could be encompassed on a case-use/diagnosis basis in order to control costs. The central funds could be differentiated, favouring high-focus states which receive higher grants in order to ensure similar benefits.

Thus, one needs to build upon incumbent institutions and reorganize risk pools, if needed, to achieve the underlying objectives of India's health policy, be it access, financial protection, service quality—instead of focusing only on the delivery structure (central or state, single or multiple pools, etc.). Complete overhauls cannot be ruled out, but one needs to prefer existing structures with modifications to achieve stated health objectives.

—

TOWARDS UNIVERSAL HEALTHCARE

Healthcare in India is a story of insufficient resources and poor outcomes. Investment is well below WHO guidelines in both qualitative and quantitative terms. Bed density is low (less than 1.5 beds per 1,000 persons as compared to the WHO guideline of 3.5), doctors few (less than 1.8 per 1,000 as compared to WHO guideline of 2.5), and out-of-pocket spend high (86 per cent as compared to an average of around 40 per cent for low-income countries). Rural India lags even further behind, with around 30 per cent of the rural population having to travel more than 30 km for treatment.

Significant inequality in access is worsened as the existing healthcare workforce is inadequate and under-utilized. With low salaries, insufficient incentives, lack of career growth, inadequate training and inconsistent policies, the majority of the medical workforce chooses not to practise in the formal sector. India's regulatory system hardly keeps up with the very diverse set of medical practitioners.

Meanwhile, infectious and chronic diseases continue to prevail. Health indicators continue to lag, healthcare spending is growing slower than GDP growth, out-of-pocket spending continues to be high, and infrastructure gaps remain substantial.

Universal healthcare offers one solution, by extending access to healthcare as widely as possible and providing quality care through minimum standards. The Soviet Union implemented it in 1937, with the UK following nearly a decade later. Most nations have funded it through general taxation, supplementing it by specific levies and private payments. Compulsory insurance utilizing common risk compensation pools and a choice of insurance funds, such as in the US and Switzerland, have helped reduce inequality and increase access. Lives have been saved, with resultant growth.

The idea of providing universal healthcare sounds almost utopian. Provisioning equitable access to affordable and reliable healthcare through an institutional mechanism is an age-old dream across any welfare state, one that would serve to reduce inequality by providing healthcare at affordable rates.

The formulation of a healthcare policy requires adherence to certain principles— access should be as universal as possible, ensuring comprehensive treatment is offered in an equitable manner, without excluding anyone (on the basis of caste, community, ethnicity, regional bias, gender or class). Such treatment should be rational and of good quality, while incorporating protection of patients' rights, enabling portability and continuity of care even if switching doctors or hospitals. There must be robust accountability and transparency in healthcare administration and pricing, in a manner that ensures community participation. Such a system requires foundations of solidarity and recognition of the common interest, with a pursuit of cross-subsidization.

India's regional diversity, with differential needs of the population, ensures that any system of universal healthcare would have to be flexible; a one-size template will not do. India's multiple transitions—urbanization, demographic change and nutritional trends—will increase systemic challenges.

The service offering will be critical —universal healthcare will have to cover primary, secondary and tertiary healthcare, including all common communicable and non-communicable diseases. Such an offering would have to be served through the existing public healthcare sector, along with contracted private facilities.

India's government needs to play a stewardship role. By focusing on universal healthcare as a long-term journey, with consensus on political backing and hard choices along with secured long-term funding, universal coverage for good-quality healthcare can be achieved. By building an effective regulatory framework and consistent policies across states and the centre, workforce shortages can be overcome, along with integrating healthcare facilities across the village, town and district levels. Patient interest can be kept as a primary focus by reforming such bodies as the National Rural Health Mission and Rashtriya Swasthya Bima Yojana (RSBY).

The private sector can help improve India's healthcare infrastructure. But without faster accreditation, few private players will gain credibility, or raise standards, resulting in low customer satisfaction, longer hospital stays and poor governance. The National Accreditation Board for Hospitals and Healthcare Providers need to roll out incentives encouraging accreditation and make it a mandatory process.

The public-private partnerships or build-operate-transfer or operations and maintenance contracting schemes can utilize private capital for provisioning healthcare services. With our growing population, the need for treatment of non-communicable and lifestyle diseases will increase, particularly in Tier-2 and Tier-3 cities. Affordable healthcare programmes (rolled out as public-private partnerships) will offer significant margins (in volume) for private players, while helping address talent resourcing and under-utilization issues. Initiatives like Ayush Graham Bahawali Project, in Nainital, running in build-operate-transfer mode, provide an alternative medicine and low-cost affordable healthcare, partly based on land grants by the government.

—

PURSUING ZERO HUNGER

Universal healthcare implies a strategic focus on those who are most vulnerable. Children born in India are, on average, shorter than those born in sub-Saharan Africa. Even worse, 255 million Indians remain food insecure, eating less than 2,100 calories daily. Jharkhand reports the lowest per capita calorie intake (1,900 kcal) in rural areas, while West Bengal hovers around a similar level (1,851 kcal) in urban areas. We have attempted to meet this challenge through legislation. Aside from the Right to Food Bill, the landmark PUCL vs Union of India (2001) case has seen over sixty orders over the last decade. And yet, this judicial activism has mostly failed to translate into execution. The opportunity for India to deliver lies fallow.

Three key factors remain to be resolved. The institutional will to execute reforms enabling better food delivery nationally has been mostly missing, despite extensive legislation. India's lopsided food policy has made cereals more widely available over other foods, while the mismanaged FCI leaks our agricultural surplus. Finally, the low social status of women has kept them mostly ill-nourished, with open defecation and bad sanitation taking its toll.

Resolving hunger is not a complex issue. The last fifty years have seen a slew of international action, recognizing the right to food, providing State guarantees and institutionalizing mechanisms. While South Africa, like India, sought to explicitly guarantee the right to food, millions continue a daily struggle to quell hunger. Brazil, on the other hand, with its 'Fome Zero' programme, sought to provide three square meals to its people, without any handouts, with cross-party institutional commitment. It consolidated thirty-one programmes, overseen by its ministry of food security, into a single programme. India offers nine programmes, run under five ministries, supported by institutions like the Food Corporation of India (FCI).

A political commitment also requires a system of legal recourse. Brazil allows public prosecutors to take up the violation of human rights, including that of hunger, at the local level. National commissions predominate the landscape of countries such as Venezuela, Uganda and South Africa, acting as oversight bodies with the power to impose penalties. India's commissioners, appointed by the Supreme Court, still lack statutory powers to impose penalties. Uganda has characterized the 'head of the household' as a duty-bearer for food security, with penalties for non-fulfilment of food obligations.

India's states have shown the way. The PDS revival (NSSO, 2014) has been a result of renewed state commitment. Changes in grain entitlements (Bihar, Tamil Nadu, Andhra Pradesh and Rajasthan), universalization of the PDS scheme (Tamil Nadu and Himachal Pradesh) and better service monitoring (Chhattisgarh and Andhra

Pradesh) (Andaleeb Rahman, IGIDR, May 2014) have turned things around. Commissions for fair price shop owners and price reductions have also helped increase PDS off-take while lowering incentives to cheat.

India stores over 3 million tonnes of grain in the open, exposed to rain and pests, enough to feed Italy, with plastic sheets offering minimal protection. While the food security law entitles ~65 per cent of Indians to low-cost grains, the challenge remains in getting the grains to the poor, with wastage and corruption biting away. Despite ongoing reforms of the PDS delivery system, beneficiary households are regularly deprived of over 44 per cent of wheat and rice (Reetika Khera, IIT Delhi, 2011).

The FCI stored 68.7 million tonnes of wheat, rice and coarse grains in FY15, double its requirement of 31.9 million tonnes, and nearly double its capacity of 39m tonnes (3.3m tonnes under open sheets)—all at a cost of ₹1 lakh crore annually. Its warehouses have not expanded over the last decade, restricting themselves to just 13 million tonnes. Only 6 per cent of farmers benefit from selling rice and wheat directly to the FCI, while a majority of the farmers remain unaware of its procurement activities. Leakages, caused by poor-quality wagons, inadequate security, multiple handling, etc., can run up to 90 per cent.

As recommended by the High Level Committee (August 2014), the FCI should explore the option of outsourcing its stocking operations to other qualified entities and follow a proactive liquidation policy for offloading excess stocks in the market. It should also consider moving to states like Assam, Bihar and UP, areas of hunger discontent and distress sales for farmers, moving out of Punjab, Haryana and Andhra Pradesh. A break-up of the FCI into its constituent parts could be explored, decentralizing procurement and encouraging local storage.

The FCI was established in 1965, under PL-480, to meet major shortfalls and stabilize food markets. Given rising food inflation, and increasing volatility in other crops like onions (concentrated in Maharashtra, MP, Karnataka and Andhra Pradesh), the FCI's procurement policy must be changed to include the 23 items under the MSP policy, including pulses and oilseeds. Onions, produced in 4 months, can be stored for the entirety of the political calendar.

Forty per cent of Indian children under the age of five are stunted (IIPS, 2010) while the proportion of 'wasted children', with low weight for height, remains at 15 per cent; 28 per cent of Indian children are not breastfed and 70 per cent of children remain anaemic. However, despite a per capita GDP of 4.2 per cent between 1990 and 2005, malnutrition amongst children was reduced by just 10 per cent (against a developing country trend of 27 per cent).

We need to pursue 'Zero Hunger', ensuring zero stunted children below two years, by empowering women. A focused effort on identifying hungry and malnourished households is needed, particularly to identify those living in remote and hilly areas, or those with dysfunctional fathers. A reduction in malnutrition, the 'hidden hunger', requires a multi-pronged strategy focusing on improving agricultural productivity, empowering women through maternal and child care practices and offering nutrition education and social protection programmes. Behavioural changes can ensue through counselling and supplementation programmes. On paper, India offers such programmes for Vitamin A and iron supplementation with huge gaps in implementation (consider the shortage in iron syrups for children in most states). Sanitation remains key (Dean Spears, DSE, 2013). Despite a lack of food inadequacy in Rajasthan, malnutrition remains substantial, potentially due to poor sanitation in given non-existent sewerage systems.

A coordinated multi-disciplinary effort can work, as witnessed in Maharashtra (Haddad, Nisbett, IDS, 2014) with child stunting reduced by 15 per cent over six years (one of the fastest globally) without PDS reforms. Its nutrition mission, headed by IAS officer V Ramani, developed better protocols for treating the acutely malnourished and ensured better coordination between the nutrition and healthcare departments.

This battle against hunger, against malnutrition, will have to be a decadal one, with a multi-pronged approach and long-term political commitment. It might have to offer food coupons, cash and in-kind transfers through a variety of institutional mechanisms, to overcome India's regional diversity. The government should seek to encourage states and local bodies to try out different policy reforms, according to their local needs, institutional culture and tastes, with the centre seeking to evaluate state and district-level outcomes on a regular basis. Without such step changes in execution, India will remain an enfeebled basket case.

GENERIC DRUGS

The death of Asif Mustafa, a thirty-five-year-old from Palashi village in district Nadia of West Bengal, who worked as a cleaning staff member in a gated community in Delhi, is a sad example of our failure in reducing OOP expenditure for drug purchases. Diagnosed with chikungunya and failing to get any medical help at the PHC, he had to rush to a local private doctor and buy medicines from a nearby pharmacy. The disease weakened his body and the treatment cost weakened his finances—not only was he spending a considerable portion of his daily earnings on medicines, he was also losing out on daily revenues as he was too weak to work. Considering himself to be a burden on his family's finances, he would stop taking the medicines the moment he felt a little better, thus never completing the prescribed course of medicines. His efforts to save money proved expensive, as he paid for it with his life and gifted an insecure future to his wife and kids.

Our public healthcare drug policies remain obsolete and under-financed. The initial two decades post-Independence witnessed higher drug prices and the rise of multinational control over the Indian pharma industry, the later years, post the '70s, heralded a shift towards self-sufficiency. Yet, under-investment and under-financing of drug procurement has significantly contributed to increasing OOP expenditure on healthcare, with more than 30 per cent of Indians in rural areas discontinuing their medical treatment on account of the financial burden. In case people continue their treatment, as many as 39 million people risk getting pushed below the poverty line each year (The Lancet, 2011).

Availability of free medicine has reduced with time, for both inpatient and outpatient care. For inpatient care, while 31 per cent of patients received free medicines in 1986–87, only 9 per cent of patients received free medicine in 2004. For outpatient care, the figure falls from 18 per cent to 5 per cent. The table below describes the change in availability of free medicines from 1986–87 to 2004.

TABLE 118: SOURCE: PLANNING COMMISSION OF INDIA, NOV 2011

PERIOD	FREE MEDICINES	PARTLY FREE	ON PAYMENT	NOT RECEIVED	TOTAL
INPATIENT					
1986–87	31.2%	15.0%	41.0%	12.9%	100.0%
1995–96	12.3%	13.2%	67.8%	6.8%	100.0%
2004	9.0%	16.4%	71.8%	2.8%	100.0%
OUT-PATIENT					
1986–87	18.0%	4.4%	65.6%	12.1%	100.0%
1995-96	7.2%	2.7%	79.3%	10.8%	100.0%
2004	5.3%	3.4%	65.3%	26.0%	100.0%

SOURCE: PLANNING COMMISSION ON INDIA, NOV 2011.

In terms of inter-state variations in drug accessibility, some states do much better than others. For example, Tamil Nadu leads the way, while Bihar, Uttarakhand and Uttar Pradesh lag behind. Almost 41 per cent of inpatient cases get free or partly paid medicines in Tamil Nadu, while for outpatient cases, the figure stands at 23 per cent. Jammu & Kashmir outperforms as well, with 64 per cent of inpatient cases and 13 per cent of outpatient cases receiving free or partly free medicines at public health facilities. On the other hand, just 3 per cent of inpatient cases and 1 per cent of outpatient cases get free or partly free medicines in Bihar. Jharkhand, Uttar Pradesh and Uttarakhand are other states which outperform in terms of affordable access to drugs. In such cases, it becomes important to learn from the success of Tamil Nadu in enduring affordable access to drugs for its populace.

The Tamil Nadu Medical Services Corporation (TNMSC) follows a centralized procurement model—including tendering, evaluation and contract award to—ensure availability of essential drugs at reasonable prices, thereby reducing the OOP burden on its citizens. Such a centralized procurement model needs well-established processes, trained personnel and a robust IT infrastructure and system. The drugs post-award, are supplied from the supplier,s premises to district warehouses, from where they are supplied to medical facilities on a value-based passbook system. The passbook system maintains control of the budget allocated to a centre, and within that budget, the centre can request for any quantity of drugs in the Essential Drugs List. Procurement for more than[59] 250 drugs across the treatment spectrum begins at the year's start, and evaluation remains a two-stage process—technical qualification wherein quality is established, followed by commercial evaluation wherein the selected bidder is chosen. Quality is assured through random sampling of drugs from district warehouses in its 11 empanelled laboratories. Bulk supply of drugs has now modified into blister packing and proper labelling in multiple languages, which prevents drug pilferage. A computerized IT system keeps track of inventory levels in district warehouses and when drugs deplete, it places orders with payments being processed in fifteen days. The district warehouse is in some way akin to a bank, which then provides drugs to each user (hospitals, clinics, etc.) at a stipulated price and enters the same in the user passbook. Stringent quality criteria is maintained through constant evaluation of both supplier and laboratories, with blacklisting of suppliers (on quality issues) and laboratories (on ethical/performance issues) being fairly common.

While many states are trying to copy the Tamil Nadu model for drug procurement, it remains critical that states customize the model to cater to their population instead of trying to blindly replicate it and expect similar success. Kerala tried to replicate the TNMSC model in 2008, and barring initial hiccups, has met with reasonable success. It tweaked the procurement model to incorporate real-time monitoring of inventory levels, with even last end-user incorporated assimilated within the IT network to have a more refined method for drug usage and future requirement. Ability to order the indents several times has allowed Kerala to have a fully centralized procurement system, as opposed to TNMSC which provides for 10

---

59   http://www.forbesindia.com/article/on-assignment/tamil-nadu-medical-services-corporation-a-success-story/15562/1

per cent district level procurement for medical emergencies.[60] On the other hand, the struggle of Odisha in initial years provides invaluable lessons. Odisha had an 80 per cent centralized model, allowing for 20 per cent purchases at the district level on a discretionary basis. Demand estimation was usually carried out at the pharmacy/clerk level in the absence of any centrally established demand estimation process, and inventory management was not based on any scientific warehousing practice. Quality assurance process was lax in absence of empanelled laboratories and discretionary testing of samples before dispatch. In cases where testing was undertaken, it took considerable time (~56 days instead of ~15 days in Tamil Nadu and Kerala). Ordering and delivery of drugs had scope for improvement, in the absence of any tracking of dispatched drugs and no flexibility in terms of order management (single order issued) and order alterations (no changes allowed on order placed). The EDL was revised after two years (compared to each year in Tamil Nadu) and each revision took ~7–8 months. The tendering process in the initial years struggled due to changing the minimum bidder turnover requirements from ₹10 lakh to ₹10 crore.

Rajasthan, on the other hand, has had reasonable success emulating the Tamil Nadu model. The Mukhya Mantri Nishulk Dawa Yojana (MNDY), launched in October 2011, was aimed to provide essential medicines, free of cost, in Rajasthan's public healthcare facilities. The scheme streamlined the government's medicine purchases by centralizing procurement in line with TNMSC and the corresponding increase in government expenditure on medicine was accompanied by a reduction in OOP expenditure by its citizens. The household OOP payments declined from 85 per cent (2004–05) to 75 per cent (2012–13), accompanied by reduced frequency of shortages/stock-outs (Public Health Foundation of India, World Health Organization, 2014). The scheme also achieved success in ensuring that ~97 per cent of medicines were prescribed by doctors using their generic names, and thus provides invaluable insights as the government attempts to make all doctors prescribe medicines by their generic name. The centralized procurement was done by RMSC with a two-bid system (technical and financial), a passbook system to ensure medicine supply and formation of the e-Aushadhi platform which brought the entire supply chain on one common platform, which was further helped by setting up of new storage and distribution warehouses.

The scheme has received robust financial support in initial years, with allocation rising from ₹76 crore in 2011–12 to ₹320 crore in 2013–14, leading to a rise in per capita health expenditure from ₹5.70 in the pre-MNDY regime to ₹50.50. Such an increase has reduced the impoverishment levels due to OOP expenditure on medicines from 3.2 per cent to 2.1 per cent. Greater focus has led to an increase

---

60   Prabal Vikram Singh, Anand Tatambhotla, Rohini Rao Kalvakuntla, Maulik Chokshi, Economic & Political Weekly, September 2012

in the number of people seeking medicare—rising from a total of 3.5 million visits in 2010 to 7.8 million in 2013, mainly due to a release of 'pent-up' demand. Availability of medicines has put pressure on healthcare facilities and staff to improve job presence and performance. The mean availability of essential medicines at the PHC, CHC and the district hospital stood at 100, 180 and 300 medicines, with median availability of drugs at 70 per cent, 67 per cent and 85 per cent respectively. Stock-outs are less—with no drugs being stocked out for more than a month, and an average stock-out of twelve days at PHC level, better than most developing countries (Public Health Foundation of India, World Health Organization, 2014). Higher bidder interest, reflected in terms of a number of bids received, signals competition among manufacturers, which, combined with the purchasing position of the government in terms of volume, ensures competitive annual rates for most drugs/essential medicines. Sufficient investments in ensuring stable medical supply and prescription guideline implementation reduce irrational prescription and thus misuse of scarce resources. Flexibility in terms of frequent deliveries of slow-moving drugs can improve intermediate stock levels while improving the expenditure mix from tertiary to primary care remains an area of improvement.

The success of TNMSC and MNDY needs to be replicated in all states with their own customization by treating it as a healthcare priority, not as a political project. The MNDY was able to register annual contract rates for essential drugs in line with rates prevalent at TNMSC, and almost one-third of prevalent market prices. In certain drugs, wherein the contracted rates were higher than TNMSC and market rates, the scope for improvement remains.[61]

Besides having a robust drug procurement model, drug manufacturing needs focus as well. India, being the leading supplier of generics on the global stage, still faces issues pertaining to domestic drug security. Ensuring government presence in drug manufacturing can enable effective control on policy implementation and provide pricing power through proper 'benchmarking' of costs, while ensuring stable supply of drugs for primary and secondary healthcare facilities on a low-cost basis. Reviving our drug manufacturing PSUs through capital infusion will strengthen drug security and would also generate employment. Our pharma PSUs were established in the first half of the twentieth century, with Bengal Chemicals and Pharmaceuticals Limited (BCPL) being established by Dr Prafulla Chandra Ray in 1901.[62] Hindustan Antibiotics Ltd and Indian Drugs & Pharmaceuticals Limited (IDPL) are other pharma PSUs, established with a view to keeping drug manufacturing under public control.

---

61 https://www.thehindubusinessline.com/specials/pulse/once-crown-jewels-pharma-psus-stare-into-the-sunset/article9493627.ece

62 https://www.thehindubusinessline.com/specials/pulse/once-crown-jewels-pharma-psus-stare-into-the-sunset/article9493627.ece

While proposals for the sale of land assets of pharma PSUs keeps getting traction, one-time capital infusion under the 'Make in India' scheme for these PSU firms can be considered. The firms can then be used to augment production of essential drugs and reduce import dependency for APIs. Such firms can also ensure constant and low-cost drug supply for generic drug stores, besides participating in generic drug procurement at a state level and being a strategic player in pro-poor health programmes.[63] The short-lived success in IDPL (when its revenues increased from ₹5 crore to ₹110 crore post infusion of technical manpower and updated machinery) illustrates that policy decisiveness can play a big role in reviving our pharma PSUs.

DRUG PRICING

Cheaper drugs are an essential component of universal healthcare. While capping drug prices arouses its own set of controversies, pharma firms globally have come under pressure to reduce prices. With a minimum wage of ~₹250/day for a government worker, a basic wage worker afflicted with chronic diseases like multi-drug resistant tuberculosis faces penury. His treatment, with drug combinations, costing roughly ₹1.2–1.5 lakh can equate to nearly four to six years of savings. Even managing something like diabetes can consume the majority of his monthly income. In India's beleaguered consumers, the international pharmaceutical industry has found its cash cow.

Turing Pharmaceuticals, headed by Martin Shkreli, was castigated for buying a drug, Daraprim, used to treat HIV patients, and raising its price from $20 to $750—an increase considered 'unjustifiable' even for the drug industry (HIVMA, September 2015). In India, Glenmark has announced an EMI scheme for two anti-cancer drugs— Abirapro (250 mg 120 pack costs ₹39,990) and Evermil (10 mg 10=tablet pack costs ₹29,965). Glivec, another anti-cancer drug, saw its base price rise from ₹8,500 to over ₹1 lakh per month over the last decade. A new hepatitis C drug, Sovaldi, is priced at $1,000 per pill. Cortisporin, used to treat ear infections, was developed by Glaxo Wellcome in 1975, and has had its price rise from $10 to $195—a pricing that its formulator, Endo Health Solutions, believes is 'rational and appropriate' (David Lazarus, February 2016). Meanwhile, China's anti-monopoly regulator has fined five domestic drug firms for colluding to raise the prices of allopurinol tablets (NDRC, 2015).

---

63   https://www.thehindubusinessline.com/specials/pulse/once-crown-jewels-pharma-psus-stare-into-the-sunset/article9493627.ece

Other arrangements have drawn concern. Finalizing Voluntary Licence (VL) agreements between Gilead Science and eleven Indian generic drug makers, has evoked pricing concerns for critical drugs. The recent decision to restore the customs duty exemption on imports of around four drugs signals the critical public need that such drugs command. We cannot let critical illnesses be viewed as a goldmines for institutions.

Healthcare remains heavily skewed against the poor in India. Out-of-pocket expenses can comprise up to 80 per cent of all health financing, with 70 per cent of health spending on outpatient treatment devoted primarily to purchasing medicines (Creese A, Kotwani A, Kutzin J, Pillay A, 2004). Access to affordable medicines remains a significant concern—Delhi, at best, offers just 48.8 per cent availability (Anita Kotwani, 2013). Unskilled workers need to work an hour in India (as against 10 minutes in the UK) to afford a basic paracetamol (All India Drug Action Network (AIDAN), 2015). This spiralling cost of basic medical drugs has left little for daily life.

India's drug pricing regime has evolved—The Drugs (Display of Prices) Order 1962, froze medicine pricing, while the landmark Hathi Committee Report (1975) led to the Drug Policy (1979) which set up a National Drug Authority and selective price control on medicines. The Drug Prices Control Order (DPCO), 2013, brought 348 drugs onto India's National List of Essential Medicines (NLEM), 2011, with significant exclusions made for formulation and presentation (S. Srinivasan, EPW, 2014).

Significant loopholes remain—while 358 formulations of paracetamol are under price control, over 2,714 combinations of paracetamol (~80 per cent of the market share) are not (Sourirajan Srinivasan, 2013). Despite price controls, DPCO 2013 covers only 18 per cent of the domestic market (~55 per cent is excluded combinations of NLEM drugs), with little impact. As highlighted by the Supreme Court, India's current drug pricing policies have tended to fix the maximum price of a medicine above the retail price of the market volume leader (AIDAN, 2015).

While the National Pharmaceutical Pricing Authority (NPPA) struck down its notification on ceiling prices for fifty non-scheduled medicines in 108 formulations/dosages, the public interest in ensuring affordable access remains (S. Srinivasan, EPW, 2014). India's pharmaceutical industry suffers from a glaring lack of competition—given significant information asymmetry; customers often buy the priciest product to alleviate an immediate need. India's drug pricing regime remains ripe for change.

Price control remains an effective answer to ensuring affordability. Even free markets in the West utilize price, volume and cost effectiveness controls to mitigate healthcare inflation. Canada has its Patented Medicines Prices Review Board, while Egypt has brought all medicines under price control and Lebanon has utilized regressive margin pricing and improved transparency by publishing patient prices on its online Lebanon National Drug Index (AIDAN, 2009).

In addition, we must encourage a centralized procurement system, as utilized by Tamil Nadu, for purchasing drugs—a Tamil Nadu state government tender for albendazole 400 mg tablets have attracted prices of 35 paise per tablet; retail prices are quoted at ₹12 (AIDAN, 2009). Unethical and unfair drug selling practices, such as holiday trip offers and fancy gifts, need to be curbed from influencing doctors and key bureaucrats. As suggested by AIDAN, the National List of Essential Medicines should be revised every two to three years, with price regulation based on the therapy considered, instead of a formulation focus. VAT abolishment on essential medicines can also be considered, as in Tajikistan.

We need to create an accessible and affordable healthcare system that offers scale, multi-generational permanence (multi-generational and is supported by sustainable financing mechanisms to ensure affordability). Along with debt financing, policy interventions like cheaper loans and tax breaks on interest payments could be tried to generate funds flow. Easing RBI rules on ECBs by healthcare projects can lead to access to cheaper funds from a larger credit source; ~20 per cent of PE funds expected to be invested in healthcare (PwC, 2012).

Medicines remain overpriced and unaffordable in India. In a country riddled with poverty, medical debt remains the second biggest factor for pushing millions back into poverty. With little to no availability of basic health insurance and a preference for private practitioners, drugs engender poverty. With innovative policymaking, this troika of quality, affordability and access could be achieved.

SINGLE INSURANCE POOL

Insurance can help as well. The government's push for low-cost 'inpatient' insurance, while encouraging, should also incorporate outpatient expenses. Low-cost diagnostic capabilities, generic drug stores (Rajasthan's 'Life Line' drug stores) and lowfrills hospitals that provide affordable care (Vaatsalya) can be considered.

Insurance coverage is also abysmal in India, with just around 25 per cent of the population covered. To achieve universal access, a coverage ratio of around 75 per cent needs to be targeted, with the remainder offered access through government payments via RSBY. Access with low out-of-pocket spending can be achieved through an expansion of healthcare insurance, with the government playing a payor or guarantor role instead of providing services.

Social insurance schemes really need to be rolled out at scale, with the government deploying a greater share of healthcare funds for RSBY. Pilot programmes launched at the state level can help us determine the best model for the Indian market. Community health insurance schemes like those launched by the Karuna Trust in Karnataka help improve access and utilization of health services by the rural poor. Those left behind in India's growth should be offered a helping hand.

We see that India's health insurance provision is dominated by multiple insurance schemes, both at state and national level. As we move towards Universal Health Care (UHC), risk consolidation assumes greater significance and decisions on risk pooling and jurisdiction become important.[64]

Amidst a multitude of insurance schemes, should the focus be placed on consolidation into a single risk pool or should it be on trying to plug the gaps within different schemes? There are obvious advantages to having a single national insurance scheme in terms of efficiency—administrative costs would be lower, the risk would be spread across heterogeneous groups in diverse geographies and implementing fiscal and administrative controls becomes relatively easier. However, the existing pool of schemes is quite diverse in terms of their provisions and their geography, thereby posing significant challenges for their integration. Additionally, it would lack the geographical proximity and local familiarity that the existing state-level insurance schemes may provide.

It should be noted that other countries have achieved wider breadth (wider coverage in terms of population) and reached greater depth (coverage of benefits) without converging to a single risk pool. Thailand, for example, has made modifications to its existing legacy insurance schemes in order to close the gaps. Mexico's experience of developing risk pools at the sub-national level (Seguro Popular), while building on their existing risk pools can provide interesting insights for any country with a strong federal government mechanism.

There exists a range of options in expanding the risk pool for achieving UHC. We can look to expand the width of the existing risk pools, which is conceptually simpler as it involves pure scaling efforts while preserving existing institutional knowledge and framework. It also ensures less dramatic changes and builds upon the ready acceptability of existing schemes at multiple levels. Meanwhile, scaling leads to reduced risk and reduced administrative costs. However, this system provides less flexibility for realignment of incentives at limited cost, which would be a critical component of the UHC.

Expanding the depth can also be focused upon—new risk pools could be introduced at a state/district level, which may speed up execution, provide greater choice to citizens and build strong local linkages. However, this will increase administrative costs, and does not address the question of adverse selection, thereby may end up causing inequity among different risk pools.

In order to achieve UHC, it is critical to expand on both depth and breadth fronts—consolidation of various risk pools would reduce administrative costs, address issues of adverse selection and, most importantly, reduce healthcare costs (government being the monopsony power) coupled with optimization of benefits in service delivery.

Thailand's experience of moving towards UHC brings about a few interesting insights. Despite three decades of experience in working with publicly subsidized, community-based healthcare insurance, nearly 75 per cent of its population remained uninsured. The Social Security Scheme (SSS) meant for the private and formal sectors covered 16 per cent of the population, whereas the Civil Servant Medical Benefit Scheme (CSMBS), meant for civil servants covered 8 per cent of the population. Their means of financing were different (the CSMBS was funded by general taxation, whereas the SSS was through payroll tax) and so were their benefits. Besides these two, the Low Income Card Scheme was a tax-based programme that offered free service at public hospitals, and the publicly financed Voluntary Health Card Scheme had limited success. In 2001, despite attempts to merge all schemes into one, Thailand left SSS and CSMBS intact and merged other schemes into the Universal Coverage Scheme (UCS)—a risk pool that is tax-based and focused on prevention and primary care. Outpatient care being provided on capitation basis helps control costs and inpatient care based on diagnosis provides an incentive to improve efficiency without reducing quality.

Thus, with three different risk pools, Thailand managed to achieve near-universal healthcare coverage. Meanwhile, registration among the schemes has been standardized despite the risk pools being funded and operated separately. The payment mechanism is also being synchronized starting with the standard fee schedule, utilization reviews and medical auditing. It's interesting to note that UHC can be achieved through multiple risk pools—on the one hand preserving the existing schemes (thereby their infrastructure and institutional capability), and on the other, introducing a new risk pool for the poor and uninsured and then achieving harmonization of benefits, payments and processes amongst them.

In some ways, India's healthcare demographics also bear resemblance to Mexico when it embarked upon providing UHC—with a large proportion of the public (50 per cent) being uninsured, high dependence on publicly financed state medical facilities, huge disparities in the funding and facilities in public healthcare in different states leading to more than 50 per cent OOP expenditures. The health insurance sector was mostly dominated by the IMSS for the formal and private sectors covering 40 per cent of the population, the ISSSTE for civil servants covering 7 per cent of the population and the remaining 3 per cent opting for voluntary, private insurance. In 2004, Seguro Popular (SP) was introduced as a tax-based, voluntary insurance system, which in some respects is similar to RSBY as it aims to offer a pre-defined variety of services through national and state-level risk pooling. Funding for SP was achieved through central transfers (fixed component plus a variable redistributive component), the state governments and beneficiary households. For the bottom two income deciles, the end-user household fees were completely waived.

The flow of funds from the central government to states ensures that poorer states get improved access compared to wealthier ones. Additionally, transfers are a function of the number of households enrolled, which then acts as an incentive to provide quality services to SP members, else they may opt for other healthcare services. The programme, besides providing access to pre-defined 255 treatments (which account for ~90 per cent of service demand), also encompasses the tertiary service aspect by covering eighteen low-frequency, high-cost treatments in a separate complementary pool. However, enrolment has weakened in a few states, where active state participation is found lacking, underlining the importance of broad-level citizen and state support. Lack of state support would also lead to poor service quality in some states, thereby prompting the paid members of SP to question the viability of enrolling in the programme – an important lesson for any public institution introducing fee-based insurance for the public. Mexico's experience shows us that in order to increase width, implementation at the state level remains important. Political commitment and alignment remain essential and any cost-sharing formula needs to take care of health requirements and fiscal space of particular states, individually and collectively.

REFERENCES

Banerjee, A., Angus Deaton, Esther Duflo (2004). Health Care Delivery in Rural Rajasthan. Economic and Political Weekly. XXXIX (09), pp. 944-949 (excerpted from http://www.epw.in/special-articles/health-care-delivery-rural-rajasthan.html)

Basu, R. (n.d). Rashtriya Swasthya Bima Yojana: Pioneering Public-Private Partnership in Health Insurance, (excerpted from http://www.napsipag.org/PDF/RUMKI%20BASU.pdf)

Basu, S. and Saurabh Ghosh. (n.d). The Road to Universal Health Coverage: An Overview, (excerpted from http://www.idfc.com/pdf/report/2013-14/Overview.pdf)

Bhandari, L. and Siddhartha Dutta. (n.d.). Health Infrastructure in Rural India (accessed at www.iitk.ac.in/3inetwork/html/reports/IIR2007/11-Health.pdf)

Bhat, R. and Nishant Jain. (2004). Analysis of Public Expenditure on Health Using State Level Data. Ahmedabad: Indian Institute of Management (IIM), June 2004 (excerpted from http://www.iimahd.ernet.in/publications/data/2004-06-08rbhat.pdf)

Centre for Enquiry into Health and Allied Themes. (2005): Review of Healthcare In India (Survey No. 2804 & 2805), Mumbai: Gangolli, Leena V., Ravi Duggal and Abhay Shukla, (excerpted from www.cehat.org/publications/PDf%20files/r51.pdf)

Centre for Policy Research. (n.d.). Can Rashtriya Swasthya Bima Yojna Help Bridge the Quality Chasm? (RSBY Working Paper), Sethi, Sonam, (excerpted from www.idfresearch.org/pdf/R SBY_Hospital_quality_paper.pdf)

Chaudhury, N., J. Hammer, M Knemer, K. Muralidharan, and F.H. Rogers. (2006). 'Missing in Action: Teacher and Health Worker Absence in Developng Countries. Journal of Economic Perspectives, 20 Pittsburg (excerpted from http://siteresources.worldbank.org/INTPUBSERV/Resources/4772 50-1187034401048/ChaudhuryandothersMIA.pdf)

Chilimuntha, A.K., Kumudini R. Thakor and Jeremiah S. Mulpuri. (2013). Disadvantaged Rural Health – Issues and International Journal of Social Work and Human Services Practice 37 3(1): 29–37, Feb 2015

'Disadvantaged Rural Health – Issues and Challenges: A Review.' National Journal of Medical Research, 3 (1): 80-82, (excerpted from http://www.scopemed.org/?mno=36128)

Das, J. and Jessica Leino. (2011). Evaluating the RSBY-Lessons from an Experimental Information Campaign, Economic and Political Weekly, XLVI(32), (excerpted from http://www.epw.in/special-articles/evaluating-rsby-lessons-experi mental-information-campaign.html)

Government of India. Faster, Sustainable and More Inclusive Growth: An approach to the 12th five year plan (2012-17): (excerpted from http://planningcommission.nic.in/plans/planrel/12appdrft/approach _12plan.pdf.)

IFMR Research, Centre for Development Finance Report (2009-10): The National Rural Health Mission, (Scheme Brief) (excerpted from cdf.ifmr.ac.in/wp-content/uploads/2011/03/NRHM-Brief.pdf)

Iyengar, S. and Ravindra H. Dholakia (2011). Access of the Rural Poor to Pimary Healthcare in India, (working paper no. 2011-05-03), IIM, Ahmedabad (excerpted from http://www.iimahd.ernet.in/assets/snippets/workingpaperpdf/3937 368102011-05-03.pdf).

Infrastructure Development Finance Company Ltd. (2013). India Rural Development Report, 2012/13, New Delhi, Orient BlackSwan (excerpted fromorientblackswan.com/ebooksfree/.../content/irdr%20full%20b ook.pdf)

International Institute for Population Sciences (IIPS) and Macro International. (2007). National Family Health Survey (NFHS-3), 2005-06, India: Key Findings. Mumbai: IIPS (excerpted from http://cbhidghs.nic.in/writereaddata/linkimages/NFHS-3%20 key% 20Findings5456434051.pdf)

Kaushik, M., Abhishek Jaiswal, Naseem Shah and Ajay Mahal (2008): High-end physician migration from India, Bulletin of the World Health Organization, 86(1), (excerpted from http://www.who.int/bulletin/volumes/86/1/07-041681/en/)

Kumar, A. and Saurav Gupta. (2012). Health Infrastructure in India: Critical Analysis of Policy Gaps in the Indian Healthcare Delivery, (Occasional paper), Vivekananda International Foundation (excerpted from http://www.vifindia.org/sites/default/files/health-infrastructure-in-i ndia-critical-analysis-of-policy-gaps-in-the-indian-healthcare-deliv ery.pdf)

Ministry of Women and Child Development, Govt. of India. (2010). Indira Gandhi Matritva Sahyog Yojana-A Conditional Maternity Benefit Scheme (excerpted from wcd.

nic.in/schemes/igmsyscheme.pdf)

Murthy, M.V. R. (n.d.). Mobile based Primary
Health Care System for Rural India, (excerpted
from www.w3.org/2008/02/MS4D_WS/.../
cdac-mobile-healthcare-pape r.pdf). NRHM
Report (2014-15): Budget Briefs, 6(5), New Delhi,
Accountability Initiative, (excerpted from http://
www.climatefinance-developmenteffectiveness.org/
archive/documents/Budget_brief_the_National_
Rural_Health_Mission_% 28NRHM%29.pdf)

Patil, A.V., K.V. Somasundaram and R.C.
Goyal. (2002). Current Health Scenario in
Rural India, Australian Journal of Rural Health,
10, 129-135 (excerpted from www.sas.upenn.
edu/~dludden/WaterborneDisease3.pdf)

Rao, M. and David Mant. (n.d.). Strengthening
primary healthcare in India: white paper on
opportunities for partnership, BMJ Journals
(excerpted from www.pathfinderhealth.in/
images/BMJ_articles/BMJ_Article.pdf)

Rao, M. Govinda and Mita. Choudhury. (2012).
Health Care Financing Reforms in India, (working
paper no. 2012-100), National Institute of
Public Finance and Policy (excerpted from www.
nipfp.org.in/media/medialibrary/2013/04/
wp_2012_100.pdf). RSBY- A Report (excerpted
from http://www.rsby.gov.in/overview.aspx)

Sethi, S. (n.d). Can Rashtriya Swasthya Bima
Yojna Help Bridge the Quality Chasm? RSBY
Working Paper (excerpted fromwww.idfresearch.
org/pdf/RSBY_Hospital_quality_paper.pdf)

Singh, S. Kumar, Ravinder Kaur, Madhu Gupta
and Rajesh Kumar. (2011). Impact of National
Rural Health Mission on Perinatal Mortality
in Rural India, Indian Pediatrics, 49, 136-138,
(excerpted from medind.nic.in/ibv/t12/i2/
ibvt12i2p136.pdf). United Nations Population
Fund, India Report (2009): Concurrent Assessment
of Janani Suraksha Yojana (JSY) in Selected
States (excerpted from http://india.unfpa.
org/drive/JSYConcurrentAssessment.pdf)

Gupta, R. K., Gautam Kumra and Barnik
C. Maitra. (2005). A Foundation for Public
Health in India McKinsey Quarterly,
2005 Special Edition, pp6-8, 3p.

Montgomery, M. R., Paul C. Hewett. 2005.
'Urban Poverty and Health in Developing
Countries: Household and Neighborhood
Effects.' Demography 42(3):397-425.

Office of the Registrar General, India.
Sample Registration System Statistical
Report 2010. 2010. New Delhi: Ministry
of Home Affairs Government of India

Zimmer, Z. 2006. 'Population Aging.' Pp.
936-40. Encyclopedia of Gerontology.
R. Schulz, L.S. Noelker, K. Rockwood
and R.L. Sprott, editors. Springer.

Government of India. Bulletin on Rural
Health Statistics in India, December 1999.
New Delhi: Rural Health Division, Ministry
of Health and Family Welfare, 2000.

Kinsella, K. 2001. 'Urban and Rural Dimensions
of Global Population Aging: An Overview.'
Journal of Rural Health 17(4):314-22.

Langmore, J. 2001. 'Rural Aging: A Global
Challenge.' Journal of Rural Health 17(4):305-06.

Mukherjee, S., N. R. Bandhopadhyay and B. K.
Bhattacharya. (2007). Reasons for Non-Utilization
of Institutional Healthcare Service in Rural
West Bengal: A Perspective. Decision (0304-
0941), Jul-Dec2007, Vol. 34 Issue 2, p113-132.

Walker, J. (1999). Partnerships to Improve Rural and
Remote Health Care. Australian Journal of Public
Administration, Sep99, Vol. 58 Issue 3, p72, 4p.

Mahoney, M, Mary Mahoney, Mardie Townsend,
Erica Hallebone and Pat Nesbitt. (2001).
An 'upside-down' view of rural health care.
International Journal of Consumer Studies,
Jun2001, Vol. 25 Issue 2, p102-113, 12p.

Montgomery, M. R., Richard Stern, Barney
Cohen, Holly E. Reed, editors. 2003.
Cities Transformed: Demographic Change
and Its Implications in the Developing
World. National Academy Press.

Mishra, S. K. (2004). Telemedicine Initiatives in
Indian subcontinent Question 14-1/2: Application
of telecommunications in health care. Study
Group-2, Document RGQ14-1/2/023-E.
Rapporteur's Group Meeting On Question
14-1/2 - Hiratsuka, Japan, 25-27 June 2004.

Baleta, A. (2009). Rural Hospital Beats the
Odds in South Africa. Lancet, 9/5/2009,
Vol. 374 Issue 9692, p771-772, 2p.

Li, J., Robert A. Runderson, Judy F. Burnham,
Geneva Bush Staggs, Justin C. Robertson and
Thomas L. Williams. (2005). Delivering Distance
Training to Rural Health Care Professionals.
Medical Reference Services Quarterly,
Spring2005, Vol. 24 Issue 1, p41-54, 14p.

Roh, Chul-Young, M. Jae Moon. (2005).
Nearby, but Not Wanted? The Bypassing of
Rural Hospitals and Policy Implications for
Rural Health Care Systems. Policy Studies
Journal, 2005, Vol. 33 Issue 3, p377-394, 18p.

Jutting, Johannes P. (2004). Do Community-based Health Insurance Schemes Improve Poor People's Access to Health Care? Evidence From Rural Senegal. World Development, Feb 2004, Vol. 32 Issue 2, p273, 16p.

Nayak, A. K. J. R. (2006). Managing Health without Doctors: A Case of Mobile Health Units (MHU). Mobile Health Unit -- Managing Health Without Doctors Case Study, 2006, pp.1-18.

Chatterjee, P. (2006). India's government aims to improve rural health. Lancet, 10/28/2006, Vol. 368 Issue 9546, p1483-1484, 2p.

Chakrabarti, A. and Kausik Chaudhuri. (2007). Antenatal and maternal health care utilization: evidence from northeastern states of India. Applied Economics, 4/10/2007, Vol. 3 Issue 6, p683-695.

Murawski, L. and Richard L. Church. (2009). Improving accessibility to rural health services: The maximal covering network improvement problem. Socio-Economic Planning Sciences, Jun2009, Vol. 43 Issue 2, p102-110, 9p.

Annigeri, V. B. (2004). 'Changes in Health Care Infrastructure Manpower and Performance in Three States during Economic Reforms', CMDR Monograph Series No. – 41.

Bhandari, L. and S. Dutta. (2007). 'Health Infrastructure in Rural India'. in P. Kalra and A. Rastogi (eds) India Infrastructure Report , New Delhi: Oxford University Press : 265-285

Chaudhury, N. and J. S. Hammer. (2003). 'Ghost Doctors: Doctor Absenteeism in Bangladeshi Health Centres', Working Paper No. 3065, World Bank Policy Research

Chutani, C.S. and T.R. Gyatso. (1993). 'Health Status of Women and Children in Sikkim', UNICEF, New Delhi:

Department of Planning and Coordination. (2004). Nagaland State Human Development Report, Government of Nagaland

Deutche Gesellschaft Fur Internationale Zusammenarbeit. (2012). Compasss Due North-East: Mapping the Regional Social Enterprise Landscape. Preliminary Assessment of the Social Enterprise Sector in the North Eastern Region of India, New Delhi

Garg, S., R. Singh and M. Grover. (2012). 'India's Health Workforce: Current status and the Way Forward', The National Medical Journal of India, 25(2): 111- 113

Goel, S. L. (2009). Health Care System

and Hospital Administration: Primary. Deep and Deep Publications:

Gyatso, T. R. and B. B. Bagdass. (1998). Status in Sikkim, Department of Health & Family Welfare. Government of Sikkim. Hati, K.K. and Majumder, R. 2013.

Hazarika, I. (2013). 'Health Workforce in India: Assessment of Availability, Production and Distribution', WHO South-East Asia J Public Health, 2:106- 12. INTER-STATE VA

Kumari, R. and R. Raman. (2011). 'Inter-District Disparity in Health Care Facility and Education: A Case of Uttar Pradesh', Journal of Education and Practice, 2(1): 38-56

Kumari, R. (2013). 'Inclusive Health in India: A disaggregated Level Analysis. Journal of Community Positive Practices, (1): 45-60

Laxmi, T. S. and D. Sahoo (2013). 'Health Infrastructure and Health Indicators: The Case of Andhra Pradesh, India', IOSR Journal of Humanities and Social Science, 6(6):22-29

Martínez, J. and T. Martineau (2002). 'Human Resources in the Health Sector: An International Perspective', Issues Paper, London: DFID Health Systems Resource Centre. Ministry of Development of North East Region. (MDoNER). 2011

Human Development Report of North East States. Government of India. North Eastern Council (NEC). (2012). Health Workforce Development Plan for NER. Shillong. Government of India

Planning Commission. (2007). National Human Development Report 2001 (No. id: 1284).Govt. of India

Planning Commission. (2011). India Human Development Report 2011: Towards Social Inclusion, Oxford University Press

Prabhakar, H. and R. Manoharan. (2005). 'The Tribal Health Initiative Model for Healthcare Delivery: A Clinical and Epidemiological Approach', Medicine

Sengupta, K. (2009). Genesis of Human Development in North East India. A Diagnostic Analysis, Concept Publishing Company. New Delhi. LASARA M. LYNGDOH

Sheet, S., and T. A. Roy. (2013). 'Micro Level Analysis of Disparities in Health Care Infrastructure in Birbhum District, West Bengal, and India', IOSR Journal of Humanities and Social Science, 7 (3): 25-31

Singh, U. P. (2008). Tribal Health in North East India: A Study of Socio-Cultural Dimensions of Health Care Practices, Serials Publication. India. The World Health Report .2000. Health Systems: Improving Performance, World Health Organization. The World Health Report .2007. A Safer Future: Global Public Health Security in the 21st Century. World Health Organization.

Barros, R. (2008). Wealthier But Not Much Healthier: Effects of a Health Insurance Program for the Poor in Mexico. Palo Alto: Stanford University.

Bitran, R. A. (2008). The Politics of the AUGE Health Reform in Chile: A Case Study Prepared for the Results for Development Institute. Washington, DC.

Bitran, R., and G. Urcullo. (2008). Chile: Good Practice in Expanding Health Care Coverage—Lessons from Reforms. In P. S. Gottret, Good Practices in Health Financing: Lessons from Reforms in Low- and Middle-Income Countries. Washington, DC: World Bank.

Britrán, R., and F. X. Almarza. (1997). Las Instituciones de Salud Previsional (ISAPRE) en Chile. Santiago: Comisión Económico para América.

Frenk, J., and F. M. Knaul. (2005). Health Insurance In Mexico:Achieving Universal Coverage Through Structural Reform. Health Affairs , 1467-1476.

Frenk, J., O. Gómez-Dantés and F. M. Knaul. (2009). The democratization of health in Mexico: financial innovations for universal coverage. Bulletin of the World Health Organization

Frenk, J., E. González-Pier, O. Gómez-Dantés, M. A. Lezana and F. M. Knaul. (2006). Comprehensive reform to improve health system performance in Mexico. Lancet , 1525.

Frenk, J., F. Knaul and O. Gómez-Dantés. (2004). Fair Financing and Universal Protection. Mexico City: Ministry of Health.

Homedes, N., and A. Ugalde. (2009). Twenty-Five Years of Convoluted Health Reforms in Mexico. PLoS Medicine .

Lakin, J. (2009, June 6). Financing structure for Mexican health reform in danger. Lancet , 1948.

Lakin, J. (2010). The End of Insurance?

Mexico's Seguro Popular, 2001 – 2007. Journal of Health Politics, Policy and Law , 313-352.

Mills, A. (2007). Strategies to achieve universal coverage: are there lessons from middle income countries. Health Systems Knowledge Network.

Radich, N. A. (1995). A Single Health Care System for a Reunified Germany.

Reddy, K., S. Selvaraj and K. C. Rao. (2011). A Critical Assessment of the Existing Health Insurance Models in India. New Delhi: Public Health Foundation of India.

Shiva Kumar, A., L. C. Chen, M. Choudhury, S. Ganju, V. Mahajan and A. Sinha, et al. (2011). Financing health care for all: challenges and opportunities. Lancet , 668-679.

Smith, P. C., and S. N. Witter. (2004). Risk Pooling in Health Care Financing. Washington, DC: World Bank.

Sparkes, S. P., and W. Hsiao. (2010). Comparative Approaches To Health Financing. Kaiser Family Foundation.

The Joint Learning Network. www. jointlearningnetwork.org.

Towse, A., A. Mills and V. Tangcharoensathien. (2005). Learning from Thailand's health reforms. BMJ , 103-105.

World Bank. (2006). Seguro Popular Incidence Analysis. In J. Scott, Decentralized Service Delivery to the Poor (pp. 247-166). Washington, DC: World Bank.

World Health Organization. (2010). Health Systems Financing: The path to universal coverage. Geneva: WHO.

World Health Organization. (2000). The World Health Report: Health systems improving performance. Geneva: World Health Organization.

World Health Organization. (2007). World Health Assessment. Geneva.

Sarnsamak, P. (2011, March 24). Panel to work on reform of healthcare.

CHAPTER X

ON RURAL CREDIT

By the very nature of India's agricultural economy, with its heavy dependency on the monsoon, with agricultural activities being inherently structurally risky, rural credit has been necessary. A variety of indigenous systems of credit have helped ease the passage across seasons, helping farmers manage weather risk and rapidly shifting and yet onerous systems of taxation. High interest rates have been historically the norm, with exploitation and misery built into the fabric of rural credit. The usurious moneylender was well-known, even in colonial times. The Central Banking Enquiry Committee Report (CBEC) (1929) stated, 'The ryot cannot cultivate without borrowing because his crop goes largely to the long-term creditor.' India's poor are still highly vulnerable: 51.4 per cent of all farmers are financially excluded from both formal and informal sources. With an average debt per household of ₹3,252,2[1] about 31 per cent of rural households are indebted. This condition results from an interlocking of the credit market with imperfect markets (land, input, output, labour and land-lease markets), which is a pathway to peasantry pauperization. 'The Indian peasant is born in debt, lives in debt and dies in debt.'[2] In ideal circumstances, the moneylender, locally, is not just a source of credit, but also a crop buyer, a labour employer and a land lessor. Borrowers can only offer collaterals of land, future labour service and future harvests, all of which can be easily undervalued. Any lender quickly develops a vested interest in maintaining poverty, or even outright default.

Even the British colonial government was concerned, leading a practice of providing institutional credit in agriculture along with a variety of reports (Royal Commission on Agriculture, 1927; Malcolm Daring Report, 1935). The Cooperative Societies Act was passed in 1904, with cooperatives utilized as the

---

1   NSSO, 2014
2   Malcolm Darling, 1925

primary agency for disbursing institutional credit.[3] There was continuous attention towards provisioning rural credit, credit societies were recognized by a new Act in 1912, while the establishment of provincial cooperative banks was encouraged.[4] And yet, even then, shortfall in loan payments by farmers was routine, 60–70 per cent of all outstanding principal due was credit overdue. Even the Reserve Bank of India (RBI) in its founding Act (the Reserve Bank of India Act, 1934) had specific provisions for prioritization of agricultural credit. The RBI was required to set up an agricultural credit desk, while conducting studies on agricultural credit (such studies highlighted that most rural credit originated from moneylenders and was subject to high interest rates). The Report of the All India Credit Survey (1954) highlighted that agricultural credit often fell short, was simply not the right type and did not serve the right purpose.

Post-Independence, the Fourth Five Year Plan saw the creation of the All India Rural Credit Review Committee in 1966, chaired by B. Venkatappiah, to review the supply of rural credit. The Committee recommended that all commercial banks embrace a complementary role to extend rural credit. Nationalization of major commercial banks in 1969 inadvertently encouraged a further shift towards agricultural credit from the banking system. Agriculture was tagged as a 'priority sector', with a certain proportion of total net bank credit mandated to be deployed in such sectors. The Green Revolution, following the 1965 drought, was built on rising availability of rural credit that was utilized for purchasing agricultural inputs. Regional rural banks were also set up; creating a separate banking structure that combined a local look and feel, along with an understanding of relevant local issues.[5] This effectively created a multi-agency approach towards rural credit.

NABARD was established in 1982[6] to pick up the refinancing functions associated with the RBI in rural credit related cooperatives and rural banks. NABARD has since then played a pivotal role in providing financial assistance in rural areas. Its administration of the Rural Infrastructure Development Fund (RIDF) has helped provide a catalytic boost to self-help groups.

However, formalized rural credit remains beset with a variety of weaknesses—there has been a significant decline in the productivity and efficiency associated with rural financial institutions; meanwhile, repayment ethics have run askew, leading to significant profitability concerns. A variety of task forces and committees have been set up to solve such issues—The High-level Committee on Agricultural Credit

3　Reserve Bank of India, 1970, p.68

4　Maclagan Committee on Cooperation in India

5　Narasimham Working Group, 1975

6　Committee to Review Arrangements for Institutional Credit for Agriculture and Rural Development, 1982

through Commercial Banks (R.V. Gupta, 1998), Task Force to Study the Functions of Cooperative Credit System and to Suggest Measures for Its Strengthening (Jagdish Capoor, 1999), Expert Committee on Rural Credit (V.S. Vyas, 2001), and The Working Group to Suggest Amendments in the Regional Rural Banks Act, 1976.[7] In summary, the agricultural credit system in India has evolved.

With little access to formal financial institutions, India's poor have invested in chit funds and Ponzi schemes (Sahara, ~₹40,000 crore dues), exposed to deposit erosion. Free from regulation, over 30,000 unregistered chit funds have emerged as a source of liquidity. Financial fraud is now frequent; the ₹2,000 crore Sarada scam in West Bengal paid investor money obtained from new investors rather than profits. The group's agents charged high commissions (15–40 per cent) while promising to pay back ten times within fourteen years. Regulators such as SEBI and RBI find themselves judicially constrained from regulating such entities, while penalties remain low (₹5,000 in Delhi, while Haryana does not even penalize!).

Rural credit, ideally, would be a cushion against such practices, smoothening out the asymmetry resulting from delayed earnings. However, the moneylender dominates, with institutional agencies advancing credit to just 17 per cent of all rural households, at moderate rates of interest (6–15 per cent). Non-institutional agencies provide a further 19 per cent, comprising 69 per cent of all loans given out, at interest rates above 20 per cent for a period of 2–3 years. Only 8 per cent of Indian adults have a loan from a formal financial institution, while just 12 per cent have savings accounts with institutions. A lack of enough money and constraints of distance, cost and lack of documentation restrict India's masses from banking. Meanwhile, MFIs consider the rural markets as business opportunities, while offering professionalism, innovation and technology in credit lending. With profits the sole consideration, there is significant pressure to 'dump money on borrowers,'[8] while seeking security deposits as cash collateral.

The availability of credit in the rural economy has historically been subject to the whims and fancies of the local moneylender, along with more macroeconomic factors—the extractive policies of the ruling state, along with political stability and weather vagaries. For peasants, the Mughal Empire was fundamentally an extractive state—a protection racket run riot. The State maintained an imperial household (consuming 5 per cent of the total budget in 1595), and the central military establishment (~9 per cent) and the salaries of the mansabdars (~80 per cent), while the Mughal nobility consumed the remainder of the budget.[9] To collect

---

7   M.V.S. Chalapathi Rao, 2002

8   Ghate, 2007

9   Richards, J.F., Fiscal states in India over the long term, 2001

tax, a zamindari system was established, with each zamindar receiving an allowance of 10 per cent of the land revenue collected amidst an established domain, ranging from a few villages to entire parganas. A land revenue assessment scheme, devised during Akbar's reign, measured potential taxes, field by field, across a variety of crops, with varying yields and market prices, and irrigation requirements. Typically, the land revenue share of a crop varied between 33 per cent and 50 per cent, depending on fertility, with a further 10–25 per cent paid to the zamindar for his efforts. As mansabdar jagirs were relocated regularly, individual revenue assignees had limited interest in pursuing long-term maintenance or growth of agriculture, seeking to maximize their extraction of any agricultural surplus.[10] On an overall basis, a peasant could ideally lose up to 56 per cent of his produce to this rapacious state.[11]

Its replacement by the East India Company and later the British Government provided little respite. Colonial rule fundamentally altered the nature of property and land rights across India, with a prior system of overlapping rights of land ownership (land was generally owned by the higher castes, while the lower castes had varying rights of occupancy and produce share rights [Gupta, 1940]) replaced by one where only sole proprietary ownership rights were recognized.[12] Zamindars were now granted hereditary and proprietary rights, with the rate of assessment fixed in perpetuity. The Company's share was often fixed at two-third of the gross produce received by the zamindars from the ryots.[13] To protect ryots from extractive zamindars, the Company instituted the pattah, a document that sought to fix a ryot's rate of customary rents—this soon turned into a 'dead letter'.

Meanwhile, the Company tightened the screws further, as Cornwallis stated, 'We have a rule that if zamindars fail to pay the full tax in time, we auction their lands to get the money, according to the Sunset Law.' This Permanent Settlement helped the British rule expand in India, with the support of higher-income Indians.[14,15] In addition, the Ryotwari system, instituted mostly in Rajasthan and the Madras Presidency, sought to establish a direct relationship between the ryot and the colonial government, with the money value of the share of the estimated average annual

10 Habib, Irfan, Agrarian System of Mughal India, 1963

11 Moosvi, S., The Silver Influx, Money Supply, Prices and Revenue-Extraction in Mughal India, 1987

12 Meena, Hareet Kumar, Land Tenure Systems in the late 18th and 19th century in Colonial India, American International Journal of Research in Humanities, Arts and Social Sciences, 9(1), December 2014-February 2015, pp. 66-71

13 Parameswari, B. Bala, Abolition Of Zamindari System And It's Impact On Agriculture, Imperial Journal of Interdisciplinary Research, Vol-2, Issue-4, 2016

14 Boyce, 1987

15 Fuller, 1922

output predetermined.[16,17] This system eventually formed 51 per cent of the entire directly controlled British territory, accounting for 38 per cent of the total cultivated area.[18] The Mahalwari system, utilized mostly in the United Provinces, Awadh and Punjab, covering 30 per cent of directly controlled British territories, pushed the responsibility of providing established land revenues down to the 'mahal', the village, with the local headmen entrusted with collecting the land revenue and depositing it in the treasury, while receiving a 5 per cent take.[19] The consequences of these land revenue systems were stark—agricultural output grew at just 0.37 per cent per annum between 1891 and 1947, with food grains at just 0.11 per cent per annum, while commercial crop output rose by 1.31 per cent annually; meanwhile, the population rose at 0.67 per cent annually.[20] Greater Bengal, with the harshest zamindari settlement, actually saw its agricultural output decline at 0.45 per cent annually. By choosing to extract land revenue and maximize its take of agricultural surplus, the colonial government pushed farmers into heavy debts and eventual pauperization.

When the American Civil War ended in 1865, cotton production in the US revived, resulting in a lack of demand for Indian cotton exports. As a result, cotton uptake from farmers in the Bombay Presidency declined, settlement demands increased, with moneylenders subsequently refusing to extend credit to willing farmers or charging usurious rates (one noted lender even charged ₹ 2,000 as interest on a loan of ₹ 100). This lack of credit enraged ryots across India, with those in the Deccan revolting in 1875 in Supa, a village near Pune. The angry peasants gathered and attacked moneylenders, asking for their debt bonds and account books, while setting fire to the houses of sahukars. The revolt soon spread to Ahmednagar and eventually across 6,500 sq km, affecting over 30 villages. Police posts were soon established in villages to drive the peasants into submission, while the countryside continued to fester for months.

The Government of the Bombay Presidency soon established the Deccan Riots Commission (1878), which makes for rivetting reading. Instead of condemning the farmers for lacking foresight, the report states, 'The constantly recurring small items of debt for food and other necessaries, for seed, for bullocks, for the Government assessment, do more to swell the indebtedness of a ryot than an occasional marriage' (ISE Pune, 2010). To reduce their burden, the report recommended abolition of

---

16   Baden-Powell, 1972

17   Banerjee, 2002

18   Blyn, 1966

19   Meena, Hareet Kumar, Land Tenure Systems in the late 18th and 19th century in Colonial India, American International Journal of Research in Humanities, Arts and Social Sciences, 9(1), December 2014-February 2015, pp. 66-71

20   Blyn, 1966

the provision of imprisonment for debt, exemption of small residential quarters for sale for recovery of debt, along with provisions to prevent court processes from being abused to extort excessive amounts from debtors. The state of peasants, it seems, has rarely changed in India.

Post-Independence, the national and state governments sought to redress this historic injustice by abolishing the zamindari system. The Madras Legislative Council passed an Act termed Madras Estates Land (Reduction of Rent) Act (1947), withdrawing the zamindar's right to collect taxes from the ryots. The Agrarian Reforms Committee of 1949 sought a programme of land reforms that would transform the actual tillers into owner-cultivators on a large scale, with a significant redistribution of land amongst peasants and labourers, while encouraging actual landlords to take up cultivation themselves. Instead, a step-by-step approach was adopted to abolish intermediaries, which encouraged zamindars to evict existing tenants instead, pauperizing them further.[21] The central government did its part by seeking to not tax agricultural income, with most states following suit.

Now, with growth in agriculture rising, a demand for taxing agriculture income has arisen. Agricultural income declared by taxpayers, in returns filed till end-2014, for exemption stood at ₹9,338 crore, with over 2,746 income tax cases declaring ₹1 crore agricultural income in the 2014–15 assessment year. In the very same year, nine of the top ten claimants for agricultural income tax exemption were corporations, with the tenth being a state department (Live Mint, 4 May 2017). The estimated total annual agricultural income from cultivation and livestock, as estimated by the NSS, is at ₹416,092.5 crore, with the total income of the top bracket at ₹16,084 crore and that of the first two brackets, including households with over 4 hectares, at ₹83,433 crore. Taxing such an income, of the top 4.1 per cent of agricultural households, could yield ₹25,000 crore of agricultural income tax.[22]

We have tried this before. The Committee on Taxation of Agricultural Wealth and Income (the Raj Committee) (1972) sought to institute a progressive agriculture tax on agricultural income in a norm-based manner, with regional average crop yields defining levy rates in a universal manner. The recommendations were not accepted, given limited political and grassroots support. Most states have instead sought to tax plantations in order to compensate for their inability to tax farmers.

However, there remain significant pitfalls with this demand. Given the level of informal occupation prevalent in agriculture, implementing an agricultural tax will

---

21 Parameswari, B. Bala, Abolition Of Zamindari System And It's Impact On Agriculture, Imperial Journal of Interdisciplinary Research, Vol-2, Issue-4 , 2016

22 Awasthi, Rajul, The Wire, 2 May 2017

not be easy. Any agricultural tax system would have to evolve crop specific norms of return to the land, while accommodating external shocks like drought, floods or pests. Without provisions to exempt farmers from income tax during catastrophes, any land-based revenue system would be inequitable and harken back to our colonial and Mughal era extractive taxation systems. Instead of raising agricultural income, we would trend back to age-old farmer pauperization.

In addition, any crop specific taxation would have to be traded off against input subsidies, which are nationally uniform for fertilizers and vary on a statewise basis for water and electricity.[23] Should input subsidies, assumed to be high at the institution of the crop tax rate, fall in the future, the farmer would effectively lose out on both ends of the value chain. Any crop specific taxation would be locally based, with a national crop register not necessarily linked to which crops would be taxed in specific regions or states. The tax rates for the same crop in different regions could be different, inequitably ensuring arbitrage for some farmers. The taxable threshold yield would have to be different across states, given differing input costs, soil conditions and yields, while the lack of crop insurance would increase the impact of exogenous shocks in the agricultural taxation system.

Amidst all this, it is hard to determine if there would be net benefit to taxing agricultural revenues, even for rich farmers (defined by local thresholds), compared to cost of monitoring and rolling out such a system. Even a progressively structured taxation system would encourage fictitious ownership splits amongst rich farmers and their relatives. Assuming a net take of ₹25,000 crore, the potential increase in the central government's taxation revenues would be by ~2 per cent, while input subsidies, currently totalling ₹35,784 crore in 2016–17, would face significant upward pressure. Is this truly worth the effort?

Agricultural taxation has historically been considered the third rail of Indian politics. This is not a Gordian knot, open to solution through a simple manoeuvre. While we harken about improving economies of scale in agriculture, such efforts send discouraging messages to large and medium farmers who seek to increase their produce through utilization of better techniques, differing crop patterns and more judicious use of agricultural inputs. Perhaps this is a problem best left to the next generation.

Restructuring rural credit has always been difficult. The historic All India Rural Credit Survey (1954) highlighted that formal credit institutions provided 9 per cent of rural credit needs, with moneylenders, traders and rich landlords accounting for more than 75 per cent (Mihir Shah, 2007). Cooperative credit societies

---

23   Rajaraman, Indira, Taxing Agriculture in a Developing Country, World Bank, Jan 2004

were encouraged, rising to 50 per cent coverage by 2007, servicing farm input distribution, crop production, processing and marketing activities. However, these societies ended up becoming a 'borrower-driven system', dominated by the state governments and the richer rural elite, beset by conflict of interest and lacking mutuality. These systems have faced regular losses and deposit erosion, and have a poor portfolio quality.

Banking pushed through priority lending and social coercion, has not met expectations. Banks continue to have an urban bias, with the distribution of credit skewed in favour of large borrowers (Sen and Vaidya, 1997). With greater profitability requirements, servicing illiterate customers with high cash requirements would lead to higher idle cash reserves and lower profitability.

Moral hazard has prevailed. The Integrated Rural Development Programme offered cheap bank credit for over 4 million households (1987), promoting a deep dependence on corrupt government officials (Dreze, 1990), while classifying millions as bank defaulters, barring their access to the formal credit sector. The official loan waiver of 1989 destroyed all credit discipline. Public sector banks, already burdened by low profitability and high non-performing assets, utilized liberalization and consolidation trends to march away from rural credit markets. The state withdrew from rural credit.

―――

NATURE OF RURAL CREDIT

Bimaljeet Singh, a 32-year-old farmer in Hans Kalan village of Jagraon district in Punjab did know a thing or two about earning his livelihood as a farmer. However, his skills in managing debt were not as deft as handling his farms. His recently deceased father left them with his one-acre farm and a 'pucca house', but these possessions were mortgaged to obtain a loan of ₹11 lakh from a commission agent. Unable to pay the interest due to failed crops, he committed suicide in April 2016 by consuming the same insecticide meant for the pests on his farm. In the same week itself, unofficial estimates for the number of suicides due to mounting loans in Punjab were pegged at 20, while another 45 had died the previous month.

Pratap Singh, a 50-year-old farmer in Bakalpur village (Etah district, Uttar Pradesh) had decided to grow potatoes in the winter of 2017–18, just like he had been doing for many years. Though his potato crop had not been successful for the last couple of years, he didn't lose hope. However, the status quo decision turned out to be very costly for him—the state's cold storages were flush with the previous year's produce, and a bumper crop meant that he was stuck between high input prices and low market prices. In order to grow these crops and support his daughter's medical costs, he raised a total loan of ₹5 lakh—₹4 lakh from banks and Self-Help Groups (SHGs) and ₹1 lakh from the local moneylender, the only person in his knowledge who would offer him a high-interest yet unsecured loan. Unable to pay for a few months and with his daughter's operation due the next month, he thought it was simpler to end his life for his troubles to stop—with insecticide being the poison of choice. His 25-year-old son seemed lost—with debt and increased family costs looming large.

Shiv Jadhav, a farmer in Pimpodi village (Ahmednagar district, Maharashtra) had recently turned to being a cattle trader in order to supplement his income. With farming returns dwindling, he sought to augment his income by dealing in purchase and sale of cows, buffaloes and cattle. In order to make these purchases and also to sow his farmland, he had racked up loans from moneylenders and cooperative banks. He left home in the evening, only for his dead body to return the next day— he had hanged himself from a tree on the outskirts of the village.

Nearly 70 per cent of India's estimated 90 million agricultural households end up spending more than their earnings, thereby being caught in a spiral of ever-increasing debt. An analysis of National Crime Records Bureau (NCRB) data reveals indebtedness to be the majority cause of farmer suicides, accounting for more than 50 per cent of such deaths. Many of our countrymen find themselves in the same plight as Kusum Devi wherein they are forced to take on debt for urgent matters (a wedding, bereavement or any ailment in the family) after having their savings wiped out due to a prolonged spell of marginal farm economics. Such events also severely hampers a farmer's ability to invest in farming.

At a rural level, 31.4 per cent of rural households were debt-stricken with average debt size per household being ₹103,457—accounting for almost 8.5 per cent of their total asset value (inclusive of land, buildings, livestock, equipment, cash and bank deposits). The table below illustrates the incidence of debt, its average size per household and average household asset size, based on occupational categories.

TABLE 119: INCIDENCE OF INDEBTEDNESS, AVERAGE VALUE OF ASSET, AVERAGE VALUE OF DEBT AND DEBT-ASSET RATIO (%) PER INDEBTED HOUSEHOLD FOR DIFFERENT OCCUPATIONAL CATEGORIES

OCCUPATIONAL CATEGORY	INCIDENCE OF DEBT (%)	AVG. VALUE OF ASSET PER HOUSEHOLD (₹)	AVG. VALUE OF DEBT PER INDEBTED HOUSEHOLD (₹)	DEBT TO ASSET RATIO
RURAL				
CULTIVATOR	35.0	15,52,914	110,438	7.1
NON-CULTIVATOR	25.6	4,68,078	87,938	18.8
RURAL - OVERALL	31.4	12,16,361	103,457	8.5
URBAN				
SELF-EMPLOYED	24.7	31,38,381	4,14,689	13.2
OTHERS	21.3	22,35,795	3,58,917	16.1
URBAN - OVERALL	22.4	25,48,486	378,238	14.8

SOURCE: HOUSEHOLD INDEBTEDNESS IN INDIA, 70TH NSSO ROUND, MOSPI

Despite having a smaller quantum of debt per household, non-cultivators have a higher debt to asset ratio in rural areas—a similar scene gets played out in urban areas where non-self employed have a higher debt to asset ratio despite lower quantum of debt per household. The subdivisions of the average asset value and average debt according to their asset holding become more interesting.

TABLE 120: INCIDENCE OF DEBT, AVERAGE VALUE OF ASSETS AND DEBT PER INDEBTED HOUSEHOLD AND DEBT/ASSET RATIO FOR INDEBTED HOUSEHOLD

DECLIE CLASS	RURAL				URBAN			
	INCIDENCE OF DEBT	AVG VALUE OF ASSET OF INDEBTED HOUSEHOLD	AVG VALUE OF DEBT OF INDEBTED HOUSEHOLD	DEBT TO ASSET RATIO	INCIDENCE OF DEBT	AVG VALUE OF ASSET OF INDEBTED HOUSEHOLD	AVG VALUE OF DEBT OF INDEBTED HOUSEHOLD	DEBT TO ASSET RATIO
	(%)	(₹)	(₹)	(%)	(%)	(₹)	(₹)	(%)
1	19.62	29,004	49,478	171%	9.34	-	-	-
2	22.3	93,851	39,554	42%	14.63	10,405	81,587	784%
3	27.05	151,588	51,053	34%	20.16	67,916	99,572	147%
4	27.46	230,917	57,077	25%	24.16	224,521	117,662	52%
5	30.95	325,059	60,746	19%	21.67	449,076	138,076	31%
6	32.99	456,504	71,047	16%	23.44	775,672	156,807	20%
7	32.69	638,710	88,006	14%	23.77	1,250,627	233,609	19%
8	37.33	920,224	100,877	11%	25.42	1,994,510	358,212	18%
9	42.64	1,563,253	132,867	8%	29.41	3,493,049	572,822	16%
10	41.32	5,378,022	270,747	5%	31.74	11,094,503	1,255,405	11%
ALL	31.44	1,216,361	103,457	9%	22.37	2,548,486	378,238	15%

SOURCE: HOUSEHOLD INDEBTEDNESS IN INDIA, 70TH NSSO ROUND, MOSPI

We witness that as we move up higher deciles based on average asset value, the average value of debt per indebted household increases in absolute terms, but their debt-asset ratio declines. Mostly, the poorest decile witnesses the highest debt to asset ratio (as much as 171 per cent).

In terms of assets owned, land and building formed the bulk of rural assets, jointly holding around a 94 per cent share in the total value of assets at the national level for all households, while accounting for 93 per cent of assets owned for households with debt. In urban areas as well, land and buildings comprise the bulk of assets owned, with a 92 per cent share in the total value of assets at the national level and an 89 per cent share in assets owned by indebted households.

TABLE 121: PERCENTAGE SHARE OF DIFFERENT COMPONENTS OF ASSETS IN THE TOTAL VALUE OF ASSETS AMONG INDEBTED HOUSEHOLDS VIS-À-VIS ALL HOUSEHOLDS

ASSET TYPE	% SHARE OVER TYPE OF ASSETS BY HOUSEHOLDS			
	RURAL		URBAN	
	INDEBTED	ALL	INDEBTED	ALL
LAND & BUILDING	93.3	93.7	88.8	91.8
LAND	72.4	72.6	51.1	46.9
BUILDING	20.9	21.1	37.7	44.9
LIVESTOCK & POULTRY	1.6	1.6	0.1	0.1
MACHINERY & EQUIPMENT	3.4	2.8	4.9	3.3
FINANCIAL ASSETS	1.7	1.9	6.2	4.8
TOTAL	100	100	100	100

SOURCE: HOUSEHOLD INDEBTEDNESS IN INDIA, 70TH NSSO ROUND, MOSPI

Overall, the pattern of asset ownership doesn't change vastly for indebted and non-indebted households. While rural households have a higher share of assets owned in machinery and equipment compared to urban households, their share is lower in financial assets (all deposits with bank, non-banking companies, PF, etc., insurance, amount receivable and value of shares) compared to urban counterparts. Gold holdings, which is a significant aspect of any savings for any Indian household, have not been incorporated into the survey.

The following table illustrates the change in incidence of debt along with the share of debt as percentage to total debt with time (over 1991, 2002 and 2012).

TABLE 122: TREND OF INCIDENCE OF INDEBTEDNESS AND PERCENTAGE SHARE OF OUTSTANDING DEBT BY OCCUPATIONAL CATEGORIES OF HOUSEHOLDS

| | RURAL | | | | URBAN | | | |
| | CULTIVATOR | | NON-CULTIVATOR | | SELF EMPLOYED | | OTHERS | |
YEAR	INCIDENCE OF DEBT	% SHARE OF TOTAL DEBT	INCIDENCE OF DEBT	% SHARE OF TOTAL DEBT	INCIDENCE OF DEBT	% SHARE OF TOTAL DEBT	INCIDENCE OF DEBT	% SHARE OF TOTAL DEBT
1991	25.9	79.5	18.5	20.5	19.9	41.7	18.9	59.3
2002	29.7	73.3	21.8	26.7	17.9	37.3	17.8	62.7
2012	35.0	73.6	25.6	26.4	24.7	38	21.3	62

SOURCE: HOUSEHOLD INDEBTEDNESS IN INDIA, 70TH NSSO ROUND, MOSPI

Thus, the percentage of cultivator households in rural India having debt increased from ~26 per cent in 1991 to 35 per cent in 2012, while their share in total debt decreased from 79.5 per cent to 73.6 per cent.

| | RURAL | | | URBAN | | |
STATE	FORMAL	INFORMAL	ALL	FORMAL	INFORMAL	ALL
ANDHRA PRADESH	35.2	32.2	54.1	27.7	22.2	39.8
ASSAM	4.4	5.9	10.1	14.8	3.6	17.6
BIHAR	5.6	25.3	29.1	5.8	8.1	13.2
CHHATTISGARH	6.7	8.9	13.9	6.6	5.3	11.8
GUJARAT	14.6	13	26	13.7	6.3	19.4
HARAYANA	13.2	14.8	23.9	7.7	5.3	12.5
JHARKHAND	6.1	13.4	18.5	7.3	4.8	11.6
KARNATAKA	26.7	29.7	46.4	18.2	12.2	26.5
KERALA	43	15	49.5	41.5	13.7	47
MADHYA PRADESH	11	15.6	24.7	10	6.4	15.3
MAHARASHTRA	24.4	11.6	31.3	14.6	5.6	18.9
ODISHA	15.4	14.4	25.7	12.2	7.8	18.7
PUNJAB	15.4	22.3	33.1	9.5	10.2	18.3
RAJASTHAN	13.2	29.1	37.4	10.1	13.8	22.6
TAMIL NADU	26.6	21.3	39.7	23.8	17.4	34.8
TELANGANA	38.9	38.6	59.1	15.8	19.1	30.5
UTTAR PRADESH	12.9	19.5	29.6	8.9	11.1	18.9
WEST BENGAL	13.2	13	23.6	9.6	6.1	14.7
ALL-INDIA	17.2	19	31.4	14.8	10.3	22.4

It is also interesting to note that there are inter-state discrepancies on how credit is availed of from different sources. Incidence of debt in rural areas is higher in Andhra Pradesh, Telangana, Kerala and Karnataka—with incidence of debt in these southern states being higher than 40 per cent, with Tamil Nadu marginally lower than 40 per cent. Similarly, for urban areas, the incidence of debt for southern states ranges from ~27 per cent to 47 per cent, much higher than the all-India average of 22.4 per cent.

In rural areas, seven of the aforementioned states have incidence of debt higher than the national average while just two states—Assam and Jharkhand—have rural incidence of debt at less than 20 per cent of households. Eight states have incidence of debt recorded between 20 per cent and the national average of 31.4 per cent for rural areas. In urban areas, six of the aforementioned states have incidence of debt higher than the national average, while five states have rural incidence of debt at less than 15 per cent of households. Eight states have incidence of debt recorded between 15 per cent and the national average of 31.4 per cent for rural areas.

It is also pertinent to note the change in mix of formal and informal sources along with time. The table below illustrates the change in share of formal credit sources over the past three to four decades in rural and urban areas.

TABLE 123: PERCENTAGE SHARE OF INSTITUTIONAL AGENCIES IN OUTSTANDING CASH DEBT FOR VARIOUS OCCUPATIONAL CATEGORIES OF HOUSEHOLDS

OCCUPATIONAL CATEGORY	1971	1981	1991	2002	2012
RURAL					
CULTIVATOR	32	63	66	61	58
NON-CULTIVATOR	11	37	55	46	49
RURAL – OVERALL	29	61	64	57	56
URBAN					
SELF-EMPLOYED	-	58	69	67	79
OTHERS	-	62	74	80	88
URBAN – OVERALL	-	60	72	75	85

SOURCE: HOUSEHOLD INDEBTEDNESS IN INDIA, 70TH NSSO ROUND

For rural areas, the share of formal credit increased rapidly from 29 per cent in 1971 to 61 per cent in 1981, followed by muted increase to 64 per cent in 1991, followed by decline till 57 per cent in 2002 and has stayed almost the same since then. On the other hand, urban areas have witnessed an increase in availing of credit from formal sources—rising from 60 per cent in 1981 to 85 per cent in 2012.

The following table illustrates the inter-state variations in percentage share of institutional agencies in outstanding cash debt for selected states:

TABLE 124: PERCENTAGE SHARE OF INSTITUTIONAL AGENCIES IN OUTSTANDING CASH DEBT FOR SELECTED STATES

STATE	RURAL					URBAN			
	1971	1981	1991	2002	2012	1981	1991	2002	2012
ANDHRA PRADESH	14	41	34	27	42	26	53	60	69
ASSAM	35	31	66	58	72	77	97	83	89
BIHAR	11	47	73	37	22	61	67	65	71
CHHATTISGARH	-	-	-	85	66	-	-	86	93
GUJARAT	47	70	75	67	64	86	59	74	92
HARYANA	26	76	73	50	52	66	81	56	94
JHARKHAND	-	-	-	71	51	-	-	91	83
KARNATAKA	30	78	78	67	50	54	85	83	73
KERALA	44	79	92	81	78	77	75	83	89
MADHYA PRADESH	32	66	73	59	52	72	70	84	86
MAHARASHTRA	67	86	82	85	73	65	78	91	96
ODISHA	30	81	80	74	57	83	83	93	96
PUNJAB	36	74	79	56	64	61	59	76	81
RAJASTHAN	9	41	40	34	31	47	78	52	59
TAMIL NADU	22	44	58	47	62	56	71	59	78
TELANGANA	-	-	-	-	32	-	-	-	80
UTTAR PRADESH	23	55	69	56	57	59	65	58	90
WEST BENGAL	31	66	82	68	51	55	74	75	87
ALL-INDIA	29	61	64	57	56	60	72	75	85

SOURCE: HOUSEHOLD INDEBTEDNESS IN INDIA, 70TH NSSO ROUND

Thus, we see that in seven aforementioned states—Assam, Chhattisgarh, Gujarat, Kerala, Maharashtra, Punjab and Tamil Nadu—share of formal sources of total cash due is 10 per cent over the national average of 56 per cent in rural areas. On the other hand, in five states—Andhra Pradesh, Bihar, Karnataka Rajasthan and Tamil Nadu—the share of formal sources in total cash due stood at 50 per cent or less, with the lowest being registered in Bihar at 22 per cent. The highest fall in share of total cash due to formal sources from 2002 to 2012 was witnessed in Jharkhand—a fall in share by approximately 20 per cent, followed by 17 percentage declines in Karnataka and Odisha. In fact, eleven out of the eighteen aforementioned states witnessed a decline in share of total cash due to formal sources from 2002 to 2012.

In urban areas, only Haryana, Odisha and Maharashtra have a share of formal sources in total cash due at greater than 10 per cent of the national average of

85 per cent. Rajasthan recorded the lowest share at 59 per cent in urban areas. In urban areas of Chhattisgarh, Gujarat and Uttar Pradesh, the share of formal sources in total cash due stands at 90 per cent or above.

Income-wise distribution of total cash due to formal sources is as shown below:

TABLE 125: PERCENTAGE SHARE OF INSTITUTIONAL AGENCIES TO THE TOTAL CASH DUES OF THE HOUSEHOLDS (AS ON 30 JUN'12) BY HOUSEHOLD ASSETS HOLDING CLASS)

ASSET HOLDING	RURAL			URBAN		
DECILE	FORMAL	INFORMAL	TOTAL	FORMAL	INFORMAL	TOTAL
1	28	72	100	45	55	100
2	23	77	100	40	61	100
3	35	65	100	48	52	100
4	26	74	100	55	46	100
5	35	65	100	53	47	100
6	40	60	100	62	38	100
7	53	47	100	73	27	100
8	49	51	100	79	21	100
9	62	38	100	90	10	100
10	75	25	100	95	5	100
ALL	56	44	100	85	15	100

SOURCE: HOUSEHOLD INDEBTEDNESS IN INDIA, 70TH NSSO ROUND, MOSPI

Thus, in both urban and rural areas, we see that as asset holding goes down, so does the share of institutional credit in the total debt mix. Thus, while formal sources of credit have better terms of credit compared to informal ones, their ability to serve the rural poor goes down with income levels, despite the fact that the poor would in fact need better credit terms, if not the same as enjoyed by others. As much as ~75 per cent of people in the lowest two deciles by asset holding still take recourse to informal channels for raising credit, with usurious rates and exploitative payment terms.

SOURCES AND END-USERS

When it comes to lenders, India has a dual network of credit supply in the rural markets. A large number of financial institutions (cooperatives, Regional Rural Banks, Scheduled Commercial Banks, non-banking financial institutions, self-help groups, microfinance institutions, and other government agencies) lend money to farmers depending on their short, medium and long-term needs, whereas informal channels like the moneylender, friends and family, and shopkeepers constitute the informal credit channel.

In terms of the formal-informal mix in India's rural/agricultural credit base, formal sources account for 63.56 per cent of loans, with the rest being fulfilled by informal sources. The table below illustrates the loan distribution based on source.

TABLE 126: DISTRIBUTION OF LOANS BY SOURCES

SHARE OF FORMAL SOURCES		SHARE OF INFORMAL SOURCES	
LOAN SOURCE	%AGE	LOAN SOURCE	%AGE
GOVERNMENT	3.61	EMPLOYER / LANDLORD	2.34
COOPERATIVE SOCIETY	25.37	MONEYLENDER	64.05
BANK	71.02	SHOPKEEPER	4.93
		RELATIVES / FRIENDS	24.03
		OTHERS	4.65
TOTAL	100	TOTAL	100
SHARE IN TOTAL LOANS	63.56	SHARE IN TOTAL LOANS	36.44

SOURCE: INSTITUTIONAL VERSUS NON-INSTITUTIONAL CREDIT TO AGRICULTURAL HOUSEHOLDS IN INDIA, IFPRI DISCUSSION PAPER 01614, MARCH 2017

Thus, we see that informal sources account for almost 36.4 per cent of total loans made, and amongst the informal credit source, more than half of the loans were made by moneylenders, mostly at usurious rates. Relatives/friends account for 24 per cent of informal loans, preferred as they usually don't charge interest.

The formal credit channel accounts for almost 63.6 per cent of all loans made, and bank loans form a huge chunk, ~71 per cent, in extending rural credit. Cooperatives account for 25 per cent of loans made through the formal credit channel. The following table illustrates the historical perspective of the nature of agricultural and rural credit:

TABLE 127: BREAK-UP OF INSTITUTIONAL AND NON-INSTITUTIONAL AGRICULTURAL CREDIT

SOURCES OF AGRICULTURAL CREDIT	1951	1961	1971	1981	1991	2002	2013
INSTITUTIONAL	10.2	20.9	32.0	56.2	66.3	61.1	64.0
GOVERNMENT	-	6.2	-	4.0	5.7	1.7	1.3
COOPERATIVE SOCIETIES/BANKS, ETC.	6.2	12.5	-	27.6	23.6	30.2	28.9
COMMERCIAL BANKS	4.0	2.2	-	23.8	35.2	26.3	30.7
INSURANCE, PF	-	-	-	0.8	0.7	0.5	0.1
OTHER AGENCIES	-	-	-	-	1.1	2.4	3.0
NON-INSTITUTIONAL	89.8	79.1	68.0	43.8	33.7	38.9	36.0
MONEYLENDERS	39.8	25.3	-	17.2	17.5	26.8	29.6
RELATIVES/FRIENDS, ETC.	-	-	-	11.5	4.6	6.2	4.3
TRADERS & COMMISSION AGENTS	-	-	-	5.8	2.2	2.6	
LANDLORDS	21.4	15.0	-	3.6	3.7	0.9	0.4
OTHERS	28.6	38.8	-	5.7	5.7	2.4	1.7
TOTAL	100.0	100.0	100.0	100.0	100.0	100.0	100.0

SOURCE: ALL INDIA DEBT AND INVESTMENT SURVEY, ICRIER WORKING PAPER NO. 302,
A. HODA AND P. TERWAY, JUNE 2015

TABLE 128: BREAK-UP OF INSTITUTIONAL AND NON-INSTITUTIONAL RURAL CREDIT

SOURCES OF RURAL CREDIT	1951	1961	1971	1981	1991	2002	2013
INSTITUTIONAL	7.2	14.8	29.2	61.2	64.0	57.1	56.0
GOVERNMENT	3.3	5.3	6.7	4.0	5.7	2.3	1.2
COOPERATIVE SOCIETIES/BANKS, ETC.	3.1	9.1	20.1	28.6	18.6	27.3	24.8
COMMERCIAL BANKS	0.8	0.4	2.2	28.0	29.0	24.5	25.1
INSURANCE, PF	-	-	0.2	0.6	1.4	0.6	0.3
OTHER AGENCIES	-	-	-	-	9.3	2.4	4.6
NON-INSTITUTIONAL	92.8	85.2	70.8	38.2	36.0	42.9	44.0
MONEYLENDERS	69.7	60.8	36.9	16.9	15.7	29.6	33.2
RELATIVES/FRIENDS, ETC.	14.2	6.9	13.8	9.0	6.7	7.1	8.5
TRADERS & COMMISSION AGENTS	5.5	7.7	8.7	3.4	7.1	2.6	0.1
LANDLORDS	1.5	0.9	8.6	4.0	4.0	1.0	0.7
OTHERS	1.9	8.9	2.8	4.9	2.5	2.6	1.4
TOTAL	100.0	100.0	100.0	99.4	100.0	100.0	100.0

SOURCE: ALL INDIA DEBT AND INVESTMENT SURVEY, ICRIER WORKING PAPER NO. 302,
A. HODA AND P. TERWAY, JUNE 2015

Thus, the share of institutional credit in total rural credit rose sharply from a minisucule 7 per cent in 1951 to 61 per cent in 1981, reaching a peak of 64 per cent in 1991. The decline in overall institutional credit saw its share in the rural credit mix decline post-1991, with its share declining by 8 per cent in the overall mix to be at 56 per cent in 2012. From the end-user perspective, the table below illustrates the loan type (formal or informal or both) depending on landholding:

TABLE 129: FARMERS' ACCESS TO CREDIT FROM FORMAL AND INFORMAL SECTORS, 2012–2013

LANDHOLDING TYPE	HOUSEHOLD DISTRIBUTION BY BORROWING PATTERNS (%)				SHARE OF CREDIT IN HOUSEHOLD BORROWING (%)	
	NON-BORROWER	FORMAL CHANNEL ONLY	INFORMAL CHANNEL ONLY	BOTH CHANNELS	FORMAL	INFORMAL
MARGINAL	54.7	14.8	21.7	8.9	55.0	45.1
SMALL	48.3	24.2	14.2	13.3	64.3	35.7
MEDIUM	41.5	30.0	11.6	17.0	67.1	32.9
LARGE	28.5	39.1	8.9	23.6	74.9	25.1
ALL	47.9	22.8	16.2	13.1	63.6	36.4

SOURCE: INSTITUTIONAL VERSUS NON-INSTITUTIONAL CREDIT TO AGRICULTURAL HOUSEHOLDS IN INDIA, IFPRI DISCUSSION PAPER 01614, MARCH 2017
(A. KUMAR, A. MISHRA, S. SAROJ, P.K. JOSHI)

Thus, on an overall basis, we observe that almost 48 per cent of rural households do not avail of any credit, either formal or informal. Some of it would be involuntary due to non-eligibility for availing of loans. As landholding increases, one witnesses an increase in credit levels (almost 45.3 per cent marginal households availing of credit against 71.5 per cent households with large landholding), thereby raising concerns if small/marginal landholding is a hurdle in availing credit. Despite measures to make credit available to everyone, it stays stifled by landholding constraints—small and marginal farmers lack collateral and hence, cannot avail of credit as easily as large landholders who have, on average, a higher amount of collateral for getting a loan.

The following table illustrates the loan landscape in rural India on a household and creditwise basis. In terms of access to formal credit, landholding matters, e.g., large landholding households, accounting for 6.8 per cent of total households, have a 24 per cent share in formal credit to agricultural households. On the other hand, marginal landholding households, accounting for 40 per cent of total households, account for only a 17 per cent share in formal credit. Small and marginal farmers account for 80 per cent of loans taken from informal sources, yet their share in the informal credit pie stands at 52.4 per cent. Large households, accounting for only 4 per cent of households, have only 3.8 per cent households taking loans from informal sources, yet their share of informal credit stands at a considerable 18 per cent.

TABLE 130: DISTRIBUTION OF BORROWER HOUSEHOLDS BY OPERATIONAL HOLDING

LANDHOLDING TYPE	SHARE OF HOUSEHOLDS	NON-BORROWER	BORROWING SOURCE			SHARE IN CREDIT	
			FORMAL CREDIT	INFORMAL CREDIT	BOTH CHANNELS	FORMAL CREDIT	INFORMAL CREDIT
MARGINAL	39.9	45.5	25.9	53.3	27.1	17.1	24.3
SMALL	30.5	30.8	32.5	26.7	31.0	25.3	28.1
MEDIUM	22.8	19.7	30.0	16.3	29.6	33.3	29.6
LARGE	6.8	4.1	11.7	3.8	12.3	24.3	18.0
ALL	100.0	100.0	100.0	100.0	100.0	100.0	100.0

SOURCE: INSTITUTIONAL VERSUS NON-INSTITUTIONAL CREDIT TO AGRICULTURAL
HOUSEHOLDS IN INDIA, IFPRI DISCUSSION PAPER 01614, MARCH 2017
(A. KUMAR, A. MISHRA, S. SAROJ, P.K. JOSHI)

SCHEMES FOR LENDING

While it is clear that with time, formal sources of lending gained prominence over informal ones for rural and agricultural credit, it is pertinent to note the instruments/schemes through which credit is disbursed.

TABLE 131: NUMBER PER THOUSAND HOUSEHOLDS REPORTING INSTITUTIONAL CASH LOANS
OUTSTANDING (AS OF 30 JUNE '12) BY SCHEME OF LENDING

SCHEME NAME	NUMBER (PER 1000) HHS REPORTING CASH LOAN		PERCENTAGE SHARE	
	RURAL	URBAN	RURAL	URBAN
DRI	7	10	4%	7%
PMRY	1	0	1%	0%
SGSY	4	1	2%	1%
SJSRY	0	1	0%	1%
ADVANCES TO MINORITIES	0	2	0%	1%
SCHEME FOR LIBERALIZATION AND REHAB. OF SCAVENGERS	0	0	0%	0%
EXCLUSIVE STATE SCHEMES	7	5	4%	3%
OTHER SCHEMES	85	116	49%	78%
KISAN CREDIT CARD	29	2	17%	1%
CROP LOAN	34	4	20%	3%
NOT COVERED UNDER ANY SCHEME	15	14	9%	9%
ALL	172	148	100%	100%

TABLE 132: NUMBER OF HOUSEHOLDS REPORTING CASH LOANS OUTSTANDING (AS OF 30 JUNE '12) TO INSTITUTIONAL AGENCIES UNDER SPECIFIC SCHEMES OF LENDING PER THOUSAND HOUSEHOLDS FOR EACH HOUSEHOLD ASSET HOLDING CLASS ACROSS RURAL INDIA

RURAL AREAS	PER 1000 HOUSEHOLDS OF HOUSEHOLD ASSET HOLDING CLASS WITH OUTSTANDING LOANS AS OF 30.06.2012										
SCHEME NAME	1	2	3	4	5	6	7	8	9	10	ALL
DRI	4	5	6	4	4	5	9	8	11	11	7
PMRY	0	0	1	1	2	0	1	1	0	1	1
SGSY	1	2	4	7	4	5	4	6	4	4	4
SJSRY	0	0	0	0	0	0	0	0	0	0	0
ADVANCES TO MINORITIES	0	0	0	0	0	0	0	0	0	1	0
SCHEME FOR LIBERALIZATION AND REHAB. OF SCAVENGERS	0	0	0	0	0	0	0	0	0	0	0
EXCLUSIVE STATE SCHEMES	7	7	9	6	7	4	8	6	6	6	7
OTHER SCHEMES	47	38	57	60	70	97	94	101	133	155	85
KISAN CREDIT CARD	1	3	6	14	14	24	30	45	71	82	29
CROP LOAN	4	10	13	21	22	29	39	48	72	80	34
NOT COVERED UNDER ANY SCHEME	17	12	16	15	12	12	15	16	21	16	15
ALL	79	74	108	124	130	169	191	222	292	326	172
EST. AMOUNT OF CASH LOAN (₹LAKH)	156,177	156,137	156,009	156,345	156,100	156,064	156,129	156,159	156,121	156,147	1,561,387
EST. NO. OF HHS (00) REPORTING CASH LOAN	12,415	11,528	16,848	19,342	20,360	26,425	29,840	34,597	45,581	50,886	267,822
NO. OF SAMPLE HHS REPORTING CASH LOAN	441	621	829	1,122	1,256	1,452	1,602	1,957	2,657	3,161	15,098

Thus, we see that specific rural credit schemes like Differential Rate of Interest (DRI), Prime Minister Rozgar Yojana (PMRY), Swarnajayanti Gramin Swarozgar Yojana (SGSY), Swarna Jayanti Sahari Rozgar Yojana (SJSRY) & 'Advances to Minority Communities' were not very popular when it came to availing of credit in rural areas. These schemes for advancing credit—DRI, PMRY, SGSY and SJSRY—accounted for only 7 per cent of rural credit and 8 per cent of urban credit. On the other hand, the Kisan Credit Card and crop loans accounted for 37 per cent of loans disbursed in rural areas, but understandably only 4 per cent in urban areas. Crop loans, loans through the Kisan Credit Card and 'other schemes' formed the bulk of credit disbursed in rural areas.

The Kisan Credit Card Scheme, introduced in August 1998, is an innovative credit delivery mechanism to meet the credit needs of the farmer. Apart from providing short-term and term loans, a certain component of KCC also covers consumption needs. An important feature of the scheme from the outset was that once the documentation to establish the bona fides and assets of beneficiaries is done, they could approach financial institutions for simple and hassle free sanction of credit from the second year onwards. Further progress was made in later years and now the passbook has been replaced by a plastic card, and the Kisan Credit Card is an ATM-enabled debit card. Up to 2012–13, 12.84 crore Kisan Credit Cards had been issued (RBI statistics), which far exceeds the number of agricultural households enumerated in the corresponding NSSO report, signifying many households having multiple cards.

PAYMENT TERMS

The institutional sources played an important role in disbursing credit at moderate interest rates (6–15 per cent)—nearly 89.4 per cent and 92.1 per cent of cash due in rural and urban areas was provided by institutional agencies at less than 15 per cent p.a. rate of interest. On the other hand, 68.6 per cent of total cash debt outstanding in rural areas through non-institutional agencies was at an interest rate of 20 per cent p.a. or higher.

TABLE 133: PERCENTAGE DISTRIBUTION OF OUTSTANDING CASH DEBT BY
RATE OF INTEREST AND SOURCE (INSTITUTIONAL & NON-INSTITUTIONAL)

PERCENTAGE DISTRIBUTION OF OUTSTANDING CASH DEBT BY RATE OF INTEREST AND SOURCE						
RATE OF INTEREST (%) P.A.	RURAL			URBAN		
	INSTITUTIONAL	NON-INSTITUTIONAL	ALL	INSTITUTIONAL	NON-INSTITUTIONAL	ALL
NIL	0.8	18.3	8.5	0.4	27	4.5
<6	7.1	2.3	5	1.5	1.1	1.4
6 - 10	26	0.4	14.7	14.5	0.9	12.4
10-12	12.9	0.7	7.5	41.6	1.2	35.3
12-15	42.6	4.1	25.7	34.1	7.7	30
15-20	7.3	5.6	6.6	6.2	4.3	5.9
20-25	2.1	33.9	16.1	1.2	27.3	5.3
>25	1.1	34.7	15.9	0.6	30.5	5.2
TOTAL	100	100	100	100	100	100

SOURCE: HOUSEHOLD INDEBTEDNESS IN INDIA, 70TH NSSO ROUND

TABLE 134: PERCENTAGE OF HOUSEHOLDS REPORTING CASH LOANS OUTSTANDING (AS OF 30 JUNE '12) ON CREDIT AGENCY-WISE AND RATE OF INTEREST-WISE BASIS

TYPE	SOURCE OF FUNDS	RATE OF INTEREST (IN %) PER ANNUM							
		<6	6-10	10-12	12-15	15-20	20-25	25-30	>30
RURAL	GOVT. & BANK	74.4	91	71.7	75.2	72.2	29.2	53.8	16.6
	INSURANCE & PF	0.4	0.5	1.4	0.3	0.5	0	0	0.8
	FINANCIAL INSTITUTIONS	0.4	1.2	4.7	2.2	12.9	8.2	8.9	17.1
	SHG-BANK LINKED & NBFC	23.7	7	21	21.3	11.1	51.7	28.1	37.2
	OTHER INSTITUTIONAL AGENCIES	1.2	0.3	1.1	1.1	3.2	10.9	9.2	28.3
	INSTITUTIONAL SOURCES	100	100	100	100	100	100	100	100
	LANDLORD, PROFESSIONAL MONEYLENDER	78.8	77.3	83.4	78.2	97.7	95.9	91.4	93.3
	INPUT SUPPLIER	1.3	0.8	0.5	0.5	0.4	0.3	0.1	0.4
	RELATIVES & FRIENDS	0	0	0	0	0	0	0	0
	DOCTOR, LAWYER & OTHER PROFESSIONALS	7.3	0	0.3	1.3	0.3	0.4	0.7	1.4
	OTHERS	12.6	21.9	15.8	20	1.6	3.4	7.8	4.9
	NON-INSTITUTIONAL AGENCIES	100	100	100	100	100	100	100	100
URBAN	GOVT. & BANK	68.3	83.4	88.1	81.5	76.6	18.6	15.5	7.8
	INSURANCE & PF	1.3	2.9	2.2	0.9	0.3	0.2	0	0
	FINANCIAL INSTITUTIONS	2.9	5.1	4.1	5.4	12.5	39.8	31.2	43.3
	SHG-BANK LINKED & NBFC	23.8	7.5	4.7	11	7.6	23.7	45.4	22.6
	OTHER INSTITUTIONAL AGENCIES	3.6	1.1	0.9	1.2	3.1	17.7	7.9	26.4
	INSTITUTIONAL SOURCES	100	100	100	100	100	100	100	100
	LANDLORD, PROFESSIONAL MONEYLENDER	71.8	69.5	70.3	88.9	92.5	96	82.7	93.6
	INPUT SUPPLIER	0	0.2	1.2	1	1.9	0.3	1.1	0.2
	RELATIVES & FRIENDS	0	0	0	0	0	0	0	0
	DOCTOR, LAWYER & OTHER PROFESSIONALS	2.6	0.6	3.5	0.7	0.3	0.2	0	0.6
	OTHERS	25.6	29.7	24.9	9.5	5.3	3.5	16.2	5.6
	NON-INSTITUTIONAL AGENCIES	100	100	100	100	100	100	100	100

SOURCE: HOUSEHOLD INDEBTEDNESS IN INDIA, 70TH NSSO ROUND

The following table illustrates the distribution of loans according to tenure of loan and interest rates in rural and urban India:

TABLE 135: PERCENTAGE OF HOUSEHOLDS REPORTING CASH LOANS OUTSTANDING
(AS OF 30 JUNE '12) BY TENURE AND INTEREST RATE

TYPE	LOAN DURATION (YEARS)	RATE OF INTEREST (%) P.A.									
		0	<6	6 - 10	10-12	12-15	15-20	20-25	25-30	>30	ALL
RURAL	<1	52.1	55.6	55.9	43.5	49.5	53.3	51.8	84.2	57.1	53.2
	1-2	18.9	16.3	14.5	23.8	18.9	19.9	24.7	8.7	20.9	19.7
	2-3	12.4	12.1	10.8	14.4	12.1	7.9	10.3	2.1	10.6	11.2
	3-4	5.4	5.8	6.1	5.2	6.4	4.9	4.7	1.1	4.7	5.4
	4-5	4.2	4.4	4	4.7	4.5	3.9	4.1	3	2.5	3.9
	5-10	5.9	4.2	7.2	6.1	6.8	7.3	3.8	0.5	3.3	5.3
	>10	1.1	1.5	1.5	2.3	2	2.8	0.5	0.3	0.7	1.3
	ALL	100	100	100	100	100	100	100	100	100	100
URBAN	<1	44.5	44.7	39.2	28.9	42.1	47.5	54.1	58.1	50.3	43.6
	1-2	22	13.2	19.2	21.2	20.7	21.8	25	23.3	25.9	21.9
	2-3	13.7	9.1	11.4	15.3	12.2	10.8	10.2	6.8	10.2	12
	3-4	6.8	9	7.4	8.1	6.3	5.8	3.6	7.7	5.2	6.3
	4-5	5.1	1.8	5.3	7	5.8	4.4	2.1	0	3.7	4.8
	5-10	5.8	8.2	13.7	15.4	10.4	7	4.2	4	4.2	8.7
	>10	1.9	14.1	3.8	4	2.6	2.7	0.8	0.1	0.5	2.7
	ALL	100	100	100	100	100	100	100	100	100	100

SOURCE: HOUSEHOLD INDEBTEDNESS IN INDIA, 70TH NSSO ROUND

The table above illustrates the distribution of loans based on duration and interest rates. It is pertinent to note that almost 84 per cent of loans are of duration less than three years in rural areas. Most of the high-interest loans are typically for a shorter period of time in both urban and rural areas. Informal sources of credit being the dominant source of such loans—they are typically availed of to meet any exigencies in the family, mostly on account of farming, healthcare, education or other socio-cultural factors. A meagre 1.3 per cent of the total outstanding loans were of long duration (greater than ten years).

REASONS FOR LOANS

A critical aspect of any loan is the intent or reason for the loan—if it is utilized in productive purposes, like for capital expenditures that lead to increase in appreciating assets or increase economic activity, it can lead to increased income for the household. On the other hand, loans can be detrimental for household finances if they are required for sustenance or utilized in purposes that neither lead to increased production of goods or services nor contribute to raising household income, with such loans mostly ushering in a vicious debt cycle in the household.

The following table presents the pattern of purpose of incurring debt for households based on their asset-holding status:

TABLE 136: PERCENTAGE SHARE OF DEBT BY BROAD PURPOSE OF LOAN FOR EACH ASSET HOLDING CLASS ACROSS INDIA

		DECILE OF ASSET HOLDING										
		1	2	3	4	5	6	7	8	9	10	ALL
RURAL	% SHARE OF DEBT IN NON-BUSINESS	84.6	88.6	86.4	82.2	77.2	72.4	61.6	63.3	55.4	44.5	60.0
	% SHARE OF DEBT IN BUSINESS	15.4	11.4	13.6	17.8	22.8	27.6	38.4	36.7	44.6	55.5	40.0
	FARM BUSINESS	9.4	7.7	8.1	13.2	16.7	20.2	32.6	31.1	37.2	34.3	28.6
	NON-FARM BUSINESS	6.0	3.7	5.5	4.6	6.1	7.4	5.8	5.6	7.4	21.2	11.4
	RATIO BETWEEN FARM & NON-FARM BUSINESS	157%	208%	147%	287%	274%	273%	562%	555%	503%	162%	251%
URBAN	% SHARE OF DEBT IN NON-BUSINESS	98.8	92.0	80.8	86.4	79.0	83.6	85.1	84.2	91.0	76.0	81.7
	% SHARE OF DEBT IN BUSINESS	1.2	8.0	19.2	13.6	21.0	16.4	14.9	15.8	9.0	24.0	18.3
	FARM BUSINESS	0.1	1.2	0.4	2.9	2.6	2.8	3.4	3.0	1.6	2.1	2.2
	NON-FARM BUSINESS	1.1	6.8	18.8	10.7	18.4	13.6	11.5	12.8	7.4	21.9	16.1
	RATIO BETWEEN FARM & NON-FARM BUSINESS	9%	18%	2%	27%	14%	21%	30%	23%	22%	10%	14%

SOURCE: HOUSEHOLD INDEBTEDNESS IN INDIA, 70TH NSSO ROUND

All capital and current expenditures made for farm or non-farm businesses are clubbed under business loans whereas expenditure on healthcare, education, litigation, etc., are clubbed under non-business loans. We see that, as the decile of asset holding decreases, the amount of loans undertaken for non-business purposes actually increases—more than 80 per cent of loans made to the poor and economically challenged in the bottom 4 deciles were non-business loans. Overall, 60 per cent loans in rural India are non-business loans. The situation in urban India is no better—more than 81 per cent loans were non-business loans. In rural India, household expenditures and farm loans form the bulk of all loans—accounting for 60 per cent and 29 per cent of loans, respectively. Additionally, in rural areas, loans made for farm business peaks in the seventh, eighth and ninth deciles of asset holding, while the poor are still taking on a higher proportion of debt for non-farm business compared to their counterparts in higher asset deciles.

The table below illustrates the trend in productive loans towards other loan types with time:

TABLE 137: PERCENTAGE DISTRIBUTION OF AMOUNT OF CASH DUE BY PURPOSE

	RURAL				URBAN			
	1981	1991	2002	2012	1981	1991	2002	2012
PRODUCTIVE PURPOSES	69	23	53	40	42	17	25	18
FARM BUSINESS								
CAPITAL EXPENDITURE	43	12	27	13	6	3	3	1
CURRENT EXPENDITURE	18	3	14	15	4	0	2	1
NON-FARM BUSINESS								
CAPITAL EXPENDITURE	7	6	9	9	23	11	17	8
CURRENT EXPENDITURE	2	2	3	3	8	4	3	8
NON-PRODUCTIVE PURPOSES	31	78	47	60	56	83	75	82
ALL	100	100	100	100	100	100	100	100

SOURCE: VARIOUS ALL INDIA DEBT AND INVESTMENT SURVEYS

Thus, we see that the most prominent change in both rural and urban areas occurred in the share of debt incurred for productive purposes. The share of cash debt, in the rural areas, settled at the 40 percentage point in 2012 after seeing considerable oscillation from 69 percentage point in 1981 to the 23 percentage point in 1991 and then to the 53 percentage point in 2002. The movement in the share of the debt for productive purposes, in the urban areas, was from 42 per cent in 1981 to 17 per cent in 1991, and then to 25 per cent in 2002 and finally dropped to 18 per cent in 2012. This fall appears to stem from a higher portion of debt being incurred to meet non-productive expenditure, particularly household expenditure.

COST AND IMPACT OF CREDIT DELIVERY

When it comes to delivering credit in rural areas, multiple channels are followed—each with its varying cost of delivering the rural credit. When lending through Public Sector Banks (PSBs), the credit can be delivered directly to the farmer through its branches, or through self-help groups (wherein the PSB lends to a self-help group, which in turn provides credit to its members) or through Micro-Finance Institutions (MFIs).

Private banks also deliver credit through rural branches, in turn lending to MFIs which can then lend to end-user. The cost of delivering credit is dependent on various factors—the cost of debt (signifying the cost at which banks raise money), the cost of equity, provisions for loan loss (the riskier the loan, higher the premium) and transaction costs, which is the cost of delivering credit and is highly dependent on the channel preferred. Transaction costs pose a challenge in rural credit, as they consist mainly of fixed costs and seem huge in percentage terms, especially in the wake of small per unit loan size.

Provisions for loan loss are a reflection of loan quality—research reveals that rural credit underwritten through the self-help group (SHG) channel is the lowest, thereby incurring the highest costs while AA rated MFIs have the lowest provisions for loan loss.

Studies (Anand Sahasranaman & Deepti George, IFMR Foundation, April '13) have shown that credit supplied through rural branches have the lowest cost to customer, but the highest cost to the banks. Thus, when banks are mandated to provide loans at stipulated rates from rural branches, many banks opt to pay for financial penalties for not meeting priority sector lending obligations instead of expanding rural banking operations. In some cases, the total cost for credit delivery ranged from ~14 per cent (AA rated MFI) to ~41 per cent (by PSBs through rural branches)—implying that for every ₹1 crore loan made through the rural branch of a PSB, ~₹27 lakh is spent due to higher channel costs.

Thus, banks would incur lower cost of credit delivery if they were advised to eschew the use of branches and instead, work exclusively through low-cost partners. It also suggests that creation of branches in remote areas for meeting small loan requirements would not be advisable because it would increase the overall cost of financial intermediation infrastructure. In other words, providing MFIs with the same cross subsidization as banks would reduce the cost of credit delivery even further.

The pre-1991 reforms era in India was witness to an administered interest rate regime with the RBI stipulating the range of interest rates applicable to loans and deposits. However, for the agriculture and priority sectors, these regulations did not apply and thus agriculture enjoyed lower rates of interest, made possible not with a direct contribution from the government but through cross-subsidization. By 1995, cross-subsidization of credit for agriculture (and other priority sectors) had been terminated.

However, the food crisis of 2006–07 saw the government taking a number of initiatives and one of them was subvention to enable lending institutions to advance credit to agriculture at a lower rate of interest. Farmers were thus offered short-term credit at 7 per cent (against the prevailing rate of 9 per cent), with an upper limit of ₹3 lakh on the principal amount with the policy coming into effect from the 2006–07 kharif crops. The differential interest was provided by the government of India as interest subvention to banks in order to enable banks to lend to farmers at lower interest rates.

In 2009–10, the Government of India introduced an additional interest subvention of 1 per cent to farmers who repaid their loans on or before the due date; interest rate subvention for timely repayment was raised to 2 per cent in 2010–11 and further to 3 per cent in 2011–12, taking the total subvention to 5 per cent. The benefit of interest subvention (but not of additional subvention for prompt payment) is also available for post-harvest loans against negotiable warehouse receipts provided by banks to small and marginal farmers with Kisan Credit Cards.

However, subsiding credit needs a relook as well, especially when gaps do exist in effective administration of the interest subvention scheme. The scale of expenditure on credit subsidies in agriculture may not be comparable to that on other input subsidies, such as fertilizer, power and irrigation. However, credit subsidies also have an incremental effect on the mounting fiscal burden and we need to analyse and evaluate the benefits of these subsidies.

One of the primary intents of credit subsidy is to reduce the interest burden on the farmer and reduce their working capital requirement. The following table presents the working capital as a percentage of the cost of cultivation for nine major crops for 2006–07 to 2011–12. It is seen that, except in the case of cotton (in which the percentage is about 3 per cent), interest on working capital constitutes between 1 and 2 per cent of the cost of cultivation.

TABLE 138: INTEREST ON WORKING CAPITAL AS PERCENTAGE OF TOTAL COST OF CULTIVATION FOR VARIOUS CROPS (DIRECTORATE OF ECONOMICS & STATISTICS, DEPARTMENT OF AGRICULTURE & COOPERATION, MINISTRY OF AGRICULTURE)

YEARS	PADDY	WHEAT	MAIZE	SUGAR CANE	POTATO	ONION	COTTON	JUTE	SUNFLOWER
2006-07	1.59	1.54	1.46	3.15	1.96	1.52	1.56	1.38	1.78
2007-08	1.53	1.5	1.48	3.19	2.12	1.9	1.51	1.43	1.77
2008-09	1.52	1.46	1.52	3.01	1.84	1.74	1.5	1.49	1.79
2009-10	1.54	1.48	1.52	2.66	2.03	1.61	1.48	1.46	1.78
2010-11	1.6	1.43	1.49	2.94	1.77	1.69	1.41	1.36	1.9
2011-12	1.58	1.46	1.52	3.23	1.8	1.84	1.48	1.35	1.72

Given the low share of cost of the working capital in overall cost of cultivation, credit subsidy, while important is not the most important determinant of decision-making for a farmer, for whom the timely availability of adequate credit may hold better value. Timely availability and adequate loan amount are what drive a farmer to informal channels and such funds used in providing credit subsidy could be used to provide small and marginal farmers with timely and adequate credit on improved terms.

Granting loans at highly concessional rates also presents a moral hazard, wherein a farmer can avail of a concessional loan and deposit it with a financial institution to receive a higher interest. There is arbitrage opportunity here as the farmer can make a risk-free profit of 2–2.5 per cent. Thus, the production loan granted to farmers for a productive purpose may not be used for agricultural production or may be so used only partially.

Figures of month-wise disbursement of agricultural credit also raise questions on the utilization of such credit. Since the main requirement in agriculture is for short-term crop loans, the normal expectation would be for the maximum credit disbursement to take place up to the time of sowing in the rabi season. However, analysis (R. Ramakumar, Pallavi Chavan, 2014) illustrates that as much as 46 per cent of the annual disbursement was made in the months of January to March in 2008–09, after the rabi sowing had ended. A similar backloading is noticed in 2013–14—the share of annual disbursement in the last quarter of the financial year was even higher at 62 per cent. The fact that the monthly credit flows are skewed against the months in which there is peak agricultural operations, heightens the suspicion that short-term credit is being diverted for non-agricultural purposes. The latest AIDIS (2013) report that only 64 per cent of the outstanding agricultural debt was owed to institutional sources also casts doubts on how subsidized agricultural credit is being utilized.

One might presume that removing credit subsidies would be effective, yet, it is also pertinent to note that a bulk of farmer suicides occur due to indebtedness to institutional channels.

TABLE 139: FARMER AND AGRI-LABOUR SUICIDES IN 2015

NO.	DESCRIPTION	AGE GROUP					TOTAL	%AGE
		<18	18-30	30-45	45-60	60 & ABOVE		
1	FARMING RELATED ISSUES	2	268	631	501	160	1562	20%
1.1	CROP FAILURE	2	262	629	499	160	1552	19%
1.1.1	DUE TO CALAMITY	0	171	342	261	105	879	11%
1.1.2	OTHER REASONS	2	91	287	238	55	673	8%
1.2	INABILITY TO SELL	0	6	2	2	0	10	0%
2	BANKRUPTCY/INDEBTEDNESS	1	491	1382	1001	222	3097	39%
2.1	LOAN TAKEN FROM FORMAL SOURCES	1	395	1121	786	171	2474	31%
2.2	LOAN TAKEN FROM INFORMAL SOURCES	0	46	138	90	28	302	4%
2.3	LOAN TAKEN FROM BOTH SOURCES	0	50	123	125	23	321	4%
	TOTAL SUICIDES	42	1513	3332	2398	722	8007	

NO.	DESCRIPTION	AGE GROUP					TOTAL	%AGE
		<18	18-30	30-45	45-60	60 & ABOVE		
1	BANKRUPTCY/INDEBTEDNESS	2	40	116	80	17	255	3%
1.1	LOAN TAKEN FROM FORMAL SOURCES	1	24	72	44	14	155	2%
1.2	LOAN TAKEN FROM INFORMAL SOURCES	1	16	44	36	3	100	1%
	TOTAL SUICIDES	116	1270	1668	1093	448	4595	

Farmer suicides in 2015 were recorded at 8,007—~42 per cent increase from 5,650 suicides in 2014. Bankruptcy and indebtedness witnessed an almost 3x increase—from 1,163 suicides in 2014 to 3,097 suicides in 2015. It is interesting to note that despite 36 per cent of people taking money from moneylenders, it accounted for only 4 per cent of suicides, whereas institution loans caused 31 per cent of all farmer suicides and ~80 per cent of all farmer suicides were due to bankruptcy/indebtedness.

One important reason is that informal channels offer flexibility—institutional sources of credit cannot offer the same due to rules. In some cases, the MFI and SHG sector fare even worse as they put pressure on the entire group by threatening to cut their share if one defaulter doesn't pay up. This creates additional social pressure over and above the economic pressure.

One cannot ignore the fact that a majority of the farmer suicides occur due to indebtedness to institutional credit sources; thus, removal of any credit subsidy becomes untenable. One needs to reform disbursal of subsidized credit in a timely manner to those who need it the most, especially small and marginal farmers.

Over the years there has been a significant increase in the access of rural cultivators to institutional credit and, simultaneously, the role of informal agencies, including moneylenders, as a source of credit has declined.

RBI studies suggest that the direct agriculture credit amount has a positive and statistically significant impact on agriculture output and with immediate effect. Meanwhile, indirect agriculture credit also has a positive significant impact on agriculture output, but with a year's lag. Agriculture credit delivery has its own flows—its heavy dependence on borrowed funds with most credit being short-term in nature plagued by service delivery gaps and inadequate provisioning to the needy, it is still playing a critical role in supporting agriculture production in India. The role of agricultural credit can be further enhanced with greater financial inclusion by the involvement of region-specific market participants and credit suppliers ranging from public sector banks, cooperative banks, the new private sector banks and micro-credit suppliers, especially self-help groups (Mohan, 2006).

One of the other reasons why greater farm credit cannot be an overall solution is that not all of our rural credit is agricultural credit, as evident from a persisting agrarian distress despite increased rural credit. The '90s were a decade of muted agricultural credit, with many believing that agrarian distress in the late '90s and early 2000s was a result of increased indebtedness—the All India Debt and Investment Survey (AIDIS) points out that the share of formal sources of debt for cultivator households fell from 64 per cent in 1992 to 57 per cent in 2003, with the share of professional moneylenders almost doubling from 10.5 per cent to 19.6 per cent during the same period. The agricultural credit growth during 1990 and 2000 from commercial banks and regional rural banks stood at 1.8 per cent, whereas the same increased to 19.1 per cent from 2000 to 2007, with the lead being taken by commercial banks and regional rural banks evident from their share in credit increasing from 30 per cent in 2000 to 52 per cent in 2007. Not all of this increased credit went to farms. Firstly, a significant proportion of this increased credit flow was through the indirect credit route. Thus, it contains loans given to institutions/firms that support agriculture, be it equipment suppliers, input suppliers or even NBFCs that lend to farmers. Secondly, definitional changes are also responsible for such seemingly impressive numbers—the definition of agricultural credit as a priority sector also started to include financing commercial/export-oriented and capital-intensive agriculture, while raising the credit limit of many forms of agricultural lending. Additionally, a sharp increase in the number of loans with ₹10 crore credit limit also drove the agricultural credit numbers. This was elaborated by the increase in credit supply from urban and metropolitan branches—more than doubling share from 16.3 per cent in 1995 to 37.6 per cent in 2006, with more than three times' increase in the share of only metropolitan branches—from 7.3 per cent to 23.8 per cent during the same period. While all the credit eventually flows into agriculture, the urban-centric nature of agricultural credit benefits mostly the corporations, not the actual small and marginal farmer, who is least likely to benefit from the urban-focused credit growth.

YEAR	SHARE OF TOTAL AGRICULTURAL CREDIT SUPPLIED BY				
	RURAL + SEMI-URBAN BRANCHES	ONLY RURAL BRANCHES	URBAN + METROPOLITAN BRANCHES	ONLY METROPOLITAN BRANCHES	ALL BRANCHES
1990	85.1	55.5	14.9	4.0	100.0
1994	83.4	54.6	16.6	5.6	100.0
1995	83.7	52.7	16.3	7.3	100.0
2005	69.3	43.0	30.7	19.0	100.0
2006	62.4	37.1	37.6	23.8	100.0
2008	66.0	38.4	34.0	20.0	100.0

FARM LOAN WAIVERS

In post-Independence India, farm loan waivers have been a regularly used policy instrument. In 1989, the Janata Dal government floated an agriculture loan write-off scheme, which waived loans up to ₹10,000 issued to farmers. By 1992, the scheme benefited over 44 million farmers at the cost of ₹6,000 crore. In 2008, the Agricultural Debt-Waiver and Debt Relief (ADWDR) Scheme benefitted over 36.9 million small and marginal farmers, along with 5.97 million large farmers, at a cost of ₹71,600 crore Even at a state level, such measures have been taken—Tamil Nadu has waived loans for small and marginal farmers in the recent past; in 2017, the outgoing state government in Uttar Pradesh too waived ₹50,000 crore worth of crop loans taken from state cooperative banks.

Consider the context. Of India's 121 million agricultural holdings, 99 million are with small and marginal farmers, with a land share of just 44 per cent and a farmer population share of 87 per cent. With multiple cropping prevalent, such farmers account for 70 per cent of vegetable and 52 per cent of cereal output. With seed application rising, given an intensified cropping pattern, farmers are also seeing a rise in seed costs. Arhar prices nearly tripled from ₹27/kg in 2004 to ₹73/kg in 2013. Cotton saw a massive five-time jump from ₹396/kg to ₹1,860/kg, courtesy of the switch to Bt cotton. Maize, riven with crop failure, saw a similar jump from ₹20/kg to ₹99/kg. Even staple crops like paddy (₹6/kg to ₹31/kg), soyabean (₹20/kg to ₹40/kg) and sugar cane (₹89/kg to ₹230/kg) have seen a significant increase. The old days of farmers handing seeds as family heirlooms to their sons are long gone. Fertilizer prices have seen a similar rise, with NPK fertilizers for cotton jumping from ₹14/kg to ₹26/kg, while plain barley saw a sudden jump from ₹9/kg in 2004-05 to ₹26/kg by 2012-13. The cost of human labour, a substitute often for agricultural machinery has also shot up substantially. Hiring a labourer can now cost at least ₹20/hour, excluding rates when NREGA is prevalent, compared to ₹9/hour previously. Animal hire rates have also increased in a similar manner. The cost paid of ensuring plant protection through pesticides has gone through the roof, jumping nearly five times for arhar (from ₹281/hectare in 2004–05 to ₹1,138/hectare in 2012–13). Given this jump in input costs, the cost of cultivation has gone up substantially, rising from ₹20,607 per hectare for Paddy in 2004–05 to ₹47,644.5 per hectare in 2012–13. Similarly, the total cost of cultivation for wheat has risen thrice from ₹12,850 per hectare in 2004–05 to ₹38,578 per hectare in 2012–13. Fixed costs (cost of land, etc.) have had a significant part to play in this rise, along with a rise in variable costs like seeds, fertilizers and insecticides.

India's fiscal pundits seem to have a rather curious penchant for decrying the offering of any fiscal sops (grants, right to food, loan waivers) offered to farmers, while discounting those offered to the industry. Let the facts speak for themselves: according to the RBI, between 2000 and 2013, over ₹1 lakh crore worth of corporate loans were written off, with 95 per cent of them being large loans; in comparison, the recent settlement scheme by the State Bank of India for tractor and farm equipment (a 40 per cent haircut on such farm loans) for loans up to ₹25 lakh each is expected to cost ₹6,000 crore India's NPAs are not the result of the lack of a credit culture with farmers; over 50 per cent of all NPAs are those allocated to medium and large enterprises.

Well-meaning critics, with a righteous belief in fiscal probity, should consider the historicity of agriculture loan waivers in India before critiquing them for destroying an embryonic credit culture. In my travels across this desiccated hinterland, the consequence of usury has long been marked in distended bellies and orphaned children. Without such corrective action, the fate of our farmers will continue to remain uncertain and Hobbesian.

SOCIAL BUDGETING

We also need to shift our budgetary allocations further towards the rural economy. While the last decade's fiscal budgets were rhetorically pronounced pro-poor, the Asian Development Bank's Social Protection Index (SPI) has ranked India 23rd in social protection across APAC, with spending at 1.7 per cent of GDP, while China, ranked 12th, spent 5.4 per cent of its GDP on such measures—even Mongolia had a better figure (9.6 per cent of its GDP). Our fiscal budgets, particularly in the last decade, have focused on tax incentive tinkering and ill-funded welfare schemes, all while spending on agriculture has declined (₹27,041 crore in 2014 vs ₹36,355 crore in 2005, Planning Commission, CBGA). We have announced grand schemes—the National Urban Health Mission (2013), but provided no budgetary allocations.[24]

Rural India's economic health requires an increase in social investments, with a particular focus on agriculture, education and malnutrition. Targeted spending, on social ailments, can help build economic confidence and power a double-digit growth rate. A socially progressive budget, which brings back a social safety net, remains necessary. Much remains to be done—agriculture, accounting for 16 per cent of the GDP and employing nearly 50 per cent of the population, faces dismal returns and rising input costs.[25] Labour productivity in India has risen anaemically over the past four decades, held down by limited innovation in agriculture—we lag significantly behind South Korea, China and even Vietnam.[26] Our performance, across various social infrastructure indicators, remains unsatisfactory—education (3.35 vs Thailand's 5.21); employment (3.14 vs Vietnam's 4.70), etc.

Over half of all agricultural households face an average loan amount of ₹47,000—borrowed heavily from moneylenders (26 per cent of all rural credit) at usurious rates (>20 per cent)—and a life of everlasting penury (NSSO Survey, 2015). Input costs have risen to 30 per cent of total output, a consequence of rising labour cost and fertilizer price inflation. Meanwhile, India's irrigation system is heavily inadequate, with high capital investment costs preventing farmers from adopting better groundwater pumps and drip irrigation techniques.

Any fiscal budget should bolster the Agricultural Demand-Side Management Program, which seeks to replace existing irrigation pumps with energy-efficient models (potentially reducing electricity consumption by 20 per cent). Fiscal incentives for drip irrigation can help improve water coverage, while rainwater

---

24   Urmi Goswami, Yojana, 2013,
25   Gemma Corrigan, WEF
26   Gronigen Growth & Development Centre, 2015

harvesting and groundwater recharging initiatives can improve productivity—building extensive resilience to El Nino-like events.

Agriculture remains the key. Our budget needs to heavily align towards bolstering a long-term rural credit policy, offering flexibility for droughts and flooding events. Crop insurance, as proposed by the government, would be a welcome move to institutionalize the habit of insuring against market and weather volatility. Subsidy policies, particularly in food procurement, should be realigned to incentivize conservation and modernization, with better support prices for water-efficient crops driving their adoption.

A change in our budgeting process is also called for. Participatory budgeting, a process in which citizens present their civic policy preferences and priorities to negotiate local budget allocations is fast becoming the norm. In Brazil, since 1989, the city of Porto Alegre has approved budget allocations for public welfare works only after recommendations of public delegates participating in the budgetary process.[27] To initiate such conversations, the city administration shares its economic and financial position with its citizens, offering a forum for popular demands, constrained by its financial resources. Shifting from a culture of clientelism to one with transparency in city, budgeting has enabled accountability in the municipal system.

In consequence, the city's budgetary spending is now closely tied to actual needs—with sewerage connections doubling, public housing units rising from 1,700 units to 27,000 units (1986–89) and the number of participants in the budgeting process jumping to 40,000 over a decade. Long-term, local, policy decisions are now markedly influenced by public choices—a five-star hotel plan was replaced with one encompassing public parks, a convention hall and other amenities.[28]

Poverty, our eternal bane, defined at $2/day, still remains at 68.7 per cent.[29] A shift in political culture must take place; responsible welfare economics makes for good politics. Our budgetary allocations should first and foremost seek to heavily address the needs of the most desperate amongst us. The fiscal budget must ensure that social progress is here to stay.

---

27 World Bank, Empowerment Case Studies
28 Souz, Celina, 2002; Jacobi, Pedro, 1999
29 Gemma Corrigan, WEF

MICROFINANCE

Microfinance provides another avenue for expanding rural credit. However, its extreme consequences, as attested by suicides in Andhra Pradesh, can lead to an explosive situation with reports of farmers borrowing from moneylenders to pay MFIs. Abusive collection practices can create huge pressure on the indebted. These can include holding weekly meetings in front of the defaulter's house, putting up loan overdue notices and encashing signed blank cheques. Freedom from poverty has a huge cost apparently.

The vacuum left by the State's limited presence in the rural credit market has encouraged microfinance, broadly defined as Self Help Group (SHG)-Bank Linkage (SBL) and microfinance institutions (MFIs). SHGs, piloted by NABARD in 1992, rapidly expanded to 7.5 million savings linked SHGs with aggregate savings of ₹70.16 billion and 1.19 million credit-linked SHGs with credit of ₹145.57 billion.[30] India's regulated microfinance market today has over 28 million clients, served by around 50 regulated institutions. The sector grew its gross loan portfolio by 35 per cent in FY14, attracting 4.7 million new clients, despite its murky record in Andhra Pradesh (2007).

Microfinance offers several strengths, making finance accessible and available for consumption needs, along with 'freedom from collateral'. However, it is no magic bullet for poverty eradication and rural empowerment. MFIs need high interest rates to justify their transaction costs and low scale of operations, which attract high-risk customers—with consequentially higher default rates. This market failure, with information provision a natural monopoly,[31] requires intermediation.

The Malegam Committee Report (RBI, 2011) sought a separate category of NBFC-MFIs, with margin and interest rate caps on individual loans, along with restrictions on multiple lending to the same individual and the establishment of credit information bureau. The Micro Finance Institutions Bill (2012, now lapsed) envisaged the RBI providing a statutory framework to regulate the industry. Further reforms are necessary. Monitoring can be done through councils and committees at the central, state and district levels. An RBI-managed Micro Finance Development Fund could be used for loans, refinancing and investments in MFIs. Every MFI would have to create a reserve fund, with the RBI specifying the percentage of net profit added annually to the fund and providing permissions for appropriations. An annual balance sheet and profit and loss account for audit for each MFI should be sent to the RBI, along with any changes in the corporate structure. The RBI

---

30 NABARD, 2011
31 Sen & Vaidya, 1997

could set the maximum annual percentage rate charged by MFIs and the maximum margins that can be made. The prospect of banking licences for MFIs (as offered in April 2014), would incentivize them to engage in institutional development, with success linked to further options such as deposit-taking.

The SBL approach requires the formation of self-help groups, usually women, who save money that is placed in a local bank. By creating a safe avenue for savings,[32,33] the SHG functions like a small bank, lending money to members. Its positive economic impact is well attested, particularly on indicators such as average net income and employment,[34] while inculcating a banking habit.

However, by virtue of being a government-'pushed' model, it suffers from bureaucratic infirmity. Banks have mostly failed to recognize their self-interest in promoting SHGs, given the lower information costs of lending to the poor through SGHs, avoiding adverse selection and moral hazards.[35]

The linkage between SHGs and the banking sector is critical for providing economies of scale. Studies in Andhra Pradesh and Tamil Nadu[36] have shown that SHGs can become financially viable by forming federations, achieving enormous economies of scale. Bank branches can become economically viable entities by doing business with SHG federations.[37] The SHG-bank linkage model can be scaled for specific requirements—distress cash needs, food scarcity, etc., while bolstering women's empowerment.

BASIC INCOME

In 1974, the Canadian government conducted a randomized controlled trial in Winnipeg, Dauphin and rural Manitoba. Lower-income households across the region were randomly allocated into seven treatment groups, along with a control. Families gained an income guarantee, dependent on their family size, constrained by their working income. The trial excluded families earning above a predetermined amount (~$13,000 in 1975; Derek Hum, Wayne Simpson, 2001). Everyone else

---

32   Hashemi et al, 1996
33   Rajasekhar, 2000
34   Puhazhendi and Satyasai, 2000
35   SPS, 2006
36   Nair, 2001
37   SPS, 2006

in the treatment groups was given a base amount ($3,386 equivalent to $16,094 now), while 50 cents was subtracted for every dollar earned from other sources.[38] This negative income tax experiment, termed 'Mincome', helped over a thousand families below the poverty line in Dauphin earn a liveable income. It offered financial predictability—food insecurity vanished, bills were paid, education was not compromised.[39] With stability in place, overall hospitalization, particularly for accidents and injuries, declined, along with physician contact for mental health diagnoses.[40] A guaranteed annual income (GAI) system had brought about social stability and improved healthcare outcomes. With the onset of '70s stagflation, induced by the oil crisis, such schemes were abandoned and any insights ignored. But, briefly, there was a town with no poverty.

The idea that every individual should have access to a minimum guaranteed basic income is not new.[41,42] Thomas Paine sought an equal inheritance for everyone, 'a national fund' which would pay every adult a sum of 'fifteen pounds sterling as compensation' for the introduction of the system of landed property (Agrarian Justice, 1797; Evelyn L. Forget, 2011). Thomas More sought to reduce poverty by giving money to all, instead of simply executing thieves. The 'Speenhamland system', critiqued much later for 'impeding labour mobility', introduced a means of tested assistance for the poor in the town of Speenhamland in Berkshire County, England in 1795. Whenever bread prices rose, the working poor with large families were subsidized with poor relief funds. Relief was no longer limited to the sick or elderly, but to those who were able but struck with misfortune. Bertrand Russell built the 'social credit' movement, which was transformed by the Labour Party into the famed 'social dividend'.[43]

The Great Depression brought about the relinquishment of the employable. Welfare policy was transformed with minimum wage legislation, while Keynesianism meant that the government would attempt to stimulate the economy during downturns, by directly financing public employment and public works. Long-term support was offered to the aged, the disabled and single mothers while unemployment insurance sought to support the temporarily unemployed. The 1960s brought about the war on poverty, waged through federally funded social service and healthcare programmes. Milton Friedman sought a negative income tax, eliminating the need for a minimum wage and potentially the 'welfare trap',

---

38   Leroy O. Stone, Michael J. MacLean, Josée Ouellet Simard, 1979
39   Zi-Ann Lum, 2014
40   Evelyn L Forget, 2011
41   Williams, 1943, 1953
42   John Cunliffe, Guido Erreygers, 2004
43   David H. Freedman, 2016

while bureaucracy could be curtailed.[44] Richard Nixon supported and yet failed to push through a 'Family Assistance Plan' while George McGovern's 1972 campaign sought a $1,000 'demogrant' for all citizens. This decadal struggle against poverty in the West cut the number of those in poverty in the US to 26 million from 36 million in twelve years.[45] Education and healthcare were improved, but the employability and the income of the poor remained stranded. With the rise of neo-liberalism, opinion shifted. Existing welfare systems had grown too cumbersome, without eliminating poverty.

Now, however, the idea of an unconditional annual income is gathering momentum. Y Combinator of Silicon Valley fame is testing a new business model—handing out money, without any strings, in an unnamed US community; an attempt to replace safety net welfare policies that often fail to help those with the greatest need.[46] Finland is considering a plan to give 100,000 citizens $1,000 a month, while four cities in the Netherlands are starting trial programmes. While Switzerland rejected its referendum on giving its citizens about $2,500 a month, the Canadian province of Ontario is planning a trial run. Progressives are hailing it as an escape route for workaholics, from oppressive jobs and situations, giving individuals greater time to build relationships and pursue education or artistic endeavours. The Conservatives applaud its potential to shrink bureaucracy. A $10,000 basic income in the US, while adding $2 trillion in annual expenses, at double the cost of existing welfare schemes, would raise the vast majority of poor Americans above the poverty line. Such individuals could use a basic income to invest in training that equips them for higher-skilled jobs. As job concerns about automation grow, the basic income stands out as a panacea.

Even India has seen its share of basic income experiments. A pilot in eight villages in Madhya Pradesh provided over 6,000 individuals a monthly payment (₹100 for a child; ₹200 for an adult, later raised to ₹150 and ₹300, respectively).[47] The money was initially paid out in cash while transitioning to bank accounts three months later. The transfer was unconditional, save the prevention of substitution of food subsidies for cash grants. The results were intriguing. Most villagers used the money on household improvements (latrines, walls, roofs) while taking precautions against malaria—24.3 per cent of households changed their main source of energy for cooking or lighting; 16 per cent of households made changes to their toilet.[48] There was a seeming shift towards markets, instead of ration shops, given better financial liquidity, leading to improved nutrition, particularly amongst SC and ST households,

---

44   Friedman, Milton, Capitalism & Freedom, 1962
45   Harris, 2005
46   David H. Freedman, 2016
47   Guy Standing, 2014
48   Sewa, Unicef, 2014

and better school attendance and performance.[49] There was an increase in small-scale investments (better seeds, sewing machines, equipment repairs, etc.). Bonded labour decreased, along with casual wage labour, while self-employed farming and business activity increased. Financial inclusion was rapid—within four months of the pilot, 95.6 per cent of the individuals had bank accounts. Within a year, 73 per cent of the households reported a reduction in their debt. There was no evidence of any increase in spending on alcohol.

Before moving ahead, we would need more data to prove its applicability in the Indian context. There have only been 8 large-scale pilot programmes testing the impact of a universal basic income on human well-being. Social context too matters—what might have worked in Manitoba or Kenya might not necessarily be applicable to India. We need a greater depth of pilot studies, focused on ensuring universal access, over a long term (at least a decade) and covering minimum living expenses.[50] With more pilots planned in Oakland, the Netherlands, Germany and even India, insights developed should be used to modify welfare policy.

A regular unconditional basic income, scaled up through pilots, and rolled out slowly and carefully, seems ideal for India. It can help improve living conditions, including sanitation, in our villages, providing them with access to better drinking water, while improving children's nutrition. Regular basic income payments can help institute rational responses to illness or hunger, enabling households to fund their health expenses instead of encountering a vicious cycle of debt. It can help reduce child labour, while facilitating an increase in school spending. It can transform villages, enabling the growth of productive work, leading to a sustained increase in income.[51] It could cut inequality; grow the economy; all while offering the pursuit of happiness.

CROP INSURANCE

Crop insurance matters as well. The Pradhan Mantri Fasal Bima Yojana (PMFBY), launched with effect from April '16, replaced the two existing schemes—the National Agricultural Insurance Scheme (NAIS) and the Modified NAIS (MNAIS), while also setting up premium benchmarks for the Weather-Based Crop Insurance

---

49   Guy Standing, 2014
50   Michael J. Coren, 2016
51   Sewa, Unicef, 2014

Scheme (WBCIS). With our farming increasingly at the mercy of natural elements, our farmers need an inclusive, effective and universal insurance scheme for their crops. The PMFBY did a commendable job of being affordable for farmers—with farmers' share of premia for kharif, rabi and horticulture crops being capped at 2 per cent, 1.5 per cent and 5 per cent, respectively. The balance premium payment was to be paid and shared by the state and central governments equally—thereby signaling a collective responsibility for ensuring payments. Additionally, removal of premium capping has also led to the removal of sum insured—thus, a farmer facing a higher risk can pay a higher premium and still get insurance. The earlier schemes (NAIS and MNAIS) also limited the maximum payout to an affected farmer—capped at credit limit for an indebted farmer or in case of a debt-free farmer, capped at maximum pre-defined liability borne by the insurance company. The PMFBY also brought the sum insured closer to the cost of production, e.g., the sum insured increased from ₹20,500 per hectare to ₹34,370 per hectare for kharif crops from 2015 to 2016.

While modifications to some key aspects like sum insured and premium payments are welcome, there are still some areas of improvement remaining. Insurance unit, for one, remains a debatable issue. It remains based on an administrative unit (block, mandal, panchayat, etc.), and thus remains prone to inaccuracies on account of large insurance units. Thus, for an equitable payment at insurance unit level, some farmer may get more than the damage incurred, by short-changing another who doesn't receive commensurate payment. It also presents a lot of room for corruption, made worse with empanelling of untrained staff for crop loss estimation. With the increased use of technology, our aim should be to make a farm as one insurance unit, thereby assisting in realistic damage estimation and timely payouts. The smaller farm-level insurance unit also suffers complications—with land being registered in the name of the father or forefathers and, with time, being subject to multiple sub-divisions.

On account of a larger insurance unit, the PMFBY doesn't link the farmer with the insurance company directly—causing a chasm between the two parties, ultimately leading to compromised service delivery. A direct linkage between the farmer, the company and the bank in case of an indebted farmer will lead to improved service delivery, and reduced hassles for interest payments from the bank in case of failed/destroyed crops. Competition between various insurance providers will offer increased choice for farmers. Additionally, croppers/cultivators who have taken land on lease cannot avail of benefits under the PMFBY scheme, due to lack of proper documents, proving their right to cultivate a particular piece of land. Some provisions need to be designed in order to enable croppers to get insurance and receive benefits in case of damage.

In terms of actuarial rates, the national rate for kharif 2016 was recorded at the highest ever at 12.6 per cent, with other areas like Gujarat, Rajasthan and Maharashtra registering actuarial rates of 20.5 per cent, 19.9 per cent and 18.9 per cent, respectively. Despite high premia, insurance payments were delayed, if at all approved and given. Even when many states had paid their share of premium payments, only 32 per cent of claims were honoured—and when honoured, payments were delayed by more than 6 months, with kharif payments not paid till April '17 in 14 out of 21 states. Such practices have led insurance firms to reap bumper profits—during the 2017–18 kharif season, the empanelled insurance firms (5 public and 12 private) collected ₹17,796 crore as premium while paying out claims of only ₹2,767 crore–a margin of ₹15,029 crore or ~85 per cent. In the WBCIS scheme with rates benchmarked to PMFBY, the insurance companies registered collections of ₹1,694 crore (as premium) against payments of ₹69.9 cr—a margin of ₹1624 crore or ~96 per cent. While profits in one year cannot be the basis of revision in rates (as a good monsoon and bumper crops would reduce claims), one cannot equally ignore the percentage of claims honoured. The actual payments of ₹2,767 crore came against claims of ₹5,052 crore—thus, only 54.77 per cent of claims were passed/approved.

TOWARDS FINANCIAL INCLUSION

To meet rural credit requirements, India needs to focus on four key reforms. Public sector banking needs to focus on high-quality credit, by de-bureaucratizing procedures and personnel and infusing new talent. It should reform the cooperative credit structure (Task Force on Revival of Rural Cooperative Credit Institutions), towards democratic, member-driven, professional organizations focused on mutuality. The SHG-bank linkage programme needs to be strengthened, with NABARD bearing promotional costs initially. MFIs should be encouraged to expand on a level playing field.

India's financial sector is currently undergoing fundamental changes, with the RBI playing a leading role in driving its development. Taking bold decisions such as promoting MFIs and SHGs as vehicles for financial inclusion across India's 800 million adults are necessary to consolidate this growth. MFIs need to be encouraged to evolve into well-regulated institutions that can offer a full range of financial services to the low-income segment. Replicating the successful model followed by Kenya and Peru, this sector's expansion could lead to broad financial inclusion.

REFERENCES

Household Indebtness in India, 70th NSS Round

Report of the Task Force on Credit Related Issues of the Farmers, Ministry of Agriculture, June 2010

Anand Sahasranaman & Deepti George, Cost of Delivering Rural Credit in India, IFMR Finance Foundation

Abhiman Das, Manjusha Senapati & Joice John, Impact of agricultural credit on agriculture production: an empirical analysis in India, Reserve bank of India, January 2009

Anjani Kumar, Ashok K Mishra, Sunil Saroj, P K Joshi, Institutional versus Non-institutional Credit to Agricultural Households in India, Evidence on Impact from a National Farmers' Survey, IFPRI Discussion Paper 01614, March 2017

Key Indicators of Debt and Investment in India, 70th NSS Round

Income, Expenditure, Productive Assets & Indebtness of Agricultural Households in India, Report No 576, 70th NSS Round

Ulrich Hess, Monsoon-Indexed Lending and Insurance for Smallholders, Innovative Financial Services for Rural India, Agriculture & Rural Development Working Paper 9, World Bank

New Trends in Agricultural Finance, Oct 2015, Global Partnership for Financial Inclusion

Rural Finance Innovations, Topics & Case Studies, Report No. 32726-GLB, April 2005, World Bank

Rangarajan Committee Report on Financial Inclusion, January 2008

Sudha Narayanan, Report No. 32726-GLB, WP-2015-01, Indira Gandhi Institute of Development Research, January 2015

Anwarul Hoda & Prerna Terway, Credit Policy for Agriculture in India – An Evaluation, Working Paper 302, June 2015, Indian Council For Research On International Economic Relations

National Crime Records Bureau data, Chapter 2A – Suicides in farming sector

All India Rural Credit Review Committee (Chairman:B.Venkatappiah)

Capoor, J (1999), 'Structural Reforms in Agricultural and Rural Development Banks', Reserve Bank of India Bulletin,

October, Vol.53 No.10, pp.1185-1190

Desai, Bhupat M. and N.V. Namboodri (1993), Rural Financial Institutions: Promotions and Performance, Oxford, New Delhi

Food and Agriculture Organization (2004), FAOSTAT (website), Rome

Government of India: Economic Survey, Various Issues Ministry of Finance, New Delhi

NSSO, Various Rounds, New Delhi

(1991), Report of the Committee on the Financial System (Chairman: Shri M. Narasimham), Ministry of Finance, New Delhi

(1998), Report of the Committee on the Banking Sector Reforms (Chairman: Shri M. Narasimham), Ministry of Finance, New Delhi

(2001), Indian Horticulture Database, New Delhi

(2002), Report of the Working Group to Suggest Amendments in the Regional Rural Banks Act,1976 (Chairman: Shri M.V.S. Chalapathi Rao), Ministry of Finance, New Delhi

Goletti Francesco (1999), Agricultural Diversification and Rural Industrialisation as a Strategy for Rural Income Growth and Poverty Reduction in Indochina and Myanmar; IFPRI, June

Indian Banks' Association (2002), Report of the Working Group on Agricultural Credit

Mohan, Rakesh (2002), A Decade After 1991: New Challenges Facing the Indian Economy: 28th Frank Moraes Lecture delivered at Chennai on July 26, Organized by United Writers Association and the Frank Moraes Foundation. Reserve Bank of India Bulletin, November

NABARD, Annual Report, Various issues, Mumbai

(1999), Report of the Task Force on Supportive Policy and Regulatory Framework for Microfinance, October

(2001), Report of the Expert Committee on Rural Credit (Chairman Dr. V.S. Vyas)

Pant Joshi, Deepali (2003), 'Indian Agriculture Perspectives', Prajnan, Vol 32(1), pp7-36

Reddy, Y.V. (1998), 'RBI and Banking Sector Reform', Speech delivered at Indian Institute of Management, Ahmedabad

Reserve Bank of India (1970), History, Annual Report, various issues, Mumbai

Functions and Working, 1983, 2001.

Handbook of Statistics on the Indian Economy, Various Issues, Mumbai

Monthly Bulletin, Various Issues, Mumbai

Report on Currency and Finance, Various Issues, Mumbai

Report on Trend and Progress of Banking in India, Various Issues, Mumbai

(1985), Report of the Committee to Review the Working of the Monetary System in India (Chairman: Prof. Sukhamoy Chakravarty)

(1998), Report of the High Level Committee on Agricultural Credit through Commercial Banks (Chairman: Shri R.V. Gupta)

(1999), Report of the Task Force on Revival/ Restructuring for Co-operating Banks (Chairperson: Shri. Jagadish Capoor), Mumbai

(2000), All-India Rural Debt and Investment Surveys, Reserve Bank of India Bulletin, February

(2004), Report of the Advisory Committee on Flow of Credit to Agriculture and Related Activities from Banking System (Chairman: Prof. V. S.Vyas), June

All-India Debt and Investment Survey, Various Issues

Armendáriz De Aghion, B. and J. Morduch (2000): 'Microfinance Beyond Group Lending', Economics of Transition, Vol 8, No 2

Baker, C.J. (1984): The Tamilnad Countryside, Oxford University Press

Banerjee, A. (2001): Contracting Constraints, Credit Markets and Economic Development, Working Paper 02-17, Department of Economics, Massachusetts Institute of Technology

Banking Services: Basic Statistical Returns, various issues, Reserve Bank of India

Basu, P. and P. Srivastava (2005): 'Exploring Possibilities: Microfinance and Rural Credit Access for the Poor in India', Economic and Political Weekly, April 23

Besley, T. (1995) 'Saving, Credit and Insurance,' in Behrman, J. and T.N. Srinivasan (ed)

Handbook of Development Economics, Vol. IIIa Amsterdam: North Holland

Bhaduri, A. (2006): 'Provision of Rural Financial Services', in Employment and

Development: Essays from an Unorthodox Perspective, Oxford University Press

Binswanger, H.P., S.R. Khandker and M.R. Rosenzweig (1993) 'How Infrastructure and Financial Institutions Affect Agricultural Output and Investment in India', Journal of Development Economics, 41: 337-366

Bose, S. (2005): 'Regional Rural Banks: The Past and Present Debate', Macro Scan, URL: http://www.macroscan.com/fet/ jul05/fet200705RRB_Debate.htm.

Burgess, R. and R. Pande (2002): Do Rural Banks Matter? Evidence from the Indian Social Banking Experiment

Catanach, I.J. (1970); Rural Credit in Western India, 1875-1930, Berkeley

CGAP (2004): Interest Rate Ceilings and Microfinance: The Story So Far, Occasional Paper, Washington

Chandavarkar, A. (1984): 'Money and Credit, 1858-1947' in D. Kumar (ed) (1984)

Chandrashekhar, C.P. and S.K. Ray (2005): 'Financial Sector Reform and the Transformation of Banking', in Ramachandran, V.K. and M. Swaminathan (ed)

Chavan, P. (2005): 'How 'Inclusive' Are Banks under Financial Liberlisation?', Economic and Political Weekly, 22 October

Chavan, P. (2005): 'Banking Sector Liberalisation and the Growth and Distribution of Regional Banking', in Ramachandran, V.K. and M. Swaminathan (ed)

Chavan, P. and R. Ramakumar (2005): 'Interest Rates on Micro-Credit', in Ramachandran, V.K. and M. Swaminathan (ed)

Ciravegna, D. (2005): The Role of Microcredit in Modern Economy: The Case of Italy, www.flacso.or.cr/fileadmin/documentos/ FLACSO/auCiravegna2.DOC

Dandekar, V.M. and F.K. Wadia (1989): 'Development of Institutional Finance for Agriculture in India', Journal of Indian School of Political Economy, I, 2.

Darling, M. L. (1925): The Punjab Peasant in Prosperity and Debt, Oxford University Press

Diamond, D. (1984): 'Financial Intermediation and Delegated Monitoring', Review of Economics Studies, Vol. 51, pp. 393-414

Dichter, T. (2004): Remarks to the Microfinance Club of New York

Drechsler, W. (2005): 'The Rise and Demise of the New Public Management', Post-Autistic Economics Review, http://www.paecon.net/PAEReview/issue33, September

Dreze, J. (1990): 'Poverty in India and the IRDP Delusion', Economic and Political Weekly, XXV, 39, 29 September

EPW Research Foundation (2007): 'Need for Calibrated Policy in Interest Rates and Credit',

Economic and Political Weekly, February 24

Fernandez, A.P. (2007): 'Sanghamithra – An MFI with a Difference: Are SHGs Only Financial Intermediaries?', Economic and Political Weekly, Vol. XLII, No. 13

Fisher, T. and M.S. Sriram (2002): Beyond Micro-Credit: Putting Development Back into MicroFinance, Vistaar, New Delhi

Ghate, P. (2006): Microfinance in India: A State of the Sector Report, 2006, CARE & Ford Foundation, New Delhi

CHAPTER XI

A WAY FORWARD

We had started this discussion by asking whether the village economy in India is sustainable. The short answer, in the near term, is that it isn't—India's urbanization is a direct consequence of this. However, answering this query requires delving into the levers associated with farmers, especially in the case of marginal farmers, and exploring avenues for a rise in non-farm income.

India's farmers currently are a stretched lot. It is reflective of India's farming miasma that farmer distress is only noted when farmers with a heavy crop loss commit suicide at a political party rally, bringing with it a crescendo in the rising chorus for farmer compensation. Consider Ram Sahey, from Dhanawa village, near Sultanpur in UP, who lost over 50 per cent of his wheat harvest to hail, losing over ₹2 lakh of potential income. With a heavy additional debt of ₹3.5 lakh, he expects compensation to be around ₹5,000. Unseasonal rainfall during February and March 2017 damaged crops over 8.5 million hectares across 14 states, including Uttar Pradesh, Haryana, Madhya Pradesh and Punjab—about one-sixth of the rabi sowing area. About 3.9 million hectares of wheat was potentially damaged, with yield loss reported at 15 per cent. Farmer distress quickly peaked, with at least 100 reported cases of farmer suicide in Uttar Pradesh alone. The central and state governments did undertake mitigation measures, with compensation amount for crop damage raised by 50 per cent, while eligibility norms were lowered to 33 per cent crop damage, along with prodding of insurance and financial firms to play a proactive role through payouts and restructured loans. And yet, compensation identification and dispersal remains a challenge, effectively insulting farmers with a pittance of compensation. This is farming in India today.

Let's consider the primary symptom first. In 2016, the sluice gate on the Bhakra mainline canal (159 km, 1.1 per cent of Punjab's total canal length), diverging from the Sutlej, in Khanauri-Kalan village in Sangrur district, became famous, reported on by various newspapers.[1] Families of farmers who have committed suicide by jumping into the Sutlej come there from Patiala and Ropar districts, seeking their bodies, if washed up along the sluice gates. Private divers have benefitted, charging around ₹5,000 to ₹15,000 for retrieving corpses, typically found at a frequency of thirty to forty-five a month. Over 2,632 farmers are reported to have committed suicide in Punjab between 1995 and 2015, according to state government records,[2] with Mansa district accounting for 1,334 alone, while Ludhiana had an additional 638. Adding farm labourers to this total raises it to 4,687 reported, a stark statistic in a land famed for its Green Revolution. Other surveys highlight larger numbers—7,000 estimated by the Punjab Agricultural University, Punjabi University and Patiala University between 2000 and 2010, with a third choosing to drown in canals, and the trend continuing in 2016. The reasons vary—the cotton crop was whittled by whiteflies, basmati's market price declined from ₹5,000 per quintal to ₹1,450 per quintal,[3] the local moneylender hiked up rates to 20 per cent. The farmer ekes his way to penury.

Farmer suicides in India have reached alarming rates. The decade between 1997 and 2006 saw as many as 166,304 farmers committing suicide in India—potentially an underestimate, given that landless rural labourers and women were not included.[4] As per the National Crime Records Bureau (NCRB), 5,650 farmers committed suicide last year, with marginal farmers accounting for 75 per cent, while Telangana, Chhattisgarh, Madhya Pradesh and Karnataka account for 90 per cent of national farmer suicides. Maharashtra has seen over 10,000 farmer suicides between 2011 and 2013, while the Marathwada region alone this year has seen over 200 farmer suicides. Farmer suicides have grown at a CAGR of over 2 per cent, with every fifth male suicide in the country being a farm suicide. To them the thought of suicide has now become a great consolation, a means to 'get through the dark night' (Friedrich Nietzche).

Farmer suicides are not a new trend. According to the NCRB, 2,195 marginal farmers reportedly committed suicide in 2015, of whom 834 were in Maharashtra, while 3,618 'small farmers' undertook such drastic steps, with Maharashtra seeing 1,285. More curious, a larger number of small farmers reportedly committed suicide in states like Maharashtra, Telangana and Karnataka than marginal farmers. Somehow, small farmers are also bedevilled by the agricultural crisis. And this is not the case in just the traditional drought-stricken states.

1   Vasudeva, V., Hindu, 28 May 2016
2   Kaur, D., May 2016
3   Patel, A.K., February 2016
4   Nagaraj, K., Madras Institute of Development Studies, 2008

Beyond the numbers, the human tragedy is poignant. Consider the family of Umesh Chandra Sharma (Nadhi village in Seetapur district) who committed suicide on 10 May 2015 and his son, unable to manage the situation, hanging himself from a mango tree a week later. Or that of Ch Ashok, son of Kirpal Singh (of Sahpur Dhamedi village in Bijnore district) who was driven to suicide by bank loans and non-receipt of mill dues. Or that of the late Laxmi Narayan Shukla (Sarsa village in Bahraich district) whose family I met in 2016 and had the opportunity to help. As a representative of these beleaguered families, I have contributed all of my parliamentary salaries for the next five years to the cause of farmers in UP while encouraging others to pitch in. Farmers now need more courage to live than to kill themselves.

India's acute agrarian crisis has led to this turmoil, increasing vulnerability while offering few alternative livelihood opportunities. India's agricultural landholdings are dominated by small and marginal farmers (99 million of 121 million), holding a land share of 44 per cent and a farmer population share of 87 per cent, while accounting for 70 per cent of all vegetables and 52 per cent of all cereals. According to the NSSO, one-third of all farmers hold less than 0.4 hectares of land, while 50 per cent of all agricultural households are indebted, with (average loan amount of ₹47,000. Within Sultanpur, in Uttar Pradesh, input costs per hectare have increased by 33 per cent over five years, while the government has limited agricultural subsidies. Such farmers now face rising penury, given diminishing returns and growing land fragmentation—yield deceleration taken to its logical end. Farming no longer offers a living wage.

India's misaligned cropping pattern and compensation system intensify such woes. Farmers living in arid areas, have been encouraged to plant high-yield wheat and rice, despite declining groundwater (61 per cent of irrigation depends on this). Rajasthan and Maharashtra have gone past sustainable levels, with the majority of their blocks categorized as 'over-exploited'. Given poor soil quality, this skewed cropping pattern, dictated by backwardness, has added to instability. The existing method for crop failure compensation is heavily skewed in favour of landowners over labouring farmers; dependent as it is on land ownership records (less than 0.4 per cent of the total cultivable land is registered under existing tenancy laws). In addition, reforming the process of crop damage estimation and consequent fund disbursal remains critical.

Given the lack of proper documentation, a corrupt bureaucracy and an inept local administration, providing compensation, cheap credit or insurance in time has become challenging. Increasing transparency on property rights and land-focused judicial reforms could strengthen such institutional systems. Effective use of satellite images and cheap drones can reduce the estimation time to a fraction.

Indebtedness correlates with farmer suicides. Farmers are driven to such an extreme step due to imprudent borrowing from high-interest rate sources for mostly non-productive uses where the increase in net incomes falls far below expectations. Numerous suicide afflicted households speak of borrowing while awaiting high yields and robust prices.[5] With Bt cotton, the input costs are very high, while the performance of these varieties depends on the availability of adequate and reliable irrigation. When farmers invest in wells and pump sets in the hope of striking water—when groundwater levels fall or rain is limited—such high investments turn out to be infructuous. Cultivation has become more variable, despite rising irrigation. When the market or the weather fails, penury rises. While traditional stereotypes cast blame on the usurious local moneylender, NCRB data shows that 2,474 of the 3,000 farmers who were reported to have committed suicide in 2015 had loans from local banks, while those that had loans from just moneylenders were only 9.8 per cent of the total. Maharashtra reported 1,293 such suicides due to indebtedness, while Karnataka had 946. Meanwhile, farmers in Punjab are estimated to have an outstanding debt of ₹69, 355 crore Somehow, the traditional moneylender is seemingly more 'flexible' than local banks.

Such a situation would merit opening up avenues for compensation and financing. Institutional financing needs to be more available and accessible—preferred over informal moneylending by sahukars. To reduce the possibility of a cyclical debt trap, benefit provision needs to be simplified while disbursed funds require effective monitoring.[6] Early warning signals need to be established, monitoring farmers that push past their default spreads and garner unsustainable loans. Village-wise lists of farmers who have availed of large amounts of loans in relation to their assets and earnings can be prepared on a periodic basis and be used to identify candidates who have large exposure to unsustainable debt and thus potential suicide candidates. The RBI and NABARD can analyse such lists for macro policy interventions, while the local administration can utilize them to provide timely loan restructuring initiatives, insurance claim settlements and better counselling.

Revamping irrigation remains critical. Drip irrigation remains an obvious solution—able to accommodate irregular field sizes and unlevelled topography, while keeping water application efficiency high (>70 per cent), providing high yield (up to 230 per cent) and improving fertilizer efficiency (up to 30 per cent). The high initial cost ($500-$1500 per acre) remains a significant barrier, with banks reluctant to provide loans on small ticket sizes. Land pooling, wherein marginal farmers can pool their land together to form an economically cultivable chunk of land and achieve economies of scale, could help utilize its economies of scale. In addition,

---

5   Vaidyanathan, A. , 2006
6   PD Jeromi, 2006

subsidy schemes like SGSY can help structure such transactions. In cases where sanction delays and supplier reticence can push back installation, banks could be encouraged to advance full loans, without insisting on sanction and release of subsidy.

For beleaguered farmers, categorizing their suicide as 'killing themselves' is a misnomer. They are simply defeated by the long, hard struggle to stay alive. Changing this pattern will require the government to pay deeper attention to grassroots issues and the unique needs of marginal agriculture. Strong social and institutional mechanisms can change their dismal economics. The marginal farmer can be given more hope.

AGRARIAN SEASONALITY

Some would argue that this is primarily due to bad or unpredictable weather. At its heart, the village economy continues to be dependent on seasonality. Seasonal vulnerability in Indian agriculture is a historical actuality. Even a modest decrease of 10 per cent of mean rainfall can lead to a significant decrease in rice production across India. The potential for future seasonal variations remains. During the period 1877–2009, India experienced twenty-four major droughts. During 2009, a rainfall deficit of 23 per cent was recorded and about 59 per cent of the area was affected. Seasonal vulnerability remains Indian agriculture's dark underbelly. And yet, weather prediction remains troublesome. In India, weather forecasts are valid only up to four to five days, while other extra-tropical regions have forecasts till two weeks. Studies on the impact of day-to-day variations of rainfall, particularly close to the harvest stages, have been mostly neglected. The accuracy of rainfall prediction in India has been error-prone, with forecasts in 1994, 1999, 2002 and 2004 seeing significant prediction error. An estimate of 20 per cent deficit rainfall nationally means little for a local farmer, given wide district-level variation. Blanket agro-met advisories at a district level need to be converted into block and village-level advisories.

When you translate this down to a marginal farmer, the consequences are significant. Bundelkhand is where India's marginal farming dream has died. Famed for the Chambal's dacoits and Jhansi's eponymous Rani, the 70,000-sq-km region, occupying thirteen districts of UP and MP, is a hotspot for climatic variability. Over the last decade, the region has faced a drought from 2003 to 2010, then floods in 2011, delayed monsoons in 2012 and 2013 and drought again since 2014.[7] The farmers tried everything to adapt—growing a mix of dry crops during the kharif season, while irrigating the winter rabi wheat with cash crops like chickpeas and mustard. With limited irrigation facilities, they invested heavily in borewells, tractors, threshers and inputs such as seeds and fertilizers through formal and informal credit. The past two winters, with hailstorms and unseasonal rain, destroyed crops (chickpea yields dropped by 90 per cent, the arhar crop failed completely), leading to farmer suicides (3,500 since 2003) and mass migration (18 lakh over the past decade). Compensation from the UP government has remained lacking, benefitting contractors, instead of farmers, and building warehouses instead of crop insurance. Bereaved families, hoping for government aid (₹7 lakh on death), were instead offered wheat bundles. A failed crop on a 4-hectare land was compensated with just 100 rupees.

India remains uniquely vulnerable to rising temperatures. A country like India, with limited arable land and a significant dependence on seasonal rainfall for rain-fed agriculture, is likely to face severe consequences from climate change (Stern, 2006; Nelson, 2009). India ranks in the top 20 in the climate change vulnerability index—with rising urbanization, there is increasing competition for land and water. India's average surface temperature, over the past four decades, while seeing significant variability, has risen by 0.3° C over the last four decades—as witnessed by a rising incidence of floods, droughts and cyclones.[8] Meanwhile, its net sown area has stabilized at 162 million hectares, of which 120 million hectares suffers from some form of degradation.[9] With over 67 per cent of all landholdings in India measuring less than 1 hectare, such marginal farmers face a 24–58 per cent decline in household income and 12–33 per cent rise in household poverty through exacerbated droughts.[10,11] Climate change would impact soil health, with increasing surface temperatures leading to higher CO_2 emissions and reducing natural nitrogen availability. Mitigating this by increasing chemical fertilizer usage could impact long-term soil fertility, leaving the soil open to greater erosion and desertification. Marginal farmland will increasingly be useless for agriculture.

And our dependency on rain will amplify. Rainfed agriculture is practised in 67 per cent of the total cropped area, supporting 40 per cent of the national food basket—55 per cent of rice, 90 per cent of pulses, 91 per cent of all coarse grains are all grown in rainfed areas. Such areas receive low and erratic rainfall (400 mm to 1,000 mm) which is unevenly distributed and uncertain[12]—greater variability

---

7   Bera, S., 2015
8   Goswami, 2006
9   NAAS, 2010, 2011
10 Bhandari, 2007
11 Birthal, Negi, Agarwal, Tajuddin Khan, 2014
12 Gopinath, Bhat, Latha K.V, 2012

would easily impact food production. Our regional crop patterns assume a specific range of weather variability—of late, high periods of heavy rainfall with long dry intervals have disturbed such established cropping patterns. In 2013, large crops of wheat, chana, lentils and mustard, weeks away from harvesting, were destroyed in untimely rains.[13] India's flood-affected area has doubled from 5 per cent to more than 12 per cent since Independence, despite generous State spending on flood protection schemes. Flood-resistant crops like paddy also face a high mortality rate (~50 per cent) as submergence increases to a week, leading to full mortality in two weeks. A predicted 70 per cent decline in summer rains by 2050 would devastate Indian agriculture.[14]

Groundwater resources, a temporary salve, have already declined beyond replenishing limits, particularly in the northwest (Punjab, Haryana) while there are longer drought periods in regions of Western India, UP, Odisha and Bihar. Our water reservoirs now stand at only 29 per cent of their capacity,[15] while continuing to deplete at 1 ft/year[16] resulting in farmers digging deep wells with expensive equipment, worsening their agricultural debt.

Research has highlighted the deleterious impact of climate change[17,18] on crop production. By 2100, the kharif season will face a varying temperature rise (0.7°–3.3°C) with rainfall concomitantly impacted (7 per cent–37 per cent). Similarly, the rabi season is expected to face a significant temperature rise (1.4°–3.7°C) with rainfall varying (-14 per cent to 28 per cent). Such limited temperature rises could lead to a 22 per cent decline in wheat yield in the rabi season, while rice yield could decline by 15 per cent. Other staple crops (sorghum: 7 per cent; groundnut: 11 per cent, chickpeas: 26 per cent) could see a sharp decline. Higher day temperatures would reduce grain filling while warmer nights would reduce yields. Its impact is already prevalent, without rising temperatures and rain variability, India's rice production over the past decades (1969–2007) could have been 8 per cent higher.[19] A future rise of just 1°C would reduce the yield of wheat by 8.1 per cent, rice by 5.4 per cent and maize by 10.4 per cent.[20] India is home to the largest hungry population—falling agricultural yields will only make matters worse.

Some would say that the issue is simply about mitigating risk. Recording losses

---

13   Damodaran & Iyer, 2013

14   ICRIER, 2016

15   Central Water Commission, 2016

16   NASA, 2016

17   IPCC, 2013

18   Birthal, Negi, Agarwal, Tajuddin Khan, 2014

19   Pattanayak, Kumar, 2013

20   Kalra, 2007

quickly and accurately is necessary. While there have been some local solutions, the Belgaum district carries out data generation through field information facilitators, an example of decentralization of responsibility and local capacity building, there remains significant risk. The utilization of open software like Google Earth to speed up compensation claims, as advocated by BM Hanasi, could be another avenue.

The obvious solution has been tried out, Weather Based Crop Insurance Schemes (WBCIS) have been introduced, with the National Agriculture Insurance Scheme (NAIS) insuring over 25 million farmers. However, challenges remain, with 95 million remaining uninsured and just 6 per cent of farmers purchasing cover voluntarily. Assistance and insurance payouts for crop damage are often delayed by a year, subject to the whims of local officers.

Agricultural risk-related data quality too varies considerably between states—given differing levels of accountability, capacity and expertise of relevant agencies. Worldwide experience suggests agricultural insurance is most efficient and effective when the private sector is encouraged to participate. Ideally, sampling error should be reduced by conducting sufficient crop cutting experiments per insurance unit, while the area yield index insurance should accurately reflect aggregate shocks. The insurance unit should be reduced from the level of a block to that of a village, as in Telangana. Risk classification is also variable with WBCIS and NAIS rules for designing and pricing products leading to the coverage value varying significantly across regions and years. Poor risk classification leads to significant adverse selection, with the farmers voluntarily purchasing cover in high-risk insurance units while promoting inequitable distribution of public subsidies and providing poor agriculture policy signalling.

Basis risk too remains considerable. A farmer can experience a large crop loss but receive no claim payments because the average yield in the insurance unit is not low enough to trigger a payment. Poor and risk-averse farmers are hindered, as a purchase worsens the worst that could happen. Weather and area yield indices need to be combined, pooling the strengths of modified NAIS and WBCIS, leading to more accurate loss estimates and faster claim settlement. Risk classification should provide flexibility to determine premium rates and threshold yields on an actuarial basis, instead of inflexible rates determined by simple formulae leaving significant inequity across regions. Basis risk can be reduced by combining farmers into local and semiformal mutual institutions.

The Indian government should reconsider overall agricultural risk mitigation infrastructure while assessing the merits of alternative models. For example, Mexico utilizes a public reinsurance company (Agroasemex) to offer technical assistance and reinsurance capacity to the domestic insurance companies involved in agricultural insurance. Spain, on the other hand, deploys a lead insurer as part of an agricultural coinsurance pool (Agroseguro).

A shift to a timely and affordable market-based crop insurance programme with actuarially sound premium rates can shield farmers from the vagaries of unseasonal rainfall. It can lead to significant benefits for farmers, including faster claims settlement, a more equitable allocation of subsidies and a lower basis risk, all the while lowering adverse selection, improving agricultural policy signalling and reducing dependency on government bailouts. Such large-scale reforms could alleviate farmer distress in the short term.

However, the village economy is bedevilled with issues far beyond risk mitigation. Our low agricultural productivity remains a key constraint—for rice, we produce 2,929 kg per hectare (China–6,321 kg; Indonesia–4,261 kg; Vietnam–3,845 kg). For other staples, we remain woeful, producing 913 kg of groundnut per hectare (2,799 kg; Indonesia–1,523 kg).[21] We use far more in inputs; a tonne of cotton takes 2.3 times the global water input average.[22] Our production inefficiencies and cropping patterns are misaligned by political interests—water-intensive crops like cotton and paddy get sown in water-starved areas. We need to amplify our investments in agriculture infrastructure, particularly in irrigation, rainwater harvesting and a national network of soil testing laboratories.[23] Simple water harvesting and conservation measures (micro-irrigation, watershed management and insurance coverage) can reduce 70 per cent of the potential loss due to drought.[24,25,26]

Indian agricultural policy has made us structurally vulnerable to climate change. Our agriculture procurement policy will have a generational impact—Punjab registers the highest share (30.6 per cent) of rice procurement despite having a high water footprint (Water Footprint, WF: 3.65, higher than 1 is inefficient); UP (WF–0.97) with a lower water footprint for wheat cultivation registers a lower procurement share (8.1 per cent) than Madhya Pradesh (WF–2.27) (26 per cent).[27,28] Such inefficient procurement policies and cropping patterns have caused stress to water reservoirs.[29] We need to promote conservation farming and dryland agriculture, helping farmers conserve and improve soil health, water quantity and

21 Swaminathan Committee on Farmers, 2006

22 Water Footprint Network 2016

23 NCF, 2002

24 ECA, 2009

25 IPCC, 2013

26 Birthal, Negi, Agarwal, Tajuddin Khan, 2014

27 Water Footprint Network, 2016

28 Food Corporation of India, 2015

29 Paper No. 04/2014-DEA, 2014, Ministry of Finance

biodiversity.[30] Drought strategies should be extended to the village level, each village should have a village pond, created under **MGNREGA**.[31] Each village should be provided timely rainfall forecasts, along with weather-based forewarnings regarding crop pests and epidemics in various seasons. Afforestation, in a bio-diverse manner, should be encouraged to help modify regional climates and prevent soil erosion.

Our agricultural research programmes need to be retooled towards dryland research, focusing on breeding for stress tolerance. Adoption of drought-tolerant breeds can help reduce production risks by 30–50 per cent,[32,33] while offering attractive returns (29 per cent–167 per cent) to breeders.[34,35,36] There remain a wide variety of other adaptation measures. Take planting dates—research highlights that planting wheat earlier than usual can help reduce climate change-induced damage by 60–75 per cent.[37] Zero tillage and laser-based levelling can also help conserve water and land resources. Crop planning should be conducted as per the agro-climatic zones of different regions while utilizing better genotypes for rainfed conditions.

Mitigation will require insurance coverage and supply of credit. We should focus on expanding our formal credit system to reach all marginal farmers. Insurance coverage should be expanded to all crops while reducing the rate of interest to nominal levels, with government support and an expanded Rural Insurance Development Fund. A debt moratorium policy on drought distressed hotspots and areas facing climate change calamities should be announced, waiving interest on loans till farming incomes are restored. We need to launch an integrated crop, livestock and family health insurance package while instituting an Agriculture Credit Risk Fund to provide relief in the aftermath of successive natural disasters.[38]

---

30   NCF, 2002
31   Swaminathan Committee on Farmers, 2006
32   Kostandini, 2008
33   Birthal, 2012
34   Mottaleb, 2012
35   Pray, 2011
36   Gautam 2009
37   Aggarwal, 2009
38   NCF, 2002

REVIVING MARGINAL AGRICULTURE

Reviving India's village economy requires reviving marginal agriculture. Of India's 121 million agricultural holdings, 99 million are with small and marginal farmers, with a land share of just 44 per cent and a farmer population share of 87 per cent. With multiple cropping prevalent, such farmers account for 70 per cent of vegetable and 52 per cent of cereal output. According to an NSSO survey, 33 per cent of all farm households have less than 0.4 hectares of land. About 50 per cent of agricultural households are indebted (average loan amount of ₹47,000). In Sultanpur district, cultivation cost per hectare for wheat has increased by 33 per cent in five years. Such farmers face an uncertain Hobbesian life–poor, brutish and short.

Rainfed agriculture has been practised since antiquity in India with Indus Valley farmers growing peas, sesame and dates. Herodotus, of the Histories, noted that 'India has many vast plains of great fertility. Since there is a double rainfall, the inhabitants of India almost always gather in two harvests annually'. With the British era came zamindars, ryots and penury. As Tirthanker Roy notes,[39] 'From 1891 to 1946, diminishing returns coupled with growing land-shortage and yield deceleration led to an acute crisis, particularly in Bengal.' India's marginal farmers have been worse off for centuries.

Our policymakers recognized this dependence on rain and attempted alleviation. India's agricultural policy focused on supporting canal-fed crops and improving agricultural productivity, coupled with incentive structures, pricing regimes and input subsidies. A bewildering array of schemes was launched—Small Farmers Development Agency (1974), Integrated Rural Programme Development (1980), Swarnjayanti Gram Swarozgar Yojana (SGSY, 1999) and National Rural Employment Guarantee Act (NREGA). Skewed by a bureaucratic approach, they focused on creating yearly jobs and roads while being resistant to decentralizing and localized decision-making. Individual symptoms were mitigated while long-term food security and ecological sustainability were ignored.

The Drought Prone Area Programme (1974) was 'concerned with drought proofing rather than livelihoods and growth-focused development'.[40] The National Policy on Farmers (2007) focused on improving farmer income through better risk management and an improved price policy. Implementation, sadly, was lacking, with <30 per cent of small and marginal farmers borrowing from institutional

---

39   Economic History of India, 1857 – 1947

40   http://planningcommission.gov.in/aboutus/committee/wrkgrp12/wr/wg_migra.pdf

credit systems.[41]

The Rashtriya Krishi Vikas Yojana (2011) allocated 10 lakh to each district to prepare and implement comprehensive district agriculture plans through local panchayats. The majority were chaired by the local minister or district collector, with little reflection of farmer needs, and limited implementation. Adoption of best practices was mostly ignored.

Farmers in arid geographies were encouraged to plant high yielding wheat instead of Malwi Ghehu, while relying on declining groundwater. Sixty-one per cent of irrigation is now from groundwater, with the proportion of districts with semi-critical and overexploited groundwater rising to 33 per cent.[42]

Punjab is well past unsustainability with 110 blocks out of 137 coming under the 'over-exploited' category. The Punjab State Farmers Commission (2013) recommended a substantial crop diversification to cotton, pulses and vegetables, decreasing area under paddy by 40 per cent over five years. Of the ₹5,300 crore suggested for diversification to dryland crops, the centre allocated ₹500 crore.[43]

A shift back to dryland agriculture, particularly in Western India, is much needed. Rajasthan, despite the lowest rainfall in the country, is buffering by integrated farming, having subsidiary farm enterprises like dairy, poultry, sericulture and goat rearing. States like Haryana, with little in rainfall, can be encouraged to shift back towards oilseeds and coarse cereals. Rice cultivation could be increased in rainfed Odisha and Assam, while incentives promoting wheat and rice are realigned.

With conventional irrigation mostly tapped, drip irrigation is an obvious solution. By accommodating irregular field sizes and unlevelled topography, water application efficiency (>70 per cent) can be kept high, lessening soil erosion. Yield can be increased up to 230 per cent, while fertilizer efficiency rises up to 30 per cent.

However, the high initial cost ($500-$1,500 per acre) has been a significant barrier. With individual loan sizes too small for transaction costs, banks have been reluctant to provide loans. Bundling farming households through subsidy schemes like SGSY can help structure such transactions. Tamil Nadu offers a 100 per cent subsidy for small and marginal farmers for taking up micro-irrigation, up to a maximum of

---

41 http://www.indianexpress.com/news/almost-75-of-small-marginal-farmers-may-not-benefit-from-loan-waiver/283365/1

42 http://economictimes.indiatimes.com/opinion/special-report/how-to-solve-the-problems-of-indias-rain-dependent-agricultural-land/articleshow/8845170.cms?curpg=4

43 http://www.thehindu.com/news/national/other-states/punjabs-new-agro-policy-will-be-a-drain-on-hope/article4960714.ece?ref=relatedNews

60,000 acres. With high monetary ceilings in irrigation projects, drip irrigation can be mostly funded through a revolving subsidy fund based around local self-help groups.[44]

Even with existing subsidies, sanction delays can cause installation delays, with suppliers reluctant unless full cost is paid. Banks could be encouraged to advance full loans to government-authorized self-help groups, without insisting on sanction and release of subsidy. Subsidy adjustment can occur later while repayment periods are kept between ten and fifteen years.

The Indian Council for Agricultural Research (ICAR) has been primarily focused on breeding higher yielding varieties for rice and wheat, while mostly ignoring coarse cereals. Funding for research, for ICAR and state agricultural universities (SAUs), has been dismal, with wages consuming most of it. Most SAUs are in overdraft, with little accreditation and a growing dependence on ICAR. Such dependence leads to an increasing focus on higher yielding varieties that ignore local ecological conditions and natural resource allocation.

A restructured funding scheme, with a focus on R&D in ten to twelve different crops in dryland agriculture, can be encouraged. The Kelkar Maharashtra Committee suggested that funding to SAUs could be increased by at least 100 crore, to upgrade research facilities and set up agriculture labour training schools. Mechanization needs to be encouraged by creating institutions for design and training, along with popularizing field tools.

The (NMSA) has been hit by a funds crunch, resulting in the Mission being subsumed into major existing programmes. This mission would have focused on mitigating risks associated with climate change and ensuring food security, with a particular focus on organic farming and System SRI propagation. Such initiatives need to be encouraged.

The Working Group on Marginal Farmers (2013) recommended that marginal cultivators could be encouraged to join FPOs. Such organizations can be provided interest subvention on loans for a five-year period and exempted from the APMC cess. Procurement from small and marginal farmers should be prioritized particularly through regulation for multi-brand retail. Enhancing their investment credit and matching their working capital requirements should be a priority. FPOs could be extended collateral-free loans of up to ₹25 lakh, along with creating a

---

44   http://www.thehindu.com/todays-paper/tp-national/tp-tamilnadu/100-subsidy-for-small-marginal-farmers/article2651629.ece

Credit Guarantee Fund for financial institutions to lend to such institutions.[45]

To foster these shifts, comprehensive ground-up regulatory and social action is essential. A shift to drip irrigation can be instituted by mandating it for all sugar cane plantations and fruit orchards. Combining this with micro-irrigation and horticulture incentives might create on-ground demand. Agriculture can be further customized through soil test labs at the ground level by giving advice to farmers on a personalized basis while promoting greater water efficiency. Taxes on agricultural machinery should be removed and agro-based industries fostered, with commodity parks created at a district level. Such social and governmental action can change this dismal agricultural future, taking us to a new growth era. The marginal farmer might be encouraged to peer beyond penury.

RETAILORING AGRICULTURE

Some of this retailoring will require a shift in the way agriculture is currently conducted. Agriculture in states like Punjab is typically a monoculture of wheat and paddy. When input costs associated with fertilizers, crop protection chemicals and seeds rose, along with fixed costs associated with agricultural equipment like tractors and submersible pumps, agriculture became economically unviable. Arhar seed prices have risen from ₹27/kg in 2004 to ₹73/kg in 2013 while those for staple crops like paddy (₹6/kg to ₹31/kg) and sugar cane (₹89/kg to ₹230/kg) have also seen a significant increase.[46] The old days of farmers handing seeds as family heirlooms to their sons are long gone. Fertilizer prices have seen a similar rise, with NPK fertilizers for cotton jumping from ₹14/kg to ₹26/kg, while plain barley saw a sudden jump from ₹9/kg in 2004–05 to ₹26/kg by 2012–13.

Hiring a labourer can now cost at least ₹20/hour, excluding rates when NREGA is prevalent, compared to ₹6–₹9/hour previously. Animal hire rates have also increased in a similar manner. With increased application of crop protection chemicals, soyabean has seen a massive jump in pesticide cost from ₹89/hectare in 2004–05 to ₹1,281/hectare in 2012–2013. The cost of labour, associated with both animal and machine labour, has also undergone a substantial jump. Hired animal labour for paddy cost ₹532/hectare in 2012–13 vs just ₹241/hectare in

---

45   http://www.thehindu.com/todays-paper/tp-national/nac-to-discuss-report-on-market-integration-of-small-marginal-farmers/article4346642.ece

46   Department of Economics and Statistics, 2016

2004–05. The cost of machine labour for wheat rose from ₹1,721/hectare in 2004–05 to ₹4,695/hectare in 2012–13. Given this jump in input costs, cultivation costs have gone up in multiples—for paddy, it rose from ₹20,607 per hectare in 2004–05 to ₹47,644.5 per hectare in 2012–13.[47] Similarly, the total cost of cultivation for wheat rose three times from ₹12,850 per hectare in 2004–05 to ₹38,578 per hectare in 2012–13.

Solving this requires an inclusive approach. We should encourage integrated pest management (IPM), an approach that focuses on combining biological, chemical, mechanical and physical means to combat pests, with a long-term focus on eliminating or significantly reducing the need for pesticides. In Vietnam, over 2 million of the Mekong Delta's rice farmers adopted a 'no spray early rule', curbing insecticide applications within the first forty days of rice planting. Predatory beetles that commonly prey on rice pests were sustained, encouraging the crop while cutting pesticide use by over 50 per cent.[48]

The local fertilizer industry needs support—timely delivery of subsidy would improve working capital requirements, enabling them to manage costs through internal sources rather than external loans. Delayed payments can cause an interest outgo of ₹3,500 crore for fertilizer firms annually.[49] State seed policies should focus on encouraging contract farming, along with identification of new genotypes for treating pest and disease syndromes and adverse weather conditions. Precision farming techniques, like Systematic Rice Intensification (SRI), can help increase seed production in this regard.[50]

Our farm equipment policy needs to be re-tailored, with a 'Make in India' focus on manufacturing farming equipment and implements that are currently imported. We should reroute subsidies to ensure lower collateral requirements, longer moratoriums and payback periods, for farmers seeking to buy equipment and entrepreneurs seeking to set up Custom Hiring Centres for agricultural equipment. Companies with a CSR focus on agriculture can be further encouraged to invest in capacity building initiatives, skill development and the establishment of CHCs.

We need to ensure that institutional financing is available and accessible; benefit provision is simplified while disbursed funds are effectively monitored (P.D. Jeromi, 2006). States should seek to establish early warning signals, monitoring farmers who go past set limits and seek unsustainable loans. Village-wise lists of deeply

---

47   Ibid
48   Pretty, Jules, Bharucha, Zareen Perves, March 2015
49   Datta, Kanika, February 2016
50   Poonia, T.C., 2013

indebted farmers must be prepared annually to identify farmers on the flight path to penury and potential suicide. NABARD, along with the local administration, should be tasked with analysing such lists for macro and local policy interventions, along with devising timely loan restructuring initiatives, insurance claim settlements and better counselling.

Finally, we should treat such individuals with the dignity and respect they deserve. Given the hard struggle of making a living in agriculture these days, such farmers face long odds for sustaining their families and educating their children. Travelling through the sullen bylanes of suicide-stricken villages in Bijnor, Bahraich, Kheri, Pratapgarh, Aligarh and Sitapur is a humbling and disconcerting experience. Even distributing ₹50,000 per distraught marginal farmer family, totalling my entire Parliamentary salary for the last 7.5 years, has had little impact, so deep is the scale of agrarian distress. Our elected representatives, often sitting in the lush environs of New Delhi, should experience this more often. We need systemic change.

We have models at a state level for progress, particularly with regard to the village economy. In the last decade, Madhya Pradesh increased its per capita state domestic product to ₹50,000 in 2015, a 300 per cent increase, with double-digit GDP growth rates in the last few years. While GSDP data can be inconsistent and MP's rise was on a low base, there is no doubt its growth has been powered by a spurt in agricultural productivity—a combination of good policies, the application of effective technology and sheer good fortune in weather patterns have helped this stage break through the BIMARU log jam. The state government has, in a decade of stability, focused on agriculture financing issues—providing interest-free loans to marginal farmers while keeping principal payment requirements relatively flexible. Subsidies have been better targeted, with particular focus on agricultural equipment and fertilizers. Irrigation, in particular, drew significant attention—increasing the irrigated area to 2.5 million hectares, a three-fold increase within the last decade. The state's Dewas model—under which over 4,000 monsoon ponds, one hectare wide and about eight to ten feet deep, in Dewas district, are being used to irrigate over eight to ten hectares of land, boosting agricultural productivity is replicable. Farmers across states have started travelling to Madhya Pradesh to understand how dryland agriculture is being managed, with the centre seeking to replicate the Dewas model across the country. Soil health cards, now being considered nationwide, are another policy action that MP initiated early on.

Rajasthan has transformed itself in the last decade—it now ranks 6th in the nation in 'ease of doing business' (DIPP, Assessment of State Implementation of Business Reforms, 2016), while ranking fifth in setting up a business, third in complying with environmental norms and being third in registration and compliance with taxation norms. According to recent surveys, Jaipur is now the second most emerging city for investment in India. Despite marginal, if any, rainfall, the state has sought to scale up its traditional nous for business into facilitating entrepreneurs. A single-window system for local entrepreneurs, integrating eleven government departments, has allowed for integration and monitoring of business applications, offering over fifty-three services for investment clearances, while communicating through SMS and helplines. Even getting electricity connections is now a matter of online applications, while e-governance has been boosted through e-mitras, kiosks that help provide government services in rural and urban areas. The Inspector Raj has been limited by the launch of self-certification schemes for industrial sectors, while documents are submitted online. Labour management has been eased through amendments to the state's Industrial Disputes Act (1947), Contract Labour (Regulation & Abolition) Act (1970) and the Apprentices Act (1961). Land records are now available online, boosting accountability while allowing for mutation. The Rajasthan State Industrial Development & Investment Corporation (RIICO) has bolstered industrial development, by offering land for industrial use without the requirement of construction permit/building plan approvals (up to 40,000 square m). This has led it to develop over 327 industrial areas, covering 74,228 acres across the state. Education has not been ignored—with over forty-five universities and technical institutes educating 355,000 students annually. As a consequence, SEZs across the state have drawn investment—263 acres in Ghiloth have drawn interest from South Korean firms, while 1,167 acres in Neemrana have been populated by Japanese firms.

Two different growth models, resulting in double-digit growth. Such states have understood that the key to broad-based growth is offering economic stability and basic infrastructure while pushing through structural reforms in certain key areas. Madhya Pradesh sought to sign up power purchase agreements in advance between 2009 and 2013 for wheat farmers. Such farmers were offered a 40 per cent subsidy on electricity costs but guaranteed supply during the winter months, resulting in over 3 million connections. With visibility on electricity access, farmers were happy to take advantage of the state's agricultural mechanization initiatives. Further investment in irrigation allowed for the provision of sufficient water to remote villages. The creation of an all-weather road network (comprising over 80,000 km) linked agricultural hubs like Harda and Betul districts to commercial markets.

States that take advantage of the powers granted to them under the Concurrent List, like labour law regulation to pursue structural reforms that allow entrepreneurs to employ workers in factories and SME units, have benefitted. With redundancy policies relaxed for medium enterprises, such firms are instilled with new-found economic dynamism, allowing them to become globally competitive. Welfare-focused reform, like allowing eligible citizens to opt for direct subsidies, like Rajasthan's

Bhamashah card (offering healthcare benefits covering over 1,700 illnesses, along with cashless treatment up to ₹30,000 at private hospitals), can improve coverage, while keeping costs under control. Reforms to agricultural marketing can lead to significant economic boost—with modified state APMC Acts increasingly allowing marginal farmers to have greater freedom in who to and at what price they sell while allowing contract farming for bulk buyers. Bolstering local governance is also important, with educational qualifications key—Rajasthan requires minimum qualifications for nominees for the sarpanch (class VII), panchayat samitis and Zila Parishads (class X) while requiring a functional toilet inside each contestant's house. Scaling up such initiatives across states, while pursuing low hanging reforms can help make the daily lives of citizens easier, at the same time providing incentives for businesses to invest. Instead of seeking grandiose summits, our states should be persuaded to continue tinkering away.

IMPROVING ACCESS TO WATER AND ENERGY

One particular aspect that policymakers need to consider is improving access to both water and energy. Many farmers have sought to change their cropping patterns, in response to water shortages. Such farmers have been able to go back to multi-cropping, while local aquifers get recharged. The influx of rainwater has also helped improve the quality of the local water, with a decrease in solids and toxins, making hard water increasingly usable. Topsoil erosion has been contained by directing the run-off to the borewell. Greater community stewardship of water resources would go a long way too.[51]

Improving access to water remains a critical need for placing the village economy on an even keel. While water as an agricultural resource in India is virtually free of cost, access to it is not. Part of this is due to geography and part of this is simply a case of exploiting water resources beyond our requirements, leaving little for those down-river. Water pricing, particularly for irrigation, needs a rethink. It is imperative that canal irrigation water and groundwater irrigation water are priced appropriately, either on a cost plus or a proxy basis. Such a policy will require additional support from the Deen Dayal Upadhyaya Gram Jyoti Yojana to separate electric feeders for agricultural and non-agricultural purposes. Such pricing should also be cognizant of the socio-economic status of marginal farmers.

---

51 Anand, Nikhil, 'Hiware Bazaar: Community Stewardship of Water Resources', Seeds of Hope, India Water Portal, 2004. Sourced from: http://www.indiawaterportal.org/sites/indiawaterportal.org/files/Seeds%20of%20hope_Case%20studies_Lokayan_Planning%20Commission_2004.pdf

Pricing water should no longer be a taboo topic. When you don't have access to water, it's a hidden cost for a marginal farmer. This reduction in income, coupled with the rising cost of medical care, is a primary factor in eroding the economic sustainability of villages.

Similarly, when providing grid-based connections to un-electrified villages, we tend not to consider the true cost of such connections. The true cost of energy should be reflected in our pricing (whether or not it includes a feed-in tariff). The discovery of this true cost can enable us to make the right decisions about which localized business models will work for electrifying our villages. Frankly speaking, we lost momentum in our push for biogas over the last few decades. It remains a viable proposition for providing cooking fuel in our hinterland, allowing the village economy to continue to function based on its bovian assets. These are the kind of models that we need to work towards. Ensuring that our farmers have access to affordable electricity so that their households continue remains our primary policy focus.

TENANCY REFORMS

We also need to change our fragmented landholding pattern. The average landholding size is 1.13 hectares; a far cry from the global average of 3.7 hectares, with the size of landholding having decreased marginally from 1.41 hectares in 2000.[52] Nearly 72 per cent of our farmers are small and marginal, owning just 6 per cent of agricultural land. If semi-medium farmers are also included, we witness that 80 per cent of our farmers own just 11 per cent of India's agricultural land. On the other hand, large landholdings account for 8 per cent of total number of landholdings but a staggering 80 per cent of the total land.

This fragmentation has ensured that we have an imperfect market for the purchase of agricultural inputs and agricultural marketing. Farmers consequently have low access to credit leading to overdependence on informal sources causing sub-optimal investment decisions and reduced access to extension services and technical know-how, besides poor access to public infrastructure like irrigation facilities and electricity. And this problem will get acute over time. Consolidation of landholdings remains a critical need. Simply put, land consolidation is the process of converting a number of small fragmented landholdings into one big continuous farm and then re-allotting them in a manner so that each farmer gets a single farm of the

---

52   http://agcensus.dacnet.nic.in/nationalholdingtype.aspx

same total size as that of his earlier landholding. It also could be implemented for convincing farmers to get one or two compact farms in place of their fragmented landholdings. However, any reform needs to be cognizant of background issues like varying soil fertility, ancestral memories and varying land pricing, along with disputes over ownership.

Meanwhile, land tenancy has its own issues. With tenants having legal rights on the land they lease, most landlords ended up evicting tenants, mostly through finding loopholes in the legislation—as much as 33 per cent of India's agricultural land had tenants being evicted as an adverse consequence of land lease reforms (Land Reforms in India, P.S. Appu, 1996). The laws have also incentivized informal tenancy, wherein owners typically get into oral agreement with the tenant farmers, bereft of any legal status, leaving them disfranchised of availing of cheaper formal credit, input subsidies, crop insurance, market access and Minimum Price support, and other public benefits.

It is imperative to reform land tenancy laws—although land ownership still remains the primary goal, access to land via leasing reforms will promote an alternative to ownership and provide legal validity to the work of millions of informally working agricultural tenants. This assumes greater significance with many farmers ageing and the youth migrating in search of better opportunities, mostly to cities rather than towns. Land market reforms would facilitate the migrants, urban areas and provide economic security, thereby increasing economic opportunities for those who rent out and those who rent in. The Model Agricultural Land Leasing Act will provide ownership security over their land to multiple landowners, especially small and marginal farmers, and enable work in the non-farm sector without fear of losing their land. We need structural reforms to revive rural India, amidst a shift of labour away from agriculture. If such tenancy regulations were relaxed, the viability of mechanization would improve, along with improving farmer access to credit and raising net returns per farmer. Pursuing tenancy reform would enable rural households that are better suited for non-farm jobs to lease out their land for productive use, unlocking land for productive use.

OVERHAULING AGRICULTURAL MARKETING

Our traditional marketing system is ripe for an overhaul. Farmers are increasingly seeking alternative channels to dispose of agricultural produce. The shorter the marketing channel, the higher the gains that accrue to a farmer. It is important to understand that increased efficiency in one channel doesn't mean that we abandon the other alternative or existing channel, it signals that the regulated markets respond to competition and traders are encouraged to modernize the operations as demonstrated by emerging channels. This needs policy support and financial resources to sustain the traditional channel based on regulated markets and upgrade the traditional channel to compete with the emerging channel.

At the same time, policy reforms need to be cognizant of the rural economy's existing structure. Any policy reform in this sector, considering its size, reach and impact, can have significant consequences. In any new system, there is potential for an oligopoly to form a number of small intermediaries with limited functions could be replaced by a few large entities, monopolizing the value chain, hurting the roadside vendor and pushcart vendors the most. Additionally, the single large entity will have greater experience, larger resources and legal firepower to take on farmers, and this can cause large-scale permanent damage to rural entrepreneurs. Discrimination against farmers is a real fear, as evidenced from high regulation of private bodies and greater public participation. While relaxing norms, we must put in caveats to prevent farmer exploitation. Our policies need to be designed to encourage private participation while ensuring safety and prosperity for the farmer.

We have to watch out for inequality—using emerging marketing channels can lead to a focus on only high-margin yielding high-quality products, which to a certain extent are a function of technology adopted by the farmer and geographical advantages and not of the farmer's efforts. Keeping in mind transaction costs for small and marginal farmers, the channels may prefer only large farmers and thus drive many marginal farmers out of farming, which would have far-reaching socio-economic consequences. Policies should be designed and programme implementation monitored closely to ensure that small and marginal farmers are empowered to participate and reap the benefits of emerging channels and not be left behind.

We need to promote long-termism in our agricultural marketing structure. If the objective of such channels, especially corporate/contract farming, deteriorates to just making short-term high profits from land, then with a monoculture focus and predescribed cultivation techniques, the Indian farmer will just become an implementation agent, with no freedom to think or innovate or act for the betterment of his land, his soil and his crop, with holistic farm management practice being taken for a ride. The capability of a farmer for traditional food grain farming and long-term food security may be compromised as farmers move en masse to lucrative cash crops. Our policies need to ensure that the farmer does not sacrifice recommended farm management practice and become a pawn in the partnership whose fate rests solely with the channel partner.

We have discussed multiple sources of potential growth in farmer income, including raising crop productivity, increasing livestock value-add, improving input resource efficiency, raising crop intensity while promoting crop diversification and pursuing agricultural marketing reforms. Making this happen will require a significant reform of the current way agriculture is managed in India. Increasing agricultural productivity will require increasing the coverage of high yielding varieties, particularly in cereal crops (e.g. for rice, high yielding varieties cover 62 per cent of the total rice growing area. Secondly, the provision of institutional credit can help improve credit supply in rural areas, leading to higher uptake of agricultural inputs. Greater collectivization, for lack of a better word, is also needed. India's agriculture, as mentioned earlier, is dominated by marginal and small farmers—small farm size is a significant deterrent for farmers in diversifying towards fruits and vegetables, given the uneconomic size of the lot for agricultural marketing along with price risk. Organizing farmers in an institutional mechanism like a FPO can help increase the benefits for farmers from the agricultural value chain.[53] But beyond this, India's policymakers also need to consider avenues for diversifying sources of income for marginal farmers.

NON-FARM INCOME

While agriculture remains the dominant source of income for rural households, non-farm sources are increasingly contributing a larger share of the pie. While this share does decline with landholding size, diversification towards it can serve as a mechanism for making the village economy viable and stemming urban-wards migration. Encouraging farmers and landless labourers to diversify towards non-farm activities will mostly be influenced by the landholding size, further decline in profits associated with marginal farming and rising educational levels, along with access to credit. Increasing the share of income from regular or casual wages (associated with construction) and livestock (mostly associated with marginal farmers and landless labourers) could help reduce inequality and transform the village economy. Livestock will lead to a regular source of income, helping to boost household incomes during times of drought and famine, while performing an informal banking role, considering how livestock can be stores of value. Creating sustainable employment opportunities in the rural non-farm sector will go a long way in helping India's rural poor in overcoming barriers to economic prosperity. India's rural development policies should increasingly focus on developing markets,

53   Singh, 2008

infrastructure and institutions that can help sectors like livestock and construction grow, while allowing migration, across states and nations, to occur.

HANDICRAFTS

India's handicrafts sector (including handlooms and textiles) needs to have its stereotype changed from a 'sunset' industry with peripheral and decorative use, made worse by lack of well-implemented policies and schemes to strengthen artisans. Development of craft-based entrepreneurship remains the need of the hour. Craft-based income has historically been a significant supplement to farm incomes for most rural households, yet in current times, we witness craft suffering from declining skills, disinterest in hand-crafted products and general lack of interest in skills handed down from one generation to the other. Firstly, having seen their parents barely manage their finances despite being skilled in crafts dissuades the new generation as they fail to see any point in picking up the profession/skills. The present-day school system fails to integrate any knowledge about local crafts into school curricula even on an optional basis, thus the children of artisans are pushed towards potentially lower skilled, low-paying jobs.

Productivity remains a big challenge for India's handmade handicrafts industries. With most production being family governed, it lacks economies of scale. Thus, it suffers from problems of economic production, warehousing, workspace, storage sheds, packing and shipping inefficiencies. The unorganized nature of the sector translates into little or no investments in tools and technologies. Meanwhile, competitors, mostly China, use updated manufacturing technologies for mass production, bringing down production costs, both in terms of time and money.

Inputs of various kinds are also a problem for most craft skills—raw material being the most important of all. The unorganized nature of the industry means most craftsmen have low volume requirements and thus have limited negotiating leverage if at all the raw material is provided to them. A fragmented marketing value chain has evolved as the bane of today's craftsmen. While craftsmen remain limited to the rural/semi-urban areas, they have limited means to approach the malls/retail stores to reach the clientele, which is increasingly becoming urbanized. In addition, artisans in most cases suffer from working capital limitations due to lack of credit access—many times unable to take on bulk orders as they would not have financial resources to purchase the requisite raw materials.

At a macro level, the inclusion of Non-Banking Finance Companies (NBFCs) in the fold of schemes supported by NABARD and SIDBI can help in improving access for India's millions of artisans, with loan disbursal remaining a core area where such skills and reach could be capitalized. Efficient and timely loan disbursal of loans would enable artisans to undertake bigger orders and provide timely products to the market. For providing relief under the AHVY scheme, NGOs, NBFCs (including microfinance companies) and social sector firms could also be empanelled thereby improving fund circulation.

An integrated approach is needed wherein each craft can be encouraged and developed in clusters—thus benefitting from common infrastructure and resource pooling. The crafts sector has to evolve into a Creative & Cultural Industry, which integrates various aspects—diverse markets for growth, industry sustainability, IPR and efficient production and value-add across the value chain. Certain preconditions need to be met in order for craft clusters to develop into creative industries—the cluster development approach needs to be strengthened focusing on creation of common assets, infrastructure and capability building of the artisans. The NSDC needs to be leveraged for skill development of cluster artisans. The tax regime for the crafts sector could be liberalized to provide higher margins during initial stages of cluster development.

Craft education could be taught in schools to create awareness among the youth and give them chances to pursue their studies in crafts through specialized courses on craft design and craft businesses. The gradual rise in incomes among the cluster members in a geographic area, besides adding stability to their lives, would usher in ground-level broad-based economic growth. Success in handicrafts would augment rural incomes and can potentially make the craft-rich village, a lively self-sustaining economic entity.

UTILIZING MGNREGA AND SKILL DEVELOPMENT SCHEMES

Instead of having an ideological opposition to the idea of MGNREGA, one must consider how best to use the programme's scale to drive non-farm income upwards. Despite significant shortfalls in its implementation, the programme has had a positive impact on the provision of livelihood security, with migration reduced significantly in a number of villages in Andhra Pradesh, Chhattisgarh, Odisha and Rajasthan during the second year of the programme. Since its inception, ~51 per cent of its works until 2014 have been focused on water, with an emphasis on water conservation, irrigation and flood control, while an additional 19 per cent stress on improving rural connectivity.[54] Such activities have helped reduce rural vulnerability to exogenous shocks, improving livelihood in areas with uncertain rainfall and poor soil fertility.[55] The programme has helped increase the employment capacity of the rural economy with a focus on expanding activities like the construction of ponds and wells.

We also need to acknowledge that as India urbanizes, a population shift away from villages is inevitable. Therefore, it is important that greater linkages be developed between our skill development systems (through the National Skill Development Corporation) and skills in demand in the international markets, which will eventually improve migration outcomes for Indian workers. For semi-skilled and unskilled labour, pre-migration skill development can cause vastly different outcomes. For vulnerable migrants, pre-employment training can provide higher wages and improved working conditions.

Any encouragement for migration has to be matched in efforts and outcomes to protect the rights and well-being of the potential migrants. The government needs to work closely with its counterparts in GCC countries to ensure that the rights of migrant workers are protected. This would include collaboration with the local government to abolish systems that enable exploitation of workers' rights.

SOCIAL POLICY

There are other hidden costs for the common man in the rural economy—education and healthcare come up first, along with issues like marriage, communication and general household needs. Any social policy in India should seek to lower the cost of big-ticket items, like education and healthcare, while providing a safety net for anyone who is unable to provision for such basic needs. In addition, the development of a viable rural credit market would help cover emergencies, shortfalls and requirements for entrepreneurship.

---

54   Gulati, 2013
55   Tiwari, 2013; Verma 2011

EDUCATION

As discussed previously, sending a child to a rural private school can be an expensive proposition. Many of these costs are borne by the State, through direct or indirect mechanisms. Education policy needs to consider that the cost of schooling (including such things as examination fees, books, stationery, uniforms and private tuition) can often be much higher than the cost of the school tuition.

There are three key policy changes that are required to change the state of education in India. The government needs to increase public spending on basic education. Education sector-wide planning policies should continue to be strengthened, along with a focus on increasing opportunities for alternative pathways to basic education. Such sector-wide planning needs to be focused on explicitly announced objectives, with coordinated action mixed with integrated programming and financing mechanisms. Any sectoral plans need to have adequate resource provision to enable equity and in order to drive a significant scale up in the number of alternative pathways to basic education. We also need to implement more large-scale holistic interventions to address the multiple barriers to schooling that currently prevail. While the past few decades have seen concerted efforts to address economic barriers, there are other systemic barriers that still prevail, preventing children (primarily from minority groups) from being able to access quality education. Any policy responses that address these barriers need to be cross-sectoral in order to improve efficacy.

We must promote a vision for education that is diverse and inclusive, including multiple learning paths—academics-oriented schools that focus on delivering formal learning across disciplines for students; vocational schools that seek to enhance employment prospects; globally ranked schools that set the bar for everyone else, and offer knowledge based on global standards. A third party rating framework should be established for all schools. Students need to be encouraged to make diverse subject combinations, enabling a choice-based approach to learning, along with the adoption of an interdisciplinary approach to K-12 and higher education.

HEALTHCARE

India's healthcare delivery remains a troika of poor accessibility, limited affordability and variable quality. Despite the presence of a well-defined structure, our inadequate per capita public healthcare remains plagued by crumbling infrastructure and lack of maintenance while construction of new facilities lags behind national needs. Healthcare facilities face a shortage of doctors, nursing staff and resources like equipment and medicines, while staff amenities present a huge scope for improvement. Our healthcare policy has primarily been policing in nature, without focusing on consolidated public health outcomes. Our priorities are also skewed—spending on tertiary care is higher than on secondary care, indicating a proclivity for hospitalization, mostly on account of failure to tackle the disease at primary and secondary care stages. It has become critical to align policy incentives with improved quality of service delivery and healthcare spends. Healthcare expenditure management remains shackled in bureaucratic shenanigans and needs reform in order to better respond amidst modern-day's changing needs. India's demand-side healthcare financing presents a host of complex issues on its own.

We need to capitalize on the inherent strengths of public insurance systems, coupled with design and policy changes, to overcome the inherent weaknesses, in order to drive improved health outcomes for the same levels of demand-side financing. Generic manufacturing by PSUs of essential drugs can increase competition and employment, steadily reducing the overarching need for ever-increasing price controls. Our public healthcare spends need to focus more on prevention (primary care) than cure (tertiary care). Finally, we need to keep in mind the long term mission of universal healthcare, supported by political consensus on hard choices, sustained long-term funding and efficient regulations, consistent and supporting policies at the centre and the state level and integration of healthcare facilities across villages, towns and districts. All this can help in universal coverage, providing good quality healthcare.

Ultimately, any of the policies that seek to address the causes of economic malaise in our rural economy needs to address issues associated with agriculture, while encouraging a shift towards non-farm income and provisioning social policy to create a safety net for meeting or subsidizing high capital needs like education and healthcare in the rural economy.

INDEX

F

M

S